FOURTH EDITION

Chemical Dependency

A Systems Approach

C. Aaron McNeece

Florida State Universit

Diana M. Di

University of Texas

D1239610

PEARSON

Boston   Columbus   Indianapolis   New York   San Francisco   Upper Saddle River
Amsterdam   Cape Town   Dubai   London   Madrid   Milan   Munich   Paris   Montreal   Toronto
Delhi   Mexico City   São Paulo   Sydney   Hong Kong   Seoul   Singapore   Taipei   Tokyo

Dedicated to all
who struggle with addiction and all who help them.

Editorial Director: Craig Campanella
Editor in Chief: Dickson Musslewhite
Executive Editor: Ashley Dodge
Editorial Product Manager: Carly Czech
Director of Marketing: Brandy Dawson
Senior Marketing Manager: Wendy Albert
Managing Editor: Maureen Richardson
Project Manager, Production: Shelly Kupperman
Operations Supervisor: Mary Fischer
Senior Operations Specialist: Sherry Lewis

Director of Cover Design: Jayne Conte
Cover Designer: Bruce Kenselaar
Cover image: Kentoh/Shutterstock
Text Research and Permissions: Margaret Gorenstein
Digital Media Editor: Felicia Halpert
Full-Service Project Management and Compostion:
 Saraswathi Muralidhar/PreMediaGlobal
Printer/Binder: R.R. Donnelley & Sons
Cover Printer: R.R. Donnelley & Sons
Text Font: 9.5/12 Photina MT Std

Credits and acknowledgments borrowed from other sources and reproduced, with permission, in this textbook appear on the appropriate page within text.

Library of Congress Cataloging-in-Publication Data

McNeece, Carl Aaron.
  Chemical dependency: a systems approach/C. Aaron McNeece, Diana M. DiNitto.—4th ed.
     p. cm.
  Includes bibliographical references and index.
  ISBN-13: 978-0-205-78727-2 (alk. paper)
  ISBN-10: 0-205-78727-4 (alk. paper)
 1. Substance abuse.   I. DiNitto, Diana M.   II. Title.
  HV4998.M46 2012
  362.29'18—dc23

                                                        2011018721

9 2023

ISBN-10: 0-205-78727-4
ISBN-13: 978-0-205-78727-2

CONTENTS

7   Preventing Alcohol and Drug Problems   171

By C. Aaron McNeece and Machelle D. Madsen

12   Substance Abuse Treatment with Sexual Minorities   336

By Catherine Lau Crisp and Diana M. DiNitto

13   Substance Use Disorders and Co-Occurring Disabilities   354

By Diana M. DiNitto and Deborah K. Webb

14   Alcohol and Drug Misuse and Abuse in Late Life   407

By Linda Vinton and Nicole Cesnales

15   Gender, Substance Use, and Substance Use Disorders   424

By An-Pyng Sun

PREFACE

The fourth edition of *Chemical Dependency: A Systems Approach* continues our comprehensive, systems-oriented approach to addressing alcohol and other drug problems. In our combined experiences in various aspects of the chemical dependency field, which have spanned almost four decades, we have heard many opinions on the causes of substance use disorders and the remedies to these problems, but often there has been a lack of critical reflection and evidence to back those views. With that in mind, we have tried to ground this text in evidence. Granted, we have our own opinions on the state of affairs, but we and the other contributors to this volume have done our best to incorporate current knowledge derived from research and theory.

Many of the issues addressed in the first three editions of the book have changed very little, but new issues and problems continue to surface. More attention is directed in this edition to abused prescription drugs, new designer drugs, and steroids. The development of new medication-assisted treatments is described and discussed. Likewise, new policy questions have developed since the last edition. What effect will health care reform have on substance abuse treatment programs? What is the environmental impact of drug eradication programs, and are they cost-effective? Will the lifting of the federal ban on funding needle and syringe exchange programs lead to their increased use at the local level? Have drug forfeiture laws had a significant impact on drug trafficking? Meanwhile, the "drug war" (law enforcement and interdiction) continues unabated, despite signals from the White House of a "softer" approach, and despite the fact that there is no evidence that the drug war has stopped a single individual from using drugs or encouraged anyone to pursue recovery.

Like many others in the field, we are concerned that much of what goes on in treatment is not based on scientific evidence of effectiveness or efficacy, and we have included current information on the most rigorous scientific studies of treatment effectiveness. The evidence tells us that some individuals do benefit from treatment, and we are committed to informing helping professionals—particularly social work students and others preparing for careers in the helping professions—about approaches that may help their clients avoid or address substance use disorders. We are as committed to addressing policy interventions as we are to individual and family interventions, because we believe that interventions at all systems levels can be useful in preventing problems and encouraging recovery once a problem has developed. Every helping professional should be informed about at-risk drinking and substance use disorders, including how to identify these problems, how to intervene once they have been identified, and how to make referrals. Given the devastation that substance use disorders can bring, there is an ethical imperative to do so.

All too often, clients are described as rationalizing or minimizing their alcohol and drug problems, but clinicians, program administrators, and policymakers are just as likely to rationalize. Not only do these professionals often blame clients for not taking advantage of available services, but they also frequently fail to sufficiently consider the impact of program design in connecting clients to services, or the effect of health care policies that may encourage more people to seek services. Our hope is that this book will encourage people to keep abreast of the growing literature in the field and to give more serious consideration to how we can better address these pervasive problems.

Plan for the Text

Part One of this text addresses theories, models, and definitions of substance use disorders. Chapter 1 covers definitions and epidemiology and discusses the process of becoming addicted. Chapter 2 summarizes most of the current theories on the etiology of addiction. Chapter 3 addresses the biology of the brain and biological explanations of alcohol and other drug disorders. With the current emphasis on brain biology as an explanatory factor in alcohol and drug disorders, social service professionals need to know more about this topic. (The authors of this chapter have tried to make the chapter as user friendly as possible.) There is an amazing array of ideas about what causes abuse and dependence. Many people believe there is no single or simple cause, that multiple factors are implicated, and that the cause may vary from one person to the next. Chapter 4 describes the physiological and behavioral consequences of substance abuse, identifying the effects of a wide range of substances. It is important for all human service professionals to know about these common symptoms and conditions.

Part Two addresses intervention, broadly defined. Chapter 5 describes screening, diagnosis, assessment, and referral—important skills for most helping professionals. The chapter also considers confidentiality and other ethical issues in substance abuse treatment. The stages of change model and motivational interviewing, which have become increasingly common and well-recognized tools in the field, are also discussed in Chapter 5. Chapter 6 looks at the system or continuum of care for people with alcohol and drug problems and describes a broad cross-section of the treatment approaches that are used, from detoxification to aftercare and maintenance of sobriety. Chapter 6 also addresses controversial strategies such as moderation and other harm-reduction approaches, as well as the mainstays of chemical dependency treatment and treatment innovations. Twelve-Step and other mutual-help approaches are also discussed in this chapter. Chapter 7 presents prevention theories and describes current programs designed to prevent abuse or dependency, sorting out the more effective from the less effective approaches. Chapter 8 takes a macro approach to intervention, dealing with public policies regarding the manufacture, distribution, and use of psychoactive substances, as well as the social, economic, and political consequences of chemical abuse and dependency. Drug-related crime also gets serious consideration in this chapter.

Part Three is devoted to substance use, abuse, and dependence among particular population groups. The subject of Chapter 9 is treating children and adolescents with alcohol and other drug problems; prevention and family-based models are two of the options discussed. The family systems perspective and chemical dependency is the topic of Chapter 10, which also considers the most prominent family therapy theories and models and their applicability to alcohol and drug treatment. Chapter 11 considers culture and ethnicity and their effects on abstention, substance use, and substance use disorders. Much of the chapter addresses chemical use and related problems among the major ethnic groups in the United States; information necessary for developing culturally-relevant prevention strategies and treatment services is provided as well. Sexual minorities and substance abuse is the subject of Chapter 12. This chapter focuses on the use of gay affirmative practice, a strengths-based approach to assisting gay men, lesbians, and other sexual minorities. Additional information on assisting bisexual and transgendered individuals is also provided. Chapter 13 covers substance use disorders and co-occurring disabilities, including mental illness, intellectual disabilities, and various physical disabilities or illnesses. The literature on co-occurring mental illness and substance use disorders has grown rapidly, but there has been relatively little research on the substance abuse problems of other groups, such as people who are blind or visually impaired or deaf or hard of hearing. Alcohol and drug use and related problems among people in later life, the topic of Chapter 14, is another area that is often overlooked or ignored. Awareness of these issues among the growing population of older adults is particularly important with the aging of the "baby boomers." Chapter 15 examines gender, comparing the prevalence, etiology, risk factors, and consequences of substance abuse among men and women. This chapter also provides information on gender-specific and gender-responsive treatment.

Part Four, which comprises Chapter 16, covers important topics such as financing chemical dependency treatment and the effects of managed care and health care reform on treatment. Chapter 16 also addresses the futility of the "drug war," and we believe that our objections to this unconscionable assault on American families are grounded in evidence. We conclude with a look at implications for the future of research, education, practice, and policy in the field of substance use disorders.

We sincerely hope that the questions raised and the information reported in this book will assist the reader in more effectively responding to the problems resulting from substance use and abuse in the twenty-first century. We are optimistic that as knowledge increases, we can more effectively address these issues.

Thanks to all the contributing authors and to Tara Alexander, Kim Comstock, Shulamith Lala Ashenberg Straussner, and Mary Marden Velasquez for helpful comments on sections of this book. We also would like to thank the individuals who reviewed this edition and offered useful comments and suggestions: Margaret Cretzmeyer, University of Iowa; Melinda Hohman, San Diego State University; Susan Robbins, University of Texas; and Wanda Spaid, Brigham Young University.

C. A. M.
D. M. D.

PART ONE

Theories, Models, and Definitions

One of the most puzzling questions about chemical dependency is: Why can one person drink socially for a lifetime and never develop a so-called drinking problem, whereas another person will become addicted to alcohol after a very short period of social drinking? Similarly, why can most teenagers experiment with illicit drugs and then become totally abstinent, whereas some of their peers will become quickly and perhaps fatally addicted? The complexity of the addiction process is why we devote the first four chapters to theories, models, and definitions.

Chapter 1 covers the most common definitions of terms such as *drug use, drug abuse, addiction, dependency, alcoholism, problem drinking,* and so on. At the heart of these different definitions is the ongoing dispute about the nature of addiction: Is it a disease, a behavioral disorder, or something else? In addition, this chapter describes the major legal and illicit drugs and examines the epidemiology of alcohol and drug use.

In Chapter 2, we take a closer look at the major etiological theories of abuse and addiction (i.e., psychological, biological, and sociocultural) as well as some alternative explanations. We also present a multi-causal model for the reader's consideration in an attempt to link all the major factors that are thought to influence drug use. It is unlikely that one single factor will ever provide an explanation for abuse or dependence.

Given the amount of new research in the neurobiology of addiction, we have updated Chapter 3, which examines the biochemistry and anatomy of the brain. Part One concludes with Chapter 4, a description of the physiological and behavioral consequences of alcohol and drug abuse. In both of these chapters, we attempt to break down some of the more common myths and stereotypes regarding addiction and addicts.

CHAPTER 1

Definitions and Epidemiology of Substance Use, Abuse, and Disorders

C. Aaron McNeece
Florida State University (Emeritus)

Lisa B. Johnson
Kennesaw State University

Introduction

In 1999, the 139 medical examiners in 40 U.S. metropolitan areas participating in the same ongoing study reported 11,651 drug-abuse deaths involving 29,106 drug mentions. The most frequently cited drug in these reports was cocaine (4,864), followed by opiates (4,820) and alcohol in combination with other drugs (3,916). In episodes in which the manner of death was accidental, heroin and morphine were the most frequently mentioned drugs (51 percent). Among suicides, alcohol in combination (34 percent) and cocaine (24 percent) were most frequently mentioned. The total number of drug-abuse deaths reported increased 15 percent between 1998 and 1999 (SAMHSA, 2000).

In 2006, hospitals in the United States reported 958,164 estimated drug-related emergencies in which illicit drugs were involved and 741,425 emergency room visits involving "nonmedical use of prescription or OTC pharmaceuticals or dietary supplements" (SAMHSA, 2008a, p. 9).

Tobacco use remains the most serious substance problem in the United States, with 443,000 tobacco-related deaths annually (CDCP,

2008). According to Breslau, Johnson, Hiripi, and Kessler (2001), nicotine dependence is not only a common psychiatric disorder, but it is the leading preventable cause of death and morbidity.

Given these statistics, it is not unreasonable to say that there is an epidemic of *substance disorders* in the United States. In the following pages, we will demonstrate that there are also high rates of *substance use* and *abuse.* Problems with alcohol- and drug-related overdoses and suicides are due at least in part to their widespread use among the population.

Alcohol Use

In 1999, the estimated per capita consumption of alcoholic beverages by adults in the United States was 25.4 gallons, which was comprised of 22.3 gallons of beer, 1.9 gallons of wine, and 1.3 gallons of distilled spirits (U.S. Department of Agriculture, 2001). In the 2007 National Survey on Drug Use and Health (NSDUH) slightly more than half (51.1 percent) of all Americans aged 12 or older reported being current users of alcohol (SAMHSA, 2008b).

Although heavy drinkers make up only about 10 percent of the drinking population, they account for more than half of all alcohol consumption in the United States. *Heavy drinking* is defined in this context as having more than two standard drinks per day for a man and more than one per day for a woman (NIAAA, 2000). However, there is no universally accepted or standard definition of the term *drink* (Dufour, 1999).

What is surprising is that despite the pervasiveness of health, social, and economic problems associated with the use of alcohol, experts have yet to agree on just what alcoholism really is. Is it a disease, a behavior problem, an addiction, or something completely different?

Drug Use

According to the same report (NSDUH, 2007) about 19.9 million Americans reported being current users of illicit drugs, and 28.6 percent of those 12 years or older reported using tobacco products. Another 2.5 million persons said that they used pain relievers non-medically for the first time within the past year (SAMHSA, 2008b).

Even though the estimated percentage of high school seniors who had used marijuana dropped in the 1990s, according to the Monitoring the Future study (Johnston et al., 2000), cocaine use remained disturbingly high. In 1995, 41.7 percent of 12th graders had at some time used marijuana and 6.0 percent had at some time used cocaine. In 1999, those numbers rose to 49.7 percent for marijuana use and 9.8 percent for cocaine (Johnston et al., 2000). By 2008 those rates had dropped slightly, but nearly 5 percent of seniors had used OxyContin, and almost 10 percent had used Vicodin. Anabolic steroids were used by 2.2 percent of high school seniors (Johnston et al., 2009) (see Table 1.1).

Generally, attention to other drugs has been focused on illicit mood-altering substances, but there is growing concern with the use of prescription drugs (such as Valium and OxyContin), over-the-counter (OTC) drugs, and drugs that have only slight mood-altering properties but present substantial health risks, such as tobacco, dietary supplements, and steroids. NSDUH reports, "The numbers of new users of specific classes of psychotherapeutics in 2007 were 2.1 million for pain relievers, 1.2 million for tranquilizers, 642,000 for stimulants, and 198,000 for sedatives" (2008, p. 55). They further noted that the number of new nonmedical users of OxyContin aged 12 or older was 554,000, and the average age of first use was 24.0 years. (2008b, p. 55).

There are other substances that might not ordinarily be considered as drugs–inhalants and solvents (toluene, paint thinner, glue, etc.) and naturally occurring plants such as mushrooms, morning glory, and yage. Perhaps it might be more technically appropriate to speak of *substances* rather than *drugs.* On the other hand, the reasons that people generally use or abuse a particular substance are related to the specific drug contained in that substance. Tobacco is smoked because of its nicotine; khat (i.e., the leaves of a shrub used in some parts of Africa) is chewed because it contains cathinone; and mushrooms are eaten for their psilocybin. Our primary focus in this book is with the most commonly used psychoactive drugs—those that alter mood, cognition, and/or behavior—whether obtained through legal or illegal means.

Definitions and Myths

Alcohol is a chemical compound that when ingested has the pharmacological property of altering the functioning of the central nervous system. Along with barbiturates and benzodiazepines, alcohol belongs to a class of chemicals called *central nervous system (CNS) depressants.* These drugs are used medically in the induction of anesthesia and the reduction of anxiety. They are often referred to as *sedative-hypnotics.* There are several different types of alcohol, but the two most common types are *methyl alcohol* or *methanol* (the type used as antifreeze or as a solvent) and *ethyl alcohol* or *ethanol* (the type that is drunk). Alcoholic beverages generally consist of ethyl alcohol (C_2H_5OH), by-products of fermentation known as congeners, colorings, flavorings, and water (Levin, 1989).

TABLE 1.1   Past Month and Lifetime Usage by Grade Level

Drug	Past Month				Lifetime Use			
	8th Grade	10th Grade	12th Grade	8th–12th Grade	8th Grade	10th Grade	12th Grade	8th–12th Grade
Illicit Drugs	7.6	15.8	22.3	14.6	19.6	34.1	47.4	32.6
Marijuana	5.8	13.8	19.4	12.5	14.6	29.9	42.6	27.9
Tobacco	6.8	12.3	20.4	12.6	20.5	31.7	44.7	31.3
Alcohol	15.9	28.8	43.1	26.1	38.9	58.3	71.9	55.1
Cocaine	0.8	1.2	1.9	1.3	3.0	4.5	7.2	4.8
Crack	0.5	0.5	0.8	0.6	2.0	2.0	2.8	2.2
Heroin	0.4	0.4	0.4	0.4	1.4	1.2	1.3	1.3
Hallucinogens	0.9	1.3	2.2	1.4	3.3	5.5	8.7	5.6
Ecstasy	0.8	1.1	1.8	1.2	2.4	4.3	6.2	4.1
Inhalants	4.1	2.1	1.4	2.6	15.7	12.6	9.9	13.1
Amphetamines	2.2	2.8	2.9	2.6	6.8	9.0	10.5	8.6
Vicodin	2.9*	6.7*	9.7*	—	2.9*	6.7*	9.7*	6.1*
OxyContin	2.1*	3.6*	4.7*	—	2.1*	3.6*	4.7*	3.4*
PCP	—	—	0.6	—	—	—	1.8	—
Methamphetamine	0.7	0.7	0.6	0.7	2.3	2.4	2.8	2.5
Ritalin	1.6*	2.9*	3.4*	—	1.6*	2.9*	3.4*	2.6*
Steroids	0.5	0.5	1.0	0.6	1.4	1.4	2.2	1.6
Sedatives (Barbiturates)	—	—	2.8	—	—	—	8.5	—
Tranquilizers	1.2	1.9	2.6	1.9	3.9	6.8	8.9	6.3
Rohypnol	0.1	0.2	—	—	0.7	0.9	1.3*	0.7*
Ketamine	1.2*	1.0*	1.5*	—	1.2*	1.0*	1.5*	1.2*

*No Monthly or Lifetime Data available, only Annual.

Source: Johnston, L. D., O'Malley, P. M., Bachman, J. G., & Schulenberg, J.E. (2009).

Beverage alcohol has been used by almost every known culture. Since any type of sugary fluid will ferment when exposed to omnipresent yeast spores, spontaneous fermentation is a common occurrence, yielding alcohol as a readily available pharmacological substance.

Technically, *cannabis* is also a CNS depressant, but it is usually treated separately in texts such as this because of the magnitude of the problems associated with it. The National Institute of Justice (NIJ, 1997) estimated that Americans would spend as much as $100 billion for marijuana by the year 2000. NIJ (2003) subsequently reduced that estimate to $11 billion. However, the overall cost of drug abuse to society rose almost $60 billion from 1992 to 2000 (NIJ, 2003).

CNS stimulants are drugs that in small doses produce an increased sense of alertness and energy, elevated mood, and decreased appetite. Included in this group are caffeine, cocaine, amphetamines, methamphetamines, and amphetamine-like substances such as Ritalin and Preludin.

Opiates are substances such as heroin, morphine, codeine, opioids, and synthetic morphine-like substances such as pethidine, methadone, and dipipanone. Small doses will produce an effect similar to that of the CNS depressants but with somewhat less impairment of the motor and intellectual processes (Drugtext, 2001).

Hallucinogens have the capacity to induce altered perceptions, thoughts, and feelings. Lysergic acid diethylamide (LSD), mescaline, and "magic mushrooms" (which contain the ingredient psilocybin) all produce these effects. Volatile solvents such as gasoline, benzene, and trichlorethylene can also produce effects similar to CNS depressants and hallucinogens when their vapor is inhaled (Drugtext, 2001).

Disease, Addiction, or Behavioral Disorder?

The major definitional issue concerning chemical dependency is whether it is a bad habit, a disease, or a form of moral turpitude. It has been variously described as a product of the genes, the culture, the devil, and the body. Disagreement persists among professional groups as well as the public at large. The various definitions of addiction are frequently driven by political motives, ideology, personal interest, and professional training. We will have much more to say about the nature of addiction throughout this chapter. The major reason for concern is that appropriate and effective treatment of addiction must be predicated on a reasonably accurate description of the etiology of the phenomenon. Practitioners cannot effectively diagnose or treat that which they cannot define. The best that they can do is deal with the outward symptoms of the problem.

The reader may have noticed terms in the chemical dependency literature have not been precisely defined—terms such as *alcoholism*, *addiction*, *use*, *misuse*, *abuse*, *dependency*, and *problem drinking*. Such terms are more often used as descriptions of a state of affairs rather than explanations of these phenomena, and there are considerable variations in the meanings attached to these terms by different writers. We will do the best we can in the following pages to define these terms; however, there will still be some ambiguity. *Problems* and *abuse* frequently exist only in the eye of the beholder.

We are also concerned that when the term *disease* is used in a metaphorical sense, it may actually make treatment more problematic, especially when the metaphoric aspect is forgotten—as it usually is. If a phenomenon is a *disease*, then we expect a cure in the form of a drug or other medical treatment. Over the years, poverty, pornography, obesity, family violence, and "gangsta rap" have all been portrayed as diseases. It is doubtful that the disease label has helped to facilitate a so-called cure for any of these conditions. The origins of the disease model of addiction have their roots in Alcoholics Anonymous (AA) (Yalisove, 1998).

Alcoholism and drug addiction also are frequently regarded as family diseases. The implication is that chemical dependency impacts the *family system*. We will discuss this idea at some length in Chapter 10. Whether it is a disease or not, there is little doubt that chemical dependency dramatically affects not only the family but also all other systems of which the family is a subsystem or with which families interact, such as the school and the workplace.

Alcoholism is one of those peculiar phenomenon for which every layperson usually has his or her own working definition; many think an alcoholic is "anyone who drinks more than I do." However, the layperson's definition of *alcoholism* usually does not differentiate *alcohol abuse* and *alcohol dependence*. Professionals working in this field do need to make these distinctions and perhaps even finer ones. One astute observer commented that it makes about as much sense to treat all alcoholics alike as to treat all persons having a rash alike. Imagine visiting the "rash ward" at your local hospital!

Contemporary scholars of alcoholism owe much to the earlier contributions of Jellinek and Bowman, who insisted that there were important differences between *chronic alcoholism* and *alcohol addiction*. The former was described as including all physical and psychological changes resulting from the prolonged use of alcoholic beverages. The latter was described as a disorder characterized by an urgent craving for alcohol (Bowman & Jellinek, 1941). According to their model, chronic alcoholism could exist without addiction, and addiction could occur without chronic alcoholism. Jellinek is usually identified as the most important researcher in making the disease concept of alcoholism scientifically respectable, but he also identified five separate types of alcoholism, thus demonstrating that the disease model was not a clear, unitary concept (Jellinek, 1960).

According to Jellinck, *alpha* alcoholics use alcohol to relieve physical or emotional pain more frequently and in greater amounts than is used under normal social rules. *Beta* alcoholics drink heavily and experience a variety of health and social problems because of their drinking, but they are not addicted to alcohol. *Gamma* alcoholics are characterized by loss of control over the amount consumed and by increased tissue tolerance to alcohol, adaptive cell metabolism, withdrawal symptoms, and craving. *Delta* alcoholics are similar to the gamma type, but they do not lose control over the amount consumed even though they cannot abstain from continuous use of alcohol. *Epsilon* alcoholics are similar to gammas but are binge or periodic drinkers (Jellinek, 1960).

It should be noted that Jellinek's research was based on a questionnaire designed by members of AA, distributed in the AA magazine *The Grapevine*, and completed by only 98 AA members. It could be very misleading to assume that all alcoholics would fall into the same patterns as these AA members (McKim, 1991, p. 105). In his book *The Disease Concept of Alcoholism*, Jellinek (1960) also noted that a *disease* is anything the medical profession agrees to call a disease.

The World Health Organization (WHO, 1952) first defined *alcoholism* as "a chronic behavioral disorder manifested by repeated drinking of alcoholic beverages in excess of the dietary and social uses of the community and to the extent that it interferes with the drinker's health or his social or economic functioning" (Keller, 1958, pp. 1–11). This definition, stressing cultural deviance and damage to the drinker, avoided the alcoholism-as-a-disease controversy. The WHO also distinguished between *alcohol addicts* and *symptomatic drinkers*. The latter group was described as similar to Jellinek's beta alcoholics.

The WHO (1952) committee on alcohol-related disabilities subsequently published a report endorsing the use of the term *alcohol dependence syndrome*. The use of this term suggests that a number of clinical phenomena occur with sufficient frequency to constitute a recognizable pattern, but the different elements are not always expected to appear with the same magnitude or frequency. The following are features of alcohol dependence syndrome:

1. Regularity in the repertoire of drinking behavior
2. Emphasis on drink-seeking behavior

3. Increased tolerance to alcohol
4. Repeated withdrawal symptoms
5. Repeated relief or avoidance of withdrawal symptoms by further drinking
6. Subjective awareness of a compulsion to drink
7. Reinstatement of the syndrome after periods of abstinence (Mandell, 1983)

The WHO's current thinking about substance dependence, including alcohol dependence, seems to have embraced the disease model. Specifically, dependence "is a brain disorder and people with drug dependence have altered brain structure and function" (WHO, 2001, p. 2).

A committee of medical authorities commissioned by the National Council on Alcoholism and Drug Dependence (NCADD) in the 1970s developed a set of guidelines to facilitate the diagnosis and evaluation of alcohol dependence at multiple levels. The criteria that were developed consisted of 86 symptoms grouped into three major diagnostic levels, with each level divided into separate tracks based on physiologic symptoms, behavior, and attitudes (National Council on Alcoholism, 1972). An experimental evaluation of the use of these criteria on 120 male alcoholics concluded that 38 items did not differentiate between alcoholics and non-alcoholics and that only four items explained 90 percent of the variance between the two groups. These items were gross tremor, regressive defense mechanisms, morning drinking, and blackouts (Ringer et al., 1977).

As we mentioned earlier, a major issue in defining chemical dependency is whether it is a *disease.* Medical professionals tend to define both alcoholism and drug addiction as diseases, but professionals with other types of backgrounds are not usually so sure. However, Vaillant (1983, p. 15) points out quite clearly that members of the medical community are not united in their conceptualization of alcoholism. In the early 1980s, about 85 percent of general practitioners agreed that alcoholism was a disease, whereas only 50 percent of medical school faculty considered

alcoholism (or coronary thrombosis, hypertension, and epilepsy) a disease.

Pattison, Sobell, and Sobell (1977) believed that alcoholism is a collection of various symptoms and behaviors related to the inappropriate use of alcohol with harmful consequences. In other words, describing a person as an alcoholic is no more useful than describing someone as having a cough. Pattison and colleagues argue that there is no single factor that explicitly defines and delineates alcoholism and that there is not a clear dichotomy between alcoholics and non-alcoholics. Furthermore, the sequence of appearance of adverse symptoms associated with drinking is highly variable, and there is no conclusive evidence to support the existence of a specific biologic process that predisposes a person toward alcoholism. Their most controversial assertion, however, is that for many supposed alcoholics, alcohol problems are reversible. In other words, some alcoholics may safely return to social drinking. This clearly puts Pattison and colleagues at odds with the majority of alcoholism professionals as well as with AA, which regards alcoholism as an incurable illness for which recovery is possible only through total abstinence (Curlee-Salisbury, 1986).

The current criteria of the American Psychiatric Association (APA) in its *Diagnostic and Statistical Manual of Mental Disorders,* or *DSM* (4th ed., text revision) distinguish between *substance abuse* and *substance dependence.* Both are classified as substance use *disorders,* but the word *disease* is not mentioned. Substance *abuse* is defined as "a maladaptive pattern of substance use leading to clinically significant impairment or distress" (APA, 2000, p. 199). This pattern must be manifested by *one* or more of the following behaviors within a 12-month period:

1. Recurrent substance use resulting in a failure to fulfill major role obligations
2. Recurrent substance use in situations in which it is physically hazardous
3. Recurrent substance abuse legal problems

4. Continued substance use despite having persistent or recurrent social or interpersonal problems caused or exacerbated by the effects of the substance

Reprinted with permission from the *Diagnostic and Statistical Manual of Mental Disorders*. Text Revision, Fourth Edition, copyright © 2000. American Psychiatric Association.

Substance *dependence* is defined in the same manner as a "maladaptive pattern of substance use, leading to clinically significant impairment or distress" (APA, 2000, p.199). However, *three* or more of the following behaviors must be manifested within a 12-month period:

1. Tolerance, as defined by either
   a. a need for markedly increased amounts of the substance to achieve intoxication or desired effect
   b. markedly diminished effect with continued use of the same amount of the substance
2. Withdrawal, as manifested by either
   a. the characteristic withdrawal syndrome for the substance
   b. the same (or a closely related) substance is taken to relieve or avoid withdrawal symptoms
3. The substance is often taken in larger amounts or over a longer period than intended
4. There is a persistent desire or unsuccessful efforts to cut down or control substance use
5. A great deal of time is spent in activities necessary to obtain the substance
6. Important social, occupational, or recreational activities are given up or reduced because of substance use
7. The substance use is continued despite knowledge of having a persistent or recurrent physical or psychological problem that is likely to have been caused or exacerbated by the substance

Not all use of a drug should be classified as *abuse* or *dependence*. If a person is using a drug without harming himself or herself or others, then it is simply drug *use*. The differentiation between use and abuse has important implications. If one has no moral or religious objections, drug use per se would not seem to be a bad thing. However, if the user is damaging himself or herself or others, drug use becomes *abuse*. (The reader should remember that society has legalized the use of two major drugs, alcohol and tobacco, even though both frequently lead to abuse and dependence.)

If chemical dependency is a disease, is it a physical, emotional, or mental disease? How does one "catch" or "get" it? Is it transmitted by certain genes? Is there a physiological pathology that leads to alcoholism? There is a vast literature devoted to these and similar questions, but it is likely to be more confusing than enlightening to most readers, and the questions are likely to remain unanswered. (A more comprehensive discussion of etiology is found in Chapter 2, and Chapter 3 addresses neurobiological models of addiction.) Some of the most interesting and convincing evidence for the disease model comes from the studies of genetically identical (i.e., monozygotic) twins.

Kaij (1960) studied 174 male twin pairs in Sweden and discovered a 54 percent concordance for alcoholism in one-egg twins versus a 28 percent concordance for alcoholism in two-egg twins. Since both types of twins were raised within the same social environment, it is assumed that any differences in rates of concordance between the two types of twins are the result of genetic factors. However, in a recent longitudinal study of children of alcoholics, Harburg, Difranceisco, Webster, Gleiberman, and Schork (1990) found a much weaker relationship between their drinking and their parents' drinking problems. This issue is unlikely to be resolved in the near future.

There is no doubt that cirrhosis, pancreatitis, Korsakoff's psychosis, and any other such *effects* that are a result of excessive drinking can properly and indisputably be called *diseases*. However, these are diseases that *result* from drinking. The debate concerns the etiology of alcoholism, and that is where we turn our attention in the subsequent sections of this chapter as well as in Chapter 2.

Is there an identifiable disease called *alcoholism* that causes a person to engage in excessive and inappropriate drinking? As important a question as this would seem to be, some contemporary scholars of alcoholism see this debate as a rather futile and useless waste of energy. Levin (1989) argues that any behavior as dysfunctional and self-destructive as alcoholism is a disease, regardless of etiology. "For an organism to destroy itself is pathological, regardless of the source of the pathology" (p. 63).

The same arguments concerning the disease concept of alcoholism are found in the literature on addiction to other drugs, as well. Psychiatrists hold many different opinions about the relationship between drug abuse and disease or mental illness. The most consistent opinion is that several different forms of physical disease or mental illness may *result* from drug abuse (Raistrick & Davidson, 1985).

Substance dependence is not described by the APA (2000) as an all-or-nothing condition but one that exists in varying degrees. There is no attempt to weigh or prioritize the syndrome components, and not all of them need to be present for a person to be labeled *dependent*.

As with alcoholism, proponents of the disease model of drug addiction can neither demonstrate a clear etiology for addiction nor predict its course or symptoms with any accuracy. It has even been suggested that the disease model is an elaborate and sinister hoax (Krivanek, 1988a, pp. 31–38). An important reason for labeling alcoholism and drug addiction as *diseases* is that it seems to reduce or alleviate the guilt or stigma associated with addiction and to make medical resources available for treatment. The recent decriminalization of public intoxication was undoubtedly related to the acceptance of the disease model.

Although most people view these events as improvements, we must allow the possibility that the disease model may also serve as an impediment to *scientific* research and to effective treatment. As we will discuss later in Chapter 6, the "track record" in providing effective treatment to chemically addicted clients is not impressive.

Epidemiology

Alcohol

There is evidence that alcohol use was widespread by the Neolithic Age. Stone pots dating from the old Stone Age in Clairvoux, Switzerland, have been discovered that once contained beer or wine. Ancient civilizations of the Near East, India, and China made copious use of alcohol. In addition, myths frequently depicted alcohol as a gift from the gods. Some societies even worshipped specific gods of wine: Osiris (Egypt), Dionysius (Greece), and Bacchus (Rome). Priests also frequently used alcohol as a part of religious rituals (Levin, 1989).

The consumption of alcohol spread from ritual use to convivial use, and before long, it was a regular part of meals. For example, the Assyrians received a daily allotment of bread and barley beer from their masters, and bread and wine were used by the Hebrews after a successful battle. By the Middle Ages, alcohol was an important staple in the diet and was used to celebrate births, marriages, coronations, diplomatic exchanges, and the signing of treaties.

Beverage alcohol came to the New World with the explorers and colonists. The *Mayflower* landed at Plymouth Rock because, according to the ship's log, "We could not now take time for further search or consideration, our victuals having been much spent, especially our beer" (Kinney & Leaton, 2000, p. 4). Spanish missionaries brought grapevines to America and were making wine in California before the United States was a nation. In 1640, the Dutch opened the first distillery of the New World (in what is known today as Staten Island, New York). Jamaican rum became the most popular drink in America under British rule, with New England bankers financing the slave trade that was used to produce the molasses needed to make rum. After the American Revolution, the preference for rum was eventually replaced by one for sour-mash bourbon whiskey (Rorabaugh, 1979).

Drinking in the United States was largely a family affair until the beginning of the nineteenth century.

With increasing immigration, industrialization, and greater social freedom, alcohol use (and abuse) became more open and more destructive. The opening of the American West brought the saloon into prominence, with the frontier hero gulping his drinks as his foot rested on the bar rail (Kinney & Leaton, 2000).

During the 1820s, the founders of the Temperance movement sought to make Americans into a clean, sober, godly, and decorous people whose values and lifestyles would reflect the moral leadership of New England federalism. In the next few decades, abstinence became a symbol of middle-class membership and a way to distinguish the ambitious and aspiring from the ne'er-do-well, the Catholic immigrant from the native Protestant, gradually losing its association with the New England upper classes and becoming democratized. By the 1850s, Temperance was allied with Abolition and Nativism to form a trio of major movements (Gusfield, 1988).

Threatened by increasing urbanization, political defeats in both the North and the South, and a steady flow of Catholic immigrants, the Populist wing of the Temperance movement adopted a theme of coercive reform. With the development of the Anti-Saloon League in 1896, reform pitted traditional rural Protestant society against urban Catholicism and industrialism, culminating in 1919 in that grand experiment known as Prohibition. Since the repeal of the Eighteenth Amendment in 1933, the Temperance movement generally has been fighting a losing battle. Today, so-called dry counties and precincts are rare and not even Protestant churches and respectable, upper-middle-class citizens can safely be counted on to support abstinence.

Estimating the prevalence of alcohol abuse, problem drinking, or whatever else we may choose to call it is very difficult. The first and most obvious difficulty is that there is no widely accepted definition of just what kind of drinking behavior constitutes a problem. Next, as all experienced researchers know, the choice of investigative method may be the overriding factor in arriving at an estimate of this phenomenon. It is widely assumed that most respondents underreport their actual alcohol consumption, either because they do not know or remember how much they drink or because they fear that their admitted use may seem excessive.

The first national survey of the prevalence of drinking problems was conducted in 1967 (Calahan, 1970), and three other nationwide surveys were completed within the next decade (Calahan & Roizen, 1974). Using Plaut's (1967) definition of *problem drinking* as "repetitive use of beverage alcohol causing physical, psychological, or social harm to the drinker or to others," 15 percent of the men and 4 percent of the women in the samples were judged to have a problem with alcohol. Another interpretation of the data viewed 43 percent of the men and 21 percent of the women as having experienced some degree of problem drinking at some time within the preceding three years (Calahan & Cisin, 1976, p. 541). A more recent study has reported that 16 percent of males and 6 percent of female drinkers disclosed personal problems associated with alcohol use (Malin, Wilson, Williams, & Aitken, 1986, pp. 56–57).

Using criteria from the *DSM* (3rd ed., rev. APA, 1987), Grant and colleagues (1991) administered the National Health Interview Survey (NHIS) to estimate an alcohol dependence rate within the preceding year of 8.63 percent in the general population. White males aged 30 to 45 were found to have the highest rate (26.14 percent). For nonwhite males, the rate was 9.29 percent; for nonwhite females, 2.50 percent. The rate for all men was 13.35 percent, and for all women it was 4.36 percent. The rate for white women was slightly higher, at 4.68 percent.

As we mentioned earlier, slightly more than half (51.1 percent) of all Americans aged 12 or older reported current alcohol use (i.e., having at least one drink in the past 30 days) in the 2007 NSDUH study, with males more likely to have used alcohol (see Table 1.2). Of those persons, over one-fifth (23.3 percent) participated in binge drinking (i.e., having five or more drinks on

TABLE 1.2   Past Month and Lifetime Usage by Gender

| | Past Month | | | | | | Lifetime Use | | | | | |
| | All Ages | | Age 12–17 | | Age 18 and Older | | All Ages | | Age 12–17 | | Age 18 and Older | |
	Male	Female	Male	Female	Male	Female	Male	Female	Male	Female	Male	Female
Illicit Drugs	10.4	5.8	10.0	9.1	10.4	5.4	50.6	41.8	27.1	25.4	53.5	43.6
Marijuana	8.0	3.8	7.5	5.8	8.1	3.6	45.2	36.2	17.3	15.0	48.5	38.5
Tobacco	35.2	22.4	14.1	10.6	37.8	23.7	77.2	62.4	30.5	24.9	44.6	27.8
Alcohol	56.6	46.0	15.9	16.0	61.5	49.2	85.5	79.3	39.7	39.2	91.0	83.6
Cocaine	1.2	0.5	0.4	0.5	1.3	0.5	17.8	11.3	2.0	2.3	19.8	12.3
Crack	0.4	0.1	0.0	0.1	0.4	0.1	4.9	2.1	0.3	0.5	5.4	2.3
Heroin	0.1	*	0.0	0.0	*	*	2.3	0.8	0.2	0.2	*	*
Hallucinogens	0.6	0.2	0.8	0.6	0.5	0.2	17.2	10.6	3.7	3.4	18.8	11.4
Ecstasy	0.3	*	0.3	0.3	*	*	5.8	4.2	1.7	1.9	*	*
Inhalants	0.3	0.2	1.2	1.1	0.2	0.1	11.9	6.4	9.5	9.7	12.2	6.1
Prescription Drugs (non medically)	3.2	2.3	3.0	3.5	3.3	2.2	22.0	18.8	11.1	12.3	23.3	19.5
Methamphetamine	0.2	0.2	0.1	0.2	*	*	6.3	4.3	0.6	1.1	*	*
OxyContin	0.2	0.1	0.2	0.2	*	*	2.3	1.3	1.3	1.5	*	*
Stimulants	0.4	0.5	0.4	0.6	*	*	9.9	7.6	2.3	1.1	*	*
Steroids	*	*	2.5	0.6	*	*	*	*	*	*	*	*
Pain Relievers (no medical use)	2.6	1.7	2.5	2.8	2.6	1.5	15.0	11.7	9.3	10.2	15.7	11.9

*Data unavailable.

Source: SAMHSA (2008c).

the same occasion at least once in the previous 30 days) and 6.9 percent reported being heavy drinkers (having five or more drinks on the same occasion at least five different times in the past 30 days) (SAMHSA, 2008b). This means that 126.8 million Americans use alcohol, 57.8 million are binge drinkers, and 17 million are heavy drinkers.

Age.   Alcohol use, heavy use, and binge drinking peak at age 21. In 2007, the reported use of alcohol increased with age from 3.5 percent among ages 12 or 13 to 68.3 percent among ages 21 to 25. After age 21, there is a steady pattern of alcohol use, with a decline in binge drinking and heavy drinking. There were also 10.7 million underage drinkers in 2007 (27.9 percent of persons aged 12 through 20), 7.2 million underage binge drinkers (18.6 percent), and 2.3 million underage heavy drinkers (6.0 percent). Binge drinking increased from 1.5 percent for ages 12 to 13 to 7.8 percent for ages 14 to 15(SAMHSA, 2008b).

Gender.   More males than females use alcohol, with 56.6 percent of males and 46.0 percent of females aged 12 years or older reporting current use in 2007. However, among the 12- to 17-year-old age group, females (16.0 percent) were slightly more likely to drink than males (15.9 percent). Males in the 12- to 20-year-age group were more likely to binge drink than females (21.1 percent compared to 16.1 percent).

Perhaps the most disturbing statistic from the NSDUH study was on female drinking, given the problem of fetal alcohol syndrome (see Chapter 15), is that "among pregnant women aged 15 to 44, an estimated 11.6 percent reported current alcohol use, 3.7 percent reported binge drinking, and 0.7 percent reported heavy drinking" (SAMSHA, 2008b, p. 33). While alcohol use for women in this age group is generally no more problematic than that for men, women who plan to become pregnant should carefully consider their use of alcohol.

Race/Ethnicity.   Whites (56.1 percent) are more likely than people from any other racial or ethnic group to report the current use of alcohol. In 2007, among persons reporting two or more races 23.2 reported current alcohol use. The rate for Hispanics was 42.1 percent; for American Indians or Alaska Natives, 44.7 percent; for African Americans, 39.3 percent; and for Asian Americans, 35.2 percent. Binge drinking was most often reported by American Indians or Alaska Natives (28.2 percent) and least often by Asian Americans (12.6 percent) (SAMHSA, 2008b). Differences in alcohol and drug use among racial/ethnic groups are explored in detail in Chapter 11 (see Tables 1.4 and 1.5).

Education.   The rate of current alcohol use increases with level of education. In 2007, 68.5 percent of college graduates reported drinking compared to only 36.5 percent of adults with less than a high school education. Persons aged 18 to 22 enrolled full time in college were more likely than others in this age group to report alcohol use (63.7 to 53.5 percent), binge drinking (43.6 to 38.4 percent), and heavy drinking (17.2 to 12.9 percent). One-half of all male college students and one-third of all female college students reported binge drinking (SAMHSA, 2008b). Persons employed full-time were slightly more likely to have used alcohol than those who were employed part-time or unemployed (see Tables 1.1 and 1.3).

Geographic Area.   The reported use of alcohol was lowest in the South (46.8 percent) and highest in the Northeast (56.0 percent). It was also lower in nonmetropolitan areas (44.0 percent) than in large metropolitan areas (53.5 percent). However, there were some interesting differences among subgroups within geographic areas. For example, among people aged 12 or older, the rate of binge drinking was the same in small, large, and nonmetropolitan areas (23.4 percent, 23.3 percent, and 23.0 percent respectively) (SAMHSA, 2008b).

TABLE 1.3 Past Month and Lifetime Usage by Education and Employment

Past Month

	Education				Employment			
	High School	High School Graduate	Some College	College Graduate	Full-time	Part-time	Unemployed	Other
Illicit Drugs	9.3	8.6	8.9	5.1	8.4	10.1	18.3	4.7
Marijuana	6.8	6.4	6.6	3.5	6.3	7.6	13.9	3.0
Tobacco	36.4	36.7	31.4	19.0	33.4	27.6	50.0	24.0
Alcohol	36.5	50.0	58.9	68.5	62.8	56.4	56.9	40.0
Cocaine	1.2	0.9	1.1	0.5	0.9	1.0	3.1	0.6
Crack	0.5	0.4	0.2	0.1	0.2	0.3	1.4	0.2
Hallucinogens	0.5	0.4	0.4	0.2	0.4	0.6	1.5	0.2
Inhalants	0.2	0.1	0.1	0.1	0.1	0.3	0.2	0.1
Prescription Drugs (non medically)	3.7	2.8	3.0	1.7	2.9	3.5	5.5	1.8
Pain Relievers (no medical use)	2.9	2.4	2.1	1.1	2.2	2.7	4.2	1.2

Lifetime

	Education				Employment			
	High School	High School Graduate	Some College	College Graduate	Full-time	Part-time	Unemployed	Other
Illicit Drugs	36.0	46.1	55.2	51.8	56.7	49.7	59.7	30.8
Marijuana	31.2	41.5	49.8	46.5	51.7	43.5	53.6	26.3
Tobacco	68.0	74.6	77.1	75.1	77.3	72.5	75.0	69.3
Alcohol	74.5	85.9	91.2	92.4	91.4	85.9	85.5	80.0
Cocaine	14.4	15.5	18.4	14.8	19.4	14.7	22.6	8.9
Crack	5.7	4.8	3.9	1.5	4.2	3.4	8.8	2.8
Hallucinogens	11.8	14.2	17.8	15.1	18.6	14.6	21.4	7.5
Inhalants	7.1	7.7	10.4	10.4	11.1	9.0	11.8	4.7
Prescription Drugs (non medically)	17.7	20.6	24.7	21.1	24.5	23.2	28.9	13.6
Pain Relievers (no medical use)	13.1	14.0	16.4	11.3	15.7	15.9	23.0	8.1

Source: SAMHSA (2008c).

TABLE 1.4   Past Month Usage by Race and Age

| | Past Month | | | | | | | | | | | |
| | Age 12–17 | | | | | | Age 18 and older | | | | | |
	White	Black or African American	American Indian or Alaska Native	Asian	Two or More Races	Hispanic or Latino	White	Black or African American	American Indian or Alaska Native	Asian	Two or More Races	Hispanic or Latino
Illicit Drugs	10.2	9.4	*	6.0	9.2	8.1	8.0	9.5	12.0	4.0	12.3	6.4
Marijuana	7.3	5.8	*	4.2	6.9	5.7	5.8	7.5	7.4	2.4	11.1	4.3
Tobacco	15.5	7.5	16.7	4.3	9.9	8.4	32.2	29.7	45.6	16.6	39.8	24.9
Alcohol	18.2	10.1	*	8.1	12.5	15.2	59.8	43.8	47.8	38.0	53.9	46.3
Cocaine	0.5	0.1	*	*	0.1	0.5	0.9	0.9	0.7	0.1	1.3	1.1
Crack	0.1	*	*	*	0.1	0.1	0.3	0.6	0.4	0.0	0.4	0.1
Hallucinogens	0.8	0.1	0.8	0.3	0.9	1.0	0.3	0.7	*	0.0	0.6	0.5
Inhalants	1.2	1.2	1.6	0.5	0.5	1.3	0.1	0.0	0.1	0.1	0.1	0.2
Prescription Drugs (non medically)	3.6	3.1	*	1.4	3.2	2.7	3.0	2.0	4.0	1.5	4.3	2.2
Pain Relievers (no medical use)	2.8	2.6	*	0.8	2.8	2.2	5.7	3.0	*	1.6	6.2	2.5

*Low precision; no estimate report.

Source: SAMHSA (2008c).

15

TABLE 1.5　Lifetime Usage by Race and Age

	Lifetime											
	Age 12–17						Age 18 and older					
	White	Black or African American	American Indian or Alaska Native	Asian	Two or More Races	Hispanic or Latino	White	Black or African American	American Indian or Alaska Native	Asian	Two or More Races	Hispanic or Latino
Illicit Drugs	27.0	26.7	43.1	16.3	28.4	24.7	52.6	45.5	56.3	23.5	55.6	35.7
Marijuana	17.3	15.4	23.5	8.0	18.6	14.4	47.9	41.5	50.4	17.2	49.5	28.8
Tobacco	31.5	21.3	32.5	14.8	25.4	24.0	80.6	63.7	80.8	44.2	76.9	59.8
Alcohol	41.9	34.0	*	25.3	38.7	39.1	91.4	80.9	86.6	65.6	89.6	77.2
Cocaine	2.4	0.7	*	0.2	1.7	3.0	17.7	11.4	17.7	5.7	18.3	13.1
Crack	0.5	0.0	0.1	*	0.8	0.6	3.7	6.1	5.3	1.2	4.6	3.0
Hallucinogens	4.2	1.2	10.8	2.4	4.1	3.5	17.6	7.4	28.3	5.8	21.8	9.6
Inhalants	10.3	7.6	11.1	6.1	11.7	9.5	10.7	3.1	12.9	4.0	13.3	6.2
Prescription Drugs (non medically)	12.7	10.1	17.0	6.4	10.7	10.8	24.5	12.3	23.3	9.1	28.8	15.9
Pain Relievers (no medical use)	10.6	8.2	15.2	4.6	9.0	9.1	30.0	14.2	*	10.6	31.3	18.3

*Low precision; no estimate report.

Source: SAMHSA (2008c).

Illicit Drugs

About 19.9 million Americans—8.0 percent of the population aged 12 or older—reported using an illicit drug in the previous 30 days in the 2007 NSDUH study (SAMHSA, 2008b). Marijuana was the most commonly used illicit drug, used by 72.8 percent of illicit drug users. About 53.3 percent of illicit drug users used marijuana only, 19.4 percent used another illicit drug and marijuana, and 27.2 percent used an illicit drug other than marijuana. The majority of those using illicit drugs other than marijuana (6.9 million users) were using psychotherapeutics non-medically. These drugs include pain relievers (5.2 million users), tranquilizers (1.8 million users), stimulants (1.1 million users), and sedatives (346,000 users) (SAMHSA, 2008b).

Marijuana.   Marijuana was a legal drug and was grown as a cash crop in parts of the United States until its use and possession were prohibited by federal law in 1937. (It is still an important but illicit cash crop in many states today.) The plant was probably brought into Texas and California by Mexican immigrants in the early part of the twentieth century. Marijuana smoking was commonly accepted in many Mexican communities as a relaxant, a remedy for headaches, and a mild euphoriant. Cultivation of the plant was a major industry in the area around Mexico City and in several of the provinces, and it extended rapidly to border towns such as Laredo, El Paso, and Nogales. A direct railroad link between Mexico City and San Antonio facilitated marijuana trade between those cities, and for a while, a druggist in Floresville, Texas, established a mail-order marijuana business with customers in Texas, Arizona, New Mexico, Kansas, and Colorado (Bonnie & Whitebread, 1998).

Smoking marijuana spread quickly to New Orleans, where it was popular among many African American jazz musicians by the early 1920s (Goode, 1969). They carried it with them as they immigrated to the urban centers of the North. Anecdotal accounts of its history indicate that marijuana was soon adopted by many so-called deviant groups: professional criminals, prostitutes, and so on. In the 1960s, it became one of the symbols of the hippie movement (Kelleher, MacMurray, & Shapiro, 1988, p. 249). Very few hard data exist regarding its use until the mid 1970s, however.

Cannabis is generally regarded as the most commonly used illicit drug. During the 1970s, 16 million Americans used marijuana at least once a month, of whom about 4 million were between 12 and 17 years of age and 8.5 million between 18 and 25 years of age (Executive Office of the President, 1978). Marijuana use seems to have peaked between 1979 and 1981, with more than 10 percent of high school seniors being daily users. By 1986, daily use by this group had dropped to 4 percent (Johnston, O'Malley, & Bachman, 1987). By 1988, it had dropped further to 3.3 percent (4.5 percent for males and 2.2 percent for females) (Johnston et al., 1987). By 1995, 4.6 percent of seniors were using marijuana daily (*Drug use*, n.d.). In 2007, 14.4 million people were identified as past month users (SAMSHA, 2008b). SAMSHA (2008b) reports, "In 2007, marijuana was used by 72.8 percent of current illicit drug users and was the only drug used by 53.3 percent of them" (p. 16).

In 1999, the number of 12th graders using marijuana daily was 6.0 percent (Johnston et al., 2000). In 2007, marijuana was the most commonly used drug among 14 or 15 year olds and 16 or 17 year olds (5.7 percent and 13.1 percent respectively) (SAMHSA, 2008b). A 1999 estimate by the National Institute on Drug Abuse (NIDA) put the total percentage of the U.S. population who had ever used marijuana at 34.6 percent. This rate was highest for the 18- to 25-year-old age group (46.8 percent). In the population aged 26 or older, 34.7 percent had used this drug. In a study of high school seniors in the class of 1995, 49.7 percent had reportedly used marijuana at some time (SAMHSA, 2001).

According to the Office of National Drug Control Policy (ONDCP, 2001), the availability of marijuana is stable through most regions of the United States. The most widely available form of outdoor-grown marijuana ("bio") is *commercial* grade, with a tetrahydrocannabinol (THC) content of 4 to 15 percent.[1] *Sinsemilla*, a seedless variety with 5 to 30 percent THC, was available in only about one-third of the reporting areas. *Hydroponic* marijuana ("hydro") can be even more potent than sinsemilla and is available in most metropolitan areas. In 2009, prices of commercial-grade marijuana varied from $700–$1000 per pound in Birmingham, Alabama, to as little as $250–$450 per pound in San Diego, California (Narcotic News, 2010).

Narcotics.   Opium, morphine, codeine, and heroin are the major drugs included in the category of narcotics. They are derived from the variety of poppy known as *papaver somniferum*. Under federal law, cocaine is classified as a narcotic, but it is actually a stimulant (see next section). Narcotics have the effect of depressing the activity of the brain and the central nervous system.

The earliest reference to opium is a Sumerian idiogram dated about 4000 B.C., referring to it as "joy plant." Hippocrates and Pliny both recommended the use of opium for a number of conditions. Since it was not banned in Muslim countries, Arab traders carried it from the Middle East to India, China, and finally Europe. By the early sixteenth century, it was prescribed by physicians throughout Europe. By 1875, the British consumption rate for opium was 10 pounds per 1,000 population (McKim, 1991).

Before 1900, opium was available in the United States as an ingredient in a number of prescription drugs such as laudanum and "black drop." It was also available in a number of patent medicines. It had a relatively mild psychological effect when taken by mouth, and it was freely prescribed by physicians.

Morphine, an opiate, was found to be an exceptionally effective painkiller, and it came into common medical usage during and after the Civil War. The importation of opium continued to rise

and finally peaked in 1896. Smoking opium, which had no medicinal value, was banned in the United States in 1909 (Musto, 1973). The Harrison Act made it illegal for physicians to prescribe morphine and opium to addicts in 1914 and made addiction to opiates a crime. Heroin, which had not been discovered until 1898, soon became a substitute for morphine users. This loophole was closed when Congress finally banned all opiate use, including heroin, in 1924 (McKim, 1991). Heroin addiction continued to climb, however, until 23 of every 10,000 Americans were addicted in 1978 (Wilkner, 1980). In 2007, about 153,000 persons identified themselves as current heroin users (SAMHSA, 2008b).

Both morphine and opium addiction have at times posed serious problems in the United States, but today, heroin is regarded as the most dangerous of all existing narcotics. Heroin can be smoked, snorted, injected under the skin ("skin-popping"), or injected directly into a vein ("mainlining"). In the mainlining case, there is an imminent danger of overdosing or contracting the human immunodeficiency virus (HIV) from the use of dirty needles (DesJarlais & Friedman, 1988).

Heroin use has long been associated with deviant groups such as criminals, prostitutes, jazz and rock musicians, and poor African Americans living in the ghettos of large urban centers (Stewart, 1987). However, many veterans of the war in Vietnam returned home addicted to heroin (Krivanek, 1988b).

One of the most controversial opioids today is OxyContin, a synthetic form of morphine. SAMSHA (2008b) reports, "in 2007, the number of new nonmedical users of OxyContin aged 12 and older was 554,000, with an average age at first use of 24.0 years among those aged 12 to 49" (p. 55).

Another psychotherapeutic drug among persons aged 12 and older is methamphetamine. SAMSHA (2008b) reports the number of recent new users aged 12 and older was 157,000 in 2007, with the average age being 19.1 years.

Inhalants.   SAMSHA (2008b) reported data on several types of inhalants. These include nitrous oxide, amyl nitrite, cleaning fluids, gasoline, spray paint and other aerosol sprays, and glue. SAMSHA (2008) reports that in 2007 there were 775,000 individuals aged 12 or older who had used inhalants for the first time within the past 12 months. Almost 12 percent of all males had used inhalants during their lifetime (See Table 1.2). In 2007, 10.7 percent of persons aged 12 or older reported using inhalants as their "first" drug. The average age of first use of inhalants in 2007 was 17.1 years (SAMSHA, 2008b).

Stimulants.   Results of a 2007 NIDA survey showed that 1.1 million individuals aged 12 or older were current users of stimulants (SAMHSA, 2008b). One of the most popular is cocaine, which made its way into the United States from Latin America, but with a very different history from that of marijuana. Coca leaves have been found in burial middens in Peru that date back to 2500 B.C. Under the Incas, coca became sacred and was used primarily by priests and nobility for special ceremonies. Widespread daily use of the coca leaf did not appear until the Spanish conquest, when it was used to pay for labor in the gold and silver mines in the Andes. The Spanish soon discovered that the Indians could work harder and longer and required less food if they were given coca (McKim, 1991).

Samples of the plant were sent to Europe in 1749, but the anesthetic effects of cocaine were not discovered until 1862. By 1884, it was in widespread use as a local anesthetic for the eye. In 1885, Sigmund Freud delivered a lecture based on his observations of the effects of cocaine on mood and behavior (Imlah, 1989). The use of cocaine was a common theme in the literature of the day, with such popular heroes as Arthur Conan Doyle's Sherlock Holmes favoring a "seven percent solution." (Holmes once mysteriously disappeared for three years and returned to his Baker Street residence cured of his cocaine addiction.)

In addition to its legitimate medical uses, cocaine was an ingredient in patent medicines and beverages such as Coca-Cola until the passage of the Harrison Tax Act of 1914. Coca-Cola now uses only the decocainized coca leaves as a flavoring agent (Cohen, 1981).

The rediscovery and reintroduction of cocaine to modern American culture is sometimes attributed to the rock musicians of the 1960s. Until recent years, the form of cocaine generally available for illicit use in the United States was the white, bitter-tasting, crystalline powder of cocaine hydrochloride. It could be smoked or injected but was most commonly *snorted* (i.e., ingested intranasally). More recently, another more dangerous form of cocaine, called *crack*, has come into use. It is made by cooking the powder with baking soda to remove its impurities. The resulting product is smoked and provides a much more rapid and intense "high" (Imlah, 1989). Unfortunately, most statistics on cocaine use have only recently distinguished cocaine powder from crack cocaine. However, in 2007, some 2.1 million Americans reported having used cocaine, and 610,000 were reported crack users (SAMHSA, 2008b).

In general, amphetamines have an effect similar to cocaine but with a slower and less dramatic action. An amphetamine is a synthetic stimulant synthesized in 1927 as a replacement for ephedrine, a common ingredient in asthma, cold, and hay-fever remedies. Drinamyl, for many years the most widely prescribed drug for symptoms of anxiety and depression, was a combination of amphetamine and barbiturates. Amphetamines were widely used in World War II for keeping the troops alert and overcoming fatigue. During the 1960s, many people unknowingly became addicted to a Benzedrine inhaler sold without a prescription for the treatment of colds, allergies, and sinusitis. Until new rules were adopted by the Food and Drug Administration in 1970, many others became addicted while using amphetamine-based diet pills (Imlah, 1989). Amphetamines were also widely used in the 1960s and 1970s in both amateur and professional sports. One report in 1978 revealed that 75 of 87 professional football players interviewed admitted using *speed*, a common name for amphetamines (Cooter, 1988, pp. 37–40).

Ice, a particularly strong and dangerous form of amphetamine, appeared in Hawaii and California in the early 1990s and rapidly spread to other parts of the country. Although the data are largely anecdotal at this point, ice seems to be responsible for an alarmingly high number of hospital emergency room admissions (Lerner, 1989, pp. 37–40). No separate national statistics of use are kept for this particular drug.

The most commonly used stimulant, caffeine, is found in coffee, tea, and certain soft drinks. Although withdrawal effects are not uncommon, caffeine does not ordinarily present a threat to health or impairment to functioning. For this reason, we will not devote much space to it in this text.

Methylphenidate (Ritalin) is still widely sought after by narcotic addicts who are maintained on methadone injections, since methadone has no antagonist effect on amphetamines. Ritalin is a drug commonly prescribed to control attention-deficit/hyperactivity disorder [ADHD] in children. Since 2001, the NIDA has assessed the extent of drug use among 8th through 12th graders each year in their *Monitoring the Future* (MTF) survey. For amphetamines and methylphenidate, the survey measures only past-year use, however (NIDA, 2009b, p. 2). Nonmedical use of stimulants in this age range has been falling since 2001, with the total declines between 25 percent and 42 percent at each grade level surveyed (NIDA, 2009b, p. 3). NIDA (2009b) further states that "the MTF data for 2008 indicate past-year nonmedical use of Ritalin by 1.6 percent of 8th graders, 2.9 percent of 10th graders, and 3.4 percent of 12th graders" (p. 3). The MTF data also indicate that amphetamine use peaked in the mid-1990's, then fell by one-half among 8th graders to 4.5 percent and by nearly one-half among 10th graders to 6.4 percent in 2008 (NIDA, 2009b, p. 3). Further, amphetamine use peaked later among 12th graders and fell by more than

one-third to 6.8 percent by 2008 (NIDA, 2009b, p. 3). It is also interesting to note that when asked, "What amphetamines have you taken during the LAST year without a doctor's order?" 2.8 percent of all 12th graders survey in 2007 reported they had used Adderall (NIDA, 2009b, p. 3).

Steroids.   Anabolic-androgenic steroids (AAS) are "synthetically produced variants of the naturally occurring male sex hormone testosterone" (NIDA, 2009a, p. 1). NIDA (2009a) explains that "'anabolic' refers to muscle-building, and 'androgenic' refers to increased male sexual characteristics" (p. 1). While these drugs can be legally prescribed to treat various conditions, they are also being abused to enhance performance and/or improve physical appearance (NIDA, 2009a). NIDA's annual Monitoring the Future (MTF) survey, among 8th, 10th, and 12thgraders, has shown that while steroid use has remained stable among all grades from 2007 to 2008, there has been a significant reduction in rates since 2001 (NIDA, 2009a). In 2008, the past-year use was the same for both 8th and 10th graders (0.9%) and was 1.5 percent for 12th graders (NIDA, 2009a). NIDA (2009a) also reports, "males consistently reported higher rates of use than females: for example, in 2008, 2.5 percent of 12th grade males, versus 0.6 percent of 12th grade females, reported past-year use" (p. 3) (see Table 1.1).

Rates of Illicit Drug Use.   There were no substantial changes in the rates of use in the major illicit drug categories between the 2007 (8.0 percent) and the 2006 (8.3 percent) NSDUH surveys, and it has remained stable since 2002 (8.3 percent). The use of new so-called *club drugs* has continued to grow, however. About 12.4 million persons have now tried ecstasy at least once in their lifetime, with 2.1 million reported users in the past year (SAMHSA, 2008b).

Data analogous to those for rates of heavy drinking and binge drinking are not collected for illicit drugs, but there are other ways to estimate the extent of problematic drug use. As mentioned earlier in this chapter, U.S. hospitals reported 958,164 drug-related emergency department episodes in 2006 in which illegal drugs were involved and 741,425 emergency room visits involving "nonmedical use of prescription or OTC pharmaceuticals or dietary supplements" (SAMHSA, 2008a, p. 9). Cocaine is the most frequently mentioned illicit drug in emergency room visits (548,608) with marijuana second (290,563), and heroin third (189,780). Stimulants, including amphetamines and methamphetamine, were involved in 107,575 emergency room visits (SAMSHA, 2008a).

Age. As with alcohol use, the rate of illicit drug use increases with age, peaking in the 18- to 20-year-old age group (21.6 percent) and then declining to around 0.7 percent for adults aged 65 and older (SAMHSA, 2008b). In 2007, use by youths aged 12 or 13 was 3.3 percent compared to those ages 14 or 15 (8.9 percent) and ages 16 or 17 (16.0 percent) (SAMHSA, 2008b). The rate of illicit drug use among 12 to 17 year olds decreased from 11.6 to 9.5 percent between 2002 to 2007 (SAMHSA, 2008b). The drugs favored by 16- and 17-year-old youths were marijuana (13.1 percent), prescription-type drugs used nonmedically (4.9 percent), hallucinogens (1.2 percent), inhalants (1.0 percent), and cocaine (0.9 percent) (SAMHSA, 2008b).

Club drugs—including methylenedioxymethamphetamine (MDMA or ecstasy), gamma hydroxybutyrate (GHB), ketamine ("Special K"), and phencyclidine (PCP)—seem to be favored by teenagers and young adults, but until recently there were few reliable national statistics on their usage, other than hospital emergency department reports. According to the Community Epidemiology Work Group in 2001, ecstasy use increased in 13 of its 21 reporting communities and GHB use has increased in 9 areas and decreased in 1. In 2008, Ketamine use was reported by 1.5 percent of 12th graders (see Table 1.1), but current usage rates for other club drugs were not available. According to the ONDCP (2001), ecstasy was seen as the most

available club drug, with more than 90 percent of respondents indicating that it was either "somewhat" or "widely" available. Ecstasy prices ranged from $10 to $40 per pill (purity unknown). Cities in the west and the south reported both GHB and Rohypnol as being widely available.

The same ONDCP report stated that about half of all illicit drug users (49 percent) in 2000 were under the age of 26, but 83 percent of all hallucinogen users and 62 percent of inhalant users were under age 26. Club drug users tended to be adolescents and young adults, mostly white, and generally from urban and suburban areas. These drugs were most commonly used at "raves," nightclubs, private parties, and outdoor concerts (ONDCP, 2001). Older illicit drug users (aged 26 and over) favored marijuana, psychotherapeutics, and cocaine, rather than hallucinogens and inhalants (SAMHSA, 2001).

In 2006, SAMHSA decided to include questions about the following drugs: GHB, Adderall, Ambien, OTC cough and cold medicines, ketamine, dimethyltrypatamine (DMT), alpha-methyltryptamine (AMT), 5-methoxydiisopropyltryptamine (5-MeO-DIPT, or "Foxy"), and Salvia divinorum (SAMHSA, 2008b). This was a result of an increase mentioning of these drugs (except for GHB) dating back to the 1999 survey (SAMHSA, 2008b).

Gender. Men (10.4 percent) reported a higher rate of illicit drug use than women (5.8 percent) in 2007 (SAMHSA, 2008b). However, in the 12- to 17-year-old age group, females (3.5 percent) were more likely than men (3.0 percent) to use psychotherapeutic drugs. On the other hand, boys (7.5 percent) in this age group were more likely than girls (5.8 percent) to use marijuana. Among women of childbearing age (15 to 44 years), 5.2 percent reported using illicit drugs in the previous 30 days, based on combined 2006 and 2007 NSDUH data (SAMHSA, 2008b) (See Table 1.2).

Race/Ethnicity. Current illicit drug use was highest among American Indians or Alaska

Natives (12.6 percent), followed by persons re-
porting two or more races (11.8 percent), African
Americans (9.5 percent), whites (8.2 percent),
Hispanic Americans (6.6 percent), and Asian
Americans (4.7 percent) (SAMHSA, 2008b)(see
Tables 1.4 and 1.5).

Education.   The rate of reported illicit drug use
in the 2007 NSDUH was lower in the college-age
population (aged 18 to 22 years) for those who
were full-time students (19.8 percent) than those
who were not (22.8 percent). Those who were
not full-time included part-time, students in other
grades, and nonstudents (SAMHSA, 2008b). Although adults who were college graduates were
more likely to report having used illicit drugs during their lifetime (51.8 percent) than adults who
had not completed high school (36.0 percent), the
college graduates had a lower rate of current use
(5.1 percent compared to 9.3 percent) (SAMHSA,
2008b) (see Table 1.3).

Geographic Area.   In 2007, current illicit drug
use was highest in the west (9.3 percent), followed
by the midwest (7.9 percent), the northeast (7.8
percent), and the south (7.4 percent) (SAMHSA,
2008b). It was also highest in large metropolitan
counties (8.3 percent), followed by small metropolitan counties (8.2 percent), and nonmetropolitan counties as a group (6.7 percent). Within the
non metropolitan areas, the rate was highest in
urbanized counties (7.5 percent) followed by less
urbanized counties (6.7 percent) and completely
rural counties (4.1 percent) (SAMHSA, 2008b).

Tobacco

The only known natural source of nicotine is tobacco, a plant cultivated in temperate climates all
over the world. The origin of *nicotiana tabacum* is
America, and it is thought that the first and only
users of the drug at the time of the European discovery of the New World were the aboriginal peoples of North and South America. A stone carving
in an ancient Mayan temple depicts a priest

smoking what appears to be a cigar. Christopher
Columbus was greeted at San Salvador in 1492
with a gift of dried tobacco leaves.

Native Americans smoked or chewed the tobacco leaf. The practice of smoking soon spread
to Europe (along with "snuffing"), but chewing
was confined largely to America. Early proponents
of tobacco use hailed its medicinal qualities, but
almost from the beginning, there were vigorous
antismoking movements. The Roman Catholic
Church forbade smoking in churches on pain
of excommunication; Muslim countries defined
tobacco as an intoxicant and held that its use
was contrary to the Koran; Dr. Benjamin Rush,
founder of the Temperance Union, claimed that
the use of tobacco created a desire for "strong
drink" (McKim, 1991).

Early smoking was practiced by burning
the tobacco in pipes or reeds or by wrapping it in
the form of a cigar. The discovery of a low-nicotine,
sweet flue-cured tobacco in North Carolina in the
mid-nineteenth century led to the popularity of cigarette smoking. By the 1880s, machines were mass
producing millions of cigarettes a day. More than
100 years later, cigarettes still constitute the bulk
of tobacco usage throughout the world (Brooks,
1952).

Most textbooks of this type do not deal with
tobacco as an addictive substance. We think it
deserves special attention for two compelling reasons. First, it is the second most commonly used
legal drug, with about 70.9 million Americans
reporting current use of a tobacco product in the
2007 NSDUH study, representing 28.6 percent
of the population aged 12 or older (SAMHSA,
2008b). SAMHSA (2008b) states, "In addition,
60.1 million persons (24.2 percent of the population) were current cigarette smokers; 13.3 million
(5.4 percent) smoked cigars; 8.1 million (3.2 percent) used smokeless tobacco; and 2.0 million (0.8
percent) smoked tobacco in pipes" (p. 41). Second,
as we mentioned earlier, about 443,000 Americans die annually from tobacco-related illnesses,
making tobacco use the nation's leading cause of
death (CDCP, 2008).

Age. As with the use of alcohol and other drugs, the rate of cigarette use increases with age, peaks in the 18- to 25-year-old group, and then generally declines. Between 2006 and 2007, cigarette use declined among the young adult age group (from 38.4 to 36.2 percent). However, the rate of cigar use in the same category (young adults) was higher in 2007 (11.8 percent) than in 2002 (11.0 percent) (SAMHSA, 2008b). The use of smokeless tobacco was higher (2.4 percent) in 2007 than it was in 2002 (2.0 percent) for users aged 12 to 17 years. The rates of past month cigarette use declined in the 12- to 17-year-olds from 2002 to 2007 (13.0 and 9.8 percent, respectively) (SAMHSA, 2008b).

Gender. Reported tobacco use was higher for males (35.2 percent) than for females (22.4), but among the 12- to 17-year-old group, there was no significant difference between the males and females (10.7 vs. 9.7 percent). Between 2006 and 2007 the rates declined for females but remained unchanged for males (SAMHSA, 2008b). Also interesting to note, "from 2002 to 2007, the rate of current cigarette smoking among youths decreased for both males (from 12.3 to 10.0 percent) and females (from 13.6 to 9.7 percent)" (SAMHSA, 2008b, p. 44). Males were approximately 16 times more likely than females to use smokeless tobacco and five times more likely to smoke cigars. Women of childbearing age (15 to 44 years), who were pregnant, smoked less (16.4 percent) than women of the same age who were not pregnant (28.4 percent) (SAMHSA, 2008b).

Race/Ethnicity. The highest rate of tobacco use (all forms) reported in 2007 was by American Indians or Alaska Natives (41.8 percent) followed by persons who reported two or more races (35.2 percent), whites (30.7 percent), blacks (26.8 percent), Hispanics (22.7 percent), and Asians (15.4 percent) (SAMHSA, 2008b). Also interesting to note is that cigarette smoking was more prevalent among whites than blacks in both the 12- to 17-year-olds (12.2 vs. 6.1 percent) and

18- to 25-year-olds (40.8 vs. 26. 2 percent), but not the 26 or older group (24.8 and 25.7 percent, respectively) (SAMHSA, 2008b).

Education. In 2007, young adults (18 to 22 years) enrolled full time in college reported less cigarette use (25.6 percent) than others in this age group (41.2 percent). Level of education is negatively correlated with cigarette smoking. Persons who lacked a high school diploma reported a rate of 32.9 percent; high school graduates who did not attend college, 31.9 percent; some college, 26.8 percent; and college graduates, 14.0 percent (SAMHSA, 2008b).

Geographic Area. There is less variation in cigarette use by region than for alcohol use and other drug use. In 2008, reported cigarette use ranged from 21.1 percent in the west to 27.2 percent in the midwest. Rates of smoking also tended to be higher in less densely populated areas. In large metropolitan areas, 22.7 percent reported having smoked in the previous 30 days, while 23.6 of those in rural areas had smoked (SAMHSA, 2008b).

Frequency of Use. SAMHSA (2008b) reports that among the 60.1 million current cigarette smokers aged 12 or older in 2007, 36.8 million (61.3 percent) used cigarettes daily (p. 18). This percentage increased with age, ranging from 26.3 percent for users aged 12 to 17 to 66.3 percent for users aged 26 or older. Furthermore, over half (50.9 percent) of daily smokers aged 12 or older reported smoking approximately one pack a day (i.e., 16 or more cigarettes).

Polydrug Use/Comorbidity

According to the 2007 NSDUH study, the rate of current illicit drug use for both adults and youths was higher among those who were currently using cigarettes or alcohol, compared with persons not using cigarettes or alcohol. While only 4.1 percent of nonsmokers aged 12 to 17 reported current use of illicit drugs, the rate of illicit drug use for smokers in this age group was 20.1 percent. Also, past-month alcohol use was reported by 66.9 percent of current cigarette smokers, compared with 46.1 percent of those who did not use cigarettes in the past month (SAMHSA, 2008, p. 48).

Not only is it becoming increasingly unusual for a person to use (or abuse) only one substance, it is also common for both mental health and substance disorders to co-occur. Sheehan (1993) states that dual diagnosis, or *comorbidity*, is said to exist "when a patient is suffering with more than one disease. Psychiatry and the addictive medicines refer to the co-existence of a psychoactive chemical use disorder with another major psychiatric disorder" (p. 108). Two comprehensive studies have considered the prevalence of dual diagnoses: the Epidemiologic Catchment Area (ECA) study, which began in 1978, and the National Comorbidity Survey (NCS), which was conducted between 1990 and 1992. According to the ECA study, having a mental disorder more than doubles a person's chances of having an alcohol diagnosis and increases his or her chances of a drug abuse diagnosis by more than four times (Regier et al., 1990). The NCS revealed rates of substance abuse and dependence exceeding 50 percent among those with both affective and anxiety disorders (Kessler et al., 1994). Chapter 13 presents a more thorough discussion of comorbidity.

Summary

The most widely used drugs in the United States are legal drugs. Tobacco and alcohol are by far the most popular drugs among both genders and all races and ethnic groups. Marijuana is the most popular illicit drug, preferred by about three-fourths of all illicit drug users. Recent surveys indicate that tobacco use continues to slowly decline, while consumption of alcohol remains relatively stable.

The first national survey to estimate the incidence of illicit drug use was conducted in 1971, but estimates of drug use based on retrospective reports indicate that an upward trend began in the mid 1960s (Gfroerer & Brodsky, 1992). Annual marijuana use increased from about 553,000 new users in 1965 to a peak of around 3.2 million new users in 1976 and 1977. Total illicit drug use peaked in 1979, at about 25 million users (SAMHSA, 2000). Illicit drug use among youths doubled between 1992 and 1995, declined in 1997 and 1998, and has held relatively stable since then (SAMHSA, 2001 and 2008b). Club drugs and steroids continue to be popular among younger users, although the usage rates of any single club drug are highly variable from year to year, with newer "designer" drugs displacing many of the older drugs.

CHAPTER 2

The Etiology of Addiction

Almost everyone has an easy answer to the question: Why do people use drugs? According to Stewart (1987), heroin addicts use "junk" the first time because they are curious. Heroin has a mystique. It is used by pop stars, writers, and glamorous people, and they like its effect. For those who find daily life to be fairly humdrum, heroin can be the ultimate filler of gaps—it can substitute for career, religion, romance, or virtually anything else. Weil and Rosen (1993) believe that drug use (and addiction) results from humans' longing for a sense of completeness and wholeness, and searching for satisfaction outside of themselves. As noted author (and addict) William S. Burroughs (1977) indicated in *Junky,* "Junk wins by default. I tried it as a matter of curiosity. I drifted along taking shots when I could score. I ended up hooked" (p. xv). This notion of *drift* is a recurrent theme in theories of addiction.

People begin using cocaine for some of the same reasons. According to Baum (1985), his clients provided these excuses for using cocaine:

> "The mystical reputation aroused my curiosity." . . .

> "It's available and being offered all the time." . . .

> "It gave me a sense of well-being, like I was worth something." . . .

> "It felt good to be a part of a group." . . .

> "It was a great way to escape." (pp. 25–42)

The reasons why people continue to use drugs to the point of becoming physically and/or psychologically dependent on them are more complex. Some have attempted to explain this phenomenon as a deficit in moral values, a disease, conditioning or learned behavior, or as a genetic propensity. Still others see it as a "rewiring" of the brain (see Chapter 3). At this point, there is no one single theory that adequately explains addiction.

Jacobs (1986) attempted to develop a general theory of addiction, drawing on his experience and research with gamblers. In his view, addiction is a dependent state acquired over time to relieve stress. Two interrelated sets of factors are required to predispose persons to addiction: an abnormal physiological resting state, and childhood experiences producing a deep sense of inadequacy. He argues that all addictions (drugs, sex, alcohol, etc.) follow a similar three-stage course of development.

Most models of addiction assume that an addiction is an "addictive disease" (Washton, 1989, p. 55). As such, it continues to exist whether or not the addicted person continues to use the drug. Even if a person who has the disease is abstinent for a long period of time, the symptoms of addiction will appear again from renewed contact with the drug. The disease model of addiction rests on three primary assumptions: predisposition to use a drug, loss of control over use, and progression (Krivanek, 1988, p. 202). Johnson (1973) put it somewhat differently in saying, "The most significant characteristics of the disease [*alcoholism*] are that it is primary, progressive, chronic, and fatal" (p. 1). There are others, such as Peele (1985), who question the validity of this model. Speaking of the complex nature of addiction, he rejects all strictly biological explanations and says that addiction cannot be resolved biologically because "lived human experience and its interpretation are central to the incidence, course, treatment, and remission of addiction (see Preface)." An adequate theory would have to synthesize pharmacological, experiential, cultural, situational, and personality components.

Drummond (2001) provides an interesting perspective on theories of drug craving, most of which can be classified into three categories: (1) *phenomenological models,* which are based on clinical observation and description; (2) *conditioning* or *cue-reactivity models,* which are useful in the exploration of craving and relapse; and (3) *cognitive models,* which are based on social learning theory. He concludes that no one theory provides an adequate explanation of the phenomenon of craving. *Addiction, drug dependence,* and *craving* are all terms used to identify the phenomenon of loss of control over drug-taking behavior, although each has a slightly different meaning.

Etiological Theories

Addiction is not easily defined. For some, it involves the "continued, self-administered use of a substance despite substance-related problems, and it results in tolerance for the substance, withdrawal from the substance, and compulsive drug-taking behavior due to cravings" or drives to use the substance (Schuckit, 1992, p. 182). However, the American Psychiatric Association's criteria for dependence do not require that tolerance or withdrawal be present (see Chapter 5).

There are at least as many explanatory theories of addiction as there are definitions. We will focus on three broad theoretical categories—psychological theories, biological theories, and sociocultural theories—as well as discuss some alternative explanations. These theories are not mutually exclusive, and divisions sometimes seem quite arbitrary. None is presented as the correct way of explaining this phenomenon. We do have preferences, and we lean more toward

certain models than others, but no single theory adequately describes the etiology of addiction or dependence. (For a more comprehensive treatment of etiology, see Ott, Tarter, and Ammerman [1999].) As social workers, it seems fitting to suggest that the "person-in-environment" model may ultimately provide the best mechanism for an understanding of addiction. We will return to this perspective at the end of the chapter.

The Moral Model

One of the earliest theories offered to explain the etiology of addiction is humankind's sinful nature. Since it is difficult to show empirical evidence of a sinful nature, the *moral model* of addiction has been generally discredited by modern scholars. However, the legacy of treating alcoholism and drug addiction as sin or moral weakness continues to influence public policies regarding alcohol and drug abuse. Perhaps this is why needle/syringe exchange programs have been so strongly opposed in the United States.

Psychological Theories

Another explanation for the origins of craving alcohol and mind-altering drugs lies in the psychological literature—that is, the literature that deals with one's mind and emotions. Psychological models define *addiction* as an individual phenomenon but do not necessarily exclude or minimize social factors or other elements in the development of an addiction. There are actually several different psychological theories of alcoholism and drug addiction; they include cognitive-behavioral, learning, psychodynamic, and personality theories, among others.

Cognitive-Behavioral Theories.   The cognitive-behavioral theories offer a variety of motivations for taking drugs. One such explanation states that humans take drugs to experience variety (Weil & Rosen, 1993). The need for variety is demonstrated in cross-cultural expressions such as singing, dancing, running, and joking. Drug use is associated with a variety of activities—for example, religious services, self-exploration, altering moods, escaping boredom or despair, enhancing social interaction, enhancing sensory experience or pleasure, and stimulating creativity and performance. A study on inner-city youths revealed that youths are motivated to take drugs out of a desire for variety, citing curiosity, celebration, getting high, and rebelling as reasons for drug use. (In the study, the youths celebrate or explore drugs by using alcohol at home, whereas they choose to use illegal marijuana away from the home [Esbensen & Huizinga, 1990].) Assuming that people enjoy variety, it follows that they repeat actions that bring pleasure (positive reinforcement).

The desire to experience pleasure is another cognitive explanation for drug use and abuse. Some animals seek alcohol and even work for it (by pushing a lever) to repeat a pleasant experience. Alcohol and other drugs are *chemical surrogates* of natural reinforcers such as eating, drinking, and reproductive behavior. Social drinkers and alcoholics both report using alcohol to relax, even though tests of actual tension-reducing effects of alcohol have yielded quite different results; scientific observations of persons using alcohol actually show them to become more depressed, anxious, and nervous (NIAAA, 1996). The dependent behavior is maintained by the degree of reinforcement the alcohol provides, and this, in turn, depends on the actor's perception of his or her need hierarchy and "the likelihood that this course of action will meet the most important needs better than other available options" (Krivanek, 1989, p. 96). Since alcohol and drugs are more powerful and persistent than natural reinforcers to which the human brain is accustomed, they set the stage for addiction.

With time, the brain adapts to the presence of the drug or alcohol. The removal of the substance from the host reveals certain abnormalities experienced by the brain. The host experiences unpleasant withdrawal symptoms, such as anxiety, agitation, tremors, increased blood pressure, and in severe cases, seizures. Naturally, one wants to avoid painful stimuli; by consuming the substance anew, an individual can avoid the unpleasant symptoms of withdrawal. Repetitive action motivated by the avoidance of unpleasant stimuli is called *negative reinforcement.* (In an alcoholic, the need to avoid withdrawal symptoms generally occurs from 6 to 48 hours after the last drink.) Another source of negative reinforcement may lie in the avoidance of unpleasant things other than withdrawal. There is a high correlation between traumatic events and subsequent substance abuse (Janoff-Bulman, 1992). The traumatized individual may take drugs to avoid unpleasant memories or heightened physiological states such as startle responses.

Learning Theory.   Closely related to cognitive-behavioral theories is learning, or reinforcement, theory. Learning theory assumes that alcohol or drug use results in a decrease in psychological states such as anxiety, stress, and tension, thus positively reinforcing the user. This learned response continues until physical dependence develops, at which time the aversion of withdrawal symptoms becomes a prime motivation for drug use (Tarter & Schneider, 1976).

There is a considerable amount of evidence to support that part of learning theory related to alcohol use and physiological aversion. Abrupt cessation of drinking will lead to unpleasant symptoms of withdrawal (A & DRCC, 1995). For the alcoholic, withdrawal can lead to trembling, shaking, hallucinations, and tonic-clonic seizures, formerly known as grand mal seizures. Similarly, for the heroin addict, abrupt withdrawal may lead to symptoms much like a case of severe flu. In each case, the addict quickly learns that these symptoms may be avoided by resuming use of the drug.

An interesting view of becoming a heroin addict is provided by Krivanek (1989). Dependencies that involve drug use follow the same basic principles of learning theory, as all other dependencies. Krivanek views drug dependence as a psychological phenomenon that can vary in intensity from a mild involvement to an addiction that seriously restricts the user's other behaviors. Pattison, Sobell, and Sobell (1977) view alcoholism as a continuum. That is, "An individual's use of alcohol can be considered as a point on a continuum from nonuse, to nonproblem drinking, to various degrees of deleterious drinking" (p. 191).

Learning theory is helpful in treatment planning because it addresses the adaptive consequences of drinking. (For a more extensive discussion of adaptation and addiction, see Peele [1998].) Also, behavioral treatments have incorporated learning theory into a treatment framework based on the premise that what has been learned can be unlearned (Bandura, 1969). It follows that intervening early is important, since there will be fewer behaviors to unlearn. Learning theory is also quite adaptable to the systems view, which is followed throughout this book.

Psychodynamic Theories. Psychodynamic theories are more difficult to substantiate than most other psychological theories because they deal with hard to operationalize concepts and with events that may have occurred many years before the onset of addiction. Although Dr. Sigmund Freud never devoted a single paper to the subject of alcoholism, his disciples were not the least bit reluctant to apply psychoanalytic theories to alcohol addiction. The earliest explanations linked alcoholism with the "primal addiction" of masturbation (Bonaparte, Freud, & Kris, 1954). Later, most explanations linked alcoholism to ego deficiencies, suggesting that alcohol is used to attain a sense of security. This theory assumes that during childhood, inadequate parenting, along with the child's individual constitution, caused the child to form weak attachments to significant others, resulting in a need to compensate for or dull the insecurity. This is accomplished in the consumption of alcoholic beverages (Chordokoff, 1964). Alcohol abuse has also been explained by psychoanalytic theorists as an expression of hostility and of homosexuality. Still others view alcoholics as self-destructive, narcissistic, or orally fixated (Schuckit, 1986). Psychoanalytic theory has even blamed the development of alcoholism on the failure of mothers to provide milk (Menninger, 1963).

A major problem with psychoanalytic theories is that experiences such as early childhood deprivation are not specific to alcoholism or addiction to other drugs. In fact, they are commonly reported by non-addicted adults with a variety of other psychological problems. Perhaps the most serious shortcoming is in the psychodynamic theories' implications for the treatment of alcoholism or drug addiction. Many counselors warn that a nondirective approach that focuses solely on the patients' development of insight into their problems neglects the addictive power of alcohol or other drugs (Cunynghame, 1983).

Nevertheless, there is a feeling among some scholars (Collins, Blaine, & Leonard, 1999) that psychodynamic approaches should not be dismissed because they serve "to guide a substantial portion of clinical practice" (p. 162). Even though the empirical support of psychodynamic theory is scanty, it has shown a remarkable resiliency and the ability to capture the imagination of practitioners.

Personality Theories. Personality theories, which frequently overlap the psychodynamic theories, assume that certain personality traits predispose an individual to drug use. An individual with a so-called alcoholic personality is often described as dependent, immature, and impulsive (Schuckit, 1986). Other personality theorists have described alcoholics as highly emotional, immature in interpersonal relationships, having low frustration tolerance, being unable to express anger adequately, and confused in their sex-role orientation (Catanzaro, 1967). After reviewing these personality theories, Keller (1972) summarized them in *Keller's law*: The investigation of any trait in alcoholics will show that they have either more or less of it. However, the many scales that have been developed in an attempt to identify alcoholic personalities have failed to distinguish consistently the personality traits of alcoholics from those of non-alcoholics. One of the subscales of the Minnesota Multiphasic Personality Inventory (MMPI) does differentiate alcoholics from the general population, but it may actually detect only the results of years of alcohol abuse, not underlying personality problems (MacAndrew, 1979).

There is some evidence that individuals with an antisocial personality (as defined in the *DSM-IV*, APA, 1994) have a higher incidence of alcoholism than the general population. There is no evidence that this personality disorder caused the alcoholism, but these individuals were more disposed to develop alcohol problems because of their antisocial personality. Apart from this relatively rare occurrence of the antisocial personality, alcoholics have not been found to exhibit a specific cluster of personality traits (Sherfey, 1955). Vaillant (1994) argues persuasively that personality (as well as psychological) factors are, at most, of minimal consequence as a cause of alcoholism. There have been similar attempts to link a constellation of certain personality traits to drug addiction as well as alcoholism (Gossop & Eysenck, 1980). A consensus seems to have evolved that personality traits are not of much importance in explaining drug dependence. In fact, most of those who work in this field agree that an individual can become dependent irrespective of personality attributes (Raistrick & Davidson, 1985). One book lists 94 personality characteristics that have been attributed to drug addicts by various theorists (Einstein, 1983). These include many characteristics that are polar opposites of one another—for example: poor self-image and grandiose self-image, ego inflation and ego contraction, self-centered and externalization, pleasure-seekers and pleasure avoiders, and several dozen other contradictory pairs.

A report to the National Academy of Sciences ("Addictive Personality," 1983) concludes that there is no single set of psychological *characteristics* that embraces all addictions. However, there are, according to the report, "significant personality *factors* that can contribute to addiction." These factors number 4 (not 94) and are as follows:

1. Impulsive behavior, difficulty in delaying gratification, an antisocial personality, and a disposition toward sensation seeking.
2. A high value on nonconformity combined with a weak commitment to the goals for achievement valued by the society.

3. A sense of social alienation and a general tolerance for deviance.
4. A sense of heightened stress. (This may help explain why adolescence and other stressful transition periods are often associated with severe drug and alcohol problems.) (pp. 11, 15).

Research on personality theories of addiction seems to have waned during the 1990s, and there are few recent empirical studies that focus on this explanation for addiction.

Biological Theories

Biophysiological and genetic theories assume that addicts are constitutionally predisposed to develop a dependence on alcohol or drugs. These theories support a medical model of addiction. Their advocates apply disease terminology and generally place responsibility for the treatment of addicts in the hands of physicians, nurses, and other medical personnel. In reality, the medical model is generally practiced only during the detoxification phase.

Generally speaking, biological theories branch into one of two explanations: neurobiological and genetic. There has been such an explosion of knowledge in recent years in the neurobiology of addiction that we have devoted a separate chapter to it (see Chapter 3). But at this point, we will briefly review the research on genetics.

Genetic Theories.   Recent studies supported by the National Institute on Drug Abuse (NIDA, 2008) found that a variant in the gene for a nicotinic receptor subunit doubled the risk for nicotine addiction among smokers. This is the first evidence of a genetic variation influencing both the likelihood of nicotine addiction and an individual's risk for the severe health consequences of tobacco use. National Institute on Alcohol Abuse and Alcoholism (NIAAA) has funded the Collaborative Studies on Genetics of Alcoholism (COGA) since 1989, but specific genetic factors have never been established as a definite cause of alcoholism, although the statistical associations between genetic factors and alcohol abuse are very strong (NIAAA, 2009). A great volume of research has been amassed in this area over the last several decades, and much of the evidence points toward alcoholism as an inherited trait. It has been observed that (1) adopted children more closely resemble their biological parents than their adoptive parents in their use of alcohol (Goodwin, Hill, Powell, & Viamontes, 1973), (2) alcoholism occurs more frequently in some families than in others (Cotton, 1979), and (3) concurrent alcoholism rates are higher in monozygotic twin pairs (53.5 percent) than in dizygotic pairs (28.3 percent) (Kaij, 1960). Children of alcoholics are three to seven times more likely to be at risk of alcoholism (Koopmans & Boomsina, 1995). Having an alcoholic parent (but not necessarily both parents) can increase the risk of becoming an alcoholic. Yet even in the presence of elevated risks, only 33 percent sons and 15 percent daughters of alcoholics demonstrate evidence of the disorder.

Some genetic theorists speculate that an inherited metabolic defect may interact with environmental elements and eventually lead to alcoholism. This genetotrophic theory posits an impaired production of enzymes within the body (Williams, 1959). Others hypothesize that inherited genetic traits result in a deficiency of vitamins (usually of the vitamin B complex), which leads to a craving for alcohol as well as cellular or metabolic changes (Tarter & Schneider, 1976).

It is important to remember that, despite the impressive statistical relationships in these studies implying a genetic link, no specific genetic marker that predisposes a person toward alcoholism has ever been isolated. The first biological marker established for alcoholism was thought to be color blindness, but a few years later, it was demonstrated that color blindness was actually a result of severe alcohol abuse (Valera, Rivera, Mardones, & Cruz-Coke, 1969). Several other genetic discoveries have met a similar fate. A workshop on genetic and biological markers in drug and alcohol abuse suggests promising areas for genetic research, such as polymorphisms in gene products and DNA polymorphisms (Nichols, 1986). A more recent study reports that the so-called dopamine D2 receptor gene, which affects the capacity of cells to absorb dopamine, was present in 77 percent of the brains of alcoholics and only 28 percent of nonalcoholics (Blum et al., 1990).

In 1990, the front page of an edition of *The New York Times* hailed the discovery of a gene claimed to be directly linked to alcoholism. Two years later, this so-called alcoholism gene, formally known as the dopamine D2 receptor gene, had become the focus of a bitter controversy. Blum and Noble insisted that their finding had been amply documented by subsequent research, and they took steps to market a test for genetic susceptibility to alcoholism. Blum suggested that job applicants, children, and perhaps even fetuses could be tested.

In Blum and Noble's experiments, the D2 gene was shown to have at least two variants, or *alleles*, called A1 and A2. They found the A1 allele in the genetic material of 69 percent of the alcoholics studied, compared to only 20 percent of the controls. Blum and Noble theorized that A1 carriers may use alcohol or other drugs excessively to compensate for a reduced ability to absorb pleasure-inducing dopamine.

A study of 862 men and 913 women who had been adopted early in life by nonrelatives identified two types of alcoholism (Boham, Cloninger, von Knorring, & Sigvardsson, 1984). Type I, or milieu-limited, alcoholism is found in both sexes and is associated with alcoholism in either biological parent, but an environmental factor—low occupational status of the adoptive father—also had to be present as a condition for alcoholism to occur in the offspring. Type II, known as male-limited alcoholism, is more severe but accounts for fewer cases. It is found only in men, and it does not appear to be affected by environmental factors.

Vaillant (1983), however, points out the potential biases in the preceding study. He says that the study failed to control for the environmental effect of parental alcoholism. He continues by pointing out that antisocial personality disorder must be distinguished from alcohol dependence and that developmental effects of abusing individuals must be controlled. Furthermore, for his studies, Vaillant excludes individuals with other major psychiatric disorders that could, by themselves, directly contribute to alcohol dependence. Such cases (direct and uncomplicated cases) are estimated to represent 60 to 70 percent of the alcohol-dependent population (Schuckit, 1986).

The notion of Type I and Type II alcoholics hangs, in part, on the age of the onset of alcoholism. Vaillant (1983) found in a study of alcohol-abusing men in inner cities and in college that age of onset and degree of antisocial symptomatology correlated with disturbed family environments but was independent of positive or negative heredity for alcoholism. In other words, this negated the hypothesis that heredity predicts the age of onset. "Alcoholic abuse began 11 years earlier for the socially disadvantaged men with a heredity negative for alcoholism than for the college men with two or more alcoholic relatives." In other words, early-onset alcohol abusers in inner cities had no more alcoholic relatives than did late-onset alcohol abusers in college. Furthermore, inner-city men were 10 times as likely as the college men to come from multi-problem families, to exhibit traits of sociopathy, to have delinquent parents, and to have spent time in jail.

These findings lead one to ask: "How do biological factors interact with environment to contribute to heavy enough drinking over long enough periods of time to produce physical and psychological dependence?" (Schuckit, 1986). Vaillant (1983) suggests that rather than there being two kinds of alcoholism, there may be (1) genetic loading (predicting whether one develops alcoholism) and (2) an unstable childhood environment (predicting when one loses control of alcohol). (Late onset is less associated with dependence, substance-related problems, hyperactivity, and dysfunctional families in one's youth.)

Genetic research on addiction shows promise, but it is an incredibly complex activity. Even the most sanguine recent studies still use phrases such as "the gene that may influence alcoholism and addiction" (Science Daily, 2007). The Human Genome Project (HGP), supported by the National Institutes of Health and the U.S. Department of Energy, has been an important impetus in the search for genes related to alcohol behavior (NIAAA, 2000). The research was completed in 2003, but analysis of the data may take several additional years (HGP, 2008).

Sociocultural Theories

There is little high-quality research regarding the macrovariables that seek to explain addiction (Esbensen & Huizinga, 1990). Yet, as we mentioned earlier, almost every known culture has discovered the use of beverage alcohol. "All societies establish a quota of deviance necessary for boundary setting"; rules around alcohol and drug use are a part of boundary setting. The ways in which different societies encourage, permit, or regulate the use of alcohol varies considerably, however.

For the most part, sociocultural theories have been generated by observations of differences or similarities between cultural groups or subgroups. Sociocultural theorists are prone to attribute differences in drinking practices, problem drinking, and alcoholism to *environmental factors*. For example, socially disorganized communities often fail to realize the common values of their residents and to maintain effective social controls. Therefore, inner-city drug use is more rampant than in the suburbs.

We know that differential rates of alcohol use between genders vary greatly between nations (Bloomfield, Gmel, & Wilsnack, 2006). Unless greater biological differences occur between women, from country to country, or between men, from country to country (a remote possibility), it seems logical that culture is a strong influence on alcohol use.

According to Goode (1972), the social context of drug use strongly influences, perhaps even determines, "four central aspects of drug reality" (p. 3): drug definitions, drug effects, drug-related behavior, and the drug experience. The sociocultural perspective stands in direct opposition to what is called the *chemicalistic fallacy*—the view that drug A causes behavior X.

Because no object or event has meaning in the abstract, all these central aspects must be interpreted in light of social phenomena surrounding drug use. For example, morphine and heroin are not very different pharmacologically and biochemically. Yet heroin is regarded as a dangerous drug with no therapeutic value, whereas morphine is defined primarily as a medicine. Definitions are shaped by the social milieu surrounding the use of each substance.

People using morphine as an illegal street drug experience a "rush" or a "high" generally unknown to patients using the same drug in a hospital setting. Psychedelic drugs, such as peyote, which are taken for religious purposes (as in some Native American churches), do not typically result in religious or mystical experiences when taken simply to get high. Drugs, according to Goode (1972), only potentiate certain kinds of experiences; they do not produce them. It is important to distinguish between *drug effects* and the *drug experience*. Many changes may take place in the body when a chemical is ingested, not all of which are noted and classified by the user. A drug may have a more or less automatic effect of dilating the pupils, causing ataxia or amblyopia, and so on, but the experience is subject to the cognitive system of the user's mind. A person must be attuned to certain drug effects to interpret them, categorize them, and place them within appropriate experiential and conceptual realms (Goode, 1972). One's propensity to use drugs, the way one behaves when one uses drugs, and one's definitions of *abuse* and *addiction* are all influenced by one's sociocultural system. Why else would someone define heroin and LSD as dangerous drugs, yet almost never perceive social drinkers and smokers as drug users?

Supracultural Theories.   The pioneering work of Bales (1946) provides some general hypotheses regarding the relationships among culture, social organization, and the use of alcohol. He proposed that a culture that produces guilt, suppressed aggression, and sexual tension and that condones the use of alcohol to relieve those tensions is likely to have a high rate of alcoholism. Bales also believed that collective attitudes toward alcohol use dramatically influence rates of alcoholism. He classified these attitudes as favoring (1) abstinence, (2) ritual use connected with religious practices, (3) convivial drinking in a social setting, and (4) utilitarian drinking (drinking for personal, self-interested reasons). The utilitarian attitude, especially in a culture that induces much inner tension, is the most likely to lead to problem drinking, whereas the other three mitigate against alcohol problems.

Also important in Bales's (1946) theory is the degree to which a society offers alternatives to alcohol use for the release of tension and for providing a substitute means of satisfaction. A social system with a strong emphasis on upward economic or social mobility will excessively frustrate an individual who has no available means of achieving success. In such a system, high rates of alcohol use would be expected (Tarter & Schneider, 1976).

Unfortunately, few alternatives to alcohol or drugs seem to exist in most modern societies. In traditional societies, such as the hill tribes of Malaysia, a shaman may assist tribesmen in achieving a trancelike state in which endorphin levels are altered (Laderman, 1987). Also at the supracultural level, Bacon (1974) theorizes that alcoholism is likely to be a problem in a society that combines a lack of indulgence of children with demanding attitudes toward achievement and negative attitudes regarding dependent behavior in adults. Another important factor in sociocultural theories is the degree of societal consensus regarding alcohol use. In cultures in which there is little agreement regarding drinking limits and customs, a higher rate of alcoholism is expected (Trice, 1966). Cultural ambivalence regarding alcohol use results in weak social controls and allows the drinker to avoid being labeled as a deviant.

Culture-Specific Theories.   According to Room, in "wet" drinking cultures, alcohol is used almost daily, with few restrictions on availability. Conversely, although legal and social restrictions govern drinking in "dry" cultures, binge drinking and even violent drunken behavior may be seen as acceptable (2001). Levin (1989) describes two examples of cultural contrast in attitudes toward drinking: the contrast between French and Italian drinking practices and the contrast between Irish and Jewish drinking practices.

There are many similarities between the French and Italian cultures; both are heavily Catholic and both produce and consume large quantities of alcohol. The French, however, drink wine and spirits, both with meals and without, and both with and away from the family. The French do not strongly disapprove of drunkenness, and they consider it bad manners to refuse a drink. On the other hand, the Italians drink mostly with meals and mostly with family, and they usually drink wine. They strongly disapprove of drunkenness, and they do not pressure people into drinking. As one might expect, France has one of the highest rates of alcoholism in the world, whereas Italy's rate is only one-fifth as great. (In 1952, Italy had the second-highest rate of wine consumption in the world, consuming only half of the amount of wine consumed in France [Kinney & Leaton, 1987].) The strong sanctions against drunkenness and social control imposed by learning to drink low-proof alcoholic beverages in moderation seems to have something to do with the lower rate of Italian alcoholism.

In a fashion, studies of Irish and Jewish drinking practices draw some sharp contrasts. The Irish have high proportions of both abstainers and problem drinkers, whereas Jews have low proportions of both (Levin, 1989). The Irish drink largely outside the home in pubs; Jews drink largely in the home with the family and on ceremonial occasions. The Irish excuse drunkenness as "a good man's fault"; Jews condemn it as something culturally alien. Bales found Irish drinking to be largely convivial on the surface, but purely utilitarian drinking was a frequent and tolerated pattern. Jewish drinking, on the other hand, was mostly ceremonial. Again, it is no surprise that the Irish alcoholism rate is one of the highest in the world, and the Jewish rate is one of the lowest (Bales, 1946).

Subcultural Theories. There have been many investigations of sociological and environmental causes of alcoholism at the subcultural level. Within the same culture, a great diversity in alcoholism rates has been related to age, sex, ethnicity, socioeconomic class, religion, and family background (Bloomfield, Gmel & Wilsnack, 2006; Tarter & Schneider, 1976). One of the landmark studies of social variables at this level was conducted more than three decades ago by Calahan (1970). He specified that social environment determines to a large extent whether an individual will drink and that sociopsychological variables also determine the level of drinking. In becoming a problem drinker, variables such as age, sex, ethnicity, and social position influence the probability that a person will learn to drink as a dominant response. Labeling the person as a heavy drinker then reinforces the probability of that response.

Of course, these processes do not occur in isolation from other factors, such as the process of physical addiction. Goode (1984), Laurie (1971), Imlah (1971), and many others have examined the sociocultural context of drug addiction and found there to be many similarities to alcoholism. A major difference is in the outcast nature of certain illicit drug users such as heroin addicts. Users of illegal drugs such as heroin may be more socially isolated than alcoholics because of their addiction. Also, certain types of drug addiction seem to thrive within specific subcultures. Heroin addiction is a persistent problem among jazz musicians. Inner-city youths frequently "huff" spray paint or sniff glue. With three feet of hose and an empty can, Native American youths on certain reservations can easily get high on gasoline fumes.

The impact of gender on drug use presents an interesting perspective on sociocultural theories. Either a culture-specific or subcultural model can be used in explaining the differences between male and female drug-related behaviors in the United States. Historically, female drinking has been less accepted than male drinking in the United States, and being intoxicated is clearly more disapproved of for women than for men (Gomberg, 1986). Similar gender differences exist throughout the world (Bloomfield, Gmel, & Wilsnack, 2006). These double standards may account for the much lower rate of problem drinking noted among women. Social pressure and social stigma may result in less problem drinking by women as a subgroup of the larger U.S. culture.

Some aspects of this phenomenon may be culture specific, however. The fact that men seem to drink more and have more problems because of alcohol in some cultures and not in others fits into a supracultural model of drug use. The degree of female problem drinking appears to be related to cultural norms regarding the overall status of women within different societies. Bear in mind that the vast majority of the research on alcohol and drug abuse has been conducted on men only. Only recently have gender-related issues in this area begun to be systematically examined.

Alternative Explanations

Fingarette (1985) sees alcoholism as "neither sin nor disease." Instead, he views it as a lifestyle. According to Fingarette, proponents of the disease model describe alcoholism as a disease characterized by loss of control over drinking. Recovery is possible only if one voluntarily seeks and enters treatment and voluntarily abstains from drinking. Only then can one be cured. Cured from what? From a disease that makes voluntary abstention impossible and makes drinking uncontrollable! This, says Fingarette (1985), is an amazing contradiction.

His alternative explanation views the "persistent heavy drinking of the alcoholic as a central activity" of the individual's way of life. Each person develops his or her unique way of life, which consists of a number of central activities. Some will adopt parenting as a central activity, while others will place sex, physical thrills, or their careers at the center. Why do some people choose drinking as a central feature? Fingarette (1985) says that

there is no general answer but that the explanation lies not only in motives but also in a person's cultural background, life circumstances, special life crises, and physical abnormalities. No single item will be the reason.

Fingarette (1985) believes that it is no harder for the alcoholic to choose to stop drinking than it is for others to abandon activities central to their ways of life. "We should see the alcoholic, not as a sick and defective human being, but as a human being whose way of life is self-destructive. The difficulty we face is stubborn human nature, not disease" (p. 63).

In a similar fashion, Peele (1988) has examined the evidence on addiction and concluded that "we have disarmed ourselves in combating the precipitous growth of addictions by discounting the role of values in creating and preventing addiction and by systematically overlooking the immorality of addictive misbehavior" (p. 224). This is not a revival of the *addiction as sin* model but an argument that addicts and alcoholics do differ from other people in the ways in which they prioritize their values.

As noted at the outset of this chapter, William S. Burroughs (1977) attempted to answer the question, "why does a person become a drug addict?" in his book *Junky*. "The answer is that he usually does not intend to become an addict. You don't wake up one morning and decide to be a drug addict … You become a narcotics addict because you do not have strong motivations in any other direction" (p. xv). Schaler (2000) has a similar view of addiction. He denies that there is any such thing as *addiction*, in the sense of a "deliberate and conscious course of action which the person literally cannot stop doing" (p. xv). He views addiction as a *metaphorical* disease, not a *physical* disease.

Stages of Alcoholism

One of the first attempts to describe the development of alcoholism is found in Jellinek's (1952) study of 2,000 male members of Alcoholics Anonymous. He characterized alcoholism as an insidious disease that progresses through well-defined phases, each with symptoms that develop in the majority of persons in an additive, orderly fashion. In Jellinek's (1960) model, the drinker progresses through four distinct stages: (1) prealcoholic symptomatic phase; (2) prodromal phase; (3) crucial phase; and (4) chronic phase (see Figure 2.1).

In the *prealcoholic symptomatic phase*, drinking is associated with rewarding relief from tension or stress, something almost all drinkers engage in occasionally. The person who is more predisposed toward alcoholism (due to chromosomes, culture, or other factors) will tend to increase the frequency of relief drinking over a period of time. At the same time, the drinker develops a physical tolerance to alcohol, so that increasingly larger amounts are needed to bring the same degree of relief from stress or tension.

The onset of blackouts marks the beginning of the *prodromal phase*. These are periods of amnesia not associated with the loss of consciousness. The drinker may seem to be acting normally, but later have no recall of those events that occurred while in a blackout. This phase is also characterized by an increase in the need for alcohol (and attempts to hide the need for alcohol), surreptitious drinking, and increasing guilt.

The primary hallmark of the *crucial phase* is loss of control over drinking, as evidenced by the inability to abstain from drinking or the inability to stop once started. During this stage, the drinker often will begin the day's drinking in the morning, will experience behavior problems in relation to employment and social life, and will frequently seek to avoid family and friends.

The final stage, or *chronic phase*, finds the drinker intoxicated for several days at a time. Drinking becomes obsessive, and both serious physical and emotional problems are evident. According to Jellinek's (1960) original model, this is where the alcoholic hits bottom. Although this work was a pioneering effort in the field of alcoholism research, we must remember that Jellinek's samples were

(1) all AA members, (2) all in the latter stages of alcoholism, and (3) all males.

This traditional view of alcohol addiction was supported by many other prominent scholars, however. Mann (1968) described alcoholism as a "progressive disease, which, if left untreated, grows more virulent year by year" (p. 3). Others seem to have conveniently ignored available scientific evidence in making assertions such as "the true alcoholic is no more able to metabolize ethanol than a diabetic can handle sugar" (Madsen, 1974, p. 94). Others conclude that alcoholism is the result of an allergy and that "one does not become an alcoholic: One is *born* an alcoholic" (Kessel, 1962, p. 128).

Vaillant (1995) was involved in one of the most comprehensive studies of alcoholism. Two samples were observed over a 45-year period, and a third group was observed for 8 years. Among the sample of 110 core-city alcohol abusers, Vaillant identified four patterns: (1) progressive alcoholism; (2) return to asymptomatic drinking; (3) stable abstinence; and (4) atypical, nonprogressive alcoholism. Although this study generally supports the developmental or progressive nature of Jellinek's (1960) model, it is important to note that Vaillant's study observed both reversibility and non-progressive alcoholism among a substantial proportion of subjects. Over the period of the study, 18 of the 110 subjects returned to social or asymptomatic drinking. (Jellinek himself identified several patterns of problematic drinking as *not* fitting into a disease model.)

The traditional concept of the nature and progress of addiction to alcohol was also challenged by Pattison, Sobell, and Sobell (1977). Perhaps the major difference in their view of alcohol *dependence* (a more precise, less value-laden term than *addiction*), is found in the following two assertions:

- The development of alcohol problems follows variable patterns over time and does not necessarily proceed inexorably to severe final stages.
- Recovery from alcohol dependence bears no necessary relation to abstinence, although such a concurrence is frequently the case. (pp. 4–5)

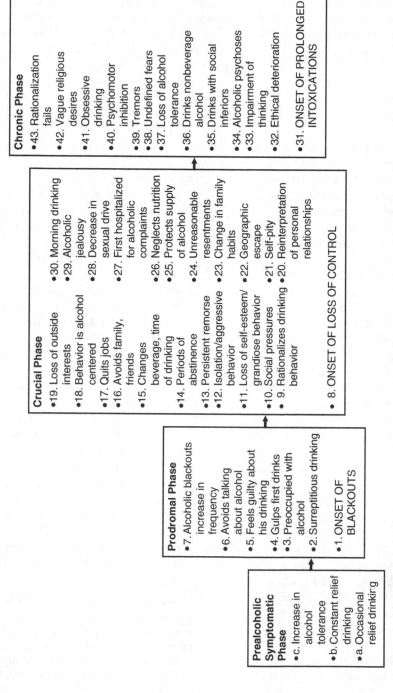

PREPATHOGENIC PERIOD

PERIOD OF PATHOGENESIS

FIGURE 2.1   The Natural History of Alcoholism According to Jellinek's Model Based on Male Members of AA.

Source: From *Alcoholism: Development, Consequences, and Interventions, 3/e* by N.J. Estes and M.E. Heinemann. Copyright © 1986 Elsevier Ltd.

Thus, a controversy was launched that continues today. Not only did Pattison, Sobell, and Sobell *not* believe in the disease model, but they also felt that alcohol dependence could be reversed. They pointed to some evidence that certain alcoholics had been able to return to social drinking. They also felt that the unproven assumptions that formed the basis for the traditional concept of alcoholism as a disease had been an *impediment* to proper treatment.

The Course of Cocaine Addiction

Other models of drug abuse/addiction reduce the number of stages to three: early, middle, and late. Washton's (1989) model of cocaine addiction describes it as a chronic disease that grows progressively worse if it is not treated. (*Chronic* indicates that cocaine addiction is never a single-acute episode but is marked by a permanent condition, with a continued vulnerability to recurring symptoms.)

According to Washton (1989), cocaine addiction is progressive and predictable in its course. "The disease of cocaine addiction is chronic, never reverses, and grows progressively more severe if left untreated" (p. 55). In the *early* stage of addiction, the user's brain chemistry is altered, withdrawal from normal activities is usually observed, and mood swings occur with increasing frequency. The *middle* stage of addiction is characterized by loss of control over cocaine use, impaired school or work performance, and denial of the problem. ("I'm not an addict; I just use the stuff a lot!") One can see that this is roughly comparable to the crucial phase in Jellinek's (1960) model of alcoholism. The *late* stage of addiction brings serious behavioral and emotional problems to the user, and it can terminate in severe depression, cocaine psychosis, and death.

A Multicausal Model

Which of these etiological models or explanations of drug abuse is correct? All are probably helpful, at least in a heuristic sense, but no single model or theory adequately explains the phenomenon of dependency or addiction. A significant advance in the study of chemical dependency is the realization that it is probably not a unitary disorder (West, 2006). Pattison and Kaufman (1982) made a strong case for a multivariate model of alcoholism more than two decades ago. Even though there may be similar behavioral topography in all addicted individuals, the etiology and motivation for drug use may differ widely. Available evidence points strongly to the possibility that addiction may be manifest through different mechanisms. Therefore, a model such as the one in Figure 2.2 may be helpful in understanding this phenomenon.

For some individuals, a genetic predisposition or physiological dysfunction is a necessary condition for drug use, drug abuse, and subsequent addiction. On the other hand, some people with disturbances in their personal development or interpersonal orientation but with no known genetic predisposition or biochemical aberration may become addicted to a drug. This debate over which model is really best is valuable only in the sense that it leads one to see the utility in an interdisciplinary, multicausal model.

This model is similar to the public health model, promoted in recent years by health care and other human service professionals. The model conceptualizes the problem of chemical dependency in terms of an interaction among three factors: the agent, the host, and the environment. In most public health areas, the agent is an organism (e.g., a virus), but in this case, it is ethanol. The second factor is the host—the chemically dependent person, including the person's genetic composition, cognitive structure, expectations about drug experiences, and personality. The last factor consists of the social, cultural, political, and economic variables that affect the use of alcohol or drugs and the resulting consequences. The public health approach involves the examination of the complex interaction of the multitude of variables affecting the agent, the host, and the environment (Hester & Sheehy, 1990).

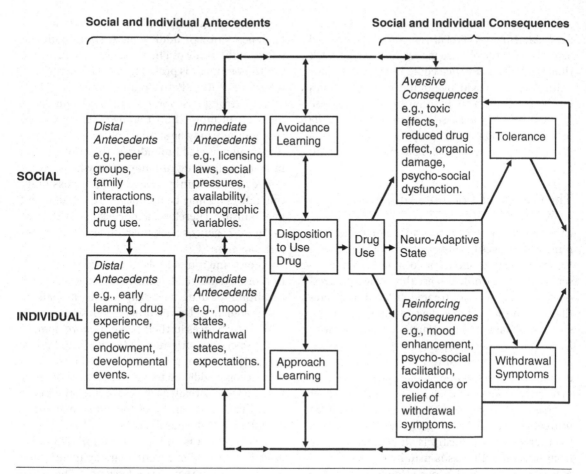

FIGURE 2.2   A Model of Drug Addiction.

Source: From *Alcoholism and Drug Addiction* by D. Raistrick and R. Davidson. Copyright © 1985 Elsevier Ltd.

Summary

The most obvious fact about alcohol and drug addiction is that there is no single theory that explains this phenomenon. Some people may be more genetically predisposed than others to become addicted. Others may be more prone to addiction because of their social environment, peer pressure, role models in the family, societal values, and so on. Still others may have one or more personality traits that make them more likely to use or abuse alcohol or drugs. Once use begins, physiological processes such as withdrawal and tolerance make the individual even more prone to continue use.

CHAPTER 3

The Brain Biology of Drug Abuse and Addiction

Richard E. Wilcox
University of Texas at Austin

Carlton K. Erickson
University of Texas at Austin

Introduction: Background on Abuse, Addiction, and Treatment

Chapter 1 provided the reader with the intellectual and social contexts in which the addicted (chemically dependent) person today finds himself or herself. The acronym *SPAM* (i.e., stigma, prejudice, and misunderstanding) (Erickson & Wilcox, 2001a, 2001b) summarizes the current popular view of addiction and of addicts. SPAM is also the major reason that funding from the National Institutes of Health for addiction research, education, treatment, and prevention continues to lag behind that for other mental disorders. It is essential that health care professionals, lawmakers, and the general public understand (a) what the disease of addiction is, (b) how the addictive process develops, and (c) why treatments based on drugs and nondrug approaches work. Current understanding of addiction is solidly based on the biochemistry and anatomy of the brain.

In this chapter, we provide the reader with an integrated model of the addictions and their treatments based on brain anatomy and brain chemistry. This information will be further integrated into the total treatment of addicted people in Chapters 5 and 6.

Terminology

As presented in Chapter 1, the clinical differentiation between *abuse* and *dependence* means that we may envision two subpopulations of drug-using people. One subpopulation may be viewed as retaining some voluntary control over drug seeking and drug taking; they are willful abusers. As noted in Chapter 1, drug abuse typically does not require intense social intervention and treatment (either behavioral or pharmacotherapeutic). The other subpopulation may be viewed as having a medical disease in which changes in brain structure and brain chemistry play a central role. These people are drug dependent (drug addicts). They have impaired control over their drug-seeking/drug-taking behavior.

In this chapter, we provide a brief introduction to concepts that will be elaborated in Chapters 5 and 6. Currently, the major defining characteristics of abuse versus dependence are psychosocial ones. The chief psychosocial characteristic of addiction is *impaired control over drug use,* or the inability to stop using when faced with adverse consequences. It took decades of research using behavioral, molecular, anatomical, and physiological methods to reach this understanding. However, the consequences of this finding are striking. A person may be dependent (addicted) without showing significant physical signs as a consequence of drug use (tolerance and physical withdrawal). *Tolerance* refers to a requirement for more drugs to achieve the same effect. *Physical withdrawal* refers to uncomfortable physiological responses after the drug leaves the body. Psychostimulants (cocaine and the various amphetamines) lead to relatively little tolerance and to modest physical withdrawal signs in most people. However, they are among the most addicting compounds known (which means they produce significant impaired control over drug use). Just as significantly, people may exhibit important clinical signs of tolerance and withdrawal to certain drugs without risking any chance of becoming addicted to them. For instance, the drugs used to treat recurrent seizures (epilepsy) alter people's consciousness, but people do not become addicted to such drugs. However, there is some tolerance to their effects and a strong possibility of withdrawal seizures if the therapeutic agents are stopped suddenly.

Drug addiction is "*not* a 'too much, too often' disease, but an 'I-can't-stop' disease" (Erickson, 1998). By reminding ourselves that addictions are "I-can't-stop" diseases, we can more easily focus on their identity as brain chemistry disorders (Leshner, 1997; Wilcox & Erickson, 2000; Wilcox & McMillen, 1998). As we will explore in the following paragraphs, it is precisely the changes in brain chemistry brought about by a combination of genetic predisposition, drug effects on the brain, and environmental effects on the brain that cause the impaired control over the person's behavior. Thus, *addiction* (chemical dependence) is best defined as occurring when the person can no longer stop using drugs even when faced with severe consequences (loss of spouse, job, life, or freedom). To give an example, an alcohol abuser can stop drinking when faced with a life-threatening diagnosis of alcohol-induced liver cirrhosis, but the alcohol-dependent person (the alcoholic) cannot do so without help.

The Genetics of Addiction

Many chemical dependency counselors report stories about addicts in recovery describing their first drink or drug exposure. These individuals noticed with the first dose that they had a special connection with the drug (Erickson & Wilcox, 2001a). That is, they realized that the drug experience made them feel more normal than ever before. Other addicts have reported that they initially felt that they could "take it or leave it" but that following repeated doses, they could no longer "leave it." Now that we understand that impaired control over drug use is the defining characteristic of the addictive process, a central question for researchers in the field immediately follows: How does this impaired control develop and evolve from normally controlled behavior?

Recent studies on the genetics of alcoholism have demonstrated that alcoholism runs in families—that is, that the tendency to become alcoholic is inherited (Cloninger, 1999). Genetic mutations may result in the abnormal formation of crucial brain regulatory proteins or the alteration of proteins such that they are less able to function correctly. Genetic mutations lead to the formation of altered proteins, which results in altered brain functioning that manifests as impaired control over drug use—the brain disease of dependence.

Brain Chemistry and the Anatomy of Addiction

Transmitters (neurotransmitters) serve as the chemical messengers of our brains (Wilcox, Gonzales, & Miller, 1998). Virtually all addictive drugs seem to have primary transmitter targets for their actions. The area of the brain in which addiction develops is the limbic system. This is the emotional brain, the part that is phylogenetically related to olfaction (smell). Emotion and smell have been linked to survival of the species and the organism in lower organisms and in humans. The term *limbic* refers to an inner margin of the brain just outside the cerebral ventricles. In humans, the nerve cells of the limbic system are surrounded by the neocortex (cerebral cortex) (Wilcox and Levitt, 1981). Limbic structures are remarkably similar when compared in species as diverse as mice and men. The limbic system contains structures (such as portions of the hypothalamus) that regulate behaviors necessary for survival of the individual and the species (eating, drinking, and sex). These links provide such vital behaviors with the emotional/motivational significance required to ensure that they will be carried out.

The transmitter *dopamine* is one of the major modulators in the development of addiction. When active in a specialized portion of the limbic system, the so-called pleasure pathway (mesolimbic dopamine system), the organism experiences pleasure or reward. Many proteins (in the form of enzymes) are involved in the production, metabolism, utilization of dopamine, or binding to its receptors in the pleasure pathway. A mutation in the genes for any of these proteins can influence the ability of dopamine neurons to utilize dopamine in a normal way. Deficiencies in functioning are most likely the result of such mutations, and they can render a person less able to experience happiness, to be motivated to do things, and to have other positive feelings, since these are all functions in which dopamine plays a role (Wilcox, 2001; Wilcox et al., 1998). As we will see later in this chapter, certain addictive drugs can counteract this deficiency, thereby making the person feel normal when they are taking the drug.

A highly schematized view of three of the major sites at which addiction develops is given in Figure 3.1: (1) the ventral tegmental area (VTA), (2) the nucleus accumbens (ACC), and (3) the frontal cortex. Thus, amphetamines and cocaine have dopamine as their major target because the primary action of each of these drugs is to increase the levels of dopamine in the spaces between nerve cells (synaptic cleft). This is shown as site 5 in Figure 3.1. Nicotine is a natural substance that mimics the transmitter acetylcholine at a subset of its receptors to stimulate them.

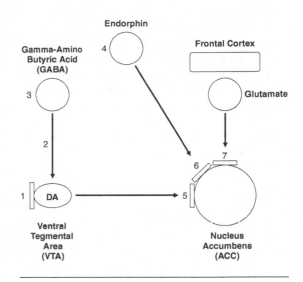

FIGURE 3.1   Sites and Actions of Addictive Drugs. The figure shows three limbic system areas for which research has shown an involvement in various drug addictions. These are the VTA (ventral tegmental area), nucleus accumbens (ACC), and frontal cortex. A few of the key transmitters are also shown: dopamine (DA), gamma-amino butyric acid (GABA), endorphin(s), and glutamate. *Site 1* represents one site for nicotine action. Nicotine acts on nicotinic receptors to increase dopamine release in the VTA. *Site 2* represents one site for ethanol action. Ethanol can increase the actions of GABA on DA neurons in the VTA, thus reducing DA release. *Site 3* represents one site of action for opioid drugs. Opioids such as morphine can inhibit the GABA interneuron (lies entirely in the VTA) within the VTA that normally regulates the DA neuron. *Site 4* represents other sites for action of nicotine and ethanol to enhance the release of natural opioids (the endorphins). *Site 5* represents the site of action of stimulants including cocaine and amphetamines. They increase the level of DA in the synapse leading to an increased stimulation of DA receptors. *Site 6* represents a site of action for opioid drugs in the ACC. Here, they act to activate endorphin receptors resulting in a net inhibition of ACC activity. *Site 7* represents one site of action of dissociative anesthetics (such as phencyclidine, PCP, or ethanol). These drugs inhibit the effects of glutamate on the ACC.

Source: From MOLECULAR NEUROPHARMACOLOGY: A FOUNDATION FOR CLINICAL NEUROSCIENCE by Eric J. Nestler, Steven E. Hman, and Robert C. Malenka is reprinted by permission of McGraw-Hill. Copyright © 2001 by the McGraw-Hill Companies, Inc.

These nicotinic receptors control smooth and skeletal muscle in the periphery and play a role in almost everything from motor function to cognition in the brain. One action of nicotine is to release dopamine in the VTA, which is site 1 in Figure 3.1.

Endorphin transmitters are small peptides that are very morphine-like in their actions. Heroin is converted in the brain to morphine and mimics the effects of endorphins at certain endorphin receptors (see site 6 in Figure 3.1). For many years, the analogous actions of alcohol (ethyl alcohol or ethanol) were difficult for investigators to understand. Today, we know that this small, simple molecule has selective effects on several brain transmitters. However, ethanol is less selective in its actions than is cocaine, nicotine, or heroin. Ethanol has major immediate effects on at least two major transmitters of the brain: the amino acid transmitters glutamate and gamma-amino butyric acid (GABA). Glutamate controls brain excitation, while GABA controls brain inhibition. Ethanol ingestion inhibits brain glutamate while enhancing brain GABA functioning (see, for example, sites 2 and 7 in Figure 3.1). Ethanol also has important actions on several other transmitters involved in the addictive process, including dopamine (Edwards et al., 2002; Wilcox & McMillen, 1998).

One of the most significant conclusions among addiction researchers is that virtually all addictive drugs act through a final common pathway from the VTA to the ACC and frontal cortex (see Figure 3.1). Furthermore, there is considerable interest in the possibility that the dopamine projections to the limbic (emotional brain) system constitute the anatomical basis for this final common pathway for addiction (Koob, Sanna, & Bloom 1998; Self, 1998; Self & Nestler, 1998; Wilcox & McMillen, 1998). Figure 3.1 provides a diagrammatic summary of a few of the important connections within this pathway. These include the VTA, the ACC, and the frontal cortex, collectively known as the *mesolimbic dopamine system* or *medial forebrain bundle.*

The medial forebrain bundle (MFB) is one of the most important pathways of the addictive process because it is a major pathway for reward/punishment, pleasure/pain, motivation, and emotion. Its name is derived from the fact that this pathway runs through the middle portion of each side of the brain. Cell bodies within the midbrain send long projections (axons) to the limbic forebrain to both subcortical and cortical structures (see Figure 3.2). The MFB is a major component of the limbic system. This dopaminergic pathway carries the feeling states that allow us to function effectively. A half-century ago, a behavioral scientist noticed that small electrical currents applied to this pathway were pleasurable to rodents (i.e., the animal would perform work to receive this stimulation) (Olds & Milner, 1954). Later investigators noted that the direct application of tiny amounts of dopaminergic drugs along this same pathway had similar positively reinforcing effects (German & Bowden, 1974).

Figure 3.2 shows the projection from the VTA to the ACC and frontal cortex (FC) in relation to the structure of the human brain. Also shown is the lateral hypothalamic area (LH), through which the MFB passes. Some of the earliest work on brain reward pathways involved measurement of the marked reinforcing actions of dopaminergic drugs microinjected along the medial forebrain bundle in the LH region (Wilcox & Levitt, 1981). Whereas only a few schematized projections are shown in Figure 3.2 for clarity, one significant aspect of VTA projections is their widespread nature. These pathways deliver dopamine to most areas of the limbic system, cortical and subcortical, and each nerve cell body gives rise to thousands of nerve endings (Wilcox, 2001; Wilcox et al., 1998). Neurons within the frontal/prefrontal cortex with glutamate as transmitter may be modulated by and modulate dopamine neurons of the MFB system.

One important aspect of the MFB pathway is that much of it does not directly involve the cerebral cortex and is thus unconscious in its actions. Another is that the portion of the cortex that receives the most indirect input is the frontal/prefrontal cortex. This portion of the brain carries

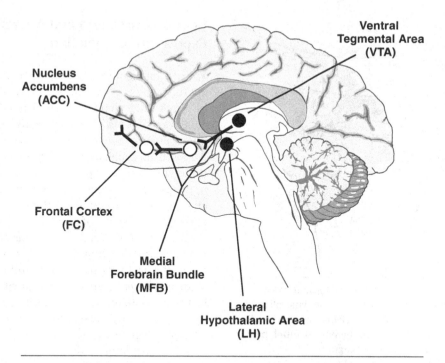

FIGURE 3.2   The Medial Forebrain Bundle and Associated Limbic System Structures. Functional parts of the medial forebrain bundle (MFB), which is part of the mesolimbic dopamine system. The bundle consists of nerve pathways, and drug-induced activity runs from the VTA to the ACC to the FC (frontal cortex). DA is the major transmitter for the MFB.

Source: Erickson, C.K. and O'Neill, J. *Your Brain on Drugs* (Hazelden Foundation, 1996). Copyright © 1997 by Hazelden Foundation. Reprinted by permission of Hazelden Foundation Center City, MN.

out the executive functions of decision-making (Nestler, Hyman, & Malenka, 2001; Wilcox & Erickson, 2000). When the addictive process spreads to the frontal cortex, people lose the ability to make rational decisions about their drug taking.

The idea of a final common pathway for addiction is supported by direct observations of the actions of addictive drugs and of drugs that appear to fight addiction (so-called anti-craving agents). Thus, cocaine and the amphetamines act directly on dopamine to yield a similar effect (i.e., more dopamine in the synapse), but they do this in different ways. Cocaine blocks the reuptake of dopamine back into the nerve terminal after its release (see Figure 3.3). It does this by

binding to and blocking the membrane transport protein that normally takes dopamine back inside the nerve terminal (the dopamine transporter, or DAT). This is shown in Figure 3.3 by the greater number of dopamine (DA) molecules (see step 5 in Figure 3.1). The amphetamines work in a slightly different way. They also bind to the membrane transport protein for dopamine and are taken inside the neuron instead of dopamine. However, the amphetamines can diffuse back outside the neuron to rebind and repeat this process. Meanwhile, the transport protein is in the open position inside the nerve terminal, where it picks up dopamine and takes it back outside the nerve cell, thus dramatically increasing

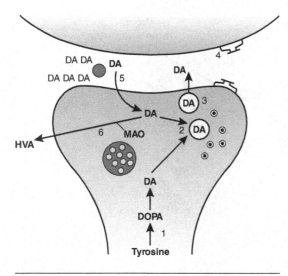

FIGURE 3.3 Cocaine Effects on Dopamine (DA)
Transcription. Cocaine blocks step 5 in synaptic transmission, the reuptake of DA back into the nerve ending.
This keeps the levels of DA in the synapse much higher
than normal (as shown in this figure).

Source: From MOLECULAR NEUROPHARMACOLOGY:
A FOUNDATION FOR CLINICAL NEUROSCIENCE by
Eric J. Nestler, Steven E. Hman, and Robert C. Malenka is
reprinted by permission of McGraw-Hill. Copyright ©
2001 by the McGraw-Hill Companies, Inc.

dopamine release (Wilcox & McMillen, 1998).
Acetylcholine and nicotine can increase the release of dopamine in the limbic system by binding to nicotinic receptors located on dopamine
nerve terminals. These receptors normally regulate dopamine release. When activated, they induce a greater release of dopamine (which is why
that first cigarette of the day may be rewarding
to many addicted people). The endorphins and
morphine bind to endorphin receptors on dopamine cell bodies that can also regulate dopamine
release. Heroin is converted to morphine in the
brain so its actions are like those of morphine.
When these receptors are stimulated, they facilitate dopamine release within the medial forebrain bundle system (Self, Barnhart, Lehman, &
Nestler, 1996; Self & Nestler, 1995).

Gene Transcription and Altered Protein Expression in Addiction

The development of improved methods for studying the regulation of gene and protein expression
has in essence blended together portions of the
genetics and brain chemistry fields. In turn, this
has opened new vistas for addiction research.
An essential problem in addiction science lies in
understanding how periodic, chronic exposure
to drugs can, in some people, yield permanent
changes in the functions of their brains. It now
appears that some of the same fundamental
processes that underlie such things as learning/
memory and development may also be operating in the brains of people becoming dependent
on drugs. Whereas chronic treatment with many
drugs is able to induce changes in gene and protein expression, those drugs associated with
chemical dependence may induce some changes
that are very long lasting. The hypothesis that
underlies this work is that the long-term changes
in the activity of dopaminergic and glutamin-
ergic nerve cells in the limbic system induced in
chemically dependent people are mediated in
part by changes in gene expression.

Transcription factors are proteins that bind
to specific regions in target genes (response elements within promoter regions) and turn on or
turn off the activity of those genes (Nestler, 2008).
Well-studied examples include CREB (the cAMP-
response element-binding protein; cAMP is an
intracellular "second messenger") and deltaFosB.
cAMP is a key second messenger inside nerve cells
in that its production is regulated by the activation
of many receptors including those for dopamine.
cAMP has a number of roles inside cells including helping to regulate the activity of many genes.
CREB is one such protein regulated by cAMP with a
number of highly important functions. For example, CREB activity is altered as a result of learning in
a manner that varies with the strength of the stimulus (Johannessen et al., 2004). Similarly, CREB activity is increased in several of the "reward" areas
of the brain following treatment with opioid drugs

(such as heroin) or psychostimulants (such as cocaine or amphetamine) (McClung & Nestler, 2008). Furthermore, genetic modifications that alter CREB activity up or down can also alter the conditioned preference for these drugs in rodents up or down (Barrot et al., 2002; McClung & Nestler, 2003).

Members of the Fos family of transcription factors (of which deltaFosB is one example) are increased within the nucleus accumbens as a result of the immediate administration of many drugs of abuse, but for most of these proteins the effects are transient (Graybiel et al., 1990; Young et al., 1991; Hope et al., 1992). Furthermore, with repeated drug administration there is a tolerance to the induction of these proteins. In contrast, abused drugs induce accumulation of deltaFosB and the high levels not only persist but also are further enhanced upon repeated drug dosing (Alibhai et al., 2007; McClung & Nestler, 2008) While much more work remains to be done, these investigations are consistent with the idea that CREB and deltaFosB may represent molecular substrates for the addictive process.

Sensitization in Addiction

It is a logical assumption (supported by evidence) that those persons who become addicted when very young or following minimal drug exposure (by objective standards) are those who are most heavily "loaded" genetically for addiction. That is, these individuals may have the misfortune to have multiple gene mutations that produce altered protein functions within the MFB and associated brain regions. For example, some people may not only produce abnormally small amounts of dopamine, but they may also break down dopamine more efficiently than average. If they are exposed to cocaine or one of the amphetamines, they may have normal dopamine levels for the first time. (This is because these drugs enhance the amount of dopamine in the synapse.) The drug high in these people might well be the first emotional high they have ever experienced. Other people may

have more subtle genetic defects, due perhaps to mutations that allow the normal production of dopamine (or the endorphins, etc.) but render one type of dopamine receptor slightly less responsive to dopamine activation. These individuals might tend to feel more normal than those just discussed but never really experience the exhilaration that most people feel upon hearing good news, for example. These persons might require a much longer period of drug exposure before they have impaired control over their drug use.

Implicit in this discussion is the idea that adaptations occur within the brain of a drug-exposed person to the first dose of a drug and to later doses. Furthermore, it would appear that such adaptations within the brain are what must constitute the development of addiction (the addictive process). Let's use cocaine exposure in a young man as an example.

Suppose that a young college student has an addiction-related genetic problem. As a consequence of this problem, he has a much-reduced amount of dopamine in the limbic system. As a child, he may have had unusual difficulty in making friends because he seemed moody. His first exposure to cocaine (in middle school) resulted in feelings of intense pleasure that he had never experienced before. Within his brain, the cocaine-induced increases in dopamine levels were much higher than he had ever felt. He liked the effects of cocaine. Because the dopamine levels in his limbic system were higher than normal, the young man's brain shows rapid and marked adaptations. As a result, even one day after a single high dose of cocaine, repeating the same dose yielded a smaller increase in dopamine in some parts of the brain. This is called *tolerance* (Riffee, Wanek, & Wilcox, 1987; 1988; Riffee & Wilcox, 1985; Riffee & Wilcox, 1987).

However, this adaptation has also caused other changes within the young man's brain—specifically, in his limbic system. Here, the same dose of cocaine taken on a second day may result in a larger increase in dopamine than was observed the day before. This adaptation is termed *sensitization*. It appears to be biochemically similar to those changes that occur within the memory areas of the brain during learning. Sensitization represents an emotional learning (learning within our emotional brain) in the nerve cells of the limbic system, especially the MFB portions (Robbins & Everitt, 1999; Robinson & Berridge, 1993, 2000, 2008; Robinson, Browman, Crombas, & Badiani, 1998). Our sensitized college student now has a greater limbic system response (high) to certain aspects of the cocaine experience. He now wants the cocaine.

There is always a price to be paid for drug use (neurochemically speaking). This is illustrated in Box 3.1, which presents the story of a 40-year-old woman who had been smoking for 30 years. Even after developing emphysema, she was unable to quit.

For individuals using cocaine, the high is followed by a low, in which the cocaine level declines and the dopamine level falls below its original baseline. The cocaine high may be enhanced with chronic drug exposure as a result of sensitization. The cocaine low may also be larger. The low may be properly defined as a *rapid rebound*, as the brain attempts to return the dopamine level to the original baseline (set-point) for that individual. Together, these highs and lows establish a molecular memory of the drug experience. An increased (sensitized) demand or urge for the drug may initiate the addictive process in these people (Robinson & Berridge, 1993, 2000, 2008).

Addicts often report that they need drugs. This means that the addict's body requires the drug to function normally (as it needs food, water, and air). A need can occur in someone who no longer wants to take the drug or derives pleasure from its use (Wilcox & Erickson, 2000). The path taken by the MFB goes through the hypothalamus, a critical area of the brain that regulates activities such as eating, drinking, and sex (Wilcox & Levitt, 1981). Addicted people and animals will take their drug in preference to food, water, or sex. Referring back to our example of the young college student, he now needs the cocaine.

The narrative in Box 3.2 indicates the extent to which a highly educated man can delude himself about his addiction ("I only drink beer, so I can't be an alcoholic"). The questions in the box, when answered truthfully, indicate that the man is alcohol dependent and suggest that recovery may be difficult, for a number of reasons.

Recent work on changes in gene expression following exposure to addictive drugs suggests that some neurochemical effects of these agents can be enhanced by the exposure—a neural substrate for "addiction learning."

BOX 3.1   *Controlling Smoking Behavior*

Richard Knox reported on National Public Radio (2001) that lung cancer kills more Americans each year than breast, colon, and prostate cancer combined. Over 90 million people are at risk for lung cancer, mostly from smoking. In addition, Knox asked, "But what if there were a test, like a mammography or a Pap smear, that could detect lung cancers when they're tiny and potentially curable?"

In fact, there is such a test. *Spiral CT* is a type of computerized axial tomography (CAT) scan that examines the region of the body in question—for example, the lung area. It is somewhat controversial but can potentially detect small lung nodules much earlier than other methods, leading to earlier detection of lung cancers.

Knox told the story of a 40-year-old woman who had decided to have the test. As a 30-year smoker who was about to remarry, she had decided to quit smoking one way or the other when she found out the results of the test. The test yielded some mixed results. She had no signs of cancer. However, she did have severe (and nonreversible) damage from emphysema.

At the time of Knox's report on National Public Radio, the woman had still been unable to quit smoking, even though she knew for sure that she had caused damage to her lungs. She explained that stress (from moving, getting married) kept her smoking. This is an example of impaired control over smoking behavior.

Source: Based on Wilcox & McMillen (1998).

Suppose that Dr. Gibbons, a 50-year-old professor of pharmacology, was brought to the emergency room by several of his graduate students on an icy winter afternoon. Because of the inclement weather, Gibbons had been unable to get to a liquor store to purchase his drink of choice: beer. He reported that he had been without alcohol for approximately two days, which one of his students tentatively confirmed. Because of this period of abstinence, Gibbons displayed upon examination signs and symptoms of severe ethanol withdrawal (which are not discussed here). Gibbons became agitated in the ER, experienced auditory hallucinations, and had to be physically restrained. He also required thiamin, magnesium replacement, and fluid and electrolyte replacement with dextrose-containing intravenous solutions.

Once Gibbons's withdrawal symptoms were brought under control with medication, a more complete history of his drinking was obtained by the medical staff based on information provided by his graduate students. Gibbons consumes only beer and is thus under the impression that he cannot be an alcoholic, as this is his only drink. He has drunk heavily for at least the last five years (the tenure of his most senior student), consuming about a case of beer a day. Four years ago, Gibbons had to leave a tenured position at a major university because he was not fulfilling his academic duties (i.e., failed to meet classes, etc.). However, some three years ago, he obtained a new academic position at a small private college on the strength of his research record and current grant funding.

Two of his four graduate students had elected to come with him because he is an extremely charismatic individual. Gibbons's two other students were recruited at his new university.

Initially following the move, Gibbons's drinking appeared to decline to about one to two 6-packs per day. During this period, he seemed relatively sober and functioned fairly well. This improvement was short lived, however. Soon, his students had to begin covering for him by teaching his classes, meeting with his students, and so on. Some two weeks prior to Gibbons's admission, his graduate students had tried an intervention with him but were unsuccessful, given their relative positions.

Following several discussions with an addiction medicine specialist, Gibbons was finally beginning to accept the fact that he might have a problem. However, upon further discussion, he also admitted that he had tried to stop drinking several times during the past 15 years but had been completely unsuccessful each time.

What steps should be taken by members of the health care team to assist Gibbons in remaining sober during the first few weeks following his release from the hospital? (Note that his insurance will not cover more than a seven-day hospital stay, and this length of stay has been permitted only because of some of the medical complications [chronic malnutrition, early cirrhosis, etc.] that were found upon Gibbons' physical examination.) What steps should Gibbons take to remain sober beyond the first few weeks following his release from the hospital?

Emotional Learning in Addiction

The preceding discussion presented a model termed the *medial forebrain bundle (MFB) model of impaired control*. This model focuses on just a portion of the limbic system. Recent research suggests that other limbic brain areas may also play important roles in the addictive process.

For example, the *extended amygdala* is envisioned as a larger brain system that also includes the amygdala (Koob et al., 1998; Nestler et al., 2001, Koob, 2008). The amygdala helps us to remember and orient to emotionally significant (salient) stimuli. Rodents with damage to the amygdala (especially its central nucleus) no longer remember that a conditioned stimulus was paired with food, for example. These recent studies were inspired by earlier studies showing that damage to a small portion of the amygdala could make rodents angry (showing aggressive behavior such as chasing other rats around a cage) and by studies in which the microinjection of tiny amounts of chemicals mimicking various transmitters into the amygdala also produced strong emotional responses (Wilcox & Levitt, 1981; Myers, 1978).

More recent studies by addiction scientists have extended this view to a regulation of emotional memory by the amygdala. In other words, the amygdala plays an important role in recording and replaying the significance of prior drug use to the person. To return to our example involving a cocaine-dependent individual, the sensitization to cocaine's effects on dopamine (with repeated exposure) is coupled with the person's learning that cocaine fulfills a need (normal emotion), which is a memory associated with the amygdala.

Addiction Therapy without Medication

As discussed more fully in Chapter 6, Alcoholics Anonymous (AA), the traditional recovery program for alcoholism, is based on the Twelve Steps, or a group-support process (Wilson, 1939). Most communities have such recovery programs for people addicted to various drugs. (See the "Big Book" of Alcoholics Anonymous [Wilson, 1939].) The Twelve Steps is founded on giving oneself over to a higher power to deal with one's own recognized weaknesses. Twelve-step programs are not only based on lifelong abstinence from addictive drugs but from most other types of mood-altering drugs, as well. However, the very success of these programs has helped maintain the misconception that addiction is a process that can be reversed solely through an act of will. This is true only in the sense that an addict must make a decision to understand that he or she is an addict and needs help. Paradoxically, it is the realization of

impaired control over drug use that causes an addict to seek treatment. He or she understands that willpower alone cannot cure this disease. Even so, research, especially over the last 25 years, has strongly suggested that "working" the Twelve Steps (like other spiritual and learning activities) may change the brain's chemistry (Erickson, 1997b; Erickson & Wilcox, 2001a, 2001b; Wilcox & Erickson, 2000).

Today, a variety of nondrug therapies are available to addicts, including structured treatment approaches (inpatient, outpatient, coping skills, and behavioral modification). For example, cognitive-behavioral therapy (CBT) involves having the person learn adaptive behaviors in therapy sessions by working through responses to hypothetical scenarios and then practicing these responses between sessions (Foreyt & Goodrick, 2001). Twelve-step programs and other psychosocial treatments may alter brain chemistry in an adaptive direction. Furthermore, they appear to do so by the same means through which we normally learn (Kandel, Schwartz, & Jessell, 2000). In other words, following therapy, a new type of learning has occurred within the limbic system of the addict, and this new learning can at least partially substitute for the drug-associated changes in brain chemistry (Nestler et al., 2001).

Part of the reason for the success of these so-called psychosocial programs lies in placing the dependent person in a controlled environment, away from the stimuli associated with drug taking. We know that such drug-associated stimuli are important because they can provide cues that prompt drug-seeking behavior many years after someone has stopped drug use (or become clean). A brain imaging study highlights this. Subjects in recovery from cocaine addiction were shown several video clips while their brain activities were monitored using positron emission tomography (PET; Wang et al., 1999). One video clip was a control scene. It elicited a neutral pattern of brain activation in control subjects and recovered addicts. Another film clip showed cocaine paraphernalia (razor blade, glass plate, and white powder). The cocaine addicts showed a very different pattern of brain activity in response to this compared to the controls. Finally, a third clip showed sexual activity. While the cocaine addicts and controls showed activity within the same brain regions in response to the sex stimulus, the cocaine addicts showed markedly less activity than the normal subjects.

Another important aspect of prevailing treatment programs is that they facilitate the relearning of adaptive social interactions (e.g., nonaggressive behavior, getting up and going to work) and, of course, provide patients the incentive and tools for remaining abstinent. Various other ancillary measures (e.g., detoxification, exercise, and nutritional counseling) are able to facilitate normal brain function and contribute to sobriety. A growing body of preclinical literature suggests that when drug craving is reduced (by giving other drugs, as noted later), the brain's chemistry has been somewhat normalized. Functional imaging studies have compared the brain activity within the limbic system of people who are actively addicted and using drugs (including ethanol) with the brain activity of the same people at various stages of the recovery process. Such research demonstrates that exposure to addictive drugs alters brain functions in people.

Changes in brain chemistry appear to cause addiction. Given this, changes in brain chemistry that are the opposite of those during the development of addiction may lead to recovery. Psychosocial treatment programs, including those that improve self-esteem and encourage a more positive outlook on life, may produce these and other beneficial effects by altering limbic system activity via changes in transmitter functioning in the brain. As the addict regains (or perhaps gains for the first time) a relatively normal brain dopamine function (for example) in the absence of addictive drugs, he or she also regains behavioral control over drug taking.

We hear on the news almost daily that some celebrity previously treated for addiction has relapsed. Because many people have access only to short-term treatment, relapse is a predictable occurrence for the addict. We need to develop a new awareness that the addictive process is a prolonged one. Months, even years, are spent creating addiction in most people. Why would we expect that therapy could reverse in a few weeks what took months or years to develop? Imagine a child who is overweight, progresses to being an obese teen and then a morbidly obese young adult. Who would expect them to trim 100 extra pounds acquired over decades in a 28-day treatment program?

Drug Therapy for Addiction

Somewhat effective drug therapies have become available for the treatment of addiction per se (i.e., not merely the physical withdrawal symptoms). The treatment of craving in the addicted person is roughly where the treatment of other major mental illnesses (e.g., schizophrenia, bipolar disorder, and depression) was in 1970. Scientists and clinicians working together have begun to apply the knowledge gained from pharmacological work with rodents to addicted people.

Like the first antipsychotic agents (chlorpromazine and haloperidol) and the first treatment for bipolar disorder (lithium), current anti-craving agents are a great deal better than nothing but are far from "magic pills" (Schatzberg & Nemeroff, 1998). Traditionally, drugs have been really good at resetting the baseline brain chemistry of the person to a new, more malleable level. Drugs will probably never be the entire answer to effective addiction treatment. They are coarse instruments, rather than delicate ones. Adjusting a person's brain chemistry toward a more normal level of functioning might be more easily achieved with therapeutic drugs. These effects could be enhanced by the more subtle adjustments achievable through behaviorally based therapeutic approaches.

Table 3.1 lists some of the medications being used to increase long-term abstinence, typically through a reduction in craving (Wilcox & McMillen, 1998). Craving is, of course, difficult to quantify because it is a subjective experience. Human studies use an objective measure—relapse—to assess craving.

TABLE 3.1 Drugs Currently Used to Treat Drug Craving

Drug Craved	Drug (Trade Name)
Cocaine	None approved, but in use:
	Desipramine (Norpramin)
	Bromocriptine (Parlodel)
	Amantadine (Symmetrel)
	Carbamazepine (Tegretol)
	In trial:
	Selegiline (Eldepryl)
	Disulfiram (Antabuse)
	Several antidepressants
Alcohol	Naltrexone (ReVia)
	Acamprosate (in trial)
	Nalmefene (in trial)
	Ondansetron (Zofran, in trial)
Heroin	Methadone (Dolophine)
	Naltrexone (ReVia)
	Buprenorphine (Buprenex)
Nicotine*	Bupropion (Zyban)
	Nicotine patches and gum (Nicorette)
	Low nicotine devices

*Technically, these drugs reduce the severity of withdrawal. However, it is not known whether these agents reduce the craving for nicotine or smoking. There are no FDA-approved medications for treating dependence on PCP, marijuana, methamphetamine, and other stimulants, inhalants, or anabolic steroids. Vaccines for treating cocaine and nicotine dependence are currently under investigation.

Source: Based on Wilcox & McMillen (1998).

Role of Detoxification in Treating Addiction

A more comprehensive discussion of the treatment of drug withdrawal and the detoxification process is found in Chapter 6. Logically, the successful treatment of an addiction caused by drug exposure can only begin when the drug exposure ceases and the drug has been removed from the body. Most medications prescribed in addiction treatment are used in *detoxification*. Generally, any drug (addicting or not) produces some adaptations during its time within the body. The response immediately after the drug leaves the body tends to be the opposite of that of the drug. To use a common example,

ingesting caffeine perks us up but we tend to feel down a few hours after our last dose. (By the way, caffeine is not addicting because it does not have a major action on the mesolimbic dopamine system.) Thus, addictive drugs, which initially can make people high, produce an opposite low during withdrawal. If at least some of these untoward symptoms can be relieved, then the addict will be more likely to complete the detoxification process as a first step to recovery (Wilcox & Levitt, 1975).

Clonidine (Catapres) and guanfacine (Tenex) are used to treat aspects of heroin withdrawal (also refer to Chapter 6). Both drugs act to lower blood pressure and reduce other signs of sympathetic nervous system hyperactivity that coincide with drug removal. These drugs act as *physiological antagonists* of heroin withdrawal. This means that they produce a beneficial action through a very different chemical pathway from that associated with heroin (Galanter & Kleber, 1999). Although these drugs reduce withdrawal signs, they have little effect on dependence. This highlights the fact that *dependence* is not *withdrawal.*

Other types of drugs may also aid in detoxification by acting through the same chemical pathway that the addictive drug utilizes. The best example is the use of some of the benzodiazepine tranquilizers (chlordiazepoxide [Librium] and diazepam [Valium]) in the detoxification of alcoholics. These types of drugs are basically ethanol in capsule form. They act on some of the same transmitters in the brain and can produce the same type of addiction, if taken inappropriately. They are used in detoxification because they can substitute for ethanol, thereby prolonging the detoxification period and rendering it less of an ordeal. Of course, these agents must be used with discretion.

Drug Therapy for Reducing Craving

Alcoholism

Efforts to find medications that can reduce alcohol craving are now extensive and at least partially successful (Wilcox & Erickson, 2000; Wilcox & McMillen, 1998). Interestingly, several basic types of drugs that have been used have very different ways of acting. Disulfiram (Antabuse) reduces ethanol metabolism, allowing a toxic metabolite (acetaldehyde) to build up in the blood. The acetaldehyde produces unpleasant effects that can actually be lethal if the drug is taken when there is a substantial amount of alcohol in the body. Although disulfiram has no effect on craving, it can make the alcoholic sufficiently afraid to drink so that he or she will remain abstinent until nondrug treatment approaches have had time to work.

Another type of drug, naltrexone (ReVia), is an example of one that may actually reduce the craving for alcohol. It is known as an *abstinence enhancer* (since it is normally given only to people who have already begun abstinence-based therapy) and a *relapse reducer* (since it blocks relapse in about half of the people who take it after abstinence-based therapy). Naltrexone blocks endorphin (morphine) receptors, which normally help to regulate mood, motivation, and reward by controlling dopamine within the MFB portion of the limbic system. The blockade of these receptors in an alcoholic by naltrexone prevents some of the subjective effects of having a drink. Alcoholics also report that it is easier to remain abstinent when they are being treated with naltrexone because they have less of an urge to drink, especially when they are stressed. Moreover, naltrexone can reduce the likelihood that a person will drink heavily. Naltrexone also reduces the number of drinks someone will take if he or she

relapses. Thus, whereas naltrexone administration may not completely prevent drinking, it seems to reduce the amount consumed at one time and overall. Both of these effects are objective signs of a reduction in the craving for alcohol. Naltrexone is available in a slow release form (Natrel).

Nalmefene (Revex) has a mechanism of action that closely resembles that of naltrexone. Nalmefene blocks additional subtypes of endorphin receptors over and above those blocked by naltrexone. Thus, nalmefene also reduces relapse in alcoholics. Nalmefene appears to have less liver toxicity than naltrexone and is currently available in a slow release form and an oral form but as of this writing is awaiting approval by the Food and Drug Administration for use in treating alcohol dependence.

Ondansetron (Zofran) is another drug with anti-craving potential (see Box 3.3). It blocks a type of receptor for the transmitter serotonin (i.e., the serotonin-3 receptor), which plays a major role in emotion, motivation, and reward (Wilcox & Erickson, 2000; Wilcox & McMillen, 1998). A recent series of studies demonstrated that ondansetron is quite effective in reducing craving among a subpopulation of alcoholics—namely, those who have the more severe (early onset) variant of the disease (Meert, 1994; Sarhan, Cloez-Tayarani, Massot, Fillion, & Fillion, 1999; Wilson, Neill, & Costall, 1998). Among its many actions in the brain, serotonin controls the release of dopamine. Some of

---

BOX 3.3   *Treating Severe Alcoholism Using a Drug for Nausea*

Cancer patients have severe nausea from the disease itself. Such nausea can be reduced by a drug that blocks a type of receptor for serotonin: the serotonin-3 receptor. Nausea occurs both peripherally and in a portion of the brain outside the so-called blood brain barrier, the area postrema.

One such drug, ondansetron, has recently been used to reduce the craving in alcoholics who have a strong genetic predisposition to drink. Serotonin, acting within the emotional brain (or limbic

system), normally plays an important role in one's ability to experience pleasure. When genetic problems lead to an imbalance in serotonin, this can predispose an individual to develop an addiction. Conversely, blocking the serotonin-3 receptor can partially restore the serotonin balance, reducing the urge to drink. Whereas ondansetron reduces nausea by acting on one part of the brain, it can reduce craving by acting on another part: the limbic system.

Source: Based on Johnson (August 23, 2000, http://news.bbc.co.uk/2/hi/health/891840.stm).

this modulation within the limbic system occurs via the serotonin-3 receptor. By blocking this receptor, ondansetron seems to remove an inhibition of dopamine release, leading to a lowered craving.

Since ondansetron and naltrexone have very different mechanisms of action in the brain, giving the two drugs together may elicit a stronger anti-craving response than giving either drug alone. Studies combining these two drugs or giving them to people undergoing psychosocial treatments have been published (Ait-Doud, Johnson, Prihoda, & Hargita, 2001).

An additional anti-craving agent is acamprosate (Campral; calcium acetyl homotaurinate). In clinical trials lasting one to two years, acamprosate appeared to reduce relapse. It may act as a modulator at a subtype of glutamate receptor (NMDA receptor) and also at a subtype of receptor for GABA (GABA-A receptor). The MFB dopamine pathway feeds into (synapse on) neurons that release either glutamate (excitatory transmitter) or GABA (inhibitory transmitter), thus providing an output for the emotional brain. Agents that can modulate glutamate or GABA may have some direct actions on this output. Also, glutamate neurons regulate dopamine neurons (and vice versa) in many parts of the brain (Edwards et al., 2002). Thus, an agent such as acamprosate may also alter limbic system dopamine release (Wilcox, Gonzales, & Miller, 1998). Studies comparing the effectiveness of acamprosate versus naltrexone have been reviewed (Kranzler & Van Kirk, 2001). The two drugs appear to be somewhat effective in the treatment of alcohol-dependent patients.

Topiramate (Topamax) is a well-known anticonvulsant drug that regulates the release of GABA and, thereby, may modulate the release of dopamine within the limbic system. Recent data suggests that topiramate may improve abstinence in alcohol-dependent patients (Rubio et al., 2009; Kenna et al., 2009).

Finally, Aripiprazole (Abilify) is a fairly new antipsychotic drug that acts by being a partial agonist at the D2 dopamine receptor. Thus, in people with schizophrenia, Aripiprazole can replace deficient dopamine with the frontal cortex and, thus, reduce "negative" symptoms (reduced emotion, apathy)

while simultaneously displacing excess dopamine from its receptors within the sub-cortical portions of the limbic system, thereby reducing "positive" symptoms (delusions and hallucinations). Aripiprazole may reduce the euphoric effects of alcohol while enhancing its sedating actions in alcoholic patients (Vergne & Anton, 2009).

Stimulant Addictions: Cocaine and the Amphetamines

Finding medications to reduce the craving for cocaine has been a challenge for pharmacologists. To date, no drugs stand out as being clearly effective in the treatment of cocaine dependence. The discussion that follows highlights attempts to find new medications that can be useful in treating this dependence.

The major types of therapeutic medications used to reduce craving in stimulant addicts are drugs used to treat symptoms of depression and Parkinson's disease. Antidepressant drugs have been widely studied as potential agents to reduce craving in a variety of drug addictions. They have certainly been found effective in addicts who are also depressed (Wilcox & Erickson, 2000; Wilcox & McMillen, 1998), but they have been found only mildly beneficial in treating cocaine and amphetamine addicts. As a group, antidepressants inhibit the reuptake of serotonin and norepinephrine. This action directly leads to higher levels of the transmitter in the synapse and to more stimulation of receptors on the receiving nerve cells. Serotonin regulates dopamine release in the limbic system, and norepinephrine has similar actions. In fact, the ascending (to the forebrain) projections of dopamine, serotonin, and norepinephrine tend to travel closely together and intertwine. With the marketing of new-generation antidepressants that have mechanisms of action that are distinct from those of earlier agents (e.g., mirtazepine [Remeron] versus fluoxetine [Prozac]), an interest in studying the effects of such treatments on craving continues.

The drugs used to reduce the symptoms of Parkinsonism also alter dopamine functions

(Wilcox et al., 1998). By definition, drugs that require an intact dopamine neuron for their effect are *indirect agonists,* while those that require only dopamine receptors are *direct agonists.* (An *agonist* mimics the actions of a transmitter.) Amantadine (Symmetrel) is a dopamine-releasing agent that works in early Parkinson's disease. As such, it is an indirect dopamine agonist. This agent appears capable of reducing relapse in a subpopulation of cocaine addicts. Bromocriptine (Parlodel) is an example of a direct dopamine agonist in that it mimics dopamine at a subtype of dopamine receptor, the D2 receptor (Wilcox et al., 2000). Bromocriptine can reduce relapse to cocaine, but it can also be abused by some at-risk individuals. These people report (and the effects are confirmed in rodent studies) that bromocriptine's subjective effects are somewhat similar to those of other addictive agents.

Recently, discoveries have been made that link several brain diseases, thus providing implications for the drugs used to treat them. For instance, epilepsy is a devastating set of neurological disorders that have in common runaway brain activity (seizures). Years ago, only a few types of drugs were available to treat these disorders, but more recently, at least nine effective classes of drugs (based on mechanism of action) have been identified (see for example, Table 3.2). What these drugs have in common is their ability to dampen excess brain activity. Another example is bipolar disorder, a major psychiatric condition in which the person has episodes of severe depression that alternate with episodes of

mania (i.e., the person loses judgment and is generally hyper in word and deed). As an oversimplification, someone who is bipolar has too little serotonin and norepinephrine within his or her limbic system during the depressive phase of the illness and too much during the manic phase.

Research has shown that some of the newer drugs effective in reducing the excess brain activity in epileptic patients are also effective in reducing the more selective excess brain activity within the limbic system of bipolar patients. Significantly, some of these drugs may also reduce craving in addicts! For example, as mentioned earlier, topiramate is an epileptic drug that may be of benefit in reducing craving. Similarly, GVG (gamma-vinyl-GABA [Sabril]) is an antiepileptic agent that is also effective in treating bipolar disorder. GVG acts by blocking the metabolism of GABA—less breakdown means a higher GABA level in the brain. In rodents, GVG also blocks the rapid increases in dopamine within the MFB that typically follow dosing with alcohol, heroin, or amphetamines (Dewey et al., 1998).

Another type of treatment for cocaine addiction is a vaccine (TA-CD) that reduces cocaine's effects by lowering the amount of cocaine reaching the brain. In turn, this action of the vaccine prevents at least some of the increase in dopamine level that normally follows ingestion of cocaine (Haney et al., 2010; Kosten & Biegel, 2002). The TA-CD vaccine substantially decreased smoked cocaine's intoxicating effects in those cocaine-dependent men who had generated a high level of the antibody.

TABLE 3.2 Drugs Currently Used for Epilepsy with Potential for Use in the Treatment of Drug Craving

Generic Name	Mechanism	Trade Name
Lamotrigine	Slows sodium channel recovery	Lamictal
Topiramate	Slows sodium channel recovery	Topamax
Fosphenytoin	Slows sodium channel recovery	Cerebrex
Valproic acid	Stimulates GABA synthesis and inhibits metabolism	Depakene
Gabapentin	Increases GABA release	Neurotonin
Tiagabine	Blocks GABA reuptake	Gabatril
Gamma-vinyl-GABA	Inhibits GABA metabolism	Sabril
Felbamate	NMDA receptor antagonist at glycine site	Felbatol

Heroin and Other Opioid Addictions

We noted earlier that the brain converts heroin to morphine. The effects of heroin, therefore, are the same as those of morphine. In turn, morphine is an agonist at some types of endorphin receptors. The mainstay of current treatment for heroin addiction is *methadone*, a direct (orally active) agonist at endorphin receptors. Methadone is a substitute for heroin and produces the same basic effect in the body (over the long term), thus lowering the craving for heroin. However, because it acts more slowly relative to heroin (due to the oral route of administration), methadone produces much less of a high. In other words, methadone binds to and activates the same receptors and induces the same effects inside nerve cells, as does heroin. Another endorphin agonist, called *LAAM* (L-alpha-acetyl-methadol), has the same mechanism of action as methadone but has an even longer duration in the body. LAAM and methadone can both reduce relapse in heroin addicts and are reported to reduce the craving for heroin, as well. However, the use of methadone and LAAM with addicts remains somewhat controversial because they are not abstinence-based therapies.

We have already seen that good clinical use can be made of drugs that block opioid (endorphin) receptors, such as naltrexone and nalmefene. These drugs have as their basic action the ability to prevent the endorphin (or any endorphin-type agonist) from binding to the receptors. Such drugs might also be effective in maintaining abstinence in heroin addicts because they can effectively reduce the effects of a (fairly expensive) heroin dose to zero! These drugs are so effective in displacing endorphins and heroin from their receptors that they can precipitate a withdrawal syndrome in an active heroin user. A short-acting antagonist (blocker) of opioid receptors, naloxone (Narcan), and the longer-acting naltrexone (ReVia) have both been used in heroin detoxification. This is directly due to the ability of these agents to remove morphine from its brain receptors.

Even more interesting is the fact that (as we saw in discussing the treatment of alcoholics) naltrexone and related compounds can help to maintain abstinence after heroin has been eliminated from the body. Some of the effect is no doubt due to the addict's knowledge that he or she cannot afford to buy enough heroin to get high in the presence of naltrexone. However, heroin addicts report a reduced need for heroin after a few weeks of naltrexone administration. Currently, a long acting (depot) form of naltrexone (Vivitrol) that allows the drug to be delivered to the body for up to 30 days following one injection has become available (Fishman, 2008).

In the preceding paragraphs, we have referred to *direct agonists* several times (bromocriptine, methadone, etc.). These drugs can be more accurately described as *full agonists*, in that they produce an effect inside the neuron that is as great as that of a neurotransmitter. In contrast, a *partial agonist* is a drug that yields a smaller effect than the transmitter inside the nerve cell. Buprenorphine (Buprenox), a recently approved treatment for heroin addicts, is a partial agonist at endorphin receptors. Thus, although buprenorphine binds to the endorphin receptors as well as does morphine, methadone, or LAAM, buprenorphine cannot fully mimic the magnitude of the effects of these drugs inside the neurons. This makes buprenorphine and related drugs potentially unique. They have enough similarity to heroin to prevent withdrawal (partially substituting for the heroin) but act enough like a blocking drug (antagonist) that they may reduce relapse and craving. A depot form of buprenorphine has been evaluated (Sigmon et al., 2006) that delivers the drug for several weeks. The drug's ability to block opioid receptors persists even at fairly low drug doses. To date, buprenorphine is available as an injectable solution and a sublingual tablet.

Nicotine Addiction

Executives of the tobacco industry have described (in revealed memos) the cigarette as "the perfect delivery system for nicotine." Currently, there are several ways that a nicotine addict can prevent relapse to smoking. First, he or she can try a form of *substitution* therapy; that is, the addict can take nicotine in a different (and less harmful) form, such as a nicotine patch or gum. Three clinically useful things happen with this change in nicotine delivery. First, the addict gets the nicotine but not as quickly (less of a high) as occurs with smoking. Second, the individual avoids inhaling the carcinogens contained in tobacco smoke (and also sharing them with others in the same room). The nicotine craving will still be present but can be addressed using a somewhat safer delivery method. (Note that nicotine in any form is toxic to the heart.) Third, nicotine substitution provides the motivated individual with a way to gradually reduce daily nicotine intake to zero.

A second type of drug therapy for nicotine addicts is the antidepressant drug, bupropion (Zyban). Bupropion acts differently from nicotine substitution. Bupropion enhances limbic system dopamine levels because it inhibits transmitter reuptake into dopamine and norepinephrine neurons. Nicotine also enhances dopamine levels, as mentioned earlier. Thus, bupropion seems to have an anti-craving action based on its ability to partially substitute for one of nicotine's major actions. Of course, as a marketed antidepressant (under a different trade name: Wellbutrin), bupropion also reduces the depression that smokers frequently face during withdrawal.

A third type of anti-craving agent is varenicline (Chantix) that is a partial agonist at a particular type of nicotinic acetylcholine receptors (alpha 4/beta 2 subunits). By partially mimicking nicotine at these sites, varenicline can induce a modest level of limbic system dopamine release and thus can reduce cravings (Crunelle et al., 2010).

Several nicotine vaccines have been evaluated. Of these, one called NicVAX appears able to prevent nicotine from entering the brain (Maurer & Bachmann, 2007).

Summary

People today accept that schizophrenia, depression, and bipolar disorder are as much medical diseases as are heart disease, diabetes, and tuberculosis. We hope that the reader now understands the reasons to include chemical dependencies on this list, as well.

Many addicted people can benefit from the use of appropriate anti-craving medications in combination with nondrug therapies (twelve-step programs, psychosocial treatments, etc.). We have noted that drugs can more easily help to reset the baseline of neural activity within the limbic system (alter the set-point), whereas nondrug therapies are better able to fine-tune brain activity. Furthermore, such combinations of drug and nondrug therapies are now part of standard psychiatric practice with other brain and behavior disorders, including depression and attention-deficit/hyperactivity disorder.

The analogy to other types of psychiatric treatment also holds with respect to the duration of treatment for the addict. Schizophrenia and many cases of depression are treated as lifelong disorders because they reflect fundamental genetic errors that have led to enduring changes in the brain chemistry of afflicted individuals. We have already asked how one could reasonably expect a few weeks of any treatment mode to alter brain chemistry that were months or years in the making (and superimposed on a background of genetically based alterations, as well). Thus, addiction may well require lifetime treatment. It is no coincidence that people who have not had a drink in many years still describe themselves as "alcoholics in recovery," implying that the process of regaining their mental health (and control) takes place every day. That is, of course, also the basis for the philosophy one hears from people in recovery: "One day at a time." However, it remains to be seen whether drug therapy needs to be continued for the life of the individual.

It is now accepted as a fundamental tenet of modern medicine that a holistic (whole-person) approach is more effective than any single therapeutic modality in treating a disease. This is perhaps even more the case for the major psychiatric disorders because of their complexity.

The modern health care team is comprised of a social worker, pharmacist, physician, nurse, and patient. Each of these people has a valuable contribution to make in managing the long-term care of the recovering addict.

CHAPTER 4

The Physiological and Behavioral Consequences of Alcohol and Drug Abuse

This chapter discusses the major physiological and behavioral consequences of abusing alcohol and certain drugs. It will not address the more technical details on such disorders as leukopoiesis and thrombopoiesis, which are better handled by the medical professions, but it will outline the more common consequences. Any professional person who has the responsibility of assisting clients with alcohol and drug problems must be able to recognize common symptoms and make appropriate referrals. In fact, it will undoubtedly be advantageous to the practicing social worker or other human service professional to be capable of deciphering a physician's report on an alcoholic or drug-abusing client. We will attempt to keep the medical terminology to a minimum, but it is essential to understand such terms as *cardiomyopathy, hepatic dysfunction,* and *fetal alcohol syndrome.*

Certain classes of drugs, such as central nervous system (CNS) depressants, will have common effects on the users' behavior. Individual CNS depressants often will have very different physiological effects, however. In some cases, the same drug will have different physiological effects, depending on the particular method of ingestion. Those who snort cocaine may have very different physical problems than those who inject the same drug with a hypodermic needle. In fact, it is frequently observed that some addicts who inject drugs often

seem to be more addicted to the process of "shooting up" than to the effects of a particular drug.

We will pay somewhat more attention to the effects of alcohol in the following pages, since it is the most widely used of all the drugs covered here. Because of its long history, we also know more about the consequences of alcohol abuse. Much less is known about the long-term consequences of abusing some of the newer drugs, such as ecstasy, GHB, or zolpidem. Greater detail about these and other drugs are discussed by Kuhn, Swartzwelder, and Wilson (2008) and on the National Institute on Drug Abuse website. The effects of tobacco/nicotine are discussed only in relation to pregnancy and fetal development.

The Effects of Alcohol

Ethyl alcohol is almost exclusively ingested in the form of a potable beverage. (In relatively rare instances, it is used for medical reasons and may be administered intravenously by a physician.) One of the most dangerous and widely used drugs throughout the world, it has the potential for causing deleterious effects on every part of the digestive system as well as every major organ in the human body (Agarwal & Seitz, 2001). Figure 4.1 provides an illustration of alcohol's effects on the body.

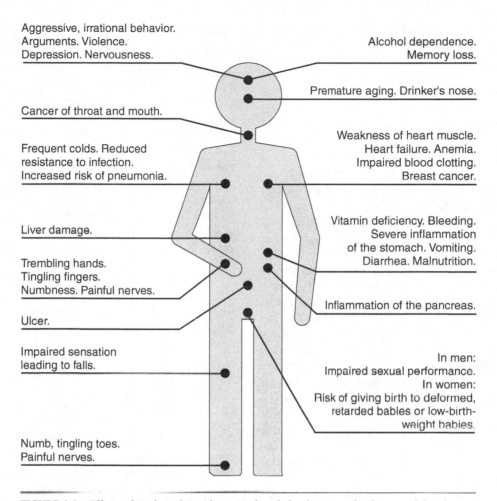

Aggressive, irrational behavior.
Arguments. Violence.
Depression. Nervousness.

Alcohol dependence.
Memory loss.

Premature aging. Drinker's nose.

Cancer of throat and mouth.

Weakness of heart muscle.
Heart failure. Anemia.
Impaired blood clotting.
Breast cancer.

Frequent colds. Reduced
resistance to infection.
Increased risk of pneumonia.

Vitamin deficiency. Bleeding.
Severe inflammation
of the stomach. Vomiting.
Diarrhea. Malnutrition.

Liver damage.

Trembling hands.
Tingling fingers.
Numbness. Painful nerves.

Inflammation of the pancreas.

Ulcer.

Impaired sensation
leading to falls.

In men:
Impaired sexual performance.
In women:
Risk of giving birth to deformed,
retarded babies or low-birth-
weight babies.

Numb, tingling toes.
Painful nerves.

FIGURE 4.1   Effects of High-Risk Drinking. High-risk drinking may lead to social, legal, medical, domestic, job, and financial problems. It may also cut your lifespan and lead to accidents and death from drunken driving.

Source: Babor, T. F.; Higgins-Biddle, J. C.; Saunders, J. B.; & Monteiro, M. G. *The Alcohol Use Identification Test: Guidelines for Use in Primary Care.* (WHO) http://www.who.int.substance_abuse/PDPfiles. auditbro.pdf.

The Metabolization of Alcohol

As soon as alcohol is ingested, the body begins to metabolize and eliminate it, primarily through oxidation. Not long ago, it was thought that approximately 95 percent of all alcohol was eliminated through oxidation and 5 percent through bodily processes such as respiration, urination, and perspiration. It was recently discovered that much of the alcohol that is consumed in small doses is actually metabolized in the stomach (Julkunen, DiPadora, & Lieber, 1985). Gastric metabolism acts as a barrier to toxicity with moderate doses of alcohol.

The major organ that metabolizes larger amounts of alcohol is the liver. Small amounts are also eliminated in the feces, and nursing mothers release some alcohol in their milk. The initial step is the conversion of alcohol to acetaldehyde by the enzyme *alcohol dehydrogenase (ADH)*. Next, the acetaldehyde is converted by another liver enzyme to an active acetate that is further broken down into carbon dioxide and water. The metabolism of alcohol results in significant changes in the ratio of important chemicals within the liver cells—changes that affect the rate of the metabolism.

Depending on the mass of functioning liver that is available, the average adult can oxidize from 10 to 15 grams of alcohol per hour. (This is approximately the amount of pure ethanol in one alcoholic beverage.) An average person can therefore consume about one drink per hour without accumulating alcohol in the body. However, there is tremendous variation in individual rates of metabolism, depending on such factors as other contents of the stomach at the time of ingestion, the body's proportion of fat, and the proportion of healthy versus cirrhotic liver tissue. Alcohol is approximately 30 times more soluble in water than in fat, a fact that accounts for the some of the gender and body weight differences in the rate of metabolism (Loomis, 1986). For example, women tend to metabolize alcohol at a slower rate than men because of the higher ratio of fat to water content in their bodies.

It is common knowledge that the experienced drinker may show some resistance to the effects of alcohol, a phenomenon known as *tolerance*. Such an individual requires larger and larger doses of alcohol in order to reach a high, or a desired state of intoxication. This phenomenon is one of the most reliable physical signs of alcoholism, and it may occur because of (1) altered distribution and/or metabolism of the alcohol, leading to lower concentrations at the receptor site; (2) altered receptor sensitivity to alcohol; and (3) the development of alternative pathways for bypassing the receptor system (Loomis, 1986; See also Chapter 3 of this volume). Heavy use of alcohol may lead to increased rates of ethanol oxidation up to 100 percent (Tewari & Carson, 1982).

Intoxication

Alcohol affects the brain in several ways. It alters the neurons' membranes as well as their ion channels, enzymes, and receptors. It also binds directly to certain receptors (Canadian Institute of Neurosciences, Mental Health and Addiction, 2009; NIAAA, 2009). It appears that although the actions on specific cells are quite selective, alcohol has a very nonspecific effect on the physiochemical systems that regulate the functions of neurons (Loomis, 1986). The five basic effects of alcohol on the CNS are (1) euphoria, (2) removal of inhibitions, (3) impairment of vision, (4) muscular incoordination, and (5) lengthened reaction time (Forney & Harger, 1971).

Intoxication and alcoholism are two completely different concepts. *Intoxication* will occur whenever alcohol is ingested. In small amounts, it may produce euphoria and a decrease in inhibitions; at a blood-alcohol concentration (BAC) of 0.10 percent, ataxia and dysarthria generally occur (Seixas, 1986). Between 0.20 and 0.25 percent, many people cannot sit or stand upright without support. The average person may fall into a coma when the BAC is between 0.3 percent and 0.4 percent, and death normally occurs beyond the 0.5 percent level (Loomis, 1986). These averages may be misleading, however, because of the development of *tolerance* in the chronic user. There have been persons arrested for driving under the influence (DUI) with a blood-alcohol level (BAL) of 0.4 percent—a level that would put the so-called average drinker in a coma. There also have been reports of persons surviving a BAL of more than 0.7 percent.

Withdrawal

The earliest and most common effects of alcohol withdrawal are anxiety, anorexia, insomnia, and tremor. In the early stages of withdrawal, a person will also be irritable and easily startled and have a subjective feeling of distress, sometimes described as internal shaking. These symptoms peak within

6 to 48 hours and then rapidly disappear (NIAAA, 2008). The pulse rate is typically elevated during withdrawal and may reach 120 to 140 beats per minute.

Some people going through withdrawal will experience alcoholic hallucinosis, a generally benign state that is not associated with paranoia or panic. Delirium tremens is the most severe state of withdrawal, characterized by marked tremor, anxiety, insomnia, anorexia, paranoia, and disorientation. The symptoms peak about three days after withdrawal, but may persist for two or three weeks. It may also be accompanied by fever, tachypnea, hyperpnea, diarrhea, diaphoresis, and vomiting. Tachycardia is almost always present (Bellenir, 2000; Palmstierna, 2001).

Grand mal convulsive seizures may also occur during withdrawal but not usually as a part of delirium tremens. Anticonvulsant therapy should be used with any patient with a past history of seizures. Seizures occurring after more than two weeks of abstinence suggest a dependency on CNS depressants other than alcohol (Brown, 1982; NIAAA, 1998).

The Digestive System

As mentioned earlier, practically every part of the body is adversely affected by the use of alcohol. Cancer occurs with alarming frequency in the mouth, tongue, pharynx, esophagus, stomach, intestines, liver, and pancreas of an alcoholic (NIAAA, 1993). Alcoholics are also susceptible to inflammation of the esophageal mucosa. This may be caused by increased acid production induced by drinking alcohol, impaired esophageal peristalsis, the direct toxic effects of alcohol on the mucosa, and frequent vomiting (Fenster, 1986). A laceration of the gastroesophageal junction (known as the *Mallory-Weiss syndrome*) frequently results from alcohol-induced gastritis. Rupture of the lower esophagus, or *Boerhaave's syndrome,* is sometimes caused by vigorous vomiting, coughing, or seizures. This condition is fatal if not promptly treated (Bellenir, 2000).

Another common outcome of heavy alcohol use is inflammation of the mucosal lining of the stomach, or *erosive gastritis.* If this condition is severe enough, it may also produce gastric ulcers. Erosive gastritis may be associated with nausea, vomiting, and distention. Occasionally, it may result in upper intestinal bleeding, a potentially life-threatening situation (Bode & Bode, 1997).

One of the most common symptoms experienced by alcoholics is diarrhea (Hermos, 1972). This condition may be caused either by the direct toxic effects of alcohol on the small intestine or by alcohol-related nutritional deficiencies that affect the functioning of the small intestine, most notably a folic acid deficiency. Even moderate amounts of alcohol may cause blisters in the small intestine (Millan, Morris, Beck, & Henson, 1980). A much more serious problem, colon cancer, is also higher than normal among alcoholics (Longnecker, 1992).

Alcohol can cause a number of changes in the liver. Alcoholic liver disease has three phases. The first, *fatty liver,* can usually be reversed with abstinence. *Alcoholic hepatitis* (liver inflammation) and *cirrhosis* (scarring of the liver tissue), the other two phases, are more serious, with a 60 percent death rate over a four-year period. Most of those deaths occur within the first 12 months of diagnosis (Chedid et al., 1991). Women are at greater risk for cirrhosis than men, and smokers and obese persons are also more prone to cirrhosis (NIAAA, 2005).

A number of studies in the last two decades have confirmed an interaction effect between acetaminophen use and alcohol consumption (USDHHS, 2000), which may lead to liver toxicity.

The Food and Drug Administration (FDA) recently proposed much tighter restrictions on the sale of acetaminophen, and a possible ban on some painkillers that contain acetaminophen, such as Vicodin, Percocet, and Darvocet (Tanner, 2009). Persons with alcohol-related liver disease are also at higher risk for hepatitis C. It is thought that the interaction of alcohol and the hepatitis C virus may impair immune response to the virus (Geissler, Geisen, & Wands, 1997).

Alcohol consumption can also lead to both acute and chronic pancreatitis. Acute pancreatitis is manifested by upper abdominal pain, nausea, and vomiting. In addition to these symptoms, chronic pancreatitis may be associated with malnutrition, weight loss, diarrhea, and foul-smelling, bulky stools. The chronic condition is so painful that victims often become addicted to analgesics or narcotics (Fenster, 1986). The exact causal mechanism is not clear, but alcohol is thought to have a direct, toxic effect on the pancreas, in addition to causing simultaneously an increase in pancreatic stimulation and obstructing the flow of pancreatic juice to the duodenum (Kalant, 1969). Acute pancreatitis is generally self-limiting, and most people will recover within a few days. Chronic pancreatitis, on the other hand, is thought to be irreversible. Abstinence may reduce the pain, but the inflammation and scarring process will continue (Ammann et al., 1984).

The Cardiovascular System

In nonalcoholic, healthy people, alcohol causes an increase in the heart rate as well as lessened stroke power. In other words, the heart simply functions less efficiently as a pump (Markiewi & Cholewa, 1982). In such individuals, alcohol also decreases resistance to blood flow throughout the body, resulting in a reduction in blood pressure (NIAAA, 1999). Other studies have found a strong relationship between alcohol use and elevated blood pressure among drinkers with hypertension (NIAAA, 2000). Acute alcohol consumption causes dysfunctional changes in heart tissue, even in young, healthy adults (Lang, Borrow, Neumann, & Feldman, 1985). In many chronic alcoholics, there is a form of cardiomyopathy that is characterized by an actual wasting away of the heart muscle (NIAAA, 2000).

Congestive heart failure associated with alcoholic cardiomyopathy, diseases involving thromboses (blood clots obstructing blood vessels), and low platelet counts are additional cardiovascular problems encountered in alcoholics. Among men,

the average alcoholic has almost *twice* the chance of death from atherosclerotic and degenerative heart disease, compared to a nonalcoholic. Among heavy drinkers, women are more likely to suffer from alcohol-related heart disease, even though women drink less alcohol than men (NIAAA, 2008). Women alcoholics are more than *four* times as likely to die from these diseases as nonalcoholics (NIAAA, 1999; Schmidt & deLint, 1972). Several studies have reported that *moderate* drinkers (i.e., no more than two drinks a day for men and one drink per day for women) have a *lower* risk of coronary heart disease (Camargo et al., 1997; Keil et al., 1997; McElduff & Dobson, 1997). However, research has not been able to confirm that alcohol itself causes the lower risk. It could result from yet unidentified factors associated with lifestyle, diet, exercise, or additives to alcoholic beverages.

The Endocrine and Reproductive Systems

Again, alcohol has both direct and indirect effects on the endocrine and reproductive systems. The spreading of endocrine effects is due in part to the organization of the endocrine glands into functional hierarchies called *axes*. Every endocrine axis has numerous feedback controls, and changes in one component may affect other components on that axis (Fink, 1979). The most common effects of alcohol on the hypothalamic-pituitary-thyroid (H-P-T) axis are a modest decrease in the levels of the hormone thyroxine and a marked decrease in the level of triiodothyronine. These changes are associated with serious liver disease, primarily through an inhibition of liver oxygen consumptions (Israel, Walfish, Orrego, Blake, & Kalant, 1979).

Alcohol also has serious consequences on the hypothalamic-pituitary-gonadal (H-P-G) axis in men, impairing the reproductive function and altering physiology (Cicero, 1981). These consequences include testicular atrophy, abnormal morphology of sperm cells, an increase in estrogen levels, and a decrease in testosterone. The relationship between liver disease and sexual dysfunction is extremely complex, but it is widely recognized that alcoholics with cirrhosis are more likely than not to be sexually impotent (Cornely, Schade, Van Thiel, & Gavaler, 1984). Noncirrhotic alcoholics are also likely to lose sexual function for other reasons, such as a decrease in testosterone or psychological impairment.

In women, alcohol-induced endocrinal failure is likely to result in early menopause, heavy menstrual flow, menstrual discomfort, infertility, and a higher frequency of obstetric and gynecologic problems. In both sexes, heavy alcohol consumption is associated with the loss of secondary sex characteristics. Men may develop female hair patterns and gynecomastia (breast enlargement) (USDHHS, 1987). Another major health problem associated with alcohol use is *fetal alcohol syndrome* or *fetal alcohol effects.* Because of the severity and prevalence of the consequences of maternal drug abuse on the newborn, we have provided a separate section on this problem later in this chapter.

The Neurologic System

Excessive use of alcohol is known to lead to acute and chronic brain damage, as well as peripheral nerve dysfunction. The neuronal membrane is the location where the biochemical effects of alcohol on the CNS begin. Alcohol is believed to disrupt normal membrane function by penetrating into the membrane, expanding its volume, and disordering the lipid components. These changes can have profound effects on neurotransmission: the electrical signaling that occurs within and between neurons. This happens because the neurons are no longer capable of transmitting the ions through the neuronal membranes. The overall consequence is a disruption of the flow of information within the brain (NIAAA, 2008).

Autopsy studies of alcoholic patients have found both cerebral and cortical atrophy to be quite common. In addition to being atrophied, the brains of alcoholics also have significant cell loss in many regions (Porjesz & Begleiter, 1983).

CAT scans have also revealed that alcoholics have a larger brain cavity, wider grooves on the brain's surface, and wider fissures (Ron, 1983). The exact mechanism by which alcohol damages the brain is not known. One theory is that alcohol triggers a CNS antigen that leads to an autoimmune response that produces brain damage (Tkach & Yoshitsugi, 1970). Another is that higher concentrations of alcohol in the blood lead to occlusion of vessels in the brain. The ensuing edema and hemorrhaging are responsible for the damage to brain tissue (Moskow, Pennington, & Knisely, 1968). Still another is that brain damage is produced by alcohol-induced interference with protein synthesis (Tewari & Noble, 1971).

There are also a number of other secondary factors that may lead to brain damage in alcoholics. Oxygen deprivation related to such things as coma with hypoventilation or vomiting and aspiration of gastric contents can be responsible for such damage. Alcoholic hypoglycemia may also cause blood glucose levels to fall to dangerous levels. Brain cells (which have no capacity for regeneration) cannot function for long periods of time without both glucose and oxygen. In chronic alcoholics, nutritional deficiencies may cause brain damage. Both Wernicke's syndrome and Korsakoff's psychosis are associated with thiamin deficiency. (Thiamin is a primary link in the production of energy for brain cells [Smith, 1986].) However, as late as 1999, there had been no studies of the natural history of alcohol-related brain damage. Factors other than thiamin deficiencies may provide a partial explanation (Homewood & Bond, 1999).

Common Neurologic Disorders.   *Acute brain syndrome* is marked by a rapid onset and a high degree of reversibility. It is manifested simply as acute intoxication or hallucinosis. *Chronic brain syndrome* is characterized by a generally slow onset and is usually irreversible. Some of the symptoms of both acute and chronic brain syndrome are a decrease in complex intellectual functioning, alteration in memory, impaired judgment, and shallowness of affect (Page, 1983). Alcoholics with chronic brain syndrome suffer from recent memory loss, confusion, disorientation (for time, place, and person), and difficulty in concentration (Miller & Orr, 1980). These symptoms may be preceded by months or even years of other symptoms, such as fatigue, listlessness, loss of interest, depression, and anxiety or agitation. Unless the brain damage is halted, the person's speech will become monosyllabic and motor controls will fail. Eventually, he or she will be unable to manage even basic tasks, such as eating or dressing, and sphincter control will fail (Smith, 1986).

A majority of alcoholics have a thiamine deficiency, and a number of those will develop serious brain disorders such as Wernicke-Korskoff syndrome. This is a disease that consists of two separate syndromes. Wernicke's encephalopathy is a severe, short-lived condition characterized by mental confusion, oculomotor dysfunction, and difficulty with motor coordination. Korsakoff's psychosis is found in as many as 90 percent of alcoholics with Wernicke's encephalopathy. It is a chronic and debilitating syndrome characterized by problems remembering old information and retaining new information (both retrograde and anterograde amnesia), and difficulty with walking and coordination. Patients are forgetful and easily frustrated (NIAAA, 2004).

Oliver Sacks (1985) described such a patient in his fascinating book of clinical tales. The patient was 49 years old in 1975, but he believed that he was still 19. In a conversation with Sacks, Jimmie related the names of the different submarines on which he had served in World War II, as well as their missions, where he was stationed, and the names of shipmates. He remembered Morse code, was still fluent in touch typing, and could do complex mathematics (including algebra) in his head. Yet when Sacks left the room for two minutes and then reentered, Jimmie did not recognize him. On one occasion, Sacks laid out his watch, tie, and glasses on the desk, covered them, and asked Jimmie to remember them. "Then after a minute's chat, I asked him what I had put under the cover. He remembered none of them—or indeed that I had even asked him to remember" (Sacks, 1985).

Alcoholic pellagra is the result of a thiamin deficiency characterized by a clouding of consciousness, rigidity, and uncontrolled sucking and grasping reflexes. Other symptoms associated with pellagra in nonalcoholics (dementia, dermatitis, and diarrhea) usually do not occur in alcoholics because of the rapid onset of the disease (Jolliffe et al., 1940).

Peripheral neuropathy can also occur in alcoholics who do not have Wernicke-Korsakoff's syndrome. Hospital reports indicate that alcoholic peripheral neuropathy is more common than all other forms of peripheral neuropathy combined (Ammendola et al., 2001). Problems occur first in the feet, the most distal parts of the longest peripheral nerves. Initial symptoms are usually burning, tingling, or prickling sensations, along with pain in the calf muscles or feet. Discomfort and numbness begin in the feet and gradually work up the legs, and muscle weakness and wasting occur as the process continues. A treatment consisting of abstinence, a nutritious diet, and supplementary vitamin B will usually allow most patients to recover (Smith, 1986).

Alcohol and Other Disorders

Alcohol use is a common cause of malnutrition, partly because alcoholic beverages are often substituted for other, more nutritional food and partly because alcohol disrupts the body's ability to absorb and properly utilize some vitamins (Leiber, 1984). In one study, *all* 41 patients with alcoholic liver disease were also found to suffer from thiamin deficiency (Majumdar et al., 1982). Long-term alcohol intake commonly results in deficiencies in fiber, protein, calcium, iron, vitamins A and C, and thiamin (Hillers & Massey, 1985).

People who have not eaten within the past day may experience a drop in blood sugar and hypoglycemia, with a potential for coma and death. Insulin-dependent diabetics are extremely vulnerable to both hypoglycemia and ketoacidosis (Arky, 1984). Alcohol consumption has also been associated with a reduction in bone mass and with osteoporosis in men (Bikle et al., 1985).

Chronic alcohol abuse is associated with higher susceptibility to several different types of infectious diseases due to a suppression of the body's immune system, including tuberculosis, pneumonia, peritonitis, and hepatitis B. Equally disturbing is the fact that alcoholics are at a much higher risk for almost every form of cancer—from the mouth to the rectum! In fact, about one-fourth of all cancer of directly exposed tissue (lip, oral cavity, pharynx, stomach, etc.) is attributed to the effects of alcohol (NIAAA, 1993, 2000).

From a medical perspective, almost nothing good can be said about the effects of alcohol on the human body, except that moderate drinkers may have slightly lower risks of atherosclerosis and coronary heart disease. This may be because alcohol reduces the oxidizability of low-density lipoprotein (LDL), which may result in the lowering of so-called bad cholesterol (Witztum & Steinberg, 1991). Experts in cardiology recommend against the use of alcohol, however. Even if moderate alcohol intake does provide this benefit, it is far outweighed by other health risks, and it makes more sense to control cholesterol levels by choosing a healthy diet (NIAAA, 2000).

The Effects of Cannabis

Compared to alcohol, the purely physiological effects of marijuana and hashish use are relatively few (see Table 4.1). However, there is still much controversy concerning the scientific evidence on the consequences of using this drug (Zimmer & Morgan, 1995). Most of the proven health risks associated with cannabis come from the common method of ingesting the drug: smoking (Barsky, Roth, Kleerup, Simmons, & Tashkin, 1998; Kuhn, Swartzwelder, & Wilson, 2008). Since marijuana smoke also contains carcinogens, regular users are also exposed to an increased risk of lung cancer. Just as in tobacco smoking, there is also an increased risk of heart disease (Imlah, 1989).

A person smoking marijuana will experience a reddening of the eyes (inflammation of the conjunctiva of the eye from the irritant effect of the smoke), slight tachycardia, and a dryness of the mouth. For a long time, it was commonly accepted that dilation of the pupils was a common side effect of marijuana smoking, but that notion has been discredited. Blood sugar level also seems to be unaffected by marijuana, despite the long-standing impact of this drug on subjective feelings of hunger ("munchies") (Goode, 1972).

No conclusive evidence supports damage to other organs related to marijuana usage (Cohen, 1981). One of the major problems in conducting research in this area, however, is that it is difficult to isolate the effects of marijuana *alone*, apart from other drugs, since marijuana users commonly use other illicit drugs as well as alcohol and tobacco.

It has long been suspected that heavy marijuana use may result in suppression of the immune system, and studies have confirmed this (Weber, 1988). Reduced sperm counts, erectile dysfunction, disrupted ovarian cycles, and diminished ovulation have also been found among regular users (Imlah, 1989; Nahas, 1984). There is scant evidence of brain damage except among the very heaviest users, but problems with learning and memory are associated with long-term use (Kuhn, Swartzwelder, & Wilson, 2008).

Cannabis generally produces a state of euphoria, in which inhibitions are relaxed and thoughts appear to come more rapidly and to be more profound than normal thoughts. Users often report feeling an exaggerated sense of ability, despite a loss of critical faculties and distorted timing. The primary personality change for regular users has been called the *amotivational syndrome.* The user loses ambition and becomes passive, apathetic, increasingly introspective, and disinterested in anything outside his or her dreamy fantasies (Imlah, 1989; Solowij, 1998).

The psychological effects of cannabis have been studied and reported since the second century, when the use of hashish was reported by a Chinese investigator, Pen-Ts'ao Ching, to produce mental illness (Nahas, 1984). Hashish use was also associated with a certain form of psychosis

TABLE 4.1   Commonly Abused Drugs

Substance: Category and Name	Examples of *Commercial* and Street Names	DEA Schedule*/ How Administered**	*Intoxication Effects*/Potential Health Consequences
Cannabinoids			*euphoria, slowed thinking and reaction time, confusion, impaired balance and coordination*/cough, frequent respiratory infections; impaired memory and learning; increased heart rate, anxiety; panic attacks; tolerance, addiction
hashish	boom, chronic, gangster, hash, hash oil, hemp	I/swallowed, smoked	
marijuana	blunt, dope, ganja, grass, herb, joints, Mary Jane, pot, reefer, sinsentilla, skunk, weed	I/swallowed, smoked	
Depressants			*reduced pain and anxiety; feeling of well-being; lowered inhibitions; slowed pulse and breathing; lowered blood pressure; poor concentration*/confusion, fatigue; impaired co-ordination, memory, judgment; respiratory depression and arrest, addiction
barbiturates	*Amytal, Nembutal, Seconal, Phenobarbital;* barbs, reds, red birds, phennies, tooies, yellows, yellow jackets	II, III, V/injected, swallowed	
benzodiazepines (other than flunitrazepam)	*Ativan, Halcion, Librium, Valium, Xanax;* candy, downers, sleeping pills, tranks	IV/swallowed	*Also, for barbiturates—sedation, drowsiness*/depression, unusual excitement, fever, irritability, poor judgement, slurred speech, dizziness
*flunitrazepam***	*Rohypnol;* forget-me pill, Mexican Valium, R2, roche, roofies, roofinol, rope, rophies	IV/swallowed, snorted	*for benzodiazepines—sedation, drowsiness*/dizziness
			for flunitrazepam—visual and gastrointestinal disturbances, urinary retention, memory loss for the time under the drug's effects
*GHB***	*gamma-hydroxybutyrate;* G, Georgia home boy, grievous bodily harm, liquid ecstasy	under consideration/ swallowed	*for GHB*—drowsiness, nausea/vomiting, headache, loss of consciousness, loss of reflexes, seizures, coma, death
methaqualone	*Quaalude, Sopor, Parest;* ludes, mandrex, quad, quay	I/injected, swallowed	*for methaqualone—euphoria*/depression, poor reflexes, slurred speech, coma
Dissociative Anesthetics			
ketamine	*Ketalar SV;* cat Valiums, K, Special K, vitamin K	III/injected, snorted, smoked	*increased heart rate and blood pressure, impaired motor function*/memory loss; numbness; nausea/vomiting

TABLE 4.1 *Continued*

Substance: Category and Name	Examples of *Commercial* and Street Names	DEA Schedule*/ How Administered**	*Intoxication Effects*/Potential Health Consequences
PCP and analogs	*phencyclidine*; angel dust, boat, hog, love boat, peace pill	I, II/injected, swallowed, smoked	*Also, for ketamine—at high doses, delirium, depression, respiratory depression and arrest* *for PCP and analogs—possible decrease in blood pressure and heart rate, panic, aggression, violence*/loss of appetite, depression
Hallucinogens			
LSD	*lysergic acid diethylamide*; acid, blotter, boomers, cubes, microdot, yellow sunshines	I/swallowed, absorbed through mouth tissues	*altered states of perception and feeling; nausea*/chronic mental disorders, persisting perception disorder (flashbacks)
mescaline	buttons, cactus, mesc, peyote	I/swallowed, smoked	*Also, for LSD and mescaline— increased body temperature, heart rate, blood pressure; loss of appetite, sleeplessness, numbness, weakness, tremors*
psilocybin	magic mushroom, purple passion, shrooms	I/swallowed	*for psilocybin—nervousness, paranoia*
Opioids and Morphine Derivatives			
codeine	*Empirin with Codeine, Fiorinal with Codeine, Robitussin A-C, Tylenol with Codeine*; Captain Cody, Cody schoolboy; (with glutethimide) doors & fours, loads, pancakes and syrup	II, III, IV/ injected, swallowed	*pain relief, euphoria, drowsiness*/respiratory depression and arrest, nausea, confusion, constipation, sedation, unconsciousness, coma, tolerance, addiction *Also, for codeine—less analgesia, sedation, and respiratory depression than morphine*
fentanyl	*Actiq, Duragesic, Sublimaze*; Apache, China girl, China white, dance fever, friend, goodfella, jackpot, murder 8, TNT, Tango and Cash	II/injected, smoked, snorted	*for heroin—staggering gait*
heroin	*diacetylmorphine*; brown sugar, dope, H, horse, junk, skag, skunk, smack, white horse	I/injected, smoked, snorted	
morphine	*Roxanol, Duramorph*; M, Miss Emma, monkey, white stuff	II, III/injected, swallowed, smoked	
opium	*laudanum, paregoric*; big O, black stuff, block, gum, hop	II, III, V/ swallowed, smoked	

(continued)

TABLE 4.1 *Continued*

Substance: Category and Name	Examples of *Commercial* and Street Names	DEA Schedule*/ How Administered**	*Intoxication Effects*/Potential Health Consequences
Stimulants			
amphetamine	*Adderall, Biphetamine, Dexedrine*; bennies, black beauties, crosses, hearts, LA turnaround, speed, truck drivers, uppers	II/injected, swallowed, smoked, snorted	*increased heart rate and blood pressure, increased metabolism; feelings of exhilaration, energy, increased mental alertness*/rapid or irregular heart beat; reduced appetite, weight loss, heart failure
cocaine	*Cocaine hydrochloride*; blow, bump, C, candy, Charlie, coke, crack, flake, rock, snow, toot	II/injected, smoked, snorted	*Also, for amphetamine—rapid breathing; hallucinations*/tremor, loss of coordination; irritability, anxiousness, restlessness, delirium, panic, paranoia, impulsive behavior, aggressiveness, tolerance, addiction
MDMA (methylenedioxy-methamphetamine)	*DOB, DOM, MDA*; Adam, clarity, ecstasy, Eve, lover's speed, peace, STP, X, XTC	I/swallowed	*for cocaine—increased temperature*/chest pain, respiratory failure, nausea, abdominal pain, strokes, seizures, headaches, malnutrition
methamphetamine	*Desoxyn*; chalk, crank, crystal, fire, glass, go fast, ice, meth, speed	II/injected, swallowed, smoked, snorted	*for MDMA—mild hallucinogenic effects, increased tactile sensitivity, empathic feelings, hyperthermia*/impaired memory and learning
methylphenidate	*Ritalin*; JIF, MPH, R-ball, Skippy, the smart drug, vitamin R	II/injected, swallowed, snorted	*for methamphetamine—aggression, violence, psychotic behavior*/memory loss, cardiac and neurological damage; impaired memory and learning, tolerance, addiction
nicotine	bidis, chew, cigars, cigarettes, smokeless tobacco, snuff, spit tobacco	not scheduled/ smoked, snorted, taken in snuff and spit tobacco	*for methylphenidate—increase or decrease in blood pressure, psychotic episodes*/digestive problems, loss of appetite, weight loss
			for nicotine—tolerance, addiction; additional effects attributable to tobacco exposure—adverse pregnancy outcomes, chronic lung disease, cardiovascular disease, stroke, cancer

TABLE 4.1   *Continued*

Substance: Category and Name	Examples of *Commercial* and Street Names	DEA Schedule*/ How Administered**	*Intoxication Effects*/Potential Health Consequences
Other Compounds			
anabolic steroids	*Anadrol, Oxandrin, Durabolin, Depo-Testosterone, Equipoise;* roids, juice	III/injected, swallowed, applied to skin	*no intoxication effects*/hypertension, blood clotting and cholesterol changes, liver cysts and cancer, kidney cancer, hostility and aggression, acne; adolescents, premature stoppage of growth; in males, prostate cancer, reduced sperm production, shrunken testicles, breast enlargement; in females, menstrual irregularities, development of beard and other masculine characteristics
inhalants	*Solvents (paint thinners, gasoline, glues), gases (butane, propane, aerosol propellants, nitrous oxide), nitrites (isoamyl, isobutyl, cyclohexyl);* laughing gas, poppers, snappers, whippets	not scheduled/ inhaled through nose or mouth	*stimulation, loss of inhibition; headache; nausea or vomiting; slurred speech, loss of motor coordination; wheezing*/unconsciousness, cramps, weight loss, muscle weakness, depression, memory impairment, damage to cardiovascular and nervous systems, sudden death

*Schedule I and II drugs have a high potential for abuse. They require greater storage security and have a quota on manufacturing, among other restrictions. Schedule I drugs are available for research only and have no approved medical use; Schedule II drugs are available only by prescription (unrefillable) and require a form for ordering. Schedule III and IV drugs are available by prescription, may have five refills in 6 months, and may be ordered orally. Most Schedule V drugs are available over the counter.

**Taking drugs by injection can increase the risk of infection through needle contamination with staphylococci, HIV, hepatitis, and other organisms.

***Associated with sexual assault.

Source: Retrieved December 22, 2003, from http://www.nida.gov/DrugsofAbuse.html

among the followers (called assassins) of an eleventh-century Moslem leader. Jacques-Joseph Moreau, an officer in Napoleon's army, reported similarities between cannabis intoxication and mental illness in 1845.

Although there may be some debate regarding whether a true cannabis psychosis exists, there is evidence that long-term heavy use has resulted in temporal disintegration, delusional-type ideation, panic reactions, dysphoric reactions

(disorientation, immobility, acute panic, heavy sedation), problems with memory, and inability to follow or to maintain a conversation. Such use also has been associated with acute brain syndrome and delirium, characterized by confusion prostration, disorientation, derealization, and sometimes auditory or visual hallucinations (Nahas, 1984). Several studies suggest that cannabis users may either cause or exacerbate psychoses and increase the risk of developing schizophrenia by inducing changes in the cannabinoid system of the brain (Dean, Sundram, Bradbury, Scarr, & Copolov, 2001).

In recent years evidence has accumulated supporting some legitimate medical uses for cannabis, such as preventing weight loss among cancer, AIDS, and other patients by preventing nausea. It has also proven effective in reducing pressure within the eyes of glaucoma patients (Kuhn, Swartzwelder & Wilson, 2008). These developments and other arguments for the legalization of marijuana are discussed in Chapter 8.

The Effects of Stimulants

Cocaine

Until recently, the most common method for ingesting cocaine among users in North America was the inhalation of refined coca paste, cocaine hydrochloride (otherwise known as *coke* or *snow*). This drug can also be injected (alone or in combination with heroin) intravenously or intramuscularly. In other parts of the world, users prefer to chew coca leaves or to smoke coca paste (Arif, 1987). In the United States, the most popular method seems to be smoking a form of solidified cocaine that has been treated with baking soda, known as *crack*. This form is also known as *freebase cocaine*, since it is the cocaine alkaloid that has been chemically separated from cocaine hydrochloride. Crack or freebase is more suitable for smoking because more of the cocaine in the freebase form volatizes without decomposing (Brower & Anglin, 1987). Different methods of ingestion are frequently associated with different types of physiological problems.

Overdoses from smoking, inhaling, or injecting cocaine may be fatal as a result of ventricular fibrillation, cardiac arrest, apnoea, or hyperthermia. Heavy use may also result in extreme hypertension, cerebrovascular bleeding, stroke, and elliptiform fits. Heart failure is a risk, even among young, otherwise healthy users of cocaine (Qureshi, Suri, Guterman, & Hopkins, 2001).

Chronic use also affects vision. Users may experience "snow lights," which are patches or flashes of white light darting in and out of their field of vision. Others may report fuzzy or double vision.

Cocaine's behavioral effects do not differ much from those produced by amphetamines; their duration is simply much shorter (Hofmann, 1975). The quality and intensity of the cocaine-induced high vary markedly from one user to the next, depending on the mood, personality, and expectations of the user and the setting and circumstances under which the drug is taken. The acute positive state generally is characterized by euphoria, feelings of increased energy and confidence, mental alertness, and sexual arousal. With continued use, tolerance develops, making it more difficult to achieve a satisfactory high and bringing rebound effects that are dysphoric. When not high, the user feels anxious, confused, depressed, and often paranoid (Yoslow, 1992).

Ironically, only 20 years ago, common wisdom held that cocaine was *not* an addictive substance. Now it is regarded as being both physically and psychologically addictive, as well as one of the most dangerous of all addictive drugs. We now have evidence of neuronal injury in the frontal cortex as the result of prolonged cocaine use (Chang, Ernst, Strickland, & Mehringer, 1999). A recent study indicates that dependence rates for cocaine are second only to that of heroin (SAMHSA, 2008). Although withdrawal from cocaine does not produce physical symptoms as severe as withdrawal from some other drugs, its psychological hold on the user is one of the strongest. There are also considerable physical risks associated with prolonged use or overdosing (Washton, 1989).

Although regarded by some to be an aphrodisiac, continued cocaine use generally produces sexual dysfunction. Men suffer from a reduced sexual drive and erectile and ejaculatory functions, while women experience a reduction in sexual desire and lose the ability to produce vaginal lubrication. Weight loss, insomnia, and hallucinations are also frequently reported (Cohen,

---

BOX 4.1   *A Little-Known Hazard of Smoking Crack*

A 34-year-old female was examined in a hospital emergency room seven hours after drinking beer and smoking crack. She was concerned that she might have inhaled the "screen" from her crack pipe: a piece of a steel wool scouring pad the size of her fingertip. She complained of burning in her throat, a foreign body sensation, and a change in her voice but no shortness of breath, difficulty swallowing, or abdominal pain. She was tearful and spoke in a whisper.

On physical examination, her temperature was normal but her pulse and respiratory rate were both somewhat elevated. There were no visible burns to the mouth or throat and listening to the lungs revealed no abnormal internal sounds. However, she made a harsh sound intermittently when breathing, indicating a possible obstruction to the air passage. No foreign body or burn was seen on indirect laryngoscopy (or internal examination of the larynx). A lateral neck X-ray study showed a normal epiglottis and no foreign body. Chest X-ray studies were unremarkable, as well. Fiberoptic laryngoscopy showed fluid buildup and swelling in the left posterior arytenoid. An abdominal X-ray revealed a foreign body in the right-lower quadrant consistent with the steel wool filter. The next morning, the patient was asymptomatic and was discharged, recovering without further treatment.

While crack pipe screen aspiration is a rarely reported event, physicians should be aware of the potential for foreign body aspiration and ingestion by this mechanism.

Source: Moettus & Tandberg (1998).

1981). Magnon's syndrome, for instance, is the sensation that bugs are crawling under the skin. Chronic cocaine users may suffer sores or lesions from scratching (Abadinsky, 2001).

Since cocaine enters the blood relatively quickly from mucous membranes, the nose is a favorite site for the ingestion or snorting of cocaine hydrochloride. The habit of snorting or sniffing cocaine eventually causes a perforation of the nasal septum, and users are sometimes referred to as "sniffy" (Imlah, 1989). When the nasal membrane is beginning to be damaged, the user will appear to have a stuffy or runny nose, and the mucous will be very watery. As the condition becomes more severe, the user will have difficulty breathing. Eventually, breathing through the nose becomes impossible, and the wall dividing the halves of the nose will disintegrate (Paredes & Gorelick, 1992).

The effects of ingesting cocaine take about three minutes to reach the brain by snorting. Freebasing or smoking crack can deliver the same effects in about six seconds (Baum, 1985). This form of administration can produce minor lung irritation, a sore chest and neck, swollen glands, and a raspy voice. The high produced from smoking crack lasts from two to five minutes and ends as abruptly as it began. After the "crash," the user is irritable, anxious, and depressed and has increasingly severe cravings for more of the drug. Reports from addicts indicate that addiction occurs *much* more quickly from the use of crack than from any other form of cocaine use (Washton, 1989). The narrative in Box 4.1 tells the story of another hazard of crack use.

Intravenous injection of cocaine hydrochloride in a water solution delivers a euphoric feeling almost as quickly as smoking crack—about 14 seconds (Baum, 1985). Some cocaine users prefer injecting a mixture of cocaine and heroin, a combination known as a *speedball*. (The heroin is said to dampen the unpleasant jitteriness and crash from the cocaine.) Taken together, these two drugs sometimes completely halt the user's respiration or cause brain seizures. The danger of a cocaine overdose cannot be overemphasized. Deaths from cocaine or cocaine/heroin combinations have exceeded heroin overdoses at least since 1983 (SAMHSA, 2000).

There are many other risks associated with any type of intravenous drug use, such as hepatitis or HIV infection. Although the new user may begin by scrupulously maintaining sterile needles and syringes ("works"), the chronic user will seldom exercise such care. One former user tells about "a day when I drove all the way across Liverpool to borrow a wornout works from an addict who had recently had syphilis" (Stewart, 1987). Since bacteria and viruses don't impede the addict's high, they are generally disregarded.

Finally, there is the issue of babies that have been exposed to cocaine in utero. A much greater incidence of miscarriages, low-birth-weight infants, premature deliveries, and birth defects have been associated with cocaine use during pregnancy (Livesay et al., 1988). However, it is difficult to separate the effects of cocaine abuse and the effects of other drugs. As these children mature, the effects of their mothers' cocaine abuse appear to have few long-term consequences on their development or behavior (Frank, Augustyn, Knight, Pell, & Zuckerman, 2001).

Amphetamines and Methamphetamines

Amphetamines are one of the most preferred drugs of so-called normal Americans—students cramming for exams, truck drivers working 24-hour days, and athletes competing for national and international records. Millions of people have legally used amphetamines for anxiety, depression, and obesity.

As mentioned earlier, millions of soldiers were given amphetamines in World War II to enhance combat performance. German Panzer troops used the drug to eliminate fatigue and maintain physical endurance. Because of the

aggressive and violent behavior frequently noted in chronic users, some historians believe that many German atrocities were linked to the use of amphetamines (Lukas, 1985). Ten years after the war ended, 200,000 cases of amphetamine psychosis, one of the most extreme side effects of this drug, were reported in Japan (Imlah, 1989). As late as 1969, the U.S. armed forces were still purchasing massive amounts of amphetamines, with the U.S. Navy dispensing 21.1 pills per person per year, followed by the U.S. Air Force (17.5) and the U.S. Army (13.8) (Lukas, 1985).

Low dosages of this drug will normally produce the following effects (Innes & Nickerson, 1970):

1. Heightened competence in motor skills and mental acuity
2. Increased alertness
3. A feeling of increased energy
4. A stimulation of the need for motor activity (particularly walking or talking)
5. A feeling of euphoria
6. Increased heartbeat
7. Inhibition of appetite
8. Constriction of the blood vessels
9. Dryness of the mouth
10. A feeling of confidence and even grandeur

Amphetamines are usually taken orally by new users in dosages of 50 to 150 milligrams (mg) daily. Addicts soon discover that a high is obtained faster by snorting or injecting the drug. During a "speed run," a "speed freak" may inject as much as 1,000 mg in one dose and up to 5,000 mg during a 24-hour period. During a run, a user will be disinclined to eat or sleep and may lose 10 pounds or more during a week. Some users prefer the "balling" technique, in which a form known as *crank* is instilled into the vagina prior to intercourse. Low dosages of amphetamine may slightly enhance sexual performance, but higher dosages consistently disrupt sexual function (Lukas, 1985). Orgasm and ejaculation are either delayed or impossible to achieve while using large doses of speed (Cohen, 1981).

After "crashing," the user may experience marked depression, apathy, a variety of aches and pains, and a ravenous appetite. The person may be so exhausted that he or she will sleep for long periods. Some users will begin another speed run as soon as they feel they are beginning to crash. It is not unusual for some users to inject amphetamines in combination with other drugs, such as sedatives or heroin. (Although the original speedball was cocaine and heroin, the "poor man's speedball" is methamphetamine and heroin [Cohen, 1981].)

Chronic amphetamine use may lead to cerebral hemorrhage, tachycardia, hypertension, cardiac arrhythmias, and liver damage. Combining amphetamine use with drinking alcohol has a multiplicative effect that puts the user at a high risk for heart failure (Higgins et al., 1988). The anorexia produced by chronic use coupled with the high caloric intake required to sustain unusually high levels of motor activity often results in malnutrition. Paranoia inevitably comes with heavy and continued use. Violent behavior, including suicide, may come during or at the end of a run (Imlah, 1989).

The repeated use of amphetamines leads to addiction, tolerance, and the need for increasingly larger doses. During the initial phase of withdrawal, the user may sleep almost continuously for up to three days. This is usually followed by a state of depression lasting up to two weeks. During this time, the individual may be irritable and apathetic and experience episodes of anxiety, extreme fear, and obsessions. Sleep disturbances may occur for the next several months. An additional problem for amphetamine users is that they frequently begin using alcohol, barbiturates, or other depressants in order to mitigate the stimulation effects of amphetamines. This is particularly dangerous because of the possibility of drug interaction effects (Kuhn, Shwartzwelder, & Wilson, 2008)

Chronic users develop *amphetamine toxicity,* which is manifested in physical, mental, and behavioral symptoms. General health and personal hygiene deteriorate, and intravenous users may show track marks, infections, and abscesses. Behavioral signs include nervousness, irritability, and restlessness due to the constant overstimulation induced by the drug. This may lead to stereotypic compulsive behavior such as taking an object apart and putting it back together again. Users may pace back and forth across a room, and their conversation will be quite repetitive. The most extreme form of this toxicity is a state of paranoia called *amphetamine psychosis.* The individual becomes suspicious of everyone, is physically exhausted, and appears to be quite confused. Delusions or hallucinations may occur, and violent, aggressive behavior is frequently noted. The paranoia of an amphetamine addict may be identical to that observed in someone with schizophrenia (Kuhn, Shwartzwelder, & Wilson, 2008).

A unique feature of amphetamine psychosis is the occurrence of tactile hallucinations. Users may feel that they have worms or lice on their bodies (similar to "cocaine bugs"). Constant picking or scratching often results in sores and abrasions. Some users have even used knives or razor blades to remove the imagined organisms from their skin.

Another particular feature of amphetamine psychosis is the quickness with which it can occur. Studies have shown that it can be induced in human volunteers, who were carefully screened to ensure they did not have a previous history of psychosis, in approximately four days (Lukas, 1985).

Methamphetamine comes in forms that can be smoked, snorted, taken orally, or injected. A single high dose of the drug can damage nerve terminals in the dopamine-containing regions of the brain. High doses can result in dangerously high body temperatures. Long-term abuse leads to compulsive drug seeking and drug use, accompanied by functional and molecular changes in the brain. Withdrawal symptoms may include depression, anxiety, paranoia, aggression, fatigue, and an intense craving for the drug (NIDA, 2001e).

Crystalline methamphetamine, which is known as *crystal meth* or *ice,* has become one of the most popular drugs in Asia and in the western United States (NIDA, 2001d). The basic ingredients for this drug can be easily obtained over the Internet. Just a few hundred dollars' worth of ingredients will produce thousands of dollars of ice in its most highly refined form (Koch Crime Institute, 2001). The drug's popularity grew quickly because of the enormous profits, because it can be easily manufactured, and because the high from smoking ice lasts 8 to 24 hours, compared to the 15-minute high from crack (Bishop, 1989).

Ice produces feelings of euphoria followed by severe depression, just as crack does, but the high lasts much longer and the crash is much worse. Addicts call the sensation from smoking ice "amping," for the amplified euphoria it provides them (Lerner, 1989). Ice users may also experience symptoms of acute psychosis that are not normally associated with crack use. Severe paranoia, hallucinations, delusions, and incoherent speech may also make the behavior of ice addicts indistinguishable from that of paranoid schizophrenics. Extremely violent and aggressive behavior is common among addicts.

Other symptoms associated with use of this drug are weight loss, insomnia, irregular heartbeat, convulsions, and body temperatures that can reach 108 degrees, frequently resulting in kidney failure. Devastating effects have been noticed in children born to mothers using ice: They tend to be asocial and incapable of bonding. Some have tremors and cry for 24 hours without stopping. Nurses report that the problems of these so-called ice babies are much more severe than the problems of babies born addicted to cocaine (Lerner, 1989).

Methamphetamine users are more likely to engage in risky sexual behavior, both among gay and bisexual men (MSM) and heterosexual populations. This may be due to the action of methamphetamine on the brain in a way that increases libido. On the other hand, long-term methamphetamine abuse is associated with decreased sexual functioning, at least in men. The combination of injecting drugs and sexual risk-taking may result in HIV becoming a greater problem among methamphetamine users (NIDA, 2006).

MDMA

A *designer drug* is generally defined as a substance tailor-made to produce specific effects. It also usually involves the process of chemically engineering existing controlled substances to create a drug that is not currently illegal (Christophersen, 2000). One of today's more popular designer drugs is *MDMA* (methylenedioxymethamphetamine). It was created to replace its cousin, MDA, methylenedioxyamphetamine, which was classified as a Schedule I drug under the 1970 Controlled Substances Act. It was sold openly, especially in bars in the Dallas, Texas, area until it also became a controlled substance in 1985 ("Trouble with Ecstasy," 1985). Another related drug is MDE, methylenedioxethlyamphetamine, sometimes known as *Love* (Kuhn, Shwartzwelder, & Wilson, 2008).

Also known as X, *XTC, ecstasy, clarity, essence,* and *Adam,* MDMA has a chemical structure similar to that of the stimulant methamphetamine and the hallucinogenic mescaline, and it can produce both stimulant and psychedelic effects (NIDA, 2001a). MDMA stimulates the release of serotonin in the brain, producing a high that lasts from several minutes to three hours (NIDA, 2001a). As with other drugs, contaminants are frequently a problem for MDMA users. Ingredients from cough syrup, caffeine, and even ketamine are found in pills sold as MDMA. One survey found only 40 percent of pills sold as Ecstasy consisted entirely of MDMA (Kuhn, Shwartzwelder, & Wilson, 2008).

MDMA is described as an aphrodisiac, a "party drug," and a "yuppie psychedelic." It is generally taken orally in doses of 100 to 150 mg. A mild euphoria may appear between 20 and 60 minutes later. The rush levels off to a plateau lasting two to three hours. Users report being in an altered state of consciousness, but still in control, having expanded mental perspective and insight into personal problems or patterns (Morland, 2000). Researchers have noted that the drug tends to enhance the pleasure of touching but interferes with erection in men and inhibits orgasm in both men and women. Users seem to develop a tolerance quickly to the positive effects of the drug but not to its negative effects (Barnes, 1988).

MDMA users may experience confusion, depression, sleep problems, anxiety, and paranoia during and even sometimes weeks after taking the drug. They may also experience physiological symptoms such as increased heart rate and blood pressure, muscle tension, involuntary teeth clenching, nausea, blurred vision, fainting, chills, and sweating. Dehydration, hyperthermia, and heart or kidney failure sometimes result (NIDA, 2001a). It has caused seizures, heart attacks, and strokes in some users (Kuhn, Shwartzwelder, & Wilson, 2008).

Brain imaging studies (i.e., PET or positron emission tomography) have found significant reductions in serotonin transporters in MDMA users (McCann, Szabo, Scheffel, Dannals, & Ricaurte, 1998), and examinations of brain tissue in animal studies have confirmed this phenomenon (Hatzidimitriou, McCann, & Ricaurte, 1999). Compared to nonusers, MDMA users also may exhibit significant impairments in visual and verbal memory (Bolla, McCann, & Ricaurte, 1998; McCann, Mertl, Eligulashvili, & Ricaurte, 1999). There is also some evidence that MDMA may suppress the immune system, with regular users experiencing more sore throats, colds, influenza, and herpes outbreaks (Beck, 1986).

Methylphenidate

Methylphenidate, better known as Ritalin, may just be the most controversial drug in America today. Although it is not the most dangerous, not the most abused, almost everyone has an opinion about it (Kuhn, Shwartzwelder, & Wilson, 2008). Not only is it the most frequently prescribed drug for treating Attention Deficit/Hyperactivity Disorder, it is also becoming increasingly popular among college students as a "study" drug and a "party" drug (CESAR Fax, 2003). Ritalin produces effects similar to those of cocaine and amphetamines. Ritalin is most often used illicitly by crushing the tablets and snorting them, causing

a rush by entering the blood stream more quickly. The result is that it simulates the feeling users of cocaine and amphetamines get. Ritalin used in this way can lead to addiction. Ritalin also can be easily dissolved and injected. Used this way, it can be much more dangerous, since these tablets include talc as a filler. The introduction of talc into the blood stream can result in serious health problems such as pulmonary fibrosis and pulmonary hypertension, which can lead to respiratory problems. Heavy or long-term abuse can result in agitation, tremors, euphoria, increased or irregular heart rate, hypertension, sleeplessness, and a loss of appetite. More serious but less frequent effects include manic or psychotic episodes, paranoid delusions, hallucinations, and, in rare instances, death. Repeated abuse can result in addiction, and Ritalin is listed as a Class II controlled substance (CESAR Fax, 2003).

The Effects of Sedatives

One of the greatest problems associated with abusing either barbiturate or nonbarbiturate sedatives is the danger of overdose. Although some drugs, such as cannabis and amphetamines, have very large "safety zones," an overdose of only one or two seconal or methaqualone pills can cause death. This danger is even further heightened when the sedative is used in combination with alcohol. In the mid 1970s, over 10,000 hospital admissions and 2,000 deaths per year were attributed to sedative overdoses, many of them in combination with alcohol (Imlah, 1989). Barbiturates are also the most frequent chemical agent used in committing suicide (Cohen, 1981).

Barbiturate intoxication is quite similar to alcohol intoxication: Speech is slurred, thinking is confused, and movements are uncoordinated with a staggering gait. Addicts fall frequently, suffering many injuries and bruises. Barbiturates also cause a shift in sleep patterns, and many users experience nightmarish, sleep-disrupting dreams upon withdrawal. Many return to using barbiturates or other sedatives in order to deal with insomnia. Barbiturates also depress the respiratory center, and apnea is a common danger to users with marginal pulmonary reserves. A more common problem is the effect of barbiturates on other drugs. Drugs such as phenobarbital induce liver enzymes that cause other drugs to be more rapidly degraded. This can reduce the effectiveness of anticoagulants, or it can speed the effect of drugs such as alcohol. With other drugs, it is simply impossible to predict the effect of the interaction (Cohen, 1981).

Withdrawal from barbiturates can be especially dangerous, much more so than heroin withdrawal. No one who has been using barbiturates over a long period of time should be withdrawn suddenly, and anyone who has taken addictive quantities should withdraw in a hospital. A condition much like delirium tremens occurs within 24 hours in a majority of cases. Three-fourths of people going through abrupt withdrawal will experience major epileptic convulsions between the sixth and eighth day. Without close medical supervision, death is a distinct danger—frequently from exhaustion or pneumonia (Imlah, 1989).

Nonbarbiturate sedatives, such as methaqualone (Quaaludes), may produce many of the same respiratory problems as the barbiturates. Other effects of methaqualone may include nausea, weakness, indigestion, numbness and tingling, and rashes. Withdrawal may resemble the symptoms of alcohol or sedative withdrawal, including delirium and convulsions (Cohen, 1981).

One of the most popular sedatives in recent years has been *flunitrazepam hydrochloride,* a drug legally prescribed in most of the world under the trade name of *Rohypnol.* (It is sometimes referred to as the "date-rape drug.") It is a benzodiazepine in the same category as Valium (DEA, 2001b). Its abuse in the United States, where it is an illegal drug, was first reported in Florida in 1993. It is commonly known by its street name, *roofies* (also known as *rophies, ruffies, rope, rib, R2, roofenol, roche, roachies,* and *Mexican valium*).

Despite the publicity about Rohyphol and its role in date rape, it does have three common patterns of use. First, it appears to have a synergistic effect when used with alcohol; it produces disinhibition and amnesia. In addition, heroin users sometimes use it to enhance the effect of low-quality heroin. Finally, cocaine users may take Rohypnol to "come down" from a cocaine high (NIDA, 2009b).

Lethal overdoses from Rohyphol are rare. Sedation occurs 20 to 30 minutes after ingesting a 2-mg tablet and lasts about eight hours. Like other sedatives, continued use may cause addiction. Withdrawal symptoms include headache, muscle pain and ache, and confusion. Severe withdrawal may result in hallucinations, convulsions, and seizures. (Seizures have been reported up to one week after withdrawal [CESAR, 1995].)

In recent years, there has been an increase in the use and abuse of prescription drugs designed specifically to treat sleep disorders. Some of the most common are Ambien (zolpidem), Lunesta (eszopiclone), and Rozerem (ramelteon), used to induce sleep. While there is a potential for dependence, research has not yet documented serious physiological problems from their use. GHB is used legally to treat narcolepsy (Xyrem) and was once sold in health food stores for "bodybuilding." GHB made in illegal labs has become a popular "club" drug. GHB overdose can cause unconsciousness, slowed heart rate, respiratory depression, seizures, hypothermia, nausea, vomiting, and coma, and it has been known to result in death with extreme use (Kuhn, Shwartzwelder, & Wilson, 2008; NIDA, 2001f).

The Effects of Narcotics

True narcotic drugs (which do *not* include marijuana and cocaine) depress the activity of the brain and the central nervous system. Their chief uses in medicine are to relieve pain and to induce sleep (Imlah, 1989). Narcotics may be divided into two groups: (1) opium and opium derivatives and (2) synthetic and semi-synthetic substances that produce effects similar to opiates. These two groups together are called *opioids*.

Opioids attach to specific proteins called opioid receptors, which are found in the brain, spinal cord, and gastrointestinal tract. By doing so, they block the perception of pain and may produce drowsiness, nausea, constipation, and decreased respiration. Opioids also can induce euphoria by affecting regions in the brain that mediate perceptions of pleasure. These feelings are often intensified by administering the drug by routes not medically recommended. For example, oxycodone is frequently snorted or injected to enhance its euphoric effects, thereby increasing the risk of serious consequences, such as death by overdose (NIDA, 2009a).

Opiates (opium, heroin, morphine, dilaudid, laudanum, paregoric, and codeine) are naturally produced substances derived from the opium poppy. The poppy produces a white, milky substance that dries in contact with air. When further dried into a powder, this substance becomes opium. Morphine is the major alkaloid of opium. Heroin is a synthetic derivative of opium produced by exposing morphine to acetic acid. Codeine is a separate alkaloid found in opium. Raw opium contains about 10 percent morphine, and heroin is derived from morphine on roughly a 1-to-5 ratio (Goode, 1972).

Opium is generally smoked, whereas the preferred method of administration for morphine and heroin is injection. Heroin may also be taken orally, snorted, or smoked (Platt & Labate, 1976). Among U.S. soldiers in Southeast Asia during the Vietnam War, smoking was the most commonly used method of ingesting heroin (Rosenbaum, 1971). Regular heroin users who shoot (inject) the drug have a characteristic slate-colored line along the veins into which they have been injecting. Frequent injection destroys superficial veins, and it becomes increasingly difficult to find healthy veins. Addicts will inject in sites such as the groin, the temples, and the penis. Gangrene,

blood clots, HIV/AIDS, hepatitis, and venereal diseases are all common risks among addicts who share needles without paying adequate attention to cleaning their needles and syringes (Imlah, 1989).

Heroin reaches the brain from the blood-stream and is transformed into morphine (NIDA, 2001c). Heroin actually has minimal central nervous system effects per se, and it is only after being changed through hydrolysis to 6-mono-acetylmorphine (MAM) and then to morphine that the major CNS effects are produced. Heroin is preferred to morphine by addicts, since it has an analgesic effect two to four times greater (Platt & Labate, 1976). The effect of an injection is described by a former self-described junky:

> The rush is so hard to describe. It's like waiting for a distant thunderstorm to move overhead. A strange foreboding. A bizarre, awesome calm. It's in your blood, moving towards your brain, relentlessly; unstoppable, inevitable. A feeling starts to grow like a rumble from the horizon. The feeling swells, surging, soaring, crashing, screaming to a devastating crescendo. The gear [heroin] smashes against the top of your skull with the power of an uncapped oil well. You won't be able to bear the intense ecstasy. It is all too much. Your body may fall apart. The rock that is your head shatters harmlessly into a million sparkling, tinkling smithereens. They tumble at a thousand miles an hour straight back down over your body, warming, insulating, tingling, denying all pain, fear, and sadness. You are stoned, you are high. You are above and below reality and law. (Stewart, 1987)

Morphine and heroin are cleared within six hours, and their subjective effects last four to five hours. With a large dose, the new user "nods out" or enters a dream state moments after an injection. As with other drugs, tolerance develops to a degree that the addict ends up taking the drug simply to avoid the consequences of withdrawal, and increasingly larger doses have to be taken to accomplish this (Imlah, 1989). Other more purely physiological effects also are produced on the body.

All opiates act on the gastrointestinal tract, resulting in dehydration of the feces and constipation in the majority of addicts. Contraction of the pupils is also obvious during chronic use (Krivanek, 1988; NIDA, 2005). Other major physical problems are common in addicts.

The Digestive System

Both peptic and duodenal ulcers are common in heroin addicts. Obstruction of the intestinal tract and hemorrhoids are also frequently associated with their chronic constipation problems (Platt & Labate, 1976).

The Endocrine System

Morphine and heroin have been demonstrated to decrease the production of hormones and gonadotrophin (Eisenman, Fraser, & Brooks, 1961). Diabetes and hypoglycemic conditions are also frequently found in opiate addicts (Sapira, 1968).

Integument

As mentioned earlier, the "tracks" seen on the bodies of heroin addicts are the result of repeated injections of heroin into the veins. These tracks are most often noticed on the sclerosed veins of the forearms, hands, and feet but may occur anywhere on the body—including the dorsal vein of the penis and external jugular and sublingual veins (Hofmann, 1975). Dark pigmentation may also occur as a result of heating the tip of the "spike" with a match flame in order to supposedly sterilize it. The resulting carbon accumulation is deposited under the skin during injection (Baden, 1975).

Abscesses and lesions of the skin frequently result from the practice of "skin-popping" (subcutaneous injection) (NIDA, 2001c). These are usually found on the thighs and back. Another type of lesion commonly found on addicts is a "rosette" of cigarette burns on the chest resulting from nodding out while having a lighted cigarette in the mouth. Tattoos are also frequently found on heroin addicts, usually over the site of tracks they wish to conceal (Sapira, 1968).

The Genitourinary System

There is some evidence of an increased risk of both venereal disease and renal disease associated with heroin addiction, but these problems are not the direct result of the action of the drug. These diseases occur because of the contamination of the heroin or an addict's "works" and because of high-risk sexual behavior (NIDA, 2005; Platt & Labate, 1976).

Other Problems

Perhaps the greatest risk facing the heroin or morphine addict is the possibility of an overdose. Drugs such as this bought illegally on the street are always cut with some other substance such as quinine, domestic cleaning compounds, or even brick dust (Imlah, 1989; NIDA, 2005). It is impossible for the addict to know what the strength of his or her "gear" is, and there is not a large margin of safety for intravenous injection. Death from overdose is a constant risk.

As mentioned earlier, tolerance develops rapidly, especially for the intravenous user. Many addicts purposefully go through withdrawal from time to time in order to reduce their tolerance. A substantial number of overdoses occur when addicts who have abstained for a period of time return to taking their usual dosage. Death or coma can also result from the combined use of opiates with either alcohol or barbiturates. The additive effect of these drugs may depress respiration to a life-threatening level (Krivanek, 1988).

See Table 4.2 for an overview of the short- and long-term effects of heroin use.

Synthetic and Semisynthetic Opioids

According to the manufacturer Purdue Pharma, U.S. doctors wrote 6 million prescriptions for OxyContin in the year 2000. This drug, heralded as a

TABLE 4.2   Short- and Long-Term Effects of Heroin Use

Short-Term Effects	Long-Term Effects
• "Rush"	• Addiction
• Depressed respiration	• Infectious diseases (e.g., HIV/AIDS and hepatitis B and C)
• Clouded mental functioning	• Collapsed veins
• Nausea and vomiting	• Bacterial infections
• Suppression of pain	• Abscesses
• Spontaneous abortion	• Infection of heart lining and valves
	• Arthritis and other rheumatologic problems

Source: NIDA (2001c).

breakthrough in the treatment of severe, chronic pain, is the nation's best-selling narcotic pain medication (Martin, 2001). A synthetic version of morphine, OxyContin also has become nationally known due to its abuse in Appalachia and other rural parts of the eastern United States. It has been linked to dozens, perhaps hundreds, of deaths.

OxyContin is a new sustained-release formulation of *oxycodone*, a semi-synthetic opioid that is structurally related to codeine and approximately equipotent to morphine in producing opiate-like effects. Meant to be swallowed whole in order for its effects to be released over a 12-hour period, OxyContin can be crushed or liquefied to provide a quick and intense high. Oxycodone was first sold under the brand name Eukodal in the early 2000s and then later under the trade names Tylox and Percodan. Abuse of the drug was minimal until it arrived in the form known as OxyContin. This sustained-release formulation has a much higher dosage (160 mg per tablet) than previous forms (10 mg per tablet). Thus, the number of emergency room episodes involving oxycodone has more than doubled in recent years: from 3,190 in 1996 to 6,429 in 1999 (DEA, 2001a). In 2006, one in ten 12th grade students reported nonmedical use of Vicodin and one in 20 reported nonmedical use of OxyContin (NIDA, 2008).

The physiological consequences of oxycodone, hydrocodone (Vicodin), and hydromorphone (Dilaudid) abuse are much the same as for the abuse of the other opiates and opioids. The most serious dangers, compared to the opiates, are associated with the strong dosages that are available in synthetic form. Fentanyl is a very fast-acting drug that can result in death through the suppression of breathing (Kuhn, Shwartzwelder, & Wilson, 2008).

The Effects of Hallucinogens

The main property of a *hallucinogen* is to create an alteration of normal perceptions or to induce abnormal perceptions. These types of drugs are called *psychotomimetic,* but they also came to be known as *psychedelic* drugs in the hippie culture of the 1960s (Imlah, 1989). The term *psychedelic* is also applied to the philosophy of that particular generation of the drug culture, generally in a positive manner. This philosophy is that "man is a creature who has been lied to and blinded by the propaganda socialized into him from infancy" (Goode, 1972). The essential function served by psychedelic drugs, according to this line of thought, is to strip away the impediments that block a direct confrontation with reality and to allow the user to see things clearly. Under the influence of mescaline, Aldous Huxley (1963) described the awesome "isness" of his trousers, his bookshelf, and the legs of a chair, "This is how things really are; how things really are."

A much different point of view is summed up in the term *hallucinogen.* It brings forth images of something illusory—a deception, a fallacy, or perhaps the ravings of a madman or hallucination of someone in imminent need of treatment. Actually, a true hallucination (a perception without an object) is relatively rare during a drug experience. Much more common is a *distortion* of perception (Imlah, 1989). There is nothing mystical about the action of LSD; it is that of a toxic chemical that disrupts the brain's normal process. It is no more mystical than the hallucinations of an alcoholic, the delusions of a schizophrenic, or the dreams of an opium eater.

Hallucinogens do not cause the physical dependence of alcohol or opiates and do not have the psychological compulsion of drugs such as cocaine, although a psychological need to repeat the experience of "tripping" is common. In the true sense, these are not drugs of dependence, but they are substances that can as easily result in disaster on the first and each subsequent use (Imlah, 1989).

Some commonly used hallucinogens are LSD, mescaline (the main alkaloid of the peyote cactus), psilocybin (from a mushroom that flourishes in Mexico), and fly agaric (*amanita muscaria,* a common toadstool). LSD is the strongest of these, having a strength approximately 200 times that of psilocybin and 4,000 times that of mescaline! In recent years, both PCP ("Angel Dust") and ketamine ("Special K") have become quite popular. Dextromethorphan, an ingredient in cough syrup also produces a dissociative state, hallucinations, and out-of-body experiences when taken in high doses (Banken & Foster, 2008).

D-lysergic acid diethylamide 25 (*LSD* or *acid*) is one of the most commonly used hallucinogens. It is usually taken orally via a pill or capsule or by chewing and swallowing a "paper" soaked in an LSD solution (frequently decorated with a tattoo or psychedelic design). During the 1960s, it was commonly taken in a sugar cube impregnated with the chemical, but this method is not generally used today. In some areas, LSD is still taken by placing a small amount in an eye dropper and

depositing it on the eyes. A quantity as small as 25 micrograms (µg) is psychoactive for most people (Goode, 1972). (An aspirin tablet is approximately 300,000 µg.)

A "trip" on LSD may last between 5 and 12 hours, although reactions may last for days, and flashbacks may occur indefinitely (NIDA, 2001b). During the trip, the user will experience distortions of the senses, especially vision. Loss of a sense of space and distance and the relationship of self to these dimensions is common. The user may describe colors, smells, and sounds as though they are being experienced for the first time. These experiences range from extremely pleasant to nightmarish (Imlah, 1989). A commonly reported effect is called *eidetic imagery,* or *eyeball movies,* in which the user (with the eyes closed) sees physical objects, usually in motion, as sharply as if he or she were watching a movie. These images are abstract and usually lacking in any dramatic content, and they usually represent repetitions of a pattern or design—such as moving wallpaper—but with the patterns constantly changing (Goode, 1972).

One of the most common hazards of LSD use is related to the distortion of visual perception. Users sometimes fall through windows above ground level, later explaining that they thought they had left through the front door or a ground-level window. Normal physical changes that occur with use are related to overstimulation of the sympathetic nervous system. These include trembling, sweating, dilated pupils, goose bumps, changes in blood pressure and pulse rate, nausea, and bowel problems (Imlah, 1989). Asthma attacks are sometimes precipitated by LSD in the predisposed individual. Loss of appetite is also common. Convulsions occur rather infrequently, but depression may occur either during or immediately after a trip (Cohen, 1981). A special hazard is the flashback phenomenon, especially when it occurs when victims are in a situation where they are at risk to themselves or others—such as driving an automobile.

Ketamine is a dissociative anesthetic, used mostly in veterinary practice. As a hallucinogen it is either snorted or injected intramuscularly. Low doses result in impaired attention, learning ability, and memory. Higher doses can cause dreamlike states and hallucinations; and at much higher doses ketamine can cause delirium and amnesia. Such high doses may also result in impaired motor function, high blood pressure, and potentially fatal respiratory problems (NIDA, 2009b).

PCP (phencyclidine) was developed in the 1950s as an intravenous anesthetic but has since been discontinued due to serious adverse effects. It is a white, crystalline, water soluble powder that can be smoked snorted, or taken orally. At low doses, it produces a dissociative state, like other hallucinogens. At higher doses, blood pressure, pulse rate, and respiration drop, and may be accompanied by nausea, vomiting, blurred vision, flicking up and down of the eyes, drooling, loss of balance, and dizziness. PCP abusers may become violent or suicidal. High doses of PCP can also cause seizures, coma, and death. Because PCP may also have sedative effects, interactions with other depressants, such as alcohol and benzodiazepines, can also lead to coma (NIDA, 2009c).

The Effects of Inhalants

Most of the *inhalants* commonly abused today are solvents, aerosols, gases, and volatile nitrates (NIDA, 2009d). These include commonly available products such as paint, gasoline, lacquer thinner, airplane glue, lighter fluid, and trichloroethylene. Inhalants have very little in common with each other, except that inhalation is the route of administration. Most of the users who sniff or "huff" these substances are under the age of 15, possibly because the sources are so much more easily available to children. Glue sniffers will typically empty the contents of a tube into the bottom of a paper bag, hold the bag tightly over the mouth (or mouth and nose), and inhale the vapors until the desired effect is reached. Liquid materials may be inhaled directly from a container or from saturated cloth (Hofmann, 1975).

Some easily obtained solvents used by children are paint thinners and removers, dry-cleaning fluids, degreasers, gasoline, glues, correction fluids, and felt-tip marker fluids. Aerosols include spray paints, deodorant and hair sprays, vegetable oil sprays for cooking, and fabric protector sprays. Household or commercial products containing gases include butane lighters, propane tanks, whipped cream dispensers, and refrigerants. Other gases are somewhat more difficult to obtain: ether, chloroform, halothane, and nitrous oxide (laughing gas). Nitrous oxide is the most commonly abused gas and can be found in whipped cream dispensers and products used to boost the horsepower in racing cars (NIDA, 2009d).

Most materials used in sniffing contain volatile or gaseous substances that are primarily generalized CNS depressants. The immediate effects may range from somnolence and dizziness to delusions of unusual strength or supernatural abilities (such as the ability to fly). Visual and auditory hallucinations similar to those associated with the hallucinogens are frequently noted. Other symptoms are slurred speech, ataxia, impaired judgment, and feelings of euphoria (Kurtzman, Otsuka, & Wahl, 2001). Excessive or prolonged sniffing of high vapor concentrations will ultimately lead to loss of consciousness. Too much solvent can also cause paralysis of the breathing center and death. Other sniffers may die from ventricular fibrillation induced by central respiratory depression. Deaths have also resulted from damage to the liver, kidneys, and bone marrow among chronic sniffers. Occasional deaths from asphyxiation also result from the practice of inhaling a solvent in a closed space or with one's head in a plastic bag (Kurtzman et al., 2001).

Nitrites are more likely to be used by adults, especially in enhancing sexual pleasure (NIDA, 2009d). Amyl nitrite was introduced into medicine over a century ago when it was found to relieve angina pectoris by dilating coronary arteries and temporarily improving the perfusion and oxygenation of heart muscle (NIDA, 2001b). It also has the effect of expanding the meningeal arteries over the surface of the brain and producing feelings of suffusion and fullness in the head. The action of amyl nitrite on the brain results in a subjective experience of time being slowed down, and it is this perception that began a modest amount of recreational use of the drug during the 1930s. Taken just before climax, it may extend the sensation of orgasm.

Although some use by heterosexual men and women has been reported, amyl nitrite is more popular as an orgasm expander among homosexual men (Kurtzman et al., 2001). Originally available in a capsule or pearl that was crushed and inhaled (called *snappers* or *poppers*), it was later sold in aerosol form (either as amyl or isobutyl nitrite) under trade names such as Locker Room, Aroma of Men, Kick, Bullet, Jac, and Rush, ostensibly as room deodorizers (Cohen, 1981).

Other symptoms accompanying use of this drug are nausea, dizziness, mild sensory intensification, a diminution of ego controls, and an increase in aggressive behavior. A drop in blood pressure and an increase in the heart rate are usually noted. Pulsating headaches also are frequently mentioned by regular users (Dewey et al., 1973). There is still a lingering controversy about whether butyl nitrite depresses the body's immune system and weakens its ability to fight the HIV virus, which causes AIDS (Vandenbroucke & Pardoel, 1989). The Centers for Disease Control (CDC) in Atlanta cites evidence that Kaposi's sarcoma is much more common among people with AIDS who use poppers than among those who do not use them. Other research indicates that 87 percent of the 290 compounds in the nitrite family have proven to be carcinogenic in tests of laboratory animals ("Trendy chemical," 1986).

The Effects of Steroids

Steroids are unusual drugs in the sense that they are not used in order to achieve a euphoric rush or "high." They are used primarily by athletes to build muscle tissue. Anabolic steroids are the common name for synthetic substances related to the male sex hormones (e.g., testosterone). They promote both the growth of skeletal muscle and the development of male sexual characteristics in males as well as females. Steroids have gained much attention in recent years because of their use by high school, college, and professional athletes. Steroidal supplements could be legally purchased in health food stores until they became illegal with the passage in 2004 of amendments to the Controlled Substances Act (NIDA, 2009e).

In terms of serious physiological and psychological consequences, steroids may be one of the most dangerous drugs to abuse, especially since abuse by adolescents has serious negative effects. Use among 12th graders was at 2.5 percent in 2004 and decreased to 1.5 percent in 2005, where it remained in 2008 (NIDA, 2009f).

Anecdotal reports and small studies indicate that anabolic steroids, when used in high doses, may increase irritability and aggression. The research on behavioral consequences is still incomplete (Kuhn, Shwartzwelder, & Wilson, 2008). The most serious consequences of steroid abuse are physiological and are well documented. They include (NIDA, 2009e):

- infertility (men)
- breast development (men)
- shrinking of the testicles
- male-pattern baldness (both men and women)
- enlargement of the clitoris
- excessive growth of body hair
- short stature (if taken by adolescents)
- tendon rupture
- increases in LDL
- decreases in HDL
- high blood pressure
- heart attacks
- enlargement of the heart's left ventricle
- liver cancer and tumors
- peliosis hepatis
- severe acne and cysts
- oily scalp
- jaundice
- fluid retention

Steroid abusers who inject the drug, the common method of administration, also run the same risks of infection as all other intravenous drug users, including STDs, hepatitis, and HIV/AIDS. There are questions about whether steroids are truly addictive, since there is no euphoric "rush" from taking the drug, and changes in the brain associated with other drug use does not occur. However, users do develop a compulsive reliance on steroids, and they experience withdrawal symptoms (fatigue, depression, loss of appetite, insomnia, and headaches) when they stop (Kuhn, Shwartzwelder, & Wilson, 2008).

The Effects of Drugs on Offspring

Most pregnant women do not abuse illicit drugs based on combined 2006 and 2007 data. However, a surprising finding from the National Survey on Drug Use and Health was that pregnant women ages 15 to 17 had a higher rate of use than women of the same age who were not pregnant (NIDA, 2009g). Offspring may be damaged by drug use by either parent, although the greater risks are generally associated with maternal drug use (Joffe, 1979). Drug use by females may affect offspring when it happens prior to conception, during gestation, or following birth—if the baby is breastfed. The most severe consequence of drugs taken by a pregnant woman is prenatal or perinatal death. Many of the causes of drug-related prenatal death are not well understood, and they may not be noticed if they occur early in pregnancy (Jones-Webb, McKiver, Pirie, & Miner, 1999). The most commonly identified teratogenic drug is alcohol, but opiates, barbiturates, benzodiazepines, amphetamines, cocaine, tobacco, and marijuana are also frequently implicated in birth defects, pre- and postnatal growth deficiency, and cognitive development (White, 1991).

Alcohol

Alcohol-related birth defects (ARBD) are the leading cause of known mental retardation in the western world (Maier & West, 2001). ARBD includes both fetal alcohol syndrome (FAS) and fetal alcohol effects (FAE), as well as alcohol-related neurodevelopmental disorder. Although the specific effects of maternal alcohol use on the fetus was not officially recognized and given a label until 1973, alcohol has been suspected as a teratogenic agent at least since biblical times. Judges 13:7 provides the injunction, "Behold thou shalt conceive and bear a son: now drink no wine or strong drink." Other early societies also recognized the danger of alcohol on offspring (Streissguth, Herman, & Smith, 1978). It was not until 1973, however, that Jones and colleagues (Smith, 1986) described the children born to chronic alcoholic mothers as having *fetal alcohol syndrome (FAS)*. These children were characterized by prenatal and postnatal growth deficiency, a pattern of physical abnormalities (including short palpebral fissures, epicanthic folds, ear anomalies, and cardiac defects), and mental retardation. In a subsequent review of 245 cases, Clarren and Smith (1978) described the three primary characteristics of FAS as growth deficiency, characteristic facial dysmorphology, and central nervous system damage. Cardiac defects occur in 30 to 40 percent of FAS children.

The incidence of FAS varies considerably among various subpopulations, but there is little doubt that the teratogenic effects of alcohol are dose related. One study concluded that between 11 and 13 percent of pregnant women who drink two to three drinks a day will give birth to children with FAS (Hanson, Streissguth, & Smith, 1978). Careful studies conducted in Göteborg, Sweden, and Roubaix, France, found the rate of FAS to be 1 in 690 births. The rate in Seattle, Washington, was 1 in 750 births, and studies conducted on Native American reservations in southwestern United States indicated a rate of 1 in 100 births (Streissguth et al., 1978). Maier and West (2001) estimate that about 1 percent of all births in the United States are affected by ARBD.

Children born with FAS are usually not grossly malformed, but they do have a particular cluster of facial characteristics that, along with their small stature and slender build, give them a readily identifiable appearance. Mental handicaps are the most debilitating aspect of FAS, with those individuals affected having an average IQ of 65 (Streissguth et al., 1978). FAS is one of the few types of mental retardation that is entirely preventable. Since there is no specific treatment for FAS, and its effects are permanent, the primary focus must remain on prevention. No safe level of drinking by pregnant women has ever been established (Little, Graham, & Samson, 1982). The only way to eliminate the risk of FAS is to be abstinent during pregnancy (Floyd, Decouflé, & Hungerford, 1999).

Opiates

Although it has been difficult to separate the effects of opiates from other factors associated with the living conditions and general lifestyles of opiate users, studies indicate that the offspring of heroin-dependent mothers tend to be low in birth weight, more frequently premature, and often experience perinatal complications and a range of abnormalities (White, 1991). Neonatal narcotic withdrawal is a common problem of offspring exposed to opiates *in utero*. Hypoxia, hyperactivity, and fetal death have also been noted (Kreek, 1982).

Tobacco

Tobacco use during pregnancy reflects a dose-dependent relationship with slowed fetal growth and low birthweight—the more a woman smokes during pregnancy, the more infant birth weight is reduced. The negative effects also include problems with cognition and postnatal behavioral problems. In addition, smoking more than a pack a day during pregnancy nearly doubles the risk of the child becoming addicted to tobacco if he or she starts smoking (NIDA, 2009g).

Spontaneous abortion is much higher in pregnant women who smoke than in nonsmokers (Jones-Webb et al., 1999). Smoking can induce malformations sufficiently severe to cause fetal death at an early stage of pregnancy. Fetuses that do survive are 10 to 15 percent lighter at birth than are those born to nonsmokers (White, 1991). The combination of both smoking and drinking entails a much higher risk to the fetus and its postnatal development (Little et al., 1982).

Amphetamines and Cocaine

A wide range of abnormalities have been associated with maternal amphetamine and cocaine administration. Among the consequences of maternal use of stimulants are spontaneous abortion, low birth weight, cleft palate, urogenital anomalies, and an increase in excitability (White, 1991). When a pregnant woman uses crack, it results in a constriction of the blood vessels and a decrease in the flow of oxygen and nutrients to the fetus. Methamphetamine use during pregnancy has been associated with fetal growth restriction, decreased arousal, and poor quality of movement in infants (NIDA, 2009g). As indicated earlier, the long-term effects of maternal cocaine abuse may not be as severe as once believed (Frank, Augustyn, Knight, Pell, & Zuckerman, 2001).

Other Drugs

There is some evidence that maternal *barbiturate* use may result in both morphological and behavioral impairment. This is especially disturbing, since many people have to use this drug to keep their epilepsy under control. *Benzodiazepine* use (especially diazepam) by pregnant women is reported to have caused a number of birth defects, including cleft palate. High levels of maternal *caffeine* use may result in higher rates of spontaneous abortion and certain congenital abnormalities. *Hallucinogens* such as LSD are capable of inducing chromosomal damage, but this does not seem to occur at normal human dosage levels. Structural abnormalities, especially of the limbs, have been more frequent in the offspring of LSD users. *Marijuana* also has been observed to induce chromosomal damage at high doses, but there is little evidence that this occurs at lower doses (Imlah, 1989). In animal studies, behavioral differences have been noted in the offspring of marijuana-treated mothers. Heroin abuse during pregnancy has been associated with low birth weight, an important risk factor for later developmental delay. If the mother is regularly abusing heroin, the child may be born physically dependent on heroin and could suffer from serious medical complications requiring hospitalization (NIDA, 2009g). There is little reliable evidence on the maternal effects of *inhalants* (White, 1991). A few animal studies designed to simulate human patterns of inhalant abuse suggest that prenatal exposure to toluene or trichlorethylene (TCE) can result in reduced birth weights, skeletal abnormalities, and delayed neurobehavioral development (NIDA, 2009d).

Summary

This chapter described the most commonly observed physiological and behavioral consequences of alcohol and drug abuse. The common effects of illicit drugs are summarized in Table 4.1. In some cases, scientists have isolated a direct relationship between drug use and a specific effect, as in the case of alcohol abuse and cirrhosis of the liver. In other cases, such as LSD, the specific mechanism for the drug's effect is not known. In still other cases, the negative consequences of drug use are not a direct effect of the drug. For instance, abscesses, venereal disease, and hepatitis all may result from using injectable drugs, but they are not results of the drug itself; rather, they are results of using contaminated needles or practicing risky sexual behavior. Marijuana and crack cocaine users may develop respiratory problems, not as a direct effect of using the drugs, but as a result of inhaling other contaminants with these drugs. While the long-term consequences of using traditional drugs, such as alcohol and tobacco, are well documented, the consequences of using newer drugs, such as MDMA and GHB, are just beginning to be understood. Needless to say, it will take time to discover the effects of these newer drugs on users as well as the offspring of users.

The reader must bear in mind that individuals vary markedly in their reactions to specific doses of particular drugs, and the same reaction cannot be expected even within the same individual over a period of time. The development of tolerance and chemically induced trauma to organs such as the brain make predictions of behavior even more difficult than predictions of physiological consequences.

One final caveat: Much of the research in this field is clouded by the phenomenon of *polydrug use*. Most of today's research indicates that a person who is abusing one drug is very likely abusing one or more other drugs. Separating the effects of one drug from another can be quite difficult.

PART TWO

Intervention, Prevention, and Public Policy

Part One of this book introduced substance use and substance use disorders, both abuse and dependence, and addressed many related topics, such as the neurobiology of addiction and the physiological and psychological effects and consequences of substance use, abuse, and dependence. The chapters in Part One also touched on social and cultural aspects of alcohol and other drug use and described the myriad etiological theories that purport to explain why people use alcohol and other drugs and develop substance use disorders. With this foundation in place, Part Two describes attempts to control substance use and to prevent and treat abuse and dependence using a perspective that involves many social systems—health, mental health, educational, legislative, judicial, and criminal justice—as well as the specialty sector that treats individuals who have substance use disorders.

Chapter 5 discusses the tools and processes that are used to identify individuals who have substance use disorders. The chapter includes a number of screening instruments, as well as diagnostic criteria, and describes screening, diagnosis, assessment, and referral to appropriate resources. The chapter also considers a number of ways to look at denial and how individuals can be motivated to change their thoughts and behaviors with regard to alcohol and other drug use. Other important topics in this chapter are ethical considerations in treating individuals who have alcohol and drug problems, such as confidentiality, maintaining professional boundaries, and treating individuals only within the realm of one's expertise.

Chapter 6 covers the components of the system for treating substance use disorders, including detoxification, intensive treatment, residential services, outpatient services, medications, education, aftercare, and maintenance. A range of mutual- and self-help resources, including twelve-step programs and other alternatives are also described. An important feature of this chapter is that it considers the evidence (or empirical literature) about the effectiveness of various treatment approaches. For instance, we know that some of the approaches for treating substance use disorders work for some of the people some of the time, that relapse rates remain high, and that we still have a great deal to learn about how better to help individuals with substance use disorders using professional treatment and mutual- and self-help approaches. In addition to the services typically offered to individuals who have alcohol and other drug problems, alternative approaches are also considered, even some that engender quite a bit of controversy, such as controlled or moderated drinking. Also discussed are attempts at matching clients to treatment based on their personal characteristics and treatment needs, using a combination of pharmacotherapy and psychosocial services to improve treatment effectiveness, and the roles that the therapist and service characteristics (e.g., length of treatment, types, and amounts of services) play in promoting better treatment outcomes.

Chapter 7 begins by looking at attempts to prevent alcohol and other drug problems through educational programming. Various approaches to education are discussed, but we find that these efforts are not nearly as effective as people might hope. The chapter also introduces various strategies to prevent alcohol and drug problems through regulatory and public policy measures. Many regulatory measures target alcohol, since it is legally available to those old enough to purchase it, including restrictions on advertising, taxes levied on alcoholic beverages, required warning labels, hours of sale, and regulation of drinking establishments. The chapter also considers successful efforts to curb tobacco use through public education and social norms.

Chapter 8 considers additional regulatory measures, many of which are hotly debated. At one end of the spectrum, we discuss decriminalization, legalization, and harm-reduction approaches such as providing safe rides home to intoxicated drivers and facilitating needle exchanges for intravenous drug users. At the other end, we address the so-called war on drugs, or attempts to curb drug problems through law enforcement and interdiction, rather than education and treatment. Some interventions fall in between these extremes, such as drug courts, which attempt to use the leverage of the courts to get people into treatment with the promise of deferred adjudication contingent on successful completion of the treatment program and avoiding relapse. The effects of the drug war, including the phenomenal increase in incarceration, are also discussed, as are controversies over topics such as providing much stiffer sentences for offenses involving crack cocaine (more often used by individuals in poorer communities) versus powdered cocaine (more often used by more affluent individuals).

Taken together, the strategies discussed in Chapters 5 through 8 suggest that many social systems are involved in attempts to control substance use and to address substance use disorders. Tradition and political considerations seem to play as big, if not bigger, part in determining what strategies are pursued than does the empirical literature on effectiveness. We return to these points in Part Four of this book.

CHAPTER 5

Screening, Diagnosis, Assessment, and Referral

This chapter presents a systems or bio-psychosocial approach to determining whether an individual has a chemical abuse or dependency problem. The first steps in this approach are screening and diagnosis. The chapter also considers the extension of this process, called *assessment*, to examine the client's needs further. A thorough assessment is generally needed to develop a treatment plan and to make referrals to appropriate resources.

Some individuals with alcohol and drug problems experience medical emergencies (intentional overdoses, accidental alcohol or drug poisoning, pancreatitis, delirium tremens, seizures, etc.) that require immediate attention. Social workers, psychologists, and other human service professionals should know what these emergencies are, but these problems can be diagnosed and treated only by qualified medical personnel. This chapter focuses primarily on the work of helping professionals once such medical crises have been resolved or when a client is seen by a helping professional before these medical complications arise.

We begin by discussing *screening*, which may be defined as the use of rapid assessment instruments and other tools to determine the likelihood that an individual has a chemical abuse or chemical dependency problem. In practice, much screening is informal and is not done with structured or standardized instruments. For example, after reviewing a parolee's "rap sheet"

containing repeated alcohol- or drug-related arrests, a parole officer may feel that is all the screening necessary for referring the client to a chemical dependency treatment program or insisting on participation in a mutual-help group as a condition of parole.

Diagnosis is the confirmation of a chemical abuse or dependency problem based on established clinical criteria. The diagnostic process generally involves an interview with the patient or client and often includes information from other sources such as a medical examination, including laboratory tests, and previous medical, psychological or psychiatric, criminal, school, and other records. Consultation with other professionals might also be used as is information from collaterals (e.g., family) who know the patient or client well.

The term *assessment* is sometimes used synonymously with the term *diagnosis*, but we use it to mean an in-depth consideration of the client's chemical abuse or dependency problems as they have affected his or her psychological well-being, social circumstances (including interpersonal relationships), financial status, employment or education, health, and so forth. This process also includes consideration of the individual's strengths and resources that may be assets in treatment and recovery. Going beyond a confirmatory diagnosis, this type of multidimensional or biopsychosocial assessment provides the basis for treatment planning.

The cornerstones of screening, diagnosis, and assessment are knowledge of substance use disorders and good interviewing skills, including the ability to establish some level of rapport with clients in a relatively brief period. Denial is a pervasive issue in work with clients who have alcohol and drug problems. Helping professionals must frequently work with clients and their significant others to reduce defensiveness and resistance; thus, this chapter addresses these topics. The assurance of confidentiality in treatment and research settings can increase the validity of clients' reports of their alcohol and drug problem (National Institute on Alcohol Abuse and Alcoholism [NIAAA], 1990), but the extent to which confidentiality can be guaranteed varies and should be represented fairly to the client. Confidentiality, as well as other aspects of ethical or professional conduct, also warrants attention in this chapter.

In addition to chemical dependency treatment, clients often need the services of other agencies. The final section of this chapter discusses the process of referring clients to other services, including mutual-help groups.

Screening

Screening for alcohol and drug problems is done in many types of settings in addition to chemical dependency programs, such as in health care facilities, mental health programs, and correctional facilities.

Although much work is being done, there is currently no biological testing procedure that most human service professionals can easily use to identify people with substance use disorders or those who have the potential to develop these problems (see Allen, Sillanaukee, Strid, & Litten, 2003; Substance Abuse and Mental Health Services Administration, 2006). Instead, human service professionals generally inquire about family history of alcohol and drug problems, the quantity and frequency of the individual's own drinking or drug use, and especially the individual's alcohol- and drug-related problems. To do this, they often

use one of a number of the paper-and-pencil or verbally administered tests specifically designed to screen for chemical abuse or dependence problems. Some of the many screening instruments available are the CAGE (defined shortly), the Michigan Alcoholism Screening Test (MAST), the Alcohol Use Disorders Identification Test (AUDIT), the Drug Abuse Screening Test (DAST), the Problem Oriented Screening Instrument for Teenagers (POSIT), and the Substance Abuse Subtle Screening Inventory (SASSI). Before these instruments are administered, there should be some interaction between the client and the treatment professional in order to explain the purpose of the screening, to put the client at ease, to encourage honest responses, and to answer questions the client might have about the procedure.

CAGE

Screening devices as short as one or two items have been tested for use in busy medical practices (Brown, Leonard, Saunders, & Papasouliotis, 2001; Smith, Schmidt, Allensworth-Davies, & Saitz, 2009), but the CAGE, developed by John Ewing and Beatrice Rouse, is the briefest of the most widely used screening instruments (see Ewing, 1984; Mayfield, McLeod, & Hall, 1974). The CAGE consists of four questions asked directly to the patient:

1. Have you ever felt you should Cut down on your drinking?
2. Have people Annoyed you by criticizing your drinking?
3. Have you ever felt bad or Guilty about your drinking?
4. Have you ever had a drink first thing in the morning to steady your nerves or get rid of a hangover (Eye opener)?

The letters in bold type in each question make up the acronym that serves as the instrument's name; the letters also serve as a mnemonic device so that the instrument is easily committed to memory. A positive response to one or more of the questions indicates the need to explore problems the patient or client may be experiencing with the use of alcohol. Two or more positive responses generally indicate a positive test (Buchsbaum, 1995; Liskow, Campbell, Nickel, & Powell, 1995). This tool is easily used in many types of clinical settings. The CAGE is generally reported to be effective in identifying adults with alcohol problems (Bush, Shaw, Cleary, Delbanco, & Aronson, 1987; Liskow et al., 1995). Since the CAGE inquires only about alcohol, the CAGE Adapted to Include Drugs (CAGE-AID) may be used with instructions to the patient or client that "when thinking about drug use, include illegal drug use and the use of prescription drugs other than as prescribed" (Brown, Leonard, Saunders, & Papasouliotis, 1998, p. 102; also see Lanier & Ko, 2008). These instructions are useful in screening individuals who are taking pain medication and those who have been prescribed medications for psychiatric disorders and are using them inappropriately.

Michigan Alcoholism Screening Test (MAST)

Another widely used screening instrument for alcohol problems is the Michigan Alcoholism Screening Test (MAST) (Selzer, 1971). It has been shown to have good validity and reliability (Lettieri, Nelson, & Sayers, 1985; Skinner, 1979). The original MAST contains 25 items and is usually self-administered (i.e., the client is asked to read and complete it). As with most screening instruments, clarifying clients' responses can be helpful. For example, question 3 on the MAST is "Does your wife, husband, a parent, or other near relative ever worry or complain about your drinking?" Drinkers married to teetotalers may respond positively to this question even if their drinking is not problematic, or an individual with ties to a religious group that prohibits drinking may respond positively to question 5 ("Do you ever feel guilty about your drinking?") regardless of how much he or she drinks.

Shorter versions of the MAST are also available (see Connors & Volk, 2003). One, called the Short MAST or the SMAST, contains 13 questions (Selzer,

Vinokur, & van Rooijen, 1975). Another is the Brief MAST (B-MAST), which contains ten questions (Pokorny, Miller, & Kaplan, 1972). The shorter versions are often used with slower readers. These instruments may also be tape-recorded or read to the client or patient by the person administering the test. The MAST has been used as a screening tool in many settings, such as in programs for those convicted of driving under the influence (DUI).

Alcohol Use Disorders Identification Test (AUDIT)

The World Health Organization (WHO) developed the Alcohol Use Disorders Identification Test (AUDIT) as a screening instrument for use by primary health care providers (Babor, Higgins-Biddle, Saunders, & Monteiro, 2001). Social service providers can also use it. As Figure 5.1 shows, the AUDIT contains ten items. Items 1 through 3 concern hazardous drinking (frequency and quantity), items 4 through 6 concern alcohol dependence, and items 7 through 10 refer to harmful alcohol use (alcohol-related problems). The AUDIT can be administered as a self-report questionnaire or as an interview. Clinical screening procedures (a physical exam and laboratory tests), which can only be administered by qualified health care providers, are also recommended, especially when an individual may not be candid about alcohol use or cannot provide answers to questions or when additional information is needed. The clinical indicators include blood vessels appearing in the face, hand and tongue tremor, changes in mucous membranes and mouth, and elevated liver enzymes observed through tests such as the serum gamma-glutamyl transferase (GGT). The AUDIT is available in a number of languages. Since drinking preferences and customs vary among cultures, these factors must be taken into account when administering the AUDIT. For example, the number of drinks specified in items 2 and 3 may require adjusting, since serving size and alcohol strength vary among countries. As Figure 5.1 also shows, the patient's score indicates the type of intervention needed.

FIGURE 5.1   The Alcohol Use Disorders Identification Test (AUDIT): Interview Version

---

Read questions as written. Record answers carefully. Begin the AUDIT by saying "Now I am going to ask you some questions about your use of alcoholic beverages during this past year." Explain what is meant by "alcoholic beverages" by using local examples of beer, wine, vodka, etc. Code answers in terms of "standard drinks." Place the correct answer number in the box at the right.

1. How often do you have a drink containing alcohol?

   (0) Never (Skip to Questions 9-10)
   (1) Monthly or less
   (2) 2 to 4 times a month
   (3) 2 to 3 times a week
   (4) 4 or more times a week

2. How many drinks containing alcohol do you have on a typical day when you are drinking?

   (0) 1 or 2
   (1) 3 or 4
   (2) 5 or 6
   (3) 7, 8, or 9
   (4) 10 or more

3. How often do you have six or more drinks on one occasion?

   (0) Never
   (1) Less than monthly
   (2) Monthly
   (3) Weekly
   (4) Daily

Skip to Questions 9 and 10 if Total
Score for Questions 2 and 3 = 0

4. How often during the last year have you found that you were not able to stop drinking once you had started?

   (0) Never
   (1) Less than monthly
   (2) Monthly
   (3) Weekly
   (4) Daily or almost daily

5. How often during the last year have you failed to do what was normally expected from you because of drinking?

   (0) Never
   (1) Less than monthly
   (2) Monthly
   (3) Weekly
   (4) Daily or almost daily

6. How often during the last year have you needed a first drink in the morning to get yourself going after a heavy drinking session?

   (0) Never
   (1) Less than monthly
   (2) Monthly
   (3) Weekly
   (4) Daily or almost daily

7. How often during the last year have you had a feeling of guilt or remorse after drinking?

   (0) Never
   (1) Less than monthly
   (2) Monthly
   (3) Weekly
   (4) Daily or almost daily

8. How often during the last year have you been unable to remember what happened the night before because you had been drinking?

   (0) Never
   (1) Less than monthly
   (2) Monthly
   (3) Weekly
   (4) Daily or almost daily

9. Have you or someone else been injured as a result of your drinking?

   (0) No
   (2) Yes, but not in the last year
   (4) Yes, during the last year

10. Has a relative or friend or a doctor or another health worker been concerned about your drinking or suggested you cut down?

   (0) No
   (2) Yes, but not in the last year
   (4) Yes, during the last year

Record total of specific items here

FIGURE 5.1 *Continued*

Risk Level	Intervention	AUDIT Score*
Zone I	Alcohol Education	0–7
Zone II	Simple Advice	8–15
Zone III	Simple Advice plus Brief Counseling and Continued Monitoring	16–19
Zone IV	Referral to Specialist for Diagnostic Evaluation and Treatment	20–40

*The AUDIT cut-off score may vary slightly depending on the country's drinking patterns, the alcohol content of standard drinks, and the nature of the screening program. Clinical judgment should be exercised in cases where the patient's score is not consistent with other evidence, or if the patient has a prior history of alcohol dependence. It may also be instructive to review the patient's responses to individual questions dealing with dependence symptoms (see Questions 4, 5, and 6) and alcohol-related problems (see Questions 9 and 10). Provide the next highest level of intervention to patients who score 2 or more on Questions 4, 5, and 6, or 4 on Questions 9 or 10.

Source: T. F. Babor, J. C. Higgins, J. B. Saunders, & M. G. Monteiro, AUDIT: The Alcohol Use Disorders Identification Test: Guidelines for Use in Primary Care, 2nd ed. (Geneva, Switzerland: World Health Organization, 2001), Reprinted with permission of the World Health Organization.

Drug Abuse Screening Test (DAST)

Some instruments, such as the Drug Abuse Screening Test, are used to screen for drug problems other than alcohol (Skinner, 1982; also see Lanier & Ko, 2008). The DAST was patterned after the MAST. Like the CAGE, MAST, and ten-item AUDIT, the DAST relies on the client or patient's responses to questions. The 10-, 20-, and 28-item versions of the DAST are reported to have good psychometric properties (Yudko, Lozhkina, & Fouts, 2007). Figure 5.2 contains the 20-item version.

Problem Oriented Screening Instrument for Teenagers (POSIT)

An instrument often used with adolescents is the Problem Oriented Screening Instrument for Teenagers (POSIT) (Winters, 1999, 2003; also see Knight, Sherritt, Harris, Gates, & Chang, 2003). POSIT is a screening tool for substance use problems and social, behavioral, and learning problems. The 139-item POSIT is longer than other tools described thus far and takes 20 to 30 minutes to complete. It is self-administered, requiring a fifth-grade reading level, and is available in English and Spanish.

Substance Abuse Subtle Screening Inventory (SASSI)

The Substance Abuse Subtle Screening Inventory (SASSI) is another instrument the client completes (Lazowski, Miller, Boye, & Miller 1998; Miller & Lazowski, 1999, 2001, 2005). There is a version for adults and one for adolescents. The SASSI differs from many instruments available in the field because most of the true/false items on one side of the form do not inquire directly about alcohol or drug use. The reverse side of the SASSI form contains another set of questions (formerly called the Risk Prediction Scales) (Morton, 1978) that do inquire directly about alcohol and other drug abuse. The SASSI therefore contains both face-valid items and subtle items that are empirically derived. Administration of the subtle true/false items before the more obvious alcohol- and drug-related questions may help minimize client defensiveness. Since the denial or defensiveness common among many persons with chemical dependency problems may result in failure to provide accurate information on face-valid, self-report measures, there has been interest in less obtrusive measures of substance use disorders such as the SASSI.

FIGURE 5.2   Drug Abuse Screening Test (DAST-20)

The following questions concern information about your potential involvement with drugs not including alcoholic beverages during the past 12 months. Carefully read each statement and decide if your answer is "Yes" or "No." Then, circle the appropriate response beside the question. In the statements "drug abuse" refers to (1) the use of prescribed or over-the-counter drugs in excess of the directions and (2) any non-medical use of drugs. The various classes of drugs may include: cannabis (e.g., marijuana, hash), solvents, tranquilizers (e.g., Valium), barbiturates, cocaine, stimulants (e.g., speed), hallucinogens (e.g., LSD) or narcotics (e.g., heroin). Remember that the questions do not include alcoholic beverages. Please answer every question. If you have difficulty with a statement, then choose the response that is mostly right.

These questions refer to the past 12 months. Circle your response.

1. Have you used drugs other than those required for medical reasons?	Yes	No
2. Have you abused prescription drugs?	Yes	No
3. Do you abuse more than one drug at a time?	Yes	No
4. Can you get through the week without using drugs?	Yes	No
5. Are you always able to stop using drugs when you want to?	Yes	No
6. Have you had "blackouts" or "flashbacks" as a result of drug use?	Yes	No
7. Do you ever feel bad or guilty about your drug use?	Yes	No
8. Does your spouse (or parents) ever complain about your involvement with drugs?	Yes	No
9. Has drug abuse created problems between you and your spouse or your parents?	Yes	No
10. Have you lost friends because of your use of drugs?	Yes	No
11. Have you neglected your family because of your use of drugs?	Yes	No
12. Have you been in trouble at work because of drug abuse?	Yes	No
13. Have you lost a job because of drug abuse?	Yes	No
14. Have you gotten into fights when under the influence of drugs?	Yes	No
15. Have you engaged in illegal activities in order to obtain drugs?	Yes	No
16. Have you been arrested for possession of illegal drugs?	Yes	No
17. Have you ever experienced withdrawal symptoms (felt sick) when you stopped taking drugs?	Yes	No
18. Have you had medical problems as a result of your drug use (e.g., memory loss, hepatitis, convulsions, bleeding, etc.)?	Yes	No
19. Have you gone to anyone for help for a drug problem?	Yes	No
20. Have you been involved in a treatment program specifically related to drug use?	Yes	No

Source: Drug Abuse Screening Test (DAST-20) is reprinted by permission of the Centre for Addiction and Mental Health, Toronto, ON, Canada. Copyright © 1982.

The SASSI includes a set of decision rules to determine if the respondent fits the profile of a chemically dependent individual. Additional guidelines can be helpful in identifying some substance abusers who are not dependent. Separate profiles are used to score results for men and women. In addition to its basic function as a substance abuse and dependence screening instrument, the SASSI may provide other useful information. Clinical experience indicates that elevations on specific scales that comprise the SASSI reflect such things as defensiveness, willingness to acknowledge problematic behavior, depressed affect, focus on others, and relative likelihood of legal problems. The SASSI can be administered as a paper-and-pencil test or on a computer.

MacAndrew Alcoholism Scale

Another device included under the category of screening tools is the MacAndrew Alcoholism Scale (MacAndrew, 1965). It is a subscale of the well-known Minnesota Multiphasic Personality Inventory (MMPI), which psychologists often use to detect a wide range of mental disorders. The items are unobtrusive and have been used for more than four decades. Special training and approval are required to interpret the MMPI.

Utility of Screening Instruments

The screening instruments discussed thus far are generally reported to have good validity and reliability by their authors, and for the most part, other researchers have provided evidence of their utility. Other factors to recommend them are that most are easy to administer, and they generally take from about 1 to 20 minutes to complete (depending on the instrument). Except for the MMPI and the AUDIT's clinical screening procedures, they can be administered and scored by most human service professionals who need relatively minimal special training in their use.

We have discussed just a few of the instruments that may be useful to human service professionals in screening for substance abuse and dependence. Allen and Wilson (2003) and several volumes in the Substance Abuse and Mental Health Services Administration's Treatment Improvement Protocol Series provide additional discussion of screening devices and screening methods. In conducting screenings and assessments for alcohol and drug problems, treatment providers often use instruments to detect other problems the client may be experiencing, such as depression, suicidal ideation, or other psychiatric problems.

Can People with Alcohol and Drug Problems Be Believed?

In our section on screening, we mentioned the terms *validity* and *reliability* (see, for example, Allen, 2003; Connors & Volk, 2003). These are basic social science concepts. An instrument is *reliable* if it produces the same results with the same person at different times and under different circumstances. For example, if the MAST or the SASSI were administered to a client today during a visit to an outpatient clinic, one would expect the same or very similar results if it were administered to the client next week at his or her home. If an instrument does not consistently produce the same results, it is not very reliable.

Validity refers to whether an instrument measures what one wants it to measure. In this case, human service professionals want to be sure they are using an instrument that will detect alcohol or drug problems, not some other concept such as bipolar disorder or antisocial personality disorder. Professionals may also be interested in these problems, but they clearly want to know which instruments should be used to screen for each of these problems.

An instrument can be reliable but not valid. For example, an instrument may consistently or reliably measure the same concept over and over, but it may not be the concept in which one is interested. To be valid, however, an instrument must be reliable. If an instrument fails to measure consistently the same concept, it is not valid, because one cannot be sure it is measuring what one wants it to measure.

Also of concern is that the instrument has good sensitivity and specificity (Connors & Volk, 2003). *Sensitivity* refers to the instrument's ability to identify correctly someone with an alcohol or drug problem (called *true positives*). Clinicians want to avoid instruments that are likely to classify an individual as having a substance use disorder when he or she does not have such a problem (*false positives*). The professional also tries to select instruments that have high *specificity*. They maximize the likelihood that people who do not have alcohol or drug problems will be correctly classified (*true negatives*), and they minimize the likelihood that people who have alcohol or drug problems will be misclassified as not having such a problem (*false negatives*).

Unfortunately, as sensitivity increases, specificity is likely to decrease and vice versa. One key to selecting appropriate instruments is in knowing the prevalence of the problem in the population. For example, sensitivity is greater when there is a greater likelihood of a problem occurring in a given population group (see Lanier & Ko, 2008). In a study using the Brief MAST to detect alcoholism in three groups (a general population sample, general medical patients, and people in inpatient alcoholism treatment), Chan and colleagues (1994) found that sensitivity was lowest for the general population sample, "probably because most of the B-MAST questions deal with severe alcohol problems, and they are not sufficiently sensitive to detect those who drank heavily but who had not yet developed these alcohol problems" (p. 695). Similarly, Heck and Williams (1995) found that the CAGE may not be as sensitive in identifying problem drinking among college students, especially women, as it generally is with adults.

To improve sensitivity and specificity of instruments with various populations, changes may be required in cutoff scores or in how items are weighted (Fleming & Barry, 1989, 1991). Wording changes may also provide more valid responses. Research helps to clarify whether modifications are useful. It may also be that another instrument is better suited to the population of interest. Various studies have compared the utility of the commonly used screening instruments, and some are more easily administered or more accurate with various types of clients in particular types of setting than others (see Connors & Volk, 2003). Staff, however, may be unaware of the psychometric properties of the instruments they routinely use. In selecting appropriate instruments, clinicians are advised to consult the available literature and to be mindful of the caveats discussed in this chapter.

Clinicians are concerned about selecting instruments with good psychometric properties, not only in screening and assessment but also in other situations such as measuring the client's progress during and after treatment and in evaluating the effectiveness of chemical dependency treatment programs. Factors such as the client's ability to recall past behaviors or events can affect accurate reporting. Questions that are ambiguous or poorly worded also present a problem.

Professionals also want to know if an instrument has been validated on the populations of interest to them. Many instruments have been validated on men. Some work has been done to develop instruments that are more sensitive to detecting alcohol problems in women. For example, Russell (1994) developed the TWEAK by using some items from other instruments, eliminating others, and making wording changes that better reflect the situation of women. For example, asking women whether they have had fistfights may not accurately reflect the drinking-related behavior they tend to exhibit. The TWEAK was developed to screen for problem drinking during pregnancy, but it may also be useful with women in other situations (Chan, Pristach, Welte, & Russell, 1993).

Another issue is whether the instrument has been tested with members of various ethnic and cultural groups. Language may be a particular concern. Terms commonly used by one ethnic group may have no meaning or a different meaning for other ethnic groups. Some efforts have been made to develop instruments that are sensitive to specific cultural groups (see, for example, Carise & McLellan, 1999), but instruments that are valid across ethnic groups are particularly useful. Language can also be a problem when an instrument is used with individuals from different age cohorts, since words can take on different meanings over time. Some instruments are designed specifically for use with adolescents and others with adults. Items should be relevant to the client's age group. For example, an adult may be asked about job and family responsibilities, whereas a child or adolescent may be asked about school.

Many of the instruments discussed so far rely on the client's self-report. Many of them are also face valid, because they clearly ask clients about their alcohol or drug use. When using a face-valid instrument, what confidence does one have that clients are telling the truth about their behavior? When asked about the amount of alcohol or drugs they consume or whether they have had an alcohol-related blackout or lost a job due to drug use, clients can easily lie, but are they likely to do this?

Based on research to determine the reliability and validity of clients' self-reports, many think that clinicians can have confidence in them (Fuller, 1988; Hesselbrock, Babor, Hesselbrock, Meyer, & Workman, 1983; NIAAA, 1990). Some also believe that direct questions about substance use "provide the logical basis for one to evaluate with the assessed person their alcohol and drug consumption and its consequences" (Svanum & McGrew, 1995, p. 212). Some researchers have correlated clients' self-reports with information from other sources, such as collateral contacts

and laboratory (medical) tests, and have found good agreement among them. Fuller (1988) agrees that the balance of evidence favors their usefulness. He also notes that some studies raise serious enough questions that self-reports should be used in combination with other evidence to gain the most accurate picture of the client's problems and functioning. Skinner (1984) describes the situations or conditions that influence the validity of clients' self-reports. These factors include whether the client is detoxified and psychologically stable at the time of the assessment, the rapport established by the interviewer with the interviewee, the clarity of the questions asked, whether the client knows that his or her responses will be corroborated with other sources of information (particularly laboratory tests [NIAAA, 1993]), and the degree of confidentiality that can be promised to the individual.

Hesselbrock and colleagues (1983) also suggest that the "demand characteristics of the situation" affect the accuracy of client self-reports. For example, individuals who have little to lose from reporting problem behaviors accurately are more likely to do so. In many situations in which alcohol- and drug-dependent individuals are found, such as criminal justice or child welfare settings, this is not the case. A diagnosis of chemical abuse or dependence may have serious consequences for them. In these cases, it may be particularly important for the clinician to utilize additional sources of information to obtain a complete picture of individuals' alcohol and drug use and any related problems in order to serve them appropriately.

There has been an interest in the use of less obtrusive (i.e., nonface-valid) instruments, such as the MacAndrew scale and the SASSI, in situations where demand characteristics might inhibit clients from giving accurate responses to face-valid questions. Even when less obtrusive measures are used, ethical, professional conduct generally requires that clients be told the purpose of the screening or assessment in which they are participating.

Diagnosis

For those individuals who screen positive, the next step is often to determine if there is sufficient evidence to confirm a diagnosis of a substance use disorder. Ideally, diagnosis is accompanied by a multidimensional, biopsychosocial assessment, which includes not only an in-depth understanding of clients' alcohol- and drug-related problems but also their strengths, support systems, and other factors that may help promote recovery.

Various authors have recounted the history of attempts to reach agreement on the criteria needed to define and diagnose alcohol and drug problems (see, for example, *Alcohol Health & Research World* 15[4], 1991; 20[1], 1996). In the last few decades, considerable progress has been made in helping clinicians and researchers grapple with these issues. An important step was the work of the Criteria Committee of the National Council on Alcoholism (NCA), now the National Council on Alcoholism and Drug Dependence (NCADD). In 1972, it simultaneously published "Criteria for the Diagnosis and Treatment of Alcoholism" in the *American Journal of Psychiatry* and *Annals of International Medicine.*

Today, the criteria of the American Psychiatric Association (APA, 2000) and the World Health Organization (WHO, 1992) are the most widely used diagnostic tools in the field. Edwards and Gross's work (1976) played an important role in the APA and WHO's efforts to define alcohol dependence. The *Diagnostic and Statistical Manual of Mental Disorders (DSM-IV-TR)* delineates the current APA criteria for diagnosing substance (alcohol and other drug) use disorders. The WHO's tenth edition of the *International Classification of Diseases (ICD-10)* contains its current criteria for alcohol and drug disorders. Table 5.1 compares the APA's criteria for alcohol dependence and abuse with the WHO's criteria for alcohol dependence and harmful use of alcohol, respectively. In the United States, the *DSM-IV-TR* is widely used to diagnose substance use disorders and other

mental disorders. Over the years, substantial changes have been made in *DSM* criteria for substance use disorders. For example, tolerance or withdrawal symptoms are no longer required for a diagnosis of dependence.

As another example from the *DSM-IV-TR*, Figure 5.3 contains its descriptions of cocaine abuse and dependence. The *DSM-IV-TR* also contains descriptions and diagnostic criteria for other types of substance use disorders (amphetamines, cannabis, opioids, etc.) and for substance-induced disorders (e.g., intoxication, withdrawal, psychosis, sleep, mood, anxiety, sexual dysfunction, etc.).

Professionals in the United States are often required to use *DSM* diagnoses to request third-party (insurance) payments for treating mental health problems, including substance use and dependence. Interview protocols (First, Spitzer, Gibbon, & Williams, 1997) and study guides (Fauman, 2002) are available to assist in applying the *DSM* diagnostic criteria.

A fifth edition of the *DSM* is being developed. Though not yet finalized, the proposed criteria are based on clinical experience and research and may differ in many ways from the current criteria. For example, given that research indicated that the reliability of the abuse diagnosis was much weaker than the dependence diagnosis, the recommendation is to replace dependence and abuse with a single diagnosis of substance use disorder. The diagnosis of substance use disorder would be specified as either moderate or severe depending on whether two to three or four or more criteria are met, respectively. The idea that alcohol and other drug problems fall along a continuum has been suggested for some time. Another significant proposed change is to add a new criterion described as "craving," given that it is a common clinical symptom or indicator of a substance use problem that is often categorized as severe (American Psychiatric Association, 2010).

A historical controversy in the field of treatment for alcohol problems centered on

TABLE 5.1 Comparison of the Diagnostic Criteria for Alcohol Dependence and Alcohol Abuse or Harmful Use in Two Diagnostic Schemes: The *ICD-10*[a] and the *DSM-IV-TR*[b]

ICD-10	DSM-IV-TR
Comparison of Criteria for Alcohol Dependence	
Symptoms of Alcohol Dependence	
Essential: Drinking or a desire to drink; the subjective awareness of compulsion to use is most common during attempts to stop or control drinking.	A maladaptive pattern of alcohol use leading to clinically significant impairment or distress, as manifested by three or more of the following:
At least three of the following:	1. Tolerance defined as (a) a need for markedly increased amounts of alcohol to achieve intoxication or desired effect or (b) markedly diminished effect with continued use of the same amount of alcohol.
1. Evidence of tolerance to the effects of alcohol.	2. Withdrawal, as manifested by (a) the characteristic alcohol withdrawal syndrome or (b) alcohol or a closely related substance taken to relieve or avoid withdrawal symptoms.
2. A physiological withdrawal state (characteristic alcohol withdrawal syndrome or drinking to relieve or avoid withdrawal symptoms).	
3. Difficulties in controlling drinking behavior in terms of onset, termination, or levels of use.	3. Drinking in larger amounts or over a longer period than intended.
4. Progressive neglect of alternative pleasures or interests because of drinking, increased amount of time to obtain or to drink alcohol, or to recover from its effects.	4. Persistent desire or unsuccessful efforts to cut down or control drinking.
5. Persisting in drinking despite clear evidence of harmful consequences which may be physical, psychological, or cognitive.	5. A great deal of time spent obtaining alcohol, using alcohol, or recovering from its effects.
6. A strong desire or compulsion to drink.	6. Important social, occupational, or recreational activities given up or reduced because of drinking.
Also a consideration: a narrowing of the repertoire of drinking patterns (e.g., drinking in the same way, regardless of social constraints that determine appropriate drinking behavior).	7. Continued drinking despite knowledge of a persistent or recurring physical or psychological problem caused or exacerbated by alcohol use.
Duration Criteria for Alcohol Dependence	
At least three of the above criteria have been met during the previous year.	Three or more symptoms have occurred at any time in the same 12-month period.
Specifiers for Alcohol Dependence	
None.	*With physiological dependence.* Evidence of tolerance or withdrawal (i.e., symptoms 1 or 2 above are present).
	Without physiological dependence. No evidence of tolerance or withdrawal (i.e., neither symptom 1 nor 2 is present).
Course Modifiers or Specifiers for Alcohol Dependence	
Currently abstinent.	**Remission Specifiers**
Currently abstinent, but in a protected environment.	(Do not apply if individual is on agonist therapy or in a controlled environment.)
Currently on clinically supervised maintenance or replacement regime.	*Early remission.*
Currently abstinent, but receiving aversive or blocking drugs (e.g., disulfiram).	1. *Early full remission.* No criteria for abuse or dependence met in last 1 to 12 months.
Currently drinking.	2. *Early partial remission.* Full criteria for dependence not met in last 1 to 12 months, but at least one criterion for abuse or dependence met, intermittently or continuously.

(*continued*)

TABLE 5.1 *Continued*

ICD-10	DSM-IV-TR
Course Modifiers or Specifiers for Alcohol Dependence *(continued)*	
Continuous drinking.	*Sustained remission.*
Episodic drinking.	Twelve months of early remission have passed.
	1. *Sustained full remission.* No criterion for abuse or dependence met at any time in past 12 months or longer.
	2. *Sustained partial remission.* Full criteria for dependence not met in past 12 months or longer, but at least one criterion for abuse or dependence met.
	Additional Specifiers
	No criteria for alcohol dependence or abuse have been met for at least one month.
	On *agonist therapy.*
	In a *controlled environment.*

Comparison of Criteria for *ICD-10* Harmful Use of Alcohol and for *DSM-IV-TR* Alcohol Abuse	
Symptoms	
Harmful Use of Alcohol	**Alcohol Abuse**
Clear evidence that a pattern of alcohol use was responsible for:	A maladaptive pattern of alcohol use leading to clinically significant impairment or distress, as manifested by one or more of the following:
1. Actual physical damage to the user.	1. Recurrent drinking resulting in failure to fulfill major role obligations at work, school, or home (e.g., repeated absences or poor work performance).
or	2. Recurring drinking in situations in which it is physically hazardous (e.g., driving an automobile).
2. Actual mental damage to the user.	3. Recurrent alcohol-related legal problems (e.g., arrests for alcohol-related disorderly conduct).
	4. Continued alcohol use despite persistent or recurrent social or interpersonal problems caused or exacerbated by the effects of alcohol (e.g., arguments, physical fights).
Duration Criteria for Harmful Use and Alcohol Abuse	
None.	One or more symptoms have occurred at any time during the same 12-month period.
Exclusionary Criteria Related to Alcohol Dependence	
Does not presently meet criteria for alcohol dependence, a psychotic disorder, or other drug- or alcohol-related disorder.	Never met criteria for alcohol dependence.

Sources: From ICD-10. Classification of Mental and Behavioural Disorders, Clinical Descriptions and Diagnostic Guidelines, World Health Organization, 1992, is reprinted by permission of WHO. From *The Diagnostic and Statistical Manual of Mental Disorders,* Fourth edition, Text Revision, Copyright © 2000 American Psychiatric Association. Reprinted with permission of the American Psychicatric Association.
[a]From World Health Organization, *The ICD-10 Classification of Mental and Behavioural Disorders, Clinical Descriptions and Diagnostic Guidelines* (Geneva: World Health Organization, 1992). Reprinted with permission of the World Health Organization.
[b]Reprinted with permission from the *Diagnostic and Statistical Manual of Mental Disorders,* Text Revision, Copyright 2000 American Psychiatric Association.

FIGURE 5.3   Cocaine Dependence and Abuse

Cocaine Dependence

Cocaine has extremely potent euphoric effects, and individuals exposed to it can develop dependence after using cocaine for very short periods of time. An early sign of Cocaine Dependence is when the individual finds it increasingly difficult to resist using cocaine whenever it is available. Because of its short half-life, there is a need for frequent dosing to maintain a "high." Persons with Cocaine Dependence can spend extremely large amounts of money on the drug within a very short period of time. As a result, the person using the substance may become involved in theft, prostitution, or drug dealing or may request salary advances to obtain funds to purchase the drug. Individuals with Cocaine Dependence often find it necessary to discontinue use for several days to rest or to obtain additional funds. Important responsibilities such as work or child care may be grossly neglected to obtain or use cocaine. Mental or physical complications of chronic use such as paranoid ideation, aggressive behavior, anxiety, depression, and weight loss are common. Regardless of the route of administration, tolerance occurs with repeated use. Withdrawal symptoms, particularly hypersomnia, increased appetite, and dysphoric mood, can be seen and are likely to enhance craving and the likelihood of relapse. The overwhelming majority of individuals with Cocaine Dependence have had signs of physiological dependence on cocaine (tolerance or withdrawal) at some time during the course of their substance use. The designation of "With Physiological Dependence" is associated with an earlier onset of dependence and more cocaine-related problems.

Cocaine Abuse

The intensity and frequency of cocaine administration is less in Cocaine Abuse as compared with dependence. Episodes of problematic use, neglect of responsibilities, and interpersonal conflict often occur around paydays or special occasions, resulting in a pattern of brief periods (hours to a few days) of high-dose use followed by much longer periods (weeks to months) of occasional, non-problematic use or abstinence. Legal difficulties may result from possession or use of the drug. When the problems associated with use are accompanied by evidence of tolerance, withdrawal, or compulsive behavior related to obtaining and administering cocaine, a diagnosis of Cocaine Dependence rather than Cocaine Abuse should be considered. However, since some symptoms of tolerance, withdrawal, or compulsive use can occur in individuals with abuse but not dependence, it is important to determine whether the full criteria for dependence are met.

Source: Reprinted with permission from the *Diagnostic and Statistical Manual of Mental Disorders,* Text Revision, Copyright 2000 American Psychiatric Association.

whether identifying and treating the underlying causes of alcoholism (e.g., various psychological problems) would result in remission of alcohol problems. This approach has not proven satisfactory for two reasons. First, scientists have yet to discover the exact etiologies of substance use disorders, and second, even if the underlying causes were known, substance use disorders often become problems in their own right. Our discussion of diagnosis generally refers to substance abuse or dependence as a major or primary problem presented by the client, requiring specific treatment. The reader may

have also encountered the term *secondary* diagnosis. In 1972, the Criteria Committee of the NCA (1972a,b) wrote:

> Reactive, secondary, or symptomatic alcohol use should be separated from other forms of alcoholism. Alcohol as a psychoactive drug may be used for varying periods of time to mask or alleviate psychiatric symptoms. This may often mimic a prodromal [early] stage of alcoholism and is difficult to differentiate from it. If the other criteria of alcoholism are not present, this diagnosis must be given. A clear relationship between the psychiatric symptom or event

must be present; the period of heavy alcohol use should clearly not antedate the precipitating situational event (for example, an object loss). The patient may require treatment as for alcoholism, in addition to treatment for the precipitating psychiatric event.

It may even be that excessive alcohol or drug use that developed following a traumatic event, such as loss of a loved one, may remit without specialized substance abuse treatment once an adjustment is made to the new life circumstance. But this is different from the situation in which alcohol or drug use itself has become a problem for the individual. Take, for example, the case of an individual who blames his diagnosis of alcohol dependence on a divorce that occurred ten years ago. Although it may be true that his drinking escalated at that time, alcohol dependence itself has become a problem, requiring it to be addressed as such. Exploring the issues that caused the client to fixate on his divorce may also be helpful at some point, but this alone is unlikely to resolve his years of alcohol problems. Many practitioners believe that treatment must first focus on arresting the alcohol dependence.

Today, we recognize that a substantial number of people with mental disorders also have diagnoses of alcohol or drug disorders. Although their drinking or drug use may have been precipitated by the desire to relieve symptoms of mental disorders (hallucinations, anxiety, etc.), many of them require treatment for substance use disorders as well as treatment for mental illness. The subject of dual or co-occurring diagnoses has become of such importance that we devote Chapter 13 to it.

Assessment

The APA and the WHO's diagnostic criteria are important in establishing whether an individual has a substance use disorder, but more information is needed to plan for the client's treatment. The *DSM-IV-TR* (APA, 2000) recommends a multiaxial assessment, which also considers factors such as the individual's cognitive abilities, medical condition, psychosocial and environmental problems, and overall level of functioning.

Addiction Severity Index

A multidimensional assessment tool widely used in the chemical dependency field is the Addiction Severity Index (ASI) (McLellan et al., 1985). The ASI is a structured interview accompanied by a numerical scoring system to indicate the severity of the patient's or client's problems in seven life areas: alcohol, drugs, vocational, family and social supports, medical, psychological or psychiatric, and legal. Chemical dependency professionals and other human service professionals who have been trained in its use can administer the ASI. The ASI has a follow-up version that has also contributed to its use in treatment and research to measure client progress and to assess the effectiveness of treatment programs. Similar instruments for use with adolescents have also been developed (Friedman & Utada, 1989; Kaminer, Wagner, Plummer, & Seifer, 1993).

Drug Use Screening Inventory

Another tool designed to assess the severity of adults and adolescents' problems on multiple dimensions and to rank these problems is the Drug Use Screening Inventory-Revised (DUSI-R) (Tarter & Hegedus, 1991; Tarter & Kirisci, 2001; also see Allen & Wilson, 2003). The 10 domains of the DUSI-R are frequency of and degree of involvement in drug and alcohol use (including drug preference), behavior patterns (such as anger and self-control), health status (including accidents and injuries), psychiatric disorder, social competence, family system, school performance/adjustment, work adjustment, peer relationships, and leisure/recreation. The DUSI-R contains 159 items requiring yes or no answers.

The DUSI is used in three phases. First, each domain is assessed using the basic assessment instrument. This instrument is written at a fifth-grade level and takes about 20 minutes to complete as a paper-and-pencil test or by computer, and it can be read to those with lower reading levels. Second, instruments are available to assess further those areas that appear to be problematic in order to provide a more comprehensive evaluation. Third, the information from stages one and two is used to develop an individualized treatment plan for the client.

Versions of the DUSI-R are available to provide information for the past week, past month, and past year. There are no scores that distinguish between types of treatment needed; instead, this is left to clinical judgment once the DUSI-R and other assessment information is compiled to give a full picture of the client's needs. Like the ASI, the instrument may be used to chart the client's progress, and client information can be aggregated for program evaluation studies. The DUSI-R's developers report that it has good ability to classify adults and adolescents with *DSM* substance disorders and that it also has good ability to identify those with no psychiatric disorders.

The information obtained from screening, diagnosis, and assessment is used to determine the type of substance abuse or dependence treatment the client needs. Chapter 6 describes the components of the chemical dependency treatment system, indicating clients' situations that are likely to warrant the various services. Since many alcoholics and addicts initially seek help for marital, family, job, legal, or health problems rather than for alcohol or drug problems, it is incumbent on helping professionals from all disciplines and in various treatment settings to be knowledgeable about screening, diagnosis, and assessment for chemical abuse and dependency problems. Similarly, tools such as the ASI are important to professionals in the chemical dependency field because they are concerned with the client's overall quality of life. A unidimensional approach indicates that the treatment goal of abstinence (or reduced use) is expected to result in improvement in other areas of the client's life, whereas a multidimensional approach suggests that each of the client's major problems be targeted for treatment since abstinence (or reduced use) alone may not resolve them (Babor, Dolinsky, Rounsaville, & Jaffe, 1988; McLellan, Luborsky, Woody, O'Brien, & Kron, 1981). The

multidimensional or systems view of assessment and treatment seems to have taken precedence over the view that chemical dependency is a unitary phenomenon and that chemical dependency professionals need be concerned only about clients' alcohol and drug problems (Babor et al., 1988; Callahan & Pecsok, 1988; Pattison, Sobell, & Sobell, 1977).

Taking a Social History

Taking a client's social history is particularly important because it is the type of assessment that exemplifies the systems or ecological perspective of this book.* Our discussion is intended to alert the new professional to some of the issues involved in doing a thorough assessment, focusing on the client's strengths as well as problems. There are many formats for doing social histories, from checklists to structured interviews to more open-ended formats. The social history outline found in Figure 5.4 can be used to structure an assessment or intake interview with adults who recognize that alcohol and/or drugs are a problem in their lives. A skillful interviewer may also be able to use this tool to reduce defensiveness in clients who are less willing to discuss their alcohol or drug use and to begin to engage the client in the treatment process and increase motivation for change (see Donovan, 1988; Miller, 1985). Although not exhaustive of all the avenues that can be explored with a client, the topics and questions suggested in the outline can help the interviewer capture information both about problems in the client's life and about the assets the client brings to the recovery process. The social history format is flexible and can be adjusted depending on the client and treatment setting. Sometimes, a comprehensive intake interview or social history is done at an initial session. In other cases, the material is obtained over several sessions. Clients may initially give limited answers to questions but reveal more information

*Thanks to William J. McCabe, who taught me a great deal about many of the elements of the social history.

FIGURE 5.4   The Social History as It Relates to Drinking and Drug Use

---

I. Education

A. How long did the client stay in school?
B. How did the client like or feel about school?
C. Did the client do well in school?
D. Did the client have a history of alcohol and/or other drug use or abuse during the school years?
E. Did the client have friends and close relationships during the school years? If so, were these individuals alcohol or drug users/abusers?
F. What work is the client educated to do?

II. Employment

A. What is the client's current job or when did the client last work?
B. What other jobs has the client held?
C. How often has the client changed jobs?
D. What is the client's favorite type of work?
E. Has the client experienced job difficulties? If so, what seems to be the cause of these problems?
F. If the client is not working, is he or she obtaining financial support from other sources?

III. Military History (if applicable)

A. If not currently in the military, what type of discharge did the client receive?
B. What was the client's last rank in the military?
C. What were the client's patterns of socialization in the military?
D. How long did the client remain in the military?
E. If the client experienced problems in the military, were they related to alcohol, other drug use, or other factors?

IV. Medical History

A. Does the client have current or past medical problems?
B. Has the client ever been hospitalized for medical problems?
C. Are past medical records available?
D. Is the client currently taking medications or has the client taken medications in the past?
E. Has the client abused prescription or nonprescription drugs?
F. Are any of the client's medical problems directly related to or exacerbated by alcohol or other drug use?
G. Will participation in treatment for alcohol or drug problems require any accommodation for medical disabilities?

V. Drinking and Drug Use History

A. If the client uses drugs, what drugs does he or she use; if the client drinks alcohol, what beverages does the client drink, and has the client consumed products containing alcohol that are not meant for human consumption?
B. How often does the client consume alcohol or other drugs?
C. How much alcohol and/or drugs does the client use?
D. What is the client's drinking or drug use pattern (daily, weekend, periodic, etc.)?
E. When did the client's drinking or drug use begin?
F. Does the client give a "reason" for his or her drinking or drug use?
G. Has the client experienced periods of abstinence?
H. Has the client experienced blackouts or other indications of chemical abuse problems?
I. Has the client experienced withdrawal symptoms from alcohol or other drugs?
J. Has the client ever received treatment for a drinking or other drug problem?
K. Are past treatment records available?

VI. Psychological or Psychiatric History

A. Does the client express feelings of being tense, lonely, anxious, depressed, etc.?
B. Has the client ever contemplated, threatened, or attempted suicide?
C. Has the client received any counseling or psychiatric treatment on an outpatient basis?
D. Has the client ever had a psychiatric hospitalization?
E. Are records of past treatment available to determine the exact nature of the problem and treatment received?
F. Will participation in treatment for alcohol or drug problems require any accommodation for mental disabilities?

VII. Legal Involvement (if applicable)

A. Is the client currently on probation or parole or incarcerated?
B. What types of charges or other legal problems has the client had?
C. Were any legal charges related to alcohol or other drug use directly (sale, possession) or indirectly (e.g., embezzlement, theft)?

D. Does the client have any charges pending? If so, what are they, and does the client believe that chemical dependency treatment will result in reduced legal penalties?

E. If the client was arrested for DWI or DUI, what was his or her blood-alcohol level or are other tests results available indicating the presence of drugs?

VIII. Family History

A. What are the drinking and drug use habits of members of the client's family of origin (mother, father, grandparents, siblings, aunts, uncles, etc.)?

B. Do members of the client's family of origin have alcohol or other drug problems?

C. What were the attitudes toward drinking alcohol and other drug use in the client's family of origin?

D. How does the cllent describe his or her relationship with family of origin members?

E. Was there a history of psychological or physical (including sexual) abuse in the family? What was the client a direct victim?

F. What is the client's current relationship with family members?

IX. Relationship with Spouse, Children, and Other Significant Individuals

A. What is the client's current marital status and marital history?

B. If the client has a spouse/partner and/or children, what is the quality of the relationship with them?

C. What are the spouse/partner's or children's drinking and drug-taking habits?

D. Are the client's spouse/partner and/or children experiencing problems (psychological or physical abuse, etc.)?

E. What are the client's living arrangements?

F. What is the extent of the client's other social relationships?

X. Religion/Spirituality

A. In what religious or spiritual tradition, if any, was the client raised?

B. Does the client have a particular religious preference or spiritual beliefs at this time?

C. Does the client view his or her religion or spiritual beliefs as a source of strength or a source of difficulty in his or her life?

XI. Why the Client is Seeking Help Now (e.g., are there legal, medical, family, work, or other pressures to do so?)

---

over time as comfort and trust with the treatment professional increases. Assessment is not a single event; it takes place throughout the treatment process as clients' needs and circumstances change.

In conducting a social history, the interviewer determines which questions to ask at a given time and the order of the questions. In approaching each section of this social history with the client, the interviewer might begin by commenting not only on the type of information that might be gathered but also on the reasons for gathering it. Often, the social history starts with information considered to be least threatening to the client. The sections on education and employment may be good starting points. Basic questions about how much education the client has had and whether the client has professional or vocational education are generally considered routine and are usually easily answered by clients without resistance.

Education. School adjustment may be a useful avenue to explore, especially for younger clients, as it may be particularly relevant to their current situation. With older clients, the interviewer may ask whether he or she liked school, did well, and fit in, or if school was a frustrating or unsatisfactory experience. Did the client initiate alcohol and/or other drug use or abuse in primary or secondary school or in college? Were his or her friends involved in alcohol and drug use in the same way? These questions may help establish the time frame and circumstances during which alcohol or drug use first became a problem. If the client has no high school diploma or no college or vocational education and wishes to pursue further education, the chemical dependency professional may note the client's need for a referral to a general equivalency diploma (GED) program or other educational or vocational program. If the client did well in school and has substantial education, these may be noted as assets to recovery.

Employment. Questions about employment often follow logically after questions about education. Is the client currently employed and is the client's job secure or has it been threatened by substance abuse or dependence? During assessment interviews, individuals (such as those referred by an employee assistance program or by the correctional system) may deny employment problems related to alcohol or drug use. The pattern of employment—whether it is stable or erratic—is important to note. An erratic employment history is not necessarily the result of a substance use disorder, but it may be an indication of it or other problems in the client's life. Discussion of employment may provide an opportunity for the assessment specialist to help clients identify how alcohol or drug use has negatively affected their work.

Another clue to problems may be the client's employment in a job that is well below his or her educational level. For example, an individual with a graduate degree may be working in a convenience store. Perhaps this work is what the individual prefers, perhaps this is the only work available, or perhaps a substance use disorder has interfered with other employment. Seeming incongruities in the individual's life such as these can be explored to help determine if substance abuse or dependence is a problem.

The client may have a job that is an obstacle to recovery. An obvious example is working as a bartender, where constant exposure to alcohol presents a problem for the client. Or perhaps the individual spends long periods on the road alone and is used to going to bars at night to relieve loneliness or boredom. Some clients frequently find themselves in situations where alcohol or perhaps other drug use is common or expected. For some of these individuals, learning how to engage in alternative activities or assertiveness training to learn how to refuse drinks or drugs may prove useful. For others, a key to attaining sobriety may include employment changes. A referral to a vocational rehabilitation agency, an employment counselor, or an employment agency may be appropriate. These referrals may be made at the time of the intake or assessment interview or at a later date, depending on the client's circumstances.

Some clients are in immediate need of a job. Professionals who work with clients who are homeless or living in very impoverished circumstances generally know the street corners or programs in town where a client can try to get a day labor job, or they know employers who hire and pay individuals by the day. The professional's interest in the whole client, not just the client's substance abuse or dependency problem, is reflected in addressing employment concerns. Productive employment can be a useful tool in maintaining sobriety. For some clients, current employment may be identified as an asset. For example, an individual referred by an employee assistance program may have a job that he or she is anxious to keep. The interviewer may also ask questions about work hours or work habits to determine whether the client is currently working to the detriment of other aspects of his or her life.

When clients are not working, it may be appropriate to inquire about their current means of support. They may be receiving public assistance or Social Security payments, or they may need a referral to apply for these benefits. Some clients may be getting help from family or friends, or they may be dealing drugs or engaging in other criminal activity to support themselves.

Military History. Questions about military service are often not asked unless the client is currently in the service or is in a Veterans Administration facility. However, these questions may be important, because young adults may be introduced to alcohol and other drugs while in the military. A problematic military history may have been the result of alcohol or drug problems. Questions that might be asked to probe into this area involve the rank or ranks the client held in the military and the type of discharge the individual received. For example, being demoted in rank or receiving a medical, general, administrative, or dishonorable discharge may have been a consequence of alcohol or drug problems.

Medical History. An obvious reason that questions about medical problems are asked is to determine if they may be related to substance use. The client may not have made a connection between his or her medical problems (e.g., sores, gastritis, or neuropathy) and alcohol or other drug use. Some medical problems are not caused by substance use, but alcohol and drug use may be contraindicated if the client has a particular condition (e.g., diabetes or epilepsy). Another reason to ask these questions is to determine if the client is receiving appropriate care for any current conditions. If the client does not have personal resources to obtain medical attention, the interviewer may act as a referral source to community clinics, the local health department, or other services, although many communities lack the resources to provide anything but emergency medical care to those who do not have health insurance.

Also important are any prescribed or over-the-counter (OTC) medications the client is taking. Some clients are taking medication but do not understand what it is, only that the doctor told them to take it. Many are unaware of the adverse consequences that alcohol can have when combined with common OTC medications such as ibuprofen, acetaminophen, and aspirin, or the additive effects of combining alcohol with other sedative drugs (Weatherman & Crabb, 1999) or the contraindications of combining illicit drugs with OTCs or prescribed medications.

An important reason health questions are asked, especially in inpatient and residential programs, is for staff to be prepared if the client experiences medical problems. For example, a history of epilepsy would be of concern in order for staff to be prepared for seizures, and it is important to know if a history of seizures is related to epilepsy or to alcohol or drug withdrawal. There is a growing body of literature on those who are dually diagnosed with chemical dependency problems and major physical disabilities (see Chapter 13).

A release or consent form signed by the client is generally needed to obtain information about prior health history and medical treatment.

This information should be requested if it would be useful in assisting the client in the chemical dependency treatment setting.

Legal History. Questions about the client's legal problems are also important. Many referrals to chemical dependency treatment programs are motivated by the legal system. A brush with the law may help the client confront a chemical dependency problem, or a client may seek treatment in the hope of obtaining a lighter or deferred sentence. Probation and parole officers and attorneys frequently refer clients to chemical dependency programs. The courts may routinely require those convicted of a driving while intoxicated (DWI) or DUI offense to submit to a screening or assessment to determine whether they have an alcohol or drug problem.

Often, a client admits to getting into legal difficulties as a result of using alcohol or drugs but denies an inability to control alcohol or other drug use. An important clue to a drinking problem in these cases may be blood-alcohol level (BAL) or blood-alcohol content (BAC). A breathalyzer or intoxilizer is frequently used to measure BAL or BAC, typically following arrest on suspicion of DWI or DUI. A high level may be an indication of tolerance to alcohol or alcohol dependence. For example, a person with a 0.20 percent BAL may deny a problem, but 0.20 is at least twice what is commonly referred to as the "legal limit" of 0.08 in most states. Most people would be unable to drive at a 0.20 level, yet those with a high tolerance may be able to do so despite its recklessness.

Asking how much alcohol was consumed before the arrest may be another clue to the client's candidness in responding to questions. When an individual says she had two cocktails but her BAL is 0.20, something is amiss. Two cocktails (of the type typically served in a bar) would not produce such a high BAL. Sometimes a blood test is used to determine BAL or the presence of other drugs. In accidents where a person is seriously injured and is taken to the hospital, the use of a blood test is common. Previous DWI or DUI arrests or other history of alcohol- or drug-related arrests are also strong clues to consider. Most people would not make the mistake of getting a second DWI or DUI because the consequences can be severe. The person with an unrecognized problem is far more likely to make this costly misjudgment.

Other common types of alcohol- and drug-related arrests are public intoxication (in locations where this offense is still a crime), disorderly conduct, and offenses related to the possession and sale of controlled substances. Transients who have chemical dependency problems are frequently arrested for vagrancy. Arrests for family violence may be due to alcohol abuse. White-collar crime, such as embezzlement and forgery, may also result from having a drug habit. With the advent of drug screening in the workplace, urinalysis, previously used most by the criminal justice system and in therapeutic communities, has become an increasingly common tool to identify job applicants or employees who use illicit drugs.

Clients may bring other legal problems to the interviewer's attention, such as fears that past behavior may result in prosecution if discovered. Other legal matters worrying clients may be how to deal with an abusive partner or civil matters such as eviction, child custody, and child support. Referrals to legal services may help clients address these problems so that they can better avail themselves of treatment.

Drinking and Drug History.   Naturally, the individual's drinking and drug history are paramount in conducting an assessment for substance use disorders. What psychoactive substances has the client used in his or her life? What drug or drugs is the individual currently using, including frequency and amount of use? Many clients have problems related to alcohol and drugs or more than one drug. Clients may also be asked if they have ingested technical products that contain alcohol but are not meant for human consumption (e.g., rubbing

alcohol, after-shave lotion, Sterno, etc.) or sniffed or inhaled other household products (e.g., paint, glue, etc.). What problems has the individual experienced as a direct result of alcohol or other drug use, such as blackouts or violent behavior or withdrawal symptoms like tremors, seizures, hallucinations, or delirium tremens?

In obtaining information from or about clients who are not detoxified, it is especially helpful to know about previous withdrawal symptoms that the client has experienced. Such information may indicate the need for immediate referral to a detoxification program and can be very helpful to the medical staff assisting the client through withdrawal. The client may be intoxicated or otherwise unable to provide this information, and others who know the information may not be available. This is frequently the case when a transient individual is brought to a hospital emergency department or to a community detoxification center (see Chapter 6).

It is also important to know if the individual has made attempts to stop using alcohol or other drugs in the past and if he or she has had periods of abstinence (no alcohol or drug use, often referred to as "sober time" or being "clean"). These periods may also indicate that the individual is an alcohol or drug abuser, since others usually do not need to make special efforts at abstinence. Periods of abstinence should be considered an asset, and the chemical dependency counselor can discuss with the individual behaviors or circumstances that may have contributed to the ability to remain alcohol or drug free. Another question is whether the client has had previous treatment for alcohol or other drug problems. The client may be asked to give consent to obtain treatment records or to talk with previous treatment providers in order to provide a better understanding of his or her progress and setbacks in treatment. Information of this nature may also be helpful in determining whether the client is best served in an inpatient, residential, or outpatient chemical dependency treatment program.

A possible avenue to explore is whether the individual perceives that his or her alcohol or drug problems were precipitated by particular events or circumstances. This may seem like an unusual question since no one really knows what causes substance use disorders. Asking the question is not done to give the client an opportunity to place blame on some internal or external factor. It is done to understand better the client's own perception of his or her substance abuse or dependence. This is a reflection of the principle of "starting where the client is." Many clients need help in understanding the dynamics of chemical abuse and dependence. Remember the client mentioned earlier who blamed his drinking on a divorce that occurred ten years ago? He may be correct in identifying that drinking or other drug use escalated at that point, but he is probably incorrect if he thinks that reuniting with his former spouse will solve the problem. The professional taking the social history may make note, however, that this will be an important point to which to return with the client. Additionally, knowing events that generally precede episodes in which the client drinks or uses drugs may help to establish plans that can avert relapse (see Chapter 6 regarding relapse).

Psychological or Psychiatric History. Psychological or psychiatric history is yet another aspect of diagnosis and assessment. Does the client have one or more mental disorders? Of immediate concern are current and serious psychological or psychiatric problems the client is experiencing, especially thoughts or plans related to suicide. Some individuals, particularly those who have made past suicide attempts or are dependent on depressant drugs such as alcohol, are at high risk for suicide. An immediate referral for psychiatric evaluation or to an inpatient psychiatric unit may be needed. Some clients with chemical dependency problems have serious mental disorders such as schizophrenia, or they may have personality disorders or other mental illnesses (also see Chapter 13).

If adequate information on psychiatric history is not available and mental health problems are suspected, a psychological or psychiatric evaluation should be obtained. An accurate diagnosis is necessary to determine the range of services the client needs and who may best treat the client. A referral to a mental health program or, where available, a program specifically for those with co-occurring chemical dependency and mental disorders may be the best alternative. Individuals with co-occurring disorders may also be directed to mutual-help or other support groups designed specifically for them.

Family History. The family history section of the assessment refers to the client's family of origin. These questions should probably be asked after some rapport has been established because they can be particularly emotionally charged for the client. Many people who become dependent on alcohol have a parent who was dependent on alcohol (this may even be the case for both parents). It has also become more common to see families with intergenerational drug problems. If so, it is useful to know whether the client's parent is (or was) in recovery and, if so, at what point in the client's life this happened. Do other family members (such as siblings, aunts, uncles, and grandparents) have drinking or drug problems?

Other useful information concerns family attitudes about alcohol and drug use. Was there an intolerant attitude toward any use of alcohol? Were drinking or drug use seen as acceptable, and how was abuse of these substances viewed? To what extent were family attitudes related to particular cultural or religious beliefs (also see Chapter 11)? Knowing whether there was a history of psychiatric or other problems among family members may also be helpful in understanding the client's situation.

Questions about the client's current relationship with members of his or her family of origin are also important. Is the client in contact with other family members or estranged from them? Are family members seen as potentially supportive of the client's recovery, or might they present obstacles by reinforcing or encouraging the client's alcohol or other drug use? It may be appropriate to consider involving family members in the client's treatment. How much the client is asked to reveal about his or her family of origin will depend on the treatment setting and its purpose. In a brief detoxification program, medical history is more important than family history. In an intensive inpatient or extended outpatient treatment setting, the social history may delve further into family matters.

Not so long ago, chemical dependency professionals were unlikely to ask clients questions about previous physical, sexual, and emotional abuse inflicted on them by family members or others. However, as professionals began hearing about this from clients, particularly women, it could not continue to be overlooked. These problems may surface during treatment and can present serious obstacles to recovery if not addressed appropriately. The topic of physical, sexual, and psychological abuse may or may not be broached in the initial assessment interview, depending on professional judgment. Unless the client offers this information, it may be premature to do so because it may be too distressing for the client to address very early in the process of alcohol or drug treatment. These problems may be better addressed once a relationship between client and professional has developed, and they may require referral to a qualified mental health practitioner.

Current Family and Social Relationships.　Other vital questions concern the client's relationship to any current or former spouse, other partners, or children. If the client's sexual orientation is not clear, the professional should take care not to make an erroneous assumption about the gender of the client's partner (also see Chapter 12 on gay men, lesbians, and bisexual and transgendered individuals). How do the client's significant others perceive his or her drinking or drug use? Are they aware that the client has come for help? Are they similarly engaged in alcohol or drug use, or have they pushed the client to contact the treatment program? Including significant others in the treatment process can be helpful for all parties involved. The interviewer should explore whether significant others are likely to be supportive and inquire as to whether the client wishes to involve them in treatment. Clients are

often encouraged to include them, though in some cases it is not advisable (e.g., when there are concerns about retaliation from an abusive partner). In other cases, the client may be threatened with an unwanted separation or divorce, and his or her partner may wish to sever all ties rather than participate in treatment. Sometimes, child abuse or neglect becomes apparent or is suspected, or threats on a partner's life are made and may have to be reported in keeping with state statute or the "duty to warn."

Stable living arrangements make the process of becoming alcohol and drug free easier, but some clients have no suitable home or are living with others who have active substance use disorders. Professionals in the alcohol and drug rehabilitation fields have always worked with individuals who are drifters or find themselves with no roof over their heads. Deinstitutionalization of people with mental illness, unemployment, and lack of affordable housing in addition to alcohol and drug disorders have added to the ranks of people who need housing or residential treatment in order to make rehabilitation a viable option.

Questions about close friends, other social relationships, and involvement with organizations and associations also help to determine the extent of social supports the client has in the community. Many clients need assistance in establishing friendships with sober or "clean" individuals and with pursuing activities not centered on alcohol and drug use.

Religion and Spirituality.　Religious affiliation and spiritual beliefs are addressed to determine if they may be an avenue of support and strength for the client or if they are causing the client difficulty. Some clients find solace in their religious and spiritual beliefs, and their priest, minister, rabbi, or other clergy member may be a resource to whom they turn in times of crisis. Church groups may also be of assistance to the client in recovery. In other cases, the church or religious group in which the individual has participated over the course of his or her life may hold punitive attitudes toward people with alcohol problems that have contributed to the client's guilt or denial. Clients may also feel that if only their faith was stronger, they could overcome their problem with alcohol or drugs, and do not take other steps needed for recovery.

The role of religion and spirituality in the recovery process has become an area of empirical study. Clients who do not subscribe to a particular religion may have deeply held spiritual beliefs. More treatment providers are including the religious or spiritual dimension in the client assessment and treatment process (see Hodge, 2001).

Why the Individual Is Seeking Services.   Finally, if it is not clear why the individual is seeking services at this particular time, the interviewer may want to inquire about this. Many clients have abused psychoactive drugs for a long time but have not previously sought help. Is there some particular concern, such as threat of job loss, divorce, or legal consequences, that has motivated the individual to seek help at this time? Or perhaps, as the saying goes, the individual is just "sick and tired of being sick and tired."

Initial appointments or assessment interviews may be done free of charge even by private-for-profit treatment programs as a way of encouraging people to consider some type of treatment or to encourage use of a particular program. For clients who want further services, the initial appointment usually also involves determining whether the individual has insurance or another means of paying for treatment. If the client does not have the financial resources required by the program or needs services the program does not offer, professionalism generally requires that a referral to another resource be offered.

Denial, Resistance, and Motivation for Recovery

It is probably impossible to work in a substance abuse or treatment program without hearing the terms *denial* and *resistance* during the course of the workday. Tarter, Alterman, and Edwards

(1984) describe the ways in which the term *denial* has been used in the chemical dependency field:

> Denial ... has frequently been used to explain an alcoholic's failure to recognize the role of his feelings in instigating and sustaining drinking. Denial has also long been believed to reflect a conscious refusal by an alcoholic to recognize the effects of continued and excessive drinking on himself and his environment, thereby contributing to the alcoholic's resistance to initiating treatment, as well as ensuring poor treatment prognosis. Within the rubric of psychodynamic theory, denial has been conceptualized as an ego defense, and as such is considered to be indicative of an unconscious attempt by an alcoholic to protect himself from the threatening or aversive aspects of drinking behavior. (pp. 214–215)

As a largely unconscious process, denial differs from lying or an outright attempt at deceit (George, 1990). Tarter and colleagues (1984) propose a biopsychological interpretation of denial, suggesting that some alcoholics have a "disturbed arousal regulation process" in which they fail "to perceive or label internal cues accurately" (pp. 214–215; also see Donovan, 1988). This causes them to underestimate the severity of stress in their lives, thereby promoting denial.

Everyone employs defense mechanisms to cope with life's stresses and strains. For example, news of the death of a family member or that one has a serious illness may be initially met with denial (see Kinney, 1996). In these cases, denial initially serves a protective function until the individual can begin to integrate the event and move along to the next stages of the grief process. Clearly, it is necessary to utilize some level of defenses in order to maintain healthy psychological functioning, but when one is unable to move past denial, well-being is jeopardized. This is frequently the case with the individual who has a substance abuse or dependence problem. As Weinberg (1986) puts it:

> Denial is a way the human mind often deals with a situation involving incompatible perceptions, thoughts, or behaviors. In the case of drinking

problems, the two elements are the powerful reinforcement derived from the drug and the unwanted side effects produced at the same time. The former is comprised of positive reinforcement (euphoria and energy) and/or negative reinforcement (temporary reduction of such unwanted feelings as tension, depression, self-hate, boredom, and sexual inadequacy). (p. 367)

Another function of denial is to shield substance abusers from feelings of hopelessness (George, 1990). Kinney (1996) notes that many patients are actually unaware that their problems are a result of substance abuse.

Weinberg (1986) and Kinney (2000) recommend helping clients reduce their denial gradually, since it is serving an important, protective function. A critical task of the treatment professional is to help clients recognize the relationship between their drug use and its negative consequences. To facilitate this process with cocaine abusers, Washton (1989) developed the Cocaine Assessment Profile (CAP), which can be useful in assessment and in addressing denial. The CAP questions about drug use and its consequences help clients understand the magnitude of their substance abuse and the need for treatment.

Family members and other loved ones are also likely to engage in denial. It is equally painful for them to recognize that someone they care about is chemically dependent. They may blame themselves for the client's problem or they may just be plain embarrassed about the situation. Consequently, people with alcohol and drug problems and their significant others reinforce each other's denial. In a well-known pamphlet published by Al-Anon (1969), Reverend Joseph L. Kellerman likened the process of denial to being on a merry-go-round, but he noted that "the alcoholic cannot keep the Merry-Go-Round going unless the others [family, friends, employers, etc.] ride it with him and help him keep it going" (p. 13). When more than one member of the family is chemically dependent, denial can be especially strong.

In addition to denial, clients and their significant others may use a variety of other defenses.

These include rationalization (attempts to find reasons to explain or excuse the chemical use), projection (blaming or attacking others for problems), avoidance or evasion of discussions of chemical use, recollection of the positive effects and experiences associated with chemical use, minimization of chemical use and its effects, and repression of painful events and feelings (George, 1990; Johnson, 1973). But George notes that "denial is a more prominent approach, because it blocks the need for the use of the other defense mechanisms entirely" (p. 36). It is also important to remember that the individual's defensiveness may result in behaving in grandiose, aggressive, and belligerent ways when often his or her feelings, especially during periods of sobriety, are actually remorse, guilt, inferiority, and helplessness.

Just as clients vary in their expression of denial and other defenses, they also vary in the extent to which they enter treatment voluntarily. Individuals who call a 24-hour crisis line asking for help with a drug problem or those who walk into a treatment program are generally considered voluntary clients. Of course, external factors may have motivated them to request help—for example, fear that their marriage or their work is suffering. Less voluntary clients may be those who have been committed or ordered to treatment through civil procedures (these laws and procedures vary by state). In these cases, family members or others have appealed to the court because the individual has refused to seek help and is in serious danger due to alcohol or other drug use. Other clients have been referred through their employer because their jobs are at stake, or their probation officer has told them to get help. These clients may recognize the problem and may participate willingly in treatment. Others may attend simply to remain employed or to fulfill the terms of their court order. Even so, there is ample evidence that some degree of pressure or coercion may be helpful in prompting treatment entry and promoting better client outcomes (Burke & Gregoire, 2007; Center for Substance Abuse Treatment, 2005; Hiller, Knight, Broome, & Simpson, 1998; Leukefeld & Tims, 1992; National Institute on Drug Abuse [NIDA], 2009; Perron & Bright, 2008; Trice & Beyer, 1982).

Clearly, individuals differ in their willingness or ability to terminate substance use and desire to engage in the treatment process. It may take some time for treatment providers to develop rapport with clients and to help them work through their defenses, but clients who come to counseling sessions or stay in halfway houses or therapeutic communities and never engage in the treatment process may be told that there is nothing more that the treatment program can do for them at this time.

Many individuals make an initial appointment at a treatment program to satisfy others but are not seeking long-term services. Following the assessment interview, they may thank the interviewer, saying they now understand the problem and are sure they can quit or control alcohol or other drug use on their own. Sometimes a brief intervention can help problem drinkers reduce their drinking (see Chapter 6). But many individuals have substance use disorders that are more serious than a brief intervention can address. Even so, unless the individual is in an immediate life-threatening situation, treatment providers cannot force someone to receive services. Some professionals object to the idea that a client would be pressured or coerced at all. Treatment providers generally consider their services voluntary, even if a client is under a civil court order or a parole or probation officer requires them to attend.

If an individual appears to have an alcohol or drug problem but resists treatment, the assessment specialist may encourage him or her to attend an educational program, a few individual or group counseling sessions, or some meetings of a mutual-help group before rejecting the notion of treatment entirely. If none of these alternatives is accepted, the professional should be supportive of the individual for his or her willingness to come in at all, being sure to leave the door open should he or she want to return later. Sometimes individuals are willing to make an agreement with the assessment specialist—if they are unable to stay clean or sober, use more than specified amounts of alcohol or drugs during a given time period, or encounter negative consequences of alcohol or drug use, they will concede that they cannot control their use, and they agree to re-contact the assessment specialist for treatment. This approach sometimes works in helping individuals identify alcohol and drug problems, especially those who are certain that they can control their use. Some chemical dependency specialists may use more direct approaches, depending on the client and the situation, but there is a growing interest today in less confrontational and more supportive approaches, such as those described in Box 5.1 called The Motivation to Change.

Finally, it may be useful to remember that labeling a client unmotivated or resistant to treatment may be unfair or unwarranted. There is a great deal experts do not know about how to treat substance use disorders. Some individuals are able to maintain sobriety or stay "clean" only after dozens of detox admissions. Others try hard but never achieve long periods of clean and sober time. The types of approaches available to treat substance abuse and dependence are relatively limited. Professionals rely heavily on cognitive- and behavior-based strategies, though there is increasing evidence of a genetic component to chemical dependence. There may be many types of alcoholism and drug addiction, each with its own complex etiology. In sum, clinicians do not yet have the tools to treat all individuals successfully, and this, rather than lack of client motivation, may be at the heart of why so many struggle with recovery.

Ethics of Chemical Dependency Treatment

Ethical dilemmas arise each day in the chemical dependency field that warrant professionals' careful attention (see Taleff, 2010). The professional organizations and licensing and certification bodies that represent social workers, psychologists,

BOX 5.1 *The Motivation to Change*

Most people want to change something about themselves. They might want to study harder, spend more time with loved ones, lose weight, exercise more, reduce drinking, or stop smoking or using other drugs. Many won't make substantial changes in these areas. They may think about it or they may try, while others will be only marginally aware that a problem even exists.

What makes people change is an important question in psychotherapeutic treatment. When it comes to alcohol and other drug problems, some people think that a serious crisis must occur before a person develops sufficient motivation to change. Others contend that professionals can intervene before a client "hits bottom" and help motivate him or her to change.

Stages of Change

Prochaska, DiClemente, and Norcross (1992) have devoted a great deal of study to the process of change—the type that is made on one's own and the type that takes place in the psychotherapeutic process. They believe that a series of stages typifies the change process in both types of situations, regardless of the behavior the individual wishes to change (also see Prochaska & DiClemente, 1982). Much of their initial research was done with smokers. Considerable research on the model has also been conducted with people who have alcohol and other drug problems (see, for example, Connors, Donovan, & DiClemente, 2001). They call their model **transtheoretical** because they believe it is compatible with a wide range of treatments. The five stages of change they identified are:

1. **Precontemplation,** in "which there is no intention to change in the foreseeable future" and people may be "unaware or underaware of their problems."
2. **Contemplation,** "in which people are aware that a problem exists and are seriously thinking about

overcoming it but have not yet made a commitment to take action" (in this stage, the pros and cons of the problem and solution are weighed).
3. **Preparation,** in which individuals intend "to take action in the next month."
4. **Action,** in which individuals have successfully modified their situation "from one day to six months."
5. **Maintenance,** in which people continue to change and prevent relapse. (Prochaska et al., 1992, pp. 1103–1104)

Prochaska and colleagues note that change is generally not a linear progression through these five stages but often involves reverting to an earlier stage before additional progress is made. Although some people may remain stuck at the first or second stage, the researchers note that individuals usually learn something at each point and generally do not regress completely. The techniques that will be successful with clients depend on the stage at which they are.

Just how does one move from one stage to the next, and how can treatment providers facilitate this process? Table 5.2 indicates the processes that seem to facilitate movement between stages.

Motivation, Not Confrontation

Miller and Rollnick (1991, 2002; Miller, 1999) also address the process of change in their work on **motivational interviewing:**

> Motivational interviewing is a particular way to help people recognize and do something about their present or potential problems. It is particularly useful with people who are reluctant to change and ambivalent about changing. It is intended to help resolve ambivalence and to get a person moving along the path to change. (Miller & Rollnick, 1991, p. 52)

Miller and Rollnick stress the importance of the therapist's role in the treatment process, saying that

TABLE 5.2 The Right Change Process at the Right Time: What Helps Clients Move from Here to There?

Stage of change				
Precontemplation to contemplation	Contemplation to preparation	Preparation to action	Action to maintenance	Staying in maintenance
Most relevant change processes				
Consciousness raising	Self-reevaluation	Self-liberation	Self-liberation	Self-liberation
Dramatic relief	Environmental reevaluation	Stimulus control	Stimulus control	Stimulus control
Self-reevaluation		Counter-conditioning	Counter-conditioning	Counter-conditioning
Environmental reevaluation	Social liberation	Helping relationships	Helping relationships	Helping relationships
			Reinforcement management	Reinforcement management
			Helping relationships	Social liberation

Experiential Processes

Consciousness raising: Individual gains knowledge about him/herself and his/her behavior through discussion, reading, etc.

Dramatic relief: Individual experiences and expresses feelings about the problem and solutions through grieving losses, role playing, etc., or may have a significant emotional experience related to the problem.

Self-reevaluation: Individual recognizes how a current behavior conflicts with his/her goals and values (values clarification).

Environmental reevaluation: Individual recognizes effects his/her behavior has on others and his/her environment through empathy training, other processes.

Self-liberation: Individual decides to make commitment to change often with specific goals; may share decision with others and ask for their support.

Behavioral Processes

Stimulus control: Individual avoids or counters stimuli ("triggers") that elicit problem behavior through restructuring environment (e.g., avoiding bars), avoiding high risk cues (e.g., arguments), etc.

Counter-conditioning: Individual substitutes healthy behaviors for problem behavior using relaxation, desensitization, assertion, positive self-statements, etc.

Helping relationships: Individual utilizes therapeutic alliance (open, trusting relationship), social support, mutual-help groups to discuss/address problem.

Reinforcement management: Individual rewards self or is rewarded (directly or indirectly) by others for making changes.

Social liberation: Individual works for changes in society through policies/political action, advocating for rights of oppressed, empowerment.

Sources: Based on tables in "In Search of How People Change" by James Prochalska from *American Psychologist,* vol. 7, # 9, Sept 1992 and from Mary Marden Velasquez et al., *Group Treatment for Substance Abuse: A Stages-of-Change Therapy Manual,* Table, 1.1., p. 10. Guilford Press (2001). Used by permission.

(continued)

therapists have widely varying success rates with clients. They advocate the use of non-possessive warmth, genuineness, and particularly *accurate empathy* (reflective listening, rather than identification with the client, as described by noted psychotherapist Carl Rogers [1959]), and they see accurate empathy as much more productive than confrontation. Miller and Rollnick also consider reasons that alcohol and drug treatment providers have used confrontation. For example, myths developed that alcoholics and drug abusers were especially defensive and that leaders in the field of addiction treatment advocated confrontation to break down those defenses. Miller and Rollnick call both these ideas erroneous. Denial, they contend, is not more characteristic of alcoholics than of others; it is a normative reaction in the face of strong confrontation. In addition, neither Vernon Johnson (1973), who developed the technique called "The Intervention" (see Chapter 10 of this text), nor the Minnesota Model nor Alcoholics Anonymous (see Chapter 6) advocate heavy, aggressive confrontation. Education of helping professionals generally does not include aggressive or authoritarian confrontation. Table 5.3

describes the "spirit" of motivational interviewing and contrasts it with an opposite approach to counseling, and Table 5.4 describes the four general principles of motivational interviewing.

Change and a Systems Approach

The models we have reviewed rely primarily on individual factors to promote change. Using a social work perspective, Barber (1995) recommends a **holistic** or **systems model** to address addictions because it better captures "the role of supply-side and demand-side drug prevention policies (mesosystem) or the (sub)cultural (exosystem) factors surrounding the overuse of certain drugs. If only because drug use is not randomly distributed within society, sociocultural factors, such as socioeconomic deprivation, norms, and anomie, *must* have explanatory and predictive utility" (p. 44) in our work with people who experience alcohol and drug problems.

Barber believes that his model focuses more on what can be done to promote change among precontemplators, such as the use of

TABLE 5.3   The Spirit of Motivational Interviewing

Fundamental Approach of Motivational Interviewing	Mirror Image Opposite Approach to Counseling
Collaboration. Counseling involves a partnership that honors the client's expertise and perspectives. The counselor provides an atmosphere that is conducive rather than coercive to change.	**Confrontation**. Counseling involves overriding the client's impaired perspectives by imposing awareness and acceptance of "reality" that the client cannot see or will not admit.
Evocation. The resources and motivation for change are presumed to reside within the client. Intrinsic motivation for change is enhanced by drawing on the client's own perceptions, goals, and values.	**Education**. The client is presumed to lack key knowledge, insight, and/or skills that are necessary for change to occur. The counselor seeks to address these deficits by providing the requisite enlightenment.
Autonomy. The counselor affirms the client's right and capacity for self-direction and facilitates informed choice.	**Authority**. The counselor tells the client what he or she must do.

Source: From MOTIVATIONAL INTERVIEWING, 2/e, by William R. Miller and Stephen Rollnick. Used by permission of Guilford Press.

TABLE 5.4   Principles of Motivational Interviewing

Principle 1.
Express empathy:
  Acceptance facilitates change.
  Skillful reflective listening is fundamental.
  Ambivalence is normal.

Principle 2.
Develop discrepancy:
  The client rather than the counselor presents the arguments for change.
  Change is motivated by a perceived discrepancy between present behavior and important goals or values.

Principle 3.
Roll with resistance:
  Avoid arguing for change.
  Resistance is not directly opposed.
  New perspectives are invited but not opposed.
  The client is a primary resource in finding answers and solutions.
  Resistance is a signal to respond differently.

Principle 4.
Support self-efficacy:
  A person's belief in the possibility of change is an important motivator.
  The client, not the counselor, is responsible for choosing and carrying out change.
  The counselor's own belief in the person's ability to change becomes a self-fulfilling prophecy.

Source: From MOTIVATIONAL INTERVIEWING, 2/e, by William R. Miller and Stephen Rollnick. Used by permission of Guilford Press.

environmental strategies. Thus, the text you are reading considers not only pharmacological interventions and psychosocial interventions with individuals, families, and groups, but it also considers cultural perspectives (see Chapters 11 and 12), prevention strategies (see Chapter 7), and policy approaches (see Chapter 8) that might affect alcohol and other drug problems.

chemical dependency counselors, and other human service professionals generally have codes of ethics to which members are expected to subscribe. For example, the code of ethics of NAADAC, the Association for Addiction Professionals (2011), covers areas such as the counseling relationship, confidentiality, cultural diversity, supervision and consultation, and policy and political involvement. According to this code, NAADAC members should provide clients "only that level and length of care that is necessary and acceptable." Members governed by the code are encouraged to be proactive in seeing that individuals and groups of all ethnic and social backgrounds have access to treatment. The code also addresses factors such as culture or disability that require consideration in working with clients. Members of other human service professions are bound by similar codes of ethics.

Human service professionals are expected to represent their credentials fairly, to treat clients only within their areas of expertise, and to make referrals when needed. Licensing and certification boards generally require that members participate in continuing education in order to keep their knowledge and skills current.

Perhaps the most frequent complaint filed with licensure and certification boards is that professionals have violated professional ethics by engaging in sexual relationships with current or former clients. Professionals should also not provide services to individuals with whom they have had prior sexual relationships. There are also taboos against other *dual relationships* with clients, such as not engaging with them in business ventures and other activities for profit.

Another issue that arises in the human service professions (and that has special import in the fields of chemical dependency and mental illness) is that of impaired professionals (Bissell & Royce, 1994) since a substantial number of chemical dependency professionals are themselves in recovery. Codes of ethics require that professionals address their own problems when these issues might prove to be detrimental to clients. Some professional organizations have peer-assistance programs that help professionals obtain treatment for such problems. When a professional does not take steps to rectify his or her own problems, colleagues who are aware of these problems may be obligated to report them to the appropriate licensing or certification authority. For professionals who are also in recovery, another issue is whether or how much information to disclose to clients about their own status as a recovering individual. Some professionals refrain from revealing this personal information. There is no absolute way to handle such disclosure, and the professional may address it on a case-by-case basis, especially if clients ask about it directly.

Respect for client confidences is an important aspect of the codes of ethics of human service professionals. Professionals working in alcohol and drug programs should be aware of the portion of the *Federal Register* called "Confidentiality of Alcohol and Drug Abuse Patient Records" (42 CFR, Part 2) as well as the Health Insurance Portability and Accountability Act (HIPAA). Generally 42CFR is more restrictive than HIPAA and was intended to provide strong protections for client confidentiality in order to encourage people

to seek treatment (see Brooks, 2004, for information on legal aspects of confidentiality). Chemical dependency professionals need to know this information to protect their clients and themselves. We describe some of its major points and discuss other issues relevant to confidentiality. These comments are no substitute for good legal counsel and are meant only to suggest some of the issues in the field.

Without an individual's written permission, treatment providers are usually prohibited from revealing whether or not the person is a patient or client in a chemical dependency treatment facility or any other information about the individual or his or her treatment. Providing information to those outside the treatment program and requesting information from other sources generally require the client's written permission. A client's written authorization to release information must state the name of the agency, program, or individual requesting the information; the agency, program, or individual from which the information is requested; the type of information that the client wishes to be provided; the purpose for which the information will be used; the date the release is signed and the date on which the release expires; and the client's signature and a witness's signature as proof of permission.

As noted earlier, staff may wish to obtain certain types of information, such as medical or psychological information, that may help them better serve the client. A consent or release-of-information form is also required for the staff to communicate with the client's spouse or other loved ones, since it should not be assumed that these individuals know that the client is receiving treatment or that the client wants the staff to communicate with them. Professional conduct also suggests that information about the client not be shared or discussed with other staff in the facility, unless they have a need to know this information to serve the client or in cases where a consultation is needed. Clients should be informed of the extent to which staff may need to share information with each other.

Sometimes a client requests that the treatment program give information to others. For example, a client may want his employer to know that he is attending treatment, or a client may be anxious for her probation officer to hear that she is making progress in treatment.

Exceptions to the right to confidentiality should be explained to the client. For example, under certain circumstances, treatment records of alcohol and drug abuse patients may be subject to subpoenas or court orders. Attempts may be made to subpoena records in cases where there are criminal charges against the client, in child custody cases, and under other circumstances. The issue of what to record in clients' charts or files is an important one. Many helping professionals do not enjoy privileged communication with their clients; that is, they may be ordered by the courts to provide information even about matters not contained in the client's case record. When a professional thinks that releasing information would not be appropriate, he or she should be given an opportunity to explain that to the court so that the court can decide the matter.

In a medical emergency, information necessary to save the client's life may be released. If the individual may be harmful to himself or herself, such as in the case of a client with a plan to commit suicide, the professional usually has a responsibility to seek protection for the client through an appropriate mental health referral. Sometimes this involves asking the local mental health crisis team or law enforcement agency that handles these problems to intervene. If a client threatens serious harm to another, there may be a "duty to warn" and the professional may be liable for injury sustained if appropriate steps are not taken. Child abuse and neglect must be reported according to state statutes. State laws may also require reporting of elder abuse and other crimes. Knowledge of state and federal law is thus necessary in the chemical dependency field.

Chemical dependency researchers may be afforded special confidentiality protections by obtaining a *certificate of confidentiality* from a federal agency such as NIAAA or NIDA. The certificate covers information obtained for research (not treatment) purposes only, but it does not provide an exemption from reporting child abuse and neglect. The certificate is particularly useful when subjects are asked about substance use or illegal activity (e.g., illicit drug use or crimes committed); since it is designed to protect researchers from having to release such information in any type of court (administrative, civil, criminal, etc.). The research must be legitimate, but the federal government or other external source does not have to fund the research for it to qualify for a certificate of confidentiality.

Legal issues arise more frequently than ever in the chemical dependency field, as they do in most fields, yet the appropriate responses are not always clear. Questions about what procedures to follow if law enforcement officers arrive at the door with an arrest warrant for a client or a subpoena for a file are not unusual. Good legal counsel is important—so is education about legal matters, since staff may be pressed to respond quickly.

Legal obligations are not always synonymous with *ethical* obligations. For example, a state may not have a legal "duty to warn," but a professional may feel morally obligated to do so. The highest calling may be to one's own ethical standards, but that may result in legal repercussions, such as being held in contempt of court for not releasing information if there is a proper court order to do so.

Referrals

Human service professionals of all types and in virtually all settings encounter individuals with substance use disorders and their loved ones. From elementary and secondary schools to the child welfare agency to the workplace to the nursing home, substance use disorders appear. Although social workers, psychologists, and other human service professionals should be prepared to screen for these problems, they may not be qualified to diagnose and treat them. When this is the case, a referral for further assessment or services is indicated. Some agencies—for example, family service agencies—may be able to provide these services in house. In other cases, knowing the local alcohol and drug abuse treatment agencies, their purposes, and their staff members can facilitate a referral. For example, a child protective services worker suspects that a child neglect case is due to alcohol abuse, but he needs a confirmatory diagnosis to help the mother get treatment so that she can retain custody of her children. Knowing the woman's limited financial resources, he refers her to a community mental health center with a substance abuse treatment component. An adult protective services worker contacts an inpatient chemical dependency treatment to assist with a client whose dependence on alcohol and benzodiazepines is preventing her from living independently. Or a parole officer makes sure a bed in a therapeutic community for offenders with chemical dependency problems will be available before a parolee who is addicted to heroin is released from prison.

Chemical dependency professionals not only accept referrals, they also make referrals to other agencies. As indicated in the discussion of assessment, clients with alcohol or other drug dependence often need additional services, such as vocational guidance, parent education, medical care, public assistance, and legal assistance. Keeping abreast of the services available in the community and developing cooperative working relationships with those who provide them are important professional responsibilities. Some agencies, such as the local offices of the state vocational rehabilitation agency, may designate a particular counselor or counselors to work with clients who have alcohol or other drug problems, or counselors may have general caseloads that include clients with substance use disorders. Informal knowledge of staff of other agencies that are most favorably disposed to working with clients who have substance use disorders can be a

big help, and it usually does not take long to learn who these individuals are.

Making a referral on which the client follows through can involve more than writing a name and a phone number on a piece of paper. No one wants to act as an enabler (in the negative sense of the word) or increase a client's dependency. However, informing the client of the referral's purpose and what the referral source may or may not be able to do, calling ahead for a client, and letting the client know specifically for whom to ask can be helpful. Clients who have mental or physical disabilities in addition to alcohol and drug problems may need extra support or assistance. This may mean providing transportation, accompanying them to the referral agency, or helping them complete application forms and compile necessary information. Clients who are desocialized or particularly unassertive may also benefit from someone to accompany them until they can develop the skills to negotiate these situations themselves.

Additional obstacles, such as lack of child care and language barriers, may also need to be addressed before a client can take advantage of referrals. In making referrals for health care, it is particularly helpful to know if the client has traditional private health insurance; belongs to a health maintenance organization (HMO) or other managed-care program; receives Medicaid or Medicare; has another type of coverage; or is entitled to services from the U.S. Department of Veterans Affairs.

Many professionals also refer clients to mutual-help groups like Alcoholics Anonymous (AA) and Narcotics Anonymous (NA) (see Chapter 6), but making these referrals is different. These groups do not have a staff of professional human service workers, and arrangements for clients generally cannot be made in advance. Anonymity of mutual-help group members is stressed, so there is no list of members' names and telephone numbers. The professional can give the client a list of meeting times or a website address or encourage the client to call the group for information. Some mutual-help groups have telephone lines that are staffed 24 hours a day; others have 24-hour answering services. Some have limited hours when telephones are staffed, and they may use a recording to give callers information or allow them to leave messages at other times.

Providing a list of meetings is not necessarily an effective way of encouraging clients to visit mutual-help groups. Many individuals do get to their first meetings on their own, but clients are frequently hesitant to go to a group about which they know very little. Professionals can make the process considerably easier. One way is to educate clients about what to expect in advance.

Some professionals "wear two hats"—they are human service professionals *and* they are members of mutual-help groups. Initially, they might accompany clients to a meeting or two (perhaps a meeting they usually do not attend) and explain what "working" a mutual-help program is about. Professionals who are not members of these groups may assist by accompanying the client to an open meeting, where those who are not "alcoholics" or "addicts" are welcome.

Many communities have a number of mutual-help groups. Even professionals who are recovering from alcohol or drug problems do not attend all the groups in their community. Some groups are only for men or only for women, some are for Spanish speakers, some are for nurses and doctors, and some are for gay men or lesbians. It is not possible for someone who wears two hats to fit in all the groups that his or her clients might need. Neither is it healthy for counselors to fill all these roles for clients. It may blur the professional-personal boundary in ways that raise ethical concerns. Professionals also do not have time to fill this function for all their clients, and clients can benefit from widening the circle of recovering individuals they know. "Twelve-step work" refers to the desire of AA and NA members to take the message of these programs to others. It may be more effective for professionals to maintain contact with recovering individuals in the community who wish to assist newcomers to the many mutual-help groups that have emerged for individuals who have alcohol and drug problems. Clients may be more likely to follow through on a referral when arrangements have been made for someone to accompany them to a meeting or they have been in contact with a member.

There are also mutual-help groups for loved ones (spouses, partners, children, and other family members and friends), such as Al-Anon and Naranon. Similar procedures can be used to make referrals to these groups.

Mutual-help groups regard themselves as strictly voluntary programs. Many do allow the secretary of the group to sign slips of paper so that attendees can verify their presence at the meeting if the courts or probation or parole officers require this.

Summary

This chapter discussed screening, diagnosis, assessment, and referral, which are the first steps in treating individuals with substance use disorders. Many tools are available to assist professionals in determining whether an individual has an alcohol or drug problem. Clients and their loved ones may, however, be resistant to these processes, and helping them overcome denial is often a prerequisite to their accepting help. Engaging clients during these early stages of treatment requires not only knowledge of substance use disorders but also the skills necessary to develop rapport and build relationships with clients.

There is much to be learned about an individual before a treatment plan can be developed. A thorough assessment includes knowledge about medical, psychiatric, family, legal, educational, and employment history, as well as other aspects of social functioning. The information obtained will help health care professionals determine whether the client needs medical detoxification and whether this should be done in a hospital, community detoxification center, or on an outpatient basis. It will also help other treatment staff determine whether intensive inpatient treatment, outpatient care, or other chemical dependency services are most appropriate for the individual. The assessment process is also used to identify other client needs so appropriate referrals can be made. Whether to include family or other individuals in the assessment and treatment process are still other decisions to be made in conjunction with the client. Professionals continue to use their assessment skills throughout the treatment process as the client's needs and circumstances change. The next chapter looks more closely at the components of the treatment system that can benefit clients and their loved ones during recovery.

CHAPTER 6

Treatment:
The System of Care

This chapter describes the system of care for those with alcohol or drug problems. Following diagnosis and assessment, the next step is to help clients select the types of treatment and other services that will meet their needs as closely as possible. The phrase *matching clients to treatment* has been used to describe this part of the helping process. It requires knowledge about all components of the system of care available to those with substance abuse or dependence, as well as mutual- or self-help programs. Professionals want to provide clients with the most optimal treatments and services, but many limitations can prevent this from happening. Particular services may not be available in a given locale. Clients may not have the financial resources to obtain services. Clients and the professionals they encounter may not be aware of resources. Clients may get whatever is available without sufficient regard for their particular needs and circumstances. Client preferences also play a role in selecting treatment modality. This chapter presents treatment options and discusses the treatment outcome evaluation literature—just how successful is treatment for substance use disorders?

Components of the Treatment System

We conceptualize approaches for treating chemical abuse and dependence using a continuum of care comprised of nine major components that are most commonly offered to clients: (1) detoxification, (2) intensive treatment, (3) residential programs, (4) outpatient services, (5) medication, (6) aftercare, (7) maintenance, (8) education and psychoeducation, and (9) adjunctive services. Some individuals may utilize each of these services over time, whereas others need only particular components. The continuum represents a comprehensive or ideal service delivery system designed to meet the range of clients' biopsychosocial needs. We also discuss some less traditional methods of treatment for those who have alcohol or drug problems.

Detoxification

Detoxification is often the first and usually the briefest step in the recovery process. Individuals often need these services if they have a physical dependence on alcohol or other drugs that results in withdrawal symptoms when drug use is reduced or terminated. Those with very mild symptoms may not require medical attention, and many of these individuals withdraw on their own. Others use drugs like hallucinogens that usually do not produce a physical dependence (Drug Enforcement Administration, 2004), although serious reactions such as psychosis require intervention. For those who need assistance with detoxification, the type of drugs on which they are dependent, the severity of their symptoms, and their medical, psychological, and social situations will help determine whether detoxification is done on an inpatient basis in a hospital, in another inpatient setting, or on an outpatient basis.

Medical, Hospital Detoxification.   Medical, hospital detoxification takes place in a general hospital or in a hospital or hospital unit specifically designed for chemical dependency treatment. In some cases, an individual's private physician will direct them to a hospital for admission for detoxification. Other times, those dependent on alcohol or other drugs have medical emergencies such as acute withdrawal symptoms, overdoses, or accidents related to alcohol or drug use that cause them to use hospital emergency departments. In emergencies, hospitals must usually treat individuals, whether or not they have the means to pay for their care. The presence of medical and social service staff knowledgeable about alcohol and drug problems increases the likelihood that patients will be referred to treatment programs or other services for chemical dependency following detoxification or other emergency treatment.

Hospitals with chemical dependency treatment units and specialty hospitals devoted to chemical dependency treatment may also provide detoxification services. Immediately following detoxification, clients can begin intensive inpatient or outpatient chemical dependency treatment at these facilities (or other appropriate specialty programs). State psychiatric hospitals that treat individuals with serious mental illness and other psychiatric hospitals may also offer addiction treatment services, and some include detoxification services.

Medical, Nonhospital Detoxification.   Detoxification is also conducted in inpatient community-based detoxification centers, sometimes referred to as *medical, nonhospital* (or *social setting*) *detoxification.* The staff includes physicians, nurses, and other professionals who provide psychosocial services to patients. These detoxification facilities sprang up around the country following passage of the federal Comprehensive Alcohol Abuse and Alcoholism Prevention, Treatment and Rehabilitation Act of 1970 (also known as the Hughes

Act, after its primary sponsor, Senator Harold Hughes). They were intended to stop the *revolving door* for those whose lives consisted of cycles of drinking, arrests for public intoxication, and short jail terms. These facilities may focus on treating alcohol withdrawal or assist with withdrawal from other types of drugs as well.

Patients in community detoxification centers may be self-referred, brought by a relative or friend, or referred by community gatekeepers such as the police, probation or parole officers, health department staff, the clergy, or social agency personnel (see Box 6.1). Some centers require that a physician screen patients before they are admitted to prevent inappropriate admissions. For example, some individuals may be experiencing a psychiatric emergency requiring care in a psychiatric hospital or a medical crisis that requires treatment in a general hospital. Some community "detox" centers permit nurses to admit patients and provide most of the medical care. There are "standing orders" that provide instructions for the care of patients with varying degrees of withdrawal symptoms. Each day a physician examines patients and provides any special instructions needed. The physician is also on call for emergencies. There are some limitations to the assistance that community detoxification centers can provide. For instance, if patients do not arrive at the detoxification center early enough to receive medical attention that will prevent the most serious withdrawal symptoms, such as seizures or delirium tremens (DTs), they may have to be transferred to a hospital.

Since the primary concern of community detoxification programs is chemical dependency treatment, more is usually done to link the client to additional services needed for recovery than in general hospitals, where the staff may be overwhelmed with medical emergencies or is not as well versed in serving patients with alcohol or drug problems. While at the detoxification program, patients are often provided alcohol and drug education and receive initial counseling and referral services. They are usually expected to participate in educational group sessions as soon as they are physically able. Loved ones may also be briefly counseled about the need for additional services for themselves as well as the patient.

Patients served in community detoxification programs often have limited financial resources. They may be charged on a sliding scale, based on their ability to pay, though recent federal legislation would give more Americans access to health insurance. The number of beds in a center usually varies with the size of the city or community served. Rural areas may have no community detox center, and those needing services may have to travel long distances to obtain care (Lenardson, Race, & Gale, 2009).

Whether detoxification occurs in a hospital or in a community program, medical personnel observe the patient and assess the severity of withdrawal symptoms to determine the medical regimen needed. Often, the medical personnel do not know what substances the patient has ingested, how much has been ingested, and over what period of time. They may be unaware of the withdrawal symptoms the patient has experienced in the past. Therefore, they must proceed cautiously before administering medications for withdrawal (such as benzodiazepines for alcohol withdrawal [Myrick & Wright, 2008] or methadone

or buprenorphine for heroin withdrawal [see National Institute on Drug Abuse, 2008; Polydorou & Kleber, 2008]). Treatment—including the type and amount of medication, if any, to be administered—will depend on whether the patient's withdrawal symptoms are mild, moderate, or severe. Patients often ask for or demand additional medication to further mitigate physical and psychological discomfort. Kasser and colleagues (1998) emphasize that "every means possible should be used to ameliorate the patient's withdrawal signs and symptoms" (p. 424). When medical staff feel that additional medication is not warranted, they generally respond with verbal encouragement and support that the symptoms will pass, but sometimes a patient attempts to bring alcohol or drugs to the facility or have someone bring alcohol or drugs to them.

The stay in detoxification programs is generally brief but depends on the drugs on which the patient is dependent. For example, the acute problems associated with alcohol withdrawal are likely to pass in a few days, whereas the period for barbiturate withdrawal is longer. Withdrawal from sedative-hypnotic drugs presents particular dangers due to the possibility of seizures or DTs.

BOX 6.1 *A Community Detoxification Center Patient*

Ed Welch,* a white male in his late forties, was well known at the community detox center. He had been admitted about six times in the last year as a result of his dependence on alcohol. Ed's most prominent withdrawal symptom was severe tremors. His medical history also included several bouts of gastritis. The medical staff was always able to manage Ed's care without referral to the hospital, and it was amazing how much better he looked after a five-day stay. Ed was a cooperative and quiet patient. He worked as a welder and his boss would bring him in when he got drunk. As soon as he was sober, Ed's boss would put

him back to work. Ed was divorced, never saw his grown children, and didn't seem to have any friends. He had no trouble downing two fifths of whiskey when he went on a binge. The detox staff was never able to get Ed to enter the halfway house or to attend outpatient groups. It seemed that the thing Ed liked least was talking. He came to AA sometimes but never said much. Ed did get an AA sponsor, a member with a history a lot like Ed's. Ed often managed to put a few months of sobriety together, but his binges, although less frequent, continued, and he returned to the detox center intermittently.

*The clients described in this chapter are fictitious or represent composite cases.

Withdrawal from more than one drug further complicates matters. Patients are detoxified from each drug sequentially, beginning with the drug that produces the most serious withdrawal symptoms (Center for Substance Abuse Treatment, 2006).

Since there is usually a high demand for the beds in community detoxification programs, patients may be referred to an inpatient or outpatient treatment program, a halfway house, the Salvation Army, or a mission as soon as withdrawal dangers have passed. Some patients are reluctant to leave, especially those who are homeless. For them, the detox center is a safe shelter and a temporary home. Others do not wish to be treated in the detoxification center at all and may leave or try to leave prematurely. Although some patients are referred by the courts or are under pressure from other authorities (e.g., probation department or child welfare agency) to enter the center, patients are generally considered to be there voluntarily. Voluntary patients cannot be required to stay, but local law enforcement may be called if a patient considered dangerous to himself or herself or to others attempts to leave. Some patients are mandated to treatment involuntarily under civil procedures. Should these patients "elope" or otherwise leave against medical advice or without permission, staff may be required to notify the appropriate authorities.

Outpatient Detoxification.   When withdrawal can be medically managed without the need for inpatient treatment, outpatient (ambulatory) care may be an economical alternative (Mee-Lee, Shulman, Fishman, Gastfriend, & Griffiths, 2001; Rawlani, Vekaria, & Eisenberg, 2009). The use of outpatient detoxification is also contingent on the patient's social and psychological states. Suicidal or severely depressed patients are obviously not good risks for outpatient detoxification, and outpatient detoxification is not a viable option if the patient lacks the ability or supervision to comply with the treatment protocol. Whether the patient has housing and emotional supports should also be considered. Various resources provide guidelines for making referrals for outpatient detoxification

(see Center for Substance Abuse Treatment, 2006; Mee-Lee et al.). Outpatient detoxification may be accomplished through chemical dependency treatment programs or physicians' offices.

Effectiveness of Detoxification Services.   From a purely medical standpoint, detoxification can be successfully accomplished on an inpatient basis in a hospital and often in other inpatient settings, or on an outpatient basis in appropriate circumstances. Community detoxification centers have been highly successful in helping patients detoxify safely, and their costs are substantially less than hospital care. Although there are advantages of inpatient detoxification, such as continual medical supervision, Hayashida and colleagues (1989) found that patients requesting detoxification for mild to moderate alcohol withdrawal syndrome can be successfully detoxified on an outpatient basis if they are screened to ensure that they do not have complicating medical and psychiatric problems. These findings are particularly interesting, given the low socioeconomic status of the patients who participated in the study and their lack of social supports, including some with unstable living arrangements. Others emphasize that "out-patient detoxification for homeless and severely drug- and alcohol-dependent populations is unrealistic. For this group, access to residential detoxification is vital as it provides an environment where potentially serious medical and psychological complications can be managed" (Silins, Sannibale, Larney, Wodak, & Mattick, 2008). Empirical evidence to determine when outpatient detoxification can be successfully used is lacking (Day, Ison, & Strang, 2010).

In addition to the procedures that have traditionally been used to help patients withdraw from alcohol or other drugs, rapid and ultra-rapid detoxification for opiate withdrawal is also being used. These procedures may have appeal for patients because they are intended to reduce the lengthy and uncomfortable withdrawal period from opiates. Ultra-rapid detoxification is usually conducted in a hospital, where the patient receives general anesthesia or heavy sedation in addition to medications for withdrawal. These procedures are costly, and thus available only to those with the means to pay for them. They are controversial because of safety concerns and lack of evidence to support their use (American Society of Addiction Medicine, 2005; Collins, Kleber, Whittington, & Heitler, 2005; Gowing, Ali, & White, 2010).

Medically safe withdrawal is the immediate goal of detoxification programs. Of importance in the long run is whether participation in a detoxification program promotes patients' further use of treatment and rehabilitation services. There is widespread agreement in the field that "medically assisted detoxification is only the first stage of addiction treatment and by itself does little to change long-term drug abuse" (National Institute on Drug Abuse [NIDA], 2009a, p. 4; also see Center for Substance Abuse Treatment, 2006, and see Box 6.2). Often, disappointingly small numbers of alcoholics and addicts continue in treatment following detoxification (Haley, Dugosh, & Lynch, 2011).

Intensive Treatment

Intensive treatment was once synonymous with inpatient care, but it is now frequently offered on an outpatient basis.

Intensive Inpatient Care. Intensive inpatient treatment programs originated primarily to assist people with alcohol use disorders but now include those with other drug problems. These programs typically lasted for 28 or 30 days, the maximum period that many health insurers would pay for this care, though some programs were longer. In recent years, managed health care has had a major impact on intensive inpatient treatment, with insurers often limiting inpatient stays (also see Chapter 16). Among the best-known intensive treatment programs is the Betty Ford Center. It is often those who have the financial resources and can be absent from work or family responsibilities who are able to avail themselves of inpatient care. Intensive inpatient treatment may be the logical choice when an individual is unlikely to remain alcohol or drug free in his or her current environment.

Intensive inpatient chemical dependency treatment programs may be located in a special unit of a general hospital or offered by a specialty hospital or other inpatient facility devoted to psychiatric or chemical dependency treatment. Some intensive inpatient treatment facilities are privately owned and intended to earn profit; others are private, not-for-profit or public facilities. The number of these programs increased tremendously during the 1970s and 1980s, along with wider recognition that chemical dependency can be successfully treated and as insurers succumbed to pressure to cover treatment. Since inpatient care is quite expensive (a stay in a private inpatient treatment program can cost as much as tens of thousands of dollars), managed health care and other cost constraints have taken their toll, resulting in the closing of many of these inpatient programs (Roman, Johnson, & Blum, 2000).

Clients who have insurance or other resources can usually get immediate admission to for-profit intensive inpatient programs, but not-for-profit and public programs often have waiting lists. Maintaining sobriety while awaiting admission to a public or not-for-profit program can be a challenge for clients. A basic tenet of addiction treatment is that it should be readily available to those who need it (NIDA, 2009a). With changes in federal laws governing health insurance parity for alcohol and drug treatment and greater access to health insurance for Americans, there is hope that more people will be able to avail themselves of alcohol and drug treatment.

Although the treatment services in inpatient programs vary to some degree, many are similar to what is called the *Minnesota model*, which has been described as "an abstinence oriented, comprehensive, multi-professional approach to the treatment of the addictions, based upon the principles of Alcoholics Anonymous" (Cook, 1988a, p. 625; also see McKay & Hiller-Sturmöhfel, 2011; Owen, 2000). The model originated at the Willmar State Hospital in Minnesota in the late 1940s and was adopted for use in other

---

BOX 6.2   *Principles of Effective Drug Addiction Treatment*

1. Addiction is a complex but treatable disease that affects brain function and behavior.
2. No single treatment is appropriate for everyone.
3. Treatment needs to be readily available.
4. Effective treatment attends to multiple needs of the individual, not just his or her drug abuse.
5. Remaining in treatment for an adequate period of time is critical.
6. Counseling—individual and/or group—and other behavioral therapies are the most commonly used forms of drug abuse treatment.
7. Medications are an important element of treatment for many patients, especially when combined with counseling and other behavioral therapies.
8. An individual's treatment and services plan must be assessed continually and modified as necessary to ensure that it meets his or her changing needs.
9. Many drug-addicted individuals also have other mental disorders.
10. Medically assisted detoxification is only the first stage of addiction treatment and by itself does little to change long-term drug abuse.
11. Treatment does not need to be voluntary to be effective.
12. Drug use during treatment must be monitored continuously, as lapses during treatment do occur.
13. Treatment programs should assess patients for the presence of HIV/AIDS, hepatitis B and C, tuberculosis, and other infectious diseases as well as provide targeted risk-reduction counseling to help patients modify or change behaviors that place them at risk of contracting or spreading infectious diseases.

Source: National Institute on Drug Abuse. (2009, April). *Principles of drug addiction treatment: A research-based guide, 2nd ed.* Bethesda, MD: U.S. Department of Health and Human Services.

---

settings, such as the Hazelden rehabilitation center in Center City, Minnesota (see White, 1998).

The services these programs most commonly provide are education about chemical dependency, group and individual counseling or therapy, and an introduction to mutual-help programs. Other services promote general health and well-being. Examples are learning to reduce stress, improving communication skills and other social skills, lectures or consultation on adopting good nutritional habits and other healthy routines, and social and recreational alternatives to drug use. There are, of course, limits on what can be accomplished in a few weeks. Many clients are just coming to grips with their chemical dependency problem. In this early stage of recovery, only so much information can be processed and retained, especially by those with long-term dependency who are newly detoxified. A criticism of the traditional Minnesota model is that services are "bundled"; that is, every client receives the same regimen of services, regardless of his or her individual needs (Miller, 1998; also see Mee-Lee et al., 2001).

Intensive inpatient programs vary in the methods used to involve clients' significant others. Education is one means, beginning with basic information on alcohol and drugs and what constitutes "addiction" or "dependence." Topics such as chemical dependency as a family disease and codependency generally receive attention (see Chapter 10). Loved ones may also be introduced to mutual-help groups such as Al-Anon and Naranon. Therapy sessions may be scheduled for individual families, or families may meet in groups. Some family groups are just for spouses and other adult partners; others include children, parents, and others important in the client's life. Though it is relatively rare, in some programs, family members, particularly spouses and other adult partners, spend a week or so in residence at the program.

Intensive Outpatient Care.   Reliance on intensive inpatient treatment for chemically dependent individuals has been questioned with regard to costs and effectiveness. Professionals often directed chemically dependent individuals to inpatient treatment because they assumed it was the best alternative or because of the lack of other treatment alternatives. In the early years of insurance coverage for substance use disorders, insurers often limited coverage to inpatient care. Patients were told that inpatient treatment came first, regardless of their personal circumstances. But insistence on inpatient treatment may have alienated potential clients concerned about disruption to their work and family lives. Single parents, those with limited financial resources, and those concerned about explaining a long job absence may see outpatient care as their only viable treatment option. Intensive outpatient treatment is now the preferred service for those who can continue to function at home and in the community.

The services provided in intensive outpatient treatment are the same as those provided during inpatient treatment, but clients work at their regular jobs or care for their families during the day and usually attend treatment in the evenings or on weekends. A typical program for clients with alcohol use disorders may involve participation four evenings a week over a 10- to 12-week period.

The *Matrix Model* is a longer-term intensive outpatient treatment approach developed to treat those who abuse stimulant drugs (Huber et al., 1997; National Institute on Drug Abuse, 2009a & b; Rawson et al., 1995). A focus of the model is the client's development of a positive relationship with a master's-level therapist, who provides individual counseling and serves as the client's "primary treatment agent." Multiple treatment modalities are used. The first phase of treatment, which lasts six months, includes individual treatment, a stabilization group, Twelve-Step meetings, breath and urine testing, relapse prevention groups, family education groups (which may include other members of the client's support system), and conjoint or couples counseling (with

a spouse or significant other). The second phase lasts an additional six months and involves a weekly support group and expectation of continued participation in a Twelve-Step program. Individual therapy and conjoint therapy are also available during this phase.

In addition to the cost savings and flexibility that intensive outpatient care affords over intensive inpatient services, it may also have "clinical advantages by allowing patients to practice relapse prevention and management skills while being in a highly structured treatment setting" (McCaul & Furst, 1994, p. 254). However, some clients may need relief from the stresses of their current environment to benefit from treatment, and others have psychiatric disorders that may contraindicate outpatient services in this early stage of recovery. Matching clients to the least restrictive treatment suitable to their needs is an appropriate goal of treatment planning.

Day Treatment.   Another type of intensive outpatient treatment is known as *day treatment* or *partial hospitalization.* One definition of a partial hospital or day treatment program is "a freestanding or hospital-based program that provides services for at least 20 hours per week, and can be used to treat Substance-Related Disorders or can specialize in the treatment of co-occurring mental health conditions and Substance-Related Disorders" (U.S. Behavioral Health Plan, California, 2010). Participation in a day treatment program may last longer than other forms of intensive treatment and is often appropriate for clients who are not—at least at this point—able to function in the community by holding jobs or caring for their families. Some of these clients have both psychiatric disorders and substance use disorders. Others have substantial physical impairments that may require a longer period of rehabilitation or substantial cognitive impairments (from substance abuse or other causes such as traumatic brain injuries) and need additional time to learn relapse prevention, communication, vocational, and independent living skills before complete reintegration to the community can be achieved. Some clients attend day treatment following intensive inpatient chemical dependency treatment or inpatient psychiatric treatment.

Though many programs throughout the country offer day treatment or partial hospitalization services, research on this treatment modality is lacking. Guydish et al. (1995) describe a day treatment program called Walden House that was designed for clients with serious alcohol and other drug problems in order to meet the growing demand for substance abuse treatment. It includes individual, group, and family therapy and employment, legal, and other services and can be used as a stand-alone treatment or to help those awaiting residential treatment. The staff and clients are regarded as a surrogate family. The program operates from 8:00 A.M. to 8:00 P.M. on weekdays with more limited weekend hours. Alterman and McLellan (1993) also discuss a Veterans Administration (VA) day hospital program for those addicted to alcohol or cocaine.

Effectiveness of Intensive Treatment.   In a review of the effectiveness of Minnesota model intensive treatment programs, Cook (1988b) found few rigorously conducted studies. He did conclude that "despite exaggerated claims of success, [the Minnesota model] appears to have a genuinely impressive 'track record' with as many as two-thirds of its patients achieving a 'good' outcome at 1 year after discharge" (p. 746). Many questions about the effectiveness of intensive treatment remain unanswered. For example, when patients do well, are particular components or combinations of components of these programs the keys to their success, or is the total package of services necessary to promote recovery?

Interest in whether inpatient treatment produces better results than outpatient treatment spawned several notable studies in the 1980s and 1990s. These studies generally showed no differences in the outcomes associated with inpatient and outpatient care (including partial hospitalization and day treatment) of alcoholics (Connors, 1993a; McKay & Maisto, 1993; NIAAA, 1987). Even one group of researchers who found that hospital treatment

for alcoholism produced better overall results than community treatment wrote, "Noteworthy ... were the findings that the IC (in community) treatment was effective for some patients and that both IH (in hospital) and IC treatment were relatively ineffective for other patients" (Wangberg, Horn, & Fairchild, 1974, p. 174). A meta-analysis of drinking outcomes in 14 studies found a slight positive effect for inpatient over outpatient alcoholism treatment at three months following treatment but not after three months (Finney & Moos, 1996). Finney, Hahn, and Moos (1996) note that while outpatient programs are appropriate for many people with alcohol problems, those with more serious psychiatric, medical, and social disadvantages should be afforded the necessary inpatient or other residential services (also see NIAAA, 2000). Treatment setting may be more important for those with drug problems other than alcohol because of its relationship to treatment retention. For example, studies of treatment for cocaine addiction show "*greater engagement and retention of patients in inpatient settings,*" although treatment completers did as well regardless of whether they were treated in an inpatient or outpatient program (McLellan & McKay, 1998, p. 330, italics in original).

Residential Programs

Also on the continuum of care are a number of residential services. These communal living environments are intended to increase the likelihood that individuals will remain clean or sober during the early days of recovery. For some individuals, they may also be the preferred type of residence in the long-run, since living alone can be isolating and may promote drinking or drug use. Residential services include halfway houses, therapeutic communities, domiciliaries, and missions. Each has a unique role in helping people with alcohol and drug problems.

Halfway Houses.   *Halfway houses* (sometimes called *rehabilitation facilities* or *recovery homes*) are another part of the continuum of care for many alcoholics and addicts (see White [1998] for an early history of halfway houses). Rubington (1977) defined a halfway house "as a transitional place of indefinite residence of a community of persons who live together under the rule and discipline of abstinence from alcohol and other drugs" (p. 352). These houses may be publicly subsidized, privately owned, or church sponsored.

Some halfway houses are solely for those who are mandated to become residents by the criminal justice system. Many halfway house residents have lost their jobs and financial assets, are estranged from family and friends, or lack social and independent living skills, and turn to halfway houses when they lack other living arrangements. In other cases, individuals specifically seek a living environment that is focused on supporting their sobriety. Despite their presence in many communities, halfway houses per se have attracted little scholarly study.

The structure of halfway houses and the services they offer vary considerably (see, for example, Orford & Velleman, 1982). Some are highly structured, with a specific treatment regimen that consumes almost all the residents' time. Others are loosely structured and are more like boarding homes with some supervision or requirements to get a job and attend mutual-help group meetings. The structure of many halfway houses falls in between these two extremes and incorporates treatment and mutual-help groups along with expectations that residents seek and maintain employment. The staff and their credentials also vary. Some halfway houses are supervised 24 hours a day by managers who are themselves in recovery. Some employ professional staff (therapists, counselors, etc.). In some halfway houses, a case manager or primary counselor coordinates the services each client needs.

Some halfway house programs require residents to have at least weekly individual counseling sessions and to participate in group treatment. Seeing that clients get a job is often a priority in these programs (Campbell, 1997). Other services may include education about independent living skills and communication as well as nutritional counseling, exercise, and instruction on maintaining good health and mental health. Participation in recreational activities and developing social skills is usually encouraged because of the desocialization of clients whose problems are severe enough to warrant referral to a halfway house. Attendance at Alcoholics Anonymous or other mutual-help meetings, often several times a week, is a frequent requirement. Halfway house staff often work closely with other community agencies to ensure that their clients receive services such as vocational rehabilitation and health care. Residence in a halfway house provides an opportunity to address many client needs.

A resident may be admitted to a halfway house on the recommendation of an individual staff member, or there may be a client *staffing* where the client meets with a small group of staff members who ask the client questions about his or her motivation to enter the halfway house and determine whether to offer the individual admission (see Rubington, 1985). Residents must usually agree to participate in all halfway house activities and to abide by other rules, which include no drinking of alcohol and no use of drugs except as approved by his or her doctor or medical staff. Residents are generally not allowed to keep their own medications but are given access to them by staff. Other rules are no violence and no sex in the house. Residents are usually obligated to report violations of the rules by other residents. They are also expected to keep their personal living area clean, and general household chores such as cooking and cleaning are often shared or rotated. Visitors and personal telephone calls may be restricted to specific times. Passes or leaves of absence are generally limited at first, but increase as the residents makes progress. Policies regarding readmission after rule violations, especially drinking or drug use, differ among programs, with some more lenient than others. As residents move through recovery, they usually take on more responsibilities and earn more privileges in the halfway house.

Some programs have resident or community governments. Residents may take turns chairing weekly meetings held to discuss and solve problems in the house, such as neglecting chores, drinking or drug use, and interpersonal conflicts between residents. Resident governments are established to help clients learn rational means of problem solving. Staff may participate in all or some of these meetings to work out problems, especially conflicts between residents and staff. This gives staff an opportunity to model problem-solving and discussion skills for residents.

The length of time clients are allowed to remain in halfway house programs varies and may be 30, 60, or 90 days or more. If demand for admission is high, the maximum stay may be shorter. In other houses, the stay is open ended because the program's philosophy is that residents need a period of treatment commensurate with the length and severity of their chemical dependency before they can achieve sufficient stability to live independently. In some cases, the stay may be determined by the terms of a resident's probation or parole.

Clients may be charged modest fees for their room, board, and treatment. In addition to the need to defray program costs, reasons commonly used to support charging halfway house residents are that (1) it helps them learn or relearn responsible behavior, (2) services that involve a fee are more highly valued than those that are free, and (3) those individuals who are not interested in treatment will be deterred from entering the program. Some clients are employed and pay the fees themselves. Others may be sponsored for a period by treatment or rehabilitation agencies such as a state's vocational rehabilitation program. Many halfway houses serve men only or women only, but some are co-ed. Some halfway houses are especially for mothers and allow them to bring their young children. The children usually receive services, too.

One particular recovery house model is Oxford House, established in Silver Spring, Maryland, in 1975 (Molloy, 1992).[1] Oxford Houses serve those with alcohol or other drug problems. They do not use paid staff and are financed and democratically run by the residents. The Oxford House charter requires that a member who uses alcohol or drugs be expelled immediately. Residents elect the officers of each house who serve six-month

terms. New residents are admitted upon approval of at least 80 percent of the current residents. There is no minimum length of clean or sober time required before a new resident can be admitted and no maximum length of stay. Although Oxford House is not affiliated with Alcoholics Anonymous or Narcotics Anonymous, residents are expected to participate in these programs. Each home houses 6 to 15 residents. There are homes for men, women, and women with children (co-ed homes are not permitted). Any group of recovering individuals can apply to start a house. The federal Anti-Drug Abuse Act of 1988 provides loans for those wishing to start new houses. There are several hundred Oxford Houses in the United States.

Effectiveness of Halfway Houses.   Rigorous studies of halfway house programs are lacking, though there is "evidence that chronic alcoholic patients have a reasonable chance for recovery if they are willing to become involved in a residential treatment setting" (Fischer, 1996, p. 163). Van Ryswyk and colleagues (1981–82) analyzed data on 641 former residents of eight halfway houses. Compared with their preadmission functioning, these individuals had fewer detox admissions, used public assistance less, had fewer encounters with the criminal justice system, had greater abstinence, and had better employment outcomes. Hitchcock, Stainback, and Rogue (1995) present some evidence that military veterans discharged from inpatient alcohol and drug treatment to a halfway house had better retention and completion in a VA after-care program than those discharged to live in the community independently or with family or friends.

Another study, based on a sample of 499 indigent clients with serious alcohol and drug problems, found they had greater increases in earnings when they participated in 28 days of inpatient treatment followed by 60 days of halfway house treatment, rather than inpatient treatment only (Wickizer, Longhi, Krupski, & Stark, 1997). These gains were also greater compared to clients who received outpatient treatment. In a more recent study, clients dependent on alcohol, drugs, or both participating in either a day hospital program or community residential treatment fared similarly in abstinence outcomes at six and twelve months (Witbrodt et al., 2007).

One group of researchers also studied 150 individuals who were assigned randomly to an Oxford House recovery home or usual after-care following inpatient treatment. After two years, those who lived in Oxford Houses for at least 6 months had less substance abuse than those who stayed less than 6 months and those assigned to usual after-care, which consisted of outpatient treatment, mutual-help groups, or other services (Jason, Olson, Ferrari, & Lo Sasso, 2006; Jason, Olson, Ferrari, Majer, Alvarez, & Stout, 2007). Other positive benefits accrued in the areas of employment, criminal activity, and child custody.

Therapeutic Communities. While halfway houses were originally designed to serve alcoholics, *therapeutic communities (TCs)* have focused on treating those addicted to heroin and other illegal drugs. Traditional TCs are highly structured residential programs that provide learning experiences in which changes in the user's conduct, attitudes, values, and emotions are continuously monitored and reinforced (De Leon, 1986; 2000). The first therapeutic community for drug addicts, Synanon, began in 1958. It combined ideas from Alcoholics Anonymous and therapeutic communities for those with psychiatric problems. (See De Leon, 1986; Kurth, 2009; Ray & Ksir, 1990; White, 1998 for descriptions of TCs.) Daytop Village and Odyssey House are also well-known TCs. TC residents often began drug involvement at a young age, which has stultified mastery of the developmental tasks of adulthood (see Box 6.3). As a result, TCs are likely to focus on habilitating as well as rehabilitating residents (De Leon, 2008; Gerstein & Harwood, 1990). These residential programs may be thought of as a combination of intensive treatment and residential care. The recommended stay is often longer than in halfway houses, though in recent years the recommended stay has decreased from as much as two years to 9 to 15 months (De Leon, 2008).

TC staff members are often addicts with substantial periods of recovery. TCs rely on group process and peer pressure to get residents to address their problematic behaviors. *Reality therapy* (Glasser, 2000) is often the underlying treatment philosophy. Confrontation is used to break the denial that is generally a part of chemical dependency. Many professionals are initially quite surprised at the intensity of the confrontation in individual and group counseling sessions, but both TCs and other chemical dependency treatment programs seem to have toned this down in recent years. The dropout rate from TCs is high, due perhaps to the rigors of these programs (De Leon, 1999, 2000, 2008). Many halfway houses expect clients to obtain jobs quickly, but therapeutic communities tend to believe a longer period of treatment is needed before the resident is capable of holding an outside job and has earned the privilege of working outside the facility. To teach employment behaviors and skills, some TCs operate cottage industries where residents work in enterprises such as a greenhouse, duplication service, and other small business.

Clients start with few privileges and earn additional privileges as they progress in the TC program. New residents are often assigned the most menial household chores. Progress is measured by abstinence from drugs, active participation in treatment, and adherence to program rules. Urine "drops" may be used to monitor abstinence. Moving up to the next level in the program may be based on a vote of residents and staff. Residents may graduate to become staff of therapeutic communities.

To address criticisms of high dropout rates, inhibition of residents' autonomous functioning, weak community ties, misdiagnosis and improper treatment of mental illness, and potential for abuse and mismanagement because leadership is invested in a few individuals, today's TCs have modified their practices to better serve residents (White, 1998). In fact, there is no single TC model, as programs have undergone many modifications due to funding realities and changing client populations, with some TCs focusing on serving women

---

BOX 6.3   *A Therapeutic Community Resident*

Susan Murphy was 18 when she entered a therapeutic community. She was skinny with long, scraggly black hair and a tattoo of a former boyfriend's name on her left hand. She had run away from home at least a dozen times during her teen years because she never got along with her mother and stepfather. Susan spent many nights on the streets and in runaway shelters. She was a high school dropout and had never held a job for more than a few weeks. Susan was convinced by staff of a criminal justice diversion program to enter the TC after she was picked up on a vagrancy charge and her "rap" sheet indicated several other infractions. Susan had used many types of drugs. She was particularly fond of amphetamines but did not want to start mainlining drugs like her current boyfriend. Susan hated the TC at first and found it difficult to take the strong feedback from staff and other residents about her attitude of blaming others for her problems. She almost left several times, but she did manage to remain for a year and earned a GED along with 12 months of "clean" time. Susan is now a graduate of the TC and is in vocational school learning computer technology. She attends Narcotics Anonymous regularly and likes to sponsor new members.

(including those with children), youth, and people dually diagnosed with mental illness and drug disorders (De Leon, 2000).

Among the developments in the history of therapeutic communities is the growth of modified TCs in correctional settings, where staff has much greater control than in more traditional TCs (Springer, McNeece, & Arnold, 2003). In fact, TCs have been called "the primary treatment for substance abuse in American prisons" (Wexler, Melnick, Lowe, & Peters, 1999, p. 3). Prison-based TCs include New York's Stay'n Out program (Wexler & Williams, 1986) and Oregon's Cornerstone program (Field, 1992). Gerstein and Harwood (1990) call today's therapeutic communities "a remarkable merger of the therapeutic optimism of psychiatric medicine and the disciplinary moralism of the criminal perspective" (p. 352).

Effectiveness of Therapeutic Communities.
In summarizing the literature on the effectiveness of TCs, De Leon (2000, 2008) notes that (1) they result in improvements in employment, criminal behavior, alcohol and drug use, and psychological adjustment; and (2) longer stays are associated with better outcomes. The research designs used in many studies do not allow concluding with confidence that this treatment approach is superior to others

in reducing drug use or providing other benefits for residents, including those who have been incarcerated (Smith, Gates, & Foxcroft, 2010; Mitchell, Wilson, & MacKenzie, 2006). A Campbell Collaboration review did find that with regard to incarcerated participants, "programs that intensively focus on the multiple problems of substance abusers, such as TCs, are most likely to reduce drug use and recidivism" (Mitchell et al.). Others also note that "when combined with close supervision and monitoring after clients leave the TC, this model does seem to work for certain 'hard core' addicts who have failed in other programs" (Springer et al., 2003, p. 123).

The effectiveness of TCs for incarcerated individuals may also be related to participation in services post-release (Olson, Rozhon, & Powers, 2009). One study of 448 subjects at 18 months after their release from prison compared the effects of (1) a prison-based TC called *KEY*, (2) a work-release TC with an aftercare component called *CREST*, (3) the Key TC followed by CREST, and (4) a comparison group that did not receive TC treatment (although some did receive some type of service) (Inciardi & Martin, 1997). The KEY and no-TC treatment groups had similar outcomes and did not fare as well as the other two groups. The CREST and KEY-CREST participants were more likely to have had no arrests and no drug use, indicating the utility of the re-entry work-release TC program as part of the TC treatment continuum. However, a five-year follow-up study of 690 individuals who participated in a multistage TC in Delaware that included residential treatment during work release prior to community release found that TC graduates had higher probabilities of being drug free and arrest free whether or not they participated in aftercare compared to a no treatment group that participated in regular work release (Inciardi, Martin, & Butzin, 2004). Welsh (2007) also found evidence of drug treatment TCs' effectiveness two-years post release, even without an aftercare participation requirement.

Domiciliaries.   A *domiciliary*, another type of residential facility, generally assists those with severe physical or mental debilitation from alcohol or other drug dependency. Some individuals referred to a domiciliary need an extensive period of recovery before they move to a halfway house. For others, the domiciliary will become their long-term home because the permanent nature of their impairments make a successful return to independent living unlikely.

Domiciliaries usually have 24-hour staff supervision. Residents are given responsibilities or participate in activities commensurate with their abilities. The care provided may be largely custodial but there may be some group treatment, especially to promote socialization. Domiciliaries are generally more lenient in reaccepting a client following alcohol or drug use than halfway houses or therapeutic communities. The U.S. Department of Veterans Affairs operates domiciliaries and supported housing programs for homeless veterans debilitated by substance use disorders or other physical and mental disorders (Ross, Booth, Russell, Laughlin, & Brown, 1995). Some communities also support domiciliary-type facilities. Residents whose conditions deteriorate to the point that they become nonambulatory or need psychiatric or nursing home care are referred to appropriate facilities.

Effectiveness of Domiciliaries.   In one of the few studies that mentions domiciliaries, Ross et al. (1995) found that male veterans who entered a

domiciliary following a 28-day inpatient alcoholism treatment program were more likely to be abstinent 12-months later compared to those who were discharged to the community. The groups did not differ on alcohol-related hospital re-admissions, and the study controlled for baseline characteristics. At baseline, those who entered the domiciliary had less social support and more depression. Following the domiciliary stay, they had increased social support and reduced depressive symptoms.

Shelters and Missions.   Shelters and rescue missions operated by the Salvation Army, religious organizations, and other entities have long assisted those who are homeless, transient, or living on the streets due to a variety of problems such as substance abuse, mental illness, or inability to secure a job (Fagan, 1986; Katz, 1966; White, 1998). Some of these facilities are better classified as halfway houses because residents spend several months at them receiving treatment and working (perhaps in one of their thrift shops). A religious program is often a component of services. In many cases, the stay at one of these facilities is brief (a night or two). In street lingo, brief stays are often referred to as "three hots and a cot" (three meals and a bed in which to sleep). Those staying overnight receive an evening meal and may be expected to attend a prayer or spiritual service designed to motivate them to find a new way of life. Following an early breakfast (sometimes toast, coffee, and grits), they are generally expected to leave the premises, and those planning to spend another night usually are not permitted to return until evening check-in time. They may be assisted in finding a few hours or a day's work. The cost of staying overnight might be a few dollars. Some facilities do not charge, or they may give a free night once every month or two.

The staff of public and not-for-profit substance abuse programs frequently refers individuals with alcohol and drug abuse problems who have no other residence or who decline treatment to these facilities. These individuals may stay at a mission or shelter while they try to find a job, make arrangements to get a bus ticket home if they are from another area, or await admission to an inpatient chemical dependency treatment center or a halfway house.

Chemically dependent individuals also utilize homeless shelters. Missions and shelters generally do not admit those who are obviously intoxicated or who are experiencing serious withdrawal symptoms. Some missions have been criticized for their moralistic approach to substance abuse and for their exploitation of clients' labor; however, they have historically provided a safe haven for those who would otherwise be sleeping on the streets or in the woods (Jacobson, 1982).

Effectiveness of Shelters and Missions.   Evaluating the effectiveness of shelters and missions in helping people with alcohol or drug problems is particularly difficult because of the transient nature of the clientele served by these programs. Jacobson (1982) concluded that despite the limited number of studies, experience shows that the short-term effects of shelter residence are generally positive. Namely, drinking is interrupted, meals and safety are provided, and individuals may be referred to other helping resources such as employment services, medical services, halfway houses, mutual-help and spiritual programs, or other services.

Outpatient Services

Outpatient services are the most often used component of the continuum of care. Some clients use outpatient services following detoxification, intensive treatment, or halfway house services. Those with less severe impairments may begin treatment with this component. Outpatient services are usually some type of counseling—individual, couple, family, or group. The theoretical orientations and treatment philosophies of those who provide these services vary as does the frequency with which clients receive outpatient services. Sessions are often scheduled weekly but may be more or less frequent and taper off as progress is made.

The content of outpatient treatment sessions is quite similar to intensive and residential treatment. Examples are how to remain alcohol and drug free, dealing with loneliness and sadness, fostering positive social relationships, and increasing self-esteem. Other services may involve teaching relaxation or stress-reduction techniques. Issues such as previous physical or sexual abuse may also be addressed. Since no single human service professional is equipped to treat all the problems clients may present, referral to other professionals may be needed.

Many types of providers offer outpatient chemical dependency services including psychiatrists, psychologists, nurses, social workers, marriage and family therapists, various types of counselors (such as rehabilitation and pastoral), and chemical dependency counselors (some who have degrees in the helping professions and others who do not). State laws regulating these providers vary. Increasingly, state laws (and community norms) have required that human service professionals, including those who treat people for alcohol and drug problems, be licensed or certified. State laws and insurance companies determine which professionals can collect third-party insurance payments for their services.

Outpatient services are provided by (1) public agencies, (2) private, not-for-profit organizations, (3) private, for-profit corporations, and (4) churches or other religious organizations. Some outpatient programs are stand-alone entities; some are attached to hospitals; others are part of community mental health centers, community alcohol and drug treatment centers, or faith-based organizations. Private practitioners in the chemical dependency field may also offer their services in individual or group practices. Health maintenance organizations (HMOs) and employee assistance programs (EAPs) may offer outpatient chemical dependency services directly, using their own personnel, or through arrangements with community agencies or individual practitioners.

Like other services, outpatient chemical dependency treatment may be covered under the individual's health care plan, or the client may pay for it directly. In public or not-for-profit programs, a sliding fee scale may be used, or clients may not be charged if they lack health insurance or other means to pay. Private practitioners usually charge fees based on local market rates; some use sliding scales or provide some treatment on a *pro bono* basis as a community service.

Individual Counseling.   Individual outpatient counseling involves only the client and the human service professional. The preference in chemical dependence treatment has been for group therapy with individual treatment used as an adjunct (NIAAA, 1990; Rounsaville, Carroll, & Back, 2009) or to treat specific problems such as trauma or sexual dysfunction that are not necessarily appropriate for the chemical dependency treatment group.

Although group treatment is often recommended, there are reasons for using individual therapy (Rounsaville et al., 2009; Washton, 2005). Clients may feel that individual treatment will be more effective, as it permits more focus on the individual's problems and greater flexibility to do so. Some clients have difficulty engaging in the group process and may find it threatening; protecting one's anonymity may also be an issue. Clients may also find it easier to schedule individual appointments, and practitioners may not have enough clients at a given time to establish a treatment group. This is especially true in rural areas, where the lack of anonymity in groups is also a problem.

Group Treatment.   Group treatment is frequently offered as the "treatment of choice" to those with alcohol and drug problems. In addition to its economy, group therapy can reduce clients' denial and increase acceptance of alcohol and drug problems and meet their "intense needs" for "acceptance and support" (Levine & Gallogly, 1985; see also Washton, 2005). Clients also receive comfort and support from others with the same problem; group members with greater recovery experience serve as role models and offer coping strategies, and admission of one's problems to the other members may promote abstinence and

deter relapse (Rounsaville et al., 2009). For those who have few positive social contacts, it can help restore relationships with others (Brook, 2008; Morrell & Myers, 2009). See Box 6.4.

Groups are almost always a component of intensive inpatient chemical dependency treatment programs. Outpatient programs also offer them. There are many forms of group therapy, and a number of theoretical approaches used in individual therapy have been adopted for group treatment such as cognitive behavioral therapy (Morrell & Myers, 2009) and the stages of change or transtheoretical model (Velasquez, Maurer, Crouch, & DiClemente, 2001).

The composition of outpatient chemical dependency treatment groups varies. Groups usually have several members, but more than 12 is generally considered too large to allow everyone to participate. Participation may be restricted to clients who share certain characteristics. For example, a group may be composed of only male or only female members, gay men or lesbians, or those in a particular age group. There is usually one group leader but sometimes two. Co-ed groups may have male and female leaders, but when groups are for men only or women only, someone of the same gender is usually the leader.

Groups may be closed or open ended. In a closed-ended group, members usually start together and contract for a certain number of sessions. At the end of the sessions, members may be asked if they wish to contract for additional group sessions. An advantage of the closed-ended group is continuity of membership, but if there are many dropouts, those remaining may become discouraged and the number may dwindle below what is necessary to carry on effective group sessions. In an open-ended group, members may join at different times. A commitment to attend a specific number of sessions may not be required. Although open-ended groups may allow members new to sobriety to benefit from those who have more experience in managing sobriety, disruptions may occur as members leave and new members are introduced to the group and the group process.

BOX 6.4   *An Outpatient Client*

Frank Villa, a 26-year-old Mexican American male, was friendly and cheerful when sober—someone who was always described as a nice guy—but his wife would not put up with his drug use and left him. To make matters worse, he flunked out of college after changing majors three times and got a DWI. He was out of work and had little choice but to move in with his mother and to try to stay away from alcohol, marijuana (his favorite drug), and whatever else came his way. Frank got a part-time job with a moving company and also enrolled part time at the junior college. He joined an outpatient group for young people at the community alcohol and drug treatment program after deciding it was time to "grow up." Frank enjoyed attending the group. The discussions of topics among his peers always seemed relevant to

him, and the socialization before and after group sessions helped assuage his loneliness. Frank felt he really fit in with the group members, unlike those at school and at work, who had no idea what it was like to have a drug problem. He also attended AA and NA a few times a week. Frank would stay off alcohol and drugs for a few months and then get high again. After his mother became distraught over his behavior and other family members asked him to leave her home, Frank got a girlfriend he met at NA to let him move in with her. With her urging, he went back to his therapy group and to AA and NA. Frank eventually celebrated a year of sobriety. Friends have told him he would make a good counselor. After giving it serious consideration, he is now working on his licensure in chemical dependency treatment.

The amount of structure leaders of substance abuse treatment groups impose varies; however, Washton (1997) notes that "successful group treatment relies heavily on the active leadership, direction, and education supplied by the group leader" (p. 445; also see Brook, 2008). In more structured groups, the leader often presents topics for discussion and uses preplanned exercises. In less structured groups, the leader may ask clients to present topics for discussion that are of current concern to them.

Group treatment is also provided to the loved ones of chemically dependent individuals. Some groups include all types of family members—spouses or other partners, children who are old enough to participate, parents, and siblings. Membership in other groups may be limited to spouses or other partners, to young children, or to adult children (see Chapters 10 and 12). The goals of these groups are usually to help family members understand the dynamics of chemical dependency, relieve guilt, build self-esteem, avoid enabling, and focus on becoming healthier and happier individuals.

Couples Therapy.   *Couples therapy,* sometimes called *marital therapy,* is another outpatient service (the term *marital* is outmoded for many clients, given the range of relationships that people may experience). Couples therapy may occur at any time but is often offered after the client receives initial inpatient or outpatient services and has maintained some sobriety. Before participating in couples treatment, the partner who is not chemically dependent may also have attended educational sessions, individual therapy, or group therapy for family members.

Initially, this form of therapy may help the couple explore how chemical dependency or other problems have affected their relationship. Ventilation of hurt and anger may be important at this stage. The topics may then progress to improving communications, working out problems, and reacting to lapses or relapses should they occur. Couples treatment may help strengthen a relationship, but it may become a forum for determining that the relationship was never satisfactory or that it is not repairable.

Some practitioners treating chemically dependent clients and their partners are marriage and family therapists or are otherwise qualified to treat couples and families. Others are not equipped to do extensive work in these areas and refer clients when these services are needed.

Family Therapy. Still another type of outpatient service is family therapy (discussed more fully in Chapter 10). Similar to couples therapy, family therapy focuses on chemical dependency's effects on the particular family, reducing family dysfunction, and improving family communications and relationships. Family members may have participated in educational sessions or in family groups before beginning family therapy. All members of the current nuclear family are usually invited to participate, although some may decline to do so. Members of the extended family, such as the parents of an adult chemical abuser, may be included, especially if they are directly enabling the client. The client and extended family members may also be seen together if the client is working to resolve family-of-origin issues.

Multimodal Approaches. Outpatient programs may combine several treatment approaches or modalities. For example, Nathan Azrin and George Hunt developed the *community reinforcement approach (CRA)* to treat people with alcohol problems (Meyers, Roozen, & Smith, 2011; Sisson & Azrin, 1989). CRA was first used in a hospital setting and later in treating those with alcohol or drug problems on an outpatient basis. This behavioral approach emphasizes positive reinforcement to encourage behaviors such as sober or "clean" living and includes: (1) analysis of antecedents and consequences of substance use to identify alternatives to substance use, (2) for those not ready to adopt a goal of abstinence, help in moving toward this goal and trying a period of abstinence, (3) selecting goals in areas to improve life, (4) behavioral skills (problem-solving, communication, drink/drug refusal) training, (5) skills training to obtain and maintain employment, (6) social and recreational counseling, (7) relapse prevention

skills, and (8) relationship counseling to improve the relationship with one's partner (Meyers et al.).

CRA has also been used with disulfiram treatment (discussed later in this chapter), including a supportive loved one to assist in complying with the disulfiram regimen (Roozen et al., 2004), and with contingency management techniques (i.e., incentives such as take-home doses of methadone and monetary rewards, also described in greater detail later in this chapter) (Higgins, Tidey, & Stitzer, 1998; Meyers et al., 2011). CRA is thus a multimodal approach to chemical dependency treatment that addresses relevant aspects of the client's life in order to promote abstinence and general well-being. *Community reinforcement and family training (CRAFT)* is another approach that has received attention because of its focus on getting resistant alcohol and drug users into treatment by helping a family member or other significant individual modify the environment to reward sobriety (Myers et al.; Smith, Meyers, & Austin, 2008).

Another multimodal approach used in outpatient addiction treatment is *network therapy* (Galanter, 2008, 2009a). It relies on treatment coordination, cognitive behavioral strategies, and social support from family and friends who assist the therapist and help the client abstain from alcohol and other drugs and comply with pharmacological treatments for addiction (e.g., disulfiram). A network usually consists of three or four family members or friends. The client and network members are expected to maintain good relations and work together as a team. Family and friends do not enforce sobriety, but they are supposed to inform the therapist about lack of client compliance. The patient participates in individual therapy as well as initial and periodic subsequent sessions with network members. Participation in mutual-help groups is encouraged.

Brief Interventions and Brief Therapies. Brief and very brief interventions as well as brief therapies are included under outpatient services. Brief and very brief interventions typically involve one to three or four sessions, with each session ranging from a few minutes to one hour in duration (Fleming, 2000; Kaner et al., 2009; McQueen, Howe, Allan, & Mains, 2009). Brief interventions have been designed for use in primary health care settings, hospital emergency and trauma departments, and colleges and universities. They have also been used with pregnant women and older adults (see Fleming, 2000; NIAAA, 2000). Brief interventions take a variety of forms, including counseling or advice by a physician or other health or social service professional to reduce drinking, agreements to reduce drinking, monitoring or check-ins in person or by phone, self-help manuals, bibliotherapy (reading materials), and drinking diaries or logs to monitor drinking.

Used alone, the briefest interventions are generally reserved for alcohol misusers or abusers (McCaul & Furst, 1994; NIAAA, 2000). Many individuals seen by professionals in health care or social service settings do not meet the diagnostic criteria for alcohol abuse or dependence, but they may engage in risk or heavy drinking (alcohol misuse), which may portend more serious problems. In the absence of medical conditions that warrant abstention, the National Institute on Alcohol Abuse and Alcoholism (NIAAA, 2005) defines *risk or excessive drinking* as a score of 8 or more on the Alcohol Use Disorders Identification Test (AUDIT, described in Chapter 5 of this text) for men and 4 or more for women or as follows:

- For healthy men up to age 65, no more than 4 standard drinks (one standard drink equals 12 ounces of beer, 5 ounces of wine, or 1.5 ounces of 80-proof spirits) in a day and no more than 14 drinks in a week.
- For healthy women and healthy men aged 65 and older, no more than 3 standard drinks in a day and no more than 7 drinks in a week.

One approach for applying brief interventions is designated by the mnemonic FRAMES, in which the professional provides *feedback* to the patient or client on his or her drinking risks, recognizes the

individual's personal *responsibility* or decision to change, provides clear *advice* about altering drinking habits, offers a *menu* of change options, counsels in a warm and *empathic* way, and emphasizes *self-efficacy* (that the patient or client can do it) (Miller & Sanchez, 1994). The professional also helps the individual establish a drinking goal and follows-up to monitor compliance and provide encouragement. Brief interventions may also be used to motivate alcohol-dependent individuals to seek treatment. Interest has also grown in using brief interventions and brief therapies to reduce drug use. Several manuals or guides for conducting brief intervention for alcohol and drug problems are available (American Public Health Association and Education Development Center, 2008; Babor & Higgins-Biddle, 2001; NIDA, 2009c).

Another short-term approach of growing interest for addressing substance use problems is *solution-focused brief therapy* (see Berg, 1995; Trepper et al., 2010). The premise underlying this social constructivist approach is that the client's "reality is created through social interaction and validation" (Berg, p. 224). As its name implies, the focus is on solutions, rather than problems. The approach recognizes that the client has at least the beginning solutions to his or her problems and views the therapist and client as collaborators on the client's (rather than the therapist's) goals to achieve a successful outcome (Berg, 1995). Treatment may be as brief as a single session. Recovering individuals have also been taught to use this approach to help peers (Miller, 2000). Solution-focused therapy has also been used in group treatment for substance abusers (Smock et al., 2008). Little research is available on solution-focused treatment with people who have alcohol or drug problems.

Effectiveness of Outpatient Services.   Gerstein and Harwood (1990; Gerstein, 1999) found that illicit drug abusers have better compliance rates with therapeutic communities and methadone maintenance than with outpatient psychosocial treatments. The Drug Abuse Treatment Outcome Study (DATOS) funded by the National Institute on Drug Abuse included four major treatment modalities—long-term residential, short-term outpatient, outpatient methadone maintenance, and outpatient drug-free treatment. All four resulted in clients using less drugs, but generally speaking, residential and inpatient programs were more effective than outpatient programs in reducing cocaine and heroin use among heroin-dependent clients who were not daily users (Hser, Anglin, & Fletcher, 1998). Modality was not significantly related to reductions in use among daily users.

Group therapy is often used to help people with substance use disorders, but challenges to conducting research on group therapy abound. Methodological improvements have been occurring. For example, Crits-Christoph and colleagues (1999) randomly assigned 487 cocaine-dependent individuals who had stable living situations and were not taking psychotropic medications to one of four manual-guided treatments: (1) individual drug counseling plus group drug counseling (GDC); (2) cognitive therapy plus GDC; (3) supportive-expressive therapy plus GDC; or (4) GDC alone. Those who received individual plus GDC (both had a Twelve-Step orientation) improved most on a measure of drug use severity. The study did not address how effective individual therapy alone would have been for the clients. In a study of over 7,000 clients who received substance abuse treatment, researchers found that those who participated in more group than individual therapy had better outcomes (Panas, Caspi, Fournier, & McCarty, 2003). Weiss, Jaffee, de Menil, and Cogley (2004) examined approximately two dozen studies that compared group treatment to no group therapy, individual therapy, group therapy plus individual therapy, and/or another type of group therapy. In general, there were no differences in outcomes between group and individual treatment, nor did any particular type of group therapy emerge as superior. It remains debatable as to whether group or individual therapy is superior for treating substance use disorders (see Morrell & Myers, 2009). No one approach to group therapy has emerged as superior, but cognitive behavioral therapy has been studied most often and seems to produce consistently positive results (Morrell & Myers).

Marital or couples and family treatments have also shown promising results. In their meta-analysis of family/couples treatment with an adult or family member who abused illicit drugs, Stanton and Shadish (1997) found these approaches more effective than individual treatment, peer groups, and family psychoeducation. They also concluded that effectiveness is equally good whether the drug abuser is an adult or adolescent and that the effectiveness of other forms of treatment can be improved by adding family and couples treatment. Particularly promising was the ability of couples and family approaches to engage and retain clients in treatment. However, there is insufficient evidence to determine whether some schools of family therapy are more effective than others. Edwards and Steinglass (1995) also conducted a meta-analysis that showed the effectiveness of family treatment in motivating alcoholics to enter treatment; however, once the individuals were in treatment, family approaches demonstrated only a marginal advantage over individual alcoholism treatment. These authors also noted that greater spousal support for abstinence and commitment to the relationship may contribute to better family treatment outcomes.

In one of the first studies of the CRA in treating alcoholism, Azrin and colleagues (1982) found that almost all clients participating in CRA were totally abstinent at six months; however, the married and cohabitating clients also did very well in a group that received the disulfiram compliance regimen only, whereas single clients did much better with the full CRA approach (perhaps because they needed more community support). Continuing research has also demonstrated the benefits of CRA with clients who have alcohol and other drug problems (Abbott, 2009; Meyers & Miller, 2001; Meyers et al., 2011). A review of 11 high-quality randomized controlled trials that compared CRA with "usual treatment" found: (1) in treating alcohol problems, CRA and CRA with disulfiram was more effective in reducing number of drinking days than in producing continuous abstinence; (2) in treating cocaine problems, CRA with incentives (vouchers that can be used to purchase goods or services) was more effective in promoting abstinence; (3) with regard to opioid problems, the evidence is limited that CRA promotes better results for methadone maintenance clients or that CRA with incentives promotes better outcomes for detoxification patients (Roozen et al., 2004). An analysis of four controlled trials of CRAFT showed much higher treatment engagement than Alcoholics Anonymous/Narcotics Anonymous or the Johnson Intervention technique (see Chapters 5 and10) (Roozen, deWaart, & van der Kroft, 2010).

McCrady and associates (1986) randomly assigned 45 couples to one of three behavioral types of outpatient treatment: minimal spouse involvement, alcohol-focused spouse involvement, or alcohol-focused plus behavioral marital therapy (BMT). A six-month follow-up indicated positive benefits for all groups, with the alcohol-focused plus BMT group generally having the best outcomes, such as a more rapid decline in drinking and greater maintenance of reduced drinking. An 18-month follow-up indicated that adding marital therapy enhanced "treatment compliance, subject's ability to cope with drinking, marital stability and satisfaction, and subjective well being" (McCrady, Stout, Noel, Abrams, & Nelson, 1991, p. 1423).

Work in the Counseling for Alcoholics' Marriages (CALM) program at Harvard University also supports the use of BMT or behavioral couples treatment (BCT) (Fals-Stewart et al., 2000). In this approach, the couple develops a sobriety contract in which the substance abuser agrees not to use alcohol and/or drugs, and the spouse agrees to support this effort (O'Farrell & Fals-Stewart, 2000). There is also a focus on improving communications skills and encouraging the couple to engage in positive activities together. A meta-analysis of a dozen well-controlled studies found at follow-up that compared to those who received individual treatment, BCT participants used alcohol and drugs less, suffered fewer alcohol- or drug-related consequences, and reported greater relationship satisfaction (Powers, Vedel, & Emmelkamp, 2008). Some evidence also indicates that BCT may result in reduced marital violence (O'Connor, 2001; Schumm, O'Farrell, Murphy, & Fals-Stewart, 2009).

No approach has been studied more than brief interventions, perhaps because they are brief. Kaner et al. (2007) conducted a meta-analysis of 22 randomized clinical trials of brief interventions conducted with primary care patients in various countries whose drinking exceeded recommended levels. The interventions involved 5,800 participants followed for one year or longer. Study results varied, but overall, drinking behavior was lower for experimental compared to control group participants. Where results were available by gender, the meta-analysis confirmed the benefits of brief intervention in reducing drinking among men, but results for women were uncertain due to insufficient research data. Longer counseling provided little additional benefit. McQueen et al. (2009) also conducted a meta-analysis of 11 controlled trials of brief interventions with heavy alcohol users admitted to general hospitals, and found the evidence of reduced drinking inconclusive.

No treatment or intervention described in this book is a magic bullet. Substance abuse and dependence treatment professionals are still trying to address the question of what treatment works best for which individuals (see Box 6.5 entitled "Matching and Combining to Enhance Treatment Effectiveness").

Medication-Assisted Treatment

Several types of drugs or medications may assist alcoholics and addicts in recovery following detoxification (also see Chapter 3 of this text). Although no medications promise a cure, some may be helpful in maintaining abstinence, which can also help people engage in the treatment process. We focus on the drugs most often used in helping individuals who are dependent on alcohol and opiates. Though there is tremendous interest in medications useful in treating cocaine and amphetamine dependence, no drug has recognized effectiveness, though

BOX 6.5   *Matching and Combining to Enhance Treatment Effectiveness*

Matching Clients and Services

There are no magic bullets in chemical dependency treatment. Individual studies and meta-analyses tell us about the effectiveness of treatment based on group averages, not about what the effectiveness will be for a particular individual. The American Society of Addiction Medicine's (ASAM) (Mee-Lee et al., 2001) offers patient placement criteria in the form of a matrix or "crosswalk" for adults and for adolescents. The levels of care for adults are early intervention; opioid maintenance therapy; outpatient treatment; intensive outpatient; partial hospitalization; clinically managed low-, medium-, and high-intensity residential treatment; and medically managed intensive inpatient treatment. The level of care a patient needs is assessed according to the following "criteria dimensions": intoxication or withdrawal potential; biomedical, emotional, behavioral, and cognitive conditions and complications; readiness to change; relapse potential; and recovery environment. To prevent the use of unnecessary services, ASAM supports "unbundling" services; that is, rather than provide a set package of services to a client based on treatment modality or setting (inpatient, outpatient, etc.), the client should be provided the type and intensity of services that meets his or her needs. Clients should also be reassessed during the course of treatment to ensure they continue to receive appropriate services.

There is considerable interest in how professionals can better match clients to treatment to improve treatment effectiveness (McLellan et al., 1983). One approach is to consider clients' characteristics and match them to a theoretical approach to treatment that is consistent with their needs. Litt and colleagues (1992) attempted to do this by randomly assigning Type A alcoholics (e.g., those with less severe problems) and Type B alcoholics (e.g., those with more severe problems) to two different types of treatment. As hypothesized, based on their needs and coping styles, Type A's

did better in the "less structured interactional group therapy," and Type B's did better in the "more structured coping skills group treatment."

Other studies have attempted to match clients to treatment based on other personal characteristics—for example, demographic characteristics such as gender, drinking-related characteristics, intrapersonal characteristics, and interpersonal characteristics—to determine their impacts, if any, on client outcomes (Mattson, 1994; Mattson et al., 1994). Believing that client matching offered a useful direction to pursue in improving alcoholism treatment, in 1989, NIAAA launched a rigorous, eight-year, $25 million study called Project MATCH. It involved nine treatment sites run under public and private auspices. A team of prominent alcoholism researchers tested the hypothesis "that more beneficial results can be obtained if treatment is prescribed on the basis of individual patient needs and characteristics as opposed to treating all patients with the same diagnosis in the same manner" (Nowinski, Baker, & Carroll, 1995, p. ix).

Treatments provided on an individual, rather than group, basis were selected for practical reasons (e.g., being able to start treating each subject immediately) and methodological reasons (e.g., interest in matching on the characteristics of individual clients, rather than groups of clients). Other important considerations were evidence of the treatments' clinical effectiveness, potential for discerning matching effects based on previous research, and distinctiveness among the treatments. Three approaches were chosen:

> The Twelve-Step Facilitation Approach (TSF) was provided in 12 sessions. TSF "is grounded in the concept of alcoholism as a spiritual and medical disease." TSF is consistent with Alcoholics Anonymous's 12 steps and the goal was to foster the client's involvement in AA. (Nowinski et al., 1995, p. x)
>
> Motivational Enhancement Therapy (MET) was provided in four sessions. MET "is based on principles of motivational psychology

(continued)

and is designed to produce rapid, internally motivated change." Rather than guide the client step-by-step, motivational strategies are used to help clients mobilize their own resources. (Miller, Zweben, DiClemente, & Rychtarik, 1995, p. viii)

Cognitive-Behavioral Therapy (CBT) was provided in 12 sessions. CBT is based on social learning theory and addresses the range of the client's problems, not only drinking. Emphasis is placed on increasing skills and the ability to cope with high-risk situations that may precipitate relapse. (Kadden et al., 1995, p. viii)

Each treatment was highly structured and guided by a manual. The approximately 80 professionals providing the treatments were carefully selected, trained, and continually supervised to maintain adherence (fidelity) to the treatment they were to provide. The study was divided into an outpatient arm at five different sites and an aftercare arm following standard inpatient or day hospital treatment at four sites. Clients were assigned randomly to the treatments. The goal of all treatments for all the clients was abstinence from alcohol.

There were some minor differences across the treatments, but on average, in the month following treatment, patients in the aftercare arm were abstinent on 90 percent of the days, compared to 80 percent of the days for those in the outpatient arm (Project MATCH Research Group, 1997a). One year after treatment, these figures decreased only slightly. However, among aftercare arm subjects, only 35 percent were totally abstinent throughout the year after treatment, compared to only 19 percent of outpatient subjects. There were no true controls (subjects who received no treatment) with which to compare the results. In addition, patients knew they were participating in a major, nationally funded study and might have tried harder, especially given the large amount of attention paid to them during initial data collection and follow-up) ("Project MATCH," 1996). At the three-year follow-up, conducted only with outpatient arm participants, nearly 30 percent reported total abstinence in the previous three

months; those who reported drinking were abstinent an average of two-thirds of the time (Project MATCH Research Group, 1997a, 1997b, 1998b). TSF participants had somewhat higher abstention rates (36 percent) than MET (27 percent) and CBT (24 percent) participants. Two motivational variables—readiness to change and self-efficacy—were the strongest predictors of better long-term drinking outcomes.

Only 4 of 21 hypothesized matches were observed (they were for client anger, support for drinking, higher alcohol dependence, and psychiatric severity), but none was particularly robust (Project MATCH Research Group, 1997a, 1997b, 1998; NIAAA, 2000). Many methodological and other reasons have been offered to explain why the matches were not more prominent (Project MATCH Research Group, 1997b). Others have interpreted the results in a more positive light: that despite what treatment is offered, improvement can be expected regardless of client characteristics if the treatment is well delivered and sufficient attention is paid to the client.

Combining To Improve Treatment Effectiveness

NIAAA decided to sponsor another large research effort called Project COMBINE to study two medications for alcoholism treatment—naltrexone and acamprosate (see the section in this chapter on Medication Assisted Treatment)—in combination with a moderate-intensity behavioral treatment (Anton et al., 2006; NIAAA, 2001; Zweben, 2001). Participants were 1,383 alcohol-dependent volunteers from 11 sites divided into nine groups. Eight groups got medical management (nine sessions designed to promote medication adherence and abstinence that can be delivered in primary care settings) and naltrexone, acamprosate, both drugs, or placebos of one or both drugs. Four groups also got more intensive behavioral counseling provided by alcoholism treatment specialists. This moderate-intensity behavioral treatment is a hybrid of the treatments used in Project MATCH and includes participation of a supportive significant other and/or participation in mutual-help groups. Treatment was more individualized than in Project MATCH, and study participants could receive up to 20 sessions. The ninth group got the behavioral counseling without medications or medical management. *During the course of treatment,* results were:

1. Drinking was reduced among all groups.
2. In conjunction with medical management, behavioral counseling alone *or* naltrexone alone produced better results than naltrexone and acamprosate combined or any medication/behavioral counseling treatment combination.
3. Acamprosate was not associated with better results in any group.

However, one-year post-treatment most differences between groups faded, indicating the need for continuing services to maintain treatment gains. The results support the benefits of behavioral counseling and naltrexone in assisting alcohol-dependent individuals. It still leaves open many questions, including whether a medication like naltrexone can be beneficial with less intensive medical management.

---

several are being studied. In addition, there are no evidence-based drug treatments for marijuana dependence (Kampman, 2009).

None of the medications discussed is recommended for use alone; rather, they are viewed as adjuncts to psychosocial treatment. Some of these drugs are called *agonists* because they mimic the actions of natural neurotransmitters (brain chemicals). Other drugs are called *analogs* because their effects are similar to those of another drug but their chemical structures differ slightly. An *antagonist* drug counteracts or blocks the effects of another drug (NIDA, 1997).

Disulfiram. Better known by the trade name Antabuse, disulfiram was approved for use in treating individuals dependent on alcohol in 1951. Disulfiram is neither an agonist nor an antagonist drug. It is intended to deter impulsive drinking, although it does not curb the desire to drink. Instead, Antabuse is described as "buying time" or as an "insurance policy" because those taking it know they will become violently ill if they drink. Originally, it was hoped that disulfiram would be an answer for many people with alcohol use disorders. The criminal justice system was enthusiastic about its use and ordered many of its alcohol-dependent charges to take the drug if it was not contraindicated by other medical conditions, though such coerced used was questioned on several grounds (Marco & Marco, 1980).

Disulfiram interferes with the normal metabolism of alcohol, resulting in a serious physical reaction if even a small amount of alcohol is ingested (for information on disulfiram see De Sousa, 2010; Ewing, 1982; Kampman, 2009, *Nurse Practitioner's Drug Handbook,* 1998; Suh, Pettinati, Kampman, & O'Brien, 2006). Those taking it must avoid all alcohol, including that found in prescription and over-the-counter drugs and other products that may contain alcohol, such as mouthwash and skin lotions. Paraldehyde, which is sometimes used to prevent delirium tremens (DTs) in alcohol-dependent individuals, will also cause a severe reaction. Inhaling alcohol fumes in closed quarters might also cause some reaction. Disulfiram-ethanol reactions may involve a variety of symptoms, including flushing, increased pulse and respiration, sweating, weakness, decreased blood pressure, a severe headache, vomiting, and confusion. In the most severe cases, reactions may result in heart failure and other life-threatening problems, and some deaths have been reported. A patient must be completely detoxified from alcohol before beginning disulfiram treatment.

Disulfiram is contraindicated for those with certain conditions, such as serious mental illness, heart disease, diabetes, epilepsy, and pregnancy.

Before beginning this treatment, patients must fully understand the consequences of using alcohol while taking disulfiram. It should not be given to those who are intellectually unable to appreciate these consequences. Patients should also be aware that if they do decide to return to drinking, they must allow up to two weeks following the last dose of Antabuse to avoid a reaction. Since serious disulfiram-ethanol reactions can occur, patients should be screened for their desire to take this drug.

Side effects of disulfiram (not related to the ingestion of alcohol) may include skin eruptions or rashes, drowsiness, headaches, and reduced sexual performance. These symptoms often abate following an initial period of adjustment to the drug, or the dosage may be reduced to prevent these symptoms. More severe effects, such as neuritis and psychoses, generally require discontinuing the drug. Patients usually take disulfiram once a day. Originally, it was given in larger doses than prescribed today (disulfiram skin implants were used in some countries), and side effects and complications from reactions were more severe. It was then determined that lower doses were also effective. Patients should carry a card with them indicating that they are taking disulfiram to alert medical personnel should they have a reaction or other medical emergency. Some patients do attempt drinking while on disulfiram and usually end up in a hospital emergency room. Although this description of disulfiram may sound frightening, many alcohol-dependent individuals have used it, apparently successfully (NIAAA, 2005; McNichol & Logsdon, 1988). There is also interest in the use of disulfiram to treat cocaine dependence.

Methadone.   Methadone is a synthetic narcotic agonist drug. In addition to its use in narcotic detoxification, it is also used in longer-term chemical dependency treatment as a substitute for the opioid drugs. Methadone's effectiveness in treating opioid addiction was demonstrated in the mid-1960s, and it was approved for this purpose by the U.S. Food and Drug Administration in 1972 (Rettig & Yarmolinsky, 1995). According to the Centers for Disease Control (2002), methadone blocks opiates' euphoric and sedating effects, relieves cravings for opiates that can lead to relapse, and relieves opiate withdrawal symptoms.

Methadone maintenance treatment (MMT) is intended only for those with a severe narcotic dependence. Some use methadone for a short period before completely withdrawing; others use it indefinitely. Methadone can provide people dependent on opioid drugs an opportunity for life stabilization and participation in a wide range of habilitative and rehabilitative services (Kleber, 2008). Although MMT is supposed to be used with other therapeutic services, the extent to which methadone clients participate in other services varies.

Patients or clients typically take a liquid daily dose of methadone (combined with a sweet drink) at outpatient clinics that also offer other services to clients. Patients taking methadone may complain about weight gain and insomnia, but these problems have been attributed to factors such as increased alcohol consumption and to personal characteristics of users rather than to the methadone itself (Gerstein & Harwood, 1990). Methadone maintenance patients may still use alcohol, cocaine, and other illicit drugs, and this must be addressed in treatment (Rawson, McCann, Hasson, & Ling, 2000; Substance Abuse and Mental Health Services Administration [SAMHSA], 2009). The drug use of clients on methadone maintenance is usually monitored through urinalyses.

Many MMT programs use a multidisciplinary team approach to provide comprehensive services to clients and to make decisions such as whether to continue or discharge a client (New Brunswick Addiction Services, 2009). As clients make progress in treatment, they may be allowed to take a Sunday dose of methadone home or to come to the clinic every other day and take a dose home for the intervening day. In the United States, the program's medical director must make these decisions according to eight criteria outlined in federal regulations, such as no recent abuse of drugs or alcohol, regular clinic attendance, and no known recent criminal activity (SAMHSA, 2009). In 2008, 1,132 opioid treatment programs were operating in the United States, serving about 268,000 clients taking methadone and 4,280 taking buprenorphine, another medication discussed in the next section of this chapter (SAMHSA, 2010).

Methadone is helpful in deterring addicts from pursuing illegal activities to support their drug habits and allows them to lead more "normal" lives, but its use remains controversial even with its 40-year history (Centers for Disease Control, 2002; Kleber, 2008; Rawson et al., 2000). Detractors argue that it replaces one addictive drug with another, rather than promoting a goal of abstinence. Hall, Ward, and Mattick (1998) justify making methadone available because of the difficulties that addicts encounter in remaining opioid free, the failure of abstinence-oriented programs to retain addicts in treatment, and the high mortality associated with chronic opioid dependence.

Methadone maintenance treatment may also help to reduce transmission of the human immunodeficiency virus (HIV), hepatitis B and C, and other diseases (Centers for Disease Control, 2002; Stine, Meandzija, & Kosten, 1998). Even so, controversies persist about the safety and health problems of methadone maintenance and how frequently users sell it to obtain illicit drugs. Gerstein and Harwood (1990) discuss these controversies, including the issue of methadone's use as a social control mechanism versus its therapeutic value to the individual client (also see Hall, Ward, & Mattick, 1998; Ray & Ksir, 1999). Despite its cost effectiveness due to factors such as reduced crime (Ling, Rawson, & Compton, 1994), some communities do not have methadone maintenance clinics because they do not wish to attract heroin users to their area.

A 1995 Institute of Medicine report questioned the very strict federal controls on the administration of methadone to opiate addicts (Rettig & Yarmolinsky, 1995). New federal regulations issued in 2001 allow "more flexibility and greater medical judgment in treatment" ("Opioid Drugs," 2001, p. 4076). For example, patients who have two years or more of stable experience

with methadone maintenance treatment may now have take-home doses of up to 31 days, compared to 6 days with previous regulations. In addition, doses are not restricted to liquid form and may include pill form. The approval process for operating these opioid treatment programs involves a certification and accreditation system overseen by the Substance Abuse and Mental Health Services Administration (SAMHSA), with quality assurance provisions that take into account client outcomes. A stabilized patient may receive methadone from a physician in an office-based practice but only if the physician is affiliated with an opioid treatment (methadone maintenance) program. Although state and program regulations may be more stringent, they are expected to comply with the spirit of the federal regulations.

Buprenorphine. Buprenorphine is an analgesic drug that is related to morphine but is much more potent. In 2002, the FDA approved buprenorphine for treating opiate addiction, and physicians who receive training may use it in office-based treatment. Buprenorphine is a drug that combines agonist and antagonist properties (see Veilleux, Colvin, Anderson, York, & Heinz, 2010). Therefore, it mimics the effects of opioid drugs by acting on the same brain receptors, and it also inhibits the effects of opiate drugs so that they do not produce the same euphoria. Buprenorphine seems to create low physical dependence and a mild withdrawal syndrome that may make it an attractive alternative to methadone, especially for patients who wish to become drug free and transfer to naltrexone (described in the next section) (Ling et al., 1994). Although it provides patients with another treatment option (Strain, Stitzer, Liebson, & Bigelow, 1994), cases of burphrenorphine abuse have been reported (Stine et al., 1998). Buprenorphine is provided in sublingual tablet form and is also available in combination with naloxone (a synthetic narcotic antagonist) in order to reduce buprenorphine's abuse potential (Kampman, 2009; Stoller, Bigelow, Walsh, & Strain, 2001). The trade name of the combination medication is Suboxone, and it is also available in dissolving film strips. Ling and colleagues (1994) note that "some patients will have a level of opioid tolerance higher than can be achieved by buprenorphine because of its ceiling effect" (p. 126), suggesting that methadone may be a better choice for them.

Naltrexone, Acamprosate, and Nalmefene. Naltrexone (trade name ReVia), like naloxone, has played a role in detoxifying those dependent on opioid drugs. Whereas methadone, which is also used in opiate detoxification, is a substitute for narcotic drugs, naloxone and naltrexone reverse their effects. Naltrexone has also been used in the longer-term treatment of those dependent on opiates (Stine, Meandzija, & Kosten, 1998; Treating opiate addiction: Part II, 2005). Naltrexone may also improve treatment outcomes for those dependent on alcohol or cocaine. Naltrexone blocks opioid receptors that may also make the effects of drinking alcohol (as well as taking opioid drugs) less pleasurable (NIAAA, 2005). Patients may therefore consume less alcohol should they begin drinking, and the likelihood of a full relapse may be reduced (Kampman, 2009; NIAAA).

Naltrexone has also being tested in combination with acamprosate, which was approved for use in treating alcohol dependence in the United States in 2004. Acamprosate acts differently on the brain than naltrexone (Center for Substance Abuse Treatment [CSAT], 2005). Indications are that naltrexone is more effective in curtailing drinking once it begins, while acamprosate is more effective in preventing drinking in the first place (Rösner, Leucht, Lehert, & Soyka, 2008) because it may reduce post-acute (protracted) withdrawal symptoms (e.g., insomnia, anxiety, and restlessness) (CSAT, 2005). Acamprosate may have advantages over naltrexone because people with liver disease can tolerate it better.

Nalmefene is another opioid antagonist being tested for use in alcoholism treatment (Anton et al., 2004). It, too, has some advantages over naltrexone, such as the ability to bind to different types of opioid receptor sites and

perhaps further reduce alcohol's reinforcing effects (NIAAA, 2000). It also is reported to have no dose-related association with liver toxicity and to have longer duration of action. In addition to safety features, researchers and treatment providers are looking closely at which drug treatments produce the highest rates of treatment retention and effectiveness.

Effectiveness of Medications

Disulfarim.   One view of disulfiram is that for many people, its benefits far outweigh the few risks associated with its use, particularly in light of alcoholism's devastating impact (McNichol and Logsdon, 1988). Where patients do have improved outcomes, questions often arise as to whether it is patients' desire and motivation to remain sober (NIAAA, 1987), fear of becoming sick (Fuller et al., 1986), other treatment being received or other confounds that produce the positive result (Suh et al., 2006). In a review of studies, Suh et al. note that patient compliance is poor and results of disulfiram clinical trials with regard to abstention from alcohol are inconsistent. Research on disulfiram's effectiveness compared to other approaches is debatable (Garbutt et al., 1999). A key factor may be in the patient or client's motivation to take the medication to assist in maintaining sobriety (Center for Applied Research in Mental Health and Addiction, 2008). Like other forms of treatment, disulfiram may work best for those who want to use it.

Azrin and colleagues (1982; Sisson & Azrin, 1989) found good results using an "Antabuse reassurance" approach in which disulfiram's benefits are described, a supportive and helpful (rather than authoritarian and coercive) person is used to help ensure compliance, and role rehearsal is used to help address situations in which failure of the client or support person to follow through with the procedure is anticipated. In a controlled six-month study in the United Kingdom, Chick et al. (1992) also found better results with supervised disulfiram use, though during the last month of the study there was no difference between the control and experimental groups' alcohol use. Others reviewing the state of disulfiram use also suggest the benefits of supervision in increasing compliance with disulfiram, and thus its effectiveness (De Sousa, 2010; Kampman, 2009; Suh et al., 2006). The Cochrane Collaboration, which does research reviews of many treatments for substance use disorders, is conducting a new review of disulfiram's effectiveness.[2] It is yet unclear whether disulfiram is effective in treating cocaine dependence (Pani et al., 2010).

Methadone.　More is known about methadone maintenance treatment's (MMT) effectiveness than about other types of treatment for illicit drug users. MMT has been called the "most effective treatment for opiate addiction" (Centers for Disease Control, 2002; Kleber, 2008). When used properly, the benefits of methadone have been widely reported (Centers for Disease Control). Gerstein and Harwood (1990) caution that methadone maintenance is not the answer for all heroin addicts, but in spite of controversies about this treatment, it generally produces favorable results:

> There is strong evidence from clinical trials and similar study designs that heroin-dependent individuals have better outcomes on average (in terms of illicit drug consumption and other criminal behavior) when they are maintained on methadone than when they are not treated at all or are simply detoxified and released, or when methadone is tapered down and terminated as a result of unilateral client request, expulsion from treatment, or program closure. (p. 153)

Given individual client differences, higher rather than lower maintenance doses of methadone seem to produce more positive results (Centers for Disease Control, 2002; Gerstein & Harwood, 1990). In a recent systematic review, methadone maintenance therapy was found superior on treatment retention and reduced heroin use compared to drug-free treatments or methadone detoxification only, since participants generally drop out of drug-free maintenance therapies (Mattick, Breen,

Kimber, & Davoli, 2010). The benefit-to-cost ratio associated with methadone maintenance is considered substantial, but the Mattick et al. review did not find statistically significant improvements on criminal activity or mortality.

Studies support the belief that clients have better treatment outcomes when they receive psychosocial services along with the methadone (Amato et al., 2008; Kraft, Rothbard, Hadley, McLellan, & Asch, 1997; McLellan, Arndt, Metzger, Woody, & O'Brien, 1993). However, a large study found that compared to other treatment modalities, methadone programs often provided less counseling and other services (Ethridge, Craddock, Dunteman, & Hubbard, 1995).

With regard to opioid dependence, West, O'Neal, and Graham's (2000) meta-analysis suggested that buprenorphine is generally as effective as methadone; however, methadone-treated patients had fewer positive tests for illicit opioid use. Mattick, Kimber, Breen, and Davoli (2008) also found that as a maintenance medication, buprenorphine is more effective than placebo in reducing heroin use, but it was not as effective as methadone, especially when methadone is prescribed in adequate doses.

Naltrexone.　Despite interest in medications such as naltrexone to treat alcohol dependence, the treatment community has not adopted them to any significant extent (O'Malley & O' Connor, 2011; Thomas, Wallack, Lee, McCarty, & Swift, 2003). In early studies, Volpicelli and colleagues (1992) and O'Malley and colleagues (1992) investigated naltrexone as an adjunct to the short-term (12-week) treatment of alcoholism and found promising results. Among the VA medical patients studied, Volpicelli et al. noted that naltrexone's primary benefit seemed to be in preventing subjects from drinking in a particularly harmful way (a relapse) once they began to consume alcohol (a lapse). O'Malley et al. (1992) also found better outcomes for those who received naltrexone with respect to number of days drinking and relapse, as well as lower severity of alcohol-related problems. Of particular interest in O'Malley's study is that

61 percent of patients who received naltrexone in combination with supportive therapy were abstinent for the 12-week period, compared with abstinence rates of 28, 21, and 19 percent, respectively, for those who received naltrexone and coping skills treatment, the placebo and coping skills treatment, and placebo and supportive treatment. In addition, both groups of patients receiving naltrexone had relapse rates (defined as five or more drinks on an occasion for men and four for women) that were substantially lower than for the placebo groups.

O'Malley et al. (1992) suggested that patients may prefer naltrexone to disulfiram, given disulfiram's side effects if alcohol is consumed, while Volpicelli et al. (1992) suggested that the combination of naltrexone and alcohol may cause an aversive reaction of nausea in some individuals similar to disulfiram. Based on retrospective reports, Volpicelli and colleagues (1995) found that naltrexone-treated patients indicated less subjective experiences of pleasurable effects (a high) from alcohol than did placebo patients. Likewise, O'Malley et al. (1996) found that patients who took naltrexone and drank retrospectively reported less incentive to continue drinking as a reason for terminating drinking, whereas placebo patients who drank reported that they stopped due to negative consequences of drinking. (The groups did not differ on the pleasantness of the first drinking experience.)

A subsequent 12-week trial by Volpicelli and colleagues (1997) in a more naturalistic setting showed only modest benefits of naltrexone in reducing alcohol use, and there was no difference in the percentages of naltrexone and placebo subjects who sampled alcohol. Those who were more compliant with naltrexone treatment did have better outcomes, indicating the need to improve patients' treatment compliance. In an effort to determine if short-term naltrexone treatment has longer-term benefits, O'Malley and colleagues (1996) followed patients 6 months after participating in a study that offered them naltrexone or a placebo and either 12 weeks of coping skills or supportive treatment. Naltrexone's benefits in supporting abstinence diminished quickly after use ceased, indicating that longer-term naltrexone treatment may be needed. However, naltrexone-treated subjects did not drink as heavily and were less likely to meet the criteria for alcohol abuse or dependence at follow-up. Monti and colleagues (2001) followed patients for one year after they took naltrexone for 12 weeks. During the 12 weeks, they found that naltrexone resulted in less alcohol consumed once drinking was initiated, but naltrexone and placebo groups had equal numbers of relapsers and only those who were more compliant with the medication showed significant effects. Naltrexone's effects were not sustained after patients stopped taking it. In fact, those who took naltrexone were more likely to relapse than those in the placebo group in the three months after the medication trial ceased.

As noted in Box 6.5 on pages 141–143, naltrexone produced positive results in Project COMBINE while acamprosate did not (almost all study participants also received medical management to help them comply with the medication treatments). One meta-analysis of 24 randomized clinical trials found that naltrexone resulted in significantly fewer relapses during short-term treatment, but not on initiation of drinking (Srisurapanont & Jarusuraisin, 2005); however, another meta-analysis found naltrexone effective in promoting abstinence and in preventing heavy drinking once drinking commenced (Leucht et al., 2008). The latter meta-analysis found acamprosate was more effective than naltrexone in preventing initiation of drinking, while naltrexone was more effective in preventing a lapse (drinking) from becoming a relapse (heavy drinking). More study is needed to determine for whom these medications are useful, how long treatment should be continued, and under what conditions, such as their use with psychosocial treatments.

Aftercare

Aftercare, also known as *continuing care* (McKay & Hiller-Sturmöhfel, 2011), the sixth component of the treatment continuum, is an extension of intensive treatment, residential, and/or outpatient programs.

Aftercare provides an opportunity for program staff to assist clients in monitoring their progress and to address problems and obstacles to maintaining recovery before they result in serious consequences. Aftercare services are provided in many ways. Individual sessions may be used but group meetings may be more common (McKay & Hiller-Sturmöhfel). Telephone contacts may also be used. Clients may participate weekly, biweekly, monthly, or bimonthly, depending on the program or on the clients' needs. Some private treatment centers charge a flat fee for services, which includes participation in an aftercare program. In selecting a treatment program, the Center for Substance Abuse Treatment recommends asking about whether the program includes long-term aftercare. Clients participating in aftercare connected to treatment programs are usually encouraged to participate in mutual-help groups as well.

Preventing Relapse.   Perhaps the most important part of aftercare is learning and practicing the skills needed to prevent lapses and relapses and to manage them should they occur. A key to teaching relapse prevention seems to be increasing clients' perceptions that they can successfully cope with situations that pose risks of drinking and drug use (Annis & Davis, 1988; Greenfield et al., 2000; NIAAA, 1990). Authors who have written extensively on relapse prevention generally recommend a number of cognitive and behavioral techniques to help clients maintain the gains made in treatment (Daley & Salloum, 1999; Douaihy, Daley, Stowell, & Park, 2007; Gorski, 2000; Gorski & Miller, 1986; Marlatt & Gordon, 1985; Quigley & Marlatt, 1999). Clients generally exert considerable effort to alter their lifestyle to achieve sobriety, and considerable planned effort is often also needed to maintain sobriety. Clients are taught to identify their behaviors and factors such as high-risk situations and negative emotional states (e.g., anxiety, depression, social pressure, family conflicts), referred to as *triggers*, that usually precede or signal their desire to drink or use drugs or their actual use of alcohol or (Daley & Salloum; Gorski & Miller;

Marlatt & Gordon). Clients then learn techniques or coping skills to avoid or defuse the particular situations that threaten their sobriety (Huebner & Kantor, 2011). For example, a trigger may be a fight with a spouse, which may be defused by teaching clients anger-control techniques, such as absenting themselves from the situation until they have cooled off and can discuss the problem rationally. Practicing relaxation and stress-reduction techniques and other healthy lifestyle habits can also be useful in avoiding negative states and preventing relapses and are essential components of one's aftercare program (Marlatt & Gordon).

Marlatt and Gordon (1985) suggest that clients also develop plans to follow if drinking or drug use does occur, such as teaching them that consuming a small amount of alcohol or drugs (which some call a *lapse* or *slip)* need not necessarily result in a full-blown relapse and that it is possible to take measures to avert a relapse. Contracting may be used to accomplish this purpose. For example, clients may agree in writing or verbally to call a professional or another individual for assistance should they begin to drink or use drugs. Since clients are often embarrassed or ashamed or feel they have let others down once alcohol or drug use commences, they may fail to stop and seek help. The contract can help them acknowledge that there is a way to conclude the episode successfully. In fact, Marlatt suggests that although relapse prevention may not produce higher abstinence rates, relapses may be shorter and lead to earlier recovery (quoted in Foxhall, 2001).

Effectiveness of Aftercare.   Aftercare or continuing care has not been "a strong and integrated" component of drug treatment (Gerstein & Harwood, 1990). Many individuals treated for alcohol problems also do not receive sufficient continuing care, either because they do not complete the treatment program they enter or due to other barriers such as inadequate insurance to cover this phase of treatment or logistical difficulties (e.g., arranging childcare) (McKay & Hiller-Sturmöhfel (2011). NIAAA's (1987) review of the research literature "support[ed] the traditional view of the importance of aftercare services in alcoholism treatment" (p. 130). More recently, Wexler et al. (1999) found that of 478 inmates randomly assigned to Amity TC or a control group that did not get the in-prison TC services, those who completed the in-prison TC *and* voluntarily completed the TC aftercare program upon release had the lowest recidivism rate (27 percent) compared to about three-quarters of those who participated in the TC but did not complete aftercare or were in the control group.

Aftercare often seems to be comprised of mutual-help group (discussed shortly) participation, rather than formal treatment services. A study of 12 inpatient alcoholism treatment programs serving U.S. Navy personnel found that at the one-year follow-up, aftercare (primarily AA attendance) best predicted treatment outcomes (NIAAA, 2000; Trent, 1998). DATOS researchers also found that among drug users, attending mutual-help groups at least twice a week after treatment was associated with less relapse to cocaine use at the one-year follow up. DATOS researchers emphasize "the importance of connecting patients with some form of after-treatment self-help treatment as a critical ingredient of the treatment process in order to increase the likelihood that gains made during treatment are reinforced and sustained" (Ethridge, Craddock, Hubbard, & Rounds-Bryant, 1999, p. 108). A 24-month follow-up study of clients in 26 drug treatment programs in the Los Angeles area also showed that a minimum of weekly participation in Twelve-Step programs following treatment resulted in greater abstinence from illicit drugs and alcohol (Fiorentine, 1999).

There may be some circularity to the argument that aftercare participation (including attendance at mutual-help group meetings) results in greater gains. Those who are doing well may be the ones predisposed to participate in aftercare programs, while those who are not doing well may shun them. However, McKay and Hiller-Sturmöhfel (2011) indicate that of 20 controlled continuing care studies conducted since the 1980s

on alcohol or drug use disorders (most involved a cognitive behavioral approach), the later studies showed greater effectiveness, suggesting that these treatments may be improving. Those that lasted at least 12 months or made greater efforts to keep clients involved, including inclusion of significant others, also seemed to produce better results. Tailoring continuing care approaches to clients' needs and preferences should also be a priority.

Maintenance

Maintenance is a crucial part of the treatment continuum because it lasts throughout the individual's life. However, it generally receives the least attention. Approaches to maintenance vary, depending on the individual's needs and preferences. Undoubtedly the most popular method of maintenance is continued use of mutual-help groups like Alcoholics Anonymous and Narcotics Anonymous (discussed at the end of this chapter). Some people drop into aftercare services or contact a professional as they feel the need. Practicing the relapse-prevention techniques learned in intensive treatment, outpatient services, or aftercare components is also important in a long-term maintenance program.

One statement that can be made about those treated for chemical dependency is that their relapse rates are high, regardless of the type of treatment they receive. Perhaps two-thirds or more of clients with alcohol problems relapse, making the treatment effectiveness literature difficult to evaluate (NIAAA, 1987). McLellan and colleagues (2000) note that 40 to 60 percent of people with alcohol or drug problems relapse, They also note that rates of treatment noncompliance are similar for people who have asthma, diabetes, and hypertension. These are also chronic illnesses with behavioral aspects. Rather than total prevention of relapse, chemical dependency specialists have come to realize that reduced drug use and longer periods of abstinence are also indicators of success.

Studies on the efficacy of teaching relapse prevention as a maintenance strategy have yielded some positive results. Despite the difficulties in studying mutual-help groups mentioned earlier in this chapter, research on Alcoholics Anonymous as an approach to aftercare and maintenance generally suggest positive results in helping people with alcohol use disorders refrain from drinking (Bradley, 1988; Emrick, 1987; Fiorentine, 1999).

Education and Psychoeducation

Didactic *education* about chemical abuse and dependency is also part of the treatment continuum. It is an essential element of almost all the components of the service system we have discussed. Whether it is education about the physiological effects of alcohol and other drugs presented to patients during their brief stay in detoxification programs or education about the effects of chemical dependency on the family presented to clients and their loved ones during intensive treatment, accurate information can address misconceptions, present the controversies in the field, and provide a foundation for rehabilitation and recovery.

Psychoeducation has become increasingly popular in the human service professions. It combines the presentation of didactic information to increase knowledge with a variety of other techniques to help clients make desired changes and to provide support. Among the methods employed are role-plays (e.g., to practice communication or assertiveness skills), structured exercises (e.g., genograms or other family exploration exercises), homework assignments (e.g., reading, charting behaviors, or keeping journals), and group discussion.

Although education or psychoeducation are part of all the components of treatment, they can also be primary services occupying their own place on the continuum of care. For example, in addition to a fine, license suspension, and any jail term, those convicted of driving while intoxicated (DWI) or driving under the influence (DUI) are usually required to attend an educational program. These programs describe the effects of alcohol and other drugs on behavior, allow participants to review the circumstances that led to

their DWI or DUI arrest and consider ways to avoid such problems in the future, present the signs and symptoms of chemical abuse and dependency, and help participants consider whether they are comfortable with their current use of alcohol or other drugs. Students in DWI or DUI courses may be screened for substance use disorders and referred to treatment if indicated, but many do not meet the criteria for these diagnoses.

Education and psychoeducation may also be the primary services offered to youths apprehended by law enforcement on minor-in-possession-of-alcohol charges or other alcohol- and drug-related infractions. The juvenile courts may also require parents to attend educational sessions when their child has been involved in an alcohol- or drug-related incident. High schools, colleges, and universities have established alcohol and drug education courses for those referred for disciplinary action after illicit drug use, underage drinking, or causing disturbances or damaging property while intoxicated. These institutions are also using education and psychoeducation (and sometimes brief interventions) to help students explore the relationship between alcohol and other drug use and sexual behavior, including contracting sexually transmitted diseases, and the role that alcohol or other drug use can play in hazing and sexual assault. Despite the wide use and presumed beneficial effects of educational lectures, films, and groups, when used alone, they have received low marks in helping people with alcohol problems change their drinking behaviors (Miller et al., 1995; Miller & Wilbourne, 2002; Moyers and Hester, 1999). Education as a tool in preventing chemical abuse and dependency is discussed at length in Chapter 7.

Adjunctive Services

The final component of the treatment continuum is *adjunctive services* (also see Chapter 5 of this text). In addition to substance abuse or dependence, a systems or multidimensional approach requires the remediation of employment, legal, family, health, and other problems the client is experiencing. In NIDA's large-scale DATOS study, researchers found that clients were receiving less adjunctive services (medical, psychological, family, legal, educational, and employment) than indicated in earlier research, especially medical and psychological services (Ethridge et al., 1995; Ethridge, Hubbard, Anderson, Craddock, & Flynn, 1997). Although vocational rehabilitation has long been an adjunct to chemical dependency treatment, Hser and colleagues (1999) also found that only ten percent of drug abuse clients' job training and housing needs were met.

A referral is sufficient for some clients to avail themselves of adjunctive services. Others need additional assistance. For some, this may involve coordinating and monitoring adjunctive services for the client. The terms *case management* and *care management* are used to describe these coordination and monitoring functions. Some state, county, and local agencies have special case-management units to assist clients with multiple problems. Clients served by these units generally (1) have problems that are severe and persistent, (2) have a history of involvement with the chemical dependency or mental health service delivery systems or both, and (3) have had difficulty in utilizing available services. Monitoring can prevent crises through the early recognition of new and recurring problems (Weil et al., 1985). Most outpatient substance abuse treatment programs provide case-management services, although what constitutes case management differs widely across programs (Alexander, Pollack, Nahra, Wells, & Lemak, 2007).

Case management has gained more attention from chemical dependency treatment providers, primarily for populations who have multiple and long-term needs. Case-management models have been used with various drug-abusing populations: intravenous drug users, methadone maintenance clients, HIV-positive drug users, drug-abusing pregnant women, formerly homeless women, youths, and parolees (Ashery, 1992; Siegal & Rapp, 1996). Many creative attempts have been made to use case management, such as the approach Levy and associates (1992, 1995) describe to reach out

to drug abusers in a combined program of case management and peer support. In addition to its use in providing services to clients with multiple needs, private and public health insurance providers use case management to control both the services drug-abusing clients use and the costs of assisting them.

If human service professionals are to continue to support a systems, multidimensional, or biopsychosocial view of substance abuse treatment, it is necessary to demonstrate that addressing problems in addition to the substance abuse or dependence promotes better outcomes for clients. McLellan and McKay (1998) note that clients benefit from adjunctive services when their problems are severe enough to warrant services. After studying 742 male military veterans who had received substance abuse treatment, McLellan and colleagues (1981) found "little relation" between the severity of the clients' substance use and functioning in most areas of life, indicating that substance abuse treatment alone may not be sufficient to help clients address employment, housing, and other problems. These problems may require specific adjunctive interventions. DATOS supports this contention in that "client reports indicated that drug abuse counseling alone did not address their wide ranging service needs" (Etheridge et al., 1995, p. 9).

A large-scale study of supported work demonstration programs indicated that compared to controls, substance abusers participating in these programs had greater employment and less criminal activity, even though drug use did not differ between the two groups (Manpower Demonstration Research Corporation, 1980). Hser and colleagues (1999) studied 171 clients and found that, in descending order, their most frequent needs were for job training, transportation, housing, and medical services. Those clients who expressed a need for a certain service and received that service improved more on that domain than clients who expressed a need but did not get the service or who did not express a need for a service. Clients whose expressed needs were met also stayed in treatment longer. Clients who asked for and received housing services and child care to attend treatment showed more improvement on drug problem severity scores, but other services were not related to improvements in drug problems. Friedmann, Hendrickson, Gerstein, & Zhang (2004) also conducted a study, this one using data from the National Treatment Improvement Evaluation Study, with a sample of 3,100 who needed services beyond core short- or longer-term residential services, outpatient methadone, or other outpatient services. The benefits of matching services to needs in five areas (medical, mental health, family, vocational skills, and housing) were strongest for reduced drug use among those with more needs and for those in long-term residential programs, though mental health services were not related to reduced drug use.

Fiorentine (1998) provides a somewhat different view of adjunctive services. He studied 330 clients and found little evidence to support the idea that clients' *unresolved* employment, housing, health, and other needs result in poorer treatment engagement or more drug use. He suggests that even resolution of these other problems will not likely improve drug use outcomes.

Though evidence indicates that case management may be effective in helping clients access services, it is not easy to separate the effects of case management from those of the other services the client receives (Ridgely & Willenbring, 1992). A number of studies with samples of substantial size do support the use of various approaches to case management to help chemically dependent clients address their multiple needs, perhaps because they encourage clients to use more services or to make better use of those services. Siegal and colleagues (1996) found that military veterans with substance use disorders who received strengths-based case management had increased income and days employed. Conrad et al. (1998) studied residentially-based case management for homeless military veterans who were chemically dependent and found improvements in alcohol problems, employment, housing, and health. Differences between this group and a control group diminished in the year following treatment.

Among substance-abusing pregnant women, Laken and Ager (1996) and Laken, McComish, and Ager (1997) found that case management along with transportation improved treatment retention. Metja et al. (1997) found improvements in treatment access, retention, and outcomes among intravenous drug users receiving case-management services. Cox et al. (1998) also found that homeless, chronic public inebriates who received case management did somewhat better with regard to drinking outcomes and living situation, compared to a control group. A study of clients in eight Philadelphia outpatient substance abuse programs who received clinical case management found improvements in alcohol use, family relations, and medical, employment, and legal statuses (McLellan et al., 1999).

Platt et al. (1998) found that "in many ways, case management is the most valuable of adjunctive services for substance abusers in treatment" (p. 1053). Individual studies do suggest beneficial effects, but a systematic review concluded that while case management can be effective in linking clients with substance use disorders to adjunctive services, the evidence is not conclusive that it produces less substance use or other beneficial outcomes (Hesse, Vanderplasschen, Rapp, Broekaert, & Fridell, 2007).

More Treatment Effectiveness Issues

Some concerns about treatment effectiveness cut across treatment modalities, including length and intensity or amount of treatment, client and therapist characteristics, theoretical approaches to treatment, and costs.

Length of Stay

In general, Gerstein and Harwood (1990) found improvement among illicit drug users was positively related to length of stay in treatment, whether clients participate in therapeutic communities, outpatient methadone maintenance programs, or other outpatient services. Other studies support this finding. For example, DATOS researchers report that stays, or *treatment thresh-olds*, of at least three months in long-term residential treatment (including therapeutic communities) and of at least a year in outpatient methadone treatment were associated with better outcomes than were shorter stays (Simpson, Joe, & Brown, 1997). McLellan and McKay (1998) offer two ideas as to why length of stay is positively related to better outcomes. One is that positive changes may come about gradually as treatment progresses; therefore, clients should be encouraged to remain in treatment. Given high treatment dropout rates, the other explanation is that more highly motivated clients are already disposed to remain in treatment and to have more positive outcomes; thus, motivation, rather than length of stay, may be the key to their recovery. Others suggest that length of stay for those with drug disorders may not be as clear cut an issue as once thought (Wallace & Weeks, 2004).

The evidence on length of stay for clients with alcohol use disorders is equivocal. Some studies show that increased stays did not improve client outcomes, while in other studies, longer stays were associated with more positive outcomes (NIAAA, 1987; Trent, 1998). Two studies of note found that shorter stays in inpatient alcoholism treatment were as effective as longer stays. Barnett and Swindle (1997) found that 28-day programs produced only slightly better outcomes among VA patients than did 21-day programs, and Trent (1998) found no statistically significant differences in outcomes for active duty military personnel who received either four weeks or six weeks of treatment. However, intensive inpatient programs of even three or four weeks' duration have become increasingly scarce in this era of health care cost containment. Perhaps more relevant in today's world is that Project MATCH participants improved whether they received four or 12 sessions of treatment over a 12-week period (Project MATCH Research Group, 1997a; see Box 6.5 on pp. 141–143).

In addition to length of stay, whether clients complete or graduate from the treatment program may also be an issue. For example, in a study of military veterans participating in an intensive outpatient substance abuse treatment program, graduates used significantly fewer psychiatric inpatient bed days one-year after program completion compared to dropouts; they were also more likely to be abstinent and less likely to have a full blown relapse or be incarcerated at 6-month follow-up (Wallace & Weeks, 2004). The question that still begs to be answered is: How much treatment is enough for a given client?

Amount and Intensity of Services

Studies generally indicate that receiving more services promotes better treatment outcomes. McLellan, Grissom, Brill, Durell, Metzger, and O'Brien (1993) studied four private substance abuse treatment programs—two residential and two outpatient—and found that clients fared better in "the programs that provided the most services directed at a particular treatment problem" (p. 253). They also cite evidence from earlier studies that both "quantity and range of services" are positively related to client outcomes.

Similarly, in an examination of 100 treatment studies, Monahan and Finney (1996) found that higher-intensity treatments (i.e., more hours of services) produced abstinence rates 15 percent higher than lower-intensity treatments. The Project MATCH Research Group (1998b) found that intensity may be important in outpatient treatment. Overall, clients had similar drinking outcomes regardless of which of three treatments they received. However, outpatient clients who received four sessions of motivational enhancement therapy over the 12 weeks were less likely to be abstinent or drinking nonproblematically at the end of the therapy, and they took longer to achieve abstinence or to drink without problems than those who received once-weekly sessions of either cognitive behavioral therapy or Twelve-Step facilitation therapy over the 12-week treatment period. DATOS provides a somewhat different picture. Ethridge et al. (1999) found that length of time in treatment was important in improving outcomes among cocaine abusers, but the amount of counseling and self-help group participation during treatment was not, suggesting that packing more services into a shorter time period may not promote better treatment outcomes. More information is needed on the combination of setting, duration, service intensity, and amount of services in promoting better treatment outcomes.

Client Characteristics

Some of the clearest evidence from alcoholism treatment effectiveness studies is that client characteristics are much more important than treatment type or setting in predicting outcome. According to NIAAA (1990), clients who are "married, stably employed, free of severe psychological impairments, and of higher socioeconomic status" (p. 130) are more likely to have positive outcomes, perhaps because these characteristics promote treatment compliance (O'Brien & McLellan, 1998). DATOS (NIDA, 1999) also indicates that an absence of psychological problems (especially antisocial personality disorder) promotes treatment retention (and by inference, better outcomes) among clients with drug problems. Having no prior legal problems or having legal pressure to stay in treatment also promoted retention. Clients' motivation for treatment is also positively associated with treatment retention (NIDA, 1999; Project MATCH Research Group, 1998a).

These findings also suggest that treatment success may be contingent on helping clients compensate for problems—specifically, severe psychiatric problems, marital difficulties (lack of social support), unstable employment, low income, and low motivation that may hinder treatment progress. Improvements have been made in some of these areas. For example, many communities now have programs that combine psychiatric treatment with chemical dependency treatment (see Chapter 13 of this text). Some chemical dependency treatments incorporate family members and coach them in how to support the individual with an alcohol or drug problem. The previous section of this chapter on adjunctive treatment

also provides evidence of the importance of helping clients address problems such as vocational difficulties in addition to addiction. Chapter 5 addressed motivating clients in the precontemplation or contemplation stages into taking action to solve their problems.

We can also consider the relationship of client satisfaction to treatment outcomes. While patient satisfaction has been emphasized in the health care field, it has received little attention in substance abuse treatment. Findings have been inconsistent in the few studies that have been reported (Zhang, Gerstein, & Friedmann, 2008). Zhang et al. conducted a study using structured computer assisted-interviews with a sample of nearly 5,000 individuals from 68 areas in 17 states attending publicly sponsored methadone, outpatient, and short- and long-term residential drug abuse treatment programs. They found that higher satisfaction was related to less drug use at follow-up over and above length of stay and other patient and program characteristics, though the amount of variance explained was relatively small. The authors suggest that satisfaction might be affected when patients and clinicians do not agree on the course of treatment, and they emphasize that patient satisfaction is an important component of patient-centered care.

Therapist Characteristics

Surprisingly little research has been conducted on the effects of therapist or counselor characteristics on substance abuse treatment outcomes. Research indicates that substance abuse therapists vary in their effectiveness (Luborsky, McLellan, Woody, O'Brien, & Auerbach, 1985; Najavits & Weiss, 1994). However, effectiveness is apparently not related to therapists' credentials or whether they are in recovery themselves (see Hser, 1995; Najavits, Crits-Christoph, & Dierberger, 2000; Project MATCH Research Group, 1998c).

Seemingly more important in determining effectiveness is whether therapists have strong interpersonal skills and can build positive relationships with clients (Najavits & Weiss, 1994). For example, Luborsky and colleagues (1985) reported on 77 clients randomly assigned to nine therapists and found that therapist personality, "particularly the ability to form a warm, supportive relationship" (p. 609), was a key determinant of treatment effectiveness. DATOS supports the importance of counselor/client rapport in promoting treatment success with clients who abuse cocaine or other drugs (Broome, Simpson, & Joe, 1999; Fiorentine & Hillhouse, 1999). Valle (1981) also found that clients who had alcoholism counselors with higher levels of interpersonal functioning (empathy, genuineness, concreteness, and respect) had fewer relapses. Miller and colleagues (Miller & Baca, 1983; Miller, Taylor, & West, 1980) found accurate empathy (see Chapter 5) to be important in predicting client outcomes over a two-year period, although the association deteriorated over time. In general, clients in their study who received directive approaches (advice and feedback about their drinking and minimization of their problems) and those whose treatment was based on empathy and reflective listening fared equally well on drinking outcomes.

One therapist behavior deserved special note: "The more the therapist *confronted*, the more the client drank" (Miller, Benefield, & Tonigan, 1993, p. 455). Fiorentine, Nakashima, and Anglin (1999) found counselors' empathy and helpfulness and other treatment variables more important than client characteristics in predicting clients' treatment engagement and outcomes. Connors and colleagues (1997) studied *therapeutic alliance*—the bond between client and therapists and their agreement about the goals and tasks of treatment—among Project MATCH clients. After controlling for many other client, therapist, and treatment characteristics, alliance was significantly related to outpatient clients' treatment outcomes but accounted for no more than 3.5 percent of the variance for any single outcome measure. The results were even more modest among aftercare clients.

Viewing the issue from the perspective of the content of treatment providers' work, rather than their affective qualities, Costello (1975) reviewed 58 alcoholism treatment effectiveness studies and discovered that the staff in more effective programs made home visits to clients and reached out to collaterals. In Luborsky et al.'s (1985) study, in which clients were randomly assigned to therapists, therapists' fidelity to the type of therapy they were assigned to provide was also an important factor in treatment effectiveness.

Matching clients and therapists may be another approach to improving client outcomes. McLachlan (1974) studied 94 alcoholics and found that those who matched their group therapist on conceptual level (interpersonal development) did better in maintaining abstinence than those who were not well matched on this characteristic. Chemical dependency studies provide insufficient information to determine whether matching clients and therapists on gender, ethnicity, age, and other factors would improve treatment outcomes but some studies have been conducted.

A retrospective study indicated that women, Latinos, and clients over age 35 were more likely to be abstinent at follow-up if they had a counselor of the same gender, and women were more likely to be abstinent if they were of the same ethnicity as their counselor (Fiorentine & Hillhouse, 1999). However, ethnic and gender matches were not associated with treatment engagement. In addition, having a more empathic counselor (as rated by clients) resulted in greater engagement and abstinence and was more important than gender or ethnic congruence for all groups except Latinos, who benefited more from gender congruence. Suarez-Morales and colleagues (2010) note studies showing that compared to members of other ethnic groups, Hispanic clients who had a therapist of the same ethnicity tended to do better on treatment engagement, participation, and abstinence, but given the wide variation among Hispanic groups, these researchers wanted to know more about what aspects of the ethnic matching accounted for these differences. Using a sample of 16 Hispanic therapists and 235 clients randomly assigned to them for specific types of treatment, they found that matching clients and counselors on birthplace and client-counselor differences in "Hispanicism" and "Americanism" scores were not related to clients' treatment participation or days of substance use. Counselors' birthplace and their Hispanicism and Americanism scores were not related to clients' treatment participation but they were related to days of substance abuse. On average, clients whose counselors were born in Latin America and had higher Americanism scores used substance on more days, while clients whose counselors had higher Hispanicism scores used substance on fewer days. Though it is unclear why the therapists' characteristics affected substance use in this way, it was the counselors' characteristics, rather than client's ethnic or cultural match with their counselor, that had the greatest effect on substance use.

Theoretical Perspectives

A cornucopia of theoretical perspectives has been used to treat people with substance use disorders, including behavioral, cognitive, and psychodynamic (see, for example, Cohen et al., 2009; Miller & Wilbourne, 2002; Ries, Fiellin, Miller, & Saitz, 2009; Witkiewitz & Marlatt, 2011). In a review of just one major school of thought, cognitive-behavioral approaches (broadly defined), Kadden (1994) identified the following techniques of interest in treating people with alcohol problems: coping skills training, relapse prevention, behavioral marital and family therapy, community reinforcement, behavioral self-control training, aversion therapy, cue exposure therapy, and motivational interviewing.

According to NIAAA (1987), "In contrast to classical, dynamic, insight-oriented psychotherapy, alcoholism counseling is directive, supportive, reality centered, focused on the present, short term, and oriented toward real world behavioral changes" (p. 127). Much of the same can be said

for the treatment of illicit drug abusers. Traditional, insight-oriented psychotherapy has historically been viewed as ineffective in helping clients terminate drug use because psychotherapists often failed to encourage abstinence, and treatment often centered on anxiety-arousing topics, which may have prompted patients to drink or use drugs (Rounsaville, Carroll, & Back, 2009; also see Rawson, 1995). In addition, exploration of psychological, often unconscious, conflicts did little to help patients understand their addiction because to date, scientists have not discovered the causes of chemical dependency. Miller and Wilbourne (2002) found most psychotherapy ineffective in treating alcohol problems, though client-centered therapy (based on Carl Rogers's [1951] work) did show positive results in some studies. Nonetheless, in one study using random assignment of 260 male court referrals, those given rational behavior therapy or insight-oriented treatment did better in reducing drinking than those referred to an AA-focused discussion group (Brandsma, Maultsby, & Welsh, 1980). The insight group had the fewest legal problems, and those in all groups did better than controls that pursued their own treatment arrangements. Perhaps insight-oriented psychotherapy or other theoretical perspectives should not be summarily dismissed. At a minimum, people with alcohol and drug problems who wish to address additional concerns following sobriety may benefit from a variety of treatment perspectives. Though there may be a preference for cognitive-behavioral therapies in treating substance use disorders, we continue to agree with Luborsky and colleagues (1985) that there is really little evidence to suggest that some theoretical perspectives are substantially better than others.

Today, the word *psychotherapy* is used broadly to encompass many types of treatment. It is therefore important that researchers carefully describe the treatment that they are studying. One effort in this regard is the use of treatments that have been specified in manual form along with supervision and review of tapes of treatment sessions in order to ensure that therapists are maintaining fidelity to the treatment under investigation (see Box 6.5 on pp. 141–143).

Substantial work has been done to match clients with treatments based on theoretical perspectives hypothesized to be most likely to meet their needs. Although Project MATCH researchers (again, see Box 6.5 on pp. 141–143) found few benefits of matching clients to treatments based on hypothesized fits between client characteristics and theoretical treatment perspectives, this does not mean that client/treatment matching studies should be abandoned. For example, O'Malley and associates (1992) found that supportive treatment produced more abstinent patients than coping skills treatment; however, among patients who initiated drinking, those who received coping skills treatment were least likely to relapse.

Aversion therapy or counterconditiong is another theoretical perspective. Cannon and associates (1988) report that one corporation "discontinued the use of aversion therapy in all 21 of its hospitals to improve its ability to recruit patients" (p. 205). Frawley and Howard (2009), however, call aversion therapy "a powerful tool in the treatment of alcohol and drug addiction. Its goal is to reduce or eliminate the 'hedonic memory' or craving for a drug and to simultaneously develop a distaste and avoidance response to the substance" (p. 843). When used, aversion therapy is generally combined with other chemical dependency treatment services. (For a review of aversion procedures using nausea producing drugs or mild electrical stimulation to the forearm, safety contraindications, and criticisms, see Frawley [1998]). Nausea and electrical aversion have been tried in alcohol, marijuana, and cocaine/amphetamine dependence treatment. Several medical panels and scientific boards support these aversion treatments (Frawley & Howard).

A small number of studies suggest the effectiveness of apneic aversion (in which breathing is briefly ceased), nausea aversion, and covert sensitization for people with alcohol use disorders (Miller & Wilbourne, 2002), though Elkins (1975) notes serious ethical concerns about apneic aversion, which can

be traumatic. More studies have been conducted on electrical aversion, but the evidence supporting it seems relatively weak (Miller & Wilbourne). "Covert sensitization employs imagery of unpleasant stimuli to elicit the aversive responses needed to accomplish … counter conditioning" (p. 144), and Shorkey (1993) notes that it is the only aversive conditioning technique that can practically be employed by most human service professionals.

It is probably accurate to say that treatment providers bring diverse theoretical perspectives to their work. Many have developed theoretical perspectives of their own that are a combination of approaches. In many cases, treatment providers try several approaches in an attempt to find one that will work with a particular client.

The Mesa Grande project is an analysis of the research evidence for treatment approaches for alcohol use disorders by William R. Miller and colleagues (Miller et al., 1995; Miller, Wilbourne, & Hettema, 2003; Miller & Wilbourne, 2002). In 2003, Miller and his colleagues wrote that "the negative correlation between scientific evidence and treatment-as-usual remains striking, and could hardly be larger if one intentionally constructed treatment programs from those with the least evidence of efficacy" (p. 41). With more emphasis on evidence-based practice, this may be changing, though some significant gaps between research and practice remain (Herbeck, Hser, & Teruya, 2008). Meta-analyses based on statistical pooling of studies are another tool to help determine what works in the alcohol and drug treatment fields (for a discussion of the these approaches, see Heather, 2007). The Cochrane Collaboration in particular now supports a number of these meta-analyses.[2]

To bridge the gap between evidence from the treatment effectiveness literature and the treatment service programs provide, in 1999, the National Institute on Drug Abuse established the Clinical Trials Network so that researchers and community-based service providers could "cooperatively develop, validate, refine, and deliver new treatment options to patients in community-level clinical practice." In addition, the Center for

Substance Abuse Treatment, part of SAMHSA, operates 13 regional Addiction Technology Transfer Centers (ATTCs) and a national ATTC office, which work to increase practitioners' "access to state-of-the art research and education."

Cost Effectiveness of Treatment

Though national studies are limited, research continues to demonstrate that treating alcohol and drug problems produces favorable cost/benefit ratios (Cartwright, 2000; Center for Substance Abuse Treatment, 2009). For example, the widely cited California Drug and Alcohol Treatment Assessment (CalDATA) found a return of $7 for each dollar invested in treatment (Gerstein et al., 1994). Most of the savings were due to reduced crime. A subsequent study, the California Treatment Outcome Project (CalTOP), which improved on the CalDATA methodology, also found a return ratio of more than 7:1 (Ettner et al., 2006). The ratio was based on pre- and post-treatment admission data that included health and mental health care, criminal activity, and earnings.

More information is needed on the costs and benefits of particular treatments for substance-use disorders. In early work on this issue, Holder and colleagues (1991) found that generally, more expensive treatments appeared to be less effective than lower costs treatments, but a subsequent study found "no relationship between cost and effectiveness" (Finney & Monahan, 1996). Work continues on estimating the costs of various treatment modalities (French, Popovici, & Tapsell, 2008). To maximize scarce resources, research is needed on matching clients with the treatments that are most effective for them and the least costly.

Nontraditional Approaches

Nontraditional treatments, some of which are referred to as *natural, complementary,* or *alternative therapies medicine* for substance use disorders (see Boucher, Kiresuk, & Trachtenberg, 1998; Dean,

2005), include many more approaches than we are able to discuss here. Among them are the use of nutrition, vitamins, and herbal remedies (Lu, Liu, Zhu, Shi, Liu, Ling, & Kosten, 2009); hypnosis and meditation in many forms (Boucher et al., O'Connell & Alexander, 1994), including recent scholarly attention to the use of mindfulness-based therapies (Marcus & Zgierska, 2009; Zgierska et al., 2009); the application of religion, spirituality, and prayer (Boucher et al.; Galanter, 2009b; Muffler, Langrod, Richardson, & Ruiz, 1997); stress-reduction and relaxation techniques (Shorkey, 1993); biofeedback or alpha-theta brainwave training (Peniston & Kulkosky, 1989, 1992); Internet-based screening tools, interventions, and support groups (Cunningham, Kypri, & McCambridge (2011); expert systems consisting of computer feedback reports and self-help manuals gauged to the stage of change or treatment (Prochaska et al., 2001); smartphones that allow patients to check in and enter information on how they are doing and request emergency or other assistance and that provide reminders to take medications and keep appointments, motivational or inspirational messages and stories, locations of mutual-help group meetings, and other features (Gustafson et al., 2001); and node-link mapping, in which a visual or pictorial display is created of client problems or issues and potential solutions (Joe, Dansereau, Pitre, & Simpson, 1997). Readers may be interested in exploring any or all of these approaches. The discussion of nontraditional and alternative treatments that follows focuses on some of those most commonly discussed in the addiction field, including controlled or moderated drinking, acupuncture, and contingency management (incentives to promote abstinence or reduce drug use).

Controlled or Moderated Drinking

The terms *controlled drinking* and *moderated drinking* have been used to describe both the desire of some alcoholics to drink in a socially acceptable manner and the treatment goal of teaching alcoholics to drink in a socially acceptable manner. The idea of teaching alcoholics to drink in a controlled manner has been met with more than spirited debate since the goal for clients in traditional treatment programs is usually abstinence.

Many individuals reject total abstinence, and apparently some people who have drunk in an abusive or alcoholic manner go on to adopt more moderate drinking practices (Armor, Polich, & Stambul, 1978; Connors, 1993b; Pattison, Sobell, & Sobell, 1977). Some do this following treatment or after minimal contact with detoxification units or information or referral centers or without any assistance from professionals or mutual-help groups (Humphreys, Moos, & Finney, 1995; Sobell, Cunningham, & Sobell, 1996; Witkiewitz & Marlatt, 2011). In his classic longitudinal study of alcoholic men, Vaillant (1983), who supports the disease theory of alcoholism, found that a substantial number returned to non-problematic social drinking without treatment. If it were possible to determine which individuals could achieve abstinence or moderate drinking without professional assistance "limited treatment resources could be more usefully directed to persons who may need them to recover" (Humphreys et al., 1995, p. 439).

Our discussion of controlled or moderated use is limited to alcohol, since the controlled use controversy has centered on this substance. However, some people apparently use drugs such as marijuana and even heroin and other narcotics (called "chipping") in a controlled manner throughout their lives (Callahan & Pecsok, 1988).

The controversy over controlled drinking gained momentum in the 1970s when Rand Corporation researchers published a NIAAA-funded study titled *Alcoholism and Treatment* (Armor et al., 1978; also see Ray & Ksir, 1987). Similar to reports by Pattison and colleagues (1977), they found that 18 months following contact with an alcoholism treatment program, a number of the male patients in the study sample reported that they were drinking in a so-called controlled (non-problematic) fashion or were alternating between drinking and abstention, even though they had been treated in traditional, abstinence-oriented programs. A second follow-up conducted four years after treatment found that 46 percent were in remission (i.e., 28 percent were currently abstinent and 18 percent were "drinking without problems"; the remaining 54 percent were drinking "with problems") (Polich, Armor, & Braiker, 1981). As with many other research studies, this one was criticized on methodological grounds. More noteworthy was the controversy generated because the study challenged the notion that abstinence is the only viable goal for people with alcohol dependence.

The work of Mark and Linda Sobell (1973a, b) added to the consternation. The Sobells used individualized behavior therapy in an effort to teach individuals who had lost control of their drinking to drink in a controlled manner while comparing them with similar individuals who were treated with a goal of abstinence. The individualized behavior therapy used to teach patients controlled drinking included identification and practice of alternative responses to excessive drinking, electric shocks, education, comparison of videotapes of themselves when drunk and sober, and other procedures. (Another technique that has been used in controlled drinking is teaching clients to discriminate their blood-alcohol levels.) After two years, the Sobells (1976) concluded from treatment outcomes that *some* alcoholics could successfully pursue controlled drinking if they were treated by a professional skilled in using this approach. They cautioned that this did not mean that all or a majority of alcoholics would be appropriate for this treatment.

Several attacks of this work followed. In an effort to discern what later happened to the original 20 alcoholics taught controlled drinking, Pendery, Maltzman, and West (1982) conducted a 10-year follow-up. They found that only 1 person had continued to engage successfully in controlled drinking, that 8 had continued to drink problematically, that 6 had become abstinent, that 4 had died from alcoholism, and that 1 was missing. How these 20 alcoholics would have fared if treated in an abstinence-oriented program from the outset cannot be determined, and it is not known how they fared over the long run in relation to the comparison group.

After reviewing research on the subject, Connors (1993b) concluded that "in fact, moderate drinking interventions with low to moderate severity alcohol abusers may be the treatment of choice" (p. 125). He also noted that good outcomes are less likely with "severely dependent alcoholics" (p. 125), but the hypothesis that achieving moderation is "inversely related to severity of alcohol dependence" has met with mixed results in the research (p. 129). Note the word *moderation* rather than *controlled* drinking in this paragraph, which may be used to avoid the negative connotations associated with the controlled drinking controversy. In a more recent study, Dawson and colleagues (2005) found that about one-quarter of people with prior year or previous alcohol dependence ever received treatment, and of all those classified with past dependence, 25 percent were still dependent in the past year, 27 percent were in partial remission, 12 percent had no current symptoms but their drinking pattern put them at risk of relapsing, 18 percent were low-risk drinkers, and 18 percent were abstainers.

NIAAA (2010) advises those who have an alcohol use disorder to abstain, but it also recognizes that some people would prefer to cut down on their drinking. For those who wish to cut down, NIAAA has a list of suggestions such as listing reasons why one wants to change, setting goals, keeping track of the number of drinks consumed, and avoiding triggers that may result in excessive drinking.

There is considerable interest in the issue of controlled drinking in other countries. In a study of 103 alcohol-dependent patients admitted to an abstinence-based program in Germany, 43 percent reportedly remained abstinent throughout the 36-month follow-up period (Bottlender, Spanagel, & Soyka, 2007). Of the remainder, only four seemed to be able to practice controlled drinking, with the authors concluding that controlled drinking cannot be recommended to those who are alcohol dependent.

Surveys of alcoholism treatment providers in the United States and Canada indicate lower acceptance of moderated drinking as a viable treatment goal than in countries such as Britain, Norway, and Australia (Klingemann & Rosenberg, 2009; Rosenberg & Melville, 2005). In a Swiss study, controlled drinking was reportedly well accepted, but more so in outpatient than inpatient programs (Klingemann & Rosenberg). Controlled drinking was also more acceptable as an intermediate rather than final treatment goal and generally for those with less severe drinking problems and more social stability. The study's authors believe that acceptance of controlled drinking is in keeping with a trend in Switzerland toward consumer-oriented services, which may encourage more people to participate in treatment.

Interest in moderation led Kishline (1996a, b) to develop a self-help program called Moderation Management, based on the ideas that drinking problems fall along a continuum rather than being an all-or-nothing phenomenon and that "brief behavioral self-management approaches" can help people control their behavior. Kishline acknowledged that moderation is not for everyone and that some people may need to pursue the goal of abstinence. According to various accounts, in 2000, Kishline decided to pursue a goal of abstinence for herself (Anderson, 2008). However, she was subsequently involved in a drunk driving accident that took two lives, and she pleaded guilty to vehicular homicide. The Moderation Management program continues to operate as do other programs aimed at helping people drink moderately.

Acupuncture

Acupuncture has been used to treat many conditions, including alcohol and drug problems (Jordan, 2006). In theory, acupuncture, an ancient Chinese approach to treating medical and psychological problems with the use of needles, is said to work in the following way:

> Energy (Chi) from oxygen and food flows through the organs and body where it is transformed and distributed. The acupuncturist assesses (through symptoms, physical

examination and pulse diagnosis) the homeostasis of this energy and intervenes with treatment if it is out of balance. (Worner, Zeller, Schwarz, Zwas, & Lyon, 1992, p. 172)

Acupuncture may promote the production of beta-endorphins or other naturally occurring substances in the body, but the precise mechanisms through which it might work are not known (Brumbaugh, 1993).

Acupuncture has been used to treat those with alcohol, opiate, and cocaine disorders. The procedure has been used since the mid-1970s at Lincoln Hospital's Substance Abuse Division in New York. The criminal justice system, such as the drug court program in Dade County (Miami), Florida, has made extensive use of acupuncture. The National Acupuncture Detoxification Association (NADA) offers suggested protocols for the use of acupuncture as an adjunctive treatment for addictions and provides training in the techniques. NADA reports that "more than 1,500 clinical sites in the U.S., Europe, Australia and the Caribbean currently utilize these protocols."[3] The World Health Organization (2003) classifies alcohol dependence and detoxification and opium, heroin, and cocaine dependence "conditions for which the therapeutic effect of acupuncture has been shown but for which further proof is needed."

Alcohol Dependence.   Bullock and colleagues (1987, 1989) found positive results in two controlled, single-blind studies using acupuncture with severe, chronic alcoholics. The experimental groups received acupuncture at points thought to be specific for substance abuse treatment, whereas the controls received it at nonspecific points. The subjects in these studies were given a place to live during the treatment, but other than Alcoholics Anonymous, no traditional chemical dependency treatment was provided. Control subjects were less likely to complete treatment, reported a greater desire to drink, and had significantly more episodes of drinking and detoxification admissions than experimental subjects.

Several subsequent studies have been less positive. Worner and associates (1992) found no difference in treatment or control subjects, all of whom were alcoholics of lower socioeconomic status, with respect to attendance at AA or treatment, treatment completion, detox admissions, or relapses. Subjects were randomly assigned to one of three groups: point-specific acupuncture along with standard, outpatient alcoholism treatment; needleless or sham acupuncture with standard treatment; or standard treatment only. They found that many individuals were unwilling to receive acupuncture treatment. Worner reported a much higher dropout rate from the point-specific acupuncture treatment group than did Bullock. In another study, Bullock et al. (2002) randomly assigned 503 clients in a Minnesota Model-type alcoholism inpatient treatment program to receive specific acupuncture, nonspecific acupuncture, symptom-based acupuncture, or no acupuncture. In general, the acupuncture conditions did not produce greater reductions in drinking than the inpatient treatment program alone. In a systematic review of 11 studies, Cho and Whang (2009) concluded that "results . . . were equivocal, and the poor methodological quality . . . do not allow any conclusion about the efficacy of acupuncture for treatment of alcohol dependence" (p. 1305).

Opiate Dependence.   Interest in the use of acupuncture to treat drug addicts continues, and researchers have worked to find better ways of offering placebo acupuncture treatments in blind studies because needles placed within a certain area of the ear may produce results, even if thought to be in nonspecific points (Avants, Margolin, Chang, Kosten, & Birch, 1995). In a recent pilot study, researchers found positive results from using transcutaneous electric acupoint stimulation (TEAS) for opiate detoxification (Meade, Lukas, McDonald, Fitzmaurice, Eldridge, Merrill, & Weiss, 2010). However, in a study of the use of auricular acupuncture as an adjunct to standard opiate detoxification, Bearn and colleagues (2009) found no effects on withdrawal severity or craving.

In one meta-analysis of acupuncture combined with opioid agonists for opioid detoxification, the researchers found evidence of reduced withdrawal symptoms on some days of the detoxification period but not in 6-month relapse rates (Liu, Shi, Epstein, Bao, & Lu, 2009). A systematic review of clinical trials of acupuncture treatment for opiate addiction also found no benefit of acupuncture over control treatment conditions (Jordan, 2006).

Cocaine Dependence. Among the acupuncture studies that have been conducted are two concurrent studies with cocaine abusers by Bullock and associates (1999). In Study 1, 236 residential clients were randomly assigned to true acupuncture at three ear points, sham acupuncture, or conventional treatment only. In Study 2, 202 day-treatment clients received true acupuncture at five sites for either 8, 16, or 28 sessions. In total, 37 percent of the clients completed the studies. There were no treatment differences between experimental and control participants in the two studies with regard to craving or functional outcomes (physical and social functioning, emotional well-being, etc.). There were also no differences in the percentage of clients with positive urine screens in Study 2. But in Study 1, the conventional treatment-only group had fewer positive screens than the true and sham acupuncture groups. In a study with a strong research design, Margolin and colleagues (2002) randomly assigned 620 cocaine-dependent individuals (one-third also used opiates) from six cities and six treatment sites (three hospital clinics and three methadone maintenance programs) to either NADA protocol auricular acupuncture or one of two control conditions—needle-insertion or relaxation techniques. Participants were followed for six months. Retention rates for all groups were the same. In general, participants reduced their cocaine use but the reductions did not differ by treatment condition. Counseling sessions were not well attended by any group. It seems that "acupuncture cannot yet be considered an effective adjunct to existing drug treatment programs for cocaine, or other stimulants" (Lu et al., 2009, p. 7).

Contingency Management

The principles of operant conditioning or reinforcement provide a useful framework for understanding both addiction and recovery (Higgins et al., 1998; Higgins, Silverman, & Heil, 2008). Many clients are threatened with negative sanctions (e.g., jail time) for failure to attend treatment and to stay clean and sober; however, positive reinforcers or incentives rather than negative reinforcers may be more useful in treating substance abusers (Higgins et al., 1994). For example, evidence indicates that offering take-home methadone doses to clients with drug-free urine tests increases abstinence from cocaine (Stitzer, Iguchi, & Felch, 1992).

One form of contingency management, material incentives, has been used as an adjunct to other forms of treatment (e.g., the Community Reinforcement Approach) to encourage patients to cease illicit drug use (see for example, Higgins et al., 2007; Silverman et al., 1996). Rather than cash payments, vouchers or similar approaches are used in which methadone maintenance clients or cocaine abusers who produce cocaine-free urine specimens earn points or dollar values that can be applied to the purchase of items that might enhance the clients' treatment goals or quality of life (e.g., household, educational, or recreational items), contingent on the approval of a staff member. The value of the reward or vouchers often increases over time. In continuing study of the use of voucher-based incentives, Higgins et al. (2007) compared groups that could earn vouchers worth either a maximum of $1,995 or $499 over a 12-week period for producing cocaine-free urine specimens. The group that could earn more stayed in treatment longer and was more likely to produce continuous cocaine-free specimens.

A problem with using these techniques in practice is that the funds to provide cash or vouchers are not readily available. Some may ask whether the public should bear the costs of paying for such incentives. The benefits to the community, however, in reduced medical, social, and criminal justice spending from helping clients remain drug free may be worth the financial investment (Higgins et al., 1994). To reduce costs, a lottery-type procedure has been used in which clients who meet target goals draw slips of paper from a fishbowl; some slips indicate prizes of varying levels while others contain words of praise but have no monetary value (Petry, Alessi, Marx, Austin, & Tardif, 2005). Though Petry et al. demonstrated the effectiveness of the technique, the size of vouchers or other monetary incentives seems to be related to their effectiveness in promoting drug abstinence (Lussier, Heil, Mongeon, Badger, & Higgins, 2006). Lussier et al.'s meta-analysis also found that more immediate rewards produced better abstinence results, and that, in general, studies of vouchers or other monetary incentives to increase clinic attendance or medication compliance produced positive results.

Other forms of contingency management are also being utilized. For example, Kentucky residents who gave up tobacco for one month could enter a lottery to win prizes. They had to select a nontobacco-using partner to serve as a witness, and counseling, a hotline, and website were available to assist them.

Mutual- and Self-Help Programs

Since the founding of the Washingtonian Societies in the mid 1800s, individuals have banded together to address their drinking problems in mutual-support groups (White, 1998). Today, Alcoholics Anonymous and other mutual-help groups continue to be an important component of the system of care for alcoholics and addicts. They are not part of the continuum of services provided by professionals. Instead, they are composed of volunteers who both "work the program" and maintain these often loosely structured organizations. Members usually take turns chairing the meetings or acting in other capacities. Today, meetings of many mutual-help groups can be attended via the Internet as well as in face-to-face encounters.

Alcoholics Anonymous

The best-known mutual-help group is Alcoholics Anonymous (AA). AA has been described as everything from a form of psychotherapy (Brandsma & Pattison, 1985; Kanas, 1982; Zimberg, 1982) to having an "antipsychotherapy attitude" (Doroff, 1977). It has also been described in systems terms as "a model for synthesizing biomedical, psychosocial, and environmental approaches to arresting alcoholism and achieving what AA members term 'contented sobriety'" (Bradley, 1988).

Alcoholics Anonymous began in 1935, well before most health and human service professionals took a serious interest in assisting alcoholics. AA's founders were two men, a physician and a stockbroker, who shared with each other their problems with alcohol and supported each other in maintaining sobriety. Alcoholics Anonymous estimates that it now has nearly 116,000 groups and approximately 2.1 million members (AA, 2010). Groups meet throughout the United States and many other countries. A directory is available to help members locate meetings, and virtually every phone book in the United States as well as the Internet lists a local number for the organization. Local groups operate rather independently, although the General Service Office, located in New York City, provides kits to assist in starting groups and offers a great deal of literature addressed to recovering persons, their friends and family members, and the various professionals who help alcoholics.

AA is referred to as a *fellowship*. More than a series of meetings, it is a program for the recovering alcoholic to "work" on a daily basis. The program is based on Twelve Steps (see Box 6.6) that refer to the individual's powerlessness over alcohol, the need to recognize one's shortcomings and to make amends, and reliance on a higher power. Many other mutual-help groups for chemically dependent individuals, such as Narcotics Anonymous, and a wide variety of other groups concerned about problems such as compulsive overeating, gambling, and sexual behavior, have adapted the AA approach. Another important

---

BOX 6.6 *The Twelve Steps of Alcoholics Anonymous*

1. We admitted we were powerless over alcohol—that our lives had become unmanageable.
2. Came to believe that a Power greater than ourselves could restore us to sanity.
3. Made a decision to turn our will and our lives over to the care of God *as we understood Him.*
4. Made a searching and fearless moral inventory of ourselves.
5. Admitted to God, to ourselves and to another human being the exact nature of our wrongs.
6. Were entirely ready to have God remove all these defects of character.
7. Humbly asked Him to remove our shortcomings.
8. Made a list of all persons we had harmed, and became willing to make amends to them all.
9. Made direct amends to such people wherever possible, except when to do so would injure them or others.
10. Continued to take personal inventory and when we were wrong promptly admitted it.
11. Sought through prayer and meditation to improve our conscious contact with God, *as we understood Him,* praying only for knowledge of His will for us and the power to carry that out.
12. Having had a spiritual awakening as the result of these steps, we tried to carry this message to alcoholics, and to practice these principles in all our affairs.

Source: The Twelve Steps are reprinted with permission of Alcoholics Anonymous World Services, Inc. ("AAWS"). Permission to reprint the Twelve Steps does not mean that AAWS has reviewed or approved the contents of this publication, or that AAWS necessarily agrees with the views expressed herein. A.A. is a program of recovery from alcoholism only—use of the Twelve Steps in connection with programs and activities which are patterned after A.A., but which address other problems, or in any other non-A.A. context, does not imply otherwise.

---

aspect of AA is its Twelve Traditions, recognizing the group's concerns about anonymity, not taking stands on outside issues, and so forth.

Some people with drinking problems do not seek professional assistance and instead rely on AA to help guide them through recovery. Others use a combination of professional assistance and mutual-help groups. The mutual-help movement does not appeal to all recovering individuals. Some professionals question its utility, believing that it is best reserved for certain types of individuals. However, it is probably accurate to say that most human service professionals concerned about chemical dependency encourage their clients to attend meetings in order to determine if participation is of help to them.

The only requirement for AA membership is a desire to stop drinking. There are no application forms or other requirements for participation,

and there are no membership dues or fees. The groups are supported by members' contributions. Since anonymity is stressed, members generally use only first names at meetings, and members are reminded to "leave what they hear at the meeting" so as not to violate the confidences of others.

A mainstay of AA is its meetings, which are usually about one hour long. In large cities, meetings are often conducted around the clock every day of the week. Individuals who come to meetings intoxicated are usually allowed to remain unless they cause disruption or appear to need immediate medical attention. Some cities have AA clubs where members can drop in whenever they wish.

When AA began, only a few women ventured into the meetings. Today, women are 35 percent of members (AA, 2010). Some AA groups are designated for women only or men only. Other groups are for young people, although anyone young at heart is usually permitted to attend. Some groups are for members of particular ethnic groups, with meetings in the United States sometimes conducted in these members' native languages (see Chapter 11). Various ethnic groups in the United States and other countries have also adapted the principles and format of AA according to their beliefs and customs. Gays and lesbians (see Chapter 12), members of particular professions, and nonsmokers have also organized groups. Sometimes the composition of the group is defined by the location where the meeting is held—an affluent residential neighborhood, the deteriorating downtown section of a city, or a prison.

The Twelve Steps include references to *God*, but AA describes itself as a spiritual rather than a religious program (AA, 1952). God is considered a "higher power" defined according to individual preference. For some, this higher power is God in the traditional sense of organized religion; for others, it may be the AA group or virtually any other spiritual or physical entity. Religious aspects of meetings seem stronger in some groups than in others, but some atheists and agnostics have successfully recovered through the program (AA, 1952).

Groups seem to develop their own "personalities," depending on their membership. Professionals often encourage newcomers to visit several different groups and to attend meetings where they feel most comfortable. Newcomers are also encouraged to attend "90 meetings in 90 days" in order to break old patterns, to become fully immersed in the program, and to not give up too quickly.

The structure of AA meetings is generally consistent in that they begin and end with readings from the book *Alcoholics Anonymous* (AA, 2001) and prayers, but there are different types of meetings. A speaker's meeting is devoted to testimonials by a member or members from the local community or who are invited from out of town. Members sometimes call these talks "drunkalogues." Each speaker tells his or her "story," usually beginning with the circumstances surrounding his or her use and abuse of alcohol and development of alcoholism. Stories often refer to negative consequences

the individual experienced while drinking and how he or she was able to recover, including his or her introduction to and use of AA. The stories assist members, especially new members, in realizing that it is possible to recover, no matter how bad one's problems. They are also cathartic for the storytellers. Birthday meetings, at which members celebrate each year of their sobriety, are often combined with speakers' meetings.

Another format is discussion meetings. The chairperson may offer a topic for discussion (such as guilt, resentments, loneliness, or intimacy) or ask members to suggest a topic. Members may volunteer comments on their personal experiences (rather than give advice to others). The chairperson may proceed in round-robin fashion depending on the number in attendance. Members who do not wish to speak are usually not pressured to do so and may simply say "I pass" when their turn comes. Thus, AA differs from group therapy and other forms of group treatment in which members are expected to verbalize their thoughts and interact with each other during sessions.

At step meetings, the chairperson leads a discussion on one of the Twelve Steps. Members comment on points that helped them work the step or the problems they are encountering in working that step. There is no one way or even recommended ways to work each step. Members offer their thoughts, but each person is free to work the step in a manner suitable to him or her. The book *Alcoholics Anonymous* (AA, 2001), referred to as the *Big Book*, recounts the history of AA and contains the stories of various members. *Big Book* meetings focus on discussion of passages from the book.

Tokens are among the symbols used in AA meetings. For example, chips of different colors may be given to those embarking on sobriety (called a "desire" chip) and after one, two, three, and six months of continuous sobriety to recognize the progress the individual has made. At birthday meetings, members with one or more years of continuous sobriety are presented with a special memento, such as a silver dollar with a hole drilled in it to commemorate each year of sobriety.

Slogans for living, such as "One day at a time" and "Live and let live," are frequently heard at AA and are often displayed on meeting room walls. Meetings generally close with everyone saying "Keep coming back; it works."

AA conventions are held around the United States, and local groups often sponsor social and recreational activities such as dances and family picnics to provide an atmosphere where members can enjoy themselves without exposure to alcohol. For some recovering alcoholics, AA is the focus of their lives. Some criticize this as a dependence on AA or an inability to lead a normal life; others call it an individual choice. There are no rules telling a member how often to attend meetings. Some members continue to attend frequently; others attend less frequently as their sober time increases. In the early stages of sobriety, failing to attend meetings is often considered a "red flag" or a precursor to a "slip" (a lapse or relapse).

Sponsorship is another aspect of the AA program. A newcomer may ask a member to serve as his or her sponsor, and many members utilize one or more sponsors throughout their recovery. A sponsor has usually been an AA member for some time and has achieved a substantial period of sobriety, but there are no requirements to serve in this capacity. Newcomers are encouraged to select sponsors whom they feel have "solid sobriety" and with whom they feel comfortable discussing their recovery. They may also be encouraged to select a sponsor of the same gender to avoid confusing issues of recovery and sexual intimacy, although this issue is obviously different for gay men, lesbians, and bisexual individuals in recovery. The individual who is asked to be a sponsor is free to accept or decline. Sponsors can be a valuable resource, especially when they are readily available to provide support and encouragement. This is particularly important when members experience a crisis, such as a strong desire to drink, or when they want help "working" aspects of the AA program.

Why are people attracted to AA? Perhaps it is the camaraderie—that other members have been there, know the ups and downs of trying to stay sober, and are engaged in the recovery process.

The fellowship of AA is a strong one. In fact, one study suggests that fellowship may be a much more important motivator to attend than spirituality (Nealon-Woods, Ferrari, & Jason, 1995). Visitors and newcomers are often struck by the way members introduce themselves and are acknowledged by fellow members. When members speak at the meetings, they usually begin by saying "I'm so-and-so, and I'm an alcoholic," to which the group responds in chorus "Hi, so-and-so!" Members and visitors are impressed with the unconditional acceptance of the alcoholic. Visitors sometimes remark that the interaction between members was so positive, they wished they were alcoholics! On the other hand, visitors and newcomers may be concerned about some of the behavior at meetings. For example, members may come and go as they wish during meetings, which can seem rude or disruptive. Or they may share their deepest thoughts and feelings but not receive a direct response, which can seem uncaring or disrespectful. Since AA is not group therapy, this behavior is not unusual; in fact, "cross talk" is discouraged.

AA groups have "closed" and "open" meetings. Closed meetings are only for those who consider themselves alcoholics. These meetings provide greater assurance to alcoholics that they are among those who share a common problem and that their anonymity will be protected. Open meetings also serve an important purpose: They allow professionals, family members and friends, those who think they might have a problem, and others to learn more about mutual-help groups, the problems they address, and the people they help. They are an important resource for every community. Anyone considering a career working with people who have alcohol and drug problems should become familiar with these meetings.

Research and Mutual-Help Groups

Alcoholics Anonymous has been touted as having helped more people recover from alcoholism than any other program (Baekeland, 1977; Sheeren, 1988). Some call this aggrandizement "an ill-considered hyperbole" (Baekeland). Others warn that even questioning AA's effectiveness might cause "surprise, annoyance, anger, exasperation, shock, or perhaps even rage" (Glaser & Ogborne, 1982; also see Trimpey, 2003). This may be less so today, since clinicians are operating in an age of evidence-based practice, but conducting randomized controlled trials of AA and similar groups remains virtually impossible despite their unique approach and large following. This is due to the voluntary nature of the groups, concern for members' anonymity, and difficulties in establishing fidelity to the model due to variation from group to group.

Descriptive studies of AA include periodic membership surveys of the organization as well as efforts to identify those most likely to affiliate with AA. A review of studies found that characteristics predictive of AA affiliation are greater use of external supports (i.e., reliance on others) for coping, greater loss of control drinking, more daily alcohol consumption, greater physical dependence, and greater anxiety about drinking (Emrick, Tonigan, Montgomery, & Little, 1993). To this list, McCrady (1998) added greater concern about drinking, stronger commitment to abstinence, less spousal support, and a stronger need to find meaning in life. Nonetheless, it is difficult to predict who will or will not be attracted to AA, and Tonigan, Toscova, and Miller (1996) "argue against efforts to develop omnibus AA profiles" because AA groups are so diverse (p. 69). Emrick's (1987) conclusion remains useful:

> Until specific affiliation characteristics are identified, prudence suggests viewing all alcoholic patients in conventional alcoholism treatment as possible members of AA, while at the same time recognizing that many alcohol-dependent patients recover from their alcohol problems without ever joining the organization. (p. 418)

After noting selection biases in some studies (mainly subjects mandated to attend), one systematic review of controlled studies found that "attending conventional AA meetings was worse than no treatment or alternative treatment" (Kownacki & Shadish, 1999), while a more recent review concluded that "no experimental studies unequivocally demonstrated the effectiveness of AA or TSF [Twelve Step Facilitation] approaches for reducing alcohol dependence or problems" (Ferri, Amato, & Davoli, 2006). Despite other significant methodological problems such as self-selected and convenience samples, a number of individual studies over the last few decades suggest positive benefits from AA, primarily abstinence or reduced drinking, for those who do affiliate (see, for example, Vaillant [1983]; also see Miller and Hester [1980], Emrick [1987], Walsh et al. [1991]) as well as cost effectiveness (Kelly & Keterian, 2011).

Individual studies also give credence to the hypothesis that AA promotes post-treatment abstinence (see, for example, Corrigan, 1980; Cross, Morgan, Mooney, Martin, & Rafter, 1990; Pettinati et al., 1982). In one of the more recent studies, which included 416 men and women who had previously not received treatment for alcohol problems, Moos and Moos (2006) found that those who participated in treatment for 27 weeks or more or in AA for 27 weeks or more during the first year after initiating participation had better outcomes than those who did not participate in either. Those who continued in AA also had better 16-year outcomes while those who received additional treatment did not experience better outcomes.

Additional research might help to determine who affiliates with AA and how, who benefits most from AA involvement, and the mechanisms of these groups that produce change. For example, Montgomery, Miller, and Tonigan (1995) suggest it is a greater degree of involvement, rather than attendance alone that promotes better outcomes. Gossop, Stewart, and Marsden (2007) also found that five years after residential treatment for drug dependence, those who attended NA and AA more frequently had higher abstinence rates from opiates and alcohol than those who attended less often and those who did not attend. McKellar,

Stewart, and Humphreys (2003) also found that AA participation among more than 2,000 alcohol-dependent male military veterans predicted fewer alcohol-related problems that could not be attributed to initial problem severity, motivation, or psychopathology.

Narcotics Anonymous and Other Programs

Narcotics Anonymous (NA) was modeled after AA. Groups began forming in the 1950s often by AA members who were addicted to alcohol and other drugs (Nurco, Wegner, Stephenson, Makofsky, & Shaffer, 1983). NA's Twelve Steps and Twelve Traditions are almost identical to AA's, with drug terminology substituted for alcohol terminology. NA emerged separately from AA because some individuals whose sole drug of abuse was alcohol were uncomfortable with individuals addicted to illicit drugs, whom they associated with the criminal element (Nurco et al.). Today, it is common to hear attendees at AA or NA meetings introduce themselves as "alcoholics" and "addicts."

Cocaine Anonymous, begun in 1982, emerged with the increased use of this drug. The unique aspects of preference for a particular drug may have encouraged the development of this mutual-help group and others, such as Marijuana Anonymous.

There are many other mutual-help groups for people with alcohol and drug problems, some of which are not based on AA principles. Jean Kirkpatrick developed Women for Sobriety (WFS) because she felt AA had a male orientation and that women needed alternatives to help them in their sobriety. WFS is discussed further in Chapter 15, along with the more recently developed Men for Sobriety.

James Christopher founded the nonprofit organization Secular Organizations for Sobriety (SOS), also called Save Our Selves. This cognitively-based or rational thought program is an alternative to the spiritually-oriented Twelve-Step programs (Christopher, 1988, 1989, 1992; Connors & Dermen, 1996). SOS is not critical of other recovery programs. It embraces scientific inquiry about addiction and supports no single theory of addiction. SOS believes it is important for individuals to that they are alcoholics or addicts. It recommends the "Sobriety Priority" (making sobriety one's primary priority or objective) to break the cycle of addiction, which SOS believes is composed of a chemical or physiological cellular need, a learned habit, and denial. The group's philosophy is to empower oneself to live a sober life, rather than relying on a higher power or other outside force. Meetings, led by volunteers, are described as "friendly, honest, anonymous, and supportive." Members are encouraged to utilize the support of other recovering individuals. Family and friends are welcome at meetings.

SMART (Self Management and Recovery Training) Recovery, another organization that seeks to help people recover from alcohol and drug problems, describes itself as having a "scientific foundation, not a spiritual one". It avoids the labels "alcoholic" and "addict." It does not utilize the disease concept or the concept of powerlessness, and sponsors are not part of the program. The program is based on Albert Ellis's rational emotive behavior therapy, which addresses irrational beliefs and using empowerment to abstain. Volunteer coordinators run the meetings and volunteer professional advisors assist the coordinators in their efforts. Members may "graduate" from SMART Recovery, rather than attend meetings indefinitely.

Jack and Lois Trimpey founded Rational Recovery (RR) in 1986. RR is an abstinence-based, *self-help* approach. RR's founders believe there is no evidence that addiction is a disease, most people quit on their own, mutual-help recovery groups and professional treatment are harmful, and the only remedy for addiction is voluntary abstinence (Trimpey, 1996; 2003). RR describes its trademarked Addictive Voice Recognition Technique (AVRT®) as "education on planned abstinence." AVRT calls addiction a "beast" or "voice" within a person that needs to be killed. Although RR materials state that "brain chemistry and genetics are *irrelevant* to recovery," they also indicate that this beast represents a primitive part of the brain dedicated to survival and pleasure; another part of the brain, the neocortex, allows one to think, solve problems, and recognize and defeat the beast. According to RR, achieving abstinence is an event—a decision to stop using (not a process)—and that it is not nearly as difficult as many people think.

Variations of mutual-help groups, including those for people with co-occurring intellectual disability (mental retardation) and substance use disorders, are generally organized and led by a professional. Groups for those with co-occurring mental illness and substance use disorders may be led by individuals recovering from both illnesses or by a professional with a co-leader who is in recovery from one or both illnesses (see Chapter 13). There are also groups for family and friends of people who have substance use disorders (see Chapter 10). The first to emerge was Al-Anon, founded by the wife of one of AA's founders. Naranon is for the family and friends of narcotics addicts, and Co-Anon is for the family and friends of cocaine addicts. Alatot and Alateen are for the children of alcoholics.

Summary

This chapter reviewed the components of the treatment system commonly used by people who have alcohol or drug problems. A wide range of treatments is available to these individuals and their loved ones. Many of these methods show at least some promising results in helping those who seek professional assistance in their recovery. Chemical dependency professionals try to match clients with the treatments that are most likely to meet their needs, but this remains more an art than a science. Mutual-help groups were among the first humane approaches to aid individuals with chemical dependency problems. They remain an important component of the helping system and have grown in number. Researchers are addressing many questions that have been raised about the effectiveness of treatment and mutual-help approaches. More efforts are being made to see that evidence-based treatments are being applied in practice. There is still much knowledge to be gained, especially given that much about the etiology of substance abuse and dependence remains a mystery, relapse rates are high, and many people never get help at all.

CHAPTER 7

Preventing Alcohol and Drug Problems

C. Aaron McNeece
Professor and Dean Emeritus,
Florida State University

Machelle D. Madsen
Florida State University

Overview of Prevention

The concept of *prevention* can be defined in a number of different ways. At the national and international levels, the United States and the United Nations advocate one approach to prevention through lowering the available supply of drugs. The U.S. "War on Drugs," begun in 1971, aimed to prevent use by reducing the country's supply. But, as a *zero-tolerance* policy, it has been fraught with many problems (see Chapter 8). The power of attitudes has been another major focus of the change. Through the media's influences, many public and private groups have attempted to prevent substance abuse. For example, The White House Office of National Drug Control Policy (ONDCP) began the National Youth Anti-Drug Media Campaign in 1998 to place advertisements on television, radio, in print, and online. They have also partnered with national organizations such as the American Academy of Pediatrics, corporations such as Procter & Gamble and Television Networks, providing subsidies for anti-drug content (ONDCP, 2009; Forbes, 2000).

At the grass-roots level, there has been increasing involvement of volunteers in organizations and local action-oriented groups, such as Mothers Against Drunk Driving (MADD), Students Against Destructive Decisions (SADD), Partnership for a Drug Free America, and hundreds of parent and community-based antidrug organizations. These groups have succeeded in developing specific *constituencies* for prevention programs—something that was lacking in earlier efforts, which focused primarily on schoolchildren. It is difficult to disagree with their specific objectives, such as protecting the public from drunk drivers, and collaborating with communications professionals, researchers, and parents to promote drug-free lifestyles. These groups are also free of the disciplinary and procedural constraints that have handicapped many of the chemical dependency professionals working in prevention programs. For instance, MADD and SADD have taken their concerns directly to the legislative arena and the media to get their point of view across. Neighborhood groups have organized public demonstrations outside the homes of suspected drug dealers. Groups such as Neighborhood Watch have mobilized as neighborhood patrols and have notified authorities when drug transactions and impaired drivers are seen. Recognizing the capabilities of these groups, major organizations such as the National Highway Traffic Safety Administration (NHTSA, 2001) and the International Association of Chiefs of Police (IASCP, 2006) recommend to law enforcement officials that they build partnerships in the community with these types of organizations. The Community Anti-Drug Coalitions of America (CADCA) is a unifying agency for such action-oriented groups. It was created at the advice of the President's Drug Advisory Council in 1992 to respond to the growing number of substance abuse–related coalitions to help them become more effective agents of change (CADCA, 2009).

Community groups have advocated for broad changes in policies and practices at all levels, from the grass roots to Washington, and many have developed a national leadership to advocate for reform. There is evidence of the impact of this movement in such issues as Proposition 99 in California. Despite a $20 million campaign by the tobacco industry to defeat it, voters passed an initiative raising taxes on tobacco products by 25 cents and designated the money for youth-oriented preventive education, research, and health care for people with tobacco-related medical problems (Wallack & Corbett, 1990). The tobacco industry has continued to lobby against restrictions on smoking in public places (Barnoya & Glantz, 2006), despite evidence that bans on smoking in both restaurants and bars have had no detrimental impact on their revenues (Martin, 1999; Neergaard, 1997; Ponkshe & Wilson, 1999). The multistate settlement against the tobacco industry will amount to $195.9 billion in payments by the year 2025 (Wilson, 1999). Coupled with other lawsuits and issues extensively considered by Congress, a more radical approach is emerging in both preventing tobacco addiction and dealing with the adverse health consequences of smoking.

The new approach is more consistent with a *harm-reduction model* of prevention, rather than the zero-tolerance philosophy that is still favored by federal law enforcement agencies (Office of the National Drug Control Policy, 2001 also see Chapter 8). The objectives of a harm-reduction approach are to reduce the mortality and morbidity associated with alcohol and drug-related *problems* as well as to reduce the rates of abuse for alcohol and drugs. The more comprehensive view includes social, cultural, and legislative aspects of prevention, rather than simply emphasizing individual responsibility (Wallack & Corbett, 1990).

Environmentally and culturally targeted approaches focus on the social and economic aspects of substance availability and stress objectives designed to reduce the severity of substance-related injuries (Moskowitz, 1989). Some environmentally oriented programs have specifically targeted young people. A good example of the approach was the change in *minimum age of consumption* laws during the early 1980s (Wagenaar, 1986). The social aspects are stressed in the ad campaigns that tell us "Friends don't let friends drive drunk." Another example of the cultural aspects of prevention can be seen in tobacco advertising and responses by various cultural groups to that advertising. According to the Tobacco Control Research Digest (1999), tobacco advertising represents 60 percent of the advertising space for most African American newspapers, compared to 12 percent in mainstream advertising. However, a "swift and powerful backlash" by African American community groups was able to force two minority-targeted brands of cigarettes, Uptown and X, to be pulled from the market. Culturally, the use of tobacco in classrooms, boardrooms, and the workplace has become more of an exception than a tradition.

Harm reduction is a utilitarian approach, one that argues for the greatest good for the greatest number of people and one that recognizes that the indirect consequences of abuse and dependency may be far more serious and widespread than is generally believed (Blane, 1986). Perhaps the best example is the high fatality rate associated with alcohol-related automobile accidents. Another is the high rate of infection (hepatitis, AIDS, etc.) associated with sharing needles among intravenous drug users. Still another is the high crime rate associated with using certain illicit drugs, such as methamphetamines. Advocates of harm-reduction approaches assume that certain drugs will always be abused. By recognizing that many college students abuse alcohol, for example, efforts might be turned toward preventing the students from driving while intoxicated by providing free transportation. A more realistic approach to intravenous drug use might be able to halt the spread of certain diseases by providing clean needles and syringes to people addicted to heroin.

Research emerging from this broader perspective is showing that an *ecological* approach (Brofenbrenner, 1979) to substance abuse prevention is more effective in preventing substance abuse. For example, a joint four-year project of the United Nations Office on Drugs and Crime and the World Health Organization in eight rapidly changing countries found that substance abuse prevention is most effective when it includes schools, families, youth groups, law enforcement, and health service workers. Programs need to include a range of risk and protective factors across a wide intervention perspective—from reducing individual demand to reducing the availability of substances (WHO, 2007). Because of this shift, the United Nations Office on Drugs and Crime now focuses drug prevention work in three core areas rather than just youth: families, schools, and the workplace (2010).

Using a traditional public health model, prevention efforts may be classified as primary, secondary, and tertiary. Preventing new cases from occurring, such as convincing elementary school students not to smoke, is *primary* prevention. Reducing the number of existing cases, generally by identifying and treating those who have a drug or alcohol problem, is *secondary* prevention. The effort to avoid relapse and maintain the health of those who have been treated is *tertiary* prevention (Kinney & Leaton, 1987).

The Institute of Medicine has utilized a prevention paradigm consisting of three completely different categories or levels: *universal* for the general population, *selective* for particularly defined populations at highest risk, and *indicated* for persons already showing problems and requiring intervention to halt progression to more serious problems. This framework may add a more proactive dimension to community-based and individually focused prevention efforts because of its targeting preventive efforts along an operationally applied continuum (Mrazek & Haggerty, 1994). In 1998, researchers at the National Institutes of Mental Health (NIMH) revisited these categories, looking at issues such as pre-interventive research. Zerhouni uses the "four Ps" to describe preventative medicine: *predictive, personalized, preemptive,* and *participatory* to engage individuals with facts and services long before problems occur (2006, p. 3). Although the categories have not changed in places like the Substance Abuse and Mental Health Services Administration's (SAMHSA's) National Registry of Evidence-based Programs and Practices (NREPP, 2010), *protective factors* in a person's life that work to prevent drug use before an intervention takes place and ameliorate severity and relapse after a problem occurs are now being emphasized across many different prevention strategies and ecological contexts (National Research Council & Institute of Medicine, 2009; Weisz, et al., 2005).

Preventive strategies may be grouped into five major categories including: public information and education; service measures; technologic measures; regulatory, legislative, and economic measures; and family and community approaches. Some of these strategies may be directed at preventing or decreasing the use or abuse of alcohol or drugs; others focus on reducing or eliminating the harmful consequences of alcohol and drug use, both to the user and the larger society. All of these, including those that emphasize spirituality and cultural factors, will be discussed in the following pages, but first we will present a brief overview of prevention efforts.

Drug problems among U.S. youth became a public concern in the middle to late 1960s. Obviously, young people had been abusing alcohol before this time, but prevention efforts were relatively insignificant until large numbers of children began experimenting with *illicit* drugs. The early prevention efforts were based on the *information deficit* approach—that children lacked adequate education about the dangers of substances (Belcher & Shinitzky, 1998). During the early 1970s, the belief prevailed that arousing fear would stop substance abusers. Little evidence, however, supported this position, even in cases of life-endangering situations. For example, even after a heart attack, many victims soon return to previous unhealthy behaviors, including smoking (Evans, 1998). In the late 1970s through the early 1990s, the majority of prevention programs focused on ways to reduce the demand for drugs and alcohol, most often by trying to change individual behavior within the venue of social and interpersonal influence. The prevailing attitude was that youth experimented with drugs because their internal value system had not sufficiently developed to resist external pressures (Belcher & Shinitzky, 1998; Evans, 1998). Few of these programs had successful results beyond superficial and transient changes in knowledge and attitudes (Klintzner, 1988; Tobler, 1997). One can change both knowledge and attitudes concerning drugs only to discover through rigorous research that it has little effect on behavior (Kinney & Leaton, 1987). In the 1990s, more comprehensive, research-based, culturally relevant, age-appropriate, interactive, and family-based programs appeared. These types of programs demonstrated more success in the prevention of substance abuse (Belcher & Shinitzky, 1998; Kumpfer, 1998a; Tobler, 1997). Even though professional writings encouraged utilizing these newer approaches, the more traditional educational, non-interactive methods continued to be employed throughout school systems, despite lack of evidence of their effectiveness (Sager, 2000; Tobler, 1997). Some of these more traditional programs, still in use today, refer to research evidence supporting their existence; however, the research methods they utilize tend to be quite weak. A major change in the 1990s was that prevention developers and researchers began to address theoretical issues that cut across common areas of concern regarding alcohol, tobacco, and illicit drugs. They began looking at

risk and protective factors as they affect high-risk behaviors, including substance abuse (Catalano et al., 1998a; Evans, 1998; Pandina, 1996).

In the 2000s, researchers have begun looking more closely at these risk and protective factors regarding substance abuse across areas of race/ethnicity, gender, social context, spirituality, family dynamics, and education (Delva, Mathiesen, & Kamata, 2001; James, Kim, & Armijo, 2000; National Center on Addiction and Substance Abuse and Columbia University [CASA], 2001a; Paschall, Flewelling, & Faulkner, 2000; Vakalahi, 2001). This information is now being consolidated to incorporate multidimensional approaches to programs. Research has indicated that these more comprehensive programs are more effective in influencing drug use behavior (Streke, 2004).

Evidence-based programs can now be submitted to a review process by SAMHSA's National Registry of Evidence-based Programs and Practices (NREPP, 2010). This registry looks at the quality of the research supporting each intervention and the readiness for dissemination to the public. These aspects are rated independently. If approved, they are considered model programs and posted on their website with relevant information about the intervention, including costs, populations served, outcomes, and so forth. In relation to *populations* served, the large majority of the 58 interventions listed (84 percent) targeted children and adolescents; 38 percent of the interventions focused on young adults, 31 percent covered 26–55 year old adults, most of which were incorporated as families supporting their children's involvement in a program. Only six programs included older adults. Four of these were workplace interventions, and the other two were community level interventions. None focused on the specific needs of retired older adults. The greatest number of programs (50) focused on alcohol, tobacco, and marijuana. Thirty-two programs included other drugs. According to the Monitoring the Future Survey of substance use in teens, non-medical use of prescription drugs continues to be a widespread problem. Seven of the top 10 drugs most likely to be misused by 12th graders were either prescription or over-the-counter medications (National Institute on Drug Abuse, 2009).

However, only four of the NREPP-listed programs specifically addressed the misuse of prescription drugs. Two of the four were programs for athletes focusing primarily on steroid misuse. The *costs* of these programs varied widely, from a free tobacco prevention program to an intervention that costs well over $35,000 a year. The mean rating of the *quality of research* supporting the programs (on a scale of 0.0–4.0) varied from .95 for Keeping a Clear mind (which also had a low readiness for dissemination score of 1.8) to 4.0 for Project Alert (with a readiness for dissemination score of 3.8). Another very high performing program was Life Skills Training, with an experimental research mean score of 3.93 and a readiness for dissemination score of 4.0.

Some researchers question the usefulness of the evidence-based label for these programs due to data analysis procedures that capitalize on the chance of obtaining statistically significant results (Gorman & Huber, 2009). We must also consider that programs may sometimes have detrimental effects. We usually think of prevention programs as being benign, but in a review of the substance prevention literature, Werch & Owen (2002) found 17 programs that increased substance abuse among children, adolescents, and young adults. Some had statistically significant negative outcomes on increased experimentation and abuse over time. Carefully reviewing outcomes of the various prevention programs and then acting on that information is a vital process in choosing an appropriate prevention method for a specific population.

Even in light of the new evidence-based programs, several questions need attention. With the overwhelming focus on alcohol and tobacco, do the ecological influences operate in the same manner regarding the different types of substances? If a prevention program is assessed a failure, do we know *why* it failed? How are the individual

protective factors which decrease the probability of substance problems interrelated? Despite the seriousness of polydrug use, programs focusing on alcohol, tobacco, and other drugs have maintained their conceptual distinctness in practice. Until recently, professionals have tended to focus on differences in their areas of specialization, rather than seek common ground (Wallack & Corbett, 1990). On a broad scale, prevention program practice is just now beginning to catch up with new trends in the research literature. However, many outmoded, ineffective practices remain in use.

Public Information and Education

Information and education are explicit elements in most drug and alcohol prevention programs. Tremendous emphasis has been placed on public information and school-based education as a primary means of prevention throughout the United States. However, these approaches to changing behaviors rooted in deeply held social values have been marginally effective, at best (Blane, 1986; Evans, 1998; Hopkins et al., 2001). Nevertheless, it is still widely accepted that informational approaches should be included in programs designed to prevent drug use (Wallack & Corbett, 1990). Universal prevention programs aimed at education for all students in school are generally shorter and less costly. However, they are frequently not able to adequately reach racial/ethnic groups and high-risk youth and families.

While we would all like to believe that drug education will deter young people from using drugs, evaluations of most types of drug education programs from all over the developed world have shown that this is not the case. Perhaps one of the reasons for this failure is that drug education is often based not on sound educational principles but on a narrow view that skews and censors information. This is not education but *propaganda.* Young people respond to this by saying what they think parents, teachers, and politicians want to hear, rather than what they really believe (Cohen, 1996). This can lead to adults' drawing inaccurate conclusions about the effectiveness of these programs. Prevention programs and models have become somewhat of an *ideology* to those who steadfastly support them, and ideologies are very resistant to data.

Under highly specific conditions, public information campaigns can sometimes achieve certain limited goals. There is evidence that programs directed at increasing the number of people inoculated for infectious diseases, increasing the response rates for census reports, and getting taxpayers to file by the deadline all have met with a measure of success (Blane, 1986). Health education in the public schools is another matter, however (Blane, 1977; Kumpfer, 1998a). This should come as no surprise, since health education has traditionally not been accorded a high priority in the public schools. Teachers often view it as an intrusion and a drain on the so-called legitimate goals of the educational process. Programs are ill conceived, lack clear-cut objectives, and are not designed to engage student interest and involvement. Teachers generally receive little training in how to present the material. Students, perhaps reflecting school and teacher attitudes, typically regard health education as a required bore. It is no wonder that purely educational programs are, at best, marginally effective (Blane, 1986; Kumpfer, 1998a; Hopkins et al., 2001).

Public information and education efforts directed at adults have been much more limited. The primary adult educational programs are "DUI schools." These are designed for persons who generally have long histories of driving under the influence violations and even longer histories of alcohol abuse, but many of their clients are probably not alcoholics. With such a varied group of clients, it is not surprising that their effectiveness is also marginal. Paradoxically, they are probably more successful with the substantial number of students who are not really alcoholic or drug dependent.

There has been a dramatic increase in mass media campaigns dealing with alcohol, drugs, and smoking in recent years. Strategies are aimed at getting children to "just say no" to drugs, at convincing adults to drink in moderation, at convincing drivers not to get behind the wheel after drinking, and at convincing everyone to quit smoking by understanding the truth about tobacco use.

However, advertising *promoting* these tobacco and alcohol products has resulted in a stronger identification with them (such as Camel No.9). Identification is also associated with higher levels of use in children and adults (Pierce, Gilpin, & Choi, 1999; Villani, 2001; Wyllie, Zhang, & Casswell, 1998). These strategies can, however, be offset in adolescents by parental reinforcement and counter-reinforcement of messages (Austin, Pinkleton, & Fujioka, 2000). As a *prevention* tool, media campaigns appear to have had limited success in reducing the use of tobacco, alcohol, and marijuana (McCaffrey, 1999). In a meta-analysis of health-related media campaign studies only a small effect size was noted for changes in behavior relating to smoking. Approximately 2 percent of effect related to the targeted audience was thought to be due to the campaigns. However, even a small change in a large number of people can save lives. The authors suggest that the small effect may be impacted by the fact that addictive behaviors are more dependent on environmental factors than a simple media campaign can overcome (Snyder et al., 2004). For example, the authors compared their media results with a phone counseling meta-analysis which yielded a 6 percent change in smoking behavior (Lichtenstein, Glasgow, Lando, Ossip-Klein, & Boles, 1996 as quoted by Snyder et al., 2004).

But even these modest declines in consumption are difficult to tie directly to media prevention efforts alone. A meta-analysis of interventions to increase tobacco cessation demonstrated the effectiveness of media campaigns when they were implemented with other interventions of support (Hopkins et al., 2001). The campaigns have also been effective in reducing children's exposure to environmental tobacco smoke. With a few exceptions, such as the Florida "truth" campaign (Sly, Heald, & Ray, 2001; Sly, Hopkins, Trapido, & Ray, 2001), the evidence does not prompt excessive optimism (Hopkins et al., 2001; Olson & Gerstein, 1985). As discussed later, one study by Siegel (2002) found that the success of anti-tobacco advertising is threatened by the political power of the tobacco lobby.

Programs Directed at Children and Adolescents

Throughout the 1970s, most drug abuse prevention programs were educational in nature, directed at adolescents, and implemented through the schools. Early programs relied on providing information and using so-called scare tactics. These programs were generally so ineffective that they were denounced by the federal government's Special Office for Drug Abuse Prevention (SODAP). In fact, SODAP was so disillusioned that it imposed a temporary ban on the funding of drug information programs (Wallack & Corbett, 1990).

Growing evidence of the ineffectiveness of these strategies led to a trend toward use of *affective education* and other alternative approaches (Wallack & Corbett, 1990). Affective programs assumed that adolescents would be deterred from using drugs if their self-esteem, interpersonal skills, and techniques for decision making and problem solving could be improved. Recreational activities, community service projects, and involvement in the arts were stressed as a way of providing meaningful, fulfilling experiences that would counteract the attractions of drugs. The affective model was developed as a result of research on the correlates of drug-using behavior, primarily among delinquents and addicts (Dembo, 1986). These studies identified drug-abusing youths as less likely to participate in clubs, youth organizations, and religious activities. Generalizing from that population to so-called normal adolescents may have led to a faulty model for prevention efforts. However,

the community involvement aspects were a step in the right direction because less comprehensive approaches, such as those that target self-esteem alone, are no more effective than education alone in reducing drug use (Braucht & Braucht, 1984; Kumpfer, 1998a). To be effective, programs must be interactive and based in a broad framework like the Life Skills Training programs which have shown effective results in reducing alcohol, tobacco, and marijuana use (Botvin et al., 2000).

Early smoking prevention programs were also information oriented and frequently resorted to scare tactics, such as showing students photographs of cancerous and healthy lungs. Like the early alcohol and drug prevention programs, they had little impact on long-term behavior. Confronted with this lack of success, some researchers began to consider ways of addressing the social milieu in which young people begin smoking. This eventually resulted in a new generation of smoking programs that have been somewhat more successful (Hopkins et al., 2001).

Drawing on Evans et al.'s (1978) *social inoculation* theory (1978) and McGuire's (1969) concept of *cognitive inoculation*, this approach argues that if adolescents are provided with counterarguments and techniques with which to resist peer pressures to smoke, as well as factual information about smoking, they are more likely to abstain. Based on this approach, many smoking prevention programs focused on the short-term effects of smoking, rather than long-term health consequences with slogans like, "When he kisses you, do you really want your breath to smell like an ashtray?" The impact of this approach is well documented in delaying young people's use of tobacco for up to two years (McCarthy, 1985). However, long-term effects were not demonstrated, and even the short-term effects appeared to decay with time (Wallack & Corbett, 1990).

Many elements from the social inoculation and affective education models were used in developing Project D.A.R.E. (Drug Abuse Resistance Education). This program was originally developed as a joint project of the Los Angeles

Police Department and the Los Angeles Unified School District in 1983. Now, millions of children in communities across the world participate (D.A.R.E., 2009). Project D.A.R.E. was originally designed to help fifth- and sixth-grade students recognize and resist the peer pressure that frequently leads to experimentation with alcohol and drugs. Some lessons focused on building self-esteem, whereas others emphasized the consequences of using alcohol or drugs and identified alternative ways of coping with stress, gaining peer acceptance, or having fun. Most importantly, students learned and practiced specific strategies for responding to peers who offer them drugs. Ways to say "no" include changing the subject, walking away or ignoring the person, and simply saying no and repeating it as often as necessary. The original curriculum was organized into 17 classroom sessions conducted by a police officer, coupled with other activities to be taught by the regular classroom teacher (DeJong, 1987; Los Angeles Unified School District, 1996). The D.A.R.E. program happened at just the right time. With the enthusiasm for drug-free schools and the funding for prevention efforts that proved politically popular in the 1980s, the D.A.R.E. program grew exponentially. By 1991, D.A.R.E. programs were found in every state, and the Drug-Free Schools and Communities reauthorization bill of 1991 required that each state use at least 10 percent of its share of the funds to support D.A.R.E. (Ray & Ksir, 1999).

One of the earliest evaluations of the D.A.R.E. program found that students who received the full-semester D.A.R.E. curriculum during the sixth grade had significantly lower use of alcohol, cigarettes, and other drugs. The impact was much greater for boys (who used more drugs to begin with) than for girls (DeJong, 1987). A later longitudinal (three-year) study found significantly lower use rates by D.A.R.E. graduates for all drugs except tobacco (Evaluation and Training Institute, 1988). However, the most comprehensive evaluation of D.A.R.E. by the Research Triangle Institute found the

program to be ineffective in preventing or reducing drug use (Ringwalt et al., 1994). D.A.R.E. officials and the U.S. Department of Justice both disavowed the report, and D.A.R.E. tried to prevent others from publishing similar criticisms (Glass, 1997). Then, a follow-up of over 1,000 individuals 10 years after graduation from D.A.R.E. found few differences between D.A.R.E. and non-D.A.R.E. participants, and in no case did the D.A.R.E. group have a more successful outcome than the comparison group (Lyman et al., 1999). The program still shows little evidence of long-term effects on drug use (Pan & Bai, 2009).

Even in light of the more recent and comprehensive research, anecdotal evidence and lack of dissemination of research findings have kept this ineffective program alive. For example, U.S. Senator Bob Coffin of the Senate Committee on Finance for the state of Nevada supported D.A.R.E. because his son had recently finished the program, "and it seemed to work very well for him and all of his classmates" (Minutes of the Senate Committee, 1999, p. 12). Despite the absence of solid evidence, he urged continued support for D.A.R.E.

The repeated failure of D.A.R.E. to demonstrate long-term effectiveness has not resulted in its abandonment, even though costs as of 2000 were thought to be $220 million per year (Sager, 2000) and have been estimated as high as $1–$1.3 billion per year (Shepard, 2001). A number of states, however, are searching for other alternatives. D.A.R.E. America is countering with the argument that one semester of fifth- or sixth-grade prevention programming is simply not enough. It is encouraging the adoption of booster programs in junior high and high school, as well as the introduction of D.A.R.E. in earlier grades (Ray & Ksir, 1999). One such add-on program, now partnering with D.A.R.E., Keepin' it Real, has demonstrated significant results in reduced alcohol use (Kulis et al., 2007).

A number of schools have turned to alternative models of school-based prevention programs altogether. Although these programs are still education-based, they also incorporate more aspects of a child's environment. For example, the schools in Hillsborough County (Tampa), Florida, have never had the D.A.R.E. program. For about 20 years, they have used the "Too Good for Drugs" program, created by the Mendez Foundation. It is a school-based program that utilizes the latest research about resiliency, risk, protective factors, and developmental assets factors—all of which have been identified as crucial for young persons' successful growth and development (Benard, 1993; Hall & Ziglar, 1997; Hanson, 1992).

Project ALERT is a program that began in California and Oregon high schools and targets tobacco, alcohol, and marijuana use. Unlike D.A.R.E., ALERT uses trained educators with the assistance of teen leaders. The program is delivered to seventh-grade students, and three booster lessons are provided in the eighth grade. Compared to a control group, the experimental group drank less alcohol and smoked less tobacco and marijuana at the end of the program. The reduction in alcohol use diminished over a 15-month follow-up, but the decrease in tobacco and marijuana use was still significant (Ray & Ksir, 1999; Ellickson et. al, 2003). Project STAR is another program aimed at junior high students that (like both D.A.R.E. and ALERT) is based on a social influence model. STAR is delivered over a two-year period, and it includes parents in homework assignments and communication training. Seniors who had completed the program in junior high were much less likely to use alcohol, tobacco, and marijuana (Johnson, MacKinnon, & Pentz, 1996). Another successful example is the Life Skills Training Program. It is a three-year program based on the social influence model and covers resistance skills, normative education, media influences, self-management skills, and general social skills. The program's effectiveness has been demonstrated in both two-year and six-year follow-ups (Botvin, Schinke, Epstein, Diaz, & Botvin, 1995; Botvin et al., 2000).

According to Dusenbury and Falco (1995), experts believe that effective school-based drug abuse prevention programs must have these components:

1. They are research based and theory driven.
2. They provide developmentally appropriate information about drugs.
3. They utilize social resistance skills training.
4. They include normative education.
5. They are presented within a broader context of skills training and comprehensive health education.
6. They use interactive teaching techniques.
7. They provide teacher training and support.
8. They cover prevention issues adequately and provide sufficient follow-up.
9. They are culturally sensitive.
10. They include other components (family, community, media, special populations, etc.) that enhance the program's effectiveness.
11. They contain an evaluation method.

Prevention efforts are now beginning to focus on the interplay of risk factors, protective factors, and resilience. *Risk factors* are those aspects across ecological systems that increase the chance that a person will have problems with substances. They include individual issues such as mental illness and genetic tendencies towards addictions; family, school, and social issues such as a history of physical or sexual abuse and affiliations with those who use drugs; community issues such as poverty and accessibility of substances; and cultural issues, including cultural acceptance and media images of substance use (Ammerman, Ott, & Blackson, 1999). *Protective factors* are those aspects across ecological systems that increase the chance that a person will avoid problems with substances. They include individual issues such as creative problem solving and self-value; social issues such as family, school, positive adult role models, and supportive relationships; and community issues such as a safe neighborhood environment and availability of wholesome activities.

Beginning with the work of Garmezy (Garmezy, 1981; Garmezy & Newuchtrelein, 1972) and Werner and Smith (1982, 2001), models of prevention and coping with difficulties have shifted from a *deficit model* to a *resilience model*. These and other authors followed young children through adulthood, identifying risk and protective factors that lead to resilience. Resilience focuses on protective factors found in youth from high-risk situations. It is a phenomenon which empowers a person to return to functional status despite high-risk events. It is observed through adaptive functioning and enabled by protective factors which act to offset negative influences. It is most clearly demonstrated when the individual, community, and family are all working together to facilitate progress toward positive life functioning. Theoretical frameworks applying resilience specifically to substance abuse have been explored (Berlin & Davis, 1989; Brown, 2001), and programs that focus on developing these factors in youth are being encouraged to decrease drug abuse (Glantz, 1995; Hanson, 2001). Some researchers have found effective results in developing these skills (Cesarone, 1999; Kumpfer, 1999). However, more research is needed to determine if resilience related skills, when taught to youth, are effective in curbing drug use.

Programs Directed at College and University Students

In keeping with the newer ecological focus on attitudes and relationships, evidence-based programs are emerging specifically for college campuses. For example, Challenging College Alcohol Abuse is a program that began at the University of Arizona and uses social norms and environmental management through venues such as media campaigns to address misperceptions about drinking. This approach is based on evidence that college students tend to think that the drinking behavior of other students is higher than it actually is. The program provides small grants to fund alcohol free social events. They also encourage increased monitoring of student alcohol use. Students impacted by this program demonstrated significant decreases in heavy drinking, frequent drinking, and negative consequences of alcohol use (Glider et al., 2001).

A similar project is being conducted at Florida State University called the Real Project. It collects data from students at the university about actual drinking habits and publishes those around campus. The surveys show that the students' perceptions of drinking were much higher than actual drinking. The project advertises dry events and is present on social networking sites. As a result, from 2002 to 2009, a 20.9 percent reduction was found in high-risk drinking behaviors, and there was a 24.8 percent increase in students who report drinking moderately and a 17.3 percent increase in those who abstain from drinking altogether (The Real Project, 2008). Additionally, the university provides a clear substance policy and readily available services for students with substance use problems. It appears that clear policies coupled with multi-faceted approaches including social norms can be a helpful prevention strategy in the college and university setting.

The most important conclusion to be reached after 30 years of organized prevention programming is that no single strategy has consistently demonstrated a long-term impact, and many experts believe that it may be a mistake to think in terms of a single-strategy solution (Belcher & Shinitzky, 1998). In many respects, life has become more complicated for the current generation. Experimentation may be seen as a normal rite of passage for many youth—a phase that most will outgrow. The problem is that many young people find themselves in very difficult situations physically and emotionally when these experimentations go awry. Previous generations of youth experimented mostly with alcohol. The greater availability of illicit drugs provides today's youth with a greater variety of choices. Education alone does not demonstrate overwhelmingly positive results. Prevention efforts, therefore, must become more comprehensive. A mixture of community, education, family, and skills training with the other measures described shortly may result in a much more effective approach to prevention.

Service Measures

Service measures (detoxification, therapeutic communities, 28-day treatment programs, Alcoholics Anonymous, etc.) are aimed at ameliorating or reversing a condition resulting from alcohol or drug use or reducing the chances of its onset among members of a high-risk population. In traditional community health terms, such measures usually fall into the secondary or tertiary prevention category. Service measures are not generally emphasized in prevention because of their ameliorative or restorative nature. Their lack of popularity among prevention experts is due to the fact that, by definition, they are directed toward remediating an existing problem, rather than preventing new cases from occurring.

Service measures are also labor intensive and therefore comparatively expensive. They may often require large capital outlays for facilities and personnel, making them not particularly cost effective. Service measures also are usually focused on the individual, whereas prevention specialists are more comfortable with strategies that apply to large populations. Additionally, when mandated to "do prevention," providers are inclined to allocate resources to specific types of services while neglecting other types of preventive measures (Kumpfer & Kaftarian, 2000). When dealing with the serious nature of a client's alcohol or drug problem, most counselors or therapists find little time for prevention work.

Early intervention services—such as those provided in occupational alcoholism programs, "troubled worker" programs, and employee assistance programs—are a common type of secondary prevention. These programs are oriented toward employees whose work performance is impaired by the use of drugs or alcohol. Most referred employees are people addicted to alcohol or drugs with

long-standing problems, rather than individuals who are at risk for first time chemical dependency (see Gould & Smith, 1988).

According to a study by Roman and Blum (1990), only about 4 percent of the employees in a firm with an employee assistance program (EAP) utilize the services in a given year, and only 1.5 percent specifically present a substance abuse problem. Harrison and Hoffman (1988) found that the employer was mentioned as a primary motivator for treatment admission by only one-sixteenth of inpatients and one-tenth of outpatients. However, Lawenthal et al. (1996) reported that levels of improvement were similar between employees who were coerced into treatment based on urine screens and those who were self-referred Awareness of the EAP services, support for the company policies, and intolerance of coworker substance abuse may increase the utilization of EAP services (Reynolds & Lehman, 2003).

Chemical dependency manifests itself in the workplace in four ways. First, an employee may be chemically dependent. Second, an employee may be affected by a spouse, child, or other loved one who is chemically dependent. Third, an employee may be an adult child of a chemically dependent parent. Finally, an employee may be selling or using drugs in the workplace (DiNitto, 1988). To intervene at the earliest possible stage of dependency, supervisors are taught to be alert for the following common symptoms of alcohol or drug abuse:

- Chronic absenteeism
- Change in behavior
- Physical signs
- Spasmodic work pace
- Lower quantity and quality of work
- Partial absences
- Lying
- Avoiding supervisors and co-workers
- On-the-job drinking or drug use
- On-the-job accidents and lost time from off-the-job accident. (Kinney & Leaton, 1987)

Assuming that early identification and treatment are achieved in a workplace program, the chances of recovery should be increased for these reasons:

1. The threat of job loss is a significant motivator.
2. The family may still be present to provide emotional support.
3. Physical health has not deteriorated seriously.
4. The client's financial resources are not depleted.

Although studies have reported that chronic drug use negatively impacts employment status, casual drug use does not (French, Roebuck, & Alexandre, 2001). As many as 70 percent of those who admit to using illicit drugs, work regularly (Marwick, 1999). It would seem that work can therefore be utilized as a positive tool in aiding workers to seek treatment. However, ethical company policies, current research, and state and federal laws should guide employers in developing interventions that do not infringe on the rights of employees.

Workplace programs use early intervention (service) measures as one component of more comprehensive prevention efforts. Other components include information sessions, substance abuse issue discussions, posters and pamphlets, use of peer pressure, and financial incentives. Such incentives may take the form of cash benefits to employees who quit smoking or reduced insurance rates for healthy lifestyles. Employers are convinced that a healthier work force results in greater organizational efficiency and higher profits.

Although Driving Under the Influence (DUI) programs were considered earlier as educational prevention, they also could be considered as early intervention. In addition to the educational component, offenders are offered treatment and probation instead of fines, jail, and other punishment. The effectiveness of treatment offered under such compulsion is questionable, however (Homel, 1988), just as in workplace programs,

the clients are also likely to be those with long-standing problems of chemical dependency, so the appropriateness of the "early intervention" label is equally questionable.

A number of pilot early detection, screening, and treatment programs have been funded by the U.S. Department of Justice. For example, in Miami, where the first Juvenile Drug Court was founded in 1989, juvenile offenders are routinely screened at detention through urine analysis. As of the early 1990s, those who tested positive for any of five major drugs (about 85 percent) were referred for treatment by local agencies. Because of a lack of follow-up, however, fewer than half the youth referred actually went to treatment, and only about one-third of them completed a treatment program. (Miami/Dade County Juvenile Screening, 1991). Today, Miami/Dade is at the forefront again, this time with more impressive results. First, the Florida Legislature established Juvenile Assessment Centers which coordinate the agencies that work with youth who have been arrested. Partnering with researchers under federal grants, the groups determined to implement evidence-based best practices including focused service measures for differing offenders. In April 2007, the Civil Citation Program was created which allowed police officers to refer a child for services after a minor offense without making an arrest. The program became a true systemic prevention model, enlisting all 37 local arresting agencies and working in cooperation with the public schools and local treatment facilities. Between 1998 and 2008 total arrests were down by 46 percent and, of the 4,700 youths referred, 81 percent successfully completed the evidence-based interventions. Re-offenses were reduced by 80 percent (Miami-Dade County Juvenile Services Department [JSD], 2009a). Furthermore, in 2008, an economic study concluded that this reformed juvenile justice system saves the Miami community over $33 million a year. According to JSD (2009b), approximately three quarters of the clients were drug offenders. It has been hailed as an exemplary model by several U.S. and international agencies (Walters, 2009).

Service measures can be very effective in preventing substance abuse when implemented in a comprehensive and creative manner with research informing the intervention.

Technologic Measures

In the traditional public health prevention model, *technologic measures* refer to "modifications in the noxious agent or the environment in which it operates that will affect the relationships among the agent, the environment, and members of a population to reduce the rate of occurrence of a disorder" (Blane, 1986). Although relatively new in chemical dependency, technologic measures are commonplace in occupational health and safety, transportation, and water sanitation.

Efforts to alter the noxious agent itself generally have been limited to modifications of alcohol and tobacco products. Cigarette makers produce a variety of so-called light brands that are lower in nicotine. Manufacturers of distilled spirits have actually decreased the average amount of absolute alcohol in their products over the past several years, and more brands of low-alcohol beer become available each year. At first, these low-alcohol brands seemed to be socially acceptable only in Europe, but they have now become quite popular in the United States. Biomedical researchers are still searching for a breakthrough that will eliminate the negative physiologic and psychological effects of alcohol. Some even have hope of developing a practical "sobering-up" pill. On the medical front, nicotine vaccines are being developed that interact with the nicotine to prevent the reward mechanism. With the *NicQb* vaccine, it was found that patients who were able to create antibodies to the nicotine had significantly greater abstinence from tobacco, compared to those given a placebo. As of 2010, however, nicotine vaccines were still in pre-clinical developmental trials (Jupp & Lawrence, 2010).

As mentioned in Chapter 6, *antagonist* therapies have been developed for drugs such as heroin addiction. Drugs such as naloxone, naltrexone, and cyclazocine block the action of the opiate drugs. A newer drug, Suboxone, is a partial receptor *agonist*, a drug which actively binds to a receptor cell, and part receptor antagonist. But these drugs do not prevent withdrawal symptoms. Patients are withdrawn from heroin before being given these drugs. The prior user who returns to using heroin while taking a narcotic antagonist will find it impossible to get high (Blane, 1986). An agonist, such as methadone, is a drug used to prevent symptoms of heroin withdrawal, and it also diminishes the effects of heroin. The heroin addict who is taking methadone will not be able to get the same high from using heroin.

The manufacturer of OxyContin, Purdue Pharma, released a ten-point plan to make this drug less susceptible to abuse. The plan included such measures as tamper-resistant prescription pads, which include six security devices that make them almost impossible to copy ("Drug maker to help curb painkiller abuse," 2001), and the possibility of adding naloxone to the primary ingredient oxycodone to prevent abusers of that drug from getting any euphoric effect. As of early 2010, OxyContin did not contain naloxone due to variability in absorption. But, with support from the FDA, Purdue continues the study of interventions to reduce abuse, such as a plastic coating on the pill (Perrone, 2009). The naloxone/oxycodone combination is available as the drug Targinact in the United Kingdom to reduce gastric side effects (Napp Pharmaceuticals, 2009). The Food and Drug Administration (FDA) has recently moved to work towards technologic and other risk-management measures with all major pharmaceutical companies that produce opioid drugs. Antabuse (disulfiram) is a drug that prevents the normal metabolization of alcohol. A person who ingests alcohol while taking Antabuse will experience an accumulation of acetaldehyde, resulting in severe physical consequences such as difficulty in breathing, nausea, dizziness, vomiting, and blurred vision. In some cases, people are able to continue drinking despite the symptoms, however (White, 1991). A newer drug, Acamprosate, works with the GABA neurotransmitter systems to normalize alcohol disrupted brain activity and reduce craving, but has shown mixed results. Some anti-convulsion medicines are being studied in clinical trials to reduce withdrawal, craving, and overall drinking (Jupp & Lawrence, 2010).

Several additional drugs such as the psychostimulants have fewer medical treatment options. A vaccine that creates cocaine specific antibodies that sequester the cocaine molecules as they enter the circulatory system is in pre-clinical trials. One problem is that a higher dose of cocaine can still overwhelm the antibodies, and the vaccine does not help with other related stimulants (Jupp & Lawrence, 2010). Further measures for deterring addictions are on the horizon, such as genetic testing. Identifying the genetic markers that identify those individuals who have physiological weaknesses for specific addictions may show promise if coupled with counseling and support.

Other technologic measures are designed to make the environment safer for the person who uses alcohol or drugs. These measures do not prevent the use of alcohol or drugs but protect both the user and innocent people from the effects of use. Passive restraints and air bags in automobiles are perhaps the best examples. Various devices have also been developed to prevent an intoxicated person from turning on the ignition of his or her automobile. Some states, such as Pennsylvania, have passed ignition interlock device legislation, requiring repeat DUI offenders to provide breath samples before their cars will be able to start (Litchman, 2002). Fire-retardant or fireproof clothing, bedding, and furniture also protect users who pass out or fall asleep while smoking.

Many cities have established a "tipsy taxi" service for drivers who have had too much to drink. In Tallahassee, Florida, for example, the city operates a free taxi service available to anyone on major holidays, when overdrinking is traditionally a problem. In the same city, Florida State University offers a free chauffeur service to all its students on a year-round basis. Alcohol-related traffic fatalities have fallen since these services were introduced.

Many communities are providing free needles and syringes to intravenous drug users in an attempt to slow the spread of infectious diseases, such as AIDS. These programs have spread much faster in European nations, partly because of a more liberal attitude toward such prevention efforts and partly because the laws are more conducive to these approaches. Many cities, such as Melbourne, Australia, have locked boxes in public restrooms where used needles and syringes can be safely deposited.

However, in many communities in the United States, there is a feeling that providing free needles and syringes *encourages* drug use. In many states, needles and syringes are available only through a physician's prescription. Some communities have attempted to get around this problem by educating intravenous drug users in methods of cleaning their equipment before using it again or sharing it with another user. Both San Francisco and New York City launched efforts to educate these drug users to "bleach their works" before state courts eventually allowed the distribution of needles and syringes.

The Harm Reduction Coalition was organized to promote the health of those who are impacted by drug use. It supports efforts to prevent further harm to those affected by drugs. Some of their programs include syringe access to prevent HIV and Hepatitis C. They have an overdose prevention component that includes information on how to help someone who has overdosed, such as teaching laypeople to administer naloxone to prevent death from an opioid overdose. In Illinois, the first naloxone distribution program in the United States reduced overdose deaths by a third in three years (Harm Reduction Coalition, 2010). The coalition also supports treatment options such as pharmacological replacement therapies. Additionally, education is encouraged to reduce harmful interactions, such as between HIV medication and methadone, and safer use of drugs, such as safer injection techniques and early detection of deadly injection site infections.

Although their practices have saved lives, they are controversial. For example, although U.S. President Barack Obama signed into law in 2009 removing a 21-year ban restricting federal funding for needle exchange programs, some states, such as Florida, still have laws that make it illegal to deliver drug paraphernalia if it is known that it would be used for illegal substances. Of the known 211 programs running syringe exchanges nationwide, it is estimated that half operate outside the law (Adams, 2010).

Legislative, Regulatory, and Economic Measures

Legislation, judicial intervention, and administrative regulations regarding drug use can be employed to raise revenue, safeguard public health or morals, provide both political and economic rewards, and prevent drug use and abuse. This chapter discusses only the latter purposes. The others will be deferred until the next chapter, where the concept of regulation will be dealt with in considerably greater depth.

Throughout the eighteenth and nineteenth centuries, there were many local and state laws restricting the sale of alcohol, culminating in 1917 in national prohibition. Whatever the failings of this "noble experiment," one of its primary purposes was achieved—a substantial decrease in the consumption of beverage alcohol (McKim, 1991). Other legislation has controlled the hours and location of sale for alcoholic beverages, and there have been long-standing laws against serving alcohol to minors. These laws are also intended to reduce consumption, frequently among specific populations. Still other laws have placed restrictions on certain activities associated with drinking (gambling; nude dancing; driving a car, boat, or airplane; etc.) as a way of protecting the public from some of the side effects of drinking alcohol. So-called dram shop laws have been revived to make it illegal for bartenders and other servers to serve alcohol to

obviously intoxicated persons. Several lawsuits and court decisions upholding server liability laws have impressed on tavern owners the need for better training of their personnel. Perhaps this desire to reduce liability will lead to a reduction of some alcohol problems (Olson & Gerstein, 1985).

Regulation of other psychoactive drugs is much less complicated. In most cases, there is either no law restricting the use of a drug (e.g., gasoline, glue, and other inhalants) or it is simply illegal to use or possess it (heroin). However, in California, common substances utilized as inhalants, such as spray paint, are contained in locked shelving. In relatively few cases (marijuana), a drug may be illegal except for certain limited medical purposes. Regulation of most of these drugs came much later than for alcohol, however. Opiates were not made illegal until the Harrison Act of 1914. Although many states had prohibitions against its use, marijuana was not outlawed nationally until the Marijuana Tax Act of 1937. Recently, there have been many more drugs added to the list of controlled substances, but there is little evidence that these prohibitions have significantly affected drug trade or drug use. In fact, government attempts to limit the supply of drugs may have served mostly to drive up prices and increase the profits of drug dealers (Currie, 1993).

Recent Legislation

On June 22, 2009, the Family Smoking Prevention and Tobacco Control Act, (U.S. Congress, Public Law 111-31, 2009), was signed by President Obama. As a primary prevention measure, this legislation increased taxes and included larger health warnings to discourage smoking. Additionally, cigarettes targeted to minors with fruity and other pleasant flavors were banned. The measure gave the FDA authority to regulate tobacco products, something anti-smoking groups had wanted for a long time. Manufacturers must now submit all ingredients including additives, amount of nicotine, and tobacco type to the FDA. They are also required to submit any research concerning their tobacco products. It is up to the FDA to act on each distinct ingredient (U.S. Department of Health and Human Services, FDA, 2009a & 2009b). Additionally a Tobacco Products Scientific Advisory Committee now provides information on research on health and safety related to all tobacco products.

The No Child Left Behind Act of 2001, (P.L. 107-110, Title IV, Part A) was written with language that specifically encourages Safe and Drug-Free Schools (SDFS). The purpose was to provide support to "prevent the illegal use of alcohol, tobacco and drugs" (Sec. 4002). The act emphasized the need for coordinated efforts. It included funding availability of grants to improve school drug prevention programs, community-based drug prevention planning, programs and activities, and evaluation. Drug and alcohol programs that apply for the grants are required to demonstrate effectiveness. Although this legislation requires evidence-based prevention practices, research has shown that its impact varies. Of the 1,612 school districts sampled across the United States, nearly 12 percent did not receive SDFS funds, districts transferred more money out of SDFS (16 percent) than into the program (2 percent), and only a third of school districts reported using evidence-based curriculum. Additionally many of the evidence-based programs are too expensive for schools. Finally, a large majority of the state and local education agencies gave SDFS drug testing a low priority (Cho, Hallfors, Iritani, & Hartman, 2009). Drug testing in schools does not show clear evidence of effectiveness as a prevention method and can be a source of several negative outcomes. For an overview of the legal issues, assumptions, evidence, and ethical comparisons of drug testing in both the U.S. and Australian schools see Roche, Bywook, Pidd, Freemand, and Steenson, 2009.

Health Warnings.   Health warnings have been mandated for alcohol and tobacco products. As of 1989, everything from light beer to 100-proof vodka must carry a government warning concerning the risk to pregnant women of birth defects and the risk to everyone of impaired driving ability:

> *Government Warning:* (1) According to the Surgeon General, women should not drink alcoholic beverages during pregnancy because of the risk of birth defects. (2) Consumption of alcoholic beverages impairs your ability to drive a car or operate machinery, and may cause health problems.

Tobacco products warn the user of a plethora of possible diseases. The impact of the warnings is unknown, but some argue that they may actually serve to protect the manufacturers from liability by providing the consumer with an adequate warning of potential risks involved in using the product.

Stricter Enforcement

All states have legislation prohibiting the sale of both alcohol and tobacco products to under-aged youth. While the enforcement of alcohol laws have been a great concern to local and state law enforcement authorities, only recently have they put much effort into enforcing the tobacco laws. In a study in California, minors aged 14 to 16 years attempted to purchase cigarettes in 412 stores and from 30 vending machines. They were successful in 74 percent of the stores and in 100 percent of the vending machines (Altman et al., 1989). The situation may be changing, however. A large Maryland convenience store chain was convicted several years ago of routinely selling cigarettes to under-aged youths and was fined several million dollars ("Chain Fined," 1991). Today, laws relating to selling cigarettes to under-aged youth are being more strictly enforced by store owners because of government's new sensitivity to adolescent substance abuse. However, purchases on the Internet may pose a greater problem.

The Tobacco and Alcohol Lobby

A major influence on legislation is the money that large corporations and lobbying groups provide to political campaigns at both the federal and state level. For example, during the 2007–2008 election cycle, the tobacco industry contributed over $2 million directly to federal candidates (Tobacco-Free Kids Action Fund, 2010). The National Institute on Money in State Politics (2010) home page contains searchable records of state and federal contributions by corporation, candidate, political action committee, and/or ballot measure. During the 2007–2008 election cycle, the database showed the top companies that contributed to these state and federal campaigns, political parties, and ballot measure committees. The top three contributors that sell alcohol were the National Beer Wholesalers Association, Anheuser-Busch, and the Wine and Spirits Wholesalers of America. These three companies were responsible for over $14.5 million in donations. The top three contributors that sell tobacco were Philip Morris (Subsidiary of ALTRIA), Reynolds American, and U.S. Smokeless Tobacco. These three gave over $17 million to these state and federal entities during the same election cycle. Additionally, the Marijuana Policy Project, a group lobbying for medical marijuana and "sensible regulation" (Marijuana Policy Project, 2010), gave over $3 million to candidates and ballot measures in 2008. On the other hand, groups such as the American Cancer Society donated over $1 million, and the American Lung Association only contributed $25, 000 (National Institute on Money in State Politics, 2010). With financial forces like these at work, it is clear why legislation surrounding substances can become very complicated.

Workplace Regulations and Policies

Drug testing in the workplace has become a common detection and prevention effort. Federal Law now requires it for certain workers such as truck drivers and aircraft maintenance personnel (U.S. Department of Transportation, 2009). In the transportation industry, research has shown that random drug testing coupled with peer-based substance abuse prevention reduced injuries by a third, resulting in millions of dollars saved in injury-related costs (Miller, Zaloshnja, & Spicer, 2007). As of 2004, all states authorized workplace drug testing, although some, like Oregon, only allow it if there is reasonable suspicion that an employee is under the influence (ACLU, 2004).

Due to more convincing evidence of the negative effects of smoking, by the end of 1980s there had been restrictions placed on tobacco use in the workplace by 32 states and limits in other public places such as restaurants were found in 23 states. In addition, national restrictions were placed on smoking on airlines. Furthermore, smoking became almost universally prohibited in government buildings, public hospitals, and other health facilities. Tobacco companies have hotly contested these prohibitions, of course (Mosher, 1990). By 1995, 46 states and Washington, DC, required smoke-free air in some public places. By 2000, The Centers for Disease Control and Prevention (CDCP) and the National Cancer Institute (NCI) had identified 1,238 state laws that focus on tobacco-control issues (Farkas et al., 2000). The negative health consequences of environmental tobacco smoke are well documented. In 2009, the U.S. Institute of Medicine released a report concluding that even low level second-hand smoke causes an increase in cardiovascular diseases (Institute of Medicine, 2009). Yet, as of 2010, only 27 states, Washington, D.C., and Puerto Rico had passed smoke-free laws that covered both restaurants and bars, but some local municipalities have passed their own bans. As of 2002, an average of 70.9 percent of workers were protected by non-smoking policies. Nevada and Kentucky still lag behind with only half of their workers protected from second-hand smoke at worksites (Centers for Disease Control and Prevention, 2006).

Impaired Driving Prevention

Impaired driving prevention has been the subject of much legislation since the advent of the automobile. Research in the United States, England, and Scandinavia indicates that no one single approach to preventing DUI is preferable, but there is a constellation of measures that seem to be effective under various circumstances. These include vigorous enforcement of DUI laws, rapid application of sanctions, and clear-cut regulations that are widely publicized. Heavy fines appear to be about as effective as the revocation of driving privileges, mandatory "DUI schools," and treatment.

Recent research indicates that tougher laws lowering the blood-alcohol concentration (BAC) level for impaired driving from 0.10 to 0.08 has been effective in reducing the proportion of fatal crashes involving alcohol. Also, the first eight states to adopt zero-tolerance policies for drivers under the age of 21 experienced a 20 percent reduction in nighttime fatal crashes among the 15- to 20-year-old age group (Hingson, Heeren, & Winter, 2000). Some of the more controversial methods, such as roadblocks used to ferret out impaired drivers, have proven less effective (American Bar Association, 1986). Such methods also have been criticized as infringement on civil liberties, but so far the courts have generally allowed the practice to continue.

Understanding the need for empowering communities to influence the reduction of impaired driving, The National Highway Traffic Safety Administration and Community Anti-Drug Coalitions have joined efforts to create resources such as the Impaired Driving Prevention Toolkit, which gives facts and practical step-by-step instructions for community groups to be more effective in their DUI prevention efforts (2003). The toolkit includes information on how to build partnerships and work with service providers, legislators, law enforcement, and the media to produce change. It is becoming clear that legislative measures must be coupled with efforts of other groups, such as families and the community in order to be effective.

Economic Measures

The difference between legislative/regulatory measures and economic measures is primarily one of emphasis. The price of alcohol or tobacco, for example, may be a matter of a producer's competitive strategy to capture a share of the market for its product. On the other hand, price also reflects federal and state legislation governing the rate of taxation for that product. Whether it happens because of company policy or government decree, the impact of a price increase or decrease on the consumer is likely to be much the same.

Several studies have indicated that the consumption of alcohol is relatively sensitive to price and that everything from cirrhosis to traffic fatalities could be reduced by increasing prices (Olson & Gerstein, 1985). The increase in prices in the underground market after the passage of Prohibition in 1917 was undoubtedly one of the major factors in the dramatic decrease in consumption. The demand for tobacco products seems to be even more sensitive to price, especially among younger users. Increasing the taxes on cigarettes may be the most effective way of convincing novice users, such as adolescents, not to smoke (Hopkins et al., 2001; Mosher, 1990). When it comes to illicit drugs such as marijuana, there is little doubt that consumption increases as prices fall (Mosher, 1990). One of the few successes of the "war on drugs" may be in maintaining prices at a relatively high level, thereby deterring some potential users. The equation works the other direction as well. Research shows that teens with more spending money are significantly more likely to smoke and smoke more often (Zhang, Camin, & Ferrence, 2008).

In addition to pricing policies, other economic measures include such items as allocating tax revenues from the sale of drugs to prevention programs (such as California's Proposition 99), reducing insurance premiums for those who abstain from alcohol and tobacco, and tax incentives that discourage drug use. (Recent income tax reforms have disallowed the "three-martini" lunch.) It is not uncommon for government to use an economic measure as a subterfuge for prohibiting drugs. For example, the Marijuana Tax Act of 1937 placed a $100 per ounce tax on marijuana. Several states have drug tax laws that require those who buy or possess illegal drugs to purchase tax stamps for them. Failure to do so results in a tax law violation. These laws are often called *Al Capone laws* because of the prosecution of that notorious gangster, who sold bootleg liquor, under the tax evasion statutes.

Cost/Benefit Analysis

A larger, more comprehensive approach is necessary to evaluate preventive efforts. In 1999, the cost of drug abuse (including the federal drug control budget) was estimated at $110 billion annually (ONDCS, 1999). Smoking-related diseases cost the United States approximately $97 billion annually in health care costs and lost productivity (American Lung Association, 2002). The total estimated spending for health care services and treatment for alcohol abuse has been estimated at $26.4 billion a year. In addition, lost productivity and other social costs (such as DUI-related car crashes) bring the total to $184.6 billion in costs for alcohol abuse (CADCA, 2008). It would therefore seem that prevention efforts focused on reducing initiation, harm, and relapse would be beneficial from a cost/benefit perspective.

In relation to program analysis, Lille-Blanton and colleagues (1998) recommend utilizing both *cost/benefit analysis* and *cost-effectiveness analysis*, or analyzing programs for the least expensive means of producing similar outcomes. The authors concluded that out of 3,206 studies, none had applied cost analysis to prevention programs. This is beginning to change, but quite slowly. Of the 58 evidence-based programs listed by SAMHSA (NREPP) as of January, 2010, only three mentioned outcomes related to cost/benefit criteria. All program listings did report the costs of implementing each program

The UN Office on Drugs and Crime states that for every dollar spent on high quality, research-based prevention programs for youth, nine dollars can be saved in the reduced costs resulting from crime, unemployment, and health issues (UNODC, 2009). For example, the average financial cost for

each additional year of life expectancy for those completing the program Not on Tobacco (N-O-T) was $442.65. This estimate ranged from $273.60 to $1,028.90 per life-year saved. The Strengthening Families Program has also reported cost-effective outcomes. Taking into account estimated intervention costs, the number of alcohol related disorders prevented by the program, the cost of alcohol use disorders for each case prevented by the program, and the average actual benefit of preventing one case of an alcohol related disorder, the researchers estimated that $9.60 is saved for every dollar invested. For each family, the net benefit is $5,923 (NREPP, 2010). Given the high costs of treatment and law enforcement devoted to this problem, it is very important to fund prevention as a more economical alternative (Woodward, 1998).

Family and Community Approaches

Most research shows us that no single prevention tool used in isolation is capable of causing even minimal changes in the actual incidence of drug abuse. As prevention theories have continued to be developed and subjected to empirical testing, we have learned that interactive and comprehensive programs using family, schools, religious systems, ethnic groups, and workplace interventions can be effective (Belcher & Shinitzky, 1998; Wyman, 1997).

Family programs engaging parents and children have demonstrated notable changes in both the addicted individual and the potential user (Kumpfer et al., 1998). Although peers and the media can influence a child to begin using drugs, the number-one deterrent to drug initiation is parents who are involved in the child's life. Children and teens whose parents discuss the media messages along with the stress in the child's life and set rules and expectations have substantially lower risks of substance abuse (Austin et al., 2000; National Center on Addiction and Substance Abuse, 2010. According to the Substance Abuse and Mental Health Services Administration

(SAMHSA, 2001), in 2000 only 7.1 percent of young people aged 12–17 who indicated that their "parents would strongly disapprove if they tried marijuana once or twice" had used an illicit drug in the past month. But 31.2 percent of the youth in that group that felt their parents "did not strongly disapprove" of their reported use of an illicit drug in the past month. Schools that provide interactive, repeated prevention measures have a significant impact on the initiation of drug use (Belcher & Shinitzky, 1998).

In a thorough review of all the prevention programs listed on SAMHSA's National Registry of Evidence-based Programs and Practices (NREPP), more than half of the listed programs involved parents, and over a third targeted families. One such program, Families and Schools together, is a program for multi-family groups to connect with each other, the schools, and communities. It uses an ecological approach with outreach to parents and children, includes multi-family group networking, and is facilitated by professionals and school personnel. Outcomes included reduced problem behaviors in the children and increased academic functioning (NREPP, 2010). Another program encouraging family connections with the school, health service agencies and law enforcement is CASASTART, a "positive youth development program" that prevents substance abuse and violence among high-risk 8–13 year olds. Students who participate are less likely to use cigarettes, alcohol, marijuana, and hard drugs; have improved grades and attendance at school; and have fewer violent incidents (CASASTART, 2010; NREPP, 2010). The Strengthening Families Program created by Karol L. Kumpfer and associates (Kumpfer, 1998b) is another prevention program that has demonstrated long-term positive effects with families at high risk for drug use. It is a selective program that addresses the needs and skills of members of several racial/ethnic groups in relation to their families and communities. The program has been rigorously evaluated and refined, and has proven to have a positive impact on adults and children with the precursors of substance abuse.

On the community level, the Institute of Medicine (2010) has issued resources and specific recommendations for local-action groups to ban smoking in communities, improve interventions, and help implement tobacco regulation to reduce the tobacco problem in the future. Some recommendations include involving the media, law enforcement, health care, and insurance providers in supporting tobacco-free strategies. They also recommend policy action through legislatures, schools, and community agencies. The Community Anti-Drug Coalitions of America (CADCA, 2009) is an organization that provides training and education and materials for over 5,000 anti-drug coalitions across the United States. Additionally, they advocate for these groups from the grassroots level to the national public policy arena. According to their 2008 annual report, 60 percent of CADCA-trained agencies bring new practice and/or policy changes to their communities. They tend to be more comprehensive in their approach and report higher levels of effectiveness.

Community Impact: Media

Both legislation and self-regulation have resulted in restrictions on the advertising of alcohol and tobacco products. Although the long-term effects of isolated advertising restrictions appear to be minimal (Warner, 1979; Willemsen & Zwart, 1999), the advertisements and promotions coming from the companies themselves can be quite effective in shaping behavior (Villani, 2001). Industry standards prohibit the advertising of hard liquor on television, and although beer, malt liquor, and wine can be advertised, no one may be shown actually drinking it. There are strong arguments for restricting the advertising of these products in all media because they frequently appeal to young people, who are particularly susceptible to suggestions that wealth, success, and peer approval may be related to using the "right" kind of alcohol or tobacco product.

The multibillion-dollar tobacco settlement reached between the state attorneys general and the tobacco companies in 1997 resulted in an agreement by the tobacco companies to limit ads in newspapers and magazines with large youth leadership to black-and-white text only. Despite that agreement, however, tobacco companies continue to run large color ads in magazines such as *People, Rolling Stone, Glamour, Vibe,* and *Mademoiselle* (National Center for Tobacco-Free Kids, 2001). Furthermore, tobacco products continue to be marketed specifically to racial and ethnic communities: Rio and Dorado to Hispanic Americans, American Spirit to Native Americans, and Pyramid and Heritage to African Americans (Tobacco Control Research Digest, 1999). Tobacco advertisements represent 60 percent of advertising space for most African American newspapers, and three African American magazines (*Ebony, Jet,* and *Essence*) included 12 percent more cigarette advertisements than did other mainstream publications (Tobacco Control Research Digest, 1999). Apparently, attempts to reduce smoking by limiting the advertising of tobacco products through the judicial process have not succeeded.

Ads for alcoholic beverages are well researched, slickly produced, and reinforced by well-organized promotions at the local retail level. After the Coca-Cola Company bought Taylor Wines in the late 1970s, it set out to promote the image of wine as a drink to be consumed regularly, rather than just on special occasions. Within a short time, the amount of advertising in the wine industry nearly doubled, partly because of Coca-Cola's aggressive marketing techniques (Olson & Gerstein, 1985).

Images such as the Budweiser "frogs" of the 1990s became readily recognizable even to children. In 1996, one year after the frogs hit the advertising market, children 9 to 11 years old became as familiar with these characters as they were with Bugs Bunny (Mediascope, 1997). During the 2009 Super Bowl, the top three most memorable ads with middle and high school students were beer ads (Stewart, 2010).

Both the advertising and the brewing industries recently have come under heavy criticism for directing advertising campaigns at minority groups and young women. One example is the 2008 release of Virginia Slims "Purse Packs" that include thin cigarettes in teal and pink boxes to fit in a small purse. Another was the 2007 release of chic black and hot pink packaging of Camel No. 9 complete with promotional giveaways (Campaign for Tobacco-Free Kids, 2009). Another example was the advertising of PowerMaster, a high-alcohol malt liquor, in media targeted toward low-income minorities ("Real Brew HaHa," 1991). The tobacco industry also developed a new cigarette, Kool Mixx: House of Menthol, with a hip-hop theme. The marketing was complete with branded goody bags and CDs. R. J. Reynolds and the states of New York, Maryland, and Illinois entered into a settlement in October of 2004, calling for limiting any promotion of products that would target youths and a payment of $1,460,000 for programs aimed at youth smoking reduction and prevention (DocStoc, 2010). Fortunately, public opinion and political pressure resulted in the removal of some products from the shelves. A very unusual marketing ploy by Kool cigarettes was introduced in Japan in 2007. They released a cigarette with a "powerball" of menthol in the filter that could be crushed to emit a strong menthol taste. The electronic looking packs came in plastic balls with a free metal case for matches. Looking more like a video game–related toy, the "powerball" was not contested in Japan (Japan Trends, 2007).

The alcoholic beverage industry spends over *$1 billion* yearly advertising its products, and the ads continue to air more aggressively (Nelson, 2001). For example, in 2002, NBC became the first network to drop a 50-year self-imposed ban on hard liquor advertising. The American Medical Association (Hill, 2002) quickly responded with a statement urging ABC, CBS, and FOX television executives not to follow the NBC lead. The effect of advertising on actual use is a controversial issue on which outcome evidence is just beginning to build. A 2001 review of the literature on advertising concluded that (1) marginal changes in expenditures for alcohol advertising have little or no effect on total alcohol consumption, and (2) existing studies shed only minimal light on the relationship between advertising and market demand (Tremblay & Okuyama, 2001). However, one national survey of 1,200 respondents aged 12 to 22 did find a moderately strong positive correlation between the amount of day-to-day exposure to ads for alcoholic beverages, on the one hand, and alcohol consumption and drinking in dangerous situations, on the other (Federal Trade Commission, 1985).

Additionally, high quality, targeted advertising may be paying off for advertisers. For example, researchers from California found that beer advertisements that children liked also increased their likelihood of wanting to buy the brand. Elements that increased likability in youths were associated with humor and a good story, with ads such as the Budweiser Ferret-Lizard ads coming in first, and more serious ads like the Busch: Legacy of Quality ad coming in last (Chen et al., 2005). A longitudinal study of over 4,400 households in 24 American media markets conducted in 2006 found that the amount of alcohol advertising expenditures in youth-oriented media was related to greater youth drinking and steeper increases in drinking over time (Snyder et al., 2006). Similar results have been seen with youth exposure to tobacco advertising. A longitudinal study found that when youths attending to cigarette advertising and utilizing tobacco product promotions such as bags, t-shirts, etc., reliably predict progression to established smoking even when other factors are taken into account (Siegel & Biener, 2000). Evidence demonstrating that advertising increases consumption makes it clear why the American Academy of Pediatrics supports a "ban on cigarette and tobacco advertising in all media ... including sports arenas," and a restriction on alcohol advertising that allows only showing the product and no other characters (American Academy of Pediatrics, 2006).

Substance Portrayal in Film and Television

Advertising is not the only way images of alcohol use are disseminated. In his study of Hollywood's treatment of the alcoholic, Denzin (1991) found 664 movies that used alcoholism as a major theme between 1909 and 1991. Many of those, such as *Harvey* and *Arthur*, depicted the main characters as "happy alcoholics" with no particular need to deal with their alcohol problems. More recent movies (*Thank You for Smoking, Walk the Line*, and *Trainspotting*) bring the viewer to a much more realistic appraisal of substances. Researchers studying the relation between movie exposure to alcohol and tobacco and subsequent long-term use and problems in a national sample of adolescents found very interesting results. Among 532 top box office hits over the preceding 5½ years, 83 percent contained alcohol use. Increased movie alcohol exposure was significantly associated with increased adolescent alcohol use over time. Additionally, it was also related to subsequent alcohol problems (Wills, Sargent, Gibbons, Gerrard, & Stoolmiller, 2009). It was also calculated that each child could expect to be exposed to an average 594 movie smoking occurrences. Results showed that higher exposure to movie smoking was related to greater likelihood of smoking onset, even when a number of other factors were taken into account. The research also showed increases in positive expectations about smoking and more affiliation with friends who smoked (Wills, Sargent, Stoolmiller, Gibbons, & Gerrard, 2008).

Television exposure to substance use is high as well. The rate of alcohol consumption averaged 8.13 incidents per hour on the top 10 series and 2.25 per hour on the soap operas. Alcohol use was shown in an almost entirely positive context, with no indication of potential risk (Greenberg et al., 1981). Researchers have also noted that on television, alcohol was consumed more than any other food or drink (Mathios, Avery, Bisogni, & Shanahan, 1998). In research on music videos across five music genres (Adult Contemporary, Country, Rock, Rap, and Rhythm & Blues), 20 percent portrayed tobacco use and 23 percent contained alcohol use. Rap music had the highest proportion of tobacco and alcohol use, and rhythm and blues had the lowest (DuRant et al., 1997).

In 1982, three alcohol-related tragedies rocked Hollywood. Two celebrities, Mary Martin and Janet Gaynor, were critically injured when a drunk driver crashed into their taxi. Next, William Holden died alone in his room because he was too drunk to know that he was bleeding to death. Finally, Natalie Wood, after drinking "a few" glasses of wine, slipped off the side of a boat and drowned. Not long after these events, one of the major networks televised a news series called *The Hollywood Alcoholic*. The result of this new realization of the dangers of alcoholism was an effort by a caucus of producers, writers, and directors to produce these guidelines for dealing with alcohol use on television and in the movies (Gerstein, 1984):

1. Try not to glamorize the drinking or serving of alcohol as a sophisticated or an adult pursuit.
2. Avoid showing the use of alcohol gratuitously in those cases in which another beverage might be easily and fittingly substituted.
3. Try not to show excessive drinking without consequences or with only pleasant consequences.
4. Try not to show drinking alcohol as an activity that is so normal that everyone must indulge. Allow characters a chance to refuse an alcoholic drink by including nonalcoholic alternatives.
5. Demonstrate that there are no miraculous recoveries from alcoholism; normally, it is a most difficult task.
6. Don't associate drinking alcohol with macho pursuits in such a way that heavy drinking is a requirement for proving one's self as a man.
7. Portray the reaction of others to heavy alcohol drinking, especially when it may be a criticism.

There have been some notable efforts by the media since then to incorporate these guidelines into their programming. For example, the TV series *Mercy* has focused on the problems experienced by its chief character and her alcoholic parents. The movie *Requiem for a Dream* graphically illustrated the most debilitating consequences of drug abuse, and it also won rave reviews from the critics. The movie *Traffic* dealt comprehensively with the intricacies and consequences of the illegal drug trade. It was unique in addressing drug issues among many levels of government, within families, and across cultures. The well-publicized incarceration of Robert Downey, Jr., and the drug-related deaths of celebrities Heath Ledger and Michael Jackson have also brought a great deal of the entertainment industry's attention to the problem of illicit drugs and the misuse of prescription drugs. Public service announcements regularly warn young people and their parents about the dangers of alcohol, tobacco, and drug abuse, and urge parents to discuss these dangers with their children at home.

At the same time, however, it is still easy to find the gratuitous portrayal of alcohol use in the media. Research conducted by Roberts and colleagues (1999) found that of the 200 most popular movies of 1996 and 1997, alcohol and tobacco appeared in more than 90 percent of them and illicit drugs appeared in 20 percent. Many times, these movies graphically portrayed the preparation and/or utilization of these substances. Very few of the films specified motivations for use, and fewer than half portrayed short-term negative consequences.

It is the National Association of Broadcaster's position that alcohol use should be *de-emphasized* on television. The truth is that the rate of drinking on television still seems to be much greater than in real life. According to one estimate, a person under the legal drinking age will be exposed to approximately 3,000 acts of drinking during a year of television viewing (Greenberg et al., 1981). Is it any wonder that young people's T-shirts sport such popular themes as "It's Only a Drinking Problem if I'm Sober" and "Avoid Hangovers, Stay Drunk"? Obviously, television and the other mass media are not entirely to blame, and they have taken certain steps to improve programming. But, as Anderson and colleagues (2009) have concluded in a thorough review of 13 longitudinal studies of over 38,000 young people, exposure to media and commercial communications on alcohol increases the likelihood that adolescents will initiate alcohol use and drink more if they are already using. Therefore, more should be done by the media industry to decrease exposure and provide the proper messages to young people about the use of alcohol.

Product Placement

For many years, tobacco companies have had arrangements with movie studios for *product placement,* or showing the use of their products in movies. Documents released during the state of Minnesota's lawsuit against the tobacco industry showed arrangements between tobacco giant Philip Morris and the makers of 11 hit movies, all of which had large box office sales to youth (Youth Media Network, 2001). Although there are some restrictions on advertising alcoholic beverages, there are no restrictions on the use of alcohol by actors in television programs or films. Consumption of alcoholic beverages is frequent in TV programs, but, the incidence of actors smoking has decreased.

Despite protestations by the tobacco companies that they no longer paid for product placement after a voluntary movie industry ban in 1988, a study of "tobacco scenes" between 1990 and 1996 yielded some very interesting results. While the total number of tobacco scenes per movie rose slightly, the number of tobacco scenes with the film's star increased dramatically (Youth Media Network, 2001). A more recent study of tobacco presentations in 1,769 films between 1991 and 2008 showed overall reductions in tobacco incidents in movie, but total tobacco incidents on screen remains above late 1990s levels. Tobacco brands have increased on screen, with Marlboro accounting for 75 percent of brand display in 2008 (Titus,

Polansky, & Glantz, 2009). One company remains a shining example in this data. A large decrease, "36% of the drop in total tobacco impressions delivered to moviegoers in the last four years, industry wide" (Titus, et al., 2009, p. 6), can be attributed to the October, 2004, Disney Depiction of Smoking in Movies policy. The policy explains that due to awareness of "recent studies suggesting a relationship between the depiction of smoking in movies and increases in adolescent smoking," they are no longer depicting smoking in movies carrying the Disney brand, strongly discouraging "the depiction of smoking in [Touchtone] movies primarily marketed to youth," and discouraging smoking, where appropriate and practical, in those movies produced outside the United States where Disney is a coproducer. While seeking to limit smoking, they do, however, allow for the "creative vision" of those involved in the productions where smoking is important to the movie (The Walt Disney Company, 2006). However, other companies are not as helpful. About 75 percent of films released by Universal continue to include tobacco use (Titus, Polansky, & Glantz, 2009). Updated weekly, Smoke Free Movies (2010) posts the top grossing movies' and DVD rentals' tobacco status as "Promotes smoking," "Smoking with negative consequences," or "Smoke Free." On the week of January 4, 2010, for example, half of the top grossing movies promoted smoking and half were smoke free. Although all of the movies specifically directed at young children were smoke free, major motion pictures with crossover appeal such as *Avatar* depict smoking without any negative consequences. Unfortunately, attempts to curtail youth from buying substances by restricting advertising may be undone by the frequent images of those substances in television programs and film.

Community Impact: Sports

Most Americans at some point have participated in and/or have become a spectator in sports. Participation in sports has been known to be a protective factor against certain substance use in teens, but it can also be a source of stress for highly competitive athletes who enhance their ability to succeed in their sport through the use of performance enhancing substances. Steroid use came to the front of U.S. awareness in U.S. President George Bush's January 2004 State of the Union address tackled prevention in sports:

> To help children make right choices, they need good examples. Athletics play such an important role in our society, but, unfortunately, some in professional sports are not setting much of an example. The use of performance enhancing drugs like steroids in baseball, football, and other sports is dangerous, and it sends the wrong message—that there are shortcuts to accomplishment, and that performance is more important than character. So tonight I call on team owners, union representatives, coaches, and players to take the lead, to send the right signal, to get tough, and to get rid of steroids now. (Bush, 2004, para.56)

Professional athletes may be tempted to use steroids for competitive, financial, and societal gains. But, currently, major organizations such as the U.S. National Football League (NFL) are directly addressing substance abuse by their athletes. The NFL Player Development Program addresses many prevention issues surrounding substance abuse. In the four day Rookie Symposium run by NFL "League personnel, expert facilitators, trained professionals, active players, and former players are involved in delivering a program specially designed to give incoming players detailed information about what they may face during their NFL careers" (National Football League, 2009). The life-skills workshops include substance abuse and DUI training, which consists of the policy, the danger and consequences of substance abuse. Additionally, according to a spokesperson from the corporate NFL Player Development Program (Anonymous, personal communication, August 31, 2009), rookies are required to take an eight-week Conduct Management Program. One unit focuses on substance abuse prevention and policy. Each year thereafter,

all clubs require mandatory substance abuse "refreshers." All players are offered a Players Assistance benefit which provides four free counseling sessions. Finally, most clubs have a program to prevent recidivism.

Empirically-based programs are emerging specifically focusing on student athletes and substance abuse prevention. The ATHENA (Athletes Targeting Healthy Exercise & Nutrition Alternatives) is a school-based, team-centered program that attempts to deter the use of substances and encourage healthy lifestyles in middle and high-school female athletes. Young women who participated in the program demonstrated less diet pill, amphetamine, and steroid use. They also exhibited significant reductions in long-term cigarette, alcohol, and marijuana use. Additionally, they practiced healthier eating habits (Elliot et al., 2006; NREPP, 2010). A comparable program for young male athletes is ATLAS (Athletes Training and Learning to Avoid Steroids). It targets young men involved in sports to prevent substance abuse and to promote a healthy lifestyle. Athletes participating in the program were significantly less likely to initiate steroid use than were the students who did not participate in the program. The participating athletes also reported less long-term alcohol and illicit drug use (Goldberg et al., 2000; NREPP, 2010).

Despite these successful efforts, performance enhancing "doping" is present in all major athletics. Before and during the Beijing Olympics, for example, 47 athletes were caught doping. The International Olympic Committee, however, has maintained a strong anti-doping code to prevent as much drug use as possible (Wochenschr, 2009). After the 2007 reports that the dozens of professional U.S. baseball players were found to have used steroids and several athletes were banned from the Tour de France due to doping, some debated whether performance enhancing drugs would become commonplace to the point that they are accepted (Katz, 2008). Many would argue that doping for sports is wrong due to the deleterious consequences on health and the fact that it is cheating. Although substance use, including steroids, remains prevalent in athletics, several organizations are having a positive impact on the issue.

Community Impact: Social Networks

Positive social networks across ecological systems are known to act as major protective factors against negative substance abuse outcomes in teens and adults (Mayberry, Espelage, & Koenig, 2009; Garmendia, Alvarado, Montenegro, & Pino, 2008). Recognizing their importance, the American Recovery and Reinvestment Act of 2009 included grant funding for studying social networks and their influence on groups at high risk for negative health behaviors including substances (National Institutes of Health [NIH], 2009). A popular medium for networking is the Internet. It contains cutting-edge resources for social networking, as well as advertising and marketing, with advantages and disadvantages in relation to substance abuse prevention. The Internet can be a place of easy access to prevention information and support for those attempting to remain drug free for the first time or following prior substance abuse. On the other hand, it also facilitates the acquisition of prescription drugs, tobacco, and alcohol for minors and those in recovery from substance abuse issues. For example, according to a study in the Journal of the American Medical Association (Ribisl, Williams, & Kim, 2003), cigarette vendors on the Internet did not comply with laws governing tobacco sales in stores. Many sites did not screen for age, and others lacked the Surgeon General's warning. Of vendors located in the United States, minors successfully received cigarettes 93.6 percent of the time when using a credit card and 88.9 percent of the time when using a money order. Age was not verified for any of the deliveries of 1,650 packs of cigarettes to adolescents. It is difficult to adequately address this issue. Even if laws are enacted in the United States to regulate these sales, enforcement would become almost impossible, as only 88 of the 1,808 sites screened were located in the United States. Other illicit drugs and questionable prescription drugs are marketed on the Internet. In one week, a typical spam folder from a user who had never bought prescription drugs online contained over 30 requests to buy pharmaceuticals from dubious sources. Some of these advertised drugs, such as Adderall, Percocet, Vicodin, and Imovane, were controlled substances and/or drugs not available in the United States as of 2010. The Drug Enforcement Administration (DEA) attempts to close illegal internet operations to prevent easy access. In 2002, they had an "unprecedented takedown" of an Internet-based "date-rape" drug-trafficking operation that involved more than 80 U.S. cities. Finding ways to reduce the advertisements and access to these types of operations is extremely difficult, but new technology in the field of computer forensics can now track Internet traffic paths even when the messages have been password encoded and deleted. Experts are continuing to use innovative techniques to track and eliminate illegal operations (Eric K. Thompson, Chairman & CTO, AccessData Computer Forensics, personal communication, January 22, 2010).

File sharing on social networking sites such as YouTube and Facebook has impacted prevention efforts in remarkable ways. For example, one local prevention effort, Faces of Meth is a project of the Multnomah County Sheriff's Department in Oregon (2005). Deputy Bret King and the Multnomah County Classification Unit created a collection of *before* and *after* mug shots of individuals who had been booked more than once and had records of methamphetamine use in all cases. In addition, he interviewed meth users and used the photos and interview information to create the Faces of Meth prevention program. In a personal interview with the Web Administrator for the Multnomah County Sheriff's Department, Sarah Mooney, the Faces of Meth website had over 625,000 hits by the beginning of 2010 and had sold 700 copies of their CD.

However, in a thorough search of the Internet, it was found that the project is actually impacting millions more viewers worldwide. For example, the *Faces of Meth* is featured on major websites such as The Partnership for a Drug-Free America (2010). These photos and those with a similar theme have become part of a natural networking prevention effort. For example, a YouTube video entitled "Drug Abuse Pictures Before and After" using the Multnomah pictures has had over 1.5 million views (marajade619, 2006). It is most popular with young male viewers. Comments on the site range from the silly to advocating other drugs to real stories of the impact the photos have. For example one comment stated, "this was inspiring, I was heading in that direction but now I know for sure that it wasn't too late for me" (klownofdestruction, 2010). Another YouTube site using meth prevention material originating from the Montana Meth Project (2010) had over seven million views as of January, 2010 (FalseInternetName, 2006). And, the messages from similar sites such as Meth; Not Even Once (NaomiDreamStudios, 2009), a school project, are reaching worldwide viewers. Some messages actually reach out to help others. For example on the same site, "a lot of kids, thank God, are not actually stupid enough to try it nowadays. ive been addicted since i was thirteen. every day i watch these videos trying to find a reason to get clean. still trying. if your thinking about trying it, please message me and ill give you thirty reasons off the top of my head not to. it took one hit to pull me under" (breanavirgilio, 2009).

Although some posts demonstrate that these types of informational sharing have prevented some from using, the threads become a discussion for all types of viewpoints—some supporting the use of "soft" drugs, some wanting policy change, others just commenting on how sad it is, or making jokes of it all. Interestingly, since 2004, the year "Faces of Meth" was made available to others involved in methamphetamine prevention efforts, methamphetamine use in teens has steadily declined (NIDA, 2009). It would be very interesting to conduct research to see how these shared files have impacted behavior on a wide scale. The Multnomah County Sherriff's office isn't waiting. They are continuing their efforts with a broader focus on drugs other than meth, with their new project *From Drugs to Mugs*.

As discussed, the incorporation of a wider ecological view including family and community factors has been the biggest recent advancement in prevention research. Incorporating the environment in which the person interacts has a sizable impact on the results of prevention programs both long and short term. Although the outlook is promising, environmental impacts from media and social networking may also be reducing planned intervention effects. Much more research is needed to explore these macro levels of intervention.

Spirituality and Religious Factors

Spirituality and religious factors may be very helpful in deterring substance abuse. A study addressing spirituality made several interesting observations. Adults who never attend religious services are almost "twice as likely to drink, three times more likely to smoke, and more than five times likelier to have used an illicit drug other than marijuana, almost seven times likelier to binge drink, and almost eight times likelier to use marijuana than those who attend religious services at least weekly" (Foster et al., 2001). The effect for teens is also significant. Teens who do not consider religious beliefs important are almost three times more likely to drink, binge drink, and smoke; almost four times more likely to use marijuana; and seven times more likely to use illicit drugs than adolescents who strongly believe that religion is important. A limitation of this study is the heavy Judeo-Christian background of the sample. However, a southwestern study conducted with a more ethnically diverse population, including Native Americans, demonstrated findings in a similar direction (Hodge, Cardenas, & Montoya, 2001). In a review of over 105 articles addressing spirituality and substance abuse, Chitwood, Weiss and Leukefeld (2008) found in 99 of the 105 articles that one or more dimensions of religiosity or spirituality were significantly associated with reduced risk of substance use or misuse. Over 75 percent looked at teens and college students; more than half studied organized religious practices rather than spirituality in general, and the large majority looked at alcohol and marijuana use rather than other drugs. Despite these limitations, it is clear that spirituality is an important component of prevention.

Based on evidence that spirituality is protective against substance abuse, spiritually-based prevention programs are now emerging in greater numbers. For example, spiritual growth appears to be associated with the benefits of Alcoholics Anonymous, which acts in a secondary and tertiary prevention manner (Zemore, 2007). In addition to the traditional Alcoholics Anonymous broad-based spirituality, some programs focusing on more specific religious aspects of substance abuse prevention are beginning to gain momentum. For example, Celebrate Recovery is a Christian-based program based on the twelve step model, but with steps reflecting a specifically biblical focus. A typical evening will include dinner, a large group worship with a person sharing the spiritual aspect of their recovery story, prayers, and small support group breakout sessions. It originally focused on alcohol at Saddleback Church in Riverside, California, and has expanded to serve other "hurts, habits and hang-ups." Meeting in churches or community centers, its focus is providing long-term support for individuals striving to remain substance-free. It also offers concurrent support groups for families of those working through issues of recovery. Over 500,000 people have completed the program worldwide (Saddleback Resources, 2009).

Another program, Art of Living, is a yoga based Sudarshan Kriya and Pranayam deep breathing, chanting, and meditation technique that has been used for many health- and stress-related issues, including tobacco addiction. Researchers reported that at a six month follow-up, 21 percent of those who participated in the Art of Living Program had remained tobacco free. This is comparable to those who take the drug Bupropion to remain tobacco free and much better than the 11 percent who take a placebo (Art of Living, 2009; Kochupillai et al, 2005).

Another program that has targeted spirituality has been the Natural Connection Program. For this program, youths were involved in deep discussions rooted in Native American cultural values. In addition to sessions conducted in the classrooms, the participants attended presentations from traditional healers and spiritual leaders from eleven different native traditions. These elders also conducted spiritual and healing ceremonies (Navarro, Wilson, Berger, & Taylor, 1997).

Cultural Factors

Approaches addressing the specific needs of racial/ethnic subgroups have demonstrated positive responses from their respective communities. For example, Chipungu and fellow researchers (2000) reported higher rates of satisfaction and perceived program importance in African American youth exposed to Afrocentric prevention programming, compared with other prevention approaches. Strong racial/ethnic identification has been identified as a significant predictor of drug attitudes (Belgrave, Brome, & Hampton, 2000). However, confounding variables of community factors must be addressed, including poverty and neighborhood characteristics. Delva and colleagues (2001) found that prevalence of drug use among minority mothers dropped by 40 percent in black mothers compared to white mothers, once the negative effects of poverty and drug availability in the neighborhood were held constant.

Programs are emerging which focus on the needs of specific cultural groups and those at high risk due to difficult community circumstances. An example of an empirically-based program utilizing a multifaceted ecological approach as a prevention tool is Project Venture. Created by the National Indian Youth Leadership Project, the outdoor experiential curriculum specifically works with Native American youth to build self-efficacy, resilience, and decision making skills, which, in turn, facilitates resistance to alcohol, tobacco, and other drugs (National Indian Youth Leadership Project, 2008). The program specifically incorporates older peer mentors, family involvement, classroom, community service, cultural values, and spiritual awareness in these 5th-8th grade youths, resulting in significant differences in substance use over time between participants and control groups (Carter, Straits, & Hall, 2007).

Another example, Storytelling for Empowerment, uses the arts to directly address Latino teens at high risk for substance abuse living in communities with high rates of poverty and availability of drugs. Cognitive decision making, positive cultural identity, and resilience models are the basis of stories, plays, artwork, and discussions to reduce high-risk behaviors. Participants demonstrated less abuse of alcohol and marijuana over time when involved in at least 20 contact hours with the program, but hard drug use was not affected (Nelson & Arthur, 2003). Another innovative culturally targeted program, H2P, is a drug and HIV prevention program with a hip-hop based curriculum created for urban African American middle-school students. It has shown preliminary evidence of changes in risk perception of drugs (Turner-Musa, Rhodes, Harper, & Quinton, 2008). These programs are promising, but much more research is needed in this area.

Summary

Prevention sounds like a good idea, but how does one measure its effect? To know whether a prevention program *really* works, researchers must hold a number of important factors constant while an intervention is implemented. They need to randomize the target population between the program and a control group and study this cohort over a relatively long period of time. Based on these requirements, the current state of knowledge regarding prevention programs is still incomplete.

From a logical perspective, we know that if a population can be prevented from using a drug, morbidity and mortality rates will be reduced. Most indications are that education and public information approaches alone do not seem to be effective, especially for those people with the most serious problems. Those techniques that do work incorporate a wide range of interventions that include addressing problems from the individual to the community. However, most programs are still relatively limited in their scope. Swift and certain law enforcement for DUI offenses seems to work. Heavy fines are also effective. Price has a strong deterrent effect on the use of certain drugs. Minimum age of purchase legislation keeps many younger drivers alive. The next chapter discusses many other law enforcement strategies, such as long prison terms, that do not seem to be very effective prevention tools

The focus of prevention efforts seems to have shifted away from reliance on the traditional educational and public information approaches to a harm-reduction and ecologically based philosophy. Society must try not only to reduce the use and abuse of harmful drugs but also to ameliorate the consequences of those drugs and support the individual throughout the process. Preventing the spread of AIDS and decreasing traffic fatalities are just as legitimate prevention goals as reducing intravenous heroin use and the consumption of alcoholic beverages. Guided by this philosophy, there are many other approaches still to be tried. For example, it has been suggested that makers of fortified wines be required to supplement them with vitamins and minerals. Those experiencing alcoholism who buy these products are especially prone to malnutrition, partly because of their alcoholism. Another suggestion is to levy special taxes on products known to be detrimental to people's health (primarily tobacco and alcohol) and to dedicate those funds to the provision of additional health care services. Legislation, the media, and the workplace can all build on the foundation set by education, the family, religious organizations, and racial/ethnic groups. Decreasing risk factors and increasing protective factors that lead to resilience may have the greatest impact on the overall problems of substance abuse.

CHAPTER 8

Regulating Drugs
and Their Consequences

One of the major obstacles to the successful prevention and treatment of chemical dependency problems is that there is no clear understanding of the etiology of drug abuse or dependence *at the level of individual pathology* (see Chapter 2). From a clinical perspective, therefore, it is difficult (some would say impossible) to match an individual's treatment needs with a particular treatment modality that is best suited for those needs. Experts do know, however, that there are a number of social, cultural, and environmental factors that influence an individual's probability of using drugs. Unfortunately, treatment plans are often developed as if chemical dependency were only an *individual* phenomenon, frequently ignoring important *systemic* causes and consequences. Most of the previous chapters focused on clinical issues; this chapter turns to some important public policy issues related to drug availability, use, and treatment. We will continue and expand the discussion, begun in Chapter 7, regarding the types of collective action that society may employ in controlling drug use.

We also will continue the debate over the deregulation of certain drugs within the context of broad public policy issues. Public policies regarding drug use and addiction include much more than the *legality* of manufacturing, selling, and using drugs, however. Public policy is concerned with controlling or limiting the use of specific drugs, restricting use to specific

segments of the population (such as adults, cancer patients, etc.), avoiding the *misuse* of drugs, enhancing governmental revenues through the collection of taxes on drugs (especially alcohol), and protecting domestic drug producers from foreign competition. The use of marijuana for medical purposes continues to be a hotly debated issue, and we will attempt to cover various perspectives on this issue. Finally, we will turn to one of the most troubling policy issues regarding drug use: what to do about the relationship between drugs and crime. The "war on drugs" is in its fourth decade, and the end is not in sight.

Sociocultural Influences on Public Drug Policy

Public policies regarding drugs vary widely throughout the world. They have also varied widely within nations during the last few centuries. Until the early part of the twentieth century, very few drugs were strictly regulated by any government (Bean, 1974). Public policies that are now common in modern Western societies cannot be considered historical norms (White, 1991).

Variations between cultures depend partly on historical accident: Peyote grew in the American Southwest, heroin in Asia, and cannabis from the Middle East to India. Beverage alcohol is the most nearly universal psychoactive drug. As locally produced drugs were spread by international trade, the culture of the importing nation had a profound impact on public policy toward these new drugs. When it was first introduced to Europe, tobacco was used as a medicine in some countries and as a mild stimulant in others. In Russia, it was used as an intoxicant by means of deep and rapid inhalation (White, 1991).

Drugs associated with ceremonial and religious use are generally treated differently from other drugs. Alcohol commonly was used by a great many people in ceremonies and rituals, often to the point of intoxication. Until very recently, these same people rarely used alcohol outside of these rituals and ceremonies. The same can be said of marijuana use in some areas of India. Where use of a drug is a very old, traditional practice, such as opium use in Arab countries, it is usually restricted to the adult male population (Rubin, 1975).

Religious beliefs and practices may either inhibit or reinforce the use of particular drugs. Psychoactive drugs were frequently viewed in traditional societies either as a gift from God or as "the devil's brew." The native residents of both North and South America used hallucinogenic drugs as a part of religious rituals. Indeed, Native Americans in the United States are still fighting for the right to use peyote legally in ceremonies sanctioned by the Native American Church. The cactus plant from which the drug is obtained is believed to be a gift from God to man. On the other hand, the strong religious injunctions against the use of alcohol in many Muslim countries severely restrict its use. This ban was decreed by the prophet Mohammed and still carries the force of law in countries such as Saudi Arabia (White, 1991).

Sociocultural differences are also found in conceptions of the role of government regarding the health and welfare of its citizens, and these different conceptions influence public policy responses to the use of drugs (Moore & Gerstein, 1981). Thus, Sweden, Norway, and Finland introduced retail liquor monopolies as a way of limiting consumption. The former Soviet Union had

a complete state monopoly on the production, distribution, and sale of alcohol, although those functions are now mostly privatized. In the United States, several states have adopted a monopoly distribution system for distilled spirits but not for wine and beer. Other states allow competitive retailing but control the hours and location of sales. Some states allow beer and wine sales in supermarkets, convenience stores, and gas stations, whereas other states restrict such sales to liquor stores. Communities in states with local option laws may simply prohibit the sale of alcoholic beverages. Even so, some restaurants and clubs allow patrons to bring and consume their own liquor.

Economic and Political Factors

Why do societies decide to regulate some drugs, prohibit other drugs, and ignore some drugs altogether? In many cases, the production and supply of the entrenched drugs—such as alcohol, nicotine, and caffeine—are sources of wealth and power (White, 1991). Permissive policies toward other drugs may threaten business. Since coffee could not be grown in Europe, it was necessary to import it. The Germans saw this as a threat to their beer industry, and the English imposed heavy taxes on coffee as a way of protecting tea produced in British colonies.

It is easy to understand why U.S. distillers and brewers may oppose the legalization of other drugs. Depending on the degree to which newly legalized drugs could be substituted for alcohol, they could stand to lose a great deal of money. On the other hand, some say that the U.S. tobacco industry is prepared to produce marijuana cigarettes in the event that cannabis is legalized (U.S. Congress, 1988). This new market might take up some of the slack resulting from declining cigarette sales.

Economic factors also have an impact on the enforcement of existing drug laws. It would be counterproductive for the tobacco industry to favor strict enforcement of the age limitation for the purchase of cigarettes when *all* their future customers, not to mention the fastest-growing segment of their current market, are under 18 years of age.

The socioeconomic status, political position, and race of drug *users* also must be considered. Heroin and crack cocaine use are still regarded as being most common in African American ghettoes. Most experts agree that these drugs are least likely to be legalized. When marijuana was perceived to be a drug used mostly by African Americans, Hispanic Americans, and a few eccentric literary figures and musicians, there was not much support for its legalization. Now that hundreds of thousands of middle-class college students have used marijuana, there is much more support for its decriminalization—even in otherwise conservative states (Galliher, McCartney, & Baum, 1974).

Changes in Drug-Use Patterns

The types of drugs used and the manner of their use within a society vary over time. A society with few or no restrictions in one historical period may have comprehensive regulations of most drugs during another time (Morgan, 1981). Traditional societies tended to have available a rather narrow range of drugs, and they were frequently used in religious rituals and ceremonies, such as Native Americans' use of peyote. This type of limited use was not viewed as a cause for alarm. Eventually, international trade brought new types of drugs to practically every nation. New drugs became a threat because they were used recreationally, their effects were not known, and their users were regarded as deviant. This called for regulation.

Changes in the manner of use of a single drug also have resulted in pressures for regulation and control. Oral administration or smoking of drugs such as opium and heroin present fewer threats to the users' health and safety than does intravenous injection. Oral administration of OxyContin was consistent with medical practice, but crushing it for

inhalation is strictly for recreation. Little thought was given to drinking small amounts of cocaine in soft drinks such as Coca-Cola; the consequences of this type of use represented no more of a threat to the user than the chewing of coca leaves by South American aborigines. Snorting cocaine brought more immediate results, but it was not regarded as truly dangerous until users began to inject a soluble form with a hypodermic needle. Intravenous use not only produces an instantaneous high, but it also brings the risk of addiction and the additional hazards of hepatitis, HIV infection, and other diseases. Finally, the discovery of a new form of smokable crack cocaine brought even greater risks of addiction. The use of cocaine itself seems no more an issue than the form of administration.

The Nature of Drug Control

The most obvious function of drug control, and the primary reason cited by lawmakers, is to decrease the amount of a particular drug that is used. In some cases, such as heroin, the goal is complete prohibition. In other cases, such as cocaine, the goal may be to limit use of the drug to medical practice. In still other cases, such as alcohol, governments may allow general use by adults but seek to limit the amount used by monitoring price controls, taxes, number of outlets, and the hours of sale.

The Harrison Narcotics Act of 1914 was primarily a labeling and registration act, and its purpose was to restrict the distribution of narcotic drugs to physicians and pharmacists. Prior to this act, access to opium derivatives was not officially restricted. After 1914, distributors had to register with the U.S. Treasury Department.

Most legal drugs are taxed. Since they are widely used commodities in any modern economy, governments have discovered that they can be a significant source of tax revenue. In most cases, the tax is imposed primarily for the purpose of raising revenue, but taxes on drugs are also used to regulate trade in one way or another. Such was the case of Britain's tax on Jamaican rum that was destined for other colonies and thus competed with English gin. Alcoholic beverages were first subjected to federal taxation in the United States in 1791, and a liquor excise was the first internal revenue law enacted by Congress under the Constitution. As late as 1907, these revenues constituted 80 percent of all federal internal tax collections (Moore & Gerstein, 1981).

Drug taxes almost always have a dual effect of decreasing consumption and raising revenue. Sometimes the revenues from taxes on a drug are only incidental to the primary purpose of the tax, prohibiting *use* of the drug. The Marijuana Tax Act of 1937 used a tax to outlaw marijuana. Marijuana approved for medical use was taxed at $1 per ounce. Marijuana used for other purposes was taxed at $100 per ounce. Few people would voluntarily pay taxes on drugs that are being sold or used illegally (McKim, 1991).

Both the amount of revenue raised and the success of the tax in curbing consumption depend on the degree of *price elasticity* of the product being taxed. The elasticity of any particular drug depends on a number of factors, such as (1) the degree to which another drug may be substituted for it, (2) the availability of the drug, (3) the addictive power of the drug, and (4) the cost of the drug, including taxes. It is generally agreed that taxes on alcoholic beverages diminish their consumption (Moore & Gerstein, 1981) but that distilled spirits are less price elastic than beer (Ornstein, 1980). In other words, a tax on distilled spirits would result in a smaller decrease in consumption than the same tax on beer. Beer is more frequently consumed as a beverage and could be replaced by tea, coffee, soft drinks, and the like. The relative elasticity of illicit drugs is less well known.

Assumptions Underlying Regulation

A number of important assumptions underlie any government's efforts to control drug use. One is that drug use produces victims (ONDCP,

2001). Victims may be the actual users of drugs or they may be innocent bystanders—those who passively inhale cigarette smoke, those maimed or killed by drunken drivers, or those whose family life is destroyed by drug use. Others argue that use of drugs is a victimless crime that has no major adverse consequences for the rest of society, but this view is not consistent with governmental regulation.

Closely related to this is a second assumption that governments are responsible for enhancing the general welfare. A nation with a large proportion of drug users would be at an economic disadvantage in the world market because of reduced work output and the need to divert resources to handle the health and welfare needs of users. In regulating drugs as a way of promoting the general welfare, government walks a fine line between benefiting the majority of its citizens and encroaching on the individual liberties of a few. This potential conflict frequently appears when governments declare smoke-free workplaces, prohibit the possession of alcoholic beverages in a public park, subject vehicles to searches, or use drug-sniffing dogs at airports.

Governments find it just as difficult to distinguish *nonproblem* from *problem* drug use as distinguishing *use* and *misuse* (see Chapter 1), but they do it anyway. Those drugs that are perceived not to cause problems (such as caffeine) are subjected to few controls. Those that are deemed to be troublesome but are impossible to prohibit because of widespread public use and acceptance, and because they are easily produced (such as alcohol), are tightly regulated. Those perceived to be the most problematic (heroin, cocaine) are generally banned.

These divisions between problem and nonproblem use are somewhat arbitrary, and the reasons for regarding drugs as acceptable or not are largely historical rather than pharmacological. For example, alcohol produces marked changes in behavior, has dangerous physical effects, and is powerfully addictive. It is highly unlikely that the

United States would ever completely legalize any other drug with such undesirable consequences (White, 1991).

Regulation of Alcohol

Alcohol is tightly regulated in most countries and banned in a few. It remains an extremely popular drug, despite its adverse consequences and the problems of addiction associated with its use. Because of its special position in most societies as a historically controlled but legal psychoactive drug, it deserves special attention in this chapter.

The Lessons of Prohibition

Although it is widely believed that the Eighteenth Amendment to the U.S. Constitution, which prohibited the production and sale of alcohol, was a failure and that it demonstrated once and for all the futility of governmental attempts to legislate morality, this is not a completely accurate account of the effects of Prohibition (Levine, 1980). This legislation failed in the sense that it bred contempt and open defiance of law and order, and it also fostered the growth of organized crime. No one denies that the Volstead Act was widely violated and that smuggling, moonshining, and speakeasies all thrived during the Prohibition era. On the other hand, there is considerable evidence that the consumption of alcoholic beverages declined considerably, especially among the working class. The most reliable indicators of heavy consumption— including acute alcohol overdose mortalities, liver cirrhosis, and hospital admissions for alcoholic psychosis—dropped well below their pre-Prohibition levels (Warburton, 1932). These declines were related to the price of alcohol, which tripled or quadrupled in parts of the nation after the Eighteenth Amendment took effect (Olson & Gerstein, 1985). It can be expensive to deal in the underground economy!

According to Moore and Gerstein (1981), there are three principal lessons of Prohibition

that should be remembered in any future attempts to regulate the supply of beverage alcohol:

1. Drinking customs in the United States are strongly held and resistant to frontal assault. It is well beyond the will or capacity of government ever to eradicate the customary demand for alcoholic beverages.
2. A criminal supply network emerges—if not instantly, then within a few years—if production and sale of alcoholic beverages are outlawed. The prices and extent of this criminal supply depend on the degree of public support for the law and the resources devoted to law enforcement.
3. The quantity of alcohol consumption and the rates of problems varying with consumption can, however, be markedly reduced by substantial increases in real prices and reductions in the ease of availability.

The well-remembered lesson of Prohibition is that an abrupt legislative decree banning beverage alcohol will not work in U.S. society. In fact, the failure of Prohibition may be responsible for the tendency of many of those interested in alcohol problems to "disassociate themselves from the taint of temperance" (Room & Mosher, 1979–80, p. 11). An equally important lesson, but one that seems to have been forgotten, is that regulation *can* reduce consumption and alcohol-related problems.

Current U.S. Policies

Today, all states in the United States set a minimum age for the legal consumption of alcohol and prescribe penalties for retailers who knowingly sell to underage customers. Some states assess penalties even when a retailer mistakenly sells alcohol in good faith to a minor with fake identification. Under pressure from the federal government, including the threat of withholding highway trust funds, the minimum age has shifted back to 21 years. All states also impose special excise taxes on alcoholic beverages, and most have restricted advertising, hours of sale, and credit sales.

Beginning in the 1930s, 18 states chose to create state or county monopolies to control both wholesale distribution and retail sales of distilled spirits. The remaining states adopted licensing systems in which state regulatory agencies are empowered to license wholesalers and retailers and to promulgate and implement other rules and regulations regarding beverage alcohol sales.

Although the Twenty-First Amendment, which repealed Prohibition, left the "dry" option open to individual states, all of them now permit alcoholic beverage sales in at least part of the state. In most cases, dry counties are predominately rural areas, and they tend to be concentrated in the South. Even there, however, drinking usually is allowed in certain lodges, fraternal organizations, and private clubs.

Taxes and Price Controls. A fundamental law of economics is that as the price of something goes up, people will generally buy less of it. Thus, as prices for alcoholic beverages rapidly rose during Prohibition, demand decreased (Olson & Gerstein, 1985). The same effect in reverse may also be partly responsible for the increase in per capita consumption that has occurred since the last major increase in federal taxes in 1951. Between 1967 and 1984, the real price of liquor dropped by almost one-half. One reason for this dramatic decrease in price was the fact that the federal excise taxes were not based on the price of the beverage but instead were tied directly to volume. Thus, the tax on an expensive quart of vodka is the same as on a cheap quart of vodka. Some critics have argued that the most important feature of federal policy in alcohol abuse prevention during the past several decades is the failure to index excise taxes on liquor to the consumer price index (Cook, 1984).

In addition to taxes, many state governments also influence alcohol prices through fair trade laws and, in monopoly states, by administrative fiat. States with liquor monopolies may still set prices by decree in state-owned liquor stores, but the courts have eliminated price fixing by the liquor industry through fair trade laws. The method used to set prices may make a great difference to the state treasury, but it matters very little to the consumer. A price increase that arrives through taxation, price fixing, or administrative decree is all the same to the customer at the checkout stand. All three methods equally affect demand for the product.

Perhaps the most comprehensive analysis of the connection between alcohol prices, consumption, and alcohol-related problems was conducted by Philip J. Cook (1984). His examination of changes in liquor tax increases over a 15-year period demonstrated that even relatively small changes in prices influence not only the consumption of alcohol but the most serious health effects as well. Similar decreases in consumption, heavy drinking, and alcohol-related problems due to price increases also have been noted in other countries (Popham, Schmidt, & DeLint, 1976).

An especially important question is whether a decrease in overall consumption within a population affects the drinking patterns of heavy drinkers. The pioneering work of Ledermann (1956) and subsequent studies by several others confirm that even a significant proportion of problem drinkers in any population will reduce their consumption as overall consumption is reduced (Skog, 1971). Some have suggested that regulation aimed at prevention of problem drinking might be more effective if specific taxes were levied on particular beverages favored by heavy drinkers, such as cheap brands of fortified wine (Olson & Gerstein, 1985). However, this may just encourage switching to other alcoholic beverages. This argument also favors keeping the tax tied to the volume of alcohol sold, rather than the purchase price, since the former approach would have a greater impact on alcoholics, especially poor alcoholics who customarily purchase the cheaper types and greater quantities of alcoholic beverages.

Even though taxes on alcohol constitute a relatively small proportion of governmental budgets, governments closely consider the implications of these taxes on their revenues. This is especially true during serious budget crises. U.S. President George H. Bush's promise of "no new taxes" was quickly amended in 1990 to allow consideration of increases in both alcohol and tobacco taxes—so called "sin" taxes. Governments are most certainly aware of the danger of raising taxes to such a high level that revenues may actually decrease from a reduction in sales. As long as the alcoholic beverage lobby still exerts any influence in legislative circles, taxes are unlikely to rise to such levels. Still, if governments have no choice but to raise income taxes or "sin" taxes, and if the amount of additional revenue needed is moderate, the latter are politically less volatile.

There are a number of other mechanisms by which government may influence the price and thereby control demand for alcohol. Between 1986 and 1992, tax laws subsidizing alcohol consumption by allowing tax deductions for beverages purchased with business-related meals were gradually eliminated. Another example is the long-standing practice of selling alcoholic beverages at greatly discounted prices on U.S. military bases, a practice that strongly encouraged drinking by both uniformed and civilian employees and their families. Fortunately, the military establishment has realized that many problems were caused by selling cheap alcohol, and current policies have changed this practice.

Control of Distribution.   In addition to taxation and monopolistic price controls, government can do much to regulate the consumption of alcohol by controlling its distribution. It can do this by adopting and implementing policies regarding the number, size, and location of outlets, hours of business for package stores and bars, advertising practices, and the minimum legal drinking age.

The matter of licensing retailers is generally a function of state and local governments. A number of earlier studies have attempted to

determine the effect of outlet density on alcohol consumption, but there appears to be no relationship (Popham, Schmidt, & DeLint, 1978). A quasi-experimental study in Ontario compared sales to residents of two cities located some miles apart, both of which were served by a package store located in one of them. Per capita sales were roughly equal for these two cities, despite the considerable differences in accessibility (Popham et al., 1978). Outlet density may be more a result than a cause of demand in communities that treat alcohol sales as a proper function of the free market (Smart, 1977).

Monopoly distribution systems also do not seem to have any appreciable effect on alcohol sales. In the former Soviet Union, for example, consumption is high and alcoholism is a major social problem (White, 1991). A comparison of states in the United States that have monopoly distribution systems with those that allow private competition showed no difference in levels of consumption or indicators of alcohol-related health problems (Popham et al., 1978).

There is little evidence that restricting the hours of sale reduces consumption. In fact, a study of changes in the hours of sale over a 25-year period concluded that "Sunday closing" laws (sometimes called *blue laws*) and earlier closing hours had the opposite effect: more sales (Hoadley, Fuchs, & Holder, 1984). However, other changes in availability have been related to increased consumption. These include a gradual easing of restrictions on alcohol sales since World War II. Liquor-by-the-drink is now available in almost every large city, wine and beer are routinely sold in grocery stores and convenience stores, mixed drinks are available in restaurants, and sporting events often realize as much profit from the sale of alcohol as from the sale of tickets.

Blose and Holder (1989) found a significant increase in alcohol sales and alcohol-related automobile accidents immediately after North Carolina adopted liquor-by-the-drink. When Idaho, Maine, Virginia, and Washington made wine available for sale in grocery stores, wine consumption rose significantly (MacDonald, 1985). Anyone who has ever attended a professional baseball or football game where alcoholic beverages are sold can attest to their popularity. Consumption at sporting events has become such a problem in some communities that local officials have imposed beer-free games on the fans. Several major stadiums no longer sell any beer after the seventh inning of major league baseball games—with no significant effect on attendance.

The effect of increased availability on consumption is not peculiar to the U.S. culture. One study of the liberalization of alcohol laws in Finland showed a remarkable *doubling* of consumption in just seven years. The Alcohol Act of 1969 abolished restrictions on sales in rural areas, lowered the drinking age, and permitted retail shops to sell beer with a higher alcohol content. By 1975, the Finns were drinking 156 percent more beer, 96 percent more spirits, and 87 percent more wine. (Another curious fact is that Finnish drivers already had a higher rate of driving under the influence [DUI] than other Europeans *before* the liberalized liquor laws [Olson & Gerstein, 1985]. This happened despite a lower rate of drinking—indicating, perhaps, that enforcement was stricter in Finland.)

Drinking Age.   Other than Prohibition, perhaps no other area of alcohol policy has been so emotionally charged as the minimum legal age for purchasing and consuming alcoholic beverages. The most common legal age for consuming alcohol throughout the world is 18. There are currently 12 nations (including Germany, Portugal, and Poland) that have a minimum drinking age of 16 years. Another 17 nations have no minimum age at all (Alcohol Problems and Solutions, 2010). Minimum age restrictions are based on the assumption that alcohol use is more harmful for young persons than it is for adults. There always has been some variation in this age in the United States, but historically most have used the age of 21 as the minimum age for unrestricted purchases. This continues to be a point of contention

among the young, since they can vote and are eligible for military service at age 18. Between 1970 and 1973, 24 states reduced their minimum drinking ages, reasoning that 18- to 21-year-olds should have all the rights and responsibilities of adulthood (Olson & Gerstein, 1985).

During that period, an enormous amount of research was conducted on the impact of lowering the minimum age of purchase. One conclusion stood out quite clearly: Lower drinking ages were associated with significant increases in the rate of automobile crashes among young people (Public Health Service, 1987). Estimates of the increase in fatality rates were found to be 7 percent among those states that had dropped their minimum ages from 21 to 18 years of age (Cook & Tauchen, 1984).

Partly because of this evidence, 15 states raised their minimum drinking ages back to 21 between 1975 and 1982. Among 13 of these states that were studied, automobile crashes were reduced from a minimum of 14 percent to a maximum of 29 percent (Arnold, 1985). Another study of 9 states that raised their minimum drinking age between 1975 and 1979 found a *41 percent* decrease in nighttime single-vehicle fatalities (Williams, Zador, & Karpf, 1983). With such convincing evidence in hand on the effect of minimum age legislation, Congress passed the Minimum Drinking Age Act of 1984 that reduced federal highway funds for any state that did not raise its minimum drinking age to 21 years by 1986. Despite the outcry on college campuses and frantic lobbying by the alcohol lobby, most states complied by the deadline. Louisiana held out until its highway system could no longer survive without federal funds. It appears that the national minimum age of consumption will remain at 21.

One of the other arguments against a lower minimum age is that it makes it just that much easier for 16- and 17-year-old students who have 18-year-old friends to obtain alcohol. (Remember, a majority of high school seniors will be 18 years old before their graduation.)

The National Highway Traffic Safety Administration (NHTSA) credits state laws that rose the legal drinking age to 21 with preventing about 1,000 traffic deaths annually. Many states have reduced the maximum blood-alcohol concentration (BAC) level for drivers under age 21 to 0.02 percent, and this has reduced nighttime fatal crashes in this age group by 16 percent (NIAAA, 1996). Nevertheless, almost two-thirds of 16- to 19-year-old drivers who had positive blood-alcohol concentrations in 1998 were higher than 0.10 percent. More than 15 percent of them tested at more than 0.20 percent (Yi, Stinson, Williams, & Dufour, 1999).

Driving Under the Influence.   In most situations, the possession and use of alcohol by adults is completely legal. However, when a legally intoxicated individual attempts to drive an automobile, a *crime* has been committed. Driving under the influence (DUI) or driving while intoxicated (DWI) is a criminal offense in all 50 states and the District of Columbia. (Most states also have laws against having any kind of open container of alcohol in a moving motor vehicle.) Progress has been made in reducing alcohol-related crash fatalities, falling from 43.6 percent of total crash fatalities in 1986 to 30.5 percent in 1998 (Yi et al., 1999). Advances in technology (automobile engineering, airbags, etc.) and stricter public policies are thought to be responsible.

All states now have a BAC maximum level of .08 percent for adult drivers. Many have "zero tolerance" policies (usually .02, but sometimes .00) for drivers under the age of 21 (APIS, 2010). Sometimes called the *blood-alcohol level (BAL)*, this figure is determined by the ratio of the weight of alcohol to the volume of blood grams per 100 milliliters (G/100ml). In states with *per se* laws, it is an offense to drive with a BAC at or above the specified value. A defendant may be convicted on the basis of chemical test evidence alone. Moreover, a driver may be charged with a DWI or DUI at a level lower than the state's *per se* standard if impairment can be shown. Other states use a particular BAC as a *presumptive standard,* allowing the defendant to introduce evidence that he or she was not, in fact,

impaired at the prescribed limit (APIS, 2010). The question of how effective these laws are in influencing the rate of drunken driving is still unsettled. Some moderately persuasive evidence does suggest that effectively enforced drunk driving laws deter drunken driving and reduce the accidents and fatalities associated with them.

The most thorough study of drunk driving laws is possibly that of the British Road Safety Act (RSA) of 1967. This act provided a *per se* BAC limit of 0.08 percent, and the first conviction resulted in a mandatory one-year license suspension. The new law was also preceded by a great deal of publicity. Ross's (1973) evaluation of the RSA found a 23 percent decline in auto fatalities, a decline in other auto injuries, and a decline in BAC levels of injured drivers—all within the first few months after implementation. Unfortunately, these improvements gradually flattened out and then began to rise by the end of 1970. The explanation for these events was that the well-publicized passage of the RSA convinced many drivers that the risk of arrest and punishment would be much higher than it had been. Although they were deterred from drinking before driving and from driving after drinking, law enforcement did not markedly increase the certainty of either detection or punishment, and drivers gradually returned to their old habits as this became known to the public.

In the United States, an evaluation of 35 alcohol safety action programs between 1970 and 1977 concluded that 12 of the programs had produced a decrease in nighttime auto fatalities, an accepted indicator of drunken driving (Levy, Voas, Johnson, & Klein, 1978). Nevertheless, there continues to be a great deal of controversy over DUI laws. In most states, a common result of a DUI conviction is the administrative suspension of the driver's license. No one could deny the logic (and perhaps the justice) of this method. However, police report that a very large proportion of DUIs involve drivers whose licenses already have been suspended for previous DUI convictions. One reason the courts cite for not strictly enforcing DUI laws is that they impose "new and heavy demands on courts, incarceration facilities, and probation services" at a time when the criminal justice system is already overflowing with more supposedly serious crimes (ABA, 1986, p. 101). Prosecuting attorneys frequently feel that tough mandatory sentences for drunk drivers are ineffective and may actually raise public expectations to unrealistic levels (ABA, 1986, p. 105). Organizations such as Mothers Against Drunk Driving (MADD) and Students Against Driving Drunk (SADD) have reacted by bringing even greater pressure for tougher sentences, especially for drunk drivers who kill or injure other people. Such pressure has resulted in much political posturing by state and local politicians but few effective solutions. Some judges have resorted to bizarre sentences such as mandating a convicted drunken driver to place a "Drunken Driver" plate or tag on his or her automobile. Needless to say, other family members who drive this automobile suffer needless embarrassment.

Another popular approach in dealing with drunken drivers is the *sobriety checkpoint*. The typical procedure is for local police to set up unannounced roadblocks along certain routes and stop vehicles, sometimes at random, to check for indications of alcohol impairment. Earlier studies questioned their effectiveness, but recent evidence indicates that they may reduce alcohol-related crashes. Shults et al. (2001) reviewed 23 studies and concluded that following the implementation of checkpoints, crashes involving alcohol dropped by 18 percent and fatal crashes dropped by 22 percent. Although a number of states have prohibited sobriety checkpoints as an unconstitutional invasion of privacy under state law, the U.S. Supreme Court upheld their legality in *Michigan State Police Dept. v. Sitz* (1990). The American Civil Liberties Union (ACLU) continues to criticize the use of sobriety checkpoints, and there will probably continue to be additional challenges in state courts.

Like drug use and possession, drunk driving lacks the usual criminal motives of gaining property or harming another person. DUI offenses are also unique in that a physical test (breathalyzer, blood analysis, etc.) is used and compared against a state standard to determine whether a crime has been committed. Drunk-driving offenses are also frequently handled administratively rather than judicially through driver's licensing regulation. This means that a driver's license can be suspended without any judicial safeguards. In most states, when drivers receive their licenses, they agree to take a breath or blood test if they are stopped on suspicion of driving while intoxicated. Refusal to take a test upon request is a violation of the licensing agreement and can result in automatic suspension or revocation of the license through an administrative process. Most states have such sanctions (APIS, 2010).

According to the National Household Survey on Drug Abuse, one in ten Americans aged 12 or older had driven under the influence of alcohol at least once in the preceding 12 months. Among young adults aged 18 to 25 years, the rate was 19.9 percent (SAMHSA, 2001). Between 1970 and 1986, arrests for drunk driving increased by 223 percent. DUI arrests peaked in 1983, with 1.9 million persons arrested (BOJS, 1988a). From 1986 to 1997, the number of people arrested for DUI fell 18 percent, from 1.8 million to 1.5 million (BOJS, 1999). By 2008, DUI arrests had fallen again to 1.1 million (BOJS, 2010b). The decline in drunk-driving arrests is attributed partially to the aging of licensed drivers. Fifty-four percent of licensed drivers were over the age of 40 in 1997, compared to 46 percent in 1986. In both years, the older the driver over age 21, the lower the rate of DUI arrests.

In interviews conducted with DUI offenders, about half admitted that they had consumed the equivalent of at least 12 beers or 6 glasses of wine prior to their arrest. The average BAC was 0.24 among jail inmates and 0.19 among probationers. Six percent of prison inmates and 12 percent of jail inmates said that they had been previously sentenced for DUI five or more times (BOJS, 1999).

Insurance/Liability Laws. Public policy is sometimes intended to indirectly affect the consumption of alcohol through such measures as the regulation of insurance rates. Drivers with DUI convictions may face higher insurance premiums, and in some cases, they may be unable to purchase automobile insurance. Since many of these drivers will continue to drive without insurance, these laws may actually be harmful to the larger population. There is no evidence indicating that higher insurance premiums have actually reduced consumption.

Another indirect measure involves server liability, or *dramshop laws.* In 35 states, commercial establishments that serve alcoholic beverages are civilly liable to those who experience harm or injury as the result of an intoxicated or underage person's irresponsible use of alcohol (Wisconsin Bar Association, 2010). The typical dramshop law imposes civil liability for damages caused by an establishment's serving alcohol to "visibly intoxicated or underage customers" (ABA, 1986, p. 107). (Criminal liability may also be attached when a minor is involved.) The courts also have held that even without a dramshop law, civil liability can be imposed on a tavern under common law (*Rappaport v. Nichols,* 1959). One result of these laws has been the provision of better training to servers to help them learn how to recognize and "cut off" a customer who is intoxicated and to see that such a customer gets home safely. Some communities offer training programs for servers on methods of referring problem drinkers to appropriate treatment services.

Decisions in a number of states have extended common law liability from commercial establishments to social hosts who provide alcohol to their intoxicated or underage guests (*Kelly v. Gwinnell,* 1984). Eleven states have laws specifically extending liability to social hosts for intoxicated adults, and 30 states hold them liable for intoxicated minors (Wisconsin Bar Association, 2010). There have been few studies of the impact of dramshop or server liability laws on alcohol consumption and related phenomena. Wagenaar and Holder (1991) found that liability lawsuits in Texas caused significant changes in alcohol servers'

practices, resulting in fewer people driving while intoxicated and fewer vehicle crashes involving injuries. Holder et al. (1993) found that in states where servers have a relatively high level of exposure to liability, there was more publicity regarding liability, alcohol servers were more aware of liability, there were fewer low-price drink promotions, and more servers regularly checked customers' identification.

Control of Illicit Drugs

Public policies regarding illicit drugs have not reached the degree of specificity that is found in policies regarding alcohol use. The primary debate surrounding illicit drugs is whether it is possible to control their use through law enforcement. The current failure of public policy to deal with the drug problem is the logical outgrowth of policies pursued by the federal government over the past decade. Since the election of U.S. President Ronald Reagan in 1981, federal policy has been much more concerned with preventing recreational drug use than with helping habitual users. During Reagan's first term, funding for drug treatment fell by almost 40 percent, adjusting for inflation (Massing, 1992). The budget for the so-called war on drugs continued to rise, however. In 1998, 1.6 million Americans were arrested for drug law violations (FBI, 2000), and nearly one in four persons imprisoned in the United States was imprisoned for a drug offense. The number of persons incarcerated for drug offenses (458,131) that year was almost as large as the entire prison and jail population was in 1980 (474,368) (Justice Policy Institute, 2001). Between 1980 and 1997, the number of people entering prison for violent offenses increased by 82 percent; for nonviolent offenses, 207 percent; and for drug offenses, 1,040 percent (Justice Policy Institute, 2001).

The approach chosen by the U.S. President George H. Bush administration was one of *zero tolerance.* This approach emphasized law enforcement toward the end of completely eradicating illegal drugs, and it appeared to be based on the following assumptions:

1. If there were no drug abusers, there would be no drug problem.
2. The market for drugs is created not only by availability but also by demand.
3. Drug abuse starts with a willful act.
4. The perception that drug users are powerless to act against the influences of drug availability and peer pressure is an erroneous one.
5. Most illegal drug users can choose to stop their drug-taking behaviors and must be held accountable if they do not.
6. Individual freedom does not include the right to self- and societal destruction.
7. Public tolerance for drug abuse must be reduced to *zero* (Inciardi & McBride, 1989).

This policy meant that possession of even the smallest amounts of illicit drugs could result in the seizure and confiscation of an individual's automobile, home, or other property. Some saw this as a serious threat to civil liberties.

Although still woefully inadequate, the George H. Bush administration did increase treatment funding by 50 percent to $1.6 billion. At the same time, the administration continued its preoccupation with casual middle-class drug use, not with addiction or habitual use.

The candidates in the 1992 presidential race, George H. Bush and Bill Clinton, seldom mentioned the drug issue, and there would have been little more interest in the 1996 election if there had not been a report indicating an increase in adolescent drug use. The Republican Party seized this issue, despite the fact that this trend had actually started during the Bush administration.

The nation's first "drug czar" (appointed by George H. Bush), William Bennett, developed a strategy of seeking out and punishing casual, nonaddicted users. He also insisted that all drugs were equally pernicious (Zimrig & Hawkins, 1992), a somewhat incongruous philosophy for a

two-pack-a-day smoker! The next drug czar, former Florida Governor Bob Martinez, shied away from the public spotlight and made few changes in Bennett's approach. Barry McCaffrey, the next drug czar, was a retired Army general and seemed determined to continue a zero-tolerance policy. Drug policy during the Clinton administration changed very little.

The major drug issue in the 2000 presidential campaign was whether candidate George W. Bush had ever used cocaine—a question he steadfastly refused to answer (Abadinsky, 2001). Fewer changes in drug policy have been noted in the U.S. President George W. Bush administration, despite promises to take an even tougher approach. John P. Walters, the top deputy in the drug office of the current Bush administration, was appointed as drug czar by George W. Bush. Walters strongly advocated mandatory minimum sentences that would lock up drug users as well as street-level dealers ("Record of Bush Nominee," 2001). Although U.S. President Barack Obama's drug czar, Gil Kerlikowske, called to an end of the "war on drugs," there has been little change in federal enforcement efforts, and President Obama opposed the recent referendum in California to legalize marijuana (Shapiro, 2010).

Recipients of public assistance programs have not fared well in the war on drugs. While the eviction of drug users/pushers from public housing projects has received a great deal of attention, other policy changes have actually been more far reaching. The Personal Responsibility and Work Opportunity Reconciliation Act of 1996 allowed states to ban public assistance (TANF and food stamps) to individuals with drug-related felony convictions, and it also permitted states to drug test welfare recipients and sanction those who test positive (CSAT, 1998). For the 20,000 Americans who are disabled due to drug addiction or alcoholism, the Contract with America Advancement Act of 1996 did the following:

• Prohibited Supplemental Security Income (SSI) Disability Benefits
• Prohibited Social Security Disability Benefits (SSDA)

- Eliminated Medicaid eligibility
- Eliminated Medicare eligibility
- Required substance abuse treatment referral only if drug addiction and/or alcoholism is secondary to another disability and the recipient is unable to manage own benefits. (CSAT, 1998)

These punitive measures are especially hard to understand in view of the acknowledged fact that welfare clients must have substance abuse treatment in order for welfare reform to succeed. "For many current welfare recipients, substance abuse may pose the largest single obstacle in their ability to secure and keep jobs" (CSAT, 1998, p. 1).

Other nations have chosen different strategies. For example, The Netherlands has legalized the use of certain drugs, such as marijuana. The Netherlands has been the European leader in so-called harm-reduction approaches, but Switzerland, Spain, Italy, Germany, and the Czech Republic are also trying similar approaches (McNeece, Bullington, Arnold, & Springer, 2001). Although Great Britain has a reputation for legalization, its approach to controlling illicit drugs really is one of harm reduction through methadone maintenance and needle/syringe exchange programs.

Many experts feel that the United States is rather myopic in considering other options. All but six states still prohibit the distribution of hypodermic needles and syringes without a prescription, making it impossible to operate a legal needle/syringe exchange program (Abadinsky, 2001). A 1995 report by the National Academy of Sciences found that needle exchange programs reduced the spread of HIV/AIDS (Leary, 1995), and in 1997, the American Medical Association endorsed the concept of needle exchange programs (Abadinsky, 2001). Nevertheless, fear of retaliation by conservative members of Congress led U.S. President Bill Clinton to continue the federal ban on such programs, despite evidence that they did not lead to increased drug use (Stolberg, 1998). President Obama expressed support for needle exchange programs during his campaign, but reversed his position after being elected. Congress, however, removed the ban on federal funding for needle and syringe programs from the 2010 budget. Whether federal funds will ever find their way to these programs is still an open question (International Harm Reduction Association, 2010). In the United States, efforts to control illicit drugs have been hampered by the great degree of fragmentation of federal, state, and local drug enforcement programs. A report from the Comptroller General indicated that the supply and demand of illicit drugs have remained relatively constant despite the massive increase in federal drug control efforts. In fact, he seriously questioned the ability of governmental efforts to regulate illegal drugs in the absence of "factual information about which anti-drug programs work best" (U.S. General Accounting Office, 1988, p. 2). It is the recognized failure of antidrug enforcement policies that gave rise to the current debate on legalization of illicit drugs.

According to Dale Masi, an expert on employee assistance programs, the legalization of illicit drugs signals "the inevitability that use will increase." Masi testified before Congress that this approach

"cannot be reconciled with ethical principles because it would be implemented with recognition of the increased personal and social destruction connected with drug abuse that would result. We, as a civilized society, are responsible for preventing disease and destruction, not spreading them." (U.S. Congress, 1988, p. 137)

This view is not accepted by all the experts, however. A New York State Senator, Joseph Caliber, proposed the legalization of *all* drugs. His plan was intended to eliminate criminal drug trafficking by allowing the sales of currently prohibited drugs in the same place and manner as alcohol. Similar restrictions on minimum age for purchase, hours of sale, location of stores, and so on would apply to drugs sales just as to current alcohol sales (U.S. Congress, 1988).

Other testimony favored various compromise proposals, such as the legalization of the less harmful forms of illicit drugs. These advocates all favored the legalization of marijuana, and some favored legalizing certain forms of cocaine (coca leaves) and opiates (smokable opium) (U.S. Congress, 1988, p. 27). Compromise proposals frequently advocate some degree of decriminalization for particular drugs rather than complete legalization. This approach sometimes suggests a civil rather than a criminal penalty for the use or possession of a controlled substance. On other occasions, it suggests that no penalty be attached to use but that sales be subjected to criminal penalties. This leaves users in the awkward position of being legally entitled to use a drug but having no legal means to obtain it. The argument for legalization or decriminalization seems to be gaining acceptance, even among conservative politicians and writers. A major portion of an issue of the *National Review* was devoted to critiques of the war on drugs ("War on Drugs," 1996), and articles in the *Journal of the American Medical Association* have advocated decriminalization ("Change of Heart," 1994). These are other hopeful signs of change in U.S. drug policies—at both the state and federal levels. The state of Indiana repealed a provision that required a mandatory 20-year sentence for anyone caught with as little as three grams of cocaine—about the size of three Sweet-and-Low packets. A criminal justice reform bill was passed in Louisiana, which gives judges more discretion in sentencing drug offenders (Ryckaert, 2001). Proposition 36 took effect on July 1, 2001, in California, diverting low-level, nonviolent drug offenders from the criminal courts to treatment (Drug Policy Alliance, 2002). In a more recent development, more than 80 percent of the voters in Oakland approved a referendum to tax marijuana sold in the city's dispensaries, a move also backed by the city council (CNN, 2009). This is viewed not just as a revenue-raising measure for cash-strapped city government, but as a step toward normalizing the sale and use of marijuana.

On the federal level President Obama's first budget proposal allocated some $64 million to rehabilitation programs such as drug courts, making it more likely for users to get treatment rather than incarceration. Attorney General Eric Holder has also slowed down the Justice Department's raids on state-approved medical marijuana dispensaries. Finally, the "drug czar," former Seattle Police Chief R. Gil Kerlikowske, is on record as not favoring hard-line drug policies (Horwitz & Jamieson, 2009), although there has been little significant change in actual enforcement activities.

The "War on Drugs"

U.S. President Richard Nixon was the first president to declare a "war on drugs." He did this in 1971 as he also introduced stronger criminal penalties for drug dealers and proposed a rapid expansion of drug treatment facilities, especially those specializing in heroin addiction (Besteman, 1989). Subsequent presidents continued this effort, with each promising to increase the war effort against drugs. Drugs have been less of an issue in the last three presidential elections, however.

The war on drugs was simply a continuation of the policies espoused in the Harrison Act in 1914, in which the federal government relied on a variety of approaches to reduce both the demand for and the supply of illicit drugs. The major changes are seen in the massive amount of funding for law enforcement, the perceived seriousness of the problem of drug abuse, and the advanced technological strategies for controlling drugs. Americans now use Bell 209 assault helicopters, Navy EC-2 and Air Force AWACS "eye-in-the-sky" aircraft, "Fat Albert" surveillance balloons, "Blue Thunder" high-performance Coast Guard vessels, and NASA satellites to fight the drug war. The war analogy may seem appropriate in halting the operation of large drug cartels, but it seems inappropriate when it comes to dealing with other aspects of drug abuse. The war analogy seems especially inappropriate regarding efforts to prevent or treat drug abuse by the nation's children (Gustavon, 1991).

For more than a decade, critics of the war on drugs have declared it "a losing battle," "almost an afterthought," and "hype from an Administration and Congress eager to justify the expenditure of billions of dollars for law enforcement" (Shannon, 1990, p. 44). According to Doweiko (2002):

> As should be obvious by now, the government's effort to solve the drug abuse problem though law enforcement/interdiction has been a failure. Of course this does not stop law enforcement officials from trumpeting the successes of the past year from hinting that, for just a few billion dollars more, it may be possible to eliminate the problem of recreational drug use in the United States. (p. 438)

These "get-tough" efforts may sound good to the public, but no serious student of drug policy is encouraged by the efforts at law enforcement in the attempt to reduce illegal drug use. Although during the Clinton administrations, there were fewer highly publicized drug eradication efforts in nations such as Colombia, the war on drugs changed little. The Bush administration endorsed a continued policy of tough law enforcement and eradication efforts, as signaled by the appointment of the current drug czar and continuing operations in Colombia and other drug-producing Latin American countries. The Obama administration has softer rhetoric, but little change in actual enforcement policies.

Forfeiture Laws

State civil asset forfeiture laws have been growing in popularity with law enforcement agencies as a tool in dealing with illegal drugs over the last three decades. These laws allow law enforcement agencies to seize personal assets such as money, motor vehicles, and real estate and use the proceeds for their budgets, even if the owner is never convicted of a crime. This sometimes leads to policies that target property instead of crime and are subject to abuse and corruption. Civil asset forfeiture may take place without proof of the origins or ownership of the asset and without a conviction of anyone for a criminal violation. Law enforcement retains the seized assets, or the proceeds from the sale of the assets, and uses the assets to fund further law enforcement efforts. Some argue that a dangerous incentive may be created for law enforcement to seize and keep assets at the expense of due process and individual liberties (Drug Policy Alliance, 2009).

BOX 8.1   *Presumed Guilty*

Willie Jones, a second-generation nursery man on his family's Nashville business, bundles up money from last year's profits and heads off to buy flowers and shrubs in Houston. He makes this trip twice a year using cash, which the small growers prefer.

But this time, as he waits at the American Airlines gate in Nashville Metro Airport, he's flanked by two police officers who escort him into a small office, search him and seize the $9,600 he's carrying. A ticket agent had alerted the officers that a large black man had paid for his ticket in bills, unusual these days. Because of the cash, and the fact that he fit a "profile" of what drug dealers supposedly look like, they believed he was buying or selling drugs.

He's free to go, he's told. But they keep his money—his livelihood—and give him a receipt in its place.

No evidence of wrongdoing was ever produced. No charges were ever filed. As far as anyone knows, Willie Jones neither uses drugs nor buys or sells them. He is a gardening contractor who bought an airplane ticket. Who lost his hard-earned money to the cops. And can't get it back.

Source: Copyright © Pittsburgh Post-Gazette, 2010. All Rights reserved. Reprinted with permission.

The Economics of Drug War/Peace

A frequent criticism of the war on drugs is that it simply has not worked. Testifying before a Senate committee, Henry L. Hinton of the General Accounting Office said,

> "Despite long-standing efforts and expenditures of billions of dollars, illegal drugs still flood the United States. Although U.S. and host-nation counternarcotics efforts have resulted in the arrest of major drug traffickers and the seizure of large amounts of drugs, they have not materially reduced the availability of drugs in the United States." (U.S. General Accounting Office, 1998)

More than 1.8 million people were arrested on drug law violations in 2007 within U.S. borders (BOJS, 2010a). In the second and third decades of the drug war, the number of people entering prison for drug offenses increased by more than *1,000 percent* (Justice Policy Institute, 2001), with a disproportionate number coming from minority populations. Despite these enforcement and interdiction efforts, drug-related emergency room admissions grew to 827,744 in the first six months of 2000 (SAMHSA, 2001). Casual use of certain illicit drugs may have leveled off or decreased slightly, but a disturbing number of Americans still use illicit psychoactive substances (Johnston, O'Malley, & Bachman, 2000).

Another criticism is that Americans cannot afford the war on drugs. From 1981 through 1988, the federal costs for this war were $16.5 billion (Inciardi & McBride, 1989). In fiscal year 2002 alone, the enacted federal budget for the war on drugs was $18.8 billion, and the budget request for fiscal year 2003 was $19.2 billion (ONDCP, 2002). One economist estimated that the cost of prohibiting illicit drugs was $48.7 billion in 2008. Roughly $33.1 billion in savings would accrue to state and local governments, while $15.6 billion would accrue to the federal government in reduced law enforcement costs. Government would gain another $34.3 billion through the taxation of marijuana, cocaine, and heroin (Miron, 2010). A more optimistic article in

Business Week (2009) estimated that such taxes could add more than $100 billion annually to governmental revenues. Further savings would accrue from not imprisoning drug offenders. At the rate of $17.1 million per day, their care cost state governments approximately $6.2 billion in 2007 (BOJS, 2008).

The cost of abusing drugs is also very expensive. According to Office of the National Drug Control Policy, Americans spent $63.2 billion on illegal drugs in 1999 (ONDCP, 2001). There was an additional economic cost to society of $109.9 billion: $77.6 billion in lost wages, $11.9 billion in health care costs, and another $20.4 billion in related costs such as depreciated property values and property damage, environmental damage, pain and suffering, and the like (ONDCP, 2001). The economic cost of alcohol use was even higher at $165.5 billion, and tobacco use cost between $100 billion and $130 billion (Hogan, 2000; Leistikow, 2000). The total financial impact of substance abuse in the United States may be as high as $510 billion annually (Evans, 1998).

The present policies on illicit drugs have amounted to a type of regressive tax: It has dramatically increased the profits of drug dealers and at the same time placed additional economic burdens on the residents of inner cities to provide more law enforcement and to ameliorate the effects of crime. In 2005, cocaine seizures reached an all-time high of 118,331 kilograms (DEA, 2009). Politicians as well as police officers often herald such actions as proof not only of the severity of the drug problem but also of the success of the country's interdiction efforts. However, it is questionable whether such raids prevent a single person from using cocaine. Likely no drug lords or street dealers are put out of business, and no additional addicts are driven to seek treatment. These events probably have no perceptible impact on the public's attitudes toward drug use. People who want cocaine are still able to find it.

There is no reliable way of predicting how much drug use would increase or decrease under a policy of legalization or decriminalization.

In Great Britain, the number of addicts seeking treatment increased after passage of the Dangerous Drugs Act (which decriminalized the use of heroin and other illicit drugs), but it is not known to what extent drug *use* increased or decreased. There is some evidence that marijuana use decreased immediately after the Dutch government decriminalized its use in 1976, however (Dennis, 1990). Both Great Britain and the Netherlands are far different from the United States in culture and economic demographics. One cannot assume that Washington, DC, would react to legalization in the same manner as London or Amsterdam. The Netherlands has a homicide rate only one-eighth that of the United States. Important aspects of its overall drug policy are also very different.

After reviewing hundreds of drug war studies by criminologists, psychologists, sociologists, and economists, Benson and Rasmussen (1994) concluded that not only is the United States not winning the drug war, but it is essentially an *unwinnable* war. Furthermore, by engaging in this war, the nation's resources have been stretched to the point where the entire criminal justice system is in a state of crisis. Their conclusion is that the United States will have to learn to coexist with the illicit drug trade and find a rational means of allocating its criminal justice resources. For example, local courts could be assigned a quota of treatment slots for their use. Judges (and voters) would no longer be forced to face decisions that result in a rapist receiving an early release from prison so that a nonviolent crack addict could be incarcerated.

A similar conclusion was reached by the Latin American Commission on Drugs and Democracy. In a report presented in Rio de Janeiro, it concluded that

> "The war on drugs has failed. And it's high time to replace an ineffective strategy with more humane and efficient drug policies . . . The revision of U.S.-inspired drug policies is urgent in light of the rising levels of violence and corruption associated with narcotics. The alarming

power of the drug cartels is leading to a criminalization of politics and a politicization of crime. And the corruption of the judicial and political system is undermining the foundations of democracy in several Latin American countries." (Wall Street Journal, 2009)

Legalization

We must remember that in the absence of any convincing empirical data regarding the effectiveness of alternative policies toward illicit drugs, the U.S. political system encourages the use of symbolic values (e.g., increased law enforcement) that become just as important, if not more important, than any tangible outcomes. Thus, the debate over the legalization of illicit drugs has strong moral overtones.

Have Drug Laws Created Problems Worse than the Drugs Themselves?   Is it reasonable to say that present drug policies are responsible for increased corruption, violence, street crime, and disrespect for the law? There is obviously much truth in these assertions. One could easily argue that present policies have made the sale of illicit drugs a highly profitable enterprise—so profitable that "turf wars" among cartels and neighborhood dealers alike have led to remarkable increases in the homicide rate. One only has to read the headlines in any Washington, DC, newspaper to learn that the great majority of homicides in the nation's capital (also the nation's *murder* capital) are drug related. On the other hand, the evidence suggests that among the majority of street drug users who are involved in crime, their criminal careers were well established prior to the onset of their drug use (Inciardi & McBride, 1989). As mentioned in previous chapters, their drug involvement may be due primarily to their involvement in a criminal subculture.

Perhaps more important is that the present laws, coupled with the propaganda fed to children for two generations about the consequences of drugs such as marijuana, have resulted in disbelief and widespread criminal violations. There is a direct parallel between this situation and the consequences of Prohibition, during which the law made criminals of millions of otherwise honest citizens.

Has Law Enforcement Failed in Reducing the Supply and the Demand for Drugs? A closely related argument often made by advocates of legalization is that the $30 billion a year currently spent for law enforcement could be better used for the treatment and prevention of drug abuse. The use of drugs among U.S. secondary school students remains high. In 2007, 19.5 percent of state and 56.4 percent of federal inmates were incarcerated for drug offenses (BJS, 2008). It is obvious that law enforcement has failed as a solution to the problem of illicit drugs.

Can One Stop the Use of Drugs That a Significant Segment of the Population Is Committed to Using? It is simply impossible to arrest, prosecute, and punish such large numbers of people, especially in a liberal democracy in which the government must not unduly interfere with personal behavior. Attempting to enforce draconian measures against drug users not only places a great fiscal burden on the nation, but it also poses an imminent threat to the civil liberties of its citizens.

Is Illicit Drug Use as Great a Threat to Society as the Legally Sanctioned Use of Alcohol and Tobacco? The Surgeon General of the United States has estimated that cigarette smoking (the leading preventable cause of death in the United States) alone kills approximately 438,000 people a year, almost one in five deaths (CDCP, 2009a). Cigarette smoking kills more people each year than all other drugs combined and is virtually always addicting. Sales of tobacco are not just legal—they are actually *subsidized* by government programs providing price supports for tobacco growers! By comparison, from 2001–2005, there were approximately 79,000 deaths annually attributable to excessive alcohol use (CDCP, 2009b).

These figures are almost certainly conservative estimates of alcohol-related deaths. Compare these numbers with the estimated mortality rate of 15,973 deaths from illicit drug use, and one must wonder why cocaine, marijuana, and heroin are regarded as being so dangerous (ONDCP, 2001). To focus on a strong drugs/crime connection, one must remember that more than half of all people convicted of violent crimes were under the influence of alcohol at the time the crime was committed (Bradley, 1987). Alcohol abuse is also implicated in a major portion of domestic violence incidents (Lehmann & Drupp, 1983–84).

What Are the Possible Benefits of Legalization? Among the expected benefits of legalization are cheaper drug prices, a decrease in drug-related crime, less corruption of governmental officials, and a destruction of the power base of drug lords and criminal syndicates. In addition, the U.S. legal system would be free to use more of its resources to provide treatment to addicts, to prosecute and punish real criminals, and to eliminate the threat to civil liberties contained in current policies. Finally, government-sanctioned sales outlets could provide quality control to see that drug users are not harmed by tainted drugs and could collect badly needed tax revenues. We mentioned earlier that Oakland voters approved the taxation of medical marijuana (CNN, 2009). In recent years twenty states have approved legislation taxing illegal marijuana, but most of these laws are not intended as revenue raising measures. For example, in Minnesota, failure to comply with the state's drug tax law may result in a fine of up to $14,000 and seven years in jail (NORML, 2009a).

Would Legalization Result in Increased Drug Use, Loss of Productivity, and Higher Health Care Costs? Some people argue that legalization could imply approval and lead to increased use. (If arguing that drug legalization would persuade people that drugs are safe, then the obvious implication is that the country needs to reconsider its policies on alcohol and tobacco!) Even if drug use were to increase with legalization, however, the economic benefits of "drug peace" would in all likelihood pay for the additional costs of increased usage, both socially and economically. As the earlier analysis indicated, the break-even point would be close to a 100 percent increase, and not even the most severe critics of legalization are predicting such dire consequences. Most people would not want to risk the harm caused by addiction, however.

Will Drug Users Seek Greater Quantities and Higher Potencies of Drugs on the Black Market?   If the government legalized drugs but restricted the amount and potency of drugs that a person could legally purchase, it is likely that some people would seek greater quantities and higher potencies in an underground market. In order to work, legalization must make drugs available at all levels of quantity and potency. Otherwise, an underground market in drugs will continue.

Will Legalizing "Soft" Drugs Such as Marijuana Lead Its Users to More Harmful and Addictive Drugs?   If the government wants to restrict so-called *gateway drugs* (drugs that young people use that appear to be precursors of later drug use), then it should place restrictions on alcohol and tobacco, *especially* tobacco. Moreover, keeping marijuana illegal forces buyers into an underground market where they are likely to be offered other illegal drugs. Finally, some 60 million Americans have tried marijuana, and the number of cocaine addicts is estimated at 1 million. Thus, most marijuana smokers did not graduate to stronger drugs. The gateway effect is apparently not very strong. Some believe that it does not exist.

Proposals for the legalization or decriminalization of drugs are incomplete and imperfect. There are still too many unanswered questions for the country to change course abruptly on these policy issues. Before people can seriously consider radical alternatives to the war on drugs, they need to answer the following questions asked by Paul Stares (1996):

- What is the range of regulatory permutations for each drug?
- What would happen to drug consumption under more permissive policies?
- What would happen to crime under decriminalization? Legalization?
- Would a black market for drugs emerge under legalization?
- Would regulations restricting the purchase of drugs be as difficult to enforce as today's alcohol and tobacco restrictions?
- How would a decision to legalize drugs affect other countries? (pp. 18–20)

Merely asking these questions will anger many people, but the United States must begin to fashion a comprehensive, consistent, and enforceable policy regarding the use of drugs. These questions, and many others, must be answered before the political system is ready to consider an abrupt change in policy. Without serious investigation and a minimum degree of consensus on a number of these issues, the nation is not likely to deviate much from its present course.

Medical Marijuana

Beginning in April, 2009, patients in Michigan began applying to register with the Michigan Medical Marijuana Program. Patients in the program are permitted under state law to possess and grow cannabis for medical purposes. Michigan became the thirteenth state to allow the physician-supervised use of marijuana under state law (NORML, 2009b). Canada also allows some patients to possess cannabis and to grow a limited number of plants (BBC News, 2001). This issue will not be so quickly resolved in the United States, since all parties seem to be zealously committed to maintaining their respective positions (McNeece et al., 2001).

Like so many other illicit substances, marijuana has been used as a popular medication all over the world for hundreds of years. No serious concerns about its use were expressed until the late nineteenth century in England, which led to an extensive investigation and publication of *Indian Hemp Commission Report* in 1898. The commission concluded that the drug had many practical uses in medicine and that many of the stories of its dangers could not be documented (McNeece et al., 2001). As noted earlier (see Chapter 1), there was little public interest in controlling marijuana until its use became associated the "dangerous classes" of people, such as African American jazz musicians and Mexican migrant workers. In response, the Marijuana Tax Act was passed in 1937 with no debate and with no input from medical practitioners (Becker, 1967).

After two years of extensive investigation, the Schafer Commission, appointed by President Nixon, issued a report in 1972 called *Marijuana: Signal of Misunderstanding.* The report found very little in the way of toxic effects, leading the commission to conclude that decriminalization of marijuana might be the most appropriate policy. The report incensed the president, however, who stated that he would never accept legalization of marijuana (McNeece et al., 2001). Another research monograph entitled *Marijuana and Health* was produced by the Department of Health and Human Services in 1982 during the first Reagan administration. This time, the experts noted serious health problems associated with marijuana use. Given the conflicting observations by different panels of experts, the debate over the effects of smoking marijuana has continued unabated.

Even so, large numbers of medical patients, especially cancer patients, have demanded legal access to marijuana. Many claim that it is effective in alleviating the side effects of chemotherapy and radiation and that it is useful for treating both glaucoma and AIDS symptoms (Stolberg, 1999). Laws that allow its medical use do not legalize marijuana or alter criminal penalties regarding the possession or cultivation of marijuana for recreational use, nor do they establish a legal supply for patients to obtain the drug. They merely provide a narrow exemption from prosecution for defined patients who use marijuana with their doctors' recommendation. In addition, the intent was to allow physicians to prescribe marijuana to patients without the fear of arrest. The federal government responded by threatening physicians with revocation of their federal prescription-writing privileges. The matter is still under review by the courts.

Representative Barney Frank (D-Mass.) reintroduced legislation in Congress in 2001 to provide for the medical use of marijuana. House Bill 912, the Medical Use of Marijuana Act, would have moved marijuana from Schedule I to Schedule II under federal law, thereby making it legal for physicians to prescribe. The rescheduling would remove cannabis from the list of drugs alleged to have no valid medical use, such as heroin and LSD, and put it in the same category as Marinol, morphine, and cocaine. (Many marijuana users believe that the pill form, Marinol, is not as effective as smoking marijuana.) If passed, House Bill 912 would not have required any state to change its current laws. Rather, it would have allowed states to determine for themselves whether marijuana should be legal for medicinal use. The bill failed, and unfortunately, the issue will probably not be resolved on the basis of scientific research, since medical marijuana is as much a political cause as a scientific issue. The expediencies of politics are more likely to triumph over reason.

Drugs, Alcohol, and Crime

There is certainly a relationship among alcohol, drugs, and crime. The exact nature of that relationship is quite complex, however, and scholars are still putting the pieces together. Rasmussen and Benson (1990) argue that the great majority of persons who are arrested for drug offenses are *not* participating in other types of more violent criminal activity. On the other hand, research shows that the great majority of persons arrested in urban areas for all crimes test positive for illicit drug use (National Institute of Justice, 1990). The effects of substance abuse on crime depend on (1) *what* drug is being used, (2) *who* is using the drug, (3) the relationship of the user to subcultures tolerant of other forms of social deviance, (4) law enforcement policies regarding drug use, and, perhaps most important of all, (5) *who* is conducting the research.

People who use drugs (except alcohol, tobacco, and certain legal prescription drugs) are committing a criminal act. There are some very persuasive arguments that because of society's unreasonable definitions of drug use *per se* as a criminal act, society forces drug users to become criminals. Labeling theorists such as Lemert (1966) argue that the secondary deviance that attaches to a person who is arrested or incarcerated for drug offenses can be far more destructive than the consequences of the drug use itself. For the most part, however, society seems to be more concerned with whether other nondrug crime, particularly street crime, is a direct result of drug-taking behavior. Labeling, stigmatization, and secondary deviance are rather remote issues for citizens facing a crime wave.

Three hypotheses continue to dominate the drugs/crime controversy. The first maintains that the "addict of lower socio-economic class is a criminal primarily because illicit narcotics are costly and because he can secure his daily requirements only by committing crimes that will pay for them" (Tappan, 1960). According to this hypothesis, criminality is a more or less direct consequence of physical dependence and tolerance, which requires ever-increasing doses of a drug that is economically unavailable to the addict with limited financial means.

The second hypothesis maintains that the "principal explanation for the association between drug abuse and crime . . . is likely to be found in the subcultural attachment" of the drug abuser to criminal associations, identifications, and activities of other persons who are addicted (Goldman, 1981). This hypothesis is more pertinent to the hard drugs such as heroin—a drug that is closely associated with a criminal subculture. It is less useful when applied to the soft drugs such as marijuana, as most middle-class college students could eagerly testify. Even cocaine seems to be a favorite drug of some business executives and other middle-class citizens.

A third theory holds that drug dependence is functional, as opposed to casual or recreational (Alexander, 1990). The addict's behavior is an attempt to deal with his or her failure to achieve social acceptance, competence, self-confidence, and personal autonomy. This adaptive model sees drug dependence as a "strategy to remove the individual (a retreat) from competitive situations in which defeat is almost certain" (Alexander, 1990, p. 45). The addict's behavior is seen as self-directed and purposeful, although not necessarily on a conscious level (Abadinsky, 2001).

The category of crime known as *domestic violence* (spousal abuse, child abuse, etc.) has been linked to alcohol and drug abuse so frequently and so consistently that one might also hypothesize a direct, causal relationship between drug use and certain crimes of violence (Langley & Levy, 1977). Alcohol, especially, is said to have a disinhibiting effect that unleashes emotions such as rage or at least lessens the ability to control rage (Shainess, 1977). In a study of 234 abusers of women appearing before the court in Indianapolis, 60 percent had been under the influence of alcohol and 21.8 percent had been under the influence of other drugs when they physically assaulted their spouses or partners. The men who were using alcohol or drugs generally displayed greater violence toward the women (Roberts, 1987).

Nonetheless, with few exceptions, there is no evidence of a clear cause-and-effect relationship between alcohol or drug use and violent behavior. Drugs such as PCP and amphetamines are known to affect the brain in some way that triggers violent behavior (Roberts, 1988). However, central nervous system depressants and marijuana generally alter behavior in the *opposite* direction

(White, 1991). There are reasons to suspect that much of the domestic violence that occurs under the influence of alcohol or drugs is preplanned. According to the *disavowal theory,* the abuser simply gets drunk or gets high so that he will have an excuse for beating his wife or children. By doing so, both his family and society may treat him less severely (Wright, 1985).

There is much evidence that most of the current problems of the criminal justice system can be attributed, either directly or indirectly, to drugs: jail and prison overcrowding, court backlogs, increased crime, inmate violence, and the increased costs of incarceration. Strains on the system caused by the increased use of drugs have resulted in frequent crisis management and a "continuing search for more effective ways for the system to absorb the increase in drug arrests and to reduce the cycle of drug use and arrest for these defendants" (Belenko, 1990, p. 27).

The data discussed on the following pages show an undeniable relationship among alcohol, drugs, and crime. One task will be to understand whether the socioeconomic class approach, the subcultural attachment approach, or some other hypothesis best explains the nature of that relationship. First, drug law violations (manufacture, use, and sales) as crimes will be examined. Next, there will be a discussion about substance abuse and criminal histories of people arrested or incarcerated for nondrug crime. Third will be a review of the research on substance abuse and domestic violence. Finally, current trends in the drugs/crime relationship will be examined, and current policies regarding drugs and crime will be reviewed.

Alcohol and Drug Law Violations

It is no secret that crime statistics are regarded by the experts as seriously flawed. Despite such impressive titles as *Uniform Crime Reports* that fill the basements of university libraries, there is actually very little uniformity in reporting practices. Crime statistics are based on reports taken by thousands of local police officers and county sheriffs. Crime statistics in a community may change dramatically overnight with a change in reporting procedures. Police commissioners arguing for larger budgets have been known to create their own crime waves simply by altering departmental rules for reporting crime.

Anyone doing research on juvenile delinquency certainly has been frustrated by the tremendous variability in state and local reporting procedures. Only about two-thirds of the states regularly report juvenile crime data to a central national registry, and many local jurisdictions are not required to report to a central state agency. There is no way to determine how many juveniles were arrested in Texas or Illinois (or several other states), for example, for drug law violations, except by reviewing records of local police. (Imagine examining the records of 254 county sheriffs and hundreds of city police departments in a state the size of Texas!)

Crime data, although seriously flawed, can be of some help in understanding the drugs/crime relationship, however. Some categories of drug-related offenses, such as adult arrests for drug law violations, are reported with much greater regularity and consistency because of stricter federal standards for reporting. Also, one can assume that the direction of error in crime data is toward *underreporting.* On a nationwide basis, one also can assume that the degree of underreporting is fairly consistent from one year to the next. Therefore, if dramatic changes occur over a period of years, one may still be able to identify specific trends.

The increase in adult incarcerations for drug violations in recent years is clear (see Table 8.1). Does this mean that there was a comparable

TABLE 8.1 Sentenced State Prisoners for Drug Offenses by Race, 2000 and 2006

	2000	*2006*	*% Change*
White	72,000	85,800	+19.2
Black	115,700	86,100	−25.6
Hispanic	54,100	64,900	+20.0

Source: Bureau of Justice Statistics, *Prisoners in 2008.* NCJ 228417, http://bjs.ojp.usdoj.gov/content/pub/pdf/p08.pdf.

TABLE 8.2   Estimated Number of Sentenced Prisoners under State or Federal Jurisdiction, by Race and Hispanic Origin, 2000–2008

Year	Total	White	Black	Hispanic
2000	1,321,200	471,000	610,300	216,900
2001	1,344,500	485,400	622,200	209,900
2002	1,380,300	472,200	622,700	250,000
2003	1,409,300	493,400	621,300	268,100
2004	1,433,800	491,800	583,400	275,600
2005	1,461,100	505,500	577,100	294,900
2006	1,502,200	527,100	562,800	308,000
2007	1,532,800	521,900	586,200	318,800
2008	1,540,100	528,200	591,900	313,100

Source: Bureau of Justice Statistics, *Prisoners in 2008*. NCJ 228417, http://bjs.ojp .usdoj.gov/content/pub/pdf/p08.pdf.

increase in illegal drug manufacture, sale, or possession during that period? It's impossible to say. In some communities, there may actually be much smaller increases or possibly even a decrease. Other data indicate that the overall crime rate peaked and began to decrease during the 1990s (Bureau of Justice Statistics, 1996, p. 10). Despite this trend, vigorous enforcement of drug laws could still produce an increasing number of arrests and commitments in this category each year.

Juvenile arrest data also indicate an increase in juvenile drug arrests of 125 percent between 1988 and 1997 (OJJDP, October 2000b), and a disproportionate number of juvenile drug offenders who were waived to adult criminal court were African American (OJJDP, August 2000a). Our best estimates indicate that 195,700 juveniles were arrested for drug law violations in 2007 (BOJS, 2010a).

In order to more fully understand the trends in drug law violations and imprisonment, one must study the data by gender and ethnicity. While the number of female drug offenders imprisoned in state prisons grew by 35 percent between 1990 and 1999, the comparable rate for males was only 19 percent (BOJS, 2001). While women prisoners are about 7 percent of the total prison population, they account for 10 percent of incarcerated drug offenders (BOJS, 2008). Although blacks

are still being incarcerated at a rate 650 percent greater than whites, the number of incarcerated black drug offenders fell by more than a quarter in recent years (see Table 8.1). The total number of black prisoners has fallen slightly, but they are still 38.4 percent of the total prison population, and Hispanics account for 20.3 percent (see Table 8.2). The racial composition of the U.S. prison population is even more disturbing when we realize that almost 10 percent of African American males between the ages of 20 and 29 are in prison, and they are there primarily for drug offenses. Equally disturbing is the fact that 60.9 percent of the growth in the number of federal inmates between 1990 and 1999 was due to drug offenses (BOJS, 2001).

With 2,424,279 persons incarcerated in U.S. jails, juvenile detention facilities, state and federal prisons, and other detention facilities at year end 2008 (BOJS, 2009), largely as a result of drug law enforcement, we must wonder how much longer we can afford to fight the war on drugs.

Drug Use by Criminals

In 1986, almost half of all prisoners in state institutions either had been convicted of a drug crime or had been a daily user of an illegal drug in the month preceding the offense for which they were incarcerated (BOJS, 1997). Although comparable data are not available for subsequent years, there is convincing evidence that even more prisoners are drug involved. There were 1,645,500 adults and 195,700 juveniles arrested for drug law violations in 2007 (BOJS, 2010a).

In the 1986 study, 28 percent of prison inmates reported a past drug dependency. The drugs most frequently mentioned were heroin (14 percent), cocaine (10 percent), and marijuana or hashish (9 percent). At the time of the offense, 17 percent were under the influence of drugs only, 19 percent were under the influence of alcohol only, and 18 percent were under the influence of both drugs and alcohol. More than half said they had taken illegal drugs during the month before committing the crime, and 43 percent said that they had used drugs on a daily basis just prior to committing the crime (BOJS, 1988b).

The latest arrestee drug abuse monitoring (ADAM) statistics, which are for 2003, indicate that 70.3 percent of male arrestees in 39 major metropolitan areas across the United States tested positive for an illicit drug and 93.4 percent tested positive for either alcohol or an illicit drug. Marijuana remains the predominant drug among adult and juvenile male arrestees (44.1%), although cocaine is a close second (NORC, 2003).

There is ample evidence that offenders are more likely than nonoffenders to use alcohol and illegal drugs, but does that mean that the drug use *caused* the crime? Huizinga and associates (1989) examined the temporal order of drug and alcohol use and other delinquent behavior and concluded that other delinquency generally precedes the use of alcohol or drugs. Therefore, alcohol and drug use cannot be the cause of other delinquent behavior. However, the same study concludes that there may be causal relationships *within* the arena of drug law violations:

1. The onset of alcohol use precedes the onset of either marijuana or polydrug use in 95 percent of all ascertainable cases; among those

who never use alcohol, no more than 3 percent initiate marijuana use and no more than 1 percent initiate polydrug use.
2. Marijuana use precedes the onset of polydrug use in 95 percent of ascertainable cases (p. 448).

It should be stressed that this (and earlier) studies of the drugs/juvenile delinquency relationship were concerned more with alcohol and the soft drugs than with hard drugs such as heroin. Remember the earlier caveat regarding the nature of the drug having an impact on its connection with criminal behavior. Heroin and cocaine both produce a much more powerful physical craving in the addicted person than drugs such as marijuana, and these drugs are much more expensive than alcohol. The alcoholic and the regular marijuana user can ordinarily maintain his or her lifestyle through regular employment.

Research in Maryland (Baltimore), California, and New York (Harlem) indicates that criminal activity increases with higher levels of heroin use. Ball, Shaffer, and Nurco (1983) found that over a nine-year period, the crime rate of 354 heroin addicts dropped with less narcotics use and rose 400 to 600 percent with increased use. An earlier paper on the Baltimore study estimated that male opiate addicts commit crimes on an average of 178 days per year (Ball, Rosen, Flueck, & Nurco, 1982). A study of Harlem heroin users found that daily users committed about five times as many robberies and burglaries as irregular users, an average of 209 per year (Johnson et al., 1985). Obviously, users are apprehended for only a tiny fraction of these crimes.

Other research on the relationship between drugs and crime indicates that the relationship is more complicated than previously thought. For example, groups of individuals with low levels of antisocial personality and self-derogation are most directly affected by the use of drugs during adolescence. They are likely to experience loss of inhibitions and to engage in acts of violence later in life (Kaplan & Damphousse, 1995).

Drug Use by Crime Victims

There is evidence that drinking alcohol or using drugs increases the likelihood of being a crime victim. According to the lifestyle/exposure theory, routines or lifestyles involving alcohol or drug use may facilitate the spatial and temporal union of victims and criminals (Hindelang, Gottfredson, & Garofalo, 1978). Ask any police officer about hanging around bars drinking or going into inner-city crack houses to buy and/or use drugs. These are both regarded as very high-risk activities.

A study of over 6,000 cases in England strongly supports the contention that drinking at night away from home greatly increases the prospects of the drinker's suffering a personal attack or injury. For young male respondents, the probability of enduring a serious personal injury as a result of such a lifestyle was even greater (Lasley, 1989). People who use drugs or alcohol away from home are frequently in unfamiliar environments, surrounded by others who are involved in all types of criminal activities. Drug users have a diminished capacity for flight or self-protection. Women who attend raves and use club drugs such as "X" or "Special K" may be particularly vulnerable to rape (NIDA, 2008).

Domestic Violence

There has traditionally been a high degree of family violence in the United States, as well as an unwillingness to look too closely at the serious incidents of physical abuse that occur in many homes. Shame, guilt, fear of reprisal, and lack of appropriate community responses have prevented many victims from reporting these crimes. Today, public attitudes allow more and more victims of abuse to take a stand against their abusers, as prison convictions have increased and the number of "safe houses" has grown. Even so, reports of alcohol- and drug-related family violence remain high, with an estimated 826,000 child victims of family violence in 1999 (National Clearinghouse, 2001).

Public opinion has long held that the wife beater or child abuser is a "lower class, beer-drinking, undershirt-wearing Stanley Kowalski brute" (Langley & Levy, 1977). Family violence is not confined to any social, geographic, economic, or racial/ethnic group, but it *is* strongly connected to the use of alcohol and drugs. More than three decades ago, Dr. Henry Kempe estimated that alcohol plays a role in about a third of all cases of child abuse (Kempe & Helfer, 1972). A study conducted at an Arkansas alcoholism treatment center indicated that more than half of the parents being treated were also child abusers (Spieker, 1978). Another study in New York found that the husband's alcohol or drug abuse was an underlying factor in over 80 percent of wife-beating cases (Roy, 1977). More recently, research in Indianapolis showed that more serious physical abuse is likely to be committed by men with alcohol or drug problems (Roberts, 1988). According to the National Institute on Alcohol Abuse and Alcoholism (NIAAA, 2000), as many as 60 percent of male alcoholics were violent toward a woman partner in the last year, and alcohol is implicated in 30 percent of all child abuse cases. Liebschutz, Mulvey, and Samet (1997) found that 42 percent of a sample of women who were seeking treatment for substance use problems had been physically or sexually abused at some point in their lives. Another study of inpatients being treated for alcoholism found that 49 percent of the women and 12 percent of the men reported that they had been sexually abused (Windle, Windle, Scheidt, & Miller, 1995).

According to Cohen (1981), violence among alcohol and drug users may occur because human aggression may be increased through drug use, and this propensity is dose related. Some of the possible explanations for this phenomenon are as follow:

1. The drug might diminish ego controls over comportment, releasing submerged anger that can come forth as directed or diffuse outbursts.

2. It may impair judgment and psychomotor performance, making the individual dangerous to self and to others.
3. It might induce restlessness, irritability, and impulsivity, causing hostile combativeness.
4. The drug could produce a paranoid thought disorder with a misreading of reality. False ideas of suspicion or persecution may bring forth assaultive acts against the imagined tormentors.
5. The craving to obtain and use the drug can result in a variety of criminal behaviors, some of them assaultive.
6. An intoxicated or delirium state may result in combativeness and outbursts of poorly directed hyperactivity and violence.
7. Drug-induced feelings of bravado or omnipotence may obliterate one's ordinary sense of caution and prudence causing harm to one's self or others.
8. An amnesic or fugue state may occur during which unpredictable and irrational assaults may take place (pp. 358–359).

In the case of certain drugs, such as ice, there is an almost certain direct link between drug use and violent or aggressive behavior. With alcohol, however, this relationship is somewhat more indirect. As noted earlier, the most widely accepted viewpoint is that alcohol abuse is a disavowal technique used by abusive husbands to excuse their behavior.

Drug/Crime Trends in the 21st Century

In addition to the dramatic increase in illicit drug use that has been observed during the past decade, some other disturbing trends are developing that merit special attention.

Drug Trafficking

The massive problem of illicit drug use in the United States is not the result of independent manufacturers, growers, and drug dealers. It takes a great deal of *organized* effort to bring cocaine from Peru, heroin from Pakistan, and cannabis from Mexico into this country in a sufficient volume to satisfy current demand. Law enforcement officials' intelligence on drug distribution networks indicates that a number of well-organized, large, highly competitive regional organizations as well as hundreds of small, independent dealers are involved in the illicit drug trade. Traditional organized crime syndicates, small ethnic groups, street gangs, and motorcycle gangs are all involved in the importation, manufacture, distribution, and sale of illegal drugs (ONDCP, 2001).

The growth of nontraditional organized crime is one of the most recent phenomena in illicit drug trafficking. Outlaw motorcycle gangs have been deeply involved in Oklahoma (Outlaws), Texas (Bandidos, Scorpions, Banshees, Ghostriders, Freewheelers, and Conquistadors), and several other states (ONDCP, 2001). A shootout in Nevada between the Hell's Angels and rival motorcycle gangs (Mongols, Bandidos, Outlaws, Pagans, Sons, and Vagos) may have been mostly a dispute over drug markets (Wilborn, 2002). Los Angeles gangs, primarily the Crips and the Bloods, have developed far-reaching illicit drug networks that operate in Oregon, Washington, Missouri, Maryland, Texas, Colorado, and New York. In some communities, such as Seattle, Tacoma, and Denver, they have dominated the trade in crack cocaine.

Most of the recent attention to drug trafficking has been focused on the Medellin cartel in Columbia (Cardona, 2010) and the drug-related violence along the Mexican border. Since Mexican President Felipe Calderon's election in September 2009, newspapers estimated the number of killings at more than 13,600 persons. The violence has reached such high levels that Mexican public officials almost never appear in public without hundreds, sometimes thousands, of federal troops for protection. Many law enforcement personnel, both Mexican and American, have been killed in drug-related shootouts in cities like Ciudad Juarez (Hidalgo, 2010).

Drugs, Crime, and Prison

As indicated earlier in this chapter, the U.S. correctional population is approaching 2.5 million, due largely to an increase in admissions for drug offenses (see Table 8.2). Between 1988 and 1997, drug offenders accounted for 61 percent of the total growth in the federal prison population (BOJS, 2001). One reason for this dramatic growth in drug-related prison admissions is parole failure and revocation. Increased emphasis on drug testing and the intensive surveillance of parolees has resulted in sharp increases in the number of drug offenders who are returned to prison. Approximately one of three prison admissions is someone who has failed to complete his or her parole satisfactorily, and the primary reason for parole failure is the use or possession of drugs (Criminal Justice Estimating Conference, 1989). In several states, prison admissions for parole violations have exceeded prison admissions for new court sentences (BOJS, 2001).

The already high incarceration rate for minorities has exploded with the "get-tough" policies of the war on drugs. Drug enforcement has somewhat narrowly focused on crack, a favorite illicit drug among the poor, who are also disproportionately African American and Hispanic American. In Virginia, new drug commitments of whites *fell* from 62 percent of total drug commitments in 1983 to 34 percent in 1989, with minority commitments rising from 38 percent to 66 percent. A majority of all drug offenders in state and federal prisons are African American (BOJS, 2009).

There seems to be reasonable evidence that institutional racism has influenced drug law enforcement. Mandatory minimum sentences force judges to incarcerate many drug violators who would not otherwise be sent to prison, and these sentences appear to apply more often to blacks than whites. For example, a conviction in federal court for possessing 5 grams of crack cocaine results in a five-year mandatory sentence, but 500 grams of cocaine powder is required

to invoke to same sentence. In 1995, the U.S. Congress rejected the U.S. Sentencing Commission's recommendation that sentences for crack (more frequently used by black arrestees) and cocaine powder be equalized. However, the Supreme Court ruled in *Kimbrough v. United States* (2007) that the Guidelines for cocaine are advisory only, and that a judge may consider the disparity in the guidelines for sentencing crack and powder cocaine offenders.

Treating Substance-Abusing Offenders

Law enforcement and corrections administrators have responded to the growing number of alcohol- and drug-involved arrests by increasing the enrollment of offenders in diversion, jail-based, probation, and prison drug treatment programs. In 1979, an estimated 4.4 percent of inmates in state correctional systems were in treatment (NIDA, 1981). By 1987, this figure had grown to 11.1 percent (Chaiken, 1989). By 1995, there were 39 special state correctional facilities designed primarily for alcohol or drug treatment (BOJS, 1997). There were few such special federal facilities at that time. However, by 2008, there were 17,523 federal inmates in residential drug treatment programs, 14,208 in nonresidential programs, 23,230 in drug education programs, and 15,456 in community transitional programs (BOP, 2009).

The most common types of treatment programs in jails and state prisons are Alcoholics Anonymous (AA), Narcotics Anonymous (NA), and other Twelve-Step approaches modeled closely after AA and NA. States estimate that 70 to 85 percent of inmates need substance abuse treatment, but only 13 percent receive any (Blanchard, 1999). It is no wonder that recidivism rates for incarcerated drug offenders are high.

Professionals outside the correctional system might assume that treatment routinely would be provided to chemically dependent inmates. After all, it makes little sense to incarcerate cocaine-abusing offenders for a period of years and then send them back to the community without treatment! However, one must consider the barriers to providing treatment within a prison, such as constraints on resources, changes in priorities for specific types of programs, staff resistance, and inmate resistance (Chaiken, 1989). Prisons and jails are, first and foremost, institutions designed for control and punishment of criminal offenders.

The literature on treatment of chemically dependent offenders presents a somewhat confusing picture. Some evaluations of treatment programs sometimes indicate little or no effect (Vito, 1978); whereas others show that treatment decreased subsequent criminal activity and normalized the lifestyles of offenders (Field, 1989). One Bureau of Prisons study, conducted in 1998, indicated that federal inmates who were provided drug treatment had a 3.3 percent recidivism rate in the first six months after release, compared to 12.1 percent for those without treatment (ONDCP, 2001). Very little of the research followed offenders for a sufficiently long post-treatment phase to generate much confidence in findings of success.

However, states and communities are once more increasing the availability of treatment for incarcerated offenders (Marks, 1999), and since the Violent Crime Control and Law Enforcement Act of 1994, all federal inmates have an opportunity for treatment prior to release (Blanchard, 1999). Nevertheless, in 1998, only 11 percent of state inmates received drug treatment (ONDCP, 2001). There is also some evidence of success in diversion efforts in California, where Proposition 36 has mandated treatment rather than incarceration for first- and second-time offenders (Drug Policy Alliance, 2002).

Historically, methadone maintenance programs have been a major treatment modality for drug-involved criminal offenders. Studies of such programs in New York City since the 1950s indicate that methadone maintenance may be the most cost-effective outpatient treatment for the majority of opiate addicts under probation or parole supervision (Joseph, 1988). Unfortunately, many patients maintained on methadone also have serious alcohol and/or cocaine addictions. In such cases, a choice of other treatment alternatives should also be available.

Therapeutic communities (TCs) have a long history of providing treatment to criminally involved drug addicts. Until 1975, drug abusers were sent to TCs under civil commitment procedures by both federal and state courts. Since 1975, the civil commitment procedures have been gradually replaced with *legal referrals*, which are equally coercive. Some TCs serve criminal justice clients almost exclusively. Clients in a therapeutic community are isolated from the outside world. Their philosophy is that there is no cure, just control. Addicts are kept away from the neighborhood, friends, and situations that have been a part of their addiction. The aim of TCs sounds surprisingly similar to the early moralistic treatments: to restructure an immature, addiction-prone individual into a strong, self-reliant person who no longer needs a drug (Springer, NcNeece, & Arnold, in press). Reviews of the research indicate that TCs are effective with legally coerced clients (ONDCP, 1996; Wexler, 1994).

There are obvious explanations for many of the higher success rates claimed by treatment programs that work with legally coerced clients. First, residential programs such as TCs may require clients to be in residence for a year or more, and these clients are under constant scrutiny by staff and other residents. The risk of detection under such circumstances is quite high, and more successful outcomes are related to longer periods of treatment (Gerstein & Harwood, 1990). Second, clients in both residential and nonresidential programs may be on long-term parole or probation. Such clients may be routinely monitored either by treatment staff or by probation/parole officers for possible drug use, including unannounced urine analysis. Finally, the threat of legal coercion (being returned to jail or prison) may simply have a deterrent effect.

Whatever one may think of the appropriateness of the coerced-treatment approach, since passage of the Anti-Drug Abuse Act of 1988, the majority of illicit drug users in treatment in most communities have been treated through the justice system. Additional funding for treating criminal offenders came from the Edward J. Byrne Memorial Fund, which replaced the Anti-Drug Abuse Act. It was subsequently reauthorized under the American Recovery and Reinvestment Act of 2009 (Public Law 111-5). Without these approaches, there would have been little treatment of any kind for criminal offenders available within the community (McNeece, 1991).

Drug Courts

A promising alternative to combat the growing substance abuse problem in the United States is the establishment of diversionary programs known as *drug courts*. Among other things, drug courts are an attempt on the part of the legal system to focus on substance abuse recovery, rather than on the merits of a given case. The mission of drug courts is to eliminate substance abuse and the resulting criminal behavior. Drug court is a "team effort that focuses on sobriety and accountability as the primary goals" (NADCP, 1997, p. 8). The team of professionals generally includes the state attorney, a public defender, pretrial intervention or probation staff, treatment providers, and the judge, who is considered the central figure of the team.

Drug courts have generally processed offenders in one of two ways: (1) through the use of deferred prosecution, by which adjudication is deferred and the defendant enters treatment, or (2) through a post-adjudication process, by which the case is adjudicated but sentencing is withheld while the defendant is in treatment (U.S. General Accounting Office, 1997). In each case, the judge may reduce or eliminate criminal penalties if a defendant completes a drug court program which

includes a substantial treatment component. A major reason for drug courts' success is the power of the court to compel treatment.

A review of the research on drug courts indicates that they are at least as effective as other diversionary programs (Belenko, 2002; ONDCP, 1996), at least for adults. However, these courts have gradually moved from targeting low level and first time offenders to focusing on those whose substance abuse and criminal activity may be more serious and pose a greater threat to society—and a greater challenge to drug courts (NIJ, 2006).There is less consensus on the effectiveness of juvenile drug courts, which are still experimenting with both prevention and diversion strategies (NIJ, 2006). There were 2,301 Drug Courts in operation as of December 31, 2008 (NDCI, 2009).

Needle and Syringe Exchange Programs

Needle exchange programs (NEPs) and syringe exchange programs (SEPs) are particularly controversial because of some individuals' views that they promote drug abuse and addiction rather than direct users to the goal of abstinence. NEPs generally make clean needles available without pressuring users to accept other health and social services. In a recent U.S. survey, 94 percent of programs indicated that they do refer clients to drug treatment programs, but many do so selectively so as not to alienate clients who would otherwise use NEP services (CDC, 2001). More than a decade ago, a study conducted through the U.S. General Accounting Office (1993) lent qualified support to NEPs and SEPs, and the Secretary of the U.S. Department of Health and Human Services has agreed that research indicates that NEPs can be useful in preventing the transmission of HIV and other blood borne infections and that they do not encourage illegal drug use ("Needle Exchange Programs," 1998). However, this is such a politically charged issue that the federal government still has not lifted the ban on the use of federal funds for NEPs, saying that it prefers to leave it to states and communities to decide the issue.

Two types of laws impede needle exchange programs (Lurie et al., 1993). In the vast majority of states, *drug paraphernalia* laws make it illegal to manufacture, possess, or distribute injecting equipment for nonmedical purposes. And in some states, *prescription laws* require a doctor's prescription to purchase such equipment. Many NEP staff and volunteers believe that they are providing a life-saving service to those who would use drugs anyway, but in many cases, they risk arrest to do so.

A survey of SEPs conducted by the Beth Israel Medical Center in New York City in conjunction with the North American Syringe Exchange Network (NASEN) indicated that the number of SEPS is growing (CDC, 2001). Of the 113 members of NASEN, 100 (89 percent) participated, representing 80 cities, 30 states, the District of Columbia, and Puerto Rico. Four states—California, New York, Washington, and Connecticut—provided 52 percent of the programs. Of the SEPs, 96 reported exchanging a total of approximately 17.5 million syringes in 1997. Based on whether the state in which the SEP was provided had a prescription law or the program was covered under an exemption to the law, 52 of the SEPs were legal, 16 were illegal but tolerated (due to approval from a local body, such as a city council), and 32 were illegal (underground). In descending order, the programs operated in the following ways: syringe pickup/dropoff sites, storefronts, vans, sidewalk tables, on-foot outreaches, cars, locations where users gather (such as "shooting galleries"), and health clinics. (Some used more than one method.) Almost all the SEPs provided other services, as well. In descending order, they are condoms and dental dams (99 percent), information on safer injection techniques and/or bleach to disinfect injection equipment (96 percent), referrals to drug treatment programs (94 percent), on-site health care services (including HIV testing and counseling) (64 percent), tuberculosis skin testing

(20 percent), screening for sexually transmitted diseases (20 percent), and primary health care services (19 percent).

Although many people believe that NEPs/SEPs offer humanitarian assistance by preventing HIV transmission and providing other life-saving services, the United States is still a long way from the stance that other countries have taken to promote needle exchange programs. For example, Denmark, France, Germany, and The Netherlands have experimented with vending machines that sell clean syringes or exchange dirty syringes for clean ones (Lurie et al., 1993). Professionals that help individuals with alcohol and other drug problems should, of course, be committed to the highest ethical standards when assisting clients in determining the course of their treatment (see Chapter 5). Given the many people who go untreated and the high relapse rates even among those who seek help, it is critical that professionals remain open to scientific investigation that might lead to improved methods of helping individuals eliminate, moderate, or otherwise reduce the negative consequences of alcohol and drug use. Although the point is debatable, some believe that we are becoming more open-minded about alternative approaches to addiction (Connors, 1993; de Miranda, 1999). Removing the ban on federal funding for these programs, as mentioned earlier, may eventually stimulate their expansion (IHRA, 2010).

Summary

Public policy regarding drug use in the United States is shaped by culture, history, economic forces, and world affairs. Like most other industrialized Western nations, the United States has chosen to sanction, regulate, and tax two major drugs—alcohol and tobacco. Policies regarding the regulation of these drugs are internally inconsistent, however. Millions of dollars are spent on scientific research to show tobacco growers how to increase their yield, and the federal government provides price supports to stabilize the tobacco industry. In the past, the government has been dependent on tax revenues from tobacco and alcohol sales for a major portion of its budget. At the same time, other governmental offices issue periodic reports decrying the dangers of using either alcohol or tobacco, both strongly addicting drugs that together are responsible for more than one-half million deaths each year in the United States. Policies regarding these drugs seem paradoxical, given the policies regarding illicit drugs.

Since the Harrison Act, national policy toward most other illicit psychoactive drugs has been one of official prohibition. This policy has been, at best, a dismal failure. Some even blame the prohibition approach for the worst of the country's social ills—increasing crime, despair in inner cities, disrespect for law and the political system, and the gradual decline of moral and ethical standards throughout society. For these reasons, as well as the ever-increasing cost of the war on drugs, the nation must face the possibility of changing its policy to allow the legalization or decriminalization of at least some illicit drugs.

That criminals are heavier drug and alcohol users than other citizens is beyond dispute. How much crime is directly attributable to drug and alcohol use is an open question. In some cases, the user's physiological response to a drug might be aggressive behavior that results in a criminal act. For some individuals, illicit drug use simply may be another aspect of their criminality that coexists along with certain other criminal activities. Their drug use and their stealing both may be due to the influences of life in an impoverished ghetto, rife with crime. Illicit drug use and other criminal activities may be mutually reinforcing; it is easier to locate and obtain certain drugs if one is already a member of a deviant subculture. If one is a junkie, that status frequently provides easier access to various forms of criminal enterprise.

According to a recovering heroin addict:

> You have put yourself on the wrong side of the law and your original framework for interaction becomes shaky. You find that people you know are stealing, kiting cheques, or doing insurance jobs. The process of osmosis into this world is slow and gradual. By the time you realize what is going on, you have ceased to be shocked. (Stewart, 1987, p. 77)

For drugs such as marijuana, perhaps the major connection with crime is the secondary deviance that comes from being caught and officially labeled as a criminal. This is especially important for juveniles, since marijuana is the primary illicit drug used by the nation's children. Official court processing and referral of these cases to agencies of the juvenile justice system are not likely to curtail further delinquent acts. In fact, just the opposite is likely to occur. The deeper a youthful drug offender is immersed in the system, the *more* likely subsequent delinquent behavior is apt to be seen (Twentieth Century Fund, 1978).

It seems obvious that the answer to the nation's drug problem is not law enforcement. Law enforcement should be a vital component of any rational plan to stem the manufacture, sale, and use of illicit drugs, but as a primary strategy, it has failed miserably. At the current rate of imprisonment for drug offenses, it is doubtful that either the economy or the political system can support such high rates of incarceration much longer.

PART THREE

Chemical Dependency in Special Populations

Much of Parts One and Two of this book addressed substance use, abuse, and dependence in general terms, although some distinctions were made with regard to use by age, gender, race/ethnicity, and other factors. Part Three addresses in greater depth substance use and substance use disorders among various population groups.

Age is one factor that affects use. Younger people use alcohol and illicit substances more than older individuals. Drug use among youth always elicits great concern; thus, Chapter 9 looks at this problem. It describes the screening and assessment tools most commonly used with youth, and it considers strategies used to treat youth who develop substance use disorders, including attempts to involve their family members and community using approaches such as multi-systemic therapy and multi-family therapy groups. As one might suspect, engaging and treating youth involves different strategies than might be applied in the treatment of adults. At the other end of the age spectrum, Chapter 14 considers substance use disorders in older adults, including the high rate of prescription drug use and its implications for the development of drug problems. Strategies such as reducing isolation and increasing socialization are discussed as well as other developmental factors and treatment approaches that address the concerns of individuals in this latter phase of the life cycle.

In keeping with the systems perspective of this book, the focus of Chapter 10 is the family system as the forum for treating substance use disorders. The chapter describes the major theoretical approaches to family treatment of substance use disorders and offers some practical tools for engaging families in the treatment process, such as family sculpting. Some of the popular concepts in chemical dependency are also considered, such as codependency and adult children of alcoholics.

Given the increasing ethnic diversity of the United States, Chapter 11 addresses differences in rates of substance use and substance use disorders among members of major racial/ethnic and cultural groups, such as American Indians and Alaska Natives, African Americans and other blacks, Hispanic or Latino(a) Americans, Asian Americans, and Jewish Americans. The literature is quite convincing in claiming that culture and race/ethnicity strongly influence alcohol and other drug use and related problems. Human service professionals have been called on to increase cultural sensitivity and to adopt culturally relevant treatment approaches, especially since some groups experience more serious health and social consequences from substance use, even when their use does not differ significantly from the majority's use. What is generally lacking, however, is empirical verification of the improvements in treatment effectiveness that can be made by introducing culturally relevant approaches in treating substance use disorders or when or with whom such approaches are necessary. Many common themes connect the literature on substance use and related disorders among each racial/ethnic group: the strong influence of peers in influencing youths' substance use, regardless of ethnic background; the concerns of family members and the need to involve them in treatment; the need for community involvement in developing prevention and treatment strategies; the roles of deprivation and discrimination in promoting substance abuse; the need to utilize strengths, rather than deficit perspectives; and the importance of identifying factors that protect individuals of various cultural groups from developing alcohol and other drug problems.

A subject that gets little attention in most books on substance use disorders is sexual minorities, including gay men, lesbians, bisexuals, and transgendered individuals. Although these individuals are members of hidden populations, the literature on their substance use and related problems is growing. As described in Chapter 12, this literature tends to show that alcohol and drug use and substance disorders occur more often among gay men and lesbians, although sampling and other methodological limitations of studies makes these points debatable. Regardless of the incidence of alcohol and drug problems among sexual minorities, chemical dependency treatment providers must be mindful of these individuals' unique treatment needs. In order to do this, Chapter 12 describes gay affirmative practice and encourages its use in helping sexual minorities address substance use disorders. This chapter also includes a discussion of the use of separate and integrated treatment programs.

Many individuals who have substance use disorders also have physical or mental illnesses. The subject of Chapter 13 is diagnoses that co-occur with substance use disorders. In some cases, there is no clear cause-and-effect relationship between a substance use disorder and another disability. In other cases, a substance use disorder clearly predates and causes a disability, as may be the case when an alcohol-related traffic accident results in a spinal cord injury or a head injury. Sometimes, a physical or mental disability prompts the use of alcohol or other drugs to assuage pain that is not properly treated, to dull the loneliness or boredom that may occur because of failures of the rehabilitation system or the individual's reluctance to engage in rehabilitative activities, or to deal with the negative or inappropriate reactions of family, friends, and others who do not know how to address the individual with a disability. Mental disorders commonly co-occur with substance use disorders. The expansive literature on this topic receives considerable attention in Chapter 13, including recommendations to integrate treatment for mental and substance use disorders. Approaches to assisting individuals with substance use disorders who are blind, visually impaired, deaf, and hard of hearing are also considered, although there is very little empirical literature to assess the extent of the problem or the effectiveness of treatment. One thing that is known is that even with the Americans with Disabilities Act (ADA) of 1990, substance use disorder treatment remains inaccessible to many individuals with disabilities. The incidence of substance use disorders among individuals with mental retardation (now often referred to as intellectual *disability*) seems to be lower than in the general population, but suggestions to assist those who do develop substance use disorders are offered. The chapter concludes with a discussion of other physical disabilities (arthritis, heart disease, diabetes, epilepsy, and chronic pain), their relationship to alcohol and other drug use and related problems, and cases in which alcohol use may produce beneficial or at least no harmful effects.

Gender differences are the topic of Chapter 15. Women use alcohol and other drugs less than men and reportedly have fewer substance-related problems, but younger women have been closing this gap, and this is a cause for concern. Also of concern is that women seem to develop substance use disorders more quickly than men and that women with substance use disorders experience more physical damage than men with substance use disorders and women who do not have substance use disorders. There is some evidence that women may benefit from different treatment approaches than men and that women can benefit from treatment in settings where all the clientele are female. Some treatment considerations are obvious, such as the need to provide child care, but more research is needed to determine just what would promote better treatment outcomes for women.

The chapters in Part Three offer case examples and illustrations to highlight particular points about the development of substance use disorders and their treatment in various population groups. These chapters also recommend that treatment be tailored to the individual's needs and characteristics. Although Project MATCH (described in Chapter 6) suggested that three treatment approaches worked about equally well regardless of factors such as the subject's gender or race/ethnicity, it is unlikely that applying generic approaches to everyone will produce satisfactory results.

CHAPTER 9

Treating Substance-Abusing Youth

Katherine L. Montgomery and **David W. Springer**

University of Texas at Austin

There are no simple explanations as to why youth use licit and illicit drugs (Wills, Sandy, & Yaeger, 2000), nor is it clear that most drug-using youth meet the diagnostic criteria to justify a diagnosis of alcohol or drug dependency. Thus, social workers should guard against the casual acceptance of substance abuse or dependency diagnoses in youth. In part, the problem is one of definition. As discussed in earlier chapters, serious definitional problems exist in assessing substance abuse and dependency. With youth, in particular, these diagnoses may become a prophecy of lifetime difficulties. On the other hand, ignoring symptoms of a youth's substance abuse difficulties constitutes negligence. Thus, it is important for social workers to approach substance-abusing youth with a well-informed balance of purposeful action and caution.

The Monitoring the Future Study is a series of annual surveys of about 50,000 students in over 400 public and private secondary schools nationwide that has been conducted since 1975 by the University of Michigan Survey Research Center. According to the most recent report (Johnston et al., 2009) from 2008, adolescent substance use has been slowly declining in recent years, but is still of great concern. The 30 day prevalence of using any illicit drug was highest among 12th graders (22 percent), followed by 10th graders (16 percent). With the emergence of prescription medication abuse around the turn of the twenty-first

century, researchers have begun recording the use of Ritalin, OxyContin, Vicodin, and over the counter cough/cold medicines. The use of Ritalin and cough/cold medicines parallels the overall decline in substance use; however, OxyContin and Vicodin use remain fairly steady. Other drugs that held steady overall in 2008 include marijuana (21.5 percent), inhalants (6.4 percent), hallucinogens (3.8 percent), LSD (1.9 percent), PCP (12th grade only—1.1 percent), ecstasy (MDMA) (2.9 percent), sedatives (12th grade only—5.8 percent), tranquilizers (6.3 percent), and heroin (0.8 percent). Substances on the decline include amphetamines (5.8 percent), cocaine (2.9 percent), crack (1.3 percent), steroids (1.1 percent), cigarettes (33.1 percent), and alcohol (48.7 percent).

Johnston and colleagues (2009) note that the 2008 data reflect two important themes. The first theme is a reflection of the substance use decline. They note that all percentages in 2008 are below the peak percentage from past years. The second theme, however, is one of caution. The authors point out that the "nation must not be lulled into complacency" (p. 9). They explain that the nationwide prevention programs seem to be working, and to keep substance abuse on the decline, the continuity of these programs is essential. According to the National Household Survey on Drug Abuse (SAMHSA, 2008), 9.7 percent of persons age 12 to 17 were binge drinkers in the year 2007, and 2.3 percent were heavy drinkers.[1]

Thus, while there is reason to be optimistic regarding substance use in the United States, abuse of substances continues to be problematic for youth. (See Chapter 2 for more detailed information on the epidemiology of drug use and abuse.)

This chapter will provide a primer on walking the fine line between an uncritical acceptance of unwarranted labels and negligent practice. To accomplish this goal, the chapter examines substance abuse treatment for youth from the perspectives of risk and protective factors, thorough biopsychosocial assessment pertaining specifically to youth, and evidence-based treatment modalities.

Risk and Protective Factors

A substantial amount of research has been conducted on the concepts of risk and protective factors within developmental and contextual domains (cf. Carbonell, Reinherz, & Giaconia, 1998; Fraser, 2004; Hodge, Cardenas, & Montoya, 2001; Jenson, Anthony, & Howard, 2006) that either increase or decrease an adolescent's likelihood of using substances. According to Howell (2003), "*risk factors* are those elements in an individual's life that increase his or her vulnerability to negative developmental outcomes and also increase the probability of maintenance of a problem condition or digression to a more serious state" (p. 104). More simply stated, particular factors can increase one's risk for negative outcomes. Conversely, *protective factors* are internalizing and externalizing factors that assist youth in guarding against social problems such as substance use (Kirby & Fraser, 1997). It is believed that the greater number of protective factors present, the less likely the youth is to engage in substance use.

Worth noting is the fact that adolescents displaying particular risk factors are not assured to use substances, but are simply at greater risk than those not displaying the specific risk factor(s). Conversely, some adolescents possess multiple risk factors and never use substances. Researchers have explored explanations as to why, despite having or

not having particular risk and protective factors, some youth chose to use substances and others do not. One conclusion currently offered in the literature is the concept of *resiliency* (Turner, 2001). Resiliency is defined as "the remarkable capacity of individuals to withstand considerable hardship, to bounce back in the face of adversity, and to go on to live functional lives with a sense of well-being" (Turner, 2001, p. 441). Vaillant (1993) metaphorically presents resiliency as "the capacity to be bent without breaking and the capacity, once bent, to spring back" (p. 248). Understanding resilience and protective factors in youth assists in explaining why some youth can overcome adversity and seemingly live normal lives while other youth succumb. While there is no simple formula for predicting the effects of drug use on youth, it is indisputable that reducing risk factors and increasing protective factors are beneficial for adolescents. Researchers typically categorize each of the factors within specific domains: individual, peer, family, school, and community (see Table 9.1). Selected factors among each domain will be explored in the following section.

Individual Factors

How an adolescent responds to external factors greatly varies between individuals. Two siblings may encounter very similar environments, yet make vastly different choices. There are multiple individual factors that contribute to a youth's risk of substance use: youth's perception of substance abuse, delinquency, antisocial behavior, rebelliousness, and sensation-seeking (Beyers, Toumbourou, Catalano, Arthur, & Hawkins, 2004; NIDA, 2003; SAMHSA, 2001). As some of the factors are explored further, the reciprocal and cyclical nature of risk factors can be observed.

Perception of Risk.   Youth who perceive substance use to be harmless are much more likely to use substances (SAMHSA, 2000). For example, youth believing marijuana to be less dangerous than smoking cigarettes often use this rationale as a motive to smoke marijuana. Additionally, a

TABLE 9.1   Substance Use Risk and Protective Factors

Domain	Risk Factors	Protective Factors
Individual	Perception of risk of substance abuse Delinquency Early and persistent antisocial behavior Rebelliousness Favorable attitudes toward substance use Sensation-seeking	Religiosity Resilient temperament Social skills Belief in moral order
Peer	Friends' attitudes toward substance use Friends' use of substances Gang involvement	Friends who engage in conventional behavior
School	Poor attitude toward school Academic failure Lack of commitment to school	Recognition for involvement in prosocial activities Anti-drug use policies School opportunities for prosocial involvement
Community	Drug Availability Community laws and norms favorable to drug use, fire arms, and crime Transitions and mobility Low neighborhood attachment Community disorganization	Community opportunities for prosocial involvement Community recognition for prosocial involvement
Family	Poor family management Lack of parental supervision Parental attitudes toward substance use Family history of substance use Parental attitudes favorable toward antisocial behavior Family conflict	Family attachment Family opportunities for pro-social involvement Family recognition for pro-social involvement

Note: Adapted from SAMHSA, 2001; NIDA, 2003; and Beyers, Toumbourou, Catalano, Arthur, & Hawkins, 2004.

youth's misperceptions about how others perceive drug use and misuse may pose a hindrance to successful treatment (Christiansen, Goldman, & Inn, 1982). If, for example, a youth believes that others are morally critical of him or her, acrimonious arguments may ensue. On the other hand, if a youth thinks of drug use and misuse as a disease, then it might eliminate some of the acrimonious arguments but encourage irresponsible,

"I'm-not-responsible-because-I'm-sick" statements. In any event, understanding how the youth perceives others' evaluations of him or her may provide useful insights.

Delinquency.   It is well documented that there are many similarities in the risk and protective factors for juvenile delinquency and substance use (Hawkins, Catalano, & Miller, 1992; Jenson, 1997;

Williams, Ayers, Abbott, Hawkins, & Catalano, 1999; Rivaux, Springer, Bohman, Wagner, & Gil, 2006). Williams et al. (1999) notes six factors that predict both juvenile delinquency and substance abuse: moral beliefs, peer influence, school attachment and commitment, family relationships, academic achievement, and social skills. Thus, youth who are at high risk of using substances are often at high risk of becoming delinquent. Implications for delinquency in assessment are explored later.

Protective Factors.   Individual protective factors include religiosity, resilient temperament, social skills, and belief in moral order (Beyers, Toumbourou, Catalano, Arthur, & Hawkins, 2004; NIDA, 2003; SAMHSA, 2001). Most individual protective factors coalesce around an adolescent's belief system and the lens through which they view the world. Crucial to the process of molding ones belief structure, however, are peers and the family system. The way youth view the world is often an indication of how they are influenced by those around them.

Peer Factors

As youth move through developmental changes, they often rely on the perceptions and choices of others to guide their behavior. Risk factors associated with youth's peers are: friends' attitudes toward substance use, friends' use of substances, and gang involvement (Beyers, Toumbourou, Catalano, Arthur, & Hawkins, 2004; NIDA, 2003; SAMHSA, 2001). When youth observe specific behaviors as normative in a group setting, it is not difficult for the adolescent to adapt to a shared belief. Conversely, having peers that engage in normative behavior serves as a protective factor. Prevention efforts allowing youth opportunities to engage in healthy relationships are necessary for youth.

Family Factors

Whether it is the level of home stability, abuse or neglect, or with whom the youth lives, the impact of the family system is great. Factors within the family

domain recognized as placing a youth at risk of using substances are: poor family management, lack of parental supervision, parental attitudes favorable toward the use of substances, family history of substance use, family conflict, and family attitudes favorable toward antisocial behavior (Beyers, Toumbourou, Catalano, Arthur, & Hawkins, 2004; NIDA, 2003; SAMHSA, 2001). Families being involved and bonding with their youth often serve to protect them from the risk of using substances. Ford (2009) found that the absence of family bonding was significantly correlated with nonmedical prescription drug use. Thus, as will be further explored next, interventions designed to treat the family system are of great value when treating substance abusing and dependent youth.

Family History of Substance Use.   In a longitudinal analysis, Hops and colleagues found that parental substance use strongly predicted children's likelihood of using substances (Hops, Duncan, Duncan, & Stoolmiller, 1996). In another example, having alcoholic parents presents is a significant risk factor associated with the offspring's development of alcohol dependency (Leukefeld, McDonald, Stoops, Reed, & Martin, 2005). Again, as youth become to recognize substance use as normative among the systems they encounter, the risk of using substances increases.

Family Conflict.   Youth raised within stable family systems are less likely to use substances (Buu, DiPiazza, Wang, Puttler, Fitzgerald, & Zucker, 2009). Discussed further in the assessment section, youth often cope with familial conflict by using substances. They are additionally drawn to peers who are seeking the same escape from conflict. When parents struggle with consistency, managing their own behavioral difficulties, and positively engaging their youth, their child becomes at risk.

School Factors

In addition to the family system, a youth's school experiences form the attitudes and often provide the market that allows drug use or a meeting place for youth who engage in drug use as a social activity (Smith, Koob, & Wirtz, 1985). Risk factors in the school domain include: youth's poor attitude toward to school, academic failure, and lack of commitment toward school (Beyers, Toumbourou, Catalano, Arthur, & Hawkins, 2004; SAMHSA, 2001). During childhood and adolescence, the importance of social activity among peers cannot be overemphasized. Youth observe, learn, and speak with each other and by so doing become socialized into the common culture. Activities that include drug use may interfere with educational activities in two ways. First, performance in the classroom may suffer. Documentation of the problems caused by drug use is widespread. Recent scientific research provides overwhelming evidence that drugs interfere with normal brain functioning and have long-term effects on brain metabolism and activity (NIDA, 2001). Second, drug use is associated with conflict. Although conflict is not inevitable with drug use, it can occur with alarming frequency. For instance, disputes over payment and extortion to secure payment for drugs can result in violence that reduces confidence in the safety of the school setting for all students. Prevention efforts to increase protective factors (recognition for involvement in prosocial activities, anti-drug use policies, and school opportunities for prosocial involvement: Beyers, Toumbourou, Catalano, Arthur, & Hawkins, 2004; SAMHSA, 2001) are necessary.

Community Factors

Of the five domains, the community domain is the area with the least amount of research (Farrington, 2000). Drug availability, community norms favorable to drug use and crime, transitions and mobility, low neighborhood attachment, and community disorganization are all identified as community level factors that place a youth at risk of using substances (Beyers, Toumbourou, Catalano, Arthur, & Hawkins, 2004; SAMHSA, 2001). Different from adults, youth are required to

experience great transitional changes as they move from the security of home to school. Research has shown that as children progress through educational transitions, they are at greater risk of using substances (NIDA, 2003). While macro-level prevention and interventions are in their infancy (Thyer, 2008), it is important for social workers to keep a macro-level perspective of what might influence or provide protection against substance use.

Social workers gain benefit from understanding risk and protective factors. The first benefit is assistance in assessment. In a thorough biopsychosocial assessment, social workers can utilize risk and protective factors to identify existing or potential substance use concerns. For example, if a parent describes their own struggle or acceptance of substances, the interviewer can explore substance use with the adolescent. A second benefit is with regard to treatment planning. The social worker can support the youth and family in making goals to change specific risk factors. By reducing risk factors and assisting families in building protective factors, the social worker can assist their client and the family in potential substance use prevention.

Assessment with Substance-Abusing Youth

Assessment is the first active phase of treatment (Springer, McNeece, & Arnold, 2003). Without a thorough and complete assessment, the social worker cannot develop a treatment plan that will serve the youth and his or her family. Assessment and diagnosis with substance-abusing clients is covered in Chapter 5; however, proper youth assessment requires additional, specific areas to be explored. A social worker hoping to positively impact youth struggling with substance use must first understand how youth differ developmentally and contextually when choosing and implementing treatment. Information gathered from a youth's educational, legal, and family history will often look dramatically different than an adult's completed assessment and specific factors must be considered. Such contexts provide social workers with the necessary background in treatment planning and undertaking drug and alcohol interventions. Although drugs have specific physiological effects, their use and meaning derive from biological, psychological, and sociological contexts. It is not possible to understand substance abuse in youth without considering these biopsychosocial contexts in assessment. Failure to assess any one of the systems accurately can result in ineffective treatment that leaves the youth vulnerable to increased alcohol and drug use and the family angered by insensitive practice.

In an ideal setting, information is gathered from both the parent(s) or guardian(s) and the youth. Studies have shown that there is little agreement between youth and parental reports during assessment (Israel, Thomsen, Langeveld, & Stormark, 2007). Typically, both have offered truthful information that provides the social worker with a broader, clearer perspective. Adolescents are often untruthful with parents, particularly in regard to illegal behavior and social problems. If possible, it is important that assessments be conducted separately, by the same professional. In first gathering information from the parent, the social worker can understand valuable developmental history the youth often does not know. Parents can provide detail the youth either do not know or are not comfortable sharing. Using the parent's assessment information, the social worker can approach the youth interview with a contextual background. It is important to allow the parent's interview to assist with the youth's assessment; however, one should take caution and use appropriate clinical skills so as to not allow a parent's perspective to overshadow the voice of the youth. In addition to assessing accurately the adolescent's understanding of others' perceptions, the social worker should examine the meaning of the drug to the youth. Their understanding or *relationship* to drugs can frequently assist the social worker in planning treatment. (Chapter 2 addressed addicts' expectations about the effects

of drugs.) When youth expect and receive a specific effect, they may come to trust the drug and perceive it as a friend. In particular, a youth who may not have other friends may consider a drug to be his or her best friend. As a result, sadness is a natural consequence of drug use cessation. Treatment that focuses on resolution of the grief that follows a significant loss should be initiated.

Education.   A youth's educational assessment will often reveal what an adult's occupational assessment would. Similar to occupational assessments in adults, educational information can illuminate patterns of truancy, level of engagement in day-to-day responsibilities, and ability to function in social settings. For youth, there is often a shift in educational behavior that mimics a choice to begin using substances on a frequent basis. As a youth begins using substances, they are more likely to have diminished success in school (Bachman, O'Malley, Schulenberg, Johnston, Freedman-Doan & Messersmith, 2007). Thus, when assessing the educational domain, the social worker can inquire about changes in grades, history of disciplinary behavior, and level of engagement in school to ascertain potential timeline for substance use.

Legal History.   Due to the manner in which youth use substances, whether it be smoking cigarettes, drinking alcohol, taking their mother's prescription medication, or smoking marijuana, it is often against the law and they are thus at risk of engaging with the juvenile justice system. In a study of juvenile detainees, 56 percent of males and 40 percent of females tested positive for an illegal substance at the time of their arrest (National Institute of Justice [NIJ], 2003). Social workers assessing youth who use substances should inquire about their legal context. Are they currently on probation? If so, it is not uncommon for many states to provide therapeutic intervention as a requirement of probation. In a thorough assessment, it is important to gather information regarding treatments they may have received. Often, previous experiences will shape the lens through which they initially perceive future relationships with social workers and therapists.

Family History. With adult assessment, family history is often gathered to inquire history about substance use or psychiatric illness displayed in the immediate and extended family system. With youth, however, substances are often used as a coping strategy to survive amongst their family system. As discussed in the risk factors, youth coming from families involving high levels of conflict are likely to abuse substances. It is important that the social worker inquire about the communication and problem-solving strategies within a family system. If youth are not allowed or do not appropriately communicate difficult feelings, they will often turn to substances for self-medication.

Standardized Instruments. A necessary component to adequate assessment is the use of standardized instruments. There are several instruments currently utilized with evaluation of substance abusing youth. Table 9.2 provides selected standardized instruments that may be useful in assessment with substance-abusing youth. (For a more comprehensive review of assessment tools for youth, see Fischer and Corcoran [2007]; Shaffer, Lucas, and Richters [1999]; and Springer, [2002a].)

Having mentioned the importance of standardized assessment tools, a word of caution is in order: It is ill advised for a practitioner to rely solely on self-report measures when determining diagnostic impressions and a course of treatment for youth. Youth can easily present themselves as they wish to be perceived by others on such measures. Thus, clinical decisions should be supplemented by a thorough biopsychosocial history (which should include information gathered from external sources such as parents, physicians, and teachers, when at all possible), a mental status exam (when appropriate), and direct observation of the client. The *timeline follow-back procedure* (Sobell & Sobell, 1992) should be included in the assessment of substance abuse history with adolescents (Waldron, 1997). This structured interview technique samples a specific period of time using a monthly calendar and memory anchor points to help the client reconstruct daily use during that period. This may offer the most sensitive assessment for adolescent substance abusers (Lecesse & Waldron, 1994).

Liability

The threat of litigation significantly affects practice decisions. More than ever, social workers must be cognizant of clients' expectations and

TABLE 9.2 Assessment Tools for Substance Abusing Adolescents

Assessment Tool	*Website*
Problem Oriented Screening Instrument for Teenagers (POSIT)	www.nhtsa.dot.gov/people/injury/alcohol/juvenile/posit.pdf
Drug Use Screening Inventory-Revised (DUSI-R)	pubs.niaaa.nih.gov/publications/Assesing%20Alcohol/InstrumentPDFs/32_DUSI-R.pdf
Child and Adolescent Functional Assessment Scale (CAFAS)	www.cafas.com/
Substance Abuse Subtle Screening Inventory for Adolescents (SASSI-A2)	www.sassi.com/
Massachusetts Youth Screening Instrument Version 2 (MAYSI-2)	www.maysiware.com/MAYSI2.htm
Voice Diagnostic Interview Schedule for Children (Voice DISC)	www.promotementalhealth.org/voicedisc.htm

up-to-date practice wisdom. When youth are brought for treatment, their parents frequently expect social workers and other service providers to employ professional methods to remedy their child's social, psychological, and familial problems. Despite parents' inclination to believe therapy can "fix" their child (Kazdin, 2005), social workers do not have any single intervention that can dramatically "cure" youths' substance use and abuse. Alcohol and drug treatment in the United States is heavily influenced by twelve-step programs. Since members sometimes make dramatic claims of these programs' success, social workers should carefully explain the limitations of available treatment. Otherwise, parents may expect dramatic and lasting results from treatment and may be angered and disheartened by failure (Michels & Cooper, 1997). Parents must also understand their roles in treatment; otherwise, they may become increasingly vocal in their complaints about progress. As a partial remedy to these legal pitfalls, social workers must avoid endorsing treatment methods that run counter to published literature regarding evidence-based practice.

In any event, the youth's legal standing must be considered when planning treatment. Although the age of consent varies from state to state, parents and guardians must give explicit consent before treatment can begin with minor children. The social worker should examine closely agency guidelines on who can give informed consent for what procedures before undertaking treatment. Drug-abusing youths' relationships with parents and/or guardians may be strained, providing fertile ground for misunderstandings. By remembering that youth may in many cases be unable to give informed consent to proceed with treatment, social workers should from the very start incorporate parents into treatment planning and implementation (Springer, 2002b).

It is not always clear if a youth has been coerced into treatment. The level of compliance with treatment directives may in part hinge on the social worker's precise understanding of who initiated and who has interest in the treatment. When parents initiate their youth's entry into treatment, the social worker will be faced with the unenviable task of gaining the youth's cooperation.

Treatment with Substance-Abusing Youth

The treatment modalities discussed in this chapter are by no means the only ones available to treat substance-abusing youth. Because treatment modalities vary so widely in their implementation, it is difficult to state with full confidence that any one type of treatment is particularly more effective with adolescents than others. In considering what type of treatment modality is best suited for preventing and remediating a youth's problems, the social worker should consider many issues in addition to reputed effectiveness. Cost, predicted compliance with treatment procedures, and level of family involvement are also important. The choice of treatment methods must take into account their degree of intrusiveness.

Primary prevention efforts that consist solely of educational efforts addressing risk and protective factors are the least intrusive, require the least involvement, and can be implemented in many settings (see Chapter 7). Outpatient treatment and community self-help groups (e.g., Alcoholics Anonymous) are the next level (see Chapter 6). More intensive, and client-centered approaches, also include family therapies designed to meet the unique needs of the family system (see Chapter 10). From a systems approach, the youth using substances is only a part of what contributes to the illness. As previously explored, various domains each play a role in placing a child at risk of using substances. Inpatient treatment, which is usually implemented in a hospital setting, is a third level of treatment. The last and most intrusive level of treatment is residential treatment and treatment communities. In the last few years, this level has been used less commonly to treat substance-abusing youth and has been replaced more frequently by outpatient efforts. In fact, a dual diagnosis of substance abuse or dependence and mental illness is often required to warrant payment of inpatient or residential treatment from a third-party payer. In addition to lower costs, less intrusive treatment methods generally require less family involvement and less disruption in day-to-day activities. More intrusive treatment methods are much more expensive and typically better suited when there is a medical risk, danger of suicide or homicide, or uncontrolled behavior that might result in harm to self or others.

Dual Diagnoses

Sixty percent of adolescents who either use, abuse, or have become dependent on substances have a diagnosable mental health illness (Armstrong & Costello, 2002). The co-occurrence of severe emotional difficulties and drug abuse is not a coincidence (see Chapter 13). Adolescents may use drugs as a means of coping with the tribulations that they experience. For other youth, drug use exacerbates serious emotional disorders. There are specific mental health illnesses that often pertain to substance-abusing youth. Studies suggest a prominent role for substance use in the etiology and prognosis of psychiatric disorders such as mood disorders, conduct disorder, attention-deficit/hyperactivity disorder, and anxiety disorders (McBride, VanderWaal, Terry, & VanBuren, 1999). Conversely, psychiatric disorders also appear to play a crucial role in the etiology of and vulnerability to substance use problems in youth (Armstrong & Costello, 2002; Hawkins, Catalano, & Miller, 1992). Thus, the presence of substance abuse and dependency in youth may be a harbinger of serious emotional difficulties. Treatment should address both conditions concurrently.

Bender, Springer, and Kim (2006) conducted a systematic review on the effectiveness of current empirically supported treatments for dually-diagnosed adolescents. Studies included in this review were those that met the following selection criteria established by the researchers:

1. randomized clinical trials, allowing researchers to determine effectiveness;
2. treatment for dually-diagnosed disorders, meaning treatment for both substance abuse and mental health disorders concurrently;
3. peer reviewed in past 10 years, to provide the most current literature available;
4. treatments designed for youth with already existing dual diagnoses, excluding prevention studies;
5. studies published in English; and
6. treatment for youth ages 12 to 18, narrowing studies to those of adolescents only.

The search identified seven interventions for dually-diagnosed adolescents reported across six different studies that met these selection criteria. These included: Multisystemic Therapy (MST; Henggeler, Pickrel, & Brondino, 1999), Interactional Group Treatment (IT; Kaminer, Burleson, Blitz, Sussman, Rounsaville, 1998; Kaminer & Burleson, 1999), Family Behavior Therapy (FBT; Azrin, Donohue, Teichner, Crum, Howell, & DeCato, 2001), Individual Cognitive Problem-Solving (ICPS; Azrin, Donohue, Teichner, Crum, Howell, & DeCato, 2001); Cognitive Behavior Therapy (CBT; Kaminer, Burleson, & Goldberger, 2002), Ecologically Based Family Therapy (EBFT; Slesnick & Prestopnik, 2005), and Seeking Safety Therapy (SS; Najavits, Gallop, & Weiss, 2006).

The results were analyzed and interpreted using a statistic called an effect size. This statistic is commonly used in clinical outcome research. Effect size statistics portray the strength of association found in any study, no matter what outcome measure is used, in terms that are comparable across studies (Rubin & Babbie, 2008). Thus, they enable us to compare the effects of different interventions across studies that use different types of outcome measures. These treatment effects are interpreted as *large*, *moderate*, or *small*, which is simply a way to more easily interpret the effect size.

TABLE 9.3   Ten Preliminary Treatment Guidelines for Dually-Diagnosed Adolescents

1. Assessment is multi-pronged, ongoing, and includes practitioner, parental and self monitoring so that treatment is responsive to the changing needs of the client.
2. Treatment strategically enhances engagement and retention.
3. Treatment plans are flexible and allow for client choice and voice.
4. An integrated treatment approach is used to address both mental health and substance related disorders concurrently.
5. Treatment is developmentally and culturally sensitive to match the unique needs of the client system.
6. Treatment is ecologically grounded and systems oriented, including important individuals to the client such as family members, friends, and school personnel.
7. Treatment taps several domains of the client's functioning to enhance the client's problem solving and decision-making skills, affect regulation, impulse control, communication skills, and peer and family relations.
8. Treatment is goal-directed, here-and-now focused, and strength-based.
9. Treatment requires active participation by all members involved, and includes home work assignments.
10. Interventions aim to produce sustainable changes over the course of treatment.

Source: From "Treatment Effectiveness with Dually Diagnosed Adolescents: A Systematic Review" by Kimberly Bender et al. from *Brief Treatment and Crisis Intervention* 6(3), 2006, p. 200. Reprinted by permission of Oxford University Press.

Substance abuse effect sizes were large for the FBT, ICPS, PET, and CBT groups. Worth noting is that EBFT and SS also had moderate effect sizes at posttest and sustained moderate reductions in substance abuse at follow-up. While analysis identifying effective treatment modalities for individual outcomes is helpful, one challenge of treating dually-diagnosed youth is their likely diagnosis with several or all of these conditions. Reviewing these results, FBT and ICPS appeared to be the only interventions to produce large treatment effect sizes across externalizing, internalizing, and substance abuse domains. Furthermore, the large effect sizes for these two treatments were evident at nine-months post-treatment, demonstrating sustainability of effects over time.

After examining the common factors among treatments with demonstrated effectiveness, Bender and colleagues developed ten preliminary treatment guidelines for dually-diagnosed adolescents (see Table 9.3). These guidelines might serve as a barometer, perhaps providing a general gauge of how to tailor treatment for dually-diagnosed adolescents.

Prevention and Drug Education

The current literature on the treatment of drug use, misuse, and dependency emphasizes the complexity of preventing adolescent substance abuse.

Indeed, research on factors and processes that increase the risk of using drugs or protect against the risk of using drugs has identified a range of primary targets for preventive intervention: family relationships, peer relationships, the school environment, and the community (Physician Leadership on National Drug Policy, 2002). Successful prevention programs "will wisely address developmental as well as parental and community factors that influence drug use among high-risk youth" (Schinke & Cole, 1995, p. 228). In other words, they will use risk and protective factors from each domain to guide prevention efforts.

Such recommendations, however, only highlight the conceptual quagmire of primary, secondary, and tertiary prevention strategies (see Chapter 7). Of the three strategies, only primary prevention is intended to prevent non-using youth from beginning substance use. There is an increasing consensus that primary prevention efforts must focus on family and school environments to increase children's self-esteem and self-efficacy (Kumpfer & Turner, 1990–1991; Schaffer, Phillips, Enzer, Silverman, & Anthony, 1989). Secondary and tertiary prevention (also known as treatment) address problems of youth that are caused by varying degrees of drug involvement. Both these types of prevention strategies focus on encouraging a cessation of drug use, remediating problems, and strengthening the youth's resilience (McNeece & Springer, 1997). However, prevention works best when there is a clear target for intensive efforts. Unfortunately, there is no clear profile for identifying youth who are at greatest risk for debilitating substance use (Johnson, 1990–1991), although much research is being done in this area.

Many alcohol and drug intervention programs developed for children and adolescents are implemented within the school setting and taught by adult authority figures. Studies comparing teacher-led and peer-led prevention interventions have resulted in mixed findings (Erhard, 1999). Some of the assumptions about peer-led models, such as the fear of control/discipline difficulties, are unfounded (Erhard, 1999), and peer-led programs have yielded twice as much student self-disclosure among participants (Erhard, 1999). All in all, there are strong indications that the peer-led model may possess greater potential for primary prevention than the teacher-led model.

Historically, drug prevention has most commonly consisted of the information-education approach, which assumes that once adults make adolescents aware of the health hazards of substances, they will develop antidrug attitudes and subsequently make choices not to use. Research that questions the effectiveness of information-only prevention programs found that not only did this form of intervention fail to produce reduction in drug use, but some programs led to a subsequent increase in the use of substances (Botvin, 1995; Dryfoos, 1993; Falck & Craig, 1988).

The contributions of social theorists (cf. Bandura, 1977; Jessor & Jessor, 1977; McGuire, 1968) led prevention model developers to consider the interplay of individual, social, and environmental factors (Falck & Craig, 1988). These models incorporate the complex, multilevel interaction of children with their environment and social and family systems. Ecological models stress the concept of multiple levels of influence on child development and the complex interaction of child and environment (Tolan, Guerra, & Kendall, 1995).

They focus on social skills and general functioning, rather than on the avoidance of substance use alone. In addition, drug-resistance strategies training are considered an important component of prevention.

Schinke, Orlandi, and Cole (1992) conducted an evaluation of the effectiveness of participatory substance abuse prevention programs in Boys and Girls Clubs (BGC) located in selected public housing projects. They found that public housing projects that received such prevention services through BGC had less drug-related activity, less damage to housing units, and increased parental involvement in youth activities. These results are consistent with findings that youth benefit from school-based prevention and treatment programs that invite parents and significant others in youth's lives to participate in treatment planning and delivery (Smith, 1985).

Traditionally, drug education has consisted of school- and district-wide teaching efforts. Early drug education involved attempts to intimidate youth from any use of any illicit drug. In general, drug education embodied didactic presentations that described the drug, its use, and the consequences of its use. Such efforts were generally aimed at public school settings, in which public school teachers or other designated school staff were given a packet of materials to present to classes or to assemblies of students. In early drug education efforts, both the message and the presenter frequently provided a skewed picture of drug use and misuse.

For example, marijuana was described as causing psychotic decompensation, juvenile delinquency, and other catastrophic consequences. When youth experimented with marijuana and failed to experience these dire consequences, they questioned the credibility of scare-oriented drug education. Traditional drug education also failed because its messages were designed to scare passive participants into compliance. In many circumstances, older students were well versed in the use of drugs and had not experienced significant consequences. Younger students were intrigued by the presentations and, in some cases, became more interested in drugs as a result of the drug education attempts.

In retrospect, one mistake of early prevention efforts was to rely on a didactic approach in a setting in which teachers may not have been perceived as credible role models. Further, some teachers might have engaged in recreational use and were undoubtedly ambivalent about presenting materials that seemed incorrect. The lesson that became apparent by the beginning of the 1980s was that pure drug education campaigns needed revision, both in terms of their content and their media. The ineffectiveness of such drug education programs resulted in their becoming an object of derision in the 1960s and 1970s (Smith, 1984).

Differing views regarding the effectiveness of drug education efforts continue to persist. Some drug educators have reported success when they employed credible information sources, avoided scare tactics, began drug education efforts in primary schools, and involved adolescents through the use of role-playing and problem-solving paradigms (Smith, 1983). For additional information about the effectiveness of D.A.R.E. and other prevention programs, see Chapter 7.

Thus far, promising programs espousing social skills, effective resistance strategies, and ecological models have been implemented with youth (Wilson, Rodrigue, & Taylor, 1997). At present, few prevention approaches have proven effective in reducing substance use among adolescents, and even fewer have been tested with youth of minority cultures (Schinke & Cole, 1995). The most successful programs tend to be the most comprehensive and are tailored to the culture of the target population. *Culture,* in this respect, refers not only to racial/ethnic upbringing but also to the swiftly changing culture of youth. There is a need for cultural grounding and mechanisms to accurately ascertain such factors to create and facilitate effective prevention efforts. The reader is referred to SAMHSA's website for the Center for the Advancement of

Prevention (CSAP) Model Programs.[2] This resource is designed to bridge the gap between research and practice by developing and disseminating culturally grounded, evidence-based substance abuse prevention programs and policies.

Outpatient Treatment

As with many aspects of treatment for adolescent substance abuse, there are sharp disagreements on the usefulness of outpatient and community self-help programs. Although some writers believe that outpatient treatment is ineffective (Wheeler & Malmquist, 1987), others argue that it is a viable option for adolescents. For example, Semlitz and Gold (1986) have outlined seven criteria that they believe will justify a recommendation for outpatient treatment:

1. Absence of acute psychiatric or medical difficulties
2. Absence of chronic medical difficulties
3. Willingness to abstain from all mood-altering drugs
4. Willingness to submit random urine screens
5. A history of successful outpatient treatment
6. Family investment and involvement in the treatment process
7. Evidence of self-motivation

Some examples of outpatient treatment techniques for youth include cognitive-behavioral skills training interventions and abstinence-oriented self-help programs. Skills-training models of treatment rely on learning theories to organize practice techniques. Skills-training techniques presuppose that behaviors, whether desired or not, are learned in some social setting. By the same logic, a behavior that is once learned can subsequently be unlearned.

Skills-training models teach youth behaviors that are incompatible with drug-using behaviors. Although some mention is made in passing about personal characteristics and how skills are taught, skills training have traditionally focused on *what* is taught, not *how* it is taught. Skills-training typically includes drug education, social skills training, and problem-solving approaches (i.e., improving faulty thinking).

Highlighted in this section will be two evidence-based treatments for working with substance-abusing youth. The first approach presented is the Adolescent Community Reinforcement Approach (A-CRA). This approach was initially found to be effective in adolescent outpatient treatment; however, in recent years it has been adapted for residential treatment setting implementation and has also been used as a family-based approach. Due to the origination of A-CRA, it will be highlighted here with outpatient treatments. The second approach to be discussed is Problem-Solving and Social Skills Training (PSST). PSST is an evidence-based approach that is used as a component in A-CRA (Godly, Smith, Meyers, & Godley, 2009) and as a standalone treatment, which is how it is discussed below. For a more detailed exposition on either of these approaches, see Springer and Rubin (2009).

Adolescent Community Reinforcement Approach.   A-CRA is a treatment initially adapted from Community Reinforcement Approach (CRA), an intervention strategy for adults with severe alcohol problems (Azrin, 1976). While additional sessions may be added, A-CRA is typically offered one hour each week for 12 to 14 weeks (Godley, Smith, Meyers, & Godley, 2009). Treatment guidelines specify a combination of three types of sessions: adolescent alone, parent/caregiver and adolescent, and parent/caregiver alone. Dependent upon the adolescent's needs and the results of his or her happiness self-assessment, the therapist will choose one of 17 strategies (NREPP, 2008). Strategies include a variation of interventions such as problem-solving techniques, communication skills, job-seeking skills, and anger management (NREPP, 2008). A-CRA is now listed on SAMHSA's National Registry of Evidence-Based Programs and Practices (NREPP; www.nrepp.samhsa.gov/).

Problem-Solving and Social Skills Training.   PSST (Spivak & Shure, 1974) is a cognitive-based approach designed to decrease disruptive and inappropriate behavior in youth. The therapeutic process encourages youth to use problem-solving techniques to address the harmful behavior by generating effective responses (Springer, 2006). Multiple techniques are implemented to achieve therapeutic goals: modeling, feedback, practice, didactic teaching, teaching alternative behaviors, social reinforcement, role playing, and therapeutic games (Kronenberger & Meyer, 2001). Springer and Lynch identify five specific steps therapists utilize in assisting their client to address problematic behavior: "1) defining the problem, 2) brainstorming, 3) evaluating the alternatives, 4) choosing and implementing an alternative, and 5) evaluating the implemented option" (Springer & Lynch, 2009). PSST has been identified as a strong, empirically supported, treatment option in working with youth with disruptive and problematic behavior (Springer & Rubin, 2009).

Abstinence-Oriented Approaches

Treatment models with a goal of abstinence dominate programs in the United States. These models are most closely associated with the Alcoholics Anonymous (AA) approach. It was originally designed for mature male alcoholics, however, and may be difficult for most youth to understand, let alone embrace. Although AA is geared toward adults, some communities are making efforts to provide youth with AA-type support groups.

Abstinence models require that social workers understand the three parts of twelve-step programs: surrender steps, integrity steps, and serenity steps (Brundage & Bateson, 1985). The *surrender steps* consist of treatment personnel persuading youth that they cannot control their use of drugs. Youth surrender their attempts to control drug use to a higher power. The *higher power* is not always intended to be synonymous with God or any similar deity; rather, the emphasis is on creating a spiritual defense against drug use. The *integrity steps* focus on youth's admitting that they have caused harm to others, thus enabling them to accept personal responsibility for the conflicts precipitated by tension around drug and alcohol misuse (Brown-Standridge, 1987). Integrity steps also allow youth to apologize for difficulties that were caused by their drug and alcohol use. The last steps in the twelve-step program, *serenity steps*, are concerned with maintaining a drug-free life-style. While the surrender steps assist chemically dependent youth to cease use, the integrity steps begin the task of rebuilding relationships through apologies, and the serenity steps focus on living a life free of drugs and alcohol.

A critical treatment planning decision for practitioners to consider is which adolescents are more likely to respond positively to groups such as Alcoholics Anonymous and Narcotics Anonymous (NA). It is certainly standard practice for practitioners to refer substance-abusing adolescents to such groups. "These adolescents are not a homogeneous group, however, and it is important for clinicians to know which may benefit most from this type of referral" (Hohman & LeCroy, 1996, p. 350).

The Chemical Abuse/Addiction Treatment Outcome Registry (CATOR) is one of the most extensive longitudinal databases on adolescent drug treatment outcomes to date (Harrison & Hoffman, 1989). Results derived from interviews with 493 youth at 6- and 12-month follow-ups revealed that adolescents who remained in self-help groups (e.g., AA) for one year following treatment had better outcomes than those who attended occasionally or not at all (cited in Jenson, 1997). Alford, Koehler, and Leonard (1991) found that AA benefited adolescents who were able to understand and accept its principles and traditions. Since there was no comparison group, these findings should be interpreted with caution. Hoffman and Kaplan (1991) found that family participation during treatment and in self-help groups following treatment were strongly correlated with adolescent abstinence and participation in AA.

However, in a study that compared the characteristics of inpatient-treated adolescents who did and did not affiliate with AA, Hohman and LeCroy (1996) found just the opposite: that family participation was *not* predictive of an adolescent's affiliation with AA. In fact, Hohman and LeCroy were better able to predict characteristics of adolescents who did not affiliate with AA than those who did. Those adolescents who had friends that used drugs, who had no prior treatment, and who experienced greater parental involvement in treatment were less likely to affiliate with AA.

The findings on which adolescents will benefit from groups such as AA are equivocal. They do, however, inform practitioners that not all substance-abusing adolescents benefit equally from affiliation with such groups. Accordingly, referring adolescents to AA and NA should be based on a thorough assessment and sound clinical decision making. Given the above findings, the blanket prescription of AA or NA groups for all adolescents who have used or abused alcohol or drugs is not a judicious use of resources, nor is it effective treatment planning.

Family-Based Treatments

It is a truism that families are critical in the youth's chemical dependency treatment, and this should not be surprising. Not only do use and abuse cause family problems, but they may also be a method of coping with family conflict (Bowen, 1974). One caveat, however, should be stressed: Because all families experience conflict and not all youth experience drug dependency, the social worker must be cautious in concluding that family conflict caused a child or adolescent to abuse drugs. Severe family conflict does create a context in which the likelihood of abusive drug use increases. But due to peer influences, adolescents begin to pull away from their families and form their own networks of friends and acquaintances. Although a thorough family assessment generally should be conducted, the clinical assessment of an adolescent may also require considering the network of friends when planning treatment (Smith, 1985; Springer, 2002b).

Several models of family therapy are available for working with substance-abusing youth and their families. Models that have gained empirical support for assisting substance-abusing youth will briefly be identified and explored. Again, it is important the social worker fully evaluate and assess the client and family need in order to identify appropriate and least intensive treatment.

Family Behavioral Therapy.   Family Behavioral Therapy (FBT) aims to treat youth and adults with substance use disorders and has gained empirical support over the past two decades. From the FBT perspective, substance use has come to represent both positive and negative reinforcers; being positively reinforced by physiological pleasures and relationships with other users, yet negatively reinforced by hangovers, arguments, and becoming disconnected from healthy support systems (Donohue, Allen, & LaPota, 2009). Treatment is typically 6 months in length and occurs over a period of 15, 90-minute sessions. Central to FBT is the involvement of one or more family members, usually one or both parents. FBT utilizes multiple treatment intervention approaches: skill-based interventions that reinforce healthy behaviors, behavioral contracting, skills-training techniques targeted at decreasing impulses and urges to use substances, communication skills to assist in development of healthy relationships and avoidance of substance-abusing peers, and training associated with academic achievement (NREPP, 2006). FBT is now listed on SAMHSA's National Registry of Evidence-Based Programs and Practices (NREPP; www.nrepp.samhsa.gov).

Brief Strategic Family Therapy.   Brief Strategic Family Therapy (BSFT) was developed in response to an increase in Hispanic adolescent drug use in the 1970's (Robbins et al., 2003; Szapocznik, Hervis, & Schwartz, 2003), and has since become the primary model used to work with Hispanic families with behavior problem youth, including alcohol and other drugs (AOD). BSFT is based on three central constructs: systems, structure/patterns, and strategy. BSFT proponents believe that a family is a system comprised of individuals whose behaviors affect other family members. Structure and 47 patterns refer to the set of repetitive patterns of interactions that are idiosyncratic to a family. A maladaptive family structure contributes to behavior problems such as conduct disorder and AOD use. Strategy is the third central construct on which BSFT is based. Therapists that adhere to BSFT use family interventions that are practical, problem-focused, and deliberate (Robbins et al., 2003). Therapy sessions, which involve the entire family, are generally once a week for 8 to 12 weeks and last between an hour and an hour and a half.

Robbins et al. (2003) highlight three key assumptions to BSFT: (1) changing the family is the most effective way of changing an individual; (2) changing an individual and then returning him or her to a detrimental or negative environment does not allow the individual changes to remain in place; and (3) changes in one central or powerful individual can result in changes in the rest of his or her family. For additional information on BSFT see www.ncjrs.gov.

Multisystemic Therapy.   Multisystemic therapy (MST) was developed by Scott Henggeler and his colleagues (Henggeler & Borduin, 1990; Henggeler, Schoenwald, Borduin, Rowland, & Cunningham, 1998) at the Family Services Research Center, Department of Psychiatry and Behavioral Sciences at the Medical University of South Carolina in Charleston. MST is a family- and community-based treatment approach that is theoretically grounded in a social-ecological framework (Bronfenbrenner, 1979) and family systems approach (Haley, 1976; Minuchin, 1974). This overview of MST is included here because the "MST is consistent with the family preservation model of service delivery" (Schoenwald, Borduin, & Henggeler, 1998, p. 488).

MST is being used across the United States in communities implementing a "wraparound" approach to service delivery, where the focus is on delivering client-centered, culturally competent services in the least restrictive but clinically appropriate environment (cf. Schoenwald et al., 1998). The social-ecological model views human development as a reciprocal interchange between the client and "nested concentric structures" that mutually influence each other (Henggeler, 1999). Furthermore, the ecological perspective asserts that one's behavior is determined by multiple forces (e.g., family, school, work, peers) and is supported by causal modeling of delinquency and substance abuse (Henggeler, 1997).

There are nine guiding principles that the MST practitioner should follow (Schoenwald, Bordulin & Henggeler, 1998):

1. The primary purpose of assessment is to understand the "fit" between the identified problems and their broader systemic context.
2. Therapeutic contacts should emphasize the positive and should use systemic strengths as levers of change.
3. Interventions should be designed to promote responsible behavior and decrease irresponsible behavior among family members.
4. Interventions should be present-focused and action-oriented, targeting specific and well-defined problems.
5. Interventions should target sequences of behavior within and between multiple systems.
6. Interventions should be developmentally appropriate and fit the developmental needs of the youth.
7. Interventions should be designed to require daily or weekly effort by family members.
8. Intervention efficacy is evaluated continuously from multiple perspectives.
9. Interventions should be designed to promote treatment generalization and long-term maintenance of therapeutic change. (pp. 488–489)

These nine principles can be used to guide practice with substance-abusing youth.

Henggeler (1999) has summarized the MST model of service delivery. The MST practitioner typically carries a low caseload of five to six families, which allows for the delivery of more intensive services (2 to 15 hours per week) than traditional approaches (normally 1 hour per week). The practitioner is available to the client system 24 hours a day, 7 days a week. Services are delivered in the client's natural environment, such as his or her home or a neighborhood center. Treatment is typically time limited, lasting 4 to 6 months. Given the level of commitment required of the practitioner, MST may be difficult to implement for some agencies. For a detailed exposition on implementing MST with high-risk youth, see Henggeler and Borduin (1990).

According to Henggeler (1999), MST utilizes treatment approaches that are pragmatic, problem focused, and have some empirical support, including but not limited to strategic family therapy (Haley, 1976), structural family therapy (Minuchin, 1974), behavioral parent training (Munger, 1993), and cognitive-behavior therapy (Kendall & Braswell, 1993). Brown, Borduin, and Henggeler (2001), call MST "the only treatment for serious delinquent behavior that has demonstrated both short-term and long-term treatment effects in randomized, controlled clinical trials with violent and chronic juvenile offenders and their families from various cultural and ethnic backgrounds" (p. 458). Moreover, the potential cost savings of MST have been demonstrated with substance-abusing juvenile offenders (cf. Schoenwald et al., 1996). For additional resources and information regarding MST, consult www.mstservices.com.

Through the Campbell and Cochrane Collaborations, Dr. Julia Littell, a social work professor in Philadelphia, conducted her own systematic review on the effectiveness of MST (Littell, 2005). In her review, Dr. Littell includes both published and unpublished studies, as is standard practice for reviews conducted through the

Campbell and Cochrane Collaborations. In total, Dr. Littell and her colleagues identified 35 unique studies and included 8 in their review. Dr. Littell discovered an unpublished study by Dr. Alan Leschied, who conducted a trial of MST with 409 youth in Canada. She presented her findings at meeting of the Campbell Collaboration, suggesting that MST may not be as effective as has been previously thought. A recent development in this line of inquiry appeared in the form of letters to the editor of *Children and Youth Social Services*, both from Dr. Scott Henggeler, the developer of MST, and his colleagues (Henggeler, Schoenwald, Borduin, & Swenson, 2006) and from Littell (2006). There continues to be much debate surrounding the effectiveness of MST following Dr. Littell's review of the research; yet, we have included it here for several reasons. MST is still quite popular. It is used in many states and communities, and MST remains one of the National Institute on Drug Abuse's recommended scientifically based approaches to drug abuse treatment. Only additional research will shed additional light on its effectiveness.

Structural-Strategic Family Therapy. Structural family therapy was developed at the Philadelphia Child Guidance Clinic by Salvador Minuchin and his associates (Minuchin, 1974; Minuchin & Fishman, 1981), including Jay Haley, whose work with Cloe Madanes subsequently led to the strategic approach (Haley, 1976). Like other family therapists, structural-strategic therapists view the interactive behaviors of family members as forms of communication. The therapy is goal oriented and short term, typically lasting 10 to 20 sessions over a period of four to six months (Todd & Selekman, 1994). Therapeutic goals are consistently related to drug abuse, but they also should relate to broader issues, such as family roles and interaction patterns. A basic assumption of this approach is that problems are maintained by dysfunctional family structures and rules. Accordingly, a major goal of family therapy is to alter the family structure that maintains the substance-abusing behavior. For example, with substance-abusing youth, a goal might be to restructure the family system so that the parents are in charge. Strategic techniques tend to be very direct.

When working with youth, this model avoids the use of labels such as "addict" and "alcoholic." These labels can actually be harmful to a youth, particularly early in treatment, before the practitioner knows how responsive the youth may be to treatment (Todd & Selekman, 1994). Moreover, studies have demonstrated that youth do not accept such labels because of their developmental stage and what they value (Glassner & Loughlin, 1987). In implementing a structural-strategic model with substance-abusing adolescents, Todd and Selekman (1994) do not routinely refer an adolescent to a twelve-step recovery group when they believe that applying an "addict" or "alcoholic" label may be harmful. However, they do recommend making such a referral when an adolescent needs the support of such a group or when he or she is immersed in the drug culture.

Goal setting is a critical task early on in family treatment and must be done with each family member. Each family member should be allowed to state what he or she would like to get out of family therapy. The practitioner's job is to help the family see how their stated goals overlap and to point out common threads, even when members' stated goals differ. It is also the practitioner's job to help the family establish goals in two major areas: elimination of substance use and improved interpersonal relationships, with a clear relationship between the two (Todd & Selekman, 1994).

Additionally, should the youth relapse, a crisis will most likely follow. It often takes a crisis for people to change, so the practitioner may want to mobilize the family to meet the challenges associated with the relapse. It is important to capitalize on the family's strengths. If the family has made considerable progress and a member relapses, then the practitioner should point out that the family unit has demonstrated their ability to cope with tough problems in the past and instill a sense of hope that they will overcome this obstacle as well. In other words, it may be more therapeutic to view a relapse that occurs later on in treatment as a temporary "slip," rather than as a permanent reversion to drug use (Todd & Selekman, 1994). Readers interested in learning more about this approach to working with families are referred to the following excellent sources: Haley (1976); Minuchin (1974); Minuchin and Fishman (1981); and Todd and Selekman (1991).

The efficacy of structural family therapy with adolescent drug abusers has been demonstrated in the literature (cf. Fishman, Stanton, & Rosman, 1991; Szapocznik, Kurtines, Foote, Perez-Vidal, & Hervis, 1983, 1986). For information on the effectiveness of other family-based interventions with adolescents, see Alexander and Parsons (1973); Aponte and VanDeusen (1981); Gutstein, Rudd, Graham, and Rayha (1988); Klein, Alexander, and Parsons (1976); Szapocznik et al. (1989); and Waldron et al. (2001).

Multifamily Therapy Groups. Multifamily therapy groups (MFTGs) are also being used as a component of treatment approaches for youth with substance abuse problems. A multifamily group usually consists of several youths and their family members, including parents, legal guardians, and siblings. In other words, it is a group consisting of several families, with each family viewed as a client system. An acceptable size for such a group is anywhere from 3 to 7 families. The use of two group leaders is recommended due to the size of most MFTGs. A group session may last approximately 1½ to 2 hours.

Techniques of structural-strategic family therapy, discussed earlier, are also often used. Therefore, the facilitator must possess a working understanding of group work and family therapy and be able to integrate the two in practice. By focusing on the interactions between members and families that take place in the here-and-now of the group experience, group members learn how they impact or are perceived by others, get feedback about their behavior, learn from one another, and

practice new skills (Springer & Orsbon, 2002). This is accomplished in the context of a supportive helping system. Multifamily therapy groups have been used successfully with substance-abusing adolescents and their families (cf. Malekoff, 1997; Polcin, 1992; Singh, 1982; Springer & Orsbon, 2002).

Residential Treatment/ Therapeutic Communities

An alternative to inpatient hospital treatment is longer-term residential treatment. Therapeutic communities (TCs) are one example of long-term residential care. Once admitted to such a facility, the adolescent is encouraged to form close emotional ties with other clients. When successful, the adolescent will perceive himself or herself as part of a group of peers who act as a support network (Obermeier & Henry, 1988-1989). If a third-party payer is involved, a dual diagnosis of the youth is generally required to warrant payment for such treatment.

There is no evidence to suggest that inpatient treatment is any more effective with most youth than outpatient treatment (Gerstein & Harwood, 1990; McBride et al., 1999; McLellan et al., 1982). However, for many parents who avail themselves of extended inpatient treatment for their children, the treatment period gives them a respite. Critics of this approach suggest that for improvements to be maintained, the youth should be treated while residing in his or her home setting (as is done with MST, described earlier). Changes that occur within a residential setting frequently occur within a vacuum, and the typical frustrations and challenges that might encourage alcohol and drug use and abuse are absent in such a setting. Thus, the improvements seen in the hospital do not necessarily extend to the home setting (Joaning, Gawinski, Morris, & Quinn, 1986). Friedman and Utada (1983) found that outpatient settings devoted more staff time to individual and family counseling than residential programs, which had a heavier emphasis on art therapy, group counseling, vocational training, and medical services.

There is little doubt that extended residential communities are necessary for seriously disturbed youth. When a youth chronically endangers himself or herself with drug and/or alcohol use, extended residential treatment may be the desired alternative so his or her behavior can be monitored 24 hours a day (Downey, 1990–1991).

Research on the effectiveness of TCs for an adolescent reveals that the length of stay in treatment is the largest and most consistent predictor of positive outcomes (Catalano, Hawkins, Wells, Miller, & Brewer, 1990–91; De Leon, 1988). Positive outcomes—such as engaging in no criminal activity, using no alcohol or drugs, and having employment—are all associated with longer stays in treatment (McBride et al., 1999). "Therefore, while juvenile TCs advocate comparatively shorter treatment times than adult TCs, it is essential that programs allow adequate time for treatment effectiveness" (p. 48).

Positive Peer Culture. In the case of work with adolescent substance abusers in residential settings, such as therapeutic communities, forms of Positive Peer Culture (PPC) are often used to facilitate group treatment. Positive Peer Culture, developed by Harry Vorrath, was heavily influenced by a peer-oriented treatment model called Guided Group Interaction (GGI). Vorrath and Brendtro (1985) have called PPC "a total system for building positive youth subcultures" (p. xx).

PPC is a holistic approach to working with youth in a therapeutic setting. It is not simply a set of techniques but rather attempts to change the culture in the therapeutic setting. "PPC is designed to 'turn around' a negative youth subculture and mobilize the power of the peer group in a productive manner. . . . In contrast to traditional treatment approaches, PPC does not ask whether a person wants to receive help but whether he is willing to give help" (Vorrath & Brendtro, 1985, p. xxi). Proponents of PPC view troubled youth not as rebellious or "bad seeds" but rather as individuals that,

with nurturing, can have much to contribute. The list below synthesizes and highlights some key aspects and assumptions of the PPC approach discussed by Vorrath and Brendtro (1985):

- PPC does not seek to enforce a set of specific rules but to teach basic values.
- The peer group has the strongest influence over the values, attitudes, and behavior of youth.
- Adults have much to offer youth, but should not attempt to control or surrender to them.
- Youth feel positive about themselves when two conditions exist: the youth feel accepted by others, and the youth feel deserving of this acceptance.
- Youth are experts on their own lives.
- Youth are resilient.
- Youth possess strengths that should be recognized by practitioners and tapped throughout the treatment process (i.e., a strength perspective). When these strengths are tapped, youth are better able to help one another.
- PPC focuses on the "here-and-now" of what is happening.
- PPC views problems as opportunities rather than as trouble.
- Youth must accept responsibility for their behavior and be held accountable.
- Both youth and adults must care for and help one another.

Simply stated, the essence of PPC is captured in the following statement: "If there were one rule, it would be that people must care for one another" (Vorrath & Brendtro, 1985, p. xxi).

Vorrath and Brendtro (1985) do not recommend co-educational groups because they present barriers to relaxed and open interaction. This is because male and female adolescents often engage in courtship behavior that masks honest communication. The authors recommend a group size of nine youths.

PPC has been used effectively with adolescents presenting with a variety of problems, including but not limited to increased feelings of self-worth and reduced delinquent values and attitudes (Michigan Department of Social Services, 1983), a reduction in asocial behavior (McKinney, Miller, Beier, & Bohannon, 1978), and runaway and physically aggressive behavior in female delinquents (Quigley & Steiner, 1996). For more information about PPC, see Vorrath and Brendtro's (1985) classic text on the subject.

Case Example

Consider the following case example, which illustrates some of the material discussed thus far. The youth presented is similar to many who participated in this particular treatment program, which was an intensive outpatient program (IOP) that was part of a larger treatment network for dually diagnosed adolescents.

Mr. and Mrs. Williams had been married for 20 years and had two children: Steven, 16 years, and Sally, 13 years. The Williams' initially sought treatment for Steven, who had been clinically depressed for about two months (meeting diagnostic criteria for major depressive disorder). Steven also used alcohol (three to four nights a week), marijuana (mostly on weekends), and ecstasy when he went to clubs (about every other weekend). He had also been exhibiting angry behavior in school and at home. He recently got into a fight at school that led to a referral to an alternative learning center (ALC) located at a separate campus, which is used in lieu of expulsion for serious infractions of school rules.

As part of Steven's treatment through the IOP, he attended interactional therapy groups and psychoeducational groups, as well as individual therapy, three days a week after attending the ALC. Multifamily therapy groups and individual family sessions were each held weekly. Even though Steven's family was involved in his treatment, as should be the case with a substance-abusing youth, the focus here is primarily on Steven. (For a case example that focuses on the

family in treatment, the reader is referred to Chapter 10.)

During an initial individual session, Steven admitted that he was afraid that his alcohol and drug use were interfering with his functioning. He cited a couple of recent blackouts, episodes of fighting, and problems concentrating on schoolwork. After explaining some of the potential health problems that can be caused by excessive drinking and drug use (marijuana and ecstasy), the therapist requested that Steven undergo diagnostic tests to ascertain the level of impairment, especially to his liver, cardiovascular system, and nervous system. The therapist believed that it was ethically necessary to rule out organic difficulties by qualified medical professionals before beginning substance abuse or mental health treatment. Doing so was crucial to understanding which erratic behaviors, if any, were influenced by somatic difficulties. Steven was medically cleared.

Providing adolescent substance abusers one-on-one time with the therapist early on in treatment is helpful in establishing rapport (Todd & Selekman, 1994). By joining with Steven, the therapist did not lose him when it came time to empower his parents to set and enforce limits. Empathy and humor proved useful in helping the therapist engage Steven.

Steven's depression was targeted with a combination of cognitive-behavioral therapy and medication management with Zoloft. The psychoeducational groups proved particularly useful in getting Steven to dispel some of the common myths that surround ecstasy use among club users. A structural-strategic approach to family therapy, as discussed earlier in this chapter, was used to guide the individual family therapy sessions.

At school, Steven's behavior improved markedly and his grades were improving as well. Steven received additional counseling from a school social worker at the ALC, who was knowledgeable about teenage drug abuse. The focus of those sessions was to reconsider his peer group in an attempt to prepare him for return to his regular school.

Although Steven received support from some of his friends, other friends heavily used alcohol and other drugs. The latter group of friends were ambivalent about Steven's decision to abstain from alcohol use, although they did not explicitly criticize his choice. However, the school social worker was worried that substance-abusing friends were not diligent about schoolwork and attending class. In addition, these friends were often involved in verbal and physical fights with other students. Over time, Steven established new friendships with peers that were supportive of his drug-free lifestyle, but this initially required consistent prompting by the social worker and structured monitoring by his parents. As Steven earned back his parents' trust, he was gradually given additional privileges at home.

Although the groups ended, maintenance family therapy sessions continued once a month. Steven relapsed once during the course of treatment. This was normalized for both Steven and his family, as for many substance-abusing adolescents in treatment relapse. The social worker helped the Williams family realize the progress that they had made and how their strengths could be used to resolve the crisis.

Recall from earlier in this chapter that not all adolescents respond equally to twelve-step recovery groups and that in implementing a structural-strategic model with substance-abusing adolescents, Todd and Selekman (1994) do not recommend routinely referring adolescents to twelve-step recovery groups when they believe that applying an "addict" or "alcoholic" label may be harmful. In keeping with this philosophy, Steven was not referred to AA or NA. He continued meeting informally with the school social worker, who proved invaluable in providing information and support on a sustained basis.

Summary

Many professionals claim to have developed treatment approaches that will positively affect youth's drug and alcohol problems, but no single treatment has been consistently proved effective in treating substance-abusing youth. The literature suggests that most treatments are somewhat effective some of the time and that one of the few common features of successful treatment efforts is an empathic relationship with the client. Despite the claims of some hospitals and clinics, there is no "cure" for drug and alcohol dependency among youth.

Rather than rely on the thin reed of therapy, social workers and other human service professionals should also use their knowledge of the community to find more tangible resources for parents and their offspring. Because families with substance-abusing youth generally encounter a multitude of problems, social workers are encouraged to empower families and to utilize available community resources. Additionally, many troubled youth, like Steven in the case example, meet the criteria for a dual diagnosis (both a substance abuse problem and a *DSM* Axis I diagnosis). It is essential that addiction counselors and mental health providers increase their efforts to work collaboratively in delivering treatment, as substance abuse and mental health problems often do not occur in isolation of one another.

Traditionally, therapeutic interventions with substance-abusing youth have been driven more by practice wisdom than by scientifically based outcome studies, also known as *evidence-based practice.* Much more outcome research needs to be conducted on the effectiveness of treatment with substance-abusing youth and in particular with non-delinquent youth. Practitioners certainly should not abandon their accumulated practice wisdom; however, to the extent that it is available, they should be encouraged to also use evidence-based practice to guide their treatment planning (cf. Nathan & Gorman, 2002; Thyer & Wodarski, 1998). In short, it is critical that practitioners remain up to date on the best practices available, as that will be critical in maximizing their effectiveness in treating substance-abusing youth.

CHAPTER 10

Family Systems
and Chemical Dependency

Catherine A. Hawkins
Texas State University-San Marcos

Raymond C. Hawkins, II
Fielding Graduate University

revious chapters indicate that alcoholism and other drug addictions frequently impair an individual's physical, psychological, and social functioning. There is also recognition that alcoholism and other drug addictions adversely affect the individual's marital and family relationships. In a Gallup poll, more than a third of respondents reported that drinking had caused problems in their family (Newport, 1999). Another Gallup poll based on interviews with 902 U.S. adults with an immediate family member with a drug or alcohol addiction reported that the family member's addiction had a negative effect on their own mental health (70 percent of respondents) and their relationship with other family members (51 percent) (Saad, 2006). These negative effects are far-reaching, given the prevalence of parental alcoholism. "It can conservatively be estimated that approximately 1 in every 4 (28.6 percent) children in the United States is exposed to alcohol abuse or dependence in the family" (Grant, 2000, p. 114).

Defining *alcoholism* at the family level lacks specificity, despite its intuitive appeal. Many terms in the literature attempt to capture this phenomenon, such as *family disease, alcoholic family, addicted or chemically dependent family, alcohol impaired family,* or *family with an alcoholic member.* An understanding of the family dynamics associated

with alcoholism or other drug addiction must entail descriptions of interactive processes that occur throughout the life cycle of the family. In addition, *family* is a term that is no longer clearly defined in society. The material presented here applies to all forms of families, including nuclear, extended, single-parent, communal, kinship, and gay/lesbian.

This chapter examines some of the more noteworthy efforts to specify the etiology and treatment of the family processes associated with chemical dependency. The term *alcoholism* will be used, although theoretically, much of the scholarly literature can be reasonably generalized to other drug addiction. The literature on a family perspective of chemical dependency, including the theory, research, and treatment of alcoholism and other drug addiction in families, is discussed. Three dominant theoretical approaches—behavioral, stress coping, and family systems—are presented. The constructs of codependency, children of alcoholics, and adult children of alcoholics are explored as they relate to family dynamics. The ways in which theory shapes practice with chemically dependent family systems are addressed along with more specific treatment information. Finally, a case example is presented that illustrates some of the main concepts discussed in this chapter.

A Family Perspective in Theory, Research, and Treatment

During the early decades of the twentieth century, a scientific tradition emerged in the social sciences. The study of alcoholism, however, was restrained by the moral overtones attached to the problem, which led to the belief that alcoholism was not amenable to scientific inquiry. The growing Temperance Movement culminated in the Prohibition amendment in 1919. Attempts at treatment of alcoholism (which were almost exclusively directed at men) consisted largely of removing the individual to a residential program for detoxification and some therapy, known euphemistically as "the cure." In *Alcoholics Anonymous*, Bill W., a founder of Alcoholics Anonymous (AA), describes his "rehabilitation" as belladonna treatment, hydrotherapy, and mild exercise (AA, 1939).

In the 1930s, the disease or biological model of alcoholism began to gain acceptance. AA, founded in 1935, embraced this model. Although AA was originally oriented toward men, wives would hold meetings modeled after AA to discuss the effects of alcoholism on their lives. (Lois W., Bill W.'s wife, is credited with organizing the first meeting.) At this same time, psychoanalysis was growing in popularity, and it explained alcoholism in terms of psychopathology. Both these models were limited to an examination of the etiology of alcoholism in the individual. Psychoanalysts acknowledged the impact of family dynamics on psychopathology, and they had some interest in the family aspects of alcoholism, but they looked at psychopathology in terms of each individual partner rather than their interaction (Lewis, 1937). Psychoanalytic practice wisdom prohibited the involvement of family members in therapy with the alcoholic, as this was believed to contaminate the therapeutic transference. Another development of the 1930s was the emergence of the fields of marital therapy and child guidance, with their focus on interpersonal relationships. However, early practitioners used a collaborative approach in which separate therapists would meet with family members, and then the therapists would consult with each other on their treatment session (Goldenberg & Goldenberg, 2008).

Theory and research on alcoholism grew through the 1940s and 1950s but continued to be limited to a study of its physiological and emotional effects on the individual (predominantly middle-aged Anglo males), such as the seminal work by Jellinek (1960). Even the conceptualizations of alcoholism in the marital dyad maintained an individual focus (Billings, Kessler, Gomberg, & Weiner, 1979; Finney, Moos, Cronkite, & Gamble, 1983). For example, the *distressed personality model*, rooted in psychoanalysis, held that underlying psychopathology in the wife led to the development and maintenance of a drinking problem in the husband (Futterman, 1953; Kalashian, 1959; Price, 1945). Alternatively, the *stress personality model*, which applied to both genders, viewed personality disturbance in the spouse as resulting from the chronic stress in the home generated by the alcoholic (Jackson, 1954).

In the 1940s, the concurrent approach to marital and family therapy began to emerge. In this model, one counselor would work with a couple but would meet with them separately (Goldenberg & Goldenberg, 2008). One of the first attempts to include families in treatment involved concurrent group therapy for alcoholics and their wives (Ewing, Long, & Wenzel, 1961; Gliedman, Rosenthal, Frank, & Nash, 1956). These early programs demonstrated that involving spouses increased the completion rate of treatment and expanded the criteria of successful outcome to include both partners' psychosocial functioning as well as abstinence by the alcoholic (Steinglass, Bennett, Wolin, & Reiss, 1987). By 1948, the support groups organized by the wives of AA members had become a formal network called Al-Anon Family Groups, targeting spouses of both genders. (For a description of the Al-Anon program, see Albon [1974], Kurtz [1994], and Keinz, Schwartz, Trench, & Houlihan [1995].) In 1957, Alateen was formed for teenage children of alcoholics, and later, Alatot groups were developed for younger children. By the late 1950s, the conjoint approach to marital and family therapy was introduced, in which one counselor would meet with couples and families as a unit (Goldenberg & Goldenberg, 2008).

In the 1960s, as social science moved away from a strictly individual perspective and began to consider the influences of the environment, a third model for conceptualizing alcoholism in the marital dyad emerged. The *psychosocial model* integrated the distressed personality and stress personality models (Bailey, 1961). It focused on the consequences of the alcoholic's drinking behavior and the spouse's coping style on both the marital partners. Through the 1960s, the rise of systems theory and behavioral theory led to a broader perspective that focused on the interactive, reciprocal nature of family processes. Although conjoint family therapy developed during this time, family treatment for alcoholism continued to consist of a concurrent program for nonalcoholic spouses (i.e., wives). This was attributed to the general ignorance of alcoholism by family therapists, who often failed to identify this problem or considered it secondary to other problems. When alcoholism was recognized as a problem, family therapists frequently referred these families to alcoholism treatment programs, where alcoholism was viewed as an individual disease (Steinglass, 1987). Alcoholism counselors reportedly avoided a family perspective due to lack of training or a belief that it was incompatible with the disease model.

This situation gradually changed during the 1970s and 1980s. Today, some type of family involvement is often included in most alcoholism treatment programs. There is considerable variation across programs, however, ranging from "family night" to full-fledged family therapy. At the same time, both the self-help and clinical movements recognize that family members have problems in their own right due to the dynamics of alcoholism. This led to such concepts as codependency, children of alcoholics, and adult children of alcoholics. According to Seilhamer and Jacob (1990), Western cultures have long recognized the detrimental impact of parental alcoholism

on children. However, there was little interest in these children until the first publications identifying the clinical implications of being raised by an alcoholic parent began to appear (Ackerman, 1986; Bosma, 1972; Cork, 1969; Slobada, 1974). This was soon followed by an awareness of the impact of parental alcoholism on the adult functioning of offspring (the Adult Children of Alcoholics or ACOA movement). Being the child of an ACOA (i.e., grandchild of an alcoholic), whether the parent is alcoholic or not, also has a potentially negative impact, since alcoholism can affect families for several generations (Smith, 1988; Stein, Newcomb, & Bentler, 1993). As a result, self-help and advocacy groups (such as the National Association for Children of Alcoholics) have emerged. ACOA support groups originally began in the 1970s under the auspices of Al-Anon. Over the next few years, independent ACOA groups developed, and Co-dependents Anonymous (CODA) groups were also established.

Since the 1990s, with the advent of behavioral managed care, cost containment has affected substance abuse treatment. For example, Platt, Widman, Lidz, Rubenstein, and Thompson (1998) conducted a review of the research literature on support services, including family therapy, as an adjunct to substance abuse treatment. The authors found that despite clear evidence of the need for support services to increase treatment effectiveness, clients often do not receive these services through their health care provider or get adequate referrals to other agencies. Steinglass (2006) and Corless, Mirza, and Steinglass (2009) critique the impact of managed behavioral health care on systemic medicine and call for the family therapy field to more directly address substance misuse.

The scholarly literature on family treatment includes studies in which the alcoholic is typically a parent, spouse, or child. As described elsewhere in this book, there is a long-standing tradition of using a family perspective with adolescents, although empirical studies in which the chemically dependent person is a woman or a member of a racial or ethnic minority group are limited. There is an emerging literature on family treatment in which the alcoholic family member is elderly, mentally ill, or gay/lesbian.

Theories on Alcoholism and the Family

Chapter 2 covered many theories regarding the etiology and treatment of alcoholism. At one extreme is a strict medical model, also known as the disease model, focused on individual biological factors with virtually no consideration of familial, social, or psychological variables. At the other extreme is a strict family systems model, focused on the family as a unit, with little consideration of the individual as distinct from the family. In the middle are theories that address, to varying degrees, both the individual and the familial aspects of dysfunction, such as behavioral and stress coping models. The difference between these various theories can be quite confusing, even to a person familiar with the chemical dependency field. This section will discuss the three predominant models that address alcoholism at the family level: behavioral, stress coping, and family systems.

Family systems theory evolved in the 1950s as an outgrowth of general systems theory, which emerged in biology in the 1940s. This theory represented an epistemological shift from a reductionist, linear (cause and effect) way of thinking to one of circular causality, process orientation, and the interrelatedness of parts. The crux of systems theory, as applied to people, holds that addiction, like any other human behavior, exists in a larger context. However, the family is viewed not merely as the context for an individual's behavior but also as an entity unto itself. Rather than expressing individual pathology, the presence of problematic behavior (such as alcoholism) in a family member is considered a symptom of underlying dysfunction in the system. The alcoholic is referred to as the *identified patient* to indicate that it is the system itself that is dysfunctional. Rather than identifying the effects of alcoholism on the individual members of the family, a family systems approach

focuses on the individuals *and* the interactions among them. The structure and dynamics of the family are assessed, and intervention is planned, through applying systems concepts such as homeostasis, boundaries, triangles, and feedback. (See any basic family therapy text, such as Nichols [2009], for a discussion of these concepts.)

The behavioral and stress-coping models first developed as theories of individual behavior but now incorporate a systems perspective. They recognize that relationships among the family members are interrelated and reciprocal and that the individual both influences and is influenced by other family members. In turn, the family exists as part of the larger social system that affects both individual and family functioning. However, these models differ from family systems theory in that the family is generally seen more as a context for individual behavior than as an entity unto itself. Although all three theories share a social systems orientation, the term *family systems* is used here specifically in reference to that particular theoretical orientation, even though the term is often used more broadly in the literature. Further, it should be noted that most family systems intervention models actually treat the family as a closed system, rather than focusing on the family's interactions with the larger environment.

Family Systems Theory of Alcoholism and the Family

This section focuses on family systems theory, especially three significant areas of family systems literature on alcoholism: rituals and routines, shame, and rules and roles. A discussion of the behavioral and stress-coping models is presented later in the section on assessment and treatment.

Two criticisms of family systems theory should be noted. First, some critics claim that it is largely descriptive, non-scientific, imprecise, and virtually untestable. However, its defenders consider such criticisms to be irrelevant, since the main value of systems theory is not as a traditional scientific model but as a fundamentally different approach to the conceptualization of clinical problems and therapeutic interventions. Second, feminist theory contends that there is a gender bias in family systems theory. Goldner (1985) argues that the central tenet of *context*—defined as a boundary that can be drawn around a family, thereby making it a distinct entity—disregards the social forces that influence the family. Another central tenet, *circularity*, assumes an equal distribution of power when, in fact, women are often regarded as subordinate to men within families just as they are within the larger society. Goldner warns that ignoring the impact of the social context can lead to theorists and practitioners "blaming the victim" and "rationalizing the status quo" rather than challenging oppressive sex-role arrangements in family life.

Rituals and Routines

Steinglass and colleagues (1987) distinguish between an alcoholic family, which is tantamount to an alcoholic system, and a "family with an alcoholic member." This distinction is made by applying three core concepts of family systems theory: (1) organization, (2) morphostasis or internal regulation, and (3) morphogenesis or controlled growth. The authors cite numerous studies that demonstrate the significance of ritual invasion in the development and maintenance of alcoholism in a family.

In the *alcoholic family*, chronic alcoholism has become its central, organizing theme. According to Steinglass et al., in these families alcoholism is no longer just operating at the individual level, it has become incorporated into virtually every aspect of the family. The erratic and unpredictable behavior of the alcoholic, over time, often elicits a characteristic response from other family members. Their behavior becomes impaired and contributes to the perpetuation of the drinking behavior, thus establishing a circular, reciprocal pattern within the family. The functioning of a family organized around alcoholism can be further understood by applying the principles of family systems theory, such as wholeness, boundaries, and hierarchies.

This organization occurs through a process in which the family's regulatory behaviors (morphostasis) are altered to make them more compatible with avoiding the stress and conflict associated with alcoholism. The family accommodates to alcohol-related behaviors in an effort to achieve short-term stability (the process of morphostasis is also called *homeostasis*). However, this increases the likelihood that the drinking will continue, because the system has (inadvertently) been organized to maintain it. Family rituals offer the clearest opportunity to investigate this developmental process since they are considered to be the most meaningful shared activity.

Rituals, encompassing cultural traditions, family celebrations, and daily routines are symbolic events repeated in a systematic fashion over time that convey a sense of belonging among family members. Cultural traditions include religious and secular events that are generally observed by the larger society, such as Christmas, Thanksgiving, or Independence Day. Family celebrations, such as birthdays, graduations, weddings, vacations, and reunions, are special events that, although perhaps shared with the larger society, are practiced in unique ways by each family. Daily routines are the most distinctive form of activity and vary widely across families. Routines reveal how the family relates in terms of time and space, such as dinnertime, bedtime, and leisure time. "The one construct that more clearly encapsulates the notion of the Alcoholic Family (a family organized around alcoholism) (is the) invasion of family regulatory behaviors by alcoholism" (p. 72). For example, the family may stop having meals together if the mother drinks in the evening and does not prepare them.

The family's long-term growth and development (morphogenesis) entails three major tasks that determine the family's identity: defining boundaries, establishing a family theme, and choosing shared values. Although greatly simplified in the present discussion, families accomplish these tasks as they move through a common developmental pathway encompassing early, middle, and late phases. During each developmental phase, the alcoholic family makes crucial, usually unconscious, decisions to either challenge or accommodate the drinking behavior of a family member and thus shapes family identity. In the early phase, the family initiates its identity. A key variable is how closely a couple links with their respective families of origin (which may also be alcoholic), since this will influence how the family responds to emerging drinking behavior. If the drinking behavior is not resolved, the middle phase for alcoholic families is characterized by maintaining this established identity. For alcoholic families, this means organizing around alcohol-related behaviors (i.e., invasion of rituals by alcoholism). In the later phase, the family consolidates and defends its alcoholic identity and, if the drinking is not successfully confronted, transmits this identity to future generations. Thus, according to this model, the etiology of an alcoholic family is rooted in the sacrifice of morphogenesis (long-term growth) for morphostasis (short-term stability).

Shame

Another construct associated with alcoholic systems (which is clinically derived but lacks adequate empirical validation) is shame. Although *normative shame* is necessary for an individual to be socially functional, shame-bound families are thought to engage in pathological patterns of communication and interaction that instill a sense of *toxic shame* in their offspring. There is considerable theoretical literature on the relationship between shame and chemical dependency at both the individual and family level (Fossom & Mason, 1986; Hawkins, 1996c; Kaufman, 1985a, 1985b; Potter-Efron, 1989; Potter-Efron & Potter-Efron, 1988).

Fossom and Mason define *shame* as "an inner sense of being completely diminished or insufficient as a person...the ongoing premise that one is fundamentally bad, inadequate, defective, unworthy,

or not fully valid as a human being" (p. 5). Shame differs from guilt in that the latter comprises a painful feeling of regret for one's actions while the former is an acutely painful feeling about one's self as a person. Guilt offers the opportunity to reaffirm personal values, repair damage, and grow from the experience. Shame, however, is more likely to foreclose the possibility of growth, since it reasserts one's self-identity as unworthy. Although shame is experienced as an intra-psychic process, its development occurs primarily through the interactions of the family. A shame-bound family operates according to

> a set of rules and injunctions demanding control, perfectionism, blame, and denial. The pattern inhibits or defeats the development of authentic intimate relationships, promotes secrets and vague personal boundaries, unconsciously instills shame in the family members, as well as chaos in their lives, and binds them to perpetuate the shame in themselves and their kin. It does so regardless of the good intentions, wishes, and love which may also be a part of the system (p. 8).

Shame-bound systems can be addictive, compulsive, abusive, phobic, or exhibit some combination of these behaviors. Alcoholic families are susceptible to shame in at least two ways. First, members often construct elaborate networks for hiding the alcoholism from each other and from the community. Second, alcoholism is frequently associated with emotional, physical, or sexual abuse. Such abuse, as well as neglect, is usually cloaked in secrecy. Secrets maintain the equilibrium of the system by inhibiting family members from changing their behaviors. Thus, secrets serve to perpetuate the addiction as well as the shame of the people involved.

Kaufman (1985b) provides an explanation of how shame is transmitted from the family level to the individual. He theorizes that a single developmental process is involved that takes different pathways, either to a healthy self or to a shame-bound self. The outcome depends on the prevailing affect encountered by the child over time in his or her interactions with adults, primarily the parents. If the child's basic needs (physical and emotional) are understood and acknowledged on a consistent and predictable basis over time, the child acquires an inner sense of trust and competence in his or her ability to get needs met. Ultimately, the child develops healthy self-esteem. However, if the parent fails to meet the child's needs, the child attributes this as personal failure and feels deficient. If this pattern is repeated consistently over time, the normative experience of shame (which occurs when one's needs are not met) evolves into the person's inner experience or identity. A shame-bound self is governed by feelings of being diminished, lonely, worthless, and alienated. Given the complexity of any family system, a child is likely to experience a combination of enhancing and diminishing responses. Parents can replace a shame-inducing reaction in a child with an affirming one by accepting and explaining the parent's own responsibility for the interaction. Thus, they free the child from the sense that he or she failed to elicit the needed response from the parent. Unfortunately, many alcoholic and codependent parents fail to take this corrective step.

Rules and Roles

Wegscheider (1981) proposes a now classic model of family interactive processes. Both the alcoholic and other family members suffer from very low self-worth and reinforce it in each other. Thus, in a reciprocal process the family system does not encourage the health and wholeness of its members, nor do members encourage the health and wholeness of the family. All families, over time, establish rules and roles that determine values and goals, regulate power and authority, specify responses to change, and establish patterns of communication. These rules are seldom recognized consciously. "Alcoholic families are governed by rules that are inhuman, rigid, and designed to keep the system closed—unhealthy rules. They grow out of the alcoholic's personal goals, which are to maintain his [sic] access to alcohol, avoid pain, protect his [sic]

defenses, and finally deny that any of these goals exist" (p. 81). Wegscheider uses the analogy of a mobile, with family members suspended and held together by strings, which represent rules. Any action by the alcoholic reverberates throughout the system. The family's reactions are intended to bring stability, but they actually produce a long-term maladaptive response.

Families also adjust to alcoholism through the process of establishing roles (i.e., outward behavior patterns). All families function through roles (such as parent, child, etc.), but roles in alcoholic families take on an added dimension. Although there is little empirical study on the subject, the model suggests that these roles are a way of maintaining stability, since families fail to confront the problem of alcoholism, which threatens the system. Thus, the family may preserve its identity, but at a high price of which it is seldom aware. Wegscheider describes six typical family roles: dependent (the alcoholic), enabler (the powerless spouse or partner), hero (the overachieving child), scapegoat (the delinquent child), lost child (the isolated child), and mascot (the immature child). This is only a schema; in small families, one person may assume more than one role and, in large families, one role may be played by several people. Further, roles may shift over time. Although these roles may appear in all families at some time, in alcoholic families, they are "more rigidly fixed and are played with greater intensity, compulsion, and delusion" (p. 85).

Codependency and Related Constructs

As discussed, alcoholism can be viewed at both the individual and familial level: An alcoholic suffers from personal impairment *and* contributes to the impairment of his or her family. Likewise, other family members can develop individual impairment *and* contribute to familial impairment. In turn, family dysfunction can exacerbate each individual family member's problems. The impairment of family members (alcoholic or non-alcoholic) can encompass the three related constructs of codependency, children of alcoholics, and adult children of alcoholics.

Codependency

Several definitional issues need to be considered in a discussion of codependency. It is a ubiquitous concept in the fields of chemical dependency and mental health, yet there is no general agreement as to its meaning. The concept is clinically derived and has received limited empirical attention (e.g., Carruth & Mendenhall, 1989; Cullen & Carr, 1999; Wright & Wright, 1999). Despite its intuitive appeal, this ambiguity has led to much confusion and controversy in the appropriate use of this concept in assessment and treatment. In addition, although the term is used irrespective of gender, it is typically applied more to women (Roth & Klein, 1990). This bias raises concerns about ignoring the oppression of women, discounting gender socialization, or pathologizing what may actually be highly desirable human traits (Bepko, 1989; Frank & Golden, 1992; Jordan et al., 1991). (See Chapter 15.)

The concept originated when chemical dependency counselors first turned their attention to the spouse (i.e., wife) of the alcoholic. They used the term *enabler* since it was observed that the behavior of the spouse often served to support the alcoholic's drinking. Another early term was *co-alcoholic*, which implied that the spouse also suffered from the disease through her relationship with the alcoholic. By the late 1970s, this term was replaced by *codependent* as the term *chemically dependent* became the more popular way to describe alcoholics and addicts.

Codependency is a useful framework for explaining some of the dysfunctional behaviors observed in the spouses of alcoholics. In their efforts to cope with the stressors brought on by their spouse's drinking, they eventually become a part of the problem by enabling it to continue through their own dependence on the relationship with the alcoholic. This concept is also useful in treatment, since it provides a framework for spouses or other family members regarding their own recovery from the effects of alcoholism. The concept is often applied more broadly to describe individuals who engage in ongoing dysfunctional relationships, whether chemical dependency is present or not. Although these definitions imply that the individual is codependent in relationship to an alcoholic or other person, the individual is actually engaged in a disease process of dependency in his or her own right (Schaef, 1986). Codependent characteristics are thought to emerge from childhood abuse experienced in one's own family of origin. Hence, there is a clinically derived, theoretical relationship between the constructs of shame and codependency (Hawkins, 1996b, 1996c, 1997).

The concept of codependency defies precision (Morgan, 1991), and various authors have defined it with their own constellation of attitudes and behaviors. Two representative definitions that capture the gist of this concept are offered here. Black (1990) states that codependency is "characterized by the numbing of feelings, denial, low self-worth, and compulsive behavior. It manifests itself in relationships when you give another person power over your self-esteem" (p. 6). Whitfield (1997) defines it as "any suffering and/or dysfunction that is associated with or results from focusing on the needs and behavior of others . . . (so) that they neglect their true self—who they really are" (p. 19).

The prevailing developmental explanation is that codependency first occurs when children grow up in shaming family systems. They lose the ability to distinguish between their needs and the needs of others, and they do not develop a firm sense of self (Kaufman, 1985b). In adulthood, such individuals have difficulty managing stress, have problems engaging in mature relationships, are at increased risk for alcoholism, and are particularly vulnerable to becoming involved with an alcoholic or pre-alcoholic partner. Further, in the absence of some sort of treatment, these individuals will likely perpetuate this cycle with their own children. A term often used in the clinical literature to convey this concept is *adult child*, which implies that "within each of these adult-age individuals there is a child who has difficulty experiencing a healthy life until...recognition and healing of the past occur" (Black, 1990, p. 3). Interestingly, however, the literature on codependency and shame does not necessarily overlap. This is perhaps because codependency originated as a self-help movement, whereas conceptualizations of shame are more theoretically derived; however, knowledgeable practitioners link the two concepts.

Children of Alcoholics

A related issue to codependency is the concept of children of alcoholics (COAs). As stated previously, estimates indicate that at least one in four children under the age of 18 in the United States is exposed to alcoholism and/or alcohol abuse (NIH, 1999). There is substantial clinical and empirical literature that indicates the detrimental effects of alcoholism on all family members, especially children, regardless of developmental stage (e.g., Copello et al., 2005; Gruber & Taylor, 2006; Peleg-Oren & Teichman, 2006). This more recent data confirms patterns identified over several decades. Being the child of an alcoholic puts an individual at greater risk for alcoholism than the child of a non-alcoholic (Cadoret, 1990; Russell, 1990; Sher, Walitzer, Wood, & Brent, 1991). While there may be a genetic component to this risk (Cadoret, 1990), studies indicate that family environment is also a critical contributing factor (Cook & Goethe, 1990; Heath & Stanton, 1998; McGue, 1997; Seilhamer & Jacob, 1990; Copello et al., 2005). In addition to being at an elevated risk for alcoholism, children raised by alcoholic parents may be more vulnerable to psychosocial impairment than other children. COAs are "over-represented in the caseloads of medical, psychiatric, and child guidance clinics; in the juvenile justice system; and in cases of child abuse" (Seilhamer & Jacob, 1990, p. 169). Sher and colleagues (1991) found that in addition to being at higher risk for substance

abuse problems, COAs showed more behavioral under control, neuroticism, and psychiatric distress as well as lower academic achievement and verbal ability than non-COAs.

Ongoing research is beginning to distinguish specific risk factors in families with a history of alcoholism that are associated with COA outcomes. Windle (1997) provides a *dynamic diathesis-stress model* of developmental psychopathology for COAs that shows how parental alcoholism may or may not lead to adult disorders. In this model, a family history of alcoholism influences other numerable variables—including biopsychosocial risk factors, situational stressors, and mental/physical health problems—that are reciprocally interactive within a broader sociocultural and historical context. Hill and colleagues (1997) point out the need to consider the interaction of parental alcoholism with other familial factors that can impair adult functioning, such as childhood socioeconomic stress. In a retrospective study using an adult sample, Dube et al. (2001) explored the relationship between parental alcohol abuse and child maltreatment. They found that COAs were 2 to 13 times more likely to experience adverse childhood events than non-COAs, and for those raised by both mothers and fathers who were alcoholic, the odds were even higher. Estimates of the relationship between parental substance use problems and child abuse and neglect differ based on the different ways these problems are measured (Testa & Smith, 2009), but parents with substance use disorders involved in the child welfare system often have co-occurring problems such as mental illness, domestic violence, housing, etc., that must also be addressed if the home is to become suitable for the child (Marsh, Ryan, Choi, & Testa, 2006).

Hussong et al. (2008) recently reviewed three longitudinal studies of type and severity of negative life stressors. Their research involved 1,752 participants, 56 percent of whom were COAs, spanning the first 30 years of life. COAs were differentially more vulnerable to family-related negative stressors than non-COAs. Hussong et al. interpreted this result as indicating that COAs had experienced a disruption of the normal stable family routines that might predispose them to increased risk for psychopathology. This greater exposure to negative life stressors may be particularly detrimental to certain COAs who have temperaments characterized by impulsivity or sensation seeking (Sher et al., 2010; Dick et al., 2010). Caspi et al., 2010 recently summarized the literature on this genetic sensitivity to certain environments. Possessing a specific gene variant alone (e.g., short 5-HTTLPR allele) does not simply determine increased likelihood for negative outcomes. Protective environments may ameliorate these vulnerabilities while the invasion of the protective family rituals/routines may exacerbate them.

Family-based preventative efforts are critical in reducing the incidence of child and adolescent substance abuse. Lochman and van den Steenhoven (2002) reviewed 30 years of research and conclude that behaviorally-oriented parenting programs directed at particular risk factors can have a significant impact on improving parental disciplinary efforts and children's behavior. The literature suggests that development of alcohol and other substance misuse by COAs and adolescents in general may be prevented by a particular form of extended protective environment: parental monitoring or supervision. Several recent empirical studies (Fromme, 2006; Fromme, Corbin, & Kruse, 2008; Wetherill & Fromme, 2007; Wetherill, Neal, & Fromme, 2010) and reviews (Lockman & van den Steenhoven, 2002; Vellerman et al., 2005) have substantiated the importance of close monitoring of adolescents' exposure to risky environments where substance misuse is likely, particularly in high school and the transition to college. Close parental monitoring may be particularly important for adolescent COAs who are genetically sensitive to risky environments (e.g., teens with impulsivity and/or sensation-seeking temperaments).

The precise nature of risk or specific familial influences remains unclear. Johnson and Leff (1999) support earlier findings on negative outcome for COAs but caution that more rigorous longitudinal studies are required to provide definitive evidence for true deficits or developmental delays. Menees and Segrin (2000) found that adults who had a positive family history for alcoholism but did not have other significant family stressors reported no higher levels of family distress than adults who had a negative family history. An emerging literature has shown empirical support for the relationship between exposure in childhood to distressing parental problem drinking and the development of anxiety disorders and substance abuse in adult offspring. There is not a direct link, however, since this model identifies the mediating effect of *anxiety sensitivity* in this relationship (MacPherson, Stewart, & McWilliams, 2001).

The child or children of an alcoholic, like the substance abuser or other family members, may need to be the target of intervention. The National Association of Children of Alcoholics developed care competencies that outline the knowledge, attitudes, and skills that a professional must have to meet the needs of children and adolescents affected by family substance abuse (see Adger, 1998). There are three inclusive levels pertaining to the primary role of the professional: Level I: clinical care; Level II: prevention, assessment, intervention, and coordination of care; and Level III: long term treatment. In short, all health care professionals should be aware of COAs' complex and comprehensive needs.

Children of alcoholics often show remarkable resiliency in the face of potentially detrimental effects of parental alcoholism and grow into well-functioning adults. Family units in which a parent has an alcohol use disorder may also be described as resilient (Coyle, Nochajski, Maguin, Safyer, DeWit, & McDonald, 2009). In fact, many COAs do not display alcoholism or other psychopathology in adulthood, while many non-COAs do exhibit these problems. Nevertheless, COAs often employ coping strategies (such as suppressing feelings), which may even appear adaptive in adulthood, but are not necessarily conducive to mature functioning.

Adult Children of Alcoholics

The psychosocial difficulties experienced by children and adolescents living with an alcoholic parent do not necessarily end as the individual matures. There is strong evidence that the vulnerability of many COAs extends into adulthood (Sher, 1997). According to the Center for Substance Abuse Prevention (2010), of the estimated 27.8 million children of alcoholics in the United States, about 16.8 million are adults over the age of 18.

As indicated above, in alcoholic families, there is not a free flow of emotional expression and open communication. Black (1981) coined a phrase that captures the powerful injunctions regarding behavioral and emotional expression in these families: "Don't talk, don't trust, don't feel." Further, these family environments are often characterized by other seriously dysfunctional behaviors that contribute to individual impairment, such as conflict, stress, violence, and child maltreatment. Parental alcoholism may or may not be related to adult impairment—in particular, the so-called adult children of alcoholic (ACOA) syndrome proposed by chemical dependency counselors. This syndrome refers to a behavioral and emotional pattern displayed by some individuals from families with a history of parental alcoholism and codependency characterized by a restricted range of affect and extreme distrust of intimacy (Black, 1981, 1990; Woititz, 1990). Although widely accepted in the chemical dependency field, the ACOA syndrome has not been validated through empirical research. Only a few studies have attempted to specify the individual or family characteristics associated with the ACOA syndrome (Hawkins, 1996a; Hawkins & Hawkins, 1995, 1997).

The literature on the etiology of the ACOA syndrome lacks specificity. An internalized sense of shame is linked to the dysfunctional behaviors of many adults, including those who display the ACOA syndrome (and who may or may not be alcoholic). Individuals who grew up in "shame-bound" families, whether characterized by alcoholism or other pathology, are thought to often experience impairment in adulthood. However, coming from a family with parental alcoholism or other pathology is not sufficient for the development of characteristics of the ACOA syndrome. According to Kaufman (1985b), theory on the development of shame does not predict a particular pathogenic family process (i.e., alcoholism, incest, mental illness, etc.). He surmised that the model of a "shame-based" identity can be applied only to adults since it is presumed that children (less than age 18) have not fully developed a stable identity, healthy or otherwise.

Pathogenic processes in the family of origin are hypothesized to increase the risk of adult offspring establishing pathogenic family processes in their family of procreation. Studies suggest that the way in which rituals and routines are practiced in the family of origin may have either a detrimental or a protective influence on the development of alcoholism in offspring (Bennett, Wolin, & Reiss, 1988; Bennett, Wolin, Reiss, & Teitelbaum, 1987; Wolin & Bennett, 1984; Wolin, Bennett, & Jacobs, 1984; Wolin & Wolin, 1993). In essence, these authors found evidence that families that had a breakdown of rituals were associated with lower levels of functioning in young offspring, higher levels of alcoholism in adult offspring, and lower levels of ritual practices by adult offspring in their family of procreation. Thus, a cross-generational pattern is established that perpetuates alcoholism and its related problems.

To conclude, definitional issues complicate an understanding of the emotional and behavioral patterns of alcoholism, codependency, COA, ACOA, and shame. These terms (and the constructs that they represent) are interrelated but are poorly defined; therefore, it is difficult to distinguish them from each other. Not all ACOAs meet the profile of codependency, nor are all codependent individuals from alcoholic or addicted families. Hawkins and Hawkins (1995) developed a measurement instrument, the Adult Children of Alcoholics Tool, to clarify these concepts (see Box 10.1).

BOX 10.1 *The Adult Children of Alcoholics Tool (ACAT)*

There is evidence of the ACAT's validity and reliability as a standardized self-report measure of
current mental health functioning. It is hypothesized to reflect the internalization of shame
and the negative attributes (inhibited emotional
expression, difficulties with intimacy, and interpersonal distrust) characteristic of growing
up in an alcoholic family (Hawkins & Hawkins,
1995). None of the items in the ACAT mentions
a drinking problem or alcoholism in the family of
origin. This is because the ACAT was developed
explicitly to measure the respondent's endorsement or internalization of the core psychological
attributes of the ACOA syndrome, not merely his
or her identification with being the offspring of
an alcoholic parent. The ACAT may be a useful
tool for practitioners and researchers in assessing potential vulnerabilities in individuals with a
family history of alcoholism. It has been shown
to be a valid and reliable measure of the ACOA
syndrome. This initial identification can then be
further explored as part of an interview process.
Individuals scoring 30 or above on the ACAT,
when informally interviewed, most often reported that they had a sense of pathogenic shame
or current mental health problems.

Directions

The following questions refer to your family of origin,
the family with which you spent the most time when
you were growing up. Indicate how strongly you
agree or disagree with each statement by choosing
the appropriate letter. Fill in the blank preceding each
statement with the letter A, B, C, D, or E, depending
on your choice: A = Strongly Agree; B = Somewhat
Agree; C = Neutral; D = Somewhat Disagree; E =
Strongly Disagree. Item scoring weights are as follows, corrected for reverse scored items: A = 3, B =
2, C = 1, D = 0, E = 0. ACAT total score = Sum of
items 3, 4, 5, 6, 7, 8, 9, 10, 11, 13, 14, 15, 16, 18,
19, 20, 21, 22, 24, 25, 26, 27, 28, 29, and 30.

*These items can be deleted to form a 25-item scale.

Part I ACAT Items

1. I tend to not talk about the real problems in relationships with people I care about.*
2. I try to take a lot of responsibility for people and things.*
3. When there is a problem in my family we can talk about it. (reverse scored)
4. The idea of loss of control is intolerable to me.
5. It is hard to share problems with people I love.
6. It is easy to trust members of my family. (reverse scored)
7. It is difficult for me to set aside responsibilities for awhile and enjoy play.
8. When I have a problem with someone I care about I am reluctant to discuss it, for fear of "rocking the boat."
9. I find it easier to avoid situations where I have to take control in my family or personal relationships.
10. Consistency and predictability are usually the rule in my family.
11. I usually look out for others' needs before my own.
12. People who know me might call me a compulsive giver.*
13. There is very little predictability in my family.
14. I have always felt comfortable bringing my friends home to meet my family. (reverse scored)
15. Ever since I was young I have learned to be tough and not to cry.
16. If I can just ignore a problem it will not hurt so bad and I can handle it easier later.
17. There is something about me that seems to attract needy individuals, or people with any kind of problem.*
18. I want to trust others, but it is so much easier just to rely on myself.
19. I have trouble following a project from beginning to end.
20. I tend to overreact to changes over which I have no control.

(continued)

21. It doesn't matter much to me whether others approve of my actions or not. (reverse scored)

22. When I start a new a project I usually have no difficulty finishing it. (reverse scored)

23. Deep down I have usually felt that I am quite different from other people.*

24. I have difficulty forming intimate relationships with others.

25. I have a strong need for others' approval and affirmation of my actions.

26. It's hard for me to decide when to get close to people and when to back off from them.

27. Telling the truth about problems is encouraged in my family. (reverse scored)

28. Sometimes I find it hard to draw a line between my feelings and the feelings of people who are close to me.

29. I have a tough time being honest about my feelings toward others.

30. There are times when I think that anyone who could love me is stupid or worthless.

31. I tend to keep a cool head during a crisis, while others are getting upset.*

32. My judgments of others are not nearly so harsh as my judgments of myself.*

Part II ACAT Items**

1. My father drinks (or did drink) about ___ alcoholic drinks a week. (Note: One 12 oz. can of beer equals one 5 oz. glass of wine or 1.5 oz. of hard liquor.)

   a. 0–1   b. 2–3   c. 4–5
   d. 6–9   e. 10 or more

2. My mother drinks (or did drink) about ___ alcoholic drinks a week.

   a. 0–1   b. 2–3   c. 4–5
   d. 6–9   e. 10 or more

3. I drink (or did drink) about ___ alcoholic drinks a week.

   a. 0–1   b. 2–3   c. 4–5
   d. 6–9   e. 10 or more

4. Currently, or at any time in the past, which of the following biological relatives have been a "problem drinker"?

   a. father   b. mother
   c. father and mother   d. none

5. Currently, or at any time in the past, which of the following biological relatives have been a "problem drinker"?

   a. paternal grandparents
   b. maternal grandparents
   c. paternal and maternal grandparents
   d. none

6. Currently, or at any time in the past, I regard(ed) myself as a "problem drinker."

   a. yes   b. no

**Optional measures of problem drinking

Note: Reverse-scored items are included to minimize response-set bias, since all items are answered either "agree" or "disagree."

Source: R. Hawkins & C. Hawkins, Research for Social Work Practice (Vol. 5. Issue 3), pp. 317–339, copyright © 1995 by Sage Publications.

Assessment and Treatment of Alcoholic Families

There are many reasons for including the family in treating what has traditionally been viewed as an individual problem. Wegscheider (1981) identifies several ways that involving the family can benefit the alcoholic in his or her individual treatment: They can provide useful information about the patient, may be alcoholic or emotionally disturbed themselves (and negatively affect the patient if they are not treated), are likely to continue to enable the patient's dependency if they do not receive assistance, and may help break the cycle of drug misuse in their offspring.

There are also reasons for focusing treatment on the family itself. It is unproductive to treat an individual separate from the system if he or she will be returning to live with the family. Family members are also under stress and probably in need of help, and only through participating together in treatment can the family truly understand its dynamics and develop new behaviors. There is some evidence that alcoholics show a better response to treatment when it includes family members, especially the spouse (Collins, 1990). Edwards and Steinglass (1995), in a meta-analysis of 21 studies, conclude that family-involved treatment is particularly effective in motivating alcoholics to enter treatment. Such an approach allows the family to share a common goal and, even if problems continue, to perhaps experience some success in non-drinking areas of communication and interaction.

In family treatment, the goal of therapy is not only sobriety for the identified alcoholic but also improvement in family functioning. Elkin (1984) identifies five goals for treatment: (1) stop the drinking and/or isolate the drinking member, (2) stop life-threatening or destructive behavior of family members, (3) disengage children from parental roles and alter inappropriate parent/child alliances, (4) help re-form the parental alliance and authority, and (5) support members in obtaining necessary resources outside of the family. Kitchens (1991) recommends targeting inflexibility, boundary confusion, parent/child coalitions, scapegoating, inadequate communication, discounting feelings, and unhealthy rules. Copello et al. (2005) examined the literature on family interventions in the treatment of alcohol and drug problems and identified three broad categories: "1) working with family members to promote the entry and engagement of misusers into treatment; 2) the joint involvement of family members and misusing relatives in the treatment of the misuse; and 3) responding to the needs of the family members in their own right" (p. 371). In a review article, Rotunda, Scherer, and Imm (1995) state that successful family treatment of alcoholism requires addressing relapse prevention and the tendency toward conflict (including violence).

A family may enter treatment through several routes. Lawson and Lawson (1998) describe four ways that a therapist may come in contact with alcoholic families. First, a family may seek therapy with the undesirable behavior of a child or adolescent as the presenting problem, which may be substance abuse or a reaction to family dysfunction caused by hidden addiction in one or both of the parents. Second, a family may acknowledge a parental alcohol problem in which drinking does not lead to significant behavior changes, is not a source of major conflict, seems incidental to other problems in the family, and may diminish as other problems are addressed. Third, a family may present with alcoholism as the major problem such that the system is organized around the drinking, which is a source of severe conflict and intensifies other problems, and is typically of lengthy duration. Behavior changes in the alcoholic while drinking are extreme and frequent. Fourth, the family may seek help after the alcoholic has completed treatment, even years into recovery, due to new problems that have emerged or developmental changes.

Thus, families may enter treatment with or without the goal of directly addressing alcoholism in a spouse, parent, or child. Depending on the nature of the treatment they receive, the alcoholism may or may not be addressed. Since alcoholic families are quite adept at keeping their "secret" hidden, alcoholism may not surface unless the therapist looks for it. If the family acknowledges the problem but the alcoholic or addict does not, a process called *intervention*, developed by Vernon Johnson (1998), has been used to engage patients in treatment. There is limited empirical support for the effectiveness of this approach (Loneck, Garrett, & Banks, 1996). A description of the Johnson Institute (JI) intervention technique is presented in Box 10.2. Ethical concerns have been raised about the JI intervention, primarily around the issues of coercion and confidentiality (Conner, Donovan, & DiClemente, 2001). They contend that this

BOX 10.2 *Intervention*

Intervention is based on the premise that alcoholics who are in denial will resist any attempt to be engaged in treatment. Therefore, presenting them with the need for help must be done in a way that they can accept. Usually, conducted in conjunction with a specially trained professional, an intervention is a carefully planned and rehearsed procedure. In a nonjudgmental tone, significant persons in the alcoholic's life (such as family members, friends, employer, doctor, etc.) confront him or her with firsthand, specific, behavioral feedback regarding how the alcoholic's drinking has affected them. Once the alcoholic's denial has been weakened by the reality of his or her behavior, the interveners present acceptable treatment options to the alcoholic, permitting him or her some input in the decision making. The alcoholic's excuses for avoiding treatment

have been anticipated, so they are less likely to be successful.

Loneck, Garrett, and Banks (1996) provide a review of the literature on the effectiveness of the Johnson intervention as a therapeutic technique. They note that although the Johnson intervention (JI) is highly effective for engaging and retaining clients in inpatient treatment, the effectiveness for outpatient treatment and the differential impact of variations of the JI have not been evaluated. This review found that patients receiving JI were more likely to enter treatment than those receiving other methods of referral (coerced, noncoerced, unrehearsed intervention, and unsupervised intervention). Of patients entering treatment, those in the JI and coerced referral were equally likely to complete treatment and were more likely to complete treatment than the other groups.

---

technique requires further evaluation and offer a detailed description of several alternative approaches for engaging the substance abuser in treatment. The ARISE program (which stands for A Relational Intervention Sequence for Engagement) is a less confrontational but progressively more intense three-stage approach (Garrett et al., 1997, 1998; Landau et al., 2000). Conner et al. acknowledge that there is limited research on the effectiveness of this approach as well. They extrapolate from evaluation studies of interventions similar to ARISE, however, and suggest that this approach may be more effective than JI in terms of the rates of treatment entrance, completion, and relapse prevention. Fernandez, Begley, and Marlatt (2006) argue that JI and AA (the predominate help-seeking approaches in the United States) are more limited than ARISE and similar family-based interventions, and cite some empirical studies to support their position.

Unilateral family therapy is another approach that targets the family to engage the

substance abuser in treatment (Thomas & Ager, 1993). Conner et al. (2001) identify that the primary goal of this three-stage approach is to improve the functional level of the family, which may in turn modify the substance abuser's behavior, including his or her willingness to enter treatment. They note that while promising, this approach lacks sufficient empirical support of its efficacy. Finally, the authors describe the Community Reinforcement and Family Training (CRAFT) program, developed by Meyers, Smith, and Miller (1998). The primary goals of this approach are helping family members to encourage the substance abuser to stop drinking, to enter treatment, and to engage in better self-care. The training program occurs over several sessions, and if it is effective in getting the substance abuser to enter treatment, significant others continue active involvement through the family program. The authors note that the effectiveness of the CRAFT approach has been demonstrated through clinical evaluations.

Once the substance abuser has entered treatment, involving the family in the treatment and aftercare process appears to enhance effectiveness, regardless of the specific treatment approach used. Conner et al. describe two therapeutic approaches that include the family in treatment: behavioral marital therapy (BMT) and the community reinforcement approach (CRA). Both approaches are effective in that "contingency management and behavioral contracting, components of both BMT and CRA, have demonstrated empirical support" (p. 170). After treatment is completed, involvement of the family in the aftercare and maintenance stage leads to improved outcomes. They identify two primary family approaches for this stage: couple relapse prevention (a component of BMT) and self-help groups, such as Al-Anon.

Regardless of the specific approach utilized, to be effective the therapist must assess the stage of the family's development in the addiction/recovery process, since the focus of intervention and prognosis varies accordingly. Brown and Lewis (1999) identify four stages (drinking, transition, early recovery, and ongoing recovery) and three domains of experience (the environment, the family system, and the individual) that must be considered. Similarly, Buelow and Buelow (1998) present a developmental model based on three stages: early abusive, middle dependent, and late deteriorative. In both models, key tasks of the therapist are noted for each stage. Conner et al. synthesize theory and research on addictive behavior change, using the Prochaska, DiClemente, and Norcross (1992) five-stage process model of precontemplation, contemplation, preparation, action, and maintenance. Although this model is based on the individual, the authors observe that "the family, in its response to the substance abuser's behavior, is likely to go through stages of readiness to change that parallel those of the substance abuser" (p. 150).

In counseling families, as opposed to counseling individuals, specific ethical concerns need to be considered. Whittinghill (2002) points out that ethical guidelines have not kept pace with the rapid expansion of family therapy as an approach to substance abuse treatment. Benshoff and Janikowski (2000) discuss several concerns, some of which are common to family therapy, such as handling secrets, using diagnostic labels, and addressing conflict. In addition, special concerns may emerge in counseling chemically dependent families, especially around informed consent and confidentiality. There may be an expectation of family involvement by treatment agencies and the criminal justice system, but family members may not want to participate. Finally, the authors note the need for therapists to engage in ongoing self-awareness and values clarification, since chemically dependent families often present with complex and challenging problems.

A family-oriented perspective in the treatment of alcoholism does not imply that the family *caused* the problem. In fact, as noted throughout this book, there is likely no single cause of chemical abuse or dependency. These problems may arise from and be maintained by a combination of biopsychosocial factors in the individual, family, and community. A family-oriented approach conceptualizes the problem in terms of family functioning and directs treatment at that level. Although differing theoretically, each of the models presented here recognizes that interactive patterns maintain the drinking and contribute to family dysfunction. Therefore, each advocates family involvement in some aspect of treatment and contends that any changes will affect the system, not just individuals.

Behavioral Perspective

A behavioral approach to working with couples or families is based on principles of behavioral theory. Such principles can be used either as behavioral therapy of families or as a model of family therapy that utilizes behavioral principles (see the next section). Briefly stated, behavioral theory argues that virtually all behavior is learned (as opposed to inborn) and maintained (or conditioned) through environmental or social consequences, such as reinforcement. Social learning theory and cognitive-behavioral theory add to the conditioning theories by recognizing that cognitive processes, such as modeling, mediate between the individual and the environment.

How does behavioral therapy apply to chemically dependent families? These families often attempt intuitively to use positive reinforcement (reward drinking behavior through attention or caregiving), negative reinforcement (protect the chemically dependent individual from the negative consequences of alcohol or drug use), or punishment (inflict a penalty on the person for drinking or drugging) (McCrady, 1986). Unfortunately, each of these responses is considered to increase the likelihood of drinking. Behavioral therapy, on the other hand, attempts to apply the principles of reinforcement to achieve desirable results. "The guiding principle of the application of behavioral techniques in family treatment of alcohol abuse is to increase and reinforce positive behaviors/interactions among family members and to decrease negative behaviors/interactions related to drinking" (Collins, 1990, p. 288). Another application of behavioral theory to family treatment is modeling. For example, the therapist can model more functional interaction with the alcoholic for family members, and the non-abusing spouse can model more appropriate drinking behavior for a non-abstinent individual (O'Farrell & Cowles, 1989).

Behaviorally oriented family treatment differs from systems-oriented family therapy in several important ways. Treatment begins with a behavioral assessment of family difficulties, which identifies specific areas to target for intervention, as well as a careful analysis of antecedent and consequent events. Assessment is an ongoing process, and intervention is modified in response to changing behaviors. Treatment is directed at observable behavior, and there is no effort to address intrapsychic processes or interpersonal patterns (other than those specifically related to the target behavior). The causes and effects of the problem are seen as linear rather than circular. Further, the behavioral approach tends to focus on dyadic interactions rather than triads. Families are often educated in the principles of behavior therapy so that they can monitor and modify their own behavior and interactions.

Behavioral couples therapy (BCT) is the most common application of the behavioral perspective with families in the substance abuse field. It is demonstrably cost effective, since it reduces alcohol-related time spent in the hospital or jail, which is far more expensive than providing therapy. O'Farrell and Fals-Stewart (1999) state that in contrast to other family approaches, which are widely used but not well researched, the behavioral approaches have strong empirical support but are not widely used. There is a rapidly expanding empirical literature verifying the effectiveness of BCT (e.g., Schumm, O'Farrell, Murphy, & Fals-Stewart, 2009; Winters, Fals-Stewart, O'Farrell, Birchler, & Kelley, 2002). Fals-Steward et al. (2009) state that multiple studies over the last 30 years have consistently found the following benefits of BCT compared to individual therapy or partner-involved control groups: 1) reduced substance use, 2) improved relationship satisfaction, and 3) greater adaptive functioning (less partner violence and better custodial child adjustment).

Stress-Coping Perspective

The stress-coping and behavioral models are similar in many respects. Both were first used to address addiction in the individual, and both have been expanded to include marital and family relationships. Like the behavioral and systems perspectives, the stress-coping perspective recognizes the reciprocal nature of family interaction. However, it differs from the family system perspective since it does not view the family as a unit unto itself. Rather, the family is viewed within a larger comprehensive approach encompassing the stress, resources, and coping of individual members. For the alcoholic, this theory contends that "substance use represents an habitual maladaptive coping response to temporarily decrease life stress and strain" (Hawkins, 1992, p. 161).

Stressors may or may not precipitate drinking; this depends on a number of factors. For example, Cronkite, Finney, Nekich, and Moos (1990) identify factors that interact to influence the recovery process for the alcoholic, such as demographic characteristics, personal resources, prior functioning, treatment program and experiences, life context, and coping responses. This model can also help to understand the functioning of other family members, although treatment variables would be less directly relevant. According to Cronkite and colleagues, "An alcoholic's life context can provide a supportive milieu for continued improvement, cushion the impact of stressors, or trigger a relapse" (p. 309). For the spouse and children of an alcoholic, other factors in their lives besides the alcoholic's behavior must be considered in order to help them to adapt better, such as environmental factors, life stressors, and the functioning of the individual or other family members. For children, this particularly refers to the non-alcoholic parent.

Family involvement using the stress-coping approach can vary widely (Wills, 1990). Al-Anon can be viewed as using this model in that it emphasizes the development of skills for coping with the stress of dealing with an alcoholic loved one. Al-Anon members are encouraged to find satisfaction through their own pursuits. Edwards and Steinglass (1995) note that, while Al-Anon is the most commonly implemented aftercare program for families, there are no systematic data on its long-term effectiveness. In addition to Al-Anon, family members can learn more adaptive coping through individual therapy. These individual efforts, in turn, can have the added effect of facilitating changes in the alcoholic, since change in one member affects the whole system. Marital or family-oriented treatment assists members in identifying personal and familial stressors that impede the recovery process and shows them how to develop more adaptive cognitive and behavioral coping mechanisms, communication patterns, and problem-solving skills. Wallace (1985) identifies five coping mechanisms often employed by the spouses of alcoholics that may actually encourage

continued drinking: (1) withdrawal, (2) protection of the alcoholic, (3) attack, (4) safeguarding family interests, and (5) acting out. Encouraging the spouse to identify more effective strategies can be a complex process, since "the effectiveness of a particular coping skill will vary, in all likelihood, with (1) the situation itself, (2) the individual alcoholic, (3) the characteristics of the spouse, and (4) the strength and cohesiveness of the marital bond" (Rychtarik, 1990, p. 357).

Family Therapy Perspective

Family therapy can be contrasted to individual therapy, which views problems as internal. Family therapists "believe that the dominate forces in our lives are located externally, in the family. . . . When family organization is transformed, the life of every family member is altered accordingly. [Over time, this process] continues to exert synchronous change on each other" (Nichols, 2009, p. 5). Family therapy (including marital therapy) represents a shift from viewing people as individuals to viewing them through their relationships to others. Models of family therapy have been classified using several different theoretical frameworks, such as Bowenian, strategic, structural, experiential, psychoanalytic, cognitive-behavioral, solution-focused, and narrative. Although the models share a family systems theoretical orientation, they differ in terms of conceptualization of the problem, specific goals of treatment, strategies and techniques, and role of the therapist. (For a discussion of these models, see any basic family therapy text, such as Nichols [2009].)

Until recently there has been no model of family therapy designed specifically to address addiction (Steinglass, 1987, 2009). Rather, the philosophy, goals, and strategies of each model are applied to alcoholism as the *presenting problem* indicative of underlying dysfunction in the family system. The behavioral or stress-coping perspectives focus directly on the alcohol-related behaviors of family members, whereas the family therapy perspective focuses more on the nature of the relationships among family members, which may not be unique to alcoholism. Collins (1990) states that, "the specific nature of the individual's impairment may be a less potent contributor to family dysfunction than is the fact that the family contains an impaired member" (p. 304). Several authors provide clinical guidelines using a family systems perspective (e.g., Lawson & Lawson, 1998; Lawson, Lawson, & Rivers, 2001; McCollum & Trepper, 2001; Perkinson, 2002). For example, Lawson and Lawson address the commonly related problems of family violence, sexual dysfunction, and divorce. McCollum and Trepper examine four areas in which family therapy has been misunderstood by the general public and many mental health professionals: parental blame, biologically-based disorders, the disease model of addiction, and differences in terminology.

Steinglass and colleagues (1987) emphasize that alcoholic families are highly heterogeneous (as are families with an alcoholic member). They believe that "it is no more credible to propose that a single treatment approach will make sense for each and every alcoholic family than it is to assume that all alcoholic families follow comparable developmental courses or manifest the same personality features" (p. 364). Therapists are also heterogeneous and should match their family therapy approach to their personality, individual style, and family background (Kaufman & Kaufman, 1992).

Steinglass et al. (1987) provide a four-stage model, briefly highlighted here, for working with alcoholic families. The first stage is a careful assessment in which overall family functioning is evaluated (including the role of alcoholism) and the primary problem is identified and defined at the family level. The assessment, to determine if the system represents an alcoholic family or a family with an alcoholic member, can be accomplished through an interview focused on family rituals to ascertain the extent to which they have been invaded by alcoholism. If the family has become organized around alcoholism,

a treatment program that leads to a cessation of drinking on the part of the family's alcoholic

member will, in such families, have profound implications at almost every level of family life. Thus, in such situations, overall treatment success is likely to depend not only on efforts aimed at alcoholism *per se*, but also on a comprehensive approach to dealing with the family-level implications of the cessation of drinking (p. 333).

The developmental phase of the family also needs to be ascertained since this has implications in terms of treatment goals and outcome criteria. Alcoholism may or may not be the presenting problem for a family. Families often seek help when they are in the midst of a developmental crisis. It is possible for a family to resolve their developmental crisis without eliminating the drinking. For example, they describe a family making the transition to the later stage of its development. At this stage, one of the family's developmental tasks is to launch adult children into age-appropriate roles. The family successfully achieved this goal even though the parents' drinking pattern remained unchanged.

The outcome of the assessment determines the course of treatment. For an alcoholic family, therapy must target the alcoholism first and then the presenting problem (if it remains after the alcoholism is addressed). For a family with an alcoholic member (i.e., not organized around alcohol), the problem as presented by the family becomes the focus of treatment. The alcoholism may be addressed within this context, using traditional family therapy techniques.

On the other hand, if alcoholism is identified as the problem, the second stage is referred to as *family detoxification*, which consists of eliminating alcohol from the family system. The authors recommend that the therapist use a problem-solving approach, which entails contracting with the alcoholic to stop drinking (including completing a medical detoxification regimen, if necessary) and identifying responsibilities for each family member. The alcoholic may refuse to acknowledge a problem and to detoxify, yet the family may still decide to continue treatment. If so, the alcoholic is excluded from the therapy. Examples of tasks in the contract are removing alcohol from the home and reinstating family routines. The therapist should anticipate difficulties in negotiating and implementing the contract, since the family is attempting to change instilled patterns.

Following successful completion of the assessment and detoxification stages, drinking is no longer considered the major issue. The next two stages address family interactional patterns, using any one of the models of family therapy. The third stage addresses the family's emotional instability that follows when drinking no longer occurs in a family that has been organized around alcohol. The task of this stage is to assist the family in tolerating this shift and in establishing new patterns that are not tied to alcohol. A psychoeducational approach explaining the difficulty of making these changes can be very helpful.

The fourth stage, in which the family consolidates changes, can result in two possible outcomes. In the first, called *family stabilization,* the interactional patterns remain essentially unchanged, but the family no longer relies on drinking to regulate them. Alternatively, *family reorganization* occurs when the family fundamentally alters its interactional patterns.

The foregoing framework is a general guide, since it is possible that a family will drop out of treatment at any stage. Further, a family may slip back into alcohol use at some point. In the latter instance, the therapist can renegotiate a *detox contract* and support the family in continuing to make changes. A family systems approach is not always the treatment of choice, since family members are not always available. In addition, family therapy does not eliminate the need to include individually oriented interventions in the treatment, such as AA or Al-Anon.

Steinglass (2009) has refined his family systems treatment model for substance abuse to include motivational interviewing, calling this newly integrated approach systemic-motivational interviewing (SMI). Motivational interviewing was developed in the 1980s as an alternative to confrontational techniques that were widely used in the United States but deemed ineffective. It is regarded as more humanistic and consistent with harm reduction and relapse prevention approaches. Preliminary data indicate it is effective with individuals, but there is no research on couples or families. Since SMI is based on prior empirical evidence of both family therapy and substance abuse treatment, Steinglass contends that it has strong face validity. SMI specifically targets the underlying belief system, particularly regarding ambivalence about change, felt by all members of the family. In this model, there are three stages: assessment and consultation, family-level treatment, and aftercare and relapse prevention. Steinglass postulates that one promise of this model is that it "potentially bridges the divide currently separating the worlds of family therapy and substance abuse treatment" (p. 171).

Effectiveness of Family Treatment

As discussed in Chapter 6, data on the effectiveness of treatment for alcoholism are often equivocal, as relapses rates remain high. This same pattern applies to studies that examine the effectiveness of family-level intervention, although there is general support for the positive outcomes of family therapy for alcoholism and substance misuse (e.g., Edwards & Steinglass, 1995; Steinglass, 1987, 2009; Steinglass et al., 1987). Although acknowledging limitations of the data, these authors point out that no other treatment has been shown to be any more effective in producing desirable changes in behavior. O'Farrell, Murphy, Alter, and Fals-Stewart (2008) observe that "meta analytic reviews indicate that involving the family in the patient's treatment generally is an effective means to promote recovery from alcoholism and drug abuse" (p. 464). In another recent review, Copello, Velleman, and Templeton (2005) also conclude that family involvement in substance misuse treatment can be very effective. Austin, Macgowan, and Wagner (2005) summarize family-based intervention approaches that have shown promise in early controlled studies, but add that these findings require replication by independent investigators. They also note (as do Crespi & Rueckert, 2006), that family therapy can only be effective if it is implemented properly; both articles call for clinicians to be properly trained.

There are several earlier noteworthy studies of family-oriented approaches that indicate effectiveness. Edwards and Steinglass (1995) "reviewed findings from twenty-one studies investigating the efficacy of family therapy as a treatment for alcoholism and found evidence to support the potential usefulness of including family members in all three phases of alcoholism treatment—initiation of treatment, primary treatment rehabilitation, and aftercare" (p. 500). No single family therapy approach was shown to be more effective, and some family variables influenced the findings (i.e., gender of the identified alcoholic, commitment to and/or satisfaction with the marriage, and spousal support for abstinence). Liddle and Dakof (1995) examined controlled treatment outcome research of family therapy for drug abuse in both adolescents and adults. They found "family therapy . . . to be more effective than other treatments in engaging and retaining adolescents in treatment and reducing their drug abuse" (p. 521), although only one study provided support in the adult area. Stanton and Shadish (1997) conducted a meta-analysis of 15 experimental studies of couples and family therapy in treating substance abuse. They found that family therapy was more effective than individual therapy, peer-group therapy, or family psychoeducation. Family therapy also proved to be effective for both adolescents and adults. Involvement of family members was significantly effective in reducing drug use and treatment dropout rates as well as in increasing the length of participation in treatment. The authors attributed this finding to the more supportive stance of family therapy as opposed to the more confrontational approach of traditional chemical dependency interventions. Lipps (1999) reviewed the literature for family

therapy with alcoholism, comparing the efficacy of the behavioral versus the family systems approach, and found that neither proved superior. On the other hand, O'Farrell and Feehan (1999) reviewed the literature on behavioral couples therapy and found that it was associated with improved family functioning, which in turn was linked to better mental health and psychosocial functioning in the offspring.

Additional studies continue to support this overall trend toward effectiveness. Carise (2000) found that family involvement in treatment significantly increased the likelihood that cocaine and alcohol abusers would complete the full course of treatment, although the author did not evaluate the impact of family involvement on continued recovery. Thomas and Corcoran (2001) conducted a meta-analysis of empirical studies with adult subjects comparing two spouse/family intervention approaches, either with the abuser's involvement (primarily behavioral couples therapy) or without the abuser's involvement. Findings indicated that "family members can successfully affect the substance user's behavior in terms of inducing them into treatment and reducing chemical use" (p. 570). Stanton (2004) reviewed 19 outcome studies on engagement into treatment that compared substance abusers alone to substance abusers and a concerned person (since the vast majority of substance abusers either live with their parents or maintain close contact). The findings indicated the clear value of including family members in the engagement process, especially since only 5–10 percent of alcoholics or addicts in any given year engage in treatment or self-help groups.

Despite the clinical appeal of support groups as a resource for families with an alcoholic member, there is limited research on the efficacy of this approach (Keinz et al., 1995). Richter, Chatterji, and Pierce (2000) examined the literature on the relationship between Al-Anon membership and certain components of adaptive life functioning. They reviewed three correlational studies—McBride (1991), Humphreys (1996), and Keinz et al. (1995)—in addition to their own qualitative study. The findings suggest the effectiveness of Al-Anon in helping family members. One unique component of a day treatment program for substance abusing adolescents, called Pathway Family Center, placed early stage abstinent teens in cross-fostering "host homes" to extend the protective 12-step sponsorship to 24 hours per day (Deskovitz, Key, Hill, & Franklin, 2004). The apparent effectiveness of this innovative component remains to be validated in a controlled study.

Finally, a critical aspect of effectiveness in family-level treatment of substance abuse pertains to special populations. While there is a growing literature on family therapy with diverse populations, there is limited empirical research specific to substance abuse issues. Delva (2000) explores culturally-specific family-oriented substance abuse treatment interventions, considering group affiliation based on race/ethnicity, gender, age, class, and sexual orientation. Cuadrado and Lieberman (2002) address traditional Hispanic family values and substance abuse prevention and intervention. The Treatment Improvement Protocol 39 on substance abuse treatment and family therapy addresses special populations, including rural populations (Center for Substance Abuse Treatment, 2004). Further, clinicians must be skillful in assessing and treating clients with co-occurring psychological disorders and addictive behaviors (Barrowclough et al., 2001; Clark, 2001; Mueser et al., 2009; Rotunda and O'Farrell, 1997; see also chapter 13).

Case Example

The following case example illustrates some main points emphasized in this chapter, particularly regarding the family therapy perspective (e.g., Steinglass, 1987; 2009). The names and significant data for the family have been altered. There is considerable variation among families, therapists, and modalities; this case represents only one possible approach. Since it does not describe specific intervention techniques employed, such as family

sculpting (originally developed by Duhl, Kantor, & Duhl, 1973), an illustration of applying this technique with the family is provided in Box 10.3. (While this case pertains to an Anglo family, Wycoff and Cameron (2000) provide a case study of a Hispanic family.)

Presenting Problem. Emily is a white, 18-year-old high school senior. She was admitted to City Psychiatric Hospital in December following a suicide attempt. She had no history of prior psychiatric treatment or difficulties. She presents as an attractive, intelligent, and cooperative adolescent. Behavioral and emotional problems emerged one year ago and escalated rapidly: conflict with her parents over money, studying, household duties, and curfew; school failure and truancy; depression; and social isolation. If these problems persist, she will not graduate in May.

While in the hospital, Emily revealed extensive substance abuse, primarily alcohol, but occasional use of marijuana, cocaine, and "pills." She would use "whatever was available." She began drinking two years ago and reported that she "loved" alcohol, both the taste and the way it made her feel. Typical use consisted of daily drinking and weekend binging to the point of intoxication. She successfully hid her drinking from her parents. She described them as "preoccupied with their own problems." Emily feels that her father abuses alcohol. She claims that her suicide attempt, mixing alcohol with barbiturates, was an accident. It occurred after her boyfriend broke up with her and she felt "sad and lonely."

After being evaluated in the hospital, Emily was transferred to a residential treatment program for adolescent substance abusers. She seems to have benefited from this treatment in that she now describes herself as "in recovery." She realizes that she must remain abstinent, and she attends several AA meetings a week. She meets regularly with the high school social worker and participates in a weekly peer support group. Although she feels that she is "turning her life around," conflict has continued with her parents. She and her

BOX 10.3   *Family Sculpting*

Family sculpting is an experiential technique used by family therapists to visibly display the dynamics of a family. It allows the family to experience themselves in an active way, rather than passively discussing their relationships. Using spatial distance and physical position, one member of the family arranges the other members in relation to how he or she perceives the family's dynamics at a particular point in time. Family members are usually instructed not to speak as they complete the exercise. This nonverbal technique can be especially useful if family members seem reluctant to express their feelings or if they are unable to describe their perceptions. It can be a creative way to pull out a silent member, take full advantage of a particularly perceptive member, or bypass familiar verbal patterns. Prior to beginning, the therapist should briefly explain the process and engage the willingness of members to participate.

Consider the family described in the case example that began on page 277. Assume that Emily is the *sculptor* and that this exercise is being used early in therapy, before any significant changes have occurred. Emily might be asked by the therapist to arrange the members of the family in a scene depicting a typical evening at home in the present. Imagine that Emily motions to her mother to stand in one corner of the room facing the wall. She indicates that her father should stand in another corner facing the wall. She positions her brother in the third corner facing the wall. Finally, Emily places herself in the fourth corner of the room, also facing the wall. This sculpture graphically shows Emily's perception of the family as distant and disengaged. When they discuss the sculpture, the family might acknowledge the effect of not eating dinner together and isolating themselves in separate rooms. Thus, the sculpture conveys the powerful sense of loneliness and lack of support that Emily feels.

Through sculpting, a family might gain awareness and sensitivity in a way that would not be possible through a verbal exchange. As a result, they might be better able to modify interactional patterns. Applying the family principles discussed in this chapter, it appears that this family is an alcoholic family in the sense that alcoholism has been allowed to invade family rituals, such as eating and spending time together. The family has assumed rigid rules and roles that perpetuate the alcoholism and do not support the health and growth of individual members or the family as a whole.

Sculpting can be implemented in many variations. For example, Emily might be asked to sculpt the family again, this time depicting how she would like them to relate. Imagine in this case that she brings them together in circle at the center of the room, close together but not touching and facing each other. This could lead to further discussion about how they can change roles, rules, and so on. Alternatively, sculpting could be used at the end of the family therapy to show progress made. In another variation, a different family member could sculpt the family to show his or her perceptions. Someone could sculpt the family at a time before the alcoholism invaded the family's rituals and they interacted together. The therapist could even sculpt the family, if needed. Sculptures can become quite complex with large nuclear and extended families, especially if there have been major disruptions over time. Members often become quite enthusiastic and creative in sculpting.

---

family were referred to Mental Health Clinic for one hour a week of outpatient family therapy following her discharge from the treatment program.

Family History.   Other family members are the father, Jim, an accountant (age 42); Susan, a homemaker (age 42); and Jason, a high school freshman (age 15). They are a white, middle-class family. Both Jim and Susan described their family of origin as traditionally suburban middle class, with a breadwinner father and homemaker mother. They met in college, married immediately after graduation, and had their first child two years later. Jim described his father as a steady drinker, who was frequently verbally abusive. In retrospect, Jim believes that his father drank heavily throughout Jim's childhood and adolescence, although he believes that his mother protected him and his older brother from much of their father's alcoholic behavior. Susan reported that there was considerable conflict between her parents, who divorced when she was 16 years old. She rarely saw her father after the divorce. She reports no substance use by her parents.

The couple described their marriage as "average," although closer inspection reveals that they seldom interact. Jim, who is self-employed, has been focused on his business over the last few years. The struggling local economy had severely cut his income. Susan is actively involved in several charity and social organizations. They acknowledged having "drifted apart." In fact, there is little indication that the family as a whole has much interaction, since they do not eat meals together and spend most of their time in separate rooms. Jim acknowledges that he has three to four drinks a night but does not see this as a problem. Susan confirms this intake and feels that Jim's drinking is a way for him to relax, given his work stress. Susan drinks socially on occasion. Jason denies any drinking or drug use, and his parents believe that this is an accurate report.

Assessment. According to a family systems perspective, Emily is the "identified patient" in this family. Although she clearly has an alcohol abuse problem in her own right, underlying factors in the family appear to be contributing to her difficulty as well as to that of other family members. One pattern observed in this family is *triangulation*. This concept can refer to the tendency of a marital dyad to maintain stability in their relationship by focusing their attention on a third person, usually a child. When a child experiences difficulties, the parents' attention is diverted away from addressing the underlying problems in their relationship. From a systems perspective, all family members are participating in this pattern with the goal of reducing stress and conflict. Emily's problems could be seen as a way to keep her parents

engaged with each other through their mutual concern for her. Thus, they are spared from having to confront the lack of emotional support in their marriage. Developmentally, Emily is at an age when she should be starting to emancipate. This pattern may also serve to keep her in a non-adult role with her parents.

This family presents with at least three generations of active substance abuse. Jim is likely the adult child of an alcoholic father and a codependent mother and appears to be in denial regarding his own alcohol abuse problem. One could hypothesize that he learned the "don't talk, don't trust, don't feel" rules that are often encountered in these families. It is not surprising that he is having difficulties with intimacy in his marriage and with his children. Susan suffered a severe blow to her sense of security when her parents divorced and her father became distant. She may not recognize the potential for a similar outcome in her own marriage. They have evolved into a classic male alcoholic, female codependent pattern in which both minimize the extent of problems that alcohol is causing in their family. They are locked in behavioral patterns that are self-defeating and are actively training their children into these roles as well. It appears that alcoholism accounts for the lack of shared rituals and routines in their daily life. Thus, according to the Steinglass model, they can be described as an "alcoholic family."

Treatment. From a systems perspective, the focus of therapy will be on improving family functioning for the benefit of all family members. Since there is apparent active alcohol abuse in two family members (Emily and Jim), this will be the initial focus of treatment. Although Emily is engaged in a recovery program, numerous factors combine to jeopardize her sobriety as well as the well-being of other family members, including Jim. These include the continued presence of alcohol in the home (despite her clear request that it be removed), her father's unwillingness to admit to his own alcohol abuse, ongoing conflict with her parents, and the general lack of emotional support in the family. Therefore, the therapy begins with the immediate goal of cessation of Jim's drinking and removal of alcohol from the home. Once this is addressed, the goal will become to assist the family in developing patterns of interaction and communication that foster the growth of all family members. The therapy will be conducted following the four-stage model of Steinglass et al. (1987) discussed earlier in this chapter.

Stage one is diagnosing alcoholism and labeling it as a family problem. In the initial session, the therapist assesses the family functioning by questioning each family member in order to gain information as well as establish a therapeutic relationship with them. Jim and Susan adamantly insist that Emily's oppositional behavior is the source of their family's current problems. They feel that otherwise they would be "fine" and cite their previous successful functioning prior to Emily's difficulties as evidence of their position. Emily remains noticeably sullen throughout the session. Jason seems to make every effort to appear invisible and grudgingly agrees with his parents when asked for his perspective.

In the next session, Emily becomes more vocal. She had met with her school social worker who urged her to share her concerns about her father's drinking and her mother's acquiescence in family therapy. She defiantly reports that her father is an alcoholic and that "I should know." She and Jim immediately become entangled in a conflict. He denies that he has a problem and accuses her of trying to shift the blame for her behavior. Susan and Jason watch in silence, with evident discomfort. When questioned by the therapist, Susan expresses concerns for Jim's health, revealing her fear that he will have a heart attack due to the stress of their financial situation. She apparently attempts to deflect the focus back to Emily by adding that their daughter's difficulties have exacerbated his stress. When questioned again about Jim's drinking, she seems to minimize it by stating that he just drinks to relax.

The family is in a standoff, and it is crucial for the therapist to address this impasse openly. She presses Jason for his opinion, since the silent member of a family is often the most valuable source of information. He reluctantly agrees with both Emily's and Susan's concerns: He thinks his father drinks too much and also worries about his health. With Jason's revelation, Susan's resolve to protect Jim in his denial appears to weaken. Although she continues to waver, she and the children gradually align in their concern about Jim's drinking. They identify the following problems: embarrassment when he is drunk in public, anxiety when he wants to drive while intoxicated, fear of his angry outbursts, sadness over his emotional unavailability, concern regarding his poor health, and worry over financial instability.

Jim becomes increasingly defensive and the therapist moves to keep him engaged in the therapy. She reframes this feedback in terms of his family's honesty: Although painful, it is an indication of their love for him. She commends him for having developed such a sense of trust with his family that they were willing to be so honest. It should be noted that the therapist is not labeling Jim as alcoholic at this point. Rather, she is keeping the focus on the family members' current topic and facilitating their efforts to state directly how his drinking is causing problems in their family. This strategy reduces the possibility that the father will attack the therapist, be supported by family members, and manage to avoid this issue. The session concludes with the therapist clearly stating that Jim's drinking seems to be a major problem for the family.

On the third session, the family comes in with a crisis: Jason had gotten into a fight at school and was suspended. Some crisis was almost to be expected, since the family homeostasis had been disrupted last week. One could hypothesize that Jason (perhaps unconsciously) was assisting Emily in maintaining the family's familiar patterns, particularly in terms of keeping the focus off Jim's drinking. The therapist quickly moves to counteract this attempt to regain stability by using a psychoeducational approach with the family. She explains the idea of "family system" and how the behavior of each member affects the family as a whole. She observes that the last session disrupted their usual patterns and notes how distressing this can be. This shows that she is empathic with their situation, places this crisis in a larger context, neutralizes the diversion, and enables her to return the focus to Jim's drinking.

A long silence is broken by Jim's query as to whether the therapist thinks that he has a drinking problem. Aware of the importance of this juncture, she responds that this certainly seems to be the case, based on behavioral indicators, but primarily because she has heard the concerns of his family and cannot disregard them. Since his attendance at this session indicates how strongly he is committed to his family, she is sure that he has heard their concerns as well. (This response puts Jim in a bind, since to disagree with the therapist would suggest that he is disregarding the concerns of his family and would call into question his commitment to them.)

Jim does not respond and is obviously distressed by his predicament. Susan tries to "rescue" him by stating her concern about the problems involving Emily and Jason. The therapist explains that she has not forgotten this, but that Jim's drinking must be addressed first if the family is to resolve other problems successfully, especially since Emily is already engaged in treatment. They are reluctant to confront him further so, rather than engage in a power struggle with the family, she wonders aloud at the "power" that alcohol seemed to have over them. Jim breaks the silence, defiantly saying that alcohol has no power over him. She asks why he thinks that his family is so threatened by the topic (in this way, she highlights the process of alcoholism in the family, not Jim's alcoholism, *per se*). This provides a less threatening avenue for Susan, Emily, and Jason to once again talk to Jim about his alcohol abuse and the effect it has on them.

In the next session, Jim indicates the effect that his family's disclosure had on him. He was quite withdrawn during the ensuing week. He attempted to prove them wrong by showing that he could quit drinking whenever he wanted.

However, in the face of his family's feedback and the unexpected struggle he had in avoiding alcohol, Jim reluctantly agrees that he might have a problem. At this point, several significant events have transpired in the therapy: Jim's denial regarding his alcohol abuse has been broken and his problem has been placed within the larger context of the family. The therapy enters **stage two**: removal of alcohol from the family system.

The family and therapist agree to work together to help Jim stop drinking. The next step is to develop a detoxification contract with the entire family, since this is now regarded as a family problem. Since hospitalization is not indicated, the therapist recommends an eight-week outpatient program (only a therapist adequately trained in assessment should make treatment recommendations). Jim agrees to make an appointment with this agency for an evaluation prior to the next session. He will also remove all alcohol from the home. Jim asks that the family spend more time together and feels that this will assist him in not drinking. He becomes tearful as he talks about how he feels uninvolved in his children's lives (the therapist notes that he did not include Susan in this sentiment). The family agrees to have dinner together in the evenings. The therapist praises the family for their courage in confronting this problem together, acknowledges the difficulty of their task, but reassures them that they can succeed in making desired changes.

The therapist begins the fifth session by reviewing the family's implementation of the detox contract. Jim has removed all the alcohol from the house, enrolled in an outpatient treatment program, and abstained for the full week. Family members confirm that he has not appeared to drink. However, they did not share any meals together. Susan, although expressing her relief over Jim's adherence to the contract, feels that he has become more "moody." Jim admits to feeling unsupported by the family, particularly since Susan has not organized any meals. Susan says that there were too many different schedules among them to plan a specific time for dinner (i.e., disruption of routines). The therapist anticipated problems with the contract, since the family is attempting to change entrenched patterns. She empathizes regarding the challenges they face, commends them for their successes, and assists them to negotiate a better plan. After considerable discussion, all members agree to adjust their schedule to have dinner together three times a week and to participate in the family component of Jim's outpatient program. (It is important to recognize that the process of assisting them to develop new skills for problem solving, such as negotiation, is as important to the therapy as the product, the new contract. The therapist also notes the weak unity and authority in the parental dyad. Thus, she is continually engaged in assessment, gathering information that will be useful when they begin to address non-alcohol-specific family patterns.)

The next week, Jim enters treatment, and for six weeks, his behavior indicates that he is clearly engaged in his treatment program. He expresses a sense of camaraderie with other males that he has not enjoyed since being in the military. Nevertheless, he is finding it difficult not to drink and relies heavily on AA meetings and his sponsor for guidance. The family is actively involved in the family program. Emily is particularly enthusiastic, given her previous positive experience with treatment. She and her father have fewer conflicts as they support each other in their recovery efforts. Jim becomes more involved in Jason's sports activities. The children have developed a habit of "checking in" with Jim at least once a day. Jim frequently expresses regret that he was not more available to them due to his drinking. The family is managing to have three dinners together a week and is trying to share one activity on the weekend.

As Jim maintains sobriety, the therapy shifts into **stage three:** the emotional desert. Jim is six weeks into his treatment and has been sober for two months. The focus of therapy is to support the family as they adjust to the absence of alcohol in the family system and to tolerate these changes. For years, they have slowly altered their behavior to accommodate Jim's drinking. In turn, family members have developed maladaptive behavior, such as Emily's drinking, Susan's codependence, and Jason's withdrawal. They must learn new patterns of interaction and communication. Since Jim drank excessively for a number of years, the shift from a "wet" to a "dry" state is extremely stressful. The therapist expects this transition to be difficult and again uses a psychoeducational framework to help them understand the nature of these changes.

Susan's adjustment appears to be the most difficult. She expresses a sense of unfamiliarity with Jim and discomfort with his new behavior. Toward the end of his treatment program, she begins to express anger toward him for now being the "perfect father," despite years of being emotionally absent. Although pleased that the family is growing closer, she feels that an unfair burden has been placed on her to prepare meals and provide emotional support while Jim "has fun" with the children or is self-absorbed in his recovery. Susan reveals that she has not been attending Al-Anon meetings or reading about codependency. The therapist indicates that, although Susan and Jason do not have a drinking problem, they must also work on their recovery.

The therapist now concentrates on non-alcohol-specific areas of family functioning. Susan's concerns have touched on core problems of intimacy in the couple's relationship. To reinforce an appropriate boundary between the parental and child subsystems, the therapist requests a meeting with Susan and Jim alone. (Although marital therapy seems indicated in this case, this change in format is not always necessary.) The goal of this marital therapy is to assist them in sharing their feelings and to solving problems through the use of traditional marital therapy techniques. An early task is to set guidelines for fair fighting as they express mutual feelings of bitterness and regret. The disorganization in the relationship is punctuated by joint statements regarding the possibility of divorce; yet, both partners indicate their commitment to each other and their desire to improve the marriage. After several conflictual sessions, the therapist is effective in helping each partner take responsibility for his or her contribution to the breakdown of their marriage and to work toward conflict resolution.

The prospect of divorce is unsettling to both of them. This crisis unveils deep fears in Susan stemming from her parents' divorce, and she gains insight into the origins of her codependency. She realizes that she assumed a child-like position in the marriage, such as giving Jim full authority over financial matters and not monitoring her children's activities. This appears to be the source of many of her complaints about changes in the family (i.e., being forced into a more mature role). She held the irrational belief that being more assertive and independent would cause him to leave her. For his part, Jim acknowledges that he encouraged her dependence, since this was the model he observed in his family of origin. However, this same upbringing left him with strong unmet emotional needs and weak coping skills. Therefore, he was equally dependent on Susan and fearful of abandonment by her. He was overwhelmed by his perceived sole responsibility for the financial well-being of the family. Rather than turn to his wife for assistance, alcohol became a way of coping with his fears. Once they identified these feelings, they were able to view each other's behavior in a more positive light and to build trust in their relationship.

The therapist met with Jim and Susan for six weeks. Jim completed his eight-week treatment, participates in the weekly follow-up program, and has been sober for over three months. Emily continues to attend follow-up sessions at her treatment program and has been sober for almost six months. As Jim and Susan address their marital problems directly and change their relational patterns, the family enters **stage four**: family reorganization. The goal of this stage is to help the family in their reorganization through traditional family therapy, since their basic patterns of functioning have significantly changed. (If Jim had maintained sobriety but their interactional patterns had gone unchanged, the goal would have been family stabilization.)

A new stability in the marriage leads to overall improved functioning in the family. They remain in family therapy for two more months. As Susan and Jim continue to work on achieving mutuality in their relationship, their parenting improves. They make joint decisions regarding the children and feel more comfortable in asserting their authority. Thus, rules and expectations become clearer, and as a result, Emily and Jason show more age-appropriate behavior. Jason begins to explore an unexpressed artistic ability. In the past, Jim had tried to push him into athletic pursuits, for which he was not temperamentally suited. Although problems still arise, they offer opportunities for the family to build and practice new skills for problem solving and conflict resolution. The family interacts more and eats together on a regular basis, with Jim sharing parental responsibility with Susan. They show more effective communication, particularly pertaining to emotional expression. All family members attend support groups to address their individual needs. Jim and Susan jointly sought advice for addressing their financial problems and are implementing a plan.

Breaking old patterns and consolidating new ones is a trial and error process that transpires over the course of therapy. Yet this process will continue even after therapy is completed. One of the last issues discussed is Emily's impending graduation and her plans to attend college in the fall. She wants to begin working this summer so she can save her money and offset some of the expenses, since the family's financial situation remains uncertain. Jim's business has shown slow improvement since he quit drinking, and Susan is considering part-time employment.

At the final session, while reviewing treatment gains and looking forward to the future, the family seems to realize that the end of therapy is really a beginning. Jim voices their commitment to break the cycle of alcoholism and codependence in their family. From Emily's attempt at death, the family has begun a new life.

Summary

An overview of a family perspective on the history, theory, research, and treatment of alcoholism indicates that this perspective is widely acknowledged and accepted in the field, although there is no general agreement as to practice. Family treatment can consist of viewing the family as the context for individual behavior as well as viewing the family as a system unto itself (a family systems approach). The related constructs of codependency, children of alcoholics, and adult children of alcoholics have gained a great deal of attention by professionals as well as the public, but these concepts lack empirical investigation that might make them more valuable in producing positive treatment outcomes for family members. Three predominant models of family assessment and treatment are behavioral, stress coping, and family systems. These models share general principles but differ in specific guidelines for intervention. Systematic motivational therapy is a noteworthy integrative approach to family therapy designed specifically to address substance-abuse disorders, although it has not yet been empirically validated. Although outcome studies are inconclusive, it appears that family therapy is equally effective in bringing about desired changes as other treatment modalities.

CHAPTER 11

Ethnicity, Culture, and Substance Use Disorders

Diana M. DiNitto
University of Texas at Austin

Eden Hernandez Robles
University of Texas at Austin

This chapter addresses substance use and substance use disorders among people of various ethnic and cultural groups. We use the terms *ethnicity* and *culture* rather than *race*, because they better reflect the richness of the experiences of the groups discussed (Lum, 2003). Ethnicity and culture have important influences on social systems, including individuals and groups' attitudes and behaviors with respect to alcohol and drug use. Rebhun (1998) calls psychoactive substance use "a profoundly social act among human beings" that is "highly affected by culture" (p. 493). Heath (1999) notes "that a single substance [e.g., marijuana] can have such different uses and meanings in a single society, or in nearby societies, demonstrates that something very different from biochemistry and physiology must be involved" (p. 176). In fact, ethnicity and culture have been called "the strongest determinants of drinking patterns in a society" (Klatsky, Siegelaub, Landy, & Friedman, 1983, p. 372).

We consider groups whose ethnic roots are in many different countries—American Indians (Native Americans), blacks (African Americans), and Hispanics (Latinos/Latinas). Like Anglo Americans, these groups' alcohol and drug use is considerable. Anglos, however, are generally less likely than members of these ethnic groups to encounter alcohol- and drug-related health problems and social consequences. We also consider Asian Americans and Jewish Americans. Although many of them use alcohol, they have fewer chemical dependency problems than the members of most other major ethnic groups.

Historically, there has been considerable interest in the drinking patterns of Europeans (primarily the French, Italians, and Irish) and the Jews. As Chapter 2 indicates, the French and the Irish are reported to have higher rates of alcoholism than the Italians and the Jews. Many Americans have roots in these countries. Various sociocultural explanations may account for these differences. For example, Italians tend to drink wine moderately with meals; whereas the French reportedly drink more distilled spirits in addition to wine and do more drinking apart from meals. Jews, regardless of nationality, generally drink moderately, primarily in conjunction with religious ceremonies and at home, whereas the Irish drink to socialize, frequently outside the home in pubs. The Netherlands, the Scandinavian countries, Great Britain, Germany, the Mediterranean countries, and India all have unique histories, customs, and laws that govern alcohol and drug use (Armyr, Elmer, & Herz, 1982; Helzer & Canino, 1992).

Another concept introduced in Chapter 2 and explored further in this chapter is that cultures that have little ambivalence about chemical use and norms that promote moderation and integration of alcohol and even other drug consumption tend to have lower rates of chemical dependency problems than do countries such as the United States, in which the norms and attitudes associated with alcohol and drug use differ widely among segments of the population.

An inherent bias pervades studies of alcohol and other drug use among different cultural groups because the comparison or normative group is generally the majority group (Gutmann, 1999). Less attention has been paid to other ethnic groups' conceptualizations of these issues. Accounts of drinking and drug use among members of various ethnic groups can vary considerably, depending on who wrote them.

The need for culturally specific or culturally relevant chemical dependency programs has been widely embraced, although few studies have been conducted to determine whether they produce better outcomes than other treatment approaches. Nonetheless, virtually everyone agrees that an understanding of human service work with individuals from various cultures is necessary to function adequately in the field. The reported reluctance of some clients to seek chemical dependency services offered by mainstream providers is not surprising, given the previous insensitive treatment of many ethnic groups. For professionals who feel a lack of efficacy in working with people from different ethnic backgrounds, pursuing education about models of cultural competence and knowledge of specific cultural groups is often helpful, as is increased contacts with people of different ethnic backgrounds (see, for example, Finn, 1994).

Many volumes have been written on culturally sensitivity for health and human professionals (e.g., Fong & Furuto, 2001; Ponterotto, Casas, Suzuki, & Alexander, 2010; Streltzer & Tseng, 2008; Sue & Sue, 2008). Some are specific to substance abuse prevention and treatment (e.g., Krestan, 2000; Straussner, 2001). Models of practice with clients of different ethnic backgrounds generally emphasize the need to understand the history of the cultural group, particularly the group's experience of oppression (Devore &

Schlesinger, 1999). In the chemical dependency field, it is important to note the ways in which groups have (or have not used) alcohol and other drugs and how they have come to define alcohol and other drug problems. The group's cultural values, expectations of its members, and use of its native language are also important in developing relevant prevention, assessment, and treatment strategies. Although it is impossible to cover many of the fine points of service provision to members of different ethnic groups in this chapter, we provide an introduction to some of this material.

Before discussing various ethnic groups, three points deserve mention. First, much of the material in this chapter is illustrative of what is known about each of the groups discussed. For instance, there are 565 federally recognized American Indian and Native Alaskan tribes, each with many distinctive cultural features, including drinking and drug use, that cannot be captured in a few pages. The same is true for the many cultural groups that fall under the categories of Hispanic, Asian, Pacific Islander, and so forth. The information is intended to stimulate thinking about how to serve individuals across a wide spectrum of cultures.

Second, the cultural experiences of members of an ethnic group or subgroup differ (Green, 1999). For example, some Americans of German, Mexican, or Japanese background have little connection to their ancestors' heritage, whereas others practice traditions closely tied to their ancestors' homelands. The region of the United States or community in which one lives may also influence ethnic identification and cultural practices. The heterogeneity *within* ethnic groups makes research on culture and substance use and related problems particularly challenging (National Institute on Alcohol Abuse and Alcoholism, 2002). Indiscriminately lumping people together may result in what has been called *ethnic glossing*, especially when it involves the use of the highly questionable categorization of race (Collins, 1993). Furthermore, individuals' characteristics in addition to ethnicity should be considered. For example, what may appear to be racial or ethnic differences in substance use or abuse may diminish or disappear once socioeconomic status and environmental or contextual factors are controlled (Amey & Albrecht, 1998; Collins, 1993; Wallace, 1999).

Third, each person's experiences vary, regardless of his or her ethnic background or other characteristics. Individuals who grew up in the same family may differ in how closely they identify with their cultural heritage and whether they use alcohol or other drugs and develop related problems.

When human service professionals talk about differential diagnosis and treatment or individual treatment plans, they are addressing the need to see the client as a unique human being and not to rely on generalizations. With these cautions in mind, we now present information based on research and practice wisdom about epidemiology and the prevention and treatment of substance use disorders among members of the major ethnic groups in the United States.

Substance Use and Abuse among American Indians and Alaska Natives

History and Background

It is common knowledge, mostly as the result of Western movies, that the "white man" introduced American Indians to alcohol or "firewater" as it was called (Winkler, 1968). A small number of tribes in what is now the southwestern United States had a history of making alcohol for use in ceremonial and religious purposes, but most American Indians learned of alcohol from contact with explorers in the sixteenth and seventeenth centuries (Abbott, 1998; Indian Health Service, 1977; Lemert, 1982). These early experiences (Dailey, 1979) remain important because in addition to learning about alcohol from white men, American Indians also learned about drunkenness from them (Kelso & Dubay, 1989; MacAndrew & Edgerton, 1969). Whites initially offered American

Indians alcohol to form alliances (Indian Health Service, 1977), but alcohol was also used as a means of getting American Indians drunk and taking advantage of them in trading and other transactions (Unrau, 1996; Winkler, 1968).

Unlike alcohol, American Indians have used peyote, a hallucinogenic drug, for religious purposes with few negative consequences (Bergman, 1971). One theory is that since American Indians were unprepared for alcohol use, problems resulted following its introduction (Lemert, 1982; Ramsperger, 1989; Winkler, 1968). However, given that early accounts of American Indians' drunkenness were written by white men,

> the facts of the matter require that such talk be taken with a rather large grain of salt, for it is indisputably the case that not all North American Indians were irresistibly drawn to alcohol, nor did they, even if they drank it, always become uncontrollable as a consequence. (MacAndrew and Edgerton, 1969, p. 123; also see Unrau, 1996).

Leland (1976) studied the *firewater myth*, that American Indians have an inordinate susceptibility to alcohol abuse, and the *reverse firewater myth*, that they are less prone to alcohol abuse, and came to no definite conclusion about either. In fact, there is no convincing evidence that American Indians have a particular physiological or genetic vulnerability to alcohol (Coyhis & Simonelli, 2008; Coyhis & White, 2006; May, 1996), though the belief persists, even among Indians (May, 1994; May & Moran, 1997).

Some American Indian leaders became deeply concerned about alcohol problems. With their encouragement, a federal law was passed in 1832 that prohibited distilled liquor on reservations; later, ale, beer, and wine were included (Indian Health Service, 1977). Excessive drinking continued, however, as bootleggers and smugglers saw to it that alcohol remained available (Indian Health Service, 1977). American Indian prohibition may have inadvertently encouraged practices such as gulping and bingeing, since it was illegal to be caught with alcohol.

The 1832 law became regarded as discriminatory, but it was not abolished until 1953, 20 years after national Prohibition was repealed (Indian Health Service, 1977). Since 1953, tribal councils have been responsible for alcoholic beverage control policies on their reservations, and "over 60% of all federally recognized reservations have retained policies of prohibition" (Office of Justice Programs, 2000, p. ix). Selling or using illicit drugs on reservations is a felony (Young & Joe, 2009). Prohibition on reservations may continue to exacerbate some alcohol-related problems, such as arrests for drunken driving and auto accidents, when American Indians travel to other areas to buy alcohol (May, 1982).

Littman (1970) summarizes three psychological explanations for substance use among American Indians that permeate the literature: (1) relief from anxiety due to extreme poverty and other hardships, (2) the psychodynamic explanation of the need to release repressed anger (sometimes regarded as an outlet that prevents the development of psychiatric problems), and (3) relief from pressures resulting from forced acculturation. Weibel-Orlando (1986–87) provides one such picture of the devastation American Indians have suffered as a result of alcohol use:

> The Sioux called liquor "mni wakon" or "sacred water" in reference to its power to induce states of euphoria and to reduce pain and sadness. In the late 19th century, when the farms and the railroads of white pioneers displaced the Sioux and drastically altered their nomadic, big game-hunting way of life, they were forced to accept a lifestyle that lacks meaning for them. Alcohol, like the Vision Quest ritual, may help to fill psychological gaps left by the Sioux's loss of cultural integrity, perception of personal worth, and sense of self-esteem. (p. 8)

The long history of oppression of American Indians has resulted in what is called "historical trauma," which may be defined as the "intergenerational accumulation of risk for poor mental health status among Native peoples that purportedly originates from the depredations of past colonial subjugation, including ethnocidal policies and practices" (Gone, 2009, p. 752; see also Morgan & Freeman, 2009).

One sociological explanation of American Indian drinking is that it promotes group solidarity through a shared, social activity (Littman, 1970; Yuan et al., 2010). Weibel (1982) called American Indian drinking "part of group membership and acceptance" (p. 337). It may be considered discourteous to refuse a drink, and sharing bottles of alcohol is common (Burns, Daily, & Moskowitz as cited in Weibel, 1982). Several authors describe "drinking parties" at which cheap alcohol is consumed rapidly until there is none left or the imbibers become unconscious (Lemert, 1982; Weibel-Orlando, 1986/87). For many American Indians, drinking *alone* is what is considered aberrant (Weibel & Weisner as cited in Weibel, 1982).

A rather provocative sociological view of American Indian alcohol use and abuse is that these acts are an expression of defiance against whites (Lewis, 1982). Lurie (1979) writes that "getting drunk remains a very Indian thing to do when all else fails to maintain the Indian-white boundary" (p. 138); "thus, before giving vent to aggressive inclinations, you get drunk or convince yourself and others you are drunk, in order that no one mistakes you for acting like a white man" (p. 133). Conversely, "a case could . . . be made that the best way for Native Americans to distinguish themselves from Whites would be to leave liquor alone" (Leland, 1980, p. 38). Alcohol and drug use "destroy . . . harmony with nature and damage the ability of the mind, body, and spirit to work together. They are clearly counter to the Indian Way" (Oetting et al., 1982, p. 35).

Substance Use Disorders among American Indians and Alaska Natives

Conducting studies with nationally representative samples of the American Indian and Alaska Native population is difficult due to the number of tribes and problems such as distrust of researchers (Weaver, 2001). In summarizing the epidemiological literature, the Office of Justice Programs (2000) reported that "fewer Indian people drink and they drink less than non-Indian people" (p. ix).

Variation Across Tribes.   Some authors speculate as to why American Indians may have high rates of both abstinence and substance use disorders. Heath (1989), for example, reported that most Hopis do not drink, even though their reservation is surrounded by the Navajo reservation, where heavy drinking is practiced. The Hopis, however, have a much higher cirrhosis death rate than the Navajo, which Heath noted may be due to Hopi problem drinkers being ostracized and living in their own isolated "skid row." High rates of alcohol-related problems among western Oklahoma tribes (the Cheyenne-Arapaho, Anadarko, Wichita, and Caddo) compared to eastern tribes (the Chickasaw, Creek, Seminole, and Cherokee) may occur because western tribes were hunters who lost their means of survival when the federal government prevented buffalo hunting (Stratton et al., 1978). These tribes also reportedly had more loosely integrated social structures and were introduced to alcohol much later than members of the eastern tribes, who were primarily farmers and had more developed social and political structures. The eastern tribes also suffered displacement but were able to re-establish their farms and communities.

The American Indian Service Utilization, Psychiatric Epidemiology, Risk and Protective Factors Project (AI-SUPERPFP) found that among a Southwest tribe, 35 percent of men and 62 percent of women reported that they had never consumed alcohol, compared to 27 percent and 34 percent, respectively, of a Northern Plains tribe (Spicer et al., 2003). For both groups of American Indian men, lifetime alcohol dependence was 50 percent higher than for all men in the U.S. population. Northern Plains women had twice the alcohol dependence rate of all women in the United States, while rates for Southwest women were similar to the general population. Studies have also shown that drinking prevalence has increased in some tribes and decreased in others (May, 1994).

High Rates of Substance Use Disorders. According to the National Survey on Drug Use and Health (Substance Abuse and Mental Health Services Administration [SAMHSA], 2010a), among the country's major ethnic groups in 2009, American Indians and Alaska Natives were least likely to report current alcohol use, and they were somewhat less likely than Hispanics and whites to report binge drinking. However, they reported the highest rates of current illicit drug and tobacco use, and they were the group most likely to have a past year diagnosis of illicit drug and/or alcohol abuse or dependence (see Table 11.1; also see Office of Applied Studies, 2007).

Alcohol-related deaths have declined substantially for American Indians; however, differences among the major U.S. ethnic groups remain (see, for example, Indian Health Service, 2009). In 2006, 31 percent of traffic fatalities among whites were alcohol related compared to 48 percent for American Indians (National Highway Traffic Safety Administration, 2009). From 1995 to 1997, the rate of fetal alcohol syndrome (FAS) per 1,000 population was reported to be 5.6 for American Indians/Alaska Natives residing in Alaska compared to 1.5 for the general population (Miller et al., 2002). Across Alaska, Arizona, Colorado, and New York, the rate of FAS for American Indians/Alaska Natives was 3.2 compared to 0.4 for the general population (Miller et al.). Though the age-adjusted chronic liver disease and cirrhosis death rate for American Indians and Alaska Natives decreased from 72.4 per 100,000 population for years 1979–1981 to 39.1 for years 2002–2004, the later rate is still four times higher than the rate for the total U.S. population (Indian Health Service).

TABLE 11.1   Percent of Past Month Alcohol and Drug Use and Past Year Abuse or Dependence among Single Race and Hispanic Ethnic Groups, Aged 12 and Older, 2009

	Whites	Blacks	American Indians/ Alaska Natives	Asians	Hispanics	Native Hawaiians/ Pacific Islanders
Tobacco use	29.6%	26.5%	41.8%	11.9%	23.2%	c
Alcohol use[a]	56.7%	42.8%	37.1%	37.6%	41.7%	c
Binge drinking[b]	24.8%	19.8%	22.2%	11.1%	25.0%	c
Illicit drug use	8.8%	9.6%	18.3%	3.7%	7.9%	c
Substance abuse or dependence	9.0%	8.8%	15.5%	3.5%	10.1%	5.3%
Illicit drug abuse or dependence	2.8%	3.3%	6.0%	1.2%	3.0%	1.8%
Alcohol abuse or dependence	7.5%	7.0%	13.3%	2.6%	8.6%	4.5%

[a]At least one drink in the past 30 days.

[b]Five or more drinks on the same occasion (i.e., at the same time or within a couple of hours of each other) on at least 1 day in the past 30 days.

[c]Low precision; no estimate reported.

Sources: Substance Abuse and Mental Health Services Administration. (2010). *Results from the 2009 National Survey on Drug Use and Health: Volume I. Summary of National Findings* (Office of Applied Studies, NSDUH Series H-38A, HHS Publication No. SMA 10-4586 Findings). Rockville, MD. Retrieved March 28, 2011, from http://oas.samhsa.gov/NSDUH/2k9NSDUH/2k9ResultsP.pdf.

Accidents, liver disease/cirrhosis, and suicide are among the top ten leading causes of death for American Indians and Alaska Natives, causes that are often alcohol related. Cerebrovascular and respiratory diseases, often associated with smoking, also rank among the top ten causes (Heron, 2010). From 2001–2005, alcohol-attributable deaths (AAD) were nearly 12 percent of all deaths among American Indians and Alaska Natives, their age-adjusted AAD rate was approximately double that of the U.S. general population, and they lose 6 more years of potential life because of AADs than the general U.S. population (Centers for Disease Control, 2008).

American Indian and Alaska Native women are generally less likely than Native American men to have alcohol use disorders, though both native men and women have higher rates of alcohol use disorders than members of other ethnic groups (Office of Applied Studies, 2007). Native men and women are nearly identical in proportions that have illicit drug disorders, and their rates also exceed those of men and women of other ethnic groups. A study of Alaska Natives receiving inpatient treatment for alcohol dependence found that the men and women had "a similar early onset and rapid progression to alcohol dependence, and...a similar prevalence of alcohol-related psychological and physical problems" (Parks, Hesselbrock, Hesselbrock, & Segal, 2001, p. 286).

American Indian and Alaska Native Youth.   Over the past several decades, alcohol and drug use among American Indian youth attending schools on or near reservations is much more similar across tribes than it is among adults where rates across tribes differ substantially

(Beauvais et al., 2008). American Indian youth generally use marijuana and other drugs at higher rates than other youth, though patterns in decreases and increases in their use tend to occur at the same time as they do for other youth. Inhalant use rates among American Indian youth are now similar to rates for other youth. This may be attributed to concerted efforts to prevent inhalant use, which was considered especially rampant among Indian youth (Beauvais et al.).

Whitbeck and colleagues (2008) studied 651 indigenous adolescents from a single culture residing on four reservations in the Midwest United States and four reserves in Canada (this indigenous group is among the largest in the two countries). Like previous studies of indigenous youth, they found an earlier onset of mental disorders compared to other youth. Substance use disorders among the indigenous youth also increased substantially from ages 10–12 to 13–15, from 3 to 27 percent. Conduct disorders also increased. The rates of substance use and conduct disorders were three and two times higher among these youth, respectively, than those in surveys of the general U.S. population. In an astonishing analysis based on a sample of 525 American Indian adults residing on contiguous reservations in southwest California, Ehlers et al. (2010) found that 92 percent of those who reported their first intoxication at age 12 or younger met lifetime criteria for alcohol dependence compared to 12 percent who did not report intoxication until age 21 or later (also see Whitesell et al., 2009).

Traditional laissez-faire childrearing practices among some American Indian tribes such as the Oglala Sioux have been suggested to explain American Indian youth's substance use (Wax cited in Weibel-Orlando, 1984). Other explanations of native youths' substance use are role models who abuse drugs and reverence of elders, even if they abuse alcohol (Trimble cited in NIAAA, 1985; Yuan et al., 2010).

Walls, Whitbeck, and Hoyt (2007) studied native youth aged 10 to 13 and their female caretakers. Coercive parenting (yelling and spanking) increased the likelihood that youth used alcohol, while parental monitoring (family knows where the child is and when they came home) reduced alcohol use. The caretaker's binge drinking was associated with youth's alcohol use, suggesting a possible modeling effect. But when Sellers, Winfree, and Griffiths (1993) compared drinking among American Indian and other youth in the same rural community, youths' own permissive attitudes toward alcohol and drug use explained more of the variance than did their perception of adults' or peers' permissiveness regardless of ethnicity. Peers' permissive attitudes played a stronger role than adults' in predicting youth's permissive attitudes and their substance use. Among a sample of 400 reservation and urban youth residing in a southwestern state, risk factors for youths' alcohol use disorder symptoms were family members' substance use, having peers who misbehaved (e.g., used substances, had gotten into trouble with the police), and participating in some activities (e.g., pow wows that were sometimes followed by drinking parties) (Yu & Stiffman, 2007). Cultural pride, spirituality, and youths' identification with a religious group or church had a beneficial effect by moderating the effects of problem family members and peers on alcohol use disorder symptoms.

Treatment Services for American Indians and Alaska Natives

American Indians and Alaska Natives are about 1.6 percent of the U.S. population (U.S. Census Bureau, 2010a) and about 2.3 percent of those admitted to alcohol and drug treatment programs in 2008 (Office of Applied Studies, 2010). As in the general population, approximately one-third of American Indians and Alaska Natives admitted to treatment are women. Most admissions among native men and women were for primary alcohol problems followed by marijuana. American Indians and Alaska Natives are more likely than those of other ethnic groups to be admitted for alcohol use disorders.

Legislative Initiatives.   In 1978, the National Institute on Alcohol Abuse and Alcoholism (NIAAA) began the transfer of its 156 alcohol and drug abuse programs for indigenous groups to the Indian Health Service (IHS). The IHS is the agency primarily responsible for federal government activities designed to prevent and treat alcohol and other drug problems among American Indians and Alaska Natives, but it has been the subject of a good deal of criticism for the way it addresses American Indians' problems. Many IHS-funded programs were transferred to tribal control (Beauvais, 1998). In 1986, the Secretary of the U.S. Department of Health and Human Services convened a task force on Native American alcoholism, and the Indian Alcohol and Substance Abuse Prevention and Treatment Act, part of the Anti-Drug Abuse Act of 1986, also helped to increase the services available to American Indians, such as special treatment centers for American Indian youth. The Office of Justice Programs (2000) and other agencies and organizations also support tribal efforts to reduce alcohol and drug problems.

The peyote religion and the Native American Church use peyote in structured ceremonies (Abbott, 1998; Albaugh & Anderson, 1974; Bergman, 1971) to promote healing, including recovery from substance use disorders. The Indian Civil Rights Act of 1968 and the American Indian Religious Freedom Act of 1978 aided native people in using indigenous approaches to healing (see Coyhis & Simonelli, 2008). In 1990, the U.S. Supreme Court ruled in *Employment Division of Oregon v. Smith* that the First Amendment did not protect those using peyote for religious purposes from prosecution under state drug laws. The American Indian Religious Freedom Act Amendments of 1994 changed this by making peyote use for *bona fide* religious purposes legal in all 50 states (Botsford & Peregoy, n.d.).

Culturally Relevant Treatment.   Some American Indians and Alaska Natives may benefit from the chemical dependency treatment programs found in most communities, others from treatment grounded in their particular culture, and others from a combination of approaches (Weaver, 2001). For example, since one-fifth of the American Indian and Alaska Native population speak a language other than English at home (U.S. Census Bureau, 2010a), treatment in their native language may be necessary or preferred. The types of treatments many chemical dependency programs offer were discussed in Chapter 6 of this text; therefore, the following discussion focuses on culturally relevant approaches.

Native Americans have a long history of attempts to address alcohol's effects on their communities (Coyhis & Simonelli, 2008; Coyhis & White, 2006) dating back to the Seneca prophet Handsome Lake and his long-house religion in the early 1800s (see, for example, Moran & May, 1997; Office of Justice Programs, 2000). In the late 1950s, American Indians recovering through Alcoholics Anonymous began to reach out to other American Indians in need, and religious groups (such as the Iroquoian long-house religion, the Indian Shaker religion, and the Native American Church) and Protestant fundamentalists tried to convey the need for abstinence (Abbott, 1998). Coyhis and Simonelli describe an American Indian "Wellbriety" movement occurring since World War II, which means that a person with a substance use disorder not only becomes sober but well (see also Morgan & Freeman, 2009). It acknowledges the sociopolitical degradation Indians have suffered as well as the hard work individuals must do to become well. The sobriety movement among American Indians encourages "pride in tradition, pride in culture, (and) pride in being Indian" (Simonelli, 2000, p. 78). Many American Indians are not conversant with their tribes' cultural traditions and languages, and others have lost these connections. An important part of treatment may be reconnection and revitalization of American Indian culture (Beauvais, 1998; Coyhis, 2000; Weaver, 2001) as well as healing from historical trauma (Gone, 2009; Morgan & Freeman, 2009).

Part of beginning "where the client is at" is to consider his or her cultural values and the values of those around him or her (Weaver, 2001). The value Native Americans place on harmony with their surroundings leads them to follow the "Red Road" (the good road or right path, which involves "traditional knowledge, values, and culture") (Coyhis & Simonelli, 2008, p. 1934; also see Coyhis, 2000). However, members of the majority culture may perceive expression of some Native American cultural values as apathy (Rhoades et al., 1988). For example, Native Americans often avoid interfering in others' decisions, giving direct advice, or telling others what to do (Hill, 1989; Littman, 1970; Rhoades et al., 1988; Yuan et al., 2010). Some have suggested that American Indians' fatalistic view of illness may contribute to a pattern in which chemically dependent individuals get into treatment late (Littman, 1970). This may be due to many American Indians' belief that substance abuse is "outside the person" (Beauvais, 1998, p. 257), or externally caused; thus, personal responsibility for chemical abuse may not be recognized (Nofz, 1988). There may also be an absence of shame attached to drunkenness and a lack of sanctions against alcohol misuse (Littman, 1970; Rhoades et al., 1988; Office of Justice Programs, 2000; Spillane & Smith, 2007). Others challenge this view, noting that sanctions abound (e.g., the deep sorrow American Indians feel over the problems wrought by alcohol such as health problems, premature death, and high arrest and incarceration rates), and the punishments for alcohol-related offenses by some tribal governments can be severe (Beals et al., 2009).

In the social work tradition, Nofz (1988) describes a task-centered group approach (see Epstein, 1980; Reid & Epstein, 1972) that combines elements of Native American and non-Native American cultures to address substance use disorders. In keeping with tribal values, "The group is organized around specific tasks in managing sobriety, with special emphasis on adapting to those situations in which different values impose conflicting behavioral expectations. Thus, alcohol abuse is not framed as an 'individual problem' and introspection into group members'

personalities is avoided" (Nofz, p. 70). The group identifies the problems and the tasks to be addressed, since American Indians often prefer an active or "doing" rather than an introspective approach. This approach also emphasizes American Indian values of self-determination and of placing group welfare over individual welfare. Nofz suggests that the social worker develop a "'low key' participatory (leadership) style" and act as a "group facilitator rather than therapist" (p. 71). Confession within the groups (as well as personal stories in Alcoholics Anonymous) may be replaced with the tribal tradition of storytelling. These stories "contain metaphorical descriptions of everyday problems, along with practical and moral advice," and they take direct attention off the individual (Nofz, p. 71).

Like others, American Indian families have been accused of enabling "by paying bills, including bail, and placing responsibility on others rather than the alcohol abuser themselves" (Rhoades et al., 1988, p. 626). Family members are likely to avoid calling police because they want to avoid entanglements with authorities, especially those that may lead to incarceration, even when family violence has occurred (see Yuan et al., 2010). The American Indian family model fosters mutual obligation or interdependence among relatives, rather than independence from them (Red Horse, 1980). Service providers are advised to utilize this extended family and tribal network (Ramsperger, 1989), not only by involving families in treatment but also in Alcoholics Anonymous groups, which are usually reserved for alcoholics or addicts (Jilek-Aall, 1981; Littman, 1970). In their efforts to denigrate American Indian culture, authorities often separated American Indians from their families and sent them to be raised in foster care (Spicer, 1998). As a result, they may lack family members on whom to rely (Merker, cited in NIAAA, 1985). Other family members may also be chemically dependent. In these cases, different strategies may be needed to develop the social support systems necessary for the individual's recovery.

American Indians' concept of spirituality and religion is an integral part of most tribal programs and has been incorporated into some mainstream treatment programs and mutual-help groups (Beauvais, 1998; Carvajal & Young, 2009; Morgan & Freeman, 2009). Abbott (1998) notes: "Therapy involves restoration of harmony and balance, rituals to appease the offended deities, dream interpretation, vision quests, and curing processes that are often based on the therapeutic myth of death and rebirth" (p. 2619). Incorporation of medicine men and women and other spiritual advisors who may be on call or conduct regular spiritual meetings are other suggestions; native leaders' support of treatment programs is also important.

Some Veterans Affairs programs incorporate the traditional *sweat lodge*, a purification ritual in which the individual usually enters a small, tent-like structure heated by rocks (Drake, 2010). A patient may spend hours in the structure, chanting native songs, confessing, and seeking spiritual renewal ("VA Hospital," 1991). The *vision quest*, another ritual that may be helpful with alcohol or drug abuse, is used to find answers to personal problems and to seek the right path. Traditional dances (Abbott, 1998), as well as ceremonies and prayers, are also important (Nofz, 1988). Professionals who are not members of the tribal group may be excluded from participation in sacred activities (Nofz). Despite abundant interest in culturally relevant approaches, they "are rarely described in sufficient detail to afford appropriately tailored outcome assessment" (Gone, 2009). Researchers may also lack knowledge of culturally appropriate approaches to research and collaborations such as tribal-participatory research necessary to study cultural practices (Thomas et al., 2009).

Tribal Approaches.   Perhaps the most enthusiastic response to addressing alcohol and drug problems among indigenous people has been to tribal initiatives. Contemporary examples are the Standing Rock Sioux's "over-all program to ameliorate alcoholism and problem drinking on the Reservation" (Whittaker, 1963) and the Council of the Cheyenne River Sioux Tribe's declaration of its intentions to become alcohol and drug free (Rhoades, 1988). The Community Pulling Together: Healing of the Canoe is a collaborative project of the Suquamish Tribe and the University of Washington (Thomas et al., 2009). The Alkali-Lake community's (located in British Columbia, Canada) efforts to eliminate alcoholism are portrayed in the video *The Honour of All* (Mail & Johnson, 1993). These efforts originated when one couple in the community recovered from alcoholism and patiently waited for others to join them (Taylor, 1987; Willie, 1989; also see Coyhis & White, 2002). The Pueblo of Zuni Recovery Center offers a comprehensive day-treatment program, a driving while intoxicated (DWI) program, and an underage drinking prevention initiative that focuses on healthy lifestyles, resisting peer pressure, and making sound decisions (Office of Justice Programs, 2000). Some tribes require that elected tribal officials live sober lives (Rhoades et al., 1988).

The circle is the symbol of healing among most native tribes (Morgan & Freeman, 2009). This symbol of interconnectedness is illustrated in traditional interventions such as the Talking Circle, Healing Circle, and Four Circles (Abbott, 1998; Coyhis, 2000; Morgan & Freeman). The Four Circles, for example, represent the Creator, an individual's spouse, other immediate family, and extended family (Abbott, 1998). Circles are like a form of group treatment in which individuals can safely share their experiences and thoughts (Abbott, 1998; Coyhis, 2000). The Family Circles Program on the Lac du Flambeau reservation ties traditional American Indian culture to contemporary life to address poor self-esteem, apathy, and helplessness and includes children, parents, and grandparents (Van Steele, Allen, & Moberg, 1998). Tribal elders are consultants to the project, which focuses on the four aspects of self—physical, intellectual, emotional, and spiritual—and incorporates Ojibwe language classes and a sports program. The Seventh Generation Program refers to a time when Indian nations came together to heal (Moran, 1999). Children are considered to be at the center of the seven generations. Some American Indian nations in the United States have adopted the Four Worlds program began in Alberta, Canada; it promotes health through community development by involving community leaders and those who need services to create a shared community vision.

Mutual-Help Groups. American Indians' participation in Alcoholics Anonymous (AA) is sometimes considered controversial because AA was developed by individuals of white European descent (Coyhis, 2000). Some American Indians may object to AA's Christian overtones (Littman, 1970), but Indians' religious preferences should not be presumed. Highly acculturated American Indians may find AA more appealing (Lewis, 1982), though this may depend on their tribe's customs. Jilek-Aall (1981) notes that unlike many other tribes, the Coastal Salish Indians in British Columbia and Washington State have a tradition of confession similar to the personal disclosure that takes place in AA. She also notes that AA groups specifically for American Indians are more consistent with native culture and are useful when there is a distrust of whites. Anonymity in AA may conflict with the group's principle of openness, and American Indian AA meetings may differ from other AA meetings (Jilek-Aall). For example, beginning and ending on time may be less important, and cultural customs resembling the potlatch (giveaway) feast are sometimes incorporated at AA "birthday" meetings.

Some Alcoholics Anonymous literature is addressed specifically to American Indians. The Umatilla tribe of Oregon has reworded and explained the Twelve Steps in a culturally relevant way for American Indians by placing them in a circle like the medicine wheel (using the directions of north, south, east, and west) to help Indians regain harmony (Coyhis, 2000; see Figure 11.1). The Indian Brotherhood offers another version of the steps. According to Coyhis (also see Coyhis & Simonelli, 2008):

> It makes sense to me when I look at the Steps in an Indian way. At an Indian Twelve-Step group... I attend we meet in a circle. We take turns reading from the Big Book in one hand, holding an eagle feather in the other. We fold up the tables and sit in a circle of chairs. As soon as we started doing that, more Indians began showing up. We smudge with sage or cedar or sweet grass to start the meeting. When we do it that way, our Medicine is good. These cultural ways help us be clear and to walk in balance. (p. 109)

Smudging is a purification ritual, and the smoke from the burned sage or sweet grass is also cleansing (Morgan & Freeman, 2009). Talking circles end with the group standing in a circle and holding the hand of the person next to them and reciting a prayer or statement of closure (similar to AA) (Morgan & Freeman). White Bison in Colorado Springs, Colorado, a community-based program, and Sobriety Through the Sacred Pipe, a prison-based program, combine American Indian traditions and the AA approach (Carvajal & Young, 2009).

Prevention Programs for American Indians and Alaska Natives

Strengthening families and communities seems fundamental to preventing alcohol and drug problems among American Indians and Alaska Natives (May & Moran, 1997). Ambivalence may play a role in addressing problem drinking as a result of conflicting values (e.g., beliefs in noninterference versus recognition of alcohol's destructive effects) in native communities, but the desire for sound prevention programming, especially where youth is concerned, is evident (see, for example, Yuan et al., 2010).

Prevention Programs for Youth. Many predictors of youths' substance use (e.g., peers who use) are the same across ethnic groups. This suggests that programs successful for the

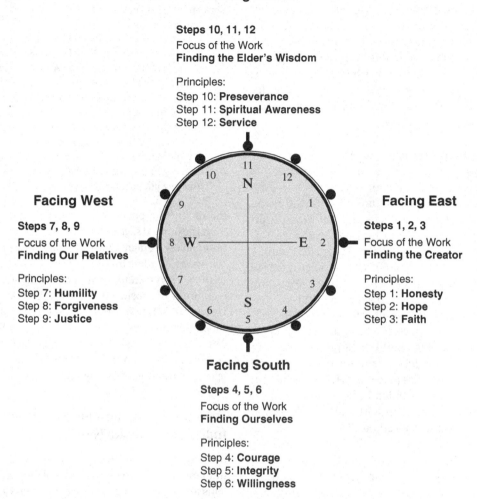

Facing North

Steps 10, 11, 12
Focus of the Work
Finding the Elder's Wisdom

Principles:
Step 10: **Preseverance**
Step 11: **Spiritual Awareness**
Step 12: **Service**

Facing West

Steps 7, 8, 9
Focus of the Work
Finding Our Relatives

Principles:
Step 7: **Humility**
Step 8: **Forgiveness**
Step 9: **Justice**

Facing East

Steps 1, 2, 3
Focus of the Work
Finding the Creator

Principles:
Step 1: **Honesty**
Step 2: **Hope**
Step 3: **Faith**

Facing South

Steps 4, 5, 6
Focus of the Work
Finding Ourselves

Principles:
Step 4: **Courage**
Step 5: **Integrity**
Step 6: **Willingness**

FIGURE 11.1   The 12 Steps in a Circle

Source: Reproduced from Coyhis, D., & Simonelli, R. (2008). "The Native American healing experience." *Substance Use & Misuse,* 43, 1927–1949. Used by permission of Informa Healthcare. Copyright © 2008.

general population may work along with cultural adaptations and strengthening for American Indian youth by focusing on peer resistance, strengthening family relationships, improving economic well-being, and encouraging school success (Beauvais et al., 2008; Oetting & Beauvais, 1989). Barlow and Walkup (2008) note that "parent training and family-based approaches have a natural fit with pan-Native American world views" (p. 843).

Many American Indian youth lack knowledge of their people's history, even if they are involved in ceremonies and practice traditions (Parker, 1990; Stivers, 1994). The four programs for American Indian youth included in the Center for Substance Abuse Prevention's Cross-Site Evaluation of High Risk Youth Programs spend much of the time devoted to culturally specific activities on traditional handicrafts, drumming, and dance in order to build cultural pride and identity. In contrast, "relatively little culturally specific program time is spent on prevention information, targeted skills development or social/emotional support" (Springer et al., 2004, p. 14). The Rhode Island Indian Council's prevention program is based on Project CHARLIE (CHemical Abuse Resolution Lies in Education), originally developed in Edina, Minnesota (Parker, 1990). The approach is designed to build self-esteem and can be adapted to meet cultural needs. Its four major components arc self-awareness, relationships, decision-making, and chemical use. In an evaluation of the Rhode Island project with a small number of participants, the cultural component seemed to be what attracted youth to it.

Preventing Birth Defects.   A number of programs address prevention and recognition of alcohol-related birth defects among American Indians (see, for example, May et al., 2008). FAS prevention efforts stress the importance of cultural relevance and the necessity to educate and involve the entire community (May et al., 2008; Streissguth, 1994). The Tuba City, Arizona, project for the Navajo utilizes a case management approach (May et al.) staffed by community residents (Streissguth). Four American Indian communities in northern Plains states have adopted the model (May et al.). Despite the serious alcohol problems of clients served, positive results have been reported—abstinence or reduced alcohol use, women entering substance abuse treatment, fewer children born with severe fetal alcohol spectrum disorders, and increased use of birth control. Indian Head Start preschool programs have also been involved in FAS awareness (Streissguth).

Whether cultural identification protects against substance use and related problems is a topic of debate (Angstman et al., 2009). Cultural *identification* may differ from cultural *pride*. In a study of native people served at a health center, smokers had a higher overall Indian cultural identification than nonsmokers (Angstman et al.). Given high rates of tobacco use for non-ceremonial purposes among Native Americans, another area for promoting health (including healthier newborns) is preventing tobacco use. Campaigns such as "Keeping Tobacco Sacred" in Montana have been developed.

Policy Approaches to Prevention.   Policy interventions (also see Chapter 8) are of particular interest because American Indian communities have the legal authority to determine whether alcohol will be sold or prohibited on their lands. May (1992) has offered numerous suggestions for limiting supply, shaping drinking practices, and reducing physical and social harm through policy. Evidence of the effects of policies such as "dry" and "wet" laws varies. In the lower 48 states, there is evidence that legalization of alcohol on some reservations is associated with fewer alcohol-related deaths and less crime, while in Alaskan villages, prohibition seems to be associated with reduced injury, violence, and crime (Office of Justice Programs, 2000). In the lower 48 states, where reservations are accessible by roads, reduced problems may be due to not having to leave the reservation and risk alcohol-related traffic accidents or hypothermia (Landen et al., 1997). In remote Alaskan villages that are not accessible by roads, the lack of access to alcohol may reduce problems, or communities with prohibition policies may be expressing cultural norms about alcohol use that act to curb problems (Berman, Hull, & May, 2000). The Cheyenne River Sioux's efforts include alcohol beverage control legislation and taxation; taxes on alcoholic beverage taxes are used to support prevention and intervention programs (Office of Justice Programs, 2000). Addressing socioeconomic factors—including poverty, unemployment, and the promotion of meaningful activity that is consistent with cultural values—is an important component of substance abuse prevention and intervention (May, 1982). Abbott (1998) notes: "Efforts to reestablish a culturally integrated community must precede or at least parallel the development of meaningful alcohol intervention; these efforts must combine basic community cultural values with the most recent advances in treatment interventions" (p. 2632).

Substance Use and Abuse among African Americans

History and Background

Africans have a long history of alcohol consumption, dating to the use of beer and palm wine in precolonial West Africa; that use was ceremonial, medicinal, and social (Christmon, 1995; Herd, 1985a).

> In traditional African cultures, as in most of the rest of the world, alcohol was widely used. Palm wine was a regular part of the diet, an important part of community celebrations, and a medicinal substance believed to be particularly effective against measles and dysentery. It was used as a medium of exchange as well. Natural substances such as Kola nuts or guinea corn were used as intoxicants or stimulants. (Gossett, 1988, p. 2)

Source: From "Alcohol and drug abuse in black America: A guide for community action" p. 2 (1988) by V. R. Gossett. Reprinted by permission of African American Family Services.

Intoxication, however, was disapproved of, and excessive drinking and related problems were apparently uncommon (Gossett, 1988; Herd, 1985a).

African Americans' history of alcohol use dates back to the seventeenth century when alcohol was provided to slaves to promote compliance and to prevent escapes (Harper, 1976, 1980; Genovese, 1974). Permission to imbibe heavily on weekends and holidays supposedly pacified the slaves and provided a respite from their oppressive existence. Genovese's finds that although slaves had easy access to cheap liquor, alcohol excess was less common among them than among the slaveholders, and that "the general sobriety of the slaves speaks well for their community strength and resistance to demoralization" (p. 644).

Some accounts indicate that once slavery ended, African Americans were anxious to test their newfound freedoms, including drinking alcohol at will (Gossett, 1988). As with Native Americans, whites tried to prevent African Americans from drinking, which they blamed for inciting problems such as violence and crime (Herd, 1985b). Herd's (1985b, 1989) analysis is that in

the nineteenth century, drunkenness and alcohol-related mortality among African Americans remained insignificant. The early U.S. Temperance movement was closely associated with the antislavery movement. Abstinence was thought to be important to freedom and equality, but African Americans withdrew from the Temperance movement when southern prohibitionists were joined by groups such as the Ku Klux Klan and adopted their racist attitudes (Herd, 1985a, 1985b). As African Americans migrated from the South to northern cities to seek employment and other opportunities, they became familiar with nightclubs, speakeasies, and other sources of alcohol. Bootlegging became a ready source of income, and alcohol abuse eventually became a problem. During the 1950s, cirrhosis among African Americans grew to epidemic proportions. Herd questions whether urbanization alone would have led to such high rates of alcohol-related problems among African Americans if the southern prohibitionists had not gone to such efforts to thwart black equality.

Today, blacks or African Americans are increasingly diverse in socioeconomic status, and they have origins in many countries (Africa, the West Indies, South and Central America, the Caribbean, etc.). Each area has a unique history, including that of alcohol and drug use. Even within the United States, African Americans' experiences vary based on the region of the country in which they reside, but some experiences—such as the knowledge of slavery and the direct effects of racism—are pervasive influences for virtually all African Americans (Ashley, 1999; Dozier, 1989; "Prevention of Alcohol Abuse," 1986–87).

Harper (1976) offers four explanations for contemporary drinking patterns among African Americans:

1. "The historical patterns of alcohol use and nonuse by Blacks have played a significant part in influencing their current drinking practices and their current attitudes toward drinking." Some African Americans drink

heavily on weekends after a hard week's work, reminiscent of the days when slaves were rewarded with alcohol and of the early days of freedom. Others, primarily women, do not drink at all, due to early prohibitions against African Americans' drinking and to religious beliefs, role expectations, and family responsibilities. Attitudes toward drinking practices continue to vary substantially among African Americans (Wallace, 1999).

2. "Many Blacks choose to drink because (a) liquor stores and liquor dealers are readily accessible and (b) Black peer groups often expect one to drink and at times to drink heavily." Drinking is highly visible in some communities. Among men, pressure to drink may be coupled with a lack of sanctions against chemical abuse. The location, number, and density of liquor stores and other establishments that sell alcoholic beverages is disproportionately high in African American communities; advertising is intense and often focuses on beverages that are large in size, high in alcohol content, and low in cost (Wallace, 1999; also see Kwate, 2009).

3. "Many Blacks, especially men, drink heavily due to the economic frustration of not being able to get a job or not being able to fulfill financial responsibilities." This chapter does not address the position of African American men in the United States or the relationships between African American men and women, but Harper and others (e.g., Reid, 2000) note that the inability to fulfill the role of breadwinner is particularly problematic for men. Drinking "is often tolerated as a stress reducer" (Dozier, 1989, p. 33).

4. "Numerous emotions and motivations influence heavy drinking among Black Americans in their attempt to escape unpleasant feelings or to fulfill psychological needs." The pain associated with the African American experience may be mitigated, at least temporarily, by alcohol use (see Bell, 1992; Williams, 2008, on cultural pain and anger).

The scholarly literature may be noteworthy for focusing more on individual and family pathology (risk and protective factors) associated with substance use disorders and less on macro-level or structural factors (Herd, 1987; Wallace, 1999). People of color disproportionately experience structural inequities (unemployment, discrimination, criminal justice involvement, etc.). Placing drinking in this structural or socioenvironmental context is important since stress and racism do not seem to explain why problems such as cirrhosis among African Americans increased after World War II (Herd, 1985a).

When 400 people in the Washington, DC, area were asked to visualize a drug user and a drug trafficker, most, including African Americans, pictured an African American individual (Watson & Jones, 1989) even though in absolute numbers and often by percentage of ethnic group, more drug users and drug traffickers are white (Burston, Jones, & Roberson-Saunders, 1995). The media reinforce these stereotypes, since crack and heroin addicts are often portrayed as being African American. Even so-called objective medical professionals may hold stereotypes. In encounters with cardiac patients, physicians rated black patients as more likely to abuse alcohol and drugs and lack social support, less educated and intelligent, and less likely to follow medical advice than white patients (van Ryn & Burke, 2000).

Substance Use and Related Problems among African Americans

In 2009, blacks, including blacks of mixed racial backgrounds, were nearly 14 percent of the U.S. population (U.S. Census Bureau, 2010b). The median income of single-race black households was approximately $17,000 less than the U.S. average. The poverty rate for blacks was nearly 26 percent compared to just over 14 percent for the U.S. population overall. In 2008, the school dropout rate for blacks aged 16 to 24 was nearly 10 percent, about twice that of whites (National Center for Education Statistics, 2010). African Americans' life expectancy has increased, but they experience poorer health and are less likely to receive needed services, including mental health services, than whites (Smedley, Stith, & Nelson, 2003). Reducing health disparities between ethnic groups is a major concern of the U.S. government's Healthy People initiative (also see Townsend & Belgrave, 2009).

Among the 10 leading causes of death for African Americans are cerebrovascular and respiratory diseases (which are often associated with smoking), as well as accidents (unintentional injuries), assault and homicide, and the human immunodeficiency virus (HIV) (which are often related to alcohol or drug use) (Heron, 2010). The picture for cirrhosis mortality has changed dramatically, though the reason is not clear. In 1968, African Americans' cirrhosis mortality rate was double that of white Americans (Singh & Hoyert, 2000). Today, the African American rate is lower than that of whites (Yoon & Yi, 2010). This change may seem less surprising if we consider that the National Comorbidity Survey-Replication (NCS-R) found that blacks were less likely to have had a lifetime substance use disorder than whites (Breslau et al., 2006). Among non-Hispanic blacks, nearly 11 percent had a *lifetime* substance use disorder compared to nearly 15 percent of whites (the rate for alcohol abuse or dependence was higher for whites than blacks; the rate for drug abuse or dependence was not statistically different between the two groups). The 2009 NSDUH found that blacks and whites had very similar rates of *past year* substance abuse and dependence; rates for Hispanics were also similar (see Table 11.1).

To determine if there are differences in substance use disorders among subgroups of the black population, Broman and colleagues (2008) compared African Americans and Caribbean blacks residing in the United States. The prevalence of substance abuse and dependence for African Americans (11.5 and 4.9, respectively) was not statistically different than the rates for Caribbean blacks (9.6 and 4.1, respectively). Substance use disorder rates for African Americans did exceed those for Caribbean blacks for

some subgroups: women, people aged 45 to 59, divorced individuals, those living in metropolitan areas, and first-generation Caribbean blacks. African American residents of the South had lower rates than Caribbean blacks, and African Americans had lower rates than second-generation Caribbean blacks. Consistent with other studies, the protective effects of immigrant status on substance use disorders seemed to weaken from first to second generation for Caribbean blacks.

Patterns of substance use may change over time. In 1984 and 1995, Black and Hispanic men were more likely to abstain from alcohol than white men, and black men's overall abstention rate increased from 29 percent in 1984 to 36 percent in 1995 with increased abstention in all age groups except for those in their forties (see Caetano & Clark, 1998; Herd, 1991). Frequent drinking declined in all groups of black men except those in their sixties. Black women and Hispanic women were also more likely to abstain from alcohol use than white women. Abstention rates for black women increased from 1984 and 1995 for all age groups except those in their forties. Black women's frequent heavy drinking rate remained the same.

Drugs, HIV/AIDS, and Criminal Justice System Involvement.   HIV/AIDS has devastated many African American communities. Though blacks are about 14 percent of the U.S. population, they account for nearly half of all new HIV infections from all transmission categories (Centers for Disease Control and Prevention, 2010a). By the end of 2008, among African American men living with HIV, 28 percent of cases were attributed to injection drug use (IDU) or a combination of having sex with a man and IDU (compared to 30 percent for Hispanics and 15 percent for whites) (Centers for Disease Control and Prevention, 2011). Among African American women, 24 percent of cases were attributed to IDU (compared to 29 percent for Hispanics and 33 percent for whites).

In 2009, the imprisonment rate of non-Hispanic black men was 3,119 per 100,000 U.S. residents—6 times higher than non-Hispanic white males and nearly 3 times higher than Hispanic males (West, Sabol, & Greenman, 2010). For a group that has rates of drug disorders that are no higher or less than whites, drug possession and drug trafficking take an inordinately high toll on blacks. For example, in 2008, blacks were 45 percent of all state prisoners sentenced for drug crimes, and among all sentenced blacks, 22 percent were sentenced for drug crimes.

A significant contributor to blacks' incarceration for drug crimes is the disparities in sentencing for crack versus powdered cocaine. It used to be that the first offense for possession of 5 grams of crack or 500 grams of powdered cocaine resulted in the same mandatory 5-year minimum penalty, a 100:1 ratio. Under the Fair Sentencing Act of 2010, the disparity in sentencing has been reduced to an 18:1 ratio with 28 grams of crack resulting in a 5-year sentence and 280 grams in a 10-year sentence. The law also eliminated the mandatory minimum sentence for simple crack possession. If the law were to be made retroactive, 85 percent of all federal prisoners affected would be black (United States Sentencing Commission, 2011).

African American Youth.   African American youth tend to start using alcohol and drugs later and use less often than white youth despite experiencing more stressors such as low income and poverty, neighborhood disorganization, and discrimination (Gibbons, Pomery, & Gerrard, 2010; also see Johnston, O'Malley, Bachman, & Schulenberg, 2011; SAMHSA, 2010a). The South Florida Youth Development Project followed a large number of males from youth into young adulthood at about age 20. Compared to non-Hispanic whites, fewer African Americans used alcohol in both life stages, and they developed fewer alcohol-related problems (Horton, 2007). The Pittsburgh Youth Study also found that by age 17, fewer blacks than whites used alcohol and hard drugs (Lee et al., 2010). This gap increased

over time, though the two groups did not differ in prevalence of marijuana use. One possible explanation for lower levels of alcohol use (and to a lesser extent, drug use) among African American youth is that many have a fundamentalist Protestant upbringing, which instructs against substance use (Harford, 1985), although Amey, Albrecht, and Miller (1996) found that being highly religious did not offer black youth as much protection against substance use as it did white youth.

Black youth are also more likely to grow up in a female-headed household, with greater exposure to female relatives who have high levels of abstention (Herd, 1990). Parker and associates (2000) found that among youth age 12 to 18, not having a father in the home predicted alcohol use in the last 30 days for Hispanic and white youth but not for black youth. Similarly, Amey and Albrecht's (1998) findings indicate that living in a single-parent household may protect black youth from using drugs, while the reverse is true for white youth. One interpretation of this finding is that black women heading households may receive more support from extended family than whites; thus, they encounter less stigma and garner more protection for their children.

In a study of approximately 300 African American school dropouts, "Positive family relationships and religiosity predicted a positive life orientation, which in turn predicted affiliations with conventional peers and avoidance of substance use" (Kogan, 2005, p. 389). Peer-related variables, such as friends' substance use, are the strongest predictors of substance use across ethnic groups. Comparing urban and suburban African American and Caucasian sixth graders in the Detroit area, Abbey et al. (2006) found that those who were more susceptible to peer pressure and had lower school commitment were more likely to use substances. In a study of nearly 7,500 African American youth in grades 7 to 12, less recent alcohol use was associated with good grades, school activity participation, church attendance, and parents and teachers who talked about alcohol's dangers and enforced rules (Vidourek & King, 2010). More use was associated with having friends who use alcohol and drugs, skipping school, and getting into other trouble. In a longitudinal study of 1,600 African American males from high school (at ages 14 to 16) to young adulthood (at ages 18 to 26), Stevens-Watkins and Rostosky (2010) suggest that while religiosity and family ties may be related to drinking, their effects may wane over time. In their study, it was close friends' perceived substance use that was significantly associated with binge drinking in high school and young adulthood.

Chemical Dependency Treatment for African Americans

Blacks may be less or no more likely to have substance use disorders than whites, but in 2009, they were 50 percent of those admitted for substance abuse treatment for smoked cocaine (crack) (Office of Applied Studies, 2010). They are also overrepresented among admissions for cocaine used through other routes, and marijuana, PCP, heroin, and hallucinogen use. Blacks are underrepresented among treatment for methamphetamine, sedative, tranquilizer, and inhalant abuse. They are most likely to be admitted for treatment of an alcohol, marijuana, or smoked cocaine problem. A study that focused on whites, African Americans, and black Caribbeans found that ethnicity was not related to delays in treatment admissions (Perron et al., 2009).

Research findings differ as to whether African Americans receive services equal in amount and quality to others and whether they fare as well in treatment. In a study of more than 13,000 individuals (18 percent were African American) admitted for substance abuse treatment in 43 programs in California, African Americans, whites, and Hispanics were compared on domains of alcohol, drug, and other problems upon entry (Niv, Pham, & Hser, 2009). African Americans had more severe employment problems. Consistent with the idea that services should be targeted to clients' specific problems (see Chapter 6), they received more employment

services. Treatment retention was similar across the groups, and African Americans had better or equal treatment outcomes in the various areas studied. Milligan, Nich, and Carroll (2004) reported on two clinical trials, one focused on treatment for cocaine dependence, the other on co-occurring cocaine and alcohol use disorders. Both trials used various treatment conditions involving cognitive behavioral therapy and the use of medications or placebos. African Americans and whites did not differ on cocaine use outcomes even though African Americans participated in fewer days of treatment.

Using a large nationally representative sample of Americans, and after controlling for demographic factors and severity of disorders, Keyes and colleagues (2008) found that blacks did not differ from whites on treatment for alcohol use disorders, though they were more likely to have received treatment for drug disorders. Marsh and colleagues (2009) found somewhat different results using data from 59 substance abuse treatment facilities that participated in the National Treatment Improvement Evaluation Study. African Americans and Latinos had higher levels of pre-treatment substance abuse but were less likely to have had previous substance abuse or mental treatment than whites. African Americans and Latinos stayed in treatment a shorter time and had fewer service needs met, but the amount of pre-treatment to post-treatment change was similar across groups. These researchers concluded that African Americans and Latinos received "fewer and lower quality services" though they had more serious substance abuse problems and fewer social and economic resources.

The Drug Abuse Warning Network (DAWN) reports emergency department (ED) visits in which illicit drug use and nonmedical use of prescription drugs are implicated, whether or not the drug use caused the visit. In 2007, approximately 1.9 million ED visits involved drug misuse or abuse. Blacks were patients in 32 percent of the ED visits involving illicit drug use (SAMHSA, 2010b). The vast majority of those incidents involved cocaine followed by marijuana and heroin use. Blacks were also overrepresented among visits involving drugs and alcohol combined (they were 22 percent of these visits). They were less likely to be involved in ED visits for nonmedical use of prescription drugs (12 percent of visits). Of nearly 140,000 ED visits of individuals seeking detoxification services, blacks were 23 percent.

Culturally Relevant Treatment. Various ethnic-specific approaches have been recommended to assist African American clients. Empowerment techniques to prevent societal victimization and to increase self-esteem (Solomon, 1976), bicultural counseling to help clients negotiate the majority culture while supporting the positives of their own culture (Beverly, 1975), and the "dual perspective" (a method for comparing clients' values and behaviors and those relevant to their immediate social systems with that of the larger society [Norton, 1978]) have all been suggested (Ziter, 1987). One definition of cultural competence is "a set of academic and interpersonal skills that allows individuals to increase their understanding and appreciation of cultural differences and similarities within, among, and between groups" (Springer et al., 2004). To assist African Americans, many authors emphasize a culturally competent strengths perspective that capitalizes on the positive attributes of clients and their significant others rather than "blaming the victim" by focusing on presumed weaknesses or deficiencies (Jackson, 1995; Reid, 2000; Wright, Kail, & Creecy, 1990).

An ecological systems perspective that includes a focus on relationships with family and other social systems to reinforce sobriety has also been recommended (Jackson, 1995; Wright et al., 1990). African Americans' extended family may include both blood and *social* relatives (such as close neighbors and friends who are referred to as "auntie" or "uncle"); these individuals can be sources of material as well as emotional support (Brisbane, 1998; Brown & Tooley, 1989; Reid, 2000). African American families are generally known as "spiritual, strong, supportive, and resilient," even in the face of adversity (Reid, 2000, p. 146), and these strengths should be a focus of

treatment. According to McGee and Johnson (1985), the so-called *superwoman myth* is very strong among African Americans, including the idea that women can endure inordinate amounts of pain when other family members are chemically dependent. Reid (2000) stresses the need to help African American women focus on their own needs in addition to those of other family members.

Feaster and colleagues (2010) studied the effects of Structural Ecosystems Therapy (SET) in preventing drug abuse relapse among African-American women who were HIV positive. SET builds on Nancy Boyd-Franklin's multisystem and culturally sensitive family therapy model developed in her practice with people of color. It is also an extension of Brief Strategic Family Therapy™ (see Szapocznik, Hervis, & Schwartz, 2003). Though SET did not specifically address substance abuse, a reduction in "family hassles" was associated with reduced relapse among the women participants.

Williams (2008) found substantial evidence of cultural pain and anger among African American men in treatment and distrust of majority-group counselors. In many treatment programs, race and racial or cultural pain are not well addressed because staff members do not want these issues to become an excuse for addiction. Staff generally encourage discussions of similarities rather than differences among clients and they often feel uncomfortable or inadequate in discussing these issues of ethnicity (Bell, 1992). Thus, this topic needs to be addressed in continuing staff education.

Perhaps the most widely discussed approach to assisting African Americans is the *Africentric* or *Afrocentric* approach (Asante, 1980, 1998), which is based on the seven principles of Kwanzaa. The principles, called *Nguzo Saba* (see Cherry et al., 1998), are unity, self-determination, collective work and responsibility, cooperative economics, purpose, creativity, and faith (Brown & John, 1999). The approach "enables people of African heritage to reassess, reclaim, recommit, remember, resurrect, and rejuvenate many of the principles used by their ancestors" (Moore, 2001, p. 29). Afrocentrism is also concerned with spirituality, eldership, and intergenerational connectedness (Brown & John, 1999).

The Healer Women Fighting Disease Integrated Substance Abuse and HIV Prevention Program is based on "culturecology," which posits that understanding African American culture is integral to behavior change. The African-Centered Behavioral Change Model attempts to bring about changes in behavior by using processes of resocialization and culturalization (Nobles, Goddard, & Gilbert, 2009). Techniques to accomplish this process are described as (1) cultural realignment with traditional African and African American values, (2) cognitive restructuring about how one thinks and feels, and (3) character refinement consistent with one's culture and well-being. Compared with women who received regular agency services, Healer Women participants made greater improvements on measures such as hopelessness and risky sexual behaviors. Roberts, Jackson, and Carlton-LaNey (2000) recommend combining black feminist theory and Afrocentric theory in serving African American women in drug treatment.

Rites of passage programs are also based on Afrocentric principles. They focus on initiation rituals that reinforce ethnic identity and allow for a healthy transition from youth to adulthood (Moore, 2001). Moore describes such a substance abuse treatment program for African American male adolescents. It combines an Afrocentric approach with *reality therapy* (Glasser, 1965) to help young people understand the immediate consequences of drug use, such as incarceration, for them and their families, and builds coping skills to deal with the world at hand.

Brinson (1995) recommends group work with black male adolescents to reduce isolation and increase connectedness. He utilizes closed groups of six to eight members that meet twice weekly during 50-minute sessions over a 12-week period. Members are encouraged to interact socially outside the group. Behaviors familiar to the youth, such as physical posturing, spontaneous participation during group sessions (rather than each person taking a turn), using cultural language, and wearing attire of their choice, are allowed or encouraged. Making direct eye contact is not demanded, since the belief is that members will do this once respect or trust has been established. Brinson considers these practices important to the youths' expression and identity formation. Many of these suggestions require that group leaders be versed in the cultural meanings of these elements. Male and female co-leaders are used for purposes of modeling appropriate male/female interactions for the young men. Other features are naming of the group, opening and closing rituals, lack of admonishment for coming late, democratic leadership style, and incorporation of each member's unique talents. A graduation ceremony, along with a certificate or plaque of recognition, is suggested as well.

Since alcohol and drug problems often present in the context of other needs, attempts are being made to apply evidence-based practices to treat co-occurring conditions. One approach being used with African American clients in residential substance abuse treatment is ACT HEALTHY. It combines two brief behavioral treatments—one to reduce depression and one to improve HIV medication adherence (Daughters et al., 2010).

Perhaps no institution in African American communities is as important as their churches (see, for example, Kogan et al., 2005). Churches serve as sources of spiritual strength, hope, and mutual aid and as outlets for expressing one's deepest emotions, including sadness and frustration (Moore, 2001; Prugh, 1986–87; Reid, 2000). The African Methodist Episcopal (AME) church has taken an active role in addressing alcoholism, including recognition of the disease concept (Prugh, 1986–87). Some churches have been resistant (McGee & Johnson, 1985), and may see substance abuse more as a sin than a disease (Bell, 1992). Developing relationships with church ministers, elders, and deacons and helping to educate them and other church members about chemical dependency are important steps in gaining allies in prevention and treatment. Appropriate messages from the pulpit are very important; education may be necessary to avoid moralistic explanations of alcohol and other drug abuse (Prugh) and to overcome ideas that accepting Jesus Christ and prayer are the only requirements for the faithful to address these problems. African Americans' religious diversity (Catholics, Muslims, etc.) should also be recognized.

Some African Americans consult spiritualists and other indigenous helpers (Prugh, 1986–87). Other individuals in the United States practice traditions such as voodoo and hoodoo (Huff, 1999). Using data from a national study, Snowden and Lieberman (1994) did not find that blacks used indigenous healers more than whites (whites were more likely than blacks to report seeking help from a religious figure). Based on a more recent national survey, Woodard and colleagues (2009) found somewhat different results. African Americans and black Caribbeans used prayer and other spiritual healing practices more than non-Hispanic whites for mood, anxiety, and substance use disorders. When use of all forms of complementary and alternative medicine (CAM) were combined, African Americans and black Caribbeans were no more likely to use CAM than non-Hispanic whites.

Physicians and other health care providers, the business community, civic groups, and fraternities and sororities, to which many African Americans belong, are also resources for addressing substance abuse. Barbers and beauticians in African American communities have been suggested as places for identifying problems and making referrals (Dozier, 1989; Wright et al., 1990). Educational films on substance abuse can be shown in these establishments.

Mutual-Help Groups. Mutual-help groups to address alcohol and drug problems have had an impact in the African American community, despite controversy about their

usefulness and sensitivity. Hudson (1985–86) traced the beginning of Alcoholics Anonymous use among African Americans to 1945 when Dr. Jim S., a black physician recovering from alcoholism, began a group in Washington, DC. According to Hudson's research, Dr. Jim's sobriety came when Ms. Ella G., a black woman and a friend of Dr. Jim's family, asked a white AA member to help him. Ms. Ella G. had learned about AA as a result of her church work and her brother's alcoholism. Alcoholics Anonymous received many requests for information from African Americans, and blacks in St. Louis, Greenwich Village, and Harlem formed other early groups. The AA office in New York, citing the policy that it would take no political stands, left it to local groups to address African Americans seeking help. Hudson defends this position as consistent with AA's view that the only requirement for membership is a desire to stop drinking. He believes that the Twelve Steps and Twelve Traditions provide the guidance necessary to help others in need, regardless of their ethnic background.

Hudson (1985–86) also rejected claims that AA is not effective with African Americans because it reflects primarily white, middle-class values and that it fails to address the deprivation and discrimination incurred by African Americans. He notes that AA has been successful in African American communities because its spiritual base is familiar, its fellowship is needed, and its traditional values appeal to members of most ethnic groups. Caldwell (1983) also believes AA is well suited to African Americans because it is consonant with the value they place on interpersonal relationships and also with their appreciation of language, metaphors, and imagery. However, Reid (2000) believes that some African Americans have difficulty with the vague way that God is defined in AA and that some may prefer treatment that is more biblically oriented.

Some individuals may need preparation to participate in mutual-help groups. For example, Harris-Hastick (2001) notes that individuals from the Caribbean closely guard their privacy. Explaining the process of Twelve-Step groups may be necessary before they will attend. Other more culturally consistent approaches should also be considered.

The question arises as to whether certain aspects of mutual-help groups, such as admitting one's powerlessness, might conflict with empowerment and strengths approaches and avoidance of the deficits perspective others recommend. Humphreys and Woods (1994) reject such concerns, noting that mutual-help organizations are democratic in nature and respect members as competent and intelligent. They also believe individuals can and should take personal responsibility for alcoholism and drug addiction, even when structural and political forces are at the root of many problems in African American communities.

Few studies of African Americans' mutual-help group participation have been conducted. Snowden and Lieberman (1994) found that only two percent of African Americans and eight percent of whites with a lifetime alcohol, drug, or mental disorder had ever used a mutual-help group. Humphreys and Woods (1994) studied 233 African Americans and 267 whites who had received alcoholism treatment. About one-third of both groups were attending Twelve-Step programs one year later. Among whites, the factor most predictive of Twelve-Step group attendance was having been treated in an inpatient program. For both groups, living in an area populated predominately by people of the same race and a longer length of stay in treatment predicted mutual-help group attendance. Several variables negatively affected white attendance, while the only factor that negatively affected African Americans' attendance was having greater psychological problems at intake. Criminal justice system involvement did not negatively affect African Americans' Twelve-Step group attendance as it did for whites. The authors suggest African American clients may view treatment rather than punishment as a relief. Living in a community of people of the same race was crudely measured, but since this variable made a strong showing in the findings, it may be that when individuals see more people like themselves at a mutual-help group meeting, they may be more likely to participate.

Prevention in African American Communities

An evaluation of prevention programs targeted at African American youth funded by SAMHSA's Center for Substance Abuse Prevention (CSAP) found that whether or not they were identified as Afrocentric, the effective ones seemed to share common "aspects of African-American experiences: values of the traditional African-American community, emphasis on extended community involvement, and emphasis on spirituality" (Gray, 1995, p. 92). CSAP also undertook a national cross-site evaluation that included 6,000 children who participated in these designated prevention programs and 4,500 youth who served as the comparison group. Youth were more satisfied with culturally specific programs and found them more meaningful than non-culturally specific ones (Springer et al., 2004). Among African Americans, the culturally specific programs also did better at preventing substance use, perhaps because they were more comprehensive, more structured, and linked cultural messages to factors that protect against substance use.

Instilling ethnic pride is as an important theme in prevention and treatment. Based on theories of behavior change, the Aban Aya Youth Project was designed as a culturally sensitive program to prevent several high risk behaviors, including substance use, among African American fifth to eighth graders (Benner, 2008). The project incorporates African American heritage; the influences of racism and stereotypes; and ethnic values, including Nguzo Saba principles. It was studied with 1,153 students in 12 schools where many of the students came from low-income households. Negative behaviors increased over time for both those in the control and experimental group, but boys in the experimental group experienced less increase in negative behaviors such as substance use (there were no significant effects for girls). Another example is NTU (pronounced "in-too"), a Bantu (Central African) word meaning "essence of life" (Cherry et al., 1998). The program originated in Washington, DC, for fifth- and sixth-grade students. Compared to those children who did not participate in NTU, a program evaluation indicated some positive effects on participants' racial identity and cultural knowledge but not on Afrocentric values (both intervention and comparison groups scored high on this factor). There were also some positive effects on variables like school interest, but drug outcomes did not differ between the groups. The children in both groups generally reported little drug use and had negative attitudes toward drugs.

Rites of passage programs emphasizing positive achievements are also being used in prevention programs (Gossett, 1988; Grant & White, 2007; Ringwalt, Graham, Sanders-Philips, Browne, & Paschall, 1999). The MATT Center for Human and Organizational Enhancement of Washington, DC, operates the Africentric Adolescent and Family Rites of Passage Program based on ecological, strengths-based, and Africentric approaches, including Nguzo Saba principles (Harvey & Hill, 2004). Another approach is the Safe Haven program, a modification of the well-known Strengthening Families program, which originated in Detroit to prevent substance abuse among children and to improve functioning in families in which one or both parents have substance use disorders (Aktan, 1999).

Churches have also been engaged in prevention. The Missouri Institute of Mental Health has teamed with African American churches in the St. Louis area using community-based participatory action research to develop several programs including Space Scouts, which uses media tools to help teach children about addiction science (Epstein et al., 2007).

Concern continues about alcohol advertising, such as billboards and magazine ads, directed to African Americans (Alaniz, 1998; Herd, 1987; see also Chapter 8). Rather than using African Americans to promote alcohol use, more emphasis is needed on African American role models who promote sobriety and recovery. Herd (1993) noted that messages about alcohol use in popular rap music and the hip-hop culture are inconsistent, although the anti-drug message is clearer. Broad strategies are needed that not only focus on substance abuse but also include "a large-scale ecological, environmental, systems-oriented approach" addressing social problems such as unemployment, failure to complete school ("Prevention of Alcohol Abuse," 1986–87), crime, health, and welfare (Grant & Moore, 1986/87). Gossett's (1988) advice, printed in a pamphlet by the Institute on Black Chemical Abuse, remains important:

> The black community must itself determine under what circumstances and at what times alcohol or other drug use is appropriate. Black people must set their own agenda on this issue. That means, for instance, formal and regulatory control on beverage control boards and zoning commissions that determine the hours, places, and location for alcohol sale. Community residents must challenge current zoning practices allowing a high density of liquor stores and advertisements in their neighborhoods. (p. 6)

Source: From "Alcohol and drug abuse in black America: A guide for community action" p. 6 (1988) by V. R. Gossett. Reprinted by permission of African American Family Services.

Substance Use and Abuse among Hispanic Americans

History and Background

The U.S. Hispanic population has grown rapidly. In 2009, more than 48 million people of Hispanic origin resided in the United States, constituting 16 percent of the population (U.S. Census Bureau, 2010c). Those of Mexican origin are 66 percent of the U.S. Hispanic population, followed by Puerto Ricans (9 percent), Cubans and Salvadorans (3.4 percent each), and Dominicans (2.8 percent). Others have origins in Central America, South America, and other countries. Most Hispanic Americans live in the West and South of the United States, particularly California and Texas. Florida and some northeastern cities also have high concentrations of Hispanics. An additional 4 million Hispanics live in the U.S. Commonwealth of Puerto Rico.

The terms *Hispanic* and *Latino/Latina* are often used interchangeably to include all people whose origins can be traced to a Spanish-speaking country, with Hispanic used often in Texas, and Latino/Latina used often in California (Suarez & Ramirez, 1999). Even the term *Hispanic*, which a Mexican American woman coined when she worked for U.S. government ("Outspoken . . . '" 2009), remains controversial (Flores, 2000; Freeman, Lewis, & Colon, 2002; Miranda, 2005). Hispanics or Latinos/Latinas also have various preferences for identifying their ethnic subgroup. A term acceptable to one individual may be offensive to another.

Hispanics are "bound by a common ancestral language and cultural history," but they "vastly differ in immigration history and settlement in the United States" (Suarez & Ramirez, 1999, p. 115). Many Hispanics are from families that have resided in the United States for generations, such as those who remained after the annexing of foreign territories. Others have escaped war, other violence, and/or extreme poverty in countries such as El Salvador, Nicaragua, Honduras, Columbia, and Mexico. Some have come in various waves from Cuba, fleeing the totalitarian regime of Fidel Castro, and sometimes risking life and limb to do so. Given the shared U.S./Mexico border, many people cross back and forth, living life in two cultures simultaneously and effectively creating a third culture. McQuade (1989) notes that "there is no typical 'Hispanic.' Representing combinations of European, African and Native American blood, each of these racial and national backgrounds influence a particular temperament and pre-disposition towards the use of alcohol and drugs" (p. 29).

Hispanics in the United States have been subject to violence, discrimination, segregation, and denied basic civil rights (Denton & Massey, 1989; Menchaca, 1993). The Treaty of Guadalupe Hidalgo of 1848 ended the Mexican-American war and granted all Mexicans residing in the annexed territory full citizenship. When the time came to honor the treaty, the United States labeled many Mexicans as Mexican Indians and denied them full rights, resulting in the loss of property, deportation, and other injustices (see, for example, Menchaca, 1993). The Jones Act of 1917 made Puerto Ricans U.S. citizens, but the U.S. government could veto any law the Puerto Rican Congress enacted (Figueroa, 2010). The U.S. Supreme Court did not recognize Hispanics' right to desegregated schools until 1973 (Prins, 2007). The Jim Crow era reinforced racial segregation of Hispanics and forced many into agricultural labor or debt servitude (Valadez, 2001). Among Hispanic immigrants, individuals coming from Cuba have received preferential immigration treatment.

In Latin America, alcohol and other substances have been used for religious or healing purposes for centuries. Alcohol use for medicinal purposes and as a remedy for sadness can be traced to Aztec times with the making of mescal (tequila is a form of mescal) (Villalobos, 2005). Acceptance of alcohol as a remedy is reflected in cultural *dichos* (sayings, metaphors, or proverbs) such as *para todo mal, mescal, y para todo bien tambien* (for all ailments, mescal, and for all good also), or *para el catarro: jarro, pero si es con tos: dos* (for a cold: a drink, but if you cough: two) (Burciaga, 1997). In the Caribbean, South America, and Mexico, there is documentation of substance use to induce religious visions and attain higher states of awareness (Valadez, 2003; Garcia-Goyco, 2007). Colonization caused many to shun the use of substances for religious purposes, but it also brought new patterns and habits of use (Valadez). Drinking is a common practice among Hispanics in the United States, but other drug use tends to be highly stigmatized (Hernandez, 2000).

As a group, the median income of the U.S. Hispanic population is considerably lower than that of non-Hispanic whites (U.S. Census Bureau, 2010c). This economic situation reflects factors such as the Hispanic population's younger average age compared to the general U.S. population and lower overall educational attainment (U.S. Census Bureau). Hispanics have greater risks for some diseases such as diabetes, but there is also a Hispanic health paradox. For example, Hispanics have a much lower infant mortality rate and a much longer life expectancy than non-Hispanic blacks despite similar poverty rates and a much lower rate of health insurance (see Centers for Disease Control and Prevention, 2010b). Although the exact reason for the Hispanic paradox is not known, some theories are that it may be related to health benefits associated with immigration status (for example, some immigrant groups such as Latinos may drink or smoke less) or to factors such as family ties and social support (Acevedo-Garcia & Bates, 2007).

Acculturation and Acculturative Stress. Acculturation has received considerable attention in the literature on alcohol and other drug use among Hispanics. One understanding of the term acculturation is that it means "assimilation into the dominant culture"; though Gutmann (1999) notes,

> "Attitudes toward drinking and actual drinking behavior do not simply reflect what people 'left behind' versus what they 'find.' ... Ethnic identity can also intensify following migration, and as part of the process alcohol use and abuse can undoubtedly change in ways not well described by simplistic acculturation theories" (p. 182).

For example, the National Latino and Hispanic Survey shows that Latino or Hispanic immigrants have a consistently lower rate of lifetime substance use disorders than those of Hispanic origin who are born in the United States (Canino, Vega, Sribney, Warner, & Alegria, 2008). Hispanic youth's drug use is also associated with greater acculturation to U.S. norms, more years in the United States, and more family generations in the United States (National Institute on Drug Abuse, 2004).

The literature is concerned not only about acculturation but also about acculturative stress, since it cannot automatically be assumed that acculturation results in stress or that stress leads to increased drinking (Caetano, 1994). Immigration stressors may vary depending on the reason for immigration (political, poverty, etc.), the financial and other human capital resources bring with them (such as education), whether immigrants are coming with or to join family, and the help they receive when entering (Caetano, Ramisetty-Mikler, & Rodriguez, 2009). These factors may affect alcohol and drug use, as may cultural values, but these topics have not been well studied.

Cultural Beliefs. Fatalism, which may be defined as "the belief that an individual has little control over personal health outcomes, is a common theme in Hispanic attitudes" (Suarez & Ramirez, 1999, p. 121). Comas-Diaz (1986) discusses Puerto Rican "folk beliefs encouraging externalization, passivity and fatalism regarding the problem of drinking" (p. 51), with alcoholism among Puerto Ricans sometimes thought to be caused by bad spirits, thus reinforcing denial of these problems. Some authors take exception to the idea that denial of substance abuse problems among Hispanics is especially strong. Gonzalez-Ramos (1990), for example, has called resistance to services by Hispanics a myth.

Rather than an illness, Hispanics may view substance use disorders as a moral weakness and rely on God or divine intervention for remediation, rather than professional help and active problem solving (Aguilar, DiNitto, Franklin, & Lopez-Pilkinton, 1991; Alvarez & Ruiz, 2001; McQuade, 1989). However, when a study of a sizable number of Hispanic and non-Hispanic respondents who "had never tried any illicit drug and were not willing to use if they had the opportunity" were asked why they felt this way, health concerns were by far the most frequently endorsed reason among the two groups (Farabee, Wallisch, & Maxwell, 1995).

Hispanic cultures also heavily influence gender norms related to drinking. Men may drink freely, although they are expected to hold their liquor (Barón, 2000). Heavy drinking may be an acceptable practice among men, and it may even be justified as part of *machismo*, although there is confusion about the meaning of this term. *Machismo* has been used to mean male virility, but it has also been used to mean honor, respect, and fulfilling family obligations (Gordon, 1989).

There is a notion that if a man "works hard and is a good family provider one then has the 'right' to drink without criticism from others" (Caetano et al., 1998, p. 234). Public disclosure of personal problems is generally unacceptable for Hispanic men and can result in feelings of emasculation and powerlessness (Figueroa & Oliver-Diaz, 1986–87). As a result, men may excuse their heavy drinking, and women may also deny that men drink excessively. A woman may take a passive role, viewing her partner's substance abuse as a behavior to be tolerated rather than changed; she may suffer in silence and not dare to seek outside help when her spouse's drinking becomes problematic (Aguilar et al., 1991; Hernandez, 2000; McQuade, 1989). Gordon (1989), however, denies any empirical support for the "widely accepted popular belief that Hispanic drinking is characterized by macho, aggressive drinking (more so than in other ethnic groups)" (p. 141). Hispanic women's relatively low rate of alcohol problems may be related to the cultural value of *marianismo*, that women should be self-sacrificing and emulate the Virgin Mary (Santiago-Rivera et al., 2002). The strongly held belief among many Hispanics that women should not drink much or exhibit substance abuse problems may prompt families to deny the possibility of chemical abuse among their female members.

Substance Use Disorders and Related Problems among Hispanic Americans

As Table 11.1 shows, the National Survey on Drug Use and Health (NSDUH) indicates that compared to the other major ethnic groups in the United States, Hispanics are less likely than all but Asians to use tobacco or illicit drugs. They are also less likely to use alcohol than whites but are similar to whites in the percent who binge drink. The NSDUH indicates that Hispanics slightly exceed whites and blacks in the percent who meet criteria for a substance use disorder, though the National Comorbidity Survey Replication found no statistically significant difference in rates of alcohol or drug use disorders between Hispanics and non-Hispanic whites (Breslau et al., 2006).

Over time, patterns of drinking among U.S. Hispanics have changed (Caetano & Clark, 1998). For example, from 1984 to 1995, frequent drinking generally declined for Hispanic men, especially for those in their twenties. Among U.S. Hispanic women, their already high rates of abstention increased for all age groups except for those in the 60 and older age group. Frequent heavy drinking, which is relatively rare for Hispanic women, decreased or remained the same for all age groups except for an increase among women aged 18 to 29.

Substance Use Disorders among Hispanic Subgroups.   Lumping all Hispanics together distorts substantial differences among the various Hispanic subgroups and between men and women in these subgroups. Table 11.2 reports data from the 2006 Hispanic American Baseline Alcohol Survey (HABLAS), which included 5,224 Hispanics selected from five U.S. major metropolitan areas. Among men, Cuban Americans had lower rates of alcohol abuse and dependence. Mexican American and Puerto Rican men had the highest rates of alcohol dependence their rates of dependence also exceed those for men in the general U.S. population. Alcohol dependence among Hispanic men does not decline as steeply with age as it does for men in the general population; this is especially true for Puerto Rican and Mexican American men (Caetano, Ramisetty-Mikler, & Rodriquez, 2008).

As in the general U.S. population, substance use disorders are less frequent among women than men (see Table 11.2). Alcohol abuse is low among all groups of Hispanic women. Alcohol dependence is highest among Puerto Rican women. Variation also occurs by age group. One anomaly in rates occurs for Cuban American women in the 18–29 age group; their abuse rate is 6.5 percent, higher than for all other subgroups of Hispanic women regardless of age (Caetano et al., 2008).

TABLE 11.2   Percent of Alcohol Abuse and Dependence among Hispanic Subgroups Aged 18 and Older by Gender, 2006 Hispanic Americans Baseline Alcohol Survey

	Men		*Women*	
	Abuse	Dependence	Abuse	Dependence
Mexican American	5.6%	15.1%	0.8%	2.1%
Puerto Rican	5.2%	15.3%	0.7%	6.4%
South/Central American	4.2%	9.0%	0.2%	0.8%
Cuban American	1.8%	5.3%	1.1%	1.6%

Source: Based on Caetano, R., Ramisetty-Mikler, S., & Rodriguez, L. (2008). The Hispanic Americans Baseline Alcohol Survey (HABLAS): Rates and predictors of alcohol abuse and dependence across Hispanic national groups. *Journal of Studies on Alcohol and Drugs*, vol. 69, #3, 441–448.

HABLAS data show that among Hispanic subgroups, those who are younger and more highly acculturated are at greater risk for alcohol abuse (Caetano, Ramisetty-Mikler, & Rodriquez, 2008, 2009). Risk factors for alcohol dependence include having less than a college education and being born in the United States. For both abuse and dependence, being male and earlier initiation of drinking are also prime risk factors. These risk factors are similar to those for individuals in the general U.S. population. Canino et al. (2008) also found that rates of substance use disorders are higher among Hispanics who speak English rather than Spanish with most of their family (often considered a measure of acculturation). Problematic family relationships were also related to substance use disorders.

Health and Social Consequences.   Death rates from chronic liver disease and cirrhosis have decreased for all race and ethnic groups but Hispanics' rate is the highest among the largest ethnic groups. In 2007, the age-adjusted alcohol-related cirrhosis death rate for Hispanic white men was 12.6 percent, nearly twice that of non-Hispanic white men (6.5 percent) and more than twice that of non-Hispanic black men (5.6) (Yoon & Yi, 2010). Among Hispanic subgroups, from 2003 to 2007, Mexican men had the highest rate followed by Puerto Ricans and other Hispanics, while Cuban

men's rate is substantially lower. The 2007 rate for all Hispanic women is much lower than the rate for Hispanic men. Mexican American women have the highest rate and Cuban women the lowest.

Using HABLAS data, Vaeth and colleagues (2009) found that as expected, men reported more alcohol-related problems (i.e., dependence symptoms such as increased tolerance, and social consequences such as problems with police, spouse, or others) than women. Mexican American men and women were most likely to report two or more problems; South/Central American men were more likely to report one problem. Cubans were least likely to report problems. Among men, Puerto Ricans and Mexican Americans reported the most dependence symptoms. Regarding social consequences, Puerto Rican men were most likely to report belligerence and Mexican Americans were most likely to report financial problems. Among women, Puerto Ricans were most likely to report dependence symptoms, social consequences, and problems with spouse.

Hispanic Youth.   In comparing Hispanic, white, and African American youth, Monitoring the Future, which samples students in school, finds that:

Hispanic students have rates of use that tend to fall between the other two groups in 12th grade—usually closer to the rates for Whites than for

African Americans. Hispanics do have the highest reported rates of use for some drugs in 12th grade—crack, methamphetamine, and crystal methamphetamine. In 8th grade, they tend to come out highest of the three racial/ethnic groups on nearly all classes of drugs (amphetamines being the major exception). One possible explanation for this change in ranking between 8th and 12th grade may lie in the considerably higher school dropout rates of Hispanic youth: more of the drug-prone segment of that ethnic group may leave school before 12th grade compared to the other two racial/ethnic groups. Another explanation could be that Hispanics are more precocious in their initiation of these types of behaviors. (Johnston, O'Malley, Bachman, & Schulenberg, p. 45)

Using Monitoring the Future data from 1991–2002, Delva et al. (2005) compared approximately 24,000 Mexican American, Puerto Rican, Cuban American, and other Latin American heritage eighth grade students. Males were more likely to report any drug use. Marijuana use was much more likely among Mexican American and Puerto Rican boys than girls, while Cuban boys and girls had similar rates of use. Cocaine use and heavy drinking did not differ by gender for any of the Hispanic subgroups. Speaking Spanish as a first language reduced the likelihood of heavy drinking and marijuana use among Mexican American youth but not among Puerto Rican and Cuban youth. Living in a household with no parents present (e.g., with other relatives or in foster care) was the most consistent predictor of heavy drinking and drug use across groups, and Puerto Rican youth were more likely to live with someone other than their parents.

Using data from the National Longitudinal Study of Adolescent Health, Wahl and Eitle (2010) found that generally speaking, first generation Hispanic adolescents are less likely to use alcohol and binge drink than their second or later generation counterparts and non-Hispanic whites. As might be expected, better grades and family relations protected against alcohol use and binge drinking for Hispanic youth of both genders. Being bilingual also protected against

alcohol use for girls. After controlling for other factors, being raised in a single-parent family and parents' education did not predict alcohol use or binge drinking. As in earlier studies, Lopez et al. (2009) and Prado et al. (2009) find that Hispanic youths' reports of their friends' substance use is closely related to reports of their own substance use. While similarities across ethnic groups and ethnic subgroups suggest common areas for preventing substance use, differences in alcohol and drug use and predictors of these behaviors among ethnic groups and subgroups and by gender also suggest the need for targeted prevention efforts.

Since Hispanic youth have higher school dropout rates than youth in other groups, they are less likely to be included in school-based surveys. The National Survey on Drug Use and Health (NSDUH) includes non-institutionalized youth whether or not they are in school. In 2007, Hispanic youth aged 12 to 17 were similar to white youth in ever having used alcohol (SAMHSA, 2008). Despite some variation in those who used various types of illicit drugs, the percent of Hispanic, black, and white youth who used any type of illicit drug was similar. For those aged 18 to 25, the pattern was somewhat different; Hispanic youth were less likely than whites to use alcohol or to have tried an illicit drug and more like blacks in the percentage who had ever tried these substances. Parker and associates (2000) used data from the precursor study to the NSDUH—which also included youth aged 12 to 18, whether or not they were in school—and found similar predictors of greater frequency or intensity of alcohol use across ethnic groups, such as being older, being male, and not being in school. Coming from a higher-income family predicted drinking by Hispanic youth but not by black or white youth.

Treatment Services for Hispanic Americans

The assumption has been that Hispanic Americans underutilize alcoholism treatment services. Studies indicate that Hispanics who get help tend to utilize AA heavily, while they use specialty alcoholism services less often than whites (Schmidt, Ye, Greenfiled, & Bond, 2007; Zemore, Mulia, Ye, Borges, & Greenfield, 2009). Similar factors predict substance abuse treatment utilization among Hispanics and other ethnic groups, such as having mental health problems and criminal justice system involvement (Cohen, Feinn, Arias, & Kranzler, 2007; Lundgren, Amaro, & Ben-Ami, 2005). Using three waves of U.S. National Alcohol Surveys, Zemore et al., found that the common predictors of whether Hispanics received any type of alcoholism treatment services, attended AA, or received institutional treatment were social pressures, legal consequences, or greater alcohol dependence symptoms, and whether they chose to be interviewed in English (rather than Spanish). Those with less than a high school education and those aged 30 to 49 were more likely than those aged 18 to 29 to have received any service and to have attended AA. Those with public insurance versus no insurance were more likely to have received institutional treatment. Studies also indicate that more highly acculturated Hispanics are more likely to use treatment services (Zemore et al., 2009; Borges, Greenfield, Mulia, Ye, & Zemore, 2009). Lesser-acculturated individuals identified both the lack of language appropriate services and professionals' lack of understanding of their unique situation as major barriers to accessing services.

In 2007, of those patients whose ethnicity was known, Hispanics made up 13 percent of emergency department (ED) visits involving illicit drugs (SAMHSA, 2010b). Half of all these visits involved cocaine use followed by marijuana (29 percent) and heroin (27 percent) (visits may involve more than one drug). Nine percent of visits involved a suicide attempt, and in 8 percent of visits, the patient was seeking detoxification services. In 2008, Hispanics were nearly 14 percent of all clients admitted to substance abuse treatment programs (Office of Applied Studies, 2010). Hispanic Americans are somewhat underrepresented in ED and treatment services compared to their representation in the general population.

Of all Hispanics admitted to substance abuse treatment, slightly more (23 percent) were admitted for heroin or other opiate use disorder compared to an alcohol use disorder only (21 percent), followed by marijuana (19 percent) (Office of Applied Studies, 2010). Admissions vary by ethnic subgroup and gender. Mexican-origin men are most likely to be admitted for an alcohol problem only followed by marijuana. Mexican-origin females are most likely to be admitted for methamphetamine disorder. Puerto Rican men and women are most likely to be admitted for heroin or other opiate use disorders.

Efforts to develop culturally relevant education, prevention, and treatment services for Hispanics include utilizing staff that reflect the community's ethnic composition and providing services in Spanish as well as English (see, for example, De La Rosa, Holleran, Rugh, & MacMaster, 2005; Santiago-Rivera, 1995). For those whose first language is Spanish, their "native tongue is needed to express the deepest feelings and longings endemic to the recovery process" (McQuade, 1989, p. 30). Santiago-Rivera's (1995) review of language importance in counseling Spanish-speaking clients suggests considering whether the client prefers to use Spanish at some times and English at others, which may depend on the nature of the material being discussed. In working with families, some members may prefer to use Spanish while others may prefer English (Sciarra & Ponterotto,1991). Dichos, such as *Dime con quién andas y te diré quién eres* (Tell me who your friends are and I will tell you who you are)," can be useful in illustrating points in prevention and treatment (Zuniga, 1991).

Familial factors must be considered in service delivery (De La Rosa et al., 2005). Given the values of *familismo* (strong family orientation) and *confianza* (interdependence and trust), family members may need to be seen together rather than individually (Aguilar et al., 1991; Comas-Diaz, 1986; Melus, 1980; Santiago-Rivera et al., 2002). Traditional chemical dependency treatment programs have stressed getting into treatment for one's own self, but other approaches might be more success-ful with Hispanic clients. Melus (1980) recom-mends appealing to Hispanics to enter treatment because family unity is being threatened, and Gilbert (1987) recommends appealing to chemi-cally dependent Hispanic mothers to improve the lives of their children. For both men and women, a key to motivating them to receive chemical de-pendency treatment is to help them see it as a way to fulfill family responsibilities (Barón, 2000). Cas-tro and colleagues (1999) recommend develop-ing systems of social support using appeals such as "*Ayundale, por que es tu hermano(a)*" ("Help him because he is your brother" or "Help her because she is your sister") (pp. 158–159). The concept of fatalism can also be used effectively in treat-ment by conveying to the client "You are here for a reason. You were meant to be helped" (Alvarez & Ruiz, 2001, p. 124).

Among Hispanics, *respeto* "is an extremely important factor in all relationships and especially in HPDP (health promotion and disease preven-tion) encounters" (Huff & Kline, 1999, p. 190). According to Barón (2000), *respeto* "denotes ele-ments of emotional dependence and dutifulness" and "indirect, implicit, or covert communication is consonant with…family harmony, on getting along and not making others uncomfortable; as-sertiveness, openly expressing differences of opin-ion, and demanding clarification are seen as rude or insensitive to others' feelings" (p. 237). *Person-alismo* generally denotes the desire to have a warm or supportive relationship with professionals. Mo-tivational interviewing techniques (see Chapter 6) may be more effective in engaging Hispanic clients in treatment than more direct or confrontational approaches (Barón, 2000). Clients may indicate agreement as a means of maintaining harmony. Rather than express an opinion they feel may alienate the therapist, Hispanics may choose not to comply or fail to follow through with treatment recommendations (Medina, 2001). But in work-ing with Puerto Ricans, Hernandez (2000) sug-gests being directive and using "a concrete plan of action" (p. 276), and Rothe and Ruiz (2001) note

that Cubans may prefer "concrete and practical solutions to their problems" rather than "long-term psychotherapies" (p. 106).

Advice about how to use social services (Comas-Diaz, 1986) and client advocacy (Melus, 1980) may also increase service utilization. Con-crete services, such as transportation to appoint-ments, can be especially important for low-income individuals from all ethnic groups (Aguilar et al., 1991; Comas-Diaz 1986). Huff and Kline (1999) emphasize the importance of removing obstacles to treatment, such as simplifying application pro-cesses, bringing services to the target population, offering the services in the target population's preferred language, and making the services rel-evant and easy to understand. They also suggest using unconventional sites for offering services. For example, Delgado (1998) suggests employing beauty parlors in Latino communities to assist in addressing alcohol problems.

Other recommendations are to target services or tailor intervention to each Hispanic subgroup as well as to age group (Caetano, 1988; De La Rosa et al., 2005). Gender norms should also be consid-ered. For example, the male is generally the head of the family, and in treatment sessions, care should be taken not to threaten his position of authority in the presence of other family members. Agui-lar and colleagues (1991) suggest using psycho-educational groups with Hispanics, particularly women, to address chemical dependency and codependency. The groups they describe are for adult family members. They are open to men and women, making them less suspect than women-only groups, which men may perceive as a threat to family cohesion. Education, group discussion, experiential exercises, and "homework" are used to educate members about chemical dependency.

Melus (1980) recommends "more sensitive and cautious" treatment approaches when His-panic women have been subject to physical or ver-bal abuse from their families. Comas-Diaz (1986) describes a group treatment approach with Puerto Rican women who are alcoholics based on literature that suggests they may feel isolated and alienated and on literature that recommends women-only groups as a forum for expressing anger and other feelings that cannot be vented directly toward family members. However, she notes that the women enrolled in the group did not attend sessions regularly and had difficulty maintaining abstinence.

Many Hispanics are Catholic, and often the first person outside the family to whom they turn for help with a problem is a priest or a nun. The clergy's support of chemical dependency treatment may facilitate recovery, as might holding mutual-help group meetings at churches. The spiritual aspects of recovery for Hispanic substance abusers and their family members must also be addressed. Hispanic women are encouraged to emulate the Virgin Mary through self-sacrifice and acceptance of suffering, but this can cause them to neglect their own well-being. With careful reframing, Mary can be discussed in a more feminist light that emphasizes her strengths and independent characteristics (Aguilar et al., 1991).

Hernandez (2000) describes several ways to incorporate spirituality in treatment by including clergy in treatment sessions, encouraging clients' religious participation, incorporating spiritual recovery as part of the overall recovery process, and "helping the family to embrace once again values that were abandoned because they were defined as old fashioned and dystonic with the new environment" (p. 281). Membership in Protestant, Pentacostal, and fundamentalist churches has grown in Hispanic communities, and some of these churches and religiously oriented groups have developed their own alcohol recovery programs (Delgado & Rosati, 2005; Figueroa & Oliver-Diaz, 1986–87; Gordon, 1991; Shorkey, Garcia, & Windsor, 2010). There has also been a mixing of Catholicism and indigenous spiritual and healing practices (Shorkey et al.). In some Hispanic cultures, folk healing practices may be combined with praying to saints (Barón, 2000).

Data on the use and effectiveness of indigenous folk healers such as *curanderas* or *curanderos* are lacking, but Hispanics may consult them about alcohol, drug, or other problems (Trotter & Chavira, cited in Gilbert & Cervantes, 1987; Shorkey et al., 2010). In fact, "traditional folk healers often are the first health practitioners consulted because they are culturally acceptable, willing to make house calls, and far less expensive than the Western health care system" (Huff & Kline, 1999, p. 192). Other indigenous recovery models are based on spiritual systems that date back to the Native American and African roots of many Latin American subcultures. These traditions incorporate a long cultural history of attempting to help people with alcohol problems through a combination of applying herbal medicine, enlisting the aid of spirits, and faith healing (Figueroa & Oliver-Diaz, 1986–87).

In a study of heavy drinking and smoking, 19 percent of the nearly 1,500 Hispanic participants reported experiences of discrimination (Borrell et al., 2010). Discrimination was related to heavy drinking but not to smoking. Hernandez (2000) recommends direct discussions of racism and oppression with clients and encouraging them to become politically active as a means of gaining a sense of control.

Although many AA groups in the United States are conducted in Spanish, little has been written about Hispanics' mutual-help group use. One study, based on data from Project MATCH (see Chapter 6), found that Hispanic and non-Hispanic clients expressed similar commitment to AA but Hispanics attended AA less often (Tonigan et al., 2002). Hernandez (2000) suggests that the spiritual nature of many mutual-help groups can be comforting to those of Hispanic origin. Aguilar and colleagues (1991) recommend preparation to participate in groups such as Alcoholics Anonymous and Al-Anon, particularly when there are few other Hispanic members. "Working the steps" of these programs can be described as taking on responsibilities and as a means of gaining respect for one's self and from others. Depending on the client, referrals to a Hispanic group may be preferable, or if one is not available, a referral can be made to a group in which participants are of diverse ethnic backgrounds (Hernandez, 2000).

Prevention Services in Hispanic Communities

Melus (1980) believes that "attitudes and perceptions must be changed in the community to make treatment and prevention of alcoholism more successful" (p. 20). An important aspect of prevention for many Hispanics is *la comunidad* (community), since many "Hispanics tend to live together, work together, and spend free time together" (Melus, p. 20; also see Comas-Diaz, 1986). The community should be involved in all aspects of prevention programming (Huff & Kline, 1999). Celebrations, or fiestas, are important in many Hispanic communities, and the use of alcohol during these occasions is common. McQuade (1989) describes fiestas as "compensation for life's suffering" (p. 30). Fiestas without the use of alcohol have been incorporated into efforts to prevent and treat alcohol use disorders among Hispanics (Aguilar et al., 1991; Comas-Diaz, 1986; McQuade, 1989). Delgado (1999) equates prevention with community development, and he emphasizes a strengths-based approach that capitalizes on community resources.

Contact with gatekeepers in ethnic, social, civic, religious, neighborhood, and church organizations, as well as parent/teacher associations and other community groups, is recommended if prevention efforts are to be successful in Hispanic American communities (Caetano, 1988). Preventing school dropout is critical (Alvarez & Ruiz, 2001). Gordon (1991) emphasizes that community health centers and clinics are important points of identification of substance abuse problems, especially for Hispanic women and children. The key is in developing relationships with those in the target community and learning about the cultural norms that guide their work. Mutual education, in which professionals learn about the community from its leaders and residents and in turn educate community leaders and groups about the dynamics of alcohol and other drug problems, is a necessary step in initiating all types of chemical dependency services (Caetano, 1988).

Various approaches have been used to reach out to children of alcoholics in Hispanic communities. *Tardes infantil* (afternoons for children) have been used to educate children about alcohol abuse by incorporating painting, movies, and dramatizations to help them express their feelings about family issues (Melus, 1980). Another program for Mexican American children has used puppets, including an *abuelita* (grandmother) puppet, because of the importance of the grandmother in Mexican American life (Rodriguez-Andrew, 1984).

The Center for Substance Abuse Prevention identifies Keepin' it REAL (kiR) as a model program. It is a ten-session culturally grounded drug prevention curriculum for children in grades 6 to 9. Evidence indicates that the program is effective in promoting anti-drug attitudes and beliefs and reducing drug use. REAL stands for Refuse, Explain, Avoid, and Leave. The program teaches children to refuse drugs and builds drug resistance strategies by enhancing decision-making and communication skills. A program component is videos developed by youth. Evidence indicates that kiR is more effective with more- rather than less-acculturated Latinos, perhaps because the less acculturated are at less risk for substance use (Marsiglia, Kulis, Wagstaff, Elek, & Dran, 2005). In tests of three versions of kiR—one geared to Latino (particularly Mexican American) culture, one to European American and African American culture, and a multicultural version—students receiving the multicultural version reported less substance use, including less alcohol and marijuana use (Kulis et al., 2005).

Crunkilton, Paz, and Boyle (2005) developed a culturally specific intervention for Hispanic families with children at risk for substance abuse incorporating language, beliefs, values, and principles to improve family functioning and increase drug knowledge. The culturally focused family intervention, which included a component for youth, was tested with a nonprobability sample of 49 Hispanic and non-Hispanic families in the rural southwest United States. No difference was indicated in pretest and posttest family functioning, but drug knowledge increased.

Prevention efforts should also target adults. An emphasis on responsible drinking, especially among men, may be accomplished through use of Spanish-language media (newspapers, magazines, TV, community newsletters, and *fotonovelas* [illustrated stories]) to prevent alcohol and drug abuse and to promote recovery (Caetano, 1988). The National Highway Traffic Safety Administration and National Latino Council on Alcohol and Tobacco Prevention Conference (2007) reported on five major projects that tested the effectiveness of strategic law enforcement efforts and culturally sensitive community education and outreach activities to reduce driving under the influence (DUI) in Hispanic communities. The culturally sensitive projects were You Drink & Drive. You Lose, *Pasa Las Llaves* (Pass the Keys), *Antes de Manejar Borracho* (Before you Drive Drunk Project), *Madrinas and Padrinos Project,* and *Promotoras.* Education alone was insufficient to reduce DUI, requiring the addition of culturally sensitive efforts. Recommendations included incorporating a focus on the family and social responsibility to others before self, especially for males. Mediums such as *promotoras* (community members trained to provide outreach to members of an ethnic minority that is otherwise difficult to reach) and *telenovelas* (a drama or story acted out on television, for example) that reflect ethnic community ideals also seem to be effective methods of reaching the community. Given the growth of the Hispanic population in the United States, it is likely that considerably more attention will be devoted to their integration into U.S. society, including the prevention and treatment of alcohol and other drug problems.

Substance Use and Abuse among Asian and Pacific Islander Americans

History and Background

A U.S. Census Bureau report lists 24 separate Asian subgroups in the United States (Barnes & Bennett, 2002). People of Asian descent now comprise 5 percent (16 million) of the U.S. population

(U.S. Census Bureau, 2011). The largest subgroup is of Chinese origin (3.8 million), followed by those of Filipino, Asian Indian, Vietnamese, Korean, Japanese, and other Asian origins. Native Hawaiians and other groups of Pacific Islanders are an additional 0.4 percent of the U.S. population. Pacific Islanders include people with origins in Malaysia, Indonesia, Micronesia, Borneo, Guam, the Philippines, Samoa, and other nations. Although Asians and Pacific Islanders are often categorized together, they have "no common ancestry, language, or religion" (Chang, 2000, p. 195).

Many Chinese and Japanese families have resided in the United States for several generations. Many more recent arrivals include Hmong, Vietnamese, Laotians, and Cambodians. Many Vietnamese came to the United States following the Vietnam War and civil war in their country. Oppressive political regimes have had dire consequences for many Cambodian immigrants (Bromley & Sip, 2001). Many immigrants from these war-torn Southeast Asian countries are poor, have not had opportunities to obtain a decent education (Makimoto, 1998), and have suffered unspeakable brutality, including witnessing the torture and murder of loved ones.

As a whole, Asian households have the highest median income of any racial group in the United States (U.S. Census Bureau, 2011). Household income may include the earnings of extended Asian family members residing together (Casken, 1999). In 2008, the poverty rate for single race Asians was 11.8 percent, lower than that of all Americans (13.2 percent) (U.S. Census Bureau, 2011). Native Hawaiians and other Pacific Islanders' poverty rate was 16.3 percent, higher than that of all Americans. Although Asians as a whole are more likely to graduate from college than members of the general U.S. population, Pacific Islanders have a substantially lower college graduation rate (U.S. Census Bureau, 2011). Data suggesting that Asian and Pacific Americans enjoy considerably better health than other groups may mask important concerns. Various subgroups of the Asian population have disproportionately high rates of tuberculosis, hepatitis B, and certain cancers (e.g., cervical, lung, liver, stomach) (Asian Americans & Pacific Islanders: Health Disparities Overview, n.d.). Smoking rates are a concern, particularly among Southeast Asians (Tran, Lee, & Burgess, 2010). Native Hawaiians and other Pacific Islanders have high rates of obesity and diabetes (Asian & Pacific Islander American Health Forum, 2010).

The Chinese Exclusion Act of 1882 and the Oriental Exclusion Act of 1924 severely restricted Asians from entering the United States. Chinese immigrants were brought to the United States in 1864 to do the backbreaking work of building the country's railroads, but as larger number of Asians entered the country and began to prosper, their presence made some Americans uneasy. Thus, the Chinese were not allowed to become naturalized U.S. citizens until 1946 (see Lai, 2001). The internment of Japanese and Japanese Americans in relocation camps after World War II erupted is another striking example of discrimination against Asians. Imperialism and colonization by a number of countries have resulted in Native Hawaiians and other Pacific Islanders losing their lands and facing efforts to destroy their culture (Mokuau, 1999; Morelli & Fong, 2000; Ogawa, 1999). These factors may influence alcohol and drug use and related problems.

Discrimination can result in stress, restricted socioeconomic mobility, feelings of inferiority, and poorer health, including the need for prescription medication use (see Gee, Delva, & Takeuchi, 2007; Tran, Lee, & Burgess, 2010). Using National Latino and Asian American Study (NLAAS) data, Chae et al. (2008a) found that higher levels of ethnic identification protected against alcohol disorders among Asians. Among Asians with low ethnic identification, racial/ethnic discrimination resulted in increased odds of an alcohol use disorder. Racial/ethnic discrimination was directly associated with smoking among Asians (Chae et al., 2008b). Tran et al., also found an association between discrimination and smoking among Southeast Asian immigrants with substantial numbers of respondents

reporting discrimination by police and in getting a job or at work. Among Filipino Americans, Gee et al. (2007) found that racial/ethnic discrimination was related to prescription drug use but not to prescription drug misuse, illicit drug use, or alcohol dependence.

The Influence of Religion and Asian Traditions on Substance Use. Alcoholic beverages have been used for centuries in the Far East. Stoil (1987/88) traced references to sake, Japan's traditional alcoholic drink, to the fifth century; to wine in the Chinese literature of the eighth century; and to social drinking in the classical literature of Vietnam and Korea. Historically, there have been few references to the problematic use of alcohol in Asian countries (Stoil, 1987/88; Sue, 1987; Wang, 1968). In China, alcohol was used for religious purposes (often in conjunction with sacrifices), as well as secular rituals celebrating the harvest; in relation to political and other important events; and for medicinal purposes, due to beliefs that alcohol is good for health (Jiacheng, 1995). Jiacheng notes that among contemporary Chinese, drinking is an important part of hospitality and that "moderate drinking is not just acceptable, it is a moral imperative. Excessive drinking, by contrast, is viewed as bad" (p. 48). Among Southeast Asians, drinking has been described as "accepted and encouraged during celebrations and when friends and relatives visit. No particular stigma is associated with males who drink to excess on these occasions" (Amodeo et al., 2004, p. 25). Alcohol is considered harmless and even "helpful for dealing with sadness and forgetting painful memories" (Amodeo et al., pp. 25–26).

Differences in the cultural, social, religious, and political backgrounds of Asian groups affect their attitudes toward alcohol use (Bromley & Sip, 2001; Kitano, 1982; Kuramoto & Nakashima, 2000; Lubben, Chi, & Kitano, 1988; Makimoto, 1998; "Old Country Values," 1986–87; Singer, 1972, 1974; Wang, 1968). The Muslim background of Indonesians and Malaysians prohibits drinking. Buddhism has a strong influence on the Chinese and Cambodians, including a proscription against alcohol use. The Confucianist and Taoist backgrounds of the Chinese emphasize that moderation (the "golden mean") be practiced in all aspects of life, including alcohol use. Buddhist, Shintoi, and Chinese philosophies influence the Japanese, but today's Japanese drinking practices reflect a more permissive, business-oriented, urban style. Buddhism and Confucianism are strong influences among Koreans. In Korea, drinking rice wine is common, drunken behavior is often tolerated, and drunk driving was not criminalized until 1989; however, drug laws are very strict (Kwon-Ahn, 2001). Asian Indians are strongly influenced by Hinduism, which recommends avoiding intoxication, although cannabis is used in religious practices (Sandhu & Malik, 2001). Muslim, Spanish, American, and Japanese colonists have all influenced Filipinos' drinking.

Substance Use and Related Problems among Asian and Pacific Islander Americans

Like Asians, Asian Americans apparently have relatively low levels of alcohol and other drug use and related problems compared to the general U.S. population. For example, using 2000–2002 household survey data from SAMHSA, Sakai et al. (2005) found that Asians aged 12 and older had low rates of substance (alcohol and drug) dependence, but when only nonabstainers were included in the analysis, the rates were comparable between Asian Americans and Caucasians.

Combining several years of NSDUH data for participants aged 12 and older, past year alcohol dependence was highest among single-race Pacific Islanders other than Native Hawaiians, followed by Native Hawaiians, Koreans, Vietnamese, Japanese, Asian Indians, and Chinese and Filipinos, while past year drug dependence was highest among Native Hawaiians followed by Koreans, other Pacific Islanders, Vietnamese, Filipinos, Asian Indians Japanese, and Chinese (Sakai, Wang, & Price, 2010). Among each ethnic group, those who

identified as multiple-race reported higher rates of alcohol dependence (multiple-race Caucasians also reported higher rates of alcohol dependence than did single-race Caucasians). Most multiple-racial groups also reported a greater likelihood of drug dependence.

Wong et al. (2007) note that distrust and the desire to not lose face may result in underreporting substance use. Additionally, since studies may not be conducted in the language in which participants are most fluent, results may be suspect.

Adults. Carpenter (2003) studied self-reports of drinking of more than one million adults in the United States from 1985–2000. Asian respondents were the least likely of all racial groups to report heavy episodic drinking. Using combined data from the NSDUH for 2004 to 2008, SAMHSA (2010c) reports that rates of past-month alcohol use, binge drinking, and illicit drug use were lower among Asian adults than in the general population. This was also true for men and for women and for those in most age groups. The percentage of Asian adults who needed treatment for a substance use problem in the past year was also lower than for adults in the general population (4.8 vs. 9.6 percent). A major U.S. study of adults found that both males and females of Asian origins had lower rates of alcohol abuse and dependence than members of the other major ethnic groups (Grant et al., 2004). Asians also have lower occurrences of many substance-related problems. For example, Asian and Pacific Islander American men have less than half the risk of cirrhosis as non-Hispanic white American men, though the rates for Asian and Pacific Islander women and non-Hispanic white women are much more similar (Singh & Hoyert, 2000).

Table 11.3 shows that among subgroups of Asian adults, Koreans and Japanese were highest in alcohol use and illicit drug use. Koreans were also highest in binge alcohol use. Asian Indians were lowest in alcohol use; along with Chinese they were lowest in binge alcohol use, and both these groups were lowest in illicit drug use.

TABLE 11.3 Percent of Past Month Alcohol and Illicit Drug Use among Asian Subgroups Aged 18 and Older: 2004 to 2008 National Survey on Drug Use and Health (NSDUH)

Subgroup	Alcohol Use	Binge Alcohol Use	Illicit Drug Use
Korean	51.9%	25.9%	5.3%
Japanese	48.3%	14.5%	6.2%
Chinese	41.3%	8.4%	2.1%
Vietnamese	38.7%	14.0%	5.3%
Filipino	38.1%	15.0%	3.2%
South Asian	32.1%	9.5%	2.1%

Source: Substance Abuse and Mental Health Services Administration, Office of Applied Studies. (May 20, 2010). *The NSDUH report: Substance use among Asian adults,* Rockville, MD: U.S. Department of Health and Human Services. Retrieved May 2, 2011, from http://oas.samhsa.gov/2k10/179/SUAsianAdults.htm.

Within subgroups, variation can also be considerable. For example, the Filipino American Community Epidemiological Study indicates that 12 percent of adult participants in San Francisco had an alcohol use disorder compared to 5 percent in Honolulu, suggesting that socioenvironmental factors as well as ethnicity may impact substance use disorders (Kim, Kim, & Nochajski, 2010). Risk factors for alcohol use disorders (abuse or dependence) for Honolulu residents were more education and lower social support; for San Francisco residents they were higher psychological distress, being U.S. born, and lower religiosity.

Youth. Studies generally find that Asian American youth drink and use other drugs less frequently and have fewer substance-related problems than other American youth (see, for example, Au & Donaldson, 2000; Office of Applied Studies, 2002). Many of these studies do not include school dropouts. SAMHSA's (2009) household survey, which samples a broad cross section of the population, also found that Asians aged 12 to 17 reported the lowest incidence of lifetime, past-year, and past-month use of any illicit drug among the groups studied. They were also least likely to report any alcohol use or binge drinking in the past month and were nearly identical to black youth in heavy alcohol use, with both groups reporting the lowest levels of heavy alcohol use among racial and ethnic groups.

Asian youths' low levels of use may be related to their beliefs about these substances. For example, they were more likely than other groups to perceive risk from drinking (Office of Applied Studies).

Some studies indicate that Asian youth are not always the lowest in use (Moloney, Hunt, & Evans, 2008). For example, using a nationally representative sample of students in grades 9 through 12 from the Youth Risk Behavior Survey, which contained approximately 1,850 Asians and Pacific Islanders, Grunbaum and associates (2000) found both male and female Asian and Pacific Islander students lowest on alcohol and marijuana use in the last 30 days, but the Asian and Pacific Islander females were no different from black females (though they were significantly less likely than Hispanic and white females) to have consumed five or more drinks at least once during the past 30 days. The male and female Asian and Pacific Islanders did not differ from black and white students on cocaine use in the last 30 days (though they were less likely than the Hispanic students to have used this substance).

Nagasawa, Qian, and Wong (2000) studied nearly 6,000 students of Asian and Pacific Islander backgrounds in California. When asked about alcohol, cigarette, marijuana, and cocaine use, Chinese and Southeast Asian students (35 percent of each group) were most likely to be nonusers, followed by

Asian Indians (30 percent), Japanese (29 percent), Koreans (27 percent), Filipinos (19 percent), and Pacific Islanders (17 percent). But the patterns of use varied. For example, while the Chinese students were the least likely to use any of the four drugs combined, they were the most likely of the subgroups to have used alcohol (33 percent) and the least likely to have used marijuana (8 percent) and cocaine (1 percent). Pacific Islanders were the least likely to be non-users and the most likely to have used marijuana (46 percent) and cocaine (7 percent, but they were the least likely to drink (14 percent) and smoke (16 percent). Using NSDUH data, SAMHSA (Office of Applied Studies, 2002) also found differences by subgroups. Filipino youth (30 percent) were most likely to have used alcohol in the past year and Asian Indian youth the least likely (16 percent), but these groups were nearly identical in the percent reporting binge drinking (5.8 and 5.4 percent, respectively).

Based on a sample of nearly 4,600 students at a Midwestern research university, McCabe et al. (2006, 2007) found that Asian and African American students were generally less likely to use drugs, to be classified as drug abusers, and to simultaneously use alcohol and prescription stimulant medication "not prescribed by a doctor" than white and Hispanic students. Iwamoto et al.'s (2010) findings indicate that although Asians rates of heavy episodic drinking (HED) were generally lower compared to those of other racial and ethnic groups, the majority of Asian American students' HED increased by the end of their junior year. Consistent with the literature on Asian youth, Liu and Iwamoto (2007) found that among male Asian American college students attending a large West Coast university, having peers who used substances was the strongest predictor of binge drinking, marijuana use, and other substance use. This study found that the Asian American men engaged in substance use at rates similar to or higher than those of male college students nationally.

Segments of the Asian American youth population are involved in the club (electronic music)/drug (e.g., ecstasy) scene (Moloney et al., 2008).

Others report gang involvement or partying that includes alcohol, drugs, and violence (Lee et al., 2008). Youth residing in poor neighborhoods with high rates of violence may be at risk, since controls on substance use in homelands (e.g., Cambodia and Laos) may be lacking in the United States (Lee et al.).

Sociocultural and Genetic Influences on Asian Americans' Substance Use

Discussions of Asian Americans' drinking and drug use have largely been concerned with explaining why their substance use and abuse rates are generally lower than most other ethnic groups. Sociocultural and genetic explanations have both received attention.

Sociocultural Influences

Alcohol and Drug Problems as Organic, Moral, or Supernatural Phenomena. Problems many Westerners would label personal or behavioral, like mental and substance use disorders, Asians may consider organic (biological or medical) (Fong & Tsuang, 2007; Ishisaka & Takagi, 1995). Asian clients may somatize these problems (Fong & Tsuang), presenting with complaints such as fatigue, insomnia, and headaches (Amodeo, Robb, Peou, & Tran, 1996; D'Avanzo, 1997; Inouye, 1999; Matsuyoshi, 2001). The holistic medicine of Eastern cultures treats the mind and body as functioning together, not separately as Western cultures do. Asian and Pacific Islanders' views of substance use problems as biological illness may relieve the individual and family of personal blame and allow them to save face (Ishisaka & Takagi, 1995).

Amodeo and associates' (1996) literature review indicates that Southeast Asians tend to view alcohol use as harmless or even helpful to relieve sadness and painful memories, unless it results in behavior that causes the family shame. Southeast Asians (Vietnamese, Cambodians, and Laotians) may turn to drugs and alcohol to relieve physical or psychic pain (Amodeo et al.; D'Avanzo, 1997). In a study using a nonprobability sample of 164 Southeast

Asians, many adults reported self-medication with alcohol, tobacco, or other drugs, and older adults were often described as "drinking alone and/or drinking to be drunk" and as being isolated, depressed, and anxious as a result of "traumatic pasts and unhappy presents" (Lee et al., 2008).

Kitano's 1982 study of mental illness among Japanese and Japanese Americans found that families tended to see these problems as moral issues, such as laziness, or as Matsuyoshi (2001) suggests, as a lack of willpower. Fong and Tusang (2007) also note that substance abuse may be viewed as an inability to resist Western temptations. Southeast Asians may also see substance use disorders "as the result of moral weakness and fate" (Amodeo et al., 2004, p. 26). Many Pacific Islanders believe illness results from moral transgression (Loos, 1999). The moral view is also prevalent among the Chinese, and addicts may be deemed "unworthy of help" (Lai, 2001).

Asians may also attribute their problems to spiritual and supernatural forces (Inouye, 1999). Destiny or fate is a frequent explanation for life's circumstances (including alcohol and drug problems) rather than individual behavior or lack of self-control (Sandhu & Malik, 2001). Pacific Islanders have "a cosmic view of health and disease" (Loos, 1999, p. 442). Many Asians and Pacific Islanders believe that the body, mind, and spirit are interconnected and that re-establishing harmony and balance with nature is necessary to overcome unhealthy states (Kline & Huff, 1999; Yee 1999).

Social Control, Peer Clusters, and Social Learning. Nagasawa and colleagues (2000) tested whether social control theory (which focuses on social bonds to traditional institutions such as family, school, and friends and moral values) or peer cluster theory (which is concerned with the direct influence of peers who use alcohol and other drugs) predicted students' alcohol or drug use. There was support for both theories, but peers' influence was particularly strong. Teachers played a significant role in keeping only the Southeast Asian students from using substances, while the family

was significant in keeping only the Chinese and the Asian Indian students from using. Attitudes toward school was a significant factor in reducing drug use among all but the Korean students, and having high moral standards was related to less use for all but the Asian Indian students.

Au and Donaldson (2000) also found strong peer influences on drinking, but Asian American adolescents spent significantly less time with friends than European American adolescents. Cook et al. (2009) examined sociocultural determinants of alcohol use among 202 Korean American adolescents in Southern California. Alcohol use was greater for students also smoked and had low scholastic achievement or aspirations. Friends' influence was particularly strong, and affiliation with non-Korean peers was positively correlated with the total number of drinks consumed.

Acculturation.   Compared to Asian immigrants, drinking among U.S.-born individuals of Asian descent is more similar to that of the general U.S. population, and acculturation may reduce the protective effects of ethnic-related health behaviors (Gfroerer & Tan, 2003; Makimoto, 1998). SAMHSA (2010c) also finds that regardless of age, past month substance abuse is lower for foreign-born than U.S.-born Asians.

The National Latino and Asian American Study included five measures of immigration or acculturation (nativity, English-language proficiency, years in the United States, age at time of immigration, and generation in the United States). Variables that predicted a lower lifetime likelihood of a substance use disorder in Asian men were being foreign-born, being in the United States 6 to 10 years or more than 21 years, and being 18 to 34 at the time of immigration (Takeuchi et al., 2007). For Asian women, the variables associated with a lower likelihood of a lifetime substance use disorder were being foreign-born and having immigrated at 12 years of age or younger or at ages 18 to 34. The likelhood of having a substance use disorder was greater for those of second or later generations, especially women.

For Native Hawaiians and other Pacific Islanders, the issue is Western influences on one's homeland rather than acculturation to a new environment (Mokuau, 1999). Depending on the extent of encroachment, traditional ways that may have limited alcohol and other drug use may be lost.

Acculturation also seems to play a role in college students' drinking, though studies vary on some findings. Lo and Globetti (2001) compared three groups (each containing approximately 100 individuals) of high school students in Hong Kong, Chinese-origin students in Chicago, and American students in Michigan. The Chinese-origin students in the United States were the most moderate drinkers of the three groups. Lo and Globetti speculate that the image of Asians as a so-called "model minority" (being hard working, having few problems, etc.) may act as a mechanism of social control because members of the group wish to maintain a positive image in their host country. Yi and Daniel (2001) studied 412 Vietnamese college students. Compared to low-acculturated males and females, those who were more highly acculturated were more likely to use alcohol and marijuana. Acculturation was not related to smoking among the females and the only acculturation variable related to males' smoking was length of residence in the United States. Those affiliated with Buddhist or Catholic faiths were at less risk for alcohol problems. Lum, Corliss, Mays, Cochran, and Lui (2009) explored the effects of acculturation (place of birth) on drinking behaviors among 753 Chinese, Filipino, Korean, and Vietnamese college students. U.S.-born females were more likely to drink than foreign-born females, though birthplace was not a significant factor for men.

Genetic Influences. The way individuals metabolize alcohol may influence drinking behavior and the likelihood of developing drinking problems. Acetaldehyde, a highly toxic substance, is a by-product of alcohol metabolism. When acetaldehyde is not converted into a nontoxic form due to a gene deficiency in the aldehyde dehydrogenase (ALDH) liver enzyme, it causes the discomfort associated with the flushing response, which has been likened to a disulfiram reaction (Stoil, 1987/88; see Chapter 6 for a discussion of disulfiram).

Luczak et al. (2002) found that both Asian American men and women with this genetic deficiency had greater sensitivity to alcohol, as measured by an increased pulse rate and flushing, and they were more likely to report being dizzy and high and felt less capable of driving after consuming alcohol than subjects without the gene deficiency. Tu and Israel (1995) studied American- and Canadian-born individuals of Asian ancestry and found that the ALDH gene variant explained two-thirds of men's drinking behavior, while measures of acculturation (e.g., language use, friends) explained a significant but much smaller portion of the variance. The Asian-ancestry women drank considerably less than the men, and being female conferred a greater protection against increased drinking than the ALDH gene deficiency. Hendershoot et al. (2009) found that among a sample of Korean and Chinese undergraduate students, the ALDH2*2 allele was significantly higher for the Chinese than the Koreans. Consistent with expectations, the Korean students consumed more alcohol, reported less sensitivity to alcohol, and scored higher on the Alcohol Use Disorders Identification Test (see Chapter 5).

Despite interest in the flushing response as a protective factor against drinking and alcohol-use disorders, Towle (1988) reported that about three-quarters of the Japanese Americans he studied who flushed could continue to drink after the onset of this response. Similarly, Johnson's (1989) review indicated that "flushing is only marginally related to reduced alcohol use" (p. 383). Cultural norms to engage in drinking may override any discomfort caused by flushing (also see Lee et al., 2008). Many Alaska Natives and American Indians have some Asian ancestry and also flush, but these groups have high rates of alcoholism and do not have the particular ALDH gene deficiency present in many Asians (see, for example, Tu & Israel, 1995). The jury is not fully in on the extent of genetic protection offered by flushing in reducing alcohol use and its relationship to socio-cultural factors that might also inhibit or promote drinking, or to psychological and sociocultural factors that may make independent contributions to substance use disorders or offer protection against these problems (Lee et al., 2004).

Treatment Services for Asian and Pacific Islander Americans

There is a lack of special chemical dependency services for Asian Americans (Chin, 2001; Subramanian & Takeuchi, 1999), which may be due to two factors: Asians are still a small percentage of the U.S. population, and they apparently have a low incidence of chemical dependency problems. In addition, Asians often learn to be stoic and to suffer in silence (Bromley & Sip, 2001; Matsuyoshi, 2001), and they prefer not to attract attention to themselves—factors that may also inhibit the development of special services to meet their needs (Kitano, 1982). The model-minority myth may also have "effectively disenfranchised Asian immigrants and Asian Americans from forms of social welfare and attention that would otherwise ameliorate certain conditions" (Subramanian & Takeuchi, p. 191).

Asian and Pacific Islander Americans were only one percent of those admitted for substance abuse treatment in 2008 (Office of Applied Studies, 2010), but contrary to what some believe, indications are that Asians do not wait until their substance abuse problems are very severe before they seek professional treatment. Data from the California Treatment Outcome Project (CalTOP) show that Asian American and Pacific Islander (AAPI) clients entered treatment with less severe alcohol and drug problems compared to other clients, but they rated alcohol and drug treatment as less important than other clients (Niv, Wong, & Hser, 2007). AAPI clients were just as likely as other clients to remain in treatment (but only about one-quarter of each group completed treatment), and their treatment outcomes

were comparable to other clients except for alcohol problems, where AAPI clients' outcomes were better than other clients. The AAPI received more legal services but fewer medical and psychiatric services (and fewer services overall while in treatment). The reasons for these differences were not clear since they had comparable levels of legal, medical, and psychiatric problems at admission and AAPI clients had fewer lifetime convictions and incarcerations. In a comparison of Chinese and Korean Americans receiving treatment for alcohol use disorders, three-quarters of both groups were referred by the legal system with DWI being by far the most common legal problem they experienced (Park, Shibusawa, Yoon, & Son, 2010). Grouped together, Asian/Pacific Islanders are about equally likely to be admitted for a primary alcohol, marijuana, or methamphetamine problem (Office of Applied Studies, 2010).

Service Underutilization.   Researchers and clinicians have identified a number of reasons for Asian Americans' underutilization of mental health and substance abuse treatment services. They include cultural attitudes (e.g., loss of face, stigma, shame; bringing dishonor to one's family; a strong preference for handling problems within the family or one's immediate community; distrust of other cultural groups) or cultural beliefs about the causes of mental health or substance use problems (including lack of recognition of substance abuse as a problem), as well as cultural inaccessibility or insensitivity (e.g., language barriers, lack of ethnic understanding or sensitivity, limited outreach to Asians, cost or lack of insurance to pay for services, lack of awareness of services or lack of familiarity with social service agencies and what services entail [see Abe-Kim et al., 2007; D'Avanzo, 1997; Matsuyoshi, 2001; Phin & Phillips, 1981]). In the NLAAS, language proficiency was not related to service use, satisfaction, or perceived helpfulness, though the findings do not indicate the language in which services were provided (Abe-Kim et al., 2007). NLAAS findings do suggest that intensive outreach is needed given Asian Americans' service underutilization.

The NLAAS also indicates that U.S.-born respondents were more likely to use services than foreign-born (13 vs. 7 percent), and third or later generation respondents were also more likely to receive services than first or second generation respondents (19 vs. 7 and 8 percent, respectively) (Abe-Kim et al., 2007). Those who immigrated at ages 13 to 17 or at 35 or older were more likely to use general medical services for these problems than those who immigrated at age 12 or younger or at age 18 to 34. In Lee et al.'s (2004) study, Asian American participants reported positive attitudes about substance abuse treatment, but they would prefer to use personal, informal resources should such problems arise. In each subgroup they studied, the largest percentage of respondents said they would attempt to quit on their own, ranging from 53 percent of Asian Indians to 36 percent of Chinese. Nevertheless, substantial numbers of members of each ethnic group thought that at least some professional services would be helpful to them if they did have a problem. Except for Vietnamese respondents, confidence in support groups like AA and NA to help was much lower.

Kitano (1982) reported that Asian Americans say that they would prefer to receive services from an ethnic agency, but specialized services for problems may not be available, causing them to turn to religious leaders, doctors, family, and friends for help. Provides who speak the same language as the client may be difficult to find. Chinese immigrants who have resided in large cities such as Hong Kong and in Taiwan may be more familiar with the types of chemical dependency services offered in the United States (Lai, 2001). To initiate participation in Western treatment programs, Asians clients with low degrees of acculturation will need education about what this treatment entails and how they are expected to participate (Sandhu & Malik, 2001). When Western treatment is not acceptable or preferred, the provider must help the client search for an approach that is.

Communication Patterns.   In Asian cultures, maintaining inner peace and tranquility and harmonious interpersonal relations, even in the face of great adversity, is highly valued, and expressing strong emotions is to be avoided (Chang, 2000; Inouye, 1999; Kwon-Ahn, 2001). Communication among Asians is generally indirect and subtle so as to avoid offending others, and confrontation is not appropriate (Bromley & Sip, 2001; Matusyoshi, 2001; Sandhu & Malik, 2001). Like Native Americans, Asians may avoid eye contact, and their shame and guilt may cause them to appear subdued, with little enthusiasm for the treatment process (Sandhu & Malik). Asian American clients may say what they think the professional would like to hear as a sign of respect (Ishisaka & Takagi, 1995), and a client's nod of the head might mean that he or she is "hearing, but not necessarily agreeing with, what is being said" (Ishida, 1999, p. 380). If Asians feel that the treatment provider is not picking up on their facial expressions and other nonverbal communication, they may consider him or her incompetent (Kwon-Ahn). Unless the client is prepared for them, very personal or intimate questions can cause great consternation and will be considered highly unprofessional (Sandhu & Malik).

One indirect approach to communication is storytelling and the use of legends about individuals who have overcome great adversity (Amodeo et al., 1996). The alcohol or drug problem must still be addressed, although "in the most nonconfrontational way possible," so that the client does not lose face (Bromley & Sip, 2001, p. 336). Kwon-Ahn (2001) notes that until trust is established, it may be best to focus on concerns that the client or family present, such as health complaints or not doing well in school. Many Asians prefer a quick and authoritative solution to problems (Sandhu & Malik, 2001), even though alcohol and drug problems are often not so easily resolved. According to D'Avanzo (1997), "perceptions of proper respect and deference may dictate that the 'expert' is expected to solve the problem with little input from the person using substances or their families"

(p. 843), a perception that is quite different from the models used to treat chemical dependency in the United States.

The Family and Treatment.   Not enough can be said about the primacy of the family in Asian life (see, for example, Au & Donaldson, 2000; Kwon-Ahn, 2001; Lai, 2001; Rastogi & Wadhwa, 2006; Sandhu & Malik, 2001). The family is generally defined as the extended family, and members may live in close physical as well as emotional proximity (Chang, 2000). Individual needs are subordinate to the family's collective needs (Rastogi & Wadhwa; Yee, 1999). Family structure is hierarchical and gender roles are often well defined, with men taking the dominant role (Bromley & Sip, 2001; Matsuyoshi, 2001; Sandhu & Malik). Male offspring are accorded higher status, and marriages may still be arranged (Bhattacharya, 1998; Chang Rastogi & Wadha). Younger members are bound to respect the wishes of parents and other elders (filial piety), and fulfilling family responsibilities is paramount (Chang). Thus, the family must be considered in addressing an individual's alcohol or drug problem. The father's authority should not be compromised. It may be necessary to consult him on treatment decisions (Sandhu & Malik). When he is the family member with the alcohol or drug problem, it is important to allow him to maintain face within the family (Matsuyoshi).

Since chemical dependency results in great shame for the individual and the family, families generally try to conceal such problems. Failure to resolve a family member's alcohol or drug problem may be considered a failure of the entire family or of the parents or spouse, and families need help to relieve this guilt (Matsuyoshi, 2001). The desire to save face and to show respect to family members, particularly elders, may also result in concealing a problem until it escalates. Chang (2000) says that "families either pretend that there is no problem or admonish and severely criticize the offending individual" (p. 200; also see Lee et al., 2004). The Japanese response may

be to solve the problem within the family and "to shore up the person with encouragement" (Matsuyoshi, p. 405). The double bind is that although the family is the core Asian social institution, it may be the last place where one can turn for help (Chang). Families themselves need assistance in understanding substance use disorders and to refrain from enabling by covering up the problem (Fong & Tusang, 2007). Mainstream chemical dependency programs in the United States tell clients to get sober for themselves, but with Asian clients, the strategy may to be get sober to restore honor to the family (Amodeo et al., 1996).

In working with Asian American families, Mercado (2000) recommends Bowen's family systems approach, saying this "modest approach to problem solving, remaining detached but interested, calm and intellectual, is congruent with Asian American's belief in modest communication and behavior" (p. 270). She suggests maintaining Asian families' "communication hierarchy" by having "each family member speak directly to the therapist and using positive reframing and reflecting" (p. 270).

Culturally Relevant Approaches.   The suggestions Phin and Phillips (1981) offer for treating Asian American drug abusers include support of traditional values and cultural identification; use of Asian American staff; emphasis on commonalities among Asian groups rather than on unique cultural factors; involvement with the larger Asian community; family therapy; and for women, consciousness raising and identity building. Asian Americans who are hesitant to seek mental health services may be more willing to go to an agency that also offers other social services. To help clients save face and to meet the multiple needs they may have, the multiservice model, in which agencies locate together or a single agency offers multiple services, may make services more appealing (Ishisaka & Takagi, 1995; Chow, 2002). As is true for all ethnic and cultural groups, sanction from respected members of the ethnic community is useful in encouraging service utilization. Agencies may garner support by including board members who are representative of the Asian American groups to be served and by gaining the backing of Asian American organizations and churches.

Since Asians may turn to family doctors when they have substance abuse problems, providing substance abuse services through general health facilities and utilizing a holistic (mind-body) treatment approach may be useful (Lee et al., 2004). Treatment by a primary health care provider who can offer medications or direct advice may be more appealing than less directive treatment by psychiatrists or other mental health professionals (Fong & Tsuang, 2007). Herbalists may also be consulted. The pharmacotherapies discussed in Chapter 6 of this textbook may also be culturally acceptable for Asian clients (Chang, 2000; Fong & Tsuang, 2007; Matsuyoshi, 2001).

Little has been written on mutual-help groups for Asians, but studies indicate substantial reluctance on the part of Asians to use these groups (Lee et al., 2004). In fact, Park et al. (2010) found that only 2 percent of 211 Korean and Chinese individuals receiving substance abuse treatment said they knew what AA was. Some groups in the United States conduct their meetings in Japanese, and there is a version of Alcoholics Anonymous in Japan called Danshukai (Kitano, 1982; Matsuyoshi, 2001). Since Asians have been taught to be stoic and endure problems without complaining (Ishisaka & Takagi, 1995), the self-disclosure used in AA is not consistent with their cultural values (Fong & Tsuang, 2007; Kwon-Ahn, 2001; Lee et al., 2004; Sandhu & Malik, 2001). However, participants may "listen and observe without revealing themselves" (Matsuyoshi, 2001). Culturally relevant adaptations of these meetings or development of alternative support groups are options to consider (Amodeo et al., 1996), such as education and support groups led or co-led by a pastor or respected elder and held in locations that protect anonymity (Fong & Tsuang, 2007). Zane and colleagues (1998) emphasize the use of educational interventions because of the importance that Asians place on education, and Sandhu and Malik

(2001) suggest that educational or psychoeducational strategies may take pressure off Asians to disclose more than they wish.

Additional culturally relevant suggestions for treatment for some Asians include assistance by Buddhist monks and residence at a Buddhist temple, rather than the residential chemical dependency treatment typically used in the United States, or the use of Catholic nuns for Asians who follow Catholicism (Amodeo et al., 1996; Bromley & Sip, 2001; D'Avanzo, 1997). Bromley and Sip discuss a women's support group at a Buddhist temple. One of the few culturally acceptable places for Koreans in the United States to seek help is at their church (which is often a Protestant church), but Kwon-Ahn (2001) found that pastors may not feel capable of addressing alcohol and drug problems; thus, there is a need for chemical dependency specialists to work closely with these clergy members.

Asians commonly use acupuncture to maintain health and to treat ailments, and some may use herbal medications or religious healers (see, for example, Amodeo et al., 2004; Fong & Tsuang, 2007). Chemical dependency treatment programs in the United States also use acupuncture for detoxification and relapse prevention. Challenges in establishing control conditions have made the effects of acupuncture difficult to discern (see Chapter 6 of this text), but it may be an acceptable and culturally consistent approach for Asian clients (Amodeo et al., 1996). Meditation and the martial arts (Chang, 2000) may also help to restore harmony and balance (Amodeo et al., 1996) as well as self-discipline and self-control.

Calling alcohol and drugs "the fuel implicated in the disintegration of culture and health among Pacific Islanders" (p. 274), Ogawa (1999) offers three guiding principles for health care to rectify the situation: "'right behavior' (referring to group harmony, support, and well-being), 'work for justice' (referring to the social and legal problems facing Pacific Islanders), and 'strive for righteousness' (referring to one's connection to the homeland)" (p. 249). Morelli and Fong (2000) describe a program for substance-abusing pregnant and postpartum women in Hawaii that has a strong cultural component capitalizing on the use of Hawaiian elders (*kūpuna*). The five-phase program begins with participation in a *ho'oponopono*, a healing practice for restoring harmony among family members. Clients in this phase are expected to demonstrate total commitment to treatment participation. In the *Mahiki-Hihia* phase, clients begin taking greater responsibility for their actions, and in the *Hala-Mihi* phase, they ask for forgiveness and make restitution and amends. The fifth phase ends with *Pani*, the closing meal, and with *hi'uwai*, a purification ritual. Periodically, the *kūpuna* lead six-hour deep cultural sessions, in which program participants re-enact Hawaiian legends, followed by discussions to help them heal from hurt and pain. *I Mua Mau Ohana* (Moving Families Forward) is a culturally based substance abuse treatment program for adolescents that uses a multisystemic family therapy approach (Kim & Jackson, 2009).

Prevention Services in Asian and Pacific Islander American Communities

With regard to prevention strategies, Kuramoto (1991) reviewed results of forums held in Chinese, Japanese, Korean, Filipino, Vietnamese, Cambodian, Laotian, Hmong, and Thai communities in California. A few of the issues and suggestions that arose were unique to particular ethnic communities, but most of the concerns that emerged were common across the groups, such as lack of bilingual and bicultural materials and culturally competent services. Other barriers often identified were stigma and lack of recreational opportunities. Family-oriented approaches were also emphasized, as was the need for better referral systems. A review of 18 programs used with Asian youth assessed by National Asian Pacific American Families Against Substance Abuse, Inc. (cited in Kuramoto, 1991) indicated themes that seemed to make programs successful, such as sponsorship by established and credible ethnic agencies in the community, bilingual and bicultural staff, youth involvement, pride in culture, emphasis on group activities, and a comprehensive approach to addressing the needs of youth.

In Asian American families, conflicts may occur when parents discourage their children from developing close relationships with peers of other ethnic groups, and dating and marriage may be considered a family rather than an individual decision (Bhattacharya, 1998). Zane and associates (1998) note that "the development of what are considered Western-oriented social skills, such as open self-expression and assertiveness, might cause intra-familial tensions for Asian Americans because these individualistic-oriented behaviors may conflict with the emphasis placed on saving face and avoiding confrontations within such families" (p. 108). An important component of prevention may be assisting parents and children to address the intergenerational conflicts that may result from young people's interest in more rapid acculturation (Bhattacharya, 1998; Kuramoto, 1991; Matsuyoshi, 2001), as well as the general strains of adolescence and young adulthood.

Young Asian Americans may use drugs to fit in to their new culture and to make friends, and gang involvement is a concern (Kwon-Ahn, 2001; Nakashima & Wong, 2000). In developing media campaigns to prevent substance use, Kuramoto and Nakashima (2000) recommend that they focus on educating parents about alcohol and other drug use and empower them to educate and nurture their children. The focus should also be on bolstering youth's self-esteem, viewing their ethnic heritage with pride, and seeing biculturalism as an advantage. Competence Through Transitions (CTT) is a prevention program that was developed so that it could be adapted for use by Chinese, Filipino, Japanese, Korean, and Vietnamese communities (Zane et al., 1998). CTT builds on the importance of family and the strength inherent in the Asians parents' desire for the youth's success by directly involving and strengthening the parents' role in school settings. By supporting parental competence as well as embedding workshops and recreational activities in ethnic-specific neighborhood youth and community centers, youths' competencies are strengthened in a culturally affirming way.

One prevention strategy for Pacific Islander communities is the Kamehameha Schools/Bishop Estate Native Hawaiian Drug-Free Schools and Community Program, which incorporates cultural themes and messages such as *He Hawai'i au; 'ai 'ole i ka la 'au 'ino* ("Hawaiian and drug free") (Mokuau, 1997). Another is the *Hui Malamo o ke Kai* (caring group from the ocean) project, with also focuses on violence prevention and is based on cultural components such as "grow, mature, and love the child" and family strengthening (Akeo et al., 2008). This after school program for 5th and 6th graders serves mostly children of Native Hawaiian ancestry and incorporates study-hall tutoring sessions followed by fun activities.

Clan groupings are very important to Pacific Islanders, and maintaining community health is considered a collective responsibility (Loos,1999). Loos recommends an indigenous model based on community empowerment in which learning is often accomplished in groups. Local artists, performers, and comedians can play an important role. Prevention messages can be conveyed informally in settings such as churches, clubs, and festivals, as well as in clinics, and in the language of the target group is important because "Pacific Islanders will not engage HPDP concepts or sustain HPDP practices if they are not their own" (Loos, p. 444).

Substance Use and Abuse among Jewish Americans

History and Background

Jews are a cultural and ethnic as well as a religious group. Participating in Jewish traditions and direct experience or awareness of anti-Semitism and historical traumas such as the Holocaust unite Jews regardless of where they reside (Straussner, 2001) and whether or not they are religious (Teller, 1989).

In Israel, over the last three decades, concerns about excessive drinking and related problems have mounted (see, for example, Kaptsan, Telias, Bersudsky, & Belmaker, 2006; Weiss, 1988, 1995). The number of pubs and the number of alcohol-related traffic accidents grew substantially (Isralowitz & Peleg, 1996). Beer and wine cost little more than soft drinks, the minimum legal drinking age of 18 is poorly enforced, there are no restrictions of hours of sale of alcoholic beverages or the location of outlets, and there are few advertising restrictions (Weiss, 1999).

The 1980s marked the first time that Israel had enough alcoholics to be included in international rankings on rates of alcoholism (Weiss, 1988, 1995; Weiss & Eldar, 1987). The Israel Society for the Prevention of Alcoholism (see Weiss & Gefen, 2003) estimated that in 2001, about 1.6 percent of Israeli residents were alcoholics (cited in Eurocare, 2001). In an Israeli survey of people age 18 to 40, 0.7 percent reported that they had received treatment for an alcohol or drug problem (Giora Rahav, personal communication, 2002). One source reports that it is worrisome that young children are now using alcohol—"75% percent of boys and 25% of girls in elementary school drink over the weekend at home, or during the week while celebrating outside the house" (Ravid, 2009). Drinking and alcohol-related problems in Israel have been blamed on "increased secularization" (Weiss, 1995, p. 144), including "adoption of foreign norms" that encourage drinking "for pleasure and fun" (Weiss, 1988, p. 220; also see Weiss & Eldar, 1987). It is apparently "fashionable nowadays for adolescents to sit in pubs and drink alcoholic beverages" (Weiss, 1995, p. 146). Other explanations offered for increased drinking in Israel are Holocaust survivors' adjustment difficulties, newer immigrants' challenges in earning a living and finding a place in the society, and immigrant groups' (e.g., Russians') drinking norms (Hasin, Rahav, Meydan, & Neumark, 1999; Weiss, 1995; Weiss & Eldar, 1987). Still, the reported rates of alcohol problems in Israeli are low compared to those for the general U.S. population.

U.S. Jews also seem to have relatively low rates of alcohol problems even though they reportedly have high rates of alcohol use (Hilton, 1988), perhaps the highest among religious groups (Cahalan & Cisin, 1968). No studies, however, provide an adequate picture of substance use among Jews in the United States. Using National Institute of Mental Health Catchment Area Study data, Levav and associates (1997) did find significantly less lifetime alcohol abuse and dependence among the Jewish men (11 percent compared to 29 percent for all other men combined). *Jewish* in this study was defined as "one's religion." There was no statistically significant difference in the lifetime rate of alcohol abuse and dependence for the Jewish women compared to all other women combined. Studies in the United States (Levav et al., 1997) and the United Kingdom (Loewenthal, MacLeod, Cook, Lee, & Goldblatt, 2003; Loewenthal, Lee, MacLeod, Cook, & Goldblatt, 2003) indicate that rather than alcohol problems, Jewish men have high rates of depression.

Prescription drug abuse may be more problematic for Jews than alcohol abuse (Carpey, 1985; Ellias-Frankel, Oberman, & Ward, 2000). Glatt (1970) noted that unlike alcohol, there are no proscriptions against drug use in the Jewish culture. An unpublished study of drug use in New York State conducted in both 1986 and 1994 showed slightly but not significantly higher drug use among Jews compared to non-Jews (cited in Straussner, 2001). Vex and Blume (2001) surveyed 379 members of an organization called Jewish Alcoholics, Chemically Dependent Persons, and Significant Others (JACS) (the response rate was approximately 45 percent and the numbers of men and women were approximately equal). Orthodox, conservative, reform, and nonaffiliated Jews were represented among the sample. Fifty-five percent identified themselves as primarily dependent on alcohol. The remainder identified themselves as primarily dependent on other drugs—most commonly, cocaine, opiates, and marijuana. Seventy-one percent reported dual addictions. Forty-eight percent had family members with alcoholism.

The evidence on Jewish college students' alcohol and other drug use has been mixed. In their study, Eisenman and colleagues (1980) found support for earlier studies that Jewish college students used marijuana more frequently than Catholic and Protestant students, but the length of marijuana use was not related to religious affiliation. Based on data from a sample of 704 male students and staff ages 18 to 25 at the University of California at San Diego, Monteiro and Schuckit (1989) found no statistically significant differences in lifetime drug use or related problems and no substantial pattern of differences in drug use between the Jews and Christians. There were also no differences in average quantity and frequency of alcohol consumption. The Jewish men did report less heavy drinking and fewer drinking problems and had fewer relatives with histories of alcoholism. Similarly, in a sample of 279 college students, Luczak and colleagues (2002) found that fewer Jewish students (33 percent) engaged in binge drinking compared to other students (45 percent). The non-Jewish students who attended religious services more frequently tended to do less binge drinking, but there was no relationship between binge drinking and religious service attendance for the Jewish students. The religiously affiliated Jewish students had one-third the risk of engaging in binge drinking as the non-religiously affiliated Jews, but there was no relationship between Jewish cultural identification and binge drinking.

Cultural Explanations of Low Rates of Alcohol Problems among Jewish Americans

There is evidence that some Jews have a genetic protection against excessive drinking through the ADH2*2 allele (Fischer et al., 2007; Hasin et al., 2002). Cultural factors have, however, been the major focus of explanations for Jews' seemingly low rates of alcohol use disorders (Neumark, Friedlander, Thomasson, & Li, 1998).

More than 200 years ago, Immanuel Kant noted protective cultural factors concerning

Jews and alcohol (Jellinek, 1941). Glatt (1970) noted that it is curious that Jews, who have been exposed to many strains and stressors and who exhibit at least as much neuroticism as the rest of the population, tend not to develop alcohol problems. Keller (1979) also noted that while the Bible contains a number of accounts of Jewish drinking and drunkenness, three reasons may explain why alcoholism did not become a problem for them: (1) They denounced pagan gods who had been worshiped with orgiastic drinking; (2) they developed a religious culture with a focus on the Torah and with worship and education taking place at synagogues; and (3) they confined drinking to rituals practiced at the synagogue and at home.

In the mid-1900s Glad (1947) and Snyder (1958) conducted notable studies of differences in drinking between Jewish Americans and other groups. Glad (1947) tested several hypotheses based on 49 male adolescents from each of three groups—American Jews, American Irish-Catholics, and a control group of third-generation Americans of Central and Northern European descent. He defined Jews as those who had a "Jewish self-consciousness" and concluded that differences in "inebriety" could be explained by the reasons for drinking: Jews drink alcohol primarily for symbolic and religious reasons while the Irish more often drink for personal and social reasons, including alcohol's effects.

Snyder's (1958) comparison of Jewish subgroups in the United States found the lowest to highest frequencies of intoxication in the following order: orthodox, conservative, reform, and secular Jews. Later work by Snyder and colleagues (1982) in Israel also indicated that alcoholism occurs less frequently among the more orthodox Ashkenasi Jews (those of German or Eastern European background) than the Sephardi (those of Spanish, Portuguese, and North, Central, and South American background) and Oriental Jews but that other factors, such as economic status and cultural stress, might also influence these rates. Snyder emphasized the

importance of adherence to Jewish religious orthodoxy in encouraging sobriety: "Through the ceremonial use of beverage alcohol religious Jews learn how to drink in a controlled manner; but through constant reference to the hedonism of outsiders, in association with a broader pattern of religious and ethnocentric ideas and sentiments, Jews also learn how not to drink" (p. 182). Bales (1946) also discussed the protections afforded because drinking among Jews is ritualized or sacred.

In a more recent effort to investigate religious and cultural issues in alcohol use disorders, Glassner and Berg (1984) conducted a qualitative study of 88 Jews in central New York State. The orthodox Jews drank as part of rituals and tended to view alcoholism as a disease. Reform and nonpracticing Jews drank more as part of socialization and were more likely to view alcoholism with condemnation and blame. Conservative Jews (who incorporate both aspects of orthodoxy and reformism) were less clear in their views of alcoholism. Flasher and Maisto's (1984) review of studies revealed no consistent picture of whether religious orthodoxy promotes sobriety.

Preserving the image of a sober people may be important to Jews (see Glad, 1947). A study in the United Kingdom found that compared to Protestants, Jews drank less and had less favorable attitudes toward alcohol (Loewenthal, MacLeod, Cook, Lee, & Goldblatt, 2003). Jews were more likely to believe that alcohol use leads to loss of self-control. Jews also noted differences between drinking behavior that is appropriate for Jews and drinking behavior that is appropriate for others (Loewenthal, Lee, MacLeod, Cook, & Goldblatt, 2003). Cultural norms suggest that drunkenness is a behavior of Gentiles (Christians & other non-Jews), not Jews (see Spiegel & Kravtiz, 2001), and that drunkenness, especially among Jewish women, is strongly condemned (Blume, Dropkin, & Sokolow, 1980; Steiker, 2011; Straussner, 2001). Disapproval of drunkenness (also see Kohn, 2004)—along with factors such as the well-defined role of alcohol in religious ceremonies and on holidays (see Bales, 1946) and "the importance of moderation in all life activities" (Teller, 1989, p. 27)—may continue to provide Jews in the United States (and other countries) with a degree of insularity from the high rates of alcoholism found in this country.

Glassner and Berg (1980) identified four factors that they believe, taken together, continue to help Jews in the United States to avoid alcohol problems: (1) Jews continue to believe that they are not susceptible to alcohol problems; (2) even with a trend away from religious orthodoxy, Jews continue to practice ritualistic drinking during events like religious observances; they drink moderately, mostly while eating, and they continue to teach these practices to their children; (3) the bulk of Jews' social relationships are with others (primarily Jews) who drink moderately and do not have alcohol problems; (4) rather than rationalize excessive drinking, Jews avoid drinking too much by practices such as nursing a single drink at a party. Ullman (1958) has also discussed the protective nature of drinking customs that are well integrated within the cultures of orthodox Jews, Italians, and Chinese.

Treatment and Prevention Services for Jewish Americans

Being Jewish does not, of course, offer complete protection against alcohol problems. Increased acculturation, with a concomitant move away from traditional Jewish life and religious practices, has been offered as a possible explanation for alcohol problems among Jews today (Blume et al., 1980; Straussner, 2001; Teller, 1989; Weiss, 1995).

There are indications that Jews voluntarily use mental health services more than others (Monteiro & Schuckit, 1989; Straussner, 2001). The same has not been said of chemical dependency treatment services. Respondents in Blume and associates' (1980) study of individuals with alcohol and drug problems indicated that their Jewish identity played a role in delaying diagnosis and treatment. According to Vex and Blume

(2001), the prevailing impression that Jews are highly unlikely to become alcoholics

> is disturbing because: (a) it contributes to the denial process in active alcoholics and their families, delaying intervention and treatment, (b) it discourages accurate diagnosis by health professionals, who fail to consider alcoholism in Jewish patients, (c) it inhibits leaders of the Jewish community from addressing the problem, and (d) it hinders members of individual congregations from seeking help within the Jewish community. (p. 74)

Or as one rabbi put it, "The general impression is that there are no Jewish alcoholics, so in addition to the low self-esteem that is often attached to alcoholism, there is the additional feeling of failure as a Jew. The way you deal with that is to deny your Jewishness. 'If I were really Jewish, I wouldn't be an alcoholic' " (quoted in Carpey, 1985, p. 47). Ellias-Frankel and associates (2000) emphasize that "Jewish addicts often feel their addiction is a betrayal of their Jewish community, if not their identity" (p. 136). In Vex and Blume's study of JACS members, 64 percent of respondents regarded Jewish culture as very important, and 50 percent regularly attended religious services. Of the respondents, 113 had sought assistance for their addiction from the Jewish community, but 83 percent of them reported receiving little or no assistance from this source, supporting the idea of community denial of alcohol and drug problems. Jewish parents place a great deal of emphasis on their children and may enable their children's substance use due to feelings of guilt and lack of understanding of alcohol and drug problems (Straussner, 2001).

Rabbis' understanding of alcohol and drug problems is particularly important, but they may accept the stereotype that Jews do not become alcoholics (Blume et al., 1980; Teller, 1989). Suggestions for assisting Jews with chemical dependency problems are to hold mutual-help group meetings in synagogue facilities (Blume et al., 1980, Carpey, 1985) and for rabbis to more openly discuss such problems with their congregations (see, for example, Spiegel & Kravitz, 2001). Treatment providers should inquire as to clients' religious practices, if any, and the role that religious beliefs may play in defining alcohol and drug problems and pursuing recovery (Straussner, 2001). Rabbi Abraham Twerski is among the best known authors addressing religion and recovery. Kravitz also offers suggestions for placing addiction and recovery in a spiritual context (see Spiegel & Kravitz, 2001). For example, the word Egypt in Hebrew means the double narrow place, and recovery from addiction can also be thought of as an escape from enslavement, as was the Jews' escape or Exodus from Egypt in the face of great difficulties in order to reach a better place where one can be serene and spiritual. Rabbi Nachman notes that spirituality is antithetical to addiction and that being in God's presence aids in overcoming addiction (see Spiegel & Kravtiz).

Jewish Alcoholics, Chemically Dependent Persons, and Significant Others (JACS) operated by the Jewish Board of Family and Children's Services of New York, is a resource center and clearinghouse for information on alcoholism and Jewish family life (Vex & Blume, 2001). JACS sponsors spiritual retreats for Jews who have substance use disorders and their family members. Another resource is the Alcohol and Drug Action Program (ADAP) of the Jewish Family Service of Los Angeles. In addition to offering mainstream alcoholism services, ADAP helps Jews who would benefit from incorporating their religious beliefs in their recovery (Teller, 1989). Rabbinic counseling and L'Chaim workshops are some of ADAP's services. L'Chaim (the Yiddish word for "to life") workshops emphasize the compatibility of Twelve-Step programs with Judaism and act as a bridge to participation in these groups. L'Chaim workshops begin with "We believe that people are neither all good nor all bad. We must constantly make choices between good and evil—between life and death. We are a people of survivors so we choose life. L'Chaim" (see Spiegel & Kravitz, 2001, p. 273). ADAP also offers a special program for adolescents with alcohol and drug problems and their families.

Other suggestions for better serving observant Jews include such obvious but often overlooked practices as making Kosher food available during inpatient treatment (Teller, 1989). Inpatient treatment staff must also be aware of religious holidays and other religious practices that may affect treatment participation. Ellias-Frankel et al. (2000) note that "even for non-religious Jews, an environment that contains other recovering Jews will more likely enable clients to deal with the intense isolation and shame that they may carry" (p. 137).

Straussner (2001) provides additional suggestions for treating Jews. For example, many Jews are well educated and bibliotherapy may be appealing to them. There is a substantial recovery literature addressed to Jews. The Rational Recovery mutual-help program may also be appealing because of its cognitive orientation (see Chapter 6 of this text). Jews are likely to be verbal and to question treatment recommendations when they feel the need to do so, and they may prefer to utilize private rather than public treatment resources. Given the denial of substance abuse in the Jewish community, shame and guilt among those in recovery must be addressed. Humor is important to Jews, as is being charitable, and these strengths may be important in recovery.

Although Alcoholics Anonymous is often seen as having a Christian orientation, Jews have successfully used the program (Steiker, 2011; see also Olitzky & Copans, 1991, on AA and Jews). Rabbi Daniel Grossman emphasizes that powerlessness in AA need not be associated with the Holocaust and that surrender is to God and to one's self (see Master, 1989). Jewish pastoral caregivers can act as guides to helping Jews in recovery utilize the 12 Steps. For example, Spiegel and Kravtiz (2001) note that steps four to ten are similar to *teshuvah*, the Jewish process of repentance, and they connect Step 12 with *gemilut chasadim*, or deeds of loving-kindness. In Vex and Blume's (2001) study of JACS members, by far the most used method of recovery was one of the Twelve-Step groups followed by psychotherapy. Of those participating in AA, 91 percent reported increased commitment to Judaism. There were no differences among the Jewish denominational subgroups in their ratings of the usefulness of different recovery services (Twelve-Step, psychotherapy, residential, rabbinical, etc.).

In the area of prevention, the Orthodox Union has published a workbook to prevent teen drinking that includes passages from biblical and *talmudic* writings and addresses misconceptions that teens might have about the place of drinking and drunkenness in religious versus secular life. For example, the booklet includes a scenario in which a teenager asks a parent why there is a difference in sharing a couple beers with friends and drinking wine on Shabbat (the Jewish Sabbath) (Levy, 1998).

Summary

Several themes have emerged from the foregoing discussion of ethnicity, culture, and substance abuse:

1. There is considerable variation in alcohol and drug use and related problems, both among and within the major cultural and ethnic groups in the United States. For example, Native Americans are more likely than whites to die from alcohol-related causes, but among Native American tribes, rates of drinking and related problems vary widely.

2. There are similarities in alcohol and drug use among the major cultural and ethnic groups. For example, the importance of peer influences in the use of alcohol and other drugs among youth, regardless of ethnicity, suggests a common pathway for prevention.

3. Writers express concern that the literature on groups such as Native Americans is replete with stereotypical notions such as the "drunken Indian." Other are concerned that substance problems are overlooked among groups such as Asian Americans and Jewish Americans because these groups are often described as model citizens.

4. Among all ethnic groups, women use alcohol and drugs less than men, but women who have substance use disorders are more stigmatized.

5. Discrimination and deprivation are thought to be related to substance abuse problems, particularly to the more severe health and social consequences experienced by members of certain ethnic groups, even when their patterns of use are similar to those of the majority.

6. Genetic factors have thus far not explained the differences in alcohol consumption and its consequences among ethnic groups.

7. Ethnic minority youth often report less alcohol and drug use than white youth, but methodological problems in studies of youth (such as exclusion of school dropouts and institutionalized individuals) may cloud the true picture of use across groups.

8. Strong family ties are important among most ethnic groups, but even well-meaning families can present obstacles to recovery by being overprotective or denying alcohol and drug problems among their members. Educating family members and incorporating them in treatment are universally suggested.

9. A consistent theme in the prevention literature is that ethnic communities must take an active role in defining social norms and promoting responsibility in alcohol and drug use.

10. Community gatekeepers (such as members of ethnic, religious, business, and educational organizations and institutions) should be recruited and educated to provide pathways to prevention and treatment.

11. Professionals should consider indigenous helpers (medicine men, *curanderas*, etc.) as viable helping resources.

12. There is a need for greater understanding of the mechanisms that protect members of ethnic groups from alcohol and drug problems, especially in the face of discrimination, poverty, and attempts to destroy their cultural traditions.

13. Differences in rates of alcohol and other drug problems among the various ethnic groups

should not obscure the need to provide appropriate treatment to members of each ethnic group and to provide individualized treatment to any person in need.

14. Prevention and treatment service providers should capitalize on the strengths of ethnic groups in designing programs and in offering services to individuals.

15. Ethnic sensitivity and competence are necessary to function effectively as a professional in the field of alcohol and drug prevention and treatment.

16. Major questions remain unanswered. There are no good epidemiological studies of substance abuse and related problems among many ethnic groups. Few studies have adequately tested culturally specific treatment and prevention approaches. Measuring concepts such as acculturation and their affects on substance use is difficult.

CHAPTER 12

Substance Abuse Treatment with Sexual Minorities

Catherine Lau Crisp
University of Arkansas at Little Rock

Diana M. DiNitto
University of Texas at Austin

In the last 30 years, significant changes in attitudes and policies affecting lesbian, gay, bisexual, and transgendered (LGBT) individuals have occurred, and an increasing body of literature has begun to address the health, mental health, and substance use of these groups. Whereas so-called conversion therapies aimed at changing the sexual orientation of gay, lesbian, and bisexual clients were once an accepted form of treatment, groups such as the American Psychiatric Association, the American Psychological Association, and the National Association of Social Workers now explicitly condemn these practices. Practitioners' focus has now shifted to providing culturally competent treatment for gays and lesbians that considers the challenges they face in the context of today's world. That world continues to be homophobic in many ways, but great progress towards equality is also being made. This chapter addresses substance abuse problems among gay and lesbian individuals. Where appropriate, the needs of bisexual and transgendered clients, groups often neglected in the literature, are also discussed.

Historical Overview

On June 27, 1969, police raided the Stonewall Inn, a popular gay bar in New York City's Greenwich Village. Although the bar had been raided several times and police frequently harassed patrons, this night was different. Rather than accept the raid, patrons fought back, leading to several days of protests, commonly referred to as the Stonewall Riots. Many consider this the beginning of the gay rights movement. One year later, on June 28, 1970, the first gay pride march was held in New York City. These events lead to significant changes in a variety of areas that affected LGB individuals, including changes in the mental health and substance abuse fields. In 1973, the American Psychiatric Association (APA) made its landmark decision to remove *homosexuality* from its classification as a mental illness in the *Diagnostic and Statistical Manual of Mental Disorders (DSM)*, 3rd edition. In 1974, *Social Work*, the flagship journal of the National Association of Social Workers, published its first article that focused on gay and lesbian issues. In the same year, the American Psychological Association created task forces to address gay and lesbian issues. The National Association of Social Workers did the same in 1977. In 1979, the National Association of Lesbian and Gay Addition Professionals, the first organization to address substance abuse problems among gays and lesbians, was founded.

In 1972, Weinberg (1972) coined the term *homophobia* to describe "the dread of being in close quarters with homosexuals" (p. 4), a term that is now widely used to describe the broad range of negative attitudes about gays and lesbians (Hudson & Ricketts, 1980). While treatment with gay and lesbian individuals with substance abuse problems once focused on treating homosexuality (Israelstam, 1986), this treatment now reflects the focus on homophobia as a problem that contributes to the stress that gay and lesbian clients experience. According to the Substance Abuse and Mental Health Services Administration (SAMHSA, 2001), "A provider who understands and is sensitive to the issues surrounding sexual and gender identity, homophobia, and heterosexism, can help LGBT (lesbian, gay, bisexual, and transgender) clients feel comfortable and safe while they confront their substance abuse and start their journey of recovery" (p. xxiii). In fact, as homosexuality came to be viewed as "a normal, healthy, life-style choice…a new question arose: What are the etiology of, associated features of, and cure for individuals who have negative attitudes and reactions toward homosexuals and homosexuality?" (O'Donahue & Caselles, 1993, p. 180).

Substance abuse treatment providers who see LGB sexual orientation rather than addiction as the problem to be treated can harm clients. That does not mean that providers should ignore sexual orientation. In fact, failure to acknowledge clients' sexual orientation and related issues may make recovery from alcohol or drug problems more difficult and increase the chances of relapse (O'Hanlan, Cabaj, Schatz, Lock, & Nemrow, 1997). When sexual orientation and substance abuse are related, providers must be equipped to help clients understand the relationship in order to effectively assist them.

Substance Abuse in Lesbians and Gay Men

Many challenges arise in describing the prevalence of substance abuse in lesbians, gay men, and bisexuals. Chief among them is identifying who is lesbian, gay, or bisexual. Although the terms *lesbian*,

gay, and *bisexual* are generally understood, studies may not distinguish those who identify as gay or lesbian from those who have sex with persons of the same gender but do not identify themselves as gay, lesbian, or bisexual (Crisp, 2003; Gay and Lesbian Medical Association, 2000; McCabe, Hughes, Bostwick, West, & Boyd, 2009). Different methods of assessing sexual orientation may yield different results in both the number of lesbians, gay men, and bisexuals identified in the general population and their characteristics. In recent years, researchers have begun to address these challenges. For example, some of the large-scale studies conducted by the Centers for Disease Control and Prevention (CDC) now ask about both respondents' sexual identity and behavior. In a 2002 study of 12,571 men and women aged 15 to 44, the CDC (Mosher, Chandra, & Jones, 2005) asked "Do you think of yourself as heterosexual, homosexual, bisexual, or something else?", a question that reflects an interest in *identity*. In order to learn more about same sex *behavior*, the CDC asked study participants about their "sexual experiences" with someone of the same sex. Research that inquires about both identity and behavior helps practitioners distinguish who and what is actually being assessed and will lead to greater understanding about the relationship between identity, sexual behavior, and concerns such as substance abuse.

In addition to challenges in identifying who is gay, lesbian, or bisexual, it is often difficult to identify the extent of substance abuse in the general population as well as in the LGB population. The lack of standard criteria used across studies of gay men and lesbians, and more recently bisexuals, to assess substance use, misuse, abuse, and dependence (Gay and Lesbian Medical Association, 2000) impacts what has been reported about these groups. In addition, due to stigma and other fears, gays, lesbians, and bisexuals may be reluctant to report their sexual orientation in studies and surveys (Cabaj, 2000) even when confidentiality is assured, and as an already stigmatized group, they may be reluctant to report problems that could further support negative perceptions of them.

Early studies suggested a higher rate of substance abuse among gay men and lesbians, particularly when compared with men and women in the general population (Fifield cited in Bickelhaupt, 1995; Lohrenz, Connelly, Coyne, & Spare, 1978; Saghir & Robins, 1973), but they were subject to many weaknesses such as the use of small convenience samples rather than probability samples. Later studies also found relatively high rates of substance use and abuse in various samples of gay men and lesbians (Bradford, Ryan, & Rothblum, 1994; McKirnan & Peterson, 1989; Skinner & Otis, 1996), but such studies were still not representative of the gay and lesbian population at large.

An analysis of data from the 1996 National Household Survey on Drug Abuse (now called the National Survey on Drug Use and Health), which is based on a representative sample of the population, did support findings of earlier studies that homosexually "active" women are more likely than other sexually "active" women to be drug or alcohol dependent (Cochran & Mays, 2000). "Active" was defined as having had at least one sexual partner in the past year. There were no significant differences in the prevalence of drug or alcohol dependence between the homosexual men and women, or between people who reported only same-gender partners and those who reported both male and female partners. Both homosexually active men and women were more likely than other sexually active respondents to have received mental health or substance abuse services in the past year. McCabe et al. (2009) used another approach to study substance use based on another representative sample obtained from the National Epidemiological Survey on Alcohol and Related Conditions that found that 2 percent of the population identified themselves as gay, lesbian, or bisexual; 4 percent reported a same sex sexual partner; and 6 percent reported attraction to those of the same sex. These groups generally tended to report more substance use or substance use or dependence than those who identified as heterosexual, had not had a same sex sexual partner, or reported attraction only to those of the

opposite sex. Once again, differences among the groups of women tended to be greater than the differences among the groups of men. However, in many cases, rates of substance use and dependence varied depending on whether the categorization was by identity, behavior, or attraction.

Other large scale national studies have also supported findings that gays, lesbians, and bisexuals may be at greater risk for substance abuse. In a 2003 study of 8,850 Australian women aged 25–30, Hughes, Szalacha, and McNair (2010) found that lesbian and bisexual women were more likely to use illicit drugs than women who identified as exclusively heterosexual. A study of 34,653 individuals in the United States found that lesbian and bisexual women and gay and bisexual men were twice as likely as heterosexual men and women to meet the criteria for a substance use disorder in the past year (Hughes et al.).

Inconsistent findings about substance use and abuse in gay, lesbian, and bisexual communities, particularly when rates were compared to those in the heterosexual population, are likely due to methodological differences and study limitations (Cabaj et al., 2001). Nevertheless, a systematic review of the stronger studies also supported earlier findings. Compared to heterosexuals, substance dependence was estimated to be 1.5 times higher in gay, lesbians, and bisexual individuals with lesbian and bisexual women at especially high risk for substance use disorders while gay and bisexual men had the highest suicide risk (King et al., 2008).

Some studies have focused on particular sexual minority groups or on particular aspects of alcohol or drug problems among these populations. For example, Halkitis, Green, and Mourgues (2005) found that 65 percent of a sample of 450 gay and bisexual men in the New York City area had used methamphetamine in the four months prior to the study. African-American respondents were significantly less likely to use methamphetamine than were whites, Latinos, and Asian/Pacific Islanders, while more educated respondents were more likely to use than less educated respondents. Thiede and colleagues (2003) found that of 3,492 men aged 15 to 22 who have sex with men recruited through community venues, 76 percent reported any illicit drug use, and 28 percent reported using three or more illicit drugs during the past 6 months. The authors also found that men who self-identified as bisexual or heterosexual had a higher prevalence of drug use than men who identified as gay. In a Washington state study, lesbian and bisexual women reported poorer health and mental health than other women, including a greater likelihood of smoking and excessive drinking (Dilley, Simmons, Boysun, Pizacani, & Stark, 2010). In this same study, compared to the heterosexual men, gay and bisexual men also had more disadvantages, including smoking, and bisexual men were also more likely to drink heavily. Overall, bisexuals had the greatest health disparities.

Since studies are generally retrospective rather than prospective, it is unclear what factors may account for any heightened substance use, misuse, abuse, or dependence among gay, lesbian, and bisexual populations. A number of explanations have been suggested, including fewer opportunities to engage in roles that moderate substance use, such as marital partner or parent; socialization in venues that promote substance use, such as gay bars; proscriptions to hide one's sexual orientation; and exposure to stigma, discrimination, and even violence (see, for example, Grella, Greenwell, Mays, & Cochran, 2009; McCabe et al., 2009). One study that did try to tease out mechanisms among 1,141 lesbians living in the southern United States found that stressors associated with being a member of a sexual minority group were related to problematic alcohol use, though some of these relationships were not significant for the 50 and older age group (Austin & Irwin, 2010). For all age groups, depression and general life stressors were more closely related to problematic alcohol use than were stressors specifically associated with sexual minority orientation. What was not clear was the extent to which stressors related to sexual orientation contributed to depression and

general life stressors. Even less is known about the mechanisms that might protect against substance use problems among sexual minorities. Whatever the prevalence rate of substance use and abuse among gays and lesbians and its causes, one thing is clear—treatment providers need accurate information about gay, lesbian, bisexual, and transgendered populations to competently treat them.

Similarities in Identities

An important concept for both people in recovery and for those who come out as gay, lesbian, bisexual, and/or transgendered is that of *identity*. Coming-out theories explain the process by which an individual develops an identity as a gay, lesbian, bisexual, and/ or transgendered person. Comfort with that identity is considered critical to the individual's well being. In a similar vein, many consider the process of identifying oneself as an *alcoholic* or *addict* and its implications as integral to recovery. Although there are many parallels between the two different identities, one important distinction should be made: *alcohol or drug addiction is an illness, while homosexuality is not.* A discussion of the similarities between identity as an addict and identity as a gay, lesbian, or bisexual person may help treatment providers offer more effective services to addicted clients.

Denial. The concept of denial is critical in both recovery from addiction and in the coming-out process for gays and lesbians. Denial is the defense mechanism most often discussed in the chemical dependency literature (see Chapter 5) and is a common problem in most addictions (Van Den Bergh, 1991) that must be addressed before recovery can begin. Denial is also a common problem in the coming-out process for many gay, lesbian, and bisexual people. Several models of coming out discuss denial of feelings of same-gender attraction and view overcoming this denial as a key process in claiming an identity as a gay, lesbian, or bisexual person (Cass, 1979; Eichberg, 1991; Troiden, 1988). During this process, LGB individuals may resort to substance use to respond to these feelings: "Substance abuse may be the primary way they have to deal with the pain associated with an experience that breaks through their denial and shatters their sense of heterosexual identity" (McNally, 2001, p. 87).

Invisibility.   Closely related to the concept of denial is the sense of invisibility for both gay and lesbian individuals and people who have alcohol or drug problems. However, these topics are rarely discussed together: "Books about alcoholism rarely mention gay people. Books about gay people rarely mention alcoholism" (Borden, 2007, p. x). Although textbooks such as the one you are reading are working to change this, many gays and lesbians and people with alcohol and drug problems continue to feel invisible. Annette W., a lesbian with 21 years in AA, speaks to this issue when she says "Gays and lesbians are often reluctant to come out at AA meetings and it may be harder to come out the longer they've been in AA without coming out" (personal communication, July 9, 2010), despite the fact that AA requests "rigorous honesty" from those who want to be successful in their recovery (Alcoholics Anonymous [AA], 1976). Fear of coming out at AA meetings further contributes to the perception that gays and lesbians with substance use problems are invisible.

Self-Definition.   Self-identification is crucial to the process of accepting oneself as a gay or lesbian person or as a person with an addiction and marks the end of denial and the start of a different life. Although many others may have told a client that he or she is addicted to a substance, until the client acknowledges this for himself or herself, the process of recovery will be limited at best. In a comparable manner, it is not uncommon for a gay or lesbian individual to report that others thought he or she was gay or lesbian long before he or she was actually able to acknowledge it.

Disclosure.   Both addicts and LGB individuals frequently face decisions about whether to disclose their respective identities. The *decision* to disclose often varies by situation, but the *need* to disclose endures over time. Disclosure is a means of affirming an identity as a gay, lesbian, or bisexual person and as a recovering addict, and clients should be supported in making decisions about to whom to disclose each of these identities.

Shame.   Both identities are often accompanied by feelings of shame. People with substance abuse problems may experience shame when their attempts to give up substance use fail and from the losses they experience as a consequence of addiction. LGB individuals often feel shame because others often believe their identities should be condemned instead of celebrated. The shame experienced in both cases can have negative consequences and is closely related to denial. For an addict, it may lead to avoidance of treatment and reinforces the addict's natural tendency toward denial (McMillin, 1995). For a LGB individual, shame about his or her identity is closely related to internalized homophobia and can lead to denial about substance abuse (Cabaj, 1995) and difficulty in confiding in treatment providers (Appleby & Anastas, 1998).

Culture.   Both gay and lesbian communities and recovering communities have their own cultures with norms, values, and rules that newcomers must learn. Although there has been considerable debate about what constitutes the gay and lesbian culture, Wright and colleagues (2001) claim that "the gay community possesses common knowledge, attitudes, and behavioral patterns and has its own legacy, argot, folklore, heritage, and history" (p. 20), to which people new to that community may need to become familiar. Similarly, "There is a whole recovery culture consisting of people who are devoted to getting and staying clean. The 'rules' are different among members of this sub-culture from the general culture in which we live" (Sewell, 1998, para. 20).

Freedom.   Many gays and lesbians report a sense of "freedom and liberation" after acknowledging their sexual orientation (Eichberg, 1991,

p. 46). Doing so enables a more complete integration of sexuality into other aspects of one's life. Freedom is also a common theme in the recovery literature: "We are going to know a new freedom and a new happiness" (Alcoholics Anonymous, 1976, p. 83).

Loss.   Both identity as an addict and identity as a gay or lesbian person may be accompanied by loss. Disclosing that one is gay, lesbian, or bisexual may lead to the loss of family members, friends, jobs, custody of children, and/or housing. People with substance abuse problems may also experience these same losses as a consequence of their addiction. In addition, recovery often means "changing people, places, and things," and these changes are often made with an awareness of the loss that results from giving up things that were once so meaningful. Moreover, gays and lesbians with limited support systems may find it difficult to make changes in their social lives to support their recovery. Although some losses may be mourned throughout life, the hope is that newfound freedoms and other benefits of coming out will provide a much more satisfying life.

Language.   Both the gay and lesbian community and the recovering community have a unique language that those outside the community may not understand. For example, AA members often use the term *friend of Bill W.* to identify themselves. The term refers to Bill W., one of AA's founders. The term *family* may be used to describe other gays and lesbians as in "Is he/she family?" when one gay or lesbian individual wants to know if another individual is gay, lesbian, or bisexual.

Treatment: Together or Separate?

Although the first gay AA meeting was held in 1947 and AA's cofounder Bill W. supported it (Jim R., International Advisory Council for Homosexual Men and Women in Alcoholics Anonymous [IAC], personal communication, July 23, 2002), the first substance abuse treatment program that specifically focused on gays and lesbians did not open until 1986 (Ratner, 1988). A SAMHSA (2010) study found that only 6 percent (777) of 13,688 substance abuse treatment facilities survey offered specialized programs for gays and lesbians. Privately run for-profit facilities were twice as likely to offer specialized services. Facilities that offer both mental health and substance abuse services were also more likely to offer specialized services.

Basic goals of specialized treatment programs for gays and lesbians are to affirm gay and lesbian culture and to foster gay pride (Ratner, 1988) so that clients in treatment can disclose their sexual orientation without fear of ostracism or homophobia. According to Hicks (2000), among the many benefits of specialized treatment programs for gay and lesbian clients are that they (1) provide a safe place for gays and lesbians to talk about all aspects of their lives without being criticized or judged, (2) have experience addressing the needs that substance abuse fills in the LGBT community, (3) can readily identify ways for gays and lesbians to socialize without using drugs and alcohol, (4) can provide safe-sex education that is unique to gays and lesbians, (5) understand the coming-out process and how conflicts in coming out may be connected to substance use and abuse, and (6) understand the role of spirituality in the lives of gays and lesbians, including helping clients heal from previous harms caused by homophobic religious organizations.

There are potential difficulties in using separate programs, however. For instance, clients' insurance may not cover specialized treatment programs (Hicks, 2000). Moreover, entering a specialized program will result in disclosure of a gay, lesbian, or bisexual identity, and clients may fear discrimination by insurance companies as a result.

In a survey conducted in Ontario, Canada, of 85 substance abuse professionals, Israelstam (1988) found that respondents were divided on the issue of whether gay men and lesbians needed specialized treatment for their drinking problems. In fact, very little research has addressed whether specialized treatment programs are more effective than mainstream programs for gays and lesbians with substance abuse problems (Anderson, 2009). In one of the few studies on this issue, Senreich (2007) found that those who received treatment in specialized programs for LGBT clients or attended LGBT groups in treatment were more likely to report being abstinent than those who did not attend specialized treatment programs or groups. They also reported higher levels of therapeutic support and connection and were less likely to leave treatment due to their needs not being met.

Arguments for integrated treatment are that it "offers a richness of experience, maintains a proper focus on alcoholism as the primary disease, and facilitates adjustment to the real world after treatment" (Nicoloff & Stiglitz, 1987, p. 288). When staff in integrated programs are knowledgeable about sexual orientation, they can assist those unsure of their sexual identity and those who do not seek specialized programs because they are concerned about exposure of their gay or lesbian identity (Hellman et al., 1989). Mainstream programs must ensure a safe environment for gay, lesbian, and bisexual clients as well as heterosexual clients by addressing homophobia and heterosexism in both clients and staff. For example, a heterosexual client may misinterpret a gay man or lesbian's social interaction with him or her as "coming on" (Nicoloff & Stiglitz). Homophobia may also lead to different standards and expectations for LGB clients. For example, a gay man who discusses his relationship with his same-sex partner may be seen as flaunting his sexuality while a married heterosexual male who shares in a similar way is simply talking about his marriage.

Both integrated and separate substance abuse treatment programs are needed. As with other underserved groups, gays and lesbians should be afforded the opportunity to attend specialized treatment (SAMHSA, 2010). To make both options more viable, Anderson (2009) recommends that the content of specialized programs be more explicitly defined and based on research about the effectiveness of such programs. In one such attempt,

Shoptaw and colleagues (2008) randomly assigned 128 gay men to treatment designed to reduce substance (primarily stimulant) abuse and associated risky sexual behaviors. One treatment was gay-specific cognitive-behavioral therapy; the other was gay-specific social support therapy. The treatments were equally effective in reducing both drug use and sexual risk behaviors. In addition to treatments specifically for LGB individuals, it is important that integrated treatment programs strive to be more sensitive to LGB clients' needs (Anderson). As Blume (1985) noted, existing programs should be modified so that *all* clients can be served effectively. Senreich (2010) further supports this in stating that treatment programs should take steps to ensure that staff members are trained to work with gay and lesbian clients and that gay and lesbian clients are not subjected to homophobic remarks. In addition, when possible, specialized treatment groups should be provided for gay and lesbian clients. Rowan and Faul (2011) also emphasize the importance of addressing LGB clients' needs in all treatment programs: "Without more substantive movement toward culturally competent treatment provisions, the LGBT population may be left in a vulnerable position in mainstream facilities" (p. 113). On what may be considered a positive note, in a study based on a representative sample of Californians, Grella and colleagues (2009) found that lesbian and bisexual women who had an alcohol or drug disorder were just as likely to have received treatment as heterosexual women; there were also no statistically significant differences when gay or bisexual men were compared to heterosexual men.

Gay Affirmative Practice

Practitioners should always treat gay and lesbians clients in ways that support their identity as gay and lesbian individuals. In the last 25 years, *gay affirmative practice* has become the preferred method for treating LGBT clients. Gay affirmative practice "affirms a lesbian, gay, or bisexual identity as an equally positive human experience and expression to heterosexual identity" (Davies, 1996, p. 25). Appleby and Anastas (1998) explain:

> the concept of *gay- or lesbian-affirmative practice* is becoming the goal to which those practicing in the mental health and substance abuse fields are striving. There is no particular approach to psychotherapy or other forms of mental health treatment nor any particular modality of treatment— individual, couple, family, or group—that cannot be made useful for lesbian, gay, or bisexual people if approached affirmatively. (p. 286)

Gay affirmative practice consists of applying the following knowledge, attitudes, and behaviors in treating gays and lesbians.

Practitioners' Knowledge

Practitioners who work with sexual-minority clients need a specific knowledge base from which to approach their treatment with these clients. Key knowledge areas are terminology, impact of oppression, policies that impact sexual minorities' lives, lifespan issues, and community resources.

Terminology.   Fellin (1998) stresses that "a central concern is the need to avoid heterosexual bias in language, so that negative stereotypes are not perpetuated and language is not offensive" (p. 20). Language can affirm one's LGBT identity, but since there is tremendous variation in the terminology that LGBT people use to describe themselves and others like them, practitioners should be sensitive to clients' preferences. The terms *gay, lesbian,* and *bisexual* are preferred over the term *homosexual,* and the term *sexual orientation* is preferred over *sexual preference* (Hunter, Shannon, Knox, & Martin, 1998) because many gays and lesbians believe that their sexual orientation, like that of heterosexuals, is not a choice. Treatment providers who are unclear about what terms to use should ask clients what they prefer and be responsive to clients' feelings and reactions about language that is used to describe their identities, relationships, and behaviors.

Impact of Oppression.   Practitioners should be knowledgeable about how sexual orientation and gender identity affect LGBT clients' lives and about the consequences of living in an environment in which discrimination against LGBT individuals is common. Many people are aware of the more obvious forms of oppression—for example, in employment, in housing, and in adoption laws. Practitioners should also be aware of the oppression that LGBT clients experience continuously, such as not being able to show affection to one's partner in public without fear of violence, constantly deciding about to whom to disclose their sexual orientation, and censoring what they share about their lives as LGBT individuals. Providers may need to help LGBT clients address these forms of oppression during the course of chemical dependency treatment.

Policies That Impact Gays and Lesbians' Lives. Many judicial decisions—as well as policies of national, state, and local governments and public and private organizations—negatively affect LGBT individuals. For example, federal law does not prohibit employment discrimination on the basis of sexual orientation, and many states do not consider crimes targeted at gays and lesbians as hate crimes. However, states that recognize gay marriage and civil unions such as Massachusetts, Connecticut, and Iowa offer gays and lesbians many statewide protections and rights that have historically been limited to heterosexually married couples such as hospital visitation and the right to make decisions about health care issues if one party becomes incapacitated. Knowledge of these policies will assist practitioners in validating the experiences of gay and lesbian clients and in making appropriate referrals and recommendations that may arise during treatment. Practitioners who want to learn more about national, state, and local policies can turn to resources such as the National Gay and Lesbian Task Force[1] and the Human Rights Campaign.[2]

Coming Out and Identity Issues.   Knowledge about lifespan and developmental issues is also key to effective treatment with LGBT clients and their families. Clinicians need "information about gay and lesbian identity development, coming out, and the relationship between a positive gay or lesbian identity and psychological adjustment" (Murphy, 1991, p. 237). Having such knowledge will help practitioners assist LGBT clients and make appropriate referrals based on the individual client's developmental stage. For example, a client in the beginning stages of the coming-out process may not be ready to attend Alcoholics Anonymous (AA) meetings for gays and lesbians, whereas a client who has progressed through more of the coming-out process may find this very useful. Knowledge of the stage the client's family is in with regard to his or her coming out and his or her chemical dependency may also provide helpful information about the degree to which the family accepts and supports the client and the degree to which the client may be able to look to his or her family for support.

Community Resources.   Practitioners should be familiar with resources that support and affirm LGBT clients (Hunter, Shannon, Knox, & Martin, 1998) and that can directly help clients' in recovery from substance abuse problems. Practitioners should create a list of resources that includes

> health, legal, religious, social service agencies, and AIDS programs that work with gay men and lesbian women and are lesbian/gay affirmative. It is also valuable to provide a list of support groups, such as coming out groups at the local women's center; gay fathers' support groups; local gay/lesbian Alcoholics Anonymous meetings; support groups for heterosexual spouses of gay, lesbian, or bisexual partners, or activity groups for gay and lesbian youth. (Murphy, 1991, p. 238)

Given the role of spirituality in recovery and the history of discrimination by religious organizations against gays and lesbians, practitioners should take special care in researching religious organizations and groups before referring LGBT clients to them. Many religious organizations now use terms such as *welcoming* and *affirming* to

indicate that they openly support gay men and lesbians, and they can often be found on the Internet.

Before referring LGBT clients to any organization, practitioners should be knowledgeable about the degree to which the agency and/or its staff are sensitive to LGBT clients' needs. Issues to consider are whether the organization (1) includes sexual orientation in its nondiscrimination policies for staff and clients, (2) has staff that are well educated about LGB issues, (3) has openly identified LGB staff members, and (4) explicitly condemns the use of reparative or conversion therapies in treatment with LGBT clients.

Practitioners' Attitudes

Only a few surveys, each confined to a particular geographical area, have examined substance abuse treatment providers' attitudes toward and work with gay and lesbian clients (Cochran, Peavy, Cauce, 2007; Eliason, 2000; Hellman, Stanton, Lee, Tytun, & Vachon, 1989; Israelstam, 1988). In general, these surveys found that although few providers had any formal education, training, or supervision about assisting gay or lesbian clients, providers generally (1) had positive attitudes about gay and lesbian clients, (2) reported knowing about many of the issues LGBT clients faced or were comfortable helping them even if they lacked specific knowledge, and (3) felt LGBT clients had unique needs or that sexual orientation should be considered in treatment.

Hellman et al., also found that therapists' academic degrees and years of practice were not related to their knowledge of working with gay and lesbian alcoholics, and many thought that achieving sobriety was as difficult, if not more difficult, for them compared to heterosexuals. More recently, Cochran, Peavy, and Cauce (2007) found support for previous studies which indicate that substance abuse counselors (and others) who are heterosexual and those with fewer LGBT friends have more negative attitudes towards LGBT individuals, but their attitudes were more positive than other groups that have been studied.

A key component in providing treatment to gay and lesbian clients is the practitioner's feelings and attitudes about people who identify themselves as gay, lesbian, bisexual, and/or transgendered. Many practitioners deny being homophobic or having anti-LGBT attitudes, feelings, and beliefs. Nevertheless, practitioners may unwittingly express to clients homophobia and its related construct, *heterosexism,* defined as the "promotion and valuing of heterosexuality over nonheterosexuality" (Morrow, 1996, p. 2). Practitioners show signs of homophobia or heterosexism when they are not comfortable hearing about LGB clients' sexual behavior; change the topic or cut clients off when they discuss LGB issues; view LGB clients strictly in terms of their sexual behavior; suggest that clients should not identify as gay, lesbian, or bisexual because they fail to meet some arbitrarily defined criterion; minimize or exaggerate the importance of sexual orientation on clients' lives; or believe that LGB people are not equal to heterosexuals. Practitioners should address these attitudes before working with LGB clients.

Berkman and Zinberg (1997) note that practitioners' homophobia may (1) interfere with counseling, (2) affect transference and counter-transference, (3) lead to inappropriate choices of treatment modality, and (4) result in treatment errors with clients. The result is a lower quality of services that may do more harm than good (Peterson, 1996; Travers, 1998). Many LGBT clients already have a deep sense of internalized homophobia. Experiences with homophobic practitioners may perpetuate this self-hatred (McHenry & Johnson, 1993) and result in noncompliance with treatment (O'Hanlan et al., n.d.). Internalized homophobia and denial of identity as a gay, lesbian, or bisexual person may extend to denial about substance use and abuse (Cabaj, 1995) and prevent a LGB individual from seeking services for alcohol or drug problems.

Practitioners' Skills

Practitioner skills are another element of gay affirmative practice. When providing substance abuse treatment to gay and lesbian clients, the following guidelines may provide a useful framework for practice.

Do not assume that all clients are heterosexual. Practitioners may be unaware that they assume clients to be heterosexual; however, failing to ask about a client's sexual orientation and using opposite gender pronouns when discussing clients' relationships are evidence of this assumption. Such behavior may inhibit clients from disclosing their LGB identity when it would be beneficial to their treatment to do so. Inquiring about sexual orientation is beneficial for both LGB clients and heterosexual clients, as their responses may yield information that is useful at different points in treatment.

Create a safe environment for all clients, regardless of sexual orientation. Programs should require that all staff and clients respect others and that derogatory comments about characteristics such as race/ethnicity, gender, appearance, physical ability, and sexual orientation will not be tolerated. Such comments should be addressed directly. Placing brochures and literature from gay affirmative organizations in public areas also sends the message that the agency supports LGB individuals.

Treat the substance abuse as the problem, not the client's sexual orientation. Regardless of the client's sexual orientation, the practitioner should treat his or her substance abuse or dependence, not his or her sexual orientation (Appleby & Anastas, 1998). In this way, LGB clients will be treated no differently than heterosexual clients. Many factors may cause alcohol and other drug problems, but practitioners should not assume that LGB identity is one of them. Focusing on sexual orientation as the presenting problem can result in the client's minimizing the magnitude and consequences of his or her addiction and what is required for recovery.

Examine the substance abuse in the *context* of the client's life as a gay or lesbian person. A client's identity as a LGBT person is one of many contexts in which his or her substance abuse occurs and should be considered that way. Treatment providers should neither exaggerate nor underemphasize the role of a client's sexual orientation in treating his or her substance abuse (Messing, Schoenberg, & Stephens, 1984). As practitioners gain experience working with LGB clients, they may become more comfortable in determining the appropriate emphasis to place on these issues.

Support clients who are struggling with their sexual orientation, and accept their identification as a LGB person as a positive outcome of any process in which clients have questioned their sexual orientation.   Clients who are struggling with or questioning their sexual orientation need a safe and supportive environment in which to fully explore these feelings (Appleby & Anastas, 1998). Although alcohol and drug problems should be the focus of substance abuse or dependence treatment, practitioners should treat these problems in the context of any uncertainty clients have about their sexual orientation. Regardless of how they choose to identify, clients who receive positive messages about their self-identification may spend less time struggling with sexual orientation and devote more energy to their alcohol and drug problems.

Recognize internalized homophobia.   Clients who openly identify as gay, lesbian, or bisexual, as well as those who question their sexual orientation, may struggle with internalized homophobia. Internalized homophobia can affect clients' expectations of treatment, make it difficult to talk openly with treatment providers (Appleby & Anastas, 1998), and contribute to denial about substance use and abuse (Cabaj, 1995). Given this potential, practitioners should openly confront expressions of internalized homophobia and help clients improve their feelings about their identity as a gay, lesbian, or bisexual person.

When conducting assessments with clients, discuss the extent to which they are out, to whom they are out, and the level of support these people have shown.   Clients who are out to more people or at later stages of the coming-out process may be more receptive to socializing in a variety of venues, may feel more comfortable using gay affirmative resources, and may be more open about their sexual orientation in Twelve-Step meetings and other support groups. These clients may also look to those to whom they are out to support them in their recovery. Identifying these supportive resources may help practitioners better serve the client and make appropriate referrals.

Include significant others and family members in treatment when appropriate.   As with heterosexual clients, family members and significant others may be useful sources of information about LGBT clients' drug and alcohol problems. Although the policies of some treatment organizations preclude contact with individuals who are not legally recognized as family members, treatment providers should advocate for the inclusion of LGBT clients' partners in treatment when indicated. In one of the few studies to specifically consider treatment outcomes for gay and lesbian clients, behavioral couples therapy (BCT), an evidence-based treatment that has been studied with heterosexual couples (see Chapter 6), was used with 52 gay and 48 lesbian clients with alcohol use disorders and their partners who were randomly assigned to either individual-based treatment (IBT) or IBT plus BCT (Fals-Stewart, O'Farrell, & Lam, 2009). Both treatment conditions were equally intensive. In the year after treatment, both the gay and lesbian clients that received BCT had fewer heavy drinking days and better relationship adjustment than those who received IBT only.

In addition, when other family members are included in treatment, practitioners should be mindful that some LGBT clients may not be out to all family members and should be careful not to disclose a client's sexual orientation without his or her permission. To more effectively treat LGBT clients, practitioners should also strive to understand the dynamics of their clients' interpersonal relationships, the problems that same-gender couples may experience, and the diversity and variety of relationships in the LGBT community (McCabe, 2001).

Refer clients to gay affirmative resources. Practitioners should take caution in referring clients to outside agencies and groups, and using the guidelines discussed earlier in this chapter, they should do so only after assessing the degree to which an organization supports sexual-minority clients.

Obtain supervision to deal with negative feelings about gay, lesbian, and bisexual clients. Most practitioners, regardless of their own sexual orientation, have some negative feelings about clients who identify as gay, lesbian, bisexual, and/or transgendered. Rather than deny or hide these feelings, practitioners should use supervision to explore their negative feelings and reactions and to take steps to minimize their impact on treatment (Hunter, Shannon, Knox, & Martin, 1998).

Treatment with Transgendered and Bisexual Clients

As with gay and lesbian clients, treatment providers' awareness of their attitudes toward bisexual and transgendered clients is crucial to effective treatment. Transphobia, negative attitudes toward transgender individuals, and biphobia, negative attitudes towards bisexual individuals, have many of the same origins as homophobia and may influence treatment with transgender and bisexual clients. In one of the only studies to examine substance abuse treatment providers' attitudes about transgendered and bisexual people, Eliason (2000) found treatment providers to be less familiar with bisexual and transgendered issues than with gay and lesbian issues. They were also more likely to report "ambivalent" and "negative" attitudes about bisexual and transgendered clients than they were about gay and lesbian clients. Given previous research that found that contact with gays and lesbians improves attitudes toward them (Hansen, 1982; Millham, Miguel, & Kellogg, 1976), it may be helpful for treatment providers to

acquaint themselves with bisexual and transgendered individuals. Moreover, practitioners should be familiar with the unique issues that need to be considered in treatment with transgender and bisexual clients.

Transgendered Clients

The term *transgendered* refers to people who do not conform to traditional conceptions of gender and sex (Lombardi & van Servellen, 2000) and includes transsexuals, cross-dressers (Tewksbury & Gagne, 1996), and others who identify as gender variant in some way. Leslie, Perina, and Maqueda (2001) have defined these terms that are important in working with transgendered individuals:

Transgender: A continuum of gender expressions, identities, and roles that challenge or expand dominant cultural values of what it means to be male and female.

Gender identity: The gender with which one identifies; this may differ from the gender with which one is born.

Sexual orientation: The gender to which one is attracted; this is distinct from *gender identity*. For example, a person may be a biological male, have a gender identity as a female, be attracted to females, and thus identify as lesbian.

Transsexual: A person whose biological gender and gender identity differ. Many but not all transsexuals desire to change their biological identity through sex reassignment surgery to reflect their gender identity.

Cross-dresser or transvestite: A person whose gender identity and biological gender are the same but who prefers to dress in clothing of the other gender.

Bigendered: A person who identifies with both genders or some combination of both.

The incidence of transgenderism is hard to quantify, as prevalence rates vary by country (Lombardi & van Servellen, 2000) and few prevalence studies have been conducted. A review of studies on transsexualism found that its incidence is approximately 1 in 9,000 to 50,000 individuals (Weitze & Osburg, 1996); however, most of these studies reflect only those individuals who sought sex reassignment surgery. The challenges in identifying how many people identify as transgendered lead to similar challenges in assessing the extent of substance abuse in this group. Whatever the incidence of substance abuse may be, practitioners need to be equipped to address the unique issues of transgendered individuals.

Although the literature about treating people who identify as transgendered is sparse, Leslie and colleagues (2001, p. 97) have created a list of "Dos and Don'ts" for practitioners who provide substance abuse treatment to transgender clients:

DO:

- Use the proper pronouns based on **their self-identity** when talking to/about transgender individuals.
- Get clinical supervision if you have issues or feelings about working with transgender individuals.
- Allow transgender clients to continue the use of hormones when they are prescribed. Advocate that the transgender client using "street" hormones get immediate medical care and legally prescribed hormones.
- Require training on transgender issues for all staff.
- Find out the sexual orientation of all clients.
- Allow transgender clients to use bathrooms and showers based on their gender self-identity and gender role.
- Require all clients and staff to create and maintain a safe environment for all transgender clients. Post a nondiscrimination policy in the waiting room that explicitly includes sexual orientation and gender identity.

DON'T:

- Don't call someone who identifies himself as a female he or him or call someone who identifies herself as male she or her.
- Don't project your transphobia onto the transgender client or share transphobic comments with other staff or clients.
- Never make the transgender client choose between hormones and treatment and recovery.
- Don't make the transgender client educate the staff.
- Don't assume transgender women or men are gay.
- Don't make transgender individuals living as females use male facilities or transgender individuals living as males use female facilities.

In addition, treatment providers should be aware of relapse triggers that are unique to transgender individuals, such as employment difficulties due to transgender status, difficulty obtaining sex reassignment surgery, the overall lack of sober social supports and positive role models, and stress that may result when transgender individuals have to "pass," or deny their transgender identity (Leslie et al., 2001). Practitioners who want more information about treatment with transgender clients are encouraged to read the World Professional Association for Transgender Health's (2001) *Standards of Care for Gender Identity Disorders.*

Bisexual Clients

According to Matteson (1996), people who are bisexual "desire sexual relations with some persons of both genders, whether or not they have yet had sexual experiences with both" (p. 434). Bisexuality is frequently misunderstood, as many people believe that sexual orientation is dichotomous (either gay/lesbian or heterosexual) and that bisexuals are psychologically maladjusted (Fox, 1996). Thus, bisexuals often lack support from both the heterosexual community and the gay and lesbian community (Dworkin, 2001).

In clinical and research studies, including studies of the incidence of homosexuality, bisexual men are frequently grouped with gay men, and bisexual women with lesbian women. Consequently, there is little information about the incidence of bisexuality and the prevalence of substance abuse in those who identify as bisexual. Despite this difficulty, studies conducted by the Centers for Disease Control and Prevention (Mosher et al., 2005) in 2002 found that 2.8 percent of women and 1.8 percent of men aged 18 to 44 identified as bisexual.

Although attitudes towards gays, lesbians, and bisexuals are changing, substance abuse treatment providers may harbor the same beliefs about bisexuals as the rest of the population. These beliefs may also include the perceptions that bisexuals are confused about their sexual orientation, are "stuck" in the coming-out process, have trouble making relationship commitments, need simultaneous relationships with individuals of both genders in order to be content, will have sex with anyone, and will leave a partner of one gender for someone of the other gender (Dworkin, 2001; McVinney, 2001).

To effectively serve bisexual clients, practitioners should view bisexuality as an identity that is stable, fixed, and not pathological. As with gay, lesbian, and transgender clients, practitioners should take care to focus on the addiction rather than on bisexual identity as the presenting problem. Few authors make recommendations for working specifically with bisexual clients, but practitioners are encouraged to do the following (Fox, 1996; McVinney, 2001):

- Recognize that clients may be attracted to both men and women at the same time.
- Work to develop positive attitudes toward bisexual clients.
- Validate the client's experience of attraction to both genders.
- Help the client find information on bisexuality that is not biphobic and develop networks that support his or her identity as a bisexual.
- Recognize that bisexuality may develop early in one's life and may remain intact across the lifespan.

- Work with the client to determine whether referral to gay/lesbian, heterosexual, or both types of Twelve-Step programs and support group is appropriate.
- Help the client to heal his or her internalized biphobia.

Lesbian, Gay, and Bisexual Youth

In recent years, researchers' interest in sexual-minority youth has increased. After a 1989 report by the U.S. Department of Health and Human Services (DHHS) (Gibson, 1989) suggested that gay and lesbian youth are two to three times more likely than their heterosexual peers to attempt suicide, additional resources have been targeted to assist LGBT youth. Although conservatives have widely criticized the DHHS report, other studies have supported the findings. For example, a 1995 study found that youth who experience same-sex attraction are two times more likely to attempt suicide and that 15 percent of all youth that reported suicide attempts also reported same-sex attraction or relationships (Russell & Joyner, 2001). A study of 1,960 LGBT youth, age 25 years and under, found that 68 percent had seriously considered taking their own lives and that 63 percent of these respondents believed these feelings were related to being LGBT (Kryzan & Walsh, 1998).

In addition to increased risk for suicide, research suggests that LGBT youth may face greater stress and have less access to social supports than their heterosexual peers (Hart & Heimberg, 2001). A 2007 nationwide study of 6,209 LGBT students aged 13-21 found that 74 percent reported hearing homophobic remarks often or frequently in their schools. Moreover, 86 percent had been verbally harassed, 44 percent has been physically harassed (pushed or shoved), and 22 percent had been physically assaulted due to their sexual orientation. The majority of these students (60 percent) did not report these incidents to school staff due to concerns that little action would be taken or that the situation would get worse if reported (Gay, Lesbian, and Straight Education Network, 2008). Additional research has found increased rates of dropping out of high school, substance abuse, physical illness, and family discord among gay youth; and these youth may also be at increased risk for victimization, sexual risk-taking behaviors, and multiple substance abuse (Lock & Steiner, 1999). Researchers find that LGBT youth are more likely than their heterosexual peers to use alcohol, marijuana, and cocaine and more likely to use alcohol and cocaine prior to age 13 (Garofalo, Wolf, Kessel, Palfrey, & DuRant, 1998).

Bisexual youth may be at even greater risk for harassment, feelings of sadness and hopelessness, and tobacco and drug use than their gay or lesbian peers (Glazier, 2009). In a longitudinal study of more than 12,000 youth conducted from 1999 to 2005, youth who identified their sexual orientation as other than "completely heterosexual" were more likely to use illicit drugs and to misuse prescription drugs, with bisexual females the group most likely to do so (Corliss, Rosario, Wypij, & Wylie et al., 2010). Though differences among the groups diminished between adolescence and early adulthood, there is concern about the risks drug use poses during adolescence. In another longitudinal study of nearly 11,000 youth, the self-identified LGB youth were more likely to engage in substance use, and their substance use escalated more rapidly than heterosexual youth's during their school years (Marshal, Friedman, Stall, & Thompson, 2009). A meta-analysis of studies also finds that LGB youth were at twice the risk for substance use as heterosexual youth, bisexual youth were at nearly 3.5 times the risk, and lesbian and bisexual females at 4 times the risk (Marshal et al., 2008). In another study based on a sample of more than 14,000 youth, results suggest that youth who were questioning or less certain about their sexual orientation reported the highest levels of substance use, victimization, and suicidal thoughts (Poteat, Aragon, Espelage, & Koenig, 2009). Rosario, Schrimshaw, and Hunter (2009) found that in a sample of 156 LGB youth,

rather than the number of disclosures of sexual orientation or the number of accepting or neutral responses to these disclosures, it was the number of rejecting reactions that was associated with cigarette, alcohol, and drug use. Recent research by Talley, Sher, and Littlefield (2010) suggests "that self-identification as a sexual minority may, in and of itself, impose heightened risk for the acquisition and maintenance of alcohol-related behaviors during emerging adulthood" (p. 240).

In response to the U.S. Department of Health and Human Services' 1989 study on LGBT youth, support groups and services were created across the United States to address the needs of this vulnerable group. Many of these groups have been created in the school system and are referred to as gay-straight alliances (GSAs). Under the Equal Access Act of 1984, any school that provides meeting space for voluntary student organizations must also provide space for GSAs (Gay, Lesbian, and Straight Education Network, 2008). Consequently, GSAs have proliferation (Walls, Kane, & Wisneski, 2010). As of 2008, over 4,000 GSAs were registered with the Gay, Lesbian, and Straight Education Network (GLSEN, n.d.). GSAs provide valuable assistance to gay, lesbian, bisexual, transgender, and questioning youth, can be a useful adjunct to treatment, and offer LGBT adolescents a substance-free environment in which to meet similar youth. As Robinson (1991) describes:

> Support groups for gay youths offer the opportunity to develop social skills, to learn more about others than the familiar stereotypes, and to gain positive gay-affirming information . . . Support groups are safe, positive environments for youths to gather. (p. 458)

Additional research has found several benefits of GSAs. For example, LGBT students in schools with GSAs hear fewer homophobic remarks, experience less harassment and assault because of their sexual orientation and gender expression, are more likely to report harassment and assaults, have a greater sense of belonging, feel safer, have better grades, and are less likely to skip school than their peers in schools without GSAs, and they reported a greater sense of belonging to their school community (GLSEN, n.d.; Walls, Kane, & Wisneski, 2010).

While support groups provide face-to-face resources for LGBT youth, the Internet has also become a good resource for LGBT youth as they can obtain information about LGBT issues anonymously and confidentially. Youth may also connect with others with similar interests through social networking sites such as Facebook and MySpace. National organizations that specifically focus on LGBT youth such as Youth Resource[3]; the National Youth Advocacy Coalition[4]; the Trevor Project[5]; and the Gay, Lesbian, and Straight Education Network[6] provide youth with information on topics such as coming out, sexuality, STDs, violence, substance abuse, and mental health issues. Other national organizations such as the Human Rights Campaign, the National Gay and Lesbian Task Force, and Parents and Friends of Lesbians and Gays have subcommittees dedicated to advocacy on behalf of LGBT youth.

Practitioners who treat LGBT youth should be familiar with the variety of local and national resources available to them but should also note that many communities and schools remain homophobic and are not supportive of LGBT youth. Treatment should thus begin with a thorough assessment of the client's support systems, including those to whom the client has disclosed his or her sexual orientation and those individuals' responses to this information. Knowledge about their responses will provide additional information about the degree to which they support the client as a LGBT person and to what degree the client may be able to look to them for support in his or her recovery from substance abuse. The assessment should also examine the client's degree of comfort with his or her sexual orientation and the degree to which he or she is struggling with internalized homophobia. Treatment providers should work with youth to help them develop a positive identity as LGBT youth.

Treatment providers should also take extra precautions to protect LGBT youth's confidentiality and to avoid inappropriate disclosure of sexual orientation without a client's explicit permission to do. The disclosure of sexual orientation to parents, for instance, may result in the youth being asked to leave home, even without having another place to go (Hunter et al., 1998) and may subject the youth to harassment or other physical or emotional harm because of her or his LGBT identity. When the client has given permission to discuss his or her sexual orientation, providers should advocate with school systems and other service providers to ensure the LGBT youth's safety.

Twelve-Step Groups for Gays and Lesbians

As with much of society, gays and lesbians have not always been widely accepted in Twelve-Step groups such as AA. Although gay AA meetings began in 1947 (Jim R., International Advisory Council for Homosexual Men and Women in Alcoholics Anonymous [IAC], personal communication, July 23, 2002), they were not listed in meeting directories until 1974 and the decision to do so followed arduous debate (Thompson, 1994). In 1989, AA World Services published *A.A. and the Gay/Lesbian Alcoholic*, a 23-page pamphlet on gays in AA. The pamphlet became conference approved literature; however, it does not appear to have been updated since its initial printing. As with much of its literature, this pamphlet can be downloaded at no charge from the Alcoholics Anonymous website. Although it is difficult to identify how many gay AA meetings there are, one figure suggests as many as 1,800 meetings throughout the world every week (Borden, 2007). An Internet search for "gay AA meetings" will lead practitioners to a variety of websites that list gay and lesbian friendly AA meetings. These meetings "are invaluable because they allow people to be completely honest about who they are" (Borden, 2007, p. 127), a key AA principle.

Although anecdotal evidence indicates that gays and lesbians are increasingly accepted at AA meetings, Twelve-Step meetings continue to have their critics. Bittle (1982) notes reasons why gay men and lesbians may not be attracted to Twelve-Step groups:

1. Even though AA emphasizes the similarities rather than the differences among members, gay men and lesbian members may feel that their sexual orientation is a difference that cannot be ignored.
2. The feeling that many members are not comfortable with gay and lesbian issues may cause gay men and lesbians to hide their sexual orientation, which is harmful to their well being. Doing so also conflicts with AA's emphasis on honesty.
3. Although the fellowship of AA encourages each member to develop a program of recovery unique to his or her lifestyle, individual members sometimes offer their own approaches as preferred methods. As a result, the program often appears to be orthodox and rigid to gay men and lesbians (as it can to heterosexuals as well).
4. In the early stages of recovery, sexual abstinence is often promoted to members, as is deferring sexuality issues until more stable sobriety is achieved. However, the issues of sexuality and alcohol abuse are often inextricably linked and may need to be addressed together.
5. Gay men and lesbian members may encounter difficulty with the concepts of God, a higher power, and spirituality, since traditional religious groups have often condemned their sexual orientation and practices (and perhaps their alcoholism). However, the spiritual dimension of recovery is important to many LGBT individuals and should not be overlooked. (see also Ratner, 1988)

Despite these concerns, many support the use of both Twelve-Step and gay Twelve-Step meetings for gays and lesbians in recovery. Saulnier (1994) describes the role that Twelve-Step groups may play in lesbians' lives: "The lesbian Twelve-Step movement has functioned as a way of defining oneself within a community of similar others, as a means of finding a lesbian place in a heterosexual world and a feminist place in AA, and, not to be underestimated, an alternative source of socializing and perhaps a place to meet a life partner" (pp. 267–268). Kominars (1995) further suggests that Twelve-Step programs help both gays and heterosexuals with alcohol and drug problems because they address the four obstacles that block the path to recovery: anger, fear, guilt, and isolation.

Kus and Latcovich (1995) identify 10 benefits of specialized Twelve-Step groups for gay men:

1. They provide an environment in which to establish trust.
2. They bring together a group of people who have shared a common journey as gay men and provide an environment in which one does not have to continually teach non-gay group members about gay culture.
3. They offer a safe place to work through internalized homophobia, which is considered critical to recovery for gays.
4. They enable participants to meet other gay men who are not drinking.
5. They provide the opportunity to openly adapt the AA experience to their experiences as gay men.
6. They may enable participants to rediscover spirituality—a key component of Twelve-Step programs—which they may have rejected because of the antigay bigotry they have experienced in other religious organizations.
7. They help gay men grow in their service work for other gay men and for AA as a whole.
8. They increase participants' sense of social and community awareness to nonalcoholic gay men and to others in general by listing these groups in meeting directories and other resources.
9. They help gay men learn how to experience the fullest in all realms of their lives, including sexuality, leisure, work, school, friendships, and spirituality.
10. They help gay men reduce the anti-male feelings that all men experience.

Source: From Kus, R. J., & Latcovich, M. A. (1995). "Special interest groups in Alcoholics Anonymous: A focus on gay men's groups" from *Journal of Gay and Lesbian Social Services,* 2(1), 67–82. Reprinted by permission of the publisher Taylor & Francis Group. www.informaworld.com.

Many of these benefits may also be applicable to lesbians in recovery.

Very few studies have examined the impact of Twelve-Step programs on abstinence in LGBT individuals. Recently, Rowan and Faul (2011) reported on 125 respondents who had previously received treatment for alcohol and other drug disorders at a specialized treatment center for LGBT individuals. They found that level of AA affiliation (participation in basic AA practices and agreement with AA tenets) was one of two significant predictors of abstinence.

To use Twelve-Step meetings more effectively, Bittle (1982) encourages gays and lesbians to seek out gay and lesbian sponsors or sponsors who are knowledgeable about gays and lesbians, to use additional support groups to address issues not addressed in Twelve-Step meetings, and once they have achieved sobriety, to foster education about gay and lesbian issues in Twelve-Step meetings. Regardless of whether gay, lesbian, bisexual, and transgendered individuals who are recovering from alcohol and drug addiction utilize a Twelve-Step program in recovery, they should seek environments that support their identities as both a LGBT individual and as an individual in recovery.

Summary

Although several studies suggest that gays and lesbians have higher rates of substance use and abuse than people in the general population, the methodological limitations of these studies and the way in which sexual orientation is defined suggest caution when making claims about substance abuse rates in the gay and lesbian population. Whatever the rate of substance use and substance use disorders among this group, treatment providers should be prepared to assist members of these groups.

Gay affirmative practice is increasingly espoused as the preferred method for helping gays and lesbians who seek treatment for a variety of problems. In employing these principles, the clinician considers the client's alcohol or drug problem in the context of his or her experiences as a gay or lesbian person while validating the client's identities as both an individual with a substance abuse problem and as a lesbian or gay individual. In order to work affirmatively with lesbian and gay clients, treatment providers need to acquire the knowledge, attitudes, and behaviors discussed in this chapter.

Providers should also be prepared to treat bisexual and transgendered clients, who face many of the same issues in recovery as gay and lesbian clients but have issues unique to their identities as members of these groups. The literature addressing the special needs of these groups is limited, but much of the information about gay affirmative practice can be applied to treatment with these individuals. Special issues also emerge when treating LGBT youth or youth questioning their sexual identity. When working with a member of any of the groups discussed in this chapter because of an alcohol or drug problem, it is important to focus on that as the presenting problem and not the client's sexual orientation or gender identity.

Although there are some detractors of Twelve-Step groups for gays and lesbians in recovery, these groups can be an important part of recovery, and clients should be encouraged to use them in conjunction with other treatment modalities. Treatment providers should help clients select Twelve-Step groups that will support their identities as LGBT individuals and to identify which type of group or groups (gay men, lesbian women, gay and lesbian, or a general group) may be best suited for them at different points in their recovery.

It is incumbent on all practitioners to develop the knowledge, attitudes, and skills to treat gay, lesbian, bisexual, and transgendered clients. Acquiring such a skill base stands to improve the quality of services provided not only to these clients but to all clients with diverse identities who seek treatment.

CHAPTER 13

Substance Use Disorders and Co-Occurring Disabilities

Diana M. DiNitto
University of Texas at Austin

Deborah K. Webb
St. Edward's University

Nearly 16 percent of the U.S. population aged 5 and older has a sensory, physical, mental, or self-care disability (U.S. Census Bureau, 2008). Beginning in the 1980s, the National Institute on Alcohol Abuse and Alcoholism began to raise awareness about people with substance use disorders who also have other disabling conditions. Several terms have been used to describe the condition of having more than one disability. The National Institutes of Health often use the term *comorbidity,* despite its unpleasant sound. The terms currently in vogue are *co-occurring* or co-existing *disabilities.*

A major study found that people with disabilities had dramatically higher alcohol-related hospital discharge rates than the general population (Dufour, Bertolucci, Cowell, Stinson, & Noble, 1989), but health care providers have not paid sufficient attention to substance abuse among people with disabilities (Office of Surgeon General, 2007). As this chapter illustrates, many people who have substance use disorders *and* other disabilities face barriers in accessing services for alcohol and drug problems (de Miranda, 1999; Krahn, Farrell, Gabriel, & Deck, 2006; Moore, 1998; National Association on Alcohol, Drugs, and Disability, 1999; West, 2007; West, Graham, & Cifu, 2009).

Identification and Attitudes

One barrier to assisting people with co-occurring disorders is helping professionals' failure to identify or intervene in substance use disorders. For example, researchers at the Rehabilitation Research and Training Center (RRTC) on Drugs and Disability at Wright State University found that of approximately 950 vocational rehabilitation (VR) customers who volunteered to participate, 21 percent were identified as having a substance use disorder using a diagnostic interview, but across states, the median percent of VR customers identified as having a substance use disorder was only 10 percent (Heinemann, Lazowski, Moore, Miller, & McAweeney, 2008; Heinemann, McAweeney, Lazowski, & Moore, 2008). In another study, the RRTC (2002) found that 43 percent of respondents with a self-reported alcohol and/or drug problem said that their VR counselor did not know about the problem. Often clients felt the problem was not relevant to their rehabilitation, even though many of them were currently using alcohol or drugs.

People with disabilities have much higher unemployment rates than those without a disability (U.S. Census Bureau, 2007). Given the importance of work in American society, "attainment of employment is both an important motivation for abstinence and an incentive for maintaining it" (Corrigan, Rust, & Lamb-Hart, 1995, pp. 43–44). Researchers find, however, that rehabilitation counselors may have less than optimal attitudes toward clients with alcohol and drug problems (West & Miller, 1999) and that substance abuse treatment facilities often do not aid clients with vocational needs (West, 2008).

A good deal of finger-pointing has occurred among professionals who assist clients who have multiple disabilities. Professionals in the chemical dependency field have accused those in the fields of mental illness and physical disabilities of overlooking (or even tacitly condoning) alcohol and drug misuse in their clientele (Greer, 1986; Nelipovich & Buss, 1991). Conversely, chemical dependency professionals have been blamed for being uninformed about other disabilities and insensitive to the special treatment needs of clients with multiple disabilities.

Section V of the Rehabilitation Act of 1973, as amended, prohibits discrimination against people with disabilities, including alcohol and drug disorders, by health care and other service agencies that receive federal funds. The Anti-Drug Abuse Act of 1986 drew attention to people with disabilities as a group that may have increased susceptibility to substance abuse (Moore & Ford, 1996). The Americans with Disabilities Act (ADA), which passed with overwhelming congressional and presidential support in 1990, put further pressure on public and private facilities to serve those with disabilities. Still, substance abuse treatment programs are often not fully accessible to many people with disabilities. Based on responses from staff at 147 substance abuse treatment programs who reported on 800 individuals with physical disabilities seeking treatment, denials ranged from 87 percent of those with multiple sclerosis to 65 to 75 percent of those with other physical disabilities (muscular dystrophy, traumatic brain injury, spinal cord injury, and other mobility disabilities) (West, Graham, & Cifu, 2009). Medicaid is a major source

of health care for many people with low incomes, including those with severe disabilities. Using the Medicaid database in the state of Oregon, Krahn et al. (2007) found that though adults with disabilities had greater need, they utilized substance abuse treatment at only half the rates of other Medicaid participants.

West (2007) also found that among substance abuse treatment programs willing to respond to a mail survey, three-quarters did not have power-assisted entrance doors, one-fifth lacked accessible restrooms, and nearly one-quarter lacked accessible doorways and halls and auditory and visual fire alarms; of facilities that were more than one story, 40 percent had no elevator or lift. Few facilities had a staff member who knew American Sign Language, and most did not have materials in Braille.

To improve services, chemical dependency prevention and treatment specialists not only need knowledge of disabilities, they need to know the *individual* who has a disability. It is often important to know, for example, whether the individual's disability is congenital and a life-long part of his or her identity or acquired at another stage of development; similarly, it is important to know whether the onset was acute (sudden) or gradual, providing more time for adjustment (Smart, 2001). Understanding the individual's response to disabilities in general and the meaning he or she ascribes to his or her own disability is also important (Smart). Familial, cultural, and societal reactions to a person with a disability also affect the individual's response and adaptation.

In some cases, an alcohol or drug problem precedes a disability and may have been a direct cause of it. For example, HIV/AIDS is often a direct result of illicit drug use, or the connection with drug use can be indirect as a result of sexual relations with an infected drug user. In other cases, excessive alcohol or drug use may be an attempt to adjust to a disability. Even if there is no direct cause-effect relationship, a pre-existing substance use disorder can hinder an appropriate response to a disability, and a substance use disorder that develops following a disability can hinder the acquisition of skills necessary to adjust to the disability and cause previously acquired skills to deteriorate (Koch, Nelipovich, & Sneed, 2002). Professionals often disagree about whether one disability should be treated before the other, which disability should be treated first, or whether substance use disorders and co-occurring disabilities should be treated at the same time.

Substance Use Disorders as a Disability

Many of the controversies over passage of the Americans with Disabilities Act (ADA) reflect ambivalence "about whether to view alcoholism/addiction as a 'real' disability" (de Miranda, 1990), and this may be the reason that federal disability legislation regarding alcohol and drug problems is so complex (Koch, 1999). Today, alcohol and drug disorders are considered disabilities under some federal legislation but not others. For example, as part of welfare reform in 1996, individuals with alcohol or drug disorders are no longer considered disabled under the Social Security Disability Insurance program or the Supplemental Security Income program (a public assistance program for those with little or no income who are disabled). However, an individual who has another disability in addition to a substance use disorder may qualify for benefits under these programs.

Under the ADA, a *disabled individual* is one who has "(a) a physical or mental impairment that substantially limits one or more major life activities of such individual; (b) a record of such an impairment; or (c) being regarded as having such an impairment." The act prohibits health care providers from discriminating against alcoholics and illegal drug users who are otherwise eligible for services. However, under ADA employment provisions, those who use illegal drugs are "specifically

excluded from the definition of a 'qualified individual with a disability'" (see U.S. Equal Employment Opportunity Commission, 2005).

A Cornell University publication helps explain ADA employment provisions with regard to alcohol and drug use, because these provisions are not always easy to understand (Weber & Moore, 2001). The ADA may provide employment protections to individuals who are undergoing rehabilitation and those with past alcohol and drug problems as long as they are not currently using illegal drugs. Alcohol is not considered a drug under the ADA; thus, employment protections include those with alcohol problems who can perform their jobs. Individuals who have been rehabilitated from alcohol and drug addiction may be considered disabled and may be entitled to job accommodations such as work schedule adjustments to participate in treatment (see, for example, Job Accommodation Network, 2010a&b; U.S. Commission on Civil Rights, 2000). The U.S. Equal Employment Opportunity Commission is the authoritative source of information on ADA compliance.

Bruckman, Bruckner, and Calabrese (1996) and Shaw, MacGillis, and Dvorchik (1994) provide information on ADA compliance for alcohol and drug treatment programs and consumers. Of particular importance in meeting the spirit of the law is that treatment programs adopt and include in their materials and outreach efforts a statement of their genuine interest in accommodating individuals with co-occurring disabilities (Moore, 1998). Too often, programs have focused on how to exclude rather than include individuals with co-occurring disabilities. When individuals with co-occurring disorders do not succeed in chemical dependency treatment, insufficient attention to accommodations may be to blame (Moore, 1998). This chapter focuses on the incidence of substance use disorders among those with co-occurring disabilities, who should treat them, the optimum settings for treatment, and the treatment techniques and modalities that might produce the best results.

Mental Illness and Substance Use Disorders

Interest in co-occurring mental and substance use disorders has surged. The *Diagnostic and Statistical Manual of Mental Disorders (DSM) 4th ed., text revision* (American Psychiatric Association, 2000) divides mental disorders into two broad categories: Axis I and Axis II. Axis I includes substance use disorders (dependence and abuse), severe mental disorders (e.g., schizophrenia, schizoaffective disorder, major depression, bipolar disorder), and other mental disorders such as anxiety disorder, phobias, and posttraumatic stress disorder (PTSD). Axis II contains the ten personality disorders and mental retardation (the preferred term is now *intellectual disability*, discussed later in this chapter). Box 13.1 contains brief descriptions of common Axis I and II mental disorders. The treatment of mental illness and substance use disorders is also called *behavioral health care*, though this term may be a misnomer because these disorders often have a neurobiological basis, and health problems often affect behavior as do mental and substance use disorders.

Mental illnesses affect a significant number of Americans. In 2008, 9.8 million adults (18 years of age and older) had severe mental illnesses (Substance Abuse and Mental Health Services Administration, 2009). Of these adults, 2.5 million had severe mental illnesses in combination with substance use disorders. Of them, 40 percent received no treatment at all; 45 percent received treatment for their mental illness only, 4 percent got substance use disorder treatment only, and only 11 percent received treatment for both disorders.

The literature on helping clients with co-occurring mental and substance use disorders (also called *dual diagnoses*) can sound discouraging. Clinicians often report that it is much more difficult to treat clients with co-occurring disorders compared to those with one type of disorder. Studies indicate that clients with dual disorders have more negative outcomes: "severe financial problems resulting from poor money management;

unstable housing and homelessness, medication noncompliance (lack of adherence), relapse, and re-hospitalization; violence, legal problems, and incarceration; depression and suicide; family burden; and high rates of sexually transmitted diseases" (Drake & Mueser, 2000, p. 106). Professionals who become frustrated in working with clients who have dual diagnoses may lack understanding of the symptoms and behaviors associated with mental illness or substance use disorders and have insufficient knowledge of how to best treat each type of disorder and combinations of disorders. Other frustrations may stem from separate data systems and public funding streams for each type of disorder that create significant barriers to helping clients with co-occurring disorders obtain the services they need (Coffey et al., 2008; Ziedonis et al., 2005). Work in the field is challenging, and clients often face a difficult course. Helping professionals must convey the message of hope for recovery.

Prevalence of Co-Occurring Mental Illness and Substance Use Disorders

The Epidemiologic Catchment Area (ECA) study found that "having a lifetime mental disorder is associated with more than twice the risk of having an alcohol disorder and over four times the risk of having another drug abuse disorder" (Regier et al., 1990, p. 2514). The National Comorbidity Survey (NCS) and the National Comorbidity Survey Replication (NCS-R) identified even higher rates of dual disorders; for example, 51 percent of those with a lifetime mental disorder also had a lifetime addictive disorder (substance abuse or dependence), and 41 to 66 percent of those with a lifetime addictive disorder had a lifetime mental disorder (Kessler et al., 1996; also see Kessler, Berglund, Demier, Jin, & Walters, 2005a; Kessler, Chiu, Demier, & Walters, 2005b). The National Longitudinal Alcohol Epidemiologic Survey also found high rates of comorbidity; for instance, "The risk of having a drug use disorder among those with major depression was about seven times . . . as great as among

BOX 13.1   *Examples of Axis I and Axis II Mental Disorders*

Axis I Mental Disorders

Psychotic Disorders

- *Schizophrenia* is a disorder that lasts for at least six months and includes at least one month of active-phase symptoms (i.e., two or more of the following: delusions, hallucinations, disorganized speech, grossly disorganized or catatonic behavior, negative symptoms).
- *Schizophreniform disorder* is characterized by a symptomatic presentation that is equivalent to schizophrenia except for its duration (i.e., the disturbance lasts from one to six months) and the absence of a requirement that there be a decline in functioning.
- *Schizoaffective disorder* is a disorder in which a mood episode and the active-phase symptoms of schizophrenia occur together and were preceded or are followed by at least 2 weeks of delusions or hallucinations with prominent mood symptoms.

Mood Disorders

- *Major depressive disorder* is characterized by one or more major depressive episodes (i.e., at least two weeks of depressed mood or loss of interest accompanied by at least four additional symptoms of depression).
- *Bipolar I disorder* is characterized by one or more manic episodes (abnormally and persistently elevated, expansive, or irritable mood for one week, or less with hospitalization) or mixed episodes for at least one week (criteria for both a manic episode and a major depressive episode are met nearly everyday), usually accompanied by major depressive episodes.
- *Bipolar II disorder* is characterized by one or more major depressive episodes accompanied by at least one hypomanic episode (abnormally and persistently elevated, expansive, or irritable mood that lasts at least four days), accompanied by at least three other symptoms (e.g., inflated self-esteem or decreased need for sleep).

- *Dysthymic disorder* is characterized by at least two years of depressed mood for more days than not, accompanied by additional depressive symptoms that do not meet the criteria for a major depressive episode.
- *Cyclothymic disorder* is characterized by at least two years of numerous periods of hypomanic symptoms that do not meet the criteria for a manic episode and numerous periods of depressive symptoms that do not meet the criteria for a major depressive episode.

Anxiety Disorders

- *A panic attack* is a discrete period in which there is the sudden onset of intense apprehension, fearfulness, or terror, often associated with feelings of impending doom. During an attack, symptoms such as shortness of breath, palpitations, chest pain or discomfort, choking or smothering sensations, and fear of "going crazy" or losing control are present.
- *Agoraphobia* is anxiety about or avoidance of places or situations from which escape might be difficult (or embarrassing) or in which help may not be available in the event of having a panic attack or panic-like symptoms.
- *Panic disorder without agoraphobia* is characterized by recurrent, unexpected panic attacks about which there is persistent concern.
- *Panic disorder with agoraphobia* is characterized by both recurrent, unexpected panic attacks and agoraphobia.
- *Obsessive compulsive disorder* is characterized by obsessions (which cause marked anxiety or distress) and/or by compulsions (which serve to neutralize anxiety).
- *Posttraumatic stress disorder* is characterized by the re-experiencing of an extremely traumatic event, accompanied by symptoms of increased arousal and by avoidance of stimuli associated with the trauma.
- *Generalized anxiety disorder* is characterized by at least six months of persistent and excessive anxiety and worry.

Axis II Personality Disorders

Cluster A

- *Paranoid personality disorder* is a pattern of distrust and suspiciousness, such that others' motives are interpreted as malevolent.
- *Schizoid personality disorder* is a pervasive pattern of detachment from social relationships and a restricted range of expression of emotions in interpersonal settings.
- *Schizotypal personality disorder* is a pervasive pattern of social and interpersonal deficits marked by acute discomfort with reduced capacity for close relationships and cognitive or perceptual distortions and eccentricities of behavior.

Cluster B

- *Antisocial personality disorder* is a pattern of disregard for and violation of the rights of others.

- *Borderline personality disorder* is a pattern of instability in interpersonal relationships, self-image, and affects and marked impulsivity.
- *Histrionic personality disorder* is pervasive and excessive emotionality and attention-seeking behavior.
- *Narcissistic personality disorder* is a pervasive pattern of grandiosity, need for admiration, and lack of empathy.

Cluster C

- *Avoidant personality disorder* is a pattern of social inhibition, feelings of inadequacy, and hypersensitivity to negative evaluation.
- *Dependent personality disorder* is a pattern of submissive and clinging behavior related to an excessive need to be taken care of.
- *Obsessive-compulsive personality disorder* is a preoccupation with orderliness, perfectionism, and mental and interpersonal control at the expense of flexibility, openness, and efficiency.

Source: Reprinted with permission from the *Diagnostic and Statistical Manual of Mental Disorders*, Fourth edition, Text Revision, Copyright © 2000 American Psychiatric Association.

---

those without major depression" (Grant, 1995, p. 489). Researchers continue to report similarly high rates of co-occurring disorders (Watkins et al., 2004; Havassy, Alvidrea, & Mericle, 2009). In clinical samples, the prevalence may even be higher, especially among younger people who have had greater exposure to illicit drugs (Wise, Cuffe, & Fisher, 2001).

The NCS also found that individuals with mental disorders are more likely to have diagnoses of substance dependence rather than substance abuse (Kessler et al., 1996; see Chapter 5 of this text for the distinctions between *abuse* and *dependence*). Among those with any Axis I mood (affective) disorder, 41 percent had some type of addictive disorder, including 71 percent of those diagnosed with mania. Among those with any anxiety disorder, 38 percent also had an addictive disorder. Those with an Axis II conduct disorder or adult antisocial personality disorder were most likely to have an addictive disorder

(82 percent). Although causal relationships cannot be established from these data, the NCS found that mental disorders tend to precede addictive disorders rather than vice versa. Only among men with affective disorders and alcohol use disorders did the addictive disorder generally precede the mental disorder. When mental and addictive disorders co-occurred, the mental disorder often began during adolescence. However, the order of occurrence of mental and substance use disorders has become harder to discern as young people have initiated alcohol and drug use at increasingly earlier ages (Pepper & Ryglewicz, 1982).

Evidence also indicates that the order of occurrence of mental and substance use disorders may not be a simple one. Among a sample of 425 clients receiving drug treatment, antisocial personality disorder and phobias (which typically begin during childhood) were most likely to precede drug dependence, while the majority of generalized anxiety disorder cases postdated drug dependence (Compton, Cottler, Phelps, Abdallah, & Spitznagel, 2000).

Studies conducted in multiple countries also find generally strong associations between substance use disorders and mood, anxiety, conduct, and antisocial personality disorders across sites (Merikangas et al., 1998; Rodriguez–Llera et al., 2006; Pozzi et al., 2006). Among individuals with comorbidity, drug disorders are associated with greater severity of psychiatric and substance problems than are alcohol disorders, and the severity of comorbidity is generally greater for substance dependence than substance abuse (Merikangas et al.). Hasin et al. (2007) also found that disability (i.e., impaired psychosocial functioning) increases with the severity of alcohol dependence. Clients with dual or multiple disorders often report abusing more than one substance (DiNitto, Webb, & Rubin, 2002). In a longitudinal study, Booth et al. (2010) found strong associations between multiple substance use and increased psychological distress (decreases in substance use correlated with decreased psychological distress).

When it comes to gender, "the magnitude of comorbidity tended to be greater for females, particularly at lower levels of severity of substance use" (Merikangas et al. 1998, p. 899). NCS analyses of co-occurring alcohol use disorders and mental disorders also find that "co-occurrence is stronger among women than men" and "that the anxiety and affective disorders constitute the largest proportion of lifetime co-occurring cases among women, while the substance disorders, conduct disorder, and antisocial personality disorder account for the majority of co-occurrence among men" (Kessler et al., 1997, pp. 318, 320).

Theories of Co-Occurring Mental Illnesses and Substance Use Disorders

It is not clear why some people develop mental disorders, others substance use disorders, and some both types of disorders. Mental disorders and substance use disorders may have separate etiologies and courses (Alterman, 1985), but given the substantial level of co-occurrence of these disorders, we must ask why.

Mueser, Drake, and Wallach (1998a) grouped the various theories of why these disorders may co-occur into four models. The first model suggests that factors such as genetics and having antisocial personality disorder (ASPD) contribute to both mental disorders and substance use disorders. They found more support for the ASPD explanation than shared genetic vulnerability.

The second model includes Khantzian's (1985, 1997) widely debated self-medication hypothesis:

> The self-medication hypothesis...derives primarily from clinical observations of patients with substance use disorders. Individuals discover that the specific actions or effects of each class of drugs relieve or change a range of painful affect states. (Khantzian, 1997, p. 231)

For example, it has long been hypothesized that nicotine may augment dopamine release which "could be especially appealing to psychiatric patients in whom these systems are deficient (Glassman, 1993). Stasiewicz et al. (1996) suggested that people who have bipolar disorder may use alcohol (a central nervous system depressant) to control a manic episode or slow rapid thoughts. Treffert (1978) found that people with paranoid schizophrenia had a propensity for using marijuana, a phenomenon Khantzian (1985) called "nonrandom self-medication." McLellan, Childress, and Woody (1985) reported that patients with depression preferred barbiturates, and patients with paranoid schizophrenia preferred amphetamines and hallucinogens (even though these drugs may exacerbate hallucinations, confusion, and suspicion). Others have not found a relationship between drugs selected and type of mental illness (Aharonovich, Nguyen, & Nunes, 2001; Ogborne et al., 2000).

Mueser et al. (1998a) found less support for the self-medication hypothesis and more support for a *general alleviation of dysphoria theory*, in which people with severe mental illness begin using alcohol and other drugs for the same reasons that other people do—to feel better. Minkoff (2002), for example, suggests that people with severe mental illness use drugs to escape isolation, boredom, loneliness, and despair and to improve peer relations and socialization. In the long-run, however, substance abuse produces negative rather than positive outcomes.

The idea that mental disorders contribute to the risk of substance use disorders also includes a *supersensitivity theory*, in which genetic factors interact with early life events and other environmental stressors, making people with major mental illnesses vulnerable to the effects of even small amounts of alcohol and other drugs (Mueser et al., 1998a; also see Ziedonis et al., 2005), an idea similar to Ryglewicz and Pepper's (1990; 1996) "substance vulnerability" hypothesis.

McLellan and colleagues (1985) considered the third theory that chronic drug use may result in mental illness, perhaps by producing biological changes in the individual. But as discussed earlier in this chapter, the National Comorbidity Survey conducted in the United States found that a mental illness often precedes a substance use disorder (rather than vice versa). In addition, alcohol disorders are common among individuals with severe mental illness, but alcoholism does not seem to cause severe disorders such as schizophrenia and bipolar disorder (Mueser et al., 1998b).

The fourth theory suggests that mental and substance use disorders exacerbate each other. Mental health and chemical dependency practitioners use this theory by repeatedly instructing clients that substance abuse can produce mental distress or precipitate episodes of mental illness, which can increase drug use and, in turn, create more mental distress (see, for example, Bakdash, 1983). They also instruct clients that failure to manage mental illness with prescribed medications and self-care routines can precipitate substance use, also resulting in a cycle of more distress and more substance abuse (DiNitto & Webb, 2001; Webb, 2004).

Whatever the explanation for why mental and substance use disorders co-occur, when a person has *bonafide* mental and substance use disorders, both illnesses must be addressed. Whether the mental illness precedes the substance use disorder or vice versa, once expressed, the substance use disorder is unlikely to disappear by treating the mental illness, and the mental illness is unlikely to disappear by treating the substance use disorder. Both illnesses should be considered primary and treated simultaneously (Minkoff, 2001a).

Assessment of Co-Occurring Mental Illness and Substance Use Disorders

Substance Vulnerability. Helping professionals generally believe that substance abuse or dependence can exacerbate mental disorders, but there is less awareness that many individuals with mental disorders have such fragile brain chemistry that so-called social use can also cause psychotic episodes. Take the case of a young man who had three psychiatric hospital admissions in one year. His mental health workers assumed it was non-adherence with medications that precipitated his episodes, but none asked him about his alcohol use. Prior to each hospital admission, he had drunk up to a six-pack of beer. When the client himself recognized the association between his drinking and his psychotic episodes and decided to quit drinking altogether, he was not hospitalized for several years. In another example, a caseworker was asked at a staffing about a female client with whom she had worked closely for three years. The client had had multiple psychiatric hospitalizations. The caseworker gave a long list of observations about the client's daily behaviors, but none indicated intoxication or addiction. Subsequently, the client met with the mental health team and was asked what symptoms she had noticed before her admissions. Much to her caseworker's surprise, the client replied that every time she drank even one beer, the next thing she knew, she was in the hospital. Her use of alcohol was so minimal that it had gone undetected, but its effects were powerful enough to precipitate re-hospitalizations. These examples demonstrate the need to screen clients with mental disorders for substance *use* as well as abuse and dependence, even though such minimal use does not meet criteria for substance use disorders.

Other difficulties in identifying individuals with co-existing disorders have been mental health professionals' tendency to overlook substance use and abuse problems (perhaps rationalizing that "everyone drinks" or "they are just self-medicating") (Ryglewicz & Pepper, 1990). Substance abuse professionals may also have a tendency to minimize mental illness symptoms ("they will clear up with sobriety") (Weiss & Mirin, 1989; Winter, 1991).

Clinicians may find behavioral assessment useful in helping clients identify relationships between increases and decreases in substance use and symptoms of mental illness, including the antecedents and consequences of both types of behaviors (Stasiewicz et al., 1996). A behavior chain generally includes the following: "Trigger/ Thought/ Feeling/Behavior/Consequence" (Stasiewicz et al., p. 97). To break the chain and avoid negative consequences, behavioral therapists help clients work backward by identifying the negative consequence first, then the behavior that prompted the consequence, the feeling that prompted the behavior, and so forth.

Screening Tools.   Few screening tools for substance use disorders have been developed specifically for people with mental disorders, but the tools described in Chapter 5 of this text may be utilized (see also DiNitto & Crisp, 2002; Ziedonis et al., 2005), especially with higher functioning clients.

- When screening time is limited, the four-question CAGE (Ewing, 1984) has been suggested (Sciacca, 1991). The CAGE Adapted to Include Drugs (CAGE-AID) may also be used with instructions to the client that "when thinking about drug use, include illegal drug

use and the use of prescription drugs other than as prescribed" (Brown, Leonard, Saunders, & Papasouliotis, 1997, p. 102). These instructions may assist in screening clients who have been prescribed medications for their psychiatric disorders but may not be taking them precisely as intended by the doctor.

- A meta-analysis found that the Michigan Alcoholism Screening Test (MAST; Selzer, 1971) had sufficient validity in psychiatric settings (Teitelbaum & Mullen, 2000). The instrument worked equally well whether respondents had schizophrenia or other psychiatric disorders.

- The Drug Abuse Screening Test (DAST; Skinner, 1982) is often used to screen for drug problems other than alcohol. Rosenberg, Drake, Wolford and Mueser (1998) found that it might not classify hospitalized patients with severe mental illness as well as some other instruments, but Cocco and Carey (1998) found that it had good reliability and validity with outpatients who had major psychiatric disorders.

Screening patients who have severe mental disorders for alcohol and other drug problems may be best accomplished with interviews rather than self-administered paper-and-pencil tests (Carey & Correia, 1998; RachBeisel, Scott, & Dixon, 1999). Clear and simplified wording and response options also makes it easier for clients to answer (Carey & Correia). More validation of the commonly used alcohol and drug screening instruments is needed for people with major psychiatric disorders, as well as better tools and improved screening techniques for those with co-occurring disorders.

Toxicologies (tests of urine, blood, or hair) may be used to corroborate information obtained from client records as can information obtained with the client's written consent from family, friends, and other service providers, especially if the client is unable or unwilling to provide accurate information. The conditions that improve screening for clients with substance use disorders discussed in Chapter 5 of this text also pertain to people with dual diagnoses. For example, be non-judgmental, build rapport with the client, and verify that the client is free of intoxicating substances and psychiatrically stable (Skinner, 1984). Responses are also generally more accurate when the client does not fear negative repercussions, such as mandated chemical dependency treatment or psychiatric hospitalization.

Practitioners should maintain a healthy skepticism when patients whose behavior indicates problematic use deny they use alcohol or drugs (Drake & Mueser, 2000; Mueser et al., 1999). While underreporting substance use is common, over-reporting may also occur as a way to gain access to desired services and other resources (Carey & Correia, 1998).

Failing to recognize mental disorders in clients receiving treatment for substance use disorders is a risk for treatment dropout (Schulte et al., 2010). Many tools are available for screening adults for mental disorders, such as the Brief Psychiatric Rating Scale (BPRS), used to assess the severity of current psychiatric symptoms (Miller & Faustman, 1996), and the Beck Depression Inventory (BDI) (Beck, 1978; Steer & Beck, 1996).

Diagnosis. In the United States, mental and substance use disorders are diagnosed based on criteria found in the *Diagnostic and Statistical Manual of Mental Disorders* or *DSM* (American Psychiatric Association, 2000). The Structured Clinical Interview (SCID) (First, Spitzer, Gibbon, & Williams, 1997) and the Psychiatric Research Interview for Substance and Mental Disorders (PRISM; Hasin et al., 1996), which are based on *DSM* criteria, are tools to aid in making these diagnoses. The brief Alcohol Use Scale (AUS) and Drug Use Scale (DUS) also rely on *DSM* criteria and utilize practitioners' ratings to assess (and monitor changes in) the alcohol and drug use of clients with major psychiatric disorders (Drake, Mueser, & McHugo, 1996).

A critical skill, especially in acute situations, is being able to differentiate substance use disorders from psychiatric illnesses. During emergencies, accurately diagnosing can be difficult because the effects some drugs produce appear very similar to the manifestations of psychoses (Turner & Tsuang, 1990; Ziedonis et al., 2005). For example, stimulants such as cocaine can produce an episode that appears to be paranoid schizophrenia, but if drug induced, the episode will usually remit within a few days (Zweben, 1996). Individuals dependent on alcohol and other sedative/hypnotic drugs may exhibit depressive symptoms during detoxification, but such symptoms will usually ease within a few weeks (Zweben). When they do not, a diagnosis of major depressive disorder may be supported.

In criminal justice settings and in emergency health and mental health settings, urine toxicologies or other laboratory procedures are often used to detect alcohol and other non-prescribed or street drug use. Many outpatient mental health and chemical dependency service providers do not use them, despite their usefulness in detecting substance use and differentiating symptoms of use from psychiatric disorders. Zweben (1996) reported a situation in which this testing may have been very helpful: "a staff member in a social model community recovery center prepared to discharge a participant who was talking loudly to herself, on the grounds that she was intoxicated. The director, observing the interchange, asked the participant if she was hearing voices" (p. 348). The client was indeed hearing voices as a result of her co-occurring mental illness. In a similar vein, mental health staff may misdiagnose patients with substance-induced psychoses as having an acute exacerbation of a severe mental illness.

Diagnostic errors may result in inappropriate treatment; in particular, mistaking a substance-induced psychosis for a primary psychotic disorder could cause a client to receive antipsychotic medication for a needlessly long period (Carey & Correia, 1998). A firm diagnosis often cannot be established until the patient is alcohol and drug free, but when the patient is known to have a psychiatric disorder requiring psychotropic medication, it is usually administered. An expert panel appointed by the Substance Abuse and Mental

Health Services Administration (SAMHSA) recommends that "medication for known serious mental illness should never be discontinued on the grounds that the patient is using substances" (Minkoff, 2001a, p. 599).

Ongoing Biopsychosocial Assessment.   People who have major psychiatric disorders and substance use disorders need comprehensive, ongoing, biopsychosocial assessment. In addition to the *DSM's* Axis I and II diagnostic criteria, Axes III, IV, and V are used for biopsychosocial assessment (American Psychiatric Association, 2000). Axis III is used to document physical illnesses. Many physical illnesses can affect the course and treatment of Axis I psychiatric disorders. For example, the insulin level of a client with diabetes must be carefully monitored, as it may be affected by medications used to treat mental illness. Liver and kidney damage (which may or may not be alcohol or drug related) can complicate the treatment of psychiatric disorders because some medications used to treat mental illness are contraindicated in the presence of these physical illnesses. Many people being treated for chemical dependency and mental illness are also receiving treatment for HIV or hepatitis C, requiring the monitoring of medications for each condition. Comprehensive and coordinated mental health, substance abuse, and health services are critical for people with co-occurring disorders (Ziedonis et al., 2005; Sterling, Chi, & Hinman, 2011).

Axis IV covers psychosocial and environmental problems that may affect the course and treatment of Axes I and II diagnoses, such as lack of social supports, discrimination, illiteracy, unemployment, housing and financial difficulties, lack of access to health and social services, and legal concerns (similar to the assessment process described in Chapter 5 of this text). Problems on Axis IV may also result from positive changes, such as a job promotion that the client has difficulty handling due to low self-esteem or difficulty with stress and anxiety. These problems are common among people who have major psychiatric and substance use disorders and must be addressed if a person is to achieve and maintain recovery from multiple disorders.

Axis V is based on the Global Assessment of Functioning (GAF) Scale that clinicians use to describe clients' overall functioning (American Psychiatric Association, 2000). It is especially useful in documenting urgent situations such as persistent danger of severely harming others or intent to commit suicide.

The Addiction Severity Index (ASI) (also described in Chapter 5 of this text) is a client assessment and progress-monitoring tool widely used in chemical dependency assessment, treatment, and research (McLellan et al., 1985). The ASI covers seven domains (medical, employment, alcohol, drug, legal, family/social, and psychiatric problems). Few other tools assess all these domains. The ASI has been used with people who have severe mental illness and substance use disorders with varying degrees of success (Appleby, Dyson, Altman, & Luchins, 1997; Carey, Cocco, & Correia, 1997). Administering it to persons with mental illnesses or dual disorders may take a little longer, but the information obtained can help develop a thorough treatment plan, and the follow up version can be used to track progress on client outcomes over time.

The Substance Abuse Treatment Scale (SATS) (Drake, Mueser, & McHugo, 1996) is a brief 8-point scale that can help clinicians identify the client's stage of or need for substance use disorder treatment (ranging from an active substance use disorder and no contact with treatment providers to remission from a substance use disorder) in order to match the client with appropriate services. Few other instruments have been developed specifically for clients with co-occurring psychiatric and substance use disorders.

Treatment of Co-Occurring Mental Illness and Substance Use Disorders

Alcohol and drug treatment programs may exclude clients whose psychopathology is evident following detoxification, using excuses such as the client's "lack of motivation" (which is a symptom of mental illness called *amotivation*) or "inability to benefit from treatment" (which is a biased and pessimistic prognosis). Though some clients with severe mental illness are, indeed, too fragile or confused to participate in chemical dependency treatment (Harrison, Martin, Tuason, & Hoffman, 1985), most can and do benefit if given the opportunity. Despite increased knowledge of co-occurring disorders, many clients continue to encounter serious gaps in services (Drake & Mueser, 2000) or receive little or no help.

Integrated Treatment. Initial attempts to treat individuals with co-occurring mental and substance use disorders involved providing services *sequentially* or *in tandem*, first by a mental health professional and then by a chemical dependency treatment provider or vice versa. This approach seemed reasonable a quarter of a century ago, but it did not prove to be very successful (Minkoff, 1989; Osher & Kofoed, 1989).

The problems with sequential treatment likely stem from chemical dependency and mental health treatment providers' different perspectives and approaches. Chemical dependency treatment has relied on peer counseling, mutual-help meetings, group treatment, an abstract spiritual approach, confrontation, detachment, abstinence from all substances (including psychotropic and antidepressant medications), and episodic treatment following relapse (Minkoff, 2002). Chemical dependency professionals may have considered alcohol and drug use the *cause* of most mental illness symptoms. Mental health treatment has been quite different, relying on professional service providers, scientifically based treatment, liberal use of medications, individualized treatment, case management, and continuous care (Minkoff). Mental health professionals have often considered substance use a *symptom* of mental illness. These different and often conflicting approaches have made it difficult for clients with co-occurring disorders to figure out how to best use services, and may have caused them to avoid services.

Clients who have a substance use disorder (and no mental illness or no severe mental illness) may feel uncomfortable with individuals who are also struggling to control symptoms of severe mental illness (e.g., mania, severe depression, hallucinations, and other thought disorders) and who may need more structured and concrete approaches to substance abuse education and group therapy. Individuals with co-occurring disorders who are treated in chemical dependency programs may sense this and be inhibited from talking about their psychiatric problems and either directly or indirectly reinforced to deny them. Similarly, clients with co-occurring disorders who are treated in psychiatric programs may deny or minimize their substance use disorders because other clients are unaware of their need to address this problem or do not understand the dynamics of chemical dependency. Treating clients with dual or multiple disorders together with clients who have a single diagnosis presents challenges, though they are not insurmountable.

Parallel or *concurrent* treatment was designed to overcome the shortcomings of sequential treatment. In parallel treatment, a chemical dependency professional and a mental health professional treat the client simultaneously. By coordinating services and approaches to treatment, they avoid sending the client conflicting messages about recovery. Parallel treatment generally requires extra time on the part of providers to communicate with each other, though electronic client records in "real time" can aid in the process. Parallel treatment can be costly because it requires two providers rather than one. Funders are often unwilling to pay for such care. Another variation of parallel services is to treat patients in a psychiatric program and to invite a chemical dependency professional to provide education and conduct group therapy as an add-on to mental health treatment (Hendrickson, 1988).

Parallel treatment programs are also called partially integrated care. Chemical dependency professionals and mental health professionals learn from each other and in effect cross-train each other on-the-job. For at least the last decade, chemical dependency treatment programs and mental health treatment programs have been implored to include services for persons with dual disorders (Minkoff, 2001b).

Parallel or partially-integrated approaches can help, but they still rely on practitioners whose expertise is in chemical dependency or mental illness, rather than in the special needs and problems of persons who have co-occurring illnesses. The newest models used to treat dual diagnoses are called *integrated* treatment. In the ideal design, specialists in co-occurring disorders provide clients fully integrated services. This saves time and money and is less potentially confusing for clients since what treatment providers say and advocate is more likely to be consistent and congruent with the treatment plan (instead of having multiple plans and providers) (Watkins et al., 2005; Primm et. al., 2000; Timko et al., 2003).

In an integrated setting, mental illnesses and substance use disorders are generally considered similar or parallel illnesses. Minkoff (2002) describes the following similarities between the two disorders: (1) they are physical (biological), mental, and spiritual diseases but are often seen as moral issues; (2) they are partly hereditary but are seen as diseases of denial that are chronic, incurable, and worsen without treatment; (3) they can lead to depression and despair; (4) they can result in lack of emotional and behavioral control; (5) they can produce feelings of guilt, failure, shame, and stigma; (6) they can have positive and negative symptoms; (7) they can affect the entire family; and (8) their symptoms can be controlled with treatment. Mee-Lee (2002) also notes that "addiction illness and many psychiatric disorders are chronic, potentially relapsing illnesses often needing on-going process of treatment, rehabilitation and recovery, with brief episodes of acute care and stabilization." He believes that a biopsychosocial perspective of mental and substance use disorders provides a common language that can be used for assessing and treating mental and substance use disorders. Integrated treatment requires staff well-versed in both disorders, including the challenges that co-occurring disorders present to clients and their families. Webb

(1992) communicates this perspective directly to clients, noting that it makes sense to treat all illnesses simultaneously because what works for one illness helps wholistically.

There is no single definition of integrated treatment (Mee-Lee, 2002), but the American Society of Addiction Medicine (ASAM) (Mee-Lee, Shulman, Fishman, Gastfriend, & Griffiths, 2001) suggests that the following elements are necessary for programs that accept clients with co-occurring mental and substance use disorders:

- M.D. and Ph.D. level staff skilled in diagnosing psychopathology.
- A majority of staff are cross-trained to deal with both mental and substance-related disorders.
- Psychoeducational components of treatment address both mental and substance-related disorders.
- A psychiatrist is available on site in acute settings and through coordination in all other settings.
- Medication management is integrated into the treatment plan.
- Counselors are trained to monitor and promote medication adherence.
- In programs that work with persons who are severely mentally ill, intensive case management and assertive community treatment services are available. (p. 11)

Stein and Test (1980) developed Assertive Community Treatment (ACT) for people with severe and persistent mental illness. Over the past 30 years, this evidence-based approach has been widely adopted (see Co-Occurring Center for Excellence, 2008). ACT relies on teams of service providers to keep clients involved in services in attempts to improve their social functioning, quality of life, and other outcomes and reduce lengths of stay in psychiatric hospitals.

Minkoff (2002) reminds providers of the necessity for individualized treatment planning dependent on the client's situation and available supports. In 2001, he published service planning guidelines for persons with co-occurring disorders in conjunction with his work with the Behavioral Health Recovery Management Project.

In a study conducted by SAMHSA, two-thirds of programs that provided mental health and chemical dependency services reported that they offered dual-diagnosis services, while 57 percent of mental health service programs and 38 percent of substance abuse treatment programs reported that they provide services for dually diagnosed clients (Office of Applied Studies, 2002). Using data from the National Survey of Substance Abuse Treatment Services, Mojtabai (2004) reports that half of all chemical dependency treatment facilities in the United States provide dual diagnoses services (p. 525), though it is not clear what program components are provided or how comprehensive the services are. There has been considerable progress in the dual diagnosis field, but many communities still do not have a full continuum of care or any integrated services for persons with dual disorders (Hendrickson, Schmal, & Ekleberry, 2004).

Diagnostic Distinctions in Treatment Planning and Service Delivery. Although there is no consensus on the optimal psychotherapeutic treatments for clients with combined mental and substance use disorders, some diagnostic distinctions seem to be important in determining the course of treatment. In treating clients with personality disorders, Ekleberry (see, for example, Ekleberry, 1996; Hendrickson et al., 2004) advises that treatment approaches consider the client's specific personality disorder and functional ability. For example, she considers some degree of confrontation an appropriate aspect of treatment for persons with antisocial personality disorder and finds it useful with high-functioning persons who have borderline or histrionic personality disorders. She does not recommend such an approach with people who have borderline personality disorder combined with a low global assessment of functioning or with people who have narcissistic or avoidant personality disorders.

Personality disorders can complicate chemical dependency treatment when they result in impulsiveness, unstable affect, and identity confusion (Naegle, 1997). Naegle suspects that health care providers may avoid individuals with narcissistic personality disorders because they complain and are never satisfied. Individuals with untreated personality disorders, especially borderline personality disorder, may also elicit negative reactions among staff (Zweben, 1996). Linehan, an expert on Borderline Personality Disorder (BPD), and her colleagues (Linehan et al., 1999) conducted a one-year study and follow up of women with BPD and substance dependence. The women were randomly assigned to Linehan's Dialectical Behavior Therapy (DBT), a form of behavioral therapy and cognitive behavioral therapy, or to treatment as usual (TAU). Those who received DBT achieved more improvement on a variety of variables. The development of specialized approaches like DBT lends hope to the treatment of persons with dual or multiple diagnoses, including severe personality disorders and chemical dependency.

Many clients with Axis I severe mental illnesses are at risk of decompensating from the confrontation used in traditional chemical dependency treatment programs (Daley, 1996; Ekleberry, 1996; Sciacca, 1991). They may regress, withdraw, or become delusional (Evans & Sullivan, 2001). Thus, dual-diagnosis experts use only gentle confrontation combined with a great deal of support and take care to maintain appropriate therapist-client boundaries to address denial and inappropriate behavior. Confrontation should always be utilized with care, regardless of a client's diagnosis.

One way to determine the type of treatment people with co-occurring disorders need is to think of their illnesses as falling into one of four categories or quadrants (Rosenthal & Westreich, 1999):

1. Clients who rate high on both disorders are chemically dependent and have a severe mental illness (e.g., schizophrenia, bipolar disorder, or another psychotic disorder) or a certain

personality disorder (e.g., borderline, antisocial) and are functioning poorly. They are likely to need stabilization of the mental illness and substance use disorder, including detoxification, in an inpatient treatment setting followed by efforts to retain them in services, such as case management and residential treatment, until ready to progress to outpatient services.

2. Clients who rate high on mental illness severity and low on substance use disorder severity have a severe mental illness and generally a substance abuse diagnosis. Following stabilization after an acute psychiatric episode with intensive mental health treatment, the recommended services are integrated treatment in a day-treatment setting or with well-coordinated parallel services.

3. Clients who rate low on mental illness and high on substance use severity have substance dependence and often a substance-induced mood, anxiety, or personality disorder. They generally need inpatient detoxification following relapse of their substance use disorder, but when clean, sober, and stable, their functioning is not severely impaired. They can utilize regular chemical dependency treatment program services with additional services to address other problems.

4. Clients who rate low in severity of both disorders have a milder psychopathology (e.g., dysthymia, generalized anxiety, an adjustment disorder, situational stress, or a Cluster C or less severe Cluster B personality disorder) and misuse or abuse substances (they are not chemically dependent). Upon refraining from substance use, these higher-functioning individuals are often good candidates for outpatient treatment.

Source: Based on "Treatment of persons with dual diagnoses of substance use disorder and other psychological problems" by R.N. Rosenthal and L. Westreich, from B.S. McCrady & E.E. Epstein, eds., ADDICTIONS: A COMPREHENSIVE GUIDEBOOK, pp. 439–476. (New York: Oxford University Press, 1999).

Clients in all four groups may benefit from medication-assisted treatment for mental and/or substance use disorders (also see Chapters 3 and 6 of this text).

The American Society of Addiction Medicine (ASAM) (Mee-Lee et al., 2001) also suggests that patients or clients with the following types of mental disorders can receive substance use disorder treatment in more traditional chemical dependency treatment programs: moderate severity mental disorders (e.g., stable mood or anxiety disorders), severe antisocial personality disorders or other personality disorders of moderate severity, and mental illnesses symptoms that are not severe. Those with high-severity mental disorders (e.g., "schizophrenia-spectrum disorders, severe mood disorders with psychotic features, severe anxiety disorders, or severe personality disorders, such as fragile borderline conditions") should be treated in "dual diagnosis specialty programs that can offer integrated mental health and addiction treatment" (Mee-Lee et al., 2001, p. 8).

ASAM uses the term *dual-diagnosis capable* to describe programs that focus on treating substance use disorders but can accommodate clients who have relatively stable severe or less severe mental illnesses and who are able to function independently. *Dual-diagnosis enhanced* programs provide integrated treatment to those with more unstable or disabling mental disorders in addition to substance use disorders and are staffed by mental health, addiction, and dual-diagnosis professionals, including psychiatrists (Mee-Lee et al., 2001).

Some chemical dependency programs are not capable of serving clients with mental illness, and many communities lack programs that are dual diagnosis enhanced or capable. Thus, treatment providers often have to scramble to put a package of services together for clients with co-occurring disorders. More chemical dependency treatment programs are responding to the increased demand for dual-diagnosis treatment by hiring professional staff who are qualified to treat both illnesses.

Stages or Phases of Treatment.   Engaging people with co-occurring disorders to accept treatment often takes a good deal of effort and time (Hellerstein, Rosenthal, & Miner, 2001; Kofoed & Keys, 1988; Osher & Kofoed, 1989). Engagement may be "conceptualized as therapeutic effort specifically aimed at combating the extreme demoralization and resultant nihilism so frequently encountered in patients with a dual diagnosis" (Kofoed, 1997, p. 216). Engagement is the first and therefore the most critical stage in dual-diagnosis treatment. In fact, one job that has emerged in the mental health and dual diagnoses fields is called *engagement specialist.*

Meeting basic survival needs consumes the energy of many individuals with co-occurring disabilities, particularly those who are homeless and living on the streets. Engagement strategies may begin by helping them obtain food, shelter, medical and dental care, and other services they need or desire (Mueser et al., 1998b). Kofoed (1997) calls these strategies "remoralizing." Engagement specialists and members of assertive community treatment teams and continuous treatment teams (Drake et al., 1993) go to the client rather than expecting the client to come to them. Once an alliance has been established, the client can be encouraged to obtain mental health and chemical dependency treatment.

Clients engaged in services may eventually decide to adopt a goal of abstinence (Kofoed, 1997), or the client may chose to reduce alcohol or drug use, also called the harm reduction model. Harm reduction can have many benefits. For example, it can help prevent the spread of diseases common among drug-injecting individuals, such as hepatitis C and HIV, through the use of clean needles instead of dirty ones. One approach to persuading clients to adopt a goal of abstinence or participate in more services or positive activities is a specialized psychoeducational group, which is also used to complement other treatment modalities (Pepper, 1991). Psychoeducation may be most useful when it begins by describing a problem in a way that makes sense to the client. For example, a substance use disorder may be defined as "a loss of consistent control over substance use" (Atkinson, cited in Kofoed & Keys, 1988) or substance use that results in serious life problems (family, social, psychological, job, and legal) (Keller, 1958). Like others with substance use disorders, many clients with co-occurring disorders do not necessarily connect their alcohol and other drug use with the life problems they are experiencing unless they learn about such correlations in a psychoeducation group.

Attending an educational, cognitive support group can be a positive experience that may evoke less psychological resistance compared to one-on-one work with a professional. Osher and Kofoed (1989) describe the Substance Abuse Group Experience (SAGE) with psychiatric inpatients to help persuade them to "acknowledge their drug addiction and to seek continued substance abuse treatment" (p. 1210). Peer-group discussions are used to address denial and to encourage outpatient follow-up after discharge. Psychoeducation combined with therapy groups are being used as catalysts for engagement and change in settings such as homeless shelters, soup kitchens, and "housing first" settings where many currently or recently homeless people with dual and multiple disorders spend time (Webb, 1992, 2004). The outreach efforts and forbearance required of professionals to engage some individuals to recognize their illnesses and accept services cannot be overstated, but it must be done to alleviate needless suffering and save lives.

Osher and Kofoed (1989) originally conceptualized the recovery process from substance use disorders for people with co-occurring mental disorders, and McHugo, Drake, Burton, and Ackerson (1995) expanded on it. Eight stages are delineated:

1. *pre-engagement:* no contact with mental health or substance abuse service providers;
2. *engagement:* some but not regular contact with service providers;
3. *early persuasion:* regular contact with service providers but little or no substance use reduction;
4. *late persuasion:* regular contact and movement toward reducing substance use;
5. *early active treatment:* regular contact and progress toward non-problematic use or abstinence;
6. *late-active treatment:* greater acknowledgement of a substance use problem and a period of non-problematic use or abstinence;
7. *relapse prevention:* the client is engaged in treatment and has attained non-problematic use or abstinence for at least six months;
8. *remission* or *recovery:* the client has no substance-related problems for over one year and has "graduated" from substance abuse treatment.

Relapse often occurs during the course of recovery. Clients in most residential chemical dependency treatment programs are subject to automatic discharge if they relapse to alcohol or drug use, though they can often be readmitted after having returned to a clean and sober state. The clients in dual diagnosis treatment programs are generally not discharged if they relapse, because relapse is considered a natural part of the recovery process. Clients with co-occurring disorders should not fear discharge when a relapse occurs as long as they process it honestly and learn from it. Dual diagnosis experts realize that abstinence is generally achieved slowly and that reducing substance use is an achievement deserving of reward.

Many chemical dependency treatment providers in the United States take exception to the idea that any substance use is acceptable for those diagnosed with substance dependence. Abstinence is widely supported, and rightly so, for many. Abstinence and reduced use (harm reduction) are not mutually exclusive goals; they can be thought of as different parts of a continuum in the recovery process. Individuals who initially agree to a goal of harm reduction may eventually adopt a goal of abstinence. The "experts" may have their opinion, but clients have a right to self-determination, including the right to pursue the goal they are willing to work toward achieving at any given point in time.

The *transtheoretical* or *stages of change model* (Connors, Donovan, & DiClemente, 2001; Prochaska, DiClemente, & Norcross, 1992), described in Chapter 5 of this text, has been widely applied in treating people with dual diagnoses (Rosenthal & Westreich, 1999; DiClemente, Nidecker, & Bellack, 2008). The most critical stages of the transtheoretical model for clinicians in the dual diagnoses field are probably precontemplation and contemplation because these are the stages that clients must work through before they will accept services. It is important to note that people with dual disorders may be in one stage with regard to their mental illness and another with regard to their substance use disorder and need services that are geared

accordingly (Velasquez, Carbonari, & DiClemente, 1999). The ASAM patient placement criteria (Mee-Lee et al., 2001), also described in Chapter 5 of this text, and Rosenthal and Westreich's (1999) four-quadrant model provide clinical wisdom about the services clients may need given their biopsychosocial functioning. Clinical wisdom also suggests that the services offered to clients should be consistent with their current stage of treatment or change and researchers have been studying whether this can be verified empirically (see James et al., 2004). For example, a person with less motivation for recovery needs more proactive assistance from service providers, and clients in the engagement stage are unlikely to accept intensive chemical dependency treatment geared to those in the active treatment phase.

Psychotropic Medication Adherence. Medication adherence (taking medication in the prescribed manner) is a complicated matter. For example, Freudenreich and Tranulis (2009) find that there are five different types or degrees of medication adherence among persons with schizophrenia ranging from those who take medications as directed and for the "right" reasons to those who are militantly opposed to taking them. People with mental illnesses and their caregivers often hold very different opinions about medication adherence, and this can result in power struggles, distrust, and animosity. An important part of recovery is encouraging clients who need psychotropic and anti depressant medications to stick with their medication regimen and discuss medication problems and concerns with their psychiatrist. Sometimes this encouragement or "coaching" is more acceptable coming from a third-party professional, such as a case manager or therapist, rather than a family member.

An essential task of professionals who assist clients with dual diagnoses is monitoring medication adherence (Mee-Lee et al., 2001). Helping clients who are able and willing to improve their medication adherence is a respectful and valuable treatment tool (Velligan et al., 2006; Webb, 2004). Some clients have brain damage, called "anosognosia," that decreases or prevents them from understanding that they have mental illnesses and need medications (Torrey, 2006, p. 51). A small number who are at risk of being a danger to themselves or others when non-adherent to medications may benefit from being placed on an outpatient commitment that allows them to live in the community if they take their medications but returns them to a psychiatric hospital if they do not and begin to decompensate. This proactive approach is designed to prevent the suffering that results from severe decompensation. Some states like New York have established laws such as "Kendra's Law" to force such treatment for clients who meet specified criteria. Some positive outcomes have been reported (Swartz et al., 2010). Psychiatrist, advocate, and author E. Fuller Torrey, whose sister had severe mental illness, founded Treatment Advocacy Centers, which advocate the judicious use of such Assisted Outpatient Treatment (AOT).

Clients who take psychiatric medications, and their loved ones, need education about the medications they are prescribed, including their potential side effects. Clients are often reluctant to question their psychiatrists, but it is important that the psychiatrist and the client work together to identify the best medication(s) for the client and to modify the regimen when needed. Case managers, social workers, counselors, nurses, nurse practitioners, and others can mediate and advocate when necessary. Helpful medication resources for nonphysicians include Preston, O'Neal & Talaga (2010). Pharmacists can also answer many questions about medications and side effects. When used wisely, the Internet offers a great deal of educational material about medications, especially from the manufacturing pharmaceutical companies.

Education about the potential adverse effects of co-using alcohol, street drugs, and other non-prescribed drugs, including over the counter drugs, and some homeopathic remedies and supplements should be made clear and consistent: (1) the use or abuse of alcohol, street drugs, and/or other non-prescribed drugs can adversely affect mental stability, and (2) the interactions of non-prescribed and prescribed drugs can be harmful or lethal. For some patients, treatment staff must consistently differentiate between *improper drug use* (i.e., street drugs, alcohol, and over-the-counter and prescription drugs not used as directed) and *medications* (i.e., drugs used by the client exactly as prescribed by a psychiatrist or other physician) (Bricker, 1995; Webb, 1994).

Comprehensive Services. Clients with co-occurring disorders generally have multiple needs that must be met to promote recovery (Drake et al., 1993; Drake & Mueser, 2000; Mueser, Drake, & Noordsy, 1998b; Rosenthal & Westreich, 1999). Treatment approaches commonly used are motivational interviewing, case management, skills training, cognitive behavioral therapy, behavioral therapy (including contingency management), and relapse prevention (Horsfall, Cleary, Hunt, & Walter, 2009). Clients may require psychiatric stabilization, health care, intensive case management services, residential care that promotes independent living skills, and help in obtaining a regular source of income through work or governmental aid, food, shelter, transportation, and once stable, decent permanent housing.

Many people with single diagnoses have functioned well in the past (they held a job and lived independently). Many with severe co-occurring disorders, especially those who have been living on the streets, need help with independent living skills. These skills are generally taught through training and educational programs that use showing and doing rather than lecturing. Though recovery usually does not occur in a linear fashion (Rosenthal & Westreich, 1999) since clients may regress at times, treatment providers should help clients make smooth transitions through the continuum of care to promote long-term, successful client outcomes.

Those who lack supportive social networks may find residential treatment programs such as halfway houses, modified therapeutic communities,

Oxford Houses, and single room occupancy (SRO) subsidized housing, especially those with added onsite services, particularly beneficial (Daley, Moss, & Campbell, 1987; De Leon, Sacks, Staines, & McKendrick, 2000). In fact, therapeutic communities originated to assist people with psychiatric problems but grew in popularity among those with drug addictions (see Chapter 6). Most communities lack the housing and services to meet the need.

A number of residential programs now operate specifically to help people with co-occurring disorders. Residents of these programs typically participate in individual and group therapy, psychiatric and chemical dependency services, educational classes, services to promote their independent living skills, and social and recreational activities geared to promote social functioning. An increasing number of residential programs for people who have mental illnesses are also available to those who have co-occurring disorders. Before referring clients with co-occurring disorders to these programs, clinicians should ensure that abstinence from alcohol and other non-prescribed drugs is a program requirement ("dry" environment), or at least that such consumption is not allowed on premises ("damp" environment).

Halfway houses designed for people who are chemically dependent may also accept individuals with co-occurring disorders, especially if their mental illness is in remission. Before making referrals to these programs, it is necessary to determine if they accept clients taking psychotropic medications, harm reduction medications such as methadone, and/or pain medications that are carefully prescribed and monitored. Some residential programs do not. People with mental illnesses should not be expected to do without life-saving mental health medications in order to qualify for residential chemical dependency treatment services. Residential programs in which the length of stay is based on individual need are particularly desirable, since individuals who have co-occurring disorders may need longer treatment than individuals with single diagnoses or permitted by halfway

houses that serve individuals with substance dependence or mental illness.

Day treatment may be an alternative to residential treatment when the individual can live with a supportive, enlightened relative or friend in a drug-free environment or in a community support residential program. Sciacca (1987) and Aliesan and Firth (1990) describe model day-treatment programs that offer integrated services for people with co-occurring mental and substance use disorders.

Most people who have severe mental illness and chemical dependency are served on an outpatient basis. Intensive case management, offered by ACT teams or continuous treatment teams, is an important component of outpatient treatment for many of these individuals. Families are not always able to respond to the multiple needs of members with co-occurring disorders, so case managers act as guides who help clients navigate the maze of mental health, chemical dependency, health, and social services (Rosenthal & Westriech, 1999). Close monitoring of clients with impaired functioning is recommended to ensure that they continue to utilize services and sustain a decent quality of life (Drake et al., 1993). In treating clients with co-occurring disorders, program administrators should select staff who are especially interested in providing long-term, comprehensive, and integrated services to this clientele (Doub, 2002).

Family Involvement.   When able to assist, and clients give permission for them to do so, family members can be a treatment team's most important allies. Family members can provide valuable information for constructing a social history. They are often able to identify subtle nuances of behavioral change (i.e., early warning signs) that their loved ones' symptoms of mental illness and/or substance use disorders are returning. Family members can be involved in creating treatment goals. They can also help by being as consistent and predictable as possible in their responses to the client, practicing "tough love," positively reinforcing accomplishments, shaping and extinguishing behaviors, not enabling, and refraining from use of high expressed emotion or EE (e.g., criticism, hostility, or yelling when their loved one does not comply) (Leff & Vaughn, 1980; Vaughn & Leff, 1976).

Family members often feel alone, ashamed, and suffer in isolation or blame themselves when their loved one has mental and substance use disorders. Stigma and embarrassment often prevent them from sharing their fears and challenges with others. Family support groups—such as Al-Anon for those with alcohol-dependent loved ones and Naranon for those with loved ones dependent on other drugs— can offer tremendous relief through understanding and fellowship. These groups encourage family members to take care of themselves and maintain healthy boundaries with their loved ones, such as avoiding preoccupation with attempts to "control" others' behavior. These groups also provide a wealth of useful literature. The National Alliance on Mental Illness (NAMI) also offers support and advocacy groups for family members of persons with mental illness in many communities. A few groups focus specifically on the concerns of families with members who have severe mental illnesses (such as the National PLAN Alliance created by NAMI in 1997) or dual diagnoses (Sciacca, 1991).

Psychoeducation is being used to help family members understand dual disorders and recovery; decrease their own stress, worry, guilt, anger, and enabling behaviors; promote their coping and communication skills; and instill hope for their loved one's improvement (Daley, 2002). The application of multifamily group (MFG) treatment (Anderson, Reiss, & Hogarty, 1986; McFarlane et al., 1993) for those with co-occurring disorders has also been important (Dixon, McNary, & Lehman, 1995; Drake et al., 2008; Mannion, Mueser, & Solomon, 1994). As its name implies, MFG brings clients and their families and other support persons together, so they can learn to assist the person with severe mental illness.

Mutual-Help Groups. Twelve-Step programs may be helpful to people with dual or multiple disorders (Bogenschutz, Geppert, & George, 2006), though little research has been conducted on the topic. DiNitto et al. (2001) found substantial mutual-help group attendance (primarily AA) among a group of 79 dually diagnosed clients, most of whom had mood rather than thought disorders as well as chemical dependency. The only factors studied that predicted the number of meetings clients attended were education (the more years of education, the more meetings attended) and major substance problem (those whose major problem did *not* include alcohol attended more meetings, though the reason for this is not clear).

Kurtz et al. (1995) also found substantial AA attendance among a group of 40 clients with dual diagnoses. About half of the participants reported feeling nervous in meetings, but 58 percent felt supported and 68 percent felt close to other group members (although only the support variable correlated with level of AA involvement). As in the DiNitto et al. (2001) study, the only demographic variable that correlated with AA involvement in the Kurtz et al. study was education. Participation in mutual-help groups and activities can lead to the development of a network of sober peers. Without sober peers with whom to identify and socialize, many clients find it difficult to impossible to stay sober and clean.

Individuals whose mental illness does not involve thought disorders (e.g., those with major depression), may be better able to utilize groups such as Alcoholics Anonymous (AA) (DiNitto et al., 2001). Noordsy and colleagues (1996) suggest that people with schizophrenia (a thought disorder) might be deterred from attending mutual-help groups because they often have difficulty sitting still during meetings, fear crowds, and believe that others are watching them. In addition, slogans such as "Let go and let God" may activate delusional religious ideation (Noordsy et al., 1996), and phrases such as "Restore us to sanity" may lead a person with mental illness to believe that medications can be abandoned as long as he or she follows the program (Wallen & Weiner, 1989).

At times, well-meaning but misinformed AA members (as well as relatives and friends at church, etc.) have told individuals with dual disorders to stop taking psychotropic medications, which they lump together with all other drugs. In 1984, at the request of Alcoholics Anonymous World Services (AAWS), a group of physicians who are members of AA wrote *The AA Member— Medications and Other Drugs* (AAWS, 1984). This AA pamphlet, often referred to as *P11*, includes examples of people who use medications properly as well as improperly and clearly admonishes that "No AA Member Plays Doctor." A similar Narcotics Anonymous pamphlet is called *In Times of Illness* (Narcotics Anonymous World Services, 1992). Professionals who make referrals to AA and Narcotics Anonymous (NA) can use these materials to prepare clients with co-occurring disorders for the possibility of misguided advice and how to deal with it.

In many communities, the number of mutual-help meetings specifically for people with co-occurring disorders is insufficient to meet clients' needs or desires. Coaching individuals with co-occurring disorders on how to participate in regular AA or NA groups can help address this gap (Minkoff, 1989; Webb, 1992, 2004) and provides additional sources of support. Professionals and individuals with dual diagnoses who are knowledgeable about meetings in their communities can assist others in selecting the most appropriate and supportive meetings.

Adaptations of the original AA Twelve-Step program (see Chapter 6) are being used to help people with co-occurring mental disorders. In 1982, professionals and volunteers from AA joined together to start Double Trouble groups in New Jersey (Caldwell & White, 1991; Noordsy, Schwab, Fox, & Drake, 1996; Woods, 1991). Bricker (1995) developed a support group for individuals with schizophrenia and chemical dependency problems called Support Together for Emotional and Mental Serenity and Sobriety (STEMSS). STEMSS consists of six steps that Erickson and Bricker adapted from the original Twelve Steps of AA to include mental illness. They deleted references to a "higher power" due to the abstract nature of the concept. Weekly meetings focus on

chemical dependency and mental illness as parallel disorders and offer direction and social interaction for those with dual problems. Similar groups continue to develop across the United States. Dual Recovery Anonymous (DRA) is another mutual-help organization dedicated to helping people who have "chemical dependency and emotional or psychiatric illnesses." Hamilton and Samples (1994, 1995) published a blueprint for Dual Recovery Anonymous and an easy to read workbook to help people with dual disorders accept their illnesses and work the Twelve Steps.

Mutual-help programs are run by individuals in recovery from various illnesses. Good Chemistry Groups (Webb, 1990, 1992, 2004) differ from mutual-help groups in that they are hybrid groups which are led or co-led by mental health, chemical dependency, or dual-diagnoses professionals. Certified Peer Specialists who have been sober, clean, and stable for at least a year assist in conducting the group sessions. The peer co-leaders serve as role models who inspire hope and lend expertise and credibility to the groups. Since 1990, Good Chemistry groups have offered clients a safe and supportive atmosphere in which to explore and address their illnesses. The groups, which have also been modified for use in a variety of settings (e.g., homeless shelters, psychiatric hospitals, and meal sites), generally combine 15 minutes of psychoeducation with 45 minutes of group therapy.

One way Good Chemistry Groups help clients accept their severe mental illnesses and substance use disorders is by teaching them how professionals use the *DSM-IV-TR* (American Psychiatric Association, 2000) to objectively diagnose illnesses. During this process, participants may come to recognize their symptoms in the *DSM*. Participants also learn how to utilize mutual-help groups, treatment options, and other supports and consider the benefits of staying clean, sober, and mentally and physically stable (which often include the need for medications). In AA and NA, members ask another member to sponsor them. In Good Chemistry, sponsors are the group as a whole or the groups' leaders rather than individual Good Chemistry members so as not to overtax individuals who are managing their own multiple disorders. Good Chemistry does give individual members the opportunity to be of service to their peers by supporting each other during group meetings and providing other assistance (e.g., suggesting other helpful community resources). The structure of Good Chemistry groups promotes feelings of familiarity, and the acceptance of participants promotes a sense of belonging. "Overlearning" is central to Good Chemistry. Certain concepts are repeated at the beginning of each meeting to help clients remember what to do in times of crisis or when they are making decisions independently. Good Chemistry II groups are open-discussion, mutual-help meetings for people with dual diagnoses who have at least one year of clean, sober, and stable time and who have previously attended Good Chemistry Groups. The Good Chemistry Group model is available free of charge. Some Good Chemistry Group guidelines are provided in Box 13.2 that follows.

Research on Integrated Treatment for Co-Occurring Mental Illness and Substance Use Disorders.   Although seemingly sound in theory, most experimental and quasi-experimental studies provide only modest support for the superior effectiveness of integrated dual diagnosis treatment versus treatment as usual in improving mental health and substance abuse outcomes, though this may differ depending on the outcomes being measured

(Blankertz & Cnaan, 1994; Bond et al., 1991; Burnam et al., 1995; De Leon et al., 2000; DiNitto, Webb, & Rubin, 2002; Drake et al., 1997; Drake et al., 1998a; Jerrell & Ridgely, 1995; Lehman et al., 1993; Nuttbrock et al., 1998). The positive news is that existing treatment models, originally designed for persons with either a mental disorder or substance use disorder, also appear to benefit people with co-occurring disorders, *if they gain access to them.*

A review of 45 studies assessing psychosocial interventions for persons with dual disorders (22 experimental and 23 quasi-experimental) found that some integrated group treatment methods helped with substance use disorders, especially group counseling, when clients become engaged and keep attending (Drake, O'Neal, & Wallach, 2008). Individual counseling, mostly using motivational interviewing (Miller & Rollnick, 2002), produced equivocal results. Some studies found individual counseling helpful, especially when delivered in more than one session; other studies did not find it effective or that it lost effectiveness over time. Integrated case management approaches seem to work as well for persons with dual diagnoses as those with a single diagnosis of mental illness, but in the studies reviewed, findings on effectiveness were not consistently superior. Most studies find that contingency management (behavior modification in conjunction with rewards and disincentives, see chapter 6), has positive effects on the substance use of persons with

---

BOX 13.2   *Good Chemistry Do's and Don'ts*

1. Don't buy alcohol or drugs for myself or others.
2. Don't hang out with people who use or deal.
3. Don't give others my meds.
4. Don't go to liquor stores, bars, or places that make me want to use.
5. Do take my medications as prescribed.
6. Do discover my own cues: recognize and avoid things and situations that make me want to use.

7. Do learn to have "natural highs" and "good chemistry" by socializing and doing fun things without using.
8. Do participate in healthy activities like going to AA meetings, church, shopping, playing or watching sports, and listening to music (whatever makes me feel good without using).

Source: Copyright 1990 Deborah K. Webb, Ph.D. Reprinted by permission.

co-occurring mental and chemical dependency disorders. Intensive outpatient treatment and family therapy interventions for persons with dual disorders have not been studied sufficiently to comment on their effectiveness. A review of 25 randomized controlled trials to reduce substance use among people with severe mental illness also "found little support for integrated, nonintegrated, or skills training programs as being superior to standard care," though comparisons were difficult to make due to issues such as "use of unvalidated measures" or "unclear reporting" (Cleary et al., 2008).

Much has been learned in 25 years of practice and research on dual diagnosis, but the field is still in its infancy. Studying treatment interventions is complicated by the many combinations of mental and substance use disorders with which clients present, the personal and socioenvironmental characteristics of these individuals, and the range, frequency, and intensity of the treatments offered. Treatments often provided to people with substance use disorders (motivational interviewing, group therapy, intensive residential treatment, and contingency management), can also help people with co-occurring disorders address mental and substance use disorders. Likewise, adherence to psychiatric medications and remaining involved in mental health treatment is beneficial to persons with single diagnosis mental illness as well as to those with dual disorders, often allowing them to work on recovery from their substance use disorder for the first time. Until such time as empirical evidence shows otherwise, integrating treatment for mental and substance use disorders seems to make the wisest sense from therapeutic and economic standpoints.

As in most other areas of human services research, dual disorder studies will be improved by increasing sample sizes, minimizing study attrition rates, increasing the length of follow-up periods, studying larger and more homogeneous samples, and more clearly specifying program treatment components (Horsfall et al., 2009). It is especially important to discern how studies

operationally define "recovery" or "remission" (e.g., "abstinence" from substances versus "non-problematic use"). Research may also benefit by assessing the knowledge, skills, and attitudes of providers delivering services in dual diagnoses studies prior to initiating services with clients.

Developmental Disabilities and Substance Use Disorders

According to Public Law (PL) 106–402, the Developmental Disabilities Assistance and Bill of Rights Act of 2000, developmental disabilities are severe, chronic disabilities that are manifest before age 22, are likely to continue indefinitely, and that limit functioning in several areas, such as self-care, self-direction, communication, learning, moving about, earning a living, and living independently. The law also indicates that individuals who are developmentally disabled are likely to require an array of services to ensure that they are able to function at the highest level possible.

Intellectual Disability

Intellectual disability (formerly called *mental retardation*) is prominent among these developmental disabilities. An estimated 7 to 8 million Americans (approximately 3 percent of the population) meet the criteria for intellectual disability (President's Committee for People with Intellectual Disabilities, 2010). The American Association on Intellectual and Developmental Disabilities (AAIDD) (2010) defines intellectual disability as "characterized by significant limitations both in intellectual functioning and in adaptive behavior, which covers many everyday social and practical skills." Intellectual disability begins before age 18, and generally indicates an IQ of 70 to 75 or below, but of critical importance in assessment is the individual's functional capabilities. Chemical dependency treatment providers are concerned primarily with those whose intellectual disability is in the mild to moderate range, because they are most likely to reside in the community and have access to alcohol and nonprescribed drugs. Fetal alcohol spectrum disorders are widely regarded as the leading preventable cause of intellectual disability in the western world,[1] but our interest here is in the drinking and drug-taking behavior of people who have intellectual disability.

Discussions about the drinking habits of people with intellectual disability began early in the last century, and by mid-century there was disagreement as to whether these individuals were more or less likely to have alcohol problems (for an overview, see Krishef & DiNitto 1981; Westermeyer, Phaobtong, & Neider, 1988). During the next few decades, the literature offered no comment on the topic, perhaps because so many people with intellectual disability lived in institutions with little access to alcohol and illicit drugs or with family members who protected them from exposure to these substances. The deinstitutionalization movement that gained impetus in the 1960s and 1970s changed this (Christian & Poling, 1997; Krishef & DiNitto). Many individuals with intellectual disability now live rather independently in the community, with access to alcohol and nonprescribed psychoactive drugs like other community residents. Studies indicate that many of these individuals smoke and/or drink alcohol, and, to a lesser extent, use other drugs (see, for example, Burgard Donohue, Azrin, & Teichner, 2000; Slayter, 2010).

Wenc (1980–81) and Selan (1981) discussed the isolation of those with intellectual disability, their need for socialization, their desire to fit in with the rest of the community, and the possible connection of these factors with substance use and abuse. Wenc noted that people with intellectual disability tend to frequent the same spots—restaurants, stores, and even bars—and the proprietors often know them. According to Selan, like others who drink, people with intellectual disability learn "that alcohol performs important psychological and social functions" (p. 6). In the words of some of her clients, "When I am drunk, I am just like everybody else," and in bars, "I am less lonely; there is always someone to talk with"

(p. 5). Moore and Ford (1991) also noted that special education students may gain easier access to peer groups that use alcohol and other drugs.

Selan (1981) and others (Westermeyer et al., 1988, Westermeyer, Kemp, & Nugent, 1996) also reported that individuals with intellectual disability may be particularly vulnerable when drinking or intoxicated and may suffer victimization, such as physical and sexual abuse and robbery. The lower socioeconomic status of many people with intellectual disability may also cause them to reside in areas with greater exposure to health risks such as substance abuse and violence (Pack, Wallander, & Browne, 1998). Textbooks have stressed that individuals who are intellectually disabled are prone to suggestibility or easily influenced and exploited (see, for example, Baroff & Olley, 1999; Pack et al., 1998), but only recently have textbooks on intellectual disability mentioned substance use disorders among this population (Baroff & Olley; Wehmeyer & Patton, 2000), and chemical dependency texts rarely mention intellectual disability.

Substance Use among People with Intellectual Disability. There are no sound estimates of the number of individuals with intellectual disability who drink, use drugs, or have substance use disorders. Most information comes from a handful of studies that lack nationally representative samples, use different definitions of intellectual disability and substance use or abuse, and have other methodological shortcomings (McGillicuddy, 2006). Studies that rely on samples of individuals with intellectual disability living in supervised facilities may be biased toward findings of less alcohol and drug use than may be present among those living independently in the community. Group homes or other supervised residences may prohibit drinking or do not accept individuals who use psychoactive substances, especially when problematic use is indicated.

The limited available evidence suggests that people with intellectual disability are less likely to use alcohol and drugs than the general population (McGillicuddy, 2006). This may be an accurate picture, or it may be due to close supervision and hesitance to report use (Myers, 1987), parents and professionals' admonishments not to drink and use drugs, limited income (Edgerton, 1986), religious proscriptions against use (Halpern et al., 1986), or other reasons such as reluctance to emulate people with alcohol and drug problems (Delaney & Poling, 1990; Edgerton, 1986; Halpern et al.).

Youth.   Generally speaking the small body of literature on the topic suggests that youth with intellectual disability are less likely to use alcohol; the literature on other substance use is less consistent. Gress and Boss (1996) compared developmentally handicapped (DH) students receiving special education and students not enrolled in special education. About one-quarter of both groups had ever used marijuana and about one-quarter had smoked cigarettes in the past 30 days. The DH students were less likely to have consumed alcohol in the past year (55 percent compared to 72 percent of other students), and they were less likely to use other drugs such as amphetamines and inhalants. Emerson and Turnbull (2005) studied somewhat younger children (aged 11 to 15) living in the community in the United Kingdom based on a nationally representative study of children's mental health. They found that children with intellectual disability were more likely to be current smokers than students without an intellectual disability (14 vs. 8 percent, respectively). The best predictors of smoking among the children with intellectual disabilities were living in poverty and having a psychiatric disorder. Like Gress and Boss, Emerson and Turnbull found that the students with intellectual disability were less likely than other children to use alcohol (12 vs. 22 percent, respectively, drank at least once a month). Factors predictive of the disabled students at least monthly alcohol use were a primary parent/caregiver who had higher psychiatric impairment and parents who were less likely to use punitive forms of punishment.

Huang (1981) compared 190 junior and senior high school students with intellectual disability with 187 other students. He, too, found that fewer students with intellectual disability reported drinking: 32 percent reported drinking at least twice in the past year, compared with 59 percent of the other students. However, among those who drank, the students who were intellectually disabled reported that they drank more often than the other students. There was also evidence of greater peer pressure to drink among the students with intellectual disability or that they were more easily led to drink.

Pack and associates (1998) found results for alcohol use similar to Huang's in their study of risky behaviors conducted in an urban area in Alabama with African American adolescents (male and female) who had intellectual disability and were receiving special education services. Although the adolescents with intellectual disability were less likely to report lifetime alcohol use than the general population of African American adolescents in the state, those who drank in the last 30 days reported more binge drinking. Like Huang (1981), Pack and associates (1998) suggest this alcohol use may be indicative of "deficits in judgment, planning, and means-end thinking" or of "social deficits, such as being unable to negotiate or resist pressure from peers" (p. 417). Unlike the differences in some drug use that Gress and Boss (1996) found, Pack did not find differences in other drug use between the adolescents with intellectual disability and those in the general population.

Adults.   DiNitto and Krishef (1983/84) enlisted the assistance of 24 Associations for Retarded Citizens (now called The Arc) and group care facilities that administered a brief instrument to 214 clients with intellectual disability to determine whether they drank alcohol. Some 52 percent of those respondents had drunk alcohol at some point in their lives, with 7 percent reporting daily drinking, 33 percent drinking at least once a week, and 47 percent drinking at least once a month. About half usually drank in their own homes, and about one-third drank in bars. Halpern and associates (1986) studied several hundred adults with intellectual disability living semi-independently. About 56 percent reported some level of alcohol consumption, and 3 percent reported some marijuana use (figures lower than in the general population). Rimmer, Braddock, and Marks (1995) studied 329 people age 17 to 70 with mild to severe intellectual disability who were ambulatory and resided in an institution, a group home, or with family. Alcohol and cigarette use was quite low regardless of living situation, but greatest among group home residents. Another study, using interviews with 122 individuals with intellectual disability recruited through community agencies whose average age was 27 years, also found lower use than among people in the general population (McGillicuddy & Blane, 1999). In the past month, 29 percent had used alcohol and 4 percent had used an illicit drug.

Substance Use Problems of People with Intellectual Disability.   Halpern and associates (1986) found that problems related to alcohol and marijuana use among people with intellectual disability appeared to be infrequent. Reiss (1990) also found that just 2 percent of 205 individuals with intellectual disability participating in community-based day programs had drug and alcohol problems. Using ethnographic techniques, Edgerton (1986) studied four samples of individuals with intellectual disability: (1) 48 "candidates for normalization," (2) 40 adults living independently, (3) 45 inner-city African Americans, and (4) 48 deinstitutionalized adults. Despite having ample opportunity to drink and use other drugs, these individuals were less likely to do so and less likely to develop alcohol- and drug-related problems than their families and friends. Few of those who used alcohol and other drugs became dependent on them, and they did not engage in socially inappropriate behavior when using them. Concerns that individuals with intellectual disability may be especially susceptible to substance use problems were not borne out by this investigation, despite the many other problems they faced, such as social rejection and low socioeconomic status.

Of 122 individuals with intellectual disabilities they studied, McGillicuddy and Blane (1999) found that most did not use alcohol; 21 percent

used alcohol and 18 percent misused alcohol. None of the demographic variables studied differentiated the nonusers, users, and misusers, although the misusers' average IQ was higher than that of the nonusers. The alcohol misusers were more likely to have smoked marijuana, to smoke more cigarettes, and to have poorer refusal skills, and they were less able to differentiate between "good" and "bad" role models than the nonusers and users. They also showed less internal control on a locus of control scale, but they made more accurate social inferences than the nonusers. Nonusers, users, and misusers did not differ with respect to alcohol attitudes and drug knowledge.

Others have focused on individuals who have substance use disorders and utilize treatment services (see Slayter, 2010). Using data from a nationally representative sample of U.S. residents, Larson and colleagues (2001) reported that approximately 33,000 (2 percent) of non-institutionalized individuals with intellectual disability had received services for alcohol and/or drug disorders in the past year. Slayter, Garnick, and Horgan (cited in Slayter, 2007) found that nearly 3 percent of Medicaid recipients with intellectual disability had received a substance abuse-related service.

Westermeyer and associates (1996) compared clients with and without intellectual disability admitted to chemical dependency treatment programs at two university medical centers. (Those with psychiatric diagnoses in addition to substance use disorders were excluded from the analyses.) The number of patients with intellectual disability ($n=40$) was relatively small, but they comprised 6.2 percent of the treatment population, more than twice the representation of people with intellectual disability in the general population. Compared to other patients, those with intellectual disability arrived at treatment after a shorter history of substance use, were less likely to use illicit drugs, and reported less current use and lower substance use severity. The patients with intellectual disability did not differ from other patients on measures used to determine psychological, family, interpersonal, occupational, and legal problems, and they had fewer financial and addiction-related behavior problems associated with their substance use. Nonetheless, consumption of relatively small amounts of alcohol (two or three drinks) resulted in blackouts and substantial behavior and personality changes for many.

Of the 214 respondents with intellectual disability living in community residences in the DiNitto and Krishef (1983/84) study, 92 percent had paid jobs, and of them, one-third said they had missed work due to feeling sick after drinking. Only four had received substance abuse services (AA, detox, counseling, or services from a church-sponsored program). These researchers (DiNitto & Krishef, 1987; Krishef & DiNitto, 1981) also engaged the participation of 54 Associations for Retarded Citizens (ARCs) and 50 alcohol treatment programs (ATPs) to identify clients with mental retardation and alcohol problems. These agencies identified 414 clients whom they believed to be intellectually disabled *and* had an alcohol use disorder; 82 percent were males. The alcohol-related problems these individuals experienced included employment problems (e.g., absenteeism) and legal offenses (e.g., public intoxication as well as more serious incidents). Family and social conflicts, including hostile and aggressive behavior, were the most frequently reported problems.

Westermeyer and colleagues (1988) studied substance abuse problems by identifying 40 people with intellectual disability who also had diagnoses of substance use disorders. These individuals were participating in various types of programs: a chemical dependency treatment program, an AA group for individuals with intellectual disability, and residential facilities for individuals with intellectual disability. The researchers matched these subjects with 40 individuals who were intellectually disabled but not known to have alcohol and drug problems. Those with substance abuse problems began drinking at an earlier age, had more frequent lifetime use of alcohol and other drugs, had more of some childhood acting-out behaviors (but not the most serious types), and were more likely to report substance-related problems

(psychological, family, social, and employment). During the study, five of the comparison group members were also identified as having substance abuse problems.

Like Krishef and DiNitto (1981), Westermeyer and colleagues (1988) believe that the individuals with intellectual disability experience many of the same types of problems from substance abuse as the general population, though they may experience problems at lower doses of alcohol and other drugs than individuals in the general population. Degenhardt (2000) believes that "abstinence may be a more appropriate goal for an individual with an intellectual disability" (p. 139). In particular, people with intellectual disability who take psychotropic and anticonvulsant (anti-seizure) medications should be warned of contraindications with alcohol, street drug, and over-the-counter drug use and taught to distinguish between medications that a doctor instructs them to take and other substances (Christian & Poling, 1997; Webb, 1994). Westermeyer et al. (1988) encourage professionals and families "to protect mentally retarded persons against substance abuse" (p. 122), while Slayter (2007) discusses the art of "balancing risk management with the 'dignity of risk'" (p. 651). For example, if human service professionals are to be true to the goals of inclusion and normalization, they must consider whether their responsibility is to protect people with intellectual disabilities from using alcohol and drugs or help them make better informed choices about use (on this topic, see Simpson, 1998 and Slayter).

Preventing and Treating Substance Use Disorders among People with Intellectual Disability. There are few descriptions of special substance abuse prevention programs for youth and adults with intellectual disability. McGillicuddy and Blane (1999) did test two methods of prevention designed specifically for people with intellectual disability. One focused on assertiveness skills and the other on modeling normative behaviors and identifying inappropriate role models. Each program was provided in one-hour sessions over a

10-week period, and each was aimed at education about the dangers of substance use and encouraged participants to use a "behavioral repertoire" when faced with alcohol- and drug-related situations. Didactic presentations were minimized in favor of experiential and interactive learning to better accommodate learning characteristics (e.g., shorter attention span). Similar to the school-based prevention programs typically used with youth, both programs resulted in increased knowledge and skills but not improved attitudes or less substance use, compared to a control group that did not receive the program. Slayter suggests "regular and repeated psychoeducational interventions on the consequences of both substance use and SA (substance abuse)" for people with intellectual disability (p. 657).

Based on information Lottman (1993) obtained from 19 agencies providing substance abuse services in the Cincinnati area, 12 reported routinely treating individuals with intellectual disability, but even they reported serving few clients with intellectual disability and were unsure of how many of their clients had this diagnosis. The staff of these agencies had no more than minimal education about intellectual disability, but a number expressed interest in obtaining more education. The agencies that did not routinely accept clients with intellectual disability were less interested in additional education, reported more difficulty in integrating these clients into their services, and did not accepted Medicaid reimbursement (an important source of assistance for many people with intellectual disability). The agencies that routinely accepted clients with intellectual disability said that barriers to serving these clients were lack of staff training and the time necessary to serve clients, rather than client behavior and communication difficulties. Lottman suggests that despite an emphasis in the substance abuse treatment field on addressing the needs of particular population groups, individuals with intellectual disability have been of little interest, perhaps because they are not perceived as high risk and because treatment programs are

besieged with demands for services. Thus, he believes that clients with intellectual disability and substance use disorders will continue to remain the responsibility of agencies that serve individuals with developmental disabilities, despite their lack of expertise in addressing substance abuse and dependence.

Krishef and DiNitto (1981) found that some alcoholism treatment programs modified their services to meet the needs of clients with intellectual disability. Examples were longer treatment periods, using more supportive and directive techniques and less confrontation, use of more behavioral treatment, use of more individual and less group treatment, placing greater emphasis on alcohol education, simplification and more repetition of concepts, specifying more concrete goals over shorter timeframes, working closely with the clients' families, and being more patient. Campbell, Essex, and Held (1994) found similar results in a survey of people working in the developmental disabilities and chemical dependency fields. What Westermeyer and associates (1996) found helpful were residential placements and day and evening programming geared toward clients who have intellectual disability, along with close supervision, contingency contracting, and supervised disulfiram therapy (although patients must be able to understand the consequences of taking this medication if they consume alcohol; see Chapter 6 of this text). Degenhardt (2000) recommends a focus on skills training. Westermeyer et al. (1996) also recommend fostering "rewarding lifestyles (rather than 'warehousing' clients in boring placements in which the local tavern or drug scene becomes the only alternative to 'sitting around')" (p. 30).

To better serve people with intellectual disability, communities are encouraged to conduct focus groups of agency staff specializing in services to individuals who have intellectual disability and those who specialize in providing chemical dependency services to determine what each group needs to know to better serve this clientele (Lottman, 1993). Following this dialogue, Lottman and Wenc (1980–81) recommend regular meetings of representatives from all the agencies that typically serve people with intellectual disability (including criminal justice and mental health) to ensure comprehensive and co-ordinated service delivery. Family involvement in these processes is also important (Christian & Poling, 1997; Krishef & DiNitto, 1981).

AHRC (formerly Association for the Help of Retarded Children) New York City provides one of the few programs specifically for individuals with intellectual disability who have alcohol and other drug problems and calls its approach "person centered" outpatient chemical dependency treatment. The Maine Approach (1984) is a practical, comprehensive model for assisting individuals with intellectual disabilities who have alcohol and drug problems that relies heavily on behavioral techniques and contracting. A manual describes assessment interviewing, the treatment process, aftercare, and the administrative arrangements used to establish the program, and it includes many useful tools, such as interview formats, informed consent forms, and sample treatment plans. The Maine Approach also recommends Alcoholics Anonymous to those who are intellectually capable of participating and encourages assisting clients in locating a sponsor who will work actively with them. Wenc (1980–81) stresses the importance of the socialization aspects of these groups for people with intellectual disability and the need to accompany them to group meetings, rather than simply refer them.

Although traditional AA groups are an option, individuals with intellectual disability sometimes report feeling uncomfortable in these groups, perhaps because other members do not understand intellectual disability (Small, 1980/81). To address this concern, Jim Voytilla began a group called Emotions Anonymous (EA) (Small, 1980–81). As with some other mutual-help groups for individuals with dual diagnoses, professional involvement was important in organizing EA. Voytilla combined elements of AA with education and relaxation techniques to form a long-term approach to outpatient treatment. He substituted the word *emotions* for *alcohol* in the Twelve Steps of AA because of the severe anxieties and tensions that individuals with intellectual disability may face. EA members set weekly goals for themselves and report their progress back to the group. Social reinforcement is used to reward goal achievement.

Paxon (1995) describes relapse prevention strategies for individuals who have intellectual disability, have borderline intellectual functioning, or are not literate that address their common issues, such as limited reading and writing skills. He recommends directive, structured, and cognitive strategies for use in relapse prevention, including:

> (1) self-regulatory training, which helps individuals monitor themselves as well as to anticipate and predict the effects of their behavior, and (2) skills training, which assists individuals in acquiring and gaining proficiency specific to a particular task or situation. These techniques assist clients in evaluating their own relapse behaviors and increase the probability of developing specific skills necessary to avert potential relapses. (p. 170)

Paxon prefers a group format because it is versatile, nonthreatening, and conserves scarce program resources. Both he and Selan (1981) emphasize the importance of psychotherapy and modified psychotherapy, even though many people are surprised that individuals with intellectual disability would be able to participate in individual and group psychotherapy as traditionally defined. However, Westermeyer and associates (1996) found that relapse prevention, application of the Twelve Steps, and other cognitive methods were rarely effective with individuals who had intellectual disability. Degenhardt (2000) also suggests that "alcohol education may be too cognitively demanding" (p. 140). Collaboration with special education experts can aid in designing psychoeducational programs based on the learning techniques most suitable to this population.

Other Developmental Disabilities

Addressing substance use disorders of individuals who have learning disabilities (LD) is also of concern, but studies have not produced consistent results about whether youth with LD have a greater propensity for substance use (McNamara, Vervaeke, & Willoughby, 2008; McNamara & Willoughby, 2010). For example, in a study of students in grades 4 through 12 in an urban U.S. community, there were almost no statistically significant differences in substance use between severely learning disabled youth receiving special education services and youth in the general school population (Gress & Boss, 1996). In a study conducted over a 4-year period in Belfast, Ireland, of youth ages 12 to 16, those with moderate learning disabilities attending a special school reported less tobacco, alcohol, and marijuana use compared to youth attending regular school, and they reported no other illicit drug use (McCrystal et al., 2007). In southern Ontario, Canada, McNamara and Willoughby collected data at time points nearly two years apart from high school students with and without LD. Students with LD generally reported more substance use. The two groups did not differ in alcohol use at time one or in rates of increase at time two. Though similar in smoking at time two, those with LD significantly increased smoking behavior while those without LD showed a decrease; the same pattern emerged for "hard" drug use. For marijuana at both time periods, youth with LD were more likely to use.

By the time a randomly selected group of youth in Ontario, Canada, reached young adulthood, those with LD were three times more likely than others to have developed a substance use disorder even after controlling for variables such as behavioral problems and parental marital status (Beitchman et al., 2001). Those with LD were also at greater risk for other adverse outcomes such as psychiatric disorders. Concerns are that youth with LD may fail to utilize information they receive or have not developed skills to avoid use, thus making them more susceptible to alcohol and drug use and negative consequences (Gress & Boss, 1996). Youth with LD may need more help to develop life skills, increase their self esteem, and foster strengths, healthy self-determination, and self-advocacy (McNamara et al., 2008; McNamara & Willoughby, 2010).

Attention-deficit/hyperactivity disorder (ADHD) is a common diagnosis among youth, and the risk of substance disorders among those with ADHD is substantial (Rosenthal & Westreich, 1999; Smith, Molina, & Pelham, 2002). Risk factors for substance involvement among youth with ADHD are "sensation seeking, poor academic achievement, and early disruptive behavior" (Tapert et al., 2002). In a study of 66 youth recruited from the community and followed from age 15 to 23, executive and attention deficits (though not necessarily ones that met criteria for ADHD) predicted substance use and dependence after controlling for a variety of baseline factors such as family history, substance use, and learning disabilities (Tapert et al.). Molina and Pelham (2001) followed a clinic-based sample of 109 children with ADHD into adolescence. Those with higher IQs and greater academic achievement were more likely to have tried cigarettes, to do so at an early age, and to be daily smokers, and they tried alcohol at an earlier age. Molina and Pelham suggest that higher intellectual capacity may be associated with earlier experimentation and the desire to fit in with peers and that children with ADHD and higher IQ scores may be aware of tobacco's stimulant properties and purposely seek it out. However, those with better reading scores were less likely to develop alcohol problems, supporting evidence from studies which suggest that verbal deficits are associated with school failure that lead to antisocial behavior. Alcohol problems were associated with more negative consequences than smoking.

In another comparison of high students in southern Ontario, Canada, those with LD and LD/ADHD were generally more similar to each other than those without LD (McNamara et al., 2008). The children with LD and LD/ADHD reported more smoking and marijuana use (but not alcohol or "hard" drug use) than the children without LD. Relationship with their mother and involvement in school and extracurricular activities mediated the relationship. Only 19 of the 109 children in Molina and Pelham's (2001) study of clinic-referred children with ADHD had learning disabilities, and the only suggestion of a difference in alcohol, marijuana, and cigarette use and related problems by the time of adolescence was that those without LD tried cigarettes at an earlier age.

Smith and colleagues (2002) find that cognitive treatments may be less effective for children with ADHD, even though they are widely used in school-based drug prevention programs. Supervision, behavioral contingencies, and modeling behavior may be more useful. Other considerations include providing treatment in an environment with reduced distractions (e.g., a minimum of noise and little art work on the walls) (Moore, 1998).

Mobility Impairments and Substance Use Disorders

People with substance use disorders are more likely than others to sustain traumatic injuries (see, for example, Erickson & Orsay, 1994; Tate Forchheimer, Krause, Meade, & Bombardier, 2004). In a British study of clinic outpatients, 17 percent of people with hypertension and 19 percent of those with diabetes were heavy drinkers, compared to 73 percent of those with fractures (Potamianos, Gorman, Duffy, & Peters, 1988). Schaschl and Straw (1989) reviewed patient histories and found that the vast majority of clients admitted with onset of physical disability after their tenth birthday had substance abuse problems prior to incurring the disability. One type of injury that may result from alcohol- or drug-related accidents is spinal cord injury (SCI). The main cause of SCI is motor vehicle accidents, followed by falls, violence, and sports and recreation accidents (National Spinal Cord Injury Statistical Center, 2010).

Relationship between Spinal Cord Injury and Substance Use.   A review of studies showed that the relationship between *intoxication* at time of injury and head and spinal cord injury varied greatly, from 17 to 68 percent of cases (Heinemann & Hawkins, 1995). A number of SCI patients have histories of *substance use disorders* prior

to becoming disabled (Heinemann, Goranson, Ginsburg, & Schnoll, 1989). Turner, Bombardier, and Rimmele (2003) identified three subtypes of individuals with SCI who may need interventions for alcohol problems. These individuals comprised about half their sample of 217 SCI level 1 trauma center inpatients. The three types were approximately equally divided among those who were (1) currently alcohol dependent, (2) currently alcohol abusers, or (3) in remission from alcohol dependence or had relapsed. Only about one-quarter wanted treatment. Radnitz and associates (1996) found that 37 percent of a group of 125 veterans with SCI met criteria for a lifetime substance dependence diagnosis and 6 percent for a lifetime substance abuse diagnosis, although few acknowledged current alcohol or drug problems.

In a study of 104 individuals (mostly white males) admitted to a level 1 trauma center, 39 percent were classified as problem drinkers (Bombardier et al., 2004). The problem drinkers stayed in the hospital 15.5 days longer than the non-problem drinkers. After controlling for age and injury level, problem drinking did not predict admission or discharge functioning or length of stay in the rehabilitation program. Problem drinking did predict rehabilitation efficiency or progress (i.e., change in functioning from admission to discharge divided by the length of stay in the rehabilitation hospital). The problem drinkers made less progress, though the reason for this is not clear because there was no relation between blood alcohol level at time of admission or recent alcohol consumption and injury level. The problem drinkers' longer stays in the rehabilitation hospital resulted in an additional rehabilitation cost per patient of nearly $25,000.

Post-Injury Alcohol and Drug Use.   Occasionally, alcohol or illicit or non-prescribed drug use may be initiated or escalate following spinal cord injury (Heinemann, Goranson, Ginsburg, & Schnoll, 1989). Of 75 SCI patients Heinemann and Hawkins (1995) studied, 4 developed drinking problems post injury. Patients' drinking generally

declined after SCI, but two-thirds of study participants were drinking 18 months later, with a median frequency of "four drinks one to two times each week." In another study of 121 SCI patients, the general tendency was reduced drinking following SCI (Heinemann, Schmidt, & Semik, 1994). Heavy drinking decreased from 55 percent of the sample six months prior to the injury to 20 percent one year post injury. Young et al. (1995) studied 123 individuals with SCI living in the community. Although fewer used alcohol and marijuana than in the general population, the 21 percent prevalence rate of alcohol use disorders was higher than in the general population but lower than in other studies of people with SCI. Marijuana users were younger than those who did not use marijuana. The difference in the proportion of women and men who used alcohol was not statistically significant as it is in the general population. Approximately equal proportions of men and women with SCI also used marijuana. About half of those who had abused alcohol in the past reported that they were not currently drinking.

Using data from the 16 Model Spinal Cord Injury Systems (MSCIS) across the United States, Tate et al. (2004) studied over 3,000 individuals aged 18 and older post-SCI. Although not necessarily representative of all individuals with SCI, the MSCIS is the largest database with information on alcohol and drug use. The researchers found the following:

1. Sixty percent of people with SCI reported at least some alcohol consumption. Seven percent reported consuming 5 or more drinks on days when they consumed alcohol.
2. Fourteen percent answered yes to at least one of the four CAGE items indicating a possible problem with alcohol use (see Chapter 5 of this text). Of those who currently or previously consumed alcohol, 24 percent responded positively to at least one CAGE item, and among these individuals, half responded positively to at least two items.
3. The at-risk drinkers were younger than other SCI patients. They were also younger at the time of injury. Those who scored positively on the CAGE were also younger.
4. Eleven percent reported some use of illegal drugs or prescribed drugs for nonmedical purposes.
5. Differences in the proportions who were abstainers, moderate, and at-risk drinkers differed only modestly by level of injury. Whether or not individuals used other substances did not differ by injury level.
6. Those most likely to be at-risk drinkers were men, single (who were also more likely to be CAGE positive), white (but they were least likely to be CAGE positive), had sustained injury in a sports accident (they were also more likely to be CAGE positive), and employed.
7. Abstainers reported less pain than moderate and at-risk drinkers, while CAGE positive individuals and drug users had worse pain than those who were CAGE negative and those who did not use substances.
8. Those reporting drug use were somewhat more likely to have pressure ulcers that develop from failure to shift their weight.
9. Drinking frequency and amount were not related to life satisfaction, but those who were CAGE positive and those who used other substances had lower life satisfaction.

Psychological Variables and Substance Abuse among SCI Patients. There is interest in whether SCI patients—as well as patients who have sustained other injuries, such as traumatic brain injury—have certain personality types. Some propose that many SCI patients are thrill-seekers who have shunned intellectual interests and pursued behaviors more likely to result in self-harm (O'Donnell, Cooper, Gessner, Shehan, & Ashley, 1981/82). Their inability to pursue previous physical activities seems to increase their frustration during rehabilitation.

Among the SCI patients Young and associates (1995) studied, those who abused alcohol tended to perceive their health as worse and reported more depression and stress. Alcohol use, alcohol abuse, or marijuana use were unrelated to medical conditions such as level of disability or pain. Psychological factors seemed more important in predicting substance use and abuse. Krause (2004) studied more than 1,300 former inpatients and outpatients of a specialty hospital and found that heavy drinking (the number of times patients consumed 5 or more drinks at a time), but not CAGE scores in the last 12-months, was associated with subsequent injury; however, once "impulsive sensation seeking" was considered, heavy drinking was no longer a predictor of sustaining a subsequent injury. Nevertheless, since heavy drinking and sensation seeking may go hand-in-hand, heavy drinking should be a target of efforts to prevent subsequent injuries following SCI. No other personality trait studied (e.g., aggression-hostility, locus of control) was related to subsequent injury. Alston (1994) also studied sensation seeking and drug abuse among 28 men and 16 women with SCI. Frequency of alcohol, recreational drug, and prescription drug use was significantly related to three of the four subscales used to measure sensation seeking. Alston describes study participants as "chronically underaroused and interested in engaging in behaviors to increase stimulus input" (p. 160). Like Young and colleagues (1995), Alston suggests attention to psychological characteristics of people with SCI and that certain individuals with disabilities may need assistance in committing to rehabilitation activities, such as job training, rather than less stressful and more stimulating activities, such as drinking. Heinemann et al. (1989) also reported that greater pre-injury drinking among SCI patients was associated with less time spent in productive activities such as rehabilitation.

SCI patients' expectations about the positive benefits of alcohol use have also been studied. For example, Heinemann and associates (1994) found that compared to those who had not drunk problematically before injury, pre-injury problem drinkers believed that alcohol would provide greater benefits such as improved mood and social and sexual functioning. The pre-injury problem drinkers did report drinking less over time, but their positive expectations about alcohol use

continued, although they diminished somewhat. The pre-injury problem drinkers also continued to use more escape-avoidance coping strategies than other study participants, who were more likely to use problem-solving strategies. The Heinemann research team believes that pre-injury problem drinking is especially telling in patient assessment and that pre-injury problem drinkers' persistent maladaptive responses may signal poorer adjustment to disability as well as a potential to drinking relapse.

Heinemann and Hawkins (1995) also found that patients who were currently abstinent but had pre-injury drinking problems reported more depression and less acceptance of their disability during follow-up. Concern arose that former problem drinkers who are currently abstinent may be experiencing the "dry drunk" syndrome, in which they are sober but have not made a good life adjustment.

Many factors may interfere with the rehabilitation process (O'Donnell et al., 1981–82; Radnitz & Tirch, 1995). Some SCI patients become comfortable in the institutional setting and fail to make progress because they have fears about independent living (Anderson, 1980/81). Successful rehabilitation may result in termination of Social Security, public assistance, or military veterans' benefits. These benefits can exceed what SCI patients may be able to earn from gainful employment. Disability payment systems that fail to reward the patient's progress have long been criticized as encouraging financial dependency.

Caregivers may exploit individuals with SCI by encouraging them to drink or use drugs (DeLambo et al., 2010). More often, family, friends, and even professional caregivers may offer alcohol or drugs to promote enjoyment and normalcy (O'Donnell et al., 1981/82; Radnitz & Tirch, 1995). Family members may also harbor resentment if they believe the individual was responsible for the injury that has left everyone overburdened; at the same time, they may feel guilty about their resentment and wish they could do more to help (O'Donnell et al.). For family members and caregivers, the strains of caregiving may make opening a beer or rolling a joint for the individual with SCI easier than feeling guilty or engaging in arguments (O'Donnell et al.). Given these dynamics, family education and involvement in the rehabilitation process are critical to prevent enabling.

Physical Problems Related to SCI and Problem Drinking. Many people with mobility disabilities, such as paraplegia and quadriplegia, take medications to reduce pain, control muscle spasms, prevent infections, and address other medical problems. Life-threatening consequences can ensue when medications used to control these problems are used with alcohol, over-the-counter medications, and street drugs (see, for example, Bombardier, 2003). For example, depressant drugs such as alcohol and other "downers" exacerbate depressed mood (which is common after SCI), impede motor activity, and can result in increased risk of accidents if consumed in sufficient quantities or when combined with other drugs.

The increase in urine produced by drinking alcoholic beverages can cause unnecessary dependence on catheterization (O'Donnell et al., 1981–82). Bladder overfill can also result in a dangerous increase in blood pressure, and waiting too long to empty the bladder can also overstretch the bladder, which may result in backflow that can cause kidney damage (Bombardier, 2003). Drinking alcohol lowers immune function, which can promote urinary tract, bladder, and skin infections, and it can also cause dehydration, which may promote decubitus ulcers (bed or pressure sores) (Bombardier).

Clues that SCI patients may be abusing or dependent on substances include failure to shift their weight (Bombardier, 2003) and lack of attention to other aspects of health care, nutrition, and hygiene, which can result in the development of pressure sores "aggravated by sitting in a wheelchair for days while they are stoned or drunk" (Anderson, 1980–81, p. 38). Elliott and colleagues (2002) studied 175 inpatients in a medical rehabilitation unit. Twenty nine percent

of the men and seven percent of the women were classified as having severe alcohol problems. Alcohol abuse was not associated with depression at admission or with disability acceptance at discharge; however, in the first years after rehabilitation, those with severe alcohol problems at admission were 2.5 times more likely to develop pressure sores after accounting for other possible risk factors (the reason was not clear, since information on current alcohol or other drug use and other factors such as self-care were lacking).

Sores and urinary tract infections can be very painful and debilitating and can impede participation in rehabilitation, employment, and other activities (Perez & Pilsecker, 1994). The relationship among substance use and abuse, psychosocial adjustment, and health problems may not be a simple one (Hawkins & Heinemann, 1998). For example, in a follow-up study of 71 individuals with SCI, Hawkins and Heinemann found that at 12 months following injury (but not after this time period), urinary tract infections occurred more often among previous heavy drinkers who were abstaining (most of whom also used illicit drugs prior to injury) and among those who had not used illicit drugs prior to injury. At 30 months after injury (but not before), pressure ulcers most often occurred among those who were using illicit drugs. Neither drinking nor abstaining during follow-up periods was related to pressure ulcer development. SCI patients must expend considerable energy in self-care in order to avoid medical complications that can become quite serious. Hawkins and Heinemann (1998) suggest that former heavy drinkers may not have developed good self-care habits, although it is curious that those currently using alcohol and other drugs were not at greater risk for health problems.

Prevention and Intervention with SCI Patients. Early identification and intervention with medical patients who have not experienced serious consequences but whose alcohol and drug use puts them at risk may help to deter life-altering accidents such as SCI. Medical practitioners should screen for substance use disorders, especially when accidents are involved. Though emergency rooms and trauma units are doing this more frequently, time constraints, reluctance to ask patients about alcohol and other drug abuse, and lack of knowledge of substance use disorders may prevent routine screening. Rohe and Basford (1989) found that the MacAndrew Alcoholism Scale may predict which male SCI patients have injuries related to alcohol use. The CAGE, MAST, and AUDIT (see Chapter 5 of this text) may also be useful in prevention and intervention (Turner et al., 2003). Alston (1994) recommends coupling early identification of individuals with a tendency toward sensation with psychoeducation to address potential problems.

The crisis SCI (and other serious injuries) cause may provide a prime opportunity for intervening in a substance abuse or dependency problem (Bombardier & Rimmele, 1998; Erickson & Orsay, 1994; Heinemann et al., 1989). Bombardier and Rimmele found considerable willingness to discuss drinking and motivation to change drinking behavior among patients who drank more and had more alcohol-related problems pre-injury, though Turner et al. (2003) found most in their study uninterested in treatment. Of 75 SCI patients Heinemann and Hawkins (1995) studied, 49 (65 percent) had drinking problems pre-injury, but only 11 percent of the sample had received substance abuse treatment pre- or post-injury. Several individuals who thought they needed substance abuse treatment immediately following their injury later changed their mind. "Motivationally oriented" strategies to promote interest in treatment may be needed (Turner et al.).

The Veterans Administration (VA) Spinal Cord Injury Service in Long Beach, California, developed one of the first substance abuse treatment programs for SCI patients after federal marshals conducted drug raids there because patients were using illicit drugs on the premises (Anderson, 1980–81). The program was designed to simultaneously address substance abuse and SCI using a therapeutic community model. The SCI units offered the advantages of physical accessibility and the staff and equipment needed for inpatient care, and staff structured the substance abuse program specifically for its clientele. For example, programs activities started later in the day than is the norm in most inpatient chemical dependency programs because morning hygiene and grooming routines may take extended periods of time for people with SCI, even with assistance. The program included a wide range of services, including education for independent living, assertiveness training, vocational rehabilitation, spiritual awareness, and participation in mutual-help groups.

Schaschl and Straw (1989) describe another type of chemical dependency program that incorporates individuals who have physical disabilities such as SCI with other patients. There are group sessions for individuals with physical disabilities to address their unique concerns, and special services are also provided to their family members. Heinemann and colleagues (1994) recommend a "lifestyle assessment and intervention program," which addresses substance use as well as beliefs about use and coping skills (Woll, Schmidt, & Heinemann, 1993). Facilities should be fully physically accessible, and clients should be provided transportation to treatment and mutual-help meetings when needed. A major barrier to treating substance use disorders is that SCI rehabilitation hospitals are not reimbursed for treating co-occurring substance use disorders (Bombardier et al., 2004).

Traumatic Brain Injury and Substance Use Disorders

Traumatic brain injury (TBI) can result in cognitive, motor, and psychological impairments of varying degrees (Graham & Cardon, 2008). Similar to spinal cord injury, TBI most frequently results from motor vehicle accidents and falls followed by violent incidents, and in nearly half of cases where testing is done, the patient has a positive blood alcohol level (Traumatic Brain Injury National Data and Statistical Center, 2010). In fact, Miller (1994) called alcohol and other drug disorders "the greatest risk factor" for TBI.

Relationship between TBI and Substance Use Disorders. Because alcohol is a central nervous system depressant, some people may erroneously believe an individual who has been drinking is more likely to be in an accident but less likely to suffer a traumatic injury (see Sparadeo & Gill, 1989). A positive BAL at the time of injury is a problem because "there is an increase in the volume of blood, increasing brain bleeding and agitation" (Terry, n.d., p. 1). Alcohol consumption reduces the body's ability to respond to hemorrhage and shock and is "a major anesthesia risk for those requiring emergency surgery" (Mitiguy, 1991, p. 6). Other metabolic changes induced by alcohol use also contribute to the negative effects of brain injury (Strauss, 2001). An accurate diagnosis is difficult to make immediately following a head trauma because it may be unclear whether the patient's symptoms are due to intoxication, a head injury, or both (Mitiguy, 1991; Strauss, 2001). Common symptoms are "lethargy, or agitation, confusion, disorientation, [and] respiratory depression" (Miller, 1994, p. 475).

Alcohol and Drug Use at the Time of TBI. Two reviews of studies found that approximately one-third to one-half of individuals with head injuries were legally intoxicated at the time the trauma occurred (Corrigan, 1995; Parry-Jones, Vaughan, & Cox, 2006). Data on other substance use at time of injury are sparse. After alcohol, marijuana (cannabis) use has been reported most often; cocaine use has been reported less frequently (Corrigan et al., 1995; Sparadeo, 2001; Sparadeo, Strauss, & Barth, 1990). A more recent study in Honolulu found that toxicologies most often detected alcohol, amphetamines, and cannabis (O'Phelan et al., 2008).

Weinstein and Martin (1995) note that "after trauma, if alcohol abuse or dependence remains undiagnosed during the evaluation or treatment of TBI, severe neuropsychiatric complications may ensue, including Wernicke-Korsakoff syndrome (if thiamine is not administered prophylactically), seizures, and delirium" (p. 291). Or a patient may be discharged from the emergency room with a diagnosis

of intoxication without recognition of a head injury (Miller, 1994; Strauss, 2001). While both brain injury and psychoactive drug use may result in "poor memory, impaired judgment, fine and gross motor impairments, poor concentration, decreased impulse control, and impaired language," the effects of drug use are usually reversible, whereas brain injury often is not (Miller, 1994, p. 487).

Alcohol and Drug Problems Pre-TBI. Corrigan (1995) found that the best estimates indicated that 50 to 66 percent of hospitalized TBI patients have a history of alcohol or other drug abuse. Parry-Jones et al.'s (2006) more recent review found that 37 to 51 percent of TBI patients have a history of alcohol misuse. (Conversely, Hillbom and Holm [1986] found that alcoholics were two to four times more likely than the general population to have a history of head trauma.) Regarding a history of illicit drug use, Parry-Jones et al. report that the most robust finding comes from Cherner et al. (2001) who found that 44 percent had used an illicit drug in the year preceding TBI.

Since studies of substance use often rely on self-reports (and sometimes family members' reports), underreporting may be an issue, as is the reliability and consistency of methods used to collect data across studies (Parry-Jones et al., 2006). Retrospective studies do confirm a significant history of TBI in incarcerated and treatment-seeking alcohol and other drug abusers, though the nature of the relationship needs further clarification (Graham & Cardon, 2008).

Functioning Following TBI. In studies of how pre-TBI substance use affects medical and neurological outcomes, Parry-Jones et al. (2006) found the evidence inconclusive, and studies that report poorer neuropsychological outcomes for patients with positive toxicology screens at time of admission often fail to control for history of substance use disorders. Thus, it is not clear whether it is intoxication at the time of injury or a history of an alcohol use disorder and related problems that causes poorer cognitive outcomes following TBI. Some studies show worse outcomes for those intoxicated at the time of brain injury; others do not (Bombardier & Thurber, 1998; Corrigan, 1995; Kolakowsky-Hayner et al., 1999). O'Phelan et al. (2008) even found that patients with severe brain injury admitted to a trauma center who screened positive for alcohol or methamphetamines had lower mortality than those with negative screens.

Sparadeo and Gill (1989) found that TBI patients with a BAL at 0.10 percent or above stayed in the hospital longer, had a longer period of agitation, and had lower cognitive status at the time of discharge. Dikmen and associates (1993) raise questions as to whether other variables that may precede or are associated with alcohol use disorders—such as lower levels of education and intellectual functioning and poorer neuropsychological functioning—may more adequately explain poorer outcomes. Tate and associates (1999) tried to clarify the relationship between a history of alcohol abuse (based on clinical judgment, patient records, formal diagnoses, and/or subjects' reports) and BAL at time of injury on post-acute cognitive functioning. After controlling for a history of alcohol abuse, they found that higher BALs were related to deficits in the areas of verbal memory and visuospatial abilities.

Alcohol and Drug Use Following TBI. In addition to neuropsychological changes, it has been suggested that chemical use by people following trauma may be prompted by alienation by peers, a desire to assert independence, changes in family members' behavior toward them, or just plain boredom (Kaitz, 1991; Sparadeo et al., 1990). Kreutzer and associates (Kreutzer, Doherty, Harris, & Zasler, 1990; Kreutzer, Marwitz, & Witol, 1995) found that drinkers generally curtailed their alcohol use following traumatic brain injury, with those sustaining greater injuries drinking less (Kreutzer et al., 1996). Likewise, Sparadeo (cited in Terry, n.d.) found that whereas the most severely injured do not return to drinking, those with moderate and minor injuries (30 percent and 50 percent, respectively) did return to drinking.

Kreutzer and colleagues (1996) found that post-injury, TBI patients were more likely to be abstainers than the general population, but both the Kreutzer and Corrigan (Corrigan et al., 1995) groups also found that some patients increased their drinking over time. In one study, one-fourth who were initially abstinent post-injury were using alcohol at the follow-up periods, with the most marked increase occurring between 12 and 24 months post injury (Kruetzer et al.). Younger people and those with higher BALs at time of injury drank more after injury, but there was no post-injury gender difference in drinking. Apparently, substantial numbers of patients do continue to use alcohol and other drugs, and this warrants concern. In their review of studies, Parry-Jones et al. (2006) found that post-injury rates for heavy alcohol use, abuse, or dependence ranged from 7 to 26 percent, though it could not be stated with certainty if these problems increased with time following TBI.

Reports of drug use other than alcohol post-TBI are limited, but Graham and Cardon (2008) suggest that opiate use is common due to severe, chronic pain. They also suggest that those with mild and undiagnosed TBI may be most susceptible to initiating or increasing substance use following injury because they receive little assistance and have greater mobility.

A primary concern is that alcohol and other drug consumption may interfere with cognitive functioning already impaired by brain trauma. For example, a patient may try marijuana in an attempt to control symptoms such as spasticity and ataxia, despite the drug's contraindications for TBI patients (Strauss, 2001). Dilantin, used to prevent seizures, and benzodiazipines, used to control muscle spasms, slow thought processes; consuming alcohol exacerbates this effect (Sparadeo, 2001). After TBI, the likelihood of sustaining a subsequent head injury is increased due to difficulties with coordination, balance, vision, and judgment, and substance use may contribute to these difficulties (Brain Injury Association of America, 2004).

Cognitive abilities and personality variables show marked improvement following abstinence (Corrigan et al., 1999). The Brain Injury Association of America (2004) recommends that people with TBI not consume alcohol or illicit or non-prescribed drugs, since all these substances can result in substantial difficulties. Box 13.3 provides reasons why people with TBI should refrain from substance use. Youth, in particular, may need to be dissuaded from use (De Pompei & Corrigan, 2001), because developmentally, this is a time when experimentation with alcohol and drugs is likely to occur.

TBI, Substance Use, and Mental Disorders. There may be an association among substance use disorders, antisocial personality disorder (APD), and the likelihood of sustaining a traumatic brain injury (Malloy, Noel, Longabuagh, & Beattie, 1990). Those with APD tend to act out, and alcohol may contribute to this behavior, resulting in a serious accident. One study indicated that the most frequent arrests for patients following TBI were alcohol and drug related (Kreutzer, Wehman, Harris, Burns, & Young, 1991).

Psychiatric disorders seen in people with alcohol dependence and people with TBI include "amnestic states, dementia, mood disorders, personality disorders, and delusional disorders" (Weinstein & Martin, 1995). In a study of nearly 7,000 clients entering state supported substance abuse treatment programs in Kentucky, nearly one-third had sustained at least one TBI that included loss of consciousness (LOC) (Walker et al., 2007). The number of mental health problems of these individuals increased with the number of TBI-LOCs, and clients with TBI-LOC also reported more marijuana and tranquilizer (but not alcohol) use, perhaps to dampen the effects of their mental health symptoms.

Assessment and Intervention with TBI Patients. Professionals in the head injury field agree that patient assessment for substance abuse and dependency problems should be routine (Bombardier & Davis, 2001; Frye, 2001). Professionals in the substance abuse field should also assess clients for brain injury. The task is not an easy one because both TBI and substance use disorders impair

BOX 13.3   *Top 10 Reasons Why Substance Use After Brain Injury Is a Bad Idea*

10. An individual who uses alcohol and other drugs after a brain injury will not recover as much or as fast as a person who does not use.
9. Problems of balance, walking and talking are exacerbated by alcohol and other drugs.
8. Problems of disinhibition are also exacerbated by alcohol and other drugs.
7. Difficulty with problem solving, memory, concentration and other thinking skills are made worse with the use of alcohol and other drugs.
6. Alcohol and other drugs have a more powerful and quicker effect on a person after a brain injury.
5. Alcohol increases depression because it is a depressant drug.
4. Alcohol and other drugs interact with medications often prescribed after a brain injury, especially those administered for seizure control, depression, anxiety or restlessness, and pain.
3. Use of alcohol and other drugs after an injury increases a person's risk of another injury.
2. Alcohol is a drug. (That means beer, too!)
1. The cumulative effect of the other nine reasons.

Source: Reprinted with permission of the Ohio Valley Center for Brain Injury Prevention and Rehabilitation. Available online: http://www.ohiovalley.org/abuse/prog/abrain.html.

concentration, memory, and cognitive process-ing, making it difficult to tell whether symptoms are related to TBI (especially mild TBI), substance abuse, or an interaction of the two (Iverson, Lange, & Franzen, 2005; Walker et al., 2007). Mental health problems (depression, anxiety [see Walker et al.]) are also common among individu-als with TBI, further complicating screening and diagnosis.

Given that TBI-related memory impairment may hamper an accurate assessment, Kreutzer and associates (1990, 1996) recommend us-ing multiple assessment tools, including patient records, standardized questionnaires, and inter-views with patients and collaterals in the home setting. Along with neuropsychological and reha-bilitation evaluations, Jones (1989) recommends the CAGE questionnaire for screening because it is brief and minimizes the use of abstract and com-plex concepts. The Short MAST and the Alcohol Use Disorders Identification Test have also been recommended (Bombardier, Kimer, & Ehde, 1997; Tate et al., 1999; also see Chapter 5). Profession-als should allow adequate time to conduct assess-ments, give clients breaks during the assessment if needed, and be sensitive should clients' become restless or their attention wanes (Moore, 1998).

The number and intensity of behavioral and psychological problems patients with head injuries face in recovery vary depending on the individual and the injury (Gardner, 2002). Henry (1988) described six problem areas: attention, memory, language, reasoning and judgment, executive func-tions (abilities of initiation, organization, direction, monitoring, and self-evaluation), and emotion. For example, a head injury may result in a diminution of cause-and-effect reasoning, the ability to make inferences, problem-solving skills, and determin-ing appropriate behavior. In particular, frontal lobe damage can result in minimization of prob-lems, lack of awareness, maladaptive behaviors, and impaired social functioning (Hughes-Dobles, 2001). Difficulty finding words to express one's thoughts may cause embarrassment and prevent patients from participating in group therapy and interacting in other situations (Sparadeo, 2001). Confabulation to hide memory deficits may be mis-taken as intentional dishonesty, and common be-haviors among those with TBI (such as giggling at inappropriate times) may cause those who do not understand TBI's effects to avoid these individuals (Henry). To help an individual with a head injury, Henry (1988) suggests that it is often appropriate for professionals and self-help program sponsors to openly address inappropriate behaviors with the in-dividual, discuss specific examples of these behav-iors, and give gentle yet firm advice for modifying behavior (also see DeLambo, Chandras, Homa, & Chandras, 2009).

Integrated treatment for those with sub-stance use disorders and TBI or SCI is scarce, and in recent years stays in rehabilitation programs have become shorter and service utilization more closely monitored (Corrigan et al., 1999). Reha-bilitation and chemical professionals often feel inadequate to respond to TBI and alcohol and drug problems simultaneously (Sparadeo, 2001). Insurance companies may exacerbate the prob-lem by arguing over which problem should be treated first, or patients may find themselves in chemical dependency treatment without compre-hensive head injury rehabilitation because chemi-cal dependency treatment is the less costly of the two (Sparadeo et al., 1990). Patients may be dis-charged without the skills needed to compensate for their cognitive deficits and for their risk of re-lapse to substance abuse (Lamb-Hart, 2001).

Several models have been developed to ad-dress substance abuse among individuals with TBI. The Ohio Valley Center for Brain Injury Prevention and Rehabilitation recommends screening, patient and family education, in-depth assessment, motivational therapy, treatment team planning, consultation, and referrals, along with case management by a staff member whose role is chemical dependency treatment (Corrigan et al., 1999). The center's website provides practi-cal information on TBI and substance abuse treat-ment for clients, families, and professionals (also see Brain Injury Association of America, 2004).

The Skills-based Substance Abuse Prevention Counseling (SBSAPC) program was also designed for TBI patients (Vungkhanching et al., 2007). SBSAPC utilizes learning theory to enhance coping skills that will prevent problematic substance use. Following evaluation, individuals participate in motivational enhancement to strengthen decision making abilities, coping skills training, and application to real world settings.

Miller (1994) recommends treatment that is simple, supportive, directive, focused, and concrete. Since what appears to be denial may be impaired cause-and-effect reasoning due to TBI, it may take time to engage clients in treatment, to help them accept a goal of abstinence, and to provide treatment (Blackerby & Baumgarten, 1990; Strauss, cited in Kaitz, 1991). Structured treatment and aftercare programs are important (Moore, 1998). Behavioral treatment techniques are recommended because TBI patients' cognitive deficits may make insight-oriented, psychodynamic approaches unsuitable (Jones, 1989; Miller, 1994). Behavioral approaches help clients achieve successes by working on long-term goals in small steps (Wood, cited in Jones, 1989). Material should be repeated and presented at an appropriate pace for TBI patients with cognitive deficits (DeLambo et al., 2009). Employing pictures to convey concepts, providing notes, taping sessions, and using other memory aids may be necessary to help clients recall information from treatment sessions (De Pompei & Corrigan, 2001; Moore, 1998; Sparadeo, 2001). Role-playing can also be useful.

Treatment must be individualized because TBI patients' problems vary widely. Clinicians should consider the need for ongoing prevention and intervention, since substance use may increase over time (Kreutzer et al., 1996). Post-injury reductions in substance use provide a prime opportunity to reinforce continued reductions in use (Tate et al., 1999).

The TBI Network provides comprehensive assessment to patients, makes referrals to community-based substance abuse treatment providers, and provides consultation to these agencies to help them serve clients (Corrigan et al., 1995). The Traumatic Brain Injury Model Systems program is also a source of help.

Mutual-help groups can be useful, but distractions (e.g., people arriving late, getting coffee) can make concentration difficult for people with TBI (Sparadeo, 2001). Concepts used in AA, such as that of a higher power, may be too abstract for individuals with severe cognitive impairments to grasp (Kaitz, 1991; Moore 1998). The Twelve Steps should be repeated often and concepts made as concrete as possible (Feinberg, 1991). The Twelve Steps of Alcoholics Anonymous have been worded so that individuals with head injuries can more readily understand them (Peterman cited in Henry, 1988; National Association of State Head Injury Administrators cited in Brain Injury Association of America, 2004). Providing additional explanation after AA and NA meetings can be beneficial (Terry, n.d.).

Based on a review of 14 substance abuse treatment evaluation studies with people who have TBI, Graham and Cardon (2008) believe the state of the literature suggests that (also see Corrigan, 2005):

1. Community-based treatment is essential but inpatient or residential treatment is often not available or not affordable.
2. Used alone, motivational interviewing techniques are not sufficient. Skills-based interventions seem more promising.
3. Providing financial incentives to TBI patients may increase treatment retention, at least in the short-run, and reducing barriers to treatment such as transportation and childcare may also be helpful. (Also see Corrigan & Bogner, 2007; Corrigan, Bogner, & Lamb-Hart, 2005.)
4. Both outpatient individual and group treatment can be helpful.
5. Support from peers may also be helpful.

TBI patients' alcohol and other drug use may cause caregiving relationships, especially parental care giving, to deteriorate (Gardner, 2002). Family and other caregivers should be involved in the process of rehabilitation from TBI and substance use disorders.

Sensory Disabilities and Substance Use Disorders

The sensory disabilities we focus on in this section are hearing and visual.

Deaf and Hard of Hearing

Based on nationally representative self-report data, nearly 0.4 percent of the population over 5 years of age are "functionally deaf" and nearly 4 percent are hard of hearing, i.e., they "have some difficulty hearing normal conversation even with the use of a hearing aid" (for a summary of studies, see Mitchell, 2005). More than half of those who are deaf or hard of hearing are over 65 years of age. Most hearing impairments are due to age-related causes, with less than one of every 1,000 people in the United States becoming deaf before age 18. The most common causes of congenital (at birth) hearing loss are genetic (American Speech-Language-Hearing Association, n.d.). Congenital hearing loss may also be due to prenatal illness or other conditions. Childhood diseases or illnesses such as ear infections, measles, and influenza may also result in hearing loss acquired after birth.

Sometimes the word "deaf" is written with a lower case "d" and other times with a capital "D." Those who see themselves as Deaf generally do not view deafness as a disability. Instead, they see the Deaf as a cultural group with its own language and experiences (Guthmann & Sandberg, 1999). In this chapter, we use the word deaf to include all those who cannot hear and the word Deaf to refer to the cultural group.

Few attempts have been made to study drinking, drug use, and related problems among individuals who are Deaf or deaf. Studies that have been conducted must be viewed cautiously due to many obstacles in obtaining accurate estimates of substance use and related disorders among those who cannot hear (Lipton & Goldstein, 1997). Obtaining representative samples is difficult, and the Deaf often mistrust hearing individuals who are likely to be conducting surveys. Studies often combine those who are congenitally deaf or became deaf early in life with those who developed hearing loss later in life even though their communication styles and life experiences may be quite different. Technology may help to improve the study of substance abuse in deaf populations. For the time being, the available literature suggests that substance use and substance use disorders occur at least as frequently among the deaf and hard of hearing as they do among the general population (Lipton & Goldstein, 1997; Titus, Schiller, & Guthmann, 2008). Dixon (1987) expressed surprise that estimates of substance abuse among people who are deaf are not higher given misconceptions about deafness and the poor treatment deaf people often receive.

Studies of substance use problems in deaf populations include different types of samples, and findings must be considered in that context. Concerns arise from reports such as Lipton and Goldstein's (1997) indicating that among 362 deaf individuals in New York State, 29 percent had "tried to cut down or quit drinking" and 21 percent reported the same for drug use. Fulton (1983) indicated that substance abuse was an issue for one-third to one-half of students seen at the Counseling and Placement Center at Gallaudet College for deaf students. However, in a study of 205 deaf college students and 185 hearing students participating in freshman orientation or taking freshman-oriented classes, no differences in alcohol and drug problems were reported (Lukomski, 2007).

In a study of youth in substance abuse treatment, those with and without hearing loss (118 and 4,049 individuals, respectively) were similar with regard to demographic characteristics, alcohol, marijuana, and most other drug use, peer substance use, involvement in crime and violence, and risk behaviors, but those with hearing loss entered treatment with more severe substance abuse problems (Titus et al., 2008). They also reported greater forms of all psychological distress included in the study (depression, anxiety, suicidal/homicidal thoughts, conduct problems, PTSD and other stress, AD, and HD), and they were more likely to have been victimized (abused) and to have experienced more severe victimization (also see Titus, 2010). Those with hearing loss were more likely to have initiated substance use at a younger age, to have used cocaine, and to have been diagnosed with substance dependence (including greater severity of lifetime dependence), and less likely to have been diagnosed with abuse. Speculation as to why their problems were more severe are the lack of substance abuse prevention and intervention efforts directed to Deaf youth and the isolation and communication barriers Deaf youth face (Titus et al.; also see Lukomski, 2007; Titus & White, 2008).

Moore and McAweeney (2006/2007) found that 1.8 percent of individuals receiving substance abuse treatment in New York state were deaf or hard of hearing. Though these deaf and hard of hearing clients differed from other clients on some demographic characteristics, the substances they were most likely to use were the same (alcohol, heroin, and cocaine), and they were very similar in achieving short-term substance use and vocational/educational goals. This later finding was not necessarily expected because of assumptions that deaf and hard of hearing clients are not well served in traditional treatment agencies.

Studies find conflicting results about the prevalence of substance use disorders among deaf vs. hearing psychiatric inpatients. Among all 64 deaf inpatients discharged from a northeastern state psychiatric hospital from 1999 to 2004, the most common diagnosis was PTSD (Black & Glickman, 2006). The deaf patients were less likely to be diagnosed with substance use or psychotic disorders and more likely to be diagnosed with mood, anxiety, personality, or developmental disorders than hearing patients. Nevertheless, 33 percent of the deaf had a substance use disorder (compared to 42 percent of the hearing patients). The deaf patients were substantially less likely to be diagnosed with alcohol dependence but more likely to be diagnosed with polysubstance abuse or dependence. They were also less impaired by their substance

use problems but the psychosocial and cognitive functioning of both the hearing and deaf patient groups was substantially compromised.

Deaf Culture. Since the life experiences of those who are pre-lingually deaf are substantially different from those who became deaf post-lingually, the degree to which deaf individuals relate to the Deaf culture and to hearing communities varies (Steinberg, 1991). Deaf children and adolescents may attend residential schools for the deaf, which isolates them from the larger community (Guthmann, 1998a). Families are often overprotective of their deaf members, and the Deaf community is close knit and often mistrustful of hearing individuals because of exclusion or mistreatment by them (Lipton & Goldstein, 1997; Sylvester, 1986). Deaf individuals face substantial barriers to achieving their potential in a hearing society.

Within the Deaf community, substance abuse prevention and education, including public service announcements about the dangers of drinking and drug use, and knowledge about treatment and self-help resources, are generally lacking (Guthmann & Blozis, 2001; Guthmann & Sandberg, 1995; Lipton & Goldstein, 1997; Titus et al., 2008). In one survey, deaf and hard of hearing individuals were less likely to report receiving information to prevent health problems from their doctors and to report being asked about their drinking or smoking (Tamaskar et al., 2000). The Deaf community may view chemical dependency in moralistic terms (Rendon, 1992; Rubin, 2003), perhaps because members lack information about the causes and treatment of these disorders.

Deafness carries its own stigma, and the Deaf community wants to present a positive image and avoid the additional stigma associated with alcohol and other drug problems (Boros, 1980/81; Guthmann & Blozis, 2001; Rubin, 2003). The New York State Division of Alcoholism and Alcohol Abuse (1988) commented on how insular Deaf communities often tend to be and noted that "an extensive 'grapevine' militates against persons coming forward to discuss and treat their problem" (p. 1). Giving up alcohol or drugs may alienate Deaf individuals from their circle of deaf friends (Rendon, 1992), and in many areas, the Deaf community is so small that developing new friendship networks is not feasible (Guthmann & Blozis, 2001). Isolation, culture, and communication barriers may all contribute to substance abuse among the Deaf (Rubin).

Assisting Substance Abusers Who Are Deaf.   Assisting members of the Deaf community requires the use of culturally relevant prevention and treatment approaches (Guthmann & Sandberg, 1999), particularly familiarity with communication styles. Many Deaf individuals use American Sign Language (ASL), a manual form of communication, or ASL variants such as Signed English; some prefer oration, which utilizes speech reading and English speech, while others speak and read English (Lipton & Goldstein, 1997) or use other methods (Marschark & Spencer, 2003). Individuals' language proficiency also varies, even in their preferred communication styles. Hearing professionals may misinterpret Deaf people's gestures or other movements. "For example, a subtle twitching of the nose signifies 'yeah-I-know,' and a furrowed brow may represent a question"; waving an arm is an attempt to get another's attention, but may be interpreted as abnormal by outsiders and result in misdiagnosis" (Steinberg, 1991, p. 381) and inappropriate treatment.

Whether it is an interpreter or an amplification device or other technology the individual prefers to use for communication, clients should be served in a way that best facilitates their recovery (see, for example, Moore, 1998). Researchers have found that Deaf individuals did not seek treatment because they thought others would not be able to communicate with them, or that they had sought help but were rejected because of their deafness (Lipton & Goldstein, 1997; Whitehouse, Sherman, & Kozlowski, 1991). Accommodating communication styles is challenging for prevention and treatment programs. Communication barriers are likely the major reason chemical dependency

treatment programs do not adequately serve deaf and hard-of-hearing individuals (Rubin, 2003).

AA's newsletter, the *Grapevine,* first published an article on alcoholism and hearing impairment in December 1968 (Boros, 1980–81). Special treatment programs for Deaf alcoholics emerged during the mid-1970s. Boros recounts the development of Alcoholism Intervention for the Deaf (AID), which began as a volunteer effort and later became Addiction Intervention with the Disabled. The Deaf community initially opposed AID, believing that the program "singled out Deaf people from other disabled persons as having drinking problems" (Boros, p. 29). To initiate AID, groundwork had to be laid with both the Deaf community and the chemical dependency treatment community. In 1979, NIAAA funded an alcoholism treatment demonstration project for Deaf individuals at the Cape Cod Alcoholism Intervention and Rehabilitation Unit. The program was developed following the death of a young Deaf man with a substance abuse problem (Rothfeld, 1981). No accessible services were available to him. He struggled and eventually took his own life.

The Substance Abuse and Mental Health Services Administration and the Office of Special Education and Rehabilitative Services have funded model programs, such as the inpatient Minnesota Chemical Dependency Program for Deaf and Hard of Hearing Individuals. The Minnesota program's emphasis is on accessibility, and it utilizes a Twelve-Step philosophy and other approaches, including behavioral change strategies (Guthmann & Blozis, 2001). The program sees clients who started using as early as age 10, and staff members find that clients often have untreated mental health problems. Family members are encouraged to participate. Materials the Minnesota program has developed include the "Choices" curriculum, "Staying Sober: Relapse Prevention Guide," a national information catalog, and the video *Dreams of Denial* (Sandberg, 1996). The video, which utilizes voice, sign, and captions, is about a deaf man dealing with chemical dependency. The Minnesota program has also produced a tobacco prevention program for deaf youth. There are only a few other specialized programs for Deaf individuals who have substance use disorders (Moore et al., 2009). Progress in helping Deaf and hard of hearing individuals with substance abuse problems is still described as "slow," with some programs closing due to lack of funding or low enrollments because the incidence of deafness is low (Titus & Guthmann, 2010).

Although the Americans with Disabilities Act requires that treatment programs be accessible to deaf individuals, programs often lack funds to pay for accommodations, including sign language interpreters, and "some mainstreamed substance abuse treatment programs claim to be accessible, but only provide a few hours of interpreting services per day" (Koster & Guthmann, n.d.). Though interpreters usually work at rates most would consider reasonable, the costs for individuals who wish to employ them for additional hours may be prohibitive.

In trying to maintain professional boundaries, those who work with Deaf individuals may be considered aloof, superior, or "in it for themselves," and these issues must be addressed for an effective therapeutic relationship to develop (Guthmann, Heines, & Kolvitz, 2001). Since health and social service professionals have not always treated Deaf individuals with appropriate sensitivity, it may take time to gain their confidence and that of the larger Deaf community. The websites of Substance Abuse Resources and Disability Issues (SARDI) at Wright State University and Substance and Alcohol Intervention Services for the Deaf (SAISD) at the Rochester Institute of Technology provide helpful resources for professionals assisting deaf and hard of hearing patients. SAISD provides a national directory of substance abuse and dependence services accessible to those who are deaf, as well as other services to help deaf individuals bridge the treatment gap. A centralized source of referral information and support such as a national, 24-hour hotline for deaf and hard of hearing would be helpful (Guthmann & Blozis, 2001).

Substance abuse and other human service professionals fluent in ASL remain scarce but are sorely needed. Professionals who want to be more responsive can learn to work with interpreters, although this is not as effective as direct communication. Determining a client's preferred mode of communication is important, but an appropriate interpreter may not be available. Communication is a complex process, and using an interpreter complicates it further. Interpreters' abilities vary, and qualified or certified interpreters are needed to ensure accurate communication. Interpretation in group therapy, a treatment modality commonly used in substance abuse treatment, or other group activities is particularly challenging (Moore et al., 2009).

Professional interpreters subscribe to a code of ethics that includes standards for confidentiality and objectiveness, but clients may still hesitate to reveal confidences with interpreters present (Steinberg, 1991), since they are likely to see them in other settings or have other relationships with them (Guthmann & Blozis, 2001; Lipton & Goldstein, 1997). The Registry of Interpreters for the Deaf can assist with locating qualified interpreters, but in crises, interpreters may not be readily available. Family and friends may be able to communicate well with the individual, but the client may not wish to share certain information with them. Using family and friends as interpreters may result in breaches of confidentiality and violations of the client's rights (Whitehouse et al., 1991).

Without direct communication, client assessment and treatment are challenging (Sandberg, 1996). Deaf clients may agree passively with professionals rather than express their own opinions (Grant, Kramer, & Nash, 1982) or ask for clarification when needed (Guthmann & Blozis, 2001). Since reading is generally taught phonetically, many who are pre-lingually deaf do not read at a level that allows them to fully comprehend standardized questionnaires and other program materials (Steinberg, 1991). Deaf individuals often do not understand the language used in the screening and assessment tools most commonly utilized in the chemical dependency field (Alexander,

DiNitto, & Tidblom, 2005). Thus, paper-and-pencil screening, assessment, educational, and treatment materials are often not appropriate for them (Moore, 1998). Some visual aids are available for prevention and treatment programs.

Standardized tools for assessing Deaf individuals for alcohol and drug problems are just beginning to emerge. Alexander (2005) developed the first psychometrically tested ASL video screening for this purpose called the Drug and Alcohol Assessment for the Deaf (DAAD). This brief screening tool is available free of charge.[2] Another instrument, the Substance Abuse in Vocational Rehabilitation Screener in American Sign Language (SAVR-S-ASL), based on the Substance Abuse Subtle Screening Inventory (see chapter 5), is in development (Guthmann & Moore, 2007).

In prevention and treatment programs, Steitler and Rubin (2001) recommend using multimedia—slides, posters, charts, and closed-captioned videos—along with exercises and other activities to further ensure that the material is being absorbed. To accommodate differences in clients' learning styles, the Minnesota Chemical Dependency Program for Deaf and Hard of Hearing Individuals utilizes experiential activities such as role-playing and engages clients in drawing as a way of completing program assignments (Guthmann & Blozis, 2001). To improve accessibility, written materials must be geared to the client's reading level. Presentations must be paced appropriately, since the material may be quite new to the client (Boros, 1980–81). Gestural languages like ASL often lack translations for the jargon used in chemical dependency treatment programs and mutual-help groups, presenting added challenges (Jorgensen & Russert, 1982). Fatigue may become a factor since the demands of absorbing new material are substantial and gesturing requires additional energy (Boros, 1980–81; Kearns, 1989). A sufficient length of treatment, especially in inpatient settings, may be needed to address these factors (NYSDAAA, 1988; Rubin, 2003).

To address service underutilization, methods such as "telehealth" videoconferencing technology are being used to provide mental health services to

deaf individuals (Wilson & Wells), and e-therapy programs such as Deaf Off Drugs and Alcohol (DODA) are being tested (Moore et al., 2009; Titus & Guthmann, 2010). DODA enhances community-based treatment thorough videoconferencing and video phone technology, which has advantages such as reducing travel time to treatment programs, increasing accessibility when clients are spread across a large geographical area, and providing faster communication than text-based telephone relay services known as TTY. New technologies such as text messaging have rapidly changed the way people in general are communicating. Regardless of hearing status, providing therapy using technological devices presents challenges such as obtaining informed consent; some of the equipment is costly and clients not already familiar with a particular technology must learn how to utilize it (Moore et al.).

Although interpreting all the interaction for deaf and hard of hearing individuals in traditional substance abuse programs is virtually impossible, empirical evidence is lacking as to whether mainstreaming or special services produce different outcomes. The Rochester Institute of Technology has brought together members of the hearing and hearing-impaired communities to promote mainstreaming of people who are Deaf in chemical dependency treatment programs (Dixon, 1987). However, the Illinois Task Force on Substance Abuse Among the Hearing Impaired called mainstreaming "ineffective and costly" and favors special treatment units (Whitehouse et al., 1991), which individuals who identify with Deaf culture may prefer (Moore, 1998). The task force recommends employing staff members who are deaf and hard of hearing, and, in addition to the usual chemical dependency treatment services, encourages Deaf issues groups, vocabulary enrichment, assertiveness training, independent living skills, and stress management activities. Few specialized program are available. Deaf clients may be unable to afford them or unable to use them because they may be far from their home and family and work responsibilities.

In addition to intensive treatment programs, it is generally difficult to find halfway houses, outpatient treatment groups, aftercare programs, and self-help groups specifically for the deaf, which may contribute to relapse (Guthmann & Blozis, 2001; Titus & Guthmann, 2010). Fully accessible services are sorely lacking, though some Deaf individuals do reside in Oxford Houses (see Chapter 6). Staff members from deaf community services often consult with these houses, and volunteers interpret Twelve-Step meetings and Oxford House chapter meetings for residents (Alvarez et al., 2006). In a few houses, Deaf residents communicate in sign language.

Some mutual-help groups are conducted in ASL, but they may not meet frequently enough to meet individuals' needs. Most mutual-help groups do not employ interpreters on a regular basis. Bringing one's own interpreter is costly, may draw unwanted attention, and is generally not as effective as a meeting conducted entirely in ASL (Guthmann & Blozis, 2001; Rendon, 1992; Steinberg, 1991). The Deaf community is generally small, making it difficult for newcomers to locate recovering role models who are Deaf (Guthmann & Blozis, 2001; Rubin, 2003). ASL is a gestural rather than a written language, but SAISD gives an idea of what the steps of Alcoholics Anonymous are like in ASL. For example, "We finish admit alcohol beat us—our lives messed up." Alcoholics Anonymous also offers versions of the Twelve Steps and Twelve Traditions in ASL on video and closed-caption films as well as in easy-to-read literature. Online meetings are also helpful to deaf and hard of hearing individuals. The Substance Abuse and Mental Health Services Administration is supporting Web conferencing technology in which deaf individuals in recovery are leading Twelve-Step meetings (Titus & Guthmann, 2010).

Blindness and Other Visual Impairments

Estimates of people with blindness and other visual impairments differ based on the definition used. In a 2005 U.S. population survey of individuals 15 years of age and older, "about 7.8 million reported difficulty seeing the words and letters in ordinary newsprint, even when wearing glasses or contacts (if normally worn). Of this group, 1.8 million reported being unable to see printed words at all or were blind" (Brault, 2008). The major causes of blindness and vision impairment in the United States are macular degeneration, cataract, diabetic retinopathy, and glaucoma (Prevent Blindness America and National Eye Institute, 2002). Alcohol and other drug use can aggravate health problems such as diabetes and glaucoma ("Blindness, Visual Impairment, and Substance Abuse," 2008; Watson et al., 1998).

Very little has been written about blindness and visual impairment in conjunction with alcohol and drug problems. Some materials are available to assist chemical dependency professionals in reaching out to those with visual impairments (Burns & de Miranda, 1991; Working with People, n.d.). A few have provided information to educate chemical dependency personnel about the general course of rehabilitation for individuals with visual disabilities (Glass, 1980–81). Others provide basic information about alcohol and drug problems to help rehabilitation counselors identify these problems among people who are blind or visually impaired and refer them to treatment programs and mutual-help groups (Peterson & Nelipovich, 1983).

Isolation and unemployment are major problems for those with severe visual impairments (American Foundation for the Blind, 2000; Burns & de Miranda, 1991). Nelipovich and Parker (1981) investigated state rehabilitation counselors' response to their work with individuals who were visually impaired and had substance use disorders. Of the 32 counselors who responded, half reported no success in helping this clientele secure gainful employment. The counselors felt that substance abuse was a greater obstacle to rehabilitation than visual impairment. They wanted more education in working with clients who have these co-occurring disabilities, indicating that professionals' lack of preparation may be an obstacle to rehabilitation.

Despite suggestions that one-fifth to one-half of blind and visually impaired individuals might have alcohol and drugs problems (Koch, Nelipovich, & Sneed, 2002), there are no good surveys on which to base concerns. A survey of clients of Wisconsin's state vocational rehabilitation program and centers for independent living included 271 respondents who were blind or visually impaired (Nelipovich & Buss, 1991). The sample's representativeness is not certain, but respondents who were blind or visually impaired or who had orthopedic impairments or spinal cord injuries were more often heavy or moderate drinkers than those with other disabilities. In a study of 69 individuals who were blind or had significant visual impairment (BVI) recruited through a state service agency, males, Hispanics, and those who used tobacco had a higher risk for substance dependence, but none of the BVI variables (such as onset of blindness) were significant in identifying those at risk (Brooks, 2000).

There is no research on the course of alcohol and drug problems for those with blindness and visual impairment, but Glass (1980–81) noted that those who have a drinking problem prior to the onset of their visual impairment lack adequate coping skills and require specific alcoholism treatment. For those who develop alcohol problems after the onset of visual impairment, Glass suggests that substance abuse may remit following adequate adjustment to the visual disability. Similarly, Nelipovich and Buss (1989) note:

> If the visual impairment is of long standing and if an appropriate level of acceptance of and adjustment to this impairment has been reached before alcohol abuse begins, then treatment should be geared to addressing the alcohol abuse. If the visual impairment has been more recent, then treatment should focus on helping the client to accept and adjust to the visual impairment first, and then on treating the alcohol abuse. (p. 129)

The greatest challenge may be assisting those who have accepted neither disability (Nelipovich & Buss, 1991). To assess the dual disabilities of substance abuse and blindness or visual impairment, Nelipovich and Buss recommend employing the ASK approach by determining the client's level of *acceptance* of each disability, the client's *skills* for coping with each disability, and the client's *knowledge* about each disability. When an individual's visual impairment has not been well addressed and substance abuse is present, intra-agency and interagency disagreements may arise about how to assist the individual, including which disability to treat first (Koch, Nelipovich, & Sneed, 2002).

Basic aspects of interacting with individuals who are blind or visually impaired should be respected ("Blindness, Visual Impairment, and Substance Abuse," 2008; Glenn & Dixon, 1991; Moore, 1998; Nelipovich & Buss, 1989; *Working with People*, n.d.):

- Communicate directly with the client. Do not defer to an individual who might accompany the client to the treatment center.
- Speak in a normal tone of voice and at a normal speed.
- Identify yourself to the client, and let him or her know when you are entering and leaving the room.
- Ask individuals how they prefer to acquaint themselves with new surroundings and help orient them to the physical environment of the treatment setting.
- Appoint a guide for the first few days to allow an individual entering an inpatient or residential treatment program time to learn to move about the facility independently.
- Provide large-print materials, magnification devices, and other optical aides so that clients with sufficient vision can utilize educational materials independently without relying on readers.
- Avoid the use of visual cues when giving directions.
- Provide sufficient verbal explanation of material when using a flipchart, whiteboard, or other visual aide in giving a presentation.
- Read materials aloud, and use tape-recorded materials for playback and review.

- Make program materials available in Braille (including admission and consent forms) and allot sufficient time for reading them (however, only about 10 percent of those who are blind read Braille).
- Obtain Braille playing cards, games, and leisure reading material for use during free time.

Few treatment facilities have substantially increased their accessibility for those who are blind or visually impaired. The MARCO model is a chemical dependency treatment program that reaches out to people who are blind or visually impaired and makes treatment accessible to them (Nelipovich, Wergin, & Kossick, 1998). Since chemical dependency treatment programs may be unable to provide all the services clients who are blind or visually impaired need (such as the latest technological equipment), cooperation with agencies that specialize in serving this clientele is needed (Burns & de Miranda, 1991). National Recordings for the Blind and each state's regional library for the blind are useful resources (Moore, 1998).

Mutual-help groups are also recommended for people who are blind or visually impaired and chemically dependent. If possible, have a member welcome, orient, and introduce the newcomer to others. Members can also offer transportation to individuals who are blind or visually impaired, especially in communities in which public transportation is lacking. The "Big Book" and some other AA materials are available in Braille and on audiocassette and can be ordered from AA's General Service Office or purchased at many local AA Intergroups.

Other Physical Disabilities and Substance Use Disorders

Heart Disease

There is a great deal of interest in how alcohol consumption affects the risk of cardiovascular disease (Mochly-Rosen & Zakhari, 2010). Excessive drinking can lead to alcoholic cardiomyopathy (a heart enlargement that inhibits this organ's ability to contract), hypertension (high blood pressure), hemorrhagic stroke (caused by ruptured blood vessels) and ischemic stroke (caused by blocked blood supply to the brain), some heart arrhythmias, and coronary heart disease (CHD) (Klatsky, 2001a; NIAAA, 2000). Light (Klatsky, 2001a) or moderate (NIAAA, 2000) drinking may reduce the likelihood of ischemic stroke, but there is disagreement over whether moderate alcohol consumption might have beneficial effects on blood pressure (NIAAA, 2000).

Studies using individuals as the unit of analysis provide evidence that a history of moderate alcohol consumption (generally defined in the United States as one drink per day for women and two for men) is associated with reduced risk of CHD (Hines & Rimm, 2001; Klatsky, 2001b) and even post-heart attack survival (NIAAA, 2000; also see Mochly-Rosen & Zakhari, 2010, for a discussion). While the causal mechanism is not clear, this benefit may be due in part to improved cholesterol levels (NIAAA, 2000; Mochly-Rosen & Zakhari). Studies differ as to whether it is red wine, wine, or any alcoholic beverage that confers protection (Mochly-Rosen & Zakhari). In addition, associated factors, such as socioeconomic status, lifestyle, and diet, have not been entirely ruled out as the beneficial mechanism (NIAAA, 2000; Mochly-Rosen & Zakhari).

Although studies of individuals indicate protective benefits of moderate alcohol consumption for CHD, a cross-cultural study did not find protective benefits at the population level, thus raising concerns about any policies suggesting alcohol's beneficial effects (Hemstrom, 2001). Criqui (2001) indicates that those at very low risk for CHD are unlikely to benefit from consuming alcohol, and given the risks of consuming alcohol, alcohol would not be approved for use under current regulatory mechanisms. Researchers are providing evidence, however, that may change this thinking. For example, King, Mainous, and Geesey (2008) found that middle-aged abstainers who began drinking wine in moderation had fewer cardiovascular events during a 4-year period than abstainers. Cautions, however, remain (King et al.), since drinking may be harmful when combined with the medications used to treat heart disease and may result in increased health risks following a heart attack (NIAAA, 1999). The American Heart Association (n.d.) does not encourage abstainers to begin drinking, and the World Health Organization does not recommend alcohol consumption to prevent CHD for individuals or population groups (Marmot, 2001). In light of the controversies over alcohol use and individual risk for harm from drinking, Mukamal and Rimm (2001) suggest there is no simple overall recommendation and encourage individual consultation with a physician about the safety and risks of drinking (also see Klatsky, 2001a, 2001b).

Diabetes

A body of literature notes that moderate alcohol consumption is associated with reduced risk of type 2 diabetes (Rehm et al., 2010). The relationship has been described as U- or J-shaped. In other words, moderate consumption is associated with lower risk than no, low, or heavy consumption; binge drinking is also associated with increased risk (Joosten et al., 2010; also see Pietraszek, Gregersen, & Hermansen, 2010). For example, Kao, Puddey, Boland, Watson, and Brancati (2001) studied more than 12,000 middle-aged individuals and found that heavy drinking (especially of spirits) increased the risk of type 2 diabetes among men (data were insufficient to conduct a similar analysis for women); moderate drinking (defined as 1 to 14 drinks per week) did not increase risk in either men or women. Conigrave et al. (2001) studied nearly 47,000 male health care professionals and found that "frequent low-to-moderate alcohol consumption appear(ed) to offer the greatest protection against type 2 diabetes, regardless of the type of alcoholic beverage chosen or the total amount of alcohol consumed per week" (p. 2394). Whether moderate alcohol consumption itself is a protection or if it is associated with other lifestyle choices that help to

protect people from diabetes is a topic of debate (see, for example, Joosten et al.).

Among people with diabetes, moderate alcohol consumption may reduce the risk of ischemic heart disease (Gallagher, Connolly, & Kelly, 2001). However, excessive drinking can result in a host of medical problems, such as hypoglycemia, peripheral neuropathy, and in men, erectile dysfunction (Gallagher et al.). Other consequences may be as severe as brain damage or death (Ryan, 1983–84). Ahern and Hendryx (2007) studied nearly 98,000 admissions of people with type 1 and type 2 diabetes to identify "avoidable" hospitalizations and found that alcohol and drug abuse were risks for short-term complications such as coma. Accurate diagnosis of a diabetic's situation in an emergency can be complicated by the difficulty in distinguishing many of the symptoms of hypoglycemia from those of intoxication (Ryan, 1983–84).

Conigrave et al. (2001) recommend that "decisions about alcohol consumption should consider the full range of benefits and risks to an individual" though their "data suggest that a reduction in type 2 diabetes may be among the benefits of regular moderate consumption" (p. 2394). Gallagher and colleagues (2001) caution against promoting drinking in diabetic patients. In a study of 395 patients over age 16 with either insulin-dependent or noninsulin-dependent diabetes, self-reported problem drinking appeared to be "lower than among other medical outpatient populations" but was similar to " the prevalence found in community surveys" (Spangler, Konen, & McGann, 1993). The problem drinkers were also more likely to smoke, and those identified as having a drinking problem had poorer coping responses to psychological stress and more guilt, hostility, anxiety, and depression than those without a drinking problem. Black males and those with higher negative affect were at greater risk for alcohol problems. The problem drinkers did not perceive their glycemic control as being different than the non-problem drinkers, and the actual glycemic values of the problem and non-problem drinkers did not differ. This was somewhat surprising given the negative effects excessive alcohol consumption can have on managing medical problems.

In addition to alcohol's effects on glucose metabolism, substance use disorders may result in failure to follow diabetes treatment regimens or insure proper nutrition (Saitz, 2009). Co-occurring mental illness may also be a complicating factor. Jackson and colleagues (2007) followed 197 individuals who had both substance use and psychotic disorders and had participated in a randomized clinical trial to test an intervention to treat these co-occurring illnesses. They found that 21 percent had received some treatment for diabetes; over a 12-year period, 41 percent of these individuals died compared to 10 percent of those who did not have diabetes.

Substance use among youth with diabetes has been a topic in a smattering of articles across several countries. The studies, often based on relatively small convenience samples, generally indicate that alcohol and drug use is less common among youth with diabetes than in the general population. For example, in the United States, Gold and Gladstein (1993) found less frequent alcohol and other drug use in a group of 79 campers and camp counselors with diabetes, age 11 to 25, than in the general population of young people. More similar to other young people was that 24 percent of the sample drank in a problematic way. Those who drank or used drugs tended to have family members who drank or used drugs. Most of the 79 youth did not perceive that drinking or drug use would affect diabetic control. There was no relationship between alcohol and drug use and perceived diabetic control, but those identified as problem drinkers were more likely to perceive their diabetic control as poor to fair and to believe that alcohol and other drug use altered diabetic control.

Glasgow et al. (1991) studied 101 young people, age 12 to 20, attending a diabetes clinic and found lower self-reported problem alcohol and drug use than in the Gold and Gladstein (1993) study, with 10 patients answering yes to at least one of six questions indicating an alcohol or drug problem. Only one patient had a urine specimen that tested positive for marijuana, and none tested positive for cocaine or PCP. There was no difference in diabetic control among those who had and had not tried alcohol, but those who reported occasional use of other drugs and those who reported any problem with alcohol and other drugs had higher glycohemoglobin values. Patients reporting that a parent had an alcohol or drug problem also had higher glycohemoglobin values. Glasgow and colleagues note that although drug use may not cause poor diabetic control, both drug use and poor diabetic control may be associated with risk-taking behavior. In another clinic-based study, this one of 150 youth with insulin dependent diabetes mellitus, Frey and colleagues (1997) also found lower levels of substance use than in community samples and wondered if this may be due to delayed social development or education provided to these children on the risks of alcohol and drug use.

In a Finnish study based on a nationally representative sample of patients aged 13 to 17 with diabetes, 64 percent of those who did not smoke and 68 percent of those who did not drink reported good compliance with their treatment regimens (Kyngäs, 2000). Satisfactory compliance was most common among regular and occasional smokers and drinkers. Of those with who smoked regularly, 16 percent had poor compliance, and of regular drinkers, 33 percent had poor compliance. In Chile, a sample of youth with diabetes used tobacco, alcohol, and illicit drugs less than other youth in earlier but not later adolescence (Martinez-Aguayo et al., 2007). In contrast, a study conducted in Italy compared youth with and without diabetes and found somewhat more tobacco use in male youth with diabetes, and female youth with diabetes used illicit drugs at similar or somewhat higher rates as other young women (Scaramuzza et al., 2010).

Although there seems to be no indication that diabetes is associated with higher rates of substance use problems, at least in the United States, medical personnel should evaluate and educate people with diabetes about alcohol intake and make referrals to substance abuse treatment when needed. Adolescents are particularly prone to experiment with alcohol and other drugs. Even if adolescents with diabetes are less likely to experiment, they need information about the added risks alcohol and drug use may pose for them in order to avoid medical emergencies (Kamboj & Draznin, 2006).

Epilepsy

Alcohol abuse can cause seizures in individuals who do not have other disabilities. Rhem and colleagues (2010) find "a consistent relationship between alcohol consumption and increased risk of ... epilepsy, especially for higher doses of alcohol" (p. 828). Gordon and Devinsky (2001) provide the following information on the relationship between epilepsy and alcohol use: Generally speaking, small amounts of alcohol (not more than two drinks a day and not more than three to six per week) are not associated with increased frequency of epileptic seizures or blood levels of drugs used to control epilepsy. CNS depressants such as phenobarbitol (used to control seizures) should not be used with alcohol (another CNS depressant) because of dangerous compound effects. Moderate or heavy drinking can increase seizure risk, and some epilepsy patients should not consume alcohol (e.g., those with histories of substance abuse or dependence and those who have experienced alcohol-related seizures). Alcoholics have increased rates of seizures and alcohol withdrawal lowers epilepsy and seizure thresholds. People with epilepsy seem less likely than others to use or abuse alcohol, perhaps due to physicians' warnings to avoid drinking.

Drugs such as cocaine also lower the seizure threshold (Argawal, 2011). Data on whether marijuana promotes or inhibits seizure activity are not as clear, but chronic marijuana users may suffer other health problems (e.g., cardiovascular,

pulmonary, endocrine) (Gordon & Devinsky, 2001). Some evidence indicates that marijuana may have antiepileptic effects, but its use could result in poor compliance with antiepileptic medications, and marijuana use or withdrawal might promote seizures in some individuals (Gordon & Devinksy).

Among nearly 14,000 veterans diagnosed with epilepsy, Zeber et al. (2007) found that 46 percent had a mental disorder, and 38 percent of those who had a serious mental illness and 30 percent of those who had another mental disorder also had a substance use disorder. None of those without a mental disorder had substance abuse or dependence. Zaccara (2009) suggests the possibility of helping people with co-occurring epilepsy and substance use disorders by treating them with antiepileptic drugs such as Topiramate that also show promise in treating substance use disorders.

Individuals with epilepsy who have not been drinking or using illicit drugs are sometimes mistaken as intoxicated, due to the disorientation and lack of coordination that follows a seizure. Law enforcement officers must take care not to make erroneous arrests for public intoxication or inappropriate referrals to detoxification centers. Medical personnel are certainly aware of the need to make this distinction.

Chronic Pain

In many cases, the same psychoactive drugs discussed in this book which people abuse or become dependent on are prescribed to bring relief for pain caused by serious injuries or illnesses (Compton & Volkow, 2006). For example, individuals with chronic back pain may be prescribed opioid analgesics such as hydrocodone or oxycodone for pain relief. Most individuals use medications as prescribed, but some use them in non-therapeutic ways that can result in dependence or cause or aggravate other conditions.

Concerns have been raised about the potential for addiction in patients prescribed analgesic medications. In an extensive review of studies, rates of addiction among patients with nonmalignant pain who received long-term opioid treatment varied between zero and 50 percent, and in cancer patients from zero to nearly 8 percent (rates varied depending on the definition of addiction used and the sample studied) (Højsted & Sjøgren, 2007). In another review that provided averages across studies of nonmalignant pain patients, the abuse/addiction rate was just over 3 percent, but when only the studies that had screened out those with previous or current abuse or addiction were included, the abuse/addiction rate dropped to just under 0.2 percent (Fishbain et al., 2008). This study also looked at aberrant drug-related behaviors or ADRBs (a term used in the pain medicine field to indicate behaviors, such as drug seeking, that are similar to addiction [see, for example, Fisher, 2004]). The average rate of patients with ADRBs was nearly 12 percent, but dropped to 0.6 percent in studies where patients with current or previous abuse or addiction histories had been screened out. Thus, among those without a prior or current abuse or addiction diagnosis, the potential for abuse or addiction while being treated with pain medications was low.

While some studies have looked at the number of individuals who develop abuse or addiction during the course of treatment for chronic pain, few have looked at the number of people being treated for substance abuse disorders that have chronic pain. Sheu and colleagues (2008) conducted such as study of 79 individuals with substance use disorders (mostly men, Caucasian, and employed, with a mean age of 40). Nearly one-third reported chronic, severe pain, and about one-quarter reported that high levels of pain interfered with their normal functioning. Pain was also associated with the participants' co-occurring medical and psychiatric conditions and their abuse behaviors, but only 40 percent of those with chronic severe pain had recently consulted a physician about the problem. Those "with chronic severe pain were more likely to cite pain as the impetus for first abusing alcohol or drugs and to report currently using alcohol, illicit drugs, or illicitly obtained prescription analgesics to treat their pain" (Sheu et al., pp. 914–915), indicating that pain should be better treated among recovering individuals.

A problem physicians face in prescribing medications that are used to treat various ailments but that can also be abused (including analgesic and stimulant drugs) is determining who is likely to abuse or become dependent on them (Compton & Volkow, 2006). This is a concern for both patients with and without a history of abuse or dependence. In a study of 500 patients consecutively admitted to a multidisciplinary pain management practice, during the study, 16 percent were found to be using illicit drugs based on urinalysis, and 9 percent were classified as opioid abusers (they had obtained controlled substances from a source outside the pain management practice by "doctor shopping" or trafficking) (Manchikanti et al., 2006). Illicit drug use was more common among patients with a history of illicit drug use and among those with previous pain, under 45 years of age, females, following motorcycle accidents, and among those with problems in three different body regions (as compared to one region). Opioid abuse was also more common following motorcycle accidents and among those with problems in three regions of the body, though the authors caution that there is no foolproof way of identifying abusers, and physicians must not only be cautious but treat patients appropriately.

Prior to beginning long-term opioid treatment for pain, patients should be screened for abuse or addiction potential, but often the instruments used are not well validated (Højsted & Sjøgren, 2007). Højsted and Sjøgren call the Pain Medicine Questionnaire (Adams et al., 2004) "well validated" and the Screener and Opioid Assessment for Pain Patients (SOAPP) questionnaire (Butler et al., 2004) "reasonably well validated" tools for this purpose.

When treating patients for chronic pain, adherence monitoring, which generally includes taking a history, signing a controlled substance agreement, periodic reviews of the agreement, education, random drug testing, and pill counts, is recommended (also see Højsted & Sjøgren, 2007; Wiedemer,

Harden, Arndt, & Gallagher, 2007). In Mancikanti et al.'s (2006) study, adherence monitoring was estimated to reduce opioid abuse by 50 percent among the 500 pain treatment patients studied.

Physicians' fears of promoting addiction may cause them to undermedicate patients who need and deserve pain relief (see, for example, Højsted & Sjøgren, 2007). In some cases, alternatives to medication use may be helpful (Moore, 1998). Physicians should consult approved guidelines to ensure appropriate treatment of pain patients (Højsted & Sjøgren), both those with and without addiction histories.

Summary

This chapter provided information about mental and physical disabilities that co-occur with substance use disorders and ways that service providers might better respond to the needs of individuals who have co-occurring disorders. Substance use disorders are more prevalent among people with some disabilities such as mental disorders. A substance use disorder may predate or precipitate another disability, as is often the case with spinal cord injury, traumatic brain injury, or injuries from other tragic accidents. An individual's response to a physical or mental disability may result in alcohol or drug abuse to diminish psychological anguish or physical pain or to produce euphoric affects; yet, multiple disabilities do not necessarily occur in a cause-and-effect relationship.

Researchers interested in the combination of substance use disorders and other disabilities will continue to investigate and debate statistics on prevalence rates and question the nature of the relationship between these co-occurring disorders. Preventing substance use disorders that lead to other disabilities and preventing disabilities that lead to substance use disorders is critical. Individuals with co-occurring disabilities need appropriate services. These individuals,

their loved ones, and the professionals who work with them face serious challenges because few alcohol and drug treatment programs have made treatment fully accessible to these individuals. It often takes a great deal of advocacy to get clients with substance use disorders and co-occurring disabilities the services they deserve. Many do not receive substance abuse treatment.

Although those in the field can offer some helpful suggestions, there are few cookbook-style solutions and proven approaches. Individualized treatment is necessary to meet each person's unique needs. The development of more innovative programs for people who have substance use disorders and co-occurring mental and physical disabilities and studies of the effectiveness of these programs would be particularly helpful. Meanwhile, a resourceful professional who is continually willing to be informed remains a tremendous asset to rehabilitation—second only to the tenacity of clients and their loved ones in pursuing recovery.

Acknowledgments

Excerpts from Mueser, K.T., Drake, R.E. & Wallach, M. A. (1998a) "Dual Diagnosis: A Review of Etiological Theories" from Addictive Behaviors, 23, 717–734, copyright © 1998. Reprinted with permission of Elsevier.

Adapted text from "Addictions and women with major psychiatric disorders," by D.M. DiNitto & C.L. Crisp (2002) from THE HANDBOOK OF ADDICTION TREATMENT FOR WOMEN, eds. S. L. Brown & L. A. Straussner (Wiley 2002). Copyright © 2002 by John Wiley & Sons, Inc. Reprinted with permission of John Wiley & Sons, Inc.

Adapted text from K. Steilter and J. L. Rubin (2001). "Deafness and Chemical Dependency: A Paper. Rochester Institute of Technology, Substance and Alcohol Intervention Services for the Deaf.

CHAPTER 14

Alcohol and Drug Misuse and Abuse in Late Life

Linda Vinton
Florida State University

Nicole Cesnales
Florida State University

The first Baby Boomers are reaching Social Security retirement age. Between 2010 and 2030, the population age 65 and older will increase from 35 to 72 million and grow to 20 percent of the total population (Wan, Sengupta, Velkoff, & DeBarros, 2005). Due to shorter life expectancy for men, the older population is disproportionately female. Until recently, limited attention has been paid to substance abuse among elderly people, despite their vulnerability to the effects of alcohol abuse and drug misuse and abuse. Escalating healthcare costs and changing demographics have ignited interest in substance abuse among older people in general and older women in particular.

Criteria and Prevalence Estimates

Alcohol Abuse

Often a misdiagnosed and misunderstood problem, alcohol abuse among older adults is challenging to define, measure, and identify. Johnson (2000) outlined several issues common to epidemiological research in this area including cohort effects, geographic and cultural differences in the populations being studied, diagnostic and classification criteria developed for younger populations, and physical and biological vulnerability to the effects of alcohol among elderly people.

Estimates of alcohol-use disorders (AUD) in the older population have been established based on screening instruments and diagnostic criteria developed and tested on younger populations. The use of these instruments poses several problems in estimating alcohol-use disorders in the aging population. For example, elders with memory loss may have difficulty recalling recent alcohol consumption, and a number of authors have suggested that denial of alcohol abuse and symptoms of drunkenness and dependence are greater among elders than other age groups. Another problem with using alcohol consumption as a measure to assess dependence among the elderly population is that elders have a decreased tolerance for alcohol and its effects. Older people have higher blood-alcohol levels after drinking than younger people (Letizia & Reinbolz, 2005). Measures of alcohol use and abuse have routinely been standardized on non-elderly men; thus, these measures may not recognize the particular alcohol-related health, social, and legal problems of male and female elders. Perhaps an even more fundamental issue with respect to the validity of the research in this area is that alcohol abuse has been variously defined, and the concepts of alcohol abuse, alcohol dependence, problem drinking, heavy drinking, and alcoholism (chronic and acute) have been used and operationalized differently.

Alcohol use disorders among elders have been classified as either early-onset (Type I) or late-onset (Type II). Individuals classified as having early-onset alcohol-use disorder typically develop AUD prior to the age of 25 and have survived into old age. Late-onset AUD is typically classified as a drinking problem that begins after the age of 45, and some see this behavior as a reaction to the life stressors that are present in older age such as widowhood and retirement. These classifications however, are not based on any diagnostic criteria and do not contribute to identifying prevalence rates of AUD among older people (Johnson, 2000). Given this lack of diagnostic criteria, Wetterling, Veltrup, John, and Driessen (2003) compared early onset and late onset alcoholics using ICD-10 criteria for alcohol dependence. A diagnosis of dependence is based on endorsement of at least three of the following criteria (WHO, 1992):

- A strong desire or sense of compulsion to drink alcohol
- Impaired capacity to control drinking in terms of its onset, termination, or levels of use
- Physiological withdrawal state
- Evidence of tolerance to the effects of alcohol
- Preoccupation with drinking
- Persistent substance use despite clear evidence of harmful consequences

Wetterling et al. (2003) found significant differences in ICD-10 criteria endorsement between early onset (94.1 percent) and late onset alcoholics (62.2 percent). These findings suggest that individuals with late onset alcoholism manifest symptoms of alcoholism differently than those with early onset alcoholism, with group differences present in several criteria (desire to drink, impaired capacity to control drinking, and preoccupation with drinking).

Reviewing a number of studies regarding the occurrence of late-life onset alcoholism among populations under treatment, Liberto and Oslin (1995) noted wide variation but concluded that a significant number of older alcoholics began abusing alcohol in later life. While it may change in the future, due to higher use among young females, elderly women are more likely than elderly men to fall in the late-life-onset category (Holzer, Myers, Weissman, Tischler, Leaf et al., 1986). This leaves a smaller but still sizable number of older persons who started to abuse alcohol late in life. The most common pattern among the general population, however, appears to be a decline in alcohol consumption and problem drinking for both men and women as they age (Moos, Schutte, Brennan, & Moos, 2005).

The National Clearinghouse for Alcohol and Drug Information (NCADI, 1995) brought together a consensus panel that consisted of researchers, clinicians, treatment providers, and substance abuse program directors and issued recommendations concerning detecting and treating substance abuse in people age 60 and older. The panel recommended that clinicians consider not using the DSM-IV criteria for substance abuse because the criteria may not be sufficiently sensitive to diagnosis of older adults with alcohol problems. The panel recommended that more than one drink per day for older men and more than two drinks on any special drinking occasion and somewhat lower limits for women be considered heavy or problem drinking.

The American Geriatrics Society (AGS, 2003) suggests the following clinical guidelines for AUD in older adults: greater than one drink per day, or greater than seven drinks per week, or greater than three drinks on a heavier drinking occasion. Furthermore, the AGS (2003) suggests that any drinking in combination with any score greater than a 0 on the CAGE could be indicative of at-risk drinking, and strongly cautions against drinking for those individuals with health conditions that could be worsened by alcohol use, or in combination with medications. The AGS also cautions clinicians against using DSM-IV criteria in diagnosing patients with AUD.

Given these diagnostic and measurement issues, overall prevalence rates for alcohol abuse by elders (also variously defined) have ranged anywhere from 2–4 percent, with 10 percent endorsing symptoms of heavy drinking (Ganry, Baudoin, Fardellon, Dubreuil, & the EPIDOS Group, 2001). There is evidence, however, that suggests these estimates are conservative. Prevalence of AUD among the elderly tend to be higher among men than women and higher for individuals living in hospital or institutional settings (O'Connell, Chin, Cunningham, & Lawlor, 2003). Some estimate that as many as 14 percent of elderly individuals presenting to emergency departments, 18 percent of elderly patients in hospitals, and 23–44 percent of elderly patients in psychiatric hospitals have AUD (O'Connell et al., 2003). Relying on structured interviews for case definition, Joseph, Atkinson, and Ganzini (1995) found that 49 percent of those entering a Veterans Administration nursing home met the DSM-III-R definition criteria for lifetime alcohol abuse or dependence while 18 percent were active alcoholics.

In a community-based study (Schonfeld, Rohrer, Zima, & Spiegel, 1993), social service staff providing services to elders estimated that one-fourth (25.9 percent) of their clients had alcohol abuse problems. Others have noted a high rate of alcoholism among the homeless population (Abbott, 1994). Butler, Lewis, and Sunderland (1998) caution, however, that only about 5 percent of alcoholics fit the stereotypic caricature of the inebriated individual sleeping on a sidewalk or doorstep. In a study conducted by Vinton (1991), legally competent yet self-neglectful elders were also seen to have a higher rate of alcohol abuse when compared with elders who were either abused or neglected by others (15 percent vs. 4 percent).

More recently, Breslow, Faden, and Smothers (2003) conducted a review of three large, national surveys to identify the prevalence of alcohol use in older Americans. The three studies included in the review were the National Health Interview Survey (NHIS-2000) conducted by the National Center for Health Statistics, the Behavioral Risk Factor Surveillance System (BRFSS-2001) conducted by the Centers for Disease Control and Prevention (CDC), and the National Household Survey on Drug Abuse (NHSDA-2000) conducted by the Substance Abuse and Mental Health Services Administration (SAMHSA).

The NHIS, a cross-sectional, nationally representative survey of 38,633 households in the United States, included measures of self-reported drinking behavior over the past 12 months. There were 6,180 individuals aged 65 and older who participated in the NHIS. Both the BRFSS and the NHSDA are cross-sectional, nationally representative studies that include questions about alcohol consumption in the past 30 days. The BRFSS included responses from 39,910 individuals over the age of 65 and the NHSAD included a sample of 2,946 respondents in the same age category.

Because each of these studies measured alcohol consumption differently, including duration and frequency, Breslow, Faden, and Smothers (2003) created multiple categories of alcohol use for each data set, including lifetime abstainers, former drinkers, and current drinkers for the NHIS and non-drinkers and current drinkers for the BRFSS and NHSDA. Prevalence rates of moderate alcohol consumption for individuals between the ages of 65 and 84 years ranged between 27 and 38 percent for men and 21 and 32 percent for women (Breslow, Faden, & Smothers, 2003). Heavier alcohol use in the same studies ranged between 9 and 10 percent for men and held steady around 2 percent for women (Breslow, Faden, & Smothers, 2003).

Merrick and colleagues (2008) found that male Medicare beneficiaries had higher prevalence rates (16 percent) of unhealthy drinking patterns than do women (4 percent) among community-dwelling individuals aged 65 and older. Unhealthy drinking was classified as the consumption of four or more drinks in one day or 30 or more drinks per month, and respondents were categorized as either exceeding the daily limit, the monthly limit, or both. This cross-sectional analysis of the nationally representative Access to Care file of the Medicare Current Beneficiary Survey contained a sample of 12,413 Medicare beneficiaries aged 65 and older. Nine percent (9 percent) of the respondents endorsed unhealthy drinking with higher prevalence present in those aged 65 to 70 years (Merrick et al., 2008).

While older men are less likely to abuse alcohol than younger men, it has been reported that older women are more likely to abuse alcohol than their younger counterparts (Friedman, 1996). In an extensive study that focused on "mature" women, the National Center on Addiction and Substance Abuse at Columbia University (CASA, 1995) found that approximately one out of four white women over the age of 59 drink (26.7 percent), compared with one out of six older African American women (17.5 percent) and Hispanic American women (17.2 percent). Applying the National Institute on Alcohol Abuse and Alcoholism (NIAAA, 1995) definition of heavy drinking as more than one drink per day for women, CASA found that older white and black women were equally likely to report heavy drinking (10.9 percent vs. 10.3 percent). In contrast, older Hispanic American women were less likely to drink heavily (6.9 percent). Heavy drinking among older women with higher incomes was more common than among lower-income women. Overall, CASA estimates that about 1.8 million (7 percent) of the population of women over the age of 59 may be abusing alcohol or have become dependent on it.

When compared to younger persons with alcohol dependence, older problem drinkers have been found to drink significantly more. Using data from the National Epidemiologic Survey on Alcohol and Related Conditions (NESARC), Ginzer and Richardson (2009) indicated that alcohol dependent adults aged 60 and over drank more than 40 alcoholic drinks per week on average; whereas, younger persons consumed between 25 and 35 drinks. These researchers also found that the older group reported more binge drinking episodes per month on average that younger age groups (19 vs. 13–15).

Drug Misuse and Abuse

DSM-IV (APA, 1994) outlines the continuum of prescription drug use as ranging from proper use to misuse to abuse to dependence. Any drug can be "misused" or used for a nonmedical purpose. Types of misuse include taking a lower dose than prescribed, taking more than prescribed, using a drug for a purpose other than what it is prescribed for, or combining prescription drugs with over-the-counter (OTC) drugs, herbs, certain foods, or dietary supplements. Individuals may also share prescription drugs, obtain them from a nonmedical source, or use them with alcohol without intending to experience the psychoactive effects. Prescription drug misuse and abuse are hidden problems that are under-recognized, under-screened, and under-treated in the older population (Simoni-Wastila, 2004). The problem may further be exacerbated when individuals purchase controlled substances from offshore pharmacies, neighboring countries, or via the Internet.

As a group, elders are more likely to use licit drugs than younger people. The average older person is prescribed seven medications and takes two over-the-counter medications for an average of six health conditions (Orwig, Brandt, & Grueber-Baldini, 2006). Although elderly people constitute less than 13 percent of the total U.S. population, they receive 30 percent of the prescriptions for medications and purchase 70 percent of the OTC medications (Friedman, 1996).

In a 2003 survey of 17,685 persons aged 65+, results showed that of the 89 percent that took prescription drugs, almost half (46 percent) used five or more prescription medications and 54 percent had drugs prescribed by more than one physician. Additionally, more than one-third (35 percent) purchased their medications at more than one pharmacy. Among the respondents with at least three chronic health conditions, slightly more than half (52 percent) reported not taking all of their drugs as prescribed (Safran et al., 2005).

Using data from the 2000 and 2001 NHSDA, 2 percent of survey respondents aged 50 or older met the criteria for substance abuse or dependence (Gfroerer, Penne, Pemberton, & Folsom, 2003). Of those identified, 85.8 percent abused alcohol and 10.2 percent abused illicit drugs, which also included using prescription drugs for nonmedical purposes. Illicit drug users were most likely to use marijuana (42 percent), followed by cocaine (36 percent). Among those that abused prescription drugs, the highest proportion (25 percent) used pain relievers, followed by stimulants (18 percent), and sedatives (17 percent).

As in previous large-scale surveys, the 2002 National Survey on Drug Use and Health (NS-DUH) (SAMHSA, 2003) showed that the rate of illicit drug use declined successively with age. Findings indicated that 3.4 percent, 1.9 percent, and 2.5 percent of persons age 50–54, 55–59, and 60–64, respectively, and 0.8 percent of those age 65 and older, reported using an illicit drug in the past month. NSDUH defined illicit drug use as use of marijuana/hashish, cocaine (including crack), inhalants, hallucinogens, heroin, or prescription-type drugs used for nonmedical purposes. Combined 2002 and 2003 NSDUH data (2005) showed overall that marijuana was the most common illicit drug used by persons aged 50 and over (1.1 percent), followed by prescription-type drugs used non-medically (0.7 percent) and cocaine (0.2 percent). In terms of gender, men aged 50+ were more likely to report using illicit drugs than women in the same age group (58 percent vs. 42 percent), and an even greater gender difference was seen for marijuana use (71 percent of the users were male vs. 29 percent female). For prescription drugs, older women were more likely to report using them for nonmedical purposes than men (59 percent vs. 41 percent). Simoni-Wastila & Strickler (2004) suggest that older women are at particular risk of prescription misuse and abuse because of greater likelihood for exposure—among persons aged 50 and older with at least one prescription, 59.5 percent are female (NSDUH, 2002). Women's biology and greater propensity to seek health care treatment also matter, but both older men and women may misuse medications

due to cognitive deficits, the complexity of drug treatment, sensory deficits that make it difficult to read labels and instructions or handle or cut medications, the cost of medications, and inability to get to the pharmacy on an as-needed basis.

Abrams and Alexopoulos (1988) state that provider-initiated misuse or the failure of the prescription writer to take into account the physiological (as well as psychosocial) aspects of aging, coupled with consumer limitations or the belief that OTC drugs are not harmful, may contribute to drug abuse or dependence. Allergy, cold, and sleep medications that are sold without prescriptions contain antihistamines and anticholinergic drugs that can enhance the anticholinergic effects of antipsychotic and tricyclic antidepressant medications. Some nonprescription preparations also contain amounts of alcohol and caffeine, which can lead to over-sedation and a reduction in the therapeutic effects of commonly prescribed antihypertensive, antiarrhythmic, and anxiolytic medications.

A survey of 83,321 adults aged 65–106 showed that an overwhelming majority (77 percent) have been prescribed alcohol-interactive medications and of these, 19 percent reported concomitant alcohol consumption (Pringle, Ahern, Heller, Gold, & Brown, 2005). These findings further illustrate the vulnerability of older adults to alcohol-related problems that should be addressed by health care workers. It is predicted that by 2020 the number of older adults needing treatment for substance abuse disorders will reach 4.4 million (Gfroerer et al., 2003).

Antecedents and Correlates

Models of chemical dependency are described in Chapter 2. Not all of these models have received specific attention in the literature on alcohol and drug abuse among older persons, although similar antecedent factors have been suggested. The determinants of alcohol and drug abuse among elders that have received the most attention are *sociocultural* or *psychosocial* models. Drug misuse, on the other hand, is often predicated by sensory or cognitive impairment or environmental factors.

Minnis (1988) has proposed a sociological perspective for studying the determinants of alcohol abuse that is based on social control theory. The major premise is that deviance (substance abuse) results when an individual's bond with society is weak or broken. Based on this theory, modified hypotheses to explain alcohol abuse among elders are:

1. The greater the attachment to conventional others, the less likely the elder is to engage in alcohol abuse.
2. The greater the commitment to conventional goals or aspirations, the less likely the elder is to engage in alcohol abuse.
3. The greater the involvement in conventional activities, the less likely the elder is to engage in alcohol abuse.
4. The greater the beliefs in the moral validity of conventional norms, the less likely the elder is to engage in alcohol abuse.

While it is difficult to test these hypotheses directly, demographic proxy variables have been studied. The Epidemiologic Catchment Area (ECA) project was a combination of five interrelated epidemiologic research studies conducted in New Haven, Baltimore, St. Louis, Los Angeles, and Durham and surrounding areas. An instrument to collect information covering three diagnostic systems, including *DSM-III-R*, was specially designed for these studies. The ECA project looked at socio-demographic factors such as age, sex, race, marital status, education, employment, and study site as correlates of alcohol abuse and dependence. Being male, separated or divorced, poor, and having less than a high school education were all found to be associated with a higher prevalence of alcoholism, regardless of age. Site, race, and employment status were not found, however, to have a relationship to the prevalence of alcoholism in the study sample (Robins & Regier, 1991).

In a 10-year study conducted at the Mayo Clinic, however, researchers found little difference in terms of the demographics of early- and late-onset alcoholics (Finlayson, Hurt, Davis, & Morse, 1988). The sample consisted of 216 primarily middle-class men and women age 65 and older who were patients at the clinic. In this study, early-onset alcoholism was present in 59 percent of the men and 51 percent of the women, and late-onset was seen in 39 percent of the men and 46 percent of the women (undetermined for the rest). Approximately two-thirds (67 percent) of the patients lived at home with a spouse and many continued to be active in their jobs.

Psychosocial models of addiction are less reductionistic and propose that an interrelated constellation of personal, social, environmental, behavioral, and health care system factors influence the onset, continuation, and termination of alcohol abuse (Gilliland & James, 1988). A life context or stress and coping model has been used to study alcohol use and abuse among elders and also to compare early- and late-onset alcoholism. Accordingly, loneliness, losses, physical and emotional separation from children, poor health, and lack of purposeful activity can precipitate alcohol abuse (Giordano & Beckham, 1985). As individuals age, they may become less attached to or isolated from sources of social support, such as his or her family, community, society, and peers, and instead must rely on their own coping skills to deal with feelings of grief, low self-esteem, and low status.

The evidence has been mixed in terms of empirical studies that examine the relationship between life events and alcohol use. Veenstra, Lemmens, Friesema, Garretsen, Knottnerus, et al. (2006) reviewed 12 cross-sectional studies that examined the relationship between life events and alcohol use in the general population. Positive associations were found in four of the studies, no association in three, and there were no clear findings in the remaining five studies. Health-related problems were found to be associated with lower alcohol use, but there were mixed findings in terms of divorce and financial problems (associated with both lower and higher use). These authors also reviewed four longitudinal studies. Health-related stress and financial problems were associated with decreased alcohol use, while retirement and life events related to family and friends were associated with increased use. In another longitudinal study of 1,291 community-dwelling individuals aged 55–65 at baseline, the authors found that health-related problems (e.g., medical conditions, physical symptoms, medication use, acute health events) were associated with decreased alcohol consumption over a 10-year interval (Moos, Brennan, Schutte & Moos, 2005).

Six of the 16 studies examined by Veenstra et al. (2006) only sampled persons aged 60 and older. When looking just at these studies, the results were still mixed. Role losses (retirement, hospitalization, divorce) were associated with excessive drinking (Jennison, 1992), and women losing a friend was associated with alcohol use (Glass, Prigerson, Kasl, & Mendes de Leon, 1995). But Glass et al. (1995) found that loss of a friend because of a move or having a close relative that was ill, along with nursing home admission, were all associated with decreased alcohol use. Health problems were found to either be directly or indirectly positively associated with cessation of drinking in a study that examined religiosity and abstinence (Krause, 1991). No association was found between the number of life events and alcohol use in studies by Graham and Schmidt (1999) and Welte and Mirand (1996), and small effects were seen in terms of number of stressful life events (financial problems, loneliness, poor heath, and limited access to world outside the home) by Welte (1998).

Effects

Physical Health

Numerous studies have indicated beneficial physiological effects of light to moderate alcohol consumption (e.g., 1 drink daily for women and 1–2 drinks daily for men) among older people. It is important to point out though that any amount of alcohol intake can have a negative impact given the effect of aging on the metabolism of alcohol (Kinney, 2006). Miller and Gold (1991) categorized the primary physical health effects from alcohol and drugs as metabolic, gastrointestinal, cardiovascular, and cerebrovascular. (See Chapter 4)

Looking specifically at the effect of aging and alcohol on the liver, alcohol competes with other drugs for metabolic enzymes in the liver and impairs drug clearance if acutely ingested (Scott & Mitchell, 1988). Conversely, if chronically ingested, alcohol induces additional metabolic enzymes, which can lead to increased drug clearance. These researchers conclude by saying that while routine liver tests change little with age, there may be less biochemical and metabolic reserve capacity in the older person's liver if stressed by diminished blood flow, infections, or exogenous drugs and toxins. There is also an increased incidence of malnutrition associated with abusive alcohol consumption (Smith, 1995).

In a meta-analysis of 156 studies on alcohol consumption and disease risk that included more than 116,000 subjects (selected from among 561 studies initially reviewed), Corrao, Bagnardi, Zambon, and LaVecchia (2004) found no clear pattern between alcohol consumption and gastroduodenal ulcer, but results indicated a strong trend in risk for cancers of the oral cavity, esophagus and larynx, chronic pancreatitis, and liver cirrhosis. Less strong associations were found between alcohol consumption and colon, rectum, breast, and liver cancers. While hypertension was strongly related to the amount of alcohol consumed, an association was seen between consumption and coronary heart disease. Low to moderate consumption appeared to have a protective effect, but at a certain threshold, there was a steep increase in risk (after 72 g/day and a significant increased risk at 89 g/day).

A number of studies have shown light to moderate alcohol consumption to be associated with reduced risk for ischemic stroke (Sacco, Elking, Boden-Albala, Lin, Kargman et al., 1999) cardiovascular disease (Thun, Peto, Lopez, 1997), and heart failure (Abramson, Williams, Krumholz, & Vaccarino, 2001). The J- or U-shaped association between alcohol consumption and a range of cardiovascular health outcomes, including stroke, has been replicated in more recent studies (Christie, Price, Edwards, Muldoon, Meltzer et al., 2008; Jennings, Muldoon, Ryan, Price, Green et al., 2005; Mukamal, Chung, Jenny, Kuller, Longstreth et al., 2005; O'Keefe, Bybee, & Lavie, 2007; Reynolds, Lewis, Nolen, Kinney, Sathya et al., 2003).

Despite some beneficial health outcomes of light to moderate alcohol consumption, it is important to take into account that the vast majority of older Americans take prescription medications. In one study of 92,652 elderly persons enrolled in Pennsylvania's Pharmaceutical Assistance Contract for the Elderly, 77 percent of the prescription drug users were exposed to alcohol-interactive drugs, ranging from 100 percent of those using central nervous system agents to 14 percent of those using gastrointestinal drugs (Pringle, Ahem, Heller, Gold, & Brown, 2005). As physical health worsened, however, concomitant use of alcohol and alcohol-interactive drugs decreased, but it is important to note that concomitant use increased as cognitive health worsened; thus, concomitant use may be related to memory.

Cognition

As with the literature on the physical effects of light to moderate alcohol consumption, several studies have purported positive or protective effects of alcohol use on cognition in later life. Older men (mean age = 74; range, 65–89) receiving primary care at a Veteran's Administration primary care clinic (N = 760) were sampled to test the hypothesis that light to moderate drinking conferred cognitive benefits (Reid, Van Ness, Hawkins, Towle, Concato, et al., 2006). Current and lifetime use of alcohol were determined and the men were administered various cognitive tests (Trailmaking, Symbol Digit, Controlled Oral Word Association [FAS], Hopkins Verbal Learning). Current and former drinkers were compared to abstainers. Current drinkers performed significantly

better on three of the four cognitive tests (all but the FAS). The number of years drinking seven or fewer drinks per week was independently associated with better cognitive performance.

Cognitive performance was studied in conjunction with the Framingham Heart Study, a large, prospective study of cardiovascular disease. As part of the study, men (n = 733) and women (n = 1,053) aged 55–88 were asked about their weekly intake of alcohol and were administered eight cognitive tests that measured verbal memory, learning, visual organization and memory, attention, abstract reasoning, and concept formation. After controlling for age, education, occupation, cardiovascular disease, and several other risk factors, results indicated that women who drank 2–4 drinks/day and men who drank 4–8 drinks/day showed superior performance when compared to abstainers in many cognitive domains (Elias, Elias, Agnostino, Silbershatz, & Wolf, 1999). In another longitudinal community study, individuals were assessed at two-year intervals over an average of seven years of follow-up (Ganguli, Vander Bilt, Saxton, Shen, & Dodge, 2005). Three group (no drinking, minimal drinking, and moderate drinking) trajectories were compared while controlling for age, sex, education, depression, smoking, and general mental status (Mini-Mental Examination [MMSE]). Minimal and moderate drinkers had significantly less decline on the MSSE and Trailmaking tests than abstainers, and minimal drinking was also associated with fewer declines on tests of naming and learning.

In terms of serious cognitive impairment or dementia, light to moderate alcohol use has been found to have a protective effect. Light to moderate alcohol drinkers have been found to have significantly lower rates of dementia than nondrinkers (Ganguli et al., 2005; Mukamal, Kuller, Fitzpatrick, Longstreth, Mittleman et al., 2003; Ruitenberg, van Swieten, Witteman, Mehta, van Duijn et al., 2002). In turn, heavy alcohol use has been found to increase risk of dementia (Luchsinger, Tan, Siddiqui, & Mayeux, 2004).

Alcohol-related dementia has been described in the literature as a global cognitive impairment that mimics Alzheimer's disease but does not progress after the cessation of drinking. DSM-IV (APA, 1994) states that "alcohol-induced persistent dementia" is manifested by progressive intellectual and cognitive decline in the absence of a profound amnestic disorder, but Gupta (2008) points out that the diagnosis is not often used. Studies of alcohol-related dementia have found that as age increases, there is a more severe decline in intellect among older alcoholics. Results have been supported by brain scans that reveal significant cerebral atrophy, notably frontal lobe changes, among alcoholics, especially older alcoholics (Hartford & Samorajski, 1984; Moselhy, Georgiou, & Kahn, 2001). Greater cognitive important due to neuronal damage may be related to the dementing process and it has been shown that repeated alcohol withdrawal (two or more detoxifications) among heavy users is associated with a greater degree of cognitive impairment (Duka, Townshend, Collier, & Stephens, 2003). Given the recent findings concerning binge drinking among the older population as noted above (Ginzer & Richardson, 2009), this is especially problematic. In contrast with Alzheimer's disease, however, alcohol-related dementia may be partially reversible, as evidenced by improved memory, visual-spatial functioning, problem solving, and attention in recovering alcoholics (Gazdzinski, Durazzo, & Meyerhoff, 2005). Such findings speak to the importance of treatment for alcohol abuse in the older population.

Depression and Suicide

Depression is often referred to as the most common psychiatric problem seen in the elderly population and is viewed as a response to loss (Butler, Lewis, & Sunderland, 1998). The normal aging process involves losses—loss of a spouse and other loved ones, loss of health, loss of job and income, loss of social roles, and loss of status. We grieve our losses and depression can be a part of the bereavement process.

Alcohol itself is a depressant, and alcohol abuse and depression have long been associated. Retrospective studies of mixed age individuals that committed suicide have estimated that 25–55 percent had substance dependence or

misuse (Murphy, 2000). Among 100 elderly (65+) suicide cases in a Scandinavian-born sample, a history of alcohol dependence or misuse was observed for 35 percent of the men and 18 percent of the women as compared to matched controls with rates of 2 percent for men and 1 percent for women (Waern, 2003). While some contend that virtually all alcoholics are depressed, it is difficult to compare the reported prevalence rates of depression in elderly versus younger alcoholics due to problems distinguishing between the depressive symptoms that are common in alcohol abusers and the symptoms of primary affective disorders. However, in looking at major depression in particular, Mayo Clinic researchers gave 8.3 percent of the alcoholics in their sample this diagnosis using *DSM-III-R* criteria (Finlayson et al., 1988). This is in contrast to a 3.7 percent rate determined in a study of a general elderly population in North Carolina and the 0.8 to 1.8 percent rate for the lifetime prevalence of major depressive episodes reported in another three site area (Robins, Helzer, Weissman, Orvaschel, Gruenberg, et al., 1984).

Alcohol abuse is considered a risk factor in suicide among the elderly population (Richman, 1992). Suicides in the older population represent a disproportionate amount of successful suicides when considered across the general population. The National Center for Injury Prevention and Control (2001) reported that the suicide rate steadily increases with age and peaks at age 85 and over, while the suicide rate for white males (who have higher rates at all ages than women and nonwhites) is 65 per 100,000. The rate of suicide for elderly alcohol abusers is suggested to be even higher than the rate in the general population (Atkinson, Turner, Kofoed, & Tolson, 1985; Hartford & Samorajski, 1984).

Assessment

Assessment Strategies and Problems

In clinical settings, older patients with AUD are often misdiagnosed, as health care workers may not suspect alcohol abuse among older patients. This is further compounded by patients' fears surrounding the disclosure of alcohol consumption behaviors. The symptoms of alcohol abuse present similarly to problems common in old age such as unsteady gait, falls, and forgetfulness. Evidence of provider misunderstanding of the problem of AUD in elders was seen in a study of alcohol use among nursing home residents. Klein and Jess (2002) surveyed 111 licensed intermediate care facilities regarding their alcohol use policies for residents. Just over half of the facilities conducted alcohol use histories on residents and almost three-quarters of the facilities interviewed permitted residents to consume alcohol, with some facilities (18 percent) sponsoring "cocktail hours" for residents (Klein & Jess, 2002). A study of 140 assisted living facility administrators in one state demonstrated that substance abuse counseling was associated with having a social worker on staff; however, only 17 of the 140 facilities employed a professional social worker on either a part-time or full-time basis (Vinton, 2004).

Ageist attitudes may hinder assessing alcohol abuse in the older population. Curtis, Geller, Stokes, Levine, & Moore (1989) suggest that health-care providers may hesitate to bring up alcohol use or do a less careful assessment of elders, and Blow (1998) states that some providers may believe older people would not benefit from interventions. A first step in overcoming these barriers to assessment appears to be to educate providers and to encourage them to ask older clients about alcohol use (Stewart & Oslin, 2001).

As noted in Chapter 5, there are numerous diagnostic instruments for the detection of alcoholism in clinical settings that relate to risk factors and biopsychosocial symptoms of alcoholism. The geriatric version of the MAST (MAST-G), a 24-item screening measure with a reported sensitivity of 93.9 percent and specificity of 78.1 percent, was designed specifically to identify alcoholism among older adults (Blow, Brower, Schulenberg, Demo-Dananberg, Young et al., 1992). Physicians can also use medical tests, such as lean body mass and amount of alcohol consumed, but these measures are confounded by age effects, making them less useful in assessing alcoholism

among the elderly. Bienenfeld (1987) concludes that simply becoming older may make a person begin to experience alcohol-induced problems without changing the amount of alcohol consumed.

O'Connell and colleagues (2004) conducted a systematic review of the literature to compare the sensitivity and specificity of various self-report alcohol screening instruments used in the elderly population including the CAGE, MAST, MAST-G, SMAST-G, ARPS, shARPS, and the Cyr-Wartman Questionnaire. Reviewing 18 studies, these authors found that the prevalence of AUD and clinical characteristics impact the utility of these screening instruments. The sensitivity and specificity of the most widely used instrument, the CAGE, proved to vary greatly between the studies. Interestingly, variations of the MAST, the MAST-G, and the SMAST-G, both designed for use in the geriatric population, proved to be insensitive, although the original version of the MAST demonstrated both sensitivity and specificity. An updated version of the AUDIT, the AUDIT-5, provided excellent sensitivity and specificity, surpassing that of both the original AUDIT and the CAGE. With only moderate specificity, the ARPS and shARPS provide excellent sensitivity, in contrast to the Cyr-Wartman, which is insensitive, but specific (O'Connell et al., 2004).

Letizia and Reibolz (2005) and others have noted particular difficulties in assessing elders for alcohol abuse using existing measures. Self-reports of alcohol consumption and dependence or drunkenness may be unreliable for several reasons. Denial, sense of stigma, social desirability effects, and memory loss can affect the accurate recollection or admission of alcohol problems among the elderly. And as cited earlier, physical and cognitive changes, whether due to aging itself or a disease process, confound consumption measures. The health problems and cognitive impairment related to alcohol abuse that have been used as markers have not been standardized for general elderly populations, and therefore are questionable when used to distinguish the elderly alcohol abuser.

Most health professionals would likely agree that the assessment of alcohol abuse needs to be comprehensive, interdisciplinary, and age and gender relevant. Along these lines, Graham (1986) suggests that five overlapping items should be included in screening for alcohol abuse among the elderly: 1) quantity and frequency of alcohol consumption; 2) alcohol-related social and legal problems (e.g., housing problems, falls or accidents, poor nutrition, inadequate self- and home care, lack of exercise, and social isolation); 3) alcohol-related health problems; 4) symptoms of drunkenness and dependence; and 5) self-recognition of alcohol-related problems. Beresford, Blow, Brower, Adams, and Hall (1988) add that a series of neuropsychological tests should also be conducted, including measures of concept formation and abstraction, short- and long-term memory, motor strength, speed, and dexterity, visual/motor coordination, attention, concentration and vigilance, novel problem solving, language functions, and perceptual integrity.

Outreach and Treatment

Community Education and Awareness

Educating the medical community is a crucial first step in preventing and ameliorating the effects of alcohol and drug abuse among elders. The American Medical Association (AMA, 1995) has proposed guidelines for physicians to address elderly alcoholism. More than 110,000 primary care physicians were sent a 17-page booklet entitled *Alcoholism in the Elderly: Diagnosis, Treatment, Prevention*. The Southern Medical Association (1998) has developed a *Medbytes* continuing medical education course entitled Alcohol Abuse in the Elderly. According to the authors of the course, "Physicians may be more tolerant of drinking problems as justifiable in response to the recognized stresses of aging" and therefore need information on how alcohol abuse can be treated in old age.

Several alcohol and aging educational programs have been evaluated and found to have positive impacts. In a series of workshops designed to

improve health care and social service practitioners' attitudes, knowledge, and competencies in the area of alcohol abuse among elders, the trainers used lectures, discussions, videotape analysis, and role-playing (McDonald, 1990; Peressini & McDonald, 1998). Those who attended the workshops and a comparison group who did not were asked to complete the Palmore Facts on Aging Quiz, the Cartwright Alcohol Attitudes Scale, an alcohol workshop quiz designed by the trainers, and a socio-demographic survey. The comparison group had a larger proportion of urban practitioners and nurses and hospital administrators/social service personnel than the workshop attendees, but there were no differences between the groups in terms of age, gender, organizational type, and schooling. Results indicated that the workshop did not change practitioners' attitudes toward aging or increased practitioners' knowledge of elders. In terms of alcohol attitudes, however, a significant difference was found between the workshop participants and the comparison group. The experimental group's scores improved significantly from pre- to post-test and were higher than the comparison group's scores. (Higher scores are associated with a wider range and strength of knowledge.) On the alcohol workshop quiz, which examined each area of training (attitudes, knowledge, assessment, intervention, and resources), the workshop participants' scores significantly improved with each administration and were higher than the comparison group's scores.

The Virginia Model Detection and Prevention Program for Geriatric Alcoholism also included an evaluation component. This program was designed to teach elders, practitioners, and family caregivers about aging and alcoholism and involved organizing communities to increase awareness (Coogle, Osgood, Pyles, & Wood, 1995). Individuals from the aging network of services and health, substance abuse, and mental health agencies served on a state-level steering committee that guided the project, and experts were hired to develop educational materials such as booklets, a brochure, and a video. A train-the-trainer approach was employed, which involved training volunteers who then offered workshops in their local communities.

The effectiveness of the Virginia program was evaluated through pre- and post-knowledge tests. The volunteer trainers were compared with individuals who were trained by the volunteer trainers. Of the 132 volunteer trainers, almost three-fourths were female, slightly less than one-fourth were minority-group members (primarily African American), and one-third were age 50 or over. Almost 75 percent were paid service providers, and almost all had some personal experience with an alcoholic. Among the volunteer trainers, 23 percent said they had experienced a drinking problem, and 16 percent reported being recovering alcoholics. There were 1,036 participants in the volunteer trainer workshops that completed pre- and post-tests. This group consisted primarily of women (78 percent) who were paid service providers (71 percent). More than one-third (38 percent) were minority-group members, and an identical proportion were age 50 or over. Fewer individuals reported a drinking problem in this group (13 percent), and fewer were recovering alcoholics (9 percent).

The volunteer trainers completed a 40-item instrument to assess their knowledge before and after their eight hours of training. *T*-tests revealed statistically significant increases from pre- to posttest, and 90 percent of the volunteer trainers scored 90 percent or better on the posttest. The trainees completed a similar 25-item instrument before and after training. Their scores also significantly increased. At posttest, 61 percent had scores of 90 percent or better.

Providing outreach in minority communities about alcohol and drug problems among elderly people is challenging. Kail and DeLaRosa (1998) have written about elderly Hispanic American substance abusers and suggested ways to identify, assess, and treat them. They believe that cultural values (see Chapter 11), such as sharply demarcated gender-role expectations (Delgado & Humm-Delgado, 1993) and the concept of *familismo* (Cervantes, 1993) may serve to hide alcohol abuse, particularly in the case of elderly women. Discussing alcohol problems with elderly family members may be viewed as

disrespectful, and discussing such problems with an alcohol counselor or support group members may be seen as disgracing one's image. Kail and DeLaRosa believe that Meals on Wheels programs and community recreational activities can be used to reach out to Hispanic American elders. These authors also suggest that social workers should apply their community organizing skills to informal social networks in Hispanic American communities, thereby heightening awareness of elders' alcohol problems.

The Florida BRITE (Brief Intervention and Treatment for Elders) Project began as an outreach pilot program (2004–2007) for persons age 55 and older in three counties and has since expanded. Its mission is to identify non-dependent substance use or prescription medication issues and to provide service strategies prior to the need for more extensive or specialized substance abuse treatment. The project attempts to reach underserved elders including isolated, withdrawn individuals, elders of color, and persons living in poverty. Provider agencies offer in-home screening and services for elders with problems related to alcohol, illicit substances, and prescription and OTC medications. BRITE now focuses on providing services within primary and emergency health care settings, public health clinics, retirement communities and senior housing, health fairs, and at sites coordinated by aging services. Clients may be offered screening, brief intervention, and brief treatment by these generalist providers, or they may be offered more intensive care by a substance abuse specialist provider agency.

Treatment

In a nationwide examination of alcoholism treatment programs serving 2,600 persons age 21 and over, Janik and Dunham (1983) found few age-related differences among alcoholics in treatment. These authors concluded that providing specialized alcoholism treatment programs for the elderly population was perhaps unnecessary. Beresford and colleagues (1988) disagree, and state that "...if we know little about screening elderly populations with respect to alcoholism, we know considerably less about specific treatment strategies appropriate to this age group" (p. 70). Fortunately, things have changed, and we can now point to several evidence-based alcohol treatment programs geared toward older persons.

In a review of the literature on late-life addiction, Stewart and Oslin (2001) noted that three findings have consistently been reported. First, when compared to younger people in treatment for alcohol addiction, older persons tend to have better adherence (Atkinson, Tolson, & Turner, 1993; Wiens, Menustik, Miller, & Schmitz, 1982–1983). Second, older persons have treatment outcomes that are at least as good if not better than those of younger persons (Janik & Dunham, 1983; Joseph, Atkinson, & Ganzini, 1995). Third, older persons tend to respond better to age-specific treatments (Kashner, Rodell, Ogden, Guggenheim, & Karson, 1992; Kofoed, Tolson, Atkinson, Toth, & Turner, 1987).

Project GOAL: Guiding Older Adult Lifestyles was the first large, randomized, double-blind, controlled clinical trial to test the efficacy of brief physician advice with respect to reducing alcohol use in elderly at-risk and problem drinkers (Fleming, Manwell, Barry, Adams, & Stauffacher, 1999). More than 6,000 patients were assessed with the Health Screening Survey, and at-risk and problem drinkers were randomly assigned to the control (n=71) and experimental treatment (n=84) groups. The physicians utilized a structured protocol and scripted workbook. Results indicated no significant differences at baseline between the control and intervention groups in terms of age, alcohol use, onset of alcohol use, smoking status, activity level, and use of mood-altering drugs. Following the intervention, the experimental group had significantly lower rates of seven-day alcohol use, incidence of binge drinking, and frequency of excessive drinking than the control group, and 35–40 percent had reduced consumption at the 12 month follow-up.

Numerous authors have written about the modifications needed to make traditional approaches to intervening in alcohol abuse age specific. Mellor and colleagues (1996) suggest that residential detoxification should be utilized routinely with elders because of the increased likelihood of serious complications during the process. Carstensen, Rychtarik, and Prue (1985) indicated some success with a behavioral inpatient program for older alcoholics that consisted of providing medical attention in addition to counseling and alcohol education. Participants were contacted two to four years after discharge, and results showed that beneficial effects were maintained for 50 percent of the sample; whereas, another 12 percent reported significant modification of their drinking.

Primary care-seeking adults aged 55 and over were recruited from VA clinic waiting rooms for an alcohol-reduction brief intervention (Copeland, Blow, & Barry, 2003). Hypotheses included that participants exposed to the intervention who were at-risk drinkers would have increased short-term health care use and decreased long-term health care use and that participants' stage of change would be a moderating variable. At-risk drinkers were defined using the NIAAA recommendations of no more than one drink per day for adults age 65 and older (two drinks per day for men younger than 65) and a maximum of two drinks on rare occasions. After screening, 205 were selected for the sample (at-risk) and randomly assigned to treatment (n=100) and control (n=105) groups. The average age was 65.9 (sd=6.4). Three-quarters were white, 52.8 percent were married, 35.3 percent lived alone, and roughly one-third each had less than a high school education, high school diploma, or some college or more.

The vast majority (84.2 percent) had done binge drinking in the past three months and the mean number of drinks per week was 21.25 (sd=21.51). In terms of contemplating a change in drinking, 24.6 percent were in the pre-contemplation stage, 29.5 percent in the contemplation stage, and 45.9 percent were in the preparation stage. No differences were seen in S-MAST-G and CAGE scores for the control and treatment groups. The brief intervention (one session) used was low cost, clinic-based, and consisted of behavioral self-control training strategies to reduce drinking. Participants in the treatment group used more outpatient health services in the short term than controls, but not long-term care. Stage of change was not found to moderate treatment effectiveness but was associated with differential use of medical care. Those in the preparation stage tended to use more non-diagnostic clinic stops but fewer stops after the treatment and those in the pre-contemplation and contemplation stages used fewer non-diagnostic stops after treatment.

Kaiser Permanente in northern California, a large, nonprofit health maintenance organization, operates an outpatient chemical dependency program in Sacramento that has been studied extensively. Between 1994 and 1996, 1,204 individuals utilized the program; 736 were age 18–39 (64 percent male), 379 age 49–54 (70 percent male), and 89 were age 55+ (76 percent male). Three-fourths of the young and middle-aged groups were Caucasian compared to 93 percent of the oldest group. The majority of all groups had completed high school and slightly more than half of the middle-aged and older groups were married. Compared to 28 percent of the younger group's dependence diagnosis of alcohol only, 57.5 percent of the middle-aged and 75.3 percent of the oldest group had this diagnosis. The patients were randomly assigned when possible (some were unable or unwilling to be assigned) to either a day hospital or a traditional outpatient program. Both programs were based on a total abstinence model with individual, family, and group counseling. Sessions were educational and supportive, patients were expected to attend 12-step meetings off site, and random breath analysis and urine screens were done (Weisner, Mertens, Parthasarathy, Moore, Hunkeler et al., 2000).

Several outcome studies have been conducted using the Kaiser Permanente data that contrast older versus younger and middle-aged patient group outcomes. The first study using the data (Satre, Mertens, Areán, & Weisner, 2003) asked if older patients were different from others at baseline and at 6-month follow-up. Results showed that at baseline the older group (55+) had lower rates of drug dependence and psychiatric symptoms but higher levels of alcohol dependence than younger groups. The two older groups (middle-aged and

older) were more likely to have a goal of abstinence than the youngest group and stayed in treatment longer, thus adding evidence to earlier studies that pointed to greater adherence with age. At six months post-treatment, older adults were not significantly different from young or middle-aged adults in terms of abstinence (55 percent vs. 50 percent and 59 percent, respectively). In the regression analysis that examined predictors of abstinence following treatment, age group was not a significant independent predictor. Five-year alcohol and drug treatment outcomes for the Kaiser-Permanente sample were compared across age groups (Satre, Mertens, Areán, & Weisner, 2004). In this study, alcohol and drug use and scores on the Addiction Severity Index, Alcoholics Anonymous Affiliation Scale, and social resource and self-reported health data were collected. The older group had longer retention in treatment, and they were less likely to be drug-dependent at baseline. After five years, older adults had fewer family and friends that encouraged substance use than younger adults and significantly more reported abstinence during the previous 30 days (52 percent vs. 40 percent of younger adults). Older women had even higher rates of abstinence than older men. Age-related findings disappeared, however, when looking at those who were dependent on alcohol alone, rather than drugs. Age group was not significant in the regression analysis, but variables associated with greater age that independently predicted 30-day abstinence included not having family and friends that encouraged substance use, and being female. Gender differences were again examined seven years following treatment (Satre, Blow, Chi, & Weisner, 2007). In this study, 25 older women and 59 older men were compared. The difference in prior 30-day abstinence was just barely significant (76 percent of women vs. 54.2 percent of men reported abstinence; p=.05). Treatment stay predicted abstinence in the regression model, though, and the authors concluded that length of treatment was more important than gender in predicting outcome.

The GET SMART (Geriatric Evaluation Team: Substance Misuse/Abuse Recognition and Treatment)

Program was a replication of the Gerontology Alcohol Project conducted in the late 1970s into the early 1980s (Dupree, Broskowski, & Schonfeld, 1984). The earlier project targeted late life onset alcohol abusers and used a group format. The intervention was a manualized cognitive-behavioral, self-management approach. Over a 12-month period, 75 percent of the graduates maintained their drinking goals and there was a significant increase in the size of social support networks for group members. The GET SMART Program was instituted first in a Los Angeles Veterans Administration Hospital and then parts of the curriculum were utilized in programs in Florida and other areas (Schonfeld, Dupree, Dickson-Euhrmann, Royer, McDermott et al., 2000). The 16 session three-stage cognitive-behavioral treatment/self-management approach included a behavioral analysis (antecedents and consequences of substance use), teaching clients how to identify the chain and high risk situations, and then teaching specific skills to deal with such situations.

Characteristics for 110 patients who participated in the GET SMART Program at the VA included: mean age 65 (range 53–82; sd=5.5); 98 percent male; 50.8 percent Caucasian, 41.7 percent African American, 5.8 percent, Latino, 1.6 percent Asian; 21.1 percent married, 60.6 percent divorced/separated, 10.5 percent widowed, 4.4 percent never married; mean years of education 12.94 (sd=2.7); 34.2 percent homeless; 19.8 percent living in a domiciliary. Slightly more than half the sample (51.8 percent) used alcohol only, but 26.4 percent used alcohol and street drugs and another 5.5 percent used alcohol and misused prescription medications (a total of 38.2 percent were using illicit drugs, mostly with alcohol, prior to admission). Outcomes at six-month follow-up compared those that completed the program (n=49, 44.5 percent) with those that did not (n=61, 55.5 percent). Participants (completers) were found to be significantly more likely to remain abstinent (55 percent vs. 16 percent) or be abstinent at follow-up but with at least one slip back to substance use (26.5 percent vs. 1.6 percent) than non-completers. Whereas 31.1 percent of the non-completers returned to steady alcohol use at six-month follow-up, only 2 percent of the completers did so. It should be noted that a substantial proportion of those that did not complete (41 percent) could not be located at follow-up.

In terms of the Florida BRITE Project, initial results from 3,497 screenings in four counties using the S-MAST-G (nearly 18,000 screenings were conducted through 2009 at 27 sites in 17 counties) show that prescription medication misuse was the most prevalent substance abuse issue, followed by alcohol abuse (Schonfeld, King-Kallimanis, Duchene, Etheridge, Herrera, et al., 2010). Among those with alcohol and prescription medication problems, depression (as measured by the Short Geriatric Depression Scale) was prevalent. For those who completed the brief cognitive-behavioral/self-management intervention, improvement was seen on the depression measure, and a decrease was seen in alcohol abuse and medication misuse.

A summary of best practices in working with older alcohol abusers has been used for treatment recommendations as follows (Dupree & Schonfeld, 1998; SAMHSA, 1998; Schonfeld & Dupree, 1997):

1. Age-specific, group treatment-supportive, not confrontive
2. Attend to negative emotions: depression, loneliness, overcoming losses
3. Teach skills to rebuild social support network
4. Employ staff experienced in working with elders
5. Link with aging, medical, and institutional settings
6. Slower pace and age-appropriate content
7. Create a "culture of respect" for older clients
8. Broad, holistic approach to treatment recognizing age-specific psychology, social and health aspects
9. Adapt treatment to address gender issues

BOX 14.1 *Case Examples*

Ms. A and her sister were born in Mexico and immigrated to the United States as children. Now in her early sixties, Ms. A was married briefly but has lived alone for many years. She lives near her sister and brother-in-law in a rural area. Ms. A has always been a heavy drinker but was able to hold a job until she began having chronic health problems 10 years ago. At that point she became somewhat isolated and worked sporadically in the kitchen of her sister and brother-in-law's restaurant. One day, while intoxicated, she stumbled into a pot of boiling water at the restaurant and suffered severe burns on her torso and legs. She refused medical help and drank heavily over the next few days. Her legs became seriously infected. Her relatives hesitated to call an ambulance but managed to persuade Ms. A to agree to be transported to the hospital. After being seen in the emergency room, Ms. A did not want to be admitted to the hospital. Her sister told the treating physician that the reason Ms. A fell at the restaurant and was refusing to stay at the hospital was because Ms. A was an alcoholic. The physician made a referral to the hospital's social services department.

Mr. B is an African American man in his seventies. He lives with his daughter and her husband and has a son living nearby. Mr. B has hypertension and diabetes. While he understands that his conditions require a special diet and insulin, Mr. B sometimes eats the foods he has always eaten (which are not on his diet) and drinks heavily when he is able to get to the store to buy liquor. His daughter has arranged for diabetic Meals on Wheels to be delivered to Mr. B while she and her husband are at work. When Mr. B visits his son, however, his son cooks anything Mr. B wants for dinner and often drinks with him. The family argues over who is to blame for Mr. B's health problems. Mr. B feels he is a burden to his daughter and wants to live with his son, but his daughter and son-in-law are concerned that the son will not purchase the medications Mr. B needs and will encourage him to abuse alcohol.

Mr. B has been complaining to the Meals on Wheels volunteer, who has discussed the situation with a case manager at the aging services agency.

Ms. C is a White woman in her seventies. She worked behind the bar at a local tavern for most of her adult life. A widow, she has a son who lives at a distance, and a daughter who lives nearby but with whom she has little contact. Ms. C began drinking heavily after retiring and states it is the only way to get rid of the ringing in her ears due to tinnitus. She was seen by a doctor who prescribed sedatives. She lives in a small, dark apartment and says sleeping and drinking are the only ways she finds peace. She states she often feels like dying. She came to the attention of adult protective services when she was found partially undressed, incoherent, and banging on her neighbor's door. After a brief stay in an inpatient psychiatric hospital, Ms. C returned home and was visited by a social worker. On one occasion, the social worker found Ms. C semiconscious after she had taken more than 50 sleeping pills. Her daughter, while angry with her mother, assisted with locating a specialist who was able to reduce the effects of the tinnitus. Ms. C began attending Alcoholics Anonymous (AA) meetings at the recommendation of her social worker and stated she felt comfortable at the meetings, because as a former bartender she was concerned for people who drank too much.

Mr. D is a White 80 year old man who lives in a retirement community of single-family homes with his wife. She is in excellent health. She assists Mr. D with his medications for high blood pressure, arthritis, and chronic obstructive pulmonary disease. For many years, she chided her husband about his eating, smoking, and drinking habits but now avoids speaking to him about these subjects. Mr. D comes from a large family and neighborhood where drinking is a cultural tradition. He regularly went for a drink after work and drank after returning home. When he began to take medication for hypertension, however, he found he had less tolerance for alcohol. He quit smoking in his sixties after being hospitalized for breathing difficulties but continued to drink beer and wine but not hard liquor. Mr. D fell onto the pavement as he was returning home from the retirement village's recreation center where he regularly drank a few beers before dinner with his friends. He needed 20 stitches to close a wound on his arm and received a concussion. Mrs. D has threatened to leave Mr. D if he takes another drink. To appease his wife, Mr. D asked his doctor to refer him to a counselor.

Summary

In the future, those who work in the health and aging fields are likely to see an increasing number of both male and female elderly alcoholics and drug abusers. Ideally, professionals will have at their disposal a growing body of information on the problem and which outreach and treatment approaches seem to work best for various groups of elders. The research and practice literature, along with practitioners' own experiences, will serve to inform their work in this area. One recent development in terms of disseminating such knowledge is the Gerontological Society of America's Elderly Alcohol/Drug Interest Group homepage on the Internet (see Websites in the Resources section at the end of the book.).

CHAPTER 15

Gender, Substance Use, and Substance Use Disorders

An-Pyng Sun
University of Nevada Las Vegas

Gender has a powerful influence on an individual's life both in normal development and the domains of dysfunction, diseases, and disabilities. The relationship between gender and substance abuse is complex. Biological predispositions, tradition, and culturally prescribed norms provide much of the foundation for these relationships. Social and economic realities and the constantly changing environment add further complexity. This chapter aims to facilitate gender-competent practice by presenting substance-abuse prevalence rates, identifying gender-relevant consequences and etiological or risk factors of substance abuse, and highlighting gender-based issues with respect to substance abuse treatment.

Prevalence of Substance Use and Substance Use Disorders among Men and Women

Although men continue to outnumber women in rates of substance use and substance use disorders, these gender differences have narrowed in the past several decades. In the 1980s, the alcohol abuse and dependence rate for men was five times the rate for women; since 2002, it has narrowed to two times the difference (Greenfield,

Pettinati, O'Malley, Randall, & Randall, 2010). The Substance Abuse and Mental Health Services Administration's (SAMHSA, 2010) National Survey on Drug Use and Health (NSDUH) also shows that for each year from 2002 to 2009, the male to female ratio for substance use disorders (abuse or dependence on alcohol or illicit drugs) was about 2:1. Rates are converging largely due to women's increased substance use and substance use disorder rates rather than any substantial decline in men's rates. Studies show that men from different birth cohorts in the United States do not vary much in their lifetime drinking rates, whereas women who were born between 1954 and 1963 have a significantly higher lifetime drinking rate than women born between 1944 and 1953. The female drinkers from the latter birth cohort were also more likely to develop alcohol dependence than female drinkers from the earlier birth cohort (Grucza, Bucholz, Rice, & Bierut, 2008). Gender convergence trends have also been noted internationally (Greenfield et al., 2010; Österling & Berglund, 1994).

Data from the 2009 NSDUH show that among individuals aged 12 or older, 58 percent of men were current drinkers versus 47 percent of women; 11 percent of men and 7 percent of women were current illicit drug users; and 34 percent of men and 22 percent of women reported current tobacco use (SAMHSA, 2010). Nearly 12 percent of males and just over 6 percent of females had a substance use disorder (abuse or dependence). Men clearly exceeded women in substance use and substance use disorder (SUD) rates for all age groups except the group aged 12–17, in which the SUD rates were similar for girls and boys (7.4 percent and 6.7 percent, respectively).

Given that twice as many men as women have substance use disorders and that women tend to encounter more barriers in entering alcohol and other drug (AOD) treatment, it is not surprising that men account for a much higher proportion of admissions to treatment for alcohol problems and most drug problems (SAMHSA, n.d.a). Men far outnumber women in admissions for alcohol problems only, alcohol with secondary drug problems, and marijuana, followed by heroin, cocaine (routes other than smoked), and PCP. Men are also more likely than women to be admitted for primary drug problems in the following categories: cocaine (smoked), other opiates (e.g., nonprescription use of methadone, codeine, morphine, oxycodone, opium, and other drugs with morphine-like effects), amphetamines, and other stimulants, though the gender gaps for these categories are not as wide as those for the first-mentioned categories. Women, on the other hand, outnumbered men in admissions related to tranquilizers by 0.6 percent, and they outnumbered men by 17 percent in admissions related to sedatives. The total numbers of admissions for problems related to tranquilizers and sedatives, however, are much lower than those for problems related to alcohol, marijuana, heroin, cocaine, and other opiates. Geography also affects gender ratios with respect to primary substance of abuse at admission. For example, in the past few years in the category of amphetamines, men outnumbered women slightly nationwide, but women outnumbered or were equivalent to men in the states of Florida, Texas, Nevada, Arizona, and New Mexico. In general, in 2008, the top three primary substances of abuse at admission are alcohol, marijuana, and

opiates for men and alcohol, opiates, and cocaine for women (SAMHSA, n.d.a).

Consequences of Substance Use and Substance Use Disorders among Men and Women

Substance abuse and dependence clearly create negative health and social consequences (World Health Organization, 2007). Researchers estimate that drug abuse and dependence may shorten an individual's life expectancy by about 22.5 years and that excessive drinking may reduce a person's life by about 30 years. Men and women who drink alcohol or use drugs experience similar consequences in certain domains but different consequences in other domains because different biological, psychological, social, and cultural factors impinge on the two sexes. Both substance-abusing men and women are subject to a high likelihood of negative consequences. The research also suggests the following differences:

- Substance-abusing men are more likely to report, more obvious/externally directed, and antisocial consequences than their women counterparts;
- Substance-abusing women often experience more internalized distress and long-term physical and health problems than their male counterparts;
- Substance-abusing women may progress from alcohol and other drug initiation to abuse or dependence more rapidly than substance-abusing men;
- Substance-abusing women's lack of resources, having a history of childhood abuse, and gender role expectations may put them at a higher risk for certain negative consequences than substance-abusing men;
- Substance-abusing women of child-bearing age are at risk for miscarriage or delivering a child affected by in utero exposure to

alcohol or drugs, whereas it is uncertain whether men's substance abuse affects the fetus;

• Both substance-abusing men and women may perpetrate violence toward intimate partners/significant others, but substance-abusing women may be at higher risk to be victimized.

Some of these consequences could also be the causes of substance abuse or the relationships may be reciprocal. For example, alcohol abuse may result in reduced inhibitions that precede domestic violence, while being a domestic violence victim may prompt alcohol use to dull emotions and pain. More studies are needed to confirm and clarify these relationships in order to aid practitioners in incorporating the information into substance-abuse prevention, education, screening, assessment, and treatment.

Personal, and Social Consequences

Men overall report more negative consequences from alcohol abuse than women do; this may be because men usually drink a greater amount and more frequently than women. However, after controlling for the level of drinking, men show an equal or a higher level of alcohol-related problems than women. For example, some studies find that men are either equally or more likely to report acute negative consequences (e.g., Kuendig et al., 2008; Plant, Miller, Thornton, Plant & Bloomfield, 2000). Kuendig and colleagues measured six consequences by adopting questions from the Alcohol Use Disorders Identification Test (AUDIT; see Chapter 5 for a description of this instrument). Men and women clearly and consistently differed on "blackouts" and "role failures," with men more likely to experience both. The two sexes did not differ on "injury," "loss of control over drinking," "guilt," and "pressure to cut down drinking." Graham et al. (2011) found somewhat different results. Men in their study were more than twice as likely as women to report blackouts (being "unable to remember [the]

night before)," to fail "to do what was expected" of them, and to have experienced harm to family relationships. Men were nearly three times more likely to have injured themselves or someone else, and to have experienced harm to their marriage or work, nearly four times more likely to engage in a "fight or physical fight," and more than four times more likely to drink in the morning to "get over bad effects." Although women's substance-abusing behaviors are more likely to be subjected to harsh sanctions from society than men's are, women are less likely to report alcohol-related social consequences than men (even after controlling for drinking level) (Bongers, van de Goor, van Oers, & Garretsen, 1998). Various reasons may explain this. Women may be more cautious in monitoring and controlling their behavior when drinking than men because of social norms, ascribed gender roles, and the stigma attached to drinking (Caudill et al., cited in Bongers et al.). It is also possible that women underreport their alcohol-related social consequences because of the stigma attached to their behavior (Bongers et al.).

Binge Drinking and Drunk Driving

Alcohol-impaired driving fatalities have decreased from close to half of all driving fatalities in 1982 to about one third in 2009 (U.S. Department of Transportation [DOT], n.d.a, n.d.b). Men are more likely to be the drivers in alcohol-related fatalities. In 2008, among male drivers in fatal crashes, 25 percent had a blood alcohol concentration of 0.08 percent (0.08 grams per deciliter) or above; among female drivers in fatal crashes, the figure was 13 percent (U.S. DOT, 2010). Men are more likely to engage in binge drinking than women, and male binge drinkers are also more likely to drive after binge drinking than female binge drinkers. For example, Naimi, Nelson, and Brewer (2009) analyzed data from 14,085 binge drinkers in the United States. Of all recent driving-after-binge-drinking episodes, 83 percent of the drivers were men. Thirteen percent of the men and 8 percent of the women reported driving either within two hours of or during their latest binge drinking incident. SAMHSA (2010) also found that about 16 percent of men and 9 percent of women drove under the influence (DUI) of alcohol during the past year.

Although men continue to have a far higher rate of DUI episodes than women, the gender gap in official DUI arrest rates narrowed in the past two decades. Nearly 11 percent of DUI arrests in 1982 and more than 18 percent in 2004 were of women, while men's rates declined and then stabilized. Schwartz and Rookey (2008) find evidence that the converging gender gap in DUI arrest rates may have more to do with changing laws and legal ramifications than the possibility that liberalized gender roles are prompting women to drink more heavily. Since the 1990s, many states lowered the criterion for DUI arrests from a blood alcohol level of 0.10 percent to 0.08 percent. They suggest that this may have resulted in more arrests of women, because women tend to drive under the influence of a lower level of alcohol than men do. According to Schwartz and Rookey:

> The organization of gender may not have changed all that much over time. . . . it is women who are still the primary caretakers of children and nurturing remains key to fulfilling female role obligations; standards of beauty and women's virtue have not changed all that much; and behavioral expectations for women, compared with men, remain more restrictive . . . It may also be . . . that women's lives have changed a great deal, but that these changes do not manifest themselves in drunk-driving behavior . . . Because drunk driving has the potential to affect the lives of others profoundly, it may not be as subjectively acceptable to women, even given changes in women's opportunities to commit this crime. (p. 664).

Physical Health Problems

Compared to men, women may progress faster from their initial substance use to the development of substance use disorders. Many studies have shown that, with an equivalent amount of alcohol consumption, women are more likely than men to experience the adverse effects of alcohol, and given a "drinking career" of equal length, women tend to develop alcoholism problems faster than men. This phenomenon in women has been labeled the "telescoping effect" (Piazza, Vrbka, & Yeager, 1989). Several factors may result in the telescoping effect. When an equivalent amount of alcohol is consumed, women tend to experience a higher blood alcohol concentration (BAC) than men do (Ely, Hardy, Longford, & Wadsworth, 1999). Women's higher BAC may be related to their smaller body size and proportionately less body water and more body fat than men, as alcohol is diffused in body water (Mumenthaler, Taylor, O'Hara, & Yesavage, 1999). Some research also suggests that women's lower level of the enzyme gastric alcohol dehydrogenase in the gastrointestinal system may also contribute to a higher BAC, although this idea awaits further proof (Graham, Wilsnack, Dawson, & Vogeltanz, 1998; Walter et al., 2003).

Consistent with the concept of the telescoping effect, extensive studies show that both sexes suffer alcohol-induced liver, heart, and brain problems despite the fact that women consume less alcohol than men. The female liver is more prone to the toxic effect of alcohol than the male liver, and women develop liver injuries and diseases more rapidly than do men. A large population-based study (Becker et al., 1996) indicated that compared to men consuming 1 to 6 drinks weekly, men consuming 14 to 27 drinks weekly had a higher risk of developing alcoholic cirrhosis/liver diseases. For women, an intake of 7 to 13 drinks weekly would increase such a risk. Women additionally may suffer obesity, osteoporosis, breast cancer, and reproductive system dysfunction, and pregnant women may give birth to infants with fetal alcohol syndrome or fetal alcohol spectrum disorders. Female heavy drinkers have a significantly higher mortality rate than male heavy drinkers (see reviews by Kay, Taylor, Barthwell, Wichelecki, & Leopold, 2010; Nolen-Hoeksema, 2004; Sun, 2009). Some drugs, such as cocaine and opioids, also show evidence of telescoping effects in women, although more studies are needed. Women may progress from cocaine initiation to cocaine abuse or opioid initiation to opioid addiction very quickly and experience more health-related problems than men do (Kay et al. 2010).

Fetal Alcohol Syndrome/Fetal Alcohol Spectrum Disorder

Drinking during pregnancy increases a woman's risks of prenatal death of the fetus or delivering a baby with fetal alcohol syndrome (FAS) or fetal alcohol spectrum disorder (FASD) (Gemma, Vichi, & Testai, 2007; Mattson, Crocker, & Nguyen, 2011). An FAS diagnosis requires all of the following three criteria: (a) all of the three facial abnormalities that involve the upper lip and eyelids ("smooth philtrum," "thin vermillion border," and "small palpebral fissures"), (b) growth deficits, and (c) central nervous system/neurodevelopmental abnormality (Centers for Disease Control and Prevention [CDC], 2004, p. viii; Sokol, Delaney-Black, & Nordstrom, 2003). The diagnosis for individuals who do not meet the criteria of the classic FAS may be considered under the term FASD (Sokol et al.). FAS is a medical diagnostic term, while FASD is an umbrella term, not a medical diagnosis (CDC). FASD encompasses FAS, partial FAS, alcohol-related neurodevelopmental disorder (ARND), and individuals who are affected by alcohol-exposure prenatally but without any diagnosis (Mattson et al. 2011). The prevalence of FAS in the United States is estimated to be 0.5—2.0 per 1,000 live births, and the prevalence of FAS or other FASD is about 10 per 1,000 live births (National Association of State Alcohol and Drug Abuse Directors, 2005). Box 15.1 describes tools available for screening women who plan to become pregnant or are pregnant for risk drinking.

Although changes in somatic growth and minor facial malformations may be the most common characteristics of a prenatally alcohol-exposed child, "the effects of alcohol on brain development are most significant in that they lead to substantial problems with neurobehavioral development" (Jones, 2011, p. 3). Prenatal AOD exposure may cause short- and long-term damage to an infant with respect to cognitive, physical, and behavioral development (Little & Yonkers 2001; Mattson et al., 2011; Streissguth, 1997). For prenatally exposed preschool children, the negative effects may include hyperactivity and inattention problems if moderate maternal drinking during pregnancy is involved. For prenatally exposed school-aged children, the negative effects may include memory deficit, learning problems, impulsivity problems, and psychiatric conditions such as mood disorders if moderate maternal drinking during pregnancy is involved (see the review by Sokol et al., 2003). The same review also showed that maternal binge drinking during pregnancy may result in an even more adverse effects on the fetus, causing future developmental delays. These prenatally exposed children may also show a lack of persistence in pursuing goals during their preadolescent period as well as manifest multiple neurobehavioral problems during their adolescent years. The negative effects of prenatal exposure to maternal drinking may be carried into adulthood. The problems may be related to executive-functioning insufficiency and may include difficulties with problem solving and daily life-functioning tasks as well as antisocial behavior and increased substance abuse.

No threshold has been identified indicating the level of drinking during pregnancy that will cause FAS or FASD. Generally speaking, binge and heavier drinking seem more risky than non-binge and light/moderate drinking. The professional community recommends abstinence for women who are pregnant or preconceptional, given the lack of a clear threshold for risky drinking during pregnancy (Sokol et al., 2003). Not all alcohol-exposed infants, however, will show medical complications or developmental problems. Some research shows that less than 10 percent of women who drink heavily during pregnancy give birth to babies with FAS (Gemma et al., 2007). Various factors—the type and combination of drugs/alcohol used, the amount and frequency of use, during which trimester the use occurs, the mother's reactions to

BOX 15.1 *Screening Pregnant Women for Alcohol Problems*

The *telescoping effect*, in which women tend to develop alcohol and other drug problems more quickly than men, makes it critical that women's chemical abuse problems be recognized early (Piazza, Vrbka, & Yeager, 1989). Duckert (1987) recommends routine screening for substance abuse during a woman's regular gynecological and prenatal care, and Turnbull (1989) suggests further training of medical, mental health, and social service professionals so they can recognize the signs of substance use disorders in women.

Screening Instruments

Most of the commonly used screening instruments for alcohol use disorders were developed using primarily male samples, but some screening instruments that are more sensitive to detecting alcohol problems in women have been developed. For example, the TWEAK test was developed from items on the MAST and CAGE tests and from the T-ACE (another gender-sensitive instrument) in order to better screen for risk drinking during pregnancy (NIAAA, 1993; Russell, 1994). It takes less than one minute to administer the TWEAK in an obstetrical/gynecological medical setting (Chang, 2001). To avoid causing a confrontation and triggering a denial, the TWEAK addresses tolerance to the effects of alcohol, instead of directly asking women about how much alcohol they have consumed (see the test items below).

Russell (1994) found that making these adaptations helped the TWEAK outperform the widely used MAST and CAGE with a group of pregnant African American women in the Detroit area. Simple wording changes seemed to make a substantial difference in detecting alcohol problems in this group of women (Chan et al., 1993). Testing has involved the addition of items (Dawson et al., 2001) and use with women who have different socioeconomic characteristics (Chang et al., 1999). Bradley and colleagues (1998) found the CAGE, AUDIT, and TWEAK more

sensitive with black than with white women and that the TWEAK may be a better choice than the CAGE or AUDIT with white women. These authors note the need for lower cutoff scores on the CAGE and AUDIT for women compared to men and suggest that interviewer rather than self-administered instruments may be more useful. Schafer and Cherpitel (1998) also found gender and ethnic biases on some of the items that comprise the more commonly used alcohol screening instruments (such as the CAGE, AUDIT, BMAST, and TWEAK; see Chapter 5 of this text). For example, men were more likely to endorse items on the scales regardless of diagnosis. Instruments that do a better job of screening women for drug problems in addition to alcohol problems are also needed.

The TWEAK Test

T	**Tolerance:** How many drinks can you hold?
W	Have close friends or relatives **Worried** or complained about your drinking in the last year?
E	**Eye opener:** Do you sometimes take a drink in the morning when you get up?
A	**Amnesia:** Has a friend or family member ever told you about things you said or did while you were drinking that you could not remember?
K (C)	Do you sometimes feel the need to **Cut down** on your drinking?

A 7-point scale is used to score the test. The Tolerance question scores 2 points if a women reports she can hold more than five drinks without falling asleep or passing out. A positive response to the Worry question scores 2 points, and positive responses to the last three questions score 1 point each. A total score of 2 or more points indicates the woman is likely to be a risk drinker.

Source: The TWEAK test is reprinted by permission of Marcia Russell, Ph.D., Prevention Research Center, Pacific Institute on Research & Evaluation.

the use, and the fetus's genetic vulnerabilities to alcohol and other drugs—may determine whether a baby will show severe, mild, or no symptoms (Gemma et al., 2007; Little & Gilstrap, 1998; Streissguth, 1997). Researchers have also proposed some additional maternal risk factors that may increase FASD liability: maternal age older than 30 years, genetic background, ethnic group, poor socioeconomic status, prior child with FASD, and maternal undernutrition (see Jones's review, 2011, pp. 5–6).

Sexually Transmitted Diseases and HIV/AIDS

Drug-abusing men and women are both at high risk for contracting HIV/AIDS. Injecting drugs with infected equipment makes both men and women highly vulnerable. Engaging in unsafe sex with men who are injection drug users IDUs heightens women's risk, while fewer men become infected from a female partner. Socially impoverished and marginalized women, such as homeless women and street prostitutes are at much higher risk for contracting HIV/AIDS and other sexually transmitted diseases (STD) than other women due to their lack of resources, sex trading, and high degree of exposure to violence from male partners (Elifson, Sterk, & Theall, 2007; Wenzel, Tucker, Elliott, & Hambarsoomians, 2007).

Some studies find that men have a higher rate of IDU than women (e.g., CDC, 2010; Wright et al., 2007); some find that women are more likely than men to be IDUs (Shillington & Clapp, 2003); other studies report no significant difference between the two sexes (Pugatch et al., 2000). In reconciling the inconsistency, Sun (2009) explained that in the general population, adolescent or adult women may have equivalent or lower rates of IDU than adolescent or adult men (e.g., those in the CDC's year 2009 sample and those in Wright et al.'s sample), while among clinical (treatment) samples or samples of people with severe drug problems, adolescent or adult women may be more likely to be IDUs than their male counterparts (e.g., those in the treatment programs in Shillington and Clapp's study).

Regardless of whether men or women are more likely to be IDUs, living with an IDU family member, particularly sex partners, increases the odds of sharing injecting equipment (Fitzgerald, Lundgren, & Chassler, 2007). Women are more likely to share or borrow injecting equipment because they are more likely than men to have an IDU sexual partner (Booth, Lehman, Brewster, Sinitsyna, & Dvoryak, 2007; Evans et al., 2003). Studies confirm that having a primary sex partner who is an IDU is a better predictor of syringe sharing or HIV risk behavior among women (Lum, Sears, & Guydish, 2005) than among men (Choi, Cheung, & Chen, 2006). A woman is likely to obtain used injecting equipment from her sex partner, whereas a man is likely to get it from close friends (Davies, Dominy, Peters, & Richardson, 1996). Furthermore, social norms and gender role expectations may put women at increased risk of using used needles/drug because the man usually uses the equipment first and passes it on to his female partner to use (Bennett, Velleman, Barter, & Bradbury, 2000; Lum et al., 2005). More studies illuminating gender effects on equipment use would give further insights into these behaviors that may be useful in HIV/AIDS prevention.

Even when women engage in sex with someone who is not an IDU, they are at increased risk for HIV/AIDS. Women, particularly substance-abusing women, may be in a less powerful position to practice safe sex. Women are less likely than men to report they use condoms or use them consistently during sex (Booth et al., 2007; Evans et al., 2003). Women may feel powerless to negotiate condom use because of expectations of a negative reaction or interpersonal violence by their male partner on whom they rely for financial support (Surratt & Inciardi, 2005; Witte, Batsukh, & Chang, 2010). This is especially true for substance-abusing, impoverished women including street-walking sex workers and homeless women. The women may engage in risky sex in exchange for money to meet survival needs or get a fix for their drug habit. Furthermore, substance-abusing women are more likely than substance-abusing men to trade sex for money or drugs, and sex trading may increase STD/HIV/AIDS risks because multiple sex partners are involved (Otto-Salaj, Gore-Felton, McGarvey, & Canterbury, 2002; Pugatch et al., 2000).

Even among more advantaged women, gender inequities in sexual relationships may weaken women's ability to practice safe sex. Roberts and Kennedy (2006) found that although the college women they studied were confident of their ability to ask their male partners to use a condom, half of the women did not refuse sex after their partners decline to use one. Any alcohol or other psychoactive drug use before or during sex may decrease inhibitions or prevent women from warding off unwanted sexual advances from men who can easily overpower them, further increasing women's vulnerability to unsafe sex (for a more detailed review, see Sun, 2009). Women also experience higher rates of sexual abuse during childhood and/or adulthood than men, and sexual or physical trauma may attenuate their decision-making ability to practice safe sex (Wyatt, Myers, & Loeb, 2004).

Intimate Partner Violence

Different research methods and measurements may contribute to the inconsistent findings about intimate partner violence (IPV) prevalence rates among men and women in the general population. For example, the National Violence Against Women Survey reports that the lifetime rates of IPV victimization are approximately 25 percent among women and nearly 8 percent among men (Tjaden & Thoennes, 2000); however, the National Family Violence Survey reports that men and women generally share a similar rate of IPV victimization (i.e., 11–12 percent) (see National Institute of Justice, n.d.). Archer's meta-analysis (2000) revealed that women are slightly more likely than men to perpetrate IPV if the IPV was measured based on "specific acts," whereas men are more likely than women to perpetrate IPV if the IPV was measured based on "physical consequences of aggression (visible injuries or injuries

requiring medical treatment)" (p. 664). Summarizing various studies, Stuart, O'Farrell, and Temple (2009) found that victimized women have a higher likelihood of experiencing depressive symptomatology, physical injuries, and medical attention resulting from the physical injuries, missing work, and using mental health services than victimized men.

Substance-abusing men and women are more likely to perpetrate IPV than men and women in the general population. Empirical studies have established a link between substance abuse and IPV perpetration and victimization: substance abuse problems are overrepresented among people who seek IPV treatment, and IPV problems are overrepresented among people who seek substance abuse treatment (see reviews by Kay et al., 2010; Stuart et al., 2009). Stuart et al.'s review of studies showed that the prevalence rate of male-to-female IPV in the past year was between 58 percent and 85 percent across samples of men receiving inpatient treatment for alcohol use disorders, and it was between 54 percent and 66 percent in men receiving outpatient treatment for alcohol use disorders. O'Farrell and Murphy (1995) found that the IPV perpetration rate of their sample of alcoholic men in treatment was four to six times higher compared to a demographically matched and nationally representative sample of men.

Researchers have focused on substance-abusing men when studying IPV perpetration and on substance-abusing women when studying IPV victimization (Chermack, Walton, Fuller, & Blow, 2001). Chermack et al. believe that the lack of information on substance abusing men with respect to IPV victimization and on substance abusing women with respect to IPV perpetration prevents a better understanding of gender issues in the field. Stuart et al.'s (2009) review showed that 50 percent to 68 percent of women in substance-abuse treatment perpetrated IPV in the past year, including 25 to 50 percent who were involved in severe violence perpetration. Chase, O'Farrell, Murphy, Fals-Stewart, and Murphy (2003) studied 103 female alcoholic patients seeking couples-based outpatient alcoholism treatment. Sixty-four percent of the women had been victimized by their male partner during the year prior to treatment (22 percent of the cases involved severe violence). Sixty-eight percent of the women perpetrated violence on their male partner (50 percent involving severe violence).

Research findings tend to suggest that substance abuse precedes violence. For example, Stuart et al.'s (2009) review showed that the likelihood of IPV occurrence could be 8 to 19 times higher on a day a man drinks than on a day he does not drink. Fals-Stewart, Golden, and Schumacher's study (2003) indicated that after controlling for factors of relationship dissonance and antisocial personality, the likelihood of male-to-female IPV occurrence was three times higher on a day when the man used cocaine than on a day he did not. Research shows that substance abuse can also be a result of violence, in that victims suffering emotional and physical consequences associated with IPV may self-medicate with substance use (Collins et al., cited in Stuart et al., 2009; Martino, Collins, & Ellickson, 2005). In addition, substance abuse may precipitate not only IPV perpetration among men and women but also IPV victimization among them, particularly among women. For example, Schneider, Burnette, Ilgen, and Timko (2009) found that about 47 percent of the substance-abusing women in their study (versus 23 percent of women in the general population) and nearly 10 percent of the substance-abusing men (versus eight percent of men in the general population) experienced IPV victimization. Various studies have shown that substance abuse may make women more vulnerable to sexual or nonsexual IPV or other violence (in some cases, regardless of the degree or status of the perpetrator's drinking; see National Institute on Alcohol Abuse and Alcoholism [NIAAA], 1999). Parks and Fals-Stewart (2004) studied 94 college women and found that the odds of the women encountering sexual aggression were seven times greater and the odds of the women encountering nonsexual aggression were about four times greater on days when they consumed any alcohol than on

days when they did not consume alcohol. As mentioned earlier, 64 percent of the female patients with alcohol use disorders in Chase et al.'s study (2003) had been victimized by their male partner during the year prior to treatment, and 68 percent perpetrated violence on their male partner.

To provide more effective assessment, treatment, and prevention, it is important to understand risk factors for IPV among substance-abusing clients. Research on the topic is in its infancy. Risk factors for IPV may include the type and level of substances abused, the quality of the couple's relationship, history of childhood abuse, and their social and economic resources (e.g., education and income). For example, Schneider et al. (2009) found that IPV victimization tends to happen to men and women who abuse alcohol or alcohol and other drugs more often than to those who abuse drugs only. Chase et al. (2003) found that the male partners' alcohol problem, especially an alcohol abuse/dependence diagnosis, may contribute to substance-abusing women's IPV victimization. Some studies show that cocaine use may precipitate woman-to-man IPV (Chase et al.) and man-to-woman IPV (Fals-Stewart et al., 2003). In addition, Schneider et al. found that both male and female injection drug users (IDUs) are more likely to become IPV victims than their non-IDU counterparts, possibly because of the severity of the IDUs' drug problems and their precipitation of IPV. Chase et al. report that predictors for substance-abusing female IPV victimization by male perpetrators may include "men's belief that the female alcoholic patient's drinking causes the couple's relationship problems," and men's "less positive feeling about the female alcoholic"[1] (p. 144). Chase et al. also noted that women's belief that the relationship problems caused their drinking problems and women's "poorer relationship adjustment" (e.g., desire to end the relationship with their partner) may predict their IPV perpetration toward the male partner. Among both substance-abusing women and men, a history of child physical or sexual abuse may increase IPV victimization risk (Schneider et al). Furthermore, substance-abusing women without a high school diploma/GED may be more likely to experience lifetime IPV victimization (Schneider et al.); likewise, lower education may predict substance-abusing women's IPV perpetration toward the male partner (Chase et al., 2003).

Etiology and Risk Factors

Empirical studies find that men and women share etiological and risk factors for substance abuse, though women's substance abuse may be more related to environmental factors (e.g., substance-abusing families of origin and substance-abusing male sexual partners), while men's substance abuse may be more related to genetics, impulsive behavior, pleasure-seeking, and social occasions.

Family History and Adverse Childhood Experiences

Studies consistently find that substance-abusing women are more likely than substance-abusing men to come from a dysfunctional family of origin or a family with a history of alcohol or drug problems, and/or to have had adverse childhood experiences (ACE) (Boyd, 1993; Chatham, Hiller, Rowan-Szal, Joe, & Simpson, 1999; Chermack, Stoltenberg, Fuller, & Blow, 2000; Deng, Vaughn, & Lee, 2003; Howell & Chasnoff, 1999; Langan & Pelissier 2001; Messina, Marinelli-Casey, Hillhouse, Rawson et al., 2008; Schneider, Kviz, Isola, & Filstead, 1995; Toray, Coughlin, Vuchinich, & Patricelli, 1991; Westermeyer & Boedicker, 2000; Zilberman, Hochgraf, & Andrade, 2003; Zimmer-Höfler & Dobler-Mikola, 1992). For example, in comparing 277 substance-abusing women and 365 substance-abusing men, Westermeyer and Boedicker (2000) found statistically significant differences indicating that the women were more likely to have a mother who abused substances (30 percent versus 22 percent), one or more siblings who abused substances (56 percent versus 41 percent), and one or more grandparents who abused substances (39 percent versus 29 percent).

Another study found that 42 percent of 63 methamphetamine-dependent female probationers versus 32 percent of 147 male counterparts came from a family with drug abuse problems (Rao, Czuchry, & Dansereau, 2009).

Studies have reported a proportionate relationship between the number of categories of adverse childhood experience (ACE) an individual experiences and the risk of developing substance-abuse problems later in life (Dube et al., 2002; Felitti & Anda, 2010). This relationship holds true regardless of whether the individual has an alcoholic parent or not (Dube et al.). The 10 categories included in ACE studies are childhood emotional abuse, physical abuse, sexual abuse, emotional neglect, physical neglect, domestic violence, substance abuse in the family, mental illness in the family, incarcerated family members, and parental divorce or separation (Felitti & Anda, 2010; Hillis et al., 2004). Dong et al.'s (2004) study indicates that ACE does not occur alone or independently and that 81 percent to 98 percent of their study respondents who had been exposed to one ACE reported at least a second ACE. Felitti and Anda studied a cohort of more than 17,000 Kaiser health plan patients, half of whom were women, and found that women were more likely than men to report having encountered at least five (of the 10) ACE categories. Felitti and colleagues (1998; Felitti & Anda, 2010) suggested that ACEs may first interrupt a person's neurodevelopment, which in turn may impair the person's emotional, cognitive, social, and other functioning. That impairment further precipitates engagement in health-risk behaviors and subsequently results in disability and disease, and finally, an early death.

Marital Status and Substance-Abusing Sexual Partners

Findings on the effect of marital status on an individual's alcohol and drug use and abuse are not completely consistent. Research and theory suggest that married men and women tend to report a lower rate of various problem behaviors—violence, crime, mental illness, and substance use disorders—than their non-married counterparts (see Fleming, White, & Catalano's literature review, 2010) because marriage acts as a protection or mechanism of social control and social support (Maume et al., Sampson & Laub, Umberson, cited in Fleming et al.). Married women (pregnant or nonpregnant) are less likely than non-married women to use alcohol, binge drink, use illicit drugs, or smoke (Burd, Martsolf, Klug, O'Connor & Peterson, 2003; CDC, 2009; Huang & Reid 2006; Tsai, Floyed, & Bertrand, 2007). Family responsibilities and an intimate partner's support and companionship may contribute to married women's lower substance use or abuse rate. Non-married women have more freedom to engage in various functional or dysfunctional behaviors, or feelings of boredom and emptiness may precipitate their substance use or abuse. For men and women with substance use disorders, studies also suggest that marriage helps prevent substance abuse relapses while not being married has the opposite effect. For example, Walter et al. (2006) found that at one-year follow up, "living alone" and being "separated/divorced" predicted relapse for both alcoholic men and women who received detoxification services. Walton et al. (2003) found that at two-year follow up, being single predicted relapse to alcohol or drug use among men and women who received substance abuse treatment.

Social development theory, however, further suggests that "the influence of social bonds depends on the behavior of the socializing unit to which an individual is bonded" (Catalano & Hawkins, cited in Fleming et al., 2010, p. 164). The relationship is not simply one of marital status. Fleming et al.'s study of 909 young adults revealed that "more supportive, enjoyable, and satisfying relationships were related to less use only in situations in which the intimate partner was not substantially involved in substance abuse" (p. 164). Other studies support this finding. For example, Hser, Huang, Teruya, and Anglin (2003) found "no spousal drug use during follow-up" was one factor related to abstinence for both men and women.

Many studies document that substance-abusing women are more likely to be introduced to drug use by their male sexual partner than the other way around (Hser et al., 1987; Brady & Randall, 1999; Eldred & Washington, 1976; Riehman, Hser, & Zeller, 2000; Wilsnack & Wilsnack, 1991). They are also more likely to keep using when their partner continues to use. Based on Haavio-Mannila's work, Wilsnack and Wilsnack stated "Women are more likely to imitate the drinking behavior of higher status males, whether in the family or in the work place than men are to imitate female drinking behavior" (p. 150). A recent qualitative study suggests that substance-abusing women's low self-worth with respect to their intimate relationships with men is one of four major factors contributing to relapse to substance use. The study found that many of the women based their self-worth and sense of well-being on their relationships with men, which is not atypical of women in the general population. Fear of losing "her man" may prompt a woman to engage in substance use to please her drug-using partner or to "keep him home." A woman may stop using substance because her male partner decides to stop using, and she may go back to using because he wants to use again. As one woman in that study said, "My whole world revolved around him" (Sun, 2007).

The effects of marital status on substance abuse relapse are more consistent for men than women. Being married tends to be protective with regard to treatment outcomes and usually predicts less relapse among men, whereas this is not always the case for women. For example, Schneider et al. (1995) found that at three months following treatment, being married protected against relapse for men but it was a risk factor for relapse among women. This finding perhaps can be explained from two perspectives. First, previous research has indicated that substance-abusing women may be more likely to be married to substance-abusing men than vice versa. Thus, substance-abusing spouses may adversely affect women's recovery and post-treatment outcomes. Second, regardless of their spouse's AOD-using status, substance-abusing women, compared to substance-abusing men, are more sensitive and vulnerable to negative interpersonal relationships, including their relationships with their spouses (McKay, Rutherford, Cacciola, Kabasakalian-McKay & Alterman, 1996; Sun, 2007). Weaver et al. (2000) found that women perceived "family" and "marital/intimate relationships" to be two major psychosocial stresses during both pre-recovery and recovery. Practitioners report that in working with alcoholic men who have non-using female partner, the focus seems to be on issues related to substance abuse or abstinence contract compliance, whereas when working with substance-abusing women who have non-using male partners, the emphasis more often is on communication skills, relationship issues, and enhancing positive interactions (Winters, Fals-Stewart, O'Farrell, Birchler, & Kelley, 2002). Compared to a woman who has a substance-abusing male partner and/or a (marital) relationship loaded with tension, a woman who is single or divorced may be better able to focus on her recovery, prompting better treatment outcomes (Wilsnack & Wilsnack, 1991).

Reducing Negative Emotions versus Enhancing Positive Emotions as a Substance Use Trigger

Among clinical samples, research findings suggest that women may be more likely to relapse to AOD when attempting to reduce their negative emotions, whereas men may be more likely to relapse to AOD while trying to seek pleasure or enhance their positive emotions. This seems to be consistent with at least two theories that accentuate the different traits of the two sexes. Theories suggest that women are more prone to depression and the negative implications of interpersonal conflicts and life stressors than men. Women's hormonal fluctuations and their socialization to suppress their desires to assert and express themselves and to internalize their negative feelings may contribute to this phenomenon (see Sun's review, 2009).

Noble (2005) calls depression "the leading cause of disease-related disability in women" (p. 49). Zilberman, Tavares, Blume, and El-Guebaly's (2003) review showed that women with depression have a higher likelihood of developing an alcohol use disorder later in life than their female counterparts without depression and their male counterparts with depression. The depression-drinking sequence seems consistent with the self-medication hypothesis among women.

Theories also suggest that men have a lower level of self-regulation and are more likely to engage in sensation seeking than women (Quinn & Fromme, 2010). Self-regulation is "the effortful control of thoughts, emotions, and behaviors in the service of a goal; it includes such capacities as planning and the ability to delay gratification" (Quinn & Fromme, p. 377). Sensation seeking is "a tendency to seek and enjoy novelty and excitement," which often predicts behavioral risks such as drinking and unsafe sexual practice (see Quinn and Fromme's review, p. 376).

Negative emotions or unpleasant moods may be triggers for substance abuse relapse for both men and women. Most research finds that women in clinical samples are more likely to relapse due to negative emotions than their men counterparts are, while a handful of studies find no difference between the two sexes in this regard (e.g., Annis et al., 1998, cited in Walitzer & Dearing, 2006), or that men are more vulnerable to the trigger of negative emotions than women (e.g., Hodgins et al., 1995, cited in Walitzer & Dearing, 2006). Numerous clinical studies find that women are more likely than men to use substances or relapse in order to self-medicate negative emotions, including those related to interpersonal conflicts and life stressors (e.g., Annis & Graham, 1995; Back, Brady, Jackson, Salstrom, & Zinzow, 2005; Chong & Lopez, 2008; Haseltine, 2000; Hser, Anglin, & Booth, 1987; Langan & Pelissier, 2001; McKay et al., 1996; Pisinger & Jorgensen, 2007; Thom, 1986; Zimmer-Höfler & Dobler-Mikola, 1992; Zywiak, Connors, Maisto, & Westerberg, 1996; Sun, 2007).

Positive emotions or "external situations and euphoric states" may also be relapse triggers for men and women. Research suggests either that men are more likely to relapse due to positive emotions than women are or that there is no significant difference between the two sexes concerning this trigger. Although many studies (Annis & Graham, 1995; Back et al., 2005; Haseltine, 2000; Hser, Anglin, & Booth, 1987; Langan & Pelissier, 2001; Thom, 1986; Zywiak et al., 1996) suggest that men are more likely than women to use AOD to seek pleasure, enhance positive feelings, or for social reasons, other studies (McKay et al., 1996; Pisinger & Jorgensen, 2007; Zimmer-Höfler & Dobler-Mikola, 1992) indicate no significant difference between the two sexes. Scourfield, Stevens, and Merikangas (1996) offer additional insight on the concepts of self-medication and thrill-seeking with respect to women. They divided participants of each gender (132 women and 130 men) into four groups—substance abuse only, substance abuse and comorbid anxiety, anxiety only, and a control group without any of these disorders. Among women, the "substance abuse only" group had a significantly higher thrill-seeking score than the "substance abuse and comorbid anxiety" group, whereas there was no significant difference in the thrill-seeking scores of the "substance abuse and comorbid anxiety" group, the "anxiety only" group, and the control group. Among men, there was no significant difference in the sensation-seeking score between the "substance abuse only" group and the "substance abuse and comorbid anxiety" group. Scourfield et al. stated that their findings provide some support for the self-medication theory for women and that thrill-seeking may be a stronger factor impacting women's substance abuse when self-medication of negative mental states is not an issue.

Genetics

Genetic influences may contribute to alcohol and drug disorders in a similar fashion as they do to other chronic illnesses, such as type 2 diabetes mellitus, asthma, and hypertension (McLellan, Lewis, O'Brien, & Kleber, 2000). Various factors including gender, ethnicity, types of substances used, and psychiatric comorbidity add complexity to the relationship between genetics and substance use disorders (McGue, Pickens, & Svikis, 1992). Whether genetics affect men and women equally and similarly is a controversial topic in the research on gender and substance abuse (Heath, Slutske, & Madden, 1997). Today, scholars are particularly interested in gene-environment interactions and their effects on mental disorders or psychopathology, including substance use disorders (e.g., Agrawal et al., 2010; Cadoret, Riggins-Caspers, Yates, Troughton, & Stewart, 2000; Enoch, 2011; Guo, Elder, Cai, & Hamilton, 2009; Tsuang, Stone, & Johnston, 2008; van Os, Rutten, & Poulton, 2009). While the research needed to clarify these relationships has a long way to go, available data show evidence of gene-environment interactions, with some indicating that the gene-environment interactions may be stronger for women than men.

Many twin and adoption studies indicate that genetic influences (heredity) explain about 40 to 60 percent of the variance in developing alcohol abuse or dependence (Goldman, Oroszi, & Ducci, 2005; Heath et al., 1997; McGue, 1999; McGue et al., 1992; Tyndale, 2003). Some studies find that genetic influences may be stronger for men than women (Han, McGue, & Iacono, 1999; King, Burt, Malone, McGue, & Iacono, 2005; Prescott et al., 2005). For example, Han et al. found that the proportion of variance heredity explained for liability to alcohol, tobacco, and drug use are 60, 59, and 33 percent, respectively, for men versus 10, 11, and 11 percent, respectively, for women.[2] Another line of research, however, demonstrates that genetics affect both sexes to equal degrees (Kendler et al., 1992; Heath et al., 1997; Prescott, Aggen, & Kendler, 1999; Prescott & Kendler, 1999; Kendler et al., 2003). The inconsistent research results pertaining to women may be due to methodological issues. For example, some studies contain very small samples of women (Prescott et al., 2005), and female twin studies with participants recruited from treatment programs may be less likely to discern the genetic influence than when comparisons are made with counterparts recruited from the general population (Prescott et al., 2005; Prescott & Kendler, 2000).

Although gene-environment (G x E) interaction is not a new concept, geneticists are giving more attention to the social environment in understanding human behaviors and human disorders, such as mental disorders and pathology, including substance use disorders. G x E interaction refers to "the dependence of a phenotypic trait's expression on a particular environment" (Cadoret et al., 2000, p. 253). Tsuang et al. (2008) explain that "gene-environment interactions occur when environmental influences on a trait differ according to a person's genetic predisposition, or when a person's genetic predisposition is expressed differently in different environments" (p. 27). The G x E interaction approach posits "a causal role not for either genes or environment in isolation, but for their synergistic co-participation in the cause ... where the effect of one is conditional on the other" (van Os et al., 2009, p. 19). True genetic effects and true environmental effects can be identified only if $G \times E$ interactions are considered.

Various studies provide evidence of a gene-environment interaction in understanding the effect of nature and nurture on human behavior and disorders. For example, studies have shown that children with a birth parent who has antisocial personality or sociopathy are more likely to exhibit delinquent behavior if they are adopted by parents who have had adverse experiences (psychiatric problems, divorce, or separation) than if they are adopted into more functional families (see Cadoret et al.'s review, 2000). Guo et al. (2009) studied 600 monozygotic twin pairs, dizygotic twin pairs, and full sibling pairs and found that among adolescents, a greater level of drinking by best friends (an environmental factor) is likely to lead to an increase in the level of genetic contribution to the drinking behavior, whereas a lower level of drinking by best friends is likely to restrain the genetic influence on alcohol use. Agrawal et al.'s (2010) study of 2,176 young twin women also showed that an increase in peer substance involvement is associated with a stronger expression of genetic influences.

Several researchers further pointed out that the G x E factor may influence adolescent girls or young women more than their male counterparts with respect to deviant behavior, drinking, or substance abuse. For example, Cadoret et al.'s adoption study (2000) showed that having an adoptive parent who had adverse experiences (an environment factor) does not predict much of the variance in the adopted child' aggressivity (about 2 percent for females and slightly less than 2 percent for males). When having an antisocial birth parent (a genetic factor) is added to the statistical models, the equation significantly predicts aggressivity for both sexes (about 6 percent for females and 7 percent for males). However, when the $G \times E$ interaction was added to the equation, the amount of explained variance rose to about 15 percent for females, though it remained the same for males (7 percent).

Substance Abuse Treatment for Men and Women

Chapter 11 of this text discussed the need for culturally relevant or culturally specific treatment when assisting people who identify with particular ethnic or cultural groups; Chapter 12 did the same for those who are gay, lesbian, bisexual or transgender. As Chapters 9 and 14 indicate, treatment must also be age relevant. Various evidence-based treatment methods and approaches discussed in these chapters and in Chapter 6—such as motivational interviewing/motivational enhancement therapy, brief intervention, cognitive behavioral therapy, twelve-step facilitation, contingency management, community reinforcement approach, pharmacological treatments, and so on—have been developed and validated to help substance-abusing men and women. Many issues and challenges in treatment, some old, some new, deserve further exploration and attention as we consider gender-relevant approaches.

Life Issues versus Drug Issues

One perspective with regard to gender and substance use disorders is that women's substance abuse problems are more likely to be a manifestation or consequence of dysfunction in various psychosocial domains, whereas men's substance abuse problems are more likely to be the source or cause of the dysfunction in various psychosocial domains. Numerous treatment outcome studies show that although substance-abusing women (especially drug-abusing women) present more severe and negative pretreatment psychosocial characteristics and substance use disorder symptoms than their male counterparts (e.g., Fiorentine, Anglin, Gil-Rivas, & Taylor, 1997; Messina, Marinelli-Casey, Hillhouse, Rawson et al., 2008; Pelissier, Camp, Gaes, Saylor, & Rhodes, 2003; Weiss et al., 1998), women's treatment outcomes are equivalent to or better than men's (Dawson et al., 2005; Porowski, Burgdorf, & Herrell, 2004; Pelissier et al., 2003; Pelissier & Jones, 2005; Rao et al., 2009; Walitzer & Dearing's review, 2006). More research is needed to understand the factors that affect treatment outcome success for each of the sexes. Improvement in various psychosocial domains (e.g., mental and physical health, parenting skills, vocational skills, spousal and other interpersonal relationships, and housing), which usually occurs via provision of comprehensive case management, may contribute to improving substance use problems, and improvement in substance use problems may contribute to better functioning in the various psychosocial domains among women. A bi-directional path may also be applicable to men, but it may not be as distinct.

Data collected by the SAMHSA-funded Residential Women and Children and Pregnant and Postpartum Women programs on 1,200 female clients from 32 treatment sites provide a clear picture of the harsh reality these women face. At admission, 40 percent of the women used crack cocaine, followed by alcohol (14 percent), methamphetamine (13 percent), and heroin (8 percent); 54 percent of them had 3 or more children; 52 percent had less than a high school/GED education; 49 percent had mental health problems; only 8 percent were employed; 77 percent were victims of abuse; 47 percent had children removed by the child protective services; 50 percent were involved with the criminal justice system; 60 percent had

health problems (Porowski et al., 2004). In another example, Messina, Marinelli-Casey, Hillhouse, Rawson et al. (2008) obtained pretreatment data on 236 male and 351 female methamphetamine-dependent prisoners and found that compared to men, women were significantly more likely to lack a high school education (22 vs. 15 percent), to be unemployed (30 vs. 11 percent), to have a young child (73 vs. 60 percent), to have a more severe drug problem, to report being abused before age 18 (emotional abuse, 55 vs. 37 percent; physical abuse, 42 vs. 27 percent; sexual abuse, 42 vs. 11 percent), to report familial arguments (40 vs. 26 percent), to experience "familial substance abuse while growing up" (63 vs. 50 percent), to witness "familial violence to other family members" (55 vs. 39 percent), and 9 percent of women versus 3 percent reported experiencing six types of childhood adverse events.

Despite women's adverse background characteristics at treatment admission, they tend to improve after receiving appropriate services, especially comprehensive case management and residential treatment. For example, SAMHSA's Residential Women and Children and Pregnant and Postpartum Women programs offered pregnant and parenting women three essential service components: (a) long-term (6 or 12 months) residential treatment, (b) on-site residential services for their infants and young children, and (c) a comprehensive package of services (e.g., substance abuse treatment, prenatal and pediatric care, nursery and preschool services, parenting skills, mental health care, vocational training, legal services, and transportation). Porowski et al. (2004) found that six months after discharge, 61 percent of the women reported no relapse and a significant pre-post decrease in alcohol and drug use categories. Though there was no control group for comparison purposes, Porowski et al. report that these women's treatment programs consistently produced larger reductions for each type of substance use than found in large-scale studies that included mostly men receiving residential treatment services (see Gerstein & Johnson, 1999). Not only did the women reduce their substance use during the follow up period, they also improved in the psychosocial domains. For example, among the abstainers (women who did not relapse to drug use during follow up), 44 percent lived with a substance-using partner at treatment admission compared to 5 percent post-treatment; among those who relapsed (used substances during follow up), the rate decreased from 46 percent to 24 percent. For the abstainers, the treatment admission employment rate was 7 percent compared to 44 percent at follow up; for relapsers, the employment rate increased from 6 percent to 26 percent.

Case management and comprehensive services may be more effective for substance-abusing women than substance-abusing men. For instance, Morgenstern, Hogue, Dauber, Dasaro, and McKay (2009) found that Coordinated Case Management, "a continuity-of-care intervention focused on engaging clients in drug treatment, linking them directly to needed ancillary services, and fostering transition to employment," improved employment for female substance-using welfare recipients but not for their male counterparts (p. 956). This may be due to men and women's different pre-treatment characteristics. Women may have faced significantly more employment barriers than men, and men may have been much more ready to work than women prior to treatment. Findings such as those on employment offer support for the theory that substance-abusing women, compared to their male counterparts, need "habilitation" rather than "rehabilitation."

Treatment Entry, Completion, and Success

Although substance abuse treatment benefits women and substance-abusing women tend to fare better than substance-abusing men after treatment, women are less likely than men to enter or complete treatment. Although women's treatment entry rate has improved over the last two decades—women accounted for 28 percent of the total substance-abuse treatment admissions in

1992, 30 percent in 2001, and 32 percent in 2007 (Office of Applied Studies, n.d.), women still have a lower treatment entry rate relative to their substance abuse prevalence rate. Once in treatment, women's completion rate is also lower than men's: 37 percent of women and 45 percent of the men completed treatment in 2002, 40 percent versus 46 percent in 2003, and 39 percent versus 47 percent in 2004, respectively (Office of Applied Studies, 2009). Research shows, however, that women are equally likely to participate and complete treatment when family, economic, and other barriers are addressed (Green, 2006).

Lack of child care services is a major barrier to women's treatment participation. Substance-abusing women are more likely than their male counterparts to have a child, but most treatment facilities do not accommodate women's childcare needs. Brown, Vartivarian, and Alderks's (2011) review showed that many mothers experience difficulty finding child care when seeking treatment, particularly low-income or single mothers, and that some mothers avoid treatment due to worries about losing child custody if they are unable to find child care. SAMHSA's (n.d.b) 2009 National Survey of Substance Abuse Treatment Services showed that only 8 percent of substance-abuse treatment programs offer childcare for clients' children and less than 4 percent offered residential beds for clients' children.

Since men are more likely to manifest acute and more pronounced symptoms and consequences of substance use disorders than women (Plant et al., 2000), men are more likely to attract attention and be identified and referred to treatment than women with substance use disorders (Guthrie & Flinchbaugh, 2001). A study found that when pediatricians were presented with fictional female adolescent girls with drug-abusing symptoms (e.g., runny nose, loss of appetite, worse relationship with parents, and loss of interest in school), they were more likely to render a diagnosis of depression than drug use disorder, whereas when fictional counterpart male adolescent boys with identical symptoms were presented, these pediatricians were more likely to render a diagnosis of drug use disorder than depression (National Center on Addiction and Substance Abuse [CASA] at Columbia University, 2000).

Stereotypes and stigma may also discourage women from entering treatment. Women may have internalized the stigma stemming from society's harsher sanction on their substance-abusing behavior than men's substance-abusing behavior, causing women to be more hesitant than men to acknowledge their substance-abuse problems and treatment need. For example, respondents in one study were less sympathetic to a female rape victim if she was intoxicated during the incident as they perceived that she should not have used alcohol to begin with; however, they were more merciful toward a male perpetrator who drank alcohol when victimizing a woman, since "it's not the man, but the alcohol" that created the problem (cited in Blume, 1997). Another study showed that women respondents tend to censure women's drinking more so than men's (cited in Blum, Nielsen, & Riggs, 1998). Internalized stigma may discourage women from seeking substance abuse treatment because of shame and guilt.

To more effectively identify and link women to treatment, society's overall harsh and punitive attitude toward substance-abusing women, especially women who are mothers or pregnant, must change. Strategies that are sensitive to women's dilemmas and concerns can better achieve the goal. For example, Sokol, Martier, and Ager (1989) believe that one reason their T-ACE screener outperformed the CAGE (see Chapter 5) in screening pregnant women was the use of the "tolerance" question (i.e., "How many drinks does it take to make you feel high?"), which replaces the CAGE question "Have you ever felt bad or guilty about your drinking?" Sokol et al. surmise that women may be less likely to perceive the tolerance items as an indicator of drinking; therefore, a woman who unconsciously or intentionally attempts to minimize her drinking may be more honest in answering the tolerance items. Russell et al. (1996) further point out that the T-ACE question "How many drinks can you hold?" tends to be more sensitive in detecting pregnant women's drinking than T-ACE question, "How many drinks does it take to make you feel high?" Since women are more likely to seek care in primary care or mental health facilities than specialty substance abuse treatment programs, and since they are also more likely to be referred by child protective services and income maintenance/welfare offices than men, practitioners in these settings need to be acquainted with gender-sensitive substance abuse screening tools and procedures (also see Box 15.1).

The criminal justice system is the largest source of referrals to substance abuse treatment (37 percent in 2007) (SAMHSA, 2009). More men than women are referred to substance abuse treatment by the criminal justice system. In 2007, that ratio was 3:1 (SAMHSA). Regardless of a client's gender and the source of a client's referral to treatment, a brief intervention or Motivational Interviewing (MI) component may be added to the initial screening process to facilitate the positive-screened client's following through with the referral treatment (see Chapter 6 of this text for information on MI).

Gender-Specific and Gender-Responsive Treatment Approaches

Although more research on woman-specific substance-abuse treatment is still needed, knowledge in this area has emerged in the past three decades to counteract the reality that substance-abuse treatment programs have traditionally been developed for men. On the other hand, although substance-abuse treatment is traditionally designed for men, male-specific developmental challenges have been overlooked in providing treatment and services to men (Woodford, 2012). Both men and women are "gendered beings," and they each need special considerations in treatment. Box 15.2 is presents some considerations for working with men, and Box 15.3 provides an example of a gender-relevant approach for assisting women.

Box 15.3 presents some considerations for working with men.

BOX 15.2 *How to Help Men in Substance Abuse Treatment Groups*

Men can present unique challenges when they come voluntarily or involuntarily to substance abuse groups. The following twelve considerations may be helpful in guiding practice with men who seek assistance for substance abuse.

The Context of Masculinity

In groups, men often present a "macho" veneer as a way of attempting to gain control both over their treatment requirements and over other people in the group. This is particularly true with involuntary clients who have lost control by being forced into treatment. The way men present in group (how they act, how they interact with others, what they say) has to be discussed and linked to the masculine culture that pushes men into drugs.

Setting a Context for a Male Exclusive Model or a Male Inclusive Model of Masculine Development

Discussions about masculinity must involve considerations about women's roles in helping men grow up and in the treatment of women in their lives (grandmothers, mothers, daughters, wives, sex partners, friends, and therapists). Asking men about their early and current experiences with women may be helpful in their understanding of what drove early drug-abusing behavior and what drives their behavior now in relation to significant females in their life.

Men as Clients

The socialization of men and women makes it hard for men to seek help. Men do not like to be interviewed about feelings and, arguably, are hard-wired differently so that processing emotions is more difficult. In addition, males have higher rates of oppositional defiant disorder and attention deficit disorder than females. With these characteristics, the treatment process of accepting help, sitting still, listening, and attending can make treatment a daunting task.

Men of Color Have Different Life Experiences Than White Men

Latino and African-American men believe they are treated worse by "the system" because of their race. The therapist needs to directly address race when it is raised and acknowledge that society does treat people differentially based on race, as well as gender, religion, sexual orientation, class, (dis)ability, and age. The discussion can then move on to asking the speaker to link that reality with the need to stop abusing drugs.

Female Therapists and Male Clients

Macho posturing by involuntary clients may be more evident with women therapists (though it can be argued that it is more common with some male therapists with whom they may be competing). Bringing therapist gender into the session and tying that to experiences with women outside of the group is one way to address issues the men may have about female therapists and women in their lives.

Men as Financial Providers

Whether acquired legally or illegally, money is a key conduit to drugs. When men have no money, they are devalued and feel less competent as a man. This may be the most intractable issue for men. Often undereducated and with a spotty employment history, the opportunities for change for some of these men, particularly in the current economy, are bleak. Yet job training programs have been shown to have some successes.

Men "Dissed" as Fathers

Many men in treatment may have troubled relationships with their children. Setting aside time to discuss parenting issues can be helpful for current

(continued)

as well as future fathers. The emphasis should include the nurturing aspects of parenting, not just the discipline and control issues with which parents often struggle. By emphasizing the nurturing aspects, a context of love can be set that can be a metaphor for how the men could treat other significant people in their lives.

Men and Their Own Fathers

Whether fathers were present or absent in men's lives, the legacy of fatherhood has a profound impact on future generations. Usually some of the earliest messages about masculinity, treatment of women, work, and money come from fathers. Helping men draw connections between their own behavior and their father's can be facilitated through drawing a family tree (or genogram) and seeing that some fathering patterns are intergenerational.

Men and Male Friends

Men are raised to do activities with other men (often sports-related) while women are socialized to have face-to-face interactions. Talking to men about their friendships with men can get to the core of the relationships that often lead to peer pressure and drug abuse. Men are advised to stay away from their old friendships yet may not be taught about normative friendships between men. Helping men to understand how friendships are started and maintained can lead to new, more adaptive social support systems.

Men and Violence

Without understanding the currents of violence inherent in many substance abusers' lives and how violence appears as a metaphor in group discussions, opportunities to curtail the cycle of violence will be missed. Violence can be addressed specifically by asking the men to what extent it has been a part of their life and to what extent they wish to keep it a part of their life.

Real Men Don't Cry

For men who have been raised to be tough and not show emotions, and who have learned to mask feelings with drugs, crying is the ultimate sign of weakness. An early reference to expressing emotions and crying will give men permission to cry in the group. Their behavior will be normalized. Asking men's reactions to someone else (it may be a woman) crying will further help to pave the way for a range of emotions to be expressed.

Sexual Issues

Drug use can also be connected to sexual dysfunction or a gateway to sex without responsibility. Men may hint at dysfunction overtly or metaphorically. Handling discussions about sexual functioning and sexual orientation are similar to discussions about masculinity and sharing of emotions. Information can be placed before the group (or the individual) as a form of education that can help normalize men's experiences in these realms.

Source: Adapted from "One dozen considerations when working with men in substance abuse groups" by G.L. Greif from *Journal of Psychoactive Drugs*, 41(4), 387–390, 2009. Reprinted by permission of the publisher Taylor & Francis Ltd. http://www.informaworld.com.

Co-Occurring Mental Disorders and Service Coordination

As Chapter 13 of this text demonstrates, substance use disorders often co-occur with mental disorders and other illnesses or disabilities. Among the mental disorders that often co-occur with substance use disorders are depression, anxiety, post-traumatic stress disorders (PTSD), borderline personality disorders (BPD), and antisocial personality disorder (APD). Child maltreatment and risky sexual or drug-using practices also occur in the presence of substance use disorders. To effectively serve clients, co-occurring disorders must be addressed by collaborating with other systems and professionals

BOX 15.3 *Using the Relational Model to Help Women with Substance Use Disorders*

By Sue Marriott, LCSW, CGP

The relational model, a conceptual approach to treatment that validates women's experiences, has evolved over the past few decades (Belenky et al., 1986; Gilligan, 1982; Jordan et al., 1991; Miller, 1976). The relational model provides a unique perspective on psychological growth and women's substance abuse. Theorist and clinicians at the Stone Center have sought to understand and describe psychological development, emphasizing the centrality of relationships in the lives of women. The Stone Center Working Papers* provide a more complete description of this history and details of the model. While this is a promising theory-driven paradigm, empirical research is needed to understand its efficacy as a form of treatment for women.

According to traditional psychological theories, human development is actualized from immature dependency to mature independence, leading to a sense of self that is self-sufficient, independent, and bounded. The relational model proposes a paradigm shift in which women are viewed in the context of their relationships and their environment. From a relational perspective, a woman seeks to engage in increasingly authentic and complex connections with herself, others, and her community. The desire for connection is recognized as life affirming, and problems manifested are understood as springing from the effects of nonmutuality, isolation, abuse, and disconnection (Miller, 1984).

The central paradox of the relational model is that women disconnect with significant parts of themselves in order to remain connected with others in relationships (Miller, 1990). Thus, one might see a woman develop a pattern of smiling when she is angry, inhibiting her sexuality, or saying she doesn't know (when, in fact, she knows exactly), all in an attempt to stay connected interpersonally. By shutting down true parts of themselves, women often end up feeling lonely, depressed, and disconnected.

Healthy connection is marked by an increasing ability to represent one's thoughts, feelings, and perceptions in relationships and by allowing oneself to be moved by others (Kilbourne & Surrey, 1991). In a healthy relationship, each person is compelled to grow and be enriched, and this sometimes occurs through healthy conflict. Each person impacts the other.

From a relational perspective, a woman's abuse of chemicals is often an attempt to make or maintain a connection (Covington & Surrey, 2000). Substance use is often supported by the woman's environment and the patriarchal community that promotes independence and devalues the role of women. Substance use can also insulate one from the pain of abuse, disconnection, and isolation before it spirals into addictive disease. It is often when intoxicated that women feel more able to share hidden parts of themselves, thus fostering the feeling of belonging and the sense of being known. Women often describe their drug of choice in relational terms, such as their "lover," their "enemy," or their "best friend."

The relational model's paradox is evident when women use chemicals not so much for the effects of the drug itself but in order to stay connected to their substance-abusing partner. Women's substance use often begins, renews, or markedly increases upon a significant loss—for example, the break-up of a relationship, the development of a health problem, or being disowned by one's family of origin. Relationships are also apparent in influencing women's decision to enter treatment due to entreaties of loved ones, the threatened loss of custody of their children, or when drug use begins to jeopardize a primary relationship. Take the following case example.

*Available from Wellesley Centers for Women, Wellesley College, Wellesley, MA, http://www.wcwonline.org.

(continued)

Case Example

Linda is the 31-year-old mother of two. She reported to outpatient psychotherapy with the complaint of marital problems. Linda began using alcohol at the age of 12 and began using dependently at age 23. She continued her alcohol dependency until age 28, when she quit drinking after discovering she was pregnant with her first child. (Her connection with the unborn child allowed her to expand and take care of herself in a way in which she was previously inhibited.) She had completed a substance abuse treatment program about five years previously but felt it was a waste of her time. Instead, she decided on her own to quit drinking alcohol and had abstained for two years.

As a child, Linda witnessed domestic abuse between her parents. Her mother believed it was her job to hold the family together and thus endured the battering by her husband "for the sake of the kids." Linda was sexually abused by a neighbor from the age of 8 to 10 years old. When Linda tried to tell her mother about the sexual abuse, her mother responded that she "should have known better." Her mother reminded her that she had warned her about that particular neighbor and told her not to go near him again.

Early in therapy with Jan, a relationally informed therapist, Linda mentioned several previous attempts at counseling with therapists that she felt were harmful to her. Although Linda was unaware of it, her feelings of harm from these relationships were directly related to the childhood experiences of neglect and abuse that resulted in fear and distrust of relationships, especially with anyone she perceived to be in authority. Linda also revealed to Jan that she regularly takes low doses of OxyContin, a powerful narcotic prescription pain reliever. Even so, she identified alcohol as her only problem substance and said she was proud that she hadn't had a drink since she decided to stop. When Jan questioned her current substance use, Linda seemed hurt and defensive and indicated that she was there for marital problems.

Jan was aware of Linda's refusal to discuss her substance use and her unsuccessful previous interventions. She knew that the narcotic use was a major factor needing attention in order for Linda to move forward, but she decided to enter the relationship through the door Linda had opened: her desire to work toward a better marriage. Jan saw herself as helping Linda to trust someone for the first time in her life.

Jan initially focused on supporting any small step Linda made at being authentic with her, and she supported the small, achievable changes Linda wanted to make in her marriage. Jan asked many questions about how Linda saw herself and how she felt about her life. She let Linda be her own expert and took her objections about her previous care seriously, without joining in or villainizing the previous therapists. Jan also noted that Linda was unable to discuss the problems she had with previous therapists directly with them, and this pattern would continue with her if left unchecked.

Over time, Linda revealed that her husband, Dylan, was being treated for a recently diagnosed neurological disorder with OxyContin. Jan wondered about the connection between Linda's use of this drug and her husband's disease. Linda was struck with the insight that since her husband's diagnosis, she had become his sole caregiver. She had given up much of her own life's pleasure to take care of him and would not even allow herself to question this arrangement, which allowed her to stay in the prescribed role of a "good wife." Instead, she began taking the drug with him and thus had unwittingly joined him in this mildly drugged state, providing an escape from the reality they were creating.

This insight surprised Linda, and although she continued to use the drug, she began to ask Dylan to do more things for himself. Jan and Linda's discussions about healthier connections expanded, and Linda used the safety she had created with Jan to begin to discover how she actually felt about her marriage, how to begin to say no at work and at home, and eventually how to reconnect to parts of herself she had lost years earlier. For example, Linda began to give voice to her concerns about Dylan's OxyContin use, even though it was prescribed by a doctor to whom Linda would normally have given away her own authority because of the implicit power difference.

Jan used Linda's concern for Dylan's drug use as an opening to explore Linda's own use of the narcotic. By this time, Linda had developed other safe and supportive relationships with female friends, as well as Jan, so that she could more readily explore her relationship with this drug. Although Linda did not admit to having a drug problem, she found giving up OxyContin much more difficult than her decision to stop drinking. Linda discovered that when she did not take the drug, she became irritable and depressed.

Using a relational perspective, Jan continued to assist Linda in finding parts of herself she was denying. With little prompting, Linda's anger began to emerge. In her early "relational map," Linda had learned to turn off her own feelings and to attend to others in order to keep herself safe. In witnessing how others handled anger, Linda had never even let herself near the experience of feeling anger herself. Her mother buried anger; her father acted it out. Both methods are dangerous, and in Linda's case, denying her anger became life threatening. Since the feeling had to go somewhere, Linda did what many women unwittingly learn to do: protect their connection with others by turning their feelings inward—in this case, resulting in depression.

Linda began to feel her anger and slowly tested out expressing it in treatment sessions. With Jan's support, Linda confronted Jan on several perceived instances of unfairness and insensitivity. For example, Linda told Jan she thought it was unfair when she was charged for a session after becoming sick and canceling at the last minute. This represented one of the first times in her life that Linda had felt the security of a relationship enough to directly challenge it. She and Jan were able to work out these feelings and agree on ways to resolve the issues. Eventually, Linda was able to express anger to family members. As Linda became better at addressing her feelings, she was able to completely stop her drug use. She described the experience of expressing anger as transforming.

Despite previous objections, Linda was finally willing to participate in Alcoholics Anonymous (AA) and to use the program's Twelve Steps in her overall recovery. She had come to see herself as a competent woman with an addiction problem. She had found a way to be a part of the program without feeling like she was losing herself or being compliant to it. She objected to some parts of the traditions but sought out a few safe others who could support her voice without having to defend AA. With this support, Linda engaged more fully in the recovery process and later with the recovery community, eventually going on to serve on organizing committees for the program.

Once sober, Linda continued to increase her support network and became more intimate with her husband. This intimacy included authentic, gentle confrontation of Dylan regarding his drug use and his passivity in his medical care. With her support, Dylan changed doctors and began utilizing alternative therapies, decreasing his reliance on pain relievers for his disease. Through their more secure attachment, Linda and Dylan propelled each other to grow personally and expanded their relationships with others. Although they have some rocky times, Linda and Dylan remain committed to each other, and Linda has maintained her sobriety.

Source: "The Relational Model: A New Perspective on Women's Substance Abuse." Reprinted with permission of Sue Marriott, LMSW-ACP, CGP.

(Cocozza, Jackson, Hennigan, Morrissey, Reed, Fallot et al., 2005; Farley, Golding, Young, Mulligan, Minkoff, 2004; Messina, Marinelli-Casey, Hillhouse, Ang, Hunter, & Rawson, 2008; Sacks, McKendrick, & Banks, 2008). Addressing trauma is especially critical in substance abuse treatment as it may be the root of substance use disorders and/or other co-occurring disorders such as PTSD, as well as a consequence of substance use disorders, such as intimate partner violence.

Men and women in the general population may have different propensities for specific mental disorders. For example, research shows that when both sexes experience sexual abuse during childhood, women are more likely to develop affective disorders, PTSD, and BPD in its aftermath, whereas men are more likely to develop APD. Cutajar et al.'s (2010) large, prospective study of 2,688 Australian subjects with a childhood sexual abuse record plus matched control subjects without a childhood sexual abuse record reported that abused females were nearly 2.5 times more likely, later on, to have an affective disorder diagnosis, more than 7 times more likely to have PTSD, and more than 7.5 times more likely to have BPD than their female controls; abused males were no more likely than their male controls to have any of these three disorders. Abused females were also more likely than abused males to have these three disorder diagnoses. On the other hand, abused males were nearly 4 times more likely to have an APD diagnosis than male controls; whereas there was no difference between the abused females and the female controls on APD diagnosis. Abused males were also more likely to have an APD diagnosis than abused females. Both the abused males and abused females were more likely to have a substance use disorder than their non-abused counterparts, and there was no significant difference between abused men and women regarding the likelihood of having a substance use disorder.

Substance-abusing men and women, in particular, may be susceptible to different types of co-occurring disorders. The more frequently found comorbid psychiatric disorders among addicted women are depression, anxiety, and eating disorders; among addicted men, they are APD, pathological gambling, and "residual attention deficit disorder" (Blume & Zilberman, 2005). Some studies, mostly of samples of incarcerated substance abusers, show that although women are more likely to have internalizing disorders (e.g., anxiety, depression) (Langan & Pelissier, 2001; Messina, Marinelli-Casey, Hillhouse, Rawson et al., 2008; Zlotnick et al., 2008), the sexes do not differ on APD (Langan & Pelissier, 2001; Messina et al.) or other externalizing disorders (e.g., hyperactivity, impulse control disorders,

or aggression) (Zlotnick et al.). Messina et al. reported that methamphetamine-dependent MD men with APD tended to have more adverse childhood events (ACEs) than MD men without APD, but there was no significant difference between the number of ACEs of MD men with and without depression. In contrast, MD women with depression had significantly more ACEs than MD Women without depression. MD women with APD also tended to have more ACEs than MD women without APD.

Substance use disorders and co-occurring mental disorders may be closely related to an individual's experience of childhood and adulthood trauma although identification of the specific causal mechanism between them awaits more research. Men and women seem to be prone to different traumatic events. Farley et al. (2004) studied 959 chemical-dependent outpatients and found that women were significantly more likely to have experienced "rape" or "other sexual assault" and to have been "beaten by family member" or to have experienced a "break-in while present" than men; whereas men were more likely to have been "mugged," experienced "war events," and "saw someone killed or injured" than women. The two sexes did not differ regarding the likelihood of chance meeting partner violence. Furthermore, men and women may respond to trauma differently. For example, the National Comorbidity Study reported that 51 percent of females and 61 percent of males had experienced a trauma in their lifetime, and of them, 20 percent of females and 8 percent of males manifested PTSD symptoms (Kessler et al., cited in Kubiak & Rose's review, 2007). The level of burden or intensity of the traumatic events may also affect an individual's reactions and adaptations. For example, Farley et al. found that approximately 30 percent of substance abuse treatment patients they studied who experienced zero to four traumatic events relapsed compared to 40 percent of those who experienced 5 to 13 traumatic events. An individual's previous experience and his or her resilience may also contribute to how he or she reacts to trauma.

Traumatic events are prevalent among individuals with substance use disorders. Although traumatic events do not inevitably result in PTSD, many substance-abusing clients suffer partial PTSD or other sub-clinical mental disorder symptoms, which often sabotage their substance abuse treatment, precipitate relapses, and prevent long-term recovery. Routine screening, assessment, and treatment of traumas among substance abusing clients have been emphasized in the recent decades (Farley et al., 2004). A systemic procedure and a structured screening interview for traumatic experience are recommended for eliciting reliable information (Bastiaens & Kendrick, 2002). Gender issues may also be relevant in trauma screening. For example, Ketring and Feinauer (1999) found that men and women yielded similar scores on a research tool called the Trauma Symptom Checklist-33 (TSC-33 [Briere & Runtz, 1989]) when they had experienced mild or moderate abuse. However, when the severity of abuse escalated, women's symptoms and trauma scores increased accordingly, but men's symptoms and trauma scores did not increase. Ketring and Feinauer suggest that this may be because women tend to internalize their symptoms regardless of the severity of symptoms, whereas men tend to internalize their relative mild or moderate symptoms but will externalize very severe symptoms. The TSC-33 measures only internalized symptoms. In assessing men for trauma (e.g., sexual abuse), both internalized and externalized symptoms (e.g., antisocial behavior and sexual acting out) must be addressed (Ketring and Feinauer).

Various evidence-based, trauma-informed and trauma-specific interventions and treatments have been developed in the past two decades. Among them are the Trauma Recovery and Empowerment Model for women (TREM) and M-TREM for men (Community Connections, n.d.; SAMHSA, n.d.c; Toussaint, Van DeMark, Bornemann, & Graeber, 2007) and *Seeking Safety* developed to help women who have both a substance use disorder and PTSD (Najavits, 2009). *Seeking Safety* can also be used to help men with a co-occurring substance use disorder and PTSD or traumas (Najavits et al., 2009). Messina,

Grella, Cartier, and Torres (2010) used Covington's *Helping Women Recover and Beyond Trauma* model with substance-abusing female prisoners and found that compared to women in the standard prison-based therapeutic community, women who received this treatment remained in residential aftercare longer, reduced their drug use more, and had a lower rate of re-incarceration after parole (12 months). Covington's model contains four modules (self, relationship, sexuality, and spirituality) plus a focus on "teaching women what trauma and abuse are, helping them to understand typical reactions to trauma and abuse, and developing coping skills" (Messina et al., p. 100). Citing Judith Herman, Covington (2008) stated that trauma is "a disease of disconnection" and it may take three steps to help women to establish "reconnection." The first step is helping women focus on safety issues, build a safe environment, and care for themselves "in the present." The second step involves "remembrance and mourning," with the women expressing their stories of past trauma and mourning the loss of their old selves. Self-soothing and other techniques may be added to this step to lower the possibly higher risk of relapse during this stage. The final step is to help women establish a new self and new future. Clark and Power (2005) suggest that many substance abuse treatment programs may not have staff available to provide trauma-*specific* services, but trauma-*informed* services are cost-effective and can be incorporated by enhancing providers' abilities to screen and assess women's substance abuse, mental health, and trauma-related issues. Trauma-informed services emphasize that providers must understand the effects violence and abuse have on women, value women's strengths, avoid retraumatizing the women, and respect women's participation in developing their own treatment plan. The outcomes of SAMHSA' "Women, Co-occurring Disorders, and Violence Study" showed effectiveness of a comprehensive and integrated trauma-informed approach, and suggested that more integrated counseling generates more favorable results (Cocozza et al., 2005).

Mutual-Help Groups

Today women are about one-third of Alcoholics Anonymous (AA) members (Alcoholics Anonymous World Services, 2008). Some AA meetings are for women only, and some men are holding meetings of their own. Women are featured in many more of the recovery stories in the "Big Book" of Alcoholics Anonymous, and at some meetings, "women are starting 'the Lord's Prayer' with 'Our Father and Mother'" (Davis & DiNitto, 2005, p. 530).

The Twelve Steps of Alcoholics Anonymous have helped many men and women recover, but there is also interest in mutual-help groups developed specifically for women and for men. Kasl (1990) claims that since "the steps were formulated by a white, middleclass male in the 1930s, not surprisingly, they work to break down an over-inflated ego, and put reliance on an all-powerful male God" (pp. 30–31). She believes that most women need just the opposite—to strengthen their sense of self and affirm their own inner wisdom. Earlier, Jean Kirkpatrick (1978) expressed similar sentiments about women's identity. In 1975, she introduced a self-help program called Women for Sobriety (WFS), which she believed could successfully be used alone or as a complement to AA and other programs (Women for Sobriety, 1976).

Rather than the Twelve Steps of AA (see Chapter 6), WFS uses the Thirteen Statements of Acceptance. For example, "I am a competent woman and have much to give life" (Women for Sobriety, 1989). Groups are lead by certified moderators. At the heart of WFS is its New Life Program. Kaskutas (1989) studied WFS and identified four major themes of the program: no drinking, positive thinking, believing one is competent, and growing spiritually and emotionally. She describes the program as follows: During meetings, members focus on what happened to them during the previous week and on current topics posed for discussion. But unlike in AA, members are discouraged from telling the stories of their drinking and from introducing themselves as alcoholics or addicts because these are considered examples of negative rather than positive thinking. During meetings there is much more cross-talk (back and forth conversation) than in AA. Kaskutas calls the WFS program far less directive than AA. For example, members are not told to "keep coming back," to "get a sponsor," or to "work the steps." Participants are encouraged to work the program each day.

Despite differences in the philosophies of AA and WFS, some women take what they need from each program and make good use of both. A survey of 600 WFS members revealed that approximately one-third were also current AA members, primarily for "insurance" against relapse, for the wider availability of meetings, and for sharing, fellowship, and support (Kaskutas, 1994). Kasl (1990) also offers an alternative set of steps to AA that she says emphasize empowerment—for example, "We became willing to let go of our shame, guilt, and other behavior that prevents us from taking control of our lives and loving ourselves." WFS has been adapted for use by men in a program called Men for Sobriety.

Summary

Men and women differ with regard to manifestations of substance use and substance use disorders. Men are more likely to drink and use most types of drugs than women, but the gender gap in rates of use and substance use disorders has narrowed over the decades. Compared to men, women have many heightened vulnerabilities to substance abuse such as physical health problems like liver disease. Women often progress to substance use disorders more quickly than men. Women often begin using alcohol or drugs in harmful ways as the result of having a partner who uses substance in these ways. It is much rarer for a man to begin using because his female partner uses. Power differentials in male-female relationships place women at a disadvantage in negotiating behaviors such as insisting that men practice safe sex by using condoms in order to prevent HIV infection and in sharing injection drug use equipment. Women are less likely to enter substance abuse treatment because they face barriers such as lack of child care or the greater stigma associated with women's substance use disorders. Women often have a more severe level of substance abuse and psychosocial problems than men at admission; however, once in treatment, their outcomes are generally equal to or better than men's. More research is needed to understand this disparity. Scholars have recently emphasized that males are also "gendered beings" and more research is needed to explore the significance of incorporating male-specific developmental issues into practice with substance abusing men. Men and women with substance use disorders have trauma histories that exceed those of men and women who do not have substance use disorders. Women with substance use disorders also have experienced more trauma than men with substance use disorders. In addition to the many types of treatment available for substance use disorders and mental health disorders, trauma-specific and trauma-informed therapy are approaches that may be useful for them.

PART FOUR

Summary and Conclusions

The final section of this book examines the current situation in the United States for providing treatment for alcohol and drug problems, discusses some future possibilities for additional treatment options, and questions the wisdom of continuing to fight the "war on drugs." We advise taking a close look at the legalization of at least some illicit drugs and alternatives such as decriminalizing drug use and providing treatment options, such as heroin replacement therapy, that are not now legally possible in most states. Without broad policy change, changes in treatment, incarceration, and other phenomena are not likely to occur in the drug war or in drug treatment. Because of the increasing importance of insurance coverage and managed care, we also discuss their effects on access to treatment for substance use disorders, and we conclude with some thoughts about the training of substance abuse professionals. We need to keep thinking "outside the box" in order to prevent more cases of alcohol and drug problems and to do a better job in providing treatment and promoting recovery.

CHAPTER 16

Chemical Dependency: Current Issues and Future Prospects

C. Aaron McNeece
Florida State University,
Professor and Dean Emeritus

Diana M. DiNitto
University of Texas at Austin

In the previous chapters, we discussed current knowledge about the epidemiology and etiology of substance abuse problems, approaches to diagnosis and treatment, issues of prevention and policy, and problems in specific populations. Although a great deal is known about the phenomena of substance use and abuse, much remains unknown. One thing is certain: Drug trends are in a constant state of flux, and making predictions about the future is risky. However, there are a number of important issues that substance abuse professionals and public officials should address, including the financing and provision of substance abuse and dependence treatment and fighting the "war on drugs."

That latest drug war has now gone on for four decades with little indication that it will end and no good reason to believe that it can ever be won (Gray, 2001). As Norman (2002) wrote, "Richard Nixon declared the war in 1971, and its aim, as stated later by an act of Congress, was a drug-free society by 1995. If that is still the objective, plainly we have lost. In 1980 there were 50,000 people in custody for drug-related crimes, twenty years later, the number was 400,000" (p. 66). There were actually 458,131 persons incarcerated for drug-related crimes in 2000, almost as many as the entire prison and jail population was in 1980 (474,368) (Justice Policy Institute, 2001). In 2007, there were 1,645,500 adults and 195,700 juveniles arrested for drug abuse violations (BJS, 2011a). The great majority of these arrests were for possession (BJS, 2011b). Moreover, the cost of the drug war has grown astronomically, and there is no evidence that the ever-increasing expenditures have brought us any closer to victory.

The politics of drug control have been described extensively by Goode (1997), Musto & Korsmeyer (2002), and many others. For many involved in this debate, the war on drugs is accepted as an ideology which is not to be questioned. Still others support the drug war based on statistics that are claimed to show a steady decline in drug use. On the other side are organizations such as the Marijuana Policy Project and NORML, advocating the decriminalization or legalization of "less noxious" substances. The traditional "liberal vs. conservative" labels do not always accurately predict one's stance on drug control policy. For example, U.S. Congressman Tom Tancredo (R-Colorado) and writer William F. Buckley both opposed the drug war, while U.S. President Barack Obama has strongly opposed the legalization of drugs. His administration was outspoken in opposing the recent California referendum to legalize marijuana. "Keeping drugs illegal reduces their availability and lessens willingness to use them," says Drug Czar Gil Kerlikowske. "That is why this Administration firmly opposes the legalization of marijuana or any other illicit drug" (O'Brien, 2010).

The producers of alcoholic beverages are also major players in the politics of drug control, with the major brands contributing large sums of money to both political parties. Contributions come from employees, political action committees, owners, and stockholders (Mackinder, 2011). It would be naïve to think that these contributions do not affect policy decisions.

> Consider: In 2010 the federal government spent about two-thirds of its $15.1 billion drug budget on law enforcement and interdiction (ONDCP, 2010). The combined drug enforcement budget for state governments may have been twice that amount (Action America, 2011). A result has been a sky-rocketing prison population—it has tripled in the last two decades—with at least 60 percent of inmates reporting a history of substance abuse. The cost of warehousing nonviolent drug offenders is more than twice as great as treating them. Meanwhile, a study by the RAND Corporation's drug-policy center found that for every dollar spent on treatment, taxpayers save more than seven dollars in other services, largely through reduced crime and medical fees and increased productivity. NIDA projects the savings to be $12 for every dollar spent on treatment (NIDA, 2009). A visit to the emergency room, for instance, costs as much as a month in rehab, and more than 70,000 heroin addicts are admitted to ERs annually. (Orenstein, 2002, p. 36)

Source: From "Staying Clean" by Peggy Orenstein, published in *The New York Times Magazine*, Feb. 10, 2002, is reprinted by permission of the author.

The drug war is a highly charged emotional issue for many individuals and many politically powerful groups. For example, the legalization (or decriminalization or depenalization) of any illicit drug faces a steep uphill battle as long as organized church groups and large factions of both major political parties oppose it.

Nevertheless, we conclude this book with the following observations, which suggest that a major change in strategy is needed:

• *There have always been some people in just about every society who use drugs and some people who* *become dependent on them.* The types of drugs used may vary, as well as the proportion of individuals using them, but drug use is a common historical phenomenon. This is not likely to change (Szasz, 1992).

• *Society cannot prevent all drug use; at most, it may control or regulate it—to an extent.* Various efforts to prohibit drug use, especially in a civil rights-oriented democracy such as the United States, are doomed to failure. Furthermore, the side effects of prohibition efforts may be worse than the direct effects of drug use (Szasz, 1985). The prohibition of beverage alcohol from 1920 to 1933 and the current "war on drugs" are examples of these policy failures.

• *Societal decisions about which drugs to allow and to prohibit are essentially political decisions.* Some drugs with a few positive benefits and many negative effects (e.g., alcohol) and some with unquestionably negative effects (tobacco) are readily available and regulated, while others with comparatively safe risk levels for both addiction and physiological consequences are illegal (marijuana). We have examined the cases against alcohol and tobacco at several points in this book.

• *While the popularity of other drugs has changed, the consumption of alcohol is the one great historical constant in drug use.* Undoubtedly, alcohol's popularity is related to its status as the only legal psychoactive drug that most people can use to get "high," as well as its well-established niche in the national economy.

• *New drugs that are even more debilitating than the current popular drugs will become major problems in this century.* It is impossible to outlaw all potential substances of abuse. As one designer drug is prohibited, molecular changes are made in a clandestine lab and a new drug is on the street almost immediately. Only a decade ago, almost no one had heard of "ecstasy," but in some communities today, especially among youth, it rivals crack cocaine and marijuana in popularity. As society advances in its technological capacity, the chemists who invent new psychoactive drugs will continue refining and improving their products.

• *Incarceration alone does little to break the cycle of illegal drug use and crime. Offenders who are sentenced to incarceration for substance-related offenses have a high rate of recidivism once they are released.* There is little doubt that apprehended drug users will continue to populate the expanding U.S. correctional system well into the twenty-first century. During the last 30 years, there have been record increases in the numbers of persons entering that correctional system. According to the U.S. Bureau of Justice Statistics (BJS, 2010a, p. 2), at the end of 2009, there were 7,225,800 people on probation, in jail or prison, or on parole—about 3.1 percent of adults in the U.S. resident population, or 1 in every 32 adults.

• *Drug abuse treatment has been shown to be demonstrably effective in reducing both drug abuse and drug-related crime.* There is a growing body of evidence, including some studies based on randomized clinical trials, that some people who abuse or are dependent on drugs can be successfully treated (NIDA, 2009; Noonan, 2001; Schilling et al., 2002). Although treatment is not as effective as practitioners want it to be, it is far preferable to incarceration (see Chapter 6).

• *Drug abuse is not a unitary phenomenon.* People who use drugs are diverse in terms of age and developmental level, drugs of abuse and reasons for use, presence of comorbidity, family composition and dynamics, race/ethnicity, gender, and socioeconomic status. Current research shows that understanding this behavior requires contextual knowledge about the individual, the substance(s) he or she uses, and the environment(s) in which he or she does so. As Liddle and Dakof (1995) noted, "The middle-class 14-year-old academic underachiever using alcohol and marijuana once every other week is worlds apart from the 17-year-old high school dropout living in poverty, involved in the juvenile justice system, and smoking marijuana every day. And the daily lives of these two youths are quite different from that of the adult cocaine addict" (p. 522).

• *There is great uncertainty regarding the financing of substance abuse treatment services.* Organizations that finance treatment programs have been

demanding more for their money by insisting on shorter stays and greater reliance on outpatient treatment, but there is a potential for the recent Health Care Reform Act to dramatically increase the number of persons seeking treatment and as a result, the cost of treatment. As many as 90 percent of those who seek treatment do not currently receive it because they lack insurance or other means to pay. Now an estimated 95 percent of the country's legal population may have healthcare coverage—and, thanks to the Mental Health Parity and Addiction Equity Act of 2008 (MHPAEA)-insurers who cover substance abuse treatment must do so at the same level of benefit they provide for other medical conditions (Carise, 2010).

Based on these observations, several courses of action regarding research, policy change, and the delivery of treatment services are outlined in the rest of this chapter.

Research

Research on Harm Reduction

For most harm-reduction approaches, only anecdotal evidence or case studies are available. However, there is convincing evidence of the utility of both methadone maintenance programs and needle/syringe exchange programs. Because intravenous drug users (IDUs) cannot be randomly assigned to experimental (clean needles) and control (shared needles), there are no randomized clinical trials. However, there have been hundreds of comparative, longitudinal, and case studies regarding both methadone maintenance programs and needle/syringe exchange programs. In 1991, Congress requested a study of needle exchange programs (NEP), which was conducted by the General Accounting Office, and it gave qualified support to such programs as decreasing needle sharing while causing no increase in drug use (GAO, 1993; Normand, Vlahov, & Moses, 1995). Another report (Lurie et al., 1993) identified and reviewed almost 2,000 American and foreign studies of needle exchange programs in addition to conducting site visits of 33 programs in 15 cities. The conclusion was that needle risk behavior was dramatically diminished, with no evidence of increased drug use or other public health dangers. One of the programs not only reduced HIV-risk behavior but also increased entry of IDUs into drug abuse treatment (Kaplan, 1993).

A more recent review of research on syringe exchange programs (SEP) (Gibson, Flynn, & Perales, 2001) examined 42 studies, including 23 comparative studies in which needle behavior and HIV status of users of SEPs were compared with those of IDUs not using SEPs. Another 11 of the studies were longitudinal studies of SEP clients only. Two studies were conducted with both community samples and SEP users, and 6 evaluated the ecological impact of SEPs (rate of seropositivity) on the community. The researchers concluded that "there is substantial evidence that syringe exchange programs are effective in preventing HIV risk behavior and HIV seroconversion among IDU" (p. 1338). Ljungberg et al. (1991) found a seroprevalence rate of *zero* in one Swedish city with an SEP, compared to prevalences of up to 60 percent in other cities without SEPs. Another recent study (Riley et al., 2002) concluded that a higher rate of utilization of NEP services is associated with a higher rate of drug treatment utilization. Thus, an overwhelming amount of the research evidence argues for the effectiveness of such harm-reduction approaches as NEPs and SEPs, yet they are illegal in almost all jurisdictions of the United States, and a ban on federal funding for these programs remained in effect until 2009. (Szalavitz, 2009).

The Drug Abuse Treatment Outcome Study (DATOS) found a significant reduction in drug use by clients using methadone (NIDA, 1997). A more recent review of the research on methadone maintenance programs and needle syringe exchange programs by the American Medical Association's Council on Scientific Affairs (Yoast, Williams, Deitchman, & Champion, 2001) concluded that

both have been effective in reducing heroin use and attendant problems (crime, spread of sexually transmitted diseases, etc.) in a cost-effective manner without any negative impact on public health. Other studies (McLellan et al., 1996; Metzger et al., 1993) have concluded that methadone maintenance treatment is an essential strategy for HIV prevention. Brown (1998) concluded that methadone treatment has the greatest capacity of any available treatment for reducing HIV risk behaviors. A National Institute on Drug Abuse (NIDA) review of 23 studies involving 7,900 patients also supported the effectiveness of methadone in reducing HIV infection (NIDA, 2006). Harm-minimization strategies have great potential to reduce drug problems but are some of the least often utilized approaches. We advocate the use of harm minimization strategies and increased use of needle and syringe exchange programs.

Research on Treatment

Drug treatment can also be considered a harm-reduction approach, when the intended objective is a reduction in harm to the user or the community, not an insistence on total abstinence. NIDA (NIDA, 2009) is unequivocal in stating that treatment for drug addiction is as effective as treatment for other chronic diseases, such as diabetes and hypertension. In its *Principles of Drug Addiction Treatment: A Research-Based Guide,* NIDA provides guidance on a dozen specific methods of treatment. This guidance was based on a thorough review of the research literature on various treatment approaches, including randomized assignments of clients in 10 studies (Azrina et al., 1996; Cornish et al., 1997; Crits-Christoph et al., 1999; Henggeler, Pickrel, Brondino, & Crouch, 1996; Higgins et al., 1994; McLellan et al., 1993; Silverman et al., 1996; Stephens, Roffman, & Simpson, 1994; Woody et al., 1995), as well as dozens of other studies using comparative and longitudinal designs. The most common outcome measure used in all of these studies was a reduction in drug use.

One review located in the Cochrane Library (Foxcroft et al., 2002) focused on primary prevention. It examined 56 randomized, nonrandomized, and interrupted time series designs, and found 20 of them to show evidence of effectiveness. While no firm conclusions were reached about the effectiveness of short- and medium-term prevention interventions, the Strengthening Families Program (SFP) showed promise as an effective longer-term prevention program. The Substance Abuse and Mental Health Services Administration (SAMHSA, 2003) features model prevention programs that have been tested in communities, schools, social service organizations, and workplaces across the United States and provided solid proof of having prevented or reduced substance abuse and other related high-risk behaviors.

The DATOS research, mentioned earlier in this chapter and in Chapter 6, demonstrated effectiveness not only for methadone treatment but also for long-term residential programs, short-term inpatient programs, and outpatient programs (NIDA, 1997), using posttreatment drug use as the outcome measure. A later NIDA report (1999a) found that a combination of individual and group counseling for cocaine addicts was more effective than other forms of treatment in reducing drug use. A four-year follow-up of a randomized clinical trial with 118 substance-abusing juveniles provided evidence of the efficacy of multisystemic therapy (Henggeler et al., 2002). At least 20 clinical trials have investigated the efficacy of motivational interviewing (MI) with substance abusers, and all but one found MI to be effective (Noonan, 2001). Schilling et al. (2002) found MI effective in encouraging alcohol abusers to participate in self-help programs after detoxification.

Project MATCH, a major treatment evaluation study funded by the National Institute on Alcohol Abuse and Alcoholism (NIAAA), examined three different behavioral treatments on reduced drinking: Twelve-Step facilitation therapy, cognitive-behavioral therapy, and motivational enhancement therapy (NIAAA, 1996). Overall, Project MATCH participants showed significant and sustained improvement in their number of abstinent days and a decrease in the number of drinks per drinking days, with few clinically significant outcome differences among the three treatment approaches. In a review of the literature on the cost/benefit analysis of drug treatment, Cartwright (2000) examined 18 cost/benefit studies and concluded that "a persistent finding is that benefits exceed costs, even when not all benefits are accounted for in the analysis" (p. 11).

Project COMBINE (Combining Medications and Behavioral Interventions) was a randomized controlled trial sponsored by NIAAA. It was conducted from January, 2001 to January, 2004 among 1,383 recently alcohol-abstinent patients with diagnoses of primary alcohol dependence. There were eight groups of patients who received medical management with 16 weeks of naltrexone or acamprosate or both, as well as placebo groups, with or without a combined behavioral intervention. A ninth group received a behavioral intervention only. Patients were also evaluated for up to 1 year after treatment, and all treatment groups showed substantial reductions in drinking. Patients receiving naltrexone, medical management, and CBI had the highest number of abstinent days (Anton, et al., 2006).

The outcome measures associated with almost all of the research cited above are consistent with a harm-reduction approach but not with a zero-tolerance (abstinence) approach. Measures include such items as reduction in alcohol and drug use, reduction in the rate of needle sharing and other HIV risk behaviors, reduction in the rate of contagion of various diseases, reduction in the rate of crime, increased length of time in treatment, higher treatment completion rates, and increased posttreatment employment. Although some clients do achieve abstinence, these existing programs are most successful at helping people *reduce* their drug use.

Drug abuse and drug dependence (or addiction) are not identical phenomena. The *Diagnostic and Statistical Manual of Mental Disorders* (4th ed., Text Revision) (APA, 2000)[1] constructs of abuse and dependence make these distinctions. The relationship of different treatment contexts and the interaction of different patient population characteristics and cultures are important variables to consider in treatment effectiveness. Current research has begun to focus more specifically on questions such as: What kinds of therapy delivered by what kinds of therapists are effective both in the short term and the long term, reflected by what breadth of changes, with what kinds of people with what kinds of substance use disorders, and how do those changes come about? (NIDA, 1999a).

Medication Assisted Treatment.   There is increasing concern about the appropriateness of viewing alcoholism and drug addiction as phenomena amenable to the medical model. There are, of course, many justifications for this point of view. First, it is much easier to finance treatment if chemical dependency is defined as a medical problem. Second, many of the physiological consequences of alcohol and heroin use are seemingly appropriate for medical treatment, according to Liddle and Dakof (1995).

The current treatment consensus indicates that opiate addicts who remain in methadone maintenance treatment for one year or more reduce their opiate and other drug use and reduce their involvement in illegal activity. Moreover, recent evidence indicates that methadone in conjunction with counseling and psychotherapy shows the best outcomes. Family treatment of opiate-addiction without long-term, higher dose methadone maintenance would not represent current state-of-the-science treatment. More recent clinical studies of other pharmacotherapies such as naltrexone and acamprosate demonstrate their effectiveness in treating substance abuse (Batki, et al., 2010; Science Daily, 2010). However, except for the medical detoxification of alcohol and heroin users, most treatment consists of talk therapies and self-help programs. Providers continue to use treatments out of tradition and habit, not because of evidence of their effectiveness.

Research Problems.   Too much drug and alcohol abuse and treatment research has narrowly focused on specific subpopulations that may behave quite differently from other groups. At the risk of overgeneralizing, white male alcoholics have received a great deal more attention than most other groups. Women alcoholics and drug users have been underrepresented in chemical dependency research, although that is slowly changing. Research on illicit drugs, especially opiates, has been conducted primarily on those who have been arrested and have become involved in the criminal justice system, the majority of whom are racial and ethnic minorities. Research on noncriminal substance abusers has concentrated on low-income groups and special populations, such as Veterans Administration patients.

Co-Occurring Mental Disorders.   One area of research that recently has gained more attention is the study of persons who are diagnosed with a substance use disorder and a co-occurring mental disorder, such as conduct disorder, affective disorders, antisocial behavior, depression, and schizophrenia. Given that estimates of adults with mental illness who also have a substance abuse problem range from 40 to 60 percent, the lack of research information about comorbidity prevents both the development of an accurate and complete description of the population and an understanding of the extent of the problem (Springer, McNeece, & Arnold, 2003). To date, this research has produced only a few encouraging findings about dual-diagnosis treatment (Batki, et al., 2010).

Spontaneous Recovery.   Another avenue of research that has been ignored is the study of persons who have recovered from chemical dependency without treatment. One study (Biernacki, 1990) of 101 opiate addicts who recovered without the help of any formal treatment discovered a potentially useful pattern of recovery among these persons, rather than a *spontaneous remission*. This pattern included forming a resolve, becoming abstinent, creating an alternative, dealing with the craving problem, and becoming "ordinary." Sobell, Ellingstand, and Sobell (2000) reviewed the problems in researching this area more than a decade ago. More recently Klingemann and Sobell (2007) edited a volume summarizing the issues in "self-change from addictive behaviors," but little more clinical research has been conducted.

Self-Efficacy and Treatment. Another promising line of research involves the application of the concept of self-efficacy to addictive behaviors, as outlined by DiClemente (1986). Originally conceptualized by Albert Bandura as an individual's perception of competence in his or her environment and related to Julian Rotter's concept of internal-external locus of control, the application of self-efficacy to addictive behaviors and the relapse process began with nicotine addiction and was then extended to eating disorders and alcoholic dependence (DiClemente, Fairhurst, & Piotrowski, 1995). DiClemente et al. (1995) stress that the application of self-efficacy requires practitioners to view addictive behaviors from a biopsychosocial perspective. Prochaska and DiClemente (1992) have conceptualized a four-stage typology of planned behavior change—from (1) precontemplation, (2) contemplation, (3) action, and (4) maintenance—that is common to smokers, drug abusers, persons with eating disorders, and alcoholics (see Chapter 5). A scale to measure alcohol abstinence self-efficacy (DiClemente, Carbonari, Rosario, & Hughes, 1994) has been developed and promising research efforts are now underway to expand the utility of this cognitive concept to relapse prevention in alcohol and substance abuse programs. Gwaltney et al.'s (2009) meta-analysis found that self-efficacy had a significant effect on smoking cessation.

Future Treatment Research. Innovative treatment methods are sorely needed; however, it *does* seem prudent to begin on a small scale and thoroughly evaluate the impact of each new method before allowing it to proliferate. Law enforcement and treatment professionals are so desperate for ways to deal with the growing problems of abuse and addiction that it is understandable why they might be willing to use unproven methods. The more traditional approaches have been unsuccessful with a relatively large proportion of clients, yet treatment providers seem to cling to them instead of investing in approaches that provide greater evidence of effectiveness (Miller et al., 1995). Several years ago the National Institute on Drug Abuse launched a Clinical Trials Network[1] to test the efficacy of new treatments for drug addiction using rigorous research designs. About 50 clinical trials have either been completed or are currently underway. There is hope that knowledge of drug treatment effectiveness will expand dramatically over the next decade (NIDA, 2011).

In 1998, a group of addiction clinicians and researchers formed the North American Opiate Medications Initiative (NAOMI) with the goal of scientifically examining the effectiveness of heroin-assisted therapy in treating long-term heroin addicts. Since traditional methadone maintenance therapy is not attractive to most heroin addicts, perhaps the use of heroin will draw more addicts into clinics. The controlled use of injectable heroin to treat addicts had been practiced in England as early as the 1920s (Kuo, Fisher, & Vlahov, 2000), but no systematic research was conducted on the project. There have been subsequent experiments in both the Netherlands and Switzerland, and Denmark's parliament has debated the possibility of a "heroin experiment" (Jepsen, 2001). Even though it was generally regarded as successful, critics of the Swiss experiment point out that (1) it was not a randomized clinical trial, (2) the retention rate was not much greater than for methadone maintenance programs, and (3) the heroin maintenance was combined with psychotherapy, so it is not possible to isolate the effects of heroin maintenance alone. A Canadian randomized clinical trial conducted under NAOMI auspices from 2005 to 2008 demonstrated that heroin therapy keeps patients in treatment, improves their health and reduces illegal activity (NAOMI, 2008). However, given the controversies over methadone maintenance therapy, the United States is not likely to become involved in the near future in heroin maintenance experiments or research. Other nations continue to investigate this mode of treatment, and they will eventually accumulate a body of knowledge that could possibly influence U.S. policy.

The latest promising findings come from the "decade of the brain" research on the neurobiological basis of addiction and craving. Substance abuse is known to produce physical changes in the brain—changes that reinforce addictive behaviors. Some medications have been demonstrated to be moderately effective when combined with behavioral treatment, while others have had little or no effect. (See Chapter 3 and the previous section on Project COMBINE for further information on this avenue of research.)

Delivery of Treatment Services

Chemical dependency treatment services, especially the public programs available to low-income persons, are woefully inadequate. The private tier of services is so expensive that they are generally unavailable to anyone except the wealthy or those fortunate enough to have adequate insurance. While 16 percent of Americans have no health insurance, almost 29 percent of the poor are uninsured, as they are covered neither by private insurance nor by public programs such as Medicaid (Gallup, 2009). Even those who do have health insurance are not always covered for substance abuse treatment. In the present age of *managed care*, insurance companies seem to have decided that substance abuse and mental health treatment are not essential services. All of that could change with the passage of the Patient Protection and Affordable Care Act (PPACA) of 2010. However, since this legislation is being tested in the courts, and a movement is underway to repeal it, the impact on substance abuse treatment is uncertain.

According to a Robert Wood Johnson study (2008), publicly-funded agencies offer more substance abuse treatment services than privately funded ones. So do agencies with more employees and agencies with more female clients. Government agencies, compared to privately funded nonprofits, offer more core services, as do programs that are hospital-based, have more employees, and serve more clients who were opiate-dependent. It seems essential to adequately fund public agencies that deliver substance abuse treatment services.

Third-Party Coverage

Early in its existence, the NIAAA decided that providing health insurance for alcoholism was the best way to assure a stable funding base for treatment. State alcoholism agencies joined the effort, and by 1981, 33 states had mandated group health insurance providers to offer optional coverage for treatment. The federal Health Maintenance Organization Act of 1973 required all HMOs to provide alcoholism treatment services in order to qualify for federal subsidies (Weisner & Room, 1988), and similar initiatives regarding drug abuse treatment eventually resulted in mandatory coverage laws in 18 states and the District of Columbia (Gerstein & Harwood, 1990). Growing numbers of workplace-based employee assistance programs provided chemical dependency services. By 2006, 88 percent of all insured workers were covered for substance abuse treatment (Gabel, Whitmore, Pickreign, Levit, Coffey, & Vandivort-Warren, 2007).

In 2002, the National Association of Social Workers (NASW) adopted a policy statement endorsing *parity* for substance abuse and mental health treatment (O'Neill, 2002), and the National Association of Addiction Professionals (NAADAC) also strongly endorsed parity in health insurance coverage for mental health with other medical conditions. There have been some small victories in this area. For example, a grassroots movement in New Hampshire led to the adoption of a partial parity bill by the state legislature (Curley, 2002). More recently the Mental Health Parity and Addiction Equity Act of 2008 (MHPAEA) requires insurers who cover substance abuse treatment to do so at the same level of benefit they provide for other medical conditions. The legislation, however, does not define substance abuse treatment services (Carise, 2010).

Nevertheless, the high cost of treatment for both alcohol and drug abuse, despite improvements in treatment effectiveness, has prompted insurers of all types to reconsider providing coverage. It appears that the movement toward universal coverage of chemical dependency treatment has leveled off or perhaps lost ground. Today, private coverage is likely to be optional, expensive, and more difficult to obtain, and when it is available, insurers are insisting on more effective and cheaper methods of treatment. Some third-party payers have strongly questioned the value of treatment, and there is a movement to view drug and alcohol treatment as part of the nonmedical/surgical fringe of health coverage that may be differentially limited to trim increasing overall costs. A recent study suggests that parity legislation has had no impact on the utilization of substance abuse treatment services (Azzone, et al., 2011). Partly because of current economic conditions, high unemployment, the rising cost of health care and health insurance, and new limitations on benefits, the immediate prospect for increasing insurance coverage for substance abuse treatment is not good.

Managed Care

During the 1990s, there were serious and successful attempts to cut the costs of treating drug and alcohol abuse. Stimulated by Miller and Hester (1986) and Saxe, Dougherty, Esty, and Fine's (1983) work, managed-care companies attempted to direct all drug clients away from hospital-based inpatient programs toward outpatient services. The primary motivation for this movement was evidence that inpatient programs were more expensive and generally no more effective than outpatient programs (see Chapter 6). A recent trend is for states to require Medicaid recipients to enroll in managed care programs. Sixteen states now have arrangements where a lump-sum payment is made to a private company to provide services to Medicaid recipients (Galewitz, 2011). By 2008, Medicaid programs in all states except Connecticut, Georgia, North Dakota, and Texas provided some coverage for substance abuse treatment. However, there were restrictions such as co-payment requirements, caps on payments, and limitations on types of treatment in most states (Kaiser Family Foundation, 2008).

Paradoxically, the entry of private for-profit companies into the field of inpatient substance abuse treatment contributed to the prohibitive cost of such care (Horgan & Levine, 1998). When the primary motivation is profit, cost-containment strategies can have a devastating effect on clients with substance abuse disorders. According to Roman, Johnson, and Blum (2000), private treatment agencies have had to greatly diversify their services as a way of surviving the cost-containment strategies of managed care, but the final result has been that clients have experienced increasing difficulty in obtaining services.

An important current trend is the merging of public- and private-sector care with the collapsing of boundaries between public, not-for-profit, and for-profit agencies (Paulson, 1996). There are three types of managed care plans (MedlinePlus, 2011):

- Health Maintenance Organizations (HMOs) usually only pay for care within the network. You choose a primary care doctor who coordinates most of your care.
- Preferred Provider Organizations (PPOs) usually pay more if you get care within the network, but they still pay a portion if you go outside.
- Point of Service (POS) plans let you choose between an HMO or a PPO each time you need care.

Managed-care organizations accumulate information about accepted clinical practices, their costs, and their appropriateness and effectiveness as treatment strategies and use this information to generate protocols for permitting and disallowing reimbursement for particular services. At least in theory, if managed-care strategies for drug and alcohol treatment are supported by adequate research on treatment effectiveness, they can ensure access to appropriate treatment while containing the costs (Gerstein & Harwood, 1990, p. 286). The introduction of managed care to Massachusetts Medicaid clients apparently reduced substance abuse treatment costs without cutting services or restricting access for disadvantaged groups (Magura, Horgan, Mertens, & Shepard, 2002). This case seems to be the exception, however. Most studies of managed care have indicated that it has had a severely negative impact on access to treatment for substance use disorders (Hay Group, 2000).

There are two basic types of managed-care cost-containment strategies (Fortney & Booth, 2001). *Demand-side*, or *cost-sharing*, *strategies* require clients to pay for health care costs up front through coinsurance, copayments, and deductibles in an effort to reduce the use of unnecessary services. *Supply-side strategies*—such as utilization review, prospective certification or preadmission review of hospital stays, gatekeeping, the use of preferred providers who cooperate on planned treatment approaches, and specialized case management—are also directed at cost containment, with the onus placed on the managed-care organization to provide only necessary services (Sederer & St. Clair, 1990). Cost sharing has been shown to reduce the use of mental health services, and cost sharing has increased more substantially for mental health and substance abuse services than for other health services over the last decade (Jensen, Rost, Burton, & Bulycheva, 1998). A more recent study indicates that decreases in cost sharing have little effect on utilization rates, which were "surprisingly" low (Brooks, 2011). Supply-side cost-containment strategies appear to have a greater impact on the availability of services for rural residents, since "provider choice restrictions have a more negative impact on the geographic accessibility of rural residents compared to urban residents" (Fortney & Booth, 2001, p. 191).

There are obviously many tensions between managed-care organizations and insurers, on the one hand, and residential treatment organizations (especially hospital-based programs), on the other. As discussed earlier, there is some evidence that treatment outcomes are related to length of treatment, and there is agreement that some clients need lengthy, inpatient services (Gerstein & Harwood, 1990; NIDA, 2009). Nevertheless, the types of brief interventions provided by the general health sector for drug abusers and at-risk drinkers are popular because they are relatively inexpensive. However, brief, inexpensive interventions may not be offered in cases where they are not reimbursable. Legislation regarding managed care has focused primarily on cost containment and has not adequately dealt with its potential to compromise the quality of treatment (Newman & Bricklin, 1991). Still, until service providers have evidence that the more expensive methods produce better outcomes, the cost-containment philosophies of managed-care organizations will be difficult to refute.

Public Funding

Unlike other health expenditures, the majority of both substance abuse and mental health treatment programs are financed with public funds. Public funding of substance abuse treatment rose to 77 percent in 2003 Medicaid and Medicare contributed 30 percent of the public share, with other federal programs contributing 19 percent and state and local governments providing 52 percent of the public expenditures (SAMHSA, 2007). Under current federal guidelines, states have great discretion in deciding how many (or how few) services will be provided under Medicaid, and coverage for substance use disorders is quite limited (Scanlon, 2002). Finding a service provider who will accept Medicaid can also be quite difficult. There are a few exceptions, such as Oregon, where the implementation of a capitated substance abuse benefit appears to have increased access to those services for state Medicaid clients. Nevertheless, by the year 2014, Medicaid alone is projected to pay for 20 percent of the costs for all substance abuse treatment (Levit, Kassed, Coffey, Mark, Stranges, Buck, et al., 2008). Access rates for clients admitted to substance abuse treatment increased from 5.5 percent under the fee-for-service arrangement in 1994 to 7.7 percent under the capitated system in 1997 (NIDA, 2000). The highest access rate was achieved by a managed-care plan that conducted extensive outreach among potential clients, routinely screened for substance abuse, and maintained strong ties with social service providers in the metropolitan area it served.

Within a few years of the passing of the welfare reform legislation (the Personality Responsibility and Work Opportunity Reconciliation Act of 1996), forty states had taken advantage of federal rules allowing the use of some Temporary Assistance for Needy Families (TANF) funds for nonmedical substance abuse treatment services, including screening, assessment, and residential child care (Scanlon, 2002). Even with the assistance of Medicaid, Medicare, and other state and local funding, total substance abuse treatment spending has not increased at the same rate as other health expenditures, and with state budgets tightening, public spending for these services is likely to decline. Public programs for substance abuse treatment are generally either means tested (e.g., Medicaid and TANF, which serve only very poor people) or limited to specifically eligible populations (Medicare for the elderly, the Veterans Administration for veterans, etc.), leaving the rest of the population with few options but to pay cash for services or to find an insurance company that will cover substance use disorders. The hope is that PPACA will increase access. The quality of treatment services and the form of service delivery will undoubtedly be impacted by recent changes in health care policy and the restructuring of delivery systems (Stewart & Horgan, 2011).

Policy Change

We proposed a number of policy changes in Chapter 8 that we will not repeat here. We will remind the reader, however, that we think the U.S. national drug policy should be guided not by the almost exclusive notion of zero tolerance but by the overall philosophy of harm reduction—that is, minimizing risks both to the user (micro harm reduction) and to the larger society (macro harm reduction) (MacCoun & Reuter, 2001). This does not necessarily mean that the United States should legalize or decriminalize illicit drugs, although that option certainly should be given serious consideration. As we said in Chapter 8, a harm-reduction strategy can be pursued without either legalizing or decriminalizing illicit drugs. It does mean, for instance, that methadone maintenance clinics and needle/syringe exchange programs should be expanded and that the use of medications such as buprenorphine should be pursued (e.g., buprenorphine does not have to be taken every day and can now be legally prescribed by physicians). The continuing AIDS crisis alone is enough to justify these changes. Perhaps on a less controversial level, why not require brewers and distillers to add vitamins and minerals to alcoholic beverages in order to prevent some of the nutritional problems associated with alcohol dependence?

Decriminalization should be seriously considered for another very practical reason: The financial burdens on the nation will greatly increase if the incarceration of drug offenders continues at the present rate. With the total annual expenditure for the "war on drugs" more than $40 billion (Action America, 2011), two-thirds of these funds are spent on criminal justice and interdiction and only one-third on treatment and prevention (Schmoke, 1997). Not only is this an immense financial problem, but it is also responsible for an overall increase in criminality and disrespect for society and its institutions. Just like Prohibition, the war on drugs is perceived as illogical, unfair, and unenforceable. Instead of guaranteeing high profits to those who "bootleg" alcohol, the current approach guarantees them to drug dealers.

More than 7 million Americans are currently under correctional supervision, partly as a result of severe penalties and mandatory sentencing policies. In 1994, one out of three black men between the ages of 20 and 29 was incarcerated or under court supervision (U.S. Bureau of Justice Statistics, 2001), and in 2009, African-Americans were incarcerated in state and federal prisons at a rate six times higher than whites (U.S. Bureau of Justice Statistics, 2010b), leaving large sections of the inner cities economically and socially devastated. Cocaine users who spend a year or two in prison and receive no treatment are much more likely to become involved in other criminal activity once they are returned to the community. In many states, persons convicted of murder, armed robbery, and rape are being released from prison early to make room for the dramatic increase in drug offenders. There is, of course, a large justice system industry that has a vested interest in continuing the "war on drugs." Without it, police departments, correctional institutions, and other justice system components would find it difficult to justify the sizes of their current budgets (King & Mauer, 2002).

President Obama and his drug czar have indicated that they favor a softer approach to the drug war, shifting to a more public health oriented model rather than a criminal justice model. Suggested changes include the lifting of the federal ban on needle and syringe exchange programs and stopping the raids on state approved medical marijuana facilities (Fields, 2009). However, within a year of taking office the president had "cranked up efforts" to oppose the legalization of marijuana. U.S. Attorney General Eric Holder said he would "vigorously enforce" federal narcotics laws, even if voters approved the measure (California's Proposition 19), and "is considering all available legal and policy options" (Hoeffel, 2010). Despite presidential rhetoric, we see little change in the current administration's position on the "war on drugs."

While so many people are being imprisoned for illicit drug use, the federal government continues to provide subsidies and price supports to tobacco farmers and to benefit from tax revenues on both tobacco and alcohol sales. Remember that tobacco alone kills more people each year than all illicit drugs combined! It is no surprise that many people fail to see any rationality or fairness in current U.S. policies.

Implications for Education and Training

Should the United States shift a substantial amount of its current resources from interdiction/enforcement to treatment and prevention, the demand for services would increase. This has already happened in California, where Proposition 36 requires treatment rather than incarceration for first- and second-time drug offenders (Drug Policy Alliance, 2002). Increased demand for services will clearly require a larger cadre of professionals equipped to provide those services.

The Association for Medical Education and Research in Substance Abuse (AMERSA, 2011) has developed a strategic plan for interdisciplinary faculty development in this area. Moreover, this group has chided social work, nursing, and other helping professions for not adequately preparing students with the knowledge necessary to address alcohol and other drug disorders. The helping professions have shied away from working with substance-abusing clients for four reasons:

1. Clients with substance use disorders have a reputation for being difficult to work with, and failures are more common that success stories. However, they may be similar to treating those with other *chronic* medical conditions than many realize. With the rapidly expanding knowledge about how to more effectively treat these clients (NIDA, 2009), health-related professions may be more inclined to serve people with alcohol and drug problems.

2. Many of these clients have been stigmatized by their behavior, being labeled as "criminal," and the helping professions have also shied away from working with justice system clients (Gibelman & Schervish, 1997). If the United States were to decriminalize illicit

substance use, less stigma would be attached to substance abusers, since they will no longer be criminals.

3. Appropriate insurance coverage for substance use disorders and increased public funding to treat substance use disorders could assist in encouraging medical and mental health professionals to provide these services (DiNitto, 2002). In light of current national and state budget shortfalls, there is concern that mental health and substance abuse treatment service budgets will be severely restrained and that people with substance use disorders will be unable to find services.

4. There are not enough professionals who specialize in treating substance abuse disorders to provide care to the number of people who need such services. Educating a wide variety of health and human service professionals to intervene, especially before problems become serious, is a promising strategy, especially given the demonstrated effectiveness of brief interventions and motivational enhancement approaches (Miller & Weisner, 2002).

Without the necessary training, many serious substance abuse problems will continue to go unnoticed and untreated. With the explosion of knowledge in such areas as the neurobiology of addiction, even those substance abuse professionals who have had formal training may need additional education (Erickson & White, 2009). A degree of cross-training in mental health will also be necessary because of the high proportion of clients who have both substance abuse and mental health problems (McNeece, 2003; also see Chapter 13).

Summary and Concluding Thoughts

When (or if) the "war on drugs" ends, more will be needed than simply better-trained clinicians to work with substance-abusing clients. If an end to the war were declared today, concerted action by social workers, psychologists, rehabilitation counselors, and other helping professionals still would be needed to modify or develop social policies to be consistent with a harm-reduction approach. This would include efforts to destigmatize and reintegrate clients returning from the criminal justice system and working to overturn decades of mistrust and suspicion in minority communities caused by racist drug war policies, such as harsher sentences for crack cocaine users than powder cocaine users (U.S. Sentencing Commission, 2011). Recent policy changes would somewhat lessen the adverse effects of harsher sentences for African Americans. Physicians, psychologists, counselors, nurses, social workers, and other health professionals must redouble their efforts to advocate for better access to treatment, including parity for substance treatment in third-party health coverage (O'Neill, 2002). The bans on public assistance benefits such as food stamps and public housing to persons who are convicted of drug offenses must also be eliminated (Adams, Onek, & Riker, 1998; DiNitto, 2002). Such policies are detrimental to these individuals and to their families, especially their children. Current federal legislation also does not allow drug addicts and alcoholics to receive Social Security Disability Insurance or Supplemental Security Income (Conklin, 1997). Legislation was recently changed to ease restrictions on college students convicted of drug offenders as adults to retain eligibility for federal student financial aid (Health Care and Education Reconciliation Act of 2010 [Pub.L. 111-152]). Rather than being declared ineligible for periods of time or requiring them to complete a rehabilitation program, they can now provide two drug-free urine specimens to have their aid reinstated. In addition, the termination of aid now applies only to those who were receiving student financial aid at the time of conviction.

With the explosion of knowledge about substance abuse, professionals in this area need to do a better job of translating research knowledge into clinical practice (DiNitto, 2002). Efforts such as the Clinical Trials Network, the 13 CSAT-funded regional Addiction Technology Transfer Centers

(ATTCs), and CSAT's Practice/Research Collaboratives (PRCs) are steps in the right direction.

Social work educators should think of new ways to utilize the Internet and distance-learning strategies to assist persons living in remote areas and those lacking transportation. In addition, the Internet could carry new developments in knowledge to clinicians and establish an ongoing dialog among researchers, clinicians, treatment organizations, policymakers, and consumers. This dialog should include matters of research along with their ethical implications. For example, consider the apparent possibility of discovering hard evidence of a genetic vulnerability for alcoholism (Reich et al., 1998). What should be done with that knowledge? And how should it be incorporated into educational programs? The potential for its misuse should be obvious.

The "war on drugs" also has important implications for U.S. relations with the rest of the world. It affects how the United States is perceived as a member of the family of nations. Drug eradication programs in Latin America have exacerbated human rights violations, helped forge or strengthen alliances between guerrillas and peasant growers, and strengthened undemocratic governments. Drug eradication efforts can lead to significant environmental damage, and the risks of herbicidal and biological weapons are frequently ignored by U.S. drug policy officials (Brisman, 2008).

The stakes in the United States' "war on drugs" are enormous. Generations of young people are at risk, not just for addiction but for all the associated problems that go hand in hand with drug and alcohol abuse under current policies: HIV/AIDS, domestic violence, incarceration, and the inability to function economically and socially as normal citizens.

The United States' current approach to treating chemical dependency and substance abuse has not served the nation well. A large part of the

problem is that a systemic perspective has not been used in planning treatment strategies. Too frequently, drug and alcohol abuse have been viewed as individual problems amenable to clinical solutions. Even the use of family therapy models is much too narrow a perspective for a problem of such magnitude. In many instances, practitioners have treated symptoms of drug-taking behavior rather than the underlying causes of such behavior. If the United States has the most widespread abuse of alcohol and *other* drugs of any modern industrial society, it seems likely to be related to factors at the societal level. Realistic solutions must be planned and executed at the same level.

The United States must start by shifting the emphasis from curing the disease of addiction to building personal capacities and increasing opportunities for alternatives in the workplace, in social relationships, and within families and entire communities. As Currie (1993) said,

> When we fail to deal with the underlying social issues of inadequate work, poor housing, abusive families, and poor health care that shape most addicts' lives, we virtually ensure that drug treatment will become a revolving door. And what is truly expensive is cycling drug abusers from treatment to shattered and dismal lives and back again. (p. 279)

The problems of drug abuse and dependency are of such a magnitude that new, dramatic intervention strategies are essential. These new strategies must use a systemic approach in dealing with these problems at the level of the client, the community, and the nation. As substance abuse professionals, we need to think far "outside the box." We have reached the point where program failure is no longer acceptable. No new approach should be rejected out of hand. There is no place for narrow-mindedness when so much is at stake.

ENDNOTES

CHAPTER 1

1. THC content is the measure of marijuana's potency. The higher the THC content, the more potent the drug.

CHAPTER 6

1. Oxford House, www.oxfordhouse.org.
2. Cochrane Collaboration, www.cochrane.org.
3. National Acupuncture Detoxification Association, www.acudetox.com.

CHAPTER 8

1. Alabama (S. 559); Connecticut (H.B. 5217); District of Columbia (Bill No. 4-123); Georgia (H.B. 1077); Iowa (S.F. 487); Illinois (H.B. 2625); Louisiana (H.B. 1187); Massachusetts (H. 2170); Minnesota (H.F. 2476); Montana (H.B. 463); New Hampshire (S.B. 21); New Jersey (A.B. 819); New Mexico (H.B. 329); New York (S.B. 1123-6); Rhode Island (H.B. 79.6072); South Carolina (S.B. 350); Tennessee (H.B. 314); Texas (S.B. 877); Vermont (H.B. 130); Virginia (S.B. 913); Washington (S.B. 6744); West Virginia (S.B. 366); and Wisconsin (A.B. 697).

CHAPTER 9

1. More details on the Monitoring the Future findings can be found at www.monitoringthefuture.org.
2. To learn more about the CSAP Model Programs, go to www.samhsa.gov/prevention/.

CHAPTER 12

1. To get information from the National Gay and Lesbian Task Force, go to www.thetaskforce.org.
2. To contact the Human Rights Campaign, go to www.hrc.org.

3. YouthResource, www.amplifyyourvoice.org/youthresource.
4. National Youth Advocacy Coalition, www.nyacyouth.org.
5. The Trevor Project, www.thetrevorproject.org/home1.aspx.
6. Gay, Lesbian, and Straight Education Network, www.glsen.org/cgi-bin/iowa/all/home/index.html.
7. Parents and Friends of Lesbians and Gays (PFLAG), www.pflag.org.

CHAPTER 13

1. For information on fetal alcohol spectrum disorders, see the Website of the Fetal Alcohol Spectrum Disorders Center for Excellence, www.fasdcenter.samhsa.gov/.
2. The DAAD is available free of charge from the Gulf Coast Addiction Technology Training Center, www.attcnetwork.org/regcenters/index_gulfcoast.asp; gulfcoast@ATTCnetwork.org; (512) 232-0616.

CHAPTER 15

1. The predictor of men's "less positive feeling about the female alcoholic" was a trend approaching significance (p. < .10).
2. Although the results were not statistically significant, Han et al. (1999) suggest that this could be, in part, because of low statistical power and that the "findings are certainly suggestive of weaker genetic effects in females than males" (pp. 987–989).

CHAPTER 16

1. For more information on the NIDA Clinical Trials Network, go to www.nida.nih.gov/ctn/.

RESOURCES

CHAPTER 1

Organizations

Centers for Disease Control and Prevention (CDCP)
1600 Clifton Road
Atlanta, GA 30333
Phone: (404) 639-3311
Website: www.cdc.gov

National Council on Alcohol and Drug Dependence
(NCADD)
20 Exchange Place, Suite 2902
New York, NY 10005
Phone: (212) 269-7797
Fax: (212) 269-7510
Website: www.ncadd.org

National Institute on Alcohol Abuse and Alcoholism
(NIAAA)
6001 Executive Boulevard, Room 5213
Bethesda, MD 20892-7003
Website: www.niaaa.nih.gov

National Institute on Drug Abuse (NIDA)
National Institutes of Health
6001 Executive Boulevard, Room 5213
Bethesda, MD 20892-9561
Website: www.nida.nih.gov

Substance Abuse and Mental Health Services
Administration (SAMHSA)
5600 Fishers Lane
Rockville, MD 20857
Website: www.samhsa.gov

Websites

Club Drugs: www.clubdrugs.org

Drug Abuse Warning Network: dawninfo.samhsa.gov/
default.asp

Drugtext: www.drugtext.org

Harm Reduction International: www.ihra.net

NIDA InfoFacts: Science-Based Facts on Drug Abuse and
Addiction: http://www.drugabuse.gov/infofacts/
infofactsindex.html

World Health Organization's guide to drug abuse
epidemiology: www.who.int/substance_abuse/
PDFfiles/EPI_GUIDE_A.pdf

CHAPTER 2

Organizations

Addiction Treatment Forum: www.atforum.com

Alcoholics Anonymous (AA):
www.alcoholics-anonymous.org

American Society of Addiction Medicine (ASAM):
www.asam.org

Drug and Alcohol Treatment and Prevention Global
Network: www.drugnet.net

National Council on Alcoholism and Drug Dependence:
www.ncadd.org

National Institute on Drug Abuse (NIDA):
www.nida.nih.gov

Web of Addictions: www.well.com/user/woa/

CHAPTER 3

Publications

Lovallo, W. R. Exploring the brain chemistry of people
at risk for alcohol disorders. Available online at
www. eurekalert.org/pub_releases/2002-04/
ace-etb040902.php.

National Institute of Health. *The Brain: Understanding
Neurobiology through the Study of Addiction* (NIH
Curriculum Supplement Series). Available online at
www.drugabuse.gov/Curriculum/HSCurriculum.html.

Organizations

Academic Research and Counseling

National Institute on Chemical Dependency:
www.nicd.us/thediseaseconcept.html

National Institute on Drug Abuse (NIDA):
www.nida.nih.gov

Research Society on Alcoholism: www.rsoa.org

CHAPTER 4

Websites

A National Institute on Drug Abuse (NIDA) website providing bulletins on so-called designer or club drugs: www.clubdrugs.org

The official NIDA website covering research, publications, programs, and grants: www.nida.nih.gov

The Drug Enforcement Administration (DEA) website. Provides information on specific drugs (epidemiology, physiological effect), and law enforcement programs: www.usdoj.gov/dea

Databases and publications of the National Institute on Alcoholism and Alcohol Abuse (NIAAA): www.niaaa.nih.gov

Lindesmith Center-Drug Policy Foundation, which advocates a harm-reduction approach to drug policy: www.lindesmith.org

The Partnership for a Drug-Free America: www.drugfree.org/Portal/drug_guide/Alcohol

CHAPTER 5

Publications

Allen, J. P., & Wilson, V. B., (2003). *Assessing alcohol problems: A guide for clinicians and researchers, 2nd ed.*, NIH Publication No. 03–3745. Bethesda, MD: National Institute on Alcohol Abuse and Alcoholism, retrieved May 1, 2010, from pubs.niaaa.nih.gov/publications/Assesing%20Alcohol/index.htm#contents.

Federal Register. (2000). *Confidentiality of alcohol and drug abuse patient records* (42CFR, Chapter 1, Part 2).

Lanier, D., & Ko, S. (2008, January). Screening in primary care settings for illicit drug use: Assessment of screening instruments—A supplemental evidence update for the U.S. Preventive Services Task Force. Evidence Synthesis No. 58, Part 2. AHRQ Publication No. 08-05108-EF-2. Rockville, Maryland: Agency for Healthcare Research and Quality, retrieved May 1, 2010, from www.ahrq.gov/clinic/uspstf08/druguse/drugevup.pdf.

Websites

AlcoholScreening.org (Boston University): www.alcoholscreening.org/Home.aspx

ASI (Addiction Severity Index) resources, Treatment Research Institute: www.tresearch.org/resources/instruments.htm

Association for Addiction Professionals (NAADAC): www.naadac.org

Motivational Interviewing resources: www.motivationalinterviewing.org

National Alcohol Screening Day: www.mentalhealthscreening.org/events/nasd/index.aspx

National Institute on Alcohol Abuse and Alcoholism: www.niaaa.nih.gov

Rethinking Drinking: Alcohol and Your Health: www.rethinkingdrinking.niaaa.nih.gov/

National Institution on Drug Abuse: www.nida.nih.gov

Substance Abuse and Mental Health Services Administration, Treatment Improvement Exchange: tie.samhsa.gov/externals/tips.html

Substance Use Screening & Assessment Instruments Database, Alcohol and Drug Abuse Institute Library, University of Washington: lib.adai.washington.edu/instruments/

CHAPTER 6

Federal Government Agencies

Clinical Trials Network: drugabuse.gov/CTN/

National Addiction Technology Transfer Center: www.attcnetwork.org/index.asp

National Institute on Alcohol Abuse and Alcoholism (NIAAA): www.niaaa.nih.gov

National Institute on Drug Abuse (NIDA): www.nida.nih.gov

Substance Abuse and Mental Health Services Administration: www.samhsa.gov

Mutual-Help Groups and Self-Help

Alcoholics Anonymous (AA)
Street Address:
475 Riverside Dr. at West 120th St.
11th Floor
New York, NY 10115
Phone: (212) 870-3400
Mailing Address:
P.O. Box 459
New York, NY 10163
Website: www.aa.org/?Media=PlayFlash

Al-Anon Family Group Headquarters
1600 Corporate Landing Parkway
Virginia Beach, VA 23454-5617
Toll free: (888) 4AL-ANON
Website: www.al-anon.org
E-mail: WSO@al-anon.org

Co-Anon Family Groups World Services
P.O. Box 12722
Tucson, AZ 85732-2124
Phone: (520) 513-5028
Website: www.co-anon.org
E-mail: info@co-anon.org

Cocaine Anonymous World Services
21720 S. Wilmington Ave., Ste. 304
Long Beach, CA 90810-1641
Phone: (310) 559-5833
Fax: (310) 559-2554
Website: www.ca.org
E-mail: cawso@ca.org

Marijuana Anonymous World Services
P.O. Box 7807
Torrance, CA 90504
Toll free: (800) 766-6779
Website: www.marijuana-anonymous.org
E-mail: office@marijuana-anonymous.org

Men for Sobriety
P.O. Box 618
Quakertown, PA 18951-0618
Phone: (215) 536-8026
Fax: (215) 538-9026
E-mail: newlife@nni.com

Nar-Anon
Website: www.naranon.org

Moderation Management Network, Inc.
2795 East Birdwell Street
Suite 100-244
Folsom, CA 95630-6480
Website: www.moderation.org
E-mail: mm@moderation.org

Narcotics Anonymous
World Service Office in Los Angeles
P.O. Box 9999
Van Nuys, CA 91409
Phone: (818) 773-9999
Fax: (818) 700-0700
Website: www.na.org

Rational Recovery
Box 800
Lotus, CA 95691
Phone: (530) 621-2667
Website: rational.org/index.php?id=1

Secular Organizations for Sobriety
4773 Hollywood Blvd.
Hollywood, California 90027
Phone: (323) 666-4295

Fax: (323) 666-4271
Website: www.cfiwest.org/sos/index.htm
E-mail: sos@cfiwest.org

SMART Recovery
7304 Mentor Ave., Ste. F
Mentor, OH 44060
Toll free: (866) 951-5357
Phone: (440) 951-5357
Website: www.smartrecovery.org
E-mail: srmail1@aol.com

Women for Sobriety
P.O. Box 618
Quakertown, PA 18951-0618
Phone: (215) 536-8026
Website: www.womenforsobriety.org

CHAPTER 7

Organizations

Community Anti-Drug Coalitions of America (CADCA): www.cadca.org

Harm Reduction Coalition: www.harmreduction.org

Higher Education Center for Alcohol and Other Drug Prevention: www.edc.org/hec/

Join Together Online, A national grass-roots antidrug site sponsored by Boston University: www.jointogether.org/sa/

National Institute on Drug Abuse (NIDA), Prevention Research: www.drugabuse.gov/drugpages/prevention.html

To search a non-partisan database of contributors to state and federal campaigns and policy: www.followthemoney.org

National Registry of Evidence-based Programs and Practices: www.nrepp.samhsa.gov

Substance Abuse and Mental Health Services Administration (SAMHSA), Center for Substance Abuse Prevention: www.prevention.samhsa.gov

Substance Abuse and Mental Health Services Administration (SAMHSA), National Clearinghouse for Alcohol and Drug Information including prevention: www.health.org

United Nations Office for Drug Control and Crime Prevention: www.unodc.org

Global Youth Network: www.unodc.org/youthnet/

CHAPTER 8

Organizations

Centers for Disease Control and Prevention (CDCP): www.cdc.gov

Center for Substance Abuse Treatment: www. treatment.org

Drug Policy Alliance: www.drugpolicy.org/homepage.cfm

Justice Policy Institute: www.cjcj.org

National Clearinghouse for Alcohol and Drug Issues: www.health.org/pressure/alcart.htm

National Institute on Alcohol Abuse and Alcoholism (NIAAA): www.niaaa.nih.gov

National Institute on Drug Abuse (NIDA): www.nida. nih.gov

North American Syringe Exchange Network (NASEN): www.nasen.org

Office of National Drug Control Policy: www. whitehousedrugpolicy.gov

Substance Abuse and Mental Health Services Administration (SAMHSA): www.samhsa.gov

U.S. Department of Justice, Bureau of Justice Statistics: bjs.ojp.usdoj.gov/

U.S. Department of Justice, Drug Enforcement Administration (DEA): www.usdoj.gov/dea/

CHAPTER 9

Videos

Chemical Dependency: Adolescence. (1990). Available from Insight Media. Order #14AB2423.

Drinking Apart: Families Under the Influence. (2003). Available from Films for the Humanities and Sciences. Order #HMR10952.

Getting Help. (2003). Available from Films for the Humanities and Sciences. Order #HMR8937.

Preventing Drug Abuse. (2003). Available from Films for the Humanities and Sciences. Order #HMR11409.

Supporting Kids. (2003). Available from Films for the Humanities and Sciences. Order #HMR8936.

Prescription for Trouble (2003). Available from Films for Humanities and Sciences. Order # BVL33244.

Organizations

American Academy of Youth Psychiatry: www.aacap.org/

National Institute on Drug Abuse (NIDA): www.nida.nih.gov

Office of Juvenile Justice and Delinquency Prevention (OJJDP): ojjdp.ncjrs.org

SAMHSA Center for Substance Abuse Prevention (CSAP): www.samhsa.gov/prevention/

SAMHSA Center for Substance Abuse Treatment (CSAT), csat.samhsa.gov/http://www.samhsa.gov/about/csat.aspx

CHAPTER 10

Publications

Center for Substance Abuse Treatment. (2004). *Substance abuse treatment and family therapy.* Treatment Improvement Protocol (TIP) Series, No. 39. DHHS Publication No. (SMA) 04 3957. Rockville, MD: Substance Abuse and Mental Health Services Administration. Retrieved March 1, 2010, http://www.ncbi.nlm.nih.gov/books/NBK14505/.

O'Farrell, T. J., & Fals-Stewart, W. (2006). *Behavioral couples therapy for alcoholism and drug abuse.* New York: Guilford Press.

Steinglass, P., Bennett, L., Wolin, S., & Reiss, D. (1987). *The alcoholic family.* New York: Basic Books.

Websites

Adult Children of Alcoholics: World Service Organization: www.adultchildren.org

American Academy of Child and Adolescent Psychiatry Center for Substance Abuse Prevention: www.ncadi. samhsa.gov

Children of Alcoholics: www.aacap.org/publications/factsfam/alcholic

National Association of Children of Alcoholics: www.nacoa.org

National Institute on Alcohol Abuse and Alcoholism (NIAAA), Children of alcoholics: www.niaaa.nih.gov/publications/pages/default.aspx

Substance Abuse and Mental Health Services Administration (SAMHSA), U.S. Department of Health and Human Services, Children, Youth & Families: www.samhsa.gov/families/index.aspx

CHAPTER 11

Organizations

General
Alcohol and Drug Abuse Institute
University of Washington
1107 NE 45th Street, Suite 120
Box 354805
Seattle, WA 98105-4631

Center for Substance Abuse Prevention
Substance Abuse and Mental Health Services
        Administration (SAMHSA)
Culturally relevant prevention information
Website: www.samhsa.gov/prevention

National Clearinghouse for Alcohol and Drug Information
Culture and prevention information
Website: www.higheredcenter.org/resources/national-
        clearinghouse-alcohol-and-drug-information-ncadi

National Institute on Drug Abuse (NIDA)
Special Populations Office
(301) 443-0441
Fax: (301) 480-8179
Website: www.nida.nih.gov/about/organization/SPO/
        SPOHome.html

Office of Minority Health Resource Center
Department of Health & Human Services
1101 Wootton Parkway, Suite 600
Rockville, MD 20852
(800) 444-6472
Fax: (240) 453-2883
Website: minorityhealth.hhs.gov/

African Americans
Institute on Black Chemical Abuse, African American
        Family Services
2616 Nicollet Avenue
Minneapolis, MN 55408
and
1041 Selby Avenue
St. Paul, MN 55104
(612) 871-7878
Website: www.aafs.net/ibac.asp

American Indians and Alaska Natives
American Indian Institute
Prevention Resource Center
University of Oklahoma
(405) 325-4127
Website: www.aii.outreach.ou.edu/

Four Worlds International Institute
P.O. Box 75028
White Rock British Columbia V4B 5L3
(604) 542-8991
Website: www.4worlds.org/index.htm

National Center for American Indian and Alaska Native
        Mental Health Research
Colorado School of Public Health
Nighthorse Campbell Native Health Building
13055 E. 17th Ave
Mail Stop F800
Aurora, CO 80045
(303) 724-1414
Fax: (303) 724-1474

Native American Center for Excellence, Substance Abuse
        and Mental Health Services Administration (NACE)
Information, training, and technical assistance on
        substance abuse prevention, programs, and policies
        among Native Americans and Alaska Natives
Website: nace.samhsa.gov/

White Bison, Inc.
(offers information and other resources for sobriety)
701 North 20th Street
Colorado Springs, CO 80904
(719) 548-1000
(877) 871-1495
Fax: (719) 548-9407
Website: www.whitebison.org

Videos on Native American alcohol and drug problems
include *Sucker Punched* and *Nagi Kicopi (Calling Back the Spirit)*.
These and other resources are available from the Prairielands
Addiction Technology Transfer Center, www.attcnetwork.org/
regcenters/index_prairielands.asp. *The Honour of All: The
Story of Alkali Lake* is available from the Four Worlds
International Institute (see previous information).

Asian and Pacific Islander Americans
National Asian Pacific American Families Against
        Substance Abuse, Inc.
340 East Second St., Suite 409
Los Angeles, CA 90012
(213) 625-5795
Fax: (213) 625-5796
Website: www.napafasa.org

Hispanics/Latinos
Caribbean Basin and Hispanic Addiction Technology
        Transfer Center

Serves Puerto Rico and U.S. Virgin Islands.
Website: www.attcnetwork.org/regcenters/index_
        caribbeanbasin.asp

Jewish Americans
Alcohol Drug Action Program
Jewish Family Service of Los Angeles
8838 West Pico Blvd Los Angeles, CA 90035
(310) 247-1180
Website: www.jfsla.org/page.aspx?pid=239

Jewish Alcoholics, Chemically Dependent Persons, and
        Significant Others (JACS)
Jewish Board of Family & Children's Services
135 West 50th Street, 6th Floor
New York, NY 10020
(212) 632-4600
Website: www.jacsweb.org

CHAPTER 12

Publications

*A Provider's Introduction to Substance Abuse Treatment for
    Lesbian, Gay, Bisexual, and Transgender Individuals:* A
    comprehensive overview of substance abuse issues

facing LGBT individuals. (2001). Rockville, MD: Substance Abuse and Mental Health Services Administration. Available at kap.samhsa.gov/ products/manuals/pdfs/lgbt.pdf

Healthy People 2010: Companion Document for LGBT Health: A comprehensive overview of health issues impacting LGBT individuals. Available at www. publichealth.pitt.edu/docs/healthy2010.pdf

Organizations

Alcoholics Anonymous (AA): AA has literature written for gays and lesbians concerned about their drinking as well as many helpful resources for anyone concerned about their drinking or a loved one's drinking.
www.aa.org

National Association of Lesbian, Gay, Bisexual and Transgender Addiction Professionals and Their Allies (NALGAP): An organization of addiction professionals dedicated to the prevention and treatment of alcohol and drug problems in lesbian, gay, bisexual, and transgender communities.
www.nalgap.org

International Advisory Committee for Homosexual Men and Women in Alcoholics Anonymous (IAC): Discussed earlier in this chapter, the IAC maintains a list of gay and lesbian AA meetings throughout the world.
www.iac-aa.org

CHAPTER 13

Publications

Center for Substance Abuse Treatment. (2005). *Substance Abuse Treatment for Persons with Co-Occurring Disorders.* Treatment Improvement Protocol (TIP) Series 42. DHHS Publication No. (SMA) 05-3922. Rockville, MD: Substance Abuse and Mental Health Services Administration. Available at www.ncbi.nlm. nih.gov/books/NBK14528/.

Moore, D. (1998). *Substance use disorder treatment for people with physical and cognitive disabilities* (Treatment Improvement Protocol [TIP] Series no. 29, DHHS Publication no. [SMA] 98-3249). Rockville, MD: Substance Abuse and Mental Health Services Administration. Available at www.ncbi.nlm.nih.gov/ books/NBK14408/.

Organizations

General

Americans with Disabilities Act
U.S. Department of Justice
Website: www.ada.gov

Emotions Anonymous International
P.O. Box 4245
St. Paul, MN 55104-0245
(651) 647-9712
Website: www.emotionsanonymous.org

SARDI Program: Substance Abuse Resources and Disability Issues
Boonshoft School of Medicine
Wright State University
P.O. Box 927
Dayton, OH 45410-0927
Voice/TTY: (937) 775-1484
jeremy.trim@wright.edu
Website: www.med.wright.edu/citar/sardi/

National Institute on Disability and Rehabilitation Research
Mailing: 400 Maryland Avenue, SW., Mailstop PCP-6038
Washington, DC 20202-8134
Physical: Potomac Center Building
550 12 St., S.W.
Washington, DC 20202
Voice/TTY: (202) 245-7640
Website: www2.ed.gov/about/offices/list/osers/nidrr/ index.html

Substance Abuse and Mental Health Services Administration, Treatment Improvement Exchange, Dual Disorders Special Topic
Website: tie.samhsa.gov/Topics/dual.html

Blindness and Visual Impairment

American Foundation for the Blind (AFB)
AFB Information Center
(800) AFB-LINE (800-232-5463)
afbinfo@afb.net
Website: www.afb.org

AFB Headquarters
2 Penn Plaza, Suite 1102
New York, NY 10121
(212) 502-7600

Rehabilitation Research and Training Center on Blindness and Low Vision (RRTC)
108 Herbert – South, Room 150 Industrial
Education Department Building
P.O. Drawer 6189
Mississippi State University
Mississippi State, MS 39762
(662) 325-2001
Voice/TTY: (662) 325-2694
rrtc@colled.msstate.edu
Website: www.blind.msstate.edu

Deaf and Hard of Hearing

Clare Foundation
909 Pico Boulevard
Santa Monica, CA 90405

TTY: (310) 450-4164
(310) 314-6200
Toll Free Number: (866) 452-5273
info@clarefoundation.org
Website: www.clarefoundation.org/index.html

Minnesota Chemical Dependency Program for
    Deaf and Hard of Hearing Individuals
2450 Riverside Avenue South
Minneapolis, MN 55454
Voice/TTY: Toll free 1-800-282-3323
(VP) 1-866-928-5713
Website: www.mncddeaf.org

University of Arkansas Rehabilitation Research and
    Training Center for Persons Who Are Deaf or
    Hard of Hearing
26 Corporate Hill Drive
Little Rock, AK 72205
Voice/TTY: (501) 686-9691
rehabres@cavern.uark.edu
Website: www.uark.edu/depts/rehabres

American Deafness and Rehabilitation Association
    (ADARA)
ADARA National Office
P.O. Box 480
Myersville, MD 21773
Voice/TTY: (301) 293-8969
adaraorg@comcast.net
Website: www.adara.org

National Association of the Deaf
8630 Fenton Street, Ste. 820
Silver Spring, MD 20910-3819
(301) 587-1788
TTY: (301) 587-1789
Website: www.nad.org

Substance and Alcohol Intervention Services for
    the Deaf (SAISD)
Rochester Institute of Technology
August Center
115 Lomb Memorial Drive
Rochester, NY 14623-5608
Voice/TTY: (585) 475-4978
cxphcc@rit.edu
Website: www.rit.edu/ntid/saisd/

University of California Center on Deafness (UCCD)
3333 California Street, Suite 10
San Francisco, CA 94143-1208
(415) 476-4980
TTY: (415) 476-7600
VP: (415) 255-5854
Website: www.uccd.org

*Mental Illness & Co-occurring Mental Illnesses &
    Substance Use Disorders*

National Alliance on Mental Illness (NAMI)
3803 N. Fairfax Dr., Ste. 100
Arlington, VA 22203
(703) 524-7600
Member Services: (888) 999-NAMI (6264)
Website: www.nami.org

National Institute on Mental Health
6001 Executive Blvd.
Bethesda, MD 20892
(866) 615-6464
TTY: (866) 415-8051
nimhinfo@nih.gov
Website: www.nimh.nih.gov/index.shtml

Good Chemistry Groups
Debbie Webb, Ph.D., LCSW, LPC, LCDC
2525 Wallingwood Dr., Bldg. 1, Ste. 140
Austin, TX 78746
(512) 799-9358
debbiewebb@aol.com
Website: www.drdebbiewebb.com

Dual Recovery Anonymous
World Network Central Office
P.O. Box 8107
Prairie Village, KS 66208
draws@draonline.org
(913) 991-2703
1-877-883-2332
Website: www.draonline.org

Substance Abuse and Mental Health Services Administration
Health Information Network
P.O. Box 2345
Rockville, MD 20847-2345
1-877-SAMHSA-7 (1-877-726-4727)
TTY: 1-800-487-4889
SAMHSAInfo@samhsa.hhs.gov
Website: www.samhsa.gov

Intellectual Disability/Developmental Disabilities

AHRC New York City
Administrative Offices
83 Maiden Lane
New York, NY 10038
(212) 780-2500
TDD/TTY: 1-800-662-1220
Website: www.ahrcnyc.org/services/services-by-type/
    chemicaldependency.html

The Arc
National Office
1660 L Street, NW, Ste. 301
Washington, DC 20036
(800) 433-5255
info@thearc.org
Website: www.thearc.org

Spinal Cord Injury

National Spinal Cord Injury Association
1 Church Street #600
Rockville, MD 20850
(800) 962-9629
info@spinalcord.org
Website: www.spinalcord.org

Traumatic Brain Injury

Brain Injury Association of America
1608 Spring Hill Road, Ste. 110
Vienna, VA 22182
(703) 761-0750
National Brain Injury Information Center
(Brain Injury Information Only): (800) 444-6443
Website: www.biausa.org

Ohio Valley Center for Brain Injury and Rehabilitation
Department of Physical Medicine and Rehabilitation
The Ohio State University
480 Medical Center Drive
1166 Dodd Hall
Columbus, OH 43210
(614) 293-3802
Website: www.ohiovalley.org/abuse/index.html

The Traumatic Brain Injury Model Systems National Data
and Statistical Center
c/o Craig Hospital Research Dept.
3425 S. Clarkson Street
Englewood, CO 80113
(303) 789-8202
Website: www.tbindsc.org

CHAPTER 14

Websites

Alcohol, Medications and Aging: Use, Misuse and Abuse
American Society on Aging Web-Based Training Program:
www.asaging.org/webseminars/

Gerontological Society of America
Aging, Alcohol, and Addictions Informal Interest Group
Louis de la Parte Florida Mental Health Institute, University
of South Florida: gsa-alcohol.fmhi.usf.edu/
GSA-Alcohol.htm

Substance Abuse Resource Guide: Older Americans
U.S. Department of Health and Human Services and
SAMHSA's National Clearinghouse for Alcohol &
Drug Information: ncadi.samhsa.gov/govpubs/
ms443/

NIDA Conference
September 16-17, 2004
Drug Abuse in the 21st Century: What Problems Lie Ahead
for the Baby Boomers?: archives.drugabuse.gov/
meetings/bbsr/comorbidities.html - 25k

Volunteers Working with the Elderly and Alcohol, Tobacco,
and Other Drug Problem Prevention
Substance Abuse & Mental Health Administration:
preventiontraining.samhsa.gov/VOL03/
VOL03ttl.htm

Organizations

American Association for Geriatric Psychiatry:
www.aagpgpa.org

American Geriatrics Society:
www.americangeriatrics.org

Elder Care Locator: www.eldercare.gov/Eldercare.NET/
Public/Index.aspx

National Association of Area Agencies on Aging:
www.agingcarefl.org/network/n4a

National Council on Aging: www.ncoa.org

National Institute on Aging: www.nia.nih.gov

Videos

Hidden Epidemic Conference DVD

The Alcohol and Aging Awareness Group of the Virginia
Department of Alcoholic Beverage Control is selling
DVDs from its 2008 conference, "The Hidden
Epidemic, Alcohol, Medication and the Older Adult."
www.abc.state.va.us/Education/olderadults/
aaagroup.html.

DVDs on elder alcohol abuse and alcohol abuse and
diabetes are available through National Health Video,
Inc., www.nhv.com/index.cfm?fuseaction=browse&id
=90552&pageid=55.

Alcohol & the Elderly. (1999). Families, doctors, and the
public often neglect drinking problems in older
people. Ignoring an alcohol problem in an elderly
person on the grounds that "he or she has only a few
years left so let them enjoy themselves" is a mistake.
Research has found that alcoholism definitely lowers
quality of life, even in our later years. This tape
outlines key issues that affect the elderly who abuse
alcohol. 16 minutes

Alcohol & Diabetes. (1998). Alcohol has a significant
impact on the management of diabetes. Patients
need to know just how alcohol and diabetes interact,
problems with hypoglycemia, medication effects,
and how to cope with this problem. 12 minutes

Substance Abuse in the Elderly The percentage of Americans living beyond age 70 is increasing, and there's growing concern that these people are also at risk for problems related to alcohol and prescription misuse. As the body ages, tolerance to alcohol decreases, and many people often have multiple prescriptions that, when combined, can cause problems. Aquarius Health Care Media, www. aquariusproductions.com.

CHAPTER 15
Publications

Center for Substance Abuse Treatment (2009). Substance Abuse Treatment: Addressing the specific needs of women. Treatment Improvement Protocol (TIP) Series 51. HHS Publication No. (SMA) 09-4426. Rockville, MD: Substance Abuse and Mental Health Services Administration.

Englar-Carlson, M. & Stevens, M.A. (Eds.). (2006). *In the room with men: A casebook of therapeutic change.* Washington, DC: American Psychological Association.

Furman, R. (2010). *Social work practice with men at risk.* New York: Columbia University Press.

Straussner, L. S. A. & Zelvin, E. (Eds.) (1997). *Gender and addictions: Men and women in treatment.* Northvale, NJ: Jason Aronson.

Straussner, L.S.A. & Brown, S. (2002) (Eds.). *The Handbook of addiction treatment for women: Theory and practice.* San Francisco: Jossey-Bass.

Substance Abuse and Mental Health Services Administration (n.d.). Fetal Alcohol Spectrum Disorders, the Course. Retrieved April 23, 2011, from www.fasdcenter.samhsa.gov/educationTraining/courses/FASDTheCourse/index.cfm.

Substance Abuse and Mental Health Services Administration (n.d.). Tools for Success Curriculum: Working With Youth With Fetal Alcohol Spectrum Disorders (FASD) in the Juvenile Justice System. Retrieved April 23, 2011, from store.samhsa.gov/shin/content//SMA07-4291/SMA07-4291.pdf

Sun, A.P. (2009). *Helping substance-abusing women of vulnerable populations: Effective treatment principles and strategies.* New York: Columbia University Press.

Organizations

National Center on Substance Abuse and Child Welfare
U.S. Department of Health and Human Services

Substance Abuse and Mental Health Services Administration
(866) 493-2758
Website: www.ncsacw.samhsa.gov/contactus.aspx

National Organization on Fetal Alcohol Syndrome (NOFAS)
1200 Eton Court, NW
Third Floor
Washington, D.C. 20007
(202) 785-4585
NOFAS Clearinghouse:
(202) 785-8570
(800) 66 NOFAS
Website: www.nofas.org

National Women's Health Resource Center
HealthyWomen
157 Broad Street, Suite 106
Red Bank, NJ 07701
(877) 986-9472
Website: www.healthywomen.org

Women for Sobriety, Inc.
P.O. Box 618
Quakertown, PA 18951
(215) 536-8026
Website: womenforsobriety.org/beta2/

Men for Sobriety, Inc.
P.O. Box 618
Quakertown, PA 18951
(215) 536-8026
Website: womenforsobriety.org/beta2/

CHAPTER 16
Websites

U.S. Department of Health and Human Services and Substance Abuse and Mental Health Services Administration (SAMHSA) Clearinghouse on Alcohol and Drug Abuse: www.health.org

National Institute on Drug Abuse (NIDA): www.nida.nih.gov

Food and Drug Administration (FDA): www.fda.gov

Substance Abuse and Mental Health Services Administration (SAMHSA): www.sammhsa.gov

Web of addictions: www.well.com/user/woa

Go Ask Alice: health questions on many topics, including substance abuse; sponsored by Columbia University: www.alice.columbia.edu

REFERENCES

CHAPTER 1

American Psychiatric Association (APA). (2000). *Diagnostic and statistical manual of mental disorders* (4th ed., text revision). Washington, DC: Author.

Bonnie, R. J., & Whitebread, C. (1998). The alien weed. In M. E. Kelleher, B. K. MacMurray, & T. Shapiro (Eds.), *Drugs and society: A critical reader* (2nd ed., pp. 256–267). Dubuque, IA: Kendall/Hunt.

Bowman, C. M., & Jellinek, E. M. (1941). Alcohol addiction and chronic alcoholism. *Quarterly Journal of Studies on Alcohol, 2,* 98–176.

Breslau, N., Johnson, E. O., Hiripi, E., & Kessler, R. C. (2001). Nicotine dependence in the United States: Prevalence, trends and smoking persistence. *Archives of General Psychiatry, 58*(Suppl. 9), 810–816.

Brooks, J. E. (1952). *The mighty leaf: Tobacco through the centuries.* Boston, MA: Little, Brown.

Calahan, D. (1970). *Problem drinkers.* San Francisco: Jossey-Bass.

Calahan, D., & Cisin, I. H. (1976). Epidemiological and social factors associated with drinking problems. In R. E. Tarter & A. A. Sugerman (Eds.), *Alcoholism* (p. 541). Reading, MA: Addison-Wesley.

Calahan, D., & Roizen, R. (1974). *Changes in drinking problems in a national sample of men.* Paper presented at the annual meeting of the Alcohol and Drug Problems Association, San Francisco.

Centers for Disease Control and Prevention (CDCP). (2008). *Smoking-attributable mortality, years of potential life lost, and productivity losses—United States, 2000–2004.* Retrieved January 6, 2010, from www.cdc.gov/mmwr/preview/mmwrhtml/mm5745a3.htm.

Cohen, S. (1981). *The substance abuse problems.* New York: Haworth Press.

Community Epidemiology Work Group. (2001). *Epidemiological trends in drug abuse: Advance report, June 2001.* National Institute on Drug Abuse. Retrieved December 11, 2001, from 165.112.78.61/CEWG Advanced Rep/601ADV/601adv.html.

Cooter, G. R. (1988). Amphetamine use: Physical activity and sport. In M. E. Kelleher, B. K. MacMurray, & T. M. Shapiro (Eds.), *Drugs and society: A critical reader.* Dubuque, IA: Kendall/Hunt.

Curlee-Salisbury, J. (1986). Perspectives on Alcoholics Anonymous. In N. J. Estes & M. E. Heinemann (Eds.), *Alcoholism: Development, consequences, and interventions* (3rd ed., pp. 329–335). St. Louis, MO: C.V. Mosby.

DesJarlais, D. C., & Friedman, S. R. (1988). HIV infections among IV drug users. In M. E. Kelleher, B. K. MacMurray, & T. M. Shapiro (Eds.), *Drugs and society: A critical reader* (2nd ed., pp. 311–325). Dubuque, IA: Kendall/Hunt.

Drugtext. (2001). *Substances and psychopharmacology.* International Harm Reduction Association. Retrieved December 2, 2001, from www.drugtext.org.

Drug use among 8th, 10th, and 12th graders. (1993–1995). Retrieved December 19, 2003 from http://dataguru./org/misc/drugs/drug9196.asp.

Dufour, M. C. (1999). What is moderate drinking? Defining "drinks" and drinking levels. *Alcohol Health and Research World, 23*(1), 5–14.

Gfroerer, J., & Brodsky, M. (1992). The incidence of illicit drug use in the United States, 1962–1989. *British Journal of Addiction, 87*(9), 1345–1351.

Goode, E. (1969). *Marijuana.* New York: Atherton Press.

Grant, B. F., Harford, T. C., Chou, P., Pickering, R., Dawson, D. A., Stinson, F. S., & Noble, J. (1991). Prevalence of DSM-III-R alcohol abuse and dependence: United States, 1988. *Alcohol Health and Research World. 15*(1), 91–96.

Harburg, E., DiFranceisco, W., Webster, D. W., Gleiberman, L., & Schork, A. (1990). Familial transmission of alcohol use: II. Imitation of and aversion to parent drinking by adult offspring, Tecumseh, Michigan, 1966–1977. *Journal of Studies on Alcohol, 51*(3), 245–256.

Imlah, N. (1989). *Addiction: Substance abuse and dependency.* Winslow, England: Sigma Press.

Jellinek, E. M. (1960). *The disease concept of alcoholism.* Highland Park, NJ: Hillhouse Press.

Johnston, L. D., O'Malley, P. M., & Bachman, J. G. (1987). *National trends in drug use and related factors among American high school students and young adults, 1975–1986.* Washington, DC: U.S. Government Printing Office.

Johnston, L. D., O'Malley, P. M., & Bachman, J. G. (2000). *Monitoring the future: National results on adolescent drug use: Overview of key findings, 1999.* Bethesda, MD: U.S. Department of Health and Human Services, National Institute on Drug Abuse.

Johnston, L. D., O'Malley, P. M., Bachman, J. G., & Schulenberg, J. E. (2009). *Monitoring the future national results on adolescent drug use: Overview of key findings, 2008* (NIH Publication No. 09-7401). Bethesda, MD: National Institute on Drug Abuse.

Kaij, L. (1960). *Alcoholism in twins.* Stockholm, Sweden: Almqvist and Wiksell.

Kelleher, M. E., MacMurray, B. K., & Shapiro, T. M. (1988). *Drugs and society: A critical reader.* Dubuque, IA: Kendall/Hunt.

Keller, M. (1958, January). Alcoholism: Nature and extent of the problem. *Annals of the American Academy of Political and Social Science, 315,* 1–11.

Kessler, R. C., McGonagle, K. A., Zhao, S., Nelson, C. B., Hughes, M., Eshleman, S., Wittchen, H., & Kendler, K. S. (1994). Lifetime and 12-month prevalence of DSM-III-R psychiatric disorders in the United States: Results from the National Comorbidity Survey. *Archives of General Psychiatry, 51,* 8–19.

Kinney, J., & Leaton, G. (2000). *Loosening the grip: A handbook of alcohol information* (2nd ed.). Boston, MA: McGraw-Hill.

Krivanek, J. (1988a). *Addictions.* Winchester, MA: Allen & Unwin.

Krivanek, J. (1988b). *Heroin: Myths and realities.* Winchester, MA: Allen & Unwin.

Lerner, M. A. (1989, November 27). The fire of "ice." *Newsweek,* pp. 37–40.

Levin, J. D. (1989). *Alcoholism: A bio-psychosocial approach.* New York: Hemisphere.

Malin, H., Wilson, R., Williams, G., & Aitken, S. (1986). 1983 Alcohol/health practices supplement. *Alcohol Health and Research World, 7,* 37–46.

Mandell, W. (1983). Types and phases of alcohol dependence illness. In M. Galanter (Ed.), *Recent developments in alcoholism* (Vol. 1). New York: Plenum Press.

McKim, W. A. (1991). *Drugs and behavior: An introduction to behavioral pharmacology.* Englewood Cliffs, NJ: Prentice Hall.

Musto, D. F. (1973). *The American disease: Narcotics in nineteenth century America.* New Haven, CT: Yale University Press.

Narcotics News. (2010). *Wholesale marijuana prices.* Retrieved February 6, 2010, from www.narcoticnews.com/Marijuana/Prices/USA/Marijuana_Prices_USA.html

National Council on Alcoholism. (1972). Criteria for the diagnosis of alcoholism. *Journal of Studies on Alcohol, 38*(2), 127–135.

National Institute of Justice (NIJ). (1997). *Critical criminal justice issues.* Washington, DC: U.S. Government Printing Office.

National Institute of Justice (NIJ). (2003). *ONDCP drug policy information clearinghouse fact sheet.* Washington, DC: U.S. Government Printing Office.

National Institute on Alcohol Abuse and Alcoholism (NIAAA). (2000). *Tenth special report to the U.S. Congress on alcohol and health.* Washington, DC: U.S. Government Printing Office.

National Institute on Drug Abuse (NIDA). (2000). *Anabolic steroid abuse* (Research Report Series NIH no. 00–3721). Washington, DC: U.S. Department of Health and Human Services.

National Institute on Drug Abuse (NIDA). (2009a). *Steroids (Anabolic-Androgenic) (National Institute of Drug Abuse Info Facts).* Washington, DC: U.S. Department of Health and Human Services.

National Institute on Drug Abuse (NIDA). (2009b). *Stimulant ADHD medications: Methylphenidate and amphetamines (National Institute of Drug Abuse Info Facts).* Washington, DC: U.S. Department of Health and Human Services.

Office of National Drug Control Policy (ONDCP). (2001). *Pulse check: Trends in drug abuse mid-year 2000* (Report no. NCJ186747). Washington, DC: Executive Office of the President.

Pattison, E. M., Sobell, M. B., & Sobell, L. C. (1977). *Emerging concepts of alcohol dependence.* New York: Springer.

Plaut, T. F. (1967). *Alcohol problems: A report to the nation by the cooperative commission on the study of alcoholism.* New York: Oxford University Press.

Raistrick, D., & Davidson, R. (1985). *Alcoholism and drug addiction.* New York: Churchill Livingstone.

Regier, D. A., Farmer, M. E., Rae, D. S., Locke, B. Z., Keith, S. J., Judd, L. L., & Goodwin, F. K. (1990). Comorbidity of mental disorders with alcohol and other drug abuse: Results from the Epidemiological Catchment Area (ECA) study. *Journal of the American Medical Association, 264,* 2511–2518.

Ringer, C., Kuefner, H., Antons, K., & Feuerlein, W. (1977). The N.C.A. criteria for the diagnosis of alcoholism. *Journal of Studies on Alcohol, 38*(7), 1259–1273.

Rorabaugh, W. J. (1979). *The alcohol republic: An American tradition.* New York: Oxford University Press.

Sheehan, M. E. (1993). Dual diagnosis. *Psychiatric Quarterly, 64*(2), 107–134.

Stewart, T. (1987). *The heroin users.* London, England: Pandora Press.

Substance Abuse and Mental Health Services Administration (SAMHSA). (2000). *Summary of findings from the 1999 National Household Survey on Drug Abuse.* Rockville, MD: Department of Health and Human Services.

Substance Abuse and Mental Health Services Administration (SAMHSA). (2001). *Summary of findings from the 2000 National Household Survey on Drug Abuse.* Rockville, MD: Department of Health and Human Services.

Substance Abuse and Mental Health Services Administration (SAMHSA). (2008a). *Drug Abuse Warning Network, 2006: National Estimates of Drug-Related Emergency Department Visits.* DAWN Series D–30, DHHS Publication No. (SMA) 08-4339, Rockville, MD.

Substance Abuse and Mental Health Services Administration (SAMHSA). (2008b). *Results from the 2007 National Survey on Drug Use and Health: National Findings* (Office of Applied Studies, NSDUH Series H–34, DHHS Publication No. SMA 08–4343). Rockville, MD.

Substance Abuse and Mental Health Services Administration (SAMHSA). (2008c). *Results from the 2007 National Survey on Drug Use and Health: Detailed Tables. Prevalence Estimates, Standard Errors, P Values, and Sample Sizes.* Rockville, MD: Office of Applied Studies.

U.S. Department of Agriculture. (2001). *Food consumption, prices, and expenditures.* Washington, DC: U.S. Government Printing Office.

Vaillant, G. E. (1983). *The natural history of alcoholism.* Cambridge, MA: Harvard University Press.

Wilkner, A. (1980). Opiod dependence. New York: Plenum Press.

World Health Organization (WHO), Expert Committee on Mental Health. (1952, August). *Report on the first session of the alcoholism subcommittee.* Geneva, Switzerland: Author.

Yalisove, D. (1998). The origins and evolution of the disease concept of treatment. *Journal of Studies on Alcohol, 59,* 469–476.

CHAPTER 2

Addictive personality, The: Common traits are found. (1983, January 18). *The New York Times,* pp. 11, 15.

Alcoholism and Drug Research Communications Center. (A & DRCC). (1995). *Sci-Mat: Science matters in the battle against alcoholism and related diseases* [No longer available online].

American Psychiatric Association (APA). (1994). *Diagnostic and statistical manual of mental disorders* (4th ed.). Washington, DC: Author.

Bacon, M. K. (1974). The dependency-conflict hypothesis and the frequency of drunkenness. *Quarterly Journal of Studies on Alcohol, 35,* 863–876.

Bales, B. F. (1946). Cultural differences in rates of alcoholism. *Quarterly Journal of Studies on Alcohol, 6,* 480–499.

Bandura, A. (1969). *Principles of behavior modification.* New York: Holt, Rinehart, and Winston.

Baum, J. (1985). *One step over the line: A no-nonsense guide to recognizing and treating cocaine dependency.* New York: Harper and Row.

Bloom, F. E. (1982). A summary of workshop discussions. In F. Bloom et al. (Eds.), *Beta-carbolines and tetrahydroisoquinolines.* New York: Alan R. Liss.

Bloomfield, K., Gmel, G., & Wilsnack, S. (2006). Introduction to special issue: Gender, culture, and alcohol problems—a multinational study. *Alcohol and Alcoholism, 41*(1), i3–i7.

Blum, K., Noble, E., Sheridan, P., Montgomery, A., Ritchie, T., Jagadeeswaran, P., Nogami, H., Briggs, A., & Cohen, J. (1990). Allelic association of human dopamine D2 receptor gene in alcoholism. *Journal of the American Medical Association, 263,* 2055–2060.

Boham, M., Cloninger, C. R., von Knorring, A. L., & Sigvardsson, S. (1984). An adoptions study of somatoform disorders: III. Cross-fostering analysis and genetic relationship to alcoholism and criminality. *Archives of General Psychiatry, 41,* 872–878.

Bonaparte, M., Freud, A., & Kris, E. (Eds.). (1954). *The origins of psychoanalysis: Letters to Fleiss.* New York: Basic Books.

Burroughs, W. S. (1977). *Junky.* New York: Penguin Press.

Calahan, D. (1970). *Problem drinkers: A national survey.* San Francisco: Jossey-Bass.

Catanzaro, P. (1967). Psychiatric aspects of alcoholism. In D. J. Pittman (Ed.), *Alcoholism.* New York: Harper and Row.

Chordokoff, B. (1964). Alcoholism and ego function. *Quarterly Journal of Studies on Alcohol, 25,* 292–299.

Collins, R. L., Blane, H., & Leonard, K. E. (1999). Psychological theories of etiology. In P. J. Ott, R. E. Tarter, & R. T. Ammerman (Eds.), *Sourcebook on substance abuse: Etiology, epidemiology, assessment, and treatment* (pp. 153–165). Boston, MA: Allyn & Bacon.

Cotton, N. A. (1979). The familial incidence of alcoholism. *Journal of Studies on Alcohol, 40,* 89–116.

Cunynghame, A. L. (1983). Some issues in successful alcoholism treatment. In D. Cook, C. Fewell, & J. Riolo (Eds.), *Social work treatment of alcohol problems* (pp. 49–59). New Brunswick, NJ: Rutgers Center of Alcohol Studies.

Drummond, D. (2001). Theories of drug craving, ancient and modern. *Addiction, 96*(1), 33–46.

Duster, T. (1970). *The legislation of morality.* New York: Free Press.

Einstein, S. (1983). *The drug user: Personality factors, issues, and theories.* New York: Plenum Press.

Esbensen, F. A., & Huizinga, D. (1990). Community structure and drug use: From a social disorganizational perspective. *Justice Quarterly, 7,* 691–708.

Fingarette, H. (1985, March/April). Alcoholism: Neither sin nor disease. *The Center Magazine,* 56–63.

Gomberg, E. (1986). Women with alcohol problems. In N. J. Estes & M. E. Heinemann (Eds.), *Alcoholism: Development, consequences, and interventions.* St. Louis, MO: C. V. Mosby.

Goode, E. (1972). *Drugs in American society.* New York: Alfred A. Knopf.

Goode, E. (1984). *Drugs in American society* (2nd ed.). New York: Alfred A. Knopf.

Goodwin, D. W., Hill, S., Powell, B., & Viamontes, J. (1973). The effect of alcohol on short-term memory in alcoholics. *British Journal of Psychiatry, 122,* 93–94.

Gossop, M. R., & Eysenck, S. (1980). A further investigation into the personality of drug addicts in treatment. *British Journal of Addiction, 75,* 305–311.

Hester, R. K., & Sheehy, N. (1990). The grand unification theory of alcohol abuse: It's time to stop fighting each other and start working together. In R. C. Engs (Ed.), *Controversies in the addictions field* (Vol. 1, pp. 2–9). Dubuque, IA: Kendall/Hunt.

Human Genome Project. (2008). *Post-HGP Information.* Retrieved July 29, 2009, from www.ornl.gov/sci/techresources/Human_Genome/home.shtml.

Imlah, N. (1971). *Drugs in modern society.* Princeton, NJ: Averbach.

Jacobs, D. F. (1986). A general theory of addictions: A new Theoretical model. *Journal of Gambling Studies, 2* (1), 15–31.

Janoff-Bulman, B. (1992). *Shattered assumptions.* New York: Free Press.

Jellinek, E. M. (1952). Phases of alcohol addiction. *Quarterly Journal of Studies of Alcohol, 13,* 673–684.

Jellinek, E. M. (1960). *The disease concept of alcoholism.* New Haven, CT: Hillhouse Press.

Johnson, V. E. (1973). *I'll quit tomorrow.* New York: Harper and Row.

Kaij, L. (1960). *Alcoholism in twins: Studies on the etiology and sequels of abuse of alcohol.* Stockholm, Sweden: Almquist & Wiskell.

Kaymakcalan, S. (1973). Tolerance to and dependence on cannabis. *Bulletin of Narcotics, 25,* 39–47.

Keller, M. (1972). The oddities of alcoholics. *Quarterly Journal of Studies on Alcohol, 33,* 11–20.

Kessel, J. (1962). *The road back: A report on Alcoholics Anonymous.* New York: Alfred A. Knopf.

Kinney, J., & Leaton, G. (1987). *Loosening the grip: A handbook of alcohol information.* St. Louis, MO: C. V. Mosby.

Koopmans, J. R., & Boomsina, D. I. (1995). *Familiar resemblances in alcohol use: Genetic or cultural transmission.* Amsterdam, The Netherlands: Department of Psychonomics, Vriji Univeriteit.

Krivanek, J. (1988). *Heroin: Myths and realities.* Sydney: Allen & Unwin.

Krivanek, J. (1989). *Addictions.* Sydney: Allen & Unwin.

Laderman, C. (1987). Trances that heal: Rites, rituals, and brain chemicals. In W. B. Rucker & M. E. Rucker (Eds.), *Drugs, society and behavior, 87/88* (pp. 233–235). Guilford, CT: Dushkin.

Laurie, P. (1971). *Drugs.* New York: Penguin Books.

Levin, J. D. (1989). *Alcoholism: A bio-psychosocial approach.* New York: Hemisphere.

MacAndrew, C. (1979). On the possibility of the psychometric detection of persons who are prone to the abuse of alcohol and other substances. *Journal of Addictive Behaviors, 4,* 11–20.

Mackarness, R. (1972). The allergic factor in alcoholism. *International Journal of Social Psychiatry, 18,* 194–200.

Madsen, W. (1974). *The American alcoholic: The nature-nurture controversies in alcoholic research and therapy.* Springfield, IL: Charles C Thomas.

Mann, M. (1968). *New primer on alcoholism* (2nd ed.). New York: Holt, Rinehart and Winston.

Meisch, R. A. (1982). Animal studies of alcohol intake. *British Journal of Psychiatry, 141,* 113–130.

Menninger, K. (1963). *The vital balance.* New York: Viking Press.

National Institute on Alcohol Abuse and Alcoholism (NIAAA). (1996). *Alcohol Alert* (no. 33). Washington, DC: U.S. Government Printing Office.

National Institute on Alcohol Abuse and Alcoholism (NIAAA). (2000). *Tenth Special Report on alcohol and health to the U.S. Congress.* Washington, DC: U.S. Government Printing Office.

National Institute on Alcohol Abuse and Alcoholism (NIAAA). (2009). *Collaborative studies on genetics of alcoholism.* Retrieved July 28, 2009, from www.niaaa.nih.

gov/ResearchInformation/ExtramuralResearch/SharedResources/projcoga.htm.

National Institute on Drug Abuse. (2008). *Genetics of addiction: A research update from the National Institute on Drug Abuse.* Retrieved July 28, 2009, from www.drugabuse.gov/tib/genetics.html.

Nichols, W. W. (1986). *Genetic and biological markers in drug abuse and alcoholism: A summary* (Research Monograph no. 66, Genetic and Biological Markers in Drug Abuse and Alcoholism). Washington, DC: National Institute on Drug Abuse.

Ott, P. J., Tartera, R. E., & Ammerman, R. T. (1999). *Sourcebook on substance abuse: Etiology, epidemiology, assessment, and treatment.* Boston, MA: Allyn & Bacon.

Pattison, E. M., & Kaufman, E. (1982). The alcoholism syndrome: Definitions and models. In E. M. Pattison & E. Kaufman (Eds.), *Encyclopedic handbook of alcoholism* (p. 13). New York: Gardner Press.

Pattison, E. M., Sobell, M. B., & Sobell, L. C. (1977). *Emerging concepts of alcohol dependence.* New York: Springer.

Peele, S. (1978). In B. Hafen & B. Peterson (Eds.), *Medicines and drugs* (2nd ed., p. 167). Philadelphia: Lea & Febiger.

Peele, S. (1985). *The meaning of addiction: compulsive experience and its interpretation.* Lexington: Lexington Books.

Peele, S. (Ed.). (1988). *Visions of addiction: Major contemporary perspectives on addiction and alcoholism.* Lexington, MA: D. C. Heath.

Peele, S. (1998). *The meaning of addiction: compulsive experience and its interpretation.* San Francisco: Jossey-Bass.

Raistrick, D., & Davidson, R. (1985). *Alcoholism and drug addiction.* New York: Churchill Livingstone.

Schaler, J. A. (2000). *Addiction is a choice.* Chicago: Open Court.

Schuckit, M. A. (1986). Etiological theories on alcoholism. In N. J. Estes & M. E. Heinemann (Eds.), *Alcoholism: Development, consequences, and interventions* (3rd ed., pp. 15–30). St. Louis, MO: C. V. Mosby.

Schuckit, M. A. (1992). Advances in understanding the vulnerability to alcoholism. In C. P. O'Brien & J. H. Jaffe (Eds.), *Addiction states* (pp. 93–108). New York: Raven Press.

Science Daily. (2007, September 27). Gene that may influence alcoholism and addiction identified. Retrieved July 28, 2009, from www.sciencedaily.com/releases/2007/09/070924163053.

Sherfey, M. (1955). Psychopathology and character structure in chronic alcoholism. In W. O. Diethelm (Ed.), *The etiology of chronic alcoholism.* Springfield, IL: Charles C Thomas.

Stewart, T. (1987). *The heroin users.* London, England: Pandora.

Tarter, R. E., & Schneider, D. U. (1976). Models and theories of alcoholism. In R. E. Tarter & A. A. Sugarmen (Eds.), *Alcoholism: Interdisciplinary approaches to an enduring problem.* Reading, MA: Addison-Wesley.

Trice, H. (1966). *Alcoholism in America.* New York: McGraw-Hill.

Vaillant, G. E. (1983). *The natural history of alcoholism: Causes, patterns, and paths to recovery.* Cambridge, MA: Harvard University Press.

Vaillant, G. E. (1994). Evidence that the type I/type II dichotomy in alcoholism must be re-examined. *Addiction, 89,* 1049–1058.

Vaillant, G. E. (1995). *The natural history of alcoholism revisited.* Cambridge, MA: Harvard University Press.

Valera, A., Rivera, L., Mardones, J., & Cruz-Coke, R. (1969). Color vision defects in non-alcoholic relatives of alcoholic patients. *British Journal of the Addictions, 64,* 67–71.

Washton, A. M. (1989). *Cocaine addiction: Treatment, recovery, and relapse prevention.* New York: W. W. Norton.

Weil, A., & Rosen, W. (1993). *From chocolate to morphine: Everything you need to know about mind-altering drugs.* Boston, MA: Houghton Mifflin.

West, R. (2006). *Theory of addiction.* Oxford: Blackwell Publishing.

Williams, R. J. (1959). *Alcoholism: The nutritional approach.* Austin: University of Texas Press.

CHAPTER 3

Alibhai, I. N., Green, T. A., Potashkin, J. A., & Nestler, E. J. (2007). Regulation of fosB and deltaFosB mRNA expression: In vivo and in vitro studies. *Brain Research, 1143,* 22–33.

Ait-Doud, N., Johnson, B. A., Prihoda, T. J., & Hargita, I. D. (2001). Combining ondansetron and naltrexone reduces craving among biologically predisposed alcoholics: Preliminary clinical evidence. *Psychopharmacology, 154,* 23–27.

Barrot, M., Oliver, J. D., Perrotti, L. I., DiLeone, R. J., Berton, O., Eisch, A. J., et al. (2002). CREB activity in the nucleus accumbens shell controls gating of behavioral responses to emotional stimuli. *Proceedings of the National Academy of Science of the USA 99,* 11435–11440.

Childress, A. R., Mozley, P. D., McElgin, W., Fitzgerald, J., Reivich, M., & O'Brien, C. P. (1999). Limbic activation during cue-induced cocaine craving. *American Journal of Psychiatry, 156*(1), 11–18.

Cloninger, C. R. (1999). Genetics of substance abuse. In M. A. K. Galanter (Ed.), *Textbook of substance abuse treatment* (2nd ed., pp. 59–66). Washington, DC: American Psychiatric Press.

Crunelle, C. L., Miller, M. L., Booij, J., & van den Brink, W. (2010). The nicotinic acetylcholine receptor partial agonist varenicline and the treatment of drug dependence: A review. *European Neuropsychopharmacology, 20*(2), 69–79.

Dewey, S. L., Morgan, A. E., Ashby, C. R., Jr., Horan, B., Kushner, S. A., Logan, J., et al. (1998). A novel strategy for the treatment of cocaine addiction. *Synapse, 30*(2), 119–129.

Edwards, S., Simmons, D. L., Galindo, D. G., Doherty, J. M., Scott, A. M., Hughes, P. D., & Wilcox, R. E. (2002). Antagonistic effects of dopaminergic signaling and ethanol on PKA-mediated phosphorylation of DARPP-32 and the NR1 subunit of the NMDA Receptor. *Alcoholism: Clinical and Experimental Research, 26*(2), 173–180.

Erickson, C. K. (1997a). *Your brain on drugs.* Center City, MN: Hazelden.

Erickson, C. K. (1997b). Voices of the afflicted: How does alcoholism treatment work? A neurochemical hypothesis *Alcoholism: Clinical Experimental Research, 21,* 567–568.

Erickson, C. K. (1998). Voices of the afflicted: What is impaired control? *Alcoholism: Clinical Experimental Research, 22,* 132–133.

Erickson, C. K., & Wilcox, R. E. (2001a). Neurobiological causes of addictions. *Journal of Social Work Practice in the Addictions, 1*(3), 7–22.

Erickson, C. K., & Wilcox, R. E. (2001b, Winter). Pharmacology of addiction. *Journal of the Texas Pharmacy Association,* 8–13.

Fishman, M. (2008). Precipitated withdrawal during maintenance opioid blockade with extended release naltrexone. *Addiction, 103*(8), 1399–1401.

Foreyt, J., & Goodrick, G. (2001). Cognitive behavioral therapy. In W. Craighead & C. Nemeroff (Eds.), *The Corsini encyclopedia of psychology and behavioral science* (Vol. 1, pp. 308–312). New York: John Wiley & Sons.

Galanter, M., & Kleber, H. D. (1999). *Textbook of substance abuse treatment* (2nd ed.). Washington, DC: American Psychiatric Press.

German, D., & Bowden, D. (1974). Catecholamine systems as the neural substrate for intracranial self-stimulation: A hypothesis. *Brain Research, 73*(3), 381–419.

Graybiel, A. M., Moratalia, R., & Robertson, H. A. (1990). Amphetamine and cocaine induce drug-specific activation of the c-fos gene in striosome-matrix compartments and limbic subdivisions of the striatum. *Proceedings of the National Academy of Science of the USA, 87,* 6912–6916.

Haney, M., Gunderson, E. W., Jiang, H., Collins, E. D., & Foltin, R. W. (2010). Cocaine-specific antibodies blunt the subjective effects of smoked cocaine in humans. *Biological Psychiatry. 67*(1), 59–65.

Hope, B., Kosofsky, B., Hyman, S. E., & Nestler, E. J. (1992). Regulation of IEG expression and AP-1 binding by chronic cocaine in the rat nucleus accumbens. *Proceedings of the National Academy of Science of the USA, 89,* 5764–5768.

Johannessen, M., Delghandi, M. P., & Moens, U. (2004). What turns CREB on? *Cell Signal, 16,* 1211–1227.

Johnson, B. A. (2010). Medication treatment of different types of alcoholism. *American Journal of Psychiatry, 167*(6), 630–639.

Kandel, E., Schwartz, J., & Jessell, T. (2000). *Principles of neuroscience* (14th ed.). New York: McGraw-Hill.

Kenna, G. A., Lomastro, T. L., Schiesl, A., Leggio, L., & Swift, R. M. (2009). Review of topiramate: An antiepileptic for the treatment of alcohol dependence. *Current Drug Abuse Reviews, 2*(2), 135–142.

Knox, R. (2001, September 1). *Early-warning system?* Report on National Public Radio.

Koob, G. F. (2008). A role for brain stress systems in addiction. *Neuron, 59*(1), 11–34.

Koob, G. F., Sanna, P. P., & Bloom, F. E. (1998). Neuroscience of addiction. *Neuron, 21,* 467–476.

Kosten, T. R., & Biegel, D. (2002, October). Therapeutic vaccines for substance dependence. *Expert Reviews Vaccines, 1*(3), 363–371.

Kranzler, H. R., & Van Kirk, J. (2001). Efficacy of naltrexone and acamprosate for alcoholism treatment: A meta-analysis. *Alcoholism: Clinical Experimental Research, 25*(9), 1335–1341.

Leshner, A. I. (1997). Addiction is a brain disease. *Science, 278*(5335), 45–47.

Levitt, R. (1981). *Physiological psychology.* New York: Holt, Rinehart and Winston.

Lonze, B. E., & Ginty, D. D. (2002). Function and regulation of CREB family transcription factors in the nervous system. *Neuron, 35,* 605–623.

Maurer, P., & Bachmann, M. F. (2007). Vaccination against nicotine: An emerging therapy for tobacco dependence. *Expert Opinion on Investigational Drugs, 16* (11), 1775–1783.

McClung, C. A., & Nestler, E. J. (2003). Regulation of gene expression and cocaine reward by CREB and deltaFosB. *Nature Neuroscience, 6,* 1208–1215.

McClung, C. A., & Nestler, E. J. (2008). Neuroplasticity mediated by altered gene expression. *Neuropsychopharmacology Reviews, 33,* 3–17.

Meert, T. F. (1994). Pharmacological evaluation of alcohol withdrawal-induced inhibition of exploratory behaviour and supersensitivity to harmine-induced tremor. *Alcohol & Alcoholism, 29*(1), 91–102.

Myers, R. (1978, June 12). Hypothalamic actions of 5-hydroxytryptamine neurotoxins: Feeding, drinking, and body temperature. *Annals of the New York Academy of Science, 305,* 556–575.

Nestler, E. J. (2008). Transcriptional mechanisms of addiction: Role of deltaFosB. *Philosophical Transactions of the Royal Society, 363,* 3245–3255.

Nestler, E., Hyman, S., & Malenka, R. (2001). *Molecular Neuropharmacology: A foundation for clinical neuroscience.* New York: McGraw-Hill.

Olds, J., & Milner, P. (1954). Positive reinforcement produced by electrical stimulation of the septal area and other regions of the rat brain. *Journal of Comparative and Physiological Psychology, 47*(6), 419–427.

Riffee, W. H., Wanek, E., & Wilcox, R. E. (1987). Prevention of amphetamine-induced behavioral hypersensitivity by concomitant treatment with microgram doses of apomorphine. *European Journal of Pharmacology, 135* (2), 255–258.

Riffee, W. H., Wanek, E., & Wilcox, R. E. (1988). Apomorphine fails to inhibit cocaine-induced behavioral hypersensitivity. *Pharmacology, Biochemistry & Behavior, 29*(2), 238–242.

Riffee, W. H., & Wilcox, R. E. (1985). Effects of multiple pretreatments with apomorphine and amphetamine on amphetamine-induced locomotor activity and its inhibition by apomorphine. *Psychopharmacology, 85*(1), 97–101.

Riffee, W. H., & Wilcox, R. E. (1987). Inhibition of amphetamine-induced locomotor activity by S-(+)-apomorphine: Comparison with the action of R-(-)-apomorphine [letter]. *Journal of Pharmacy and Pharmacology, 39*(1), 71–72.

Robbins, T. W., & Everitt, B. J. (1999). Drug addiction: Bad habits add up. *Nature, 398*(6728), 567–570.

Robinson, T. E., & Berridge, K. C. (1993). The neural basis of drug craving: An incentive-sensitization theory of addiction. *Brain Research Review, 18,* 246–291.

Robinson, T. E., & Berridge, K. C. (2000). The psychology and neurobiology of addiction: An incentive-sensitization view. *Addiction, 95*(Suppl. 2), S91–S117.

Robinson, T. E., & Berridge, K. C. (2008). The psychology and neurobiology of addiction: Some current issues. *Philosophical Transactions of the Royal Society, 363,* 3137–3146.

Robinson, T. E., Browman, K. E., Crombag, H. S., & Badiani, A. (1998). Modulation of the induction or expression of psychostimulant sensitization by the circumstances surrounding drug administration. *Neuroscience Biobehavior Review, 22,* 347–354.

Rubio, G., Martinez-Gras, I., & Manzanares, J. (2009). Modulation of impulsivity by topiramate: Implications for the treatment of alcohol dependence. *Journal of Clinical Psychopharmacology, 29*(6), 584–589.

Sarhan, H., Cloez-Tayarani, I., Massot, O., Fillion, M. P., & Fillion, G. (1999). 5-HT1B receptors modulate release of (3H) dopamine from rat striatal synaptosomes. *Naunyn-Schmiedeberg's Archives of Pharmacology, 359*(1), 40–47.

Schatzberg, A., & Nemeroff, C. (1998). *Textbook of psychopharmacology* (2nd ed.). Washington, DC: American Psychiatric Press.

Self, D. (1998). Neural substrates of drug craving and relapse in drug addiction. *Annals of Medicine, 30,* 379–389.

Self, D., Barnhart, W., Lehman, D., & Nestler, E. (1996). Opposite modulation of cocaine-seeking behavior by D1- and D2-like dopamine receptor agonists. *Science, 271*(5255), 1586–1589.

Self, D. W., & Nestler, E. J. (1995). Molecular mechanisms of drug reinforcement and addiction. *Annual Review of Neuroscience, 18,* 463–495.

Self, D. W., & Nestler, E. J. (1998). Relapse to drug-seeking: Neural and molecular mechanisms. *Drug and Alcohol Dependence, 51,* 49–60.

Sigmon, S. C., Moody, D. E., Nuwayser, E. S., & Bigelow, G. E. (2006). An injection depot form of buprenorphine: Extended biodelivery and effects. *Addiction, 101*(3), 420–432.

Vergne, D. E., & Anton, R. F. (2010). Aripiprazole: A drug with a novel mechanism of action and possible efficacy for alcohol dependence. *CNS Neurological Disorders Drug Targets, 9*(1), 50–54.

Wang, G. J., Vokow, N. D., Fowler, J. S., Cervany, P., Hitzemann, R. J., Pappas, N. R., et al. (1999). Regional brain metabolic activation during craving elicited by recall of previous experiences. *Life Science, 64*(9), 775–784.

Wilcox, R. E. (2001). Dopamine. In W. E. Craighead & C. B. Nemeroff (Eds.), *The Corsini encyclopedia of psychology and behavioral science* (Vol. 1, pp. 454–457). New York: John Wiley & Sons.

Wilcox, R. E., & Erickson, C. K. (2000). Commentary: Neurobiological aspects of the addictions. *Journal of Addictons Nursing, 12,* 117–133.

Wilcox, R. E., Gonzales, R. A., & Miller, J. D. (1998). Introduction to neurotransmitters, receptors, signal transduction and second messengers. In C. B. Nemeroff & A. F. Schatzberg (Eds.), *Textbook of psychopharmacology* (pp. 3–36). Washington, DC: American Psychiatric Press.

Wilcox, R. E., Huang, W. H., Brusniak, M. Y., Wilcox, D. M., Pearlman, R. S., Teeter, M. M., DuRand, C. J., Wiens, B. L., & Neve, K. A. (2000). CoMFA-based prediction of agonist affinities at recombinant wild type versus serine to alanine point mutated D2 dopamine receptors. *Journal of Medical Chemistry, 43*(16), 3005–3019.

Wilcox, R. E., & Levitt, R. A. (1975). The depressants. In R. A. Levitt (Ed.), *Psychopharmacology: A biological approach.* Washington, DC: Hemisphere/Wiley.

Wilcox, R. E., & Levitt, R. A. (1975). The neuron. In R. A. Levitt (Ed.), *Physiological psychology* (pp. 39–78). New York: Holt, Rinehart, & Winston (CBS College Publishing).

Wilcox, R. E., & Levitt R. A. (1981). The neuron. In R. A. Levitt, R. Holt, & Winston (Eds.), *Physiological psychology* (pp. 39–78). New York: CBS College Publishing.

Wilcox, R. E., & McMillen, B. A. (1998). The rational use of drugs as therapeutic agents for the treatment of the alcoholisms. *Alcohol, 15,* 161–177.

Wilson, A. W., Neill, J. C., & Costall, B. (1998). An investigation into the effects of 5-HT agonists and receptor antagonists on ethanol self-administration in the rat. *Alcohol, 16*(3), 249–270.

Wilson, W. (1939). *Alcoholics anonymous.* New York: Alcoholics Anonymous.

Young, S. T., Porrino, L. J., & Iadaerola, M. J. (1991). Cocaine induces striatal c-fos-immunoreactive proteins via dopaminergic D1 receptors. *Proceedings of the National Academy of Science of the USA, 88,* 1291–1295.

CHAPTER 4

Abadinsky, H. (2001). *Drugs: An introduction.* Belmont, CA: Wadsworth.

Agarwal, D. P., & Seitz, H. K. (2001). *Alcohol in health and diseases.* New York: Dekker.

Ammann, R. W., Akovbiantz, A., Largiader, F., & Schuele, G. (1984). Course and outcome of chronic pancreatitis: Longitudinal study of a mixed medical-surgical series of 245 patients. *Gastroenterology, 86,* 820.

Ammendola, A., Geiselhoringer, A., Hoffman, F., & Schlossmann, J. (2001). Peripheral neuropathy in chronic alcoholism: A retrospective cross-sectional study in 76 subjects. *Alcohol and Alcoholism, 36*(3), 271–275.

Arif, A. (Ed.). (1987). *Adverse health consequences of cocaine abuse.* Geneva, Switzerland: World Health Organization.

Arky, R. A. (1984). Alcohol use and the diabetic patient. *Alcohol Health and Research World, 8,* 8–13.

Baden, M. M. (1975). Pathology of the addictive states. In R. W. Richter (Ed.), *Medical aspects of drug abuse* (pp. 189–211). New York: Harper & Row.

Banken, J., & Foster H. (2008). Dextromethorphan: An emerging drug of abuse. *Annals of the New York Academy of Science, 1139,* 402–411.

Barnes, D. M. (1988). New data intensify the agony over ecstasy. *Science, 239,* 864–866.

Barsky, S. H., Roth, M. D., Kleerup, E. C., Simmons, M., & Tashkin, D. P. (1998). Histopathological and molecular alteration in bronchial epithelium in habitual smokers of marijuana, cocaine and/or tobacco. *Journal of National Cancer Institute, 90*(16), 1198–1205.

Baum, J. (1985). *One step over the line: A no-nonsense guide to recognizing and treating cocaine dependency.* San Francisco: Harper & Row.

Beck, J. (1986). The popularization and resultant implications of a recently controlled psychoactive substance. *Contemporary Drug Problems, 13,* 1.

Beck, J., & Morgan, P. A. (1986). Designer drug confusion: A focus on MDMA. *Journal of Drug Education, 16,* 287–302.

Bellenir, K. (2000). *Alcoholism sourcebook.* Detroit: Omnigraphics.

Bikle, D. D., Genant, H. K., Cann, C., Recker, R. R., Halloran, B. P., & Strewler, G. J. (1985). Bone disease in alcohol abuse. *Annals of Internal Medicine, 103,* 42–48.

Bolla, K. I., McCann, U. D., & Ricuarte, G. A. (1998). Memory impairment in abstinent MDMA "ecstasy" users. *Neurology, 51,* 1532–1537.

Bishop, K. (1989, September 16). Fear grows over effects of a new smokable drug. *New York Times,* p. 1.

Bode, C., & Bode, J. C. (1997). Alcohol's role in gastrointestinal disorders. *Alcohol Health and Research World, 21,* 76–83.

Brower, K. J., & Anglin, M. D. (1987). Adolescent cocaine use: Epidemiology, risk factors, and prevention. *Journal of Drug Education, 17,* 163–180.

Brown, C. (1982). The alcohol withdrawal syndrome. *Annals of Emergency Medicine, 11,* 276.

Butz, R. H. (1986). Intoxication and withdrawal. In N. J. Estes & M. E. Heinemann (Eds.), *Alcoholism: Development, consequences, and interventions* (pp. 103–109). St. Louis: C. V. Mosby, 9(1), 50–54.

Camargo, C. A., Jr., Stampfer, M. J., Glynn, R. J., Grodstein, F., Gaziano, J. M., Manson, J. E., et al. (1997). Moderate alcohol consumption and risk for angina pectoris or myocardial infarction in U.S. male physicians. *Annals of Internal Medicine, 126*(5), 372–375.

Canadian Institute of Neurosciences, Mental Health and Addiction. (2009). *The brain from top to bottom.* Retrieved July 10, 2009, from thebrain.mcgill.ca/flash/i/i_03/i_03_m/i_03_m_par/i_03_m_par_alcool.html#drogues.

Center for Substance Abuse Research (CESAR). (1995, June 19). *CESAR Fax, 4*(24).

Center for Substance Abuse Research (CESAR). (2003, December 1) *CESAR FAX, 12*(48).

Chang, L., Ernst, T., Strickland, T., & Mehringer, C. M. (1999). Gender effects on persistent cerebral-metabolite changes in the frontal lobes of abstinent cocaine users. *American Journal of Psychiatry, 156*(5), 716–722.

Chedid, A., Mendenhall, C. L., Gartside, P., French, S. W., Chen, T., & Rabin, L. (1991). Prognostic factors in alcoholic liver disease. *American Journal of Gastroenterology, 86*(2), 210–216.

Christophersen, A. (2000). Amphetamine designer drugs—An overview and epidemiology. *Toxicology Letters, 112–113,* 127–131.

Cicero, T. J. (1981). Neuroendocrinological effects of alcohol. *Annual Review of Medicine, 32,* 123–142.

Clarren, S. K., & Smith, D. W. (1978). Fetal alcohol syndrome. *New England Journal of Medicine, 298,* 1063–1067.

Cohen, S. (1981). *The substance abuse problem.* New York: Haworth Press.

Cornely, C. M., Schade, R. R., Van Thiel, D. H., & Gavaler, J. S. (1984). Chronic advanced liver disease and impotence: Cause and effect? *Hepatology, 4,* 1227–1230.

Dean, B., Sundram, S., Bradbury, R., Scarr, E., & Copolov, D. (2001). Studies on [3H] CP–55940 binding in the human central nervous system: Regional specific changes in density of cannnabinoid-1 receptors associated with schizophrenia and cannabis use. *Neuroscience, 103*(1), 9–15.

Dewey, W. L., Tucker, L. S., Prange, A. (1973). Some behavioral and toxicological effects of amyl nitrite. *Research Communications in Chemical Pathology and Pharmacology, 5,* 889.

Drug Enforcement Administration (DEA). (2001a). *Drugs and chemicals of concern: Oxycondone.* Drug Enforcement Administration: Diversion Control Program. Retrieved August 26, 2001, from www.deadiversion.usdoj.gov/drugs_concern/oxycodone/oxycodone.htm.

Drug Enforcement Administration (DEA). (2001b). *Drugs and chemicals of concern: Flunitrazepam.* Retrieved August 26, 2001, from www.deadiversion.usdoj.gov/drugs_concern/rohypnol.htm.

Drug Enforcement Administration (DEA). (2001c). *Drugs and chemicals of concern: Methamphetamine.* Retrieved August 26, 2001, from www.deadiversion.usdoj.gov/drugs_concern/meth.htm.

Eisenman, A. J., Fraser, H. F., & Brooks, T. (1961). Urinary excretion and plasma levels of 17-hydroxycorticoseroids during a cycle of addiction to morphine. *Journal of Pharmacology and Experimental Therapeutics, 132,* 226–231.

Fenster, L. F. (1986). Alcohol and disorders of the gastrointestinal system. In N. J. Estes & M. E. Heinemann (Eds.), *Alcoholism: Development, consequences, and interventions* (pp. 145–152). St. Louis: C. V. Mosby.

Fink, G. (1979). Feedback actions of target hormones on hypothalamus and pituitary with special reference to gonadal steroids. *Annual Review of Physiology, 41,* 571–585.

Floyd, R., Decouflé, P., & Hungerford, D. (1999). Alcohol use prior to pregnancy recognition. *American Journal of Preventive Medicine, 17*(2), 101–107.

Forney, R. B., & Harger, R. N. (1971). The alcohols. In J. R. DiPalma (Ed.), *Drill's pharmacology in medicine.* New York: McGraw-Hill.

Frank, D. A., Augustyn, M., Knight, W. G., Pell, T., & Zuckerman, B. (2001). Growth, development, and behavior in early childhood following prenatal cocaine exposure: A systematic review, *Journal of the American Medical Association, 285*(12), 1613–1625.

Friedman, H. S., Geller, S. A., Lieber, C. S. (1982). The effects of alcohol on the heart, skeletal, and smooth muscles. In C. S. Lieber (Ed.), *Medical disorders of alcoholism, pathogenesis, and treatment* (Vol. 22, pp. 436–479). Philadelphia: W. B. Saunders.

Geissler, M., Gesien, A., & Wands, J. R. (1997). Inhibitory effects of chronic ethanol consumption on cellular immune responses to hepatitis C virus core protein are reversed by genetic immunizations augmented with cytokine-expressing plasmids. *Journal of Immunology, 159*(10), 5107–5113.

Goode, E. (1972). *Drugs in American society.* New York: Knopf.

Gross, J. (1988, November 27). Speed's gain in use could rival crack, drug experts warn. *New York Times,* p. 1.

Hanson, W. J., Streissguth, A. P., & Smith, D. W. (1978). The effects of moderate alcohol consumption during pregnancy on fetal growth and morphogenesis. *Journals of Pediatrics, 92,* 457–460.

Hatzidimitriou, G., McCann, U. D., & Ricuarte, G. A. (1999). Altered serotonin innervation patterns in the forebrain of monkeys treated with MDMA seven years previously: Factors influencing abnormal recovery. *Journal of Neuroscience, 91*(12), 5096–5107.

Hermos, J. A. (1972). Mucosa of the small intestine in folate-deficient alcoholics. *Annals of Internal Medicine, 76,* 957.

Higgins, S. T., Bickel, W., & Bilenson, M. (1988). Behavioral and cardiovascular effects of alcohol and d-amphetamine combinations in normal volunteers. *Problems of Drug Dependence: Proceedings of the Fiftieth Annual Scientific Meeting, the Committee on Problems of Drug Dependence* (DHHS Publication no. 89–1605), pp. 35–36.

Hillers, V. N., & Massey, L. K. (1985). Interrelationships of moderate and high alcohol consumption with diet and health status. *American Journal of Clinical Nutrition, 41,* 356–362.

Hofmann, E. G. (1975). *A handbook on drug and alcohol abuse.* New York: Oxford University Press.

Homewood, J., & Bond, N. W. (1999). Thiamin deficiency and Korsakoff's syndrome: Failure to find memory impairments following nonalcoholic Wernicke's encephalopathy. *Alcohol, 19*(1), 75–84.

Hunt, W. A. (1985). *Alcohol and biological membranes.* New York: Guilford Press.

Hutchings, D. E. (1993). The puzzle of cocaine's effects following maternal use during pregnancy: Are there reconcilable differences? *Neurotoxicology and Treatology, 15,* 281–286.

Huxley, A. (1963). *The doors of perception and Heaven and Hell.* New York: Harper & Row.

Imlah, N. (1989). *Addiction: Substance abuse and dependency.* Winslow, England: Sigma Press.

Innes, I. R., & Nickerson, M. (1970). Amphetamine methamphetamine. In L. S. Goodman & A. Gilman (Eds.), *The pharmacological basis of therapeutics* (pp. 501–507). New York: Macmillan.

Israel, Y., Walfish, P. G., Orrego, H., Blake, S., & Kalant, H. (1979). Thyroid hormones in alcoholic liver disease. *Gastroenterology, 76,* 116–122.

Joffe, J. (1979). Influence of drug exposure of the father on perinatal outcome. *Clinics in Perinatology, 6,* 21–36.

Jolliffe, N., Karl, M., Bowman, M. D., Louis, A., Rosenblum, M. D., Harry D., et al. (1940). Nicotinic acid deficiency encephalopathy. *Journal of the American Medical Association, 114,* 307–312.

Jones, K. L., & Smith, D. W. (1973). Recognition of the fetal alcohol syndrome in early infancy. *Lancet, 2,* 999–1001.

Jones-Webb, R., McKiver, M., Pirie, P., & Miner, K. (1999). Relationships between physician advice and tobacco and alcohol use during pregnancy. *American Journal of Preventive Medicine, 16*(3), 244–247.

Julkunen, R. J. K., DiPradova, C., & Lieber, C. S. (1985). First pass metabolism of ethanol: A gastrointestinal barrier against the systemic toxicity of ethanol. *Life Sciences, 37,* 567–573.

Kahn, C. (2001, August 23). *OxyContin maker tries safeguard.* Retrieved August 26, 2001, from www.news.excite.com/news/ap/010823/21/oxycontin-task-force.

Kalant, H. (1969). Alcohol, pancreatic secretion, and pancreatitis. *Gastroenterology, 56,* 380.

Kiel, U., Chambless, L. E., Doring, A., Filipack, B., & Steiber, J. (1997). The relation of alcohol intake to coronary heart disease and all-cause mortality in a beer-drinking population. *Epidemiology, 8*(2), 150–156.

Knauer, C. M. (1976). Mallory-Weiss syndrome: Characteristics of 75 Mallory-Weiss lacerations in 528 patients with gastrointestinal hemorrhage. *Gastroenterology, 71,* 71.

Koch Crime Institute. (2001). *Methamphetamine: Frequently asked questions.* Retrieved December 21, 2003, from www.kci.org/meth_info/faq_meth.htm.

Kreek, M. J. (1982). Opiod disposition of effects during chronic exposure in the perinatal period in man. In B. Stimmel (Ed.), *The effects of maternal alcohol and drug abuse on the newborn* (pp. 21–53). New York: Haworth Press.

Krivanek, J. (1988). *Heroin: Myths and realities.* Sydney, Australia: Allen & Unwin.

Kuhn, C., Swartzwelder, S., & Wilson, W. (2008). *Buzzed: The straight facts about the most used and abused drugs, from alcohol to ecstasy* (3rd ed). New York: W. W. Norton & Company.

Kurtzman, T., Otsuka, K., & Wahl, R. (2001). Inhalant use by adolescents. *Journal of Adolescent Health, 28,* 170–180.

Lang, R. M., Borrow, K. M., Neumann, A., & Feldman, T. (1985). Adverse cardiac effects of acute alcohol ingestion in young adults. *Annals of Internal Medicine, 102,* 742–747.

Lerner, M. A. (November 27, 1989). The fire of "ice." *Newsweek,* pp. 37–40.

Lieber, C. S. (1984). Alcohol-nutrition interaction: 1984 update. *Alcohol, 1*(2), 151–157.

Lieber, C. S., Seitz, H. K., Garro, A. J., & Worner, T. M. (1979). Alcohol-related diseases and carcinogenesis. *Cancer Research, 39,* 2863–2866.

Little, R. E., Graham, J. M., & Samson, H. H. (1982). Fetal alcohol effects in humans and animals. In B. Stimmel (Ed.), *The effects of maternal alcohol and drug abuse on the newborn* (pp. 103–125). New York: Haworth Press.

Livesay, S., Ehrlich, E., Ryan, L., & Finnegan, L. (1988). Cocaine and pregnancy: Maternal and infant outcome. *Problems of Drug Dependence: Proceedings of the Fiftieth Annual Scientific Meeting, the Committee on Problems of Drug Dependence* (DHHS Publication no. 89–1605), p. 328.

Longnecker, M. P. (1992). Alcohol consumption in relation to risk of cancers of the breast and large bowel. *Alcohol Health and Research World, 16,* 223–229.

Loomis, T. (1986). The pharmacology of alcohol. In N. J. Estes & M. E. Heinemann (Eds.), *Alcoholism: Development, consequences, and interventions* (pp. 93–102). St. Louis: C. V. Mosby.

Lukas, S. E. (Ed.). (1985). Amphetamines. In *The encyclopedia of psychoactive drugs.* New York: Chelsea House.

Majumdar, R. K., et al. (1982). Blood vitamin status (B1, B2, B6, folic acid, and B12) in patients with alcoholic liver disease. *International Journal for Vitamin and Nutrition Research, 5,* 266–271.

Markiewi, K., & Cholewa, M. (1982). The effect of alcohol on the circulatory system adaptation to physical effort. *Journal of Studies on Alcohol, 43,* 812–823.

Martin, S. (2001). Abuse of painkiller OxyContin targeted: Illegal use of potent drug widening, authorities fear. *WebMD Medical News Archive.* Retrieved December 22, 2003, from my.webMD.content/article/32/1728_79798.htm.

Mathias, R. (2001). "Ecstasy" damages the brain and impairs memory in humans. *Drug Enforcement Administration: NIDA Notes.* Retrieved December 22, 2003, from www.drugabuse.gov/NIDA_Notes/NNvol14N4/Ecstasy. html.

Maier, S. E., & West, J. R. (2001). Drinking patterns and alcohol-related birth defects. *Alcohol Research & Health, 25*(3), 159–167.

McCann, U. D., Mertl, M., Eligulashvili, V., & Ricaurte, G. A. (1999). Cognitive performance in W 3, 4-methylenedioxymethainphetamine (MDMA, "ecstasy") users: A controlled study. *Psychopharmacology, 143,* 417–425.

McCann, U. D., Szabo, Z., Scheffel, U., Dannals, R. F., & Ricaurte, G. A. (1998). Positron emission tomographic evidence of toxic effect of MDMA ("ecstasy") on brain serotonin neurons in human beings. *Lancet, 352*(9138), 1433–1437.

McElduff, P. A., & Dobson, A. J. (1997). How much alcohol and how often? Population based case control study of alcohol consumption and risk of a major coronary event. *British Medical Journal, 314*(7088), 1159–1164.

Merritt, H. H. (1979). *A textbook of neurology.* Philadelphia: Lea & Febiger.

Mezey, E. (1982). Alcoholic liver disease. In H. Popper & F. Schaffner (Eds.), *Progress in liver diseases* (vol. 3, pp. 555–572). New York: Grune & Stratton.

Millan, M. S., Morris, G. P., Beck, I. T., & Henson, J. P. (1980). Villous damage induced by suction biopsy and by acute ethanol intake in normal human small intestine. *Digestive Diseases and Sciences, 25*, 513–525.

Miller, W. R., & Orr, J. (1980). Nature and sequence of neuropsychological deficits in alcoholics. *Journal of Studies on Alcohol, 41*, 325–337.

Moettus, A. T., & Tandberg, D. (1988). Brillo pad crack screen aspiration and ingestion. *Journal of Emergency Medicine, 16*(6), 861–863.

Moreau, J. J. (1972). *Du hashish et de l'Alienation mentale.* New York: Raven Press (Original work published 1845).

Morland, J. (2000). Toxicity of drug abuse-amphetamine designer drugs (ecstasy): Mental effects and consequences of single dose use. *Toxicology Letters, 112– 113*, 147–152.

Moskow, H. A., Pennington, R. C., & Knisely, M. H. (1968). Alcohol, sludge, and hypoxic areas of nervous system, liver, and heart. *Microvascular Research, 1*, 174–185.

Nahas, G. G. (1984). *Marijuana in science and medicine.* New York: Raven Press.

National Institute on Alcohol Abuse and Alcoholism (NIAAA). (1993). *Alcohol and cancer.* Retrieved December 22, 2003, from www.niaaa.nih.gov/publications/aa21.htm.

National Institute on Alcohol Abuse and Alcoholism (NIAAA). (1998). *Alcohol withdrawal.* Retrieved December 22, 2003, from www.niaaa.nih.gov/publications/arh22-1/toc22-6htm.

National Institute on Alcohol Abuse and Alcoholism (NIAAA). (1999). *Alcohol and coronary heart disease.* Retrieved December 22, 2003, from www.niaaa.nih.gov/publications/aa45.htm.

National Institute on Alcohol Abuse and Alcoholism (NIAAA). (2000). *Alcoholism.* Tenth Special Report to the U.S. Congress on Alcohol and Health. Washington, DC: U.S. Department of Health and Human Services.

National Institute on Alcohol Abuse and Alcoholism (NIAAA). (2004). Alcohol alert: Alcohol's damaging effects on the brain. Number 63, October.

National Institute on Alcohol Abuse and Alcoholism (NIAAA). (2005). Alcohol alert: Alcoholic liver disease. Number 64, January.

National Institute on Alcohol Abuse and Alcoholism (NIAAA). (2008). Neuroscience: Pathways to Alcohol Dependence Part 1—Overview of the Neurobiology of Dependence, Volume 31, Number 3, 2008.

National Institute on Alcohol Abuse and Alcoholism (NIAAA). (2008). Alcohol: A women's health issue. NIH Publication No. 03–4956.

National Institute on Drug Abuse (NIDA). (1999). *Epidemiologic trends in drug abuse: Advance report.* Retrieved October 14, 2001 from www.drugabuse.gov/CEWG/AdvancedRep/699ADV/699adv.html.

National Institute on Drug Abuse (NIDA). (2001a). *Facts about MDMA (Ecstasy).* Retrieved October 14, 2001 from www.drugabuse.gov/Infofax/ecstasy.html.

National Institute on Drug Abuse (NIDA). (2001b). *Hallucinogens and dissociative drugs.* Retrieved October 14, 2001, from 165.112.78.61/ResearchReports/ hallucinogens/halluc3.htmlOct142001.

National Institute on Drug Abuse (NIDA). (2001c). *Heroin: Abuse and addiction.* Retrieved October 14, 2001, from www.nida.nih.gov/ResearchReports/Heroin/Heroin3.html.

National Institute on Drug Abuse (NIDA). (2001d). *Methamphetatime.* Retrieved October 13, 2001, from www.nida.nih.gov/infofax/methamphetamine.html.

National Institute on Drug Abuse (NIDA). (2001e). *Methamphetamine: Abuse and addiction.* Retrieved October 13, 2001, from www.drugabuse.gov/ResearchReports/methamp/methamp.html.

National Institute on Drug Abuse (NIDA). (2001f). NIDA Notes: Conference Highlights Increasing GHG Use. Vol. 16. No 2, May.

National Institute on Drug Abuse (NIDA). (2005). *Research Report Series: Heroin Abuse and Addiction. NIH Publication Number 05–4165.* Retrieved from July 14, 2009, from www.drugabuse.gov/PDF/RRHeroin.pdf.

National Institute on Drug Abuse (NIDA). (2006). NIDA Research Report Series: Methamphetamine Abuse and Addiction. NIH Publication Number 06–4210, Revised, September, 2006.

National Institute on Drug Abuse (NIDA). (2008). *NIDA Topics in brief: Prescription drug abuse.* Retrieved July 14, 2009, from www.drugabuse.gov/pdf/tib/prescription.pdf.

National Institute on Drug Abuse (NIDA). (2009a). *NIDA Research Report Series - Prescription Drugs: Abuse and Addiction.* Retreived from July 2, 2009, from www.nida.nih.gov/Researchreports/Prescription/prescription2.html#HowDo.

National Institute on Drug Abuse (NIDA). (2009b). *NIDA Infofacts: Club drugs.* Retreived July 15, 2009, from www.drugabuse.gov/infofacts/Clubdrugs.html.

National Institute on Drug Abuse (NIDA). (2009c). *NIDA Infofacts: Hallucinogens.* Retreived July 15, 2009, from www.drugabuse.gov/Infofacts/hallucinogens.html.

National Institute on Drug Abuse (NIDA). (2009d). *Research Report Series: Inhalant abuse.* Retrieved July 15, 2009, from www.drugabuse.gov/Research Reports/Inhalants/Inhalants2.html#what.

National Institute on Drug Abuse (NIDA). (2009e). *Research Report Series: Anabolic steroid abuse.* Retrieved July 2, 2009, from www.drugabuse.gov/ResearchReports/Steroids/anabolicsteroids4.html#health.

National Institute on Drug Abuse (NIDA). (2009f). *Monitoring the Future: Overview of Key Findings, 2008.* Retrieved July 19, 2009, from www.monitoringthefuture.org/pubs/monographs/overview2008.pdf.

National Institute on Drug Abuse (NIDA). (2009g). *Prenatal exposure to drugs of abuse.* Retrieved July 16, 2009, from www.drugabuse.gov/tib/prenatal.html.

Page, R. D. (1983). Cerebral dysfunction associated with alcohol consumption. *Substance Alcohol Actions/Misuse, 4*(6), 405–421.

Palmstierna, T. (2001). A model for predicting alcohol withdrawal delirium. *Psychiatric Services, 52*(6), 820–823.

Paredes, A. A., & Gorelick, A. (1992). *Cocaine: Physiological and physiopathological effects.* New York: Haworth Press.

Platt, J. J., & Labate, C. (1976). *Heroin addiction.* New York: John Wiley and Sons.

Porjesz, B., & Begleiter, H. (1983). Brain dysfunction and alcohol. In B. Kissin & H. Begleiter (Eds.), *The biology of alcoholism* (vol. 7, pp. 415–483). New York: Plenum Press.

Potter, J. F., & Beevers, D. G. (1984). Pressor effect of alcohol in hypertension. *Lancet, 1,* 119–122.

Qureshi, A., Suri, F., Guterman, L., & Hopkins, L. (2001). Cocaine use and the likelihood of nonfatal myocardial infarction and stroke. *Circulation, 103*(4), 502–506.

Ron, M. A. (1983). *The alcoholic brain: CT scan and psychological findings.* Cambridge, England: Cambridge University Press.

Rosenbaum, B. J. (1971). Heroin: Influence of method of use. *New England Journal of Medicine, 285,* 299–300.

Sacks, O. (1985). *The man who mistook his wife for a hat.* New York: Summit Books.

Sapira, J. D. (1968). The narcotic addict as a medical patient. *American Journal of Medicine, 45,* 555–558.

Schmidt, W., & deLint, J. (1972). Causes of death in alcoholics. *Quarterly Journal of Studies on Alcohol, 33,* 171–185.

Seixas, F. A. (1986). The course of alcoholism. In N. J. Estes & M. E. Heinemann (Eds.), *Alcoholism: Development, consequences, and interventions* (pp. 67–77). St. Louis: C. V. Mosby.

Smith, J. W. (1986). Neurologic disorders in alcoholism. In N. J. Estes & M. E. Heinemann (Eds.), *Alcoholism: Development, consequences, and interventions* (pp. 153–175). St. Louis: C. V. Mosby.

Solowij, N. (1998). *Cannabis and cognitive functioning.* Cambridge, England: Cambridge University Press.

Stewart, T. (1987). *The heroin users.* London, England: Pandora Press.

Streissguth, A. P., Herman, C. S., & Smith, D. W. (1978). Intelligence, behavior, and dysmorphogenesis in the fetal alcohol syndrome: A report on 20 patients. *Journal of Pediatrics, 92,* 363–367.

Substance Abuse and Mental Health Services Administration (SAMHSA). (2000). *National Household Survey on Drug Abuse.* Washington, DC: U.S. Government Printing Office.

Substance Abuse and Mental Health Administration (SAMHSA). (2008). Substance use and dependence following initiation of alcohol or illicit drug use: The NSDUH Report. Washington, DC: U.S. Government Printing Office.

Tanner, L. (2009). *Possible Tylenol limits causing anxiety.* Associated Press, July 12. Retrieved July 12, 2009, from www.delawareonline.com/article/20090712/BUSINESS/907120329/1003.

Tewari, S., & Carson, V. G. (1982). Biochemistry of alcohol and alcohol metabolism. In E. M. Pattison & E. Kaufman (Eds.), *Encyclopedic handbook of alcoholism* (pp. 83–104). New York: Gardner Press.

Tewari, S., & Noble, E. P. (1971). Ethanol and brain protein synthesis. *Brain Research, 26,* 469–474.

Tkach, J. R., & Yoshitsugi, H. (1970). Autoimmunity in chronic brain syndrome. *Archives of General Psychiatry 23,* 61–64.

Trendy chemical, AIDS tie feared. (1986, October 12). *Miami Herald,* p. G–14.

Trouble with ecstasy, The. (1985, September). *Life,* pp. 88–94.

U.S. Department of Health and Human Services (USDHHS). (1983). *Fifth special report to the U.S. Congress on alcohol and health.* Washington, DC: U.S. Government Printing Office.

U.S. Department of Health and Human Services (USDHHS). (1987). *Sixth special report to the U.S. Congress on alcohol and health.* Washington, DC: U.S. Government Printing Office.

U.S. Department of Health and Human Services (USDHHS). (2000). *Tenth special report to the U.S. Congress on alcohol and health.* Washington, DC: U.S. Government Printing Office.

Vandenbroucke, J. P., & Pardoel, V. P. A. M. (1989). An autopsy of epidemiologic methods: The case of "poppers" in the early epidemic of the acquired immunodeficiency syndrome (AIDS). *American Journal of Epidemiology, 129*(3), 455–457.

Washton, A. M. (1989). *Cocaine addiction: Treatment, recovery and relapse prevention.* New York: W. W. Norton.

Weber, R. (1988). Immunologic effects of drugs of abuse. Problems of Drug Dependence: Proceedings of the fiftieth annual scientific meeting, The Committee on Problems of Drug Dependence (DHHS Publication no. 89–1065, pp. 99–104). Washington, DC: U.S. Government Printing Office.

White, J. M. (1991). *Drug dependence.* Englewood Cliffs, NJ, Prentice Hall.

Witztum, A., & Steinberg, D. (1991). Role of oxidized low density lipoprotein in atherogenesis. *Journal of Clinical Investigation, 88,* 1785–1992.

Yoslow, M. (1992). *Drugs in the body: Effects of abuse.* New York: Watts.

Zimmer, L., & Morgan, J. P. (1995). *Exposing marijuana myths: A review of the scientific evidence.* New York: Open Society Institute.

CHAPTER 5

Al-Anon. (1969). *Alcoholism: A Merry-Go-Round Named Denial.* Virginia Beach, VA: Author.

Allen, J. P. (2003). Assessment of alcohol problems—An overview. In J. P. Allen & V. B. Wilson, *Assessing alcohol problems: A guide for clinicians and researchers* (2nd. ed.), NIH Publication No. 03–3745. Bethesda, MD: National Institute on Alcohol Abuse and Alcoholism Retrieved March 18, 2010, from pubs.niaaa.nih.gov/publications/Assesing%20Alcohol/behaviors.htm.

Allen, J. P., Sillanaukee, P., Strid, N., & Litten, R. Z. (2003). Biomarkers of heavy drinking. In J. P. Allen & V. B. Wilson, *Assessing alcohol problems: A guide for clinicians and researchers* (2nd. ed.), NIH Publication No. 03–3745. Bethesda, MD: National Institute on Alcohol Abuse and Alcoholism, Retrieved March 18, 2010, from pubs.niaaa.nih.gov/publications/Assesing%20Alcohol/behaviors.htm.

Allen J. P., & Wilson, V. B., Eds. (2003). *Assessing alcohol problems: A guide for clinicians and researchers* (2nd. ed.), NIH Publication No. 03–3745. Bethesda, MD: National Institute on Alcohol Abuse and Alcoholism Retrieved March 18, 2010, from pubs.niaaa.nih.gov/publications/Assesing%20Alcohol/behaviors.htm.

American Psychiatric Association (APA). (2000). *Diagnostic and statistical manual of mental disorders* (4th ed., Text rev). Washington, DC: Author.

American Psychiatric Association. (2010). Rationale for changes to Substance-Related Disorders tentative new title of new combined section: Addiction and Related Disorders. Washington, DC: Author, retrieved April 3, 2010, from www.dsm5.org/ProposedRevisions/Pages/proposedrevision.aspx?rid=431#.

Babor, T. F., Dolinsky, Z., Rounsaville, B., & Jaffe, J. (1988). Unitary versus multidimensional models of alcoholism treatment outcome: An empirical study. *Journal of Studies on Alcohol, 49*(2), 167–177.

Babor, T. F., Higgins-Biddle, J. C., Saunders, J. B., & Monteiro, M. G. (2001). *AUDIT: The Alcohol Use Disorders Identification Test: Guidelines for use in primary care* (2nd ed.). Geneva, Switzerland: World Health Organization, retrieved April 18, 2011, from www.who.int/substance_abuse/publications/alcohol/en/.

Barber, J. G. (1995). *Social work with addictions.* London, England: Macmillan.

Bissell, L., & Royce, J. E. (1994). *Ethics for addiction professionals* (2nd. ed.), Center City, MN: Hazelden Foundation.

Brooks, M. K. (2004). Legal aspects of confidentiality of patient information. In J. H. Lowinson, P. Ruiz, R. B. Milman, & J. G. Langrod (Eds.), *Substance abuse: A comprehensive text book* (pp. 1361–1382). Philadelphia: Williams & Wilkins.

Brown, R. L., Leonard, T., Saunders, L. A., & Papasouliotis, O. (1998). The prevalence and detection of substance abuse disorders among inpatients 18 to 49: An opportunity for prevention. *Prevention Medicine, 27,* 101–110.

Brown, R. L., Leonard, T., Saunders, L. A., & Papasouliotis, O. (2001). A two-item conjoint screen for alcohol and other drug problems. *Journal of the American Board of Family Practice, 14*(2), 95–106.

Buchsbaum, D. G. (1995). Quick effective screening for alcohol abuse. *Patient Care, 29*(12), 56–62.

Burke, A. C., & Gregoire, T. K. (2007). Substance abuse treatment outcomes for coerced and noncoerced clients. *Health and Social Work, 32*(1), 7–15.

Bush, B., Shaw, S., Cleary, P., Delbanco, T. L., & Aronson, M. D. (1987). Screening for alcohol abuse using the CAGE questionnaire. *American Journal of Medicine, 82,* 231–235.

Callahan, E. J., & Pecsok, E. H. (1988). Heroin addiction. In D. M. Donovan & G. A. Marlatt (Eds.), *Assessment of addictive behavior* (pp. 390–418). New York: Guilford Press.

Carise, D., & McLellan, A. T. (1999). *Increasing cultural sensitivity of the Addiction Severity Index (ASI): An example with Native Americans in North Dakota: Special report.* Rockville, MD: Center for Substance Abuse Treatment.

Center for Substance Abuse Treatment. (2005). *Substance abuse treatment for adults in the criminal justice system.* Treatment Improvement Protocol (TIP) Series 44. DHHS Publication No. (SMA) 05–4056. Rockville, MD: Substance Abuse and Mental Health Services Administration.

Chan, A. W. K., Pristach, E. A., & Welte, J. W. (1994). Detection of alcoholism in three populations by the brief-MAST. *Alcoholism: Clinical and Experimental Research, 18*(3), 695–701.

Chan, A. W. K., Pristach, E. A., Welte, J. W., & Russell, M. (1993). Use of the TWEAK Test in screening for alcoholism/ heavy drinking in three populations. *Alcoholism: Clinical and Experimental Research, 17*(6), 1188–1192.

Connors, G. J., Donovan, D. M., & DiClemente, C. C. (2001). *Substance abuse treatment and the stages of change: Selecting and planning interventions.* New York: Guilford Press.

Connors, G. J., & Volk, R. J. (2003). Self-report screening for alcohol problems among adults. In J. P. Allen & V. B. Wilson, *Assessing alcohol problems: A guide for clinicians and researchers* (2nd. ed.), NIH Publication No. 03–3745. Bethesda, MD: National Institute on Alcohol Abuse and Alcoholism, retrieved March 18, 2010, from pubs.niaaa.nih.gov/publications/Assesing%20Alcohol/selfreport.htm.

Criteria Committee, National Council on Alcoholism (now National Council on Alcoholism and Drug Dependence). (1972a). Criteria for the diagnosis and treatment of alcoholism. *Annals of International Medicine, 77,* 249–258.

Criteria Committee, National Council on Alcoholism (now National Council on Alcoholism and Drug Dependence). (1972b). Criteria for the diagnosis and treatment of alcoholism. *American Journal of Psychiatry, 129*, 127–135.

Donovan, D. M. (1988). Assessment of addictive behaviors: Implications of an emerging biopsychosocial model. In D. M. Donovan & G. A. Marlatt (Eds.), *Assessment of addictive behaviors* (pp. 3–48). New York: Guilford Press.

Edwards, G., & Gross, M. M. (1976). Alcohol dependence: Provisional description of a clinical syndrome. *British Medical Journal, 1*, 1058–1061.

Ewing, J. A. (1984). Detecting alcoholism. The CAGE questionnaire. *Journal of the American Medical Association, 252*(14), 1905–1907.

Fauman, M. A. (2002). *Study guide to DSM-IV.* Washington, DC: American Psychiatric Press.

First, M. B., Spitzer, R. L., Gibbon, M., & Williams, J. B. W. (1997). *Structured clinical interview for DSM-IV axis I disorders (SCID-I) clinical version administration booklet.* Washington, DC: American Psychiatric Press.

Fleming, M. F., & Barry, K. L. (1989). A study examining the psychometric properties of the SMAST-13. *Journal of Substance Abuse, 1*, 173–182.

Fleming, M. F., & Barry, K. L. (1991). The effectiveness of alcoholism screening in an ambulatory care setting. *Journal of Studies on Alcohol, 52*(1), 33–36.

Friedman, A. S., & Utada, A. (1989). A method for diagnosing and planning the treatment of adolescent drug abusers (the Adolescent Drug Abuse Diagnosis [ADAD] instrument). *Journal of Drug Education, 19*(4), 285–312.

Fuller, R. K. (1988). Can treatment outcome research rely on alcoholics' self-reports. *Alcohol Health and Research World, 12*(3), 180–186.

George, R. L. (1990). *Counseling the chemically dependent: Theory and practice.* Englewood Cliffs, NJ: Prentice Hall.

Heck, E. J., & Williams, M. D. (1995). Using the CAGE to screen for drinking-related problems in college students. *Journal of Studies on Alcohol, 56*, 282–286.

Hesselbrock, M., Babor, T. F., Hesselbrock, V., Meyer, R. E., & Workman, K. (1983). Never believe an alcoholic? On the validity of self-report measures of alcohol dependence and related constructs. *International Journal of the Addictions, 18*(5), 593–609.

Hiller, M. L., Knight, K., Broome, K. M., & Simpson, D. D. (1998). Legal pressure and treatment retention in a national sample of long-term residential programs. *Criminal Justice and Behavior, 25*(4), 463–481.

Hodge, D. R. (2001). Spiritual assessment: A review of major qualitative methods and a new framework for assessing spirituality. *Social Work, 46*, 203–214.

Johnson, V. E. (1973). *I'll quit tomorrow.* New York: Harper and Row.

Kaminer, Y., Wagner, E., Plummer, B., & Seifer, R. (1993). Validation of the Teen Addiction Severity Index (T-ASI). *American Journal of Addiction, 2*, 250–254.

Kinney, J. (1996). *Clinical manual of substance abuse* (2nd ed.). St. Louis, MO: Mosby-Year Book.

Kinney, J. (2000). *Loosening the grip: A handbook of alcohol information* (6th ed.). Boston, MA: McGraw-Hill.

Knight, J. R. Sherritt, L., Harris, S. K., Gates, E. C., & Chang, G. (2003). Validity of brief alcohol screening tests among adolescents: A comparison of the AUDIT, POSIT, CAGE, and CRAFFT. *Alcoholism: Clinical and Experimental Research, 27*(1), 67–73.

Lanier, D., & Ko, S. (2008, January). Screening in primary care settings for illicit drug use: Assessment of screening instruments—A supplemental evidence update for the U.S. Preventive Services Task Force. Evidence Synthesis No. 58, Part 2. AHRQ Publication No. 08–05108-EF-2. Rockville, Maryland: Agency for Healthcare Research and Quality. Retrieved May 1, 2010, from www.ahrq.gov/clinic/uspstf08/druguse/drugevup.pdf.

Lazowski, L. E., Miller, F. G., Boye, M. W., & Miller, G. A. (1998). Efficacy of the Substance Abuse Subtle Screening Inventory-3 (SASSI-3) in identifying substance dependence disorders in clinical settings. *Journal of Personality Assessment, 71*, 114–128.

Lettieri, D. J., Nelson, J. E., & Sayers, M. A. (Eds.). (1985). *Alcoholism treatment assessment research instruments, treatment handbook, Series 2.* Rockville, MD: National Institute on Alcohol Abuse and Alcoholism.

Leukefeld, C. G., & Tims, F. M. (Eds.). (1992). *Drug abuse treatment in prisons and jails* (NIDA Research Monograph no. 118, DHHS Publication no. [ADM] 92–1884). Rockville, MD: U.S. Department of Health and Human Services.

Liskow, B., Campbell, J., Nickel, E. J., & Powell, B. J. (1995, May). Validity of the CAGE questionnaire in screening for alcohol dependence in a walk-in (triage) clinic. *Journal of Studies on Alcohol, 56*, 277–281.

MacAndrew, C. (1965). The differentiation of male alcoholic outpatients from nonalcoholic psychiatric outpatients by means of the MMPI. *Quarterly Journal of Studies on Alcohol, 26*, 238–246.

Mayfield, D., McLeod, G., & Hall, P. (1974). The CAGE questionnaire: Validation of a new alcoholism screening instrument. *American Journal of Psychiatry, 131*, 1121–1123.

McLellan, A. T., Luborsky, L., Cacciola, J., Griffith, J., Evans, F., Barr, H. L., & O'Brien, C. R. (1985). New data from the Addiction Severity Index: Reliability and validity in three centers. *Journal of Nervous and Mental Disease, 173*(7), 412–423.

McLellan, A. T., Luborsky, L., Woody, G. E., O'Brien, C. P., & Kron, R. (1981). Are the "addiction-related" problems of substance abusers really related? *Journal of Nervous and Mental Disease, 169*, 232–239.

Miller, F. G., & Lazowski, L. E. (1999). *The Substance Abuse Subtle Screening Inventory-3 (SASSI) manual.* Springville, IN: SASSI Institute.

Miller, F. G., & Lazowski, L. E. (2001). *The Adolescent Substance Abuse Subtle Screening Inventory-A2 (SASSI–A2) manual.* Springville, IN: SASSI Institute.

Miller, F. G., & Lazowski, L. E. (2005). Substance Abuse Subtle Screening Inventory for Adolescents—second version. In D. Seagrave (Ed.), *Handbook of mental health screening and assessment for juvenile justice.* New York: Guilford Press.

Miller, W. R. (1985). Motivation for treatment: A review with special emphasis on alcoholism. *Psychological Bulletin, 98*(1), 84–107.

Miller, W. R. (1999). *Enhancing motivation for change in substance abuse treatment* (Treatment Improvement Protocol (TIP) Series no. 35, DHHS Publication no. [SMA] 02–3629). Rockville, MD: Substance Abuse and Mental Health Services Administration.

Miller, W. R., & Rollnick, S. (1991). *Motivational interviewing.* New York: Guilford Press.

Miller, W. R., & Rollnick, S. (2002). *Motivational interviewing: Preparing people for change* (2nd. ed.), New York: Guilford Press.

Morton, L. A. (1978). *The risk prediction scales.* Indianapolis, IN: Department of Mental Health, Division of Addiction Services.

NAADAC (The Association for Addiction Professionals). (2011, March 28). NAADAC Code of Ethics. Retrieved April 18, 2011, from www.naadac.org/index.php?option=com_content&view=article&id=185&Itemid=113.

National Institute on Alcohol Abuse and Alcoholism (NIAAA). (1990). *Seventh special report to the U.S. Congress on alcohol and health.* Rockville, MD: U.S. Department of Health and Human Services.

National Institute on Alcohol Abuse and Alcoholism (NIAAA). (1993). *Eighth special report to the U.S. Congress on alcohol and health.* Rockville, MD: U.S. Department of Health and Human Services.

National Institute on Drug Abuse. (2009). *Principles of drug addiction treatment: A research based guide* (2nd ed.). NIH Publication No. 09–4180, Bethesda, MD: National Institutes of Health.

Pattison, E. M., Sobell, M. B., & Sobell, L. C. (1977). *Emerging concepts of alcohol dependence.* New York: Springer.

Perron, B. E., & Bright, C. L. (2008). The influence of legal coercion on dropout from substance abuse treatment: Results from a national survey. *Drug and Alcohol Dependence, 92,* 123–131.

Pokorny, A. D., Miller, B. A., & Kaplan, H. B. (1972). The brief MAST: A shortened version of the Michigan alcoholism screening test (MAST). *American Journal of Psychiatry, 129*(3), 342–345.

Prochaska, J. O., & DiClemente, C. C. (1982). Transtheoretical therapy: Toward a more integrative model of change. *Psychotherapy: Theory, Research, and Practice, 19*(3), 276–288.

Prochaska, J. O., DiClemente, C. C., & Norcross, J. C. (1992). In search of how people change: Applications to addictive behaviors. *American Psychologist, 47*(9), 1102–1114.

Rogers, C. R. (1959). A theory of therapy, personality, and interpersonal relationships as developed in the client-centered approach. In S. Koch (Ed.), *Psychology: The study of a science: Vol. 3: The formulations of the person and the social context* (pp. 184–256). New York: McGraw-Hill.

Russell, M. (1994). New assessment tools for risk drinking during pregnancy: T-ACE, TWEAK, and others. *Alcohol Health and Research World, 18*(1), 55–61.

Selzer, M. L. (1971). The Michigan Alcoholism Screening Test: The quest for a new diagnostic instrument. *American Journal of Psychiatry, 127,* 1653–1658.

Selzer, M. L., Vinokur, A., & van Rooijen, L. (1975). A self-administered short version of the Michigan Alcoholism Screening Test (MAST). *Journal of Studies on Alcohol, 36,* 117–126.

Skinner, H. A. (1979). A multivariate evaluation of the MAST. *Journal of Studies on Alcohol, 40,* 831–844.

Skinner, H. A. (1982). The Drug Abuse Screening Test. *Addictive Behaviors, 7,* 363–371.

Skinner, H. A. (1984). Assessing alcohol use by patients in treatment. In R. G. Smart, H. D. Cappell, & F. B. Glaser (Eds.), *Research advances in alcohol and drug problems* (Vol. 8, pp. 183–207). New York: Plenum Press.

Smith, P. C., Schmidt, S. M., Allensworth-Davies, D., & Saitz, R. (2009, July). Primary care validation of a single-question alcohol screening test. *Journal of General Internal Medicine, 24*(7), 783–788.

Substance Abuse and Mental Health Services Administration. (2006, September). The role of biomarkers in the treatment of alcohol use disorders. Substance Abuse Treatment Advisory, 5(4). Retrieved March 18, 2010, from kap.samhsa.gov/products/manuals/advisory/pdfs/0609_biomarkers.pdf.

Svanum, S., & McGrew, J. (1995). Prospective screening of substance dependence: The advantages of directness. *Addictive Behaviors, 20*(2), 205–213.

Taleff, M. J. (2010). *Advanced ethics for addiction counselors.* New York: Springer Publishing.

Tarter, R. E., Alterman, A. I., & Edwards, K. L. (1984). Alcoholic denial: A biopsychological interpretation. *Journal of Studies on Alcohol, 45*(3), 214–218.

Tarter, R. E., & Hegedus, A. M. (1991). The Drug Use Screening Inventory: Its application in the evaluation and treatment of alcohol and other drug abuse. *Alcohol Health and Research World, 15*(1), 65–75.

Tarter, R. E., & Kirisci, L. (2001). Validity of the Drug Use Screening Inventory for Predicting DSM-III-R Substance Use Disorder. *Journal of Child and Adolescent Substance Abuse, 10*(4), 45–53.

Trice, H. M., & Beyer, J. M. (1982). Job based alcoholism programs: Motivating problem drinkers to rehabilitation. In E. M. Pattison & E. Kaufman (Eds.), *Encyclopedic handbook of alcoholism* (pp. 954–978). New York: Gardner Press.

Washton, A. M. (1989). *Addiction.* New York: W. W. Norton.

Weatherman, R., & Crabb, D. W. (1999). Alcohol and medication interactions. *Alcohol Research and Health, 23*(1), 40–54.

Weinberg, J. R. (1986). Counseling the person with alcohol problems. In N. J. Estes & M. E. Heinemann (Eds.), *Alcoholism: Development, consequences, and interventions* (3rd ed.). St. Louis, MO: C. V. Mosby.

Winters, K. (1999). *Screening and assessing adolescents for substance use disorders* (Treatment Improvement Protocol [TIP] Series no. 31, DHHS Publication no. [SMA] 99–3282). Rockville, MD: Substance Abuse and Mental Health Services Administration.

Winters, K. (2003). Assessment of alcohol and other drug use behaviors among adolescents. In J. P. Allen & V. B. Wilson, *Assessing alcohol problems: A guide for clinicians and researchers* (2nd ed.). NIH Publication No. 03–3745. Bethesda, MD: National Institute on Alcohol Abuse and Alcoholism. Retrieved March 18, 2010, from pubs.niaaa.nih.gov/publications/Assesing%20Alcohol/behaviors.htm.

World Health Organization. (1992). *ICD-10 classification of mental and behavioural disorders: Clinical descriptions and diagnostic guidelines.* Geneva: Author.

Yudko, E., Lozhkina, O., & Fouts, A. (2007). A comprehensive review of the psychometric properties of the Drug Abuse Screening Test. *Journal of Substance Abuse Treatment, 32,* 189–198.

CHAPTER 6

Abbott, P. J. (2009). A review of the Community Reinforcement Approach in the treatment of opioid dependence. *Journal of Psychoactive Drugs, 41*(4), 379–385.

Alcoholics Anonymous (AA). (1952). *Forty-four questions and answers about the AA program of recovery from alcoholism.* New York: Alcoholics Anonymous World Services.

Alcoholics Anonymous (AA). (2001). *Alcoholics Anonymous: The story of how many thousands of men and women have recovered from alcoholism* (4th ed.). New York: Alcoholics Anonymous World Services.

Alcoholics Anonymous (AA). (2010). *A.A. fact file.* New York: Alcoholics Anonymous World Services. Retrieved December 23, 2010, from www.aa.org/pdf/products/m-24_aafactfile.pdf.

Alexander, J. A., Pollack, H., Nahra, T., Wells, R., & Lemak, C. H. (2007). Case management and client access to health and social services in outpatient substance abuse treatment. *Journal of Behavioral Health Services and Research, 34*(3), 221–236.

Alterman, A. I., & McLellan, T. (1993). Inpatient and day hospital treatment services for cocaine and alcohol dependence. *Journal of Substance Abuse Treatment, 10,* 269–275.

Amato, L., Minozzi, S. Davoli, M., Vecchi, S., Ferri, M., & Mayet, S. (2008, July 16). Psychosocial and pharmacological treatments versus pharmacological treatments for opioid detoxification. Cochrane Database of Systematic Reviews 1008, Issue 4. Art No.: CD005031. DOI: 10.1002/14651858.CD005031.pub 3. Retrieved December 26, 2010, from www2.cochrane.org/reviews/en/ab005031.html.

American Public Health Association and Education Development Center, Inc. (2008). Alcohol screening and brief intervention: A guide for public health practitioners. Washington DC: National Highway Traffic Safety Administration, U.S. Department of Transportation. Retrieved December 22, 2010, from www.adp.cahwnet.gov/SBI/pdfs/Alcohol_SBI_Manual.pdf.

American Society of Addiction Medicine. (2005, April 1). Public policy statement on rapid and ultra rapid opioid detoxification. Washington, DC: Author. Retrieved April 5, 2010, from www.asam.org/RapidandUltraRapidOpioidDetoxification.html.

Anderson, K. L. (2008, May 13). *What we can learn from the Audrey Kishline tragedy--the case for harm reduction.* Retrieved December 27, 2010, from ezinearticles.com/?expert=Kenneth_L_Anderson.

Annis, H. M., & Davis, C. S. (1988). Self-efficacy and the prevention of alcoholic relapse: Initial findings from a treatment trial. In T. B. Baker & D. S. Cannon (Eds.), *Assessment and treatment of addictive disorders* (pp. 88–112). New York: Praeger.

Anton, R. F. et al. (2004). A multi-site dose ranging study of nalmefene in the treatment of alcohol dependence. *Journal of Clinical Psychopharmacology, 24*(4), 421–428.

Anton, R. F. et al. for the COMBINE Research Group, (2006). Effect of combined pharmacotherapies and behavioral intervention (COMBINE Study) for alcohol dependence. *Journal of the American Medical Association, 295*(17), 2003–2017.

Armor, D. J., Polich, J. M., & Stambul, H. B. (1978). *Alcoholism and treatment.* New York: John Wiley and Sons.

Ashery, R. S. (1992). *Progress and issues in case management* (DHHS Pub. no. [ADM] 92–1946). Rockville, MD: National Institute on Drug Abuse.

Avants, S. K., Margolin, A., Chang, P., Kosten, T. R., & Birch, S. (1995). Acupuncture for the treatment of cocaine addiction: Investigation of a needle puncture control. *Journal of Substance Abuse Treatment, 12*(3), 195–205.

Azrin, N. H., Sisson, R. W., Meyers, R., & Godley, M. (1982). Alcoholism treatment by disulfiram and community reinforcement therapy. *Journal of Behavior Therapy and Experimental Psychiatry, 13,* 105–112.

Babor, T. F., & Higgins-Biddle, J. C. (2001). *Brief intervention for hazardous and harmful drinking: A manual for use in primary care.* Geneva, Switzerland: World Health Organization.

Baekeland, F. (1977). Evaluation of treatment methods in chronic alcoholism. In B. Kissin & H. Begleiter (Eds.), *The biology of alcoholism: Treatment and rehabilitation of the chronic alcoholic* (Vol. 5, pp. 385–440). New York: Plenum Press.

Barnett, P. G., & Swindle, R. W. (1997). Cost-effectiveness of inpatient substance abuse treatment. *Health Services Research, 32*(5), 615–629.

Bearn, J., Swami, A., Stewart, D., Atnas, C., Giotto, L., & Gossop, M. (2009). Auricular acupuncture as an adjunct to opiate detoxification treatment: Effects on withdrawal symptoms. *Journal of Substance Abuse Treatment, 36,* 345–349.

Berg, I. K. (1995). Solution-focused brief therapy with substance abusers. In A. M. Washton (Ed.), *Psychotherapy and substance abuse: A practitioner's handbook* (pp. 223–242). New York: Guilford Press.

Bottlender, M., Spanagel, R., & Soyka, M. One drink, one drunk—controlled drinking by alcoholics. *Psychotherapie. Psychosomatik. Medizinische Psychologie, 57,* 32–38. Retrieved December 21, 2010, from www.thieme-connect.com/ejournals/abstract/ppmp/doi/10.1055/s-2006-951918.

Boucher, T. A., Kiresuk, T. J., & Trachtenberg, A. I. (1998). Alternative therapies. In A. W. Graham & T. K. Shultz (Eds.), *Principles of addiction medicine* (2nd ed., pp. 371–394). Chevy Chase, MD: American Society of Addiction Medicine.

Bradley, A. M. (1988). Keep coming back: The case for a valuation of Alcoholics Anonymous. *Alcohol Health & Research World, 12*(3), 192–199.

Brandsma, J. M., Maultsby, M. C., Jr., & Welsh, R. J. (1980). *Outpatient treatment of alcoholism: A review and comparative study.* Baltimore, MD: University Park Press.

Brandsma, J. M., & Pattison, E. M. (1985). The outcome of group psychotherapy alcoholics: An empirical review. *American Journal of Drug and Alcohol Abuse, 11*(1 & 2), 151–162.

Brook, D. W. (2008). Group therapy. In M. Galanter & H. D. Kleber, *The American Psychiatric Publishing textbook of substance abuse treatment* (4th ed., pp. 413–427). Washington, DC: American Psychiatric Publishing.

Broome, K. M., Simpson, D. D., & Joe, G. W. (1999). Patient and program attributes related to treatment process indicators in DATOS. *Drug and Alcohol Dependence, 57,* 127–135.

Brumbaugh, A. G. (1993). Acupuncture: New perspectives in chemical dependency treatment. *Journal of Substance Abuse Treatment, 10,* 35–43.

Bullock, M. L., Culliton, P. D., & Olander, R. T. (1989). Controlled trial of acupuncture for severe recidivist alcoholism. *The Lancet, 1,* 1435–1439.

Bullock, M. L., Kiresuk, T. J., Pheley, A. M., Culliton, P. D., & Lenz, S. K. (1999). Auricular acupuncture in the treatment of cocaine abuse: A study of efficacy and dosing. *Journal of Substance Abuse Treatment, 16,* 31–38.

Bullock, M. L., Kiresuk, T. J., Sherman, R. E., Lenz, S. K., Culliton, P. D., Boucher, T. A., & Nolan, C. J. (2002). A large randomized placebo controlled study of auricular acupuncture for alcohol dependence. *Journal of Substance Abuse Treatment, 22,* 71–77.

Bullock, M. L., Umen, A. J., Culliton, P. D., & Olander, R. T. (1987). Acupuncture treatment of alcoholic recidivism: A pilot study. *Alcoholism: Clinical and Experimental Research, 11*(3), 292–295.

Callahan, E. J., & Pecsok, E. H. (1988). Heroin addiction. In D. M. Donovan & G. A. Marlatt (Eds.), *Assessment of addictive behavior* (pp. 390–418). New York: Guilford Press.

Campbell, W. G. (1997). Evaluation of a residential program using the Addiction Severity Index and stages of change. *Journal of Addictive Diseases, 16*(2), 27–39.

Cannon, D. S., Baker, T. B., Gino, A., & Nathan, P. E. (1988). Alcohol aversion therapy: Relationship between strength of aversion and abstinence. In T. B. Baker & D. S. Cannon (Eds.), *Assessment and treatment of addictive disorders* (pp. 205–237). New York: Praeger Publishers.

Cartwright, W. S. (2000). Cost-benefit analysis of drug treatment services: Review of the literature. *Journal of Mental Health Policy and Economics, 3,* 11–26.

Center for Applied Research in Mental Health and Addiction. (2008, November). *Family physician guide for depression, anxiety disorders, early psychosis and substance use disorders.* British Columbia: Faculty of Health Sciences, Simon Fraser University.

Centers for Disease Control. (2002, February). *Methadone maintenance treatment.* Atlanta, GA: U.S. Department of Health and Human Services. Retrieved April 29, 2010, from cdc.gov/idu/facts/MethadoneFin.pdf.

Center for Substance Abuse Treatment. (2005, Fall). Acamprosate: A new medication for alcohol use disorders. *Substance Abuse Treatment Advisory, 4*(1). Retrieved April 28, 2010, from www.google.com/search?hl=en&source=hp&q=when+was+acamprosate+approved+for+use+in+the+US&btnG=Google+Search&aq=f&aqi=&aql=&oq=&gs_rfai=.

Center for Substance Abuse Treatment. (2006). *Detoxification and substance abuse treatment.* Treatment Improvement Protocol (TIP) Series 45. DHHS Publication No. (SMA) 06-4131. Rockville, MD: Substance Abuse and Mental Health Services Administration.

Center for Substance Abuse Treatment. (2009, April). *Cost offset of treatment services. Rockville, MD: Substance Abuse and Mental Health Services Administration.* Retrieved December 20, 2010, from www.samhsa-gpra.samhsa.gov/CSAT/view/docs/SAIS_GPRA_CostOffset Substance-Abuse.pdf.

Chick, J., Gough, K., Falkowski, W., Kershaw, P. Hore, Mehta, B., Ritson, B., Ropner, R., & Torley, D. (1992). Disulfiram treatment of alcoholism. *British Journal of Psychiatry, 161,* 84–89.

Cho, S, & Whang, W. W. (2009). Acupuncture for alcohol dependence: A systematic review. *Alcoholism: Clinical and Experimental Research, 33*(8), 1305–1313.

Christopher, J. (1988). *How to stay sober without religion.* Amherst, NY: Prometheus Books.

Christopher, J. (1989). *Unhooked: Staying sober and drug free.* Amherst, NY: Prometheus Books.

Christopher, J. (1992). *SOS Sobriety: The proven alternative to 12-Step programs.* Amherst, NY: Prometheus Books.

Cohen, L. M., Collins, F. L., Young, A. M., McChargue, D. E., Leffingwell, T. R., & Cook, K. L. (2009). *Pharmacology and treatment of substance abuse.* New York: Taylor & Francis Group.

Collins, E. D., Kleber, H. D., Whittington, R. A., & Heitler, N. E. (2005). Anesthesia-assisted vs. buprenorphine- or clonidine-assisted heroin detoxification and naltrexone induction: A randomized trial. *JAMA, 294,* 903–913.

Connors, G. J. (1993a). *Innovations in alcoholism treatment: State of the art reviews and their implications for clinical practice.* Binghamton, NY: Haworth Press.

Connors, G. J. (1993b). Drinking moderation training as a contemporary therapeutic approach. *Drugs & Society, 18*(1), 117–134.

Connors, G. J., Carroll, K. M., DiClemente, C. C., Longabaugh, R., & Donovan, D. M. (1997). The therapeutic alliance and its relationship to alcoholism treatment participation and outcome. *Journal of Consulting and Clinical Psychology, 65,* 588–598.

Connors, G. J., & Dermen, K. H. (1996). Characteristics of participants in Secular Organizations for Sobriety (SOS). *American Journal of Drug and Alcohol Abuse, 22,* 281–295.

Conrad, K. J., Hultman, C. I., Pope, A. R., Lyons, J. S., Baxter, W. C., Daghestani, A. N., Lisiecki, J. P., Elbaum, P. L., McCarthy, M., & Manheim, L. M. (1998). Case managed residential care for homeless addicted veterans: Results of a true experiment. *Medical Care, 36*(1), 40–53.

Cook, C. C. H. (1988a). The Minnesota model in the management of drug and alcohol dependency: Miracle, method or myth? Part I. The philosophy and the program. *British Journal of Addiction, 83,* 625–634.

Cook, C. C. H. (1988b). The Minnesota model in the management of drug and alcohol dependency: Miracle, method or myth? Part II. Evidence and conclusions. *British Journal of Addiction, 83,* 735–748.

Corrigan, E. M. (1980). *Alcoholic women in treatment.* New York: Oxford University Press.

Costello, R. M. (1975). Alcoholism treatment and evaluation: In search of methods. II. Collation of two-year follow-up studies. *International Journal of the Addictions, 10*(5), 857–867.

Cox, G. B., Walker, R. D., Freng, S. A., Short, B. A., Meijer, L., & Gilchrist, L. (1998). Outcome of a controlled trial of the effectiveness of intensive case management for chronic public inebriates. *Journal of Studies on Alcohol, 59,* 523–532.

Crits-Christoph, P., Siqueland, L., Blaine, J., Frank, A., Luborsky, L., Onken, L. S., Muenz, L. R., Thase, M. E., Weiss, R. D., Gastfriend, D. R., Woody, G. E., Barber, J. P., Butler, S. F., Daley, D., Salloum, I., Bishop, S., Najavits, L. M., Lis, J., Mercer, D., Griffin, M. L., Moras, K., & Beck, A. T. (1999). Psychosocial treatments for cocaine dependence. *Archives of General Psychiatry, 56,* 493–502.

Cross, G. M., Morgan, C. W., Mooney, A. J., Martin, C. A., & Rafter, J. A. (1990). Alcoholism treatment: A ten-year follow-up study. *Alcoholism: Clinical and Experimental Research, 14*(2), 169–173.

Cunningham, J. A., Kypri, K., & McCambridge, J. (2011). The use of emerging technologies in alcohol treatment. *Alcohol Research & Health, 33*(4), 320–326.

Daley, D. C., & Salloum, I. (1999). Relapse prevention. In P. J. Ott, R. E. Tarter, & R. T. Ammerman (Eds.), *Sourcebook on substance abuse: Ethology epidemiology, assessment, and treatment* (pp. 255–263). Boston, MA: Allyn & Bacon.

Dawson, D. A., Grant, B. F., Stinson, F. S., Chou, P. S., Huang, B., & Ruan, W. J. (2005). Recovery from DSM-IV alcohol dependence: United States, 2001–2002. *Addiction, 100*(3), 281–292.

Day E., Ison J., & Strang, J. (2005, April 18). Inpatient versus other settings for detoxification for opioid dependence. Cochrane Database of Systematic Reviews 2005, Issue 2. Art. No.: CD004580. DOI: 10.1002/14651858. CD004580.pub2. Retrieved December 26, 2010, from www2.cochrane.org/reviews/en/ab004580.html.

Dean, A. J. (2005). Natural and complementary therapies for substance use disorders. *Current Opinions in Psychiatry, 18,* 271–276.

De Leon, G. (1986). The therapeutic community for substance abuse: Perspectives and approach. In G. D. Leon & J. T. Ziegenfuss (Eds.), *Therapeutic communities for addictions: Readings in theory, research and practice* (pp. 5–18). Springfield, IL: Charles C. Thomas.

De Leon, G. (1999). The therapeutic community treatment models. In B. S. McCrady & E. E. Epstein (Eds.), *Addictions: A comprehensive guidebook* (pp. 306–327). New York: Oxford University Press.

De Leon, G. (2000). *The therapeutic community: Theory, model, and method.* New York: Springer.

De Leon, G. (2008). Therapeutic communities. In M. Galanter & H. D. Kleber (Eds.), *The American psychiatric publishing textbook of substance abuse* (4th ed., pp. 485–501). Washington, DC: American Psychiatric Publishing.

De Sousa, A. (2010). The pharmacotherapy of alcohol dependence: A state of the art review. *Mens Sana Monographs, 8,* 69–82.

Doroff, D. R. (1977). Group psychotherapy in alcoholism. In B. Kissin & H. Begleiter (Eds.), *The biology of alcoholism: Treatment and rehabilitation of the chronic alcoholic* (Vol. 5, pp. 235–258). New York: Plenum Press.

Douaihy, A., Daley, D. C., Stowell, K. R., & Park, T. W. (2007). Relapse prevention: Clinical strategies for substance use disorders. In K. Witkiewitz & G. A. Marlatt (Eds.), *Therapist's guide to evidence-based relapse prevention* (pp. 37–71). Burlington: Elsevier.

Drug Enforcement Administration (DEA). (2004). *Drugs of abuse, 2005 edition.* Washington, DC: Author. Retrieved April 7, 2010, from www.justice.gov/dea/pubs/abuse/index.htm#From.

Edwards, M. E., & Steinglass, P. (1995). Family therapy treatment outcomes for alcoholism. *Journal of Marital and Family Therapy, 21,* 475–509.

Elkins, R. L. (1975). Aversion therapy for alcoholism: Chemical, electrical, or verbal imaginary? *Substance Use and Misuse, 10*(2), 157–209.

Emrick, C. D. (1987). Alcoholics Anonymous: Affiliation processes and effectiveness as treatment. *Alcoholism: Clinical and Experimental Research, 11*(5), 416–423.

Emrick, C. D., Tonigan, J. S., Montgomery, H., & Little, L. (1993). Alcoholics Anonymous: What is currently known? In B. S. McCrady & W. R. Miller (Eds.), *Research on Alcoholics Anonymous: Opportunities and alternatives* (pp. 41–76). New Brunswick, NJ: Rutgers Center of Alcohol Studies.

Ethridge, R. M., Craddock, S. G., Dunteman, G. H., & Hubbard, R. L. (1995). Treatment services in two national studies of community-based drug abuse treatment programs. *Journal of Substance Abuse, 7*, 9–26.

Ethridge, R. M., Craddock, S. G., Hubbard, R. L., & Rounds-Bryant, J. L. (1999). The relationship of counseling and self-help group participation to patient outcomes in DATOS. *Drug and Alcohol Dependence, 57*, 99–112.

Ethridge, R. M., Hubbard, R. L., Anderson, J., Craddock, S. G., & Flynn, P. M. (1997). Treatment structure and program services in the Drug Abuse Treatment Outcome Study (DATOS). *Psychology of Addictive Behaviors, 11*(4), 244–260.

Ettner, S. L., Huang, D., Evans, E., Ash, D. R., Jourabchi, M., & Hser, Y. Benefit-cost in the California Treatment Outcome Project: Does substance abuse treatment "pay for itself"? *Health Services Research, 41*(1), 192–213.

Ewing, J. A. (1982). Disulfiram and other deterrent drugs. In E. M. Pattison & E. Kaufman (Eds.), *Encyclopedic handbook of alcoholism* (pp. 1033–1042). New York: Gardner Press.

Fagan, R. W. (1986). Modern rescue missions: A survey of the International Union of Gospel Missions. *Journal of Drug Issues, 16*, 495–509.

Fals-Stewart, W., O'Farrell, T. J., Feehan, M., Birchler, G. R., Tiller, S., & McFarlin, S. K. (2000). Behavioral couples therapy versus individual-based treatment for male substance-abusing patients. An evaluation of significant individual change and comparison of improvement rates. *Journal of Substance Abuse Treatment, 18*, 249–254.

Ferri, M., Amato, L., & Davoli, M. (2006). Alcoholics Anonymous and other 12-step programmes for alcohol dependence. Cochrane Database of Systematic Reviews 2006, Issue 3. Art. No.: CD005032. DOI: 10.1002/ 14651858. CD005032.pub2. Retrieved December 23, 2010, from www2.cochrane.org/reviews/en/ab005032.html.

Field, G. (1992). Oregon prison drug treatment programs. In C. G. Leukefeld & F. M. Timms (Eds.), *Drug abuse treatment in prisons and jails* (pp. 142–155). Rockville, MD: National Institute on Drug Abuse.

Finney, J. W., Hahn, A. C., & Moos, R. H. (1996). The effectiveness of inpatient and outpatient treatment for alcohol abuse: The need to focus on mediators and moderators of treatment. *Addiction & Recovery, 91*, 1773–1796.

Finney, & Monahan. (1996). The cost-effectiveness of treatment for alcoholism: A second approximation. *Journal of Studies on Alcohol, 57*, 229–243.

Finney, J. W., & Moos, R. H. (1996). Effectiveness of inpatient and outpatient treatment for alcohol abuse: Effect sizes, research design issues, and explanatory mechanisms (Response to commentaries). *Addiction, 91*, 1813–1820.

Fiorentine, R. (1998). Effective drug treatment: Testing the distal needs hypothesis. *Journal of Substance Abuse Treatment, 15*(4), 281–289.

Fiorentine, R. (1999). After drug treatment: Are 12-step programs effective in maintaining abstinence? *American Journal of Drug and Alcohol Abuse, 25*(1), 93–116.

Fiorentine, R., & Hillhouse, M. P. (1999). Drug treatment effectiveness and client-counselor empathy: Exploring the effects of gender and ethnic congruency. *Journal of Drug Issues, 29*, 59–74.

Fiorentine, R., Nakashima, J., & Anglin, M. D. (1999). Client engagement in drug treatment. *Journal of Substance Abuse Treatment, 17*, 199–206.

Fischer, E. H. (1996). Alcoholic patients' decisions about halfway houses: What they say, what they do. *Journal of Substance Abuse Treatment, 13*(2), 159–164.

Fleming, M. (2000, November). Brief intervention to reduce alcohol use: A counseling strategy with broad implications across health care settings and patient groups. *FrontLines*, pp. 1, 2, 7.

Foxhall, K. (2001). Preventing relapse. *Monitor on psychology, 32*(5). Retrieved July 17, 2001, from www.apa. org/ monitor/jun01/relapse.htmlJune.

Frawley, P. J. (1998). Aversion therapy. In A. W. Graham & T. K. Shultz (Eds.), *Principles of addiction medicine* (2nd ed., pp. 667–674). Chevy Chase, MD: American Society of Addiction Medicine.

Frawley, P. J., & Howard, M. O. (2009). Aversion therapies. In In R. K. Ries, D. A. Fiellin, S. C. Miller, & R. Saitz, *Principles of Addiction Medicine* (4th ed., pp. 843–855). Philadelphia: Lippincott Williams & Wilkins.

French, M. T., Popovici, I., & Tapsell, L. (2008). The economic cost of substance abuse treatment: Updated estimates and cost bands for program assessment and reimbursement. *Journal of Substance Abuse Treatment, 35*, 462–469.

Friedmann, P. D., Hendrickson, J. C., Gerstein, D. R., & Zhang, Z. (2004). The effect of matching comprehensive services to patients' needs on drug use improvement in addiction treatment. *Addiction, 99*, 962–972.

Fuller, R. K., Branchey, L., Brightwell, D. R., Derman, R. M., Emrick, C. D., Iber, F. L., James, K. E., Lacoursiere, R. B., Lee, K. K., Lowenstam, I., Maany, I., Neiderhiser, D., Nocks, J. J., & Shaw, S. (1986). Disulfiram treatment of alcoholism: A Veterans Administration cooperative study. *Journal of the American Medical Association, 256* (11), 1449–1455.

Galanter, M. (2008). Network therapy. In M. Galanter & H. D. Kleber, *The American Psychiatric Publishing textbook of substance abuse treatment* (4th ed., pp. 401–412). Washington, DC: American Psychiatric Publishing.

Galanter, M. (2009a). Network therapy. In R. K. Ries, D. A. Fiellin, S. C. Miller, & R. Saitz, *Principles of Addiction Medicine* (4th ed., pp. 819–829). Philadelphia: Lippincott Williams & Wilkins.

Galanter, M. (2009b). Spirituality in the recovery process. In R. K. Ries, D. A. Fiellin, S. C. Miller, & R. Saitz, *Principles of Addiction Medicine* (4th ed., pp. 939–942). Philadelphia: Lippincott Williams & Wilkins.

Garbutt, J. C., West, S. L., Carey, T. S., Lohr, K. N., Crews, F. T. (1999). Pharmacological treatment of alcohol dependence. *Journal of the American Medical Association, 281*(14), 1318–1325.

Gerstein, D. R. (1999). Outcome research: Drug abuse. In M. Galanter & H. D. Kleber (Eds.), *Textbook of substance abuse treatment* (2nd ed., pp. 135–147). Washington, DC: American Psychiatric Press.

Gerstein, D. R., & Harwood, H. J. (Eds.). (1990). *Treating drug problems* (Vol. 1). Washington, DC: National Academy Press.

Gerstein, D. R., Johnson, R. A., Harwood, H. J., Fountain, D., Suter, N., & Malloy, K. (1994). *Evaluating recovery services: The California Drug and Alcohol Treatment Assessment (CALDATA): Annual Report.* Sacramento, CA: California Department of Alcohol and Drug Programs.

Glaser, F. B., & Ogborne, A. C. (1982). Does A. A. really work? *British Journal of Addiction, 77,* 123–129.

Glasser, W. (2000). *Reality therapy in action.* New York: HarperCollins.

Gorski, T. T. (2000). The CENAPS model of relapse prevention therapy (CMRPT). In J. J. Boren, L. S. Onken, & K. M. Carroll (Eds.), *Approaches to drug abuse counseling* (pp. 21–34). Bethesda, MD: National Institute on Drug Abuse.

Gorski, T. T., & Miller, M. (1986). *Staying sober: A guide for relapse prevention.* Independence, MO: Independence Press.

Gossop, M., Stewart, D., & Marsden, J. (2007). Attendance at Narcotics Anonymous and Alcoholics Anonymous meetings, frequency of attendance and substance use outcomes after residential treatment for drug dependence: A 5-year follow-up study. *Addiction, 103,* 119–125.

Gowing, D., Ali, R., & White, J. M. (2010). Opioid antagonists under heavy sedation of anesthesia for opioid withdrawal. *Cochrane Database of Systematic Reviews, Issue 12.* Retrieved December 22, 2010, from www2.cochrane.org/reviews/en/ab002022.html.

Greenfield, S. F., Hufford, M. R., Vagge, L. M., Muenz, L. R., Costello, J. E., & Weiss, R. D. (2000). The relationship of self-efficacy expectancies to relapse among alcohol dependent men and women: A prospective study. *Journal of Studies on Alcohol, 61,* 345–351.

Gustafson, D. H., Boyle, M. B., Shaw, B. R., Isham, A., McTavish, F., Richards, S., Schubert, C., Levy, M., & Johnson, K. (2011). An e-health solution for people with alcohol problems. *Alcohol Research & Health, 33*(4), 327–337.

Guydish, J., Werdegar, D., Sorenson, J. L., Clark, W., & Acampora, A. (1995). A day treatment program in a therapeutic community setting: Six-month outcomes: The Walden House day treatment program. *Journal of Substance Abuse Treatment, 12*(6), 441–447.

Haley, S. J., Dugosh, K. L., & Lynch, K. G. (2011). Performance contracting to engage detoxification-only patients into continued rehabilitation. *Journal of Substance Abuse Treatment, 40*(2), 123–131.

Hall, W., Ward, J., & Mattick, R. P. (1998). Introduction. In J. Ward, R. P. Mattick, & W. Hall (Eds.), *Methadone maintenance treatment and other opioid replacement therapies* (pp. 1–14). Amsterdam, The Netherlands: Harwood Academic.

Hayashida, M., Alterman, A. I., McLellan, T., O'Brien, C. P., Purtill, J. J., Volpicelli, J. R., Raphaelson, A. H., & Hall, C. P. (1989). Comparative effectiveness and costs of inpatient and outpatient detoxification of patients with mild-to-moderate alcohol withdrawal syndrome. *New England Journal of Medicine, 320*(6), 358–365.

Heather, N. (2007). How should the effectiveness of treatment for alcohol problems be evaluated? *Drugs and Alcohol Today, 7*(4), 22–32.

Herbeck, D. M., Hser, Y., & Teruya, C. (2008). Empirically supported substance abuse treatment approaches: A survey of treatment providers' perspectives and practices. *Addictive Behaviors, 33*(5), 699–712.

Hesse, M., Vanderplasschen, W., Rapp, R., Broekaert E., & Fridell, M. (2007). Case management for persons with substance use disorders. *Cochrane Database of Systematic Reviews 2007,* Issue 4. Art. No.: CD006265. DOI: 10.1002/14651858.CD006265.pub2. Retrieved December 23, 2010, from www2.cochrane.org/reviews/en/ab006265.html.

Higgins, S. T., Budney, A. J., Bickel, W. K., Foerg, F. E., Denham, R., & Badger, G. J. (1994, July). Incentives improve outcome in outpatient behavioral treatment of cocaine dependence. *Archives of General Psychiatry, 51,* 568–576.

Higgins, S. T., Heil, S. H., Dantona, R., Donham, R., Matthews, M., Badger, G. J. (2007). Effects of varying the monetary value of voucher-based incentives on abstinence achieved during and following treatment among cocaine-dependent outpatients. *Addiction, 102*(2), 271–281.

Higgins, S. T., Silverman, K., & Heil, S. H. (Eds.). (2008). Contingency management in substance abuse treatment. New York: Guilford Press.

Higgins, S. T., Tidey, J. W., & Stitzer, M. L. (1998). Community reinforcement and contingency management interventions. In A. W. Graham & T. K. Shultz (Eds.), *Principles of addiction medicine* (2nd ed., pp. 675–690). Chevy Chase, MD: American Society of Addiction Medicine.

Hitchcock, H. C., Stainback, R. D., & Rogue, G. M. (1995). Effects of halfway house placement on retention of patients in substance abuse aftercare. *American Journal of Drug and Alcohol Abuse, 21,* 379–390.

Holder, H., Longabaugh, R., Miller, W. R., & Rubonis, A. Y. (1991). The cost effectiveness of treatment for alcoholism: A first approximation. *Journal of Studies on Alcohol, 52*(6), 517–540.

Hser, Y. (1995). Drug treatment counselor practices and effectiveness: An examination of literature and relevant issues in a multilevel framework. *Evaluation Review, 19,* 389–408.

Hser, Y., Anglin, M. D., & Fletcher, B. (1998). Comparative treatment effectiveness: Effects of program modality and client drug dependence history on drug use reduction. *Journal of Substance Abuse Treatment, 15,* 513–523.

Hser, Y., Polinsky, M. L., Maglione, H., & Anglin, M. D. (1999). Matching clients' needs with drug treatment services. *Journal of Substance Abuse Treatment, 16,* 299–305.

Huber, A., Ling, W., Shoptaw, S., Gulati, V., Brethen, P., & Rawson, R. (1997). Integrating treatments for methamphetamine abuse: A psychosocial perspective. *Journal of Addictive Diseases, 16*(4), 41–50.

Huebner, R. B., & Kantor, L. W. (2011). Advances in alcoholism treatment. *Alcohol Research & Health, 33*(4), 295–299.

Humphreys, K., Moos, R. H., & Finney, J. W. (1995). Two pathways out of drinking problems without professional treatment. *Addictive Behaviors, 20*(4), 427–441.

Inciardi, J. A., & Martin, S. S. (1997). An effective model of prison-based treatment for drug-involved offenders. *Journal of Drug Issues, 27,* 261–278.

Inciardi, J. A., Martin, S. S., & Butzin, C. A. (2004). Five-year outcomes of therapeutic community treatment of drug-involved offenders after release from prison. *Crime & Delinquency, 50*(1), 88–107.

Jacobson, G. R. (1982). The role of shelter facilities in the treatment of alcoholics. In E. M. Pattison & E. Kaufman (Eds.), *Encyclopedic handbook of alcoholism* (pp. 894–906). New York: Gardner Press.

Jason, L. A., Olson, B. D., Ferrari, J. R., & Lo Sasso, A. T. (2006). Communal housing settings enhance substance abuse recovery. *American Journal of Public Health, 96*(10), 1727–1729.

Jason, L. A., Olson, B. D., Ferrari, J. R., Majer, J. M., Alvarez, J., Stout, J. (2007). An examination of main and interactive effects of substance abuse recovery housing on multiple indicators of adjustment. *Addiction, 102*(7), 1114–1121.

Joe, G. W., Dansereau, D. F., Pitre, U., & Simpson, D. D. (1997). Effectiveness of node-link mapping enhanced counseling for opiate addicts: A 12-month posttreatment follow-up. *The Journal of Nervous and Mental Disease, 185,* 306–313.

Jordan, J. B. (2006). Acupuncture treatment for opiate addiction: A systematic review. *Journal of Substance Abuse Treatment, 30,* 309–314.

Kadden, R. M. (1994). Cognitive-behavioral approaches to alcoholism treatment. *Alcohol Health and Research World, 18*(4), 279–286.

Kadden, R., Carroll, K., Donovan, D., Cooney, N., Monti, P., Abrams, D., Litt, M., & Hester, R. (1995). *Cognitive-behavioral coping skills therapy manual: A clinical guide for therapists treating individuals with alcohol abuse and dependence* (Project MATCH Monograph Series, Vol. 2, NIH Publication no. 94–3724). Rockville, MD: National Institute on Alcohol Abuse and Alcoholism.

Kampman, K. M. (2009). Biologic treatments for drug and alcohol dependence. *Primary Psychiatry, 16*(8), 47–52.

Kanas, N. (1982). Alcoholism and group psychotherapy. In E. M. Pattison & E. Kaufman (Eds.), *Encyclopedic handbook of alcoholism* (pp. 1011–1021). New York: Gardner Press.

Kaner, E. F., et al. (2009). The effectiveness of brief alcohol interventions in primary care settings: A systematic review. *Drug and Alcohol Review, 28*(3), 301–323.

Kasser, C. L., Geller, A., Howell, E., & Wartenberg, A. (1998). Principles of detoxification. In A. W. Graham & T. K. Shultz (Eds.), *Principles of addiction medicine* (2nd ed., pp. 423–430). Chevy Chase, MD: American Society of Addiction Medicine.

Katz, L. (1966). The Salvation Army men's social service center: II. Results. *Quarterly Journal of Studies on Alcohol, 27,* 636–647.

Kelly, J. F., & Keterian, J. D. (2011). The role of mutual-help groups in extending the framework of treatment. *Alcohol Research & Health, 33*(4), 350–355.

Kishline, A. (1996a, January/February). A toast to moderation. *Psychology Today,* 53–56.

Kishline, A. (1996b). *Moderate drinking: The moderation management guide for people who want to reduce their drinking.* New York: Crown.

Kleber, H. D. (2008). Methadone maintenance four decades later: Thousands of live saved but still controversial. *JAMA, 300*(19), 2303–2305.

Klingemann, H., & Rosenberg, H. (2009). Acceptance and therapeutic practice of controlled drinking as an outcome goal by Swiss alcohol treatment programmes. *European Addiction Research, 15,* 121–127.

Kownacki, R.J., & Shadish, W. R. (1999). Does Alcoholics Anonymous work? The results from a meta-analysis of controlled experiments. *Substance Use & Misuse, 34*(13). 1897–1916.

Kraft, M. K., Rothbard, A. B., Hadley, T. R., McLellan, A. T., & Asch, D. (1997). Are supplementary services provided during methadone maintenance really cost-effective? *American Journal of Psychiatry, 154,* 1214–1219.

Kurth, D. J. (2009). Therapeutic communities. In R. K. Ries, D. A. Fiellin, S. C. Miller, & R. Saitz, *Principles of Addiction Medicine* (4th ed., pp. 831–841). Philadelphia: Lippincott Williams & Wilkins.

Laken, M. P., & Ager, J. W. (1996). Effects of case management on retention in prenatal substance abuse treatment. *American Journal of Drug and Alcohol and Abuse, 22,* 439–448.

Laken, M. P., McComish, J. F., & Ager, J. (1997). Predictors of prenatal substance use and birth weight during outpatient treatment. *Journal of Substance Abuse Treatment, 14,* 359–366.

Lenardson, J. D., Race, M. M., & Gale, J. A. (2009). Few and Far Away: Detoxification Services in Rural Areas. Portland, ME: Maine Rural Health Research Center. Retrieved May 2, 2010, from muskie.usm.maine.edu/Publications/rural/pb41/Rural-Detox-Brief.pdf.

Levine, B., & Gallogly, V. (1985). *Group therapy with alcoholics: Outpatient and inpatient approaches.* Beverly Hills, CA: Sage.

Levy, J. A., Gallmeier, C. R., Weddington, W. W., & Wiebel, W. W. (1992). Delivering case management using a community based model of drug intervention. In R. S. Ashery (Ed.), *Progress and issues in case management* (pp. 12–33). Rockville, MD: National Institute on Drug Abuse.

Levy, J. A., Gallmeier, C. R., & Wiebel, W. W. (1995). The outreach assisted peer-support model for controlling drug dependency. *The Journal of Drug Issues, 25*(3), 507–529.

Ling, W., Rawson, R. A., & Compton, M. A. (1994). Substituting pharmacotherapies for opioid addiction: From methadone to LAAM and buprenorphine. *Journal of Psychoactive Drugs, 26*(2), 119–128.

Litt, M. D., Babor. T. F., Del Boca, F. K., Kadden, R. M., & Cooney, N.L. (1992). Types of alcoholics II: Application of an empirically derived typology to treatment matching. *Archives of General Psychiatry, 49,* 609–614.

Liu, T., Shi, J., Epstein, D. H., Bao, Y., & Lu, L. (2009). A meta-analysis of acupuncture combined with opioid receptor agonists for treatment of opiate-withdrawal symptoms. *Cell and Molecular Neurobiology, 29*(4), 449–454.

Lu, L., Liu, Y., Zhu, W., Shi, J., Liu, Y., Ling, W., & Kosten, T. R. (2009). Traditional medicine in the treatment of drug addiction. *The American Journal of Drug and Alcohol Abuse, 35,* 1–11.

Luborsky, L., McLellan, A. T., Woody, G. E., O'Brien, C. F., & Auerbach, A. (1985, June). Therapist success and its determinants. *Archives of General Psychiatry, 42,* 602–611.

Lussier, J. P., Heil, S. H., Mongeon, J. A., Badger, G. J., & Higgins, S. T. (2006). A meta-analysis of voucher-based reinforcement therapy for substance use disorders. *Addiction, 101,* 192–203.

Manpower Demonstration Research Corporation. (1980). *Summary and findings of the National Supported Work Demonstration.* Cambridge, MA: Ballinger.

Marco, C. H., & Marco, J. M. (1980). Antabuse: Medication in exchange for a limited freedom—Is it legal? *American Journal of Law & Medicine, 5*(4), 295–330.

Marcus, M. T., & Zgierska, A. (2009). Mindfulness-based therapies for substance use disorders: Part 1. *Substance Abuse, 30*(4), 263.

Margolin, A., Kleber, H. D., Avants, S. K., Konefal, J., Gawin, F., Stark, E. et al. (2002). Acupuncture for the treatment of cocaine addiction. *Journal of the American Medical Association, 287*(1), 55–63.

Marlatt, G. A., & Gordon, J. R. (1985). *Relapse prevention: Maintenance strategies in the treatment addictive behaviors.* New York: Guilford Press.

Mattick, R., Breen, C., Kimber, J., Davoli, M. (2010). Methadone maintenance therapy versus no opioid replacement therapy for opioid dependence. Cochrane Database of Systematic Reviews 2009, Issue 3. Art. No.: CD002209. DOI: 10.1002/14651858.CD002209.pub2. Retrieved December 26, 2010, from www2.cochrane.org/reviews/en/ab002209.html.

Mattick, R. P., Kimber, J., Breen, C., & Davoli, M. (2008). Buprenorphine maintenance versus placebo or methadone maintenance for opioid dependence. Cochrane Database of Systematic Reviews 2008, Issue 2. Art. No.: CD002207. DOI: 10.1002/14651858.CD002207.pub3. Retrieved December 26, 2010, from www2.cochrane.org/reviews/en/ab002207.html.

Mattson, M. E. (1994). Patient-treatment matching: Rationale and results. *Alcohol Health and Research World, 18,* 287–295.

Mattson, M. E., Allen, J. P., Longabaugh, R., Nickless, C. J., Connors, G. J., & Kadden, R. M. (1994). A chronological review of empirical studies matching alcoholic clients to treatment. *Journal of Studies on Alcohol,* Supplement no. 12, 16–29.

McCaul, M. E., & Furst, J. (1994). Alcoholism treatment in the United States. *Alcohol Health and Research World, 18,* 253–260.

McCrady, B. S. (1998). Recent research in Twelve Step programs. In A. W. Graham & T. K. Shultz (Eds.), *Principles of addiction medicine* (2nd ed., pp. 707–717). Chevy Chase, MD: American Society of Addiction Medicine.

McCrady, B. S., Noel, N. E., Abrams, D. B., Stout, R. L., Nelson, H. F., & Hay, W. M. (1986). Comparative effectiveness of three types of spouse involvement in outpatient behavioral alcoholism treatment. *Journal of Studies on Alcohol, 47*(6), 459–467.

McCrady, B. S., Stout, R., Noel, N., Abrams, D., & Nelson, H. F. (1991). Effectiveness of three types of spouse-involved behavioral alcoholism treatment. *British Journal of Addiction, 86,* 1415–1424.

McKay, J. R., & Hiller-Sturmhöfel, S. (2011). Treating alcoholism as a chronic disease. *Alcohol Research & Health, 33*(4), 356–370.

McKay, J. R., & Maisto, S. A. (1993). An overview and critique of advances in the treatment of alcohol use disorders. *Drugs & Society, 8*(1), 1–29.

McKellar, J., Stewart, D., & Humphreys, K. (2003). Alcoholics Anonymous involvement and positive alcohol-related outcomes: Cause, consequence, or just a correlate? A prospective 2-year study of 2,319 alcohol-dependent men. *Journal of Consulting and Clinical Psychology, 71*(2), 302–308.

McLachlan, J. E. C. (1974). Therapy strategies, personality orientation and recovery from alcoholism. *Canadian Psychiatric Association Journal, 19*(1), 25–30.

McLellan, A. T., Arndt, I., Metzger, D. S., Woody, G. E., & O'Brien, C. P. (1993). The effects of psychosocial services in substance abuse treatment. *Journal of the American Medical Association, 269*(15), 1953–1959.

McLellan, A. T., Grissom, G. R., Brill, P., Durell, J., Metzger, D. S., & O'Brien, C. P. (1993). Private substance abuse treatments: Are some programs more effective than others? *Journal of Substance Abuse Treatment, 10,* 243–254.

McLellan, A. T., Hagan, T. A., Levine, M., Meyers, K., Gould, F., Bencivengo, M., Durell, J., & Jaffe, J. (1999). Does clinical case management improve outpatient addiction treatment? *Drug and Alcohol Dependence, 55,* 91–103.

McLellan, A. T., Lewis, D. C., O'Brien, C. P., & Kleber, H. D. (2000). Drug dependence: A chronic medical illness: Implications for treatment, insurance, and outcomes evaluation. *Journal of the American Medical Association, 284*(13), 1689–1695.

McLellan, A. T., Luborsky, L., Woody, G. E., O'Brien, C. P., & Kron, R. (1981). Are the "addiction-related" problems of substance abusers really related? *The Journal of Nervous and Mental Disease, 169,* 232–239.

McLellan, A. T., & McKay, J. R. (1998). Components of successful treatment programs: Lessons from the research literature. In A. W. Graham & T. K. Shultz (Eds.), *Principles of addiction medicine* (2nd ed., pp. 327–343). Chevy Chase, MD: American Society of Addiction Medicine.

McLellan, A. T., Woody, G. E., Luborsky, L., O'Brien, C. P., & Druley, K. A. (1983). Increased effectiveness of substance abuse treatment: A prospective study of patient-treatment "matching." *The Journal of Nervous and Mental Disease, 171*(10), 597–605.

McNichol, R. W., & Logsdon, S. A. (1988). Disulfiram: An evaluation research model. *Alcohol Health & Research World, 12*(3), 202–209.

McQueen, J., Howe, T. E., Allan, L., & Mains, D. (2009). Brief interventions for heavy alcohol users admitted to general hospital wards. London: Cochrane Collaboration. Retrieved December 18, 2010, from www2.cochrane.org/reviews/en/ab005191.html.

Meade, C. S., Lukas, S. E., McDonald, L. J., Fitzmaurice, G. M., Eldridge, J. A., Merrill, N,, & Weiss R. D. (2010). A randomized trial of transcutaneous electric acupoint stimulation as adjunctive treatment for opioid detoxification. *Journal of Substance Abuse Treatment, 38,* 12–21.

Mee-Lee, D., Shulman, G., Fishman, M., Gastfriend, D., & Griffiths, J. H. (Eds.). (2001). *ASAM placement criteria for the treatment of substance-related disorders* (2nd ed., rev.) (ASAM PPC-2R). Chevy Chase, MD: American Society of Addiction Medicine.

Metja, C. L., Bokos, P. J., Mickenburg, J., Maslar, M. E., & Senay, E. (1997). Improving substance abuse treatment access and retention using a case management approach. *Journal of Drug Issues, 27,* 329–340.

Meyers, R. J., & Miller, W. R. (Eds.). (2001). *A community reinforcement approach to addiction treatment.* Cambridge, England: Cambridge University Press.

Meyers, R. J., Roozen, H. G., & Smith, J. E. (2011). The Community Reinforcement Approach: An update of the evidence. *Alcohol Research & Health, 33*(4), 380–388.

Miller, M. M. (1998). Traditional approaches to the treatment of addiction. In A. W. Graham & T. K. Shultz (Eds.), *Principles of addiction medicine* (2nd ed., pp. 315–326). Chevy Chase, MD: American Society of Addiction Medicine.

Miller, S. D. (2000). Description of the solution-focused brief therapy approaches to problem drinking. In J. J. Boren, L. S. Onken, & K. M. Carroll (Eds.), *Approaches to drug abuse counseling* (pp. 83–88). Bethesda, MD: National Institute on Drug Abuse.

Miller, W. R., & Baca, L. M. (1983). Two-year follow-up of bibliotherapy and therapist-directed controlled drinking training for problem drinkers. *Behavior Therapy, 14,* 441–448.

Miller, W. R., Benefield, R. G., & Tonigan, J. S. (1993). Enhancing motivation for change in problem drinking: A controlled comparison of two therapist styles. *Journal of Consulting and Clinical Psychology, 61*(3), 455–461.

Miller, W. R., Brown, J. M., Simpson, T. L., Handmaker, N. S., Bien, T. H., Luckie, L., Montgomery, H. A., Hester, R. K., & Tonigan, J. S. (1995). What works? A methodological analysis of the alcohol treatment outcome literature. In R. K. Hester & W. R. Miller (Eds.), *Handbook of alcoholism treatment approaches: Effective alternatives* (2nd ed., pp. 12–44). Boston, MA: Allyn & Bacon.

Miller, W. R., & Hester, R. K. (1980). Treating the problem drinker: Modern approaches. In W. R. Miller (Ed.), *The addictive behaviors: Treatment of alcoholism, drug abuse, smoking, and obesity* (pp. 11–141). Oxford: Pergamon Press.

Miller, W. R., & Sanchez, V. C. (1994). Motivating young adults for treatment and lifestyle change. In G. S. Howard & P. E. Nathan (Eds.), *Issues in alcohol use and misuse by young adults* (pp. 55–81). Notre Dame, IN: University of Notre Dame Press.

Miller, W. R., Taylor, C. A., & West, J. C. (1980). Focused versus broad-spectrum behavior therapy for problem drinkers. *Journal of Consulting and Clinical Psychiatry, 48*(5), 590–601.

Miller, W. R., & Wilbourne, P. L. (2002). Mesa Grande: A methodological analysis of clinical trials of treatments for alcohol use disorders. *Addiction, 97,* 265–277.

Miller, W. R., Zweben, A., DiClemente, C. D., & Rychtarik, R. (1995). *Motivational enhancement therapy manual: A clinical guide for therapists treating individuals with alcohol abuse and dependence* (Project MATCH Monograph Series, Vol. 2, NIH Publication no. 94–3723). Rockville, MD: National Institute on Alcohol Abuse and Alcoholism.

Mitchell, O., Wilson, D. B., & MacKenzie, D. L. (2006, September 18). The effectiveness of incarceration-based drug treatment on criminal behavior. Campbell Systematic Reviews 2006:11, DOI: 10.4073/csr.2006.11.

Molloy, J. P. (1992). *Self-run, self-supported houses for more effective recovery from alcohol and drug addiction.* Rockville,

MD: Substance Abuse and Mental Health Services Administration.

Monahan, S. C., & Finney, J. W. (1996). Explaining abstinence rates following treatment for alcohol abuse: A quantitative synthesis of patient, research design and treatment effects. *Addiction, 91,* 787–805.

Montgomery, H. A., Miller, W. R., & Tonigan, S. (1995). Does Alcoholics Anonymous involvement predict treatment outcome? *Journal of Substance Abuse Treatment, 12,* 241–246.

Monti, P., M., Rohsenow, D. J., Swift, R. M., Gulliver, S. B., Colby, S. M., Mueller, T. I., Brown, R. A., Gordon, A., Abrams, D. B., Niaura, R. S., & Asher, M. K. (2001). Naltrexone and cue exposure with coping and communication skills training for alcoholics: Treatment process and 1-year outcomes. *Alcoholism: Clinical and Experimental Research, 25*(11), 1634–1647.

Moos, R. H., & Moos, B. S. (2006). Participation in treatment and Alcoholics Anonymous: A 16-year follow-up of initially untreated individuals. *Journal of Clinical Psychology, 62*(6), 735–750.

Morrell, H. E. R., & Myers, M. G. (2009). Group therapy for substance abuse. In Cohen, L. M., Collins, F. L., Young, A. M., McChargue, D.E., Leffingwell, T. R., & Cook, K. L., *Pharmacology and treatment of substance abuse: Evidence- and outcome-based perspectives* (pp. 179–196). New York: Routledge.

Moyers, T., & Hester, R. K. (1999). Outcome research: Alcoholism. In M. Galanter & H. D. Kleber (Eds.), *Textbook of substance abuse treatment* (2nd ed., pp. 129–134). Washington, DC: American Psychiatric Press.

Muffler, J., Langrod, J. G., Richardson, J. T., & Ruiz, P. (1997). Religion. In J. H. Lowinson, P. Ruiz, R. M. Millman, & J. G. Langrod (Eds.), *Substance abuse: A comprehensive textbook* (3rd ed., pp. 492–499). Baltimore: Williams & Wilkins.

Myrick, H., & Wright, T. (2008). Clinical management of alcohol abuse and dependence. *The American Psychiatric Publishing textbook of substance abuse treatment* (4th ed., pp. 129–142). Washington, DC: American Psychiatric Publishing.

Najavits, L. M., Crits-Christoph, P., & Dierberger, A. (2000). Clinicians' impact on the quality of substance use disorder treatment. *Substance Use and Misuse, 35*(12–14), 2161–2190.

Najavits, L. M., & Weiss, R. D. (1994). Variations in therapist effectiveness in treatment. *Addiction, 89,* 679–688.

National Institute on Alcohol Abuse and Alcoholism (NIAAA). (1987). *Sixth special report to the U.S. Congress on alcohol and health.* Rockville, MD: U.S. Department of Health and Human Services.

National Institute on Alcohol Abuse and Alcoholism (NIAAA). (1990). *Seventh special report to the U.S. Congress on alcohol and health.* Rockville, MD: U.S. Department of Health and Human Services.

National Institute on Alcohol Abuse and Alcoholism (NIAAA). (2000). *Tenth special report to the U.S. Congress on alcohol and health.* Bethesda, MD: U.S. Department of Health and Human Services.

National Institute on Alcohol Abuse and Alcoholism. (2001, March 8). *NIAAA launches COMBINE clinical trial* [news release]. Retrieved December 27, 2010, from www.niaaa.nih.gov/NewsEvents/NewsReleases/Pages/COMBINE3-01.aspx.

National Institute on Alcohol Abuse and Alcoholism. (2005). *Helping patients who drink too much: A clinician's guide.* NIH Publication No. 07–3769. Bethesda, MD: National Institutes of Health. Retrieved April 25, 2011, from www.niaaa.nih.gov/Publications/EducationTrainingMaterials/Documents/guide.pdf.

National Institute on Alcohol Abuse and Alcoholism. (2010, April). *Rethinking drinking: Alcohol and your health.* NIH Publication No. 10–3770. Bethesda, MD: National Institutes of Health. Retrieved December 21, 2010, from pubs.niaaa.nih.gov/publications/RethinkingDrinking/Rethinking_Drinking.pdf.

National Institute on Drug Abuse (NIDA). (1997). *Research report series: Heroin abuse and addiction.* Bethesda, MD: U.S. Department of Health and Human Services.

National Institute on Drug Abuse (NIDA). (1999). *The sixth triennial report to Congress from the Secretary of Health and Human Services.* Bethesda, MD: Author.

National Institute on Drug Abuse (NIDA). (2008, July 22). *What are the treatments for heroin addiction?* Bethesda, MD: Author. Retrieved May 2, 2010, from www.drugabuse.gov/researchreports/heroin/heroin5.html.

National Institute on Drug Abuse (NIDA). (2009a, April). *Principles of drug addiction treatment: A research-based guide* (2nd ed.). Bethesda, MD: U.S. Department of Health and Human Services.

National Institute on Drug Abuse (NIDA). (2009b, May 13). *The Matrix Model.* Behavioral Therapies Development Program—Effective Drug Abuse Treatment Approaches. Bethesda, MD: U.S. Department of Health and Human Services. Retrieved April 10, 2010, from www.drugabuse.gov/BTDP/Effective/Rawson.html.

National Institute on drug abuse (NIDA). (2009c). *Resource guide: Screening for drug use in general medical settings.* Bethesda, MD: U.S. Department of Health and Human Services. Retrieved July 1, 2010, from www.drugabuse.gov/nidamed/resguide/index.html.

Nealon-Woods, M. A., Ferrari, J. R., & Jason, L. A. (1995). Twelve-Step program use among Oxford House residents: Spirituality or social support in sobriety? *Journal of Substance Abuse, 7,* 311–318.

New Brunswick Addiction Services. (2009, February). *Methadone maintenance treatment policies and procedures.* Canada: New Brunswick Addiction Services. Retrieved April 19, 2011, from www.gnb.ca/0378/pdf/methadone_policies-e.pdf.

Nowinski, J., Baker, S., & Carroll, K. (1995). *Twelve step facilitation therapy manual: A clinical guide for therapists treating individuals with alcohol abuse and dependence* (Project MATCH Monograph Series, Vol. 1. NIH Publication no. 94–3722). Rockville, MD: National Institute on Alcohol Abuse and Alcoholism.

Nurco, D. N., Wegner, N., Stephenson, P., Makofsky, A., & Shaffer, J. W. (1983). *Ex-addicts' self-help groups: Potentials and pitfalls.* New York: Praeger.

Nurse practitioner's drug handbook. (2nd ed.). (1998). Springhouse, PA: Springhouse.

O'Brien, C. P., & McLellan, A. T. (1998). Myths about the treatment of addiction. In A. W. Graham & T. K. Shultz (Eds.), *Principles of addiction medicine* (pp. 309–314). Chevy Chase, MD: American Society of Addiction Medicine.

O'Connell, D. F., & Alexander, C. N. (Eds.). (1994). Self-recovery: Treating addictions using transcendental meditation and Maharishi Ayur-Veda. *Alcoholism Treatment Quarterly, 11*(1/2 & 3/4).

O'Connor, E. (2001). Lean on me: Behavioral couples therapy offers addicts a path to recovery alongside a loved one. *Monitor on Psychology, 32*(5). Retrieved December 27, 2010, from www.apa.org/monitor/jun01/leanonme.aspx.

O'Farrell, T. J., & Fals-Stewart, W. (2000). Behavioral couples therapy for alcoholism and drug abuse. *Journal of Substance Abuse Treatment, 18*, 51–54.

Olson, D. E., Rozhon, J., & Powers, M. (2009). Enhancing prisoner reentry through access to prison-based and post-incarceration aftercare treatment: Experiences from the Illinois Sheridan Correctional Center therapeutic community. *Journal of Experimental Criminology, 5*, 299–321.

O'Malley, S. S., Jaffe, A. J., Chang, G., Rode, S., Schottenfeld, R., Meyer, R. E., et al. (1996). Six-month follow-up of naltrexone and psychotherapy for alcohol dependence. *Archives of General Psychiatry, 53*, 217–224.

O'Malley, S. S., Jaffe, A. J., Chang, G., Schottenfeld, R. S., Meyer, R. E., & Rounsaville, B. (1992, November). Naltrexone and coping skills therapy for alcohol dependence: A controlled study. *Archives of General Psychiatry, 49*, 881–887.

O'Malley, S. S., & O' Connor, P. G. (2011). Medications for unhealthy alcohol use. *Alcohol Research & Health, 33*(4), 300–312.

Opioid drugs in maintenance and detoxification treatment of opiate addiction. 66 Fed. Reg. 4076 (Jan. 17, 2001) (to be codified at 21 C.F.R., pt. 291, 42 C.F.R. pt. 8).

Orford, J., & Velleman, R. (1982). Alcoholism halfway houses. In E. M. Pattison & E. Kaufman (Eds.), *Encyclopedic handbook of alcoholism* (pp. 907–922). New York: Gardner Press.

Owen, P. (2000). *Minnesota* model: Description of counseling approach. In J. J. Boren, L. S. Onken, & K. M. Carroll (Eds.), *Approaches to drug abuse counseling* (pp. 103–110). Bethesda, MD: National Institute on Drug Abuse.

Panas, L., Caspi, Y., Fournier, E., & McCarty, D. (2003). Performance measures for outpatient substance abuse services: Group versus individual counseling. *Journal of Substance Abuse Treatment, 25*, 271–278.

Pani, P. P., Trogu, E., Vacca, R., Amato, L., Vecchi, S., & Davoli, M. Disulfiram for the treatment of cocaine dependence. (2010, January 20). Cochrane Database of Systematic Reviews 2010, Issue 1. Art. No.: CD007024. DOI: 10.1002/14651858.CD007024.pub2. Retrieved December 26, 2010, from www2.cochrane.org/reviews/en/ab007024.html.

Pattison, E. M., Sobell, M. B., & Sobell, L. C. (1977). *Emerging concepts of alcohol dependence.* New York: Springer.

Pendery, M. L., Maltzman, I. M., & West, L. J. (1982). Controlled drinking by alcoholics? New findings and a reevaluation of a major affirmative study. *Science, 217* (4555), 169–175.

Peniston, E. G., & Kulkosky, P. J. (1989). Alpha-theta brainwave training and beta-endorphin levels in alcoholics. *Alcoholism: Clinical and Experimental Research, 13*(2), 271–279.

Peniston, E. G., & Kulkosky, P. J. (1992). Alpha-theta EEG biofeedback training in alcoholism and post-traumatic stress disorder. *International Society for the Study of Subtle Energies and Energy Medicine, 2*(4), 5–7.

Petry, N. M., Alessi, S. M., Marx, J., Austin, M., & Tardif, M. (2005). Vouchers versus prizes: Contingency management treatment of substance abusers in community settings. *Journal of Consulting and Clinical Psychology, 73*(6), 1005–1114.

Pettinati, H. M., Sugerman, A. A., DiDonato, N., & Maurer, H. S. (1982). The natural history of alcoholism over four years after treatment. *Journal of Studies on Alcohol, 43*(3), 201–215.

Platt, J. J., Widman, M., Lidz, V., Rubenstein, D., & Thompson, R. (1998). The case for support services in substance abuse treatment. *American Behavioral Scientist, 41*, 1050–1062.

Polich, J. M., Armor, D. J., & Braiker, H. B. (1981). *The course of alcoholism: Four years after treatment.* New York: John S. Wiley and Sons.

Polydorou, S., & Kleber, H. D. (2008). Detoxification of opioids. In M. Galanter & H. D. Kleber (Eds.), *The American Psychiatric Publishing textbook of substance abuse treatment* (4th ed., pp. 265–287). Washington, DC: American Psychiatric Publishing.

Powers, M. B., Vedel, R., & Emmelkamp, P. M. G. (2008). Behavioral couples therapy (BCT) for alcohol and drug use disorders: A meta-analysis. *Clinical Psychology Review, 28*, 952–962.

Prochaska, J. O., Velicer, W. F., Fava, J. L., Ruggiero, L., Laforge, R. G., Rossi, J. S., Johnson, S. S., & Lee, P. A. (2001). Counselor and stimulus control enhancements of a stage-matched expert system intervention for smokers in a managed care setting. *Preventive Medicine, 32*, 23–32.

"Project MATCH." (1996). *News and Views* (Newsletter of the Texas Research Society on Alcoholism), 5(2 & 3), 2.

Project MATCH Research Group. (1997a). Matching alcoholism treatments to client heterogeneity: Project MATCH posttreatment drinking outcomes. *Journal of Studies on Alcohol, 58,* 7–29.

Project MATCH Research Group. (1997b). Project MATCH secondary a priori hypotheses. *Addiction, 92,* 1671–1698.

Project MATCH Research Group. (1998a). Matching alcoholism treatments to client heterogeneity: Project MATCH three-year drinking outcomes. *Alcoholism: Clinical and Experimental Research, 22,* 1300–1311.

Project MATCH Research Group. (1998b). Matching alcoholism treatments to client heterogeneity: Treatment main effects and matching effects on drinking during treatment. *Journal of Studies on Alcohol, 59,* 631–639.

Project MATCH Research Group. (1998c). Therapist effects in three treatments for alcohol problems. *Psychotherapy Research, 8,* 455–474.

Quigley, L. A., & Marlatt, G. A. (1999). Relapse prevention: Maintenance of change after initial treatment. In B. S. McCrady & E. E. Epstein (Eds.), *Addictions: A comprehensive guidebook* (pp. 370–384). New York: Oxford University Press.

Rawlani, V., Vekaria, S., & Eisenberg, S. (2009). Treatment of the hospitalized alcohol-dependent patient with alcohol withdrawal syndrome. *Internet Journal of Internal Medicine, 8*(1), 24. Retrieved April 19, 2010, from www.ispub.com/journal/the_internet_journal_of_internal_medicine/volume_8_number_1_18/article/treatment-of-the-hospitalized-alcohol-dependent-patient-with-alcohol-withdrawal-syndrome.html.

Rawson, R. A. (1995). Is psychotherapy effective for substance abusers? In A. M. Washton (Ed.), *Psychotherapy and substance abuse: A practitioner's guide* (pp. 55–75). New York: Guilford Press.

Rawson, R. A., McCann, M. J., Hasson, A. J., & Ling, W. (2000). Addiction pharmacotherapy 2000: New options, new challenges. *Journal of Psychoactive Drugs, 32,* 371–378.

Rawson, R. A., Shoptaw, S. J., Obert, J. L., McCann, M. J., Hasson, A. L., Marinelli-Casey, P. J., Brethen, P. R., & Ling, W. (1995). An intensive outpatient approach for cocaine abuse treatment. *Journal of Substance Abuse Treatment, 12*(2), 117–127.

Ray, O., & Ksir, C. (1990). *Drugs, society, and human behavior* (5th ed.). St. Louis, MO: Times Mirror/Mosby.

Ray, O., & Ksir, C. (1999). *Drugs, society, and human behavior* (8th ed.). Boston, MA: WCB/McGraw-Hill.

Rettig, R. A., & Yarmolinsky, A. (Eds.). (1995). *Federal regulation of methadone treatment.* Washington, DC: National Academy Press.

Ridgely, S., & Willenbring, M. L. (1992). Application of case management to drug abuse treatment: Overview of models and research issues. In R. S. Ashery (Ed.), *Progress and issues in case management* (pp. 12–33). Rockville, MD: National Institute on Drug Abuse.

Ries, R. K., Fiellin, D. A., Miller, S. C., & Saitz, R. (2009). *Principles of Addiction Medicine* (4th ed.). Philadelphia: Lippincott Williams & Wilkins.

Rogers, C. R. (1951). *Client-centered therapy: Its practice, implications and theory.* Boston, MA: Houghton Mifflin.

Roman, P. M., Johnson, J. A., & Blum, T. C. (2000). The transformation of private alcohol problem treatment: Results of a national study. *Advances in Medical Sociology, 7,* 321–342.

Roozen, H. G., Boulogne, J. J., van Tulder, M. W., van den Brink, W., De Jong, C. A., & Kerkhof, A J. (2004). A systematic review of the effectiveness of the community reinforcement approach in alcohol, cocaine, and opioid addiction. *Drug and Alcohol Dependence, 74*(1), 1–13.

Roozen, H. G., deWaart, R., & van der Kroft, P. (2010). Community reinforcement and family training: An effective option to engage treatment-resistant substance-abusing individuals in treatment. *Addiction, 105*(10), 1729–1738.

Rosenberg, H., & Melville, J. (2005). Controlled drinking and controlled drug use as outcome goals in British treatment services. *Addiction Research and Theory, 13*(1), 85–92.

Rösner, S., Leucht, S., Lehert, P., & Soyka, M. (2008). Acamprosate supports abstinence, naltrexone prevents excessive drinking: Evidence from a meta-analysis with unreported outcomes. *Journal of Psychopharmacology, 22*(1), 11–23.

Ross, R., Booth, B. M., Russell, D. W., Laughlin, P. R., & Brown, K. (1995). Outcome of domiciliary care after inpatient alcoholism treatment in male veterans. *Journal of Substance Abuse Treatment, 12*(5), 319–326.

Rounsaville, B. J., Carroll, K. M., & Back, S. E. (2009). Individual psychotherapy. In R. K. Ries, D. A. Fiellin, S. C. Miller, & R. Saitz (Eds.), *Principles of addiction medicine* (4th ed., pp. 769–785). Philadelphia: Lippincott Williams & Wilkins.

Rubington, E. (1977). The role of the halfway house in the rehabilitation of alcoholics. In B. Kissin & H. Begleiter (Eds.), *The biology of alcoholism: Treatment and rehabilitation of the chronic alcoholic* (pp. 351–383). New York: Plenum Press.

Rubington, E. (1985). Staff problems in halfway houses. *Alcoholism Treatment Quarterly, 2*(2), 29–47.

Schumm, J. A., O'Farrell, T. J., Murphy, C. M., & Fals-Stewart, W. (2009). Partner violence before and after couples-based alcoholism treatment for female alcoholic patients. *Journal of Consulting and Clinical Psychology, 77*(6), 1136–1146.

Sheeren, M. (1988). The relationship between relapse and involvement in Alcoholics Anonymous. *Journal of Studies on Alcohol, 49*(1), 104–106.

Shorkey, C. T. (1993). Use of behavioral methods with individuals recovering from psychoactive substance dependence. In D. K. Granvold (Ed.), *Cognitive and behavioral treatment: Methods and applications* (pp. 135–158). Belmont, CA: Brooks/Cole.

Siegal, H. A., Fisher, J. H., Rapp, R. C., Kelliher, C. W., Wagner, J. H., O'Brien, W. F., & Cole, P. A. (1996). Enhancing substance abuse treatment with case management: Its impact on employment. *Journal of Substance Abuse Treatment, 13,* 93–98.

Siegal, H. A., & Rapp, R. C. (1996). *Case management and substance abuse treatment: Practice and experience.* New York: Springer.

Silins, R., Sannibale, C., Larney, S., Wodak, A., & Mattick, R. (2008). Residential detoxification: Essential for marginalized, severely alcohol- and drug-dependent individuals. *Drug and Alcohol Review, 27,* 414–419.

Silverman, K., Higgins, S. T., Brooner, R. K., Montoya, I. D., Cone, E. J., Schuster, C. R., et al. (1996). Sustained cocaine abstinence in methadone maintenance patients through voucher-based reinforcement therapy. *Archives of General Psychiatry, 53,* 409–415.

Simpson, D. D., Joe, G. W., & Brown, B. S. (1997). Treatment retention and follow-up outcomes in the Drug Abuse Treatment Outcome Study (DATOS). *Journal of Addictive Behaviors, 11*(4), 294–307.

Sisson, R. W., & Azrin, N. H. (1989). The community reinforcement approach. In R. K. Hester & W. R. Miller (Eds.), *Handbook of alcoholism treatment approaches: Effective alternatives* (pp. 242–258). New York: Pergamon.

Smith, L. A., Gates, S., & Foxcroft, D. (2010). Therapeutic communities for substance related disorder. *Cochrane Database of Systematic Reviews, Issue 12.* Retrieved December 22, 2010, from www2.cochrane.org/reviews/en/ab005338.html.

Smith, J. E., Meyers, R. J., & Austin, J. L. (2008). Working with family members to engage treatment-refusing drinkers: The CRAFT program. *Alcoholism Treatment Quarterly, 26*(1/2), 169–193.

Smock, S. A., Trepper, T. S., Wetchler, J. L., Mc Collum, E. E., Ray, R., & Pierce, K. (2008). Solution-focused group therapy for level 1 substance abusers. *Journal of Marital and Family Therapy, 34*(1), 107–120.

Smokers in Kentucky dared to quit for cash. (2001, August 3). *Austin American-Statesman,* p. A15.

Sobell, L. C., Cunningham, J. A., & Sobell, M. B. (1996). Recovery from alcohol problems with and without treatment: Prevalence in two population surveys. *American Journal of Public Health, 86,* 966–972.

Sobell, M. B., & Sobell, L. C. (1973a). Alcoholics treated by individualized behavior therapy: One year treatment outcome.*Behaviour Research and Therapy, 11*(4), 599–618.

Sobell, M. B., & Sobell, L. C. (1973b). Individualized behavior therapy for alcoholics. *Behavior Therapy, 4,* 49–72.

Sobell, M. B., & Sobell, L. C. (1976). Second-year treatment outcome of alcoholics treated by individualized behavior therapy: Results. *Behaviour Research and Therapy, 14,* 195–215.

Springer, D. W., McNeece, C. A., & Arnold, E. (2003). *Substance abuse treatment for criminal offenders: An evidence-based guide for practitioners.* Washington, DC: American Psychological Association.

Srisurapanont, M., & Jarusuraisin, N. (2005). Naltrexone for the treatment of alcoholism: A meta-analysis of randomized controlled trials. *International Journal of Neuropsychopharmacology, 8,* 267–280.

Stanton, M. D., & Shadish, W. R. (1997). Outcome, attrition, and family-couples treatment for drug abuse: A meta-analysis and review of the controlled, comparative studies. *Psychological Bulletin, 122*(2), 170–191.

Stine, S., Meandzija, B., & Kosten, T. R. (1998). Pharmacologic therapies for opioid addiction. In A. W. Graham & T. K. Shultz (Eds.), *Principles of addiction medicine* (2nd ed., pp. 545–555). Chevy Chase, MD: American Society of Addiction Medicine.

Stitzer, M. L., Iguchi, M. Y., & Felch, L. J. (1992). Contingent take-home incentive: Effects on drug use of methadone maintenance patients. *Journal of Consulting and Clinical Psychology, 60,* 927–934.

Stoller, K. B., Bigelow, G. E., Walsh, S. L., & Strain, E. C. (2001). Effects of burprenorphine/naloxone in opioid-dependent humans. *Psychopharmacology, 154,* 230–342.

Strain, E. C., Stitzer, M. L., Liebson, I. A., & Bigelow, G. E. (1994, July). Comparison of buprenorphine and methadone in the treatment of opioid dependence. *American Journal of Psychiatry, 151,* 1025–1030.

Suarez-Morales, L., et al. (2010). Do therapist cultural characteristics influence the outcome of substance abuse treatment for Spanish-speaking adults? *Cultural Diversity and Ethnic Minority Psychology, 16*(2), 199–205.

Substance Abuse and Mental Health Services Administration. (2009, Spring). *Emerging issues in the use of methadone.* Rockville, MD: U.S. Department of Health and Human Services. Retrieved April 19, 2011, from www.kap.samhsa.gov/products/manuals/advisory/pdfs/Methadone-Advisory.pdf.

Substance Abuse and Mental Health Services Administration. (2010, January 28). *Overview of opioid treatment programs in the United States: 2008. Rockville, MD: U.S. Department of Health and Human Services.* Retrieved April 29, 2010, from http://oas.samhsa.gov/2k10/222/222USOTP2k10Web.pdf.

Suh, J. J., Pettinati, H. M., Kampman, K. M., & O'Brien, C. P. (2006). The status of disulfiram: A half of a century later. *Journal of Psychopharmacology, 26,* 290–302.

Thomas, C. P., Wallack, S. S., Lee, S., McCarty, D., & Swift, R. (2003). Research to practice: Adoption of naltrexone in alcoholism treatment. *Journal of Substance Abuse Treatment, 24,* 1–11.

Tonigan, J. S., Toscova, R., & Miller, W. R. (1996). Meta-analysis of the literature on Alcoholics Anonymous: Sample and study characteristics moderate findings. *Journal of Studies on Alcohol, 57,* 65–72.

Treating opiate addiction, Part II: Alternatives to maintenance. (2005, January). *Harvard mental health letter.* Retrieved December 26, 2010, from www.health.harvard.edu/newsweek/Treating_opiate_addiction_Alternatives_to_maintenance.htm.

Trent, L. K. (1998). Evaluation of a four- versus six-week length of stay in the Navy's alcohol treatment program. *Journal of Studies on Alcohol, 59,* 270–279.

Trepper, T. S., McCollum, E. E., De Jong, P., Korman, H., Gingerich, W., & Franklin, C. (2010). *Solution-Focused Therapy treatment manual for working with individuals,* Research Committee of the Solution Focused Brief Therapy Association. Retrieved December 18, 2010, from www.solutionfocused.net/treatmentmanual.html.

Trimpey, J. (1996). *Rational recovery: The new cure for substance addiction.* New York: Pocket Books.

Trimpey, J. (2003). Why self-recovery? Lotus, CA: Rational Recovery. Retrieved April 10, 2010, from rational.org/index.php?id=97.

U.S. Behavioral Health Plan, California. (2010). *2010 level of care guidelines: Substance abuse.* California: Author. Retrieved December 22, 2010, from www.ubhonline.com/html/guidelines/levelOfCareGuidelines/pdf/saPartialHospitalDayTreatment.pdf.

Vaillant, G. E. (1983). *The natural history of alcoholism.* Cambridge: Harvard University Press.

Valle, S. R. (1981). Interpersonal functioning of alcoholism counselors and treatment outcome. *Journal of Studies on Alcohol, 42*(9), 783–790.

Van Ryswyk, C., Churchill, M., Velasquez, J., & McGuire, R. (1981–82). Effectiveness of halfway house placement for alcohol and drug abusers. *American Journal of Drug and Alcohol Abuse, 8*(4), 499–512.

Velasquez, M. M., Maurer, G. G., Crouch, C., & DiClemente, C. C. (2001). *Group therapy for substance abuse: A stages-of-change manual.* New York: Guilford Press.

Veilleux, J. C., Colvin, P. J., Anderson, J., York, C., & Heinz, A. J. (2010). A review of opioid dependence treatment: Pharmacological and psychosocial interventions to treat opioid addiction. *Clinical Psychology Review, 30,* 155–166.

Volpicelli, J. R., Alterman, A. I., Hayashida, M., & O'Brien, C. P. (1992). Naltrexone in the treatment of alcohol dependence. *Archives of General Psychiatry, 49*(11), 876–880.

O'Brien, C. P. (1997). Naltrexone and alcohol dependence. *Archives of General Psychiatry, 54,* 737–742.

Volpicelli, J. R., Watson, N. T., King, A. C., Sherman, C. E., & O'Brien, C. P. (1995). Effect of naltrexone and alcohol "high" in alcoholics. *American Journal of Psychiatry, 152*(4), 613–615.

Wallace, A. E., & Weeks, W. B. (2004). Substance abuse intensive outpatient treatment: Does program graduation matter? *Journal of Substance Abuse Treatment, 27*(1), 27–30.

Walsh, D. C., Hingson, R. W., Merrigan, D. M., Levenson, S. M., Cupples, A., Heeren, T., et al. (1991). A randomized trial of treatment options for alcohol-abusing workers. *The New England Journal of Medicine, 325,* 775–782.

Wangberg, K. W., Horn, J. L., & Fairchild, D. (1974). Hospital versus community treatment of alcoholism problems. *International Journal of Mental Health, 3*(2–3), 160–176.

Washton, A. (1997). Structured outpatient group therapy. In J. H. Lowinson, P. Ruiz, R. B. Millman, & J. G. Langrod (Eds.), *Substance abuse: A comprehensive textbook* (pp. 440–448). Baltimore: Williams & Wilkins.

Washton, A. (2005). Group therapy with outpatients. In J. H. Lowinson, P. Ruiz, R. B. Millman, & J. G. Langrod (Eds.), *Substance abuse: A comprehensive textbook* (4th ed., pp. 671–680). Baltimore: Lippincott Williams & Wilkins.

Weil, M., Karls, J. M., & Associates. (1985). *Case management in human service practice.* San Francisco: Jossey-Bass.

Weiss, R. D., Jaffee, W. B., de Menil, V. P., & Cogley, C. B. (2004). Group therapy for substance use disorders: What do we know? *Harvard Review of Psychiatry, 12*(6), 339–350.

Welsh, W. N. (2007). A multisite evaluation of prison-based therapeutic community drug treatment. *Criminal Justice and Behavior, 34*(11), 1481–1498.

West, S. L., O'Neal, K. K., & Graham, C. W. (2000). Meta-analysis comparing the effectiveness of buprenorphine and methadone. *Journal of Substance Abuse, 12,* 405–414.

Wexler, H. K., Melnick, G., Lowe, L., & Peters, J. (1999). Three-year incarceration outcomes for Amity in-prison therapeutic community and aftercare in California. *The Prison Journal, 79,* 321–336.

Wexler, H. K., & Williams, R. (1986). The Stay'n Out therapeutic community: Prison treatment for substance abusers. *Journal of Psychoactive Drugs, 28*(3), 221–230.

White, W. L. (1998). *Slaying the dragon: The history of addiction treatment and recovery in America.* Bloomington, IL: Chestnut Health Systems.

World Health Organization. (2003). *Acupuncture: Review and analysis of reports on controlled clinical trials.* Geneva Switzerland: Author. Retrieved April 22, 2010, from apps.who.int/medicinedocs/en/d/Js4926e/1.html.

Wickizer, T., Longhi, J. J., Krupski, A., & Stark, K. (1997). *Employment outcomes of indigent clients receiving alcohol and drug treatment in Washington state.* Rockville, MD: Substance Abuse and Mental Health Services Administration.

Witbrodt, J., Bond, J., Kaskutas, L. A., Weisner, C., Jaeger, G., Pating, D., et al. (2007). Day hospital and residential addiction treatment: Randomized and nonrandomized managed care clients. *Journal of Consulting and Clinical Psychology, 75*(6), 947–959.

Witkiewitz, K., & Marlatt, G. A. (2011). Behavioral therapy across the spectrum. *Alcohol Research & Health, 33*(4), 313–319.

Worner, T. M., Zeller, B., Schwarz, H., Zwas, E., & Lyon, D. (1992). Acupuncture fails to improve treatment outcome in alcoholics. *Drug and Alcohol Dependence, 30,* 169–173.

Zgierska, A., Rabago, D., Chawla, N., Kushner, C. N., Koehler, R., & Marlatt, A. (2009). Mindfulness meditation for substance use disorders: A systematic review. *Substance Abuse, 30*(4), 266–294.

Zhang, A., Gerstien, D. R., & Friedmann, P. D. (2008). Patient satisfaction and sustained outcomes of drug abuse treatment. *Journal of Health Psychology, 13*(3), 388–400.

Zimberg, S. (1982). Psychotherapy in the treatment of alcoholism. In E. M. Pattison & E. Kaufman (Eds.), *Encyclopedic handbook of alcoholism* (pp. 999–1010). New York: Gardner Press.

Zweben, A. (2001). Integrating pharmacotherapy and psychosocial interventions in the treatment of individuals with alcohol problems. *Journal of Social Work Practice in the Addictions, 1*(3), 65–80.

CHAPTER 7

Adams, R. W. (January 16, 2010). Proven effective, needle exchange banned in Fla. *The Ledger.* Retrieved February 2, 2010, from www.theledger.com/article/20100116/NEWS/1175030/1023?p=4&tc=pg.

Altman, D., Foster, V., Rasenick-Douss, L., & Tye, J. (1989). Reducing the illegal sale of cigarettes to minors. *Journal of the American Medical Association, 261*, 80–83.

American Academy of Pediatrics. (2006). Policy Statement. Retrieved from http://aappolicy.aappublications.org/cgi/content/full/pediatrics;118/6/2563 6/26/11.

American Bar Association. (1986). *Drunk driving laws and enforcement: An assessment of effectiveness.* Washington, DC: Author.

American Civil Liberties Union. (2004). State by state workplace drug testing laws: Table 410. Retrieved August 31, 2009, from www.aclu.org/files/FilesPDFs/testing_chart.pdf.

American Lung Association. (2002, January). *Tobacco control.* Retrieved January 14, 2002, from www. lungusa.org/tobacco.

Ammerman, R. T., Ott, P. J., & Blackson, T. C. (1999) Critical issues in prevention of substance abuse. In R. T. Ammermann, P. Ott, & R. E. Tarter (Eds.), *Prevention and Societal Impact of Drug and Alcohol Abuse.* Mahwah, NJ: L. Erlbaum Associates.

Anderson, P., de Bruijin, A., Angus, K., Gordon, R., & Hastings, G. (2009). Impact of alcohol advertising and media exposure on adolescent alcohol use: A systematic review of longitudinal studies. *Alcohol and Alcoholism, 44*(3), 229–243.

Art of Living. (2009). *The art of living course.* Retrieved August 31, 2009, from us.artofliving.org/content-art-living-course?center=usa.

Atkin, C., Neuendorf, K., & McDermott, S. (1983). The role of alcohol advertising in excessive and hazardous drinking. *Journal of Drug Education, 13,* 313–326.

Austin, E. W., Pinkleton, B. E., & Fujioka, Y. (2000). The role of interpretation processes and the parental discussion in the media's effects on adolescents' use of alcohol. *Pediatrics, 105*(2), 343–349.

Belcher, H. M. E., & Shinitzky, H. E. (1998). Substance abuse in children: Prediction, protection, and prevention. *Archives of Pediatrics and Adolescent Medicine, 152*(10), 952–960.

Belgrave, F. Z., Brome, D. R., & Hampton, C. (2000). The contribution of Africentric values and racial identity to the prediction of drug knowledge, attitudes and use among African American youth. *Journal of Black Psychology, 26*(4), 386–401.

Barnoya, J., & Glantz, S. A. (2006). The tobacco industry's worldwide ETS consultants project: European and Asian components. European Journal of Public Health, 16(1), 69–77.

Benard, B. (1993). *Turning the corner from risk to resiliency.* Portland, OR: Northwest Regional Educational Laboratory.

Berlin, R., & Davis, R. (1989). Children from alcoholic families: Vulnerability and resilience. In T. Dugan & R. Coles (Eds.), *The child in our time: Studies in the development of resiliency* (pp. 81–105). New York: Brunner/Mazel.

Blane, H. T. (1977). *Health education as a preventive strategy.* Paper presented at the Tripartite Conference on Prevention, Washington, DC.

Blane, H. T. (1986). Preventing alcohol problems. In N. J. Estes & M. E. Heinemann (Eds.), *Alcoholism: Development, consequences, and interventions* (3rd ed., pp. 78– 90). St. Louis, MO: C. V. Mosby.

Bloom, M. (1996). *Primary prevention: Issues in children's and families' lives.* Thousand Oaks, CA: Sage.

Botvin, G. J., Baker, E., Dusenbury, L., Botvin, E. M., & Diaz, T. (1995). Long-term follow-up results of a randomized drug abuse prevention trial in a white middle-class population. *Journal of the American Medical Association, 273,* 1106–1112.

Botvin, G. J., Griffin, K. W., Diaz, T., Scheier, L. M., Williams, C., & Epstein, J. A. (2000). Preventing illicit drug use in adolescents: Long-term follow-up data from a randomized control trial of a school population. *Addictive Behaviors, 25*(5), 769–774.

Botvin, G. J., Schinke, S. P., Epstein, J. A., Diaz, T., & Botvin, E. M. (1995). Effectiveness of culturally focused and generic skills training approaches to alcohol and drug abuse prevention among minority adolescents: Two-year follow-up results. *Psychology of Addictive Behaviors, 9*(3), 183–194.

Braucht, G. N., & Braucht, B. (1984). Prevention of problem drinking among youth: Evaluation of educational strategies. In P. M. Miller & T. D. Nirenberg (Eds.), *Prevention of alcohol abuse.* New York: Plenum Press.

Bray, J., Zarkin, G., Dennis, M., & French, M. (2000). Symptoms of dependence, multiple substance abuse, and labor market outcomes. *American Journal of Drug and Alcohol Abuse, 26*(1), 77–96.

breanavirgilio. (2009, November). Meth not even once. Message posted to www.youtube.com/watch?v= 7fvIOUrEejg.

Brofenbrenner, U. (1979). *The ecology of human development: Experiments by nature and design.* Cambridge, Massachusetts: Harvard University Press.

Brown, J. H. (2001). Youth, drugs and resilience education. *Journal of Drug Education, 31*(1), 83–122.

Bush, G. W. (2004). *2004 State of the Union Address.* American Rhetoric Online Speech Bank. Retreived January 10, 2010, from www.americanrhetoric.com/speeches/stateoftheunion2004.htm.

Campaign for Tobacco-Free Kids. (2009). *Deadly in pink: Big tobacco steps up its targeting of women and girls.* Retrieved January 10, 2010, from www.tobaccofreekids.org/reports/women_new/.

Carter, S., Straits, K. J. E., & Hall, M. (2007). Project Venture: Evaluation of an experiential, culturally based approach to substance abuse prevention with American Indian Youth. *Journal of Experiential Education, 29*(3), 397–400.

CASASTART. (2010). *Fact sheet.* Retrieved January 15, 2010, from casastart.org/content/FactSheet.asp.

Catalano, R. F., Haggerty, K. P., Gainey, R. R., Hoppe, M. J., & Brewer, D. D. (1998a). Effectiveness of prevention interventions with youth at high risk of drug abuse. *Cost-benefit/cost-effectiveness research on drug abuse prevention: Implications for programming and policy* (NIDA Research Monograph no. 176). Rockville, MD: National Institute on Drug Abuse.

Catalano, R. F., Kosterman, R., Haggerty, K., Hawkins, J. D., & Spoth, R. (1998b). A universal intervention for the prevention of substance abuse: Preparing for the drug-free years. *Drug abuse prevention through family intervention* (NIDA Research Monograph no. 177). Rockville, MD: National Institute on Drug Abuse.

Saddleback Resources. (2009). *Celebrate recovery.* Retrieved June 30, 2009, from www.saddlebackresources.com/en-US/CELEBRATERECOVERY/CelebrateRecovery.htm.

Centers for Disease Control and Prevention (CDCP), Surveillance Summaries Preview/Abstract. (1995). State laws on tobacco control—United States (Vol. 44). Retrieved January 7, 2004, from www.cdc.gov/mmwr/PDF/ss/ss4406.pdf.

Centers for Disease Control and Prevention. (2006). *Sustaining state programs for tobacco control: Data highlights 2006.* Retrieved September 5, 2009, from www.cdc.gov/tobacco/data_statistics/state_data/data_highlights/2006/pdfs/dataHighlights06rev.pdf.

Cesarone, B. (1999). *Resilience guide: A collection of resources on resilience in children and families.* Champaign, IL: ERIC Clearinghouse on Elementary and Early Childhood Education.

Chain fined for sales to minors. (1991). *Tallahassee Democrat,* p. 2, sec. C.

Chipungu, S. S., Hermann, J., Sambrano, S., Nistler, M., Sale, E., & Springer, J. F. (2000). Prevention programming for African-American youth: A review of strategies in CSAP's national cross-site evaluation of high-risk youth programs. *Journal of Black Psychology, 26*(4), 360–385.

Chitwood, D. D., Weiss, M. L., & Leukefeld, C. G. (2008). A systematic review of recent literature on religiosity and substance use. *The Journal of Drug Issues, 38,* 653–688.

Cho, H., Hallfors, D. D., Iritani, B. J., & Hartman, S. (2009). The influence of "No Child Left Behind" legislation on drug prevention in U.S. schools. *Evaluation Review, 33,* 446–463.

Cohen, J. (1996). Drug education: Politics, propaganda and censorship. *International Journal of Drug Policy, 7*(3).

Community Anti-Drug Coalitions of America. (2008). Changing Communities: CADCA 2008 Annual Report. Retrieved January 20, 2010, from www.cadca.org/files/2008AnnualReport.pdf.

Community Anti-Drug Coalitions of America. (2009). CADCA: Building drug-free communities. Retrieved October 22, 2009, from www.cadca.org/about/institute/detail.

Community Anti-Drug Coalitions of America & National Highway Traffic Safety Administration. (2003). *Impaired Driving Prevention Toolkit.* DOT HS 809 552. Retrieved August 31, 2009, from www.nhtsa.dot.gov/people/injury/alcohol/IDPToolKit/IDP_index.html.

Currie, E. (1993). *Reckoning: Drugs, the cities and the American future.* New York: Hillard Wang.

DeJong, W. (1987). Short term evaluation of Project DARE (Drug Abuse Resistance Education): Preliminary indications of effectiveness. *Journal of Drug Education, 17*(4), 279–294.

Delva, J., Methiesen, S. G., & Kamata, A. (2001). Use of illegal drugs among mothers across racial/ethnic backgrounds in the U.S.: A multi-level analysis of individual and community level influences. *Ethnicity & Disease, 11,* 614–625.

Dembo, R. (1986). Key issues and paradigms in drug use research: Focus on etiology. *Journal of Drug Issues, 16*(1), 1–4.

Denzin, N. K. (1991). *Hollywood shot by shot: Alcoholism in American cinema.* Hawthorne, NY: Aldine DeGruyter.

DiNitto, D. M. (1988). Drunk, drugged, and on the job. In G. Gould & M. L. Smith (Eds.), *Social work in the workplace* (p. 77). New York: Springer.

DocStoc. (2010). *Settlement agreement.* State of New York, State of Maryland, State of Illinois, R.J. Reynolds Tobacco Company and Brown & Williamson Tobacco Corporation. Retrieved January 10, 2010, www.docstoc.com/docs/11154563/Kool-MIXX-Settlement.

Drug Abuse Resistance Education (D.A.R.E.). (2009). *About D.A.R.E.* Retrieved September 4, 2009, from www.dare.com/home/about_dare.asp.

Durant, R. H., Rome, E. S., Rich, M., Allred, E., Emans, S. J., & Woods, E. R. (1997). Tobacco and alcohol use behaviors portrayed in music videos: A content analysis. *American Journal of Public Health, 87*, 1131–1135.

Dusenbury, L., & Falco, M. (1995). Eleven components of effective drug abuse prevention curricula. *Journal of School Health, 65*(10), 420–425.

Ellickson, P. L., McCaffrey, D. F., Ghosh-Dastidar, B., & Longshour, D. L. (2003). New inroads in preventing adolescent drug use: Results from a large-scale train of Project ALERT in middle schools. *American Journal of Public Health, 93*, 1830–1836.

Elliot, D. L., Moe, E. L., Goldberg, L., DeFrancesco, C. A., Durham, M. B., & Hix-Small, H. (2006). Definition and outcome of a curriculum to prevent disordered eating and body-shaping drug use. *Journal of School Health, 76*, 67–73.

Evaluation and Training Institute. (1988). *DARE longitudinal evaluation annual report: 1987–88.* Unpublished manuscript, Evaluation and Training Institute, Los Angeles.

Evans, R. I. (1998). A historical perspective on effective prevention. In W. J. Bukoski & R. I. Evans (Eds.), *Cost-benefit/cost-effectiveness research on drug abuse prevention: Implications for programming and policy* (NIDA Research Monograph no. 176). Rockville, MD: National Institute on Drug Abuse.

Evans, R. L., Rozelle, R. M., Mittelmark, M. B., Hansen, W. B., Bane, A. L., & Havis, J. (1978). Determining the onset of smoking in children: Knowledge of immediate physiological effects and coping with peer pressure, media pressure, and parent modeling. *Journal of Applied Social Psychology, 8*(2), 126–135.

FalseInternetName. (2006). meth addict. Retrieved January 29, 2010, from www.youtube.com/watch?v=EWjteKYxIM8.

Farkas, A. J., Gilpin, E. A., White, M. M., & Pierce, J. P. (2000). Association between household and workplace smoking restrictions and adolescent smoking. *Journal of the American Medical Association, 284*(6), 717–722.

Federal Trade Commission, Bureau of Consumer Protection and Economics. (1985). *Omnibus petition for regulation of unfair and deceptive alcoholic beverage advertising and marketing practices* (Docket no. 209–46). Washington, DC: Author.

Forbes, D. (2000, January 13). Prime-time propaganda. *Salon Media Group.* Retrieved October 22, 2009, from archive.salon.com/news/feature/2000/01/13/drugs/.

French, M. T., Roebuck, M. C., & Alexandre, P. K. (2001). Illicit drug use, employment, and labor force participation. *Southern Economic Journal, 68*(2), 349–368.

Garmendia, M. L., Alvarado, M. E., Montenegro, M., & Pino, P. (2008). Social support as a protective factor of recurrence after drug addiction treatment. *Revista Medica de Chile, 136*, 169–178.

Garmezy, N., & Nuechterlein, K. (1972). Invulnerable children: The fact and fiction of competence and disadvantage. *American Journal of Orthopsychiatry, 42*, 328–329.

Garmezy, N. (1981). Children under stress: Perspectives on antecedents and correlates of vulnerability and resistance to psychopathology. In A. I. Rabin, J. Arnoff, A. M. Barklay, & R. A. Zucker (Eds.), *Further explorations in personality* (pp. 196–269). New York: John Wiley.

Gerstein, D. R. (Ed.). (1984). *Toward the prevention of alcohol problems: Government, business, and community action.* Washington, DC: National Academy Press.

Glantz, M. (1995). *The application of resiliency and risk research to the development of preventive interventions.* National Institute on Drug Abuse: Resiliency and Risk Workgroup Prevention Program Development. Retrieved October 14, 2001, from 165.112.78.61/ResilandRiskWG/ResilandRiskWG.html.

Glass, S. (1997, March 3). Don't you D.A.R.E. *New Republic*, pp. 18–20, 22–23, 26–28.

Glider, P., Midyett, S. J., Mills-Novoa, B., Johannessen, K., & Collins, C. (2001). Challenging the collegiate rite of passage: A campus-wide social marketing media campaign to reduce binge drinking. *Journal of Drug Education, 31*(2), 207–220.

Goldberg, L., MacKinnon, D. P., Elliot, D. L., Moe, E. L., Clarke, G., & Cheong, J. (2000). The Adolescents Training and Learning to Avoid Steroids Program: Preventing drug use and promoting health behaviors. *Archives of Pediatrics and Adolescent Medicine, 154*, 332–338.

Gorman, D. M., & Huber, J. C., Jr. (2009). The social construction of "evidence-based" drug prevention programs: A reanalysis of data from the Drug Abuse Resistance Education (DARE) program. *Evaluation Review, 33*, 396–414.

Gould, G. M., & Smith, M. L. (Eds.). (1988). *Social work in the workplace: Practices and principles.* New York: Springer.

Greenberg, B., Fernandez-Collado, C., Graef, D., Dorzenny, F., & Atkin, C. (1981). *Trends in use of alcohol and other substances on television.* East Lansing, MI: Michigan State University, Department of Communication.

Hall, N. W., & Ziglar, E. (1997). Drug abuse prevention: A review and critique of existing programs. *American Journal of Orthopsychiatry, 67*(1), 134–143.

Hanson, M. (2001). Alcoholism and other drug addictions. In A. Gitterman (Ed.), *Handbook of social work practice with resilient and vulnerable populations* (2nd ed., pp. 64–96). New York: Columbia University Press.

Hanson, W. B. (1992). School-based substance abuse prevention: A review of the state of the art in curriculum, 1980–1990. *Health Education Research, 7*(3), 403–430.

Harm Reduction Coalition. (2010). *Our programs.* Retrieved February 1, 2010, from www.harmreduction.org/article.php?list=type&type=57.

Harrison, P. A., & Hoffman, N. G. (1988). *Adult outpatient treatment: Perspectives on admission and outcome.* St. Paul, MN: Chemical Abuse/Addiction Treatment Outcome Registry, Ramsey Clinic.

Hill, J. E. (2002). *AMA asks CBS, ABC and FOX executives not to join NBC in running hard liquor ads.* American Medical Association. Retrieved March 4, 2002, from www.ama-assn.org/ama/pub/article/3289-5799.html

Hill, L., & Casswell, S. (2001). Alcohol advertising and sponsorship: Commercial freedom or control in the public interest? In N. Heather & T. Peters (Eds.), *International handbook of alcohol dependence and problems* (pp. 823–846). New York: John Wiley & Sons.

Hingson, R., Hereen, T., & Winter, M. (2000). Effects of recent 0.08% legal blood alcohol limits on fatal crash involvement. *Injury Prevention, 6,* 109–114. Retrieved January 8, 2004, from ip.bmjjournals.com/cgi/content/abstract/6/2/109.

Hodge, D. R., Cardenas, P., & Montoya, H. (2001). Substance abuse: Spirituality and religious participation as protective factors among rural youths. *Social Work Research, 25*(3), 153–167.

Homel, R. (1988). *Policing and punishing the drinking driver: A study of general and specific deterrence.* New York: Springer.

Hopkins, D., Briss, P. A., Ricard, C. J., Husten, C. G., Carande-Kulis, V. G., Fielding, J. E., Alao, M. O., McKenna, J. W., Sharp, D. J., Harris, J. R., Woollery, T. A., & Harris, K. W. (2001). Reviews of evidence regarding interventions to reduce tobacco use and exposure to environmental tobacco smoke. *American Journal of Preventive Medicine, 20*(2S), 16–66.

Institute of Medicine. (2009). *Secondhand smoke exposure and cardiovascular effects: Making sense of the evidence.* Retrieved January 2, 2010, from www.iom.edu/secondhandsmokecveffects.

Institute of Medicine. (2010). *Ending the tobacco problem: Resources for local action.* Retrieved January 21, 2010, from sites.nationalacademies.org/Tobacco/.

James, W. H., Kim, G. K., & Armijo, E. (2000). The influence of ethnic identity on drug use among ethnic minority adolescents. *Journal of Drug Education, 30*(3), 265–280.

Japan Trends. (August 2, 2007). *Crush your menthol: Kool Boost Powerball cigarettes.* Retrieved January 29, 2010, from www.japantrends.com/crush-your-menthol-kool-boost-powerball-cigarettes/.

jimbobmcfred. (2009, August). *Meth;Not even once.* Message posted to www.youtube.com/watch?v=7fvIOUrEejg

Johnson, C. A., MacKinnon, D. P., & Pentz, M. A. (1996). Breadth of program and outcome effectiveness in drug abuse prevention. *American Behavioral Scientists, 38*(84), 884–896.

Johnson, J. L., & Leff, M. (1999). Children of substance abusers: Overview of research findings. *Pediatrics, 103*(5), 1085–1099.

Jupp, B., & Lawrence, A. J. (2010). New horizons for therapeutics in drug and alcohol abuse. *Pharmacology & Therapeutics, 125*(1), 138–168.

Katz, J. (January 23, 2008). *Should we accept steroid use in sports?* National Public Radio. Retrieved January 25, 2010, from www.npr.org/templates/story/story.php?storyId=18299098.

Kinney, J., & Leaton, G. (1987). *Loosening the grip: A handbook of alcohol information.* St. Louis, MO: Times Mirror/Mosby.

Kochupillai, V., Dumar, P., Dingh, D., Aggarwal, D., Bhardwaj, N., Bhutani, M. (2005). Effect of rhythmic breathing (Sudarshan Kriya and Pranayam) on immune functions and tobacco addiction. *Annals of the New York Academy of Sciences, 1056,* 242–252.

Kumpfer, K. L. (1998a). *Identification of drug abuse prevention programs: Literature review.* National Institute on Drug Abuse, Resource Center for Health Services Research. Retrieved November 4, 2001, from 2165.2112.2061/HSR/da-pre/KumpferLitReview.htm.

Kumpfer, K. L. (1998b). Selective prevention interventions: The strengthening families program. In R. Ashery, E. Robertson, & K. L. Kumpfer (Eds.), *Drug abuse prevention through family intervention* (NIDA Research Monograph no. 177). Rockville, MD: National Institute on Drug Abuse.

Kumpfer, K. L. (1999). Factors and processes contributing to resilience: The resilience framework. In M. D. Glantz & J. L. Johnson (Eds.), *Resilience and development: Positive life adaptations. Longitudinal research in the social and behavioral sciences* (pp. 179–224). New York: Kluwer Academic/Plenum.

Kumpfer, K. L., Alexander, J. F., McDonald, L., & Olds, D. L. (1998). Family-focused substance abuse prevention: What has been learned from other fields. In R. S. Ashery, E. B. Robertson, & K. L. Kumfer (Eds.), *Drug abuse prevention through family interventions* (NIDA Research Monograph no. 177). Rockville, MD: National Institute on Drug Abuse.

Kumpfer, K. L., & Kaftarian, S. J. (2000). Bridging the gap between family-focused research and substance abuse prevention practice: Preface. *Journal of Primary Prevention, 21*(2), 169–183.

Lawenthal, E., McLellan, A. T., Grissom, G. R., Brill, P., & O'Brien, C. (1996). Coerced treatment for substance abuse problems detected through workplace urine surveillance: Is it effective? *Journal of Substance Abuse, 8*(1), 115–128.

Lichtenstein, E., Glasgow, R. E., Lando, H. A., Ossip-Klein, D. J., & Boles, S. M. (1996). Telephone counseling for smoking cessation: Rationales and meta-analytic review of evidence. *Health Education Research, 11*(2), 243–257.

Lillie-Blanton, M., Werthamer, L., Chatterji, P., Fienson, C., & Caffray, C. (1998). Issues and methods in evaluating costs, benefits, and cost-effectiveness of drug abuse prevention programs for high-risk youth. In W. J. Bukoski & R. I. Evans (Eds.), *Cost-benefit/cost-effectiveness research of drug abuse prevention: Implications for programming and policy* (NIDA Research Monograph no. 176). Rockville, MD: National Institute on Drug Abuse.

Litchman, L. (2002). Court puts the brakes on installation of ignition interlock device only court, not PennDOT, can order the penalty. *The Legal Intelligencer: Regional News, 11,* 3.

Los Angeles Unified School District. (1996). *D.A.R.E. to resist drugs and violence: Drug abuse resistance education student workbook grades 5–6.* Los Angeles: Author.

Lyman, D. R., Milich, R., Zimmerman, R., Novak, S. P., Logan, T. K., Martin, C., Leukefeld, C., & Clayton, R. (1999). Project DARE: No effects at 10-year follow-up. *Journal of Consulting and Clinical Psychology, 67*(4), 590–593.

marajade619. (2006). *Drug abuse pictures before and after.* Retrieved January 29, 2009, from www.youtube.com/watch?v=RJIjWlLa8MU.

Marijuana Policy Project. (2010). *About the marijuana policy project.* Retrieved February 5, 2010, from www.mpp.org/about/.

Martin, D. (1999, January 22). Excerpts on study of smoking ban in restaurants: Smoking ban has not hurt restaurants, analysts say. *New York Times,* p. B–7.

Marwick, C. (1999). Illicit drug users not idle; Report says 70% go to work. *Journal of the American Medical Association, 282*(14), 1320.

Mathios, A., Avery, R., Bisogni, C., & Shanahan, J. (1998). Alcohol portrayal on prime-time television: Manifest and latent messages. *Journal of Studies on Alcohol, 59*(3), 305–310.

Mayberry, M. L., Espelage, D. L., & Koenig, B. (2009). Multi-level modeling of direct effects and interactions of peers, parents, school, and community influences on adolescent substance use. *Journal of Youth and Adolescence, 38,* 1038–1049.

McCaffrey, B. R. (1999, June). *Investing in our nation's youth: National youth anti-drug media campaign: Phase II (Final Report).* Executive Office of the President, Office of the National Drug Control Policy. Retrieved December 4, 2001, from www.mediacampaign.org/publications/phasii/phaseII_appf.pdf.

McCarthy, W. J. (1985). The cognitive development model and other alternatives to the social deficit model of smoking onset. In C. S. Bell & R. Battles (Eds.), *Prevention research: Deterring drug abuse among children and adolescents* (pp. 153–169). Rockville, MD: U.S. Department of Health and Human Services.

McGuire, W. J. (1969). The nature of attitude and attitude change. In G. Lindsay & E. Aronson (Eds.), *Handbook of social psychology* (2nd ed., Vol. 3, pp. 136–314). Reading, MA: Addison-Wesley.

McKim, W. A. (1991). *Drugs and behavior* (2nd ed.). Englewood Cliffs, NJ: Prentice Hall.

Miami/Dade County Juvenile Screening, Detection, and Treatment Program Officials. (1991, June 7). Personal interview.

Miami-Dade County Juvenile Services Department. (2009). *Research and statistics: JSD facts.* Retrieved January 2, 2010, from www.miamidade.gov/jsd/library/JSD%20Facts.pdf.

Miami-Dade County Juvenile Services Department. (2009). *Research and statistics: JSD monthly report for month ending July 31, 2009.* Retrieved January 2, 2010, from www.miamidade.gov/jsd/library/July%202009.pdf.

Minutes of the Senate Committee on Finance. (1999.) *Seventieth session, April 19, 1999.* Retrieved December 18, 2001, from www.leg.state.ne.../SM-FIN-990419-Finance&20Meeting-Bills%20&20Closings.htm.

Montana Meth Project. (2010). *The meth project: View ads.* Retrieved January 29, 2010, from www.notevenonce.com/View_Ads/index.php.

Moon, D. G., Jackson, K. M., & Hecht, M. L. (2000). Family risk and resiliency factors: Substance use and the drug resistance process in adolescence. *Journal of Drug Education, 30*(4), 373–398.

Mosher, J. F. (1990). Drug availability in a public health perspective. In H. Resnik (Eds.), *Youth and drugs: Society's mixed messages.* Rockville, MD: U.S. Department of Health and Human Services.

Moskowitz, J. M. (1989). The primary prevention of alcohol problems: A critical review of the research literature. *Journal of Studies on Alcohol, 50*(1), 54–88.

Mrazek, P. J., & Haggerty, R. J. (Eds.). (1994). *Reducing risks for mental disorders: Frontiers for preventive intervention research.* Washington, DC: National Academy Press.

Multnomah County Sheriff's Department. (2005). *Faces of Meth.* Retrieved October 12, 2009, from www.facesofmeth.us/.

NaomiDreamStudios. (2009). *Meth:Not even once.* Retrieved January 29, 2009, from www.youtube.com/watch?v=7fvIOUrEejg.

Napp Pharmaceuticals. (2009). *Targinact, Oxycodone/Naloxone: Your questions answered: Information for healthcare professionals.* Retrieved February 2, 2010, from www.targetingpain.co.uk/content/your-questions-answered.pdf.

National Center for Tobacco-Free Kids. (August 15, 2001). *Special report: Big tobacco still addicting kids.* Retrieved February 11, 2002, from www.tobaccofreekids.org/reports/addicting/.

National Center on Addiction and Substance Abuse (CASA) and Columbia University. (2001a). *So help me God: Substance abuse, religion and spirituality.* Retrieved January 8, 2004, from www.casacolumbia.org/pdshopprov/files/91513.pdf.

National Center on Addiction and Substance Abuse. (2010). *Fact sheet.* Retrieved January 15, 2010 from http://casastart.org/content/FactSheet.asp.

National Football League. (2009). *Player development: Event-rookie symposium.* Retrieved August 17, 2009, from www.nfl.com/playerdevelopment/events.

National Highway Traffic Safety Administration. (2001). *Saturation patrols and sobriety checkpoints: A how-to guide for planning and publicizing impaired driving efforts* (Document no. DOT HS 809 063). Retrieved January 24, 2002, from www.nhtsa.dot.gov/people/injury/alcohol/saturation_patrols/index.html.

National Institute on Alcohol Abuse and Alcoholism. (1998). Alcohol consumption among racial/ethnic minorities. *Alcohol Health and Research World, 22*(4), 233–241.

National Institute on Drug Abuse. (2009, December 14). *Teen methamphetamine use, cigarette smoking at lowest levels in*

NIDA's 2009 monitoring the future survey. Retrieved January 4, 2010, from www.drugabuse.gov/newsroom/09/NR12–14.html.

National Institute on Money in State Politics. (2010). *Follow the money.* Retrieved February 5, 2010, from www.followthemoney.org/.

National Institutes of Health. (2009). *American Recovery and Reinvestment Act of 2009: Challenge grant applications.* Retrieved August 31, 2009, from grants.nih.gov/grants/funding/challenge_award/Omnibus.pdf.

National Institutes of Mental Health (NIMH). (1998). A framework for modern prevention science. *Priorities for prevention research at NIMH: A report by the National Advisory Mental Health Council Workgroup on mental disorders prevention research* (NIH Publication no. 98–4321). Bethesda, MD: U.S. Department of Health and Human Services.

National Registry of Evidence-Based Programs and Practices (NREPP). (2010). *Substance abuse prevention programs Search: United States Department of Health and Human Services, SAMHSA.* Retrieved December 9, 2009, from www.nrepp.samhsa.gov/listofprograms.asp?textsearch=Search+specific+word+or+phrase&ShowHide=1&Sort=1&T4=4.

National Research Council and Institute of Medicine. (2009). *Preventing mental, emotional, and behavioral disorders among young people: Progress and possibilities.* Committee on the Prevention of Mental Disorders and Substance Abuse Among Children, Youth, and Young Adults: Research Advances and Promising Interventions. Mary Ellen O'Connell, Thomas Boat, and Kenneth E. Warner, Editors. Board on Children, Youth, and Families, Division of Behavioral and Social Sciences and Education. Washington, DC: The National Academies Press.

National Indian Youth Leadership Project. (2008). *Project Venture: A tradition of excellence.* Retrieved January 9, 2010, from www.niylp.org/programs.htm.

Navarro, J., Wilson, S., Berger, L. R., & Taylor, T. (1997). Substance abuse and spirituality: A program for Native American students. *Journal of Health Behavior, 21*(1) 3–11.

Neergaard, L. (1997, November 3). *Smoke-free bars stay busy.* Associated Press. Retrieved November 28, 2001, from www.gasp.org/nyrest.html.

Nelson, J. P. (2001). Alcohol advertising and advertising bans: A survey of research methods, results and policy implications. In M. R. Baye & J. P. Nelson (Eds.), *Advances in applied microeconomics, Vol. 10: Advertising and differentiated products* (pp. 239–295). Amsterdam, The Netherlands: JAI & Elsevier Science.

Nelson, R. P., Brown, J. M., Brown, W. D., Koops, B. L., McInerny, T. K., Meurer, J. R., Wright, J. A., McManus, M., Davis, J., Jacobs, E. A., Joffe, A., Knight, J. R., Kulig, J., Rogers, P. D., Boyd, G. M., Czechowicz, D., Simkin, D., & Smith, K. (2001). American Academy of Pediatrics: Improving substance abuse, assessment, and treatment financing for children and adolescents. *Pediatrics, 108*(4), 1025–1029.

Nelson, A., & Arthur, B. (2003). Storytelling for Empowerment: Decreasing at-risk youth's alcohol and marijuana use. *The Journal of Primary Prevention, 24* (2), 169–180.

Office of the National Drug Control Policy (ONDCS). (1999). *Reducing drug abuse in America: An overview of demand reduction initiatives.* Executive Office of the President of the United States, Office of the National Drug Control Strategy. Retrieved January 24, 2002, from www.whitehousedrugpolicy.gov/publications/policy/ndcs01/chap1.html.

Office of the National Drug Control Strategy (ONDCS). (2001). *National drug control policy annual report and the national drug control strategy: An overview.* Executive Office of the President of the United States, Office of the National Drug Control Strategy. Retrieved January 24, 2002, from www.whitehousedrugpolicy.gov/publications/policy/ndcs01/chap1.html.

Olson, S., & Gerstein, D. R. (1985). *Alcohol in America: Taking action to prevent abuse.* Washington, DC: National Academy Press.

Pan, W., & Bai, H. (2009). A multivariate approach to a meta-analytic review of the effectiveness of the D.A.R.E. program. *International Journal of Environmental Research and public Health, 6*(1), 267–277.

Pandina, R. J. (1996). *Risk and protective factor models in adolescent drug use: Putting them to work for prevention.* Paper presented at the National Conference on Drug Abuse Prevention Research: Presentations, Papers, and Recommendations, Plenary Session, Washington, DC.

The Partnership for a Drug-Free America. (2010). Faces of Meth. Retrieved October 13, 2009. from www.drugfree.org/Portal/DrugIssue/MethResources/faces/index.html.

Paschall, M. J., Flewelling, R. L., & Faulkner, F. D. (2000). Alcohol misuse in young adulthood: Effects of race, educational attainment, and social context. *Substance Use and Misuse, 35*(11), 1485–1506.

Perrone, M. (2009, September 24). FDA panel backs reformulated OxyContin pill. *Associated Press Archives.* Document ID: 12B3CCF5139EF6E8.

Pierce, J. P., Gilpin, E. A., & Choi, W. S. (1999). Sharing the blame: Smoking experimentation and future smoking-attributable mortality due to Joe Camel and Marlboro advertising and promotions. *Tobacco Control Online, 8*, 37–34. Retrieved January 30, 2002, from www.tc.bmjjournals.com/cgi/content/full/2008/2001/2037.

Ponkshe, P., & Wilson, E. (1999). *Studies find Massachusetts' smoke-free ordinances having no significant effect on restaurant revenue.* U.S. Newswire. Retrieved January 8, 2004, from www.gasp.org/restaurants.html.

Ray, O. S., & Ksir, C. (1999). *Drugs, society, and human behavior* (8th ed.). Dubuque, IA: WCB/McGraw-Hill.

Real brew-haha, A. (July 1, 1991). *Time,* p. 56.

The Real Project. (2008). Florida State University. Retrieved January 15, 2010, from www.fsureal.com.

Reynolds, G. S., & Lehman, W. E. K. (2003). Levels of substance use and willingness to use the employee assistance program. *Journal of Behavioral Health Services & Research, 30*(2), 238–248.

Ribisl, K. M., Williams, R. S., & Kim, A. E. (2003). Internet sales of cigarettes to minors. *Journal of the American Medical Association, 290*, 1356–1359.

Ringwalt, C. L., Green, J. M., Ennett, S. T., Iachan, R., Clayton, R. R., & Leukfeld, C. G. (1994). *Past and future directions of the D.A.R.E. program: An evaluation review.* Research Triangle Park, NC: Research Triangle Institute, University of Kentucky.

Roche, A. M., Bywook, P., Pidd, K., Greeman, T., & Seenson, T. (2009). Drug testing in Australian schools: Policy implications and consideration of punitive, deterrence and/or prevention measures. *International Journal of Drug Policy, 20*, 521–528.

Roberts, D. F., Henriksen, L., Christenson, P. G., Kelly, M., Carbone, S., & Wilson, A. B. (1999). *Substance use in popular movies and music.* Office of National Drug Control Policy: Media Campaign, Department of Health and Human Services, Substance Abuse and Mental Health Services Administration. Retrieved December 18, 2001, from www.mediacampaign.org/publications/movies/movie_partI.html.

Roman, P. M., & Blum, T. (1990). Employee assistance and drug screening programs. In D. R. Gerstein & H. J. Harwood (Eds.), *Treating drug abuse* (Vol. 2). Washington, DC: National Academy Press.

Saddleback Resources. (2009). Celebrate recovery: freedom from your hurts, habits and hang-ups. Retrieved from http://www.saddlebackresources.com/Celebrate-Recovery-C5.aspx 6/26/11.

Sager, R. (2000). Teach them well: Drug talk that fails. *National Review, 52*(8), 30–32.

Shadel, W. G., Niaura, R., & Abrams, D. B. (2001). How do adolescents process smoking and anti-smoking advertisements? A social cognitive analysis with implications for understanding smoking initiation. *Review of General Psychology, 5*(4), 429–444.

Shelly, H. (1998). Survivors sue bar, its owners over patron's DUI death. *The Legal Intelligencer,* Suburban Edition, p. 6.

Shepard, E. M. (2001). *The economic costs of D.A.R.E.* Institute of Industrial Relations, Le Moyne College, Research Paper, No. 22.

Siegel, M. (2002). Antismoking advertising: Figuring out what works. *Journal of Health Communication, 7*(2), 157–162.

Siegel, M., & Biener, L. (2000). The Impact of Anti-Smoking Media Campaigns on Progression to Established Smoking: Results of a Longitudinal Youth Study in Massachusetts. *American Journal of Public Health, 90,* 380–386.

Sly, D. F., Heald, G. R., & Ray, S. (2001). The Florida "Truth" anti-tobacco media evaluation: Design, first year results, and implications for planning future state media evaluations. *Tobacco Control, 10*(1), 9–15.

Sly, D. F., Hopkins, R. S., Trapido, D., & Ray, S. (2001). Influence of a counter advertising media campaign on initiation of smoking: The Florida "Truth" campaign. *American Journal of Public Health, 91*(2), 233–238.

Smoke Free Movies. (2010). *The problem: Now showing.* Retrieved January 4, 2010, from www.smokefreemovies.ucsf.edu/problem/now_showing.html.

Snyder, L. B., Hamilton, M. A., Mitchell, E. W., Kwanuka-Tondo, J., Fleming-Milici, F., & Proctor, D. (2004). A meta-analysis of the effect of mediated Health Communication campaigns on behavior change in the United States. *Journal of Health Communication, 9* (Supplement 1), 71–96.

Stewart, C. (2010). *Super Bowl Sunday 2010.* Indiana Prevention Resource Center. Retrieved January 22, 2010, from www.drugs.indiana.edu/news-featured_detail.aspx?seq=35.

Streke, A. V. (2004). Meta-analysis of adolescent community-based drug prevention programs. *Dissertation Abstracts International, A: The Humanities and Social Sciences, 65*(6), 2388–A.

Substance Abuse and Mental Health Services Administration (SAMHSA). (2001). *Summary of findings from the 2000 national household survey on drug abuse: Chapter 6. Prevention-related measures.* U.S. Department of Health and Human Services, Retrieved December 6, 2001, from www.samhsa.gov/oas/nhsda/2knhsda/chapter6.htm.

The Walt Disney Company. (October, 2006). *Safety and security: Statement by the Walt Disney Company regarding the depiction of Smoking in the Movies.* Retrieved November 27, 2009, from corporate.disney. go.com/corporate/cr_safety_security_smoking.html.

The White House Office of National Drug Control Policy. (2009). *National Youth Anti-Drug Media Campaign: Frequently asked questions.* Retrieved August 31, 2009, from www.whitehousedrugpolicy.gov/media campaign/faqs.html.

Thompson, E. (2010). Personal communication, January 22, 2010.

Titus, K., Polansky, J. R., & Glantz, S. (2009). *Smoking presentation trends in U.S. movies 1991–2008.* UC San Francisco: Center for Tobacco Control Research and Education. Retrieved December 20, 2009, from escholarship.org/uc/item/30q9j424.

Tobacco Control Research Digest. (1999). *Overcoming barriers: Racial and ethnic issues in the war against tobacco.* Retrieved January 27, 2002, from www.ftcc.fsu.edu/digests/digest599/index.html.

Tobacco-Free Kids Action Fund. (2010). *Quarterly report: Campaign contributions by tobacco interests.* Retrieved February 9, 2010, from tobaccofreeaction.org/contributions/.

Tobacco industry behind smoking ban. (2000, June 4). *Billings Gazette.* Retrieved August 28, 2001, from www.billingsgazette.com/wyoming/20000604_y3tobac.html.

Tobler, N. S. (1997). Meta-analysis of adolescent drug prevention programs: Results of the 1993 meta-analysis. In W. J. Bukoski (Ed.), *National Institute on Drug Abuse research monograph series: Meta-analysis of drug abuse prevention programs* (p. 170). Rockville, MD: National Institute on Drug Abuse.

Tremblay, V. J., & Okuyama, K. (2001). Advertising restrictions, competition, and alcohol consumption. *Contemporary Economic Policy, 19*(3), 313–321.

Turner-Musa, J. O., Rhodes, W. A., Harper, P. T. H., & Quinton, S. L. (2008). Hip-hop to prevent substance use and HIV among African-American youth: A preliminary investigation. *Journal of Drug Education, 38*(4), 351–365.

United Nations Office on Drugs and Crime. (2010). *Prevention of drug use.* Retrieved February 4, 2010, from www.unodc.org/unodc/en/prevention/index.html.

U.S. Department of Health and Human Services, U.S. Food and Drug Administration. (2009a). *Tobacco products: Guidance, compliance & regulatory information.* Retrieved January 2, 2010, from www.fda.gov/TobaccoProductsGuidanceComplianceRegulatoryInformation/default.htm.

U.S. Department of Health and Human Services, U.S. Food and Drug Administration. (2009b). *Tobacco products: Guidance to industry and FDA staff: General questions and answers on the ban of cigarettes that contain certain characterizing flavors (Edition 2).* Retrieved January 2, 2010, from www.fda.gov/TobaccoProducts/GuidanceComplianceRegulatoryInformation/FlavoredTobacco/ucm183228.htm.

U.S. Department of Transportation. (2009). *Office of Drug & Alcohol Policy and Compliance.* Retrieved August 30, 2009, from www.dot.gov/ost/dapc/index.html.

U.S. Drug Enforcement Administration. (September 19, 2002). *"Date Rape" drug sold over the internet: More than 80 U.S. cities targeted by international operation.* Retrieved August 29, 2009, from www.justice.gov/dea/pubs/pressrel/pr091902.html.

University of North Carolina (UNC), School of Public Health. (2001, December 10). *Research finds Internet cigarette sales present potential threat to public health.* Retrieved March 21, 2002, from www.sph.unc.edu/news/?fuseaction=disply&press_id=1355.

Vakalahi, H. F. (2001). Adolescent substance use and family-based risk and protective factors: A literature review. *Journal of Drug Education, 31*(1), 29–46.

Villani, S. (2001). Impact of media on children and adolescents: A 10-year review of the research. *Journal of the American Academy of Child and Adolescent Psychiatry, 40*(2), 392–401.

Wagenaar, A. C. (1986). *Youth, alcohol, and traffic crashes.* Paper presented at the Prevention Research Center Workshop, Berkeley, CA.

Wallack, L., & Corbett, K. (1990). Illicit drug, tobacco, and alcohol use among youth: Trends and promising approaches in prevention. In H. Resnik, S. E. Gardner,

R. P. Lorian, & C. E. Marcus (Eds.), *Youth and drugs: Society's mixed messages* (p. 16). Rockville, MD: U.S. Department of Health and Human Services.

Walters, W. (2009). Miami-Dade County, Florida Juvenile Justice Model. International Juvenile Justice Observatory Conference, Valencia, Spain.

Warner, K. E. (1979). Clearing the airwaves: The cigarette ad ban revisited. *Policy Analysis, 4,* 435–450.

Werch, C. E., & Owen, D. M. (2002). Iatrogenic effects of alcohol and drug prevention programs. *Journal of Studies on Alcohol, 63*(5), 581–590.

Werner, E. E., & Smith, R. S. (1982). *Vulnerable but invincible: A study of resilient children.* New York: McGraw-Hill.

Werner, E. E., & Smith, R. S. (2001). *Journeys from childhood to midlife: Risk, resilience and recovery.* Ithaca, NY: Cornell University Press.

Weisz, J. R., Sandler, I. N., Durlak, J. A., & Anton, B. S. (2005). Promoting and protecting youth mental health through evidence-based prevention and treatment. *American Psychologist, 60*(6), 628–648.

White, J. M. (1991). *Drug dependence.* Englewood Cliffs, NJ: Prentice Hall.

Willemsen, M. C., & Zwart, W. M. D. (1999). The effectiveness of policy and health education strategies for reducing adolescent smoking: A review of the evidence. *Journal of Adolescence, 22*(5), 587–599.

Williamson, D. (2001). *Research finds Internet cigarette sales present potential threat to public health.* EurekaAlert Press Release. Retrieved January 30, 2002, from www.eurekalert.org/pub_releases/2001-12/unco-rfil20701.php.

Wills, T. A., Sargent, J. D., Gibbons, F. X., Gerrard, M., Stoolmiller, M. (2009). Movie exposure to alcohol cues and adolescent alcohol problems: A longitudinal analysis in a national sample. *Psychology of Addictive Behavior, 23*(1): 23–35.

Wilson, J. J. (1999). *Summary of the attorneys general master tobacco settlement agreement.* National Conference of State Legislators. Retrieved January 24, 2002, from www.udayton.edu/~health/syllabi/tobacco/summary.htm.

Wochenschr, W. K. (2009). Doping and the Olympic games: The good, the bad, and the ugly. *The Middle European Journal of Medicine, 121,* 13–14.

Woodward, A. (1998). Overview of methods: Cost-effectiveness, cost-benefits, and cost-offsets of prevention. In W. J. Bukoski & R. T. Evans (Eds.), *Cost-benefit/cost-effectiveness research of drug abuse prevention: Implications for programming and policy* (NIDA Research Monograph no. 176). Rockville, MD: National Institute on Drug Abuse.

World Bank Group. (2002). *Economics of tobacco control: Report on all topics in the United States.* Retrieved January 24, 2002, from www1.worldbank.org/tobacco/brieflist_db.asp.

World Health Organization. (2001). Substance use disorders. *The world health report 2001. Mental health: New understanding, new hope.* Retrieved January 14, 2002, from

www.who.int/whr/2001/main/en/ chapter2002/
2002e2002.htm.

World Health Organization Department of Mental Health and
Substance Abuse. (2007). *Outcome evaluation summary
report: WHO/UNODC global initiative on primary prevention of substance abuse.* Geneva, Switzerland. Retrieved
December 20, 2009, from www.who.int/substance_
abuse/publications/global_initiative_summary_report.
pdf.

Wyllie, A., Zhang, J. F., & Casswell, S. (1998). Positive responses to televised beer advertisements associated with
drinking and problems reported by 18–29 year olds. *Addiction, 93,* 361–371.

Wyman, J. R. (1997). Multifaceted prevention programs reach
at-risk children through their families. *NIDA Notes: Children on the Brink: Youths at Risk of Drug Abuse, 12*(3). Retrieved January 17, 2001, from 2165.2112.2078.2061/
NIDA-Notes/NNVol2012N2003/ Multifacet.html.

Youth Media Network. (2001). *Tobacco and advertising.*
Retrieved August 31, 2001, from www.ymn.org/
newstats/advertising.shtml.

Zhang, B., Camin, C., & Ferrence, R. (2008). The role of
spending money and drinking alcohol in adolescent
smoking. *Addiction, 103*(2), 310–319.

Zemore, S. E. (2007). A role for spiritual change in the benefits of 12-step involvement. *Alcoholism: Clinical and Experimental Research, 31,* 76S–79S.

Zerhouni, E. A. (2006). The promise of personalized medicine. *NIH Medline Plus.* Retrieved February 1, 2009,
from, www.nih.gov/about/director/int.

CHAPTER 8

Abadinsky, H. (2001). *Drugs: An introduction* (4th ed.).
Belmont, CA: Wadsworth.

Alcohol Policy Information System. (2010). *Blood alcohol concentration limits.* Washington, DC: NIAA. Retrieved April
22, 2010, from alcoholpolicy.niaaa.nih.gov/APIS_
Policy_Topics.html.

Alcohol Problems and Solutions. (2010). *Minimum drinking
ages around the world.* Retrieved April 22, 2010, from
www2.potsdam.edu/hansondj/LegalDrinkingAge.
html.

Alexander, B. K. (1990). Alternatives to the war on drugs.
Journal of Drug Issues, 20(1), 1–27.

American Bar Association (ABA), Criminal Justice Section.
(1986). *Drunk driving laws and enforcement: An assessment of effectiveness.* New York: Sage Foundation.

Arnold, R. D. (1985). *Effect of raising the legal drinking age on
driver involvement in fatal crashes: The experience on thirteen states* (NHTSA Technical Report DOT HS 806 902).
Washington, DC: National Highway Traffic and Safety
Administration.

Ball, J. C., Rosen, L., Flueck, J. A., & Nurco, D. N. (1982, Summer). Lifetime criminality of heroin addicts in the
United States. *Journal of Drug Issues, 11,* 225–238.

Ball, J. C., Shaffer, J. W., & Nurco, D. N. (1983). Day to day
criminality of heroin addicts in Baltimore: A study in
the continuity of offense rates. *Drug and Alcohol Dependence, 12,* 119–142.

Bean, P. (1974). *The social control of drugs.* London, England:
Martin Robertson.

Becker, H. (1967). *Outsiders: Studies in the sociology of deviance.* New York: Free Press.

Belenko, S. (1990). The impact of drug offenders on the criminal justice system. In R. Weisheit (Ed.), *Drugs, crime,
and the criminal justice system* (p. 27). Cincinnati, OH:
Anderson.

Belenko, S. (2002). The challenges of conducting research in
drug treatment court settings. *Substance Use and Misuse,
37*(1), 635–1664.

Benson, B. L., & Rasmussen, D. W. (1994). *The economic anatomy of a drug war: Criminal justice in the commons.*
Latham, MD: Rowman & Littlefield.

Besteman, K. J. (1989). War is not the answer. *American Behavioral Scientist, 32*(3), 290–293.

Blanchard, C. (1999, Winter). Drugs, crime, prison and treatment. *Spectrum, 72,* 26–27.

Blose, J., & Holder, H. (1989). Liquor-by-the-drink and alcohol-
related traffic crashes: A natural experiment using time-
series analysis. *Journal of Studies on Alcohol, 48,* 52–60.

Bradley, A. M. (1987). A capsule review of the state of the art:
Sixth special report to the U.S. Congress on alcohol and
health. *Alcohol Health and Research World, 4*(3).

Bureau of Justice Statistics (BOJS). (1997). *Correctional populations in the United States 1995* (NCJ-163916). Washington, DC: U.S. Department of Justice.

Bureau of Justice Statistics (BOJS). (1988a). *Report to the nation on crime and justice* (NCJ-105506). Washington, DC:
U.S. Department of Justice.

Bureau of Justice Statistics (BOJS). (1988b). *Profile of state
prison inmates* (NCJ-109926). Washington, DC: U.S. Department of Justice.

Bureau of Justice Statistics (BOJS). (1996). *Correctional
populations in the United States, 1994* (NCJ-160091).
Washington, DC: U.S. Department of Justice.

Bureau of Justice Statistics (BOJS). (1997). *Prisoners in 1996*
(NCJ-16419). Washington, DC: U.S. Department of
Justice.

Bureau of Justice Statistics (BOJS). (1999, June 13). *More than
500,000 drunk drivers on probation or incarcerated in 1997.*
U.S. Department of Justice. Retrieved March 25, 2002,
from www.ojp.usdoj.gov/bjs/pub/press/dwiocls.pr.

Bureau of Justice Statistics (BOJS). (2001). *Prisoners in 2000*
(NCJ 188207). Washington, DC: U.S. Department of
Justice.

Bureau of Justice Statistics (BOJS). (2001). *Sourcebook of
criminal justice statistics.* Washington, DC: U.S. Department of Justice.

Bureau of Justice Statistics (BOJS). (2008). *Prisoners in 2007*
(NCJ224280). Washington, DC: U.S. Department of
Justice.

Bureau of Justice Statistics (BOJS). (2009). *Prisoners in 2008* (NCJ 228417). Washington, DC: U.S. Department of Justice.

Bureau of Justice Statistics (BOJS). (2010a). *Estimated arrests for drug abuse violations by age group, 1970–2007.* Retrieved April 20, 2010, from www.bjs.ojp.usdoj.gov/ content/glance/tables/drugtab.cfm.

Bureau of Justice Statistics (BOJS). (2010b). *Sourcebook of criminal justice statistics.* Washington, DC: U.S. Department of Justice. Retrieved April 22, 2010, from www. albany.edu/sourcebook/toc_4.html.

Bureau of Prisons. (2009). *Annual Report on Substance Abuse Treatment Programs, Fiscal Year 2008, Report to the Congess.* Washington, DC: Department of Justice, January.

Business Week. (2009). *The debate room: Legalize marijuana for tax revenue.* Retrieved August 5, 2009, from www.businessweek.com/debateroom/archives/ 2009/03/legalize_mariju.html.

Canada legalises medical marijuana. (2001, July 5). *BBC News.* Retrieved March 25, 2002, from news/bbc/co/ uk/1/americas/1424798.stm.

Cardona, L. (2010). Evaristo Porras, 62; trafficked drugs for Medellin cartel. Associated Press, March 10.

Center for Substance Abuse Treatment (CSAT). (1998). *The end of welfare as we know it.* SAMHSA. Retrieved May 25, 2002, from www.treatment.org/communique/ comm98W/inthe/End.html.

Center for Disease Control. (2001, May 18). Update: Syringe exchange programs—United States, 1998. *Morbidity and Mortality Weekly Report, 50*(19), 384–388. Retrieved May 17, 2003, from www.cdc.gov/mmwrhtml/ mm5019a4.htm.

Centers for Disease Control and Prevention (CDCP). (2009a). *Smoking and tobacco use: Health effects of cigarette smoking.* Retrieved August 7, 2009, from www.cdc.gov/ tobacco/data_statistics/fact_sheets/health_effects/ effects_cig_smoking/index.htm.

Centers for Disease Control and Prevention (CDCP). (2009b). *Alcohol & public health.* Retrieved August 7, 2009, from www.cdc.gov/alcohol/index.htm.

Chaiken, M. R. (1989). *In-prison programs for drug-involved offenders.* Washington, DC: U.S. Department of Justice, National Institute of Justice, Office of Communication and Research Utilization.

Change of heart, perhaps, but not of legislation. (1994, June 1). *Journal of the American Medical Association, 271,* 1635–1639.

Cohen, S. (1981). *The substance abuse problems.* New York: Haworth Press.

Connors, G. J. (1993). Drinking moderation training as a contemporary therapeutic approach. *Drugs and Society, 8*(1), 117–134.

Cook, P., & Tauchen, G. (1984). The effect of minimum drinking age legislation on youthful auto fatalities, 1970–1977. *Journal of Legal Studies, 13,* 169–190.

Cook, P. J. (1984). Increasing the federal alcohol excise tax. In D. R. Gertein (Ed.), *Toward the prevention of alcohol problems: Government, business, and community action* (pp. 24–56). Washington, DC: National Academy Press.

Criminal Justice Estimating Conference. (1989, February 23). *Final report of the Florida consensus.* Tallahassee, FL: Office of the Governor.

de Miranda, J. (1999, May 17). Despite federal resistance, harm reduction strategies take hold. *Alcoholism and Drug Abuse Weekly, 11*(20), 5.

Dennis, R. J. (1990, November). The economics of legalizing drugs. *Atlantic Monthly,* 129.

Doweiko, H. E. (2002). *Concepts of chemical dependency* (5th ed.). Pacific Grove, CA: Brooks/Cole-Thomson Learning.

Drug Enforcement Administration (DEA). (2009). Stats & facts: 2008 successes in the fight against drugs. Retrieved August 5, 2009, from www.usdoj.gov/dea/statistics.html#seizures.

Drug Policy Alliance. (June 29, 2001). *Rand Institute study slams drug war.* Retrieved April 13, 2002, from www. soros.org/lindesmith/news/DailyNews/ 06_28_01Rand2.html.

Drug Policy Alliance. (2002). *Progress report: Substance abuse and crime prevention act of 2000.* Retrieved May 13, 2002, from www.prop36.org/progress_report.html.

Drug Policy Alliance. (2009). *Drugs, police, and the law: Illegal search and seizure.* Retrieved August 9, 2009, from www. drugpolicy.org/law/searchandsei/.

Evans, W. N. (1998). Assessment and diagnosis of the substance use disorders (SUDs). *Journal of Counseling and Development, 76,* 325–333.

Federal Bureau of Investigation (FBI). (1999). *Uniform crime report, 1998.* Washington, DC: U.S. Department of Justice.

Federal Bureau of Investigation (FBI). (2000). *Crime in the United States 1980 through 1999: Uniform crime reporting program.* Washington, DC: U.S. Department of Justice.

Field, G. (1989). The effects of intensive treatment on reducing the criminal recidivism of addicted offenders. *Federal Probation, 53*(4), 51–56.

Galliher, J. F., McCartney, J. L., & Baum, B. E. (1974). Nebraska's marijuana law: A case of unexpected legislative innovation. *Law and Society Review, 8,* 441–455.

Gerstein, D. R., & Harwood, H. J. (Eds.) (1990). *Treating drug problems* (Vol. 1). Washington, DC: National Academy Press.

Goldman, F. (1981). Drug abuse, crime and economics: The dismal limits of social choice. In J. A. Inciardi (Ed.), *The drugs-crime connection* (pp. 155–181). Beverly Hills, CA: Sage.

Gustavson, N. S. (1991). The war metaphor: A threat to vulnerable populations. *Social Work, 36*(4), 277–278.

Hidalgo, O. (2010, April 25). Mexican drug trafficking. *New York Times.*

Hindelang, M. J., Gottfredson, M. R., & Garofalo, J. (1978). *Victims of personal crime: An empirical foundation for a theory of personal victimization.* Cambridge, MA: Ballinger.

Hoadley, J., Fuchs, B., & Holder, H. (1984). The effect of alcohol beverage restrictions on consumption: A 25-year longitudinal analysis. *American Journal of Drug and Alcohol Abuse, 10,* 375–401.

Hogan, M. J. (2000). Diagnosis and treatment of teen drug use. *Medical Clinics of North America, 84,* 927–966.

Holder, H. D., Janes, K., Mosher, J., Saltz, R., Spurr, S., & Wagenaar, A. C. (1993). Alcoholic beverage server liability and the reduction of alcohol-involved problems. *Journal of Studies on Alcohol, 54,* 23–36.

Horwitz, J., & Jamieson, D. (2009, April 8). The two faces of U.S. drug policy. *The Atlantic.* Retrieved August 3, 2009, from www.theatlantic.com/doc/200904u/us-drug-policy-mexico.

Huizinga, D. H., Menard, S., & Elliott, D. S. (1989). Delinquency and drug use: Temporal and developmental patterns. *Justice Quarterly, 6,* 419–455.

Inciardi, J. A., & McBride, D. C. (1989). Legalization: A high-risk alternative in the war on drugs. *American Behavioral Scientist, 32*(3), 259–289.

International Harm Reduction Association. (2009). Retrieved April 22, 2010, from www.ihra.net/July2009#USAMovesTowardsRemovingFundingBanforNeedle Exchange.

Johnson, B., Goldstein, P., Preble, E., Schmeidler, J., Lipton, D., Spunt, B., & Miller, T. (1985). *Taking care of business: The economics of crime by heroin abusers.* Lexington, MA: Lexington Books.

Johnston, L. D., O'Malley, P. M., & Bachman, J. G. (2000). *Monitoring the future: National results on adolescent drug use: Overview of key findings, 1999.* Bethesda, MD: U.S. Department of Health and Human Services, National Institute on Drug Abuse.

Joseph, H. (1988). *The criminal justice system and opiate addiction: A historical perspective* (Research Monograph Series no. 86). Rockville, MD: National Institute on Drug Abuse.

Justice Policy Institute. (2001). Poor prescription: The costs of improving drug offenders in the United States. Retrieved September 2, 2001, from www.cjcj.org/drug/exsumm.html.

Kaplan, H. B., & Damphousse, K. R. (1995). Self-attitudes and antisocial personality as moderators of the drug use-violence relationship. In H. B. Kaplan (Ed.), *Drugs, crime and other deviant adaptations: Longitudinal studies* (pp. 187–210). New York: Plenum Press.

Kelly v. Gwinnell, Vol. 96 N.J. 538, 476 A.2d 1219. (1984).

Kempe, H., & Helfer, R. E. (1972). *Helping the battered child and his family.* New York: Lippincott.

Langley, R., & Levy, R. C. (1977). *Wife beating: The silent crisis.* New York: E. P. Dutton.

Lasley, J. R. (1989). Drinking routines/lifestyles and predatory victimization: A casual analysis. *Justice Quarterly, 6*(4), 529–542.

Leary, W. E. (1995, September 20). Report endorses needle exchanges as AIDS strategy. *New York Times,* pp. 1, 14.

Ledermann, S. (1956). Alcool-Alcoolisme—Alcoolisation. *Donnes Scientifiques de caractere physiologique, economique, et social* (Institut National d'Etudes Demographiques, Travaux et Documents, Cahier no. 29).

Lehmann, N., & Drupp, S. L. (1983/84, Winter). Incidence of alcohol-related domestic violence. *Alcohol Health and Research World,* 23–27, 39.

Leistikow, B. N. (2000). The human and financial cost of smoking. *Clinics in Chest Medicine, 21,* 189–197.

Lemert, E. (1966). *Social pathology: A systematic approach to the theory of sociopathic behavior.* New York: McGraw-Hill.

Levine, H. G. (1980). *The committee of fifty and the origins of alcohol control* (Publication no. F129). Berkeley: Social Research Group, University of California.

Levy, P., Voas, R., Johnson, P., & Klein, T. M. (1978). An evaluation of the Department of Transportation's alcohol safety action projects. *Journal of Safety Research 10*(1), 162–176.

Liebschutz, J. M., Mulvey, K. P., & Samet, J. H. (1997). Victimization among substance-abusing women. *Archives of Internal Medicine, 157,* 1093–1097.

Lurie, P., Reingold, A., Bowser, B. P., Chen, D., Foley, J., Guydish, J., Kahn, J. G., Lane, S., & Sorensen, J. L. (1993). *Public health impact of needle exchange programs in the United States and abroad.* Berkeley: University of California, School of Public Health.

MacDonald, S. (1985). *The impact of increased availability of wine in grocery stores on consumption: Four case histories.* Toronto, Canada: Addiction Research Foundation.

Marks, A. (1999, May 5). More states turn to treatment in drug war. *Christian Science Monitor.* Retrieved September 1, 2002, from www.csmonitor.com/2002.

Massing, M. (1992, June 11). Whatever happened to the war on drugs? *New York Review of Books, 39,* 42–46.

McKim, W. A. (1991). *Drugs and behavior* (2nd ed.). Englewood Cliffs, NJ: Prentice Hall.

McNeece, C. A. (1991). *Substance abuse treatment program evaluation project.* Tallahassee, FL: Florida State University, Institute for Health and Human Services Research.

McNeece, C. A., Bullington, B., Arnold, E. M., & Springer, D. W. (2001). The war on drugs: Treatment, research, and substance abuse intervention in the twenty-first century. In R. Muraskin & A. R. Roberts (Eds.), *Visions for change: Crime and justice in the twenty-first century* (3rd ed., pp. 11–36). Upper Saddle River, NJ: Prentice Hall.

Michigan State Police Dept. v. Sitz, 496 U.S. 444 (1990).

Miron, J. A. (2010). *The budgetary implications of drug prohibition.* Unpublished paper, Harvard University. Retrieved April 21, 2010, from www.economics.harvard.edu/faculty/miron/files/budget%202010%20Final.pdf.

Moore, M. H., & Gerstein, D. R. (Eds.). (1981). *Alcohol and public policy: Beyond the shadow of prohibition.* Washington, DC: National Academy Press.

Morgan, H. W. (1981). *Drugs in America: A social history 1800–1900.* Syracuse, NY: Syracuse University Press.

National Association of Drug Court Professionals (NADCP), Drug Court Standards Committee. (1997). *Defining drug courts: Key components.* Washington, DC: Author.

National Clearinghouse for Alcohol and Drug Issues. (1997). *Homepage.* Retrieved September 9, 1997, from www.health.org/pressure/alcart.htm.

National Clearinghouse on Child Abuse and Neglect Information. (2001, April 12). Highlights from *Child Maltreatment 1999.* Administration for Children and Families, Department of Health and Human Services. Retrieved April 18, 2002, from www.calib.com/nccanch/pubs/factsheets/canstats.cfm.

National Drug Court Institute. (2009). *Research findings.* Retrieved August 3, 2009, from www.ndci.org/research.

National Institute of Justice. (1990). *1988 Drug use forecasting annual report.* Washington, DC: U.S. Department of Justice.

National Institute of Justice, Office of Justice Programs. (2006). *Drug courts: The second decade.* Retrieved August 3, 2009, from www.ncjrs.gov/pdffiles1/nij/211081.pdf.

National Institute on Alcohol Abuse and Alcoholism (NIAAA). (1996). *Alcohol alert* (no. 31, PH362). Washington, DC: Author.

National Institute on Drug Abuse (NIDA). (1991). *Drug abuse treatment in prisons and jails.* (Treatment Research Reports, NIDA Research Monograph no. 118). Rockville, MD: National Institute on Drug Abuse.

National Institute on Drug Abuse (NIDA). (2008). *NIDA InfoFacts: Club drugs.* Washington: NIDA, August.

National Opinion Research Center. (2003). *Drug and alcohol use and related matters among arrestees, 2003.* Retrieved April 20, 2010, from www.ncjrs.gov/nij/adam/ADAM2003.pdf.

Needle exchange programs: Part of a comprehensive HIV prevention strategy. (1998, April 20). *U.S. Department of health and human services.* Retrieved September 1, 2002, from www.hhs.gov/news/press/1998pres/980420b.html.

NORML. (2009a). Marijuana tax laws and penalties. Retrieved August 17, 2009, from norml.org/index.cfm?Group_ID=6670.

NORML. (2009b). *Michigan: State medical marijuana program now accepting applicants.* Retrieved August 17, 2009, from norml.org/index.cfm?Group_ID=7843.

Oakland, California passes landmark marijuana tax. (2009, July 22). *CNN.com.* Retrieved August 3, 2009, from edition.cnn.com/2009/POLITICS/07/22/california.pot.tax/.

Office of National Drug Control Policy (ONDCP). (1996). *Treatment protocol effectiveness study.* Executive Office of the President. Retrieved May 5, 2002, from www.whitehousedrugpolicy.gov.

Office of National Drug Control Policy. (2001). *2000 annual report.* Washington, DC: Executive Office of the President.

Office of National Drug Control Policy (ONDCP). (2001). *Fact sheet: Drug treatment in the criminal justice system* (NCJ-181857). Washington, DC: Executive Office of the President.

Office of National Drug Control Policy (ONDCP). (2002). *National drug control strategy: FY 2003 budget summary.* Washington, DC: Executive Office of the President.

Office of Juvenile Justice and Delinquency Prevention (OJJDP). (2000a). Juvenile transfers to criminal courts in the 1990s: Lessons learned from four studies (Summary) (NCJ 181301). Washington, DC: U.S. Department of Justice, Office of Justice Programs.

Office of Juvenile Justice and Delinquency Prevention (OJJDP). (2000b). Offenders in juvenile court, 1997 (NCJ 181204). Washington, DC: Department of Justice, Office of Justice Programs.

Olson, S., & Gerstein, D. R. (1985). *Alcohol in America: Taking action to prevent abuse.* Washington, DC: National Academy Press.

Ornstein, S. I. (1980). The control of alcohol consumption through price increases. *Journal of Studies on Alcohol, 41,* 807–818.

Popham, R. E., Schmidt, W., & DeLint, J. (1976). The effects of legal restraint on drinking. In B. Kissin & H. Begleiter (Eds.), *The biology of alcoholism, Vol. 4, Social aspects of alcoholism* (pp. 579–625). New York: Plenum Press.

Popham, R. E., Schmidt, W., & DeLint, J. (1978). Government control measures to prevent hazardous drinking. In J. A. Ewing & B. A. Rouse (Eds.), *Drinking.* Chicago: Nelson-Hall.

Public Health Service, Alcohol, Drug Abuse, and Mental Health Administration, National Institute on Alcohol Abuse and Alcoholism. (1987). *Sixth special report to the Congress on alcohol abuse and alcoholism* (DHHS Publication no. [ADM] 87–1519). Washington, DC: U.S. Department of Health and Human Services.

Rappaport v. Nichols, Vol. 31 N.J. 188, 156 A.2d 1 (1959).

Rasmussen, D. W., & Benson, B. L. (1990). *Drug offenders in Florida.* Tallahassee: Florida State University.

Record of Bush nominee anchored in losing strategy. (2001, April 30). *Detroit free press.* Retrieved September 11, 2001, from www.freep.com.

Roberts, A. R. (1987). Psychosocial characteristics of batterers: A study of 234 men charged with domestic violence offenses. *Journal of Family Violence, 2*(1), 81–93.

Roberts, A. R. (1988). Substance abuse among men who batter their mates. *Journal of Substance Abuse Treatment, 5,* 83–87.

Room, R., & Mosher, J. (1979–80). Out of the shadow of treatment: A role for regulatory agencies in the prevention of alcohol problems. *Alcohol Health and Research World, 4*(2), 11.

Ross, H. L. (1973). Law, science, and accidents: The British Road Safety Act of 1967. *Journal of Legal Studies, 2*(1), 1–78.

Roy, M. (1977). Current survey of 150 cases. In *Battered women: A psychosociological study of domestic violence.* New York: Van Nostrand Reinhold.

Rubin, V. (1975). *Cannabis and culture.* The Hague, The Netherlands: Mouton.

Ryckaert, V. (2001). New law drops set time for drug dealers. *Indianapolis Star.* Retrieved July 13, 2001, from www.november.org.

Shainess, N. (1977). Psychological aspects of wifebattering. In M. Roy (Ed.), *Battered women.* New York: Van Nostrand Reinhold.

Shannon, E. (1990, December 30). A losing battle. *Time,* p. 44.

Shapiro, N. (2010, April 14). Drug Czar Gil Kerlikowske's "New Direction" in drug policy looks a lot like the old one. *Seattle Weekly Blog.* Retrieved April 22, 2010, from blogs.seattleweekly.com/dailyweekly/2010/04/drug_czar_gil_kerlikowskes_new.php.

Shults, R. A., Elder, R. W., Sleet, D. A., Nichols, J. L, Alao, M. O., Carande-Kulis, V. G., Zaza, S., Sosin, D. M., & Thompson, R. S. (2001). Reviews of evidence regarding interventions to reduce alcohol-impaired driving. *American Journal of Preventive Medicine, 21*(4S), 66–88.

Skog, O. J. (1971). *Alkoholkonumets fordeling I befolkingen.* Oslo, Norway: National Institute for Alcohol Research.

Smart, R. G. (1977). The relationship availability of alcoholic beverages per capita consumption and alcoholism rates. *Journal of Studies on Alcohol, 38*(5), 891–896.

Spieker, G. (1978). *Family violence and alcohol abuse.* Paper presented at the Twenty-Fourth International Institute on Prevention and Treatment of Alcoholism, Zurich, Switzerland.

Springer, D. W., McNeece, C. A., & Arnold, E. M. (in press). *Substance abuse treatment for criminal offenders: An evidence-based guide for practitioners.* Washington, DC: American Psychological Association.

Stares, P. B. (1996, Spring). Drug legalization: Time for a real debate. *Brookings Review,* 18–20.

Stewart, T. (1987). *The heroin users.* London, England: Pandora.

Stolberg, S. G. (1998, April 21). President decides against financing needle programs. *New York Times,* pp. 1, 18.

Stolberg, S. G. (1999, March 18). Government study of marijuana sees medical benefits. *New York Times,* pp. 1, 20.

Substance Abuse and Mental Health Services Administration (SAMHSA). (2001). *Mid-year 2000 preliminary emergency department data from the drug abuse warning network.* Washington, DC: U.S. Department of Health and Human Services.

Substance Abuse and Mental Health Services Administration (SAMHSA). (2002). *Fiscal year 2003 budget.* Washington, DC: U.S. Department of Health and Human Services.

Tappan, P. (1960). *Crime, justice, and correction.* New York: McGraw-Hill.

Twentieth Century Fund Task Force on Sentencing Policy toward Young Offenders. (1978). *Confronting youth crime.* New York: Holmes & Meier.

U.S. Congress. (1988). *Hearing before the Select Committee on Narcotics Abuse and Control* (Second Session ed.), p. 61.

U.S. General Accounting Office. (1988). *Controlling drug abuse: A status report.* Washington, DC: Comptroller General of the United States.

U.S. General Accounting Office. (1993). *Needle exchange programs: Research suggests promise as an AIDS prevention strategy.* Washington, DC: U.S. Government Printing Office.

U.S. General Accounting Office. (1997). *Drug counts: Overview of growth, characteristics, and results* (GEO/GGD-97–106). Washington, DC: Comptroller General of the United States.

U.S. General Accounting Office. (1998). *Drug control—Observations on U.S. counternarcotics activities.* GAO. Retrieved April 13, 2002, from www.fas.org/irp/gao/nsiad-98-249.htm.

Vito, G. F. (1978). The Kentucky substance abuse program: A private program to treat probationers and parolees. *Federal Probation, 15*(1), 65–72.

Wagenaar, A. C., & Holder, H. D. (1991). Effects of alcoholic beverage server liability on traffic crash injuries. *Alcoholism: Clinical and Experimental Research, 15,* 942–947.

Wall Street Journal. (2009, February 23). *The war on drugs is a failure.* Retrieved August 7, 2009, from online.wsj.com/article/SB123535114271444981.html.

War on drugs is lost, The. (February 12, 1996). *National Review,* p. 48.

Warburton, C. (1932). *Economic results of prohibition.* New York: Columbia University Press.

Wexler, H. K. (1994). Progress in prison substance abuse treatment: A 5-year report. *Journal of Drug Issues, 24*(2), 349–360.

White, J. M. (1991). *Drug dependence.* Englewood Cliffs, NJ: Prentice Hall.

Wilborn, P. (2002, May 3). Nevada shooting signals new biker gang turf war. *Tallahassee Democrat,* p. 6.

Williams, A., Zador, P., & Karpf, R. (1983). The effect of raising the legal minimum drinking age on involvement in fatal crashes. *Journal of Legal Studies, 12,* 169–179.

Windle, M., Windle, R. C., Scheidt, D. M., & Miller, G. B. (1995). Physical and sexual abuse and associated mental disorders among alcoholic inpatients. *American Journal of Psychiatry, 152,* 1322–1328.

Wisconsin Bar Association. (2010). *Dramshop liability by state.* Retrieved April 22, 2010, from www.wisbar.org/am/template.cfm?section=wisconsin_lawyer&template=/cm/contentdisplay.cfm&contentid=50672.

Wright, J. (1985). Domestic violence and substance abuse: A cooperative approach toward working with dually affected families. In E. M. Freeman (Ed.), *Social work practice with clients who have alcohol problems* (pp. 26–39). Springfield, IL: Charles C Thomas.

Yi, H., Stinson, F. S., Williams, G. D., & Dufour, M. C. (1999). *Trends in alcohol-related fatal traffic crashes, United States, 1977–1998* (Surveillance Report no. 53). Rockville, MD: National Institute on Alcohol and Alcoholism, Division of Biometry and Epidemiology.

Young, S. (1998, November 20). US WI: Re-Indictments Hit Motorcycle Gang. *Chicago Tribune.* Retrieved

December 31, 2003, from mapinc.org/drugnews/v98/n1069/a06.html.

Zimrig, F. E., & Hawkins, G. (1992). *The search for rational drug control.* Cambridge, England: Cambridge University Press.

2009 Criminal Justice Transition Coalition. (2008). *Smart on crime: Recommendations for the next administration and congress.* Retrieved August 5, 2009, from www.hsdl.org/hslog/?q=node/4482.

CHAPTER 9

Alexander, J. F., & Parsons, B. V. (1973). Short-term behavioral intervention with delinquents: Impact on family process and recidivism. *Journal of Abnormal Psychology, 81,* 219–225.

Alford, G. S., Koehler, R. A., & Leonard, J. (1991). Alcoholics Anonymous-Narcotics Anonymous model inpatient treatment of chemically dependent adolescents: A two-year outcome study. *Journal of Studies on Alcohol, 52,* 118–126.

Aponte, H. J., & VanDeusen, J. M. (1981). Structural family therapy. In A. S. Gurman & D. P. Kniskern (Eds.), *Handbook of family therapy* (pp. 310–360). New York: Brunner/Mazel.

Armstrong, T. D., & Costello, E. J. (2002). Community studies on adolescent substance use, abuse and psychiatric comorbidity. *Journal of Consulting and Clinical Psychology, 70,* 1224–1239.

Azrin, N. H. (1976). Improvements in the community reinforcement approach to alcoholism. *Behavior Research and Therapy, 14,* 339–348.

Azrin, N. H., Donohue, B., Teichner, G. A., Crum, T., Howell, J., & DeCato, L. A. (2001). A controlled evaluation and description of Individual-Cognitive Problem Solving and Family-Behavior Therapies in dually-diagnosed conduct-disordered and substance dependent youth. *Journal of Child & Adolescent Substance Abuse, 11*(1), 1–43.

Bachman, J. G., O'Malley, P. M., Schulenberg, J. E., Johnston, L. D., Freedman-Doan, P., & Messersmith, E. E. (2007). *The education-drug use connections: How successes and failures in school relate to adolescent smoking, drinking, drug use, and delinquency.* Danvers, MA: CRC Press.

Bandura, A. (1977). *Social learning theory.* Englewood Cliffs, NJ: Prentice Hall.

Bender, K., Springer, D. W., & Kim, J. (2006). Treatment effectiveness with dually-diagnosed adolescents: A systematic review. *Brief Treatment and Crisis Intervention, 6,* 177–205.

Beyers, J. M., Toumbourou, J. W., Catalano, R. F., Arthur, M. W., & Hawkins, J. D. (2004). A cross-national comparison of risk and protective factors for adolescent substance use: The United States and Australia. *Journal of Adolescent Health, 35,* 3–16.

Bloom, M., Fischer, J., & Orme, J. G. (2009). *Evaluating practice: Guidelines for the accountable professional* (6th ed.). Boston, MA: Allyn & Bacon.

Botvin, G. J. (1995). Drug abuse prevention in school settings. In G. J. Botvin, S. Schinke, & M. A. Orlandi (Eds.), *Drug abuse prevention with multiethnic youth* (pp. 169–192). Thousand Oaks, CA: Sage.

Bowen, M. (1974). A family systems approach to alcoholism. *Addictions, 21,* 3–11.

Bronfenbrenner, U. (1979). *The ecology of human development: Experiences by nature and design.* Cambridge, MA: Harvard University Press.

Brown, T. L., Borduin, C. M., & Henggeler, S. W. (2001). Treating juvenile offenders in community settings. In J. B. Ashford, B. D. Sales, & W. H. Reid (Eds.), *Treating adult and juvenile offenders with special needs* (pp. 445–464). Washington, DC: American Psychological Association.

Brown-Standridge, M. (1987). Creating therapeutic realities via responsibility messages. *American Journal of Family Therapy, 12,* 206–224.

Brundage, V., & Bateson, G. (1985). Alcoholics Anonymous and stoicism. *Psychiatry, 48,* 40–51.

Buu, A., DiPiazza, C., Wang, J., Puttler, L. I., Fitzgerald, H. E., & Zucker, R. A. (2009) Development of child substance use and other psychopathology from preschool to the start of adulthood. *Journal of Studies on Alcohol and Drugs, 70,* 489–498.

Carbonell, D. M., Reinherz, H. Z., & Giaconia, R. M. (1998, August). Risk and resilience in late adolescence. *Child and Adolescent Social Work Journal, 15,* 251–272.

Catalano, R. F., Hawkins, J. D., Wells, E. A., Miller, J., & Brewer, D. (1990/91). Evaluation of the effectiveness of adolescent drug abuse treatment, assessment of risks for relapse, and promising approaches for relapse prevention. *International Journal of the Addictions, 25,* 1085–1140.

Christiansen, B. A., Goldman, M. S., & Inn, A. (1982). Development of alcohol-related expectancies in adolescents: Separating pharmacological from social-learning influences. *Journal of Consulting and Clinical Psychology, 50,* 336–344.

De Leon, G. (1988). Legal pressures in therapeutic communities In C. G. Luekefeld & F. Tims (Eds.), *Compulsory treatment of drug abuse: Research and clinical practice* (pp. 160–177). (National Institute on Drug Abuse Research Monograph no. 86 [DHHS Publication no. ADM] 89–1578) Rockville, MD: U.S. Department of Health and Human Services, National Institute on Drug Abuse.

Donohue, B., Allen, D. N., & LaPota, H. B. (2009). Family behavioral therapy for substance abuse and associated problems. In D. W. Springer & A. Rubin (Eds.), *Substance abuse treatment for youth and adults: Clinician's guide to evidence-based practice.* Hoboken, New Jersey: John Wiley & Sons.

Downey, A. M. (1990–1991). The impact of drug abuse on adolescent suicide. *Omega Journal of Death and Dying, 22*(4), 261–275.

Dryfoos, J. G. (1993). Preventing substance use: Rethinking strategies. *American Journal of Public Health, 83,* 793–795.

Erhard, R. (1999). Peer-led and adult-led programs: Student perceptions. *Journal of Drug Education, 29*(4), 295–308.

Falck, R., & Craig, R. (1988). Classroom-oriented primary prevention programming for drug abuse. *Journal of Psychoactive Drugs, 20*(4), 403–408.

Farrington, D. P. (2000). Explaining and preventing crime: The globalization of knowledge—The American Society of Criminology 1999 presidential address. *Criminology, 38,* 1–24.

Fischer, J., & Corcoran, K. (2007). *Measures for clinical practice: A sourcebook* (4th ed., Vols. 1 & 2). New York: Free Press.

Fishman, H. C., Stanton, M. D., & Rosman, B. (1991). Treating families of adolescent drug abusers. In M. D. Stanton, T. C. Todd, and associates (Eds.), *The family therapy of drug abuse and addiction.* New York: Guilford Press.

Ford, J. A. (2009). Nonmedical prescription drug use among adolescents: The influence of bonds to family and school. *Youth and Society, 40,* 336–352.

Fraser, M. W. (Ed.). (2004). *Risk and resilience in childhood: An ecological perspective.* Washington, DC: NASW Press.

Friedman, A. S., & Utada, A. (1983). High school drug use. *Clinical research notes.* Washington, DC: U.S. Government Printing Office, National Institute on Drug Abuse.

Gerstein, D. R., & Harwood, H. J. (Eds.). (1990). *Treating drug problems* (Vol. 1). Washington, DC: National Academy Press.

Glassner, B., & Loughlin, J. (1987). *Drugs in adolescent worlds: Burnouts to straight.* New York: St. Martin's Press.

Godley, S. H., Smith, J. E., Meyers, R. J., & Godley, M. D. (2009) Adolescent community reinforcement approach (A-CRA). In D. W. Springer & A. Rubin (Eds.), *Substance abuse treatment for youth and adults: Clinician's guide to evidence-based practice.* Hoboken, New Jersey: John Wiley & Sons.

Gutstein, S. E., Rudd, M. D., Graham, J. C., & Rayha, L. L. (1988). Systemic crisis intervention as a response to adolescent crises: An outcome study. *Family Process, 27,* 201–211.

Haley, J. (1976). *Problem solving therapy.* San Francisco: Jossey-Bass.

Harrison, P. A., & Hoffman, N. G. (1989). *CATOR report: Adolescent completers one year later.* St. Paul, MN: Chemical Abuse/Addiction Treatment Outcome Registry, Ramsey Clinic.

Hawkins, J. D., Catalano, R. F., & Miller, J. Y. (1992). Risk and protective factors for alcohol and other drug problems in adolescence and early adulthood: Implications for substance abuse prevention. *Psychological Bulletin, 112*(1), 64–105.

Henggeler, S. W. (1997). The development of effective drug-abuse services for youth. In J. A. Egertson, D. M. Fox, & A. I. Leshner (Eds.), *Treating drug abusers effectively* (pp. 253–279). New York: Blackwell.

Henggeler, S. W. (1999). Multisystemic therapy: An overview of clinical procedures, outcomes, and policy implications. *Child Psychology & Psychiatry, 4*(1), 2–10.

Henggeler, S. W., & Borduin, C. M. (1990). *Family therapy and beyond: A multisystemic approach to treating the behavior problems of children and adolescents.* Pacific Grove, CA: Brooks/Cole.

Henggeler, S. W., Pickrel, S. G., & Brondino, M. J. (1999). Multisystemic treatment of substance-abusing and dependent delinquents: Outcomes, treatment, fidelity, and transportability. *Mental Health Services Research, 1*(3), 171–184.

Henggeler, S. W., Schoenwald, S. K., Borduin, C. M., Rowland, M. D., & Cunningham, P. B. (1998). *Multisystemic treatment of antisocial behavior in children and adolescents.* New York: Guilford Press.

Hodge, D. R., Cardenas, P., & Montoya, H. (2001). Substance use: Spirituality and religious participation as protective factors among rural youths. *Social Work Research, 25*(3), 153–161.

Hoffman, N., & Kaplan, R. (1991). One-year outcome results for adolescents: Key correlates and benefits of recovery. *CATOR Report,* 1–21.

Hohman, M., & LeCroy, C. W. (1996). Predicators of adolescent A.A. affiliation. *Adolescence, 31*(122), 339–352.

Hops, H., Duncan, T., Duncan, S., & Stoolmiller, M. (1996, Summer). Parent substance use as a predictor of adolescent use: A six-year lagged analysis. *Annals of Behavioral Medicine, 18,* 157–164.

Howell, J. C. (2003). *Prevention and reducing juvenile delinquency: A comprehensive framework.* Thousand Oaks, CA: Sage.

Hudson, W. W. (1982). *The clinical measurement package: A field manual.* Homewood, IL: Dorsey Press.

Israel, P., Thomsen, P., Langeveld, J., & Stormark, K. (2007). Parent-youth discrepancy in the assessment and treatment of youth in usual clinical care setting: Consequences to parent involvement. *European Child & Adolescent Psychiatry, 16,* 138–148.

Jenson, J. M. (1997). Juvenile delinquency and drug abuse: Implications for social work practice in the justice system. In C. A. McNeece & A. R. Roberts (Eds.), *Policy and practice in the justice system* (pp. 107–123). Chicago: Nelson-Hall.

Jenson, J. M., Anthony, E. K., & Howard, M. O. (2006). Policies and programs for adolescent substance abuse. In J. M. Jenson & M. W. Fraser (Eds.), *Social policy for children and families: A risk and resilience perspective* (pp. 195–230). Thousand Oaks, CA: Sage Publications.

Jessor, R., & Jessor, S. L. (1977). *Problem behavior and psychosocial development: A longitudinal study of youth.* New York: Academic Press.

Joaning, H., Gawinski, B., Morris, J., & Quinn, W. (1986). Organizing a social ecology to treat adolescent drug abuse. *Journal of Strategic and Systemic Therapies, 5,* 55–66.

Johnson, J. L. (1990–1991). Preventive interventions for children at risk: An introduction. *International Journal of the Addictions, 25,* 429–434.

Johnston, L. D., O'Malley, P. M., Bachman, J. G., & Schulenberg, J. E. (2008). *Monitoring the future: National survey results on drug use, 1975–2008. Vol. 1: Secondary school students* (NIMH Publication no. 01-4924). Bethesda, MD: National Institute on Drug Abuse.

Kaminer, Y., & Burleson, J. A. (1999). Psychotherapies for adolescent substance abusers: 15-month follow-up of a pilot study. *American Journal on Addictions, 8*, 114–119.

Kaminer, Y., Burleson, J. A., Blitz, C., Sussman, J., & Rounsaville, B. J. (1998). Psychotherapies for adolescent substance abusers: A pilot study. *Journal of Nervous and Mental Disease, 186*(11), 684–690.

Kaminer, Y., Burleson, J. A., & Goldberger, R. (2002). Cognitive-behavioral coping skills and psychoeducation therapies for adolescent substance abuse. *The Journal of Nervous and Mental Disease, 190*(11), 737–745.

Kazdin, A. E. (2005). *Parent management training: Treatment for oppositional, aggressive, and antisocial behavior children and adolescents.* New York: Oxford University Press.

Kendall, P. C., & Braswell, L. (1993). *Cognitive-behavioral therapy for impulsive children* (2nd ed.). New York: Guilford Press.

Kirby, L. D., & Fraser, M. W. (1997). Risk and resilience in childhood. In M. W. Fraser (Ed.), *Risk and resilience in childhood: An ecological perspective* (pp. 10–33). Washington, DC: NASW Press.

Klein, N. C., Alexander, J. F., & Parsons, B. V. (1976). Impact of family systems intervention on recidivism and sibling delinquency: A model of primary prevention and program evaluation. *Journal of Consulting and Clinical Psychology, 45*, 469–474.

Kronenberger, W. C., & Meyer, R. G. (2001). *The child clinician's handbook* (2nd ed.). Boston, MA: Allyn & Bacon.

Kumpfer, K. L., & Turner, C. W. (1990–1991). The social ecology model of adolescent substance abuse: Implications for prevention. *International Journal of the Addictions, 25*, 435–463.

Leccese, M., & Waldron, H. B. (1994). Assessing adolescent substance abuse: A critique of current measurement instruments. *Journal of Substance Abuse Treatment, 11*, 553–563.

Leukefeld, C. G., McDonald, H. M. S., Stoops, W. W., Reed, L., & Martin, C. (2005). Substance misuse and abuse. In T. P. Gullotta, G. R. Adams, & J. M. Ramos (Eds.), *Handbook of adolescent and behavioral problems* (439–466). New York: Springer.

Littell, J. H. (2005). Lessons from a systematic review of effects of Multisystemic Therapy. *Children and Youth Services Review, 27*, 445–463.

Malekoff, A. (1997). *Group work with adolescents: Principles and practice.* New York: Guilford Press.

McBride, D. C., VanderWaal, C. J., Terry, Y. M., & VanBuren, H. (1999). *Breaking the cycle of drug use among juvenile offenders.* Retrieved October 24, 2002, from www.ncjrs.org/pdffiles1/179273.pdf.

McGuire, W. J. (1968). The nature of attitudes and attitude change. In G. Lindzey & E. Aronson (Eds.), *Handbook of social psychology* (pp. 136–314). Reading, MA: Addison-Wesley.

McKinney, F., Miller, D. J., Beier, L., & Bohannon, S. R. (1978). Self-concept, delinquency, and positive peer culture. *Criminology, 15*, 529–538.

McLellan, T. A., Luborsky, L., O'Brien, C., Woody, G. E., & Druley, K. A. (1982). Is treatment for substance abuse effective? *Journal of the American Medical Association, 247*, 1423–1428.

McNeece, C. A., & Springer, D. W. (1997). Drug abuse prevention programs. In F. Schmalleger (Ed.), *Crime and the justice system in America: An encyclopedia* (pp. 79–81). Westport, CT: Greenwood.

Michels, R., & Cooper, A. M. (1997). *Psychiatry* (Vol. 2). Baltimore, MD: Lippincott, Williams, and Wilkins.

Michigan Department of Social Services. (1983). *The institution centers: Objectives and progress.* Lansing, MI: Institutional Services Division, O. C. Y. S.

Minuchin, S. (1974). *Families and family therapy.* Cambridge, MA: Harvard University Press.

Minuchin, S., & Fishman, H. C. (1981). *Family therapy techniques.* Cambridge, MA: Harvard University Press.

Munger, R. L. (1993). *Changing children's behavior quickly.* Lanham, MD: Madison Books.

Najavits, L. M., Gallop, R. J., & Weiss, R. D. (2006). Seeking Safety therapy for adolescent girls with PTSD and substance use disorder: A randomized controlled trial. *Journal of Behavioral Health Services and Research, 33*, 453–463.

Nathan, P., & Gorman, J. M. (Eds.). (2002). *A guide to treatments that work* (2nd ed.). New York: Oxford University Press.

National Institute on Drug Abuse (NIDA). (2001, January). *Understanding drug abuse and addiction.* Retrieved March 11, 2002, from www.nida.gov/Infofax/understand.html

National Institute on Drug Abuse (NIDA). (2003). *Preventing drug use among children and adolescents: A research-based guide for parents, educators, and community leaders: Second edition* (NIH Publication No. 04-4212(B)). Washington, DC: Author.

National Institute of Justice (NIJ). (2003). *2000 Arrestee drug abuse monitoring: Annual report.* Washington, DC: U.S. Department of Justice, Office of Justice Programs.

National Registry of Evidence-Based Programs and Practices. (2006, October). *Family behavior therapy.* Retrieved September 1, 2009, from www.nrepp.samhsa.gov/programfulldetails.asp?PROGRAM_ID=73.

National Registry of Evidence-Based Programs and Practices. (2008, March). *Adolescent community reinforcement approach (A-CRA).* Retrieved September 1, 2009, from www.nrepp.samhsa.gov/programfulldetails.asp?PROGRAM_ID=73.

Obermeier, G. E., & Henry, P. B. (1988–1989) Adolescent inpatient treatment. *Journal of Chemical Dependency, 2*, 163–182.

Physician Leadership on National Drug Policy. (2002). *Adolescent substance abuse: A public health priority. An evidence-based, comprehensive, and integrative approach.* Providence, RI: Brown University, Center for Alcohol and Addiction Studies.

Polcin, D. (1992). A comprehensive model for adolescent chemical dependency treatment. *Journal of Counseling and Development, 70,* 376–382.

Quigley, R., & Steiner, M. E. (1996). Unleashing the power of young women through peer helping groups. *Reclaiming Children and Youth, 5,* 102–106.

Rivaux, S. L., Springer, D. W., Bohman, T., Wagner, E. F., & Gil, A. G. (2006). Differences among substance abusing Latino, Anglo, and African-American juvenile offenders in predictors of recidivism and treatment outcome. *Journal of Social Work Practice in the Addictions, 6,* 5–29.

Robbins, M. S., Szapocznik, J., Santisteban, D. A., Hervis, O. E., Mitrani, V. B., & Schwartz, S. J. (2003). Brief strategic family therapy for Hispanic youth. In A. E. Kazdin & J. R. Weisz (Eds.), *Evidence based psychotherapies for children and adolescents* (pp. 407–424). New York: Guildford Press.

Rubin, A., & Babbie, E. (2008) Research Methods for Social Work, 6th ed. Belmont, CA: Brooks/Cole.

Schaffer, D., Phillips, I., Enzer, N. B., Silverman, M. M., & Anthony, V. (1989). *Prevention of mental disorders, alcohol, and other drug use in children and adolescents* (OSAP Prevention Monograph no. 2, DHHS Publication no. 89-1646). Rockville, MD: Department of Health and Human Services.

Schinke, S., & Cole, K. (1995). Prevention in community settings. In G. J. Botvin, S. Schinke, & M. A. Orlandi (Eds.), *Drug abuse prevention with multiethnic youth* (pp. 215–232). Thousand Oaks, CA: Sage.

Schinke, S. P., Orlandi, M. A., & Cole, K. C. (1992). Boys and girls clubs in public housing developments: Prevention services for youth at risk. *Journal of Community Psychology* (OSAP Special Issue), 118–128.

Schoenwald, S. K., Borduin, C. M., & Henggeler, S. W. (1998). Multisystemic therapy: Changing the natural and service ecologies of adolescents and families. In M. H. Epstein, K. Kutash, & A. Duchnowski (Eds.), *Outcomes for children and youth with emotional and behavioral disorders and their families: Programs and evaluation best practice* (pp. 485–511). Austin, TX: Pro-Ed.

Schoenwald, S. K., Ward, D. M., Henggeler, S. W., Pickrel, S. G., & Patel, H. (1996). Multisystemic therapy treatment of substance abusing or dependent adolescent offenders: Costs of reducing incarceration, inpatient, and residential placement. *Journal of Child and Family Studies, 5,* 431–444.

Semlitz, L., & Gold, M. S. (1986). Adolescent drug abuse. *Psychiatric Clinics of North America, 9,* 455–473.

Shaffer, D., Lucas, C. P., & Richters, J. E. (Eds.). (1999). *Diagnostic assessment in child and adolescent psychopathology.* New York: Guilford Press.

Singh, N. (1982). Notes and observations on the practice of multiple family therapy in an adolescent unit. *Journal of Adolescence, 5,* 319–332.

Slesnick, N., & Prestopnik, J. L. (2005). Ecologically based family therapy outcome with substance abusing runaway adolescents. *Journal of Adolescence, 28,* 277–298.

Smith, T. E. (1983, Fall). Reducing adolescents' marijuana abuse. *Social Work, 9,* 33–44.

Smith, T. E. (1984, January/February). Reviewing adolescent marijuana abuse. *Social Work, 29,* 17–21.

Smith, T. E. (1985). Group work with adolescent drug abusers. *Social Work with Groups, 8,* 55–64.

Smith, T. E., Koob, J., & Wirtz, T. (1985). Ecology of adolescent marijuana abusers. *International Journal of Addictions, 20,* 1421–1428.

Sobell, L. C., & Sobell, M. B. (1992). Timeline follow-back: A technique for assessing self-reported alcohol consumption. In R. Z. Litten & J. P. Allen (Eds.), *Measuring alcohol consumption: Psychosocial and biochemical methods* (pp. 41–72). Totowa, NJ: Humana Press.

Spivak, G., & Shure, M. B. (1974). *Social adjustment in young children.* San Francisco: Jossey-Boss.

Springer, D. W. (2002a). Assessment protocols and rapid assessment instruments with troubled adolescents. In A. R. Roberts & G. J. Greene (Eds.), *Social workers' desk reference* (pp. 217–221). New York: Oxford University Press.

Springer, D. W. (2002b). Treatment planning with adolescents: An ADHD case application. In A. R. Roberts & G. J. Greene (Eds.), *Social workers' desk reference* (pp. 324–327). New York: Oxford University Press.

Springer, D. W. (2006). Treating juvenile delinquents with conduct disorder, ADHD, and oppositional defiant disorder. In A. R. Roberts & K. R. Yeager (Eds.), *Foundations of evidence-based social work practice.* New York, NY: Oxford University Press.

Springer, D. W., & Lynch, C. (2008). Effective interventions for students with conduct disorder. In C. Franklin, M. B. Harris, & P. Allen-Meares (Eds.), *The school practitioner's concise companion to mental health.* New York, NY: Oxford University Press.

Springer, D. W., McNeece, C. A., & Arnold, E. M. (2003). *Substance-abuse treatment for criminal offenders: An evidence-based guide for practitioners.* Washington, DC: American Psychological Association.

Springer, D. W., & Orsbon, S. H. (2002). Families helping families: Implementing a multifamily therapy group with substance-abusing adolescents. *Health and Social Work, 27*(3), 204–207.

Springer, D. W., & Rubin, A. (2009). *Substance abuse treatment for youth and adults: Clinician's guide to evidence-based practice.* Hoboken, New Jersey: John Wiley and Sons.

Substance Abuse and Mental Health Administration (SAMHSA). (2000). *National household survey on drug abuse.* Retrieved February 3, 2001, from www.samhsa.gov/oas/nhsda/htm#NHSDAinfo.

Substance Abuse and Mental Health Services Administration (SAMHSA). (2001, February). *Risk and protective factors for adolescent drug use: Findings from the 1997 national household survey on drug abuse.* Retrieved on September 1, 2009, from www.oas.samhsa.gov/NHSDA/NAC97/Table_of_Contents.htm.

Szapocznik, J., Hervis, O. E., & Schwartz, S. (2003). *Brief strategic family therapy for adolescent drug abuse* (NIH Publication No. 03-4751). NIDA Therapy Manuals for Drug Addiction: Rockville, MD: National Institute on Drug Abuse.

Szapocznik, J., Kurtines, W. M., Foote, F. H., Perez-Vidal, A., & Hervis, O. (1983). Conjoint versus one-person family therapy: Some evidence for the effectiveness of conducting family therapy through one person with drug-abusing adolescents. *Journal of Consulting and Clinical Psychology, 51,* 990–999.

Szapocznik, J., Kurtines, W. M., Foote, F. H., Perez-Vidal, A., & Hervis, O. (1986). Conjoint versus one-person family therapy: Further evidence for the effectiveness of conducting family therapy through one person with drug-abusing adolescents. *Journal of Consulting and Clinical Psychology, 54,* 395–397.

Szapocznik, J., Murray, E., Scopetea, M., Hervis, O., Rio, A., Cohen, R., et al. (1989). Structural family versus psychodynamic child therapy for problematic Hispanic boys. *Journal of Consulting and Clinical Psychology, 57,* 571–578.

Thyer, B. A. (2008). Evidence-Based Macro Practice: Addressing the Challenges and Opportunities. *Journal of Evidence-Based Social Work, 5,* 453–472.

Thyer, B. A., & Wodarskit, J. S. (1998). *Handbook of empirical work practice.* New York: John Wiley & Sons.

Todd, T., & Selekman, M. (Eds.). (1991). *Family therapy approaches with adolescent substance abusers.* Englewood Cliffs, NJ: Prentice Hall.

Todd, T. C., & Selekman, M. (1994). A structural-strategic model for treating the adolescent who is abusing alcohol and other drugs. In W. Snyder & T. Ooms (Eds.), *Empowering families, helping adolescents: Family-centered treatment of adolescents with alcohol, drug abuse, and mental health problems* (Publication Series no. 6) (pp. 79–89). Rockville, MD: U.S. Department of Health and Human Services, Center for Substance Abuse Treatment.

Tolan, P. H., Guerra, N. G., & Kendall, P. C. (1995). A developmental-ecological perspective on antisocial behavior in children and adolescents: Toward a unified risk and intervention framework. *Journal of Consulting and Clinical Psychology, 63,* 579–584.

Turner, S. G. (2001). Resilience and social work practice: Three case studies. *Families in Society, The Journal of Contemporary Human Services, 82,* 441–448.

Vaillant, G. E. (1993). *The wisdom of the ego.* Cambridge, MA: Harvard University Press.

Vorrath, H. H., & Brendtro, L. K. (1985). *Positive peer culture* (2nd ed.). New York: Aldine de Gruyter.

Wagner, E. F., & Austin, A. M. (2009). Problem solving and social skills training. In D. W. Springer & A. Rubin (Eds.), *Substance abuse treatment for youth and adults: Clinician's guide to evidence-based practice.* Hoboken, New Jersey: John Wiley & Sons.

Waldron, H. B. (1997). Adolescent substance abuse and family therapy outcome: A review of randomized trials. *Advances in Clinical Child Psychology, 19,* 199–234.

Waldron, H. B., Slesnick, N., Brody, J. L., Turner, C. W., & Peterson T. R. (2001). Treatment outcomes for adolescent substance abuse at 4- and 7-month assessments. *Journal of Consulting and Clinical Psychology, 69,* 802–813.

Wheeler, K., & Malmquist, J. (1987). Treatment approaches in adolescent chemical dependency. *Pediatric Clinics of North America, 9,* 455–473.

Williams, J., Ayers, C., Abbott, R., Hawkins, J., & Catalano, R. (1999). Racial differences in risk factors for delinquency and substance use among adolescents. *Social Work Research, 23,* 241–256.

Wills, T. A., Sandy, J. M., & Yaeger, A. (2000). Temperament and adolescent substance use: An epigenetic approach to risk and protection. *Journal of Personality, 68,* 1127–1151.

Wilson, D. K., Rodrigue, J. R., & Taylor, W. C. (Eds.). (1997). *Health-promoting and health-compromising behaviors among minority adolescents.* Washington, DC: American Psychological Association.

CHAPTER 10

Ackerman, R. (Ed.). (1986). *Growing in the shadow.* Pompano Beach, FL: Health Communications.

Adger, H. (1998). Children in alcoholic families: Family dynamics and treatment issues. In A. Graham & T. Schultz (Eds.), *Principles of addiction medicine* (pp. 1111–1114). Chevy Chase, MD: American Society of Addiction Medicine.

Albon, J. (1974). Al-Anon family groups: Impetus for learning and change through the presentation of alternatives. *American Journal of Psychotherapy, 28,* 30–45.

Alcoholics Anonymous. (1939). New York: Alcoholics Anonymous World Services.

Amodeo, M., & Lopez, L. M. (2011). Social work intervention with alcohol and other drug problems. In J. R. Brandell (Ed.), *Theory and practice in clinical social work* (pp. 525–559). Los Angeles: Sage.

Austin, A. M., Macgowan, M. J., & Wagner, E. F. (2005). Effective family-based interventions for adolescents with substance use problems: A systematic review. *Research on Social Work Practice, 15*(2), 67–83.

Bailey, M. (1961). Alcoholism and marriage: A review of research and professional literature. *Quarterly Journal of Studies on Alcohol, 22*(1), 81–97.

Barrowclough, C., Haddock, G., Tarrier, N., Lewis, S., Moring, J., O'Brien, R., Schofield, N., & McGovern, J. (2001). Randomized controlled trial of motivational interviewing, cognitive behavioral therapy, and family intervention for patients with co-morbid schizophrenia and substance abuse disorders. *American Journal of Psychiatry, 158*(10), 1706–1713.

Bennett, L. (1995). Accountability for alcoholism in American families. *Social Science Medicine, 40*(1), 15–28.

Bennett, L., Wolin, S., & Reiss, D. (1988). Deliberate family process: A strategy for protecting children of alcoholics. *British Journal of Addiction, 83*(7), 821–829.

Bennett, L., Wolin, S., Reiss, D., & Teitelbaum, M. (1987). Couples at risk for transmission of alcoholism: Protective influences. *Family Process, 26*(1), 111–129.

Benshoff, J., & Janikowski, T. (2000). *The rehabilitation model of substance abuse counseling.* Pacific Grove, CA: Brooks/Cole.

Bepko, C. (1989). Disorders of power: Women and addiction in the family. In M. McGoldrick, C. Anderson, & F. Walsh (Eds.), *Women in families: A framework for family therapy.* New York: W. W. Norton.

Berenson, D., & Schrier, E. (1998). Current family therapy approaches. In A. Graham & T. Schultz (Eds.), *Principles of addiction medicine* (pp. 1115–1125). Chevy Chase, MD: American Society of Addiction Medicine.

Billings, A., Kessler, M., Gomberg, C., & Weiner, S. (1979). Marital conflict resolution of alcoholic and nonalcoholic couples during drinking and non-drinking sessions. *Journal of Studies on Alcohol, 40*(3), 183–195.

Birchler, G. R., Fals-Stewart, W., & O'Farrell, T. (2005). Couples therapy for alcoholism and drug abuse. In J. L. Lebow (Ed.), *Handbook of clinical family therapy* (pp. 251–280). Hoboken, New Jersey: Wiley & Sons.

Black, C. (1981). *It will never happen to me.* Denver, CO: MAC.

Black, C. (1990). *Double duty.* New York: Ballantine.

Bosma, W. (1972). Children of alcoholics—A hidden tragedy. *Maryland State Medical Journal, 21*(1), 31–36.

Boylin, W., & Anderson, S. A. (2005). Responsibility versus contribution in family therapy of substance abuse and other disorders. *Journal of Family Psychotherapy, 16*(4), 1–15.

Brown, S., & Lewis, V. (1998). A developmental model of the alcoholic family. In A. Graham & T. Schultz (Eds.), *Principles of addiction medicine* (pp. 1099–1110). Chevy Chase, MD: American Society of Addiction Medicine.

Brown, S., & Schmid, J. (1999). Adult children of alcoholics. In P. Ott, R. Tarter, & R. Ammerman (Eds.), *Sourcebook on substance abuse: Etiology, epidemiology, assessment, and treatment* (pp. 416–429). Boston, MA: Allyn & Bacon.

Buelow, G., & Buelow, S. (1998). *Psychotherapy in chemical dependency treatment.* Pacific Grove, CA: Brooks/Cole.

Cadoret, R. (1990). Genetics of alcoholism. In L. Collins, K. Leonard, & J. Searles (Eds.), *Alcohol and the family: Research and clinical perspectives.* New York: Guilford Press.

Carise, D. (2000). Effects of family involvement on length of stay and treatment completion rates with cocaine and alcohol abusers. *Journal of Family Social Work, 4*(4), 79–94.

Carruth, B., & Mendenhall, W. (1989). *Codependency: Issues in treatment and recovery.* New York: Haworth Press.

Caspi, A., Hariri, A., Holmes, A., Uher, R., & Moffitt, T. (2010). Genetic sensitivity to the environment: The case of the serotonin transporter gene and its implications for studying complex diseases and traits. *American Journal of Psychiatry, 167*(5), 509–527.

Center for Substance Abuse Prevention (CSAP). (n.d.). Substance abuse and mental health services administration.

Children of Alcoholics. Retrieved May 1, 2010, from ncadi.samhsa.gov/govpubs/ms417/.

Center for Substance Abuse Treatment. (2004). *Substance abuse treatment and family therapy.* Treatment Improvement Protocol (TIP) Series, No. 39. DHHS Publication No. (SMA) 04 3957. Rockville, MD: Substance Abuse and Mental Health Services Administration. Retrieved March 1, 2010, www.ncbi.nlm.nih.gov/books/NBK14505/.

Clark, R. (2001). Family support and substance use outcomes for persons with mental illness and substance use disorders. *Schizophrenia Bulletin, 27*(1), 93–101.

Collins, L. (1990). Family treatment of alcohol abuse: Behavioral and systems perspectives. In L. Collins, K. Leonard, & J. Searles (Eds.), *Alcohol and the family: Research and clinical perspectives* (pp. 285–308). New York: Guilford Press.

Conner, G., Donovan, D., & DiClemente, C. (2001). *Substance abuse treatment and the stages of change: Selecting and planning interventions.* New York: Guilford Press.

Cook, W., & Goethe, J. (1990). The effects of being reared with an alcoholic half-sibling: A classic study reanalyzed. *Family Process, 29*(1), 87–93.

Copello, A. G., Velleman, R. B., & Templeton, L. J. (2005). Family interventions in the treatment of alcohol and drug problems. *Drug and Alcohol Review, 24,* 369–385.

Cork, M. (1969). *The forgotten child: A study of children with alcoholic parents.* Toronto, Ontario, Canada: Alcoholism and Drug Addiction Research Foundation of Ontario.

Corless, J., Mirza, K. A., & Steinglass, P. (2009). Family therapy for substance misuse: The maturation of a field. *Journal of Family Therapy, 31*(4), 109–114.

Coyle, J. P., Nochajski, T., Maguin, E., Safyer, A., DeWit, D., & McDonald, S. (2009). An exploratory study of the nature of family resilience in families affected by parental alcohol abuse. *Journal of Family Issues, 30*(12), 1606–1623.

Crespi, T. D., & Rueckert, Q. H. (2006). Family therapy and children of alcoholics: Implications for continuing education and certification in substance abuse practice. *Journal of Child and Adolescent Substance Abuse, 15*(3), 33–44.

Cronkite, R., Finney, J., Nekich, J., & Moos, R. (1990). Remission among alcoholic patients and family adaptation to alcoholism: A stress and coping perspective. In L. Collins, K. Leonard, & J. Searles (Eds.), *Alcohol and the family: Research and clinical perspectives* (pp. 309–337). New York: Guilford Press.

Cuadrado, M., & Lieberman, L. (2002). *Traditional family values and substance abuse: The Hispanic contribution to an alternative prevention and treatment approach.* New York: Plenum Press.

Cullen, J., & Carr, A. (1999). Codependency: An empirical study from a systemic perspective. *Contemporary Family Therapy, 21*(4), 505–526.

Delva, J. (Ed.). (2000). *Substance issues among families and diverse populations.* New York: Haworth Press.

Deskovitz, M., Key, D. E., Hill, E. M., & Franklin, J. T. (2004). A long-term family-oriented treatment for adolescents with substance-related disorders: An outcome study. *Child and Adolescent Social Work Journal, 21*(3), 265–284.

Dick, D. M., Smith, G., Olausson, P., Mitchell, S. H., Leeman, R. F., O'Malley, S. S., & Sher, K. (2010). *Addiction Biology, 15*(2), 217–226.

Dube, S., Anda, R., Felitti, V., Croft, J., Edwards, V., & Giles, W. (2001). Growing up with parental alcohol abuse: Exposure to childhood abuse, neglect, and household dysfunction. *Child Abuse and Neglect, 25*(12), 1627–1640.

Duhl, F., Kantor, D., & Duhl, B. (1973). Learning, space, and action in family therapy: A primer of sculpture. In D. Bloch (Ed.), *Techniques of family psychotherapy: A primer* (pp. 47–63). New York: Grune & Straton.

Edwards, M. E., & Steinglass, P. (1995). Family therapy treatment outcomes for alcoholism. *Journal of Marital and Family Therapy, 21*(4), 475–509.

Elkin, M. (1984). *Families under the influence: Changing alcoholic patterns.* New York: W. W. Norton.

Ewing, J., Long, V., & Wenzel, G. (1961). Concurrent group therapy of alcoholic patients and their wives. *International Journal of Group Psychotherapy, 11*(3), 329–338.

Fals-Stewart, W., Lam, W., & Kelley, M. L. (2009). Learning sobriety together: Behavioral couples therapy for alcoholism and drug abuse. *Journal of Family Therapy, 31*(2), 115–125.

Fenster, J. (2005). Substance abuse issues in the family. In G. P. Mallon & P. M. Hess (Eds.), *Child welfare for the 21st century: A handbook of practices, policies, and programs* (pp. 335–348). New York: Columbia.

Fernandez, A. C., Begley, E. A., & Marlatt, G. A. (2006). Family and peer interventions for adults: Past approaches and future directions. *Addictive Behaviors, 20*(2), 207–213.

Finney, J., Moos, R., Cronkite, R., & Gamble, W. (1983). A conceptual model of the functioning of married persons with impaired partners: Spouses of alcoholic partners. *Journal of Marriage and the Family, 55*(45), 23–34.

Fossom, M., & Mason, M. (1986). *Facing the shame: Families in recovery.* New York: W. W. Norton.

Frank, P., & Golden, G. (1992). Blaming by naming: Battered women and the epidemic of co-dependence. *Social Work, 37*(1), 5–6.

Fromme, K. (2006). Parenting and other influences on the alcohol use and emotional adjustment of children, adolescents, and emerging adults. *Psychology of Addictive Behaviors, 20*(2), 138–139.

Fromme, K., Corbin, W. R., & Kruse, M. I. (2008). Behavioral risks during the transition from high school to college. *Developmental Psychology, 44*(5), 1497–1504.

Futterman, S. (1953). Personality trends in wives of alcoholics. *Journal of Psychiatric Social Work, 23*(1), 37–41.

Garrett, J., Landau, J., Shea, R., Stanton, M., Baciewicz, G., & Brinkman-Sull, D. (1998). The ARISE intervention: Using family and network links to engage addicted persons in treatment. *Journal of Substance Abuse Treatment, 15,* 333–343.

Garrett, J., Landau-Stanton, J., Stanton, M., Stellato-Kabar, J., & Stellato-Kabar, D. (1997). ARISE: A method for engaging reluctant alcohol- and drug-dependent individuals in treatment. *Journal of Substance Abuse Treatment, 14,* 235–248.

Gliedman, L., Rosenthal, D., Frank, J., & Nash, H. (1956). Group therapy of alcoholics with concurrent group meetings of their wives. *Quarterly Journal on Studies of Alcoholism, 17*(4), 655–670.

Goldenberg, I., & Goldenberg, H. (2008). *Family therapy: An overview.* Pacific Grove, CA: Brooks/Cole.

Goldner, V. (1985). Feminism and family therapy. *Family Process, 24*(1), 33–41.

Grant, B. (2000). Estimates of U.S. children exposed to alcohol abuse and dependence in the family. *American Journal of Public Health, 90,* 112–115.

Gruber, K. J., & Taylor, M. F. (2006). A Family perspective for substance abuse: Implications from the literature. *Journal of Social Work Practice in the Addictions, 6*(1/2), 1–29.

Hawkins, C. (1996a). Alcoholism in the family of origin of MSW Students: Estimating the prevalence of mental health problems. *Journal of Social Work Education, 32*(1), 127–143.

Hawkins, C. (1996b). Pathogenic and protective relations in alcoholic families (I): Development of the ritual invasion scale. *Journal of Family Social Work, 1*(4), 39–49.

Hawkins, C. (1996c). Pathogenic and protective relations in alcoholic families (II): Ritual invasion, shame, ACOA traits, and problem drinking behavior in adult offspring. *Journal of Family Social Work, 1*(4), 51–63.

Hawkins, C. (1997). Disruption of family rituals as a mediator of adult children of alcoholics' traits and problem drinking. *Addictive Behaviors, 22*(2), 219–231.

Hawkins, C., & Hawkins, R. (1997). Psychological type and adult children of alcoholics' traits. *Journal of Psychological Type, 41,* 17–22.

Hawkins, R. (1992). Substance abuse and stress-coping resources: A life contextual viewpoint. In B. Wallace (Ed.), *The chemically dependent: Phases of treatment and recovery* (pp. 127–158). New York: Brunner/Mazel.

Hawkins, R., & Hawkins, C. (1995). Development and validation of an adult children of alcoholics tool. *Research for Social Work Practice, 5*(3), 317–339.

Heath, A., & Stanton, M. (1998). Family-based treatment: Stages and outcomes. In A. W. Heath & M. D. Stanton (Eds.), *Clinical textbook of addictive behaviors* (pp. 496–520). New York: Guilford Press.

Hill, E., Ross, L., Mudd, S., & Blow, F. (1997). Adulthood functioning: The joint effects of parental alcoholism, gender and childhood socio-economic stress. *Addiction, 92*(5), 583–596.

Humphreys, K. (1996). Alanon self-help groups: Reconstructing the alcoholic family. *International Journal of Group Psychotherapy, 46*(2), 255–263.

Hussong, A. M., Bauer, D. J., Huang, W., Chassin, L., Sher, K. J., & Zucker, R. (2008). Characterizing the life stressors of children of alcoholic parents. *Journal of Family Psychology, 22*(6), 819–832.

Jackson, J. (1954). The adjustment of the family to the crisis of alcoholism. *Quarterly Journal of Studies on Alcohol, 15*(4), 562–568.

Jacob, T., & Johnson, S. (1999). Family influences on alcohol and substance abuse. In P. Ott, R. Tarter, & R. Ammerman (Eds.), *Sourcebook on substance abuse: Etiology, epidemiology, assessment, and treatment* (pp. 166–174). Boston, MA: Allyn & Bacon.

Jellinek, E. (1960). *The disease concept of alcoholism.* New Haven, CT: Hill House.

Johnson, J., & Leff, M. (1999). Children of substance abusers: Overview of research findings. *Pediatrics, 103*(5), 1085–2001.

Johnson, V. (1998). *Intervention: How to help someone who doesn't want help.* Center City, MN: Johnson Institute.

Jordan, J., Kaplan, A., Miller, J., Stiver, I., & Surrey, J. (Eds.). (1991). *Women's growth in connection.* New York: Guilford Press.

Kalashian, M. (1959). Working with wives of alcoholics in an outpatient clinical setting. *Marriage and the Family, 21*(2), 130–133.

Kaufman, E., & Kaufman, P. (1992). *Family therapy of drug and alcohol abuse.* Boston, MA: Allyn & Bacon.

Kaufman, G. (1985a). *The psychology of shame.* New York: Springer.

Kaufman, G. (1985b). *Shame: The power of caring.* Cambridge, MA: Schenkman.

Kienz, L. A., Schwartz, C. S., Trench, B. M., & Houlihan, D. D. (1995). An assessment of membership benefits in the Al-Anon program. *Alcoholism Treatment Quarterly, 12*(4), 31–38.

Kitchens, J. (1991). *Understanding and treating codependency.* Englewood Cliffs, NJ: Prentice Hall.

Kurtz, L. F. (1994). Self-help groups for families with mental illness or alcoholism. In T. J. Powell (Ed.), *Understanding the self-help organization: Frameworks and findings* (pp. 293–313). Thousand Oaks, CA: Sage.

Landau, J., Garrett, J., Shea, R., Stanton, M.D., Brinkman-Sull, D., & Baciewicz, G. (2000). Strength in numbers: The ARISE method for mobilizing family and network to engage substance abusers in treatment. *The American Journal of Drug and Alcohol Abuse, 26*(3), 379–398.

Lawson, G., & Lawson, A. (1998). *Alcoholism and the family: A guide to treatment and prevention.* Gaithersburg, MD: Aspen Press.

Lawson, G., Lawson, A., & Rivers, P. (2001). Family counseling: Seeing the family as the client. In G. W. Lawson, A. W. Lawson, & P. C. Rivers (Eds.), *Essentials of chemical dependency counseling* (pp. 179–220). Gaithersburg, MD: Aspen Press.

Lewis, M. (1937). Alcoholism and family casework. *Social Casework, 35*(18), 39–44.

Liddle, H., & Dakof, G. (1995). Efficacy of family therapy for drug abuse: Promising but not definitive. *Journal of Marital and Family Therapy, 21*(4), 511–543.

Lipps, A. (1999). Family therapy in the treatment of alcohol related problems: A review of behavioral family therapy, family systems therapy, and treatment matching research. *Alcoholism Treatment Quarterly, 17*(3), 13–23.

Lochman, J. E., & van den Steenhoven, A. (2002). Family-based approaches to substance abuse prevention. *The Journal of Primary Prevention, 23*(1), 49–114.

Loneck, B., Garrett, J., & Banks, S. (1996). The Johnson intervention and relapse during outpatient treatment. *American Journal of Drug and Alcohol Abuse, 22*(3), 363–375.

MacPherson, P., Stewart, S., & McWilliams, L. (2001). Parental problem drinking and anxiety disorder symptoms in adult offspring: Examining the mediating role of anxiety sensitivity components. *Addictive Behaviors, 26*, 917–934.

Marsh, J. C., Ryan, J. P., Choi, S., & Testa, M. (2006). Integrated services for families with multiple problems: Obstacles to family reunification. *Children and Youth Services Review, 28*(9), 1074–1087.

McBride, J. L. (1991). Assessing the Al-Anon component of alcoholics anonymous. *Alcoholism Treatment Quarterly, 8*(4), 57–65.

McBride, J. L. (1996). Family functioning and alcoholics anonymous attendance. *Alcoholism Treatment Quarterly, 14*(3), 103–106.

McCollum, E. E., & Trepper, T. S. (2001). *Family solutions for substance abuse: Clinical and counseling approaches.* New York: Haworth Press.

McCrady, B. (1986). The family in the change process. In W. Miller & R. Hester (Eds.), *Treating addictive behaviors* (pp. 305–318). New York: Plenum Press.

McGue, M. (1997). A behavioral-genetics perspective on children of alcoholics. *Alcohol Health and Research World, 21*, 210–217.

Menees, M., & Segrin, C. (2000). The specificity of disrupted processes in families of adult children of alcoholics. *Alcohol and Alcoholism, 35*(4), 361–367.

Meyers, R., Smith, J., & Miller, E. (1998). Working through the concerned significant other. In W. Miller & N. Heather (Eds.), *Treating addictive behaviors* (pp. 149–161). New York: Plenum Press.

Morgan, J. (1991). What is codependency? *Journal of Clinical Psychology, 47*(5), 720–729.

Mueser, K. T., Glynn, S. M., Cather, C., Zarate, R., Fox, L., Feldman, J., Wolfe, R., & Clark, R. E. (2009). Family intervention for co-occurring substance use and severe psychiatric disorders: Participant characteristics and correlates of initial engagement and more extended exposure in a randomized controlled trial. *Addictive Behaviors, 34*, 867–877.

National Institute of Health. (December 30, 1999). One in four children exposed to family alcohol abuse or alcoholism. *NIH News*. Retrieved May 1, 2010, from www.niaaa.nih.gov/NewsEvents/NewsReleases/4children.htm.

Newport, F. (1999, November 3). More than a third of Americans report drinking has caused family problems. *Gallup News Service*. Retrieved May 10, 2011, from www.gallup.com/poll/3493/More-Than-Third-Americans-Report-Drinking-Has-Caused-Family-Problems.aspx.

Nichols, M. (2009). *The essentials of family therapy*. Boston, MA: Allyn & Bacon.

O'Farrell, T. (1995). Marital and family therapy. In R. Hester & W. Miller (Eds.), *Handbook of alcoholism treatment approaches* (pp. 195–220). Boston, MA: Allyn & Bacon.

O'Farrell, T., & Fals-Stewart, W. (1999). Treatment models and methods: Family models. In B. McCrady & E. Epstein (Eds.), *Addictions: A comprehensive guidebook* (pp. 287–305). New York: Oxford.

O'Farrell, T., & Feehan, M. (1999). Alcoholism treatment and the family: Do family and individual treatments for alcoholic adults have preventive effects for children? *Journal of Studies on Alcohol, 60*, 125–129.

O'Farrell, T. J., & Cowles, K. S. (1989). Marital and family therapy. In R. K. Hester & W. R. Miller (Eds.), *Handbook of alcoholism treatment approaches* (pp. 183–205). New York: Pergamon Press.

O'Farrell, T. J., Murphy, M., Alter, J., & Fals-Stewart, W. (2008). Brief family treatment intervention to promote aftercare among substance abusing patients in inpatient detoxification: Transferring a research intervention to clinical practice. *Addictive Behaviors, 33*, 464–471.

Peleg-Oren, N., & Teichman, M. (2006). Young children of parents with substance use disorders (SUD): A review of the literature and implications for social work practice. *Journal of Social Work Practice in the Addictions, 6*(1/2), 49–61.

Perkinson, R. (2002). The family program. *Chemical dependency counseling: A practical guide*. Thousand Oaks, CA: Sage.

Platt, J., Widman, M., Lidz, V., Rubenstein, D., & Thompson, R. (1998). The case for support services in substance abuse treatment. *American Behavioral Scientist, 41*(8), 1050–1063.

Potter-Efron, R. (1989). *Shame, guilt, and alcoholism*. New York: Haworth Press.

Potter-Efron, R., & Potter-Efron, P. (Eds.). (1988). *The treatment of shame and guilt in alcoholism counseling*. New York: Haworth Press.

Price, G. (1945). A study of the wives of twenty alcoholics. *Quarterly Journal of Studies on Alcohol, 5*, 620–627.

Prochaska, J. O., DiClemente, C., & Norcross, J. (1992). In search of how people change: Applications to addictive behaviors. *American Psychologist, 47*, 1102–1114.

Richter, L., Chatterji, P., & Pierce, J. (2000). Perspectives on family substance abuse: The voices of long-term Al-Anon members. *Journal of Family Social Work, 4*(4), 61–78.

Roth, D., & Klein, J. (1990). Eating disorders and addictions: Diagnostic considerations. *The Counselor, 8*(6), 28–33.

Rotunda, R. J., & O'Farrell, T. J. (1997). Marital and family therapy of alcohol use disorders: Bridging the gap between research and practice. *Professional Psychology: Research and Practice, 28*(3), 246–252.

Rotunda, R., Scherer, D., & Imm, P. (1995). Family systems and alcohol misuse: Research on the effects of alcoholism on family functioning and effective family interventions. *Professional Psychology: Research and Practice, 26*(1), 95–104.

Russell, M. (1990). Prevalence of alcoholism among children of alcoholics. In M. Windle & J. Searles (Eds.), *Children of alcoholics: Critical perspectives*. New York: Guilford Press.

Rychtarik, R. (1990). Assessment and implications for treatment. In L. Collins, K. Leonard, & J. Searles (Eds.), *Alcohol and the family: Research and clinical perspectives*. New York: Guilford Press.

Saad, L. (2006, August 25). *Families of drug and alcohol abusers pay an emotional toll*. Gallup News Service. Retrieved May 10, 2011, from www.gallup.com/poll/24256/Families-Drug-Alcohol-Abusers-Pay-Emotional-Toll.aspx.

Schaef, A. (1986). *Co-dependence: Misunderstood—mistreated*. San Francisco: Harper & Row.

Schumm, J. A., O'Farrell, T. J., Murphy, C. M., & Fals-Stewart, W. (2009). Partner violence before and after couples-based alcoholism treatment for female alcoholic patients. *Journal of Consulting and Clinical Psychology, 77*(6), 1136–1146.

Seilhamer, R., & Jacob, T. (1990). Family factors and adjustment of children of alcoholics. In M. Windle & J. Searles (Eds.), *Children of alcoholics: Critical perspectives*. New York: Guilford Press.

Sher, K. J., Dick, D. M., Crabbe, J. C., Hutchison, K. E., O'Malley, S. S., & Heath, A. C. (2010). Consilient research in studying gene x environment interactions in alcohol research. *Addiction Biology, 15*(2), 200–216.

Sher, K., Walitzer, K., Wood, P., & Brent, E. (1991). Characteristics of children of alcoholics: Putative risk factors, substance use and abuse, and psychopathology. *Journal of Abnormal Psychology, 100*(4), 427–448.

Slobada, S. (1974). The children of alcoholics: A neglected problem. *Hospital and Community Psychiatry, 25*(9), 605–606.

Smith, A. (1988). *Grandchildren of alcoholics*. Pompano Beach, FL: Health Communications.

Stanton, M. D. (2004). Getting reluctant substance abusers to engage in treatment/self-help: Review of outcomes and clinical options. *Journal of Marital and Family Therapy, 30*(2), 165–182.

Stanton, M. D., & Shadish, W. R. (1997). Outcome, attrition, and family-couples treatment for drug abuse: A meta-analysis and review of the controlled, comparative studies. *Psychological Bulletin, 122*, 170–191.

Stein, J., Newcomb, M., & Bentler, P. (1993). Differential effects of parent and grandparent drug use on behavior problems of male and female children. *Developmental Psychology, 29*(1), 31–43.

Steinglass, P. (1987). A systems view of family interaction and psychopathology. In T. Jacobs (Ed.), *Family interaction and psychopathology: Theories, methods and findings* (pp. 25–65). New York: Plenum Press.

Steinglass, P. (2006). The future of family systems medicine: Challenges and opportunities. *Families, Systems, & Health, 24*(4), 396–411.

Steinglass, P. (2009). Systemic-motivational therapy for substance abuse disorders: An integrative model. *Journal of Family Therapy, 31(2)*, 155–174.

Steinglass, P., Bennett, L., Wolin, S., & Reiss, D. (1987). *The alcoholic family.* New York: Basic Books.

Stellato-Kabat, D., Stellato-Kabat, J., & Garrett, J. (1995). Treating chemical-dependent couples and families. In A. M. Washton (Ed.), *Psychotherapy and substance abuse: A practitioner's handbook* (pp. 314–335). New York: Guilford.

Tapia, M. I., Schwartz, S. J., Prado, G., Lopez, B., & Pantin, H. (2010). Parent-centered intervention: A practical approach for preventing drug abuse in Hispanic adolescents. In K. van Wormer & B. Thyer (Eds.), *Evidence-based practice in the field of substance abuse: A book of readings* (pp. 105–134). Thousand Oaks, CA: Sage.

Testa, M. F., & Smith, B. (2009). Prevention and drug treatment. *Future of Children, 19*(2), 147–168.

Thomas, C., & Corcoran, J. (2001). Empirically based marital and family interventions for alcohol abuse: A review. *Research on Social Work Practice, 11*(5), 549–575.

Thomas, E., & Ager, R. (1993). Unilateral family therapy with spouses of uncooperative alcohol abusers. In T. J. O'Farrell (Ed.), *Treating alcohol problems: Marital and family interventions* (pp. 3–33). New York: Guilford.

Velleman, R. B., Templeton, L. J., & Copello, A. G. (2005). The role of the family in preventing and intervening with substance use and misuse: A comprehensive review of family interventions, with a focus on young people. *Drug and Alcohol Review, 24*, 93–109.

Wallace, J. (1985). *Alcoholism: New light on the disease.* Newport, RI: Edgehill.

Wegscheider, S. (1981). *Another chance: Hope and health for the alcoholic family.* Palo Alto, CA: Science and Behavior Books.

Wetherill, R. R., & Fromme, K. (2007). Perceived awareness and caring influences alcohol use by high school and college students. *Psychology of Addictive Behaviors, 21*(2), 147–154.

Wetherill, R. R., Neal, D. J., & Fromme, K. (2010). Parents, peers, and sexual values influence sexual behavior during the transition to college. *Archives of Sexual Behavior, 39*, 682–694.

Whitfield, C. (1997). Co-dependence, addictions, and related disorders. In J. Lowinson, P. Ruiz, R. Millman, & J. Langrod (Eds.), *Substance abuse: A comprehensive textbook* (pp. 672–683). Baltimore: Williams & Wilkins.

Whittinghill, D. (2002). Ethical considerations for the use of family therapy in substance abuse treatment. *Journal of Counseling and Therapy for Couples and Families, 10*(1), 75–78.

Wills, T. A. (1990). Stress and coping factors in the epidemiology of substance use. In L. Kozlowski (Ed.), *Research advances in alcohol and drug problems* (Vol. 10, pp. 215–250). New York: Plenum Press.

Windle, M. (1997). Concepts and issues in COA research. *Alcohol Health and Research World, 21*, 185–191.

Winters, J., Fals-Stewart, W., O'Farrell, T., Birchler, G., & Kelley, M. (2002). Behavioral couples therapy for female substance-abusing patients: Effects on substance use and relationship adjustment. *Journal of Consulting & Clinical Psychology, 70*(2), 344–355.

Woititz, J. (1990). *Adult children of alcoholics.* Deerfield Beach, FL: Health Communications.

Wolin, S., & Bennett, L. (1984). Family rituals. *Family Process, 23*(3), 401–420.

Wolin, S., Bennett, L., & Jacobs, T. (1988). Assessing family rituals in alcoholic families. In E. Imber-Black, J. Roberts, & R. Whiting (Eds.), *Rituals in families and family therapy* (pp. 230–256). New York: W. W. Norton.

Wolin, S., & Wolin, S. J. (1993). *The resilient self: How survivors of troubled families rise above adversity.* New York: Villard.

Wright, P., & Wright, K. (1999). The two faces of codependent relating: A research-based perspective. *Contemporary Family Therapy, 21*(4), 527–543.

Wycoff, S., & Cameron, S. C. (2000). The Garza family: Using a structural systems approach with an alcohol-dependence family. *The Family Journal, 8*, 47–57.

CHAPTER 11

Abbey, A., Jacques, A. J., Hayman, L. W., & Sobeck, J. (2006). Predictors of early substance use among African American and Caucasian youth from urban and suburban communities. *Merrill-Palmer Quarterly, 52*(2), 305–326.

Abbott, P. J. (1998). Traditional and Western healing practices for alcoholism in American Indians and Alaska Natives. *Substance Use and Misuse, 33*, 2605–2646.

Abe-Kim, J., Takeuchi, D., Seunghye H., Appel, H., Nicdao, E., Zane, N., Sue, S., Spencer, M., Alegría, M. (2007). Use of mental health-related services among immigrant and US-born Asian Americans: Results from the National Latino and Asian American Study. *American Journal of Public Health, 97*(1), 91–98.

Acevedo-Garcia, D., & Bates, L. M., (2007). Latino health paradoxes: Empirical evidence, explanations, future research, and implications. In H. Rodriguez, R. Saenz, &

C. Menjivar (Eds.), *Latino/as in the United States: Changing the face of America* (pp. 101–113). New York, NY: Springer.

Aguilar, M. A., DiNitto, D. M., Franklin, C., & Lopez-Pilkinton, B. (1991). Mexican-American families: A psychoeducational approach for addressing chemical dependency and codependency. *Child and Adolescent Social Work Journal, 8*(4), 309–326.

Akeo, N., Bunyan, E., Burgess, K., Eckart, D., Evensen, S., Hirose-Wong, S., et al. (2008). Hui Malama o ke Kai: Mobilizing to prevent youth violence and substance use with passion, common goals, and culture. *American Journal of Preventive Medicine, 34*(3), S67–S71.

Aktan, G. B. (1999). A cultural consistency evaluation of a substance abuse prevention program with inner city African-American families. *Journal of Primary Prevention, 19*, 227–239.

Alaniz, M. L. (1998). Alcohol availability and targeted advertising in racial/ethnic minority communities. *Alcohol Health and Research World, 22*, 286–289.

Albaugh, B. J., & Anderson, P. (1974). Peyote in the treatment of alcoholism among American Indians. *American Journal of Psychiatry, 131*(11), 1247–1250.

Alvarez, L. R., & Ruiz, P. (2001). Substance abuse in the Mexican American population. In S. L. A. Straussner (Ed.), *Ethnocultural factors in substance abuse treatment* (pp. 111–136). New York: Guilford Press.

Amey, C. H., & Albrecht, S. L. (1998). Race and ethnic differences in adolescent drug use: The impact of family structure and the quantity and quality of parental interaction. *Journal of Drug Issues, 28*, 283–298.

Amey, C. H., Albrecht, S. L., & Miller, M. K. (1996). Racial differences in adolescent drug use: The impact of religion. *International Journal of the Addictions, 31*, 1311–1332.

Amodeo, M., Peou, S., Grigg-Saito, D., Berke, H., Pin-Riebe, S., & Jones, L. K. (2004). Providing culturally specific substance abuse services in refugee and immigrant communities: Lessons from a Cambodian treatment and demonstration project. *Journal of Social Work Practice in the Addictions, 4*(3), 23–46.

Amodeo, M., Robb, N., Peou, S., & Tran, H. (1996). Adapting mainstream substance-abuse interventions for Southeast Asian clients. *Families in Society, 77*, 403–413.

Angstman, S., Harris, K. J., Golbeck, A., & Swaney, G. (2009). Cultural identification and smoking among American Indian adults in an urban setting. *Ethnicity & Health, 14*(3), 289–302.

Armyr, G., Elmer, A., & Herz, U. (1982). *Alcohol in the world of the 80s.* Stockholm, Sweden: Sober Forlags AB.

Asante, M. K. (1980). *Afrocentricity.* Buffalo, NY: Amulefi.

Asante, M. K. (1998). *The Afrocentric idea.* Philadelphia: Temple University Press.

Ashley, M. (1999). Health promotion planning in African American communities. In R. M. Huff & M. V. Kline

(Eds.), *Promoting health in multicultural populations: A handbook for practitioners* (pp. 223–240). Thousand Oaks, CA: Sage.

Asian & Pacific Islander American Health Forum. (2010, August). *Native Hawaiian and Pacific Islander health disparities.* Retrieved May 2, 2011, from www.apiahf.org/sites/default/files/NHPI_Report08a_2010.pdf.

Au, J. G., & Donaldson, S. I. (2000). Social influences as explanations for substance use differences among Asian-American and European-American adolescents. *Journal of Psychoactive Drugs, 32*, 15–23.

Bales, R. F. (1946). Cultural differences in rates of alcoholism. *Quarterly Journal of Studies on Alcohol, 6*, 480–499.

Barlow, A., & Walkup, J. T. (2008). The first Americans have much to teach us. *Journal of the American Academy of Child and Adolescent Psychiatry, 47*(8), 843–844.

Barnes, J. S., & Bennett, C. E. (2002, February). *The Asian population: 2000.* Washington, DC: U.S. Census Bureau. Retrieved May 2, 2011, from www.census.gov/prod/2002pubs/c2kbr01-16.pdf.

Barón, M. (2000). Addiction treatment for Mexican American families. In J. Krestan (Ed.), *Bridges to recovery: Addiction, family therapy, and multicultural treatment* (pp. 219–251). New York: Free Press.

Beals, J., Belcourt-Dittloff, A., Freedenthal, S., Kaufman, C., Mitchell, C., Whitesell, N., et al. (2009). Reflections on a proposed theory of reservation-dwelling American Indian alcohol use: Comment on Spillane and Smith (2007). *Psychological Bulletin, 135*(2), 339–343.

Beauvais, F. (1998). American Indians and alcohol. *Alcohol Health & Research World, 22*, 253–259.

Beauvais, F., Jumper-Thurman, P., & Burnside, M. (2008). The changing patterns of drug use among American Indian students over the past thirty years. *American Indian and Alaska Native Mental Health Research, 15*(2), 15–24.

Bell, P. (1992). *Cultural pain and African Americans: Unspoken issues in early recovery.* Center City, MN: Hazelden Foundation.

Benner, T. A. (2008). Aban Aya Youth Project: Preventing high-risk behaviors among African American youths in grades 5–8. In J. J. Card & T. A. Benner (Eds.), *Model programs for adolescent sexual health* (pp. 157–164). New York: Springer.

Bergman, R. L. (1971). Navajo peyote use: Its apparent safety. *American Journal of Psychiatry, 128*(6), 695–699.

Berman, M., Hull, T., & May, P. (2000). Alcohol control and injury death in Alaska Native communities: Wet, damp, and dry under Alaska's local option law. *Journal of Studies on Alcohol, 61*, 311–319.

Beverly, C. C. (1975). Toward a model for counseling black alcoholics. *Journal of Non-White Concerns in Personnel & Guidance, 3*(4), 169–176.

Bhattacharya, G. (1998). Drug use among Asian-Indian adolescents: Identifying protective/risk factors. *Adolescence, 33*, 169–184.

Blume, S., Dropkin, D., & Sokolow, L. (1980). The Jewish alcoholic: A descriptive study. *Alcohol Health and Research World, 4*(4), 21–26.

Borges, G., Greenfield, T., Mulia, N., Ye, Y., & Zemore, S. (2009). Gender, acculturation, and other barriers to alcohol treatment utilization among Latinos in three National Alcohol Surveys. *Journal of Substance Abuse Treatment, 36*, 10.

Borrell, L. N., Diez Roux, A., Jacobs, D. R., Shea, S., Jackson, S. A., Shrager, S., et al. (2010). Perceived racial/ethnic discrimination, smoking and alcohol consumption in the multi-ethnic study of atherosclerosis (MESA). *Preventive Medicine, 51*(3–4), 307–312.

Botsford, J., & Peregoy, R. (n. d.). *Peyote and the American Indian Religious Freedom Act Amendments of 1994: National and local impact.* Retrieved March 15, 2011, from www.wisbar.org/AM/Template.cfm?Section=Home&TEMPLATE=/CM/ContentDisplay.cfm&CONTENTID=52302.

Breslau, J., Aguilar-Gaxiola, S., Kendler, K. S., Su, M., Williams, D., & Kessler, R. C. (2006). Specifying race-ethnic differences in risk for psychiatric disorder in a USA national sample. *Psychological Medicine, 36*(1), 57–68.

Brinson, J. A. (1995). Group work for black adolescent substance users: Some issues and recommendations. *Journal of Child and Adolescent Substance Abuse, 24*(2), 49–59.

Brisbane, F. L. (1998). Introduction: Diversity among African Americans. In F. L. Brisbane (Ed.), *Cultural competence for health care professionals working with African-American communities: Theory and practice* (pp. 1–8). Rockville, MD: U.S. Department of Health and Human Services.

Broman, C. L., Neighbors, H. W., Delva, J., Torres, M., & Jackson, J. S. (2008). Prevalence of substance use disorders among African American and Caribbean blacks in the National Survey of American Life. *American Journal of Public Health, 98*(6), 1107–1114.

Bromley, M. A., & Sip, S. K. C. (2001). Substance abuse treatment issues with Cambodian Americans. In S. L. A. Straussner (Ed.), *Ethnocultural factors in substance abuse treatment* (pp. 321–344). New York: Guilford Press.

Brown, F., & Tooley, J. (1989). Alcoholism in the black community. In A. W. Lawson & G. W. Lawson (Eds.), *Alcoholism and substance abuse in special populations* (pp. 115–130). Rockville, MD: Aspen.

Brown, L. S., & John, S. (1999). Substance abuse prevention in African-American communities. In S. B. Kar (Ed.), *Substance abuse prevention: A multicultural perspective* (pp. 171–184). Amityville, NY: Baywood.

Burciaga, J. A. (1997). *In few word/En pocas palabras: A compendium of Latino folk wit and wisdom.* San Francisco: Mercury House.

Burston, B. W., Jones, D., & Roberson-Saunders, P. (1995). Drug use and African Americans: Myth versus reality. *Journal of Alcohol and Drug Education, 40*(2), 19–39.

Caetano, R. (1994). Drinking and alcohol-related problems among minority women. *Alcohol Health and Research World, 18*(3), 233–241.

Caetano, R. (1988). Responding to alcohol-related problems among Hispanics. *Contemporary Drug Problems, 15*(3), 335–363.

Caetano, R., & Clark, C. L. (1998). Trends in alcohol consumption patterns among Whites, Blacks, and Hispanics: 1984 and 1995. *Journal of Studies on Alcohol, 59,* 659–668.

Caetano, R. A., Clark, C. L., & Tam, T. (1998). Alcohol consumption among racial/ethnic minorities: Theory and research. *Alcohol Health and Research World, 22,* 233–241.

Caetano, R., Ramisetty-Mikler, S., & Rodriguez, L. (2008). The Hispanic Americans Baseline Alcohol Survey (HABLAS): Rates and predictors of alcohol abuse and dependence across Hispanic national groups. *Journal of Studies on Alcohol and Drugs, 69* (3), 441–448.

Caetano, R., Ramisetty-Mikler, S., & Rodriguez, L. (2009). The Hispanic Americans Baseline Alcohol Survey (HABLAS): The association between birthplace, acculturation and alcohol abuse and dependence across Hispanic national groups. *Drug and Alcohol Dependence, 99,* 215–221.

Caetano, R., Vaeth, P., Ramisetty-Mikler, S., & Rodriguez, L. (2009). The Hispanic Americans Baseline Alcohol Survey: Alcoholic beverage preference across Hispanic national groups. *Alcoholism: Clinical and Experimental Research, 33*(1), 150–159.

Cahalan, D., & Cisin, I. H. (1968). American drinking practices: Summary of findings from a national probability sample: 1. Extent of drinking by population subgroups. *Quarterly Journal of Studies on Alcohol, 29,* 130–151.

Caldwell, F. J. (1983). Alcoholics Anonymous as a viable treatment resource for black alcoholics. In T. D. Watts & R. Wright, Jr. (Eds.), *Black alcoholism: Toward a comprehensive understanding* (pp. 85–99). Springfield, IL: Charles C Thomas.

Canino, G., Vega, W., Sribney, W., Warner, L., & Alegria, M. (2008). Social relationships, social assimilation, and substance use disorders among adult Latinos in the U.S. *Journal of Drug Issues, 38*(1), 33.

Carpenter, C. (2003). Seasonal variation in self-reports of recent alcohol consumption: Racial and ethnic differences. *Journal of Studies on Alcohol, 44*(3), 415–418.

Carpey, S. (1985, June 7). Alcoholism, new expressions of Jewish concern create climate of hope. *Jewish Exponent, 48.*

Carvajal, S. C., & Young, R. S. (2009). Culturally based substance abuse treatment for American Indians/Alaska Natives and Latinos. *Journal of Ethnicity in Substance Abuse, 8*(3), 207–222.

Casken, J. A. (1999). Pacific Islander health and disease: An overview. In R. F. Huff & M. V. Kline (Eds.), *Promoting health in multicultural populations: A handbook for practitioners* (pp. 397–417). Thousand Oaks, CA: Sage.

Castro, F. G., Cota, M. K., & Vega, S. C. (1999). Health promotion in Latino populations: A sociocultural model for program planning, development, and evaluation.

In R. M. Huff & M. V. Kline (Eds.), *Promoting health in multicultural populations: A handbook for practitioners* (pp. 137–168). Thousand Oaks, CA: Sage.

Centers for Disease Control and Prevention. (2008, August 29). Alcohol-attributable deaths and years of potential life lost among American Indians and Alaska Natives—United States, 2001–2005. *Morbidity and Mortality Weekly Report, 57*(34), 938–941. Retrieved March 13, 2011, from www.cdc.gov/mmwr/preview/mmwrhtml/mm5734a3.htm.

Centers for Disease Control and Prevention. (2010a, July 26). *HIV in the United States: An overview*. Atlanta: U.S. Department of Health and Human Services. Retrieved February 26, 2011, from www.cdc.gov/hiv/topics/surveillance/resources/factsheets/us_overview.htm.

Centers for Disease Control and Prevention. (2010b, October 13). *First report on Hispanic life expectancy released by CDC*. Retrieved March 24, 2011, from www.cdc.gov/media/pressrel/2010/a101013.html.

Centers for Disease Control and Prevention. (2011, February 16). *Diagnoses of HIV infection and AIDS in the United States and dependent areas, 2009 HIV Surveillance Report, Volume 21*. Atlanta: U.S. Department of Health and Human Services. Retrieved February 26, 2011, from www.cdc.gov/hiv/surveillance/resources/reports/2009report/index.htm#3 (See especially Table 17a).

Chae, D. H., Takeuchi, D. T., Barbeau, E. M., Bennett, G. G., Lindsey, J. C., Stoddard, A. M., & Krieger, N. (2008a). Alcohol disorders among Asian Americans: Associations with unfair treatment, racial/ethnic discrimination, and ethnic identification (the National Latino and Asian American Study, 2002–2003). *Journal of Epidemiology and Community Health, 62*, 973–979.

Chae, D. H., Takeuchi, D. T., Barbeau, E. M., Bennett, G. G., Lindsey, J. C., & Krieger, N. (2008b). Unfair treatment, racial/ethnic discrimination, ethnic identification, and smoking among Asian Americans in the National Latino and Asian American Study, 2002–2003). *American Journal of Public Health, 98*(3), 485–492.

Chang, P. (2000). Treating Asian/Pacific American addicts and their families. In J. Krestan (Ed.), *Bridges to recovery: Addictions, family therapy, and multicultural treatment* (pp. 192–218). New York: Free Press.

Cherry, V. R., Belgrave, F. Z., Jones, W., Kennon, D. K., Gray, F. S., & Phillips, F. (1998). NTU: An Africentric approach to substance abuse prevention among African American youth. *Journal of Primary Prevention, 18*, 319–339.

Chin, J. L. (2001). *Asian Americans/Pacific Islanders: Assessing the unmet need for mental health services*. Bethesda, MD: Center for Mental Health Services.

Chow, J. (2002). Asian American and Pacific Islander mental health and substance abuse agencies: Organizational characteristics and service gaps. *Administration and Policy in Mental Health, 30*(1), 79–86.

Christmon, K. (1995). Historical overview of alcohol in the African American community. *Journal of Black Studies, 25*, 318–330.

Cohen, E., Feinn, R., Arias, A., & Kranzler, H. (2007). Alcohol treatment utilization: Findings from the National Epidemiologic Survey on Alcohol and Related Conditions. *Drug and Alcohol Dependence, 86*, 214–221.

Collins, L. (1993). Sociocultural aspects of alcohol use and abuse: Ethnicity and gender. *Drugs & Society, 18*(1), 89–116.

Comas-Diaz, L. (1986). Puerto Rican alcoholic women: Treatment considerations. *Alcoholism Treatment Quarterly, 3*(1), 47–57.

Cook, W. K., Hoffstetter, R., Kang, M., Hovell, M., & Irvin, V. (2009). Rethinking acculturation: A study of alcohol use of Korean American adolescents in Southern California. *Contemporary Drug Problems, 36*(1/2), 217–244.

Coyhis, D. (2000). Culturally specific addiction recovery for Native Americans. In J. Krestan (Ed.), *Bridges to recovery: Addiction, family therapy, and multicultural treatment* (pp. 77–114). New York: Free Press.

Coyhis, D., & Simonelli, R. (2008). The Native American healing experience. *Substance Use & Misuse, 43*, 1927–1949.

Coyhis, D., & White, W. (2006). *Alcohol problems in Native America: The untold story of resistance and recovery: "The truth about the lie."* Colorado Springs, CO: White Bison, Inc.

Coyhis, D., & White, W. L. (2002). Alcohol problems in Native America: Changing paradigms and clinical practices. *Alcoholism Treatment Quarterly, 20*(3/4), 157–166.

Crunkilton, D., Paz, J., & Boyle, D. (2005). Culturally competent intervention with families of Latino youth at risk for drug abuse. In M. R. De La Rosa, L. Holleran, & S. L. A. Straussner (Eds.), *Substance abusing Latinos: Current research on epidemiology, prevention and treatment* (pp. 113–131). Binghamton, NY: The Haworth Social Work Practice Press.

Dailey, R. C. (1979). The role of alcohol among North American Indian tribes as reprinted in the Jesuit Relations. In M. Marshall (Ed.), *Beliefs, behaviors, and alcoholic beverages: A cross-cultural survey* (pp. 116–127). Ann Arbor: University of Michigan Press.

Daughters, S., Magidson, J., Schuster, R., & Safren, S. (2010). ACT HEALTHY: A combined cognitive–behavioral depression and medication adherence treatment for HIV–infected substance abusers. *Cognitive and Behavioral Practice, 17*(3), 309–321.

D'Avanzo, C. E. (1997). Southeast Asians: Asian-Pacific Americans at risk for substance misuse. *Substance Use & Misuse, 32*, 829–848.

De La Rosa, M., Holleran, L., Rugh, D., & MacMaster, S. (2005). Substance abuse among U.S. Latinos. *Journal of Social Work Practice in the Addictions, 5*(1–2), 1–20.

Delgado, M. (1998). Alcoholism services and community settings: Latina beauty parlors as case examples. *Alcoholism Treatment Quarterly, 16*, 71–83.

Delgado, M. (1999). A state of the art review of Latinos and substance abuse. In S. B. Kar (Ed.), *Substance abuse prevention: A multicultural perspective* (pp. 155–170). Amityville, NY: Baywood.

Delgado, M., & Rosati, M. (2005). Pentecostal religion, asset assessment and alcohol and other drug abuse: A case study of a Puerto Rican community in Massachusetts. In M. Delgado (Ed.), *Latinos and alcohol use/abuse revisted: Advances and challenges for prevention and treatment programs* (pp. 185–203). Binghamton: Haworth Press.

Delva, J., Wallace, J., O'Malley, P., Bachman, J., Johnston, L., & Schulenberg, J. (2005). The epidemiology of alcohol, marijuana, and cocaine use among Mexican American, Puerto Rican, Cuban American, and other Latin American eighth-grade students in the United States: 1991–2002. *American Journal of Public Health, 95*(4), 696–702.

Denton, N., & Massey, D. (1989). Racial identity among Caribbean Hispanics: The effect of double minority status on residential segregation. *American Sociological Review, 54*(5), 790–808.

Devore, W., & Schlesinger, E. G. (1999). *Ethnic-sensitive social work practice* (5th ed.). Boston, MA: Allyn & Bacon.

Dozier, C. D. (1989). The African-American and alcoholism: Roadblocks to treatment. *The Counselor, 7*(3), 33–34.

Drake, F. B. (2010, May 24). An ancient cure for recent trauma. *Mail Tribune.* Retrieved March 15, 2011, from www.mailtribune.com/apps/pbcs.dll/article?AID=/20100524/NEWS/5240316/-1/OREGONHEALTHYLIVING02.

Ehlers, C. L., Phillips, E., Gizer, I. R., Gilder, D. A., & Wilhelmsen. (2010). EEG spectral phenotypes: Heritability and association with marijuana and alcohol dependence in an American Indian community study. *Drug and Alcohol Dependence, 106,* 101–110.

Eisenman, R., Grossman, J. C., & Goldstein, R. (1980). Undergraduate marijuana use as related to internal sensation novelty seeking and openness to experience. *Journal of Clinical Psychology, 36*(4), 1013–1019.

Ellias-Frankel, J., Oberman, A., & Ward, K. (2000). Addiction treatment for Jewish Americans and their families. In J. Krestan (Ed.), *Bridges to recovery: Addiction, family therapy, and multicultural treatment* (pp. 115–144). New York: Free Press.

Epstein, J., Collins, K. K., Bailey-Burch, B., Walker-Thoth, D., & Pancella, T. (2007). Space Scouts: A collaboration between university researchers and African American churches. *Journal of Ethnicity and Substance Abuse, 6*(1), 67–79.

Epstein, L. (1980). *Helping people: The task-centered approach.* St. Louis, MO: C. V. Mosby.

Eurocare. (2001, November 26). *Israel consumption.* Retrieved June 28, 2002, from www.eurocare.org/ profiles/isconsump.htm.

Farabee, D., Wallisch, L., & Maxwell, J. C. (1995). Substance abuse among Texas Hispanics and non-Hispanics: Who's using, who's not, and why. *Hispanic Journal of Behavioral Sciences, 17*(4), 523–536.

Feaster, D. J., Burns, M. J., Brincks, A. M., Prado, G., Mitrani, V. B., Mauer, J. H., & Szapocznik, J. (2010). Structural Ecosystems Therapy for HIV+ African-American women and drug abuse relapse. *Family Processes, 49*(2), 204–219.

Figueroa, R., & Oliver-Diaz, P. (1986/87). Hispanic alcoholics' children need extra help. *Alcohol Health & Research World, 11*(2), 66–67.

Figueroa, W. (2010). *History of Puerto Rico: Sol Boricua.* Retrieved March 24, 2011, from www.solboricua.com/history2.htm#usa.

Finn, P. (1994). Addressing the needs of cultural minorities in drug treatment. *Journal of Substance Abuse Treatment, 44*(4), 325–337.

Fischer, M., Wetherill, L., Carr, L., You, M., & Crabb, D. (2007). Association of adelhyde dehydrogenase 2 promoter polymorphism with alcohol consumption and reactions in an American Jewish population. *Alcoholism: Clinical and Experimental Research, 31*(10), 1654–1659.

Flasher, L. V., & Maisto, S. A. (1984). A review of theory and research on drinking patterns among Jews. *Journal of Nervous and Mental Disease, 172*(10), 596–603.

Flores, G. (2000, January). Culture and the patient-physician relationship: Achieving cultural competency in health care. *The Journal of Pediatrics, 136*(1), 10.

Fong, R., & Furuto, S. B. C. L. (2001). *Culturally competent practice: Skills, interventions, and evaluations.* Boston, MA: Allyn & Bacon.

Fong, T., Tsuang, J. (2007). Asian-Americans addictions and barriers to treatment. *Psychiatry, 4*(11), 51–58.

Freeman, R., Lewis, Y., & Colon, H. (2002). *Handbook for conducting drug abuse research with Hispanic populations.* Westport: NOVA Research Company.

Garcia-Goyco, O. (2007). The Mapa de Cuauhtinchan No. 2 and the Cosmic Tree in Mesoamerica, the Caribbean, and the Amazon-Orinoco Basin (S. Sessions, Trans.). In D. Carrasco & S. Sessions (Eds.), *Cave, city, and eagles nest: An interpretive journey through the Mapa de Cuautinchan* (pp. 357–388). China: Everbest Printing Company, Ltd.

Gee, G. C., Delva, J., & Takeuchi, D. T. (2007). Relationships between self-reported unfair treatment and prescription medication use, illicit drug use, and alcohol dependence among Filipino Americans. *American Journal of Public Health, 97*(5), 933–940.

Genovese, E. D. (1974). *Roll, Jordan, roll: The world the slaves made.* New York: Pantheon Books.

Gfroerer, J. C., & Tan, L. L. (2003). Substance abuse among foreign-born youths in the United States: Does the length of residence matter? *American Journal of Public Health, 93,* 1892–1895.

Gibbons, R. X., Pomery, E. A., & Gerrard, M. (2010). Racial discrimination and substance abuse: Risk and protective factors in African American adolescents. In L. Scheier (Ed.), *Handbook of drug use etiology: Theory, methods, and empirical findings* (pp. 341–361). Washington, DC: American Psychological Association.

Gilbert, M. J. (1987). Program approaches to the alcohol-related needs of Mexican Americans. In M. J. Gilbert & R. C. Cervantes (Eds.), *Mexican Americans and alcohol* (Monograph no. 11, pp. 95–107). Los Angeles: Spanish Speaking Mental Health Research Center.

Gilbert, M. J., & Cervantes, R. C. (1987). Alcohol services for Mexican Americans: A review of utilization patterns, treatment considerations and prevention activities. In M. J. Gilbert & R. C. Cervantes (Eds.), *Mexican Americans and alcohol* (Monograph no. 11, pp. 61–93). Los Angeles: Spanish Speaking Mental Health Research Center.

Glad, D. D. (1947). Attitudes and experiences of American-Jewish and American-Irish male youth as related to differences in adult rates of inebriety. *Quarterly Journal of Studies on Alcohol, 8,* 406–472.

Glasser, W. (1965). *Reality therapy.* New York: Harper & Row.

Glassner, B., & Berg, B. (1980). How Jews avoid alcohol problems. *American Sociological Review, 45,* 647–664.

Glassner, B., & Berg, B. (1984). Social locations and interpretations: How Jews define alcoholism. *Journal of Studies on Alcohol, 45*(1), 16–25.

Glatt, M. M. (1970). Alcoholism and drug dependence amongst Jews. *British Journal of Addiction, 64,* 297–304.

Gone, J. P. (2009). A community-based treatment for Native American historical trauma. Prospects for evidence-based practice. *Journal of Consulting and Clinical Psychology, 77*(4), 751–762.

Gonzalez-Ramos, G. (1990). Examining the myth of Hispanic families' resistance to treatment: Using the school as a site for services. *Social Work in Education, 12*(4), 261–274.

Gordon, A. J. (1989). State-of-the-art review: Caribbean Hispanics and their alcohol use. In D. Spiegler, D. Tate, S. Aitken, & C. Christian (Eds.), *Alcohol use among U.S. ethnic minorities: Proceedings of a conference on the epidemiology of alcohol use and abuse among ethnic minority groups, September 1985* (NIAAA Research Monograph no. 18, pp. 135–146). Rockville, MD: National Institute on Alcohol Abuse and Alcoholism.

Gordon, A. J. (1991). Alcoholism treatment services to Hispanics: An ethnographic examination of a community's services. *Family and Community Health, 13*(4), 12–24.

Gossett, V. R. (1988). *Alcohol and drug abuse in black America: A guide for community action.* Minneapolis: Institute on Black Chemical Abuse.

Grant, B. F., Dawson, D. A., Stinson, F. S., Chou, S. P., Dufour, M. C., & Pickering, R. P. (2004). The 12-month prevalence and trends in DSM-IV alcohol abuse and dependence: United States, 1991–1992 and 2001–2002. *Drug and Alcohol Dependence, 74*(3), 223–234.

Grant, D., & Moore, B. (1986–87). MIBCA-sponsored conference: Groundwork for future action. *Alcohol Health & Research World, 11*(2), 18–25, 51.

Grant, D., & White, B. W. (2007). Substance abuse among African-American children: Contemporary issues and challenges for effective intervention. In L. A. Lee (Ed.), *Human behavior in the social environment from an African-American perspective* (2nd ed., pp. 393–419). New York: Haworth Press.

Gray, M. (1995). African Americans. In J. Philleo & F. L. Brisbane (Eds.), *Cultural competence for social workers: A guide for alcohol and other drug abuse prevention professionals working with ethnic/racial communities* (CSAP Cultural Competence Series no. 4, pp. 71–101). Washington, DC: U.S. Government Printing Office.

Green, J. W. (1999). *Cultural awareness in the human services: A multi-ethnic approach* (3rd ed.). Boston, MA: Allyn & Bacon.

Grunbaum, J., Lowry, R., Kann, L., & Pateman, B. (2000). Prevalence of health risk behaviors among Asian American/Pacific Islander high school students. *Journal of Adolescent Health, 27,* 322–330.

Gutmann, M. C. (1999). Ethnicity, alcohol, and acculturation. *Social Science and Medicine, 48,* 173–184.

Harper, F. D. (1976). Etiology: Why do blacks drink? In F. D. Harper (Ed.), *Alcohol abuse and black America* (pp. 27–37). Alexandria, VA: Douglass.

Harper, F. D. (1980). Research and treatment with black alcoholics. *Alcohol Health and Research World, 4*(4), 10–16.

Harford, T. C. (1985). Drinking patterns among black and nonblack adolescents: Results of a national survey. In R. Wright, Jr., & T. D. Watts (Eds.), *Prevention of black alcoholism, issues and strategies* (pp. 122–139). Springfield, IL: Charles C Thomas.

Harris-Hastick, E. F. (2001). Substance abuse issues among English-speaking Caribbean people of African ancestry. In S. L. A. Straussner (Ed.), *Ethnocultural factors in substance abuse treatment* (pp. 52–74). New York: Guilford Press.

Harvey, A. R., & Hill, R. B. (2004). Africentric youth and family rites of passage program: Promoting resilience among at-risk African American youths. *Social Work, 49*(1), 65–74.

Hasin, D., Aharonovich, E., Liu, X., Mamman, Z., Matseoane, K., Carr, L., & Li, T. (2002). Alcohol and ADH2 in Israel: Ashkenazis, Sephardics, and recent Russian immigrants. *American Journal of Psychiatry, 159*(8), 1432–1434.

Hasin, D., Rahav, G., Meydan, J., & Neumark, Y. (1999). The drinking of earlier and more recent Russian immigrants to Israel: Comparison to other Israelis. *Journal of Substance Abuse, 10,* 341–353.

Heath, D. B. (1989). American Indians and alcohol: Epidemiological and sociocultural relevance. In D. Spiegler, D. Tate, S. Aitken, & C. Christian (Eds.), *Alcohol use among U.S. ethnic minorities: Proceedings of a conference on the epidemiology of alcohol use and abuse among ethnic minority groups, September 1985* (NIAAA Research Monograph no. 18, pp. 207–222). Rockville, MD: National Institute on Alcohol Abuse and Alcoholism.

Heath, D. B. (1999). Culture. In P. J. Ott, R. E. Tarter, & R. T. Ammerman (Eds.), *Sourcebook on substance abuse: Etiology, epidemiology, assessment, and treatment* (pp. 175–183). Boston, MA: Allyn & Bacon.

Helzer, J. E., & Canino, G. (1992). *Alcoholism in North America, Europe, and Asia.* New York: Oxford University Press.

Hendershot, C., Collins, S., George, W., Wall, T., McCarthy, D., Liang, T., & Larimer, M. (2009). Associations of ALDH2 and ADH1B genotypes with alcohol-related phenotypes in Asian young adults. Alcoholism: Clinical and Experimental Research, 33(5), 839–847.

Herd, D. (1985a). Ambiguity in black drinking norms: An ethnohistorical interpretation. In L. A. Bennett & G. M. Ames (Eds.),*The American experience with alcohol: Contrasting cultural perspectives* (pp. 149–170). New York: Plenum Press.

Herd, D. (1985b). Migration, cultural transformation and the rise of black liver cirrhosis mortality. *British Journal of Addiction, 80,* 397–410.

Herd, D. (1987). Rethinking black drinking. *British Journal of Addiction, 82,* 219–223.

Herd, D. (1989). Epidemiology of drinking patterns and alcohol-related problems among U.S. blacks. In D. Spiegler, D. Tate, S. Aitken, & C. Chrisitian (Eds.), *Alcohol use among U.S. ethnic minorities: Proceedings of a conference on the epidemiology of alcohol use and abuse among ethnic minority groups, September 1985* (NIAAA Research Monograph no. 18, pp. 3–50). Rockville, MD: National Institute on Alcohol Abuse and Alcoholism.

Herd, D. (1990). Subgroup differences in drinking patterns among black and white men: Results from a national survey. *Journal of Studies on Alcohol, 51*(3), 221–232.

Herd, D. (1991). Drinking patterns in the black population. In W. B. Clark & M. E. Hilton (Eds.), *Alcohol in America: Drinking practices and problems* (pp. 308–328). Albany: State University of New York Press.

Herd, D. A. (1993). Contesting culture: Alcohol-related identity movements in contemporary African American communities. *Contemporary Drug Problems, 20*(4), 739–758.

Hernandez, M. (2000). Puerto Rican families and substance abuse. In J. Krestan (Ed.), *Bridges to recovery: Addiction, family therapy, and multicultural treatment* (pp. 253–283). New York: Free Press.

Heron, M. (2010, March 31). Deaths: Leading causes for 2006. *National Vital Statistics Report, 58*(14). Retrieved February 24, 2011, from www.cdc.gov/nchs/data/nvsr/nvsr58/nvsr58_14.pdf.

Hill, A. (1989). Treatment and prevention of alcoholism in the Native American family. In G. W. Lawson & A. W. Lawson (Eds.), *Alcoholism and substance abuse in special populations* (pp. 262–265, 268). Rockville, MD: Aspen.

Hilton, M. E. (1988). The demographic distribution of drinking patterns in 1984. *Drug and Alcohol Dependence, 22,* 37–47.

Horton, E. G. (2007). Racial differences in the effects of age of onset on alcohol consumption and development of alcohol-related problems among males from mid-adolescence to young adulthood. *Journal of Ethnicity in Substance Abuse, 6*(1), 1–13.

Hudson, H. L. (1985/86). How and why Alcoholics Anonymous works for blacks. *Alcoholism Treatment Quarterly, 2*(3–4), 11–30.

Huff, R. M. (1999). Cross-cultural concepts of health and disease. In R. M. Huff & M. V. Kline (Eds.), *Promoting health in multicultural populations: A handbook for practitioners* (pp. 23–39). Thousand Oaks, CA: Sage.

Huff, R. M., & Kline, M. V. (1999). Tips for working with Hispanic populations. In R. M. Huff & M. V. Kline (Eds.), *Promoting health in multicultural populations: A handbook for practitioners* (pp. 189–197). Thousand Oaks, CA: Sage.

Humphreys, K., & Woods, M. D. (1994). Researching mutual-help group participation in a segregated society. In T. J. Powell (Ed.), *Understanding the self help organization: Frameworks and findings* (pp. 62–87). Thousand Oaks, CA: Sage.

Indian Health Service. (1977). *Alcoholism: A high priority health problem. A report of the Indian Health Services Task Force on Alcoholism.* Washington, DC: Department of Health, Education, and Welfare.

Indian Health Service. (2009, October). *Trends in Indian health, 2002–2003 edition.* Washington, DC: Government Printing Office. Retrieved March 13, 2011, from www.ihs.gov/nonmedicalprograms/ihs_stats/files/Trends_02-03_Entire%20Book%20(508).pdf.

Inouye, J. (1999). Asian American health and disease: An overview of the issues. In R. M. Huff & M. V. Kline (Eds.), *Promoting health in multicultural populations: A handbook for practitioners* (pp. 337–356). Thousand Oaks, CA: Sage.

Ishida, D. N. (1999). Promoting health among Asian American population groups: A case study from the field. In R. M. Huff & M. V. Kline (Eds.), *Promoting health in multicultural populations: A handbook for practitioners* (pp. 375–381). Thousand Oaks, CA: Sage.

Ishisaka, H. A., & Takagi, C. Y. (1995). Social work with Asian and Pacific Americans. In J. W. Green (Ed.), *Cultural awareness in the human services: A multi-ethnic approach* (2nd ed., pp. 122–156). Boston, MA: Allyn & Bacon.

Isralowitz, R. E., & Peleg, A. (1996). Israeli college student alcohol use: The association of background characteristics and regular drinking patterns. *Drug and Alcohol Dependence, 42,* 147–153.

Iwamoto, D. K., Corbin, W., & Fromme, K. (2010). Trajectory classes of heavy episodic drinking among Asian American college students. *Addiction, 105,* 1912–1920.

Jackson, M. S. (1995). Afrocentric treatment of African women and their children in a residential chemical dependency program. *Journal of Black Studies, 26*(1), 17–30.

Jellinek, E. M. (1941). Immanuel Kant on drinking. *Quarterly Journal of Studies on Alcohol, 1,* 777–778.

Jiacheng, X. (1995). China. In D. B. Heath (Ed.), *International handbook on alcohol and culture* (pp. 42–50). Westport, CT: Greenwood Press.

Jilek-Aall, L. (1981). Acculturation, alcoholism, and Indian-style Alcoholics Anonymous. *Journal of Studies on Alcohol* (Suppl. 9), 143–158.

Johnson, R. C. (1989). The flushing reaction and alcohol use. In D. Spiegler, D. Tate, S. Aitken, & C. Christian (Eds.), *Alcohol use among U.S. ethnic minorities: Proceedings of a conference on the epidemiology of alcohol use and abuse among ethnic minority groups, September 1985* (NIAAA Research Monograph no. 18, pp. 383–396). Rockville, MD: National Institute on Alcohol Abuse and Alcoholism.

Johnston, L. D., O'Malley, P. M., Bachman, J. G., & Schulenberg, J. E. (2011). *Monitoring the Future, National results on adolescent drug use: Overview of key findings, 2010.* Ann Arbor, MI: Institute for Social Research, University of Michigan. Retrieved March 17, 2011, from www.monitoringthefuture.org/pubs/monographs/mtf-overview2010.pdf.

Kaptsan, A., Telias, D., Bersudsky, Y., & Belmaker, R. H. (2006). Ethnic origin of alcoholics admitted to an Israeli treatment center. *American Journal of Drug and Alcohol Abuse, 32*(4), 549–553.

Keller, M. (1979). The great Jewish drink mystery. In M. Marshall (Ed.), *Beliefs, behaviors, and alcoholic beverages: A cross-cultural survey* (pp. 404–414). Ann Arbor: University of Michigan Press.

Kelso, D., & Dubay, W. (1989). Alaskan Natives and alcohol: A sociocultural and epidemiological review. In D. Spiegler, D. Tate, S. Aitken, & C. Christian (Eds.), *Alcohol use among U.S. ethnic minorities: Proceedings of a conference on the epidemiology of alcohol use and abuse among ethnic minority groups, September 1985* (NIAAA Research Monograph no. 18, pp. 223–238). Rockville, MD: National Institute on Alcohol Abuse and Alcoholism.

Keyes, K., Hatzenbuehler, M., Alberti, P., Narrow, W., Grant, B., & Hasin, D. (2008, August). Service utilization differences for Axis I psychiatric and substance use disorders between white and black adults. *Psychiatric Services, 59*(8), 893–901.

Kitano, H. H. L. (1982). Alcohol drinking patterns: The Asian Americans. In *Special Population Issues* (NIAAA Alcohol and Health Monograph no. 4, pp. 411–430). Washington, DC: National Institute on Alcohol Abuse and Alcoholism.

Kim, R. J., & Jackson, D. S. (2009). Outcome evaluation findings of a Hawaiian culture-based adolescent substance abuse treatment program. *Psychological Serivces, 6*(1), 43–55.

Kim, W., Kim, I., & Nochajski, T. H. (2010). Risk and protective factors of alcohol use disorders among Filipino Americans: Location of residence matters. *American Journal of Drug and Alcohol Abuse, 36,* 214–129.

Klatsky, A. L., Siegelaub, A. B., Landy, C., & Friedman, G. D. (1983). Racial patterns of alcoholic beverage use. *Alcoholism: Clinical and Experimental Research, 74*(4), 372–377.

Kline, M. V., & Huff, R. M. (1999). Tips for working with Asian American populations. In R. M. Huff & M. V. Kline (Eds.), *Promoting health in multicultural populations: A handbook for practitioners* (pp. 383–394). Thousand Oaks, CA: Sage.

Kogan, S. (2005). Risk and protective factors for substance use among African American high school dropouts. *Psychology of Addictive Behaviors, 19*(4), 382–391.

Kohn, D. B. (2004). *Sex, drugs, and violence in the Jewish tradition.* Lanham, MD: Jason Aronson.

Krestan, J. (Ed.). (2000). *Bridges to recovery: Addiction, family therapy and multicultural treatment.* New York: Free Press.

Kulis, S., Marsiglia, F. F., Elek, E., Dustman, P., Wagstaff, D., & Hecht, M. (2005). Mexican/Mexican American adolescents and keepin' it REAL: An evidence-based substance abuse prevention program. *Children and Schools, 27*(3), 133–145.

Kuramoto, F. (1991). Asian Americans. In J. Philleo & F. L. Brisbane (Eds.), *Cultural competence for social workers: A guide for alcohol and other drug abuse prevention professionals working with ethnic/racial communities* (CSAP Cultural Competence Series no. 4, pp. 103–155). Washington, DC: U.S. Government Printing Office.

Kuramoto, F., & Nakashima, J. (2000). Developing an ATOD prevention campaign for Asian and Pacific Islanders: Some considerations. *Journal of Public Health Management Practice, 6*(3), 57–64.

Kwate, N. O. A. (2009). Association between residential exposure to outdoor alcohol advertising and problem drinking among African American women in New York City. *American Journal of Public Health, 99*(2), 228–230.

Kwon-Ahn, Y. H. (2001). Substance abuse among Korean Americans: A sociocultural perspective and framework for intervention. In S. L. A. Straussner (Ed.), *Ethnocultural factors in substance abuse treatment* (pp. 418–435). New York: Guilford Press.

Lai, T. M. (2001). *Ethnocultural background and substance abuse treatment of Chinese Americans.* New York: Guilford Press.

Landen, M. G., Beller, M., Funk, E., Propst, M., Middaugh, J., & Moolenaar, R. L. (1997). Alcohol-related injury death and alcohol availability in remote Alaska. *Journal of the American Medical Association, 278,* 1755–1758.

Lee, C., Mun, E., White, H. R., & Simon, P. (2010). Substance use trajectories of black and white young men from adolescence to emerging adulthood: A two part growth curve analysis. *Journal of Ethnicity in Substance Abuse, 9*(4), 301–319.

Lee, J. P., Battle, R. S., Antin, T. M. J., & Lipton, R. (2008). Alcohol use among two generations of Southeast Asians in the United States. *Journal of Ethncity in Substance Abuse, 7*(4), 357–375.

Lee, M. Y., Law, P., & Eo, E. (2004). Perception of substance use problems in Asian American communities by Chinese, Indian, Korean and Vietnamese populations. *Journal of Ethnicity in Substance Abuse, 2*(3), 1–29.

Leland, J. (1976). *Firewater myths: North American Indian drinking and alcohol addiction.* New Brunswick, NJ: Rutgers Center of Alcohol Studies.

Leland, J. H. (1980). Native American alcohol use: A review of the literature. In P. D. Mail & D. R. McDonald (Eds.), *Tulapai to Tokay: A bibliography of alcohol use and abuse among Native Americans of North America* (pp. 1–56). New Haven, CT: HRAF Press.

Lemert, E. M. (1982). Drinking among American Indians. In E. Lisansky-Gomberg, H. R. White, & J. A. Carpenter (Eds.), *Alcohol, science and society revisited* (pp. 80–95). Ann Arbor and New Jersey: University of Michigan Press and Rutgers Center for Alcohol Studies.

Levav, I., Kohn, R., Golding, J. M., & Weissman, M. M. (1997). Vulnerability of Jews to affective disorders. *American Journal of Psychiatry, 154,* 941–947.

Levy, F. (1998, March 20) *Orthodox Union workbook combats teen drinking.* Retrieved February 1, 2011, from www.jweekly.com/article/full/7869/orthodox-union-workbook-combats-teen-drinking/.

Lewis, R. G. (1982). Alcoholism and the Native Americans—A review of the literature. In *Alcohol and Health* (Monograph no. 4, Special Population Issues, pp. 315–328). Rockville, MD: National Institute on Alcohol Abuse and Alcoholism.

Littman, G. (1970). Alcoholism, illness, and social pathology among American Indians in transition. *American Journal of Public Health, 60*(9), 1769–1787.

Liu, W. M., & Iwamoto, D. K. (2007). Conformity to masuline norms, Asian values, coping strategies, peer group influences and substance use among Asian American males. *Psychology of Men and Masculinity, 8*(1), 25–39.

Lo, C. C., & Globetti, G. (2001). Chinese in the United States: An extension of moderation in drinking. *International Journal of Comparative Sociology, 42,* 261–274.

Loewenthal, K. M., Lee, M., MacLeod, A. K., Cook, S., & Goldblatt, V. (2003). Drowning your sorrows? Attitudes towards alcohol in UK Jews and Protestants: A thematic analysis. *International Journal of Social Psychiatry, 49*(3), 204–215.

Loewenthal, K. M., MacLeod, A. K., Cook, S., Lee, M., & Goldblatt, V. (2003). Beliefs about alcohol among UK Jews and Protestants: Do they fit the alcohol-depression hypothesis? *Social Psychiatry and Psychiatric Epidemiology, 38*(3), 122–127.

Loos, G. P. (1999). Health promotion planning in Pacific Islander Population groups. In R. M. Huff & M. V. Kline (Eds.), *Promoting health in multicultural population: A handbook for practitioners.* Thousand Oaks, CA: Sage.

Lopez, B., Wang, W., Schwartz, S. J., Prado, G., Huang, S., Brown, C. H., Pantin, H., & Szapocznik, J. (2009). School, family, and peer factors and their association with substance use in Hispanic adolescents. *Journal of Primary Prevention, 30,* 622–641.

Lubben, J. E., Chi, I., & Kitano, H. H. L. (1988). Exploring Filipino American drinking behavior. *Journal of Studies on Alcohol, 49*(1), 26–29.

Luczak, S. E., Elvine-Kreis, B., Shea, S. H., Carr, L. G., & Wall, T. L. (2002). Genetic risk for alcoholism relates to level of response to alcohol in Asian-American men and women. *Journal of Studies on Alcohol, 63,* 74–82.

Lum, D. (2003). *Culturally competent practice* (2nd ed.). Pacific Grove, CA: Brooks/Cole.

Lum, C., Corliss, H., Mays, V., Cochran, S., & Lui, C. (2009). Differences in the drinking behaviors of Chinese, Filipino, Korean, and Vietnamese college students. *Journal of Studies on Alcohol and Drugs, (70)*4, 568–574.

Lundgren, L. M., Amaro, H., & Ben-Ami, L. (2005). Factors associated with drug treatment entry patterns among Hispanic women injection drug users seeking treatment. *Journal of Social Work Practice in the Addictions, 5*(1/2), 157–174.

Lurie, N. O. (1979). The world's oldest on-going protest demonstration: North American Indian drinking patterns. In M. Marshall (Ed.), *Beliefs, behaviors, and alcoholic beverages: A cross-cultural survey* (pp. 127–145). Ann Arbor: University of Michigan Press.

MacAndrew, C., & Edgerton, R. B. (1969). *Drunken comportment: A social explanation.* Chicago: Aldine de Gruyter.

Mail, P. D., & Johnson, S. (1993). Boozing, sniffing, and toking: An overview of the past, present, and future of substance use by American Indians. *American Indian and Alaska Native Mental Health Research, 5*(2), 1–33.

Makimoto, K. (1998). Drinking patterns and drinking problems among Asian-American and Pacific Islanders. *Alcohol Health and Research World, 22,* 270–275.

Marsh, J. C., Cao, D., Geuerrero, E., & Shin, H. (2009). Need-service matching in substance abuse treatment: Racial/ethnic differences. *Evaluation and program planning, 32,* 43–51.

Marsiglia, F. F., Kulis, S., Wagstaff, D. A., Elek, E., & Dran, D. (2005). Acculturation status and substance abuse prevention with Mexican and Mexican American youth. *Journal of Social Work Practice in the Addictions, 5*(1/2), 85 111.

Master, L. (1989). Jewish experience of Alcoholics Anonymous. *Smith College Studies in Social Work, 59*(2), 183–199.

Matsuyoshi, J. (2001). Substance abuse interventions for Japanese and Japanese American clients. In S. L. A. Straussner (Ed.), *Ethnocultural factors in substance abuse treatment* (pp. 393–417). New York: Guilford Press.

May, P. A. (1982). Substance abuse and American Indians: Prevalence and susceptibility. *International Journal of the Addictions, 17*(7), 1185–1209.

May, P. A. (1992). Alcohol policy considerations for Indian reservation and bordertown communities. *American Indian and Alaska Native Mental Health Research, 4*(3), 5–59.

May, P. A. (1994). The epidemiology of alcohol abuse among American Indians: The mythical and real properties. *American Indian Culture and Research Journal, 18*(2), 121–143.

May, P. A. (1996). Overview of alcohol abuse epidemiology for American Indian populations. In G. Sandefur, R. Rindfuss, & B. Cohen (Eds.), *Changing numbers, Changing needs: American Indian demography and public health* (pp. 235–261). Washington, DC: National Academy Press.

May, P. A., Miller, J. H., Goodhart, K. A., Maestas, O. R., Buckley, D., Trujillo, P. M., & Gossage, J. P. (2008). Enhanced case management to prevent fetal alcohol spectrum disorders in Northern Plains communities. *Maternal and Child Health Journal, 12,* 747–759.

May, P., & Moran, J. R. (1997). American Indians. In J. Philleo & F. L. Brisbane (Eds.), *Cultural competence in substance abuse prevention* (pp. 1–31). Washington, DC: NASW Press.

McCabe, S. E., Cranford, J. A., Morales, M., & Young, A. (2006). Simultaneous and concurrent polydrug use of alcohol and prescription drugs: Prevlance, correlates, and consequences. *Journal of Studies on Alcohol, 67,* 529–537.

McCabe, S. E., Morales, M., Cranford, J., Delva, J., McPherson, M., & Boyd, C. (2007). Race/ethnicity and gender differences in drug use and abuse among college students. *Journal of Ethnicity in Substance Abuse, 6*(2),75–95.

McGee, G., & Johnson, L. (1985). *Black, beautiful and recovering.* Center City, MN: Hazelden Foundation.

McQuade, F. X. (1989). Treatment and recovery issues for the addicted Hispanic. *Counselor, 7*(3), 29–30.

Medina, C. (2001). Toward an understanding of Puerto Rican ethnicity and substance abuse. In S. L. A. Straussner (Ed.), *Ethnocultural factors in substance abuse treatment* (pp. 137–163). New York: Guilford Press.

Melus, A. (1980). Culture and language in the treatment of alcoholism. *Alcohol Health & Research World, 4*(4), 19–20.

Menchaca, M. (1993). Chicano Indianism: A historical account of racial repression in the United States. *American Ethnologist, 20*(3), 583–603.

Mercado, M. M. (2000). The invisible family: Counseling Asian American substance abusers and their families. *The Family Journal: Counseling and Therapy for Couples and Families, 8*(3), 267–272.

Miller, L., Tolliver, R., Druschel, C., Fox, D., Schoellhorn, J., Podvin, D., Merrick, S., Cunniff, C., Meaney, F. J., Pensak, M., Dominique, Y., Hymbaugh, K., Boyle, C., & Baio, J. (2002). Fetal alcohol syndrome. *Morbidity and Mortality Weekly Report, 51*(20), 433–435.

Milligan, C. O., Nich, C., & Carroll, K. M. (2004). Ethnic differences in substance abuse treatment retention, compliance, and outcome from two clinical trials. *Psychiatric Services, 55*(2), 167–173.

Miranda, C. (2005). Brief overview of Latino demographics in the twenty-first century: Implications for alcohol-related services. In M. Delgado (Ed.), *Latinos and alcohol use/abuse revisted: Advances and challenges for prevention and treatment programs* (pp. 9–28). Binghamton, NY: Haworth Press.

Mokuau, N. (1997). Pacific Islanders. In J. Philleo & F. L. Brisbane (Eds.), *Cultural competence in substance abuse prevention* (pp. 127–152). Washington, DC: NASW Press.

Mokuau, N. (1999). Substance abuse among Pacific Islanders: Cultural context and implications for prevention programs. In B. W. K. Yee, N. Mokuau, S. Kim, L. G. Epstein, & G. Pacheco (Eds.), *Developing cultural competence in Asian-American and Pacific Islander communities: Opportunities in primary health care and substance abuse prevention* (CSAP Cultural Competence Series no. 5, Special Collaborative Edition, pp. 221–248). Rockville, MD: Center for Substance Abuse Prevention.

Moloney, M., Hunt, G., & Evans, K. (2008). Asian American identity and drug consumption: From acculturation to normalization. *Journal of Ethnicity in Substance Abuse, 7*(4), 376–403.

Monteiro, M. G., & Schuckit, M. A. (1989). Alcohol, drug, and mental health problems among Jewish and Christian men at a university. *American Journal of Drug and Alcohol Abuse, 15*(4), 403–412.

Moore, S. E. (2001). Substance abuse treatment with adolescent African American males: Reality therapy with an Afrocentric approach. *Journal of Social Work Practice in the Addictions, 1*(2), 21–32.

Moran, J. R. (1999). Preventing alcohol use among urban American Indian youth: The Seventh Generation program. *Journal of Human Behavior in the Social Environment, 2*(1–2), 51–67.

Moran, J. R., & May, P. A. (1997). American Indians. In J. Philleo & F. L. Brisbane (Eds.), *Cultural competence in substance abuse prevention* (pp. 1–31). Washington, DC: NASW Press.

Morelli, P. T. T., & Fong, R. (2000). The role of Hawaiian elders in substance abuse treatment among Asian/Pacific Islander women. *Journal of Family Social Work, 4*(4), 33–44.

Morgan, R., & Freeman, L. (2009). The healing of our people: Substance abuse and historical trauma. *Substance Use & Misuse, 44,* 84–98.

Nagasawa, R., Qian, Z., & Wong, P. (2000). Social control theory as a theory of conformity: The case of Asian Pacific drug and alcohol nonuse. *Sociological Perspectives, 43,* 581–603.

Nakashima, J., & Wong, M. M. (2000). Characteristics of alcohol consumption, correlates of alcohol misuse among Korean American adolescents. *Journal of Drug Education, 30,* 343–359.

National Center for Education Statistics. (2010). *The condition of education 2010* (NCES 2010-028), Indicator 20. *Status dropout rates of 16- through 24-year-olds, by race/ethnicity: Selected years, 1980–2008.* Washington, DC: U.S. Department of Education. Retrieved February 28, 2011, from nces.ed.gov/fastfacts/display.asp?id=16.

National Highway Traffic Safety Administration. (2009). Traffic safety facts, 2006 data, race and ethnicity. Washington, DC: U.S. Department of Transportation.

Retrieved March 7, 2011, from www-nrd.nhtsa.dot.gov/Pubs/810995.PDF.

National Institute on Alcohol Abuse and Alcoholism (NIAAA). (1985). *Alcohol topics: Research review, alcohol and Native Americans.* Rockville, MD: Author.

National Institute on Alcohol Abuse and Alcoholism (NIAAA). (2002, January). Alcohol and minorities: An update. *Alcohol Alert, 55.*

National Institute on Drug Abuse. (2004, July). *Strategic plan on reducing health disparities. NIH Health Disparities Strategic Plan, Fiscal Year 2004–2008.* Retrieved May 2, 2011, from www.nida.nih.gov/PDF/HealthDispPlan.pdf.

National Latino Council on Alcohol and Tobacco Prevention and National Highway Traffic Safety Administration. (2007). *Priorities for reducing alcohol-related driving among Latino communities.* Retrieved January 25, 2011, from www.nhtsa.gov/staticfiles/nti/pdf/811263.pdf.

Neumark, Y. D., Friedlander, Y., Thomasson, H. R., & Li, T. (1998). Association of the ADH*2 allele with reduced ethanol consumption in Jewish men in Israel: A pilot study. *Journal of Studies on Alcohol, 59,* 133–139.

Niv, N., Pham, R., & Hser, L. (2009). Racial and ethnic differences in substance abuse service needs, utilization, and outcomes in California. *Psychiatric Services, 60*(10), 1350–1356.

Niv, N., Wong, E. C., & Hser, Y. (2007). Asian Americans in community-based substance abuse treatment: Service needs, utilization, and outcomes. *Journal of Substance Abuse Treatment, 33,* 313–319.

Nobles, W. W., Goddard, L. L., & Gilbert, D. J. (2009). Culturecology, women, and African-centered HIV prevention. *Journal of Black Psychology, 35*(2), 228–246.

Nofz, M. P. (1988). Alcohol abuse and culturally marginal American Indians. *Social Casework, 69*(2), 67–73.

Norton, D. G. (1978). *The dual perspective: Inclusion of ethnic minority content in the social work curriculum.* New York: Council on Social Work Education.

Oetting, E. R., & Beauvais, F. (1989). Epidemiology and correlates of alcohol use among Indian adolescents living on reservations. In D. Spiegler, D. Tate, S. Aitken, & C. Christian (Eds.), *Alcohol use among U.S. ethnic minorities: Proceedings of a conference on the epidemiology of alcohol use and abuse among ethnic minority groups, September 1985* (NIAAA Research Monograph no. 18, pp. 239–267). Rockville, MD: National Institute on Alcohol Abuse and Alcoholism.

Oetting, E. R., Beauvais, F., & Goldstein, G. S. (1982). *Drug abuse among Native American youth: Summary of findings* (1975–1981). Fort Collins: Colorado State University.

Office of Applied Studies. (2002, September 13). *Low rates of alcohol use among Asian youths.* Rockville, MD: Substance Abuse and Mental Health Services Administration. Retrieved January 17, 2011, from oas.samhsa.gov/2k2/AsianYouthAlc/AsianYouthAlc.pdf.

Office of Applied Studies. (2007). *Substance use and substance use disorders among American Indians and Alaska Natives.* Rockville, MD: Substance Abuse and Mental Health Services Administration. Retrieved March 12, 2011, from www.oas.samhsa.gov/2k7/AmIndians/AmIndians.pdf.

Office of Applied Studies. (2010). *Treatment Episode Data Set (TEDS), 1998–2008. National Admissions to Substance Abuse Treatment Services* (DASIS Series: S-50, HHS Publication No. (SMA) 09-4471). Rockville, MD: Substance Abuse and Mental Health Services Administration. Retrieved February 24, 2011, from wwwdasis.samhsa.gov/teds08/teds2k8natweb.pdf.

Office of Justice Programs. (2000). *Promising practices and strategies to reduce alcohol and substance abuse among American Indians and Alaska natives.* Washington, DC: U.S. Department of Justice.

Ogawa, B. K. (1999). *E hana pono:* Issues of responsibility, justice, and culture in the design and practice of prevention programs for Pacific Islanders. In B. W. K. Yee, N. Mokuau, S. Kim, L. G. Epstein, & G. Pacheco (Eds.), *Developing cultural competence in Asian-American and Pacific Islander communities: Opportunities in primary health care and substance abuse prevention* (CSAP Cultural Competence Series no. 5, Special Collaborative Edition, pp. 249–277). Rockville, MD: Center for Substance Abuse Prevention.

"Old country values" influence Asian-American drinking. (1986–87). *Alcohol Health and Research World, 11*(2), 47.

Olitzky, K. M., & Copans, S. A. (1991). *Twelve Jewish steps to recovery: A personal guide to turning from alcoholism and other addictions* (Twelve step recovery). Woodstock, VT: Jewish Lights.

Outspoken; A Conversation With Grace Flores-Hughes Hispanic wordsmith. (July 26, 2009). *Washington Post,* p. B2.

Parks, C. A., Hesselbrock, M. N., Hesselbrock, V. M., & Segal, B. (2001). Gender and reported health problems in treated alcohol dependent Alaska Natives. *Journal of Studies on Alcohol, 62,* 286–293.

Park, S., Shibusawa, T., Yoon, S. M., & Son, H. (2010). Characteristics of Chinese and Korean Americans in outpatient treatment for alcohol use disorders examining heterogeneity among Asian American subgroups. *Journal of Ethnicity in Substance Abuse, 9,* 128–142.

Parker, L. (1990). The missing component in substance abuse prevention efforts: A Native American example. *Contemporary Drug Problems, 17*(2), 251–270.

Parker, K. D., Calhoun, T., & Weaver, G. (2000). Variables associated with adolescent alcohol use: A multiethnic comparison. *Journal of Social Psychology, 140,* 51–62.

Perron, B. E., Alexander-Eitzman, B., Watkins, D., Taylor, R. J., Baser, R., Neighbors, H. W., & Jackson, J. S. (2009). Ethnic differences in delays to treatment for substance use disorders: African Americans, Black Caribbeans and non-Hispanic whites. *Journal of Psychoactive Drugs, 41*(4), 369–377.

Phin, J. G., & Phillips, P. (1981). Drug treatment entry patterns and socioeconomic characteristics of Asian American,

Native American, and Puerto Rican clients. In A. J. Schecter (Ed.), *Drug dependence and alcoholism, Vol. 2: Social and behavioral issues* (pp. 803–818). New York: Plenum Press.

Ponterotto, J. G., Casas, J. M., Suzuki, L. A., & Alexander, C. M. (2010). *Handbook of multicultural counseling* (3rd ed.). Thousand Oaks, CA: Sage.

Prado, G., Huan, S., Schwartz, S. J., Maldonado-Molina, M. M. Bandiera, F. C., de la Rosa, M., & Pantin, H. (2009). What accoutns for differences in substance use among U.S.-born and immigrant Hispanic adolescents?: Results form a longitudinal prospective cohort study. *Journal of Adolescent Health, 45,* 118–125.

Prevention of alcohol abuse among black Americans: An interview with Thomas D. Watts and Roosevelt Wright, Jr. (1986/87). *Alcohol Health and Research World, 11*(2), 40–41, 65.

Prugh, T. (1986–87). The black church: A foundation for recovery. *Alcohol Health and Research World, 11*(2), 52–54.

Prins, E. (2007). Interdistrict transfers, Latino/White school segregation, and institutional racism in a small California town. *Journal of Latinos and Education, 6*(4), 285–308.

Ramsperger, K. B. (1989). Salvation for an invisible people. *Counselor 7*(3), 21–23.

Rastogi, M., & Wadha, S. (2006). Substance abuse among Asian Indians in the United States: A consideration of cultural factors in etiology and treatment. *Substance Use and Misuse, 41,* 1239–1249.

Ravid, M. (2009, November 11). Alcohol is killing Israel. *Ynetnews.* Retrieved February 1, 2011, from www.ynetnews.com/articles/0,7340,L-3802814,00.html.

Rebhun, L. A. (1998). Substance use among immigrants to the United States. In S. Loue (Ed.), *Handbook of immigrant health* (pp. 493–519). New York: Plenum Press.

Red Horse, J. G. (1980). Family structure and value orientation in American Indians. *Social Casework, 61*(8), 462–467.

Reid, D. J. (2000). Addiction, African Americans, and a Christian recovery journey. In J. Krestan (Ed.), *Bridges to recovery: Addiction, family therapy, and multicultural treatment* (pp. 145–172). New York: Free Press.

Reid, W. J., & Epstein, L. (1972). *Task-centered casework.* New York: Columbia University Press.

Rhoades, E. R., Mason, R. D., Eddy, P., Smith, E. M., & Burns, T. R. (1988). The Indian health service approach to alcoholism among American Indians and Alaska Natives. *Public Health Reports, 103*(6), 621–627.

Ringwalt, C., Graham, P., Sanders-Philpis, K., Porune, D., & Paschall, M. G. (1999). Ethnic identity as a protective factor in the health behaviors of African American male adolescents. In S. B. Kar (Ed.), *Substance abuse prevention: A multicultural perspective* (pp. 131–151). Amityville, NY: Baywood.

Roberts, A., Jackson, M. S., & Carlton-LaNey, I. (2000). Revisiting the need for feminism and Afrocentric theory when treating African-American female substance abusers. *Journal of Drug Issues, 30,* 901–918.

Rodriguez-Andrew, S. (1984, March/April). *Los niños:* Intervention efforts with Mexican-American families. *Focus on Family and Chemical Dependency, 8,* 20.

Rothe, E. M., & Ruiz, P. (2001). Substance abuse among Cuban Americans. *Ethnocultural factors in substance abuse treatment, 30,* 368–392.

Sakai, J. T., Ho, M. P., Shore, J. H., Risk, N. K., & Price R. K. (2005). Asians in the United States: Substance dependence and use of substance-dependence treatment. *Journal of Substance Abuse Treatment, 29,* 75–84.

Sakai, J. T., Wang, C., & Price, R. K. (2010). Substance use and dependence among Native Hawaiians, other Pacific Islanders, and Asian ethnic groups in the United States: Contrasting multiple-race and single-race prevalence rates from a national survey. *Journal of Ethnicity in Substance Abuse, 9*(3), 173–185.

Sandhu, D. S., & Malik, R. (2001). Ethnocultural background and substance abuse treatment of Asian Indian Americans. In S. L. A. Straussner (Ed.), *Ethnocultural factors in substance abuse treatment* (pp. 97–110). New York: Guilford Press.

Santiago-Rivera, A. L. (1995). Developing a culturally sensitive treatment modality for bilingual Spanish-speaking clients: Incorporating language and culture in counseling. *Journal of Counseling and Development, 76,* 12–17.

Santiago-Rivera, A., Arredondo, P., & Gallardo-Cooper, M. (2002). *Counseling Latinos and la familia: A practical guide.* Thousand Oaks: Sage Publications.

Schmidt, L. A., Ye, Y., Greenfield, T. K., & Bond, J. (2007). Ethnic disparities in clinical severity and services for alcohol problems: Results from the National Alcohol Survey. *Alcoholism: Clinical and Experimental Research, 31*(1), 48–56.

Sciarra, D. T., & Ponterotto, J. G. (1991). Counseling the Hispanic bilingual family: Challenges to the therapeutic process. *Psychotherapy, 28,* 173–179.

Sellers, C. S., Winfree, L. T., Jr., & Griffiths, C. T. (1993). Legal attitudes, permissive norm qualities, and substance use: A comparison of American Indian and non-Indian youth. *Journal of Drug Issues, 23*(3), 493–513.

Shorkey, C., Garcia, E., & Windsor, L. (2010). Spirituality as a strength in the Latino community. In R. Furman & N. Negi (Eds.), *Social work practice with Latinos: Key issues and emerging themes* (pp. 85–101). Chicago: Lyceum.

Simonelli, R. (2000). Culturally specific addiction recovery for Native Americans. In J. Krestan (Ed.), *Bridges to recovery: Addiction, family therapy, and multicultural treatment* (pp. 77–79). New York: Free Press.

Singer, K. (1972). Drinking patterns and alcoholism in the Chinese. *British Journal of Addiction, 67,* 3–14.

Singer, K. (1974). The choice of intoxicant among the Chinese. *British Journal of Addiction, 69,* 257–268.

Singh, G. K., & Hoyert, D. L. (2000). Social epidemiology of chronic liver disease and cirrhosis mortality in the United States: Trends and differentials by ethnicity, socioeconomic status, and alcohol consumption. *Human Biology, 72,* 801–820.

Smedley, G. D., Stith, A. Y., & Nelson, A. R. (2003). *Unequal treatment: Confronting racial and ethnic disparities in health care.* Washington, DC: National Academies Press.

Snowden, L. R., & Lieberman, M. A. (1994). African-American participation in self-help groups. In T. J. Powell (Ed.), *Understanding the self-help organization: Frameworks and findings* (pp. 50–61). Thousand Oaks, CA: Sage.

Snyder, C. R. (1958). *Alcohol and the Jews: A cultural study of drinking and sobriety.* Glencoe, IL: Free Press.

Snyder, C. R., Palgi, P., Eldar, P., & Elian, B. (1982). Alcoholism among the Jews in Israel: A pilot study, 1. Research rationale and a look at the ethnic factor. *Journal of Studies on Alcohol, 43*(7), 623–654.

Solomon, B. B. (1976). *Black empowerment: Social work in oppressed communities.* New York: Columbia University Press.

Spicer, P. (1998). Drinking, foster care, and the intergenerational continuity of parenting in an urban Indian community. *American Indian Culture and Research Journal, 22*, 335–360.

Spicer, P., Beals, J., Croy, C. D., Mitchell, C. M., Novins, D. K., Moore, L., & Manson, S. M. (2003). The prevalence of DSM-III-R alcohol dependence in two American Indian populations. *Alcoholism: Clinical and Experimental Research, 27*(11), 1785–1797.

Spiegel, M. C., & Kravitz, Y. (2001). Confronting addiction. In D. A. Friedman, *Jewish pastoral care: A practical handbook from traditional and contemporary sources* (pp. 264–285). Woodstock, VT: Jewish Highlights Publishing.

Spillane, N. S., & Smith, G. T. (2007). A theory of reservation-dwelling American Indian alcohol use risk. *Psychological Bulletin, 133*(3), 395–418.

Springer, J. F., Sale, E., Kasim, R., Winter, W., Sambrano, S., & Chipungu, S. (2004). Effectiveness of culturally specific approaches to substance abuse prevention: Findings from CSAP's national cross-site evaluation of high risk youth programs. *Journal of Ethnic & Cultural Diversity in Social Work, 13*(3), 1–23.

Steiker, L. H. (2011). Judaism, alcoholism, and recovery: The experience of being Jewish and alcoholic. *Journal of Social Work Practice in the Addictions, 11*(1), 90–95.

Stevens-Watkins, D., & Rostosky, S. (2010). Binge drinking in African American males from adolescence to young adulthood: The protective influence of religiosity, family connectedness, and close friends' substance use. *Substance Use & Misuse, 45*(10), 1435–1451.

Stivers, C. (1994). Drug prevention in Zuni, New Mexico: Creation of a teen center as an alternative to alcohol and drug use. *Journal of Community Health, 19*(5), 343–359.

Stoil, M. J. (1987/88). The case of the missing gene: Hereditary protection against alcoholism. *Alcohol Health and Research World, 12*(2), 130–136.

Stratton, R., Zeiner, A., & Paredes, A. (1978). Tribal affiliation and prevalence of alcohol problems. *Journal of Studies on Alcohol, 39*(7), 1175.

Straussner, S. L. A. (2001). Jewish substance abusers: Existing but invisible. In S. L. A. Straussner (Ed.), *Ethnocultural factors in substance abuse treatment* (pp. 291–317). New York: Guilford Press.

Streltzer, J. M., & Tseng, W. S. (2008). *Cultural competence in health care.* New York: Springer.

Streissguth, A. F. (1994). Fetal alcohol syndrome: Understanding the problem; Understanding the solution; What Indian communities can do. *American Indian Culture and Research Journal, 18*(3), 45–83.

Suarez, L., & Ramirez, A. G. (1999). Hispanic/Latino health and disease: An overview. In R. M. Huff & M. V. Kline (Eds.), *Promoting health in multicultural populations: A handbook for practitioners* (pp. 115–136). Thousand Oaks, CA: Sage.

Subramanian, S. K., & Takeuchi, D. (1999). The complexities of diversity: Substance abuse among Asian Americans. In S. B. Kar (Ed.), *Substance abuse prevention: A multicultural perspective* (pp. 185–198). Amitiville, NY: Baywood.

Substance Abuse and Mental Health Services Administration. (2008, September). 2007 National Survey on Drug Use and Health: Detailed Tables. Rockville, MD: U.S. Department of Health and Human Services. Retrieved May 30, 2011, from http://oas.samhsa.gov/NSDUH/2k7NSDUH/tabs/TOC.htm.

Substance Abuse and Mental Health Services Administration. (2009). *Results from the 2008 National Survey on Drug Use and Health: National findings* (Office of Applied Studies, NSDUH Series H-36, HHS Publication No. SMA 09–4434). Rockville, MD: U.S. Department of Health and Human Services Retrieved April 6, 2011, from www.oas.samhsa.gov/nsduh/2k8nsduh/2k8results.cfm.

Substance Abuse and Mental Health Services Administration, Office of Applied Studies. (2010a). *Results from the 2009 National Survey on Drug Use and Health: Volume I. Summary of national findings* (Office of Applied Studies, NSDUH Series H-38A, HHS Publication No. SMA 10–4586). Rockville, MD: U.S. Department of Health and Human Services. Retrieved March 28, 2011, from oas.samhsa.gov/NSDUH/2k9NSDUH/2k9ResultsP.pdf.

Substance Abuse and Mental Health Services Administration, Office of Applied Studies. (2010b). *Drug Abuse Warning Network, 2007: National Estimates of Drug-Related Emergency Department Visits.* Rockville, MD: U.S. Department of Health and Human Services. Retrieved February 26, 2011, from dawninfo.samhsa.gov/files/ED2007/DAWN2k7ED.pdf.

Substance Abuse and Mental Health Services Administration, Office of Applied Studies. (2010c, May 20). *The NSDUH Report: Substance use among Asian adults.* Rockville, MD: Author. Retrieved February 5, 2011, from www.oas.samhsa.gov/2k10/179/SUAsian Adults.htm.

Sue, D. (1987). Use and abuse of alcohol by Asian Americans. *Journal of Psychoactive Drugs, 19*(1), 57–66.

Sue, D. W., & Sue, D. (2008). *Counseling the culturally diverse: Theory and practice* (5th ed.). New York: John Wiley & Sons.

Szapocznik, J., Hervis, O., & Schwartz, S. (2003). *Brief strategic family therapy for adolescent drug abuse.* Bethesda, MD: National Institute on Drug Abuse.

Takeuchi, D. T., Zane, N., Hong, S., Chae, D., Gong, F., Gee, G., Walton, E., Sue, S., & Alegria, M. (2007). Immigration-related factors and mental disorders among Asian Americans. *American Journal of Public Health, 97*(1), 84–90.

Taylor, V. (1987). The triumph of the Alkali Lake Indian Band. *Alcohol Health and Research World, 12*(1), 57.

Teller, B. (1989). Chemical dependency in the Jewish community. *Counselor, 7*(3), 27–28.

Thomas, L. R., Donovan, D. M., Sigo, R. L. W., Austin, L., Marlatt, G. A., & the Susquamish Tribe. (2009). The community pulling together: A tribal community-university partnership project to reduce substance abuse and promote good health in a reservation tribal community. *Journal of Ethnicity in Substance Abuse, 8*(3), 283–300.

Tonigan, S., Miller, W. R., Juarez, P., & Villanueva, M. (2002). Utilization of AA by Hispanic and non-Hispanic white clients receiving outpatient alcohol treatment. *Journal of Studies on Alcohol, 63*(2), 215–218.

Towle, L. H. (1988). Japanese-American drinking: Some results from the joint Japanese-U.S. alcohol epidemiology project. *Alcohol Health and Research World, 12*(3 & 4), 216–223, 314–315.

Townsend, T. G., & Belgrave, F. Z. (2009). Eliminating health disparities: Challenges for African American psychologists. *Journal of Black Psychology, 35*(2), 146–153.

Tran, A. G. T. T., Lee, R. M., & Burgess, D. J. (2010). Perceived discrimination and substance use in Hispanic/Latino, African-born black, and Southeast Asian immigrants. *Cultural Diversity and Ethnic Minority Psychology, 16*(2), 226–236.

Tu, G., & Israel, Y. (1995). Alcohol consumption by Orientals in North America is predicted largely by a single gene. *Behavior Genetics, 25*(1), 59–65.

Ullman, A. D. (1958). Sociocultural backgrounds of alcoholism. *Annals of the American Academy of Political and Social Science, 315,* 48–54.

United States Sentencing Commission. (2011, January 28). *Analysis of the Impact of Amendment to the Statutory Penalties for Crack Cocaine Offenses Made by the Fair Sentencing Act of 2010 and Corresponding Proposed Permanent Guideline Amendment if the Guideline Amendment Were Applied Retroactively.* Washington, DC. Retrieved February 26, 2011, from www.ussc.gov/Research/Retroactivity_Analyses/Fair_Sentencing_Act/20110128_Crack_Retroactivity_Analysis.pdf.

Unrau, W. E. (1996). *White man's wicked water: The alcohol trade and prohibition in Indian Country, 1802–1892.* Lawrence: University Press of Kansas.

U.S. Census Bureau. (2010a, November). *Facts for features: American Indian and Alaska Native Heritage Month: November 2010.* Retrieved May 2, 2011, from www.census.gov/newsroom/releases/archives/facts_for_features_special_editions/cb10ff22.html.

U.S. Census Bureau. (2010b, December 2). *Facts for features: Black (African-American) History Month: February 2011.* Retrieved February 25, 2011, from www.census.gov/newsroom/releases/archives/facts_for_features_special_editions/cb11ff_01.html.

U.S. Census Bureau. (2010c, July 15). *Facts for features: Hispanic Heritage Month 2010: Sept. 15-Oct. 15.* Retrieved May 2, 2011 from www.census.gov/newsroom/releases/archives/facts_for_features_special_editions/cb10-ff17.html.

U.S. Census Bureau. (2011, March 8). *Facts for features: Asian Pacific American Heritage Month: May 2011.* Washington, DC: U.S. Department of Commerce. Retrieved March, 2011, from www.census.gov/newsroom/releases/archives/facts_for_features_special_editions/cb11-ff06.html.

U.S. Department of Health and Human Services. (1985). *Report of the Secretary's task force on black & minority health, Vol. 1, executive summary.* Washington, DC: Author.

VA Hospital calls in "Medicine Man" to Help Indians Beat Alcoholism. (1991, August 25). *Austin American-Statesman,* p. D28.

Vaeth, P., Caetano, R., Ramisetty-Mikler, S., & Rodriguez, L. (2009). Hispanic Americans Baseline Alcohol Survey (HABLAS): Alcohol-related problems across Hispanic national groups. *Journal of Studies on Alcohol and Drugs,* 991–999.

van Ryn, M., & Burke, J. (2000). The effect of patient race and socio-economic status on physician's perceptions of patients. *Social Science and Medicine, 50,* 813–828.

Van Steele, K. R., Allen, G. A., & Moberg, D. P. (1998). Alcohol and drug prevention among American Indian families: The Family Circles program. *Drugs and Society, 12*(1–2), 53–60.

Valadez, J. (2001). *Deliberative democracy, political legitimacy, and self determination.* Boulder: Westview Press.

Valadez, J. (2003). Pre-Columbian and modern philosophical perspectives in Latin America. In R. Solomon & K. Higgins (Eds.), *From Africa to Zen* (2nd ed., pp. 67–103). Lanham, MD: Rowman & Littlefield Publishers, Inc.

Vex, S. L., & Blume, S. B. (2001). The JACS Study I: Characteristics of a population of chemically dependent Jewish men and women. *Journal of Addictive Diseases, 20*(4), 71–89.

Vidourek, R. A., & King, K. A. (2010). Risk and protective factors for recent alcohol use among African-American youth. *Journal of Drug Education, 40*(4), 411–425.

Villalobos, J. (2005). Mitos, leyendas, e historia del tequila, 1 parte. (Spanish). *Xipe Totek, 14*(1), 35–48.

Wahl, A., & Eitle, T. (2010). Gender, acculturation and alcohol use among Latina/o adolescents: A multi-ethnic comparison. *Journal of Immigrant Minority Health, 12,* 153–165.

Wallace, J. M. (1999). The social ecology of addiction: Race, risk, and resilience. *Pediatrics, 103,* 1122–1127.

Walls, M. L., Whitbeck, L. B., Hoyt, D. R. (2007). Early-onset alcohol use among Native American youth: Examining female caretaker influence. *Journal of Marriage and Family, 69,* 451–464.

Wang, R. R. (1968). A study of alcoholism in Chinatown. *International Journal of Social Psychiatry, 14,* 260–267.

Watson, B., & Jones, D. (1989). Drug use and African Americans. *Runtafac Sheet of the National Urban League, 2.*

Weaver, H. N. (2001). Native Americans and substance abuse. In S. L. A. Straussner (Ed.), *Ethnocultural factors in substance abuse treatment* (pp. 77–96). New York: Guilford Press.

Weibel, J. C. (1982). American Indians, urbanization, and alcohol: A developing urban Indian drinking ethos. In *Special population issues* (NIAAA Alcohol and Health Monograph no. 4, pp. 331–358). Washington DC: National Institute on Alcohol Abuse and Alcoholism.

Weibel-Orlando, J. C. (1984). Substance abuse among American Indian youth: A continuing crisis. *Journal of Drug Issues, 14*(2), 313–335.

Weibel-Orlando, J. C. (1986/87). Drinking patterns of urban and rural American Indians. *Alcohol Health and Research World, 11*(2), 8–12, 54.

Weiss, S. (1988). Primary prevention of excessive drinking and the Jewish culture—Preventive efforts in Israel, 1984–1985. *Journal of Primary Prevention, 8*(4), 218.

Weiss, S. (1995). Israel. In D. B. Heath (Ed.), *International handbook on alcohol and culture* (pp. 142–155). Westport, CT: Greenwood Press.

Weiss, S. (1999). Attitudes of Israeli Jewish and Arab high school students toward alcohol control measures. *Journal of Drug Education, 29,* 41–52.

Weiss, S., & Eldar, P. (1987). Alcohol and alcohol problems research. 14. Israel. *British Journal of Addiction, 82,* 227–235.

Weiss, S., & Gefen, L. (2003). The Israeli Society for the Prevention of Alcoholism. *Addiction, 98*(3), 255–259.

West, H. C., Sabol, W. J., & Greenman, S. J. (2010, December). *Prisoners in 2009.* Washington, DC: Bureau of Justice Statistics, U.S. Department of Justice. Retrieved February 26, 2011, from bjs.ojp.usdoj.gov/content/pub/pdf/p09.pdf (See especially Tables 14, 15, 16c, and 17c).

Whitbeck, L. B., Yu, M., Johnson, K. D., Hoyt, D. R., & Walls, M. L. (2008). Diagnostic prevalence rates from early to mid-adolescence among indigenous adolescents: First results from a longitudinal study. *Journal of the American Academy of Adolescent Psychiatry, 47* (98), 890–900.

Whitesell, N. R., Beals, J., Mitchell, C. M., Manson, S. M., Turner, J., & the AI-SUPERPFP Team. (2009). Childhood exposure to adversity and risk of substance-use disorder in two American Indian populations: The mediational role of early substance-use initiation. *Journal of Studies on Alcohol and Drugs, 70,* 971–981.

Whittaker, J. (1963). Alcohol and the Standing Rock Sioux tribe. II. Psychodynamic and cultural factors in drinking. *Quarterly Journal of Studies on Alcohol, 24,* 80–90.

Williams, C. (2008). Cultural pain and anger as causal factors to substance abuse in an African-American male clinical population: An exploration with implications for treatment. Dissertation, Union Institute and University, Cincinnati, OH, 2008. *Dissertation Abstracts International.* (Publication number: AAT 3321619).

Willie, E. (1989). The story of Alkali Lake: Anomaly of community recovery or national trend in Indian country? *Alcoholism Treatment Quarterly, 6*(3/4), 167–173.

Winkler, A. M. (1968). Drinking on the American frontier. *Quarterly Journal of Studies on Alcohol, 29,* 413–445.

Wong, F. Y., Huang, Z. J., Thompson, E. E., De Leon, J. M., Shah, M. S., Park, R. J., et. al. (2007). Substance use among a sample of foreign- and U.S.-born Southeast Asians in an urban setting. *Journal of Ethnicity and Substance Abuse, 6*(1), 45–66.

Woodard, A., Kai, B., Taylor, R., Chatters, L., Baser, R., Perron, B., & Jackson, J. (2009). Complementary and alternative medicine for mental disorders among African Americans, Black Caribbeans, and whites. *Psychiatric Services, 60*(10), 1342–1349.

Wright, R. J., Kail, B. L., & Creecy, R. E. (1990). Culturally sensitive social work practice with black alcoholics and their families. In S. M. L. Logan, E. M. Freeman, & R. G. McRoy (Eds.), *Social work practice with black families* (pp. 203–222). New York: Longman.

Yee, B. W. K. (1999). Strategic opportunities and challenges for primary health care: Developing cultural competence for Asian-American and Pacific Islander communities. In B. W. K. Yee, N. Mokuau, S. Kim, L. G. Epstein, & G. Pacheco (Eds.), *Developing cultural competence in Asian-American and Pacific Islander communities: Opportunities in primary health care and substance abuse prevention* (CSAP Cultural Competence Series no. 5, Special Collaborative Edition, pp. 1–38). Rockville, MD: Center for Substance Abuse Prevention.

Yi, J., & Daniel, A. M. (2001). Substance use among Vietnamese American college students. *College Student Journal, 35*(1), 13–23.

Yoon, Y., & Yi, H. (2010). *Liver cirrhosis mortality in the United States, 1970–2007.* Surveillance Report #88. Bethesda, MD: National Institute on Alcohol Abuse and Alcoholism. Retrieved April 30, 2011, from pubs.niaaa.nih.gov/publications/surveillance88/cirr07.htm.

Young, R., & Joe, J. (2009). Some thoughts about the epidemiology of alcohol and drug use among American Indian/Alaska Native populations. *Journal of Ethnicity in Substance Abuse, 8*(3), 223–241.

Yu, M., & Stiffman, A. R. (2007). Culture and environment as predictors of alcohol abuse/dependence symptoms in American Indian youths. *Addictive Behaviors, 32,* 2253–2259.

Yuan, N. P., Eaves, E. R., Koss, M. P., Polacca, M., Beletzer, K., & Goldman, D. (2010). "Alcohol is something that has been with us like a common cold": Community perceptions of American Indian drinking. *Substance Use & Misuse, 45,* 1909–1929.

Zane, N., Aoki, B., Ho, T., Huang, L., & Jang, M. (1998). Dosage-related changes in a culturally-responsive prevention program for Asian American youth. *Drugs and Society, 12,* 105–125.

Zemore, S., Mulia, N., Ye, Y., Borges, G., & Greenfield, T. (2009). Gender, acculturation, and other barriers to alcohol treatment utilization among Latinos in three National Alcohol Surveys. *Journal of Substance Abuse Treatment, 36,* 446–456.

Ziter, M. L. P. (1987). Culturally sensitive treatment of black alcoholic families. *Social Work, 32*(2), 130–135.

Zuniga, M. E. (1991). "Dichos" as metaphorical tools for Latino clients. *Psychotherapy, 28,* 480–483.

CHAPTER 12

Alcoholics Anonymous (AA). (1976). *Alcoholics Anonymous* (3rd ed.). New York: Alcoholics Anonymous World Services.

Anderson, S. (2009). *Substance use disorders in lesbian, gay, bisexual, and transgender clients.* New York: Columbia University Press.

Appleby, G. A., & Anastas, J. W. (1998). *Not just a passing phase: Social work with gay, lesbian, and bisexual people.* New York: Columbia University Press.

Austin, E. L., & Irwin, J. A. (2010). Age differences in the correlates of problematic alcohol use among Southern lesbians. *Journal of Studies on Alcohol and Drugs, 71,* 295–298.

Berkman, C., & Zinberg, G. (1997). Homophobia and heterosexism in social workers. *Social Work, 12,* 319–332.

Bickelhaupt, E. E. (1995). Alcoholism and drug abuse in gay and lesbian persons: A review of incidence studies. *Journal of Gay and Lesbian Social Services, 2,* 5–14.

Bittle, W. E. (1982). Alcoholics Anonymous and the gay alcoholic. *Journal of Homosexuality, 7*(4), 81–88.

Blume, E. S. (1985). Substance abuse (of being queer, magic pills, and social lubricants). In H. Hidalgo, T. L. Peterson, & N. J. Woodman (Eds.), *Lesbian and gay issues: A resource manual for social workers* (pp. 79–87). Silver Spring, MD: National Association of Social Workers.

Borden, A. (2007). *The history of gay people in Alcoholics Anonymous.* New York: Haworth Press.

Bradford, J., Ryan, C., & Rothblum, E. D. (1994). National Lesbian Health Care Survey: Implications for mental health care. *Journal of Consulting and Clinical Psychology, 62*(2), 228–242.

Cabaj, R. P. (1995). Sexual orientation and the addictions. *Journal of Gay and Lesbian Psychotherapy, 2*(3), 97–117.

Cabaj, R. P. (2000). Substance abuse, internalized homophobia, and gay men and lesbians: Psychodynamic issues and clinical implications. *Journal of Gay and Lesbian Psychotherapy, 3*(3/4), 5–24.

Cabaj, R. P., Gorman, M., Pellicio, W. J., Ghindia, D. J., & Neisen, J. H. (2001). An overview for providers treating LGBT clients. In *A provider's introduction to substance abuse treatment for lesbian, gay, bisexual and transgender individuals* (pp. 1–14). Rockville, MD: U.S. Department of Health and Human Services.

Cass, V. (1979). Homosexual identity formation: A theoretical model. *Journal of Homosexuality, 4*(3), 219–235.

Cochran, S. D., & Mays, V. M. (2000). Relation between psychiatric syndromes and behaviorally defined sexual orientation in a sample of the U.S. population. *American Journal of Epidemiology, 151*(5), 516–523.

Cochran, B. N., Peavy, M., & Cauce, A. M. (2007). Substance abuse treatment providers' explicit and implicit attitudes regarding sexual minorities. *Journal of Homosexuality, 53*(3), 181–207.

Corliss, H. L., Rosario, M., Wypij, D., Wylie, S. A., Frazier, A. L., & Austin, S. B. (2010). Sexual orientation and drug use in a longitudinal cohort study of U.S. adolescents. *Addictive Behaviors, 35,* 517–521.

Crisp, C. (2003). Selected characteristics of research on lesbian women: 1995–1997. *Journal of Homosexuality, 44*(1), 139–155.

Davies, D. (1996). Towards a model of gay affirmative therapy. In D. Davies & C. Neal (Eds.), *Pink therapy: A guide for counsellors and therapists working with lesbian, gay and bisexual clients* (pp. 24–40). Philadelphia: Open University Press.

Dilley, J. A., Simmons, K. W., Boysun, M. J., Pizacani, B. A., & Stark, M. J. (2010). Demonstrating the importance and feasibility of including sexual orientation in public health surveys: Health disparities in the Pacific Northwest. *American Journal of Public Health, 100*(3), 460–467.

Dworkin, S. H. (2001). Treating the bisexual client. *Psychotherapy in Practice, 57,* 671–680.

Eichberg, R. (1991). *Coming out: An act of love.* New York: Penguin.

Eliason, M. J. (2000). Substance abuse counselors' attitudes regarding lesbian, gay, bisexual, and transgendered clients. *Journal of Substance Abuse, 12,* 311–328.

Fals-Stewart, W., O'Farrell, T. J., & Lam, W. K. K. (2009). Behavioral couple therapy for gay and lesbian couples with alcohol use disorders. *Journal of Substance Abuse Treatment, 37,* 379–387.

Fellin, P. (1998). Teaching about sexual orientation from a community context. *Journal of Teaching in Social Work, 16*(1/2), 19–31.

Fox, R. C. (1996). Bisexuality: An examination of theory and research. In R. Cabaj & T. Stein (Eds.), *Textbook of homosexuality and mental health* (pp. 147–171). Washington, DC: American Psychiatric Press.

Garofalo, R., Wolf, R. C., Kessel, S., Palfrey, J., & DuRant, R. H. (1998). The association between health risk behaviors and sexual orientation among a school-based sample of adolescents. *Pediatrics, 101,* 895–902.

Gay and Lesbian Medical Association (GLMA). (2000). *Healthy people 2010: Companion document for lesbian, gay, bisexual, and transgender (LGBT) health.* Retrieved December 14, 2002, from glma.org/_data/n_0001/resources/live/HealthyCompanionDoc3.pdf.

Gay, Lesbian, and Straight Education Network (GLSEN). (2008). *Executive summary: 2007 national school climate survey.* Retrieved July 12, 2010, 2002, from www.glsen.org/binary-data/GLSEN_ATTACHMENTS/file/000/001/1306-1.pdf.

Gay, Lesbian, and Straight Education Network (GLSEN). (n.d.). *Background and information about gay-straight alliances.* Retrieved July 8, 2010, from www.glsen.org/cgi-bin/iowa/all/library/record/2336.html.

Gibson, P. (1989). Gay male and lesbian youth suicide. In *Report of the secretary's task force on youth suicide* (DHHS Publication ADM 89–1623; pp. 110–142). Washington, DC: U.S. Government Printing Office.

Glazier, R. P. (2009). Sexual minority youth and risk behaviors: Implications for the school environment. (Dissertation. University of Northern Colorado, 2009). *Dissertation Abstract International.* (Publication number: 3374860).

Grella, C. E., Greenwell, L., Mays, V. M., & Cochran, S. D. (2009). Influence of gender, sexual orientation, and need on treatment utilization for substance use and mental disorders: Findings from the California Quality of Life Survey. *BMC Psychiatry, 9,* 52. Retrieved July 30, 2010, from www.crativecommons.org/licenses/by/2.0

Halkitis, P. N., Green, K. A., & Mourgues, P. (2005). Longitudinal investigation of methamphetamine use among gay and bisexual men in New York City: Findings from Project BUMPS. *Journal of Urban Health, 82,* Supplement 1, i18–i25.

Hansen, G. (1982). Androgyny, sex role orientation, and homosexism. *Journal of Psychology, 112,* 39–45.

Hart, T. A., & Heimberg, R. G. (2001). Presenting problems among treatment-seeking gay, lesbian, and bisexual youth. *Psychotherapy in Practice, 57,* 615–627.

Hellman, R. E., Stanton, M., Lee, J., Tytun, A., & Vachon, R. (1989). Treatment of homosexual alcoholics in government-funded agencies: Provider training and attitudes. *Hospital and Community Psychiatry, 40,* 1163–1168.

Hicks, D. (2000). The importance of specialized treatment programs for lesbian and gay patients. *Journal of Gay and Lesbian Psychotherapy, 3*(3/4), 81–94.

Hudson, W., & Ricketts, W. (1980). A strategy for the measurement of homophobia. *Journal of Homosexuality, 5,* 357–372.

Hughes, T., McCabe, S., Wilsnack, S. C., West, B. T., & Boyd, C. J. (2010). Victimization and substance use disorders in a national sample of heterosexual and sexual minority women and men. *Addiction, 105*(12), 2130–2140. doi:10.1111/j.1360-0443.2010.03088.x.

Hughes, T., Szalacha, L. A., & McNair, R. (2010). Substance abuse and mental health disparities: Comparisons across sexual identity groups in a national sample of young Australian women. *Social Science & Medicine, 71*(4), 824–831. doi:10.1016/j.socscimed.2010.05.009.

Hunter, S., Shannon, C., Knox, J., & Martin, J. I. (1998). *Lesbian, gay, and bisexual youths and adults: Knowledge for human services.* Thousand Oaks, CA: Sage.

Israelstam, S. (1986). Alcohol and drug problems of gay males and lesbians: Therapy, counselling, and prevention issues. *Journal of Drug Issues, 16*(3), 443–461.

Israelstam, S. (1988). Knowledge and opinions of alcohol intervention workers in Ontario, Canada, regarding issues affecting male gays and lesbians: Parts I and II. *International Journal of the Addictions, 23,* 227–258.

King, M., Semlyen, J., Tai, S. S., Killaspy, H., Osborn, D., Popelyuk, D., & Nazareth, I. (2008). A systematic review of mental disorder, suicide, and deliberate self harm in lesbian, gay, and bisexual people. *BMC Psychiatry, 8*(70). Retrieved July 19, 2010, from www.biomedcentral.com/1471-244X/8/70.

Kominars, S. B. (1995). Homophobia: The heart of darkness. *Journal of Gay and Lesbian Social Services, 2,* 29–40.

Kryzan, C., & Walsh, J. (1998, March). !OutProud!/Oasis Internet survey of queer and questioning youth. *Oasis Magazine.* Retrieved August 31, 2001, from www.oasismag.com/survey/.

Kus, R. J., & Latcovich, M. A. (1995). Special interest groups in Alcoholics Anonymous: A focus on gay men's groups. *Journal of Gay and Lesbian Social Services, 2*(1), 67–82.

Leslie, D. R., Perina, B. A., & Maqueda, M. C. (2001). Clinical issues with transgender individuals. In *A provider's introduction to substance abuse treatment for lesbian, gay, bisexual and transgender individuals* (pp. 91–97). Rockville, MD: U.S. Department of Health and Human Services.

Lock, J., & Steiner, H. (1999). Gay, lesbian, and bisexual youth risks for emotional, physical, and social problems: Results from a community based survey. *Journal of the American Academy of Child and Adolescent Psychiatry, 38,* 297–303.

Lohrenz, L. J., Connelly, J. C., Coyne, L., & Spare, K. E. (1978). Alcohol problems in several midwestern homosexual communities. *Journal of Studies on Alcohol, 39,* 1959–1963.

Lombardi, E. L., & van Servellen, G. (2000). Building culturally sensitive substance use prevention and treatment programs for transgendered populations. *Journal of Substance Abuse Treatment, 19,* 291–296.

Marshal, M. P., Friedman, M. S., Stall, R., King, K. M., Miles, J., Gold, M. A., et al. (2008). Sexual orientation and adolescent substance use: A meta-analysis and methodological review. *Addiction, 103,* 546–556.

Marshal, M. P., Friedman, M. S., Stall, R., & Thompson, A. L. (2009). Individual trajectories of substance use in lesbian, gay and bisexual youth and heterosexual youth. *Addiction, 104,* 974–981.

Matteson, D. R. (1996). Psychotherapy with bisexual individuals. In R. Cabaj & T. Stein (Eds.), *Textbook of homosexuality and mental health* (pp. 433–450). Washington, DC: American Psychiatric Press.

McCabe, P. T. (2001). Families of origin and families of choice. In *A provider's introduction to substance abuse treatment for lesbian, gay, bisexual and transgender individuals* (pp. 69–72). Rockville, MD: U.S. Department of Health and Human Services.

McCabe S. E., Hughes, T. L., Bostwick, W. B., West, B. T., & Boyd, C. J. (2009). Sexual orientation, substance use behaviors and substance dependence in the United States. *Addiction, 104*(8), 1333–1345.

McHenry, S. S., & Johnson, J. W. (1993). Homophobia in the therapist and gay or lesbian client: Conscious and unconscious collusions in self-hate. *Psychotherapy, 30,* 141–151.

McKirnan, D., & Peterson, P. L. (1989). Alcohol and drug use among homosexual men and women: Epidemiology and population characteristics. *Addictive Behaviors, 14,* 545–553.

McMillin, S. (1995). A warning from SOAR: Stigma kills. *Addiction Letter, 95*(11), 3.

McNally, E. B. (2001). The coming out process for lesbians and gay men. In *A provider's introduction to substance abuse treatment for lesbian, gay, bisexual and transgender individuals* (pp. 85–91). Rockville, MD: U.S. Department of Health and Human Services.

McVinney, D. (2001). Clinical issues with bisexual clients. In *A provider's introduction to substance abuse treatment for lesbian, gay, bisexual and transgender individuals* (pp. 87–90). Rockville, MD: U.S. Department of Health and Human Services.

Messing, A., Schoenberg, R., & Stephens, R. (1984). Confronting homophobia in health care settings: Guidelines for social work practice. In R. Schoenberg, R. Goldberg, & D. Shore (Eds.), *With compassion toward some: Homosexuality and social work in America* (pp. 65–74). New York: Harrington Park.

Millham, J., Miguel, C., & Kellogg, R. (1976). A factor-analytic conceptualization of attitudes toward male and female homosexuals. *Journal of Homosexuality, 2*(1), 3–10.

Morrow, D. (1996). Heterosexism: Hidden discrimination in social work education. *Journal of Gay and Lesbian Social Services, 5*(4), 1–16.

Mosher, W. D., Chandra, A., & Jones. J. (September 15, 2005). Sexual behavior and selected health measures: Men and women 15–44 years of age, United States, 2002. *Advance Data No. 362.* Hyattsville, MD: Centers for Disease Control and Prevention. Retrieved July 15, 2010, from www.cdc.gov/nchs/data/ad/ad362.pdf.

Murphy, B. (1991). Educating mental health professionals about gay and lesbian issues. *Journal of Homosexuality, 22,* 229–247.

Nicoloff, L. K., & Stiglitz, E. A. (1987). Lesbian alcoholism: Etiology, treatment, and recovery. In Boston Lesbian Psychologies Collective (Ed.), *Lesbian psychologies* (pp. 283–293). Chicago: University of Illinois Press.

O'Donahue, W., & Caselles, C. (1993). Homophobia: Conceptual, definitional, and value issues. *Journal of Psychopathology and Behavioral Assessment, 15*(3), 177–195.

O'Hanlan, K. A., Cabaj, R. P., Schatz, B., Lock, J., & Nemrow, P. (1997). A review of the medical consequences of homophobia with suggestions for resolution. *Journal of the Gay and Lesbian Medical Association, 1,* 25–39.

O'Hanlan, K., Lock, J., Robertson, P., Cabaj, R. P., Schatz, B., & Nemrow, P. (n.d.). *Homophobia as a health hazard: Report of the Gay and Lesbian Medical Association.* Retrieved August 10, 2001, from www.ohanlan.com/phobiahzd.htm

Peterson, K. J. (1996). Preface: Developing the context: The impact of homophobia and heterosexism on the health care of gay and lesbian people. In K. J. Peterson (Ed.), *Health care for lesbians and gay men: Confronting homophobia and sexism* (pp. xvii–xx). New York: Harrington Park.

Poteat, V. P., Aragon, S. R., Espelage, D. L., & Koenig, B. W. (2009). Psychosocial concerns of sexual minority youth: Complexity and caution in group differences. *Journal of Consulting and Clinical Psychology, 77*(1), 196–201.

Ratner, E. (1988). A model for treatment of lesbian and gay alcohol abusers. *Alcoholism Treatment Quarterly, 5,* 25–46.

Robinson, K. E. (1991). Gay youth support groups: An opportunity for social work intervention. *Social Work, 36,* 458–459.

Rosario, M., Schrimshaw, E. W., & Hunter, J. (2009). Disclosure of sexual orientation and subsequent substance use and abuse among lesbian, gay, and bisexual youths: Critical role of disclosure reactions. *Psychology of Addictive Behaviors, 23*(1), 175–184.

Rowan, N. L., & Faul, A. C. (2011). Gay, lesbian, bisexual, and transgendered people and chemical dependency: Exploring successful treatment. *Journal of Gay & Lesbian Social Services, 23*(1), 107–130.

Russell, S. T., & Joyner, K. (2001). Adolescent sexual orientation and suicide risk: Evidence from a natural study. *American Journal of Public Health, 91,* 1276–1282.

Saghir, M. T., & Robins, E. (1973). *Male and female homosexuality: A comprehensive investigation.* Baltimore: Williams & Wilkins.

Saulnier, C. (1994). Twelve Steps for everyone? Lesbians in Al-Anon. In T. J. Powell (Ed.), *Understanding the self-help organization: Frameworks and findings* (pp. 247–271). Newbury Park, CA: Sage.

Senreich, E. (2009). Demographic, background, and treatment factors that affect gay and bisexual clients in substance abuse programs. *Journal of LGBT Issues in Counseling, 3,* 177–197.

Senreich, E. (2010). The effects of honesty and openness about sexual orientation on gay and bisexual clients in substance abuse programs. *Journal of Homosexuality, 57*(3), 364–383. doi:10.1080/00918360903542990.

Sewell, V. H., Jr. (1998). *How it works: The Twelve Steps of Narcotics Anonymous.* Retrieved March 27, 2003, from www.nawol.org/2008_12steps.htm.

Shoptaw, S., Reback, C. J., Larkins, S., Wang, P. C., Fuller, E. R., Dang, J., & Yang, X. (2008). Outcomes using two tailored behavioral treatments for substance abuse in urban gay and bisexual men. *Journal of Substance Abuse Treatment, 35*(3), 285–293.

Skinner, W. E., & Otis, M. D. (1996). Drug and alcohol use among lesbian and gay people in a southern U.S. sample: Epidemiological, comparative, and methodological findings from the Trilogy Project. *Journal of Homosexuality, 30*(3), 59–92.

Substance Abuse and Mental Health Services Administration (SAMHSA). (2001). *A provider's introduction to substance abuse treatment for lesbian, gay, bisexual and transgender individuals.* Rockville, MD: U.S. Department of Health and Human Services.

Substance Abuse and Mental Health Services Administration (SAMHSA). (2010). *New national study shows that only six percent of substance abuse treatment facilities offer specialized services for gays and lesbians.* Retrieved July 10, 2010 from www.samhsa.gov/newsroom/advisories/1006225100.aspx.

Talley, A. E., Sher, K. J., & Littlefield, A. K. (2010). Sexual orientation and substance use trajectories in emerging adulthood. *Addiction, 105*(7), 1235–1245. doi:10.1111/j.1360-0443.2010.02953.x.

Tewksbury, R., & Gagne, P. (1996). Transgenderists: Products of non–normative intersections of sex, gender, and sexuality. *Journal of Men's Studies, 5*(2), 105–130.

Thiede, H., Valleryo, L. A., MacKellar, D. A., Celentano, D. D., Ford, W. L., Hagan, B. A., et al. (2003). Regional patterns and correlates of substance use among men who have sex with men in 7 urban areas. *American Journal of Public Health, 93,* 1915–1921.

Thompson, M. (Ed.). (1994). *Long road to freedom: The advocate history of the gay and lesbian movement.* New York: St. Martin's Press.

Travers, P. (1998). *Counseling gay and lesbian clients.* Unpublished master's thesis, James Madison University. Harrisonburg, VA.

Troiden, R. (1988). *Gay and lesbian identity.* New York: General Hall.

Van Den Bergh, N. (1991). Having bitten the apple: A feminist perspective on addictions. In N. Van Den Bergh (Ed.), *Feminist perspectives on addiction* (pp. 3–30). New York: Springer.

Walls, N. E., Kane, S. B., & Wisneski, H. (2010). Gay-straight alliances and school experiences of sexual minority youth. *Youth & Society, 41*(3), 307–322.

Weinberg, G. (1972). *Society and the healthy homosexual.* New York: St. Martin's Press.

Weitze, C., & Osburg, S. (1996). Transsexualism in Germany: Empirical data on epidemiology and application of the German Transsexuals' Act during its first ten years. *Archives of Sexual Behavior, 25,* 409–425.

Wright, E., Shelton, C., Browning, M., Orduna, J. M. G., Martinez, V., & Young, F. Y. (2001). Cultural issues in working with LGBT individuals. In *A provider's introduction to substance abuse treatment for lesbian, gay, bisexual and transgender individuals* (pp. 15–27). Rockville, MD: U.S. Department of Health and Human Services.

CHAPTER 13

Adams, L. L., Gatchel, R. J., Robinson, R. C., Polatin, P., Gajraj, N., Deschner, M., & Noe, C. (2004). Development of a self-report screening instrument for assessing potential opioid medication misuse in chronic pain patients. *Journal of Pain Symptom Management, 27,* 440–459.

Addiction intervention with the disabled (n.d.). Kent, OH: Kent State University.

Agarwal, P. (2011, March 8). Neurologic effects of cocaine. *Medscape.* Retrieved April 9, 2011, from emedicine.medscape.com/article/1174408-overview

Aharonovich, E., Nguyen, H., & Nunes, E. (2001). Anger and depressive states among treatment-seeking drug abusers: Testing the psychopharmacological specificity hypothesis. *American Journal on Addictions, 10,* 327–344.

Ahern, M. M. & Hendryx, M. (2007). Avoidable hospitalizations for diabetes: Comorbidity risks. *Disease Management, 10*(6), 347–355.

Al-Anon. (n.d.). *Paths to Recovery: Al-Anon's steps, traditions and concepts (B-24).* Virginia Beach, VA: Al-Anon Family Groups Headquarters.

Alcoholics Anonymous (AA). (1984). *The AA member—Medications and other drugs.* New York: Alcoholics Anonymous World Services.

Alexander, T., DiNitto, D., & Tidblom, I. (2005). Screening for alcohol and other drug abuse problems among the deaf. *Alcoholism Treatment Quarterly, 23*(1), 63–78.

Alexander, T. L. (2005). *Substance abuse screening with deaf clients: Development of a culturally sensitive scale.* Dissertation. Austin, TX: University of Texas at Austin.

Aliesan, K., & Firth, R. C. (1990). A MICA program: Outpatient rehabilitation services for individuals with concurrent mental illness and chemical abuse disorders. *Journal of Applied Rehabilitation Counseling, 21*(3), 25–29.

Alston, R. J. (1994). Sensation seeking as a psychological trait of drug abuse among persons with spinal cord injury. *Rehabilitation Counseling Bulletin, 38*(2), 154–163.

Alterman, A. I. (1985). Substance abuse in psychiatric patients: Etiological, developmental, and treatment considerations. In A. I. Alterman (Ed.), *Substance abuse and psychopathology* (pp. 121–136). New York: Plenum Press.

Alvarez, J., Adebanjo, A. M., Davidson, M. K., Jason, L. A., & Davis, M. I. (2006). Oxford House: Deaf-affirmative support for substance abuse recovery. *American Annals of the Deaf, 151*(4), 418–422.

American Association on Intellectual and Developmental Disabilities. (2010). *Definition of intellectual disability.* Washington, DC: Author. Retrieved April 6, 2011, from www.aaidd.org/content_100.cfm? navID=21.

American Heart Association. (n.d.) Alcohol, wine and cardio-vascular disease. Dallas, TX: Author. Retrieved August 30, 2010, from www.americanheart.org/presenter.jhtml?identifier=4422.

American Foundation for the Blind. (2000). *Statistics and sources for professionals*. Retrieved December 9, 2002, from www.afb.org/info_document_view.asp?documentid=1367.

American Psychiatric Association (APA). (2000). *Diagnostic and statistical manual of mental disorders* (4th ed., Text Revision). Washington, DC: Author.

Anderson, C. M., Reiss, D. J., & Hogarty, G. E. (1986). *Schizophrenia and the family: A practitioner's guide to psychoeducation and management*. New York: Guilford Press.

Anderson, P. (1980/81, Winter). Alcoholism and the spinal cord disabled: A model program. *Alcohol Health and Research World*, 37–41.

Appleby, L., Dyson, V., Altman, E., & Luchins, D. J. (1997). Assessing substance use in multiproblem patients: Reliability and validity of the Addiction Severity Index in a mental hospital population. *Journal of Nervous and Mental Disease, 185*, 159–165.

Bakdash, D. P. (1983). Psychiatric/mental health nursing. In G. Bennet, C. Vourakis, & D. S. Woolf (Eds.), *Substance abuse: Pharmacologic, developmental, and clinical perspectives* (pp. 223–239). New York: John Wiley and Sons.

Baroff, G. S., & Olley, J. G. (1999). *Mental retardation: Nature, cause, and management* (3rd ed.). Philadelphia: Brunner/Mazel.

Beck, A. T. (1978). *Beck Depression Inventory*. San Antonio, TX: Psychological Corporation.

Beitchman, J. H., Wilson, B., Douglas, L., Young, A., & Adlaf, E. (2001). Substance use disorders in young adults with and without LD: Predicitive and concurrent relationships. *Journal of Learning Disabilities, 34*(4), 317–332.

Black, P. & Glickman, N. (2006) Demographics, psychiatric diagnoses, and other characteristics of North American deaf and hard-of-hearing inpatients. *Journal of Deaf Studies and Deaf Education, 11*(3), 303–321.

Blackerby, W. F., & Baumgarten, A. (1990). A model treatment program for the head-injured substance abuser: Preliminary findings. *Journal of Head Trauma Rehabilitation, 5*(3), 47–59.

Blankertz, L. E., & Cnaan, R. A. (1994). Assessing the impact of two residential programs for dually diagnosed homeless individuals. *Social Service Review, 68*(4), 536–560.

Blindness, visual impairment, and substance abuse: Facts for substance abuse prevention and treatment professionals. (2008, May 29). Dayton, OH: Substance Abuse Resources and Disability Issues. Retrieved January 1, 2011, from www.med.wright.edu/citar/sardi/brochure_blindness.html.

Bogenschutz, M. P., Geppert, C. M., & George, J. (2006). The role of twelve-step approaches in dual diagnosis treatment and recovery. *American Journal of Addiction, 15*, 50–60.

Bombardier, C. H. (2003, Spring). Alcohol and your health after SCI. Seattle: Northwest Regional Spinal Cord Injury System. Retrieved January 5, 2011, from sci.washington.edu/info/newsletters/articles/03sp_alco hol.asp.

Bombardier, C. H., & Davis, C. (2001). Screening for alcohol problems among persons with TBI. *Brain Injury Source, 5*(4), 16–19.

Bombardier, C. H., Kilmer, J., & Ehde, D. (1997). Screening for alcoholism among persons with recent traumatic brain injury. *Rehabilitation Psychology, 42*, 259–271.

Bombardier, C. H., & Rimmele, C. T. (1998). Alcohol use and readiness to change after spinal cord injury. *Archives of Physical Medicine and Rehabilitation, 79*, 1110–1115.

Bombardier, C. H., Stroud, M. W., Esselman, P. C., & Rimmele, C. T. (2004). Do preinjury alcohol problems predict poorer rehabilitation progress in persons with spinal cord injury? *Archives of Physical Medicine and Rehabilitation, 85*(9), 1488–1492.

Bombardier, C. H., & Thurber, C. A. (1998). Blood alcohol level and early cognitive status after traumatic brain injury. *Brain Injury, 12*, 725–734.

Bond, G. R., McDonel, E. C., Miller, L. D., & Pensec, M. (1991). Assertive community treatment and reference groups: An evaluation of their effectiveness for young adults with serious mental illness and substance abuse problems. *Psychosocial Rehabilitation Journal, 15*(2), 31–43.

Booth, B. M., Curran, G., Han, X., Wright, P., Frith, S., Leukefeld, C., Falck, R., & Carlson, R.G. (2010). Longitudinal relationship between psychological distress and multiple substance use: Results From a three-year multisite natural-history study of rural stimulant users. *Journal of Studies on Alcohol and Drugs, 71*, 258–267.

Boros, A. (1980/81). Alcoholism intervention for the deaf. *Alcohol Health and Research World, 5*(2), 26–30.

Brain Injury Association of America. (2004). *Substance abuse issues after traumatic brain injury*. Vienna, VA: Author. Retrieved January 23, 2011, from www.biausa.org/_literature_41447/2007_Accomplishments.

Brault, M. W. (2008, December). *Americans with disabilities: 2005*. Washington, DC: U.S. Census Bureau. Retrieved August 28, 2010, from www.census.gov/prod/2008pubs/p70-117.pdf.

Bricker, M. G. (1995). *The STEMSS supported self-help model for dual diagnosis recovery: Applications for rural settings*. Rockville, MD: Substance Abuse and Mental Health Services Administration. Retrieved April 6, 2011, from www.kap.samhsa.gov/products/manuals/taps/17k.htm.

Brooks, G. I. (2000). *Correlates of substance abuse among people with blindness/visual impairment*. Dissertation. Austin, TX: University of Texas at Austin.

Brown, R., Leonard, T., Saunders, L., & Papasouliotis, O. (1997). A two-item screening test for alcohol and other drug problems. *The Journal of Family Practice, 44*(2), 151–160.

Bruckman, B., Bruckner, V. T., & Calabrese, C. (1996). *Alcohol and drug programs and the Americans with Disabilities Act.* Oakland, CA: Pacific Research and Training Alliance.

Burgard, J. F., Donohue, B., Azrin, N. H., & Teichner, G. (2000). Prevalence and treatment of substance abuse in the mentally retarded population: An empirical review. *Journal of Psychoactive Drugs, 32,* 293–298.

Burnam, M. A., Morton, S. C., McGlynn, E. A., Petersen, L. P., Steche, B. M., Hayes, C., & Vaccaro, J. V. (1995). An experimental evaluation of residential and nonresidential treatment for dually diagnosed homeless adults. *Journal of Addictive Diseases, 14,* 111–134.

Burns, L. R., & de Miranda, J. (1991). *Blindness and visual impairment: Drug and alcohol abuse prevention and treatment.* San Mateo, CA: Peninsula Health Concepts.

Butler, S., Budman, S., Fernandez, K., & Jamison, R. (2004). Validation of a screener and opiod assessment measure for patients with chronic pain. *Pain, 112*(1–2), 65–75.

Caldwell, S., & White, K. K. (1991). Co-creating a self-help recovery movement. *Psychosocial Rehabilitation Journal, 15*(2), 91–95.

Campbell, J. A., Essex, E. L., & Held, G. (1994). Issues in chemical dependency treatment and aftercare for people with learning differences. *Health and Social Work, 19*(1), 63–70.

Carey, K. B., Cocco, K. M., & Correia, C. J. (1997). Reliability and validity of the Addiction Severity Index among outpatients with severe mental illness. *Psychological Assessment, 9,* 422–288.

Carey, K. B., & Correia, C. J. (1998). Severe mental illness and addictions: Assessment considerations. *Addictive Behaviors, 23*(6), 735–748.

Cherner, M., Temkin, N. R., Machamer, J. E., & Dikmen, S. S. (2001). Utility of a composite measure to detect problematic alcohol use in persons with traumatic brain injury. *Archives of Physical Medicine Rehabilitation, 82*(6), 780–786.

Christian, L., & Poling, A. (1997). Drug abuse in persons with mental retardation: A review. *American Journal on Mental Retardation, 102,* 126–136.

Cleary, M., Hunt, G. E., Matheson, S., Siegfried, N., & Walter, G. (2008). Psychosocial treatment programs for people with both severe mental illness and substance misuse. *Schizophrenia Bulletin, 34*(2), 226–228.

Cocco, K. M., & Carey, K. B. (1998). Psychometric properties of the Drug Abuse Screening Test in psychiatric outpatients. *Psychological Assessment, 10,* 408–414.

Coffey, R. M., Buck, J. A., Kassed, C. A., Dilonardo, J., Forhan, C., Marder, W. D., & Vandivort-Warren, R. (2008). Transforming Mental Health and Substance Abuse Data Systems in the United States. *Psychiatric Services, 59*(11), 1257–1263.

Compton, W. M., Cottler, L. B., Phelps, D. L., Abdallah, A. B., & Spitznagel, E. L. (2000). Psychiatric disorders among drug dependent subjects: Are they primary or secondary? *American Journal on Addictions, 9,* 126–134.

Compton, W. M., & Volkow, N. D. (2006). Abuse of prescription drugs and the risk of addiction. *Drug and Alcohol Dependence, 83S,* S4–S7.

Conigrave, K. M., Hu, B. F., Camargo, C. A., Stampfer, M. J., Willett, W. C., & Rimm, E. B. (2001). A prospective study of drinking patterns in relation to risk of type 2 diabetes among men. *Diabetes, 50*(10), 2390–2395.

Connors, G. J., Donovan, D. M., & DiClemente, C. C. (2001). *Substance abuse treatment and the stages of change.* New York: Guilford Press.

Co-occurring Center for Excellence. (2008, June). *Consensus- and evidence-based practices or treatment of persons with co-occurring disorders: Technical assistance (TA) report for the co-occurring state incentive grants (COSIGS).* Retrieved April 10, 2011, from www.coce.samhsa.gov/cod_resources/PDF/C-EBPworkgrpFinal6-19-08rslakjh.pdf.

Corrigan, J. D. (1995). Substance abuse as a mediating factor in outcome from traumatic brain injury. *Archives of Physical Medicine and Rehabilitation, 76*(4), 302–309.

Corrigan, J. D, Bogner, J., Lamb-Hart, G., Heinemann, A. W., & Moore, D. (2005). Increasing substance abuse treatment compliance for persons with traumatic brain injury. *Psychology of Addictive Behavior, 19,* 131–139.

Corrigan, J. D., & Bogner, J. (2007). Intervention to promote retention in substance abuse treatment. *Brain Injury, 21,* 343–356.

Corrigan, J. D., Bogner, J. A., & Lamb-Hart, G. L. (1999). Substance abuse and brain injury. In M. Rosenthal, J. S. Kreutzer, E. R. Griffith, & B. Pentland (Eds.), *Rehabilitation of the adult and child with traumatic brain injury* (pp. 556–571). Philadelphia: F. A. Davis.

Corrigan, J. D., Rust, E., & Lamb-Hart, G. L. (1995). The nature and extent of substance abuse problems in persons with traumatic brain injury. *Journal of Head Trauma Rehabilitation, 10*(3), 29–46.

Criqui, M. H. (2001). Alcohol, lipoproteins, and the French paradox. In D. P. Agarwal & H. K. Seitz (Eds.), *Alcohol in health and disease* (pp. 597–609). New York: Marcel Dekker.

Daley, D. C. (1996, March/April). Relapse prevention strategies for dual disorders. *Counselor,* 26–29.

Daley, D. C. (2002, March 28). *Dual diagnosis and the family.* Presentation at Building the Bridge, a national conference on integrating mental health and substance abuse services, San Antonio, TX.

Daley, D. C., Moss, H., & Campbell, F. (1987). *Dual disorders: Counseling clients with chemical dependency and mental illness.* Center City, MN: Hazelden Foundation.

DeLambo, D. A., Chandras, K. V., Homa, D., & Chandras, S. V. (2010). *Spinal cord injury and substance abuse: Implications for rehabilitation professionals.* Retrieved January 5, 2010, from counselingoutfitters.com/vistas/vistas10/Article_83.pdf.

DeLambo, D. A., Chandras, K. V., Homa, D., & Chandras, S. V. (2009, March). *Traumatic brain injuries and substance abuse: Implications for rehabilitation professionals.* Paper based on a program presented at the American Counseling Association Annual Conference and Exhibition, Charlotte, NC.

De Leon, G., Sacks, S., Staines, G., & McKendrick, K. (2000). Modified therapeutic community for homeless mentally ill chemical abusers: Treatment outcomes. *American Journal of Drug and Alcohol Abuse, 26,* 461–480.

de Miranda, J. (1990, August). The common ground: Alcoholism, addiction and disability. *Addiction and Recovery,* 42–45.

de Miranda, J. (1999, May/June). Treatment services offer limited access for people with disabilities. *Counselor,* 24–25.

De Pompei, R., & Corrigan, J. D. (2001). Double trouble: Substance abuse and traumatic brain injury in youth. *Brain Injury Source, 5*(4), 32–34.

Degenhardt, L. (2000). Interventions for people with alcohol use disorders and an intellectual disability: A review of the literature. *Journal of Intellectual and Developmental Disability, 25*(2), 135–146.

Delaney, D., & Poling, A. (1990). Drug abuse among mentally retarded people: An overlooked problem? *Journal of Alcohol and Drug Education, 35*(2), 48–54.

DiClemente, C. C., Nidecker, M. & Bellack, A. S. (2008). Motivation and the stages of change among individuals with severe mental illness and substance abuse disorders. *Journal of Substance Abuse Treatment, 34,* 25–35.

Dikmen, S. S., Donovan, D. M., Lokerg, T., Machamer, J. E., & Temkin, N. R. (1993). Alcohol use and its effects on neuropsychological outcome in head injury. *Neuropsychology, 7*(3), 296–305.

DiNitto, D. M., & Crisp, C. L. (2002). Addictions and women with major psychiatric disorders. In S. L. Brown & S. L. A. Straussner (Eds.), *The handbook of addiction treatment for women* (pp. 423–450). San Francisco: Jossey-Bass.

DiNitto, D. M., & Krishef, C. H. (1983/84). Drinking patterns of mentally retarded persons. *Alcohol Health and Research World, 8*(2), 40–42.

DiNitto, D. M., & Krishef, C. H. (1987). Family and social problems of mentally retarded alcohol users. *Social and Behavioral Science Documents, 17*(1), 31.

DiNitto, D. M., & Webb, D. K. (2001). Clinical practice with clients who abuse substances. In R. G. Sands (Ed.), *Clinical social work practice in behavioral mental health* (2nd ed., pp. 328–368). Boston, MA: Allyn & Bacon.

DiNitto, D. M., Webb, D. K., & Rubin, A. (2002). The effectiveness of an integrated treatment approach for clients with dual diagnoses. *Research on Social Work Practice, 12,* 621–641.

DiNitto, D. M., Webb, D. K., Rubin, A., Morrison-Orton, D., & Wambach, K. (2001). Self-help group meeting attendance among clients with dual diagnoses. *Journal of Psychoactive Drugs, 33,* 263–272.

Dixon, L., McNary, S., & Lehman, A. (1995). Substance abuse and family relationships of persons with severe mental illness. *American Journal of Psychiatry, 152*(3), 456–458.

Dixon, T. L. (1987, January/February). Addiction among the hearing impaired. *EAP Digest,* 41–44, 74.

Doub, T. W. (2002, March 28). *Three year study of an integrated therapeutic community: Treatment outcomes.* Presentation at Building the Bridge, a national conference on integrating mental health and substance abuse services, San Antonio, TX.

Drake, R. E., Bartels, S. J., Teague, G. B., Noordsy, D. L., & Clark, R. E. (1993). Treatment of substance abuse in severely mentally ill patients. *Journal of Nervous and Mental Disease, 181*(10), 606–661.

Drake, R. E., Mercer-McFadden, C., Mueser, K. T., McHugo, G. J., & Bond, G. R. (1998). Review of integrated mental health and substance abuse treatment for patients with dual disorders. *Schizophrenia Bulletin, 24,* 589–608.

Drake, R. E., & Mueser, K. T. (2000). Psychosocial approaches to dual diagnosis. *Schizophrenia Bulletin, 26,* 105–118.

Drake, R. E., Mueser, K. T., & McHugo, G. J. (1996). Clinician rating scales: Alcohol Use Scale (AUS), Drug Use Scale (DUS), and Substance Abuse Treatment Scale (SATS). In L. I. Sederer & B. Dickey (Eds.), *Outcomes assessment in clinical practice* (pp. 113–116). Baltimore: Williams & Wilkins.

Drake, R. E., O'Neal, E. L., & Wallach, M. A. (2008). A systematic review of psychosocial research on psychosocial interventions for people with co-occurring severe mental and substance use disorders. *Journal of Substance Abuse Treatment, 34,* 123–138.

Dufour, M. C., Bertolucci, D., Cowell, C., Stinson, F. S., & Noble, J. (1989). Alcohol-related morbidity among the disabled: The Medicare experience 1985. *Alcohol Health and Research World, 13*(2), 158–161.

Edgerton, R. B. (1986). Alcohol and drug use by mentally retarded adults. *American Journal of Mental Deficiency, 90*(6), 602–609.

Ekleberry, S. C. (1996, March/April). Dual diagnosis: Addiction and Axis II personality disorders. *Counselor,* 7–13.

Elliott, T. R., Kurylo, M., Chen, Y., & Hicken, B. (2002) Alcohol abuse history and adjustment following spinal cord injury. *Rehabilitation Psychology, 47*(3), 278–290.

Emerson, E., & Turnbull, L. (2005). Self-reported smoking and alcohol use among adolescents with intellectual disabilities. *Journal of Intellectual Disabilities, 9*(1), 58–69.

Erickson, T., & Orsay, E. (1994). Toxicology screening and substance abuse consultations in acutely traumatized patients. *American Journal of Emergency Medicine, 12*(1), 126–127.

Evans, K., & Sullivan, J. M. (2001). Antisocial & Borderline personality disorders. In *Dual diagnosis: Counseling the Mentally Ill Substance Abuser* (2nd ed., pp. 122–145). New York: Guilford Press.

Ewing, J. A. (1984). Detecting alcoholism: The CAGE questionnaire. *Journal of he American Medical Association, 252*(14), 1905–1907.

Feinberg, K. (1991, Summer). Maintaining gains through AA. *Headlines*, 16.

First, M. B., Spitzer, R. L., Gibbon, M., & Williams, J. B. W. (1997). *Structured clinical interview for DSM-IV Axis I disorders (SCID-I) clinical version administration booklet.* Washington, DC: American Psychiatric Publishing.

Fishbain, D. A., Cole, B., Lewis, J., Rosomoff, H. L., & Rosomoff, R. S. (2008). What percentage of chronic nonmalignant pain patients exposed to chronic opioid analgesic therapy develop abuse/addiction and/or aberrant drug-related behaviors? A structured evidence-based review. *Pain Medicine*, 9(4), 444–459.

Fisher, F. B. (2004). Interpretation of "aberrant" drug-related behaviors. *Journal of American Physicians and Surgeons*, 9(1), 25–28. Retrieved January 3, 2011, from www.jpands.org/vol9no1/fisher.pdf.

Freudenreich, O., & Tranulis, C. (2009). A prototype approach toward antipsychotic medication adherence in schizophrenia. *Harvard Review of Psychiatry*, 17(1), 35–40.

Frey, M. A., Guthrie, B., Loveland-Cherry, C., Park, P. S., & Foster, C. M. (1997). Risky behavior and risk in adolescents with IDDM. *Journal of Adolescent Health*, 20, 38–45.

Frye, D. (2001). Screening for substance abuse as part of the neuropsychological assessment. *Brain Injury Source*, 5(4), 20–22.

Fulton, K. (1983). Alcohol and drug abuse among the deaf: Collaborative programming for the purpose of prevention, intervention and treatment. In D. Watson & B. Heller (Eds.), *Mental health and deafness: Strategic perspectives* (pp. 365–386). Silver Spring, MD: American Deafness and Rehabilitation Association.

Gallagher, A., Connolly, V., & Kelly, W. F. (2001). Alcohol consumption in patients with diabetes mellitus. *Diabetic Medicine*, 18, 72–73.

Gardner, W. (2002). The impact of behavior problems on caregivers after traumatic brain injury. *Brain Injury Source*, 6(1), 40–44.

Glasgow, A. M., Tynan, D., Schwartz, R., Hicks, J. M., Turek, J., Driscol, C., et al. (1991). Alcohol and drug use in teenagers with diabetes mellitus. *Journal of Adolescent Health*, 12, 11–14.

Glass, E. J. (1980/81). Problem drinking among the blind and visually impaired. *Alcohol Health and Research World*, 5(2), 20–25.

Glassman, A. H. (1993). Cigarette smoking: Implications for psychiatric illness. *American Journal of Psychiatry*, 150(4), 546–553.

Glenn, M., & Dixon, S. (Eds.). (1991). *A look at alcohol and drug abuse prevention and blindness and visual impairments.* Washington, DC: Resource Center on Substance Abuse Prevention and Disability.

Gold, M. A., & Gladstein, J. (1993). Substance use among adolescents with diabetes mellitus: Preliminary findings. *Journal of Adolescent Health*, 14, 80–84.

Gordon, E., & Devinsky, O. (2001). Alcohol and marijuana: Effects on epilepsy and use by patients with epilepsy. *Epilepsia*, 2, 1266–1272.

Graham, D. P., & Cardon, A. L. (2008). An update on substance use and treatment following traumatic brain injury. *Annals of the New York Academy of Sciences*, 1141, 148–162.

Grant, B. F. (1995). Comorbidity between *DSM-IV* drug use disorders and major depression: Results of a national survey of adults. *Journal of Substance Abuse*, 7(4), 481–497.

Grant, T. N., Kramer, C. A., & Nash, K. (1982). Working with deaf alcoholics in a vocational training program. *Journal of Rehabilitation of the Deaf*, 15(4), 14–20.

Greer, B. G. (1986). Substance abuse among people with disabilities: A problem of too much accessibility. *Journal of Rehabilitation*, 52(1), 34–38.

Gress, J. R., & Boss, M. S. (1996). Substance abuse differences among students receiving special education school services. *Child Psychiatry and Human Development*, 26, 235–246.

Guthmann, D. S. (1998). *Is there a substance abuse problem among deaf and hard of hearing individuals?* Minnesota Chemical Dependency Program for Deaf and Hard of Hearing Individuals. Retrieved April 6, 2011, from www.mncddeaf.org/articles/problem_ad.htm.

Guthmann, D. S., & Blozis, S. A. (2001). Unique issues faced by deaf individuals entering substance abuse treatment and following discharge. *American Annals of the Deaf*, 146, 294–303.

Guthmann, D. & Moore, D. (2007). The Substance Abuse in Vocational Rehabilitation-Screener in American Sign Language (SAVR-S-ASL) for persons who are deaf. *JADARA*, 41(1), 9–16.

Guthmann, D. S., & Sandberg, K. A. (1995). Clinical approaches in substance abuse treatment for use with deaf and hard of hearing adolescents. *Journal of Child and Adolescent Substance Abuse*, 4(3), 69–79.

Guthmann, D. S., & Sandberg, K. A. (1999). *Access to treatment services for deaf and hard of hearing individuals.* Retrieved April 6, 2011, from www.mncddeaf.org/articles/access_ad.htm

Halpern, A. S., Close, D. W., & Nelson, D. J. (1986). *On my own: The impact of semi-independent living programs for adults with mental retardation.* Baltimore: Paul H. Brookes.

Hamilton, T., & Samples, P. (1994). *The Twelve Steps and dual disorders: A framework of recovery for those of us with addiction and an emotional or psychiatric illness.* Center City, MN: Hazelden Foundation.

Hamilton, T., & Samples, P. (1995). *The Twelve Steps and dual disorders workbook.* Center City, MN: Hazelden Foundation.

Harrison, P. A., Martin, J. A., Tuason, V. B., & Hoffman, N. G. (1985). Conjoint treatment of dual disorders. In A. I. Alterman (Ed.), *Substance abuse and psychopathology* (pp. 367–390). New York: Plenum Press.

Hasin, D. S., Stinson, F. S., Ogburn, E., & Grant, B. F. (2007). Prevalence, correlates, disability, and comorbidity of DSM-IV alcohol abuse and dependence in the United States. *Archives of General Psychiatry*, 64(7), 830–842.

Hasin, D. S., Trautman, K. D., Miele, G. M., Samet, S., Smith, M., & Endicott, J. (1996). Psychiatric Research Interview for Substance and Mental Disorders (PRISM): Reliability for substance abusers. *American Journal of Psychiatry, 153,* 1195–1201.

Havassy, B. E., Alvidrea, J., & Mericle, A. A. (2009). Disparities in use of mental health and substance abuse services by persons with co-occurring disorders. *Psychiatric Services, 60*(2), 217–223.

Hawkins, D. A., & Heinemann, A. W. (1998). Substance abuse and medical complications following spinal cord injury. *Rehabilitation Psychology, 43*(3), 219–231.

Heinemann, A. W., Goranson, N., Ginsburg, K., & Schnoll, S. (1989). Alcohol use and activity patterns following spinal cord injury. *Rehabilitation Psychology, 34*(3), 191–205.

Heinemann, A. W., & Hawkins, D. (1995). Substance abuse and medical complications following spinal cord injury. *Rehabilitation Psychology, 40*(2), 125–140.

Heinemann, A. W., Lazowski, L. E., Moore, D., Miller, F. & McAweeney, M. (2008). Validation of a substance use disorder screening instrument for use in vocational rehabilitation settings. *Rehabilitation Psychology, 53*(1), 63–72.

Heinemann, A. W., McAweeney, M., Lazowski, L. E., & Moore, D. (2008). Utilization of substance abuse screening by state vocational rehabilitation agencies. *Journal of Applied Rehabilitation Counseling, 39*(2), 5–11.

Heinemann, A. W., Schmidt, M. E., & Semik, P. (1994). Drinking patterns, drinking expectancies, and coping after spinal cord injury. *Rehabilitation Counseling Bulletin, 38*(2), 134–153.

Hellerstein, D. J., Rosenthal, R. N., & Miner, C. R. (2001). Integrating services for schizophrenia and substance abuse. *Psychiatric Quarterly, 72,* 291–306.

Hemstrom, O. (2001). Per capita alcohol consumption and ischaemic heart disease mortality. *Addiction, 96*(1), S93–S112.

Hendrickson, E. L. (1988). Treating the dually diagnosed (mental disorder/substance use) client. *TIE-Lines, 5*(4), 1–4.

Hendrickson. E. L., Schmal, M. S., & Ekleberry, S. C. (2004). *Treating co-occurring disorders: A handbook for mental health and substance abuse professionals.* Binghamton, NY: The Haworth Press, Inc.

Henry, K. (1988). *A letter to sponsors of chemically dependent head injured persons.* Washington, DC: National Head Injury Foundation.

Hillbom, M., & Holm, L. (1986). Contribution of traumatic head injury to neuropsychological deficits in alcoholics. *Journal of Neurology, Neurosurgery and Psychiatry, 49*(12), 1348–1353.

Hines, L. M., & Rimm, E. B. (2001). Moderate alcohol consumption and coronary heart disease: A review. *Postgraduate Medical Journal, 77,* 747–752.

Horsfall, J., Cleary, M., Hunt, G. E., & Walter, G. (2009). Psychosocial treatments for people with co-occurring severe mental illnesses and substance use disorders (dual diagnosis): A review of empirical evidence. *Harvard Review of Psychiatry, 17,* 24–34.

Højsted, J., & Sjøgren, P. (2007). Addiction to opioids in chronic pain patients: A literature review. *European Pain Journal, 11,* 490–518.

Huang, A. M. (1981). The drinking behavior of the educable mentally retarded and the nonretarded students. *Journal of Alcohol and Drug Education, 26*(3), 41–50.

Hughes-Dobles, E. (2001). A therapeutic approach to substance abuse recovery with individuals with traumatic brain injury in a residential neurobehavioral program. *Brain Injury Source, 5*(4), 28–31, 46–47.

Iverson, G. L., Lange, R. T., & Franzen, M. D. (2005). Effect of mild traumatic brain injury cannot be differentiated from substance abuse. *Brain Injury, 19,* 11–18.

Jackson, C. T., Covell, N. H., Drake, R. E., & Essock, S. M. (2007). Relationship between diabetes and mortality among persons with co-occurring psychotic and substance use disorders. *Psychiatric Services, 58*(2), 270–272.

James, W., Preston, N. J., Koh, G., Spencer, C., Kisely, S. R., & Castle, D. J. (2004). A group intervention which assists patients with dual diagnosis reduce their drug use. A randomized controlled trial. *Psychological Medicine, 34,* 983–990.

Jerrell, J. M., & Ridgely, M. S. (1995). Comparative effectiveness of three approaches to serving people with severe mental illness and substance abuse disorders. *Journal of Nervous and Mental Disease, 183*(9), 566–576.

Job Accommodation Network. (2010a, March 22). *Employees with alcoholism.* Accommodation and Compliance Series. Morgantown, WV: Author. Retrieved April 10, 2011, from askjan.org/media/downloads/AlcoholismA%26CSeries.pdf#search=%22employees%20with%20alcoholism%22.

Job Accommodation Network. (2010b, March 22). *Employees with drug addiction.* Accommodation and Compliance Series. Morgantown, WV: Author. Retrieved April 10, 2011, from askjan.org/media/downloads/DrugAddA&CSeries.pdf.

Jones, G. A. (1989). Alcohol abuse and traumatic brain injury. *Alcohol Health and Research World, 13*(2), 104–109.

Joosten, M. M., Grobbee, D. E., van der A. D. L., Verschuren, W. M. M., Hendriks, H. F. J., & Beulens, J. W. J. (2010). Combined effect of alcohol consumption and lifestyle behaviors on risk of type 2 diabetes. *The American Journal of Clinical Nutrition, 91,* 1777–1783.

Jorgensen, D. G., & Russert, C. (1982, February). An outpatient treatment approach for hearing-impaired alcoholics. *American Annals of the Deaf,* 41–44.

Kaitz, S. (1991, Summer). Integrated treatment: Safety net for survival. *Headlines,* 11–12, 14, 16–17.

Kamboj, M. K., & Draznin, M. B. (2006). Office management of the adolescent with diabetes mellitus. *Primary Care Clinics in Office Practice, 33,* 581–602.

Kao, W. H. L., Puddey, I. A., Boland, L. L., Watson, R. L., & Brancati, F. L. (2001). Alcohol consumption and the risk of type 2 diabetes mellitus: Atherosclerosis risk in communities study. *American Journal of Epidemiology, 154*(8), 748–757.

Kearns, G. A. (1989). Hearing-impaired alcoholics—An underserved community. *Alcohol Health and Research World, 13*(2), 162–166.

Keller, M. (1958). Alcoholism: Nature and extent of the problem. In S. D. Bacon (Ed.), *Understanding alcoholism: Annals of the American Academy of Political and Social Science* (pp. 1–11). Philadelphia: American Academy of Political and Social Science Society.

Kessler, R .C., Berglund, P. A., Demier, O., Jin, R., & Walters, E. E. (2005a). Lifetime prevalence and age-of-onset distributions of *DSM-IV* disorders in the National Comorbidity Survey Replication. *Archives of General Psychiatry, 62*(6), 593–602.

Kessler, R. C., Chiu, W. T., Demier, O., & Walters, E. E. (2005b). Prevalence, severity, and comorbidity of 12-month *DSM-IV* disorders in the National Comorbidity Survey Replication. *Archives of General Psychiatry, 62*(6), 617–627.

Kessler, R. C., Crum, R. M., Warner, L. A., Nelson, C. B., Schulenberg, J., & Anthony, J. C. (1997). Lifetime co-occurrence of DSM-III-R alcohol abuse and dependence with other psychiatric disorders in the National Comorbidity Survey. *Archives of General Psychiatry, 54,* 313–321.

Kessler, R. C., Nelson, C. B., McGonagle, K. A., Edlund, M. J., Frank, R. G., & Leaf, P. J. (1996). The epidemiology of co-occurring addictive and mental disorders: Implications for prevention and service utilization. *American Journal of Orthopsychiatry, 66*(1), 17–31.

Khantzian, E. J. (1985). The self-medication hypothesis of addictive disorders: Focus on heroin and cocaine dependence. *American Journal of Psychiatry, 142*(11), 1259–1264.

Khantzian, E. J. (1997). The self-medication hypothesis of substance use disorders: A reconsideration and recent applications. *Harvard Review of Psychiatry, 4,* 231–244.

King, D. E., Mainous, A. G., Geesey, M. E. (2008). Adopting moderate alcohol consumption in middle age: Subsequent cardiovascular events. *The American Journal of Medicine, 121*(3), 201–202.

Klatsky, A. L. (2001a). Alcohol and cardiovascular diseases. In D. P. Agarwal & H. K. Seitz (Eds.), *Alcohol in health and disease* (pp. 517–546). New York: Marcel Dekker.

Klatsky, A. L. (2001b). Should patients with heart disease drink alcohol? [Editorial]. *Journal of the American Medical Association, 285,* 2004–2006.

Koch, D. S. (1999). Protections in federal rehabilitation legislation for persons with alcohol and other drug abuse disabilities. *Journal of Applied Rehabilitation Counseling, 30*(3), 29–34.

Koch, D. S., Nelipovich, M., & Sneed, Z. (2002). Alcohol and other drug abuse as coexisting disabilities: Considerations for counselors serving persons who are blind or visually impaired. *RE:view, 33,* 151–159.

Kofoed, L. (1997). Engagement and persuasion. In N. S. Miller (Ed.), *The principles and practices of addictions in psychiatry* (pp. 214–220). Philadelphia: W. B. Saunders.

Kofoed, L., & Keys, A. (1988). Using group therapy to persuade dual-diagnosis patients to seek substance abuse treatment. *Hospital and Community Psychiatry, 39*(11), 1209–1211.

Kolakowsky-Hayner, S. A., Gourley, E. V., Kreutzer, J. S., Marwitz, J. H., Cifu, D. X., & McKinley, W. O. (1999). Pre-injury substance abuse among persons with brain injury and persons with spinal cord injury. *Brain Injury, 13,* 571–581.

Koster, T. B., & Guthmann, D. (n.d.). *Substance abuse and the Deaf/HH community.* Minneapolis, MN: The Minnesota Chemical Dependency Program for Deaf and Hard of Hearing Individuals. Retrieved August 24, 2010, from www.mncddeaf.org/articles/substance_abuse_ad.htm.

Krahn, G., Deck, D., Gabriel, R., & Farrell, N. (2007). A population-based study on substance abuse treatment for adults with disabilities: Access, utilization, and treatment outcomes. *The American Journal of Drug and Alcohol Abuse, 33,* 791–798.

Krahn, G., Farrell, N., Gabriel, R. M., & Deck, D. (2006). Access barriers to substance abuse treatment for people with disabilities: An exploratory study. *Journal of Substance Abuse Treatment, 31*(4), 375–384.

Krause, J. S. (2004). Factors associated with risk for subsequent injuries after traumatic spinal cord injury. *Archives of Physical Medicine and Rehabilitation, 85*(9), 1503–1508.

Kreutzer, J. S., Doherty, K. R., Harris, J. A., & Zasler, N. D. (1990). Alcohol use among persons with traumatic brain injury. *Journal of Head Trauma Rehabilitation, 5*(3), 9–20.

Kreutzer, J. S., Marwitz, J. H., & Witol, A. D. (1995). Interrelationships between crime, substance abuse, and aggressive behaviours among persons with traumatic brain injury. *Brain Injury, 9*(8), 757–768.

Kreutzer, J. S., Wehman. P. H., Harris, J. A., Burns, C. T., & Young, H. F. (1991). Substance abuse and crime patterns among persons with traumatic brain injury referred for supported employment. *Brain Injury, 5*(2), 177–187.

Kreutzer, J. S., Witol, A. D., Sander, A. M., Cifu, D. X., Marwitz, J. H., & Delmonico, R. (1996). A prospective longitudinal multicenter analysis of alcohol use patterns among persons with traumatic brain injury. *Journal of Head Trauma Rehabilitation, 11*(5), 58–69.

Krishef, C. H., & DiNitto, D. M. (1981). Alcohol abuse among mentally retarded individuals. *Mental Retardation, 19*(4), 151–155.

Kurtz, L. F., Garvin, C. D., Hill, E. M., Pollio, D., McPherson, S., & Powell, T. J. (1995). Involvement in alcoholics anonymous of persons with dual disorders. *Alcoholism Treatment Quarterly, 12*(4), 1–18.

Kyngäs, H. (2000). Compliance of adolescents with diabetes. *Journal of Pediatric Nursing, 15*(4), 260–267.

Lamb-Hart, G. L. (2001). "I see nothing, I see nothing." *Brain Injury Source, 5*(4), 12–14.

Larson, S., Lakin, K., Anderson, L., Kwak, N., Lee, J. H., & Anderson, D. (2001, April). *Characteristics of and service use by persons with MR/DD living in their own homes or with family members: NHIS-D analysis.* Minneapolis, MN: University of Minnesota Institute on Community Integration. Retrieved April 10, 2011, from rtc.umn.edu/docs/dddb3-1.pdf.

Leff, J., & Vaughn, C. (1980). The interaction of life events and relatives' expressed emotion in schizophrenia and depressive neurosis. *British Journal of Psychiatry. 136,* 146–153.

Lehman, A. F., Herron, J. D., Schwartz, R. F., & Myers, C. P. (1993). Rehabilitation for adults with severe mental illness and substance use disorders: A clinical trial. *Journal of Nervous and Mental Disease, 14,* 86–90.

Linehan, M. M., Schmidt, H., Dimeff, L. A., Craft, J. C., Kanter, J., & Comtois, K. A. (1999). Dialectical behavior therapy for patients with borderline personality disorder and drug-dependence. *The American Journal on Addictions, 8,* 279–292.

Lipton, D. S., & Goldstein, M. F. (1997). Measuring substance abuse among the deaf. *Journal of Drug Issues, 27,* 733–754.

Lottman, T. J. (1993). Access to generic substance abuse services for persons with mental retardation. *Journal of Alcohol and Drug Education, 39*(1), 41–55.

Lukomski, J. (2007). Deaf college students' perceptions of their social-emotional adjustment. *Journal of Deaf Studies and Deaf Education, 12*(4), 486–494.

Maine approach: A treatment model for the intellectually limited substance abuser. (1984). Augusta: The Maine Department of Mental Health and Mental Retardation.

Malloy, P., Noel, N., Longabaugh, R., & Beattie, M. (1990). Determinants of neuropsychological impairment in antisocial substance abusers. *Addictive Behaviors, 15,* 431–438.

Manchikanti, L. et al. (2006). Controlled substance abuse and illicit drug use in chronic pain patients: An evaluation of multiple variables. *Pain Physician, 9,* 215–226.

Mancikanti, L., Manchukonda, R., Damron, K. S., Brandon, D., McManus, C. D., & Cash, K. (2006). Does adherence monitoring reduce controlled substance abuse in chronic pain patients? *Pain Physician, 9,* 57–60.

Mannion, E., Mueser, K., & Solomon, P. (1994). Designing psychoeducational services for spouses of persons with serious mental illness. *Community Mental Health Journal, 30*(2), 177–191.

Marmot, M. G. (2001). Alcohol and coronary heart disease. *International Journal of Epidemiology, 30,* 724–729.

Marschark, M., & Spencer, P. E. (Eds.) (2003). *Oxford handbook of deaf studies, language, and education.* New York: Oxford University Press.

Martinez-Aguayo, A., Araneda, J. C., Fernandez, D., Gleisner, A., Perez, V., & Codner, E. (2007). Tobacco, alcohol, and illicit drug use in adolescents with diabetes mellitus. *Pediatric Diabetes, 8,* 265–271.

McCrystal, P., Percy, A., & Higgins, K. (2007). Substance use behaviors of young people with a moderate learning disability: A longitudinal analysis. *The American Journal of Alcohol and Drug Abuse, 33,* 155–161.

McFarlane, W. R., Dunne, E., Lukens, E., Newmark, M., McLaughlin-Toran, J., Deakins, S., & Horen, B. (1993). From research to clinical practice: Dissemination of New York state's family psychoeducation project. *Hospital and Community Psychiatry, 44*(3), 265–270.

McGillicuddy, N. (2006). A review of substance use research among those with mental retardation. *Mental Retardation and Developmental Disabilities Research Reviews, 12*(1), 41–47.

McGillicuddy, N. B., & Blane, H. T. (1999). Substance use in individuals with mental retardation. *Addictive Behaviors, 24,* 869–878.

McHugo, G. J., Drake, R. E., Burton, H. L., & Ackerson, T. H. (1995). A scale for assessing the stage of substance abuse treatment in persons with severe mental illness. *Journal of Nervous and Mental Disease, 183,* 762–767.

McLellan, A. T., Childress, A. R., & Woody, G. E. (1985). Drug abuse and psychiatric disorder: Role of drug choice. In A. I. Alterman (Ed.), *Substance abuse and psychopathology* (pp. 137–172). New York: Plenum Press.

McNamara, J., Vervaeke, S., & Willoughby, T. (2008). Learning disabilities and risk-taking behavior in adolescents. *Journal of Learning Disabilities, 41*(6), 561–574.

McNamara, J. K., & Willoughby, T. (2010). A longitudinal study of risk-taking behavior in adolescents with learning disabilities. *Learning Disabilities Research & Practice, 25*(1), 11–24.

Mee-Lee, D., Shulman, G., Fishman, M., Gastfriend, D., & Griffiths, J. H. (2001). *ASAM patient placement criteria for the treatment of substance-related disorders* (2nd ed. rev.) (ASAM PPC-2R). Chevy Chase, MD: American Society of Addiction Medicine.

Mee-Lee, D. (2002, March 28). *Why integrating mental health and substance abuse is hard and what to do about it.* Presentation at Building the Bridge: A national conference on integrating mental health and substance abuse services, San Antonio, TX.

Merikangas, K. R., Mehta, R. L., Molnar, B. E., Walters, E. E., Swendsen, J. D., Aguilar-Gaziola, S., et al. (1998). Comorbidity of substance use disorders with mood and anxiety disorders: Results of the International Consortium in Psychiatric Epidemiology. *Addictive Behaviors, 23,* 893–907.

Miller, L. S., & Faustman, W. O. (1996). Brief Psychiatric Rating Scale. In L. I. Sederer & B. Dickey (Eds.), *Outcomes assessment in clinical practice* (pp. 105–109). Baltimore: Williams & Wilkins.

Miller, N. S. (1994). Alcohol and drug disorders. In J. M. Silver, S. C. Yudofsky, & R. E. Hales (Eds.), *Neuropsychiatry of traumatic brain injury* (pp. 471–498). Washington, DC: American Psychiatric Press.

Miller, W. R. & Rollnick, S. (2002). *Motivational interviewing: Preparing people for change* (2nd ed.). New York, NY: Guilford Press.

Minkoff, K. (1989). An integrated treatment model for dual diagnosis of psychosis and addiction. *Hospital and Community Psychiatry, 40*(10), 1031–1036.

Minkoff, K. (2001a). Developing standards of care for individuals with co-occurring psychiatric and substance use disorders. *Psychiatric Services, 52,* 597–599.

Minkoff, K. (2001b, April). *Service planning guidelines: co-occurring psychiatric and substance disorders* (Illinois: Behavioral Health Recovery Management Project). Retrieved April 6, 2011, from www.bhrm.org/guidelines/Minkoff.pdf.

Minkoff, K. (2002, March 28). *An integrated model for treatment of people with co-occurring disorders.* Presentation at Building the Bridge, a national conference on integrating mental health and substance abuse services, San Antonio, TX.

Mitchell, R. E. (2005, February). *Can you tell me how many deaf people there are in the United States?* Washington, DC: Gallaudet Research Institute, Gallaudet University. Retrieved April 10, 2011, from research.gallaudet.edu/Demographics/deaf-US.php.

Mitiguy, J. (1991, Summer). Alcohol and head trauma. *Headlines, 6.*

Mochly-Rosen, D., & Zakhari, S. (2010). Focus on the cardiovascular system. What did we learn from the French (paradox)? *Alcohol Research & Health, 33*(1&2), 76–86.

Molina, B. S. G., & Pelham, W. E. (2001). Substance use, substance abuse, and LD among adolescents with a childhood history of ADHD. *Journal of Learning Disabilities, 34*(4), 333–342, 351.

Mojtabai, R. (2004). Which substance abuse facilities offer dual diagnosis programs? *The American Journal of Drug and Alcohol Abuse, 30*(3), 525–536.

Moore, D. (1998). *Substance use disorder treatment for people with physical and cognitive disabilities* (Treatment Improvement Protocol [TIP] Series no. 29, DHHS Publication no. [SMA] 98–3249). Rockville, MD: Substance Abuse and Mental Health Services Administration.

Moore, D., Guthmann, D., Rogers, N., Fraker, S. & Embree, J. (2009). E-therapy as a means for addressing barriers to substance use disorder treatment for persons who are deaf. *Journal of Sociology and Social Welfare, 36*(4), 75–92.

Moore, D., & Ford, J. A. (1991). Prevention of substance abuse among persons with disabilities: A demonstration model. *Prevention Forum, 11*(2), 1–3, 7–10.

Moore, D., & Ford, J. A. (1996). Policy responses to substance abuse and disability. *Journal of Disability Policy Studies, 7*(1), 91–106.

Moore, D., & McAweeney, M. (2006/2007). Demographic characteristics and rates of progress of deaf and hard of hearing persons receiving substance abuse treatment. *American Annals of the Deaf, 151*(5), 508–512.

Mueser, K. T., Drake, R. E., & Wallach, M. A. (1998a). Dual diagnosis: A review of etiological theories. *Addictive Behaviors, 23,* 717–734.

Mueser, K. T., Drake, R. E., & Noordsy, D. L. (1998b). Integrated mental health and substance abuse treatment for severe psychiatric disorders. *Journal of Practical Psychiatry and Behavioral Health, 4,* 129–139.

Mueser, K. T., Rosenberg, S. D., Drake, R. E., Miles, K., Wolford, G., Vidaver, R., & Carrieri, K. (1999). Conduct disorder, antisocial personality disorder and substance use disorders in schizophrenia and major affective disorders. *Journal of Studies on Alcohol, 60,* 278–284.

Mukamal, K. J., & Rimm, E. B. (2001). Alcohol's effects on the risk for coronary heart disease. *Alcohol Research & Health, 25*(4), 255–261. Retrieved April 6, 2011, from pubs.niaaa.nih.gov/publications/arh25-4/255-261.htm.

Myers, B. A. (1987). Psychiatric problems in adolescents with developmental disabilities. *Journal of the American Academy of Child and Adolescent Psychiatry, 26*(1), 74–79.

Naegle, M. A. (1997). Understanding women with dual diagnoses. *Journal of Obstetric, Gynecologic, and Neonatal Nursing, 26,* 567–575.

National Association on Alcohol, Drugs, and Disability (NAADD). (1999). *Access limited substance abuse services for people with disabilities: A national perspective.* San Mateo, CA: Author.

Narcotics Anonymous World Services. (1992). *In times of illness.* Van Nuys, CA: Author.

National Institute on Alcohol Abuse and Alcoholism (NIAAA). (1999). *Alcohol and coronary heart disease.* Retrieved May 11, 2011, from pubs.niaaa.nih.gov/publications/aa45.htm.

National Institute on Alcohol Abuse and Alcoholism (NIAAA). (2000). *Tenth special report to the U.S. Congress on alcohol and health.* Washington, DC: U.S. Department of Health and Human Services.

National Spinal Cord Injury Statistical Center. (2010, February). *2009 Annual report for the Spinal Cord Injury Model Systems.* Birmingham, AL: University of Alabama at Birmingham. Retrieved April 6, 2011, from www.nscisc.uab.edu/public_content/pdf/2009%20NSCISC%20Annual%20Statistical%20Report%20-%20Complete%20Public%20Version.pdf.

New York State Division of Alcoholism and Alcohol Abuse (NYSDAAA). (1988). Alcoholism and the hearing impaired. *DAAA Focus, 3*(3), 1.

Nelipovich, M., & Buss, E. (1989). Alcohol abuse and persons who are blind: Treatment considerations. *Alcohol Health and Research World, 13*(2), 128–131.

Nelipovich, M., & Buss, E. (1991). Investigating alcohol abuse among persons who are blind. *Journal of Visual Impairment and Blindness, 85*(8), 343–345.

Nelipovich, M., & Parker, R. (1981). The visually impaired substance abuser. *Journal of Visual Impairment and Blindness, 75*(6), 305.

Nelipovich, M., Wergin, C., & Kossick, R. (1998). The MARCO model: Making substance abuse services accessible to people who are visually impaired. *Journal of Visual Impairment and Blindness, 92*(8), 567–570.

Noordsy, D. L., Schwab, B., Fox, L., & Drake, R. E. (1996). The role of self-help programs in the rehabilitation of persons with severe mental illness and substance use disorders. *Community Mental Health Journal, 32*, 71–81.

Nuttbrock, L. A., Rahav, M., Rivera, J. J., Ng-Mak, D. S., & Link, B. G. (1998). Outcomes of homeless mentally ill chemical abusers in community residences and a therapeutic community. *Psychiatric Services, 49*, 68–76.

Office of the Surgeon General. (2007). *The Surgeon General's call to action to improve the health and wellness of persons with disabilities.* Washington, DC: U.S. Department of Health and Human Services. Retrieved April 10, 2011, from www.surgeongeneral.gov/library/disabilities/calltoaction/future.html.

O'Donnell, J. J., Cooper, J. E., Gessner, J. E., Shehan, I., & Ashley, J. (1981/82). Alcohol, drugs, and spinal cord injury. *Alcohol Health and Research World, 6*(2), 27–29.

O'Phelan, K., McArthur, D. L., Chang, C. W. J., Green, D., & Hovda, D. A. (2008). The impact of substance abuse on mortality in patients with severe traumatic brain injury. *Journal of Trauma, 65*, 674–677.

Ogborne, A. C., Smart, R. G., Weber, T., & Birchmore-Timney, C. (2000). Who is using cannabis as a medicine and why: An exploratory study. *Journal of Psychoactive Drugs, 32*(4), 435–443.

Osher, F. C., & Kofoed, L. L. (1989). Treatment of patients with psychiatric and psychoactive substance abuse disorders. *Hospital and Community Psychiatry, 40*(10), 1025–1030.

Pack, R. P., Wallander, J. L., & Browne, D. (1998). Health risk behaviors of African American adolescents with mild mental retardation: Prevalence depends on measurement method. *American Journal on Mental Retardation, 102*, 409–420.

Parry-Jones, B. L., Vaughan, F. L., & Cox W. M. (2006). Traumatic brain injury and substance misuse: A systematic review of prevalence and outcomes research (1994–2004). *Neuropsychological rehabilitation, 16*(5), 537–560.

Paxon, J. E. (1995). Relapse prevention for individuals with developmental disabilities, borderline intellectual functioning, or illiteracy. *Journal of Psychoactive Drugs, 27*(2), 167–172.

Pepper, B. (1991). Some experience with psychoeducation groups for clients with dual disorders. TIE-Lines, *8*(2), 4.

Pepper, B., & Ryglewicz, H. (Eds.) (1982). The young adult chronic patient. *New directions in mental health services, no. 14.* San Francisco: Jossey-Bass.

Perez, M., & Pilsecker, C. (1994). Group psychotherapy with spinal cord injured substance abusers. *Paraplegia, 32*, 188–192.

Peterson, J., & Nelipovich, M. (1983). Alcoholism and the visually impaired client. *Journal of Visual Impairment and Blindness, 77*, 345–348.

Pietraszek, A., Gregersen, S., & Hermansen, K. (2010). Alcohol and type 2 diabetes. A review. *Nutrition, Metabolism & Cardiovascular Diseases, 20*, 366–375.

Potamianos, G., Gorman, D. M., Duffy, S. W., & Peters, T. J. (1988). Alcohol consumption by patients attending outpatient clinics. *International Journal of Social Psychiatry, 34*(2), 97–101.

Pozzi, G., Frustaci, A., Janiri, L., & Di Giannantonio, M. (2006). The challenge of psychiatric comorbidity to the public services for drug dependence in Italy: A national survey. *Drug and Alcohol Dependence, 82*(3), 224–230.

President's Committee for People with Intellectual Disabilities (2010, November 5). About the committee. Washington, DC: U.S. Department of Health and Human Services. Retrieved June 27, 2011, from http://www.acf.hhs.gov/programs/pcpid/pcpid_about.html.

Preston, J. D., O'Neal, J. H. & Talaga, M. C. (2010). *Handbook of clinical psychopharmacology for therapists* (6th ed.). New Harbinger Publishers, Inc.

Prevent Blindness America and National Eye Institute. (2002). *Vision problems in the U.S.: Prevalence of adult vision impairment and age-related eye disease in America.* Schaumburg, IL: Prevent Blindness America. Retrieved April 6, 2011, from www.preventblindness.org/vpus/VPUS_report_web.pdf.

Primm, A. B., Gomez, M. B., Tzolova-Iontchev, I. et al. (2000). Mental health versus substance abuse treatment programs for dually diagnosed patients. *Journal of Substance Abuse Treatment, 19*, 285–290.

Prochaska, J. O., DiClemente, C. C., & Norcross, J. C. (1992). In search of how people change: Applications to addictive behaviors. *American Psychologist, 47*(9), 1102–1114.

RachBeisel, J., Scott, J., & Dixon, L. (1999). Co-occurring severe mental illness and substance use disorders: A review of recent research. *Psychiatric Services, 50*, 1427–1434.

Radnitz, C. L., Broderick, C. P., Perez-Strumolo, L., Tirch, D. D., Festa, J., et al. (1996). The prevalence of psychiatric disorders in veterans with spinal cord injury: A controlled comparison. *Journal of Nervous and Mental Disease, 184*, 431–433.

Radnitz, C. L., & Tirch, D. (1995). Substance misuse in individuals with spinal cord injury. *International Journal of the Addictions, 30*, 1117–1140.

Regier, D. A., Farmer, M. E., Rae, D. S., Locke, B. Z., Keith, S. J., Judd, L. L., & Goodwin, F. K. (1990). Comorbidity of mental disorders with alcohol and other drug abuse: Results from the epidemiologic catchment area (ECA) study. *Journal of the American Medical Association, 264*(19), 2511–2518.

Rehabilitation Research and Training Center (RRTC) on Drugs and Disability. (2002). *Technical Report: Summary of findings for research component R1—Continuing investigation of substance abuse, disability, and vocational rehabilitation.* Dayton, OH: Substance Abuse Rehabilitation and Disability Issues (SARDI) Program, Wright State University School of Medicine. Retrieved May 11, 2011, from www.med.

wright.edu/sites/default/files/citar/sardi/files/pdf_technicalr1.pdf.

Rehm, J., Baliunas, D., Borge, G. L. G., et al. (2010). The relation between different dimensions of alcohol consumption and burden of disease: An overview. *Addiction, 105*(5), 817–843.

Reiss, S. (1990). Prevalence of dual diagnosis in community-based day programs in the Chicago metropolitan area. *American Journal on Mental Retardation, 94*(6), 578–585.

Rendon, M. E. (1992). Deaf culture and alcohol and substance abuse. *Journal of Substance Abuse Treatment, 9,* 103–110.

Rimmer, J. H., Braddock, D., & Marks, B. (1995). Health characteristics and behaviors of adults with mental retardation residing in three living arrangements. *Research in Developmental Disabilities, 16,* 489–499.

Rodriguez-Llera, M. C., Domingo-Salvany, A., Brugal, M. T., Silva, T. C., Sanchez-Niubo, A., & Torrens, M. (2006). Psychiatric comorbidity in young heroin users. *Drug and Alcohol Dependence, 84*(1), 48–55.

Rohe, D. E., & Basford, J. R. (1989). Traumatic spinal cord injury, alcohol, and the Minnesota multiphasic personality inventory. *Rehabilitation Psychology, 34*(1), 25–32.

Rosenberg, S. D., Drake, R. E., Wolford, G. L., & Mueser, K. T. (1998). Dartmouth Assessment of Lifestyle Instrument (DALI): A substance abuse disorder screen for people with severe mental illness. *American Journal of Psychiatry, 155,* 232–238.

Rosenthal, R. N., & Westreich, L. (1999). Treatment of persons with dual diagnoses of substance use disorder and other psychological problems. In B. S. McCrady & E. E. Epstein (Eds.), *Addictions: A comprehensive guidebook* (pp. 439–476). New York: Oxford University Press.

Rothfeld, P. (1981). Alcoholism treatment for the deaf: Specialized services for special people. *Journal of Rehabilitation of the Deaf, 14*(4), 14–17.

Rubin, J. (2003). Deafness and chemical dependency. Rochester, NY: Rochester Institute of Technology, Substance and Alcohol Intervention Services for the Deaf. Retrieved May 6, 2011, from ritdml.rit.edu/bitstream/handle/1850/1165/JRubin2Article2003.pdf?sequence=6.

Ryan, K. (1983/84). Alcohol and blood sugar disorders: An overview. *Alcohol Health and Research World, 8*(2), 3–7, 15.

Ryglewicz, H., & Pepper, B. (1990). *Alcohol, drugs, and mental/emotional problems: What you need to know to help your dual-disorder client.* New City, NY: Information Exchange.

Ryglewicz, H., & Pepper, B. (1996). *Lives at risk: Understanding and treating young people with dual disorders.* New York, NY: The Free Press.

Saitz, R. (2009). Medial and surgical complications of addiction. In R. K. Ries, D. A. Fiellin, S. C. Miller, & R. Saitz (Eds.), *Principles of addiction medicine* (4th ed.,

pp. 945–967). Philadelphia: Lippincott Williams & Wilkins.

Sandberg, K. A. (1996). *Alcohol and other drug use among post secondary deaf and hard of hearing students.* Minnesota Chemical Dependency Program for Deaf and Hard of Hearing Individuals. Retrieved April 6, 2011, from www.mncddeaf.org/articles/use_ad.htm.

Scaramuzza, A. E., De Palma, A., Mameli, C., Spiri, D., Santoro, L., & Zuccotti, G. V. (2010). Adolescents with type 1 diabetes and risky behaviour. *Acta Paediatrica, 99,* 1237–1241.

Schaschl, S., & Straw, D. (1989). Results of a model intervention program for physically impaired persons. *Alcohol Health and Research World, 13*(2), 150–153.

Schulte, S. J., Meier, P. S., Stirling, J., & Berry, M. (2010). Unrecognised dual diagnosis—a risk factor for dropout in addiction treatment. *Mental Health and Substance Use, 3*(2), 94–109.

Sciacca, K. (1987). New initiatives in the treatment of the chronic patient with alcohol/substance use problems. *TIE-Lines, 4*(3), 5–6.

Sciacca, K. (1991). An integrated approach for severely mentally ill individuals with substance disorders. In K. Minkoff & R. E. Drake (Eds.), *Dual diagnosis of major mental illness and substance disorder* (pp. 69–84). San Francisco: Jossey-Bass.

Selan, B. H. (1981). *The psychological consequences of alcohol use or abuse by retarded persons.* Paper presented at the American Association on Mental Deficiency Annual Conference, Detroit, MI.

Selzer, M. L. (1971). The Michigan alcoholism screening test: The quest for a new diagnostic instrument. *American Journal of Psychiatry, 127,* 1653–1658.

Shaw, L. R., MacGillis, P. W., & Dvorchik, K. M. (1994). Alcoholism and the Americans with Disabilities Act: Obligations and accommodations. *Rehabilitation Counseling Bulletin, 38*(2), 108–123.

Sheu, R. et al. (2008). Prevalence and characteristics of chronic pain in patients admitted to an outpatient drug and alcohol treatment program. *Pain Medicine, 9*(7), 911–917.

Simpson, M. (1998). Just say 'no'? Alcohol and people with learning difficulties. *Disability and Society, 13,* 541–555.

Slayter, E. M. (2007). Substance abuse and mental retardation: Balancing risk management with the "dignity of risk." *Families in Society, 88*(4), 651–659.

Slayter, E. M. (2010). Disparities in access to substance abuse treatment among people with intellectual disabilities and serious mental illness. *Health & Social Work, 35*(1), 49–59.

Skinner, H. A. (1982). The drug abuse screening test. *Addictive Behaviors, 7,* 363–371.

Skinner, H. A. (1984). Assessing alcohol use by patients in treatment. In R. G. Smart, H. D. Cappell, & F. B. Glaser (Eds.), *Research advances in alcohol and drug problems* (vol. 8, pp. 183–207). New York: Plenum Press.

Small, J. (1980/81). Emotions anonymous: Counseling the mentally retarded substance abuser. *Alcohol Health and Research World, 5*(2), 46.

Smart, J. (2001). *Disability, society, and the individual.* Gaithesburg, MD: Aspen.

Smith, B. H., Molina, B. S. G., & Pelham, W. E. (2002). Clinically meaningful link between alcohol use and attention deficit hyperactivity disorder. *Alcohol Research and Health, 26*(2), 122–129.

Spangler, J. G., Konen, J. C., & McGann, K. P. (1993). Prevalence and predictors of problem drinking among primary care diabetic patients. *Journal of Family Practice, 37*(4), 370–375.

Sparadeo, F. R. (2001). Treating substance abuse in individuals with TBI: The lessons of experience. *Brain Injury Source, 5*(4), 24–27, 42–45.

Sparadeo, F. R., & Gill, D. (1989). Effects of prior alcohol use on head injury recovery. *Journal of Head Trauma Rehabilitation, 4*(1), 75–82.

Sparadeo, F. R., Strauss, D., & Barth, J. T. (1990). The incidence, impact, and treatment of substance abuse in head trauma rehabilitation. *Journal of Head Trauma Rehabilitation, 5*(3), 1–8.

Stasiewicz, P. R., Carey, K. B., Bradizza, C. M., & Maiston, S. A. (1996). Behavioral assessment of substance abuse with co-occurring psychiatric disorder. *Cognitive and Behavioral Practice, 3,* 91–105.

Steer, R. A., & Beck, A. T. (1996). Beck Depression Inventory (BDI). In L. I. Sederer & B. Dickey (Eds.), *Outcomes assessment in clinical practice* (pp. 100–104). Baltimore: Williams & Wilkins.

Stein, L. I., & Test, M. A. (1980). Alternative to mental hospital treatment. I. Conceptual model, treatment program, and clinical evaluation. *Archives of General Psychiatry, 37,* 392–397.

Steinberg, A. (1991). Issues in providing mental health services to hearing impaired persons. *Hospital and Community Psychiatry, 42*(4), 380–389.

Steitler, K., & Rubin, J. L. (2001). Deafness and chemical dependency. Rochester, NY: Rochester Institute of Technology, Substance and Alcohol Intervention Services for the Deaf. Retrieved April 13, 2002, from www.rit.edu/~257www/tips/paper.htm.

Sterling, S., Chi, F., & Hinman, A. (2011). Integrating care for people with co-occurring alcohol and other drug, medical, and mental health conditions. *Alcohol Research & Health, 33*(4), 338–349.

Strauss, D. (2001). An overview of substance abuse and brain injury. *Brain Injury Source, 5*(4), 8–11, 40–41.

Substance Abuse and Mental Health Services Administration (SAMHSA). (2009). *Results from the 2008 National Survey on Drug Use and Health: National findings (Office of Applied Studies, NSDUH Series H-36, HHS Publication No. SMA 09–4434).* Rockville, MD: U.S. Department of Health and Human Services. Retrieved April 10, 2011, from www.oas.samhsa.gov/nsduh/2k8nsduh/2k8results.cfm.

Swartz, M. S., Wilder, C. M., Swanson, J. W., Van Dorn, R. A., Robbins, P. C., Steadman, H. J., Moser, L. L., Gilbert, A. R., & Monahan, J. (2010). Assessing outcomes for consumers in New York's assisted outpatient treatment program. *Psychiatric Services, 61*(10), 976–981.

Tamaskar, P., Malia, T., Stern, C., Gorenflo, D., Meador, H., & Zazove, P. (2000). Preventive attitudes and beliefs of deaf and hard-of-hearing individuals. *Archives of Family Medicine, 9,* 518–525.

Tapert, S. F., Baratta, M. V., Abrantes, A. M., & Brown, S. A. (2002). Attention dysfunction predicts substance involvement in community youths. *Journal of the American Academy of Child and Adolescent Psychiatry, 41*(6), 680–686.

Tate, D. G., Forchheimer, M. B., Krause, J. S., Meade, & Bombardier, C. H. (2004). Patterns of alcohol and substance use and abuse in persons with spinal cord injury: Risk factors and correlates. *Archives of Physical Medicine and Rehabilitation, 85*(11), 1837–1847.

Tate, P. S., Freed, D. M., Bombardier, C. H., Harter, S. L., & Brinkman, S. (1999). Traumatic brain injury: Influence of blood alcohol level on post-acute cognitive function. *Brain Injury, 13,* 767–784.

Teitelbaum, L., & Mullen, B. (2000). The validity of the MAST in psychiatric settings: A meta-analytic integration. *Journal of Studies on Alcohol, 61,* 254–261.

Terry, L. (n.d.). Treating the head injured substance abuser. *New Jersey Rehab* [Reprint].

Timko, C., Lesar, M., Calvi, N., et al., (2003). Trends in acute mental health care: Comparing psychiatric and substance abuse treatment programs. *Journal of Behavioral Health Services and Research, 30,* 145–160.

Titus, J. C. (2010). The nature of victimization among youths with hearing loss in substance abuse treatment. *American Annals of the Deaf, 155*(1), 19–30.

Titus, J. C., & Guthmann, D. (2010). Addressing the black hole in substance abuse treatment for deaf and hard of hearing individuals: Technology to the rescue. *JADARA, 43*(2), 92–100.

Titus, J., Schiller, J. & Guthmann, D. (2008). Characteristics of youths with hearing loss admitted to substance abuse treatment. *Journal of Deaf Studies and Deaf Education, 13*(3), 336–350.

Titus, J. C., & White, W. L. (2008, late Fall). Substance use among youths who are deaf and hard of hearing: A primer for student assistance professionals. *Student Assistance Journal,* 14–18. Retrieved January 16, 2011, from www.williamwhitepapers.com/pr/2008Substance UseDeaf%26HardofHearing.pdf.

Torrey, E. F. (2006). *Surviving schizophrenia: A family manual* (5th ed.). New York, NY: Harper Paperbacks.

Traumatic Brain Injury National Data and Statistical Center. (2010). 2010 Model Systems Presentation. Englewood, CO: Author. Retrieved January 9, 2011, from www.tbindsc.org.

Treffert, D. A. (1978). Marijuana use in schizophrenia: A clear hazard. *American Journal of Psychiatry, 135*(10), 1213–1215.

Turner, W. M., & Tsuang, M. I. (1990). Impact of substance abuse on the course and outcome of schizophrenia. *Schizophrenia Bulletin, 16*(1), 87–95.

Turner, A. P., Bombardier, C. H., & Rimmele, C. T. (2003). A typology of alcohol use patterns among persons with recent traumatic brain injury or spinal cord injury: Implications for treatment matching. *Archives of Physical Medicine and Rehabilitation, 84*(3), 358–364.

U.S. Census Bureau. (2007). *Selected economic characteristics for the civilian noninstitutionalized population by disability status.* Washington, DC: Author. Retrieved January 11, 2011, from factfinder.census.gov/servlet/STTable?_bm=y&-geo_id=01000US&-qr_name=ACS_2007_1YR_G00_S1802&-ds_name=ACS_2007_1YR_G00_&-_lang=en&-redoLog=false&-state=st&-format=.

U.S. Census Bureau. (2008, February). *Disability status and the characteristics of people in group quarters: A brief analysis of disability prevalence among the civilian noninstitutionalized and total populations in the American Community Survey.* Retrieved January 11, 2011, from www.census.gov/hhes/www/disability/GQdisability.pdf.

U.S. Commission on Civil Rights, (2000). *Sharing the dream: Is the ADA accommodating all?* Washington, DC: Author. Retrieved April 10, 2011, from www.us ccr.gov/pubs/ada/main.htm.

U.S. Equal Employment Opportunity Commission. (2005). *Americans with disabilities act: Questions and answers.* Washington, DC: U.S. Department of Justice.

Vaughn, C. E., and Leff, J. P. (1976). The influence of family and social factors on the course of psychiatric illness. A comparison of schizophrenic and depressed neurotic patients. *British Journal of Psychiatry, 129,* 125–137.

Velasquez, M. M., Carbonari, J. P., & DiClemente, C. C. (1999). Psychiatric severity and behavior change in alcoholism: The relation of the transtheoretical model variables to psychiatric distress in dually diagnosed patients. *Addictive Behaviors, 24,* 481–496.

Velligan, D. I., Lam, Y. W., Glahn, D. C., et al. (2006). Defining and assessing adherence to oral antipsychotics: A review of the literature. *Schizophrenia Bulletin, 32,* 724–742.

Vungkhanching, M., Heinemann, A. W., Langley, M. J., Ridgely, M., & Kramer, K. M. (2007). Feasibility of a skills-based substance abuse prevention program following traumatic brain injury. *Journal of Head Trauma and Rehabilitation, 22*(3), 167–176.

Wallen, M. C., & Weiner, H. D. (1989). Impediments to effective treatment of the dually diagnosed patient. *Journal of Psychoactive Drugs, 21,* 161–168.

Walker, R., Cole, J. E., Logan, T. K., & Corrigan, J. D. (2007). Screening substance abuse treatment clients for traumatic brain injury: Prevalence and characteristics. *Journal of Head Trauma Rehabilitation, 22*(6), 360–367.

Watkins, K. E., Hunter, S. B., Burnam, M. A., et al. (2005). Review of treatment recommendations for persons with a co-occurring affective or anxiety and substance use disorder. *Psychiatric Services, 56,* 913–926.

Watkins, K. E., Hunter, S. B., Wenzel, S. L., et al. (2004). Prevalence and characteristics of clients with co-occurring disorders in outpatient substance abuse treatment. *American Journal of Drug and Alcohol Abuse, 30,* 749–764.

Watson, A. L., Franklin, M. E., Ingram, M. A., & Eilenberg, L. B. (1998). Alcohol and other drug abuse among persons with disabilities. *Journal of Applied Rehabilitation Counseling, 29*(2), 22–29.

Webb, D. K. (1994). Psychoeducation/group therapy for individuals with serious mental illnesses and chemical abuse or dependence: Testing the effectiveness of "Good Chemistry." Doctoral Dissertation, The University of Texas at Austin, Austin, TX.

Webb, D. K. (1990, 1992, 2004). *Good Chemistry Co-Leader's Manual.* Austin, TX: Author.

Weber, E. M., & Moore, D. (2001). Employing and accommodating individuals with histories of alcohol or drug abuse. Ithaca, NY: Cornell University.

Wehmeyer, M. L., & Patton, J. R. (2000). *Mental retardation in the 21st century.* Austin, TX: PRO-ED.

Wiedemer, N. L., Harden, P. S., Arndt, I. O., & Gallagher, R. M. (2007). The opioid renewal clinic: A primary care, managed approach to opioid therapy in chronic pain patients at risk for substance abuse. *Pain Medicine, 8*(7), 573–584.

Weinstein, D. D., & Martin, P. R. (1995). Psychiatric implications of alcoholism and traumatic brain injury. *American Journal on Addictions, 4*(4), 285–296.

Weiss, R. D., & Mirin, S. M. (1989). The dual diagnosis alcoholic: Evaluation and treatment. *Psychiatric Annals, 19*(5), 261–265.

Wenc, F. (1980/81). The developmentally disabled substance abuser. *Alcohol Health and Research World, Winter, 5*(2), 42–46.

West, S. L. (2007). The accessibility of substance abuse treatment facilities in the United States for persons with disabilities. *Journal of Substance Abuse Treatment, 33,* 1–5.

West, S. L. (2008). The utilization of vocational rehabilitation services in substance abuse treatment facilities in the U.S. *Journal of Vocational Rehabilitation, 29*(2), 71–75.

West, S. L., Graham, C. W., Cifu, D. X. (2009). Rates of alcohol/other drug treatment denials to persons with physical disabilities: Accessibility concerns. *Alcoholism Treatment Quarterly, 27*(3), 305–316.

West, S. & Miller, J. (1999). Comparisons of vocational rehabilitation counselors' attitudes toward substance abusers. *Journal of Applied Rehabilitation Counseling, 30*(4), 33–37.

Westermeyer, J., Kemp, K., & Nugent, S. (1996). Substance disorder among persons with mental retardation: A comparative study. *American Journal on Addictions, 5*(1), 23–31.

Westermeyer, J., Phaobtong, T., & Neider, J. (1988). Substance use and abuse among mentally retarded persons: A comparison of patients and a survey population. *American Journal of Drug and Alcohol Abuse, 14*(1), 109–123.

Whitehouse, A., Sherman, R. E., & Kozlowski, K. (1991). The needs of deaf substance abusers in Illinois. *American Journal of Drug and Alcohol Abuse, 17,* 103–113.

Winter, A. S. (1991, January/February). Dual diagnosis = double trouble. *Counselor, 9,* 34.

Wise, B. K., Cuffe, S. P., & Fisher, T. (2001). Dual diagnosis and successful participation of adolescents in substance abuse treatment. *Journal of Substance Abuse Treatment, 21,* 161–165.

Woll, P., Schmidt, M. F., & Heinemann, A. W. (1993). *Alcohol and other drug abuse prevention for people with traumatic brain and spinal cord injuries.* Chicago, IL: Rehabilitation Institute of Chicago.

Woods, J. D. (1991). Incorporating services for chemical dependency problems into clubhouse model programs: A description of two programs. *Psychosocial Rehabilitation Journal, 15*(2), 107–111.

Young, M. E., Rintala, D. H., Rossi, D., Hart, K. A., & Fuhrer, M. J. (1995). Alcohol and marijuana use in a community-based sample of persons with spinal cord injury. *Archives of Physical Medicine and Rehabilitation, 76*(6), 525–532.

Zaccara, G. (2009). Neurological comorbidity and epilepsy: Implications for treatment. *Acta Neurologica Scandinavica, 120*(1), 1–15.

Zeber, J., Copeland, L., Amuan, M., Cramer, J., & Pugh, M. (2007). The role of comorbid psychiatric conditions in health status in epilepsy. *Epilepsy & Behavior, 10*(4), 539–546.

Ziedonis, D. M., Smelson, D., Rosenthal, R. N., Batki, S. L., Green, A. I., Henry, R. J. et al. (2005). Improving the care of individuals with schizophrenia and substance abuse disorders: Consensus recommendations. *Journal of Psychiatric Practice, 11,* 315–339.

Zweben, J. E. (1996). Psychiatric problems among alcohol and other drug dependent women. *Journal of Psychoactive Drugs, 28,* 345–366.

CHAPTER 14

Abbott, M. B. (1994, Fall). Homelessness and substance abuse: Is mandatory treatment the solution? *Fordham Urban Law Journal,* p. 3.

Abrams, R. C., & Alexopoulos, G. S. (1988). Substance abuse in the elderly: Over-the-counter and illegal drugs. *Hospital and Community Psychiatry, 39,* 822–823.

Abramson, J. L., Williams, S. A., Krumholz, H. M., & Vaccarino, V. (2001). Moderate alcohol consumption and risk of heart failure among older persons. *JAMA, 285,* 1971–1977.

American Geriatrics Society (AGS). (2003). *Clinical guidelines for alcohol use disorders in older adults.* Retrieved July 30, 2009 from www.americangeriatrics.org/products/positionpapers/alcohol.shtml.

American Medical Association (AMA). (1995, October 23/30). Help combat a hidden epidemic. AMA guidelines address elderly alcoholism. Editorial in *American Medical News,* Retrieved January 4, 2002, from www.amaassn.org/sci-pubs/amnews/amn_arch/edit 1023.htm.

American Medical Association (AMA), Council on Scientific Affairs. (1996). Alcoholism in the elderly. *Journal of the American Medical Association, 275,* 797–801.

American Psychiatric Association (APA). (1994). *Diagnostic and statistical manual of mental disorders* (4th ed.). Washington, DC: Author.

Atkinson, R. M., Tolson, R. L., & Turner, J. A. (1993). Factors affecting outpatient treatment compliance of older male problem drinkers. *Journal of Studies on Alcoholism, 54,* 102–106.

Atkinson, R., Turner, J. A., Kofoed, L. L., & Tolson, R. L. (1985). Early versus late onset alcoholism in older persons: Preliminary findings. *Alcoholism, 9,* 513–515.

Beresford, T. P., Blow, F. C., Brower, K. J., Adams, K. M., & Hall, R. C. W. (1988). Alcoholism and aging in the general hospital. *Psychosomatics, 29,* 61–72.

Bienenfeld, D. (1987). Alcoholism in the elderly. *American Family Physician, 36,* 163–169.

Blow, F. (1998). Substance abuse among older Americans. In *Treatment improvement protocol* (Center for Substance Abuse Treatment). Washington, DC: U.S. Government Printing Office.

Blow, F. C., Brower, K. J., Schulenberg, J. E., Demo-Dananberg, L. M., Young, K. J., & Beresford, T. P. (1992). The Michigan Alcoholism Screening Test: Geriatric version (MAST-G): A new elderly-specific screening instrument. *Alcoholism: Clinical and Experimental Research, 16,* 172.

Breslow, R. A., Faden, V. B., & Smothers, B. (2003). Alcohol consumption by elderly Americans. *Journal of Studies on Alcohol, 64,* 884–892.

Butler, R. N., Lewis, M. I., & Sunderland, T. (1998). *Aging and mental health: Positive psychosocial and biomedical approaches* (5th ed.). Boston, MA: Allyn & Bacon.

Carstensen, L. L., Rychtarik, R. G., & Prue, D. M. (1985). Behavioral treatment of the geriatric alcohol abuser: A long-term follow-up study. *Addictive Behaviors, 10,* 307–311.

CASA (The National Center on Addiction and Substance Abuse at Columbia University). (1995). *Analysis of the National Household Survey on Drug Abuse, 1995.* Washington, DC: Substance Abuse and Mental Health Services Administration, U.S. Department of Health and Human Services.

Cervantes, R. (1993). The Hispanic family intervention program: An empirical approach to substance abuse prevention. In R. S. Mayers, B. Kail, & T. Watts (Eds.), *Hispanic substance abuse* (pp. 101–114). Springfield, IL: Charles C Thomas.

Christie, I. C., Price, J., Edwards, L., Muldoon, M., Meltzer, C. C., & Jennings, J. R. (2008). Alcohol consumption and cerebral blood flow among older adults. *Alcohol, 42,* 269–275.

Coogle, C. L., Osgood, N. J., Pyles, M. A., & Wood, H. E. (1995). The impact of alcoholism education on service providers, elders, and their family members. *Journal of Applied Gerontology, 14,* 321–332.

Corrao, G., Bagnardi, V., Zambon, A., & LaVecchia, C. (2004). A meta-analysis of alcohol consumption and the risk of 15 diseases. *Preventive Medicine, 38,* 613–619.

Copeland, L. A., Blow, F. C., & Barry, K. L. (2003). Health care utilization by older alcohol-using veterans: Effects of a brief intervention to reduce at-risk drinking. *Health Education & Behavior, 30,* 305–321.

Curtis, J. R., Geller, G., Stokes, E. J., Levine, D. M., & Moore, R. D. (1989). Characteristics, diagnosis and treatment of alcoholism in elderly patients. *Journal of the American Geriatrics Society, 37,* 310–316.

Delgado, M., & Humm-Delgado, D. (1993). Chemical dependence, self-help groups and the Hispanic community. In R. S. Mayers, B. Kail, & T. Watts (Eds.), *Hispanic substance abuse* (pp. 145–156). Springfield, IL: Charles C Thomas.

Duka, T., Townshend, J. M., Collier, K., & Stephens, D. N. (2003). Impairment in cognitive functions following multiple detoxifications in alcoholic inpatients. *Alcoholism: Clinical & Experimental Research, 27,* 1563–1572.

Dupree, L. W., Broskowski, H., & Schonfeld, L. (1984). The Gerontology Alcohol Project: A behavioral treatment program for elderly alcohol abusers. *The Gerontologist, 24,* 510–516.

Dupree, L. W., & Schonfeld, L. (1998). The value of behavioral perspectives in treating older adults. In M. Hersen, & V. B. Van Hasselt (Eds.), *Handbook of clinical geropsychology* (pp. 51–70). New York: Plenum Press.

Elias, P. K., Elias, M. F., D'Agostino, R. B., Silbershatz, H., & Wolf, P. A. (1999). Alcohol consumption and cognitive performance in the Framingham Heart Study. *American Journal of Epidemiology, 150,* 580–589.

Finlayson, R. E., Hurt, R. D., Davis, L. J., & Morse, R. M. (1988). Alcoholism in elderly persons: A study of the psychiatric and psychosocial features of 216 inpatients. *Mayo Clinic Proceedings, 63,* 761–768.

Fleming, M. F., Manwell, L. B., Barry, K. L., Adams, W., & Stauffacher, E. A. (1999). Brief physician advice for alcohol problems in older adults: A randomized community-based trial. *Journal of Family Practice, 48,* 378–384.

Friedman, L. (Ed.). (1996). *Source book of substance abuse and addiction.* Baltimore, MD: Williams & Wilkins.

Gazdzinski, S., Durazzo, T. C., & Meyerhoff, D. J. (2005). Temporal dynamics and determinants of whole brain tissue volume changes during recovery from alcohol dependence. *Drug and alcohol dependence, 78,* 263–273.

Ganguli, M., Vander Bilt, J., Saxton, J. A., Shen, C., & Dodge, H. H. (2005). Alcohol consumption and cognitive function in late life. *Neurology, 65,* 1210–1217.

Ganry, O., Baudoin, C., Fardellon, P., Dubreuil, A., & the EPIDOS Group. (2001). Alcohol consumption by non-institutionalized elderly women: The EPIDOS Study. *Public Health, 115,* 186–191.

Gazdzinski, S., Durazzo, T. C., & Meyerhoff, D. J. (2005). Temporal dynamics and determinants of whole brain tissue volume changes during recovery from alcohol dependence. *Drug & Alcohol Dependence, 78,* 263–273.

Gfroerer, J., Penne, M., Pemberton, M., & Folsom, R. (2003). Substance abuse treatment need among older adults in 2020: The impact of the aging baby-boom cohort. *Drug and Alcohol Dependence, 69,* 127–135.

Gilliland, B. E., & James, R. K. (1988). *Crisis intervention strategies.* Pacific Grove, CA: Brooks/Cole.

Ginzer, L. M., & Richardson, V. E. (2009, November). *How much are people drinking, anyway: Findings from NESARC.* Paper presented at the 62nd Annual Meeting of The Gerontological Society of America, Atlanta, GA.

Giordano, J. A., & Beckham, K. (1985). Alcohol use and abuse in old age: An examination of Type II alcoholism. *Journal of Gerontological Social Work, 9,* 65–83.

Glass, T. A., Prigerson, H. G., Kasl, S. V., & Mendes de Leon, C. (1995). The effects of negative life events on alcohol consumption among the older men and women. *Journal of Gerontology: Social Sciences, 50B,* S205–S216.

Graham, K. (1986). Identifying and measuring alcohol abuse among the elderly: Serious problems with existing instrumentation. *Journal of Studies on Alcohol, 47,* 332–326.

Graham, K., & Schmidt, G. (1999). Alcohol use and psychosocial well-being among older adults. *Journal of Studies on Alcohol, 60,* 345–351.

Gupta, S. (2008). Alcohol-related dementia: A 21st-century silent epidemic? *The British Journal of Psychiatry, 193,* 351–353.

Hartford, J. T., & Samorajski, T. (Eds.). (1984). *Alcoholism in the elderly: Social and biomedical issues.* New York: Raven Press.

Holzer, C. E., Myers, J. K., Weissman, M. W., Tischler, G. L., Leaf, P. J., Anthony, J., & Bednarski, P. B. (1986). Antecedents and correlates of alcohol abuse and dependence in the elderly. In G. Maddox, L. N. Robins, & N. Rosenberg (Eds.), *Nature and extent of alcohol problems among the elderly* (pp. 217–244). New York: Springer Publishing.

Janik, S. W., & Dunham, R. G. (1983). A nation-wide examination of the need for specific alcoholism treatment programs for the elderly. *Journal of Studies on Alcohol, 44,* 307–317.

Jennings, J. R., Muldoon, M. F., Ryan, C., Price, J. C., Green, P., Sutton-Tyrrell, M. S. K., van der Veen, F. M., & Meltzer, C. C. (2005). Reduced cerebral blood flow response and compensation among patients with untreated hypertension. *Neurology, 64,* 1358–1365.

Jennison, K. M. (1992). The impact of stressful life events and social support on drinking among older adults: A general population survey. *International Journal of Aging and Human Development, 35,* 99–123.

Johnson, I. (2000). Alcohol problems in old age: a review of recent epidemiological research. *International Journal of Geriatric Psychiatry, 15,* 575–581.

Joseph, C. L., Atkinson, R. M., & Ganzini, L. (1995). Problem drinking among residents of a VA nursing home. *International Journal of Geriatric Psychiatry, 10,* 243–248.

Kail, B. L., & DeLaRosa, M. (1998). Challenges to treating the elderly Latino substance abuser: A not so hidden research agenda. *Journal of Gerontological Social Work, 39,* 123–141.

Kashner, T. M., Rodell, D. E., Ogden, S. R., Guggenheim, F. G., & Karson, C. N. (1992). Outcomes and costs of two VA inpatient programs for older alcoholic patients. *Hospital and Community Psychiatry, 43,* 985–989.

Kinney, J. (2006). Loosening the grip: A handbook of alcohol information (8th ed.). New York: McGraw Hill.

Klein, W. C., & Jess, C. (2002). One last pleasure? Alcohol use among elderly people in nursing homes. *Health & Social Work, 27,* 193–203.

Kofoed, L. L., Tolson, R. L., Atkinson, R. M., Toth, R. L., & Turner, J. A. (1987). Treatment compliance of older alcoholics: An elder-specific approach is superior to "mainstreaming." *Journal of Studies in Alcoholism, 48,* 47–51.

Krause, N. (1991). Stress, religiosity, and abstinence from alcohol. *Psychology and Aging, 6,* 134–144.

Letizia, M. & Reinbolz, M. (2005). Identifying and managing acute alcohol withdrawal in the elderly. *Geriatric Nursing, 26,* 176–183.

Liberto, J. G., & Oslin, D. W. (1995). Early versus late onset of alcoholism in the elderly. *International Journal of the Addictions, 30,* 1799–1818.

Luchsinger, J. A., Tang, M. X., Siddiqui, M., Shea, S., & Mayeux, R. (2004). Alcohol intake and risk of dementia. *Journal of the American Geriatrics Society, 52,* 540–546.

McDonald, L. (1990). *Alcohol problems and older adults: Trainer's manual.* Edmonton, Alberta, Canada: Alberta Association on Gerontology.

Mellor, M. J., Garcia, A., Kenny, E., Lazarus, J., Conway, J. M., Rivers, R., Viswanathan, N., & Zimmerman, J. (1996). Alcohol and aging. *Journal of Gerontological Social Work, 25,* 71–89.

Merrick, E. L., Horgan, C. M., Hodgkin, D., Garnick, D. W., Houghton, S. F., Panas, L., et al. (2008). *Journal of the American Geriatrics Society, 56,* 214–223.

Miller, N., & Gold, M. S. (1991). *Alcohol.* New York: Plenum Press.

Minnis, J. R. (1988). Toward an understanding of alcohol abuse among the elderly: A sociological perspective. *Journal of Alcohol and Drug Education, 33,* 32–40.

Moos, R. H., Brennan, P. L., Schutte, K. K., & Moos, B. S. (2005). Older adults' health and changes in late-life drinking patterns. *Aging & Mental Health, 9,* 49–59.

Moselhy, H. F., Georgiou, G., & Kahn, A. (2001). Frontal lobe changes in alcoholism: A review of the literature. *Alcohol and Alcoholism, 36,* 357–368.

Mukamal, K. J., Chung, H., Jenny, N. S., Kuller, L. H., Longstreth, W. T., Mittleman, M. A., Burke, G. L., & Cushman, M., Beauchamp, N. J., & Siscovick, D. S. (2005). Alcohol use and risk of ischemic stroke among older adults: The CV Health Study, *Stroke, 36,* 1830–1834.

Mukamal, K. J., Kuller, L. H., Fitzpatrick, A. L., Longstreth, W. T., Mittleman, M. A., & Siscovick, D. S. (2003). Prospective study of alcohol consumption and risk of dementia in older adults. *JAMA, 289,* 1405–1413.

Murphy, G. E. (2000). Psychiatric aspects of suicidal behavior: Substance abuse. In K. Hawton, & K. vanHeeringen (Eds.), *The international handbook of suicide and attempted suicide* (pp. 135–146). Chichester, U.K.: John Wiley and Sons.

National Center for Injury Prevention and Control. (2001). *Suicide deaths and rates per 100,000: United States 1994–1997.* Retrieved January 4, 2002, from www.cdcc.gov/ncipc/data/us9794/Suic.htm

National Clearinghouse for Alcohol and Drug Information (NCADI). (1995). *Substance abuse resource guide: Older Americans.* Retrieved January 4, 2002, from www.health.org/govpubs/ms443/

National Institute on Alcohol Abuse and Alcoholism (NIAAA). (1986). *A guide to planning alcoholism treatment* (DHHS Pub. no. ADM 86–1430). Washington, DC: U.S. Department of Health and Human Services.

National Institute on Alcohol Abuse and Alcoholism (NIAAA). (1995). *The physicians' guide to helping patients with alcohol problems.* Bethesda, MD: U.S. Department of Health and Human Services.

O'Connell, H., Chin, A., Cunningham, C., & Lawlor, B. (2003). Alcohol use disorders in elderly people—redefining an age old problem in old age. *British Medical Journal, 237,* 664–667.

O'Connell, H., Chin, A., Hamilton, F., Cunningham, C., Walsh, J. B., Coakley, D., et al. (2004). A systematic review of the utility of self-report alcohol screening instruments in the elderly. *International Journal of Geriatric Psychiatry, 19,* 1074–1086.

O'Keefe, J. H., Bybee, K. A., & Lavie, C. J. (2007). Alcohol and cardiovascular health: The razor-sharp double-edged sword. *Journal of the American College of Cardiology, 50,* 1009–1014.

Orwig, D., Brandt, N., Gruber-Baldini, A. L. (2006). Medication management assessment for older adults in the community. *The Gerontologist, 46,* 661–668.

Peressini, T., & McDonald, L. (1998). An evaluation of a training program on alcoholism and older adults for health care and social service practitioners. *Gerontology and Geriatrics Education, 18,* 23–44.

Pringle, K. E., Ahern, F. M., Heller, D. A., Gold, C. H., & Brown, T. V. (2005). Potential for alcohol and prescription drug interactions in older people. *Journal of the American Geriatrics Society, 53,* 1930–1936.

Reid, M. C., Van Ness, P. H., Hawkins, K. A., Towle, V., Concato, J., & Guo, Z. (2006). Light to moderate alcohol consumption is associated with better cognitive function among older male veterans receiving primary care. *Journal of Geriatric Psychiatry & Neurology, 19,* 98–105.

Reynolds, K., Lewis, B., Nolen, J. D., Kinney, G. L., Sathya, B., & He, J. (2003). Alcohol consumption and risk of stroke: A meta-analysis. *JAMA, 289*, 579–588.

Richman, J. (1992). *Suicide in the elderly.* New York: Springer Publishing.

Robins, L. N., Helzer, J. E., Weissman, M. M., Orvaschel, H., Gruenberg, E., Burke, J. D., & Regier, D. A. (1984). Lifetime prevalence of specific psychiatric disorders in three sites. *Archives of General Psychiatry, 41*, 949–958.

Robins, L. N., & Regier, D. A. (Eds.). (1991). *Psychiatric disorders in America: The epidemiologic catchment area study.* New York: Free Press.

Ruitenberg, A., van Swieten, J. C., Witteman, J. C. M., Mehta, K. M., van Duijn, C. M., Hofman, A., & Breteler, M. M. B. (2002). Alcohol consumption and risk of dementia: The Rotterdam Study. *Lancet, 359*, 281–286.

Sacco, R. L., Elkind, M. S., Boden-Albala, B., Lin, I. F., Kargman, D. E., Hauser, W. A., Shea, S., & Paik, M. C. (1999). The protective effect of moderate alcohol consumption on ischemic stroke. *JAMA, 281*, 53–60.

Safran D. G., Neuman, P., Schoen, C., Kitchman, M. S., Wilson, I. B., Cooper, B., Li, A., Chang, H., & Rogers, W. H. (2005). *Prescription drug coverage and seniors: Findings from a 2003 national survey.* DOI 10.1377/hlthaff. W5.152. Retrieved from www.kff.org/medi care/med041905nr.cfm.

SAMHSA. (1998). *Substance abuse among older adults: Treatment improvement protocol (TIP) series 26.* DHHS Publication No. (SMA) 98–3179. Retrieved from www.ncbi. nlm.nih.gov/bookshelf/br.fcgi?book=hssamhsatip& part=A48302.

Satre, D. D., Blow, F. C., Chi, F. W., & Weisner, C. (2007). Gender differences in seven-year alcohol and drug treatment outcomes among older adults. *American Journal on Addictions, 16*, 216–221.

Satre, D. D., Mertens, J., Areán, P. A., & Weisner, C. (2003). Contrasting outcomes of older versus middle-aged and younger adult chemical dependency patients in a managed care program. *Journal of Studies on Alcohol, 64*, 520–530.

Satre, D. D., Mertens, J., Areán, P. A., & Weisner, C. (2004). Five-year alcohol and drug treatment outcomes of older adults versus middle-aged and younger adults in a managed care program. *Addiction, 99*, 1286–1297.

Schonfeld, L., & Dupree, L. W. (1997). Treatment alternatives for older alcohol abusers. In A. M. Gurnack (Ed.), *Older adults' misuse of alcohol, medicines, and other drugs: Research and practice issues* (pp. 113–131). New York: Springer Publishing.

Schonfeld, L., Dupree, L. W., Dickson-Euhrmann, E., Royer, C. M., McDermott, C. H., Rosansky, J. S., Taylor, S., & Jarvik, L. F. (2000). Cognitive-behavioral treatment of older veterans with substance abuse problems. *Journal of Geriatric Psychiatry & Neurology, 13*, 124–129.

Schonfeld, L., King-Kallimanis, B. L., Duchene, D. M., Etheridge, R. L., Herrera, J. R., Barry, K. L., & Lynn, N. (2010). Screening and brief intervention for substance misuse

among older adults: The Florida BRITE Project. *American Journal of Public Health, 100*, 108–114.

Schonfeld, L., Rohrer, G. E., Zima, M., & Spiegel, T. (1993). Alcohol abuse and medication misuse in older adults as estimated by service providers. *Journal of Gerontological Social Work, 21*, 113–125.

Scott, R. B., & Mitchell, M. C. (1988). Aging, alcoholism, and the liver. *Journal of the American Geriatrics Society, 35*, 255–265.

Simoni-Wastila, L., & Strickler, G. (2004). Risk factors associated with problem use of prescription drugs. *American Journal of Public Health, 94*, 266–268.

Smith, J. W. (1995). Medical manifestation of alcoholism in the elderly. *International Journal of Addictions, 30*, 1749–1798.

Southern Medical Association. (1998). *Alcohol abuse in the elderly.* Retrieved January 4, 2002, from www. sma.org/medbytes/gm_9.htm

Stewart, D., & Oslin, D. W. (2001). Recognition and treatment of late-life addictions in medical settings. *Journal of Clinical Geropsychology, 7*, 145–158.

Substance Abuse and Mental Health Services Administration. (2003). *Overview of Findings from the 2002 National Survey on Drug Use and Health* (Office of Applied Studies, NHSDA Series H-21, DHHS Publication No. SMA 03-3774. Rockville, MD. Retrieved on August 15, 2009, from www.oas.samhsa.gov/nhsda/2k2nsduh/overview/2k2Overview.htm.

Substance Abuse and Mental Health Services Administration (SAMHSA). (1999). *The sixth triennial report to congress: Research on the nature and extent of drug use in the United States.* Retrieved January 4, 2002, from 165.112.78.61/STRC/Forms.html

Thun, M. J., Peto, R., Lopez, A. D., Monaco, J. H., Henley, S. J., Heath, C. W., & Doll, R. (1997). Alcohol consumption and mortality among middle-aged and elderly U.S. adults. *New England Journal of Medicine, 337*, 1705–1714.

Veenstra, M. Y., Lemmens, P. H., Friesema, In. H., Garretsen, H. F., Knottnerus, J. A., & Zwietering, P. J. (2006). A literature overview of the relationships between life-events and alcohol use in the general population. *Alcohol & Alcoholism, 41*, 455–463.

Vinton, L. (1991). An exploratory study of self-neglectful elderly. *Journal of Gerontological Social Work, 18*, 55–67.

Vinton, L. (2004). Perceptions of the need for social work in assisted living facilities. *Journal of Social Work in Long-term Care, 3*, 85–100.

Waern, M. (2003). Alcohol dependence and misuse in elderly suicides. *Alcohol & Alcoholism, 38*, 249–254.

Wan, H., Sengupta, M., Velkoff, V. A., & DeBarros, K. A. (2005). U.S. Census Bureau, Current Population Reports, P23–209, *65+ in the United States: 2005*, U.S. Government Printing Office, Washington, DC, 2005.

Weisner, C., Mertens, J., Parthasarathy, S., Moore, C., Hunkeler, E. M., Hu, T., & Selby, J. V. (2000). The outcome and cost of alcohol and drug treatment in an HMO: Day hospital versus traditional outpatient regimens. *Health Services Research, 35,* 791–812.

Welte, J. W. (1998). Stress and elder drinking. In E. S. L. Gomberg, A. M. Hegedus, & R. A. Zuker (Eds.), *Alcohol problems and aging* (pp. 229–246). Bethesda, MD: NIAAA Research Monograph No. 33, NIH Publication No. 98–4163.

Welte, J. W., & Mirand, A. L. (1995). Drinking, problem drinking and life stressors in the elderly general population. *Journal of Studies on Alcohol, 56,* 67–73.

Wetterling, T., Veltrup, C., John, U., & Driessen, M. (2003). Late onset alcoholism. *European Psychiatry, 18,* 112–118.

Wiens, A. N., Menustik, C. E., Miller, S. L., & Schmitz, R. E. (1982–1983). Medical-behavioral treatment of the older alcoholic patient. *American Journal of Drug and Alcohol Abuse, 9,* 461–475.

WHO (1992). International classification of diseases, 10th revision (ICD-10). Geneva.

CHAPTER 15

Agrawal, A., Balasubramanian, S., Smith, E. K., Madden, P. A. F., Bucholz, K. K., Heath, A. C., & Lynskey, M. T. (2010). Peer substance involvement modifies genetic influences on regular substance involvement in young women. *Addiction, 105,* 1844–1853.

Alcoholics Anonymous (AA). (2008). *Alcoholics Anonymous 2007 membership survey.* New York: Alcoholics Anonymous World Services. Retrieved May 8, 2011, from www.aa.org/pdf/products/p-48_07survey.pdf.

Annis, H. M., & Graham, J. M. (1995). Profile types on the inventory of drinking situations: Implications for relapse prevention counseling. *Psychology of Addictive Behaviors, 9*(3), 176–182.

Annis, H. M., Sklar, S. M., & Moser, A. E. (1998). Gender in relation to relapse crisis situations, coping, and outcome among treated alcoholics. *Addictive Behaviors, 23*(1), 127–131.

Archer, J. (2000). Sex differences in aggression between heterosexual partners: A meta-analytic review. *Psychological Bulletin, 126*(5), 651–680.

Back, S. E., Brady, K. T., Jackson, J. L., Salstrom, S., & Zinzow, H. (2005). Gender differences in stress reactivity among cocaine-dependent individuals. *Psychopharmacology, 180,* 169–176.

Bastiaens, L., & Kendrick, J. (2002). Trauma and PTSD among substance-abusing patients. *Psychiatric Services, 53*(5), 634.

Becker, U., Deis, A., Sørensen, T. I. A., Grønbæk, M., Borch-Johnsen, K., Müller, C. F., et al. (1996). Prediction of risk of liver disease by alcohol intake, sex, and age: A prospective population study. *Hepatology, 23*(5), 1025–1029.

Bennett, G. A., Velleman, R. D., Barter, G., & Bradbury, C. (2000). Gender differences in sharing injecting equipment by drug users in England. *AIDS Care, 12*(1), 77–87.

Bongers, I. M. B., van de Goor, L. A. M., van Oers, J. A. M., & Garretsen, H. F. L. (1998). Gender differences in alcohol-related problems: Controlling for drinking behaviour. *Addiction, 93*(3), 411–421.

Boyd, C. J. (1993). The antecedents of women's crack cocaine abuse: Family substance abuse, sexual abuse, depression, and illicit drug use. *Journal of Substance Abuse Treatment, 10*(5), 433–438.

Blum, L. N., Nielsen, N. H., & Riggs, J. A. (1998). Alcoholism and alcohol abuse among women: Report of the Council on Scientific Affairs. *Journal of Women's Health, 7*(7), 861–871.

Blume, S. B. (1997). Women and alcohol: Issues in social policy. In R. W. Wilsnack and S. C. Wilsnack (Eds.), *Gender and alcohol: Individual and social perspectives.* New Brunswick, N.J.: Rutgers Center for Alcohol Studies.

Booth, R. E., Lehman, W. E., Brewster, J. T., Sinitsyna, L., & Dvoryak, S. (2007). Gender differences in sex risk behaviors among Ukraine injection drug users. *Journal of Acquired Immune Deficiency Syndromes, 46*(1), 112–117.

Bradley, K. A., Boyd-Wickizer, J., Powell, S. H., & Burman, M. L. (1998). Alcohol screening questionnaires in women. *Journal of the American Medical Association, 280,* 166–171.

Brady, K. T., & Randall, C. L. (1999). Gender differences in substance use disorders. *Psychiatric Clinics of North America, 22,* 241–252.

Briere, J., & Runtz, M. (1989). The Trauma Symptom Checklist (TSC-33): Early data on a new scale. *Journal of Interpersonal Violence, 4,* 151–163.

Brown, J. D., Vartivarian, S., Alderks, C. E. (2011). Child care in outpatient substance abuse treatment facilities for women: Findings from the 2008 National Survey of Substance Abuse Treatment Services. *Journal of Behavioral Health Services & Research,* published online. February, 4, 2011.

Burd, L., Martsolf, J., Klug, M.G., O'Connor, E., & Peterson, M. (2003). Prenatal alcohol exposure assessment: Multiple embedded measures in a prenatal questionnaire. *Neurotoxicology and Teratology, 25,* 675–679.

Cadoret, R. J., Riggins-Caspers, K., Yates, W. R., Troughton, E. P., & Stewart, M.A. (2000). Gender effects in gene-environment interactions in substance abuse. In E. Frank (Ed.), *Gender and its effects on psychopathology* (pp. 253–279). Washington, DC: American Psychopathological Association.

Centers for Disease Control and Prevention. (2004). Fetal alcohol syndrome: Guidelines for referral and diagnosis. Retrieved April 17, 2011, from www.cdc.gov/ncbddd/fasd/documents/FAS_guidelines_accessible.pdf.

Centers for Disease Control and Prevention. (2009, May 22). Alcohol use among pregnant and nonpregnant women of childbearing age–United States, 1991—2005. *Morbidity and Mortality Weekly Report, 58*(19), 529–532. Retrieved April 30, 2011, from www.cdc.gov/mmwr/preview/mmwrhtml/mm5819a4.htm

Centers for Disease Control and Prevention. (2010, June 4). Youth risk behavior surveillance—United States, 2009. *Morbidity and Mortality Weekly Report, Surveillance Summaries 59*, no. SS-5. Retrieved April 14, 2011, from www.cdc.gov/mmwr/pdf/ss/ss5905.pdf.

Chan, A. W. K., Pristach, E. A., Welte, J. W., & Russell, M. (1993). Use of the TWEAK test in screening for alcoholism/heavy drinking in three populations. *Alcoholism: Clinical and Experimental Research, 17*(6), 1188–1192.

Chang, G. (2001). Alcohol screening instruments for pregnant women. *Alcohol Research and Health, 25*(3), 204–209.

Chang, G., Wilkins-Haug, L., Berman, S., & Goetz, M. A. (1999). The TWEAK: Application in a prenatal setting. *Journal of Studies on Alcohol, 60*, 306–309.

Chase, K. A., O'Farrell, T. J., Murphy, C. M., Fals-Stewart, W., & Murphy, M. (2003). Factors associated with partner violence among female alcoholic patients and their male partners. *Journal of Studies on Alcohol, 64*, 137–149.

Chatham, L. R., Hiller, M. L., Rowan-Szal, G. A., Joe, G. W., & Simpson, D. D. (1999). Gender differences at admission and follow-up in a sample of methadone maintenance clients. *Substance Use and Misuse, 34*(8), 1137–1165.

Chermack, S. T., Stoltenberg, S. F., Fuller, B. E., & Blow, F. C. (2000). Gender differences in the development of substance-related problems: The impact of family history of alcoholism, family history of violence, and childhood conduct problems. *Journal of Studies on Alcohol, 61*(6), 845–852.

Chermack, S. T., Walton, M. A., Fuller, B. E., & Blow, F. C. (2001). Correlates of expressed and received violence across relationship types among men and women substance abusers. *Psychology of Addictive Behaviors, 15*(2), 140–151.

Choi, S. Y. P., Cheung, Y. W., & Chen, K. (2006). Gender and HIV risk behavior among intravenous drug users in Sichuan Province, China. *Social Science and Medicine, 62*, 1672–1684.

Chong, J., & Lopez, D. (2008). Predictors of relapse for American Indian women after substance abuse treatment. *American Indian and Alaska Native Mental Health Research* (Online), *14*(3), 24–48.

Clark, H. W., & Power, A. K. (2005). Women, co-occurring disorders, and violence study: A case for trauma-informed care. *Journal of Substance Abuse Treatment, 28*, 145–146.

Cocozza, J. J., Jackson, E. W., Hennigan, K., Morrissey, J. P., Reed, B. G., Fallot, R. et al., (2005). Outcomes for women with co-occurring disorders and trauma: Program-level effects. *Journal of Substance Abuse Treatment, 28*, 109–119.

Community Connections. (n.d.). *TREM Overview.* Retrieved May 2, 2011, from communityconnectionsdc.org/web/page/657/interior.html.

Covington, S. S. (2008). Women and addiction: A trauma-informed approach. *Journal of Psychoactive Drugs,* SARC Supplement 5, November, 377–385.

Covington, S. S., & Surrey, J. (2000). The relational model of women's psychological development: Implications for substance abuse. (Work in progress no. 91). Wellesley, MA: Stone Center.

Cutajar, M. C., Mullen, P. E., Ogloff, J. R. P., Thomas, S. D., Wells, D. L., & Spataro, J. (2010). Psychopathology in a large cohort of sexually abused children followed up to 43 years. *Child Abuse & Neglect, 34*, 813–822.

Davies, A. G., Dominy, N. J., Peters, A. D., & Richardson, A. M. (1996). Gender differences in HIV risk behaviour of injecting drug users in Edinburgh. *AIDS Care, 8*(5), 517–527.

Davis, D. R., & DiNitto, D. M. (2005). Gender and the use of drugs and alcohol: Fact, fiction, and unanswered questions. In C. A. McNeece & D. M. DiNitto, *Chemical dependency: A systems approach* (pp. 503–545). Boston, MA: Allyn & Bacon.

Dawson, D. A., Grant, B. F., Stinson, F. S., Chou, P. S., Huang, B., & Ruan, W. J. (2005). Recovery from DSM-IV alcohol dependence: United States, 2001–2002. *Addiction, 100*, 281–292.

Deng, F., Vaughn, M. S., & Lee, L.-J. (2003). Imprisoned drug offenders in Taiwan: A gender-based analysis. *Substance Use and Misuse, 38*(7), 933–964.

Dong, M., Anda, R. F., Felitti, V. J., Dube, S. R., Williamson, D. F., Thompson, T. J., et al. (2004). The interrelatedness of multiple forms of childhood abuse, neglect, and household dysfunction. *Child Abuse and Neglect, 28*(7), 771–784.

Dube, S. R., Anda, R. F., Felitti, V. J., Edwards, V. J., & Croft, J. B. (2002). Adverse childhood experiences and personal alcohol abuse as an adult. *Addictive Behaviors, 27*(5), 713–725.

Duckert, F. (1987). Recruitment into treatment and effects of treatment for female problem drinkers. *Addictive Behaviors, 12*, 137–150.

Eldred, C. A., & Washington, M. N. (1976). Interpersonal relationships in heroin use by men and women and their role in treatment outcome. *International Journal of the Addictions, 11*(1), 117–130.

Elifson, K. W., Sterk, C. E., & Theall, K. P. (2007). Safe living: The impact of unstable housing conditions on HIV risk reduction among female drug users. *AIDS and Behavior, 11* (Supplement 2), S45-S55.

Ely, M., Hardy, R., Longford, N. T., & Wadsworth, M. E. J. (1999). Gender differences in the relationship between alcohol consumption and drink problems are largely accounted for by body water. *Alcohol and Alcoholism, 34*(6), 894–902.

Enoch, M. (2011). The role of early life stress as a predictor for alcohol and drug dependence. *Psychopharmacology, 214*, 17–31.

Evans, J. L., Hahn, J. A., Page-Shafer, K., Lum, P. J., Stein, E. S., Davidson, P. J., & Moss, A. R. (2003). Gender differences in sexual and injection risk behavior among active young injection drug users in San Francisco: The UFO Study. *Journal of Urban Health: Bulletin of the New York Academy of Medicine, 80*(1), 137–146.

Fals-Stewart, W., Golden, J., & Schumacher, J. A. (2003). Intimate partner violence and substance use: A longitudinal day-to-day examination. *Addictive Behaviors, 28,* 1555–1574.

Farley, M., Golding, J. M., Young, G., Mulligan, M., Minkoff, J. R. (2004). Trauma history and relapse probability among patients seeking substance abuse treatment. *Journal of Substance Abuse Treatment, 27,* 161–167.

Felitti, V. J., Anda, R. F., Nordenberg, D., Williamson, D. F., Spitz, A. M., Edwards, V., Koss, M. P., & Marks, J. S. (1998). Relationship of childhood abuse and household dysfunction to many of the leading causes of death in adults: The adverse childhood experiences (ACE) study. *American Journal of Preventive Medicine, 14*(4), 245–258.

Felitti, V., & Anda, R. F. (2010). The relationship of adverse childhood experiences to adult medical disease, psychiatric disorders and sexual behavior: Implications for healthcare. In R.A. Lanius, E. Vermetten, and C. Pain (Eds.), *Impact of early life trauma on health and disease: The hidden epidemic* (pp. 77–87). New York: Cambridge University Press.

Fiorentine, R., Anglin, M. D., Gil-Rivas, V., & Taylor E. (1997). Drug treatment: Explaining the gender paradox. *Substance Use and Misuse, 32*(6), 653–678.

Fitzgerald, T., Lundgren, L., & Chassler, D. (2007). Factors associated with HIV/AIDS high-risk behaviours among female injection drug users. *AIDS Care 19*(1), 67–74.

Fleming, C. B., White, H. R., & Catalano, R. F. (2010). Romantic relationships and substance use in early adulthood: An examination of the influences of relationship type, partner substance use, and relationship quality. *Journal of Health and Social Behavior, 51*(2), 153–167.

Gemma, S., Vichi, S., & Testai, E. (2007). Metabolic and genetic factors contributing to alcohol-induced effects and fetal alcohol syndrome. *Neuroscience and Biobehavioral Reviews, 31*(2), 221–229.

Gerstein, D. R., & Johnson, R. A. (1999). *Prospective and retrospective studies of substance abuse treatment outcomes: Methods and results of four large-scale follow-up studies.* Rockville, MD: National Evaluation Data Services, Center for Substance Abuse Treatment.

Gilligan, C. (1982). *In a different voice: Psychological theory and women's development.* Cambridge, MA: Harvard University Press.

Goldman, D., Oroszi, G., & Ducci, F. (2005). The genetics of addictions: Uncovering the genes. *Nature Reviews Genetics, 6*(7), 521–532.

Graham, K., Bernards, S., Knibbe, R., Kairouz, S., Kuntsche, S., Wilsnack, S.C., et al. (2011). Alcohol-related negative consequences among drinkers around the world. *Addiction,* doi:10.1111/j.1360-0443.2011.03425.x

Graham, K., Wilsnack, R., Dawson, D., & Vogeltanz, N. (1998). Should alcohol consumption measures be adjusted for gender differences? *Addiction, 93*(8), 1137–1147.

Green, C. (2006). Gender and use of substance abuse treatment services. *Alcohol Research & Health, 29*(1), 55–62.

Greenfield, S. F., Pettinati, H. M., O'Malley, S., Randall, P. K., & Randall, C. L. (2010). Gender differences in alcohol treatment: An analysis of outcome from the COMBINE study. *Alcoholism: Clinical and Experimental Research, 34*(10), 1803–1818.

Grucza, R. A., Bucholz, K. K., Rice, J. P., & Bierut, L. J. (2008). Secular trends in the lifetime prevalence of alcohol dependence in the United States: A re-evaluation. *Alcoholism Clinical and Experimental Research, 32,* 763–770.

Guo, G., Elder, G. H., Cai, T., & Hamilton, N. (2009). Gene-environment interactions: Peers' alcohol use moderates genetic contribution to adolescent drinking behavior. *Social Science Research, 38,* 213–224.

Guthrie, B. J., & Flinchbaugh, L. J. (2001). Gender-specific substance prevention programming: Going beyond just focusing on girls. *Journal of Early Adolescence, 21*(3), 354–372.

Han, C., McGue, M. K., & Iacono, W.G. (1999). Lifetime tobacco, alcohol, and other substance use in adolescent Minnesota twins: Univariate and multivariate behavioral genetic analyses. *Addiction, 94*(7), 981–993.

Haseltine, F. P. (2000). Gender differences in addiction and recovery. *Journal of Women's Health & Gender-based Medicine, 9*(6), 579–583.

Heath, A. C., Slutske, W., & Madden, P. A. F. (1997). Gender differences in the genetic contribution to alcoholism risk and alcohol consumption patterns. In R. W. Wilsnack and S. C. Wilsnack (Eds.), *Gender and alcohol: Individual and social perspectives* (pp. 114–149). Rutgers, NJ: Rutgers University Press.

Hillis, S. D., Anda, R. F., Dube, S. R., Felitti, V. J., Marchbanks, P. A., & Marks, S. (2004). The association between adverse childhood experiences and adolescent pregnancy, long-term psychosocial consequences, and fetal death. *Pediatrics, 113*(2), 320–327.

Hodgins, D. C., el-Guebaly, N., & Armstrong, S. (1995). Prospective and retrospective reports of mood states before relapse to substance use. *Journal of Consulting and Clinical Psychology, 63*(3), 400–407.

Howell, E. M., & Chasnoff, I. J. (1999). Perinatal substance abuse treatment: Findings from focus groups with clients and providers. *Journal of Substance Abuse Treatment, 17*(1–2), 139–148.

Hser, Y.-I., Anglin, M. D., & Booth, M. W. (1987). Sex differences in addict careers. 3. Addiction. *American Journal of Drug and Alcohol Abuse, 13*(3), 231–251.

Hser, Y., Huang, D., Teruya, C., & Anglin, M. D. (2003). Gender comparisons of drug abuse treatment outcomes and predictors. *Drug and Alcohol Dependence, 72,* 255–264.

Huang, C.-C., & Reid, R. J. (2006). Risk factors associated with alcohol, cigarette, and illicit drug use among pregnant women: Evidence from the Fragile Family and Child Well-being Survey. *Journal of Social Service Research, 32*(4), 1–22.

Jones, K. L. (2011). The effects of alcohol on fetal development. *Birth Defects Research (Part C), 93,* 3–11.

Jordan, J. V., Kaplan, A., Miller, J. B., Stiver, I., & Surrey, J. (1991). *Women's growth in connection: Writings from the Stone Center.* New York: Guilford Press.

Kaskutas, L. (1989). Women for Sobriety: A qualitative analysis. *Contemporary Drug Problems, 16*(2), 177–200.

Kasl, C. D. (1990, November/December). The Twelve-Step controversy. Ms. Magazine, pp. 30–31.

Kay, A., Taylor, T. E., Barthwell, A. G., Wichelecki, J., & Leopold, V. (2010). Substance use and women's health. *Journal of Addictive Diseases, 29,* 139–163.

Kendler, K. S., Heath, A. C., Neale, M. C., Kessler, R. C., & Eaves, L. J. (1992). A population-based twin study of alcoholism in women. *Journal of the American Medical Association, 268*(14), 1877–1882.

Kendler, K. S., Prescott, C. A., Myers, J., & Neale, M. C. (2003). The structure of genetic and environmental risk factors for common psychiatric and substance use disorders in men and women. *Archives of General Psychiatry, 60,* 929–937.

Ketring, S. A., & Feinauer, L. L. (1999). Perpetrator-victim relationship: Long-term effects of sexual abuse for men and women. *The American Journal of Family Therapy, 27,* 109–120.

Kilbourne, J., & Surrey J. L. (1991). *Women, addiction, and codependency.* [Audiotape]. Available from WCW Publications. Stone Center. Wellesley College. Wellesley, MA 02481.

King, S. M., Burt, S. A., Malone, S. M., McGue, M., & Iacono, W. G. (2005). Etiological contributions to heavy drinking from late adolescence to young adulthood. *Journal of Abnormal Psychology, 114*(4), 587–598.

Kirkpatrick, J. (1978). Turnabout: Help for a new life. Garden City, NY: Doubleday.

Kubiak, S. P., & Rose, I. M. (2007). Trauma and posttraumatic stress disorder in inmates with histories of substance use. In D. W. Springer and A. R. Roberts (Eds.), *Handbook of forensic mental health with victims and offenders: Assessment, treatment, and research* (pp. 445–466). New York, Springer Publishing Company.

Kuendig, H., Plant, M. L., Plant, M. A., Kuntsche, S., Miller, P., Gmel, G. et al. (2008). Beyond drinking: Differential effects of demographic and socioeconomic factors on alcohol-related adverse consequences across European countries. *European Addiction Research, 14,* 150–160.

Langan, N. P., & Pelissier, B. M. M. (2001). Gender differences among prisoners in drug treatment. *Journal of Substance Abuse, 13*(3), 291–301.

Little, B. B., & Yonkers, K. A. (2001). Treatment of substance abuse during pregnancy: An overview. In K. A. Yonkers & B. B. Little (Eds.), *Management of psychiatric disorders in pregnancy* (pp. 228–252). London: Arnold.

Lum, P. J., Sears, C., & Guydish, J. (2005). Injection risk behavior among women syringe exchangers in San Francisco. *Substance Use & Misuse, 40,* 1681–1696.

Martino, S. C., Collins, R. L., & Ellickson, P. L. (2005). Cross-lagged relationships between substance use and intimate partner violence among a sample of young adult women. *Journal of Studies on Alcohol, 66*(1), 139–148.

Mattson, S. N., Crocker, N., & Nguyen, T. T. (2011). Fetal alcohol spectrum disorders: Neuropsychological and behavioral features. *Neuropsychology Review.* DOI 10.1007/s11065-011-9167-9. Published online: 19 April 2011.

McGue, M. (1999). The behavioral genetics of alcoholism. *Current directions in psychological science, 8*(4), 109–115.

McGue, M., Pickens, R. W., & Svikis, D. S. (1992). Sex and age effects on the inheritance of alcohol problems: A twin study. *Journal of Abnormal Psychology, 101*(1), 3–17.

McKay, J., Rutherford, M. J., Cacciola, J. S., Kabasakalian-McKay, R., & Alterman, A.I. (1996). Gender differences in the relapse experiences of cocaine patients. *Journal of Nervous and Mental Disease, 184*(10), 616–622.

McLellan, A. T., Lewis, D. C., O'Brien, C. P., & Kleber, H. D. (2000). Drug dependence, a chronic medical illness: Implications for treatment, insurance, and outcomes evaluation. *Journal of the American Medical Association, 284*(13), 1689–1695.

Messina, N., Grella, C., Cartier, J., & Torres, S. (2010). A randomized experimental study of gender-responsive substance abuse treatment for women in prison. *Journal of Substance Abuse Treatment, 38,* 97–107.

Messina, N. P., Marinelli-Casey, P., Hillhouse, M., Ang, A., Hunter, J., & Rawson, R. (2008). Childhood adverse events and health outcomes among methamphetamine-dependent men and women. *International Journal of Mental Health and Addiction, 6,* 522–536.

Messina, N., Marinelli-Casey, P., Hillhouse, M., Rawson, R., Hunter, J., & Ang, A. (2008). Childhood adverse events and methamphetamine use among men and women. *Journal of Psychoactive Drugs, SARC Supplement 5,* November, 399–409.

Miller, J. B. (1976). *Toward a new psychology of women.* Boston, MA: Beacon Press.

Miller, J. B. (1984). The development of women's sense of self. Wellesley, MA: Wellesley College, Stone Center for Developmental Services and Studies.

Miller, J. B. (1990). Connections, disconnections, and violations. Wellesley, MA: Wellesley College, Stone Center for Developmental Services and Studies.

Morgenstern J., Hogue, A., Dauber, S., Dasaro, C., & McKay, J. R. (2009). Does coordinated care management improve employment for substance-using welfare recipients? *Journal of Studies on Alcohol and Drugs, 70*(6), 955–963.

Mumenthaler, M. S., Taylor, J. L., O'Hara, R., & Yesavage, J. A. (1999). Gender differences in moderate drinking effects. *Alcohol Research and Health, 23*(1), 55–64.

Naimi, T. S., Nelson, D. E., Brewer, R. D. (2009). Driving after binge drinking. *American Journal of Preventive Medicine, 37*(4), 314–320.

Najavits, L. M. (2009). Seeking Safety: An implementation guide. In A. Rubin and D. W. Springer (Eds.), *The clinician's guide to evidence-based practice* (pp. 311–347). Hoboken, NJ: John Wiley.

Najavits, L. M., Schmitz, M., Johnson, K. M., Smith, C., North, T., Hamilton, N., et al. (2009). Seeking Safety therapy for men: Clinical and research experiences. In L. J. Katlin (Ed.), *Men and addictions* (pp. 37–58). Hauppage, New York: Nova Science Publishers.

National Association of State Alcohol and Drug Abuse Directors. (2005, August). Alcohol research on prenatal alcohol exposure, prevention, and implications for state AOD systems. *State Issue Brief No. 2.* Retrieved May 7, 2011, from www.niaaa.nih.gov/Publications/Education TrainingMaterials/Documents/PrenatalBrief2.pdf.

National Center on Addiction and Substance Abuse (CASA) at Columbia University. (2000). *Missed opportunities: National survey of primary care physicians and patients on substance abuse.* New York: Author.

National Institute of Justice. (n.d.). *Measuring intimate partner (domestic) violence.* Retrieved April 16, 2011, from www.nij.gov/topics/crime/intimate-partner-violence/measuring.htm.

National Institute on Alcohol Abuse and Alcoholism. (1993). *Eighth special report for the U.S. Congress on alcohol and health.* Rockville, MD: Author.

National Institute on Alcohol Abuse and Alcoholism. (1999, December). Are women more vulnerable to alcohol's effects? *Alcohol Alert,* No. 46. Retrieved May 7, 2011, from pubs.niaaa.nih.gov/publications/aa46.htm.

Noble, R. E. (2005). Depression in women. *Metabolism Clinical and Experimental, 54*(5) (Suppl 1), 49–52.

Nolen-Hoeksema, S. (2004). Gender differences in risk factors and consequences for alcohol use and problems. *Clinical Psychology Review, 24,* 981–1010.

O'Farrell, T. J., & Murphy, C. M. (1995). Marital violence before and after alcoholism treatment. *Journal of Consulting and Clinical Psychology, 63*(2), 256–262.

Office of Applied Studies. (2009). Trends in rates of treatment completion. Source: Substance Abuse and Mental Health Services Administration, Treatment Episode Data Set Discharge data set. Retrieved March 14, 2011, from www.drugabusestatistics.samhsa.gov/TXtrends.htm.

Office of Applied Studies. (n.d.). *Substance abuse treatment admissions by primary substance of abuse, according to sex, age group, race, and ethnicity.* Source: Center for Behavioral Statistics and Quality, Substance Abuse and Mental Health Services Administration, Treatment Episode Data Set. Retrieved March 14, 2011, from www.dasis.samhsa.gov/webt/quicklink/US92.htm, www.dasis.samhsa.gov/webt/quicklink/US01.htm, and www.dasis.samhsa.gov/webt/quicklink/US07.htm.

Österling, A., & Berglund, M. (1994). Elderly first time admitted alcoholics: A descriptive study on gender differences in a clinical population. *Alcoholism: Clinical and Experimental Research, 18*(6), 1317–1321.

Otto-Salaj, L. L., Gore-Felton, C., McGarvey, E., & Canterbury, R. J. (2002). Psychiatric functioning and substance use: Factors associated with HIV risk among incarcerated adolescents. *Child Psychiatry and Human Development, 33*(2), 91–106.

Parks, K. A., & Fals-Stewart, W. (2004). The temporal relationship between college women's alcohol consumption and victimization experiences. *Alcoholism: Clinical and Experimental Research, 28*(4), 625–629.

Pelissier, B. M. M., Camp, S. D., Gaes, G. G., Saylor, W. G., & Rhodes, W. (2003). Gender differences in outcomes from prison-based residential treatment. *Journal of Substance Abuse Treatment, 24,* 149–160.

Pelissier, B., & Jones, N. (2005). A review of gender differences among substance abusers. *Crime & Delinquency, 51*(3), 343–372.

Piazza, N. J., Vrbka, J. L., & Yeager, R. D. (1989). Telescoping of alcoholism in women alcoholics. *International Journal of the Addictions, 24*(1), 19–28.

Pisinger, C., & Jorgensen, T. (2007). Weight concerns and smoking in a general population: The Inter99 study. *Preventive Medicine, 44*(4), 283–289.

Plant, M., Miller, P., Thornton, C., Plant, M., & Bloomfield, K. (2000). Life stage, alcohol consumption patterns, alcohol-related consequences, and gender. *Substance Abuse, 21*(4), 265–281.

Porowski, A. W., Burgdorf, K., Herrell, J. M. (2004). Effectiveness and sustainability of residential substance abuse treatment programs for pregnant and parenting women. *Evaluation and Program Planning, 27,* 191–198.

Prescott, C. A., Aggen, S. H., & Kendler, K. S. (1999). Sex differences in the sources of genetic liability to alcohol abuse and dependence in a population-based sample of U.S. twins. *Alcoholism: Clinical and Experimental Research, 23*(7), 1136–1144.

Prescott, C. A., Caldwell, C. B., Carey, G., Vogler, G. P., Trumbetta, S. L., & Gottesman, I. I. (2005). The Washington University twin study of alcoholism. *American Journal of Medical Genetics Part B: Neuropsychiatric Genetics, 134B*(1), 48–55.

Prescott, C. A., & Kendler, K. S. (1999). Age at first drink and risk for alcoholism: A noncausal association. *Alcoholism: Clinical and Experimental Research, 23*(1), 101–107.

Prescott, C. A., & Kendler, K. S. (2000). Influence of ascertainment strategy on finding sex differences in genetic estimates from twin studies of alcoholism. *American Journal of Medical Genetics (Neuropsychiatric Genetics), 96*(6), 754–761.

Pugatch, D., Ramratnam, M., Strong, L., Feller, A., Levesque, B., & Dickinson, B. P. (2000). Gender differences in HIV risk behaviors among young adults and adolescents entering a Massachusetts detoxification center. *Substance Abuse, 21*(2), 79–86.

Quinn, P. D., & Fromme, K. (2010). Self-regulation as a protective factor against risky drinking and sexual behavior. *Psychology of Addictive Behaviors, 24*(3), 376–385.

Rao, S. R., Czuchry, M., & Dansereau, D. F. (2009). Gender differences in psychosocial functioning across substance abuse treatment. *Journal of Psychoactive Drugs, 41*(3), 267–273.

Riehman, K.S., Hser, Y.-I., & Zeller, M. (2000). Gender differences in how intimate partners influence drug treatment motivation. *Journal of Drug Issues, 30*(4), 823–838.

Roberts, S. T., & Kennedy, B. L. (2006). Why are young college women not using condoms? Their perceived risk, drug use, and developmental vulnerability may provide important clues to sexual risk. *Archives of Psychiatric Nursing, 20*(1), 32–40.

Russell, M. (1994). New assessment tools for risk drinking during pregnancy. *Alcohol Health and Research World, 18*(1), 55–61.

Russell, M., Martier, S. S., Sokol, R. J., Mudar, P., Jacobson, S., & Jacobson, J. (1996). Detecting risk drinking during pregnancy: A comparison of four screening questionnaires. *American Journal of Public Health, 86*(10), 1435–1439.

Sacks, J. Y., McKendrick, K., & Banks, S. (2008). The impact of early trauma and abuse on residential substance abuse treatment outcomes for women. *Journal of Substance Abuse Treatment, 34*, 90–100.

Schneider, K. M., Kviz, F. J., Isola, M. L., & Filstead, W. J. (1995). Evaluating multiple outcomes and gender differences in alcoholism treatment. *Addictive Behaviors, 20*(1), 1–21.

Schneider, R., Burnette, M. L., Ilgen, M. A., & Timko, C. (2009). Prevalence and correlates of intimate partner violence victimization among men and women entering substance use disorder treatment. *Violence and Victims, 24*(6), 744–756.

Schwartz, J., & Rookey, B. D. (2008). The narrowing gender gap in arrests: Assessing competing explanations using self-report, traffic fatality, and official data on drunk driving, 1980–2004. *Criminology, 46*(3), 637–671.

Scourfield, J., Stevens, D. E., & Merikangas, K. R. (1996). Substance abuse, comorbidity, and sensation seeking: Gender differences. *Comprehensive Psychiatry, 37*(6), 384–392.

Shillington, A. M., & Clapp, J. D. (2003). Adolescents in public substance abuse treatment programs: The impacts of sex and race on referrals and outcomes. *Journal of Child and Adolescent Substance Abuse, 12*(4), 69–91.

Sokol, R. J., Delaney-Black, V., Nordstrom, B. (2003). Fetal alcohol spectrum disorder. *Journal of the American Medical Association, 290*(22), 2996–2999.

Sokol, R. J., Martier, S. S., & Ager, J. W. (1989). The T-ACE questions: Practical prenatal detection of risk-drinking. *American Journal of Obstetrics and Gynecology, 160*(4), 863–870.

Streissguth, A. (1997). *Fetal alcohol syndrome: A guide for families and communities.* Baltimore: Paul H. Brookes.

Stuart, G. L., O'Farrell, T. J., & Temple, J. R. (2009). Review of the association between treatment for substance misuse and reductions in intimate partner violence. *Substance Use & Misuse, 44*(9/10), 1298–1317.

Substance Abuse and Mental Health Services Administration. (n.d.a). *Substance Abuse Treatment Admissions by Primary Substance of Abuse, According to Sex, Age Group, Race, and Ethnicity, Year=2008, United States, Treatment Episode Data Set (TEDS).* Retrieved March 14, 2011, from wwwdasis.samhsa.gov/webt/quicklink/US08.htm.

Substance Abuse and Mental Health Services Administration. (2009). Office of Applied Studies, *The TEDS Report: Substance abuse treatment admissions referred by the criminal justice system.* Rockville, MD. Retrieved March 14, 2011, from www.oas.samhsa.gov/2k9/ 211/211CJadmits2k9.htm.

Substance Abuse and Mental Health Services Administration. (2010). *Results from the 2009 National Survey on Drug Use and Health: Volume I. Summary of national findings* (Office of Applied Studies, NSDUH Series H-38A, HHS Publication No. SMA 10–4586Findings). Rockville, MD. Retrieved May 7, 2011, from oas.samhsa.gov/nsduh/2k9nsduh/2k9resultsp.pdf.

Substance Abuse and Mental Health Services Administration. (n.d.b). 2009 State Profile – United States National Survey of Substance Abuse Treatment Services (N-SSATS). Retrieved March 13, 2011, from wwwdasis.samhsa.gov/webt/state_data/US09.pdf.

Substance Abuse and Mental Health Services Administration (n.d.c). *Trauma Recovery and Empowerment Model (TREM).* National Registry of Evidence-based Programs and Practices. Retrieved May 2, 2011, from nrepp.samhsa.gov/ViewIntervention.aspx?id=158.

Sun, A. P. (2007). Relapse among substance-abusing women: Components and processes. *Substance Use and Misuse, 42*(1), 1–21.

Sun, A. P. (2009). *Helping substance-abusing women of vulnerable populations: Effective treatment principles and strategies.* New York: Columbia University Press.

Surratt, H. L., & Inciardi, J. A. (2005). Developing an HIV intervention for indigent women substance abusers in the United States Virgin Islands. *Journal of Urban Health: Bulletin of the New York Academy of Medicine, 82*(3), Supplement, 4, iv74-iv83.

Thom, B. (1986). Sex differences in help-seeking for alcohol problems—1. The barriers to help-seeking. *British Journal of Addiction, 81*, 777–788.

Tjaden, P., & Thoennes, N. (2000). *Extent, nature, and consequences of intimate partner violence: Findings from the National Violence Against Women Survey.* Washington, DC: U.S. Department of Justice. Retrieved May 8, 2011, from www.ncjrs.gov/pdffiles1/nij/181867.pdf.

Toray, T., Coughlin, C., Vuchinich, S., & Patricelli, P. (1991). Gender differences associated with adolescent substance abuse: Comparisons and implications for treatment. *Family Relations, 40*(3), 338–344.

Toussaint, D. W., Van DeMark, N. R., Bornemann, A., & Graeber, C. J. (2007). Modifications to the Trauma Recovery and Empowerment Model (TREM) for substance-abusing women with histories of violence: Outcomes and lessons learned at a Colorado substance abuse treatment center. *Journal of Community Psychology, 35*(7), 879–894.

Tsai, J., Floyd, R. L., & Bertrand, J. (2007). Tracking binge drinking among U.S. childbearing-age women. *Preventive Medicine, 44*(4), 298–302.

Tsuang, M. T., Stone, W. S., & Johnston, J. M. (2008). Gene-environment interactions in mental disorders: A current view. In H. Freeman & S. Stansfeld (Eds.), *The impact of the environment on psychiatric disorder.* (pp. 27–51). New York: Routledge.

Turnbull, J. E. (1989). Treatment issues for alcoholic women. *Social Casework, 70*(6), 364–369.

Tyndale, R. F. (2003). Genetics of alcohol and tobacco use in humans. *Annals of Medicine, 35*(2), 94–121.

U.S. Department of Transportation. (n.d.a). *Traffic safety facts 2007: A compilation of motor vehicle crash data from the Fatality Analysis Reporting System and the General Estimates System.* Washington, DC: Author. Retrieved May 5, 2011, from www-nrd.nhtsa.dot.gov/Pubs/811002.pdf.

U.S. Department of Transportation (n.d.b). *Traffic safety facts: 2009 Data.* Washington, DC: Author. Retrieved May 5, 2011, from www-nrd.nhtsa.dot.gov/Pubs/ 811385.pdf.

U.S. Department of Transportation. (2010). *Fatality Analysis Reporting System/General Estimates System 2008 Data Summary.* Washington, DC: Author. Retrieved April 27, 2011, from www-nrd.nhtsa.dot.gov/Pubs/811171. pdf.

van Os, J., Rutten, B., & Poulton, R. (2009). Gene-environment interactions for searchers: Collaboration between epidemiology and molecular genetics. In W. F. Gattaz & G. Busatto (Eds.), *Advances in schizophrenia research* (pp. 19–50). New York: Springer Science + Business Media.

Walitzer, K. S., & Dearing, R. L. (2006). Gender differences in alcohol and substance use relapse. *Clinical Psychology Review, 26*(2), 128–148.

Walter, M., Gerhard, U., Duersteler-MacFarland, K. M., Weijers, H., Boening, J., & Wiesbeck, G. A. (2006). Social factors but not stress-coping styles predict relapse in detoxified alcoholics. *Neuropsychobiology, 54,* 100–106.

Walter, H., Gutierrez, K., Ramskogler, K., Hertling, I., Dvorak, A., & Lesch, O. M. (2003). Gender-specific differences in alcoholism: Implications for treatment. *Archives of Women's Mental Health, 6*(4), 253–258.

Walton, M. A., Blow, F. C., Bingham, C. R., & Chermack, S. T. (2003). Individual and social/environmental predictors of alcohol and drug use 2 years following substance abuse treatment. *Addictive Behaviors, 28,* 627–642.

Weaver, G.D., Turner, N.H., & O'Dell, K.J. (2000). Depressive symptoms, stress, and coping among women recovering from addiction. *Journal of Substance Abuse Treatment, 18,* 161–167.

Weiss, R. D., Najavits, L. M., & Mirin, S. M. (1998). Substance abuse and psychiatric disorders. In R. J. Frances & S. I. Miller (Eds.), *Clinical texbook of addictive disorders* (pp. 291–318). New York: Guilford.

Wenzel, S. L., Tucker, J. S., Elliott, M. N., & Hambarsoomians, K. (2007). Sexual risk among impoverished women: Understanding the role of housing status. *AIDS and Behavior, 11* (Supplement 2), S9–S20.

Westermeyer, J., & Boedicker, A. E. (2000). Course, severity, and treatment of substance abuse among women versus men. *American Journal of Drug and Alcohol Abuse, 26*(4), 523–535.

Women for Sobriety. (1976). Who we are. Quakertown, PA: Author.

World Health Organization. (2007). *WHO Expert Committee on Problems Related to Alcohol Consumption. Second Report.* World Health Organization Technical Report Series, 944. Geneva, Switzerland: Author. Retrieved December 30, 2007, from www.who.int/sub stance_abuse/expert_committee_alcohol_trs944.pdf.

Wilsnack, S. C., & Wilsnack, R. W. (1991). Epidemiology of women's drinking. *Journal of Substance Abuse, 3,* 133–157.

Winters, J., Fals-Stewart, W., O'Farrell, T. J., Birchler, G. R., & Kelley, M. L. (2002). Behavioral couples therapy for female substance-abusing patients: Effects on substance use and relationship adjustment. *Journal of Consulting and Clinical Psychology, 70*(2), 344–355.

Witte, S. S., Batsukh, A., & Chang, M. (2010). Sexual risk behaviors, alcohol abuse, and intimate partner violence among sex workers in Mongolia: Implications for HIV prevention intervention development. *Journal of Prevention & Intervention in the Community, 38,* 89–103.

Woodford, M. S. (2012). *Men, addiction, and intimacy: Strengthening recovery by fostering the emotional development of boys and men.* New York: Routledge.

Wright, P. B., Stewart, K. E., Fischer, E. P., Carlson, R. G., Falck, R., Wang, J., Leukefeld, C. G., & Booth, B. M. (2007). HIV risk behaviors among rural stimulant users: Variation by gender and race/ethnicity. *AIDS Education and Prevention, 19*(2), 137 150.

Wyatt, G. E., Myers, H. F., & Loeb, T. B. (2004). Women, trauma, and HIV: An overview. *AIDS and Behavior, 8*(4), 401–403.

Zilberman, M. L., Hochgraf, P. B., & Andrade, A. G. (2003). Gender differences in treatment-seeking Brazilian drug-dependent individuals. *Substance Abuse, 24*(1), 17–25.

Zilberman, M. L., Tavares, H., Blume, S. B., & El-Guebaly, N. (2003). Substance use disorders: Sex differences and psychiatric comorbidities. *Canadian Journal of Psychiatry, 48*(1), 5–13.

Zimmer-Höfler, D., & Dobler-Mikola, A. (1992). Swiss heroin-addicted females: Career and social adjustment. *Journal of Substance Abuse Treatment, 9,* 159–170.

Zlotnick, C., Clarke, J. G., Friedmann, P. D., Roberts, M. B., Sacks, S., & Melnick, G. (2008). Gender differences in comorbid disorders among offenders in prison substance abuse treatment programs. *Behavioral Sciences and the Law, 26,* 403–412.

Zywiak, W. H., Connors, G. J., Maisto, S. A., & Westerberg, V. S. (1996). Relapse research and the reasons for drinking questionnaire: A factor analysis of Marlatt's relapse taxonomy. *Addiction, 91* (Supplement), S121–S130.

CHAPTER 16

Action America. (2011). *Drug War Cost Clock.* RetrievedFebruary 13, 2011, from actionamerica.org/drugs/wodclock.shtml.

Adams, R., Onek, D., & Riker, A. (1998). *Double jeopardy: An assessment of the felony drug provision of the welfare reform act.* San Francisco: Justice Policy Institute. Retrieved July 10, 2001from www.cjcj.org/jpi/doublejep.html.

American Psychiatric Association (APA). (2000). *Diagnostic and statistical manual of mental disorders* (4th ed., Text Revision). Washington, DC: Author.

Anton, R., et al. (2006). *Combined Pharmacotherapies and Behavioral Interventions for Alcohol Dependence.* JAMA, May 3, 2006. Vol. 295, No. 17, pp 2003–2017. Retrieved March 26, 2011, from jama.ama-assn.org/content/295/17/2003.full.

Association for Medical Education and Research in Substance Abuse (AMERSA). (2011). Project mainstream. Retrieved February 28, 2011, from www.projectmainstream.net.

Azrina, N. H. Aciernoa, R., Kogana, E. S, Donohue, B., Besalela, V. A., & McMahona, T. (1996). Follow-up results of supportive versus behavioral therapy for illicit drug use. *Behaviour Research and Therapy, 34* (1), 41–46.

Azzone, V., Frank, R., Normand, S., & Burnam, M. (2011). Effect of Insurance Parity on Substance Abuse Treatment. Psychiatr Serv 62:129–134.

Batki, S., Dimmock, J., Wade, M., Gately, P., Cornell, M., Maisto, S. & Carey, K. (2010). Monitored Naltrexone without Counseling for Alcohol Abuse/Dependence in Schizophrenia-Spectrum Disorders. *American Journal of Addictions* (On-Line), May 4, 2010. Retrieved February 15, 2011, from onlinelibrary.wiley.com/doi/10.1080/10550490701389732/full.

Biernacki, P. (1990). *Recovery from opiate addiction without treatment: A summary* (Research Monograph no. 98). Washington, DC: National Institute on Drug Abuse.

Brisman, A. (2008). Crime-environment relationships and environmental justice. *Seattle Journal for Social Justice, 6*(2). Retrieved March 30, 2011, from www.law.seattleu.edu/Documents/sjsj/2008spring/Brisman%20v.7.0_FINAL.pdf.

Brooks, M. (2011). Cutting Co-pays Has Negligible Effects on Mental Health Use. *Medscape Today,* Feb. 11, 2011. Retrieved March 29, 2011, from www.medscape.com/viewarticle/737228.

Brown, B. S. (1998). *HIV/AIDS and drug abuse treatment services: Literature review.* Retrieved October 20, 2002, from 165.112.78.61/HSR/da-tre/BrownHIVPartA.html.

Carise, D. (2010). What healthcare reform means for substance abuse treatment. Huffington Post, March 26, 2010.

Cartwright, W. S. (2000). Cost-benefit analysis of drug treatment services: Review of the literature. *Journal of Mental Health Policy and Economics, 3,* 11–26.

Conklin, M. (1997). Out in the cold: Washington shows addicts the door. *Progressive, 61*(3), 25–27.

Cornish, J. W., Metzger, G. E., Woody, D. W., McLellan, A. T., Vandergrift, B., & O'Brien, C. P. (1997). Naltrexone pharmacotherapy for opioid dependent federal probationers. *Journal of Substance Abuse Treatment, 14*(6), 529–534.

Crits-Christoph, P., et al. (1999). Psychosocial treatments for cocaine dependence: National Institute on Drug Abuse Collaborative Cocaine Treatment Study. *Archives of General Psychiatry, 56,* 493–502.

Curley, B. (2002, May 4). Grassroots alliance between mental health, addiction advocates wins N.H. parity law. *Join Together Online.* Retrieved December 8, 2002, from www.jointogether.org/sa/news/features/reader/0,1854,551330,00.html.

Currie, E. (1993). *Reckonin: Drugs, the cities, and the American future.* New York: Hill and Wang.

DiClemente, C. C. (1986). Self-efficacy and the addictive behaviors. *Journal of Social and Clinical Psychology, 4,* 302–315.

DiClemente, C. C., Carbonari, J. P., Rosario, P. G., & Hughes, S. O. (1994). The alcohol abstinence self-efficacy scale. *Journal of Studies on Alcohol, 55,* 141–148.

DiClemente, C. C., Fairhurst, S. K., & Piotrowski, N. A. (1995). The role of self-efficacy in the addictive behaviors. In James Maddus (Ed.), *Self-efficacy, adaptation, and adjustment: Theory, research, and application.* New York: Plenum Press.

DiNitto, D. (2002). War and peace: Social work and the state of chemical dependency treatment in the United States. *Journal of Social Work Practice in the Addictions, 2*(3/4), 7–29.

Drug Policy Alliance. (2002, March). Progress report: Substance abuse and crime prevention act of 2000. Retrieved May 13, 2002, from www.prop36.org/progress_report.html.

Erickson, C. K. and White, W. L. (2009). The neurobiology of addiction recovery. *Alcoholism Treatment Quarterly. 27,* 338–345.

Fields, G. (2009). White house drug czar calls for end to war on drugs. *Wall Street Journal,* May 14.

Fortney, J., & Booth, B. M. (2001). Access to substance abuse services in rural areas. *Recent developments in alcoholism, Vol. 15: Services research in the era of managed care* (pp. 177–197). New York: Kluwer Academic/ Plenum.

Foxcroft, D. R., Ireland, D., Lister-Sharp, D. J., Lowe, G., & Breen, R. (2002). Primary prevention for alcohol misuse in young people (Cochrane Review). *Cochrane Library, 3.* Retrieved September 2, 2003, from www.cochrane.org/cochrane/revabstr/ab003024.htm.

Gabel, J., Whitmore, H. Pickreign, J., Levit, K., Coffey, R. & Vandivort-Warren. R. (2007). Substance Abuse Benefits: Still Limited After All These Years. *Health Affairs,* 26, no. 4 (2007). Retrieved March 29, 2011, from content.healthaffairs.org/content/26/4/w474.full.

Galewitz, P. (2011, Feb. 23). States turn to private insurance companies for managed care. *USA Today*. Retrieved February 23, 2011, from www.usatoday.com/money/industries/health/2011-02-21-longtermcare21_ST_N.htm?csp=34news.

Gallup. (2009). About One in Six U.S. Adults Are Without Health Insurance. Gallup Poll, July 22, 2009. Retrieved March 28, 2011, from www.gallup.com/poll/121820/one-six-adults-without-health-insurance.aspx.

General Accounting Office (GAO). (1993). *Needle exchange programs: Research suggests promise as an AIDS prevention strategy.* Washington, DC: U.S. Government Printing Office.

Gerstein, D. R., & Harwood, H. M. (Eds.). (1990). *Treating drug problems* (Vol. 1, pp. 289–294). Washington, DC: National Academy Press.

Gibson, D. R., Flynn, N. M., & Perales, D. (2001). Effectiveness of syringe exchange programs in reducing HIV risk behavior and HIV seroconversion among injecting drug users. *AIDS, 15*(11), 1329–1341.

Gibelman, M., & Schervish, P. (1997). *Who we are: A second look.* Washington, DC: NASW Press.

Goode, E. (1997). Between politics and reason: The drug legalization debate. New York: St. Martin's Press.

Gray, J. P. (2001). *Why our drug laws have failed and what we can do about it—A judicial indictment of the war on drugs.* Philadelphia: Temple University Press.

Gwaltney, C., Metrik, J., Kahler, C. & Shiffman, S. (2009). Self-efficacy and smoking cessation: A meta-analysis. Psychology of Addictive Behaviors 23(1), 56–66. Hay Group. (2000). Employer health care dollars spent on addiction treatment. Retrieved December 8, 2002, from www.asam.org/pressrel/hay.htm.

Hay Group. (2000). Employer health care dollars spent on addiction treatment. Retrieved 1/8/2002 from http://www.asam.org/pressrel/hay.htm.

Henggeler, S. W., Clingempeel, W. G., Brondino, M. J., & Pickrel, S. G. (2002). Four-year follow-up of multisystemic therapy with substance-abusing and substance dependent juvenile offenders. *Journal of American Academy of Child Adolescent Psychiatry, 41*(7), 868–874.

Henggeler, S. W., Pickrel, S. G. Brondino, M. J., & Crouch, J. L. (1996). Eliminating (almost) treatment dropout of substance abusing on dependent delinquents through home-based multisystemic therapy. *American Journal of Psychiatry, 153*(3), 427–428.

Higgins, S. T., Budney, A. J., Bickel, W. K., Foerg, F. E., Donhan, R., & Badger, G. J. (1994). Incentives improve outcome in outpatient behavioral treatment of cocaine dependence. *Archives of General Psychiatry, 51*(7), 568–576.

Hoeffel, J. (2010). Drug czar criticizes proposition 19. *Los Angeles Times*, October 21.

Horgan, C. M., & Levine, H. J. (1998). The substance abuse treatment system: What does it look like and whom does it serve? Preliminary findings from the alcohol and drug services study. In *Bridging the gap between practice and research: Forging partnerships with community-based drug and alcohol treatment.* Washington, DC: National Academy of Science.

Jensen, G. A., Rost, K. M., Burton, R. P. D., & Bulycheva, M. (1998). Mental health insurance in the 1990s: Are employers offering less to more? *Health Affairs, 17,* 201–208.

Jepsen, J. (2001). What kind of science for what kind of decision? The discourse on a Danish heroin maintenance experiment.*Contemporary Drug Problems, 28*(2), 245.

Justice Policy Institute. (2001). Poor prescription: The costs of improving drug offenders in the United States. Retrieved September 2, 2001, from www.cjcj.org/drug/exsumm.html.

Kaiser Family Foundation. (2008). Medicaid Benefits: Online Database. Retrieved March 29, 2011, from medicaidbenefits.kff.org/service.jsp?nt=on&so=0&tg=0&yr=2&cat=12&sv=36.

Kaplan, E. H. (1993). Federal response to needle-exchange programs, Part II: Needle-exchange research: The New Haven Experience.*Pediatric AIDS and HIV Infection: Fetus to Adolescent, 4*(2), 92–96.

King, S., & Mauer, M. (2002). Distorted Priorities: Drug Offenders in State Prisons. Washington, D.C.: The Sentencing Project.

Klingemann, H. & Sobell, L. (Eds.) (2007). Promoting Self-Change From Addictive behaviors. New York: Springer.

Kuo, I., Fischer, B., & Vlahov, D. (2000). Consideration of a North American heroin-assisted clinical trial for the treatment of opiate dependent individuals. *International Journal of Drug Policy, 11,* 357–370.

Levit, K. R., Kassed, C. H., Coffey, R. M., Mark, T. L., Stranges, E. M., Buck, J. A., et al. (2008). Future funding for mental health and substance abuse: Increasing burdens for the public sector. *Health Affairs, 27,* 513–522.

Liddle, H. A., & Dakof, G. A. (1995). Efficacy of family therapy for drug abuse: Promising but not definitive. *Journal of Marital and Family Therapy, 21,* 522.

Ljungberg, B., Christensson, B., Tunving, K., Andersson, B., Landvall, B., Lundberg, M., et al. (1991). HIV prevention among injecting drug users: Three years of experience from a syringe exchange program in Sweden. *Journal of Acquired Immune Deficiency Syndrome, 4,* 890–895.

Lurie, P., Reingold, A. L., Bowser, B., Chan, D., Foley, J., Guydish, J., Kahn, J. G., Land, S., & Sorenson, J. (1993). *The public impact of needle exchange programs in the United States and abroad.* (Vol. 1). San Francisco: University of California.

Magura, S., Horgan, C. M., Mertens, J. R., & Shepard, D. S. (2002, March). Effects of managed care on alcohol and other drug (AOD) treatment. *Alcoholism: Clinical and Experimental Research, 26*(3), 416–422.

MacCoun, R. J., & Reuter, P. (2001). *Drug war heresies: Learning from other vices, times and places.* New York: Cambridge University Press.

Mackinder, E. (2011). Politics on Tap: Alcohol Producers Pour Out Campaign Cash for Parties. Open Secrets Blog, March 23, 2011. Retrieved March 27, 2011, from www.opensecrets.org/news/2011/03/politics-on-tap.html.

McLellan, A. T., Metzger, D. S., Alterman, A. I., Woody, G. E., Durell, J., & O'Brien, C. P. (1996). Evaluating the effectiveness of addiction treatment: Reasonable expectations, appropriate comparisons. *Milbank Quarterly, 74,* 51–85.

McLellan, A. T., Arndt, I. O., Metzger, D. S., Woody, G. E., & O'Brien, C. P. (1993). The effects of psychosocial services in substance abuse treatment. *Journal of the American Medical Association, 269,* 1953–1959.

McNeece, C. A. (2003). After the war is over: Implications for social work. *Journal of Social Work Education, 39*(2), 1–20.

McNeece, C. A., Bullington, B., Arnold, E. L. M., & Springer, D. W. (2002). The war on drugs: Treatment, research and substance abuse intervention in the twenty-first century. In R. Muraskin and A. R. Roberts (Eds.), *Visions for change: Crime and justice in the twenty-first century* (3rd ed., pp. 1–44). Upper Saddle River, NJ: Prentice-Hall.

MedlinePlus. (2011). *Managed Care.* Retrieved February 23, 2011, from www.nlm.nih.gov/medlineplus/man aged-care.html.

Metzger, D. S., Woody, G. E., McLellan, A. T. O'Brien, C. P., Druley, P. Navaline, H., DePhilippis, D., Stolley, P., & Abrutyn, E. (1993). Human immunodeficiency virus seroconversion among intravenous drug users in- and out-of-treatment: An 18–month prospective followup. *Journal of Acquired Immune Deficiency Syndromes, 6,* 1049–1056.

Miller, W. R., & Hester, R. K. (1986). Inpatient alcoholism treatment: Who benefits? *American Psychologist, 41,* 794–805.

Miller, W. R., & Weisner, C. M. (Eds.). (2002). *Changing substance abuse through health and social systems.* New York: Kluwer Academic/Plenum.

Miller, W. R., Brown, J. M., Simpson, T. L., Handmaker, N. S., Bien, T. H., Luckie, L. F., et al. (1995). What works? A methodological analysis of the alcohol treatment outcome literature. In R. K. Hester & W. R. Miller (Eds.), *Handbook of alcoholism treatment approaches: Effective alternatives* (2nd ed., pp. 12–44). Boston, MA: Allyn & Bacon.

Musto, D., & Korsmeyer, P. (2002). The Quest for Drug Control: Politics and Federal Policy in a Period of Increasing Substance Abuse, 1963–1981. New Haven: Yale University Press.

National Association of Alcohol and Drug Counselors (NAADAC). (2002). *Leading organization of addiction professionals urges Bush to endorse mental health parity.* Retrieved December 8, 2002, from naadac.org/pressroom/index.php?PressReleaseID=5.

National Institute on Alcoholism and Alcohol Abuse (NIAAA). (1996). *NIH news release: NIAAA reports project MATCH main findings.* Retrieved April 16, 2003, from www.samhsa.gov/search/search.html.

National Institute on Drug Abuse (NIDA). (1997). Study sheds new light on the state of drug abuse treatment nationwide. *Focus on Treatment Research, 12*(5). Retrieved October 18, 2002, from www.drugabuse.gov/NIDA_Notes/NNVol12N5/Study.html.

National Institute on Drug Abuse (NIDA). (1999a). Combining drug counseling methods proves effective in treating cocaine addiction. *Focus on Treatment Research, 14*(5). Retrieved July 10, 2001 from 165.112.78.61/ NIDA_Notes NNVol14N5/Combining.html.

National Institute on Drug Abuse (NIDA). (2006). *Methadone Research Web Guide.* Retrieved March 26, 2011, from international.drugabuse.gov/collaboration/guide_methadone/index.html.

National Institute on Drug Abuse (NIDA). (2009). *Principles of drug addiction treatment: A research-based guide* (NIH Publication no. 99-4180). Washington, DC: U.S. Government Printing Office. Revised April, 2009.

National Institute on Drug Abuse (NIDA). (2000). *Access to substance abuse treatment for Medicaid clients improves with Oregon model for financing treatment under managed care.* NIDA news release. Retrieved April 18, 2003, from www.drugabuse.gov/MedAdv/00/NR10-24.html.

National Institute on Drug Abuse (NIDA). (2011). *Clinical Trials Network: Research Studies.* Retrieved February 17, 2011, from www.nida.nih.gov/ctn/researchstudies.php.

Newman, R., & Bricklin, P. M. (1991). Parameters of managed mental health care: Legal, ethical, and professional guidelines.*Professional Psychology Research and Practice, 22*(1), 26–35.

Noonan, W. C. (2001). Group motivational interviewing as an enhancement to outpatient alcohol treatment. *Dissertation Abstracts International: Section B: The Sciences and Engineering.* University Microfilms International, US 2001, Vol. 61(12-B), p. 6716.

Norman, G. (2002, July). Put these guys in rehab: The government's hooked on the drug war. *Playboy,* pp. 66–135.

Normand, J., Vlahav, D., & Moses, L. E. (1995). *Preventing HIV transmission: The role of sterile needles and bleach.* Washington, DC: National Academy Press.

North American Opiate Medication Initiative (NAOMI). (2008). *Results show that North America's first heroin therapy study keeps patients in treatment, improves their health and reduces illegal activity.* Retrieved February 17, 2011, from www.naomistudy.ca/pdfs/NAOMI_release_Oct%2017-08.pdf.

Office of National Drug Control Policy. (2010). *Drug Control Policy: FY 2010 Budget Summary.* Retrieved February 13, 2011, from www.whitehousedrugpolicy.gov/publications/policy/10budget/index.html.

O'Brien, M. (2010). Obama drug plan 'firmly opposes' legalization as California vote looms. *The Hill,* May 11, 2010.

Retrieved March 26, 2011, from thehill.com/blogs/blog-briefing-room/news/97101-obama-drug-plan-firmly-opposes-legalization-as-california-vote-looms.

O'Neill, J. V. (2001, January). Expertise in addictions said crucial. *NASW News, 46,* 10.

O'Neill, J. V. (2002, June). Parity legislation likely. *NASW News, 47,* 1.

Orenstein, P. (2002, February 19). Staying clean. *New York Times Magazine, 6,* pp. 34–75.

Paulson, R. I. (1996). Swimming with the sharks or walking in the garden of Eden. In P. R. Raffoul & C. A. McNeece (Eds.),*Future issues for social work practice* (pp. 85–96). Boston, MA: Allyn & Bacon.

Prochaska, J. O., & DiClemente, C. C. (1992). Stages of change in the modification of problem behaviors. In M. Hersen, R. M. Eisler, & P. M. Miller (Eds.), *Progress in behavior modification.* Sycamore, Il: Sycamore Publishing.

Reich, T., Edenberg, H. J., Goate, A., Williams, J. T., Rice, J. P., Van Eerdewegh, P., et al. (1998). Genome-wide search for genes affecting the risk for alcohol dependence. *American Journal of Medical Genetics, 81,* 207–215.

Riley, E. D., Wu, A. W., Junge, B., Marx, M., Strathdee, S. A., & Vlahov, D. (2002). Health services utilization by injection drug users participating in a needle exchange program. *American Journal of Drug and Alcohol Abuse, 28*(3), 297–511.

Robert Wood Johnson Foundation. (2008). Service Delivery in Substance Abuse Treatment: Reexamining "Comprehensive" Care. RWJ Research Highlight, Number 28, March 2008, 1–2.

Roman, P. M., Johnson, A., & Blum, T. C. (2000). The transformation of private alcohol problem treatment: Results of a national study. *Advances in Medical Sociology, 7,* 321–342.

Saxe, L. M., Dougherty, D. M., Esty, K. & Fine, M. (1983). *The effectiveness and costs of alcoholism treatment: Health technology case study 22.* Washington, DC: Office of Technology Assessment.

Scanlon, A. (2002, December). *State spending on substance abuse treatment. National Conference of State Legislatures.* Retrieved April 17, 2003, from www.ncsl.org/programs/health/forum/pmsas.pdf.

Schilling, R. F., El-Bassel, N., Finch, J. B., Roman, R. J., & Hanson, M. (2002). Motivational interviewing to encourage self-help participation following alcohol detoxification. *Research on Social Work Practice, 12*(6), 711–730.

Science Daily. (2010). *Acamprosate prevents relapse to drinking. Science Daily, September 17, 2010.* Retrieved February 16, 2011, from www.sciencedaily.com/releases/2010/09/100907210819.htm.

Schmoke, K. (1997, January). Save money, cut crime, get real. *Playboy,* p. 128.

Sederer, L. I., & St. Clair, R. L. (1990). Quality assurance and managed health care. *Psychiatric Clinics of North America, 3,* 89–97.

Silverman, K., Higgins, S. T., Brooner, R. K., Montoya, I. D., Cone, E. J., Schuster, C. R., & Preston, K. L. (1996). Sustained cocaine abstinence in methadone maintenance patients through voucher-based reinforcement. *Archives of General Psychiatry, 53,* 409–415.

Sobell, L. C., Ellingstad, T. P., & Sobell, M. B. (2000). Natural recovery from alcohol and drug problems: Methodological review of the research with suggestions for future directions. *Addiction, 95*(5), 749–764.

Springer, D. W., McNeece, C. A., & Arnold, E. M. (2003). *Substance abuse treatment for criminal offenders: An evidence-based guide for practitioners.* Washington, DC: American Psychological Association.

Stephens, R. S., Roffman, R. A., & Simpson, E. E. (1994). Treating adult marijuana dependence: A test of the relapse prevention model. *Journal of Consulting and Clinical Psychology, 62,* 92–99.

Stewart, M. & Horgan, C. (2011). Health Services and Financing of Treatment. *Alcohol Health and Research 33*(4), 389–394.

Straussner, S. L. A., & Senreich, E. (2002). Educating social workers to work with individuals affected by substance use disorders. In M. R. Haack & H. Adger (Eds.), *Strategic plan for interdisciplinary faculty development: Arming the nation's health professional workforce for a new approach to substance use disorders.* Supplement to *Journal of the Association for Medical Education and Research in Substance Abuse,* Vol. 23, No. 3, 319–340.

Substance Abuse and Mental Health Services Administration (SAMHSA). (2000). *Health care spending: National expenditures for mental health and substance abuse treatment, 1997.* Rockville, MD: Author.

Substance Abuse and Mental Health Services Administration (SAMHSA). (2003). *SAMHSA model programs.* Retrieved April 16, 2003, from modelprograms. samhsa.gov/template.cfm?CFID=511304&CFTOKEN =87929902.

Substance Abuse and Mental Health Services Administration (SAMHSA). (2007). National Expenditures for Mental Health Services and Substance Abuse Treatment 1993–2003. DHHS Publication No. SMA 07-4227.

Szalavitz, M. (2009). *Why Obama isn't funding needle exchange programs.* Time.com. Retrieved February 15, 2011, from www.time.com/time/nation/article/0,8599,1898073,00.html.

Szasz, T. (1985). *Ceremonial chemistry: The ritual persecution of drugs, addicts, and pushers.* Holmes Beach, FL: Learning Publications.

Szasz, T. (1992). *Our right to drugs: The case for a free market.* New York: Praeger.

U.S. Bureau of Justice Statistics. (2010a). Correctional Populations in the United States, 2009. December 2010, NCJ 231681.

U.S. Bureau of Justice Statistics. (2010b). Prisoners in 2009, December 2010, NCJ 231675.

U.S. Bureau of Justice Statistics. (2011a, March 5). *Estimated arrests for drug abuse violations by age group, 1970–2007.* Washington, DC: U.S. Department of Justice. Retrieved March 5, 2011, from bjs.ojp.usdoj.gov/content/glance/tables/drugtab.cfm.

U.S. Bureau of Justice Statistics. (2011b, March 5). *Estimated number of arrests, by type of drug law violation, 1982–2007*. Washington, DC; U.S. Department of Justice. Retrieved March 5, 2011, from bjs.ojp.usdoj.gov/content/dcf/tables/salespos.cfm.

U.S. Bureau of Justice Statistics. (2001). *Prisoners in 2000* (NCJ 188207). Washington, DC: U.S. Department of Justice.

U.S. Bureau of Justice Statistics. (2002). *Prisoners in 2001* (NCJ 195189). Washington, DC: U.S. Department of Justice.

U.S. Bureau of the Census. (2001). *Health insurance coverage: 2000* (Report no. P60–215). Washington, DC: Author.

U.S. Sentencing Commission. (2011). *Analysis of the Impact of Amendment to the Statutory Penalties for Crack Cocaine Offenses Made by the Fair Sentencing Act of 2010 and Corresponding Proposed Permanent Guideline Amendment if the Guideline Amendment Were Applied Retroactively.*
Washington, DC: Author. Retrieved March 29, 2011, from www.ussc.gov/Research/Retroactivity_Analyses/Fair_Sentencing_Act/20110128_Crack_Retroactivity_Analysis.pdf.

Weisner, C., & Room, R. (1988). Financing and ideology in alcohol treatment. In M. E., Kelleher, B. K. MacMurray, & T. M. Shapiro (Eds.), *Drugs and society: A critical reader* (2nd ed., pp. 360–378). Dubuque, IA: Kendall/ Hunt.

Woody, G. E., McLellan, A. T., Luborsky, L., & O'Brien, C. P. (1995). Psychotherapy in community methadone programs: A validation study. *American Journal of Psychiatry, 152*(9), 1302.

Yoast, R., Williams, M. A., Deitchman, S. D., & Champion, H. C. (2001). Report of the Council on Scientific Affairs: Methadone maintenance and needle-exchange programs to reduce the medical and public health consequences of drug abuse. *Journal of Addictive Diseases, 20*(2), 15–40.

INDEX